ARANTE

AMERICAN ART

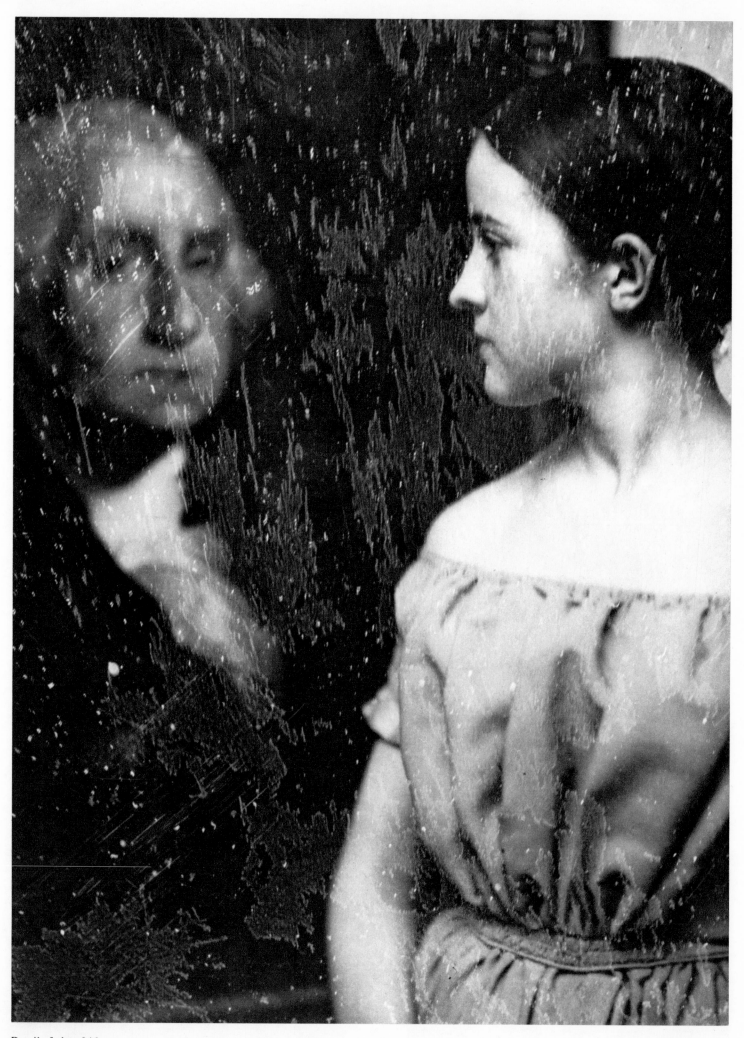

Detail of plate 346

AMERICAN ART

PAINTING · SCULPTURE · ARCHITECTURE
DECORATIVE ARTS · PHOTOGRAPHY

BY

MILTON W. BROWN

Executive Officer, Doctoral Program in Art History, City University of New York

SAM HUNTER

Professor, Department of Art and Archaeology, Princeton University

JOHN JACOBUS

Chairman, Department of Art, Dartmouth College

NAOMI ROSENBLUM

Instructor in Art History, Brooklyn College

DAVID M. SOKOL

*Chairperson of the History of Architecture and Art Department,
University of Illinois/Chicago Circle*

PRENTICE-HALL, INC., ENGLEWOOD CLIFFS, NEW JERSEY

HARRY N. ABRAMS, INC., NEW YORK

Editor: Theresa C. Brakeley

Designer: Gerald Pryor

Library of Congress Cataloging in Publication Data

Main entry under title:

American Art: painting, sculpture, architecture,
  decorative arts, photography.

  Basic text drawn from Milton Brown's American Art to 1900 and
Hunter/Jacobus' American Art of the Twentieth Century.
  Bibliography: p.
  Includes index.
  1. Art, American. I. Brown, Milton Wolf, American art to
1900. II. Hunter, Sam, American art of the twentieth
century. III. Jacobus, John M., American art of the twentieth
century. IV. Rosenblum, Naomi, photography. V. Sokol, David M.,
decorative arts.
N6505.H57   709'.73   78-12866
ISBN 0-13-024653-0

Library of Congress Catalogue Card Number: 78-12866

Published in 1979 by Harry N. Abrams, Incorporated, New York
All rights reserved. No part of the contents of this book may be
reproduced without the written permission of the publishers

Printed and bound in Japan

CONTENTS

*Decorative Arts are integrated
throughout the volume.*

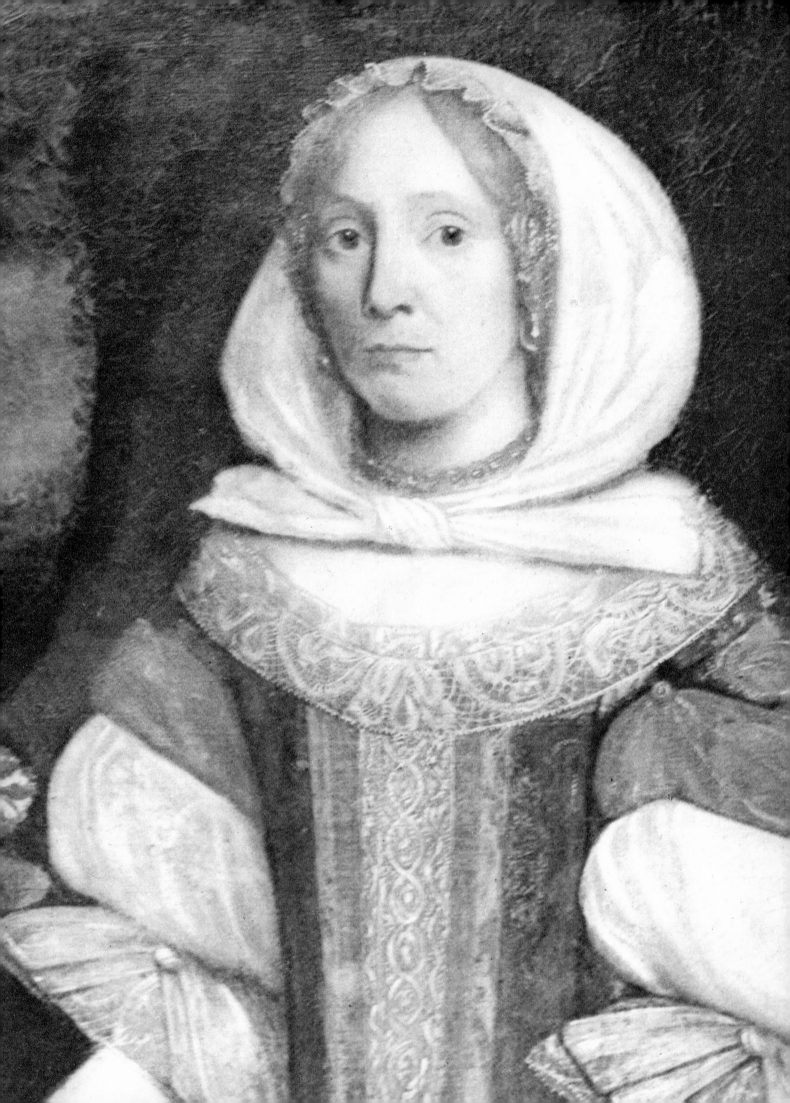

Part 1
THE COLONIAL PERIOD

The colonization of the Americas was part of the world-wide expansion of Europe beginning in the sixteenth and seventeenth centuries, a phase of a larger historical epoch which is only now coming to an end. The basic character of European colonialism was one of territorial spread and exploitation as part of an emerging mercantile capitalism. Within this general picture the American experience presents differences which have helped to form our national character, our culture, and our art.

Without denying the contributions of many national groups to American colonial life, there is no question that it was dominated by the English and their traditions. The English settlements in the New World were basically different from those of the Spanish, the French, and the Dutch. They were also different from the normal patterns of English colonialism in other parts of the world in that they were something of an anachronism for mercantile capitalism, a throwback to a more ancient form of colonization, similar to the Greek colonial expansion of the seventh and sixth centuries B.C. Both Americans and Greeks sought permanent settlement in a new land; were organized under some form of compact, charter, or constitution; thought of themselves as English or Greek; carried with them the traditions and the rights of the mother country and tried to maintain them in a new world; and had cultural and sentimental ties which tended to loosen with time. Both groups were fundamentally concerned not with the subjugation and exploitation of an indigenous population but with the conquest and exploitation of the land through their own efforts and labor. In this the English colonies in America differed most markedly from their Spanish counterparts.

The pre-Columbian inhabitants of the American land mass presented a cultural spread from the urban civilizations of the Incas and Aztecs to the Stone Age tribes of the Sioux, and comparable variations in population density. Over the centuries the overwhelming native populations absorbed the Spanish conqueror and his culture into their own, creating a synthesis in which one can still discern the divergent sources. In contrast, the English found a land sparsely settled by fairly primitive peoples, transitional from a hunting to a rudimentary agricultural economy, unwilling or unable to be exploited either through peonage or slavery. The Indian was eventually eliminated as an element in the environment. At most the colonists may have learned something about living in the wilderness from the natives, and though they readily adopted indigenous agricultural products, there was never any real cultural interplay.

Thus, English expansion in the New World was really colonization rather than colonialism, and the failure to recognize that distinction colored the relationship between the colonists and the mother country. While the former thought themselves Englishmen abroad, England could never convince herself that they were not part of her imperialist empire.

Perhaps the crucial factor in the North American colonization was the proliferation of its European population, with expanding enclaves of settlers unremittingly hacking their way into the wilderness. As time went on and the colonies grew and developed their own roots, they took on a new coloration and a more independent stance, but their ties were still with the Old World. Of all the early influences, the Spanish was the only one in which some admixture of indigenous Indian forms is apparent. However, the Spanish areas became part of the United States long after the mold of American culture had been set, so that the Spanish phase of our artistic heritage has remained largely local and not especially generative. Long before the Revolution the thirteen original colonies were thoroughly English in language, culture, and political orientation, and it is back toward England that one must look for the influences that helped shape American art.

1
Early Colonial Architecture

THE ENGLISH COLONIES

Almost immediately on arrival the settlers had to protect themselves from the weather. The makeshift shelters erected in Jamestown, Plymouth, Salem, and New Amsterdam have long since disappeared, but examples reconstructed from contemporary descriptions may be studied today in Pioneer Park, Salem, Mass. (plate 1). Among these, the *dugout* was the most primitive in form, like a cave dug into the side of a hill, sometimes built up with sod and covered over with poles and bark. Somewhat more ambitious was the *palisade hut* or *cabin*, built of upright poles driven into the ground, woven with wattles, chinked with clay, and roofed with turf or thatch. The *wigwam* may be derived from the building traditions of local Indians, although there seem to be some English antecedents in the meager hut shelters of poorer yeomen. Wigwams were constructed by bending and tying stripped saplings into a vault, interweaving them with twigs, and covering them with bark. The interior might also be insulated with straw. Fireplaces and chimneys were made of fieldstones laid in clay as high as they would remain in place and then carried upward in wood daubed with clay. They could not long withstand the accidents of weather or fire. Only the iron cooking pots they had brought with them gave any indication of the advanced technology out of which these people had come.

Yet before long the colonists began to erect more permanent *cottages,* which reveal their architectural traditions. Most of the New England settlers came from

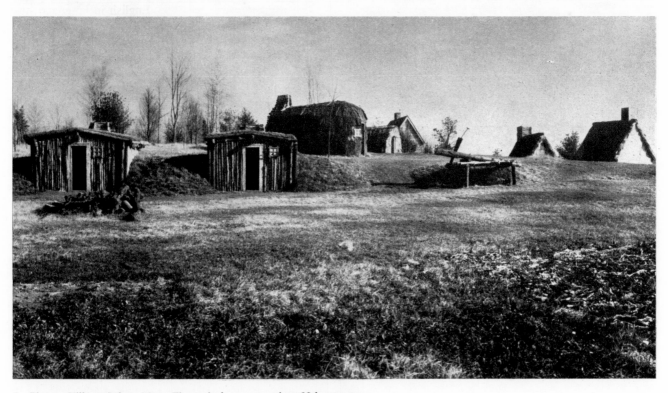

1 Pioneer Village, Salem, Mass. Theoretical reconstruction, 20th century

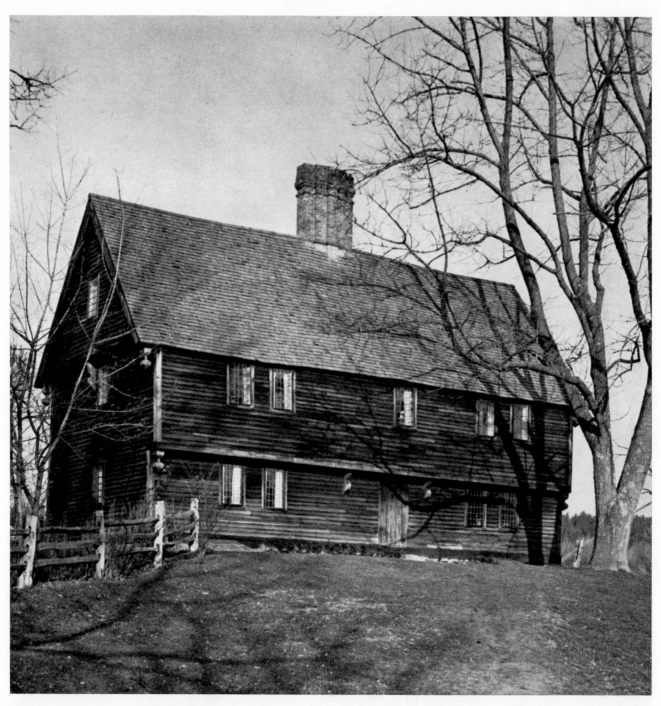

2 Parson Capen House, Topsfield, Mass. 1683

the rural areas of East Anglia, and the Gothic building forms of that region were transplanted, though modified by local conditions and materials. Houses there had been constructed of oak-beamed frames which were mortise-and-tenon jointed, the intervening spaces packed with wattle and daub (twigs and clay), cat and clay (chopped straw and clay), or brick. The common cottage in New England, perhaps because of the rigors of climate, abundance of wood, and scarcity of some materials, was of half timber with clapboarding for added insulation. The framed half-timbered house in America continued a long medieval European tradition of carpentry construction. The heavy timbers were intricately joined and pegged into a rigid interlocking frame.

In the beginning, most houses consisted of one room and an attic, with a fireplace on the short wall. Roofs were shingled or thatched and chimneys were made of logs daubed with clay. This type was long continued in use by poorer inhabitants, new arrivals, and those who pushed on into the wilderness. For the more affluent, the earlier form was soon supplanted by the so-called "classic" type, like the Parson Capen House (1683), Topsfield, Mass. (plate 2). It had two stories and an attic, two rooms to a floor, one on either side of a central firestack built of brick. Many such houses retained the Gothic overhang, with the upper stories projecting slightly beyond the lower and with carved drop ornaments, called "pendills" (pendants), at the vertical posts. Gothic and also functional in a northern climate was the steeply pitched roof running the length of the building. The attic floor was lit only by windows in the short ends, except in a few cases, such as the Whipple House (1639, plate 3), Ipswich, Mass., where cross gables were introduced. The door was centered on the long side and made of a double thickness of boards, vertical on the outside and horizontal on the inside. Windows were either stationary or casement with small diamond-shaped panes of blown glass, which had to be imported and were set in lead.

Such houses grew in response to family needs; whole sections, individual rooms, or lean-tos were added as changing circumstances demanded. Interior living space was specialized only in that daytime activities took place in the "hall," and formal entertainment or occasions in the "parlor." These two large rooms on the ground floor flanked the central firestack, which contained back-to-back fireplaces. Sleeping was confined to the attic and the two rooms on the second floor, called the "hall chamber" and the "parlor chamber." Walls and ceiling were plastered, sometimes revealing the vertical wooden members or posts and usually the major supporting "summer" beam and joists of the ceiling (plate 4). Wainscoting was also common, with vertical or horizontal boards covering the wall from floor to ceiling or forming a dado. The floor was usually a double thickness of planks in varying widths of oak or, later, of pine. In the hall the cavernous brick or stone hearth, with its great log lintel, served for cooking and was the focus of daily family life. In expanded houses cooking was often transferred to a lean-to.

(continued on page 17)

3 Whipple House, Ipswich, Mass. 1639

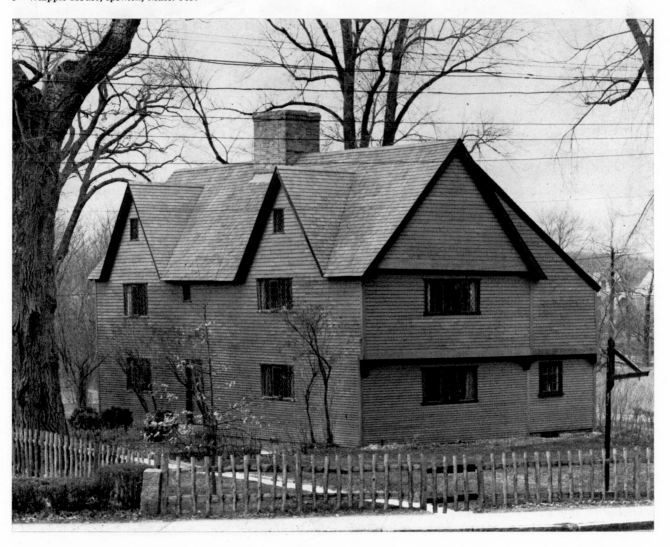

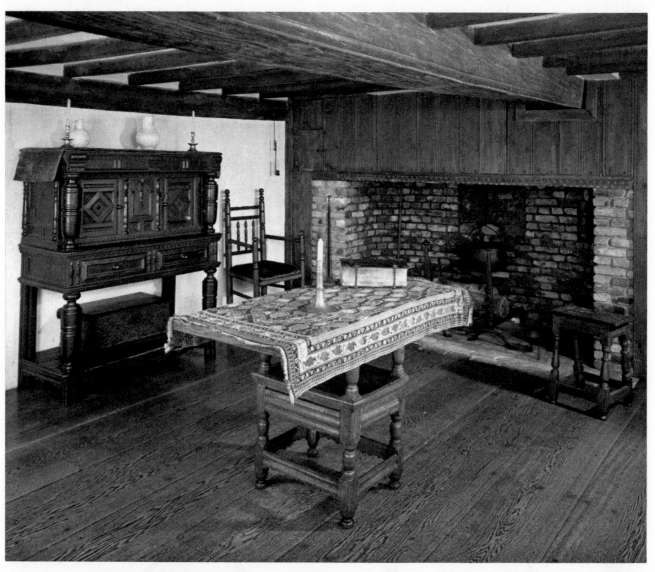

4 Room from Thomas Hart House, Ipswich, Mass. c. 1640. American Wing,
The Metropolitan Museum of Art, New York

DECORATIVE ARTS

Seventeenth-century household objects were either imported from the mother country or inexpensively homemade of local materials. The earliest surviving furniture made in America dates from the 1640s and early 50s and was made by anonymous joiners and carvers in New England. The small seventeenth-century houses did not accommodate much specialized furniture. The needs were supplied by versatile stools, chairs, trestle tables, and small chests constructed of simple horizontal and vertical members supported by stretchers. Oak had been widely used in England, and for their more important pieces the colonists continued to utilize it, but for items of everyday convenience they adopted the softer local wood, pine. Most of the furniture, regardless of the wood, was decorated by staining, glazing, or, most often, painting.

One early and major furniture form was the "great chair," based on medieval European prototypes. The "Brewster" type (plate 5), evolved here as a simplified version of the English seventeenth-century form, has two rows of turned spindles on the back and a row under the arms. The rounded members of this chair and other furniture (legs, spindles, etc.) were turned on pole lathes or on very large wheel lathes called "turners." The posts have vase-shaped decorations and incised lines provide secondary ornament. The rush seat is found on various chair types throughout New England.

As there were no closets in early Colonial homes, clothing (aside from items hung on pegs) was stored in chests or in cupboards. Chests of the period were decorated with flat carving in abstract leaf-and-scroll forms, often accompanied by brightly painted or stained colors. Very little of this color ornamentation survives to our day, because the vegetable coloring matter and mineral pigments used were unstable when mixed in distemper (a mixture of water and sizing) rather than in oil. Also, much of the finished furniture that has survived has succumbed to the taste of modern collectors, who prefer the color of natural oak and who strip away the original paint or stain.

By 1678, when the joiner Thomas Dennis (1638–1706) made a chest of drawers for his neighbors (colorplate 1), the storage chest had evolved into a more sophisticated form with drawers. The turnings on this massive piece are limited to split spindles applied as decoration rather than as architectonic elements (compare the court cupboard at the left in the Thomas Hart House, plate 4). The use of direct carving is confined to the front of a single drawer, while the black, white, and red paint is a more important part of the decorative scheme.

Two small objects frequently found in Colonial homes were the Bible or desk box and the spice cabinet. In that they usually are decorated with overall carving and have flat tops extending beyond the sides they relate both to the earlier small chests and to the later chests of drawers produced in the more rural areas.

This desk box (plate 6) is a rather carefully detailed example of the type, with thumbnail molding on all sides of the staple-hinged lid and a beveled projecting base. The

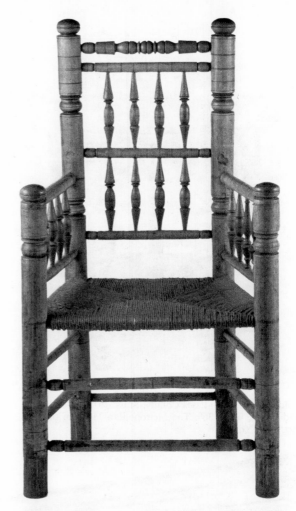

5   Great chair, from Plymouth, Mass., area. 1640–60. Oak and maple, height 45½″. Museum of Fine Arts, Boston. Frederick Brown Fund

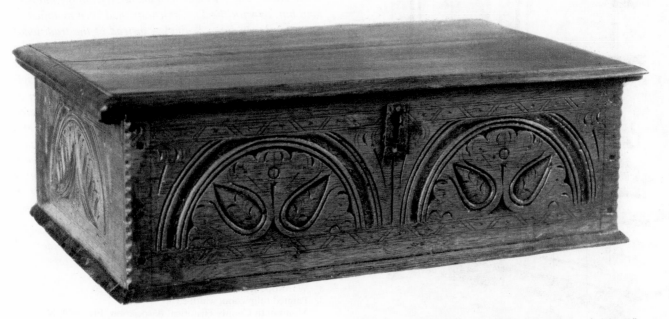

6   Desk box, from Connecticut. 1660–75. Oak and pine, height 6¾″. Museum of Fine Arts, Boston. Bequest of Charles Hitchcock Tyler

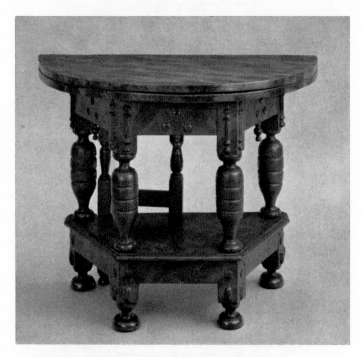

7 Folding table, from Essex County, Mass. 1675–90. Oak and maple, width 36″. The Metropolitan Museum of Art, New York

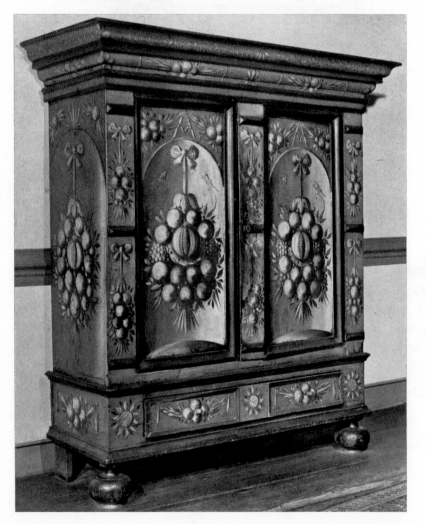

8 Wardrobe (*Kas*), from New York. 1690–1720.
Painted tulipwood, width 53″.
Monmouth County Historical Association, Freehold, N.J.

interior is fitted with a trough on one side and a till on the other and contains a divided compartment. The box was made to lock. The carved pattern—two lunettes on the front, each containing two flower buds set diagonally; lunettes on the ends containing two adjoined almond-shaped areas incised with palm leaves; and similar stamping and incising filling the voids and borders—points to an origin in the Connecticut Valley, where such motifs were common from the 1660s to quite late in the eighteenth century.

The furniture made in New England in the second half of the seventeenth century derives from the Renaissance in northern Europe, as modified in England during the hundred years preceding the colonists' departure from the mother country, and was called "Anglo-Flemish." Further modification of types popular in Jacobean England took place in the colonies, usually simplifying the form and eliminating some of the ornamentation.

The folding table (plate 7), with its bulbous "melon" supports and flat top and shelf, is a simplified variation of more intricate tables illustrated in Flemish design books known in England early in the century. The massive quality of the table and the solidity of the supports is similar to that found in the furniture shown in plate 4, particularly the cupboard. The folding table was an important space saver, because it could be stored against a wall and brought out to the center of the room only when needed. This form and its successor, the gateleg table, were hardy favorites in New England for many generations.

While the English colonists were using simple chests and, later, chests of drawers, the Dutch in New Amsterdam were building a type of large freestanding wardrobe called a Kas (plate 8), one of the most important pieces of furniture in the house. The Kas had been imported from the motherland but, as with the English chests, had been modified in the colonies. In some examples, instead of the traditional Dutch carving, the massive surfaces were covered with the earliest still-life paintings in the New World. Although Kasten were also made by German colonists in Pennsylvania and New Jersey, only the Dutch utilized these overall grisaille decorations and produced such sophisticated designs. Despite the limitations of the monochromatic approach to the representation of these panoplies of pears, apples, grapes, or (in this case) pomegranates, we see a full Baroque form of illusionistic painting. These painted symbols of fertility, accompanied by songbirds, hang in painted artificial niches, where they complement the massive yet compact overall form.

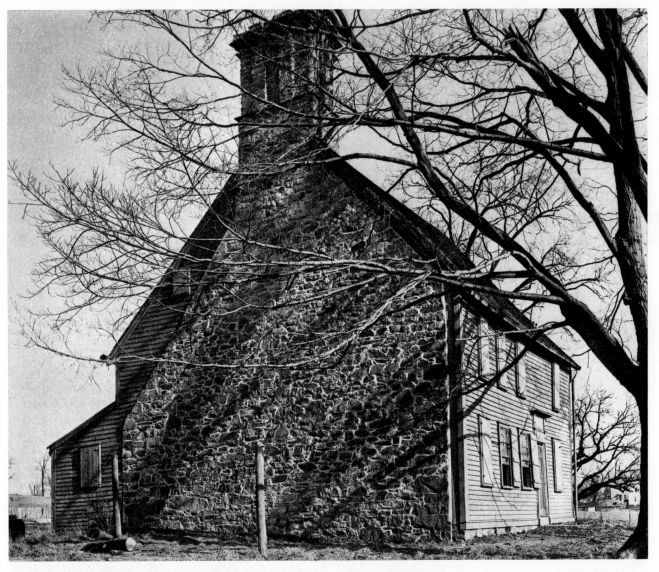

9 Eleazer Arnold House, Lincoln, R.I. 1687. View from the southwest before restoration

(continued from page 13)

Brick and stone buildings were rare at first in the colonies because of the shortage of lime for mortar. Even when masonry houses began to symbolize status, New England retained throughout the Colonial period a preference for its earlier wood tradition. Plenty of stone and mortar made from shell lime were available in Rhode Island, so that a local type of cottage called the "stone-ender" developed there, one of the best examples being the Eleazer Arnold House (1687, plate 9), Lincoln. The most famous New England stone house now extant is the Henry Whitfield House (1639–40, plate 10), Guilford, Conn., originally the minister's residence but also used as a meetinghouse and fort.

The major English variant from the New England cottage was the plantation house of the southern colonies. The same Gothic traditions prevailed there, but because of the difference in economic and social life and background of these colonists, their architecture tended to imitate the English manor house rather than the yeo-

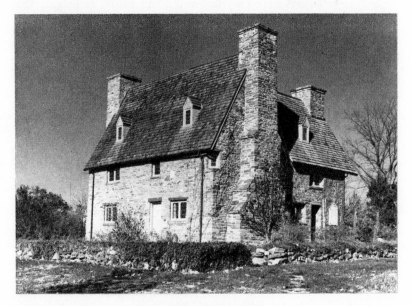

10 Henry Whitfield House, Guilford, Conn. 1639–40

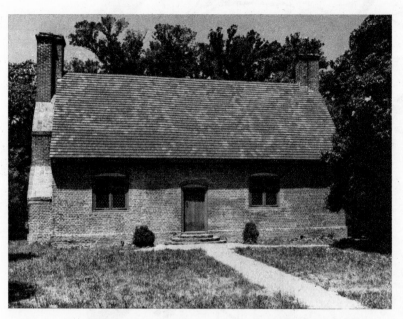

11 Adam Thoroughgood House, Princess Anne County, Va. 1636–40

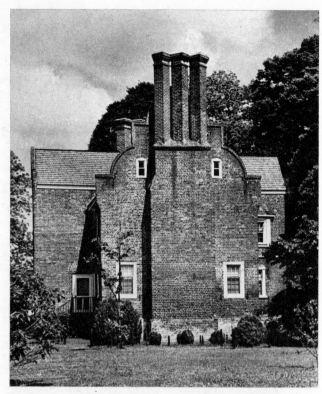

12 End view, Arthur Allen House ("Bacon's Castle"),
Surrey County, Va. c. 1655

man's cottage. Also, these settlers came from different areas of England, bringing with them a greater variety in plan and a predilection for brick rather than wooden building.

Virginia house plans ranged from the simpler single- and double-room types to a double-room type with a central hallway and finally to a cruciform plan with projecting porches at front and rear. Generally these houses were only one and a half stories in height. The chimneys were at the ends, rather than coupled in the center, and, in a characteristic type, extended beyond the end walls.

The Adam Thoroughgood House (1636–40, plate 11), the earliest extant house in Virginia, is an example of the more modest southern cottage. The Arthur Allen House (c. 1655), better known as "Bacon's Castle" because of its use as the insurgents' headquarters during Bacon's Rebellion, is the largest and most elaborate of the existing seventeenth-century southern plantation houses and one of the outstanding monuments of Colonial architecture. This two-and-a-half-story edifice was constructed of brick on a cruciform plan in the Tudor Gothic style (plate 12).

Public buildings during this early period were rather small. Only two major monuments, both religious buildings, can be dated unequivocally to the time. Old Ship Meeting House (1681, plate 13), Hingham, Mass., is the only surviving example of the Protestant meetinghouse so common in seventeenth-century New England. Four-

square in form, it was consciously conceived as breaking away from "Popery," as symbolized by English Gothic church architecture. Expressive of new anticeremonial religious attitudes is the replacement of the altar at the end of a long nave, which is the focal point of the mass, by a pulpit on the long side opposite the entrance, from which the sermon is delivered (plate 14). Old Ship Meeting House is a wooden structure, its exterior hip-roofed and clapboarded, and is capped by a simple belfry. The interior is dominated by a lofty Gothic trussed-rafter ceiling, whose curved beams, resembling the inverted hull of a ship, were probably executed by local ship carpenters and give the building its name.

On the other hand, the Newport Parish Church (plates 15, 16), in Smithfield, Va., known as the "Old Brick Church" and for a long time popularly as St. Luke's, is thoroughly Anglican in character. Now considered to have been erected in 1632, it is properly an English Gothic parish church built of brick, with wall buttresses, lancet windows under round arches, a square tower of three stages with ornamental quoins in brick at the west end, and an interior consisting of a long nave and a flat chancel with a large tracery window at the east end.

Blockhouses and garrison houses were common features of life at the edges of an unstable frontier, but except for the William Damm Garrison House (c. 1675, plate 17), Exeter, N. H., few are still standing. Although such houses were built of hewn logs, they follow closely the plan and appearance of the New England cottage.

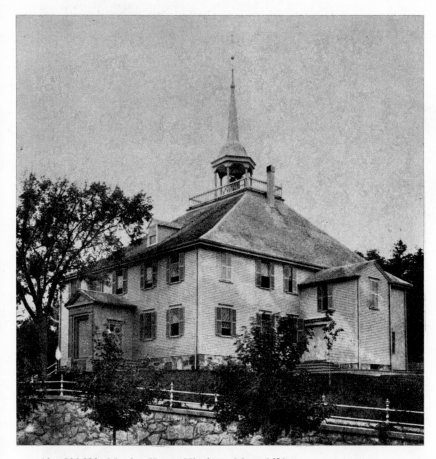

13 Old Ship Meeting House, Hingham, Mass. 1681

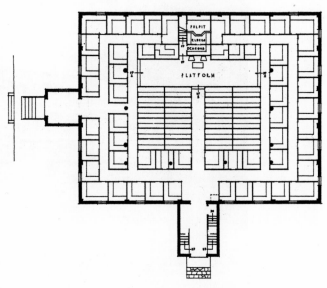

14 Main-floor plan, Old Ship Meeting House, Hingham, Mass. 1681. From *Old Time New England*, XXI, No. 1, July, 1930

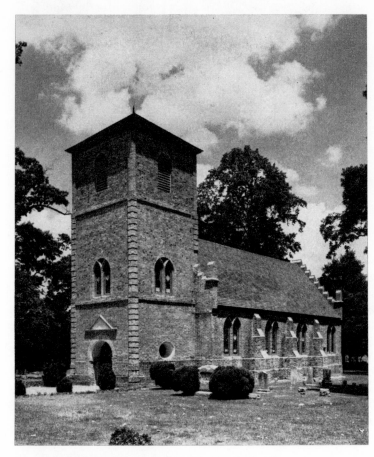

15 Newport Parish Church ("Old Brick Church," or St. Luke's), Smithfield, Va. 1632

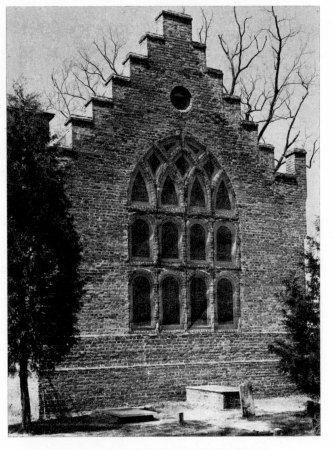

16 Southeast view of apse end, Newport Parish Church ("Old Brick Church," or St. Luke's), Smithfield, Va. 1632

Early Colonial Architecture 19

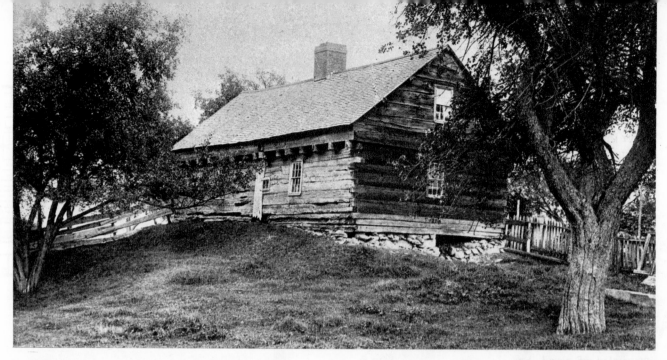

17 William Damm Garrison House, Exeter, N.H. c. 1675

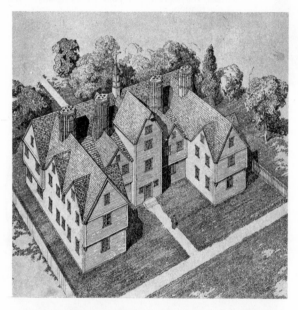

18 "Old College" at Harvard, Cambridge, Mass. 1638–42. Conjectural reconstruction, drawn by H. R. Shurtleff, 1933. Society for the Preservation of New England Antiquities, Boston

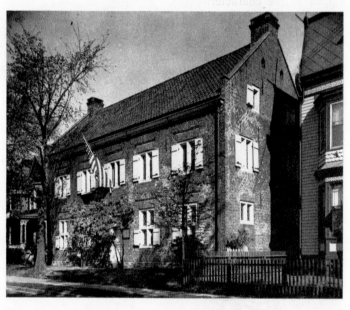

19 Fort Crailo, Rensselaer, N. Y. 1642?

Commercial buildings—stores, warehouses, trading posts, taverns, and inns—also followed the cottage form, but no examples remain.

From the outset the American concern with public education, motivated by both democratic and religious intentions, was phenomenal, and this tendency was especially strong in New England. Harvard College was established in 1636, but none of its early buildings exists today. The original "Old College" at Harvard (plate 18), the first college building in America, was begun in 1638, finished for the first commencement in 1642, and torn down in 1679. It was oak-framed and clapboarded and

probably E-shaped, as shown in the reconstruction, with gables and clustered chimneys.

No town halls or other government buildings of the seventeenth century have survived.

NEW HOLLAND

The architectural types of New Holland are actually distinguishable as two separate traditions: one Dutch, which dominated the Hudson Valley and New Amsterdam; the other Flemish, which spread through western Long Island and, in the eighteenth century, into northern New Jersey. The Dutch variety was built of brick and tile beautifully and intricately handled. Similar to houses still to be seen in Dutch cities, they were narrow, two or three and a half stories high, with stepped gables, patterned brickwork, and ornamental wrought-iron clamps which served to rivet the brick exterior to the wooden frame. There are isolated examples with straight-edged gables and elbow corners in the Hudson Valley. Of these, Fort Crailo (1642?, plate 19), Rensselaer, built to serve as an estate administrative building and fortress, is the largest and finest. There is some question as to its date, and important additions were carried out during the eighteenth century, but, with its now completely renovated interior and handsomely sturdy exterior, it is a splendid example of the Dutch style.

It is the Flemish-style house which is commonly thought of as Dutch Colonial. This type was usually constructed of wood, but a picturesque and informal admixture of stone and brick was also employed. It was topped by the characteristic "Dutch cap" roof, either peak or gambrel, curving out and projecting appreciably beyond the front and rear walls. Among the few such

homely but charming farmhouses of the seventeenth century still standing is the Pieter Wyckoff House (c. 1639–41, plate 20), Brooklyn. However, this rural style had its greatest development during the eighteenth century, long after the colony had come under English rule, in such specimens as the Ackerman House (1704, plate 21),

20 Pieter Wyckoff House, Brooklyn, N.Y. c. 1639–41

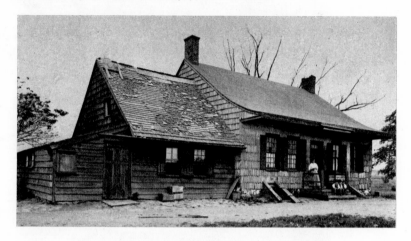

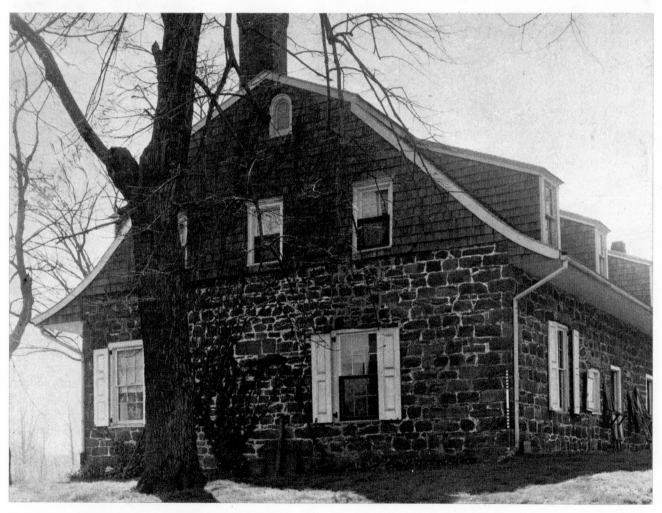

21 Abraham Ackerman House, Hackensack, N.J. 1704

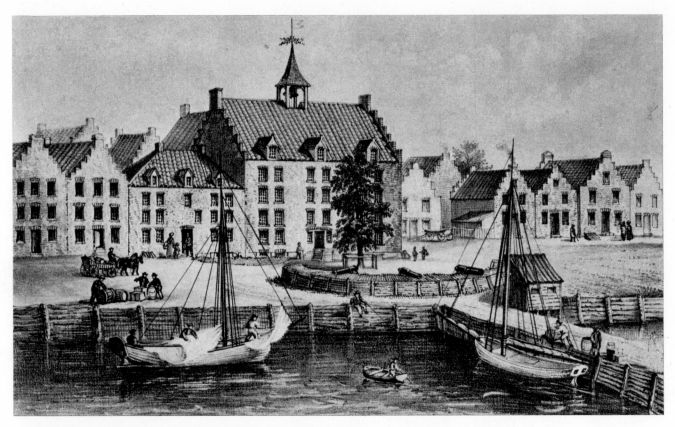

22 Stadthuys, New Amsterdam. 1679. From a print.
Museum of the City of New York. J. Clarence Davies Collection

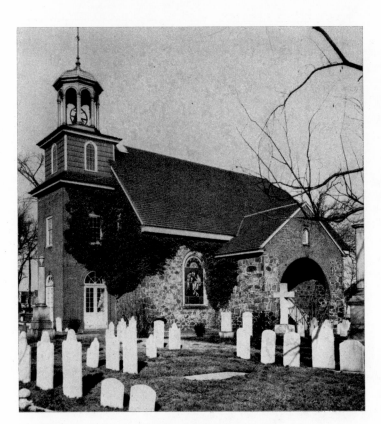

23 Holy Trinity Church ("Old Swedes"),
Wilmington, Del. 1698–99

Hackensack, N. J., a rich variant common to northern New Jersey, in which stone was used up to the eaves and wood above. In the later eighteenth century, the flaring roof projection was extended and supported by slender posts to create a "stoep," "piazza," or porch along the front.

The public buildings of the Dutch are known to us only through pictorial records. The Stadthuys (plate 22) in New Amsterdam was an overblown brick house with tiled roof and stepped gables.

NEW SWEDEN

The Swedes in Delaware had only a short-lived autonomous existence, but they brought with them a long heritage of wooden building which had a marked influence on their neighbors. They built the first log houses that later, in the hands of Scotch-Irish immigrants, became the log cabin of the frontier. Such houses were constructed of round logs fitted together by notching the corners and permitting the ends to protrude. There was also a more refined type utilizing square-hewn logs and dovetailed corners so carefully fitted that they needed no chinking. Other Swedish contributions to American building include the corner fireplace, the so-called "Quaker plan" of three rooms, which became fairly common along the migration route from Pennsylvania to North Carolina, and the awkward, steeply pitched "Swedish gambrel" roof, which one finds in the adjacent areas of New Jersey, Pennsylvania, Delaware, and Maryland.

Two Swedish Lutheran churches are still standing— Holy Trinity (1698–99, Wilmington, Del.) and Gloria Dei (1698–1700, Philadelphia), both called "Old Swedes." Although commissioned by Swedish congregations, both churches were built by Philadelphia craftsmen of English descent. Holy Trinity (plate 23) was originally a simple rectangular structure with massive stone walls three feet thick and an odd, steep-gabled, jerkin-headed roof. In the eighteenth century a south porch of stone and brick was added to buttress the buckling wall, and the west end was extended; not until 1802 were the small square tower and belfry completed. The interior has a false shallow vault of plastered wood, box pews, and a red-brick floor. Despite Scandinavian elements, both buildings are largely English in character and, in their classical ornamentation and trim, already Georgian in inspiration.

NEW SPAIN

The Spaniards were early established below the Rio Grande, but not until the seventeenth century did they expand significantly northward into what is now the United States. This area was divided for administrative efficiency into five "mission" territories—Florida, New Mexico, Arizona, Texas, and California. Though settlement began in Florida as early as the sixteenth century and in New Mexico at the very end of the century, it did not occur in Arizona until the last years of the seventeenth, and in Texas and California only in the eighteenth. Thus, only in Florida and New Mexico is there any visible evidence contemporary with the American colonies we have been discussing.

The Spanish conquest was a centralized effort of the Crown supported by a monolithic church. The Crown was looking for gold; the Church, motivated by the proselytizing zeal of the Counter-Reformation, for "souls" in the untapped human resources of heathen America. The first colonial push was with troops accompanied by priests. The native population was subjugated, strong points were established, and the priests then went about converting the Indians. Mission complexes with churches were erected by the natives under the direction of padres. After the pacification of an area settlers might move in and towns grow up, but in many cases the missions remained isolated enclaves.

The earliest Spanish settlement in Florida, in 1513, lasted only a short time, and no further efforts were made for more than half a century. Nearby, the ill-fated Fort

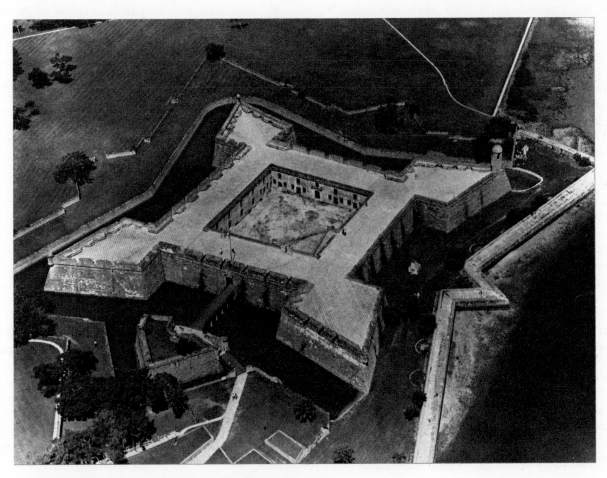

24   Castillo de San Marcos, St. Augustine, Fla. Begun 1672

Early Colonial Architecture   23

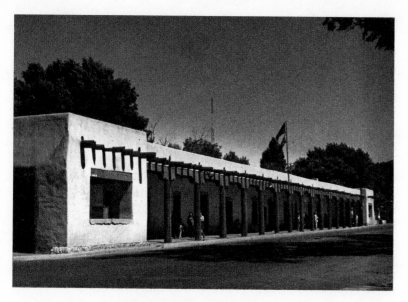

25 Governor's Palace, Santa Fe, N.M. 1610–14

(1610–14, plate 25), the oldest extant building by Europeans in the United States. The Palace is a long, low, one-story structure with a porch (*portal*) in the front, supported by wooden posts, facing the open plaza to the south. It is built of adobe, or clay, in the manner traditional with the Indians of the region in the construction of their own houses. They usually applied adobe successively in layers and allowed it to bake in the sun. The surface was then smoothed with adobe thinned in water and finished with a thin coat of white gypsum plaster. Roofs were constructed of *vigas*, or log rafters, projecting beyond the walls and carrying lighter transverse limbs, which then were laid with rushes or branches and covered with clay. The Spanish introduced a technical advance in casting the adobe in block forms, but the finishing of the surface still produced the irregular soft and fluid forms so characteristic of all adobe building.

The Spanish tried to re-create their European environment but lacked the skilled craftsmen to achieve that aim. In the outlying regions the local population was the labor force, and there was no alternative but to adapt to local materials and skills. The result was a synthesis of the European memory and the American present, and, uniquely in New Mexico, an original architectural form grew out of native traditions, naive and rudimentary but moving in its simple dignity, adjusted to terrain and climate, and organically related to the desert landscape.

By 1626 there were forty-three churches in the territory, but only a handful of them remains. Since such churches were much larger than houses, the achievement of greater height and the spanning of wider spaces presented a new challenge to their Indian builders; but they still used adobe or a mixture of stone and adobe. With such limited means the padre's memory of Baroque splendor had to be scaled down to the simplest forms and a minimum of elaboration. Walls had to be very thick at the base to carry the height and thus were battered. Large *vigas* supported by corbels projecting from the walls spanned the interior space and carried the flat roof of ceiling boards piled thick with adobe.

The best remaining church of that period is San Esteban (plates 26, 27), probably completed about 1642, on the remote and spectacular mesa of Acoma. Built of stone and adobe, its facade has only a simple doorway and, above, a window opening on the choir loft. It is flanked by two squat towers with belfries. Characteristic of the region are the barnlike interior, the bare walls with a few windows high under the eaves, and the richly painted corbels and *vigas*. San Esteban is long and narrow in plan, with a polygonal apse and no transepts.

The early phase of architecture in New Mexico was abruptly ended by the Pueblo Revolt of 1680, when the Indians, cruelly exploited, rose and in a bloody reprisal killed four hundred Spaniards and sacked the missions. It was not until 1692 that the Spanish returned to begin reconstruction.

Caroline, founded by French Huguenots in 1564, was wiped out the following year by the Spanish, who were in turn driven out by Sir Francis Drake in 1586. Not until 1593, with the arrival of twelve Franciscan monks, did the colonization of Florida begin in earnest. Of the forty missions built from the Gulf of Mexico to Miami in the years that followed, not a single one stands today, or very much else to remind us of Spanish rule, except for the great fort of St. Augustine, the Castillo de San Marcos (plate 24). The fort had been rebuilt eight times before the present structure was begun in 1672. It was not entirely completed until almost a century later. It remains today as the best example of the type of fortress developed in Europe after the introduction of gunpowder. The fortification, except for the bastions, moat, and outworks, was erected in three years through the combined labor of Indians, slaves, soldiers, and settlers. Built of coquina limestone, the stronghold contains an open plaza 100 feet square, surrounded by chambers with massive vaulted ceilings to carry the fort's sixty-four guns mounted above. Included were a chapel, a council chamber, barracks, officers' quarters, storerooms, magazines, and dungeons. The outer walls are 25 feet high, the battered sloping sides 12 feet at the base and 7 at the top, and the moat is 40 feet wide.

The Spanish venture into the American Southwest never paid off, at least financially. It was a harsh, unfriendly land, far from the centers of men and supplies. Although Francisco Vásquez de Coronado had explored New Mexico in 1540, no attempt to settle there was made until 1598, and not until 1609 was Santa Fe founded and the building of the Presidio, the fortified administrative center, begun. The Presidio was a walled enclosure, 400 by 800 feet, which included a chapel, barracks, offices, magazines, and prisons, as well as the Governor's Palace

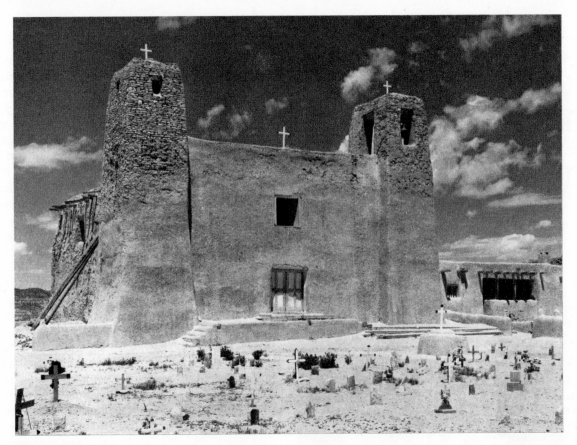

26 San Esteban, Acoma, N.M. Completed c. 1642

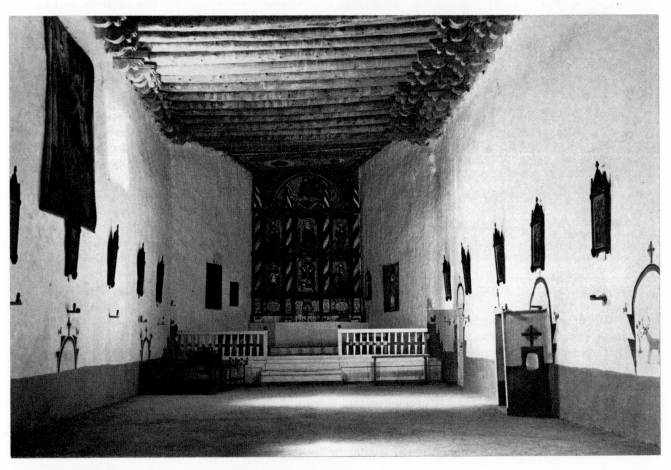

27 Nave and sanctuary, San Esteban, Acoma, N.M. Completed c. 1642

2
Early Colonial Painting and Sculpture

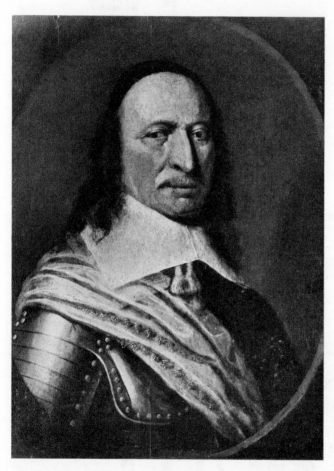

28 Anonymous. *Governor Peter Stuyvesant*. c. 1660.
Wood panel, 21½ × 17½″. The New-York Historical Society

The scarcity of painting and the practical nonexistence of sculpture during the seventeenth century were due to a variety of reasons. There was not yet much demand for luxury goods, and the average settler came from a background in which the presence of these arts was not usual. Religious attitudes in Protestant areas prohibited the idolatrous image in churches, and even in the secular field moral precepts concerning vanity and ostentation placed severe restrictions upon the production of painting

and sculpture. Then, also, the English at that time were not especially distinguished in the visual arts. On the contrary, the Dutch arrived during the golden age of Dutch painting, and the wealthier brought with them not only portraits but collections of paintings. Still, for a long time people felt that one could do better by importing luxury goods than by depending on local production. There was almost no religious art except in New Spain.

PAINTING

Throughout the Colonial period the dominant pictorial expression remained the portrait, as it did in England. During the seventeenth century only limners, anonymous artisans with no formal training, did occasional portraits. The naive character of their efforts has led to a designation of such works as "primitive" or "folk," but naive as they are, faint as the echo may sometimes become, these paintings reflect the memory of established forms carried on through prints or preserved in painted originals.

An anonymous portrait of Peter Stuyvesant (c. 1660, plate 28), governor of New Amsterdam, is probably Dutch in origin, despite some effort to assign it to a Hendrick Couturier who was listed in New Amsterdam in 1663. Dutch also are portraits of the De Peyster children (1631, plate 29).

Authentic examples of this period are extremely rare and at times over-restored and repainted. A number of such portraits from New England, dated about 1670, are charming, strongly patterned, flat, and linear. The anonymous portraits, *John Freake* and *Mrs. Freake and Baby Mary* (c. 1674, plate 30), despite the artist's obvious limitations as a draftsman and his uncertainties in three-dimensional representation, show a fine sense of composition in the boldness of the silhouettes, a feeling for decorative detail, and an intuitive felicity with color. The portrait of the mother and child even has a surprisingly authentic psychological mood. It is perhaps pretentious to designate so primitive a craftsman with the title Freake Master, as has been done, but there is no denying the presence of an artistic personality.

Very similar in spirit to the Freake family portraits are a series of portraits of children, resembling one another closely and perhaps by the same painter, although they have been attributed to two anonymous sources, the Gibbs Master and the Mason Master. The three paintings of the Gibbs children and the two Mason portraits are all similarly inscribed and dated 1670. Furthermore, they are closely connected in composition, black-and-white-squared floors and dark backgrounds, details of dress and pose, and even errors in drawing. The children all look like little china dolls, stiffly and self-consciously posed, with practically no differentiation in physiognomy or personality, except perhaps in the *Margaret Gibbs* (colorplate 2), which seems not only more forcefully realized but more carefully painted than the others. They are endearing portraits. The artist's untutored simplicity of conception and almost childish delight in detail underline the very nature and appeal of childhood.

A comparison of these portraits with the De Peyster children reveals a remarkable similarity in iconography as well as composition, but a complete variance in style. The Dutch pictures reflect, even if heavy-handedly, the newer Baroque conception of visual realism which saw such a rich development in seventeenth-century Holland.

Toward the end of the century the Baroque style was beginning to make itself felt among the New England limners, possibly as a provincial extension of the change in English painting under the impact of Sir Anthony Van Dyck. The establishment of the identity of a seventeenth-century American painter, Thomas Smith, is conjectural, but on the basis of a record of payment by Harvard College in 1680 of four guineas to a Thomas Smith for a portrait of a Dr. Ames, another portrait of a man in which the monogram TS appears has been called a *Self-Portrait* (c. 1690, colorplate 3). The connection is tenuous, but, considering the limited range of art relationships at that time, persuasive. The portrait is in the traditional form of a *memento mori,* or reminder of death, in which the man holds a skull, and the accompanying inscribed poem expresses an appropriately Puritan rejection of the vanities of life and an embracing of the glory of death. The drawn curtain on the right, a standard portrait prop, balances the view of a naval battle seen through an opening on the left. This is in all respects a stock portrait, but the direct, even crude modeling of the face projects a forcefulness and immediacy which obscure the inadequacies of the painting, as in the skull and the lace. Other portraits attributed to Thomas Smith are close to the *Self-Portrait* in composition, iconography, and style: *Captain George Corwin* (1675), *Major Thomas Savage* (1679), and his daughter *Maria Catherine Smith* (c. 1690).

In general, limners toward the end of the century were beginning to respond, probably through the medium of prints, to the changing fashion in English painting, and portraits such as *Mrs. Elizabeth Paddy Wensley* (1670–

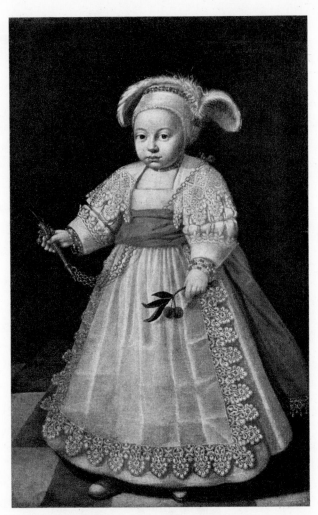

29 Anonymous Dutch. *Portrait of Jacques De Peyster.* 1631. Canvas, 39 × 24¾″. Collection James S. De Peyster, Jr., New York

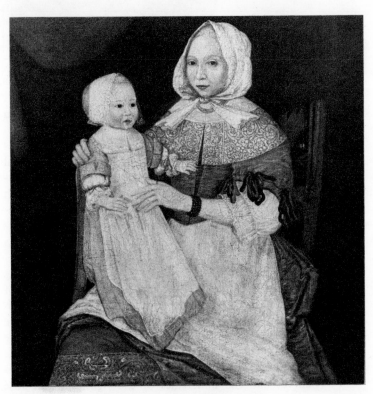

30 Anonymous. *Mrs. Freake and Baby Mary.* c. 1674. Canvas, 42½ × 36¾″. Worcester Art Museum. Gift of Mr. and Mrs. Albert W. Rice

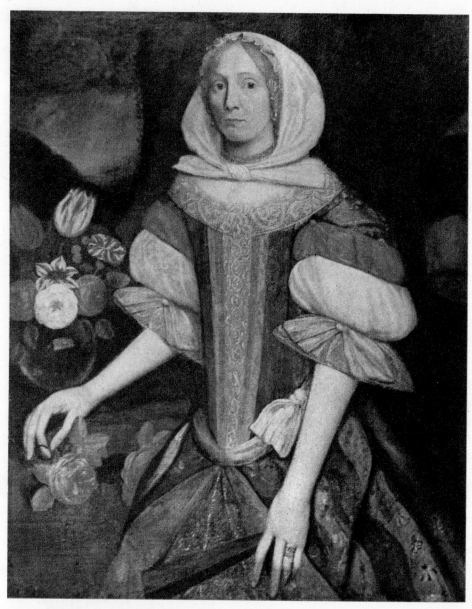

31 Anonymous. *Mrs. Elizabeth Paddy Wensley.* 1670–90. Oil on canvas,
40½ × 33″. The Pilgrim Society Collection, Pilgrim Hall, Plymouth, Mass.

90, plate 31) are distantly but unmistakably related to more current European models.

Except for portraiture, Spanish, unlike English, painting was predominantly religious. Altarpieces and mural decorations were copied from European prints by immigrant Spanish and Flemish artists. However, such activities, provincial as they may have been, were confined to the major colonial centers. In the North American outposts such artistic production as did exist was almost entirely the handwork of the local Indians.

The Indians of the Southwest, at least, had a strong painting tradition of their own, and their practice of ceremonial painting on the walls of the religious chambers known as *kivas* was adapted by the padres to the embellishment of church interiors. Employing the native palette of black, white, blue-green, yellow, and red, the Indians decorated the corbels they had carved in vigorous curves and the undersides of the *vigas*. At San José

(Laguna), which contains the most remarkable examples of New Mexican mission painting (colorplate 4), the padres permitted the Indians to cover the nave walls at dado height with their own mythological symbols. In contrast, the painting of the sanctuary walls and ceiling is an attempt to imitate the typical Spanish or Mexican *reredos* with barbaric vigor in a conglomerate of floral arabesques, representations of the Trinity and saints, symbols of the sun and moon, scrolls, and spiral columns.

In the smaller and more intimate images of religious figures the Indians of the Southwest produced a unique genre of acculturated art. Such images of saints carved in soft wood coated with gesso and painted are called *bultos,* and those painted on panels of wood, sometimes stretched with canvas or skin, and on tin, are called *santos.* Most are later in date, but they seem to retain local tradition without much change or development.

(continued on page 31)

During the latter part of the seventeenth century, the three main colonial cities and centers of social life—Boston, New York, and Philadelphia—all had dealings with London at least as frequently as they did with one another. The well-to-do citizens bought many locally made objects but often imported their prize possessions from Europe. Silverware had already been carried to the colonies by settlers who wished to keep their assets near them and who distrusted the fluctuation of currency; the metal itself was valuable and could be melted for conversion to currency. It was also a desirable indication of wealth and social status, and thus some colonists continued to purchase it from abroad through most of the eighteenth century. To repair and maintain imported silver plate (all silver objects were called "plate") and to create new cups, dishes, and spoons for local sale, the colonists needed trained silversmiths. During the early years several craftsmen migrated to the major cities; John Hull and Robert Sanderson were two who settled in Boston, where they served the Massachusetts Mint and created many important pieces based on English styles. To handle the large demand they took on young men to learn the craft as apprentices, and one of them, Jeremiah Dummer (1645–1718), represents the first production of a native-born silversmith.

Though not much survives of the large amount of work he must have done, there is enough to give us an understanding of his range and style. The silver tankard illus-

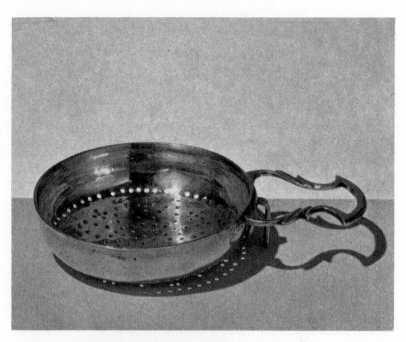

33 Cesar Ghiselin. Porringer, from Philadelphia. c. 1685–88. Silver, diameter 4". Philadelphia Museum of Art. Gift of Mrs. W. Logan MacCoy

trated (plate 32) was one of two he made for a church in Charlestown, Mass., about 1676. The height is almost equal to the width at the base, which has a low stepped molding, so that the whole presents an appearance of solidity and strength. The handle flows in an S curve almost out of the graceful, low lid, and the small thumb piece echoes the curve of the handle. As is typical of unadorned late seventeenth-century silver, dancing patterns of light are created by the gentle ripples that were intentionally hammered into the body and lid. In accordance with basic Puritan taste, Dummer adopted substantial, simple forms without applied decoration.

Many of the immigrant silversmiths of the period were French Protestants (Huguenots) who left their country after Louis XIV removed protection from them by revoking the Edict of Nantes in 1685. Some, such as Cesar Ghiselin (c. 1663–1733), left before the ax fell; he arrived in Philadelphia in 1681, having already completed his apprenticeship. He was the earliest silversmith to work in that city, and this porringer (plate 33) is certainly the oldest surviving piece from his hand. The porringer was a very popular form, being made of pewter and iron as well as silver, and was used for gruel or soup. The seventeenth-century date of this example is indicated by the almost flat bottom, as opposed to later pieces, which tend to have a raised base. The bowl is fairly shallow and has a narrow rim (later models tended to be deeper and more strongly curved toward the top). The cutout handle is decorated

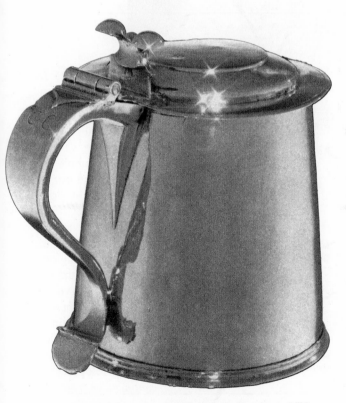

32 Jeremiah Dummer. Tankard, from Boston. c. 1676. Silver, height 6$\frac{3}{16}$". The Henry Francis du Pont Winterthur Museum, Del.

with simple patterns of Huguenot inspiration (circle, heart, and cloverleaf), differing from the piercings on objects of English derivation. The handle is flat and wide, permitting heat to diffuse and providing an easy grip.

The beaker is another basic seventeenth-century form for silver, although less popular than the tankard for everyday use. The unusually tall example shown (plate 34) is both graceful and elegant. It displays the strong Dutch tradition of rich ornamentation carried on in New York even at the end of the century. The complex base of the beaker,

with its molding, stamped square design, and engraved bands and scalloping, is only the prelude to an elaborately engraved series of pictorial scenes with their own symbolic significance. The oval motifs, surrounded by foliage, symbolize industry, integrity, and virtue, and the scenes at the base represent fidelity, humility, and magnanimity. The gently flaring lip is engraved with flowers and foliage encased in interlaced strapwork indebted to a Dutch sixteenth-century model. The richly exuberant Dutch ornamentation here and in the Kas (plate 8) contrasts sharply with the more severe work found in Boston and Philadelphia.

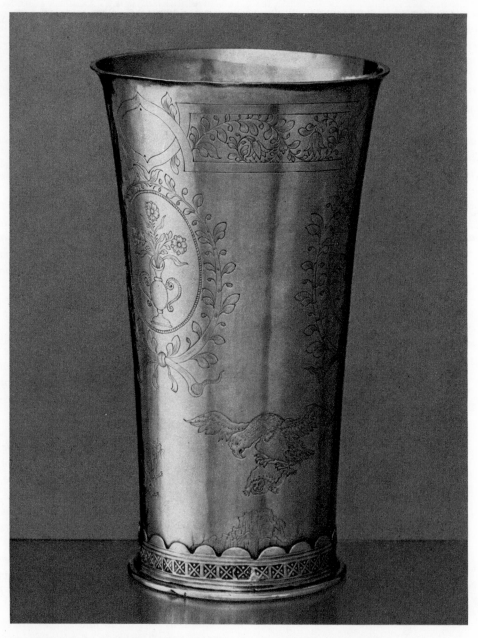

34 Cornelius van der Burch. Beaker, from New York. c. 1685. Silver, height 8".
Yale University Art Gallery, New Haven. The Mabel Brady Garven Collection

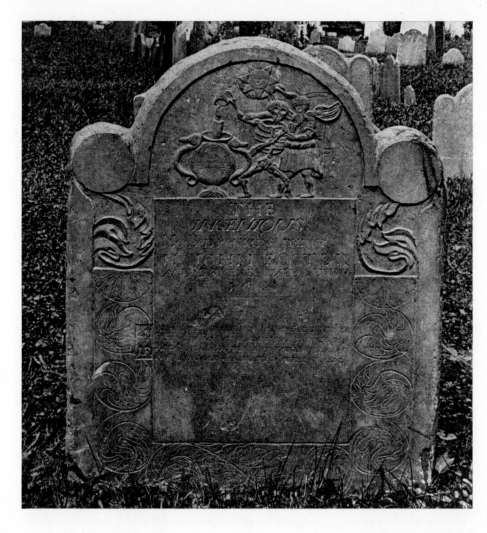

35 Anonymous. Gravestone of
John Foster (d. 1681),
Dorchester, Mass.

(continued from page 28)

SCULPTURE

For more than a century gravestone carving remained almost the only form of sculpture practiced in the colonies. It had even less relation to the sophisticated art of the period than did painting. Still, humble as it was, it was the only art of the Early Colonial era in which a religious and philosophical attitude found expression. The Protestant fixation on death was echoed in these stone warnings to the living of the vanities of the world, the passage of time, and the mortality of man. Predictably, the most striking of these gravestones are from Puritan-dominated New England.

The earliest grave markers were mostly of slate, which lends itself to easy but shallow carving. Though limestone was introduced at the turn of the century, it was some time before artisan stonecutters attempted anything but low relief. The first and simplest seventeenth-century gravestones gave only vital statistics. By midcentury such rudimentary ornamental elements as rosettes and radiating sun disks were added, and the scalloped top with a large semicircle in the center flanked by a smaller one on each side became common. This basic type saw various elaborations during the second half of the century: the transformation of the semicircles into scrolls, the development of vertical side panels with geometric and floral ornaments, and the definition of pictorial fields as the iconography became richer. Beginning with the winged skull, the earliest and most common motif, the mortuary vocabulary was soon expanded into a more detailed iconography of death—hourglass, crossed bones, winged-soul's head, coffin, symbolic plant forms, Death, Father Time, and a catalogue of appropriate homilies. Though the constant repetition of certain motifs may be ascribed to a deep-seated folk tradition going back to the Middle Ages, the particular visual imagery occurring in many cases and in complex pictorial forms presupposes graphic prototypes.

The Baroque forms of the gravestone of the publisher, printer, and sometime painter John Foster (d. 1681, plate 35) are matched by the involutions in its symbolism. It includes a pictorial elaboration representing Father Time accompanying the skeleton figure of Death, the former with his hourglass and scythe, the latter with a candle-snuffer advancing to smother the flame of life supported by the globe of the earth. Despite its comic garbling, the scene is obviously derived from a sophisticated rendering of figures moving in space. Allan I. Ludwig cites as the source a little engraving from Francis Quarles's *Hieroglyphiques of the Life of Man* (1638, London).

Ability to handle representational form and pictorial composition varied greatly among artisans, ranging from primitive incision to rich and fanciful carving.

3
Eighteenth-Century Colonial Architecture

By 1700 there were about a quarter of a million people in the English dependencies. The frontier was moving inexorably westward. Those less adventurous, more skilled, or more solvent remained in the towns of the eastern seaboard and helped transform them into burgeoning cities. By the eighteenth century Philadelphia was second in population only to London in all the English realm, and America had become an important element in the English economy.

Wealthy merchants in the towns and prospering plantation owners in the South were interested in more gracious living and financially able to support a higher level of production in the arts. While southern planters imported many of their luxuries from England, in the North merchants were finding a growing class of artisans—carpenters, cabinetmakers, silversmiths, and even portrait painters—to satisfy their demands. Crafts moved out of the home, became more diversified, and achieved a quite respectable standard of quality before the Revolution, and architecture became more formal.

The bustling towns of the New World were much like those in England, except for New York, which retained a good deal of its Dutch flavor. One gets some inkling of what such towns were like only in isolated enclaves in Salem, Annapolis, or Charleston, and in the refurbished downtown section of Philadelphia around Independence Hall or in the reconstructions of Williamsburg, Va., and Sturbridge, Mass. In most cases the natural process of growth, together with the American penchant for newness and progress, has destroyed what we now think of regretfully as our cultural heritage.

AMERICAN GEORGIAN

The so-called "Georgian style" of the eighteenth century is a Baroque manifestation and a far cry from the Gothic inspiration of the seventeenth. The English Baroque, which late in the seventeenth century followed a short period of Renaissance classicism, was dominated by the genius of Sir Christopher Wren and was carried into the eighteenth century by such followers as Sir John Vanbrugh, Nicholas Hawksmoor, and James Gibbs. But it was a restrained and classical Baroque, quite different from the florid late versions of the style in Germany or Spain.

The architecture of the pre-Revolutionary period of the eighteenth century is commonly designated as "American" or "Colonial" Georgian, to distinguish it from the English version, which was imitated in the colonies on a more modest scale because of obvious limitations of economy, craftsmanship, and materials. Since all the colonies were now under English rule, a truly homogeneous style was developed here for the first time.

There were no trained "professional" architects in the colonies, and public buildings were frequently the amateur efforts of gentlemen who had acquired some knowledge of architecture or artisans who had some skill in drawing. The new manner was introduced mostly through the medium of architectural books: Andrea Palladio's *Four Books of Architecture* in two volumes, with plates by Giacomo Leoni; *Vitruvius Britannicus* by Colen Campbell; William Kent's *Designs of Inigo Jones*; new editions of Leon Battista Alberti and Giacomo da Vignola; *Palladio Londinensis* by William Salmon; and *Vitruvius Scoticus* by William Adam. Even these were little known in the colonies except by knowledgeable amateurs such as Peter Harrison, John Ariss, and Thomas Jefferson. Most builders, artisans, and clients relied on the more popular guides or handbooks, which simplified current architectural practice with emphasis on practical application. Batty Langley was probably the most widely read, *The City and Country Builder's and Workman's Treasury of Designs* being the most famous of his more than twenty titles, but James Gibbs's *A Book of Architecture* (1728) was probably the single most popular architectural book of the century and had the greatest influence on Colonial building.

If Colonial architecture of the Georgian period owed its homogeneity to the currency of such handbooks, it owed its eccentricities to a free, naive, and often whimsical mixing of details found in them. It is possible to distinguish within the American Georgian an early or transitional phase from about 1700 to 1750 and a more fully developed one lasting until the Revolutionary War. The Early Georgian is characterized by an incomplete understanding and a tentative handling of the new style elements, with occasional throwbacks to the Gothic. Its most recognizable features are a flatter treatment of the facade; a preference for the gambrel roof—almost without exception a hallmark of the Early Georgian—or in the South a very high-pitched hip roof with necessarily taller chimneys; and detailing which is heavier, bolder, and cruder than that of the more sophisticated High Georgian.

GEORGIAN PUBLIC BUILDINGS

The impact of the Georgian style, as developed by Christopher Wren in the rebuilding of London after the great fire of 1666, made itself manifest earlier in public than in private buildings. In the colonies the earliest, largest, and most splendid secular complex was erected at Williamsburg, Va.: the College of William and Mary (1695–1702), the Capitol (1701–05), and the Governor's Palace (1706–20). All these were destroyed, but they now exist again in scrupulously authentic reconstructions. The city was laid out with rationality and pomp, the main avenue joining the Capitol with the College and affording the kind of vista made popular by Baroque planning of the seventeenth century. The buildings are Wrenian, al-

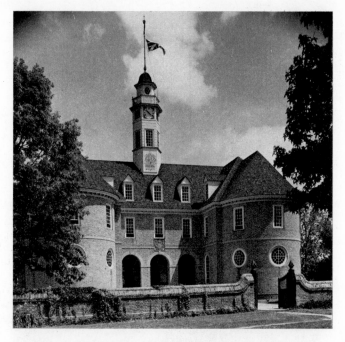

36 Capitol, Williamsburg, Va. Reconstruction begun 1927

though their attribution to him is purely conjectural.

The Capitol (plate 36), especially, is an imposing mass of Baroque formal elements rendered with uncommon decorative reticence. On the basis of the existing evidence, an eighteenth-century print in the Bodleian Library that is far from a measured drawing, the reconstruction may be a bit prim and too neat in detailing, but the handsome

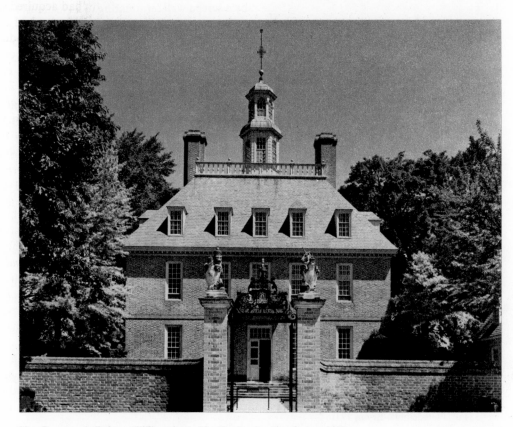

37 Governor's Palace, Williamsburg, Va. Reconstruction begun 1927

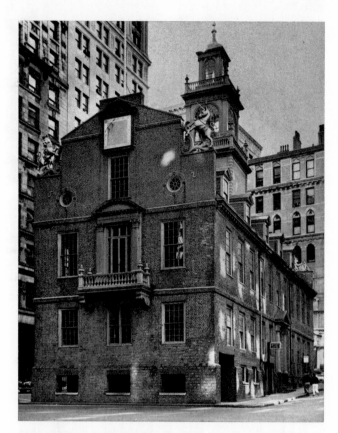

38 Old State House, Boston. 1712–13

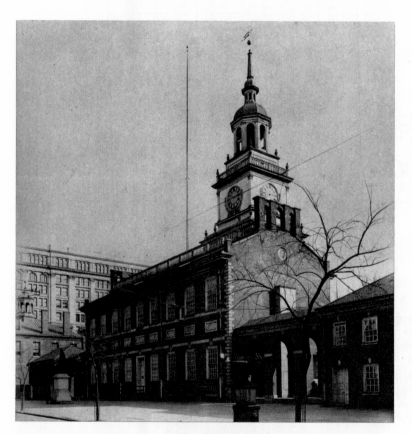

39 Andrew Hamilton. Independence Hall, Philadelphia. Begun 1731

three-arched loggia entrance, flanked by boldly projecting wings that end in semicircular turret-like masses, is a fine conception. The steeply pitched hip roof and the elongated dormers became common in Early Georgian domestic architecture in Virginia. The rather simple cupola, although a bit spindly, was obviously inspired by Wren's use of the device and became exceedingly popular in the American Georgian. The Palace (plate 37) and College, handsome as they are, are not much more than overblown houses.

The oldest extant public building of the period is Boston's charming little Town House, commonly known as the Old State House (1712–13, plate 38). The simple rectangular brick structure is capped by an ornate cupola. The stepped and ornamented end gables with their lion and unicorn decorations, the insignia of the English crown, are something of a throwback to the Tudor style. Like many Georgian public buildings, the Town House is of red brick with white trim and resembles an enlarged dwelling, even to the inclusion of dormer windows.

The most impressive of all Colonial public buildings is undoubtedly the legendary Independence Hall in Philadelphia (plate 39), Pennsylvania's Old State House, erected after a design by the Speaker of the Assembly, Andrew Hamilton. It was begun in 1731 and completed in 1753, although extensions and renovations continued beyond the turn of the century. It was a more satisfying structure before the erection of its rather heavy-handed, oversized tower in 1750. At that stage it consisted of a central building with a gambrel roof masked at the ends by a screen wall terminating in a cluster of four chimneys, an unusually rich variation of the Early Georgian form, and flanked by symmetrical smaller wings joined by loggias open to the north. The result was a well-proportioned, beautifully cadenced composition of solid masses and light arcades.

Other buildings worth attention are the historic market and "cradle of liberty," Faneuil Hall (1740–42, plate 40) in Boston, designed by the painter John Smibert and enlarged by Charles Bulfinch in 1805–06; and the remarkably advanced classical Redwood Library (1748–50) and the lovely small Brick Market (1761–72), both in Newport, R.I., and by Peter Harrison. Faneuil Hall was originally a long, narrow, two-story building with an open arcaded market on the ground floor, in the tradition of medieval guild halls, and in its altered state has continued to serve as a market center of Boston.

Peter Harrison (1716–1775), a successful sea captain, ship owner, and merchant, was the most interesting and best of the architectural practitioners of the pre-Revolutionary period. He accepted commissions at a nominal fee and, during the thirty years that he was active, designed some of the finest Colonial buildings in New England. In the Redwood Library (plate 41), based on a plate from Edward Hoppus's *Andrea Palladio*, Harrison re-

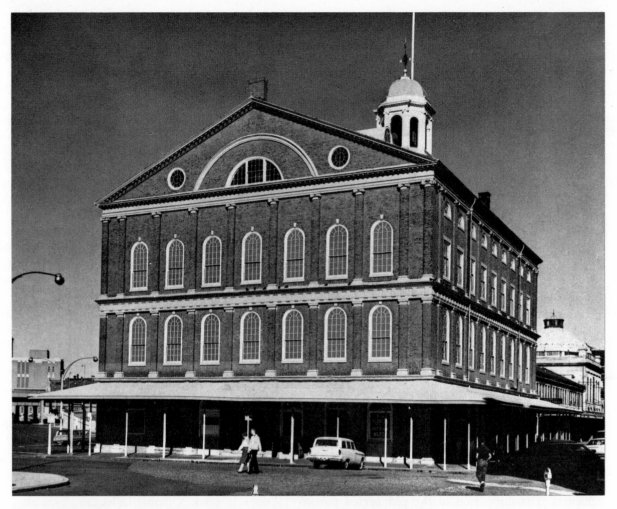

40   John Smibert. Faneuil Hall, Boston. 1740–42 (enlarged by Charles Bulfinch, 1805–06)

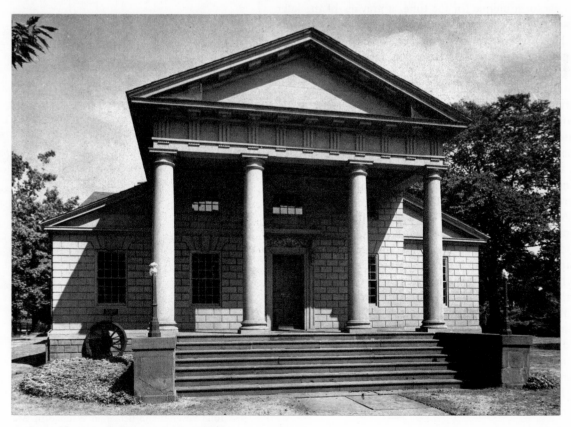

41   Peter Harrison. Redwood Library, Newport, R.I. 1748–50

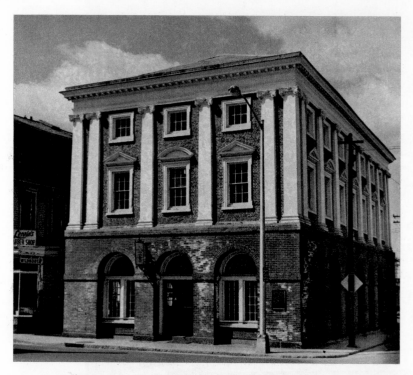

42 Peter Harrison. Brick Market, Newport, R.I. 1761-72

vealed an unexpected awareness of English neo-Palladianism. The disposition of the pedimented portico overshadowing the wings, the heaviness of proportions, and the severely restrained decoration create a quasi-temple form unique for the time, a preview of the later Classical Revival. The Brick Market (plate 42) is the gem of Harrison's architectural career. Deriving from Inigo Jones, it transforms the grandeur of the late Renaissance into something more modest without losing dignity. The lower floor is distinguished from the upper stages by a variant treatment of the brick, and its three clean arches framing the doorway and flanking windows serve as a base for the more elaborately decorated superstructure. The three-bayed facade is divided by pilasters, doubled at the ends, with alternating pedimented and arched windows on the second floor and square ones on the third level, all characteristic Palladian devices.

American concern with public education assured the construction of college buildings to house and board students as well as educate them. The earliest extant example and the model for much neo-Georgian college architecture of the twentieth century is Massachusetts Hall (1718-20, plate 43) at Harvard, planned by its president, John Leverett, and Benjamin Wadsworth. This four-story, red-brick dormitory, with its gambrel roof and masking screen walls at the ends, its six massive chimneys, and its flat and undecorated facade, differs from the typical Early Georgian house only in scale. Perhaps the most charming of Georgian college buildings

is Dartmouth Hall (plate 44), in Hanover, N.H., a clapboarded building painted white, beautifully proportioned, and capped by a delicate cupola. It was carefully reconstructed after a fire in 1904.

Since American colonization had been involved with European religious struggles of the seventeenth century, it was only natural that ecclesiastical building should be one of the primary American considerations. In the eighteenth century a greater religious tolerance was symbolized through the acceptance by practically all denominations of the basic Anglican church form developed by Wren. This was usually a long, naved structure with either a single tower and spire or cupola at the front or rising from a columnar porch. The form of the tower had been borrowed from the Gothic, but all its decorative details were now Classical, as were those of the body of the church itself. The Wrenian type was transplanted to the colonies early in the century and brought with it the Classical orders in columns and pilasters; elaborate cornices, balustrades, and urns; windows that were rectangular, roundheaded, Palladian, or bull's-eye; and columned interiors that were vaulted or made to appear so.

In the English colonies the earliest church in the Georgian mode, Bruton Parish (1711-15, plate 45) in Williamsburg, Va., is reputed to have been designed by Governor Alexander Spotswood, recently arrived from England. It is a stripped-down version of a Wren church done in brick. Unusual in its cruciform plan, it has a modest and rather ungainly square tower with a sim-

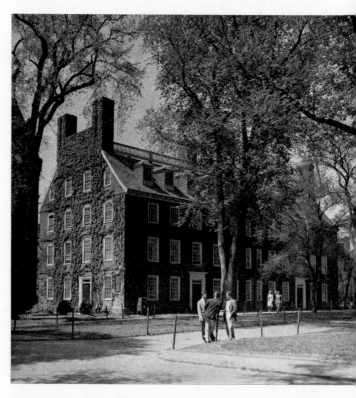

43 John Leverett and Benjamin Wadsworth. Massachusetts Hall, Harvard University, Cambridge, Mass. 1718-20

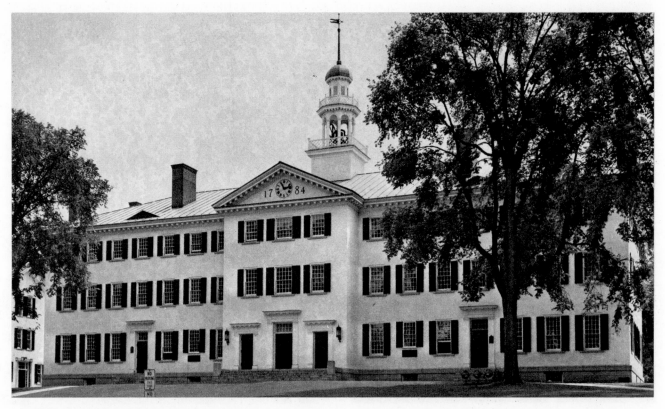

44 Dartmouth Hall, Dartmouth College, Hanover, N.H. 1784–91

plified octagonal spire, which were added in 1769, and a barnlike interior with stationary pews.

The largest of the Early Georgian churches are two in Boston: Christ Church, better known as "Old North," from whose belfry the light was flashed to Paul Revere, built in 1723 and designed by William Price, a Boston print dealer; and Old South Meeting House (plate 46), equally famous as the meeting place of the "Sons of Liberty," designed by Robert Twelves and built in 1729–30. These buildings established a type which dominated New England church architecture and was widely copied. Both are brick constructions of simple rectangular mass covered by peaked roofs and lit by two ranges of round-headed windows. The square towers in four stages separated by belt courses, which might very well be designated as "the Boston type," are capped by lofty wooden spires clearly dependent on English sources and emulating their Baroque richness in carpentry. Old South is broader in proportion and retains the meetinghouse plan with pulpit on the side: a large, open interior space with no particular focal point. The interior of Old North (plate 47) is divided into a nave and side aisles and has a gallery supported by square paneled piers and superimposed fluted ones rising to a false elliptically vaulted plaster ceiling.

A major problem facing Colonial church builders was the limited ability of local masons to cope with brick or stone vaulting. All the roofs were of wooden construction

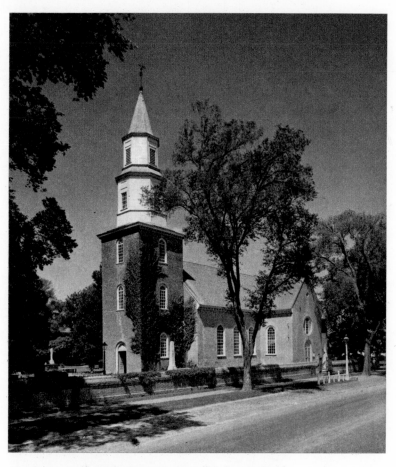

45 Governor Alexander Spotswood (attrib.). Bruton Parish Church, Williamsburg, Va. 1711–15

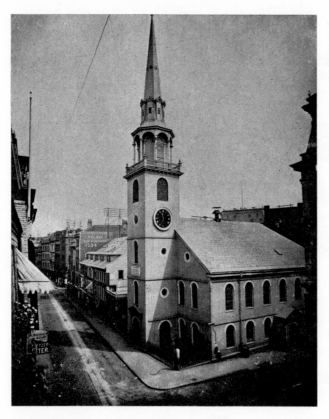

46 Robert Twelves. Old South Meeting House, Boston. 1729–30

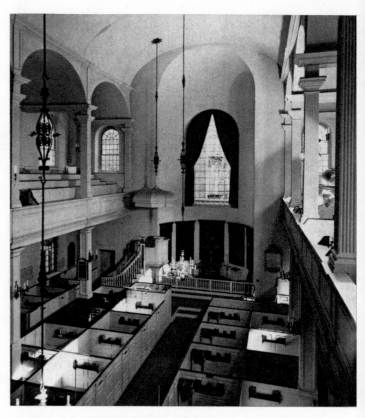

47 William Price. Interior, Christ Church ("Old North"), Boston. 1723

with hung ceilings formed and plastered to imitate vaulting. An analogous problem presented itself in the church spire. American steeples were inordinately high, and everything above the square brick tower was rendered in wood. They were crude and simplified versions of English models, but a redeeming feature is the almost spidery lightness of form, due, no doubt, to the nature of the carpentry itself.

Christ Church, Philadelphia, (1727–44), designed by Dr. John Kearsley, is the most advanced Early Georgian church. Its square tower is relatively early in character, but the rest is ornately decorated in the more lavish style of the High Georgian. The apse end exhibits an especially rich composition of Baroque architectural motifs centering on a great Palladian window flanked by niches. In the interior (plate 48), the use of giant columns and rich entablature is the first competent Colonial translation of the Wren-Gibbs manner.

High Georgian churches were larger in scale, more complex and refined in both plan and detail, and were usually characterized by the addition of a columnar portico on the west, or entrance, end. St. Michael's (1752–61, plate 49), in Charleston, S.C., is the finest of southern Georgian churches. Its attribution to Peter Harrison is about as farfetched as its occasional attribution to James Gibbs; a local builder, Samuel Cardy, is a

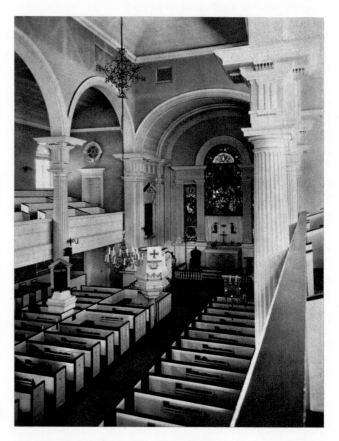

48 John Kearsley. Interior, Christ Church, Philadelphia. Begun 1727

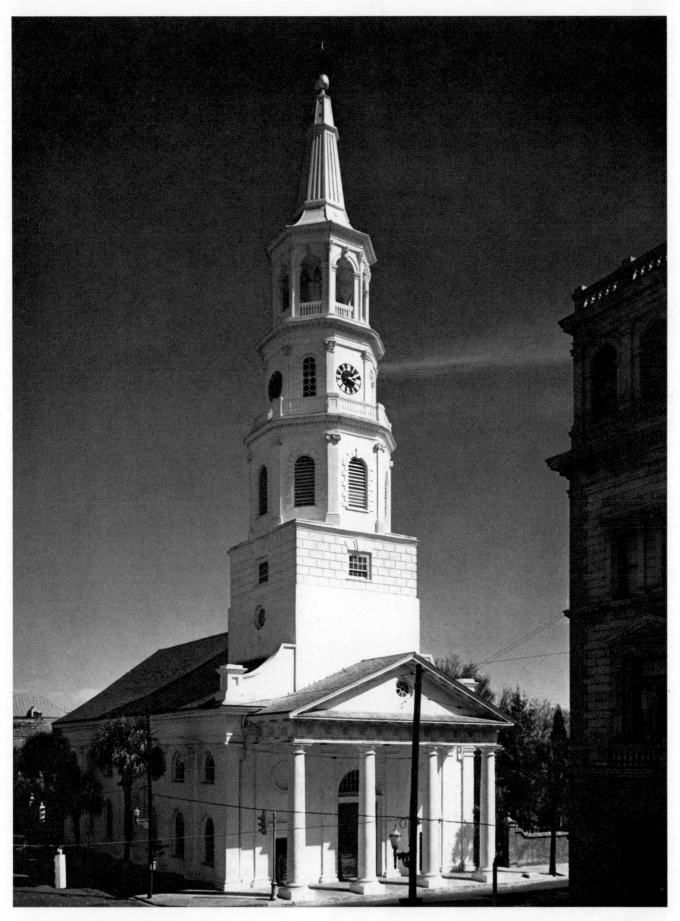

49 St. Michael's Church, Charleston, S.C. 1752–61

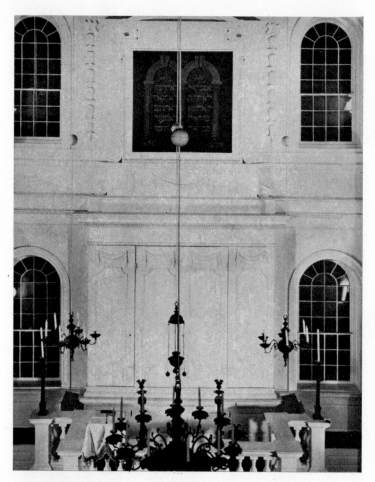

50 Peter Harrison. Interior, Jeshuat Israel (Touro Synagogue), Newport, R.I. 1759–63

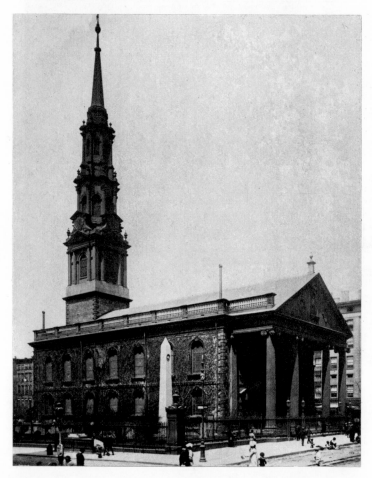

51 Thomas McBean. St. Paul's Chapel, New York. 1764–66

more likely candidate. In any case, St. Michael's has the first columnar church portico in the colonies.

Undeniably by Harrison is the unique Jeshuat Israel, or Touro Synagogue (1759–63), in Newport, R.I., the earliest extant example of its kind, built for one of the first communities of Jews in the New World. The commission presented an unprecedented problem, and Harrison approached it as a situation demanding something different both functionally and stylistically. The Jewish community's preference for a modest building influenced Harrison's design of an almost square house form of smooth stucco over brick, with large roundheaded windows, completely unaccented except for the small two-columned doorway porch on the west side. The brilliant Baroque interior (plate 50) is, however, one of the finest of the period. The plan calls for a raised and railed platform, or bema, in the center; a large, elegantly decorated Ark of the Covenant on the east wall; and a gallery to house the women and children during services. The gallery is supported by Ionic columns, the ceiling entablature by Corinthian. All the detailing is rich but restrained.

The richest and most knowledgeable High Georgian church is St. Paul's Chapel (plate 51) in New York, which was designed by Thomas McBean and was built in 1764–66 of Manhattan schist with brownstone trim. McBean, who is said to have studied with Gibbs, showed his training, or at least his acquaintance with the latter's handbook, in the design of the tall, all-brownstone belfry tower, the one Colonial tower that demonstrates some awareness of the subtle nuances of planned transition from one stage to the next in a continuous flow of geometric complexity and Baroque opulence. The interior (plate 52) also outstrips all others in richness and sophistication. The majestic columns and sumptuous decorative display are capped by a fully understood vaulting system, the only one in the colonies (but still false).

GEORGIAN DOMESTIC BUILDINGS

The American "classic" type of Georgian dwelling was a boxlike, two-story building with an attic floor lit by the newly introduced dormer windows. The plan was usually almost rigidly regular, with one room in each of the four corners and a central hallway leading to a richly balustered staircase. In place of 'the picturesque, free-form plan of the seventeenth-century house, the Georgian presented a rationally conceived, immutable shell, into which the process of living was forced. Indeed, the cultural style of the period was dominated by formal logic and elegance.

The houses of the southern landed gentry were larger and usually more sumptuous than those of affluent northerners, which were commonly town houses. The designs of these southern mansions, derived from the villa types

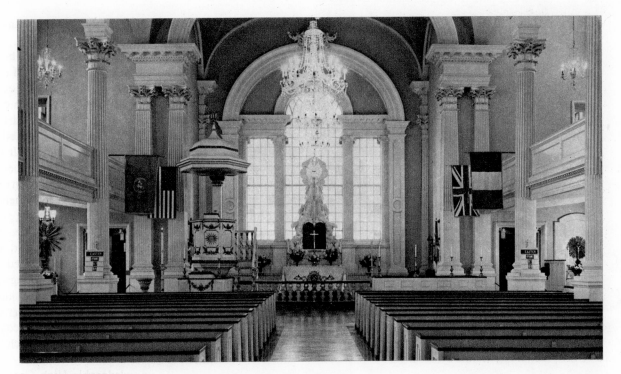

52 Thomas McBean. Interior, St. Paul's Chapel, New York. 1764–66
(restored to 18th-century appearance)

found in architectural manuals, were variously laid out in complexes consisting of a large central building, the house proper, symmetrically flanked by contiguous wings or separate structures housing kitchens, offices, and workshops, all carefully and rationally disposed amid lawns and formal gardens.

Symmetry dominated the exterior design and the plan of the Georgian house. The facade usually had five windows to a story, with additional spacing on either side of the central window for axial emphasis, and four windows on the sides. On the Early Georgian facade the center was emphasized by a richly ornamented doorway. Pilasters and engaged columns; rusticated quoins; scrolls and brackets; and pediments that might be angled, segmental, or broken with a carved ornament in the center—all were common. High Georgian had a slightly projecting central pavilion framing either the single central window or an augmented set of three, often defined by pilasters or quoins at the outer edges and capped by a pediment breaking above the cornice line. The more stately two-story columnar porch projection of the central pavilion occurred only after about 1750.

The most advanced Georgian roof type was the deck, but the earlier gambrel and hip roofs continued through the first half of the century, and an anomalous peak roof occasionally intruded. Commonly the deck roof was crowned by a balustered railing enclosing the so-called "captain's" or "widow's walk," and many houses were topped by a central cupola. Richly dentilated and bracketed cornices, as well as belt courses between stories,

tied the four sides into a unified whole, emphasizing the horizontal divisions of the structure, while pilasters and quoins reinforced the structural appearance of the corners. Since each room of the house now had its own fireplace on the outside wall or back-to-back on an interior wall, either four separate chimney stacks emerged on the exterior at the cornice line or, in the more advanced solution, two at the deck-roof line. There were, of course, many exceptions and variations.

All the detailing had a pronounced Baroque plasticity, more robust in the Early and more elegant in the High Georgian.

American building continued to translate European models in terms of local materials, though improved craftsmanship made building in brick and stone more common. New England, however, maintained a preference for wood, and the simulation of stone masonry in wood was fairly frequent. Elsewhere in the colonies brick and stone had become symbols of economic and social position, and where good stone was available, as in the Middle Atlantic colonies, it was increasingly employed, whereas brick became the preferred material in the South.

The interior was adapted to comfortable upper-class life. Compared with a seventeenth-century house, it had larger rooms and higher ceilings and was better lit. Room functions had become more specialized: a normal Georgian house had a kitchen, often relegated to an attached ell or an outbuilding; a dining room; a withdrawing, or drawing, room which also served as a

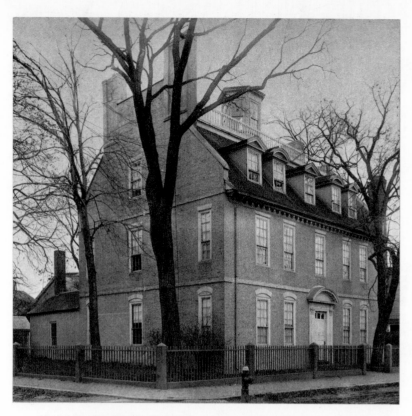

53 McPhedris-Warner House, Portsmouth, N.H. 1718–23

library; and a parlor or ballroom—all on the lower floor. The main bedrooms were on the second floor, with additional bedrooms for children and servants in the garret. In the southern plantation house the grand ballroom or saloon was occasionally on the second floor. A major distinction between Early Colonial and Georgian was the development of the modest entryway into an almost ceremonial hallway or reception room. Ceiling beams and joists were now hidden behind plastered and frequently decorated ceilings. Simple vertical wainscoting gave way in the formal rooms to richly articulated paneling in the finest walnut and mahogany. Wood was elaborately turned for balusters and carved for stair ends and overmantels with opulent Baroque motifs. Lesser rooms were painted or wallpapered, and even an occasional mural turns up.

Many authentic Georgian domestic buildings still exist. One of the earliest still standing is the McPhedris-Warner House (1718–23, plate 53), built by a merchant sea captain on the harbor of Portsmouth, N.H. This brick building, with its almost austerely simple facade, gambrel roof, and irregularity of plan, betrays its transi-

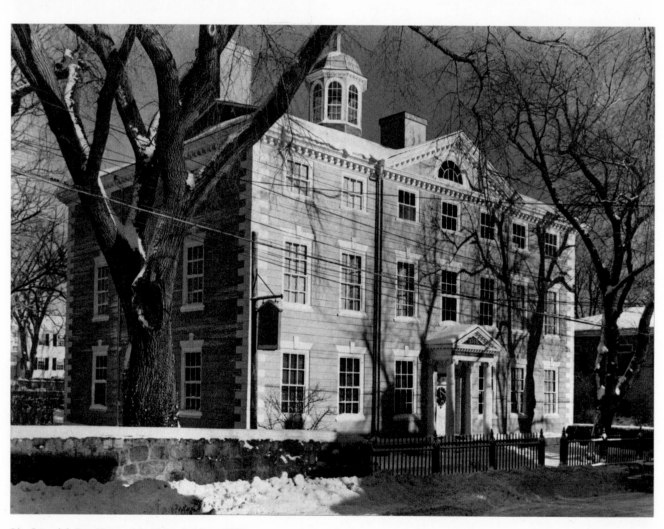

54 Jeremiah Lee House, Marblehead, Mass. 1768

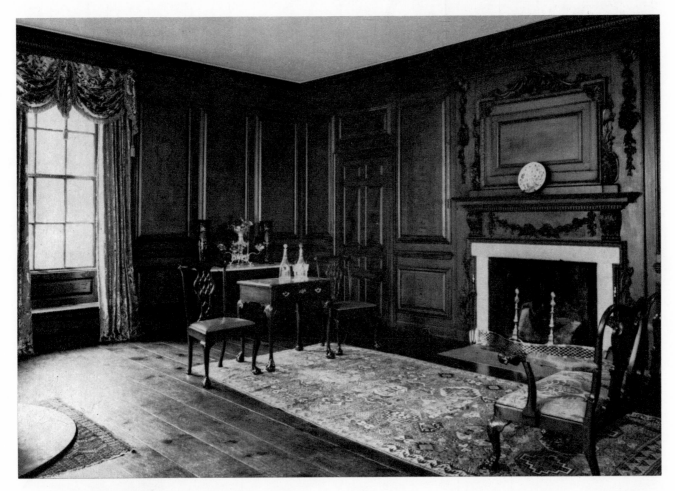

55 Parlor, Jeremiah Lee House, Marblehead, Mass. 1768

tional character. However, its alternating angular and segmental pedimented dormers and the decorated doorway reveal it to be a provincial imitation of English prototypes.

The finest High Georgian example in New England is the lavishly decorated Jeremiah Lee House (1768, plate 54), Marblehead, Mass. The wooden structure was sheathed in broad boards imitating courses of stone masonry, and the interior (plate 55) was finished in the choicest mahogany paneling and imported handpainted wallpapers. The overmantels were carved with garlands so richly executed that they could hardly have been done on this side of the Atlantic.

New York City now has few Georgian houses. The somewhat rustic Van Cortlandt Mansion (1748–49, plate 56) was built as a country house, and it is a curiously provincial building constructed of fieldstone. The interior is extremely simple, still somewhat Dutch and heavy in scale. The Morris-Jumel Mansion (1765, plate 57), built by Roger Morris, is more sophisticated. The original character of the house was probably changed by renovations during the Federal period, when an octagonal room was built onto the rear, at which time the

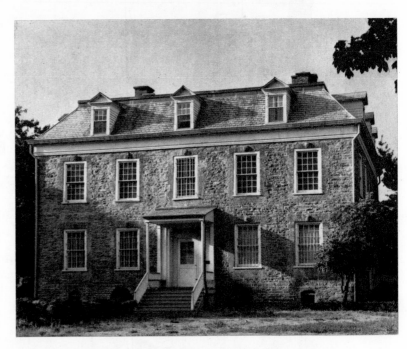

56 Van Cortlandt Mansion, New York. 1748–49

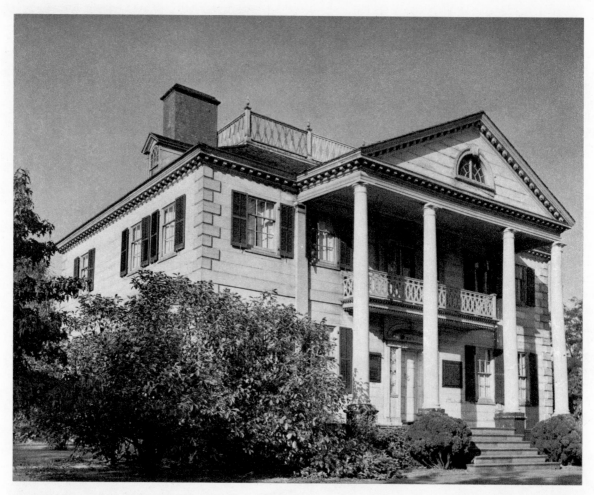

57 Morris-Jumel Mansion, New York. 1765

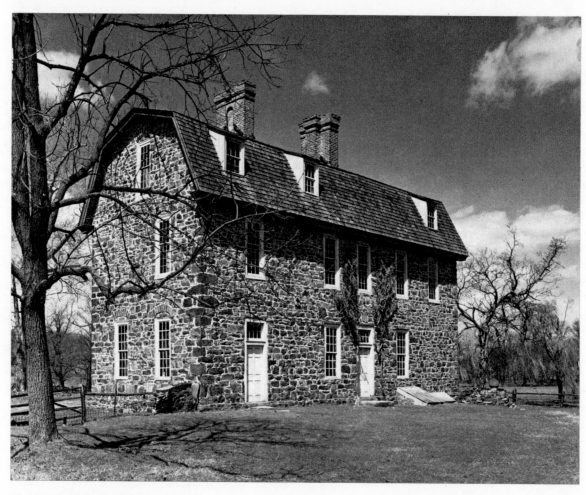

58 Graeme Park, Horsham, Pa. 1721–22

Neoclassic doorway and the railing at the cornice level may have been added. The giant portico may be original, but the slender columns seem Neoclassic in proportion.

Philadelphia, especially with its suburb of Germantown, still retains some splendid Georgian houses. Among Pennsylvania examples the deceptively rustic, barnlike Graeme Park (1721–22, plate 58) in Horsham is a long, narrow building of irregular courses of stone masonry which reflect both the limitations of local craftsmanship and the beauty of the natural material. Its ungainly gambrel roof, centrally located chimneys, and the asymmetrical spacing of its facade all hark back to the seventeenth century, but the interior is surprisingly impressive with its boldly scaled wooden paneling. In Philadelphia itself the small, brick Letitia Street, or William Penn, House (plate 59), later removed to Fairmount Park and restored, is one of the few modest houses left from this period. Dated sometime between 1703 and 1715, it is a very plain, almost nondescript box with a peaked roof. Such style as it shows is Georgian.

Among the more opulent houses of Philadelphia is the stone High Georgian Cliveden (1763–64, plate 60), in

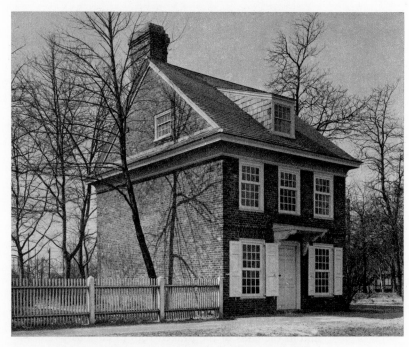

59 Letitia Street (William Penn) House, Philadelphia. 1703–15

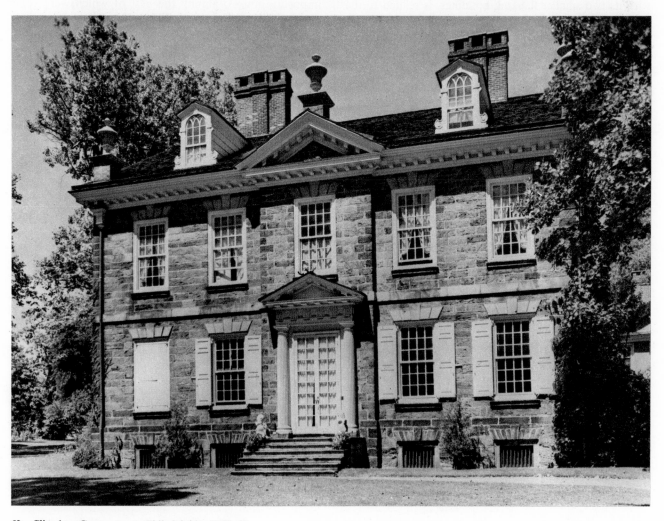

60 Cliveden, Germantown, Philadelphia. 1763–64

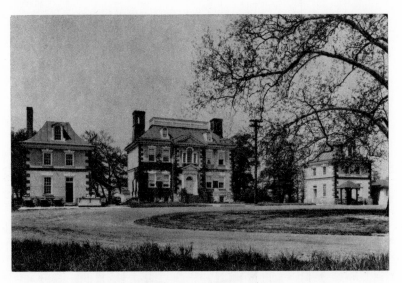

61 Mount Pleasant, Philadelphia (before restoration). 1761–62

Germantown, with its urns at the corners of the cornice and at the ends of the peaked roof (a curiously *retardataire* feature) and the scrolled dormers, which appear to have been a local Philadelphia device. The grandeur of Mount Pleasant (1761–62, plate 61), in Fairmount Park, with its two smaller flanking buildings, is related to the plantation houses of the South. It was built of rubble masonry and stuccoed, and, like Cliveden, has scrolled dormers. Its roofs are unique in the colonies, resembling the French mansard and in the side buildings flaring on the lower slope. Notable also are the two chimney stacks

on the main house, each a cluster of four joined by arches.

Virginia retains the largest number and finest examples of Georgian domestic architecture. Of the Early Georgian, Stratford (c. 1725–30, plate 62), in Westmoreland County, is exceptional in several respects. The central brick building, flanked by two smaller structures of the same material, is unusual in its H-plan, its basement and single-story elevation without dormers, its long and stately exterior stairways, and its quadruple-clustered chimneys. Yet, despite its beautiful siting and unique design, it is a strange mixture of handbook parts that hardly looks Georgian.

In contrast, Westover (c. 1730–34, plate 63), in Charles City County, is the paradigm, the most famous and perhaps the most beautiful, of all Georgian plantation houses. Set in a magnificent park, its imposing mass consists of a central building with attached wings capped by a steeply pitched hip roof and exceptionally tall chimneys. The comparatively flat facades of red brick with white trim set off the elaborately Baroque doorways of the front and rear. It has been attributed to Richard Taliaferro (1705–1779), the leading architect in Virginia during the Early Georgian.

The High Georgian in Virginia produced a series of imposing houses, among the best of which were some designed by John Ariss (c. 1725–1799). His major work, Mount Airy (1758–62, plate 64), borrowed almost literally from a plate in James Gibbs, is one of the rare stone houses of the South, distinguished by its stately entrance loggia of three arched openings on the south

62 Front (south elevation), Stratford, Westmoreland County, Va. c. 1725–30

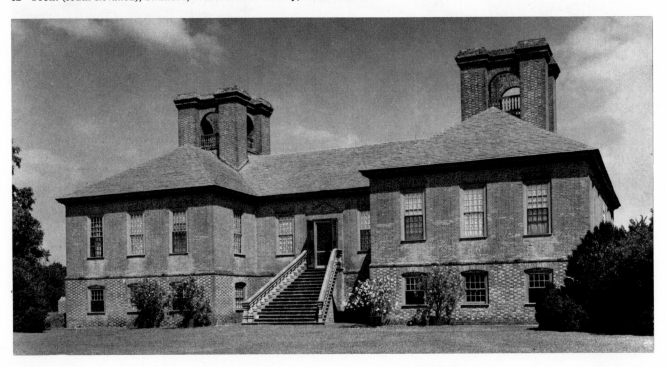

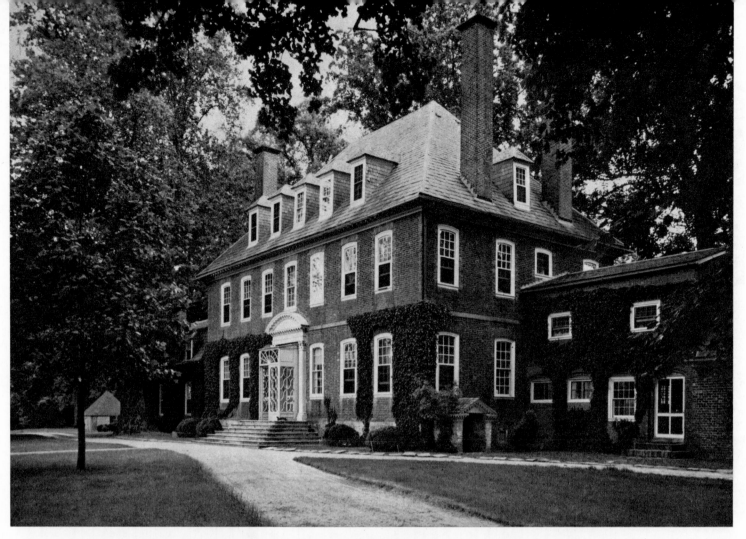

63　Richard Taliaferro (attrib.). Westover, Charles City County, Va. c. 1730–34

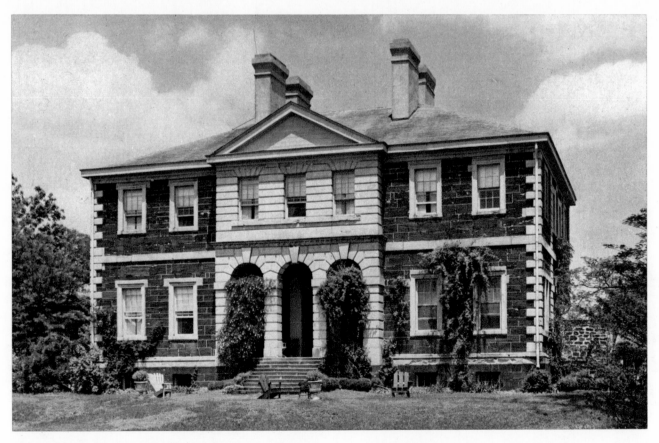

64　John Ariss. Mount Airy, Richmond County, Va. 1758–62

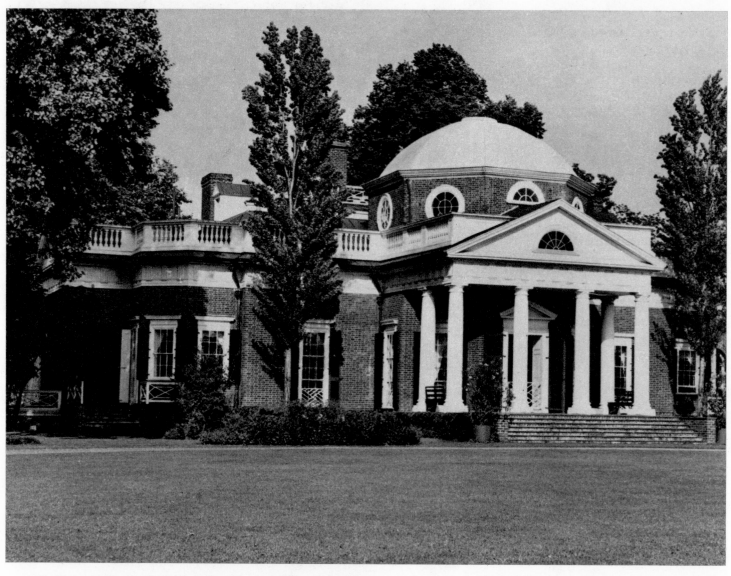

65 Thomas Jefferson. Monticello, Albemarle County, Va. 1770–1809

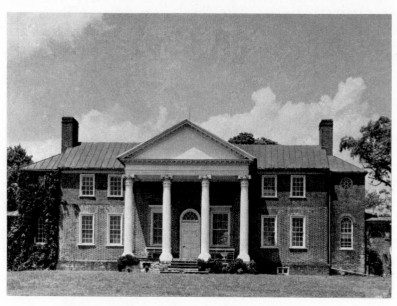

66 Whitehall, Anne Arundel County, Md. 1764

and three rectangular openings on the north facade. Thomas Jefferson's home, Monticello (1770–75, plate 65), was redone after the Revolution, but in its various earlier projections indicated a sequence of dependence on architectural handbooks and ultimately on Leoni's English edition of Palladio.

Maryland also boasts a series of handsome Georgian plantation houses. The most notable date from the middle of the century, including the majestic Whitehall (plate 66), in Anne Arundel County, built in 1764. Whitehall has one of the rare giant porticoes and an interior of architectural detailing in wood of palatial splendor. Annapolis, a thriving seaport in the pre-Revolutionary period, luckily retains many of the fine brick town houses built for its prosperous families. It produced an easily recognizable local type, with no dormer attic, a flattened roof hardly visible from below, and a front entrance raised above ground level by a half-story basement. The restrained exterior, cubical in appearance, was clear-edged and almost Neoclassic in feeling. Among the best of Annapolis houses are those attributed to William Buckland, including the three-story, boxlike Chase House (1769–74, plate 67). Buckland's houses are characterized by coherence of design and refinement of both proportion and detail, revealing a greater knowledge and experience in architectural practice than was common in the colonies.

South Carolina's prosperity was reflected in the great river plantation houses as well as the town houses of Charleston. The most imposing of the former is Drayton Hall (1738–42), and the most lavish of the latter is the Miles Brewton House (1765–69). Both have the typical Carolinian features of a comparatively wide, two-story, pedimented portico with Doric and Ionic orders and winged staircases. Drayton Hall was a spacious mansion with a basement floor given over to service and servants' quarters and a courtly reception hall on the first floor, above which was the grand ballroom. The Miles Brewton House (plate 68) presents a modest face toward the street, hidden as it is behind a high wall, but its rear garden elevation shows a rich elaboration, and its interior is one of the most succulent examples of Rococo influence in Colonial architecture.

(continued on page 57)

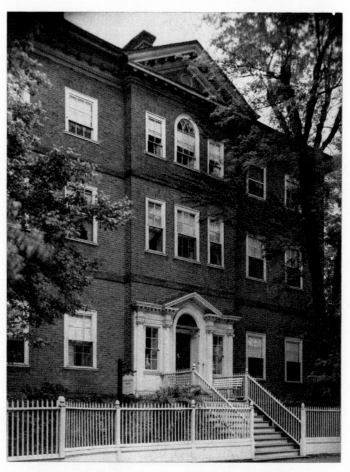

67   William Buckland (attrib.). Chase House, Annapolis, Md. 1769–74

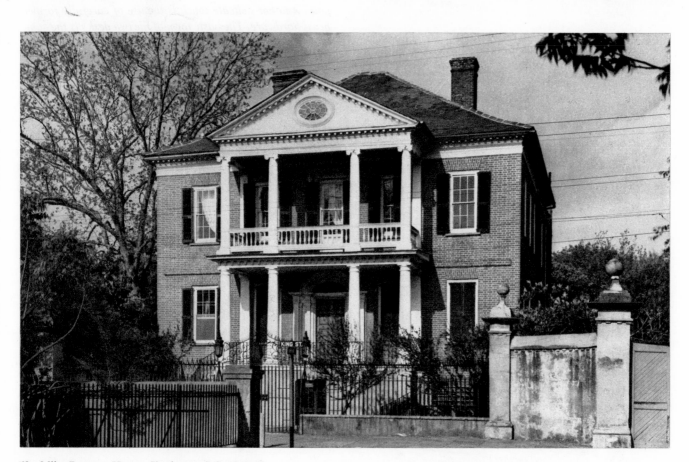

68   Miles Brewton House, Charleston, S.C. 1765–69

Eighteenth-Century Colonial Architecture   49

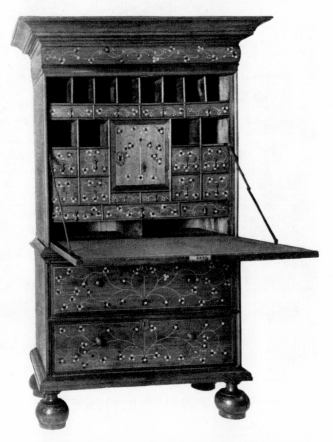

69 Fall-front desk for the Brinckerhoff family, from New York. c. 1690–1720. Cedar with inlay, height 66¾". The Museum of the City of New York. Gift of Mrs. Elon Huntington Hooker

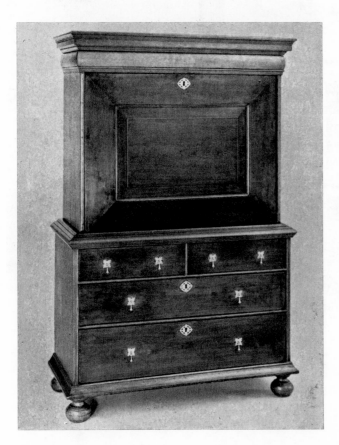

The William and Mary furniture style prevailed in the English-speaking colonies from the last decade of the seventeenth century through the first quarter of the eighteenth and was distinguished by the introduction of several new types as well as the modification of earlier forms. Several of the newer forms were derived from Dutch models, so that it is not surprising to find pieces such as the fall-front desk in both the English and former Dutch colonies. The desk made for the Brinckerhoff family of New York (plate 69) illustrates the continuity of Dutch ideals (cf. plate 8). Both of the desks illustrated have broad cornice moldings and flattened ball feet, and in both projecting moldings divide the component sections from the entablature to the base. The desk, while still massive, is more slender than earlier models, and the substitution of scroll-and-flower inlay for painting is another step away from the earliest styles.

In comparison with the Brinckerhoff desk, the one by the Philadelphia joiner Edward Evans (active 1702–19; plate 70) shows the late Baroque style noticeably refined by contact with England. Evans either copied his writing cabinet from an imported piece or, more likely, based it on a widely available pattern. As is typical of the William and Mary change of taste in woods, the cabinet is made of walnut, rather than oak, with drawer linings of cedar and pine. Another delicate touch is the use of carefully formed brass hardware. The basic form of the two desks is the same and ultimately derived from the same sources, but the work of Evans, for all its provincially severe construction, is a harbinger of the development of fine eighteenth-century American cabinetmaking.

As more rooms were added to the home and leisure time and increasing wealth permitted more specialized forms of furniture, the all-purpose stool and the trestle table gave way to new forms. Among those to achieve popularity during the William and Mary period and to continue into the Queen Anne era was the daybed, or couch (plate 71), a variation on the caned chair. It was usually from five to six feet long and had either a caned or wooden slatted back. The daybed had a thin mattress and, often, a pillow for the head, when it was being used as a recliner. When the home was filled with visitors, the parlor became a sleeping room and the daybed an emergency bed. Being fairly lightweight, the daybed was portable.

This version has eight legs of the block-and-vase variety, the two at the foot being of the type commonly (and incorrectly) called "Spanish feet." The form comes from Portugal, where it is known as a "paintbrush foot," and it is found on many William and Mary chairs. This example is a transitional piece, with the older form of turnings and feet but a later Queen Anne style head.

70 Edward Evans. Fall-front desk, from Philadelphia. 1707. Walnut, height 66½". Colonial Williamsburg, Williamsburg, Va.

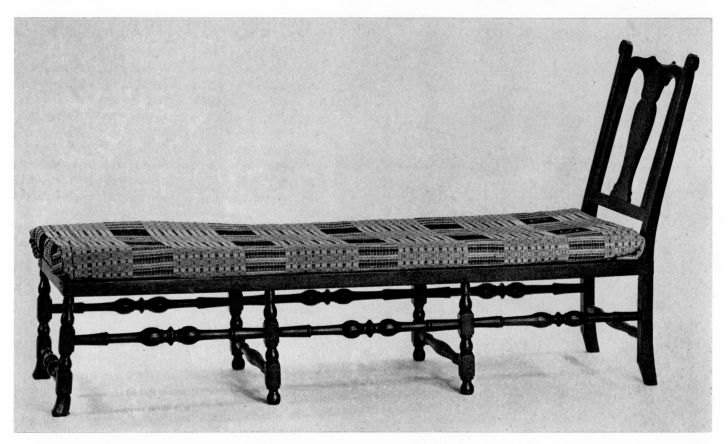

71 Daybed, from New England. c. 1725. Beech. Wadsworth Atheneum, Hartford, Conn.

The gateleg table (plate 72), another innovation in fur-niture, is an outgrowth of the space-saving furniture of the earliest Colonial days and is the cousin of the folding table (plate 7). The gateleg table was entirely the work of the turner, who skillfully balanced the proportions of the legs with those of the stretchers, while adjusting the turnings to allow sufficient room for clearance as the gates open and close. All but the frame and drawer linings of this specific table are made from the primary wood, walnut, but this was not always the case. For economy secondary woods such as pine were often used for legs and stretchers, for pine took stain readily and was much cheaper than walnut or other primary woods. This particular turner used the "paintbrush foot," which provides an interesting juxtaposi-tion with the turnings of the legs. The gateleg type soon disappeared, but its descendant, the drop-leaf folding table, has survived till our own time.

By the time this chest (plate 73) was made by a traditional joiner, walnut and maple had emerged as the major primary woods, and such elements as elongated turnings and the "paintbrush foot" had been introduced. In the smaller towns of New England, however, tradition died hard, and, except for switching from oak to the widely available tulip, most of the earlier forms and methods survived through the end of the Revolutionary period. And as rural

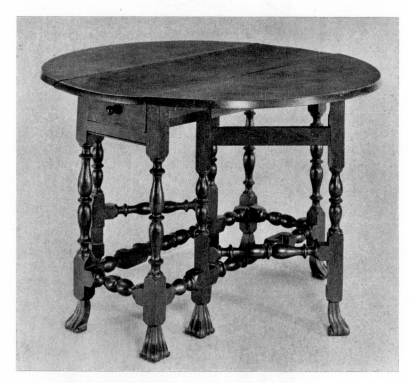

72 Gateleg table, from Massachusetts. 1700–30.
Walnut and white pine, height 27⅝", depth (open) 41⅜".
Colonial Williamsburg, Williamsburg, Va.

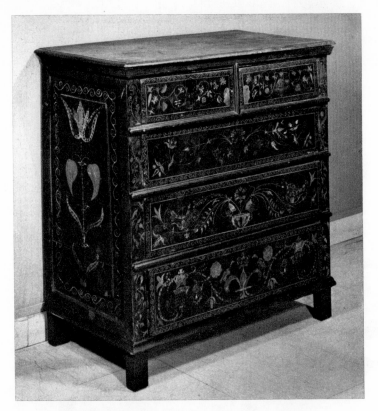

73 Chest of drawers, from Guilford area, Conn. c. 1700. Tulip, oak, and pine, width, 44¼″. Wadsworth Atheneum, Hartford, Conn. Gift of J. P. Morgan

Connecticut was to remain a center of conservatism in painting, so also along the coastline of Connecticut traditional painted furniture retained its vitality.

In this typical joined form, the native soft tulip wood was first primed with red stain and then decorated in cheery red, yellow, and white on a black background. As on so many pieces identified with the Guilford-Saybrook area, the decoration here takes the form of crowns, fleurs-de-lis, thistles, and roses, all motifs identified with the English royalty. On the margins of the frame there are delicate vines and simple bilaterally symmetrical scroll patterns. The large tulips on the sides are almost standard. Some examples have more sophisticated trumpet turnings or carved stretchers, but the style of painting and range of subjects remained fairly constant for another three generations. Throughout the eighteenth century and even the nineteenth, regional styles in rural areas would continue to survive side by side with the latest in furniture and other household arts.

The slat-back chair is usually rush-seated, like the "Brewster" type (plate 5), and has turned upright and horizontal members. In some the vertical members terminate in finely formed finials (plate 74). This refined example illustrates the difference between the basic form of the mid-seven-

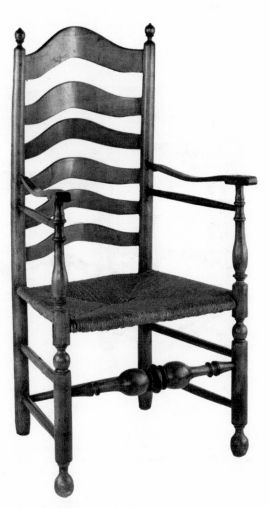

74 Slat-back armchair, from Pennsylvania. c. 1725. Maple, height 46½″. Greenfield Village and the Henry Ford Museum, Dearborn, Mich

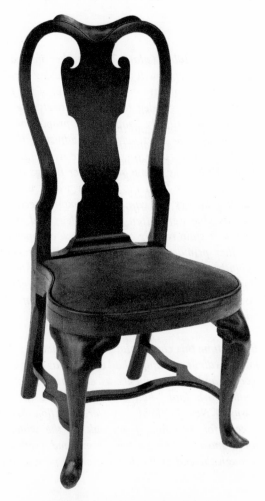

75 Side chair, from Philadelphia. 1740–50. Walnut with leather slip seat, height 40″. Philadelphia Museum of Art. Gift of Mr. and Mrs. J. Wells Henderson

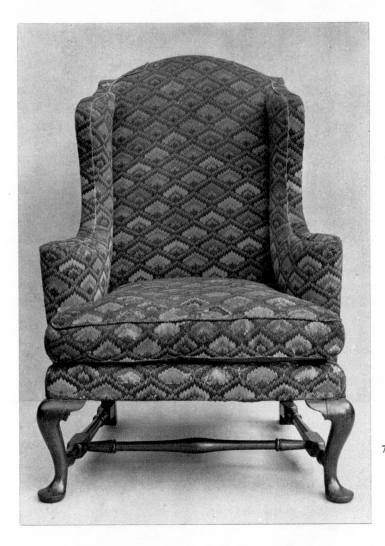

76 Queen Anne wing chair, from New
England. c. 1725–50. Walnut and
maple with needlepoint, height 46¾″.
The Metropolitan Museum of Art,
New York. Gift of Mrs. J. Insley Blair

teenth century and that of the third decade of the eighteenth. Graceful proportions are evident in the Baroque
turnings of both stretchers and arm supports, in the graduated arched slats, and in the flat arms echoing the shape
of the slats. The undulation of the slats and arms and the
contrast of the turned parts, like the light-and-dark contrasts in paintings of the period, are manifestations of the
late Baroque, which, by the 1720s, was being replaced by
the French-influenced Rococo style. As a rural survival, the
slat-back form lasted well into the nineteenth century.

In the early years of the eighteenth century, styles that
developed in England took some time to take root on these
shores. Thus the forms associated with the reign of Queen
Anne (1702–14) first appeared here about 1725, dominated
the decorative arts until at least midcentury, and in smaller
towns survived to the end of the century. During the Queen
Anne period most of the massive forms associated with the
earlier Jacobean era, modified in the William and Mary
years, were transformed into lighter and more graceful
ones. Elegant simplicity and curving outlines became the
rule, and ornament was greatly subdued. The heyday of the
joiner and turner was succeeded by the age of the cabinetmaker. The S-shaped curve, the single most important

motif, was carried through all the decorative arts — furniture, metalwork, ceramics, and so on — but its most
common use was on fine furniture. It is found in the splats
of chair backs and in cabriole legs of chairs, chests, and
desks, most of which, at this time, were made of walnut.

Of all the furniture forms in the Queen Anne period,
the chair best illustrates the attributes of the style: the
recurving line that is its basic silhouette, the repeated
curve in the vase-shaped splat, and the cabriole leg.
Either leather or textiles replaced the wooden or rush
seat of earlier years. Regional differences are important,
but all areas share the qualities already mentioned. This
example (plate 75) is from Philadelphia, and the fiddle-
back splat points to its place of manufacture. Not breaking completely with tradition, the cabinetmaker maintained
the straight line of the inside of the front legs and, even
more significant, opted for structural security by his re-
fusal to give up stretchers between the legs.

One of the forms to develop in the Queen Anne period was
the upholstered easy, or "wing," chair, a type remarkably
uniform in its appearance from area to area. Typical elements of the form, as seen in this Boston example (plate
76), include the S-curved cabriole legs, curved and rolled

arms, and the continued use of turned stretchers connecting and strengthening the legs. As well as providing simple comfort, the upholstering of the armchair was meant to soften the massiveness of the earlier chairs. Regional differences consist in matters of detail: New England chairs tend to have the square rear leg illustrated here, while New York examples, following English models, have a rounded rear leg, often ending in a square foot. Probably most of the chairs were covered with commercially made material, though some, such as this one, were covered with hand-embroidered work. The front is an overall flame-stitch pattern, and on the back the same colors are used in a fanciful landscape that includes trees and flowers, a shepherd and flock, running deer, and a variety of acrobatic birds swirling through the sky.

Both the English and the Dutch had a history of interest in the Orient, and many Eastern items were being imported into New England, New York, and the South in the early eighteenth century. Supply did not equal demand, and imitations of such goods were produced with varying degrees of success. The most desired items of furniture were lacquered wares, impossible to duplicate in the West. The English substituted a method of japanning and exported much of their work to the colonies, but before 1720 furniture makers in Boston and New York were turning out their own versions. The colonials painted the desired Oriental motifs on a fine-grained wood, building up the pictorial areas with various substances, and then varnished over the whole surface. Typical elements of the painting included real and fanciful animals, flowers, and human figures of Chinese aspect, often drawn to no particular scale but filling most of the available space. On this Queen Anne example (plate 77) the figures disport themselves on the body of the chest, and other decoration is confined to the peripheral areas of the piece. The cabriole legs, curved broken pediment, and shell forms are characteristic Queen Anne features of the period. The rage for japanned work had passed after about 1770.

The Chippendale period introduced modifications and variations of Queen Anne forms rather than entirely new

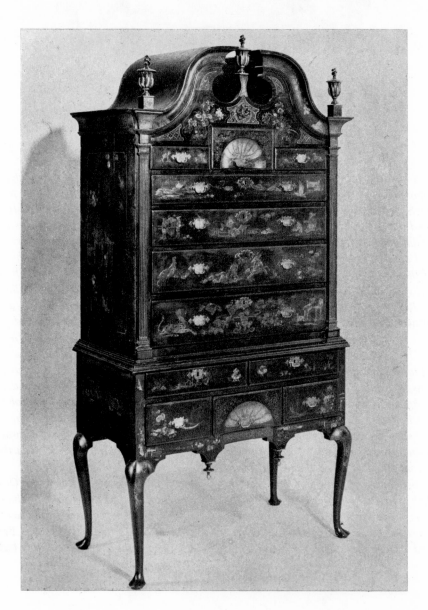

77 High chest of drawers, from Boston. 1740–60. Maple with white-pine frame, height 84½″. Colonial Williamsburg, Williamsburg, Va.

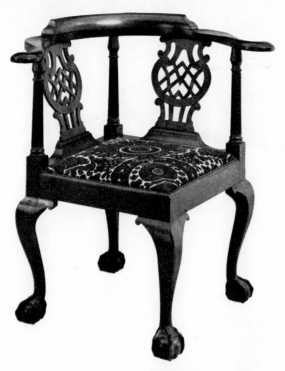

78 Corner chair, from Massachusetts or Rhode Island. 1760–90. Mahogany with maple, height 31″. Colonial Williamsburg, Williamsburg, Va.

portance, the shell and other natural forms were integrated into many patterns, whirls and spirals abounded, and the Oriental influence was undiminished. The popularity of the English cabinetmaker Thomas Chippendale was immense, and his book of furniture designs had a profound influence throughout the colonies. Carving and gilding are an important part of the Rococo style in general, and the Chippendale emphasis on those techniques caused a division of labor in the artisan class: the cabinetmaker constructing his chests and chairs, the gilder and carver producing wall brackets, picture frames, and looking glasses.

The accent on carving in the Chippendale era made woods with close grain, notably mahogany, the most popular for furniture. For gilded pieces, however, soft, easily carved woods such as pine were used. The gilded mirror (plate 79) with intricate white and gold painted

types of furniture. The corner chair, which attained popularity in this period, was in the best tradition of space-saving, and it was treated exactly like a side chair or armchair and might be part of a larger dining-room set. What was different, however, was that the splats were now not only shaped but also pierced; bow-shaped cresting rails were common; and several varieties of legs and feet were utilized. Obviously, piercing the splat provided the chairmakers with the opportunity for imaginative innovation and an almost infinite number of designs. The cresting rails had elaborately carved "ears" with shell or other natural forms. Finally, the feet could be treated in several ways. The example here (plate 78) has the extremely popular claw-and-ball foot, found from Newport to Charleston, but actually considered out of date by this time. Many straight-legged chairs had Chinese-influenced, squared Marlborough feet or other forms then in fashion.

This chair has extremely elaborate pierced splats, which are double because it fits into a corner; a very curvaceous rail and legs; and a rare form of fluted-column vertical supports. It is not so delicate as the Philadelphia mirror (plate 79) but, by contrast, has a feeling of solid and almost understated dignity. Combining features of several regions, this example illustrates the catholic appeal of the style and the diversity of decoration within a clearly defined framework.

The new wave of immigrant painters brought the Rococo style to the colonies at midcentury, and the interest in silk, lace, and satin, as seen in their portraits, was matched in the decorative arts by a similar concern for lushness of materials and ornament. The S curve retained its im-

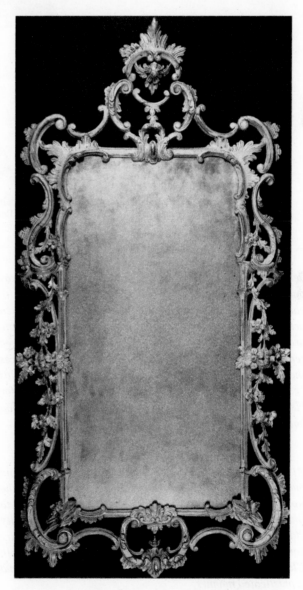

79 James Reynolds. Mirror. 1770. White pine and tulip, gilded and painted, height 55½″. The Henry Francis du Pont Winterthur Museum, Del.

Eighteenth-Century Colonial Architecture 55

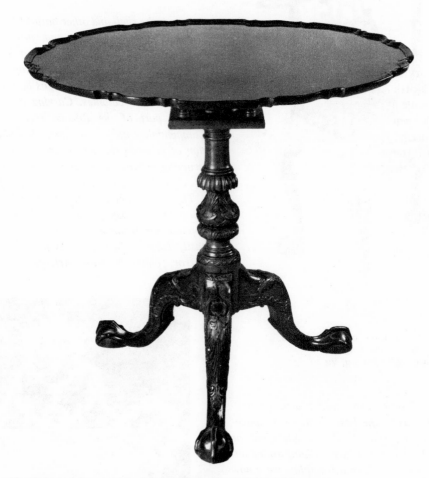

80 Chippendale tea table, from Philadelphia. 1760–75. Mahogany,
height 29″. Museum of Fine Arts, Boston. M. and M. Karelik Collection

designs illustrates the lightness and naturalism that was one side of the Rococo. The simple designs associated with earlier painted furniture have given way to a sophisticated arrangement of foliage and flowers that gently undulate around the mirror, and flat cornice-like forms have been replaced with such buoyant decoration as that which graces the top of the mirror. A craftsman such as James Reynolds (c. 1736–1794) had a finger on the pulse of his patrons, for his work was in great demand, and many a fine Philadelphia home was enriched by it.

At the time of the Revolution, Philadelphia was the second most populous city in the entire British Empire, and the work of its craftsmen was the closest in style and skill to that of London of any colonial center. In no other city did the use of carved decoration achieve such a plasticity nor did other cabinetmakers manage to combine both Classical and Rococo forms in such a successful and sophisticated manner.

The pedestal table (plate 80), used primarily for serving

tea, is a form which had developed during the Queen Anne period, but only after midcentury did it achieve the mature form shown here. The beautifully carved claw-and-ball feet flow into cabriole legs, which join at a complex multi-level pedestal. A fluted Doric column is joined to a Chinese-influenced vase which, in turn, supports a bird-cage base. The pie-crust top can both turn and fold down against the bird cage when the table is not in use, and it resembles the edging of fine silver trays and salvers. What gives this particular type its distinctly Philadelphia grandeur is not only the sensitive blend of Classical and Oriental elements but also the rich and graceful carving. The decoration is neither so sedate as that on the corner chair (plate 78) nor as frivolous as that on the mirror (plate 79), but rather blends the best of both. The legs are solid and powerful, yet have rich grass forms flowing down them, denying massiveness, and the alternating concavity and convexity of the pedestal provide a subtle transition to the otherwise austere column. Finally, the scalloped edge plays against the solidity of the circular top, continuing the rich contrast found throughout this mature example of the Chippendale style.

(continued from page 49)

SPANISH COLONIAL ARCHITECTURE

The eighteenth century saw the greatest efflorescence of Spanish building in North America and produced several monuments that in scale and aesthetic sophistication are far superior to anything achieved in the English colonies. In New Mexico some of the modest mission churches later rebuilt still exist, the most famous being San Francisco de Asís (1772), the picturesque little church at Ranchos de Taos, which continued the older New Mexican tradition of adobe building (plate 81). Primitive in plan and construction, it is most notable for the massive buttressing of its squat towers and apse. Its trapezoidal battered sides and the boldly simple cubical volumes, made soft and fluid by the adobe surfacing, give it the appearance of some primordial structure organically emerged from the desert flat.

Far different was the rich Baroque architectural expression of Texas and Arizona, a provincial but quite informed version of the Churrigueresque (that frenzied explosion of the late Baroque in Spain made popular by the architect José Churriguera). Texas was a tough and unprofitable territory, but the Spaniards managed to establish twelve missions in the south and central regions, of which five, all around San Antonio, still stand in varying states of preservation. San José y San Miguel de Aguayo (1723–31), the most splendid of them, covered 8 acres surrounded by a wall, and included facilities for administration, priests, supporting troops, and Indians.

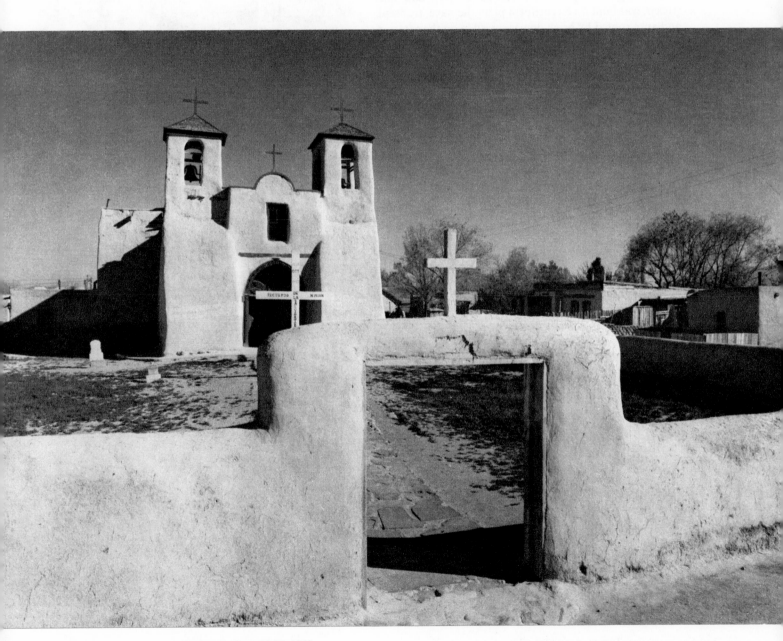

81 San Francisco de Asís, Ranchos de Taos, N.M. 1772

The mission church was built of tufa surfaced in stucco with detailing in brown sandstone. Local Indians may have supplied the labor and many of the basic skills, but the planning and technological level of building were European. The nave contained three stone groin-vaulted bays and a fourth capped by a 60-foot dome; the church was entirely restored in 1933. Its facade is typically Churrigueresque. The elaborate carving around the doorway and window of the central section (plate 82), probably the finest example of its kind in the United States, was executed by Pedro Huizar, a Mexican sculptor imported for the job.

Of more than a dozen missions founded in Arizona during the eighteenth century, only one remains intact today, but that was the most ambitious of all the Spanish missions in North America—San Xavier del Bac (1784–97). The church (plate 83), of baked brick and lime stucco, was built on a cruciform plan, the nave, transept, and apse roofed by brick domes invisible on the exterior, and the crossing marked by a high dome on an octagonal drum. Two elaborate towers flank the central facade of red brick, which is buried in a profusion of Churrigueresque ornament.

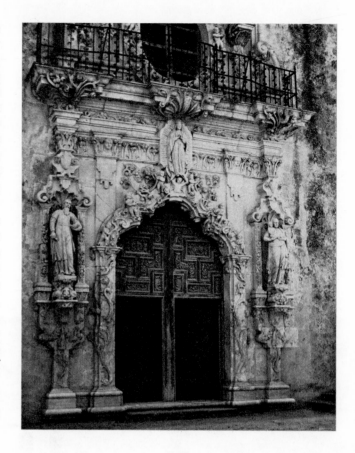

82 Pedro Huizar. Portal sculptures, San José y San Miguel de Aguayo, San Antonio, Tex. 1723–31

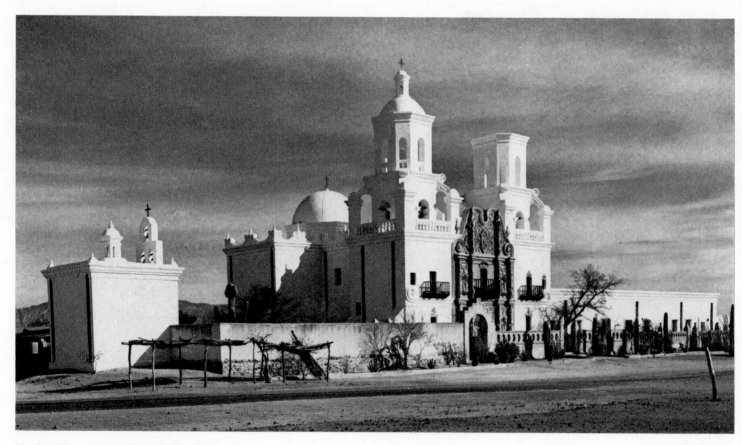

83 San Xavier del Bac, Tucson, Ariz. 1784–97

FRENCH COLONIAL ARCHITECTURE

Although France had a brilliant history of exploration in the New World, her colonial population was never large, and settlements were widely scattered. Very little remains even of this limited activity. However, New Orleans still retains something of its Creole flavor in the Vieux Carré (old quarter), and the French domestic-building type that developed in the Louisiana Territory had a belated effect on the antebellum architecture of the so-called "Black Belt."

Aside from the large public buildings of New Orleans, French architecture in the Mississippi Valley during the eighteenth century was of a frontier variety. The houses were half-timbered but unlike the English in construction. Walls were built of upright cypress or cedar logs driven several feet into the ground and spaced several inches apart, and the interstices were filled with a mixture of clay and grass or Spanish moss. A variation on this technique used rubble stone in clay for filling. However, since surfaces were left exposed, filling eroded and logs rotted in the ground. A structural improvement consisted of vertical logs resting on wooden sills supported by stone foundations. In Louisiana a soft, porous brick was used as filling, and the whole was covered with lime plaster, a building technique that became popular in New Orleans.

Frontier houses were usually one story in height, containing a row of rooms, with chimneys in the center or on the ends, the whole surrounded by a railed porch, which offered access to the rooms. The roof was a steeply pitched hip which covered the house proper and swept out at a lower angle to be supported by slender posts. The best-known example of the frontier house is the so-called Cahokia Courthouse (c. 1737, plate 84), in Illinois, originally a dwelling but sold to the town in 1793 for a courthouse and jail. It is comparatively large, with four rooms and an attic and brick chimneys on the ends.

The plantation houses in the lower parishes of Louisiana were larger, mostly two stories in height, the lower of stucco-covered brick, the upper of wood, but they had much in common with the frontier type and may have evolved from the "raised cottages" along the river bottoms, built on stilts to avoid flooding. A notable example is Parlange (1750, plate 85). A *galerie* with slender colonnettes circles the entire building, which is capped by a hip roof of cypress shingles. Such houses were essentially informal—spacious, open, and simple.

New Orleans was settled fairly early by the French, in 1718. It was a planned town, laid out on a grid along the river, with the Place d'Armes, now Jackson Square, surrounded by a church, school, and governor's palace, forming the heart of the Vieux Carré. It became the capital of Louisiana five years later and soon dominated the settlements along the river as far north as St. Louis. New Orleans remained French in character even after

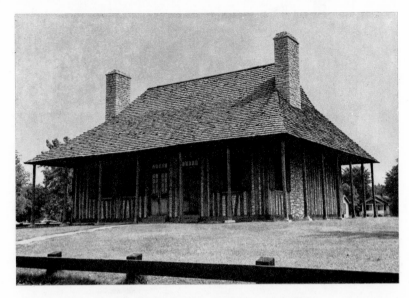

84 Cahokia Courthouse, Cahokia, Ill. c. 1737 (re-erected 1939)

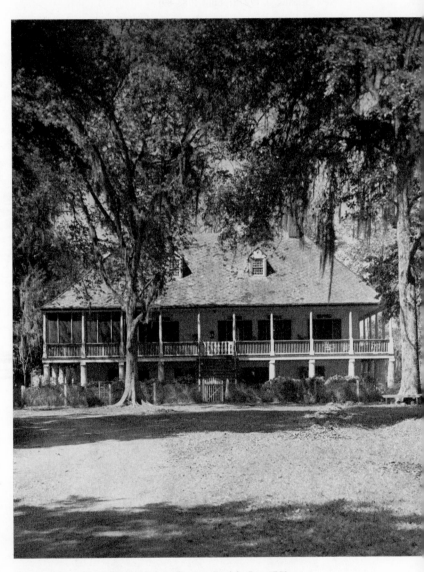

85 Parlange, New Roads, Pointe Coupee Parish, La. 1750

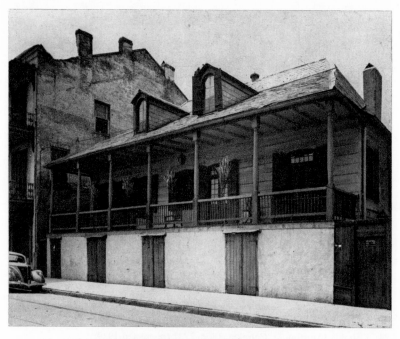

its cession to Spain in 1763, although its unusual mixture of peoples—French, Spanish, Canary Islanders, and Acadians (Cajuns)—gave it a particular flavor. Little of eighteenth-century New Orleans is left. The Jean Pascal House (c. 1727, plate 86), better known as "Madam John's Legacy," is of two stories, the lower enclosed, but deriving perhaps from the "raised cottage" type.

Among the public buildings left in New Orleans is the Cabildo (1795, plate 87). Built during Spanish rule to house the legislative and administrative council of the colony, this rather academic, classicizing Baroque stone edifice, except for its mansard roof (added in the 1850s), is an excellent example of Spanish official Colonial architecture. French, as well as Spanish, architectural monuments of the eighteenth century remain as relics of cultures aborted by the expansion of the new and independent nation of the United States of America.

86 Jean Pascal House ("Madam John's Legacy"), New Orleans. c. 1727 (rebuilt 1788–89)

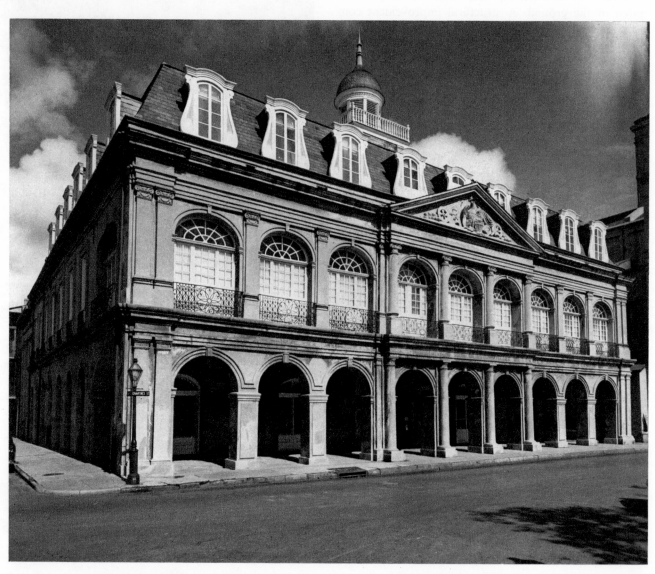

87 The Cabildo, New Orleans. 1795

4
Eighteenth-Century Colonial Painting and Sculpture

The eighteenth century brought with it a widening of the social and cultural gap between merchants and planters, on the one hand, and, on the other, workers and artisans in the cities and independent farmers in the rural areas. Those who could afford to lived in splendid houses and wore satin rather than homespun, used silver instead of pewter, bought fine china, ordered the best furniture, sat for their portraits.

As a luxury, painting required wealth, and for the first time in colonial history such wealth was available. The dominant form of painting in those years was portraiture, because, first, the portrait offered the most obvious status support and ego inflation to the nouveau riche, and second, with what remained of Puritan reserve, portraiture was more acceptable than "frivolous" forms such as landscape, still life, or genre painting. Also, the English, to whom the colonials looked for inspiration, were almost totally committed to portraiture.

For the English colonist, a collection including other forms of painting, to say nothing of sculpture, was almost inconceivable. Only among the Dutch in New York was the tradition of art collecting, so common among the burghers of Holland, to be found. In the South the remarkable Colonel William Byrd II of Virginia, who had pictures purported to be by Titian and Rubens, no doubt mementos of his sojourn in England, was exceptional.

From the early part of the eighteenth century, at least partly trained painters migrated to this country to try their luck. They were mostly marginal professionals, only slightly more adept than artisans, though conversant with academic standards and formulas. The style they brought with them was that of fashionable European portraiture of the late seventeenth and early eighteenth centuries, exemplified in England by the court painter, Sir Godfrey Kneller (1646/9–1723), a limited and unimaginative artist of German birth and Dutch training. He carried into the eighteenth century a style that went back to Van Dyck and Lely, both of whom had been in their time court painters also. Kneller's was a much more modest art, largely middle-class in attitude and pedestrian in execution, though its striving for the aristocratic ideal

is almost pitifully evident. Even before the migration of trained European painters to America some of the anonymous limners were responding, though tentatively and often in a garbled manner, to basic changes in style. It was engravings that first spread the new fashions in portraiture in the colonies, and from them were borrowed poses, gestures, dress, symbols of rank, and other obvious details.

However, many portraits of the time resemble those of the seventeenth century in their bold linearity and flat patterning, as does the *Mrs. Anne Pollard* (1721, plate 88). The hard-edged literalness in this portrait of a cen-

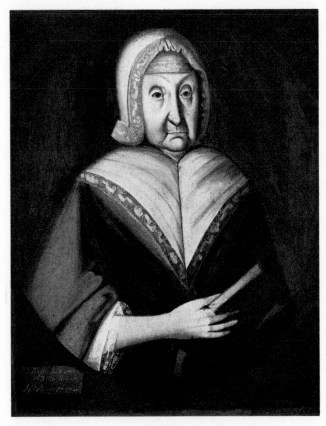

88 Anonymous. *Mrs. Anne Pollard.* 1721. Oil on canvas, 27½ × 22½″. Massachusetts Historical Society, Boston

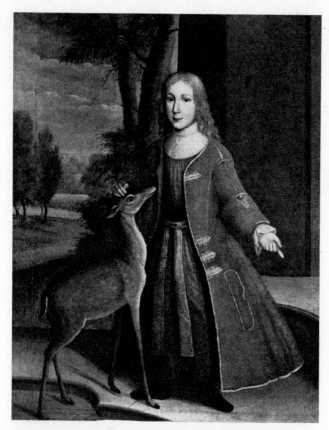

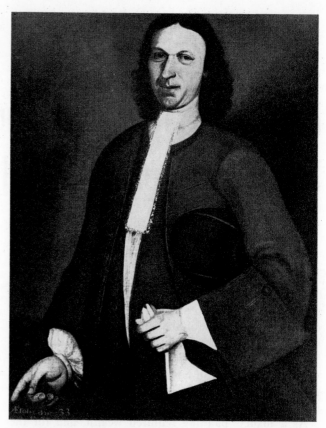

89 Anonymous. *De Peyster Boy with Deer.* 1720s.
Oil on canvas, 50¼ × 41".
The New-York Historical Society

90 Anonymous Hudson Valley artist. *"Thomas van Alstyne."*
1721. Oil on canvas, 39¼ × 30".
The New-York Historical Society

tenarian has nothing to do with the new fashionable portraiture in either a social or an artistic sense. What is remarkable about it is the unfaltering control of artisan means within the limitations of the artisan's vision, raising it to the level of an authentic image.

The richest development of artisan portraiture was in the formerly Dutch area of the Hudson Valley, from New York City to Albany. The clients were mostly Dutch patroon families, and the profusion of portraits was within the Dutch tradition, but the visual evidence is that they derive from English engravings or painted models. James Thomas Flexner, in *First Flowers of Our Wilderness,* has made a considerable contribution to early American art history in his characterization of this group of anonymous artists, whom he calls the "Patroon Painters," and by his analysis of different manners among them. One group of works was done in what he defines as the De Peyster manner and includes several portraits of the De Peyster children (c. 1728). These are clearly based on courtly models, although transformed by a naive vision which results at times in charming fantasy, as in the *De Peyster Boy with Deer* (1720s, plate 89).

Another group of portraits, most of which may be considered the work of a single painter, is described as the "Aetatis Sue" manner from the inscription giving the age and date on most of them; this painter has previously been called the Hudson Valley Master, or, on rather circumstantial evidence, Pieter Vanderlyn, grandfather of the more famous John. His is a cruder, essen-

tially realistic style, especially in the male portraits. Stock poses borrowed from the Lely-Kneller repertory are reduced to a naive artisan level—flat, heavy, and awkward. The male heads seem hacked into powerful images of personality and character (plate 90). Obviously they were painted from life, and with an almost ferocious intensity, but with such limited knowledge that the physiognomies become caricatures, the expressions grimaces.

A third group of pictures, identified with the Gansevoort Limner, are more sharply linear, flat, patterned artisan paintings in which fashionable elements are almost unrecognizable. The *Pau de Wandelaer* (c. 1730, colorplate 5) is one of the finest so-called "primitives" in American painting. Beautifully composed in an exquisite relationship of geometric shapes, it creates a sensitive mood of lyric poetry in which the young boy and the landscape blend in a muted harmony of color and form. The landscape itself—the Hudson River with its softly rounded hills—not only identifies this painter's portraits but also delineates the American terrain.

The provincial anonymity of American painting was interrupted by the arrival of the first immigrant European painters with some experience in studio practice. John Smibert (1688–1751), born in Scotland, was the best of this first wave. He started as a house painter in Edinburgh, moved on to London, where he decorated carriages, and then began copying old masters. He attended Sir James Thornhill's Great Queen Street Academy and then spent some three years studying in Italy. There he met Dean Berkeley, afterward the famous Bishop, who later recruited him to the staff of his projected university for the Indians of the New World, planned for Bermuda. Berkeley's party stayed more than a year in Newport, R.I., waiting in vain for a parliamentary grant to carry out his project. Meanwhile, Smibert had recognized the ready market for fashionable portraiture in America and had moved on to Boston with the copies, prints, and plaster casts he had collected in Italy; these were to become almost an academy for a generation of Bostonians.

Despite his superiority to any possible competition and the wealth and needs of his clientele, he had to supplement his income by selling art supplies, frames, and prints; at one time he even offered his own print collection for sale. Apparently even under the best circumstances, the artist in the colonies, at least until Copley, had to earn additional income. At his best, Smibert was a competent portraitist in the Kneller manner. He drew passably; modeled well, if somewhat pedantically; and painted materials with verve.

Smibert's first painting in America, *The Bermuda Group: Dean George Berkeley and His Entourage* (1729, colorplate 6), his most ambitious and complex undertaking, was well composed in an interlocking triangulation of forms common to academic painting of the time; though there is too much misdirected focusing of gazes, the portraits are competent and, in the case of his standing self-portrait at the left and that of Richard Dalton seated in the lower left, even interestingly handled. The generally strong modeling of the heads is weakened by a certain indecision and softness in the clothes and a repetition of formula in the poses and gestures of the sitters. At his best, as in *Richard Bill* (1740, plate 91), Smibert exhibits a strong painterly feeling for pigment, a professional handling of physiognomy, if no profound insight into character, and a commendable grace in the painting of the red velvet, the white lace, and the skin texture and color.

Gustavus Hesselius (1682–1755), born in Sweden, came to this country with his older brother, a Lutheran minister assigned to the Wilmington congregation. He worked in Delaware, Pennsylvania, and for fifteen years in Maryland, but the scarcity of extant portraits would point to a limited patronage in those colonies. As late as 1740 he was advertising that he was available for "Coats of Arms drawn on Coaches, Chaises, &c or any other kind of Ornaments, Landskips, Signs, Shewboards, Ship and House Painting. . . &c." He finally gave up painting for the making of organs and spinets.

Hesselius's manner was modest, direct, and almost puritanical in its reserve, constrained by technical inadequacies that he never overcame; yet he managed to produce a portraiture of honesty and sobriety. The uncertainty of his drawing and modeling is evident in his two Indian chieftains *Tishcohan* (1735, plate 92) and

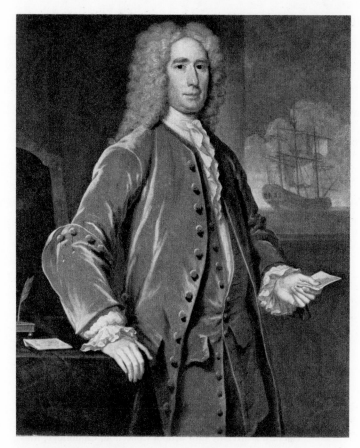

91 John Smibert. *Richard Bill*. 1740. Oil on canvas, 50¼ × 40¼". The Art Institute of Chicago

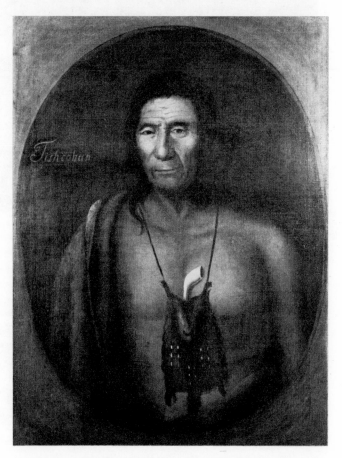

92 Gustavus Hesselius. *Chief Tishcohan*. 1735. Oil on canvas, 33 × 25". The Historical Society of Pennsylvania, Philadelphia

Eighteenth-Century Colonial Painting and Sculpture   63

Lapowinsa (1735), but these Delaware (Leni-Lenape) chiefs, aside from their historical interest, are remarkable as the first unprejudiced records of the Amerind.

Justus Engelhardt Kühn (active 1708–17), one of the earlier immigrants of the century, was so limited in ability that, had he stayed in his native Germany, he would no doubt have remained in oblivion. In Annapolis, Maryland, he found employment as portraitist, and the few works he left have some antiquarian import. Two portraits, *Eleanor Darnall* and her brother, *Henry Darnall III with Slave* (both about 1710), aside from their naive charm, are notable mostly for the fantastic landscape backgrounds, deriving either from Kühn's European memories or from prints. *Eleanor* is much like the seventeenth-century *Margaret Gibbs* (colorplate 2), even to the checkered floor, except for the modeling, which, while painfully indecisive, shows a striving for three-dimensionality.

Among other early immigrant artists were America's first woman artist, Henrietta Johnston (died c. 1728/29), wife of the rector of St. Philip's in Charleston, who did pastel portraits; and Peter Pelham (1697–1751), who was more important as engraver than painter and even more so as the stepfather and first teacher of Copley.

Jeremiah Theüs (c. 1719–1774) seems to have come from Switzerland while still in his teens. In the thirty-odd years that he dominated Charleston portrait painting and amassed a tidy fortune, he turned out many routine likenesses, all in the recognizable "pouter-pigeon pose" but somewhat redeemed by a delicate color sense.

A generation of American-born painters was influenced by these first professional artists or by engravings, but they were, on the whole, not a very prepossessing lot. It is rather hard to deal seriously with a painter like Joseph Badger (1708–1765), who rose to prominence in Boston, possibly because of the failure of Smibert's eyesight. His style is an inept imitation of Smibert's from composition to brushwork. Badger's sitters often appear to have been made of dough and to have been painted in toothpaste, but they have a clumsy forthrightness. A few of his portraits of children, especially his grandson *James Badger* (1760), have a redeeming innocence and appeal.

Painting in Boston in those years would be a story of

93 Robert Feke. *Isaac Royall and Family*. 1741. Oil on canvas, 54⅝ × 77¾". Harvard University Law School Collection, Cambridge, Mass.

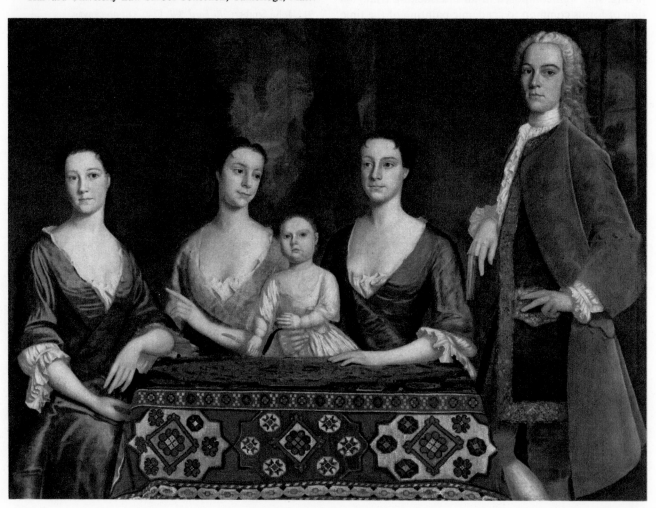

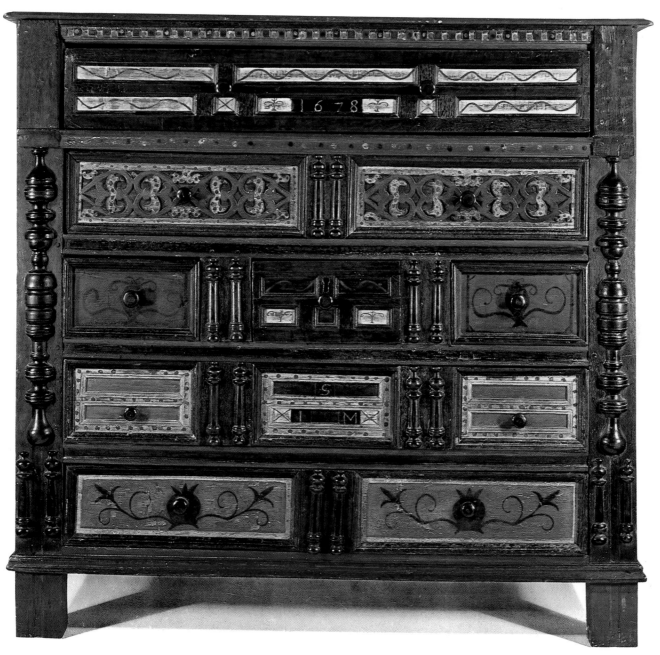

1 Thomas Dennis (attrib.). Chest of drawers. 1678. Painted red oak, height 42″, width 44¾″.
The Henry Francis du Pont Winterthur Museum, Del.

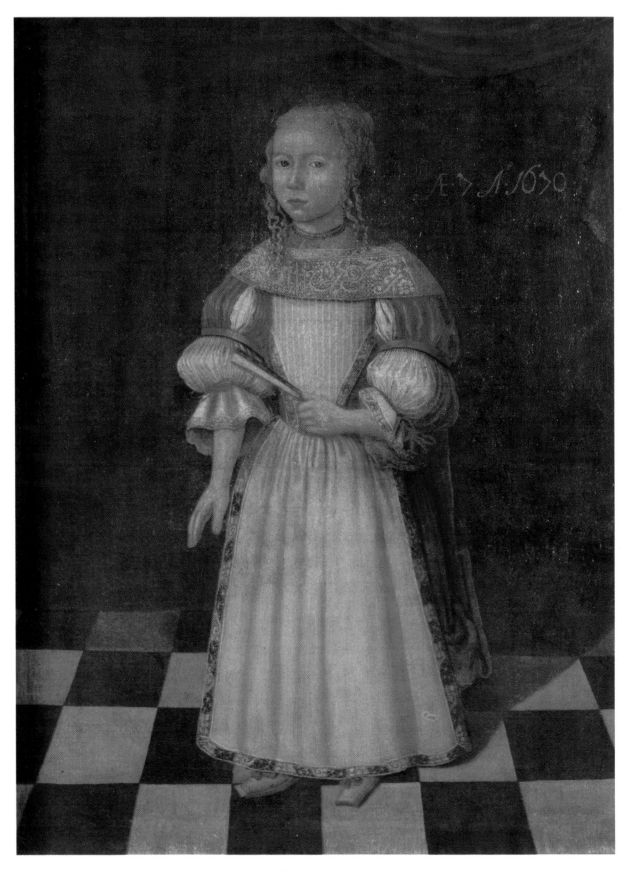

2 Anonymous. *Margaret Gibbs*. 1670. Oil on canvas, 40½ × 33″.
Collection Mrs. Elsie Q. Giltinan, Charleston, W.Va.

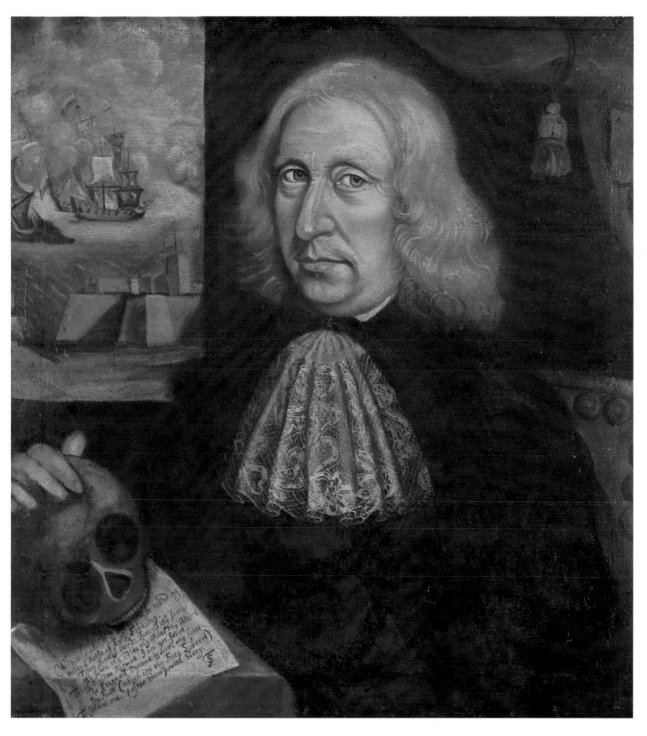

3   Thomas Smith. *Self-Portrait*. c. 1690. Oil on canvas, $24\frac{1}{2} \times 23\frac{3}{4}''$. Worcester Art Museum

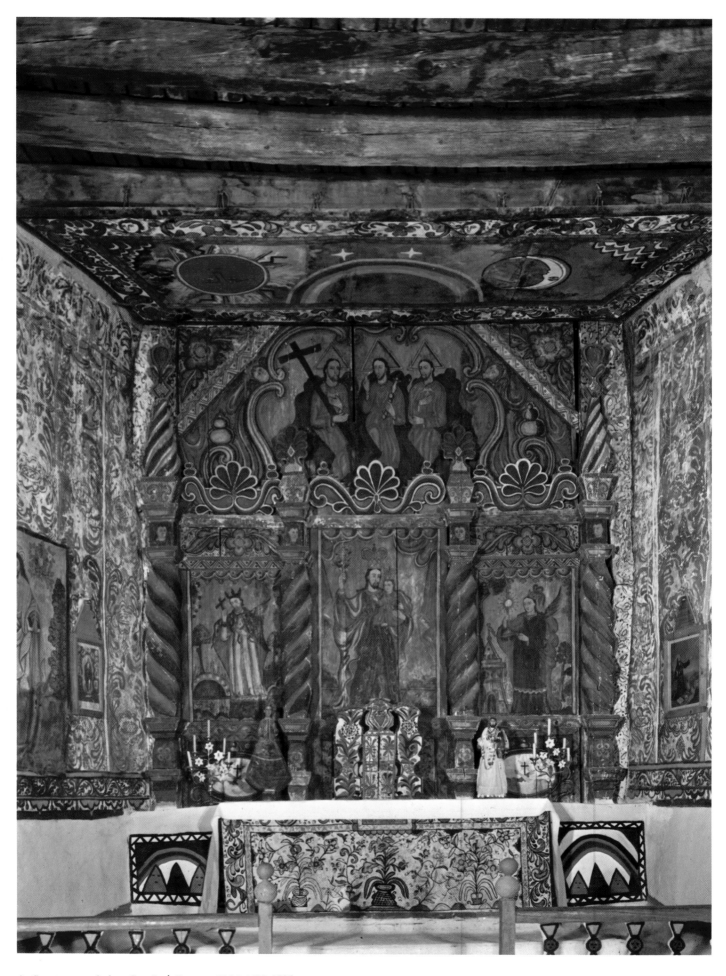

4 Sanctuary and altar, San José, Laguna, N.M. 1699–1706

5 Right: Anonymous (Gansevoort Limner). *Pau de Wandelaer*. c. 1730.
Oil on canvas, 45 × 35⅜″. Albany Institute of History and Art

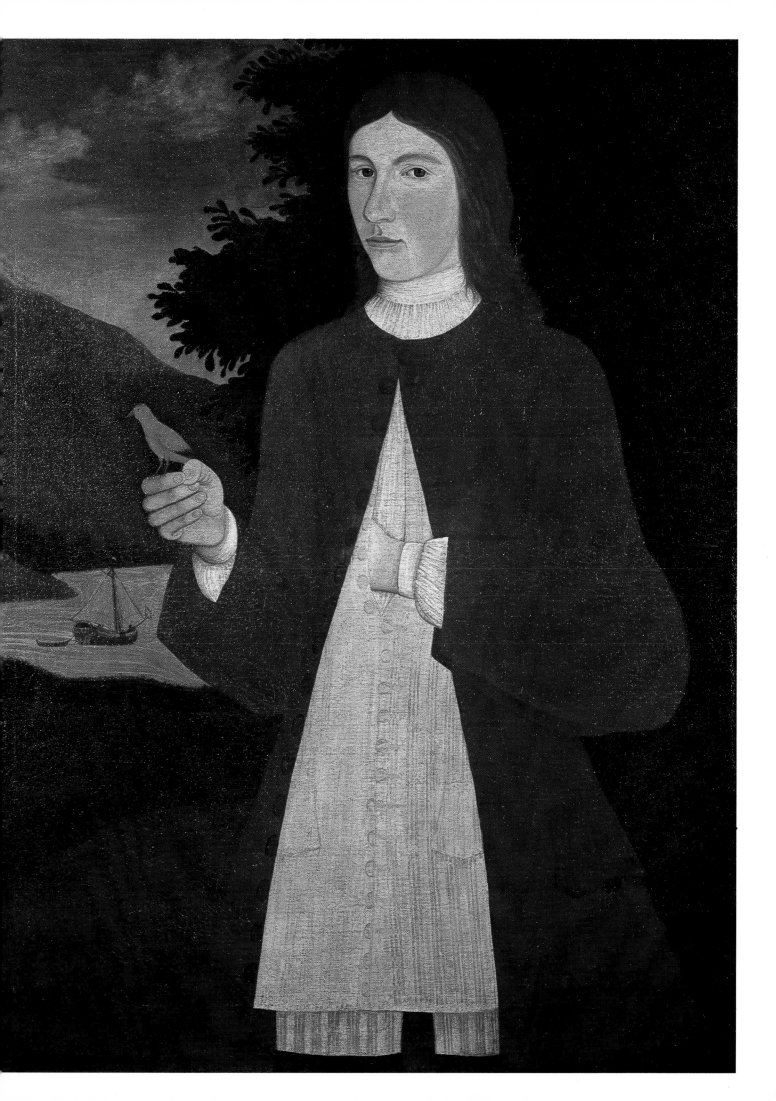

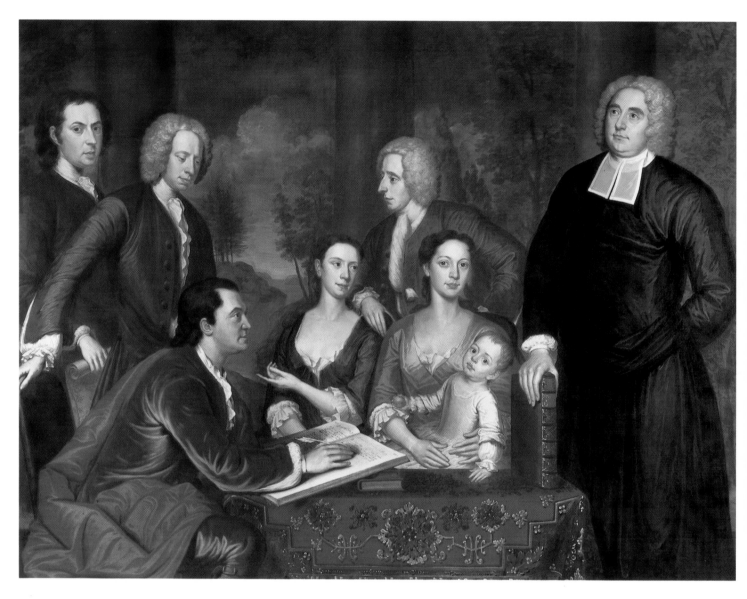

6   John Smibert. *The Bermuda Group: Dean George Berkeley and His Entourage*. 1729. Oil on canvas, $69\frac{1}{2} \times 93''$. Yale University Art Gallery, New Haven. Gift of Isaac Lothrop

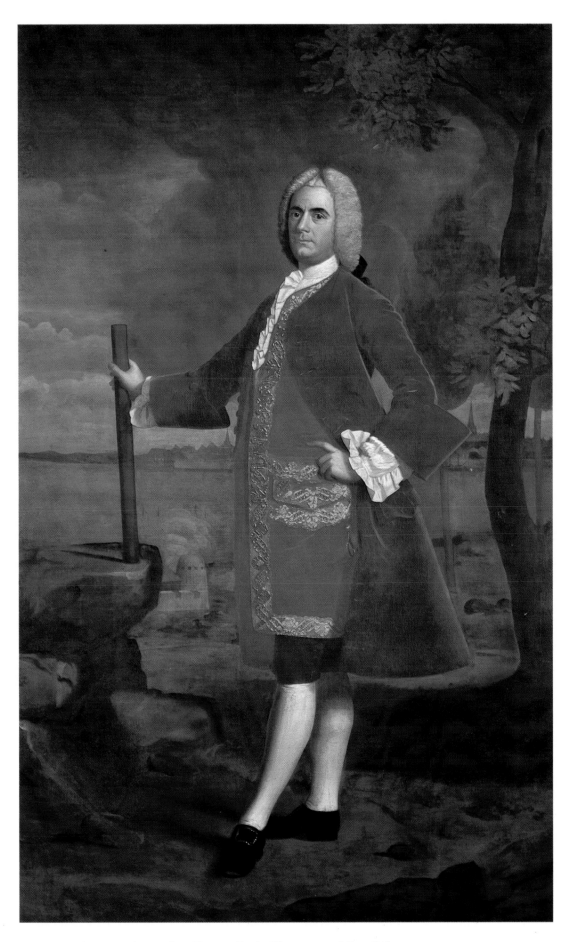

7   Robert Feke. *General Samuel Waldo*. c. 1748–50. Oil on canvas, 96¾ × 60¼″.
Bowdoin College, Brunswick, Me.

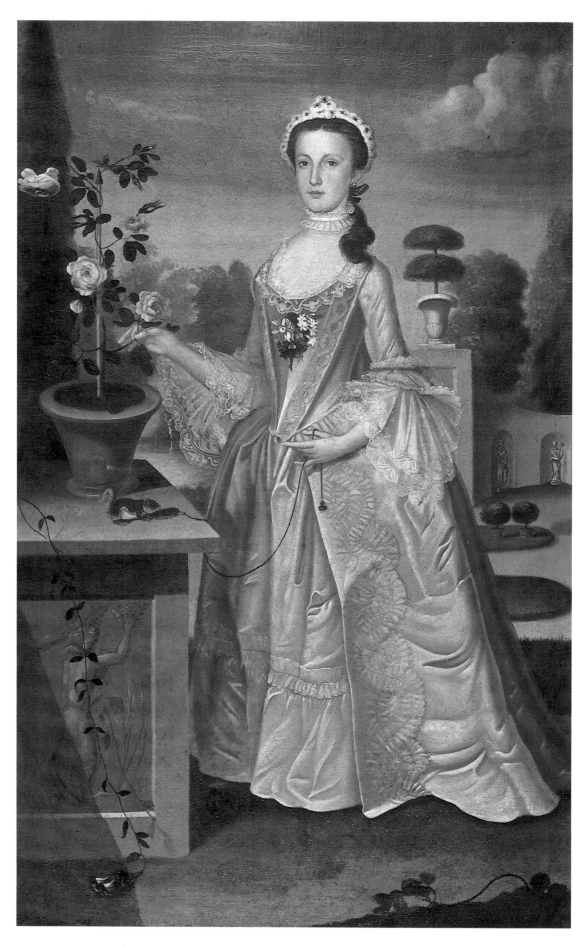

8 William Williams. *Deborah Hall*. 1766. Oil on canvas, $71\frac{1}{4} \times 46\frac{1}{2}''$. The Brooklyn Museum

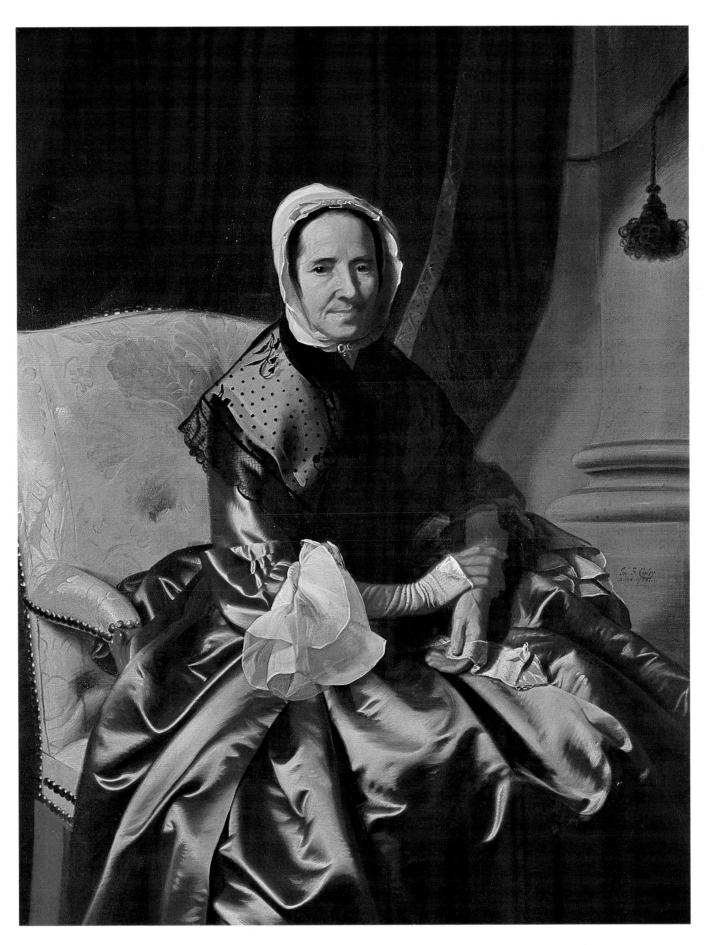

9   John Singleton Copley. *Mrs. Thomas Boylston*. 1766. Oil on canvas,
     50⅝ × 40¼″. Harvard University, Cambridge, Mass.

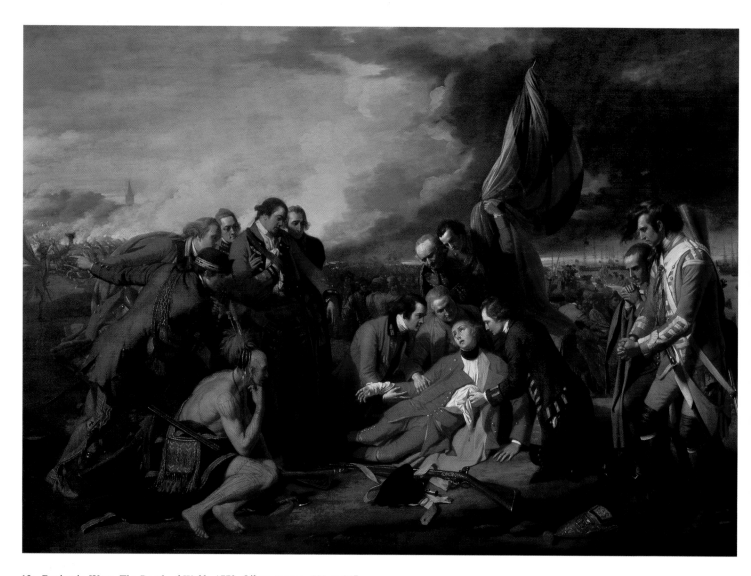

10 Benjamin West. *The Death of Wolfe*. 1770. Oil on canvas, $59\frac{1}{2} \times 84''$.
The National Gallery of Canada, Ottawa

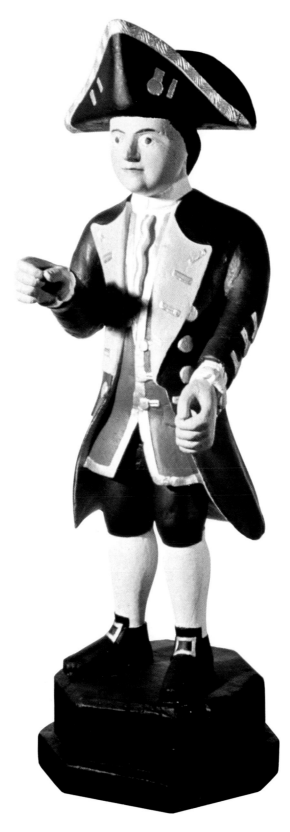

11 Shem Drowne (attrib.). *The Little Admiral*. 1750–70.
Painted wood, height 42″. The Bostonian Society,
Old State House, Boston

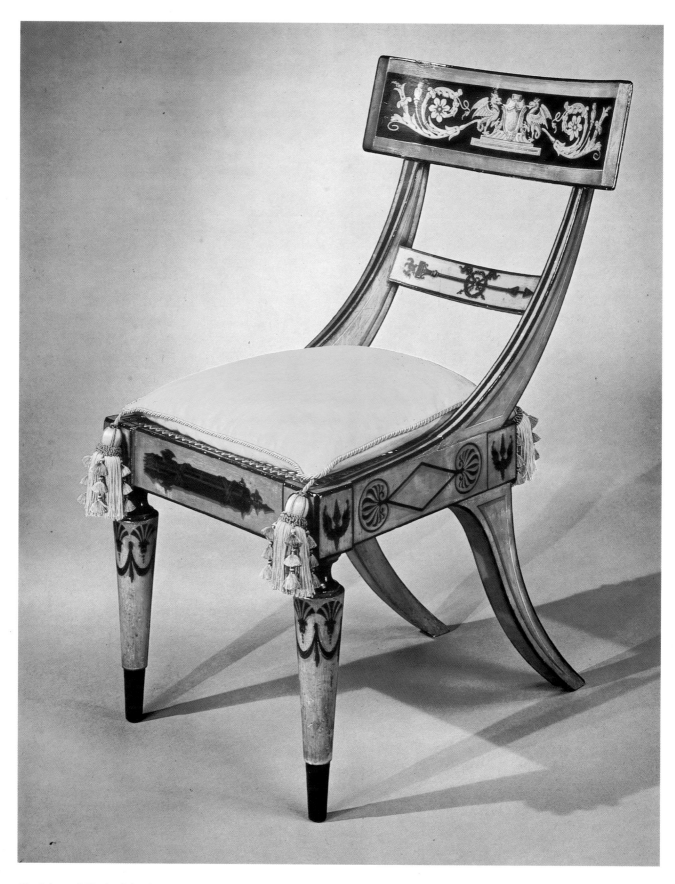

12　John and Hugh Finlay (attrib.). Side chair, from Baltimore. c. 1820. Painted maple, height 34½″.
The Metropolitan Museum of Art, New York. Purchase, Mrs. Paul Moore Gift, 1965

13 Charles Willson Peale. *Staircase Group*. 1795.
Oil on canvas, 89 × 39½″.
Philadelphia Museum of Art.
George W. Elkins Collection

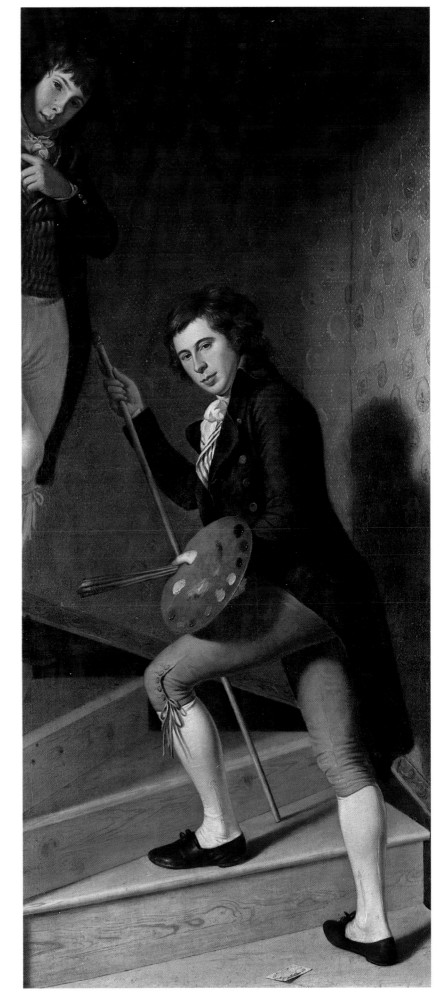

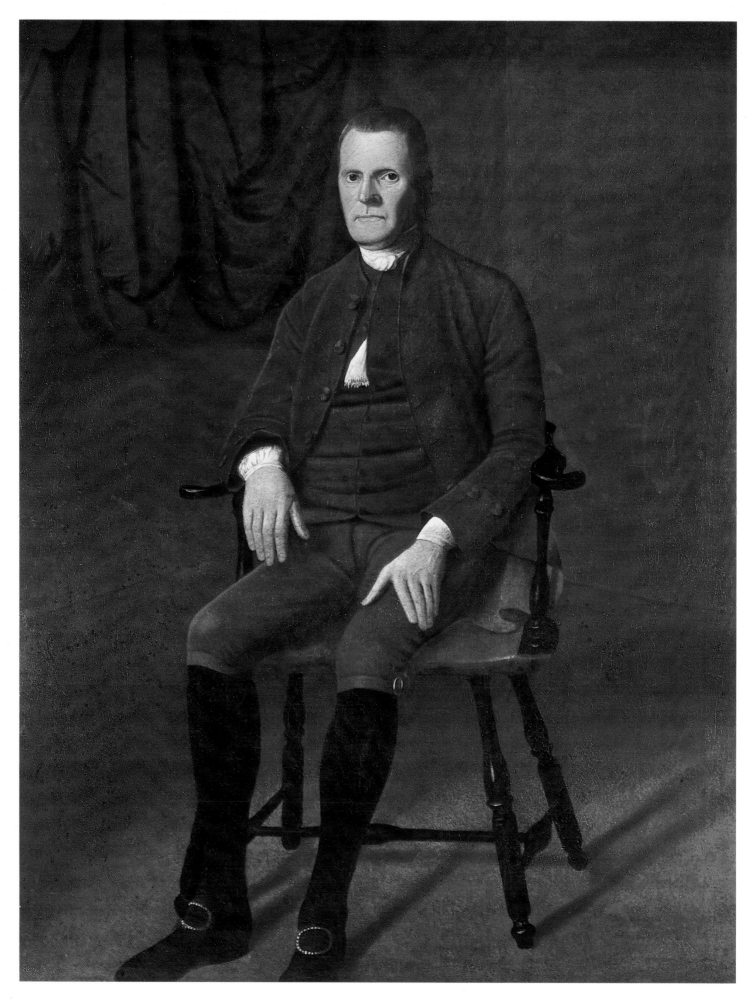

14   Ralph Earl. *Roger Sherman*. c. 1775. Oil on canvas, $64\frac{5}{8} \times 49\frac{5}{8}''$. Yale University Art Gallery,
New Haven. Gift of Roger Sherman White, B. A., 1899

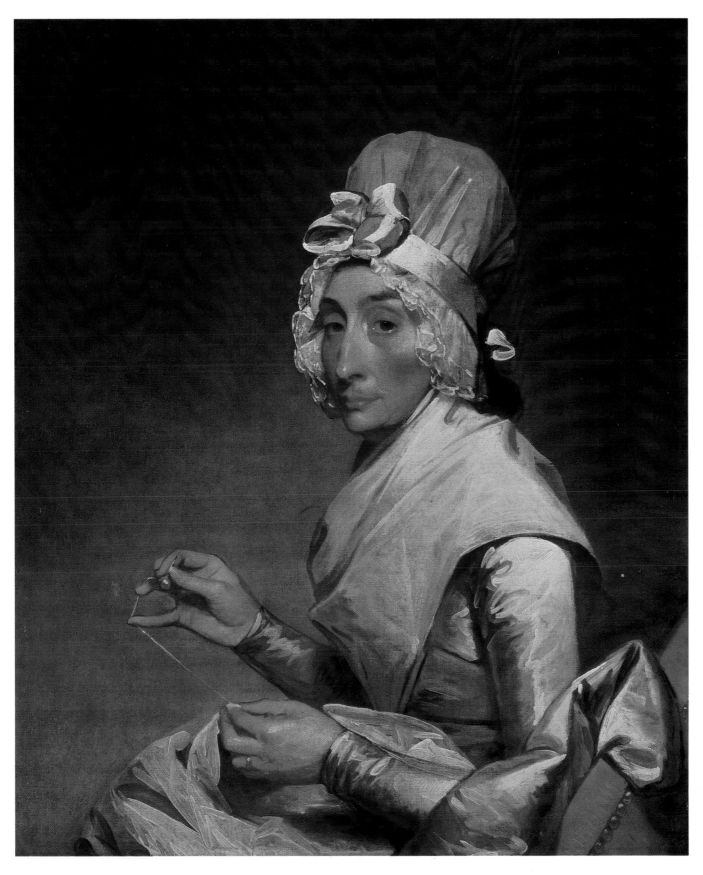

15 Gilbert Stuart. *Mrs. Richard Yates*. c. 1793. Oil on canvas, 31¼ × 25″. National Gallery of Art, Washington, D.C. Andrew Mellon Collection

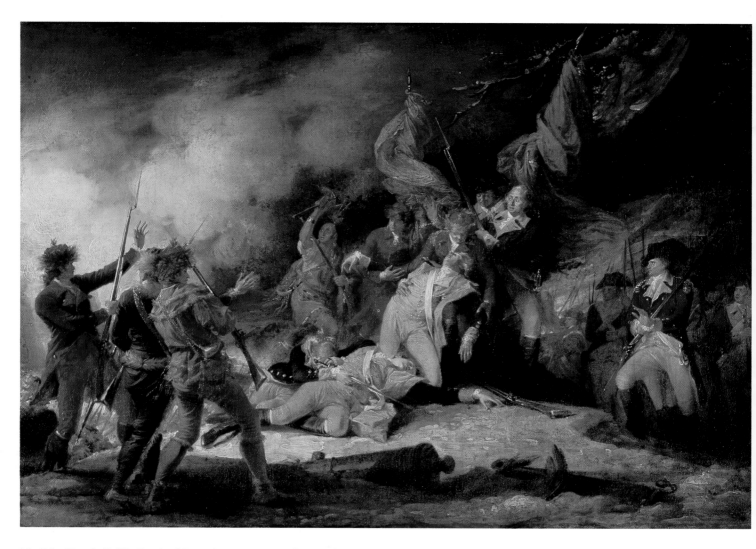

16   John Trumbull. *The Death of General Montgomery in the Attack on Quebec*. 1786.
Oil on canvas, 20¾ × 37″. Yale University Art Gallery, New Haven

abject tedium were it not for Robert Feke (1705?–1750?). Feke's life is shrouded in mystery: one can state only that he was married and lived in Newport and painted there and in Boston, in Philadelphia, and possibly on Long Island, from 1741 to 1750, and that he was a "mariner."

Feke's earliest work was clearly dependent on Smibert, witness his *Isaac Royall and Family* (1741, plate 93), based on the latter's Berkeley group, but the figures are stiff, the faces stereotyped, the movements awkward, and the painting, especially of the women's costumes, uncertain. However, the modeling is strong and volumetric in conception, and the color is more personal and original than Smibert's.

Feke stripped the fashionable portrait of its superficial stock mannerisms and at the same time invested his sitters with an air of nobility deriving from natural dignity rather than painterly flourishes. All his male portraits have the same ramrod stance of prideful elegance, their dignity increased by the low horizon and the silhouetting of the figure against the sky. The backgrounds are generally artificial, more like painted backdrops than actual spatial extensions, but it is the painting of the figure in this shallow space that identifies Feke. The crisp, nonatmospheric modeling, beautifully precise, is achieved by reducing the infinite value scale of nature to a limited and clearly defined relationship between dark, middle, and light tones. The result is an abstract but faithful rendering of reality with a crystalline sparkle. Feke is most successful in the delineation of materials, especially white linen and shining silks and braid, upon which highlights twinkle like jewels. His painting of faces is usually less satisfying, except for a few male portraits such as the *General Samuel Waldo* (c. 1748–50, colorplate 7), an impressive characterization. His usual portraits of women have nearly identical masklike faces on heads perched rigidly on columnar throats, rising above tightly corseted torsos, with rather aggressive bosoms and voluminous skirts painted in a virtuoso manner but a routine spirit. However, in a small bust portrait, the so-called *Pamela Andrews* (c. 1741, plate 94), all artificiality and pretense fall away, and the loveliness of an ideal, yet natural beauty shines through with a cool freshness of spirit and a ripe sensuosity.

Feke remained a formula painter, but out of what was available in the painted examples of Smibert or in prints, and fitted to his own personality and talents, emerged a cool elegance, a natural but remarkably subtle sense of color, and a true painter's feeling for the quality of pigment.

About 1750 a new group of immigrant painters brought with them a change of style which has generally been described as Rococo. An essentially courtly style, it had hard going among the English, who domesticated the Rococo fantasy and eliminated its frivolity, retaining

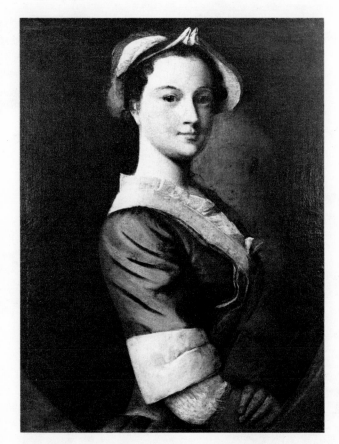

94 Robert Feke. *Pamela Andrews.* c. 1741. Oil on canvas, 30¾ × 23¾″. Museum of Art, Rhode Island School of Design, Providence

only its lightness and grace. The style imported into America still had pretensions to aristocracy but was less pompous, more natural, and more bourgeois.

Among the painters who brought it to this country in the third quarter of the century, the most influential were two English "drapery painters," John Wollaston in 1749 and Joseph Blackburn in 1753. Both were journeymen painters with a set of stock figures and a bag of fashionable painting tricks. They offered a grace, charm, and prettiness which were new for the colonies, even if the grace was a bit leaden, the charm somewhat forced, or the prettiness not always convincing. Both painters had plenty of commissions. In Blackburn's *Isaac Winslow and His Family* (1757, plate 95), the sprightly movements of the Rococo become nervously agitated; and, although he never really concerned himself with likeness, much less character, he often produced light, gay, and graceful decorations. Wollaston's style (plate 96) was coarser than Blackburn's and more dependent on a set repertory of elegant mannerisms. Among his conventions were broad faces with pudgy features, slanted eyes (he was identified as the "almond-eyed artist"), and boneless fingers. Both these artists had a great influence on colonial painters, for, despite their obvious limitations, they turned out

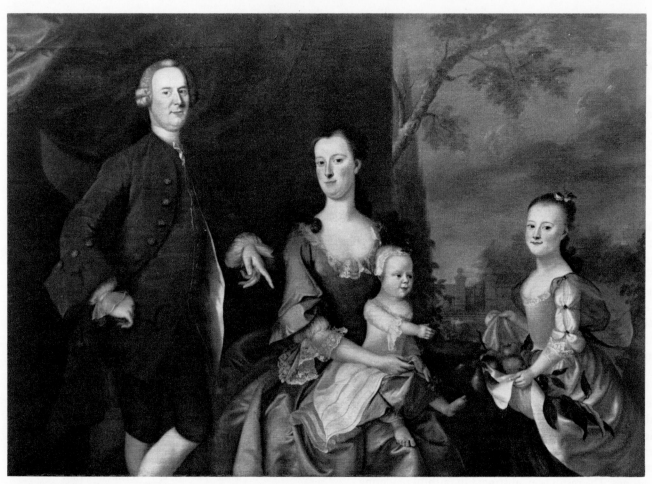

95 Joseph Blackburn. *Isaac Winslow and His Family*. 1757. Oil on canvas,
54½ × 79½″. Museum of Fine Arts, Boston. Abraham Shuman Fund

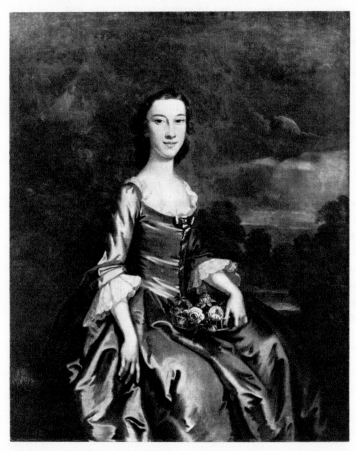

96 John Wollaston. *Mrs. Samuel Gouverneur*. c. 1750.
Oil on canvas, 48½ × 39¼″. Henry Francis du Pont
Winterthur Museum, Winterthur, Del.

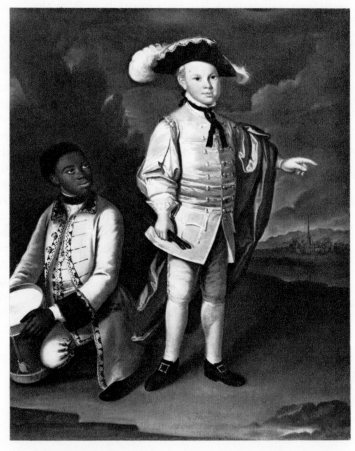

97 John Hesselius. *Charles Calvert*. 1761. Oil on canvas, 50¼ × 40¼″.
The Baltimore Museum of Art. Gift of Alfred R. and
Henry G. Riggs in memory of General Lawrason Riggs

professional portraits with all the symbols of social status and cultural refinement.

William Williams, active in Philadelphia and New York from about 1747 to the Revolution, was an artist of greater interest, if less importance. He may have been largely self-taught, mostly from prints, but he produced a charming, personal version of the Rococo. His pictures have a hard-edged, sparkling clarity and a flower-like freshness of color, as seen in one of his finest portraits, *Deborah Hall* (1766, colorplate 8). Even more interesting are his conversation pieces, unique in America at the time but characteristic of Hogarth and common among lesser-known and nonaristocratic painters in England.

Among the American-born painters, John Hesselius (1728–1778) remained essentially provincial. He spent his youth in Philadelphia and received his first training from his father, Gustavus, whose portrait-painting business he took over when the latter retired. In 1763 he settled down to paint in Annapolis for the rest of his life. His best-known work is the charming and colorful *Charles Calvert* (1761, plate 97), which manages to combine some of the elegant artificialities of Wollaston with his own sense of solid reality in the painting of three-dimensional form.

COPLEY AND WEST

The brilliant flowering of John Singleton Copley (1738–1815) in a meager soil has led writers on American art to stress his uniqueness and his self-education, when in actuality his dependence upon contemporary models is absolutely clear. Copley appears self-made only because he surpassed almost unexplainably the limitations of his sources and his environment. The fact is that, as a youth, he found himself in a most favorable situation for an incipient artist. His widowed mother married Peter Pelham in 1748, when John was eleven. Copley thus came into a household where art was a central concern, and through his stepfather he also came to know the Smibert household, its activities, and its contents. Peter Pelham had a collection of prints, and Smibert had one containing examples of Raphael, Michelangelo, Poussin, and Rubens, as well as his own copies of European masterworks. Copley's emergence as an artist was not, therefore, so remarkable; only his genius was. His earliest datable works were done when he was only fourteen or fifteen. These paintings were full of gleanings from his stepfather, Smibert, Feke, even Badger, for Copley was always an avid student, borrowing, imitating, and copying throughout his life.

The appearance of Blackburn in Boston offered a standard to strive for, and Copley's clarity in modeling, lustrous color, and sparkling textures must have derived from the older man, but Copley's sense of reality and his concern with portrait likeness were already distinguishing marks. He was driven by a fanatical search for the truth in the character of his sitters as well as in the material

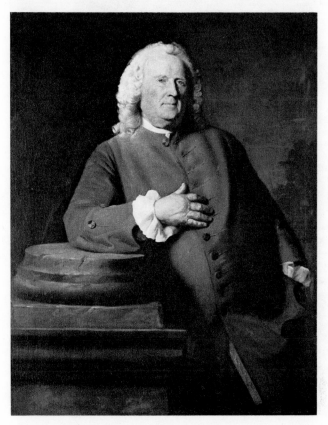

98 John Singleton Copley. *Epes Sargent*. 1760. Oil on canvas, 49⅞ × 40″. National Gallery of Art, Washington, D.C. Gift of the Avalon Foundation

things which surrounded them, and he has left us a gallery of memorable portraits of colonial Americans. Among these are the contemplative old man *Epes Sargent* of Gloucester (1760, plate 98), with his light eyes and his puffy old hand painted almost impressionistically; the sprightly, wizened dowager *Mrs. Thomas Boylston* (1766, colorplate 9), wife of a saddler and mother of eight, wryly accepting the honor of sitting for her portrait because her wealthy merchant sons had paid for it; and *Governor and Mrs. Thomas Mifflin* (1773, plate 99), the paradigm of colonial economic and social stability expressed in marital felicity and the encompassing warmth of the home.

During the sixties Copley's skill continued to grow, but all his American work exhibits certain recurring inaccuracies in anatomical drawing and proportion which reflect the narrowness of his training. His color, although bright, sensuous, vital, and even exciting in itself, is essentially naive, almost totally local, without variation in hue or atmospheric modification. This is not entirely an unmixed fault, however, for it reinforces the visual clarity as well as the forthrightness of his characterizations.

He was successful financially and had achieved unparalleled recognition. Yet he felt "peculiarly unlucky in Liveing in a place into which there has not been one

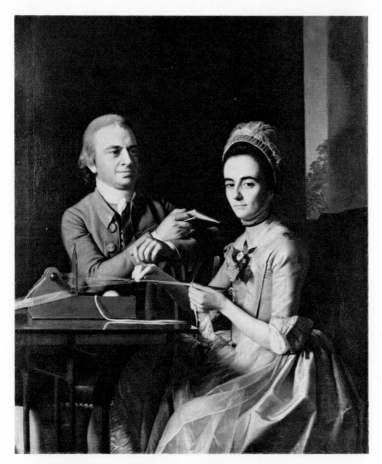

99 John Singleton Copley. *Governor and Mrs. Thomas Mifflin.*
1773. Oil on bed ticking, 61½ × 48". The Historical
Society of Pennsylvania, Philadelphia

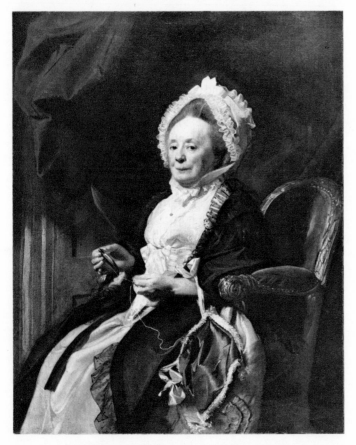

100 John Singleton Copley. *Mrs. Seymour Fort.* c. 1778.
Oil on canvas, 50 × 40". Wadsworth Atheneum,
Hartford, Conn.

portrait brought that is worthy to be call'd a Picture
within my memory." To test his true stature as an artist,
Copley sent the recently completed portrait of his half
brother, Henry Pelham, called *Boy with Squirrel* (1765),
to Sir Joshua Reynolds in London for exhibition at the
Society of Artists. This familiar masterwork, a lyrical
portrait, reveals not only his love for the boy but also
his love for everything paintable—the fuzz of the little
animal's fur, the glitter of the metal chain, the sparkle
of the glass and water, the texture of skin, and the gleam
of satin. Its skill and realism startled the London art
world, and Reynolds advised him to seek "the advantages
of the Example and Instruction which you could have in
Europe . . . before it was too late in Life, and before
your Manner and Taste were corrupted or fixed by
working in your little way at Boston." Yet, perhaps
because Copley was making "a pretty living in America,"
he continued with increasing renown and skill to turn
out resemblances at home.

In June, 1774, he finally made the break, probably
guided at least in part by political considerations, for
his family were among the first Tory émigrés from the
Revolutionary War. In London he soon achieved recognition and commissions, was elected an Associate of the
Royal Academy in 1776, and elevated to full membership in 1779. Copley's American style was provincial by
London standards, but in a short time he made himself
over into a fashionable English painter and a good one.
As a portraitist he would have to be ranked with Reynolds, Gainsborough, and Romney. A work such as his
Mrs. Seymour Fort (c.1778, plate 100), or individual
heads in his historical pictures, combines the suave handling of the English school with his own innate realism.

But Copley was no longer satisfied with portraiture.
He had come to Europe for greater things. Driven by his
own ambitions, he attempted to rival Benjamin West in
historical painting. Copley's gigantic historical canvases
brought him fame but not the rewards he had hoped for.
With time his reputation as well as his art declined; his
health failed and he spent his last years in loneliness,
frustration, regret, and tragic senility.

Benjamin West (1738–1820), though a painter of no
great talent, played an important role in the innovation
of three successive historic styles in European art:
Neoclassicism, Realism, and Romanticism. One of the
earliest of Neoclassic pictures is his *Agrippina Landing at
Brundisium with the Ashes of Germanicus* (1767, plate
101). His *Death of Wolfe* (1770, colorplate 10) is a landmark in eighteenth-century historical painting for its
choice of a contemporary event depicted in contemporary
costume. And his *Death on a Pale Horse* (1802, plate
102) was an early probe into Romantic art.

West's parents were Quaker innkeepers in what is now
Swarthmore, Pa., yet despite severe religious restrictions
his artistic interests were not impeded. Considered a
child prodigy, he was taken at the age of eight to William

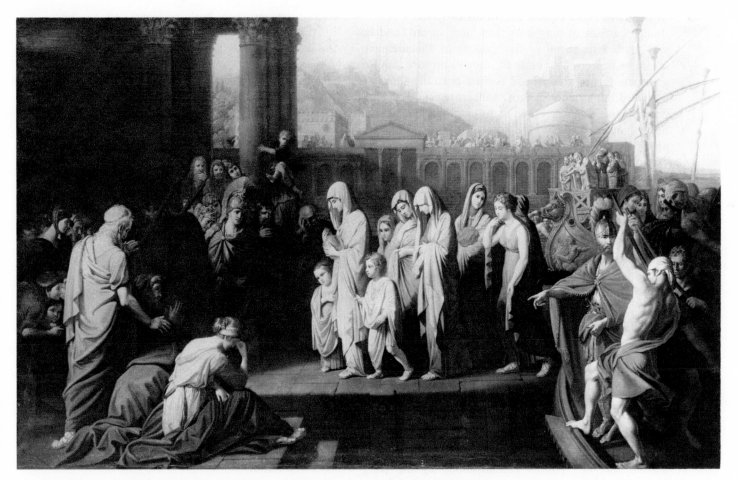

101 Benjamin West. *Agrippina Landing at Brundisium with the Ashes of Germanicus.* 1767. Oil on canvas, 64½ × 94½″. Yale University Art Gallery, New Haven. Gift of Louis M. Rabinowitz

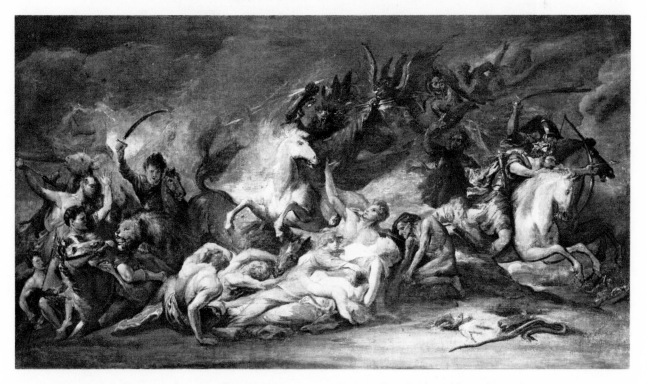

102 Benjamin West. *Death on a Pale Horse.* 1802. Oil on canvas, 21 × 36″. Philadelphia Museum of Art

Williams in Philadelphia, and in his early teens he was doing portraits of neighbors. His fame spread, and he was invited to enroll at the College of Philadelphia, where he was given a course of study to prepare him for greatness in the arts. West's earliest portraits show an awkward but straightforward manner, which soon took on the naive elegance of Williams and, before long, the heavy-handed graces of the newest arrival to Philadelphia, Wollaston. It is to West's credit that he fought his way out of this influence. Inspired by a Spanish picture reputedly of the school of Murillo, West decided to go abroad to study and finally left America late in 1759 to become a great artist. The fair stranger from America was something of a curiosity in Rome and before long became the darling of the *dilettanti*. West received private instruction from Raphael Mengs, met Johann Winckelmann, and copied old masters. By chance, his old-fashioned and sketchy education in moral precepts and classical mythology had prepared West for the academic absolutes of Mengs and the new Classicism of Winckelmann.

On the way home from Italy, West's reception in London was so enthusiastic that he remained. Portrait commissions were plentiful, but he was imbued with the idea that art had higher aims, and finally the Archbishop of York, for whom he had painted the *Agrippina*, introduced him and his work to King George III. West struck up an immediate friendship with the King, and became the only painter commissioned by the King to execute historical pictures, of which he produced a tremendous number, both religious and secular.

To handle such production West needed an atelier on the scale of a Rubens, and he welcomed many young American artists into his household—among them Charles Willson Peale, Gilbert Stuart, William Dunlap, Ralph Earl, Joseph Wright, and John Trumbull. Few of them were influenced by him stylistically. Some, including Stuart, were even contemptuous of his powers as a painter, and most remained beholden to him only as a fellow countryman who had helped them on their way and as a symbol of what an artist born in America could achieve.

Most of West's large historical pictures are studio productions and, since he was not a great master, could not be saved by his final touches. His best works are his less pretentious and less labored ones, such as the unfinished *American Commissioners of the Preliminary Peace Negotiations with Great Britain* (c. 1783, plate 103).

American painting came of age in the late Colonial period with the work of Copley and West. It had run the gamut of provincial development through the immigration of minor though professionally trained painters to American artists who, finding the provincial environment hampering, were drawn irresistibly to the center of their culture, London, there to remain. The next generation began, before the Revolution and increasingly thereafter, to go to Europe to learn, but with the idea of returning prepared for the task of building a new culture for a new nation.

(continued on page 89)

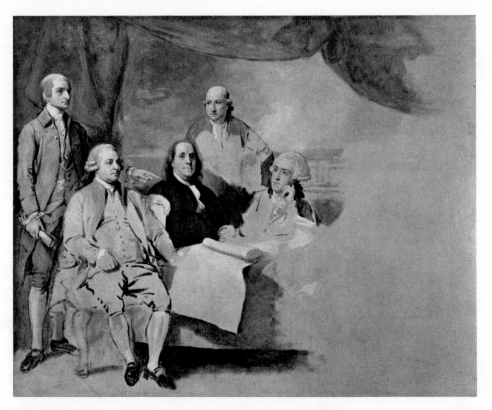

103 Benjamin West. *American Commissioners of the Preliminary Peace Negotiations with Great Britain.* c. 1783. Oil on canvas, 28½ × 37½".
Henry Francis du Pont Winterthur Museum, Winterthur, Del.

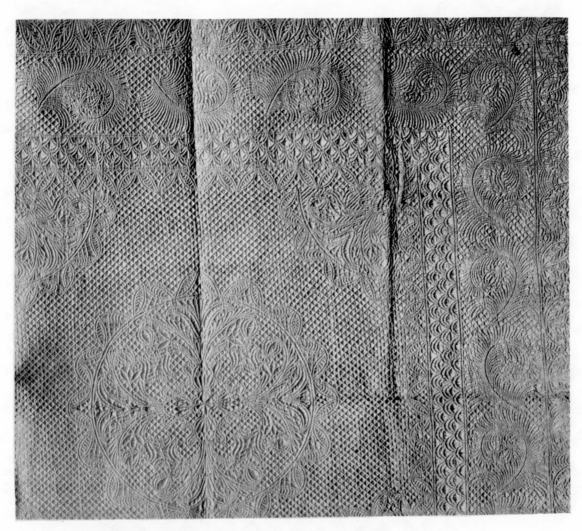

104 Quilt, from Philadelphia (detail). 1720–30. Silk and chintz with embroidery, $100\frac{3}{8} \times 101\frac{3}{16}''$. Philadelphia Museum of Art. Bequest of Lydia Thompson Morris

Students of Colonial American life have often suggested that fine needlework of the eighteenth century could not have been produced here and must have been imported. In support of that argument they have cited Britain's export regulations prohibiting the sale of India chintz to the colonies. However, there were ways to get around that law, and chintz, along with many other products, was re-exported to these shores throughout the century. The quality of work produced here was often very high, especially in Philadelphia, because needlework was an integral part of the education of Quaker women and specialization evolved early.

The quilt illustrated (plate 104) is made of narrow silk strips, each about fifteen inches long. The underside consists of three large pieces of plain-woven India chintz,

sewn together along their length and bearing repeated patterns of flowers, leaves, and small figures block-printed in brown, green, and red, with stems and outlines stenciled in black. The quilting, executed in running-stitch with silk thread, has an overall diamond design and includes conventional pineapple motifs at the center and each corner, a wreath of laurel leaves, and a series of scrolled feathers. Repetition is a key factor in the design, but it is subtle, and the whole is a masterly work of its kind.

Bed rugs were brought by colonists from England and other northern European countries and were important in wintry New England. In 1630 the governor of Massachusetts indicated their value in a letter to his son still in England, "Bring a store of Course Rugges, both to use

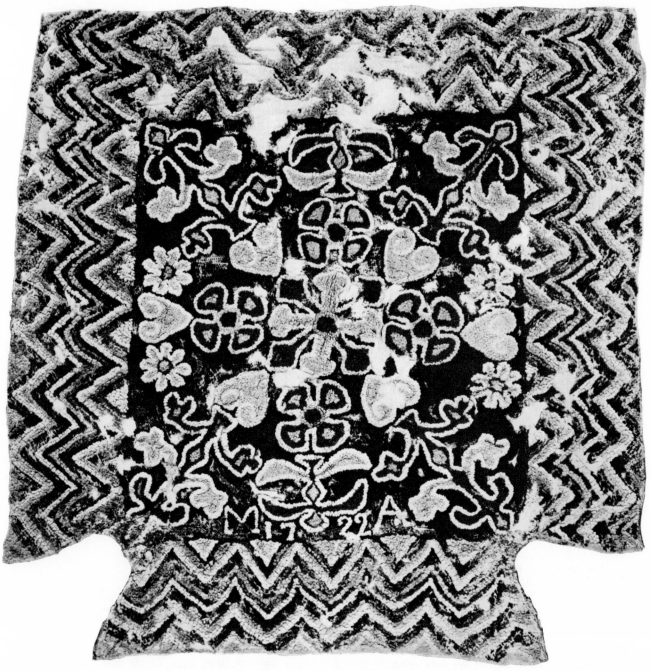

105   Mary Avery. Bed rug, from North Andover, Mass. 1722. Wool on homespun linen, 98 × 88″. Essex Institute, Salem, Mass.

and to sell." Naturally, an item of such usefulness was soon being made by the colonists and modeled after those already in use. They are all similar in that they are worked in wool over a background material of woolen homespun or, as in the case of this example (plate 105), linen. The backgrounds of almost all are dyed, usually with a butternut dye, in well set, warm earth tones. The colors of the needlework were brilliant, and the designs, such as the chevron and floral here, usually large, aggressive, and often naive.

The bed rug continued in importance for about a hundred years, and the use of hand-spun wool, tufted over the entire surface of the backing, was later to be adapted for the creation of hooked rugs. Both the bed rug and the later form were often the creation of young brides, although some were turned out by specialists in the art.

(continued from page 86)

LANDSCAPE AND OTHER GENRES

Despite a dearth of nonportrait painting during the Colonial period, literary evidence implies at least some activity in such areas. For instance, an advertisement in a Charleston newspaper in 1766 listed "History Pieces, Altar Pieces, Landscapes, Sea Pieces, Flowers, Fruit, Heraldry. . . . Rooms painted in Oil or Water in a new Taste. Deceptive Temples, Triumphal Arches, Obelisks, Statues, &c, for Groves or Gardens."

One of the genres mentioned most frequently in advertisements is the "landskip," and yet only a very few landscapes as such, and those questionable, have come down to us: for instance, four panels out of eleven for the Clark-Franklin House in Boston (c. 1712–42, plate 106). Such wall paintings were equivalent to or imitations of contemporary wallpaper—set pieces, painted by artisans following decorators' patterns, of romantic and exotic landscapes or genre scenes.

The most frequently quoted document suggesting an autonomous landscape form is the obituary of Nathaniel Emmons (1704–1740), possibly the first artist born and trained in America. It says: "His Pieces are . . . admirable Imitations of Nature, both in faces, Rivers, Banks and Rural Scenes." It is possible that time has destroyed all his landscape and subject pictures. On the other hand, the passage can also be read as a description of exactly the kind of English portrait Emmons and others copied from available prints, a figure posed in a landscape. However, all the references to landscape painting in advertisements can more easily be understood as of artisan-level production of overmantel panels or wall decorations, since they are usually listed along with other artisan jobs the painter could handle in a pinch. Most overmantel paintings still extant date from after the Revolution. Among the earlier ones are six attributed to Winthrop Chandler (1747–1790) for houses in Connecticut and Massachusetts and the *British Privateers with French Prizes in New York Harbor* (c. 1756–57, plate 107), obviously the work of a sign painter. These works actually reflect the popular topographical print.

Topographical views have a tradition as old as the print itself, since satisfying curiosity about distant and famous places was from the outset one of the print's main functions. It was in this area that the first authentic landscapes of America appeared. William Burgis (act. c. 1716–31), something of a rakehell as well as a painter and an innkeeper, did topographical views of New York, Boston, and Philadelphia between 1722 and 1736. One of Harvard College (c. 1726, plate 108) is widely known.

An occasional landscape painting may be inferred from such rare references as Smibert's writing in a letter that

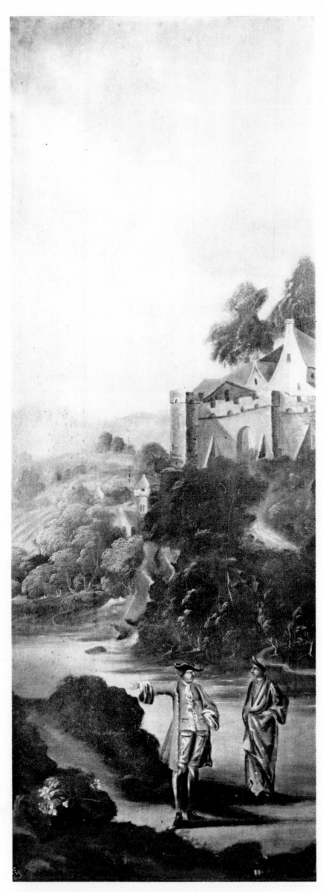

106 Anonymous. Landscape panel from the Clark-Franklin. House, Boston. c. 1712–42. Oil on panel, 60 × 22¾". Maine Historical Society, Portland

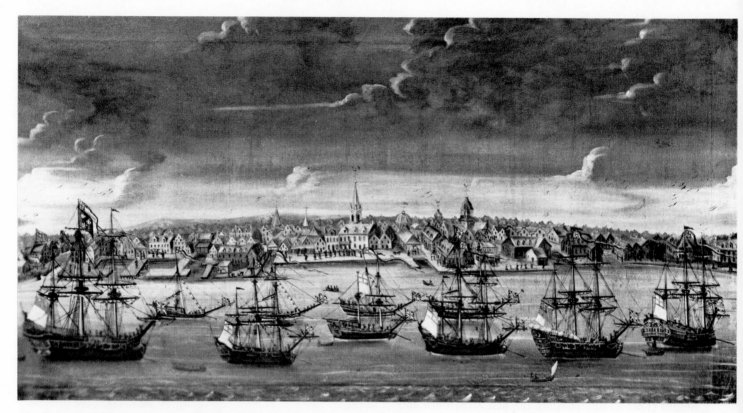

107 Anonymous. *British Privateers with French Prizes in New York Harbor.* 1756–57.
Oil on canvas, 38 × 72½". The New-York Historical Society

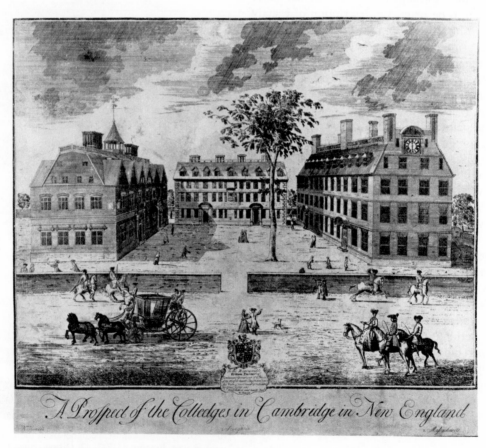

108 William Burgis. *Harvard College in 1726.* Engraving.
Massachusetts Historical Society, Boston

he was "diverting [himself] with something in the Land-skip way, which you know I always liked." The only Colonial landscapes that look like what we think of as traditional landscape painting are two small, rather naively executed pictures tenuously attributed to Benjamin West as a child.

In addition there is mention of subject pictures or landscapes in the effects of such artists as Kühn and Theüs. The interpretation of such evidence remains open to question; in no case in which landscapes or subject pictures are mentioned in inventories is it possible to assume that these were paintings and not prints or that they were by American painters.

The only true example of a genre painting from the Colonial period is one called *Sea Captains Carousing in Surinam* (c. 1758, plate 109), attributed to American-born John Greenwood (1727–1792) and said to have been painted after he had left America for Surinam at the age of twenty-five. Although there are mentions of genre pictures in collections, that in itself is not proof that they were paintings or American. On the other hand, there is incontrovertible documentary evidence of a few. There is written mention that Badger sold a "laughing boy" in 1757, that Copley sold a painting of a nun by candlelight to King's College, and that West had painted a man reading by candlelight.

History painting, which included religious, secular, and mythological themes, was considered the noblest objec-tive of the artist. Copley and West ultimately left America, at least in part because the urge to paint historical subjects could not be satisfied here. While prints dealing with such themes were available and some of them must have hung in homes, the occasional painting of this type was done by the artist for his own satisfaction. We actually have two mythological scenes by Gustavus Hesselius, but they appear to be somewhat naive and clumsy copies rather than original conceptions, and Copley has left us three allegorical scenes, copied from engravings and dated about 1753–54, which are tentative efforts of the young painter to learn by translating black-and-white prints into paint.

The only known commission for a religious painting was for a *Last Supper* by Gustavus Hesselius for Saint Barnabas' Church, Queen Anne's Parish, Prince Georges County, Md., installed in 1722 but lost after 1773. Two other religious paintings by Hesselius mentioned in literary sources no longer exist. However, a large and unique body of religious paintings by John Valentin Haidt (1700–1780), a missionary of the Moravian Brotherhood, is still extant in churches in Bethlehem, Lititz, and Nazareth, Pa. Haidt had a modicum of training in Europe, came here as a convert in 1754, and spent the rest of his life decorating the churches of the sect, but his efforts are hardly notable works of art.

One type of the historical genre which became popular before the Revolution was the journalistic print, a record

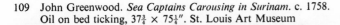

109 John Greenwood. *Sea Captains Carousing in Surinam.* c. 1758. Oil on bed ticking, 37¾ × 75¼″. St. Louis Art Museum

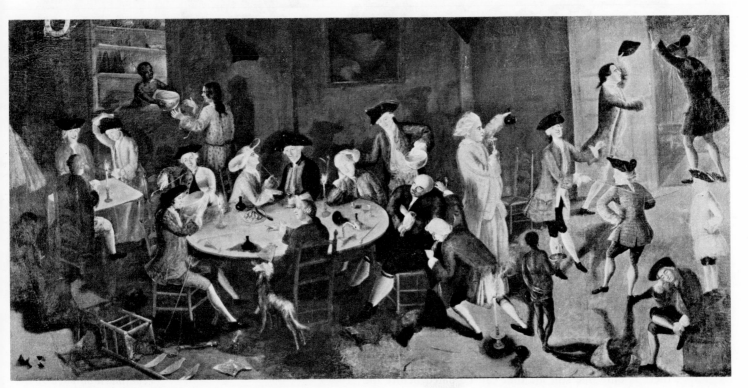

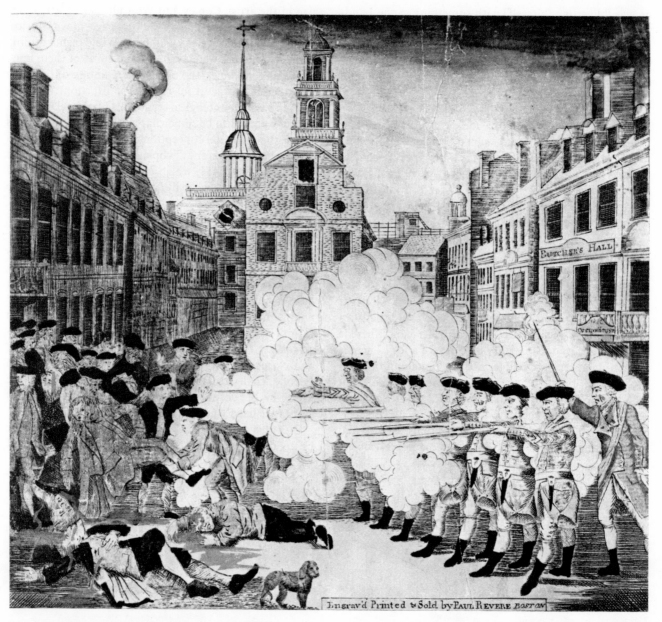

110 Paul Revere. *The Boston Massacre*. 1770. Engraving, $7\frac{7}{8} \times 8\frac{5}{8}''$. Worcester Art Museum

of some important and interesting recent event, usually a battle scene. Paul Revere's famous *The Boston Massacre* (plate 110) was issued immediately after the event in 1770. The earliest known venture of Ralph Earl (see Chapter 6) was the execution of four paintings concerned with the battles of Lexington and Concord. This early journalistic scoop was achieved when Amos Doolittle published engravings of Earl's paintings in December, 1775.

The evidence for still-life painting is even more meager than for the other types. According to Virgil Barker, there is only one still life that can be dated before the Revolution, a painting by Winthrop Chandler of a row of books, evidently intended as a *trompe l'oeil*, for a Connecticut house, where it still hangs. After that we are back to advertisements: pictures of dead game, flower subjects, still life as decorations for the home, birds.

It seems fairly obvious that Americans were aware of the kinds of art available in Europe at the time, but long before they would patronize local artists, they would buy imported prints of similar subjects, which would be cheaper and carry more cachet than the efforts of local craftsmen.

(continued on page 95)

The earliest indicators of ceramic activity in this country are the fragments of earthenware cooking vessels and tableware found at the early colony of Jamestown, Va., dating from the first half of the seventeenth century. Such objects were made of redware, still being produced in quantity into the nineteenth century. Redware was made from local red clays and kiln-fired at low temperatures. New England, especially the Boston area, was the major center of redware production in the seventeenth and early eighteenth centuries and the activities of several important potters are documented. The most common forms produced there were mugs, jugs, pitchers, and crocks. The smaller everyday objects were not usually decorated, but larger and more important pieces had some minimal treatment. This large crock (plate 111) is an example of decoration by incising lines in the clay before firing it. The contrasting color of the interior was produced by adding some local minerals to a lead glaze which, when the crock was fired, permanently adhered to the clay. We know from both records and pottery shards that there were also pieces decorated with painted designs, but because these objects were made for everyday use and, though fragile, were easily replaceable, they were not preserved. As there was no pressure to adopt new styles on such mundane household objects, and as succeeding generations continued to produce in the same areas, something about the early forms is known from later but similar examples.

The earliest glassmaking in this country was attempted by a German settler named Caspar Wistar in 1739, on a creek some miles from the future town of Glassboro, N.J. Wistar and his son imported four additional blowers from Holland and turned out windows, bottles, and other objects until the progress of the Revolutionary War put him out of business in 1781. The availability of sand, wood, and water transportation made the area suitable for glassmaking, however, and several other factories were opened during the next few years. As none of the free-blown production was signed, the individual pieces cannot be positively assigned to the manufacturer, and the entire output of the area is called "South Jersey type." During the late colonial period, when Wistar and others

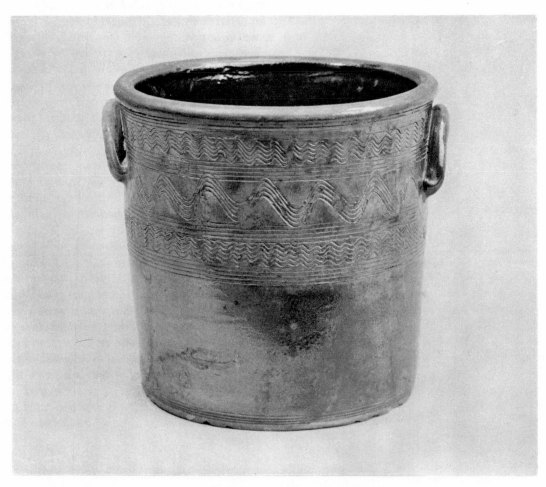

111 Crock, from Essex County, Mass. Early 18th century. Red earthenware with incised decoration. National Museum of History and Technology, Smithsonian Institution, Washington, D.C. Gift of Lura Woodside Watkins

Eighteenth-Century Colonial Painting and Sculpture 93

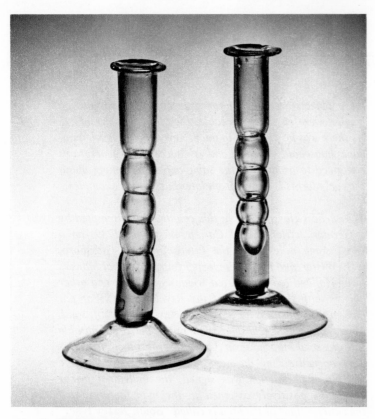

112 Candlesticks of South Jersey type. c. 1740–80. Free-blown and tooled light-green glass, height c. 7⅜″.
The Corning Museum of Glass, Corning, N.Y.

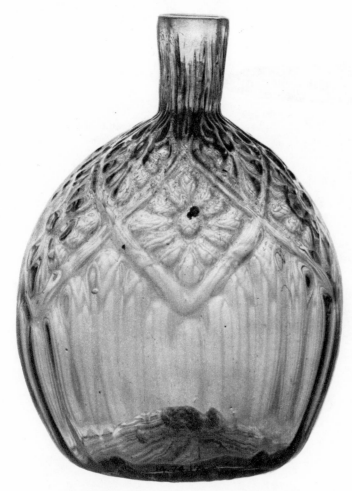

113 Flask of Stiegel type, from Pennsylvania. 1770s.
Pattern-molded amethyst glass, height 4¾″.
The Metropolitan Museum of Art, New York.
Gift of Frederick W. Hunter, 1914

were entering the field, England was discouraging manufacturing here in order to increase her exports to the colonies. British glass was too expensive for most colonials, however, and the demand for a variety of household objects was met by the South Jersey firms.

Glass candlesticks (plate 112) were cheaper than metal ones and could be as graceful as those in pewter. Like so much South Jersey work, these holders are light green and have some imperfections, due to being blown from a low grade of glass. The forms are conventional for the period with a simple classic shape and tooled work applied to the stems. It was this sort of glass, cheaply made, yet reflecting the forms of the major European styles, that kept the South Jersey glassblowers and their midwestern descendants busy for many generations.

In 1763 Heinrich Wilhelm ("Baron") Stiegel set up his first glassworks at Elizabeth Township, Pennsylvania, the beginning of what was to be his ultimately unsuccessful attempt to produce all sorts of glass in the major European traditions. He eventually had three factories, with trained cutters, enamelers, and grinders in addition to the necessary blowers, and even visited England to learn about the popular Bristol glass process. In 1772 the high-living and expansive Baron was advertising glasses, tableware, decanters, jelly glasses, and many other objects such as window glass, but by 1774 he was in debtor's prison. As his objects were eagerly bought by housewives from Maryland to Boston, they were obviously both popular and of good quality. His failure must thus be attributed to the cost of manufacture and to his well-recorded overexpansion. With so much known about his life and his glassmaking, it is quite frustrating that there is no factory mark on any of his sizable output and no single piece can stand as indisputably an authentic "Stiegel" example. Several designs of objects can be reasonably ascribed to his factory or to those later set up by his workmen, and such objects are known as "Stiegel type." Because of Stiegel's close copying of European models, it is often difficult to decide which of those surviving items were actually made in the colonies.

Some particular decorative motifs, such as that found on this small scent bottle (plate 113), are unknown in Europe and prove their American origin. Such a bottle was blown in a process called "pattern-molding," which consists of blowing a "gather" of glass into a one-piece mold that imprints the pattern on the glass. After it is removed from the mold, the glass is blown to full size, with the pattern expanding proportionately. The unique motif mentioned above, the diamond-daisy design, is a series of diamonds, each filled with one daisy, its petals shaped so as to fill each diamond completely. Such a decorated bottle, provided with a stopper, was used by colonial women to hold perfume.

(continued from page 92)

SCULPTURE BEFORE THE REVOLUTION

The gravestone still monopolized stonecutting, but increased wealth and cultural changes prepared the way for new mortuary forms. Soon after the turn of the century the relaxation in Puritan strictures became evident in the introduction on gravestones of bust portraits in place of winged skulls. Primitive as some of these are, they nevertheless were the first efforts at portraiture in stone. Among the earliest is the gravestone of the Reverend Jonathan Pierpont (d. 1709, plate 114), Wakefield, Mass. By midcentury the type was common all along the eastern seaboard. The change in both attitude and taste, with the introduction of Classical forms and motifs, is apparent in the work of Henry Emmes, a Boston grave-

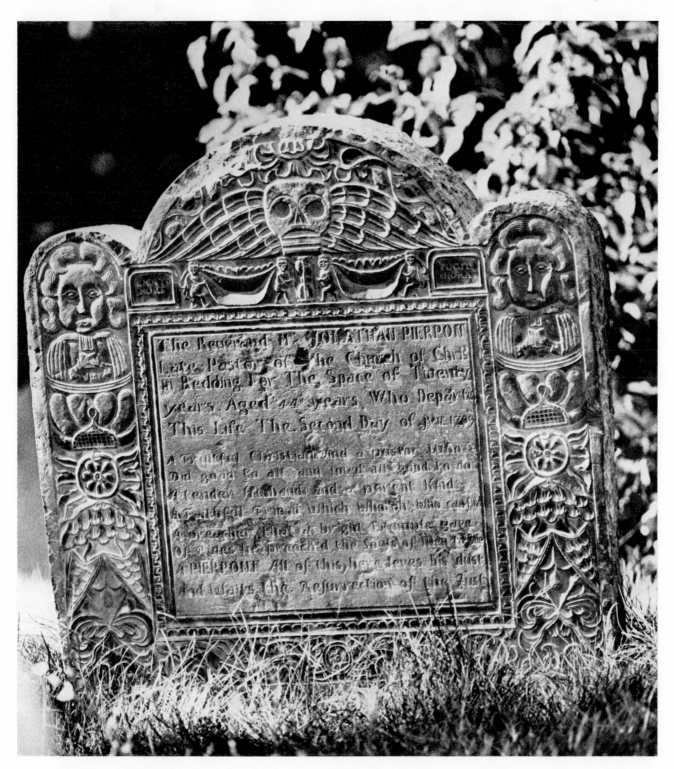

114 Gravestone of the Reverend Jonathan Pierpont (d. 1709), Wakefield, Mass.

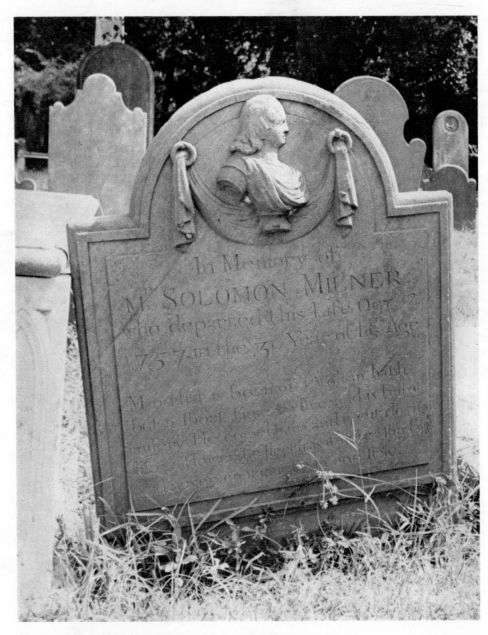

115 Gravestone of Solomon Milner (d. 1757), Congregational churchyard, Charleston, S.C.

stone cutter whose tombs can be found as far south as Charleston. There the Congregational churchyard contains the grave marker of Solomon Milner (d. 1757, plate 115), which bears a profile bust portrait with a toga in the Roman manner. Even on the highest levels of craftsmanship such tombstones remain provincial and fairly primitive imitations of English models.

Quite separate from this development toward a high style was the continuation in backwoods areas of the seventeenth-century artisan tradition, evolving from complexity of form back to simplified, almost abstract pattern, in which rudimentary signs are carved with great refinement. This typical folkloric process occurs in isolation and stems from constant reiter-

ation of a limited vocabulary of forms.

Throughout the eighteenth century carpentry remained a more extensive and highly developed craft than stone-cutting, and it was in shops that produced architectural and furniture decoration, signs, and ship figureheads that the first tentative steps toward sculpture as an independent art were made. Shipbuilding had become a major industry by the early years of the century in New England coastal towns, and with it ship carpentry in all its forms flourished. There are records that the first of the Skillins, Simeon Sr. (1716–1778), produced figureheads, but unfortunately none of these early examples has survived. The golden age of figurehead carving is post-Revolutionary.

The production of shop signs was probably the work

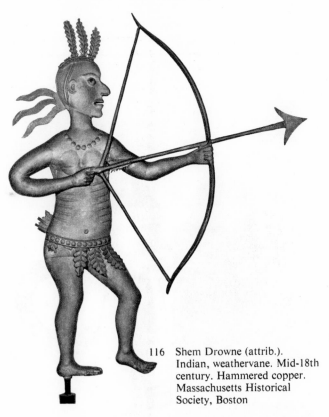

116 Shem Drowne (attrib.). Indian, weathervane. Mid-18th century. Hammered copper. Massachusetts Historical Society, Boston

of the same carvers, but, again, little remains except for a small polychromed wood figure called *The Little Admiral* (1750–70, colorplate 11), immortalized by Nathaniel Hawthorne in "Drowne's Wooden Image." Its attribution to the legendary Shem Drowne is questionable, but it seems to be the earliest extant freestanding sculpture done in America. The figure, which once held a nautical instrument (if it served as a ship chandler's sign) or a stein (if it was a tavern sign), is awkward, ill-proportioned, and crudely carved.

Although they are products of an entirely different craft, mention should be made of the earliest surviving weather vanes, both from Boston: the hammered-copper Indian (c. 1750, plate 116), which once gyrated above the cupola of the Province House (the remodeled Peter Sergeant House of the seventeenth century); and the Grasshopper (1742, plate 117), also in copper, atop Faneuil Hall. Both have been traditionally attributed to Shem Drowne. Such meager remnants are the first intimations of a sculptural figurative art.

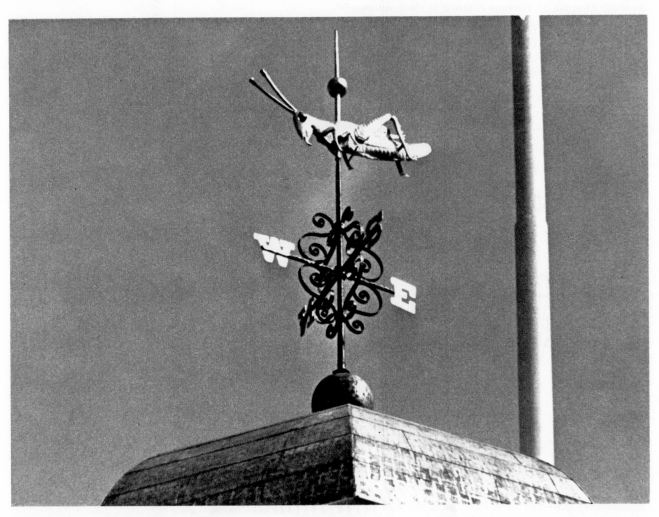

117 Shem Drowne (attrib.). Grasshopper, weathervane. 1742. Copper. Faneuil Hall, Boston

Eighteenth-Century Colonial Painting and Sculpture 97

With increasing affluence at the beginning of the eighteenth century, objects proliferated as much as varieties of furniture, and growing collections of plate began to be displayed on chests and highboys. Gradually Puritan insistence on simplicity was relaxed, and Boston silversmiths began to decorate their work with engraving and repeated patterns. Edward Winslow, who was a major pupil of Dummer, was an early and skillful practitioner of the new decorative techniques and used one of them, gadrooning, on a covered chocolate pot about 1700 (plate 118). Gadrooning, identified by its use of a parallel convex vertical design, is usually used in certain critical areas and contrasted with the otherwise plain surfaces. On the chocolate pot it appears at the widest part of the base and near the top of the lid and is supplemented with some deep cutwork related in design to textile patterns of the era. The pot itself still has the solid quality of the Dummer piece (plate 32) and balances the curve of the spout with that of the handle. A real touch of practicality is that the chain and finial can be removed so that a stick could be inserted for stirring the chocolate. Balance of form and decoration make this a classic example of Baroque contrast in the development of the early history of American silver.

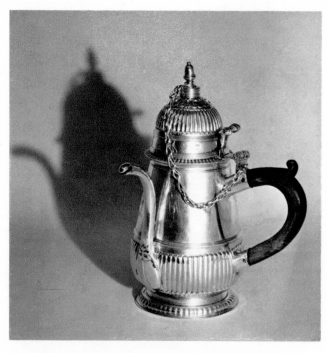

118 Edward Winslow. Chocolate pot. c. 1700. Silver, height 9½". The Metropolitan Museum of Art, New York. Bequest of A. T. Clearwater, 1933

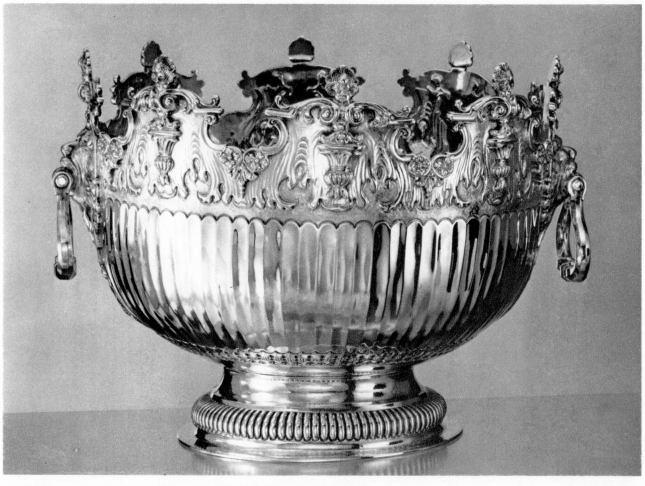

119 John Coney. Monteith. c. 1700–10. Silver, height 8⅜". Yale University Art Gallery, New Haven. The Mabel Brady Garvan Collection

Only the upper stratum of society would have owned such an object as this large bowl (plate 119). Appropriated from English prototypes, the monteith is a form that bespeaks conspicuous consumption. It was designed so that wineglasses could be hung down over the rim and chilled in the iced water inside. The form is sophisticated and the decoration is even more so. The splayed base, with its circle of gadrooning, the punched pattern at the bottom of the body, and the delicate fluting which accentuates the upward flow of the body are a prelude for the intricate and extremely rich rim. There are two swiveling handles, each attached to open-mouthed lion's-head masks, all at the base of the clearly defined rim area. Eight finials, each in the form of a cherub's head, sit atop Baroque corbels decorated with flowers, and the familiar acanthus leaves run around the whole. The Colman family arms are engraved in another common element of the period's design vocabulary, the cartouche. Most, if not all, of the decorative elements can be seen in many pieces of the period's silver and many on the furniture, but seldom have all been brought together in a piece of balanced proportions and, at the same time, incredible lushness. The bowl is perhaps the most elaborate creation of the Boston silversmith John Coney (1656–1722).

During the Queen Anne period, when the new fashion of drinking tea was sweeping the colonies, a whole new range of furniture and furnishings was developed to enhance the activity: tea tables, with delicately turned legs and scalloped rims, porcelain teacups, and, of course, silver tea services. The shapes of the teapots differ from city to city; very few survive from Philadelphia, but there are numerous apple-shaped pots from Boston and pear-shaped ones from New York. An example of the latter is a Queen Anne-inspired pot (plate 120) by Peter Van Dyck (1684–1750). The S-shaped spout and handle are related to the use of the same curve in furniture design (plate 75) and depart from the Baroque form of overblown ornamentation. The quality of the teapot lies in the sweep of its outline, with use of repeated moldings at the points of division to check, but not stop, the eye from its upward flow. The finial essentially repeats the entire shape of the bowl in miniature, adding to the fluidity of movement. Of particular interest is the balance between the handle and the spout, with the thumb piece on the handle echoing the back-slung curve of the lip. In total, outline and simple moldings produce a study in simplicity as compared to the elaborately engraved silver forms (plate 34) of the later seventeenth century in New York.

The sugar bowl of the second quarter of the eighteenth century differed substantially from the large, magnificently decorated form of a generation earlier. Taste at the later date called for a small bowl-shaped form with a lid that is a variation on the shape of the bowl, but inverted. The form was usually circular, as in this example (plate 121), but

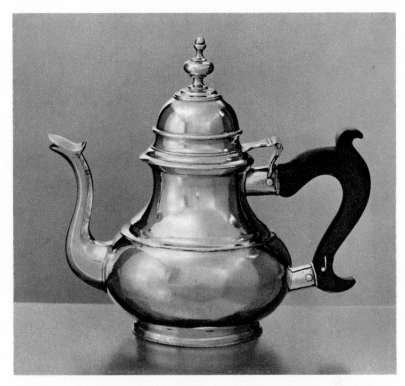

120   Peter Van Dyck. Teapot. c. 1725–50. Silver, height 7½″. Yale University Art Gallery, New Haven. The Mabel Brady Garvan Collection

121   Paul Revere, Sr. Sugar bowl. c. 1725–40. Silver, height 4¾″. Historic Deerfield, Inc., Deerfield, Mass.

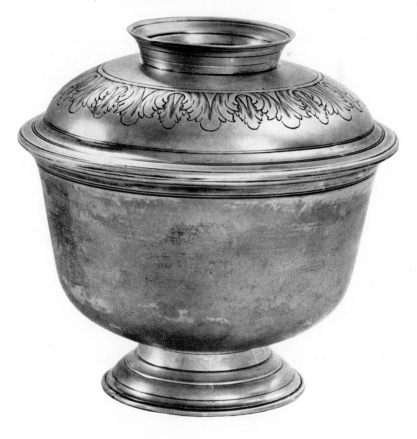

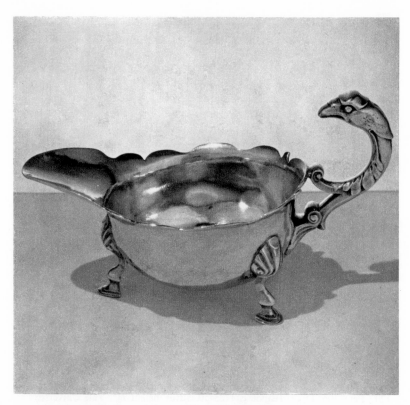

122 Elias Boudinot. Sauce boat. c. 1760. Silver, height 4¼".
Philadelphia Museum of Art. Purchase, McIlhenny Fund

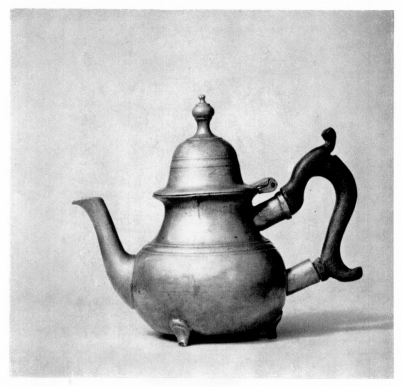

123 William Will. Teapot. 1780. Pewter, height 7". Philadelphia
Museum of Art. Gift of Lessing J. Rosenwald

some were hexagonal or octagonal in design. Paul Revere, Sr. (1702–1754), was an apprentice of Coney, and it is therefore not surprising that the engraving on the cover is indebted to the Baroque tradition in which his master had worked. The form itself is not Baroque, however, and the subtle steps of the bowl's base and at both top and base of the cover are far removed from formal qualities of the earlier era. Delicate balance is the norm here, and small variations on the Rococo line from base to top give the bowl its charm.

A late example of the Queen Anne style can be seen in this sauce boat (plate 122) designed and executed by Elias Boudinot (1706–1770), a smith who worked in both gold and silver in New Jersey near Philadelphia. The rim of the sauce boat, with its undulating form, is like those found on the few pieces of porcelain produced here during this period. The firm of Bonnin and Morris, of Philadelphia, actually produced pieces in a similar Queen Anne style, and there is little doubt that they were influenced by the metalwork of such craftsmen as Boudinot, who, in turn, derived from English models. As in the example illustrated, the silver sauce boat usually rested on three curved feet (rather than on the splayed base of ceramic pieces) and had high double-scroll handles. Boudinot twisted the scrolls upward and adapted the eagle head found on earlier English furniture for the end of the handle. Instead of the claws that one might expect to serve as the feet, the artist introduced tiny S-curved hoofs, which were also found on chafing dishes and, in a more richly carved format, on small silver saltcellars popular through the period. Boudinot's sauce boat reflects the change of direction at the end of the Rococo period by mixing the simpler hammered work of the body with the applied ornamentation of the feet and handle, incorporating many of the tendencies soon to be found in the full-blown Chippendale style.

Although the use of pewter was fairly widespread in eighteenth-century America, most was imported and very little of it, either imported or domestic, remains today. Most of the pewter was imported from England, as much as 250 tons of the finished article in 1767, but 137 pewterers are recorded as working here before the Revolution. The reason for its scarcity today is that pewter is fragile. An alloy of tin, mixed with varying quantities of copper, antimony, and lead, it has a low melting point and is easily broken or worn. Thus the items definitely ascribable to some forty-two craftsmen are all that we can speak of with authority. This teapot (plate 123) by William Will (1742–1798) is typical in that it illustrates the pewterer's use of the same forms as the silversmith, in this case, the pear shape seen also in the teapot by Van Dyck (plate 120). Originating in Philadelphia, this piece, with its claw-and-ball feet like those on furniture (plate 80), shows Will's adherence to current fashion. Aside from having feet instead of a base, the pewter pot is quite similar to the silver ones, with its S-shaped handle, narrow linear bands, and similar shape of the finial. This adaptation of furniture motifs, at the height of their popularity, was not so easy for the pewterer as for the silversmith, for pewter was not worked freely, as were silver and gold. Pewter was cast in molds, which were expensive to make, and they were not discarded for trivial changes in taste. Thus, so long as there was reasonable demand for a certain object, for economic reasons the pewterer remained a conservative force, and one should not ascribe too early a date to a pewter object that might well have been cast many years after a similar piece of known date.

Probably the best-known piece of American silver is the punch bowl made in 1768 by Paul Revere, Jr. (1735–1818), and known as the "Sons of Liberty" bowl (plate 124). It is important as a historic document, not only because so much is known about the occasion for its presentation but also because of the specific words and symbols engraved on it. As the inscription says, it commemorates a historic vote by the Massachusetts House of Representatives: Massachusetts had circularized a letter to the colonies urging resistance to British policies which were thought repressive. Pressure had been put on the House to rescind, but they voted not to do so. The praise that Revere inscribed on the bowl was specifically for the vote, as he puts it, "Not To Rescind." Also engraved are names of the patriotic leaders, in a frieze around the bowl's lip, and references to the Magna Carta, Bill of Rights, John Wilkes, and other symbols in the iconography of liberty. The overall shape is based on a type of Chinese porcelain bowl that was imported through England and was popular in the colonies. The base is conservative, and the smooth surface (necessarily left so for the extensive engraving) is fairly heavy and lacking in vitality. Revere, who was an excellent craftsman, was more concerned in this case with message than with medium.

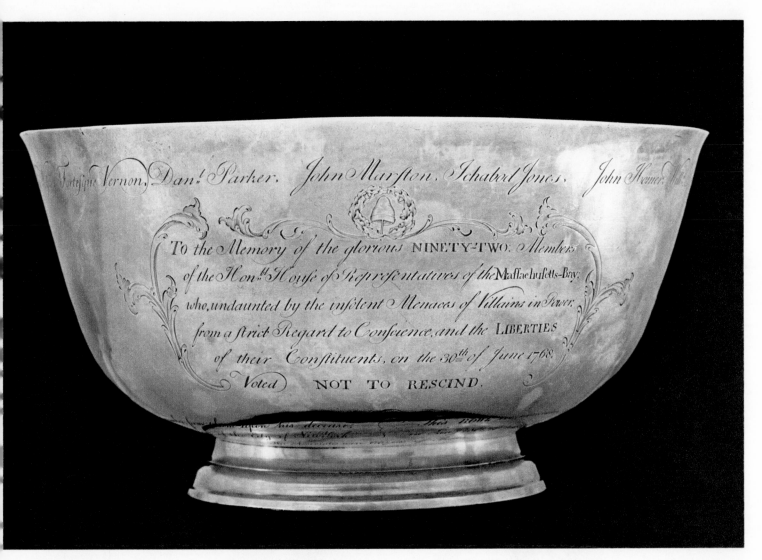

124 Paul Revere, Jr. The "Sons of Liberty Punch Bowl." 1768. Silver, diameter 11". Museum of Fine Arts, Boston. Gift by public subscription and from the Francis Bartlett Fund

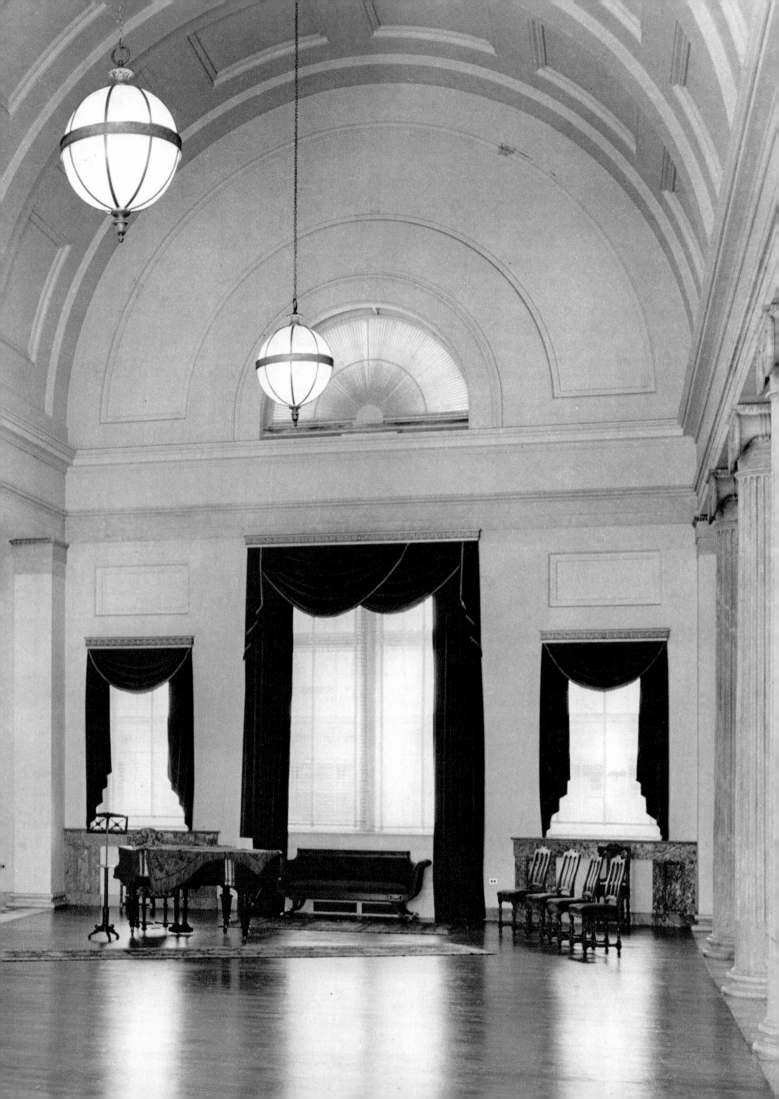

Part 2
THE EARLY REPUBLIC

When the American nation was forged in the heat of the War of Independence, the American character was transformed and its culture was given a new direction. Americans accepted their new role with a self-conscious sense of destiny which made historical necessity, moral righteousness, and patriotic fervor almost synonymous. They postulated a society based on liberty and equality. This political euphoria was bolstered by a period of economic growth, increased immigration fostered by European political unrest, and westward expansion. The Louisiana Purchase by Jefferson in 1803 underlined the growing concept of "manifest destiny." The individual merchant, artisan, or farmer might not see beyond his own self-interest, but America's political leaders, thinkers, and artists took a broader and longer view into the future. What they saw were endless vistas and only the best of auguries. It did not then seem even remotely possible that nature's gifts might be despoiled or man's ideals betrayed.

Everything had become "American" and thus was related to the total of what America meant. Architecture had to stand for something, express something American. Painting must now glorify the nation and its heroes, inform and educate the public, underline the greatness and promise of America. Sculpture, which had hardly existed before, could immortalize America's heroes in imperishable bronze and stone. America would outdo the past—the Renaissance, which because of its Popish taint was of lesser concern,

and, more important, the Romans and the Greeks.

But why were Greece and Rome ideals for a Protestant-dominated nation that had so recently been as opposed to paganism as to the Pope? The intellectual history of the eighteenth century, culminating in the Age of Reason, had undermined the earlier religious parochialism and intolerance that had dominated European culture for centuries. In the search for reason, the Greek philosophers supplanted the Church Fathers. In the search for an equitable society, the concept of representative government challenged the divine right of kings, with the city-states of Greece and the Republic of Rome as models. The Age of Reason even developed a new approach to religion for those who needed it—deism, a rational faith. All this came rather easily, because Protestantism itself had already fought the battle of reason over faith. It has been validly suggested that this whole development was really an expression of the growing strength and dynamic momentum of the middle class in its rise to power. Certainly middle-class economic, social, political, moral, and even cultural positions were being furthered.

Also, the rediscovery of Herculaneum and Pompeii during the middle of the century had initiated a fashion for the antique. The ideological formulations of Winckelmann and Mengs and the paintings of West, Hamilton, and then David had sparked a Classical Revival that swept over Europe to replace the aristocratic frivolity of the Rococo with an art which was serious and moral.

5
Neoclassic Architecture

In nineteenth-century architecture Neoclassicism was the first of a sequence of revival styles. It has therefore been characterized as part of the Romantic Movement and, along with other revivalist tendencies, as a mistaken effort to find solutions for contemporary problems in the past. But Romanticism and revivalism are not entirely escapist or negative. At that time history-mindedness was synonymous with progressivism. The past offered material, experience, and ideas that creative artists could and did employ with freedom, originality, and inventiveness. The revivalists, after all, built the first modern hospitals, prisons, factories, bridges, canals, banks, hotels, office buildings, schools, railroad stations, and government buildings. They were the first to use new materials—iron, concrete, glass—in modern ways. They worried about spatial organization, adequate sanitary facilities, circulation, and fireproofing. The buildings they designed were often successful attempts to solve basic problems of site, function, materials, and cost.

The war and unsettled conditions under the confederation of states inhibited building for more than a decade, and this hiatus helped produce a clean break between pre- and post-Revolutionary architecture. To designate the latter as "Late Georgian," as has been done, can be misleading. For the English, who still had a king named George, the designation of the Neoclassic or Adam style as "Late Georgian" reflects a reverence for historical neatness. In America, such a term for an art that was now an expression of a new nation which had won its independence from George III is ironic. Aside from ideological reasons, the Neoclassic, the Adamesque, the Federal, whatever it is called, is not a continuation of the Georgian, since its fundamental aesthetic considerations are at complete variance with those of the Baroque.

There were two wings to the Neoclassic style in America, as in Europe—one which tried to revise what had gone before, and one which tried to make a clean break with the immediate past. In New England especially there was a pronounced dependence on English architec-

ture, but that itself had changed: England was in the midst of a Classical Revival, its taste dominated by the brothers Robert and James Adam in architecture, by Josiah Wedgwood in decoration, and by Thomas Sheraton and George Hepplewhite in furniture. America received the new style through architectural handbooks by the Adams, William Paine, and James Pain, and eventually via the first American imitations by Asher Benjamin (1773–1845) in *The Country Builder's Assistant* (1797) and *The American Builder's Companion; or, A New System of Architecture* (1806).

Those who looked for a specifically American architecture went back directly to Classical sources for their inspiration: first to Palladio again, but not seen through the prism of the Baroque; then to the Roman; and finally to the Greek. This radical aspect of Neoclassicism, called Monumental Classicism (or Romantic Classicism), was fundamentally a public architecture with domestic by-products, whereas the more conservative Adamesque was a domestic architecture which produced a limited number of public buildings. The former flourished largely in Washington, D.C., and Philadelphia; the latter in New England and the South.

Extremely important to the development of the Monumental style was the influx of professional foreign architects. Although Thomas Jefferson inspired much of the style, its character and generally high level of excellence in design and execution were due to these immigrants. The variety and originality of public buildings in the Monumental style contrast with the general lack of inventiveness of Adamesque domestic architecture, which can be traced to amateur practice and the continued use of architectural books. It is more than coincidence that the Adamesque practitioners were all American and local products, while nearly all the Monumental architects were Europeans. However, the Classical Revival in its Monumental aspect was not a foreign or imported architecture; it was, in fact, the first truly American style.

(continued on page 108)

The Windsor chair originated in England, but was developed and refined to such an extent in this country that many people assume it to be an indigenous furniture form. Philadelphia was the early center of Windsor-chair production, with over 6,000 put out by the end of the Revolution. The activity then shifted to New York and, eventually, to almost all the eastern seaboard. The Windsor was made in a variety of shapes (plate 125 and colorplate 14) and was used throughout the house. The three most common shapes were high-backed, low-backed, and sack-backed, with many variations, including such extremes as

fan chairs (plate 126), used as a solution to problems of both heat and flies. The armless variety might be associated with dining and the high-back armchair with the parlor. In addition, there were Windsor settees, stools, tables, and cradles.

All were made of several woods: hardwood for the legs and stretchers, resilient woods for the spindles and curved tops, and softwoods for the indented shaped seats. Sometimes the seats were covered with leather cushions and finished with brass tacks. All were painted. Most of the eighteenth-century Windsors were green, but some had two

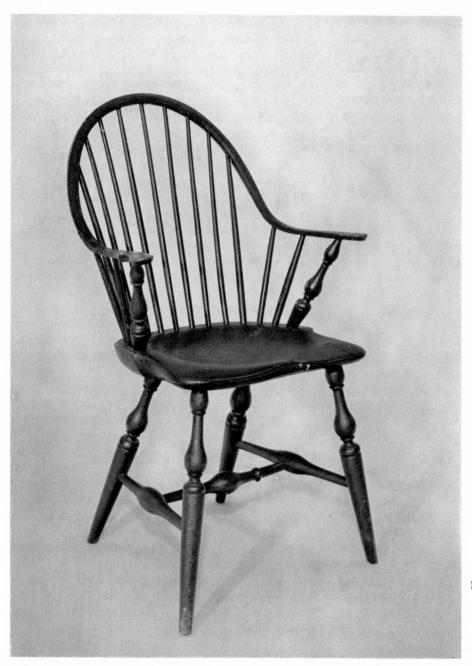

125 J. M. Hasbrouck. Windsor armchair, from New York. 1775–85. Maple and hickory, height 36¼″. The Art Institute of Chicago. Gift of Emily Crane Chadbourne

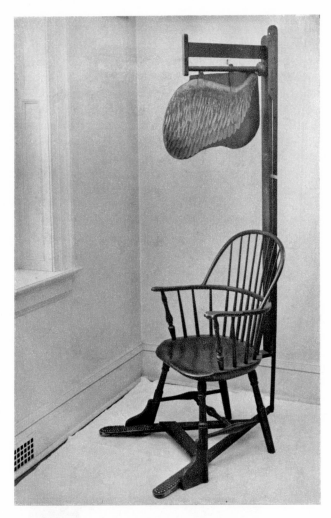

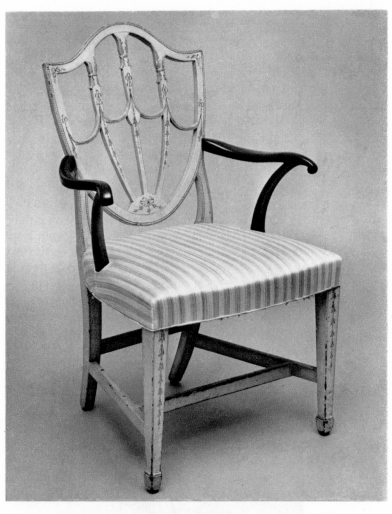

126 Windsor fan chair. 1785–90. Painted wood with
gilded fan and painted feathers, height 77".
The New Haven Colony Historical Society

127 Armchair, from Philadelphia. 1790–1800. Poplar, mahogany,
and pine, height 37½". The Museum of Fine Arts, Houston.
Bayou Bend Collection

or even three colors. Roger Sherman sits in a typical low-back armchair (colorplate 14) of the traditional green with a red seat, of about the time of the Revolution. The high-backs (or comb-backs) evolved into the fan-back after the war, and increased interstate activity spread the styles to such an extent that the discovery of a particular type of Windsor in a certain location cannot be taken as proof that it was made there. The skill and imagination of the turner were given full vent in the variation of legs and stretchers. Some popular designs were widely advertised and produced in large quantities. One Philadelphia manufacturer of Windsors had 1,200 in stock in 1775, and as late as 1796 George Washington ordered twenty-four oval-back chairs for use at Mount Vernon.

After the Revolutionary War a new style, the Early Federal, permeated the urban centers of furniture manufacture. It was part of the general Classical Revival seen also in such architecture as Bulfinch's State House in Boston (plate 131) and Jefferson's Virginia State Capitol (plate 143). Design books were still important and Chippendale's was replaced by Hepplewhite's The Cabinet-Maker and Upholsterer's Guide (1788) and Sheraton's The Cabinet-Maker and Upholsterer's Drawing Book (1793). These volumes introduced wreaths, busts, urns, and swags to American cabinetmakers and modified the frivolity of Rococo with inlay work and veneering. Painting too, which had retreated to the country during the Chippendale domination, now returned with vitality, often combined with delicate giltwork and light blond tonalities (plate 127). Philadelphia remained one of the most important furniture centers, with about one hundred cabinetmakers in the 1790s, and this example was made there near the turn of the century. It derives from a Hepplewhite model and is painted light yellow with bellflower and ribbon ornamentation in tones of blue and white, and, reflecting the taste of the times, has satin upholstery.

(continued from page 105)

THE ADAMESQUE

The Adam style was a rather particular translation of late-Roman art popularized by the rediscovery of Pompeii and Herculaneum. Robert Adam adapted the so-called "Third Style" of wall painting (itself a Roman Neoclassicism), with its small-scale decorative motifs arranged in delicately elegant patterns, to architecture as well as to interior decoration. He continued to use basic Georgian architectural elements but transformed them into something quite different. Plasticity gave way to flatness, boldness to delicacy, opulence to spareness, the heavy to the slender or even fragilely attenuated. The resulting style, unlike the rich-textured Baroque, has a clean-cut, sharp-edged purity.

The first handbooks that brought the Neoclassicism of Adam to America treated it as a vocabulary supplementing the older Georgian forms, rather than as a totally new style. It was accepted rather grudgingly at first, especially in conservative rural areas, where the Georgian died hard, but before the turn of the century the basic Adamesque house form was established. The pavilion capped by a pediment disappeared, as did columnar porches, leaving only a modest but delicately proportioned entrance porch. Windows were larger and taller in proportion, with larger panes and thinner frames. With no other focus of decoration on the facade, the doorway became more elaborate in design, with fanlight and sidelights subdivided by intricate patterns of wire-thin struts. The attic story and its dormer windows were replaced by a third story, so that the house now resembled a simple cube. This look was reinforced by reducing the roof pitch and transferring the balustrade from the deck to the cornice line, thus making the roof shape invisible from ground level.

Adamesque builders continued to use red brick and white trim, as did their Georgian predecessors, though in New England the preference for wood still persisted. Adamesque houses exhibited a greater freedom in planning and a decided advance in utility. For the first time circular, elliptical, and octagonal rooms broke through the tyranny of the rectangle. Rooms now even had elliptical or semicircular vaults, and occasionally a dome.

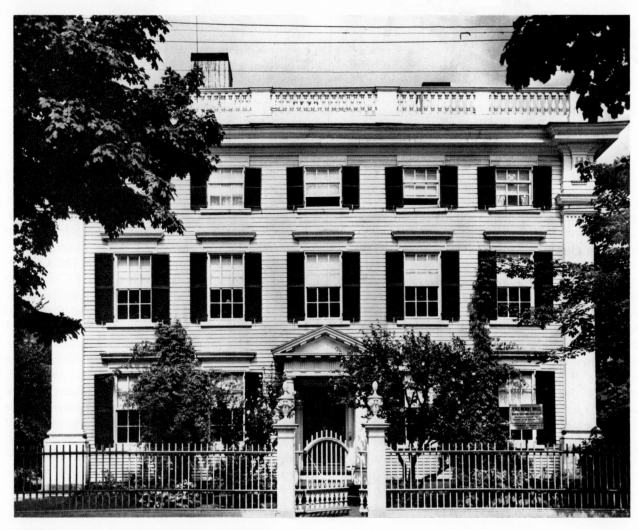

128   Samuel McIntire. Peirce-Nichols House, Salem, Mass. 1782

Many Adamesque buildings are the work of carpenters rather than architects, so that their finest expression is in detail—especially the interior decoration—rather than in planning or composition. Walls are swept clean of ornamentation and are smoothly plastered and painted in pastel colors or papered in small, discreet patterns. White becomes increasingly popular and is now used almost exclusively on woodwork. Moldings, door frames, and fireplaces are covered with an ornament of tiny elements kept strictly within the larger forms and seen only as surface sparkle of light and shade, all in extremely low relief. The ornamental vocabulary changes to impossibly elongated colonnettes and pilasters; miniature triglyphs and dentils; reedings, flutings, and beadings; decorated and fluted ovals and paterae with Classical motifs—urns, garlands, swags, palmettes, and rosettes. Classical bulls' heads and torches mingle with American eagles and sheaves of wheat.

The intricacy of the carving eventually led to the use of prefabricated decorations pressed in composition material, a development begun by the Adam brothers and Wedgwood and the first experiment in the production of "well-designed" objects at reasonable prices. Composition products were soon being manufactured also in America, moldings by the yard and plaques by the dozen. But, on the whole, Adam-style interiors kept their air of delicate and refined simplicity.

McINTIRE AND BULFINCH

The leading exponents of the Adam style, Samuel McIntire and Charles Bulfinch, were both New Englanders. They represent in their separate ways the culmination and demise of the colonial "amateur" tradition in architecture. Samuel McIntire (1757–1811) came from a family of Salem woodcarvers and carpenters and spent all his life in that city and within the framework of his craft and the family shop. The addition of the word "architect" to his gravestone indicates his achievement as well as his aspiration. Despite his impeccable craftsmanship and native sense of taste and proportion, McIntire remained more the artisan and builder than the architect, for he was dependent on handbooks and on the work of others. Yet some of his interiors and carved details are among the loveliest products of the Adam style. His mark is still to be seen in the quiet, tree-lined streets of old Salem in the houses built for the Derbys, the Peirces, and the Crowninshields during the great days of shipbuilding and sailing after the Revolution.

The earliest McIntire effort in the Adam style, perhaps the earliest in the country, is the Peirce-Nichols House (1782, plate 128). Although it is tentative and clumsy in the handling of the new elements, the basic cubical form is clearly stated. The facade is plain, the dormer story has been eliminated, and the roof is hidden by the balustrade. Decorative features of the Georgian still intrude—the

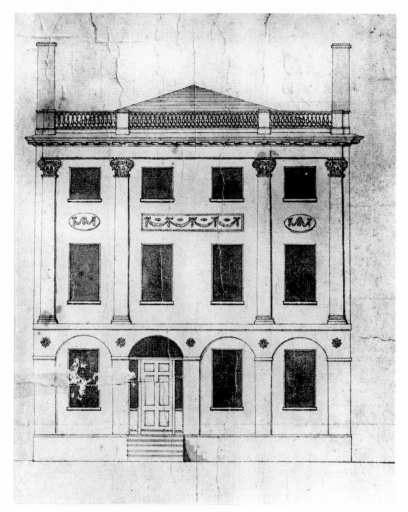

129 Samuel McIntire. Design for main facade, Ezekiel Hersey Derby House, Salem, Mass. Built 1799

heavy corner pilasters, the projecting cornice, the plastic window frames—but the refined carving of the small Classical porch and doorway, the picket fence, and the decorative urns on the gate posts are early evidence of McIntire's style and skill.

The Ezekiel Hersey Derby House (1799), said to have been done by McIntire after a design by Bulfinch, shows full acceptance of the Adam style and is one of the most elegant and original examples (plate 129). The inspiration is now fully English and Adamesque. The sensitivity of scale and proportion, the refinement of detail, and the spacing of elements on the smoothly plastered facade create an architectural bijou unique among American examples of the Adam style.

Charles Bulfinch (1763–1844) was a man of totally different stripe—urbane, sophisticated, and knowledgeable. Reverence for tradition, particularly English tradition, kept him from radical innovation, but his fastidious taste created Adamesque prototypes that dominated New England architectural expression for more than a generation.

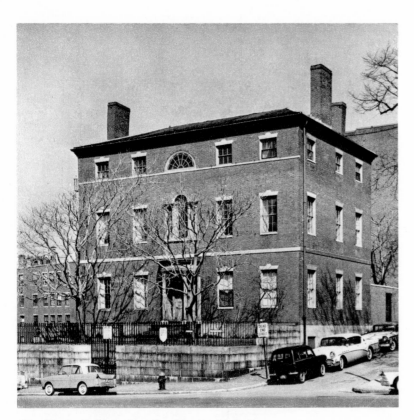

130 Charles Bulfinch. First Harrison Gray Otis House, Boston. 1795–96

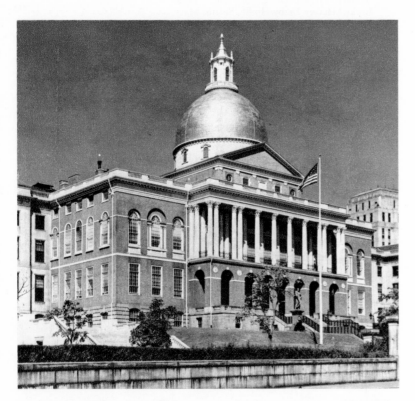

131 Charles Bulfinch. State House, Boston. 1795–98

Bulfinch transformed the Georgian town house in Adamesque terms. The first Harrison Gray Otis House (1795–96, plate 130) established the canon—a clean-cut cube of red brick (he seems to have preferred wood for rural houses) with a sharp cornice; immaculate walls with large, slender windows beautifully spaced; horizontal white-stone bands marking the story divisions; and an exquisitely rendered hemispherical porch with elongated columns and pilasters in the Corinthian mode. Bulfinch retained an old-fashioned preference for the Palladian window and what seems a consciously anachronistic insistence on the semicircular rather than the elliptical form in lunettes and fanlights. This latter, along with a window recessed in an arch, is almost a signature of the personal Bulfinch manner.

Bulfinch's work in semipublic building—the housing development as speculative building—was the first experiment of its kind in this country, and Bulfinch was both architect and entrepreneur. Franklin Place, or the Tontine Crescent, erected in Boston in 1793, consisted of sixteen attached single houses in a row, designed as a unit but purchasable singly. Bulfinch had seen such complexes in London and Bath, and his Franklin Place was an imitation of such models, with the row of houses arranged in a shallow arc facing a gardened park plot. It was a solution eagerly accepted, and it spawned the ubiquitous row houses of American cities, which unfortunately exploited only the economic advantages to the builder and sloughed off the amenities.

Bulfinch, as the dominant personality in New England architecture, naturally received many major government commissions, but his strength was not in monumentality. His most ambitious building, Boston's State House (1795–98, plate 131), a gold-domed landmark revered by Bostonians, reveals his limitations as a designer. There is no denying the logic, sophistication, and elegance in Bulfinch's handling of the central arcade surmounted by columns, but the exquisite composition of the lower part is vitiated by an inexplicable pedimented section above, capped by an even less defensible dome on a drum and topped by a cupola. The sides of the pedimented section are clumsily abutted by the hip roofs of the wings, the dome does not have enough room on the gable, and the fussy cupola is an inadequate afterthought. Inside, the chamber of the House of Representatives is one of the most imposing interiors of the period, beautifully proportioned but somewhat diminished by niggling Adamesque ornamentation.

His masterpiece is the First Church of Christ (1816–17, plate 132), Lancaster, Mass. A superb delicacy of detail is here combined with bold simplicity of form. The restraint of the whole unfolds rich recompense in the unique transformation of the Georgian porch into an arcaded loggia accented by stripped and "orderless" pilasters; in the bold, clear, geometric masses against

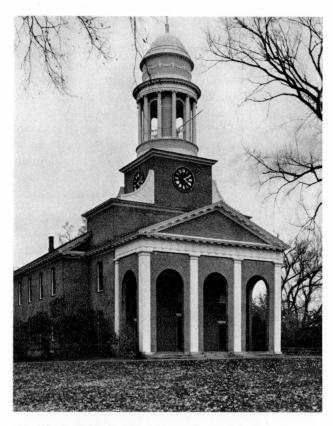

132 Charles Bulfinch. Fifth Meeting House of the First Church of Christ, Lancaster, Mass. 1816–17

which the elegance of the porch is set; in the fragile, almost ephemeral fan screen which manages to make the transition between the bare cubes; and in the exquisite cupola, like a piece of Wedgwood ware, absolutely impeccable in scale.

Unique in New England is the splendid Gore Place (1805–06) in Waltham, Mass., more like a southern plantation house than a New England country residence, with a large central section and extended arms ending in wings (plate 133). Even its hip roofs and tall chimneys are reminiscent of the Georgian and the South, but in its stately sweep, clean surfaces, elegant proportions, and precise detailing it is totally Adamesque and very English. The front facade is fairly plain, but in the rear the rectangle of the central block is broken by a graceful bow created by the magnificent oval room that overlooks the broad lawn sweeping down to the river. Although the house has been attributed to others, the recessed arches, the predilection for the semicircular window, and the strong feeling for cubical form are all Bulfinchian features. Gore Place may be, like many other American buildings, a compendium of ideas, in this case fused into a masterpiece of the Adam style. Its graceful spiral staircase, with simple fragile banisters and sweeping handrail, seems almost to float in air as it soars up the curved

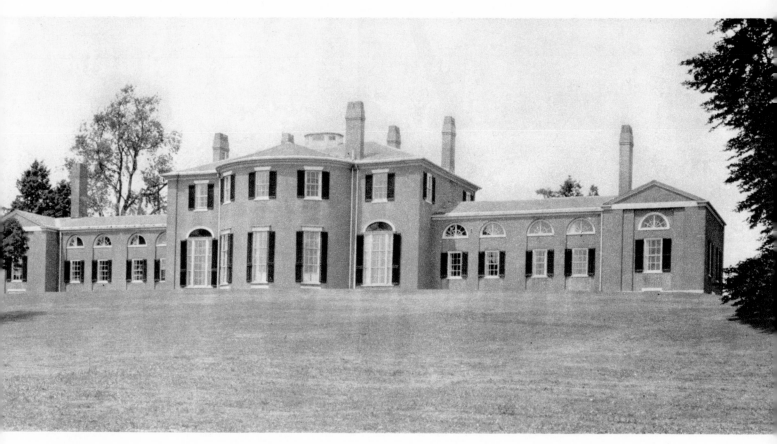

133 South facade, Gore Place, Waltham, Mass. 1805–06

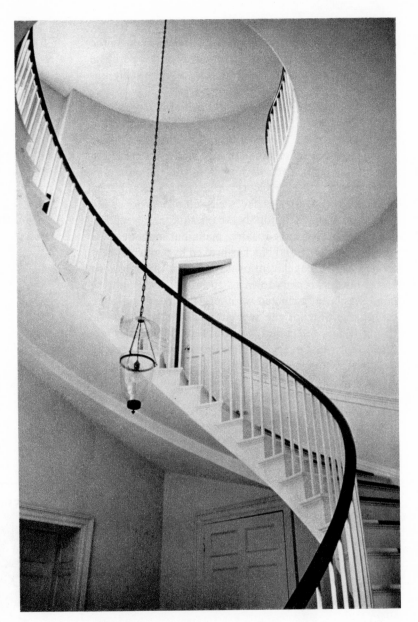

134　Spiral staircase, Gore Place, Waltham, Mass. 1805–06

Outside New England the Adamesque was not so prevalent, though there are some important survivals. For instance, Homewood (1801–03, plate 136), now part of Johns Hopkins University in Baltimore, and attributed to Dr. William Thornton (1759–1828), retains its southern Georgian plantation-house form, though all its proportions and details are Adamesque.

New York's City Hall (1802–12, plate 137) is not Adamesque, although its conservative adherence to an eighteenth-century mode brings it close. It is the only French-inspired public building of the period, perhaps because revulsion against the Reign of Terror dampened an earlier enthusiasm for things French. Joseph-François Mangin (act. 1794–1818), who, together with John McComb, Jr., submitted a design for the building in 1802, was responsible for City Hall's French air. Available evidence indicates that the original design was Mangin's, while its actual construction, as well as the adaptation of its detailing to a more English mode, belonged to McComb. Something in its total design, scale and proportions, spacing, and general vitality recalls the Rococo, but a Rococo laced with Classical restraint. Its exterior remains one of the treasures of American architecture, and its interior is no less impressive.

(continued on page 117)

135　First Congregational Church, Bennington, Vt. 1805

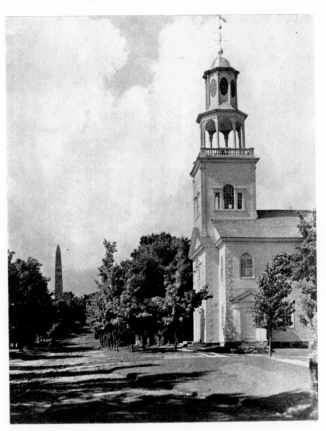

wall of the side hall, a gem of elegant simplicity (plate 134).

Bulfinch's influence in New England was pervasive, especially in Boston. Elsewhere his style was imitated directly or through the designs reproduced in handbooks by Asher Benjamin.

Although the Adamesque never became a vernacular style, perhaps because too much in it depended on subtleties of scale, proportion, and detail that carpenters could not well manage, it was still widespread, and local variations abound. For instance, in Vermont Lavius Fillmore, a local builder, probably did the charming First Congregational Church (1805, plate 135) in Bennington, copied from a plate in Benjamin.

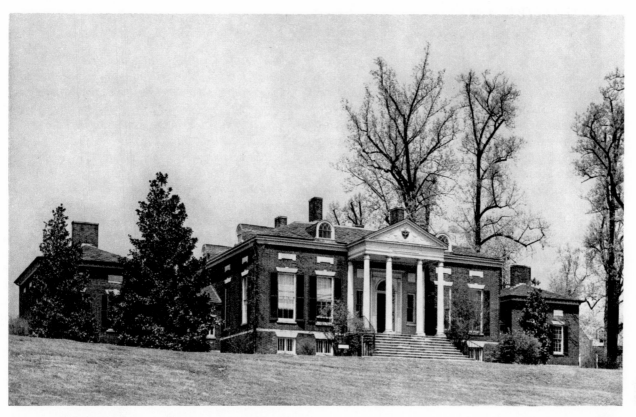

136 William Thornton (attrib.). Homewood, Baltimore. 1801–03

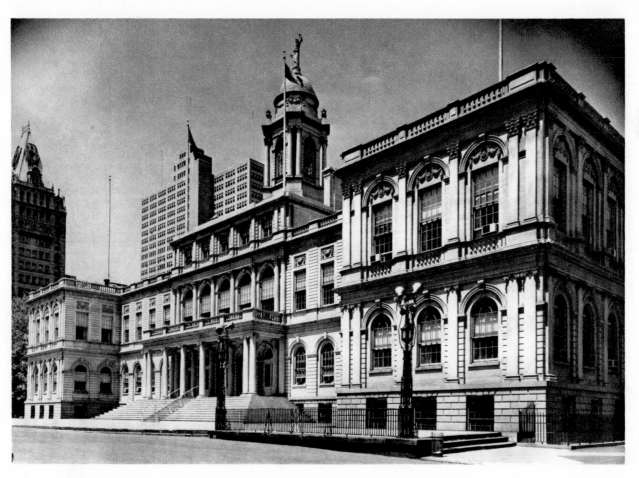

137 Joseph Mangin and John McComb, Jr. City Hall, New York. 1802–12

The high-post bed (plate 138) was popular for elegant bedrooms and was accompanied by various pieces of accessory furniture: dressing tables, basin stands, and chests of drawers. Such beds were found in all parts of the settled country and, of course, had regional differences. This bed is a southern example, made in Charleston, and incorporates the most obvious distinguishing feature, a careful carving known as "rice carving." Southern furniture has suffered more from dispersal and destruction than the work of any other area, so that generalizations about it are hazardous. It is obvious, though, in comparing the top of the bed with the lady's dressing table (plate 140), that the squared-off tops and applied arms were features common to the more elegant manifestations of Early Federal style. Four-posters from New England share the ribbed column posts, the drapery, and the valance, but tend to be plain-topped, with nothing above the valance. The difference in taste reflects the modified but still heavy reliance of the South on England in matters of art and culture; much furniture was still purchased from England and locally made works more directly reflected English forms.

During the Early Federal years, several elegant new furniture forms made their appearance in this country: the lady's work table, the sectional dining table, and, most important, the sideboard. Among forms that evolved from earlier ones were the secretary-bookcase and the lady's dressing table.

The secretary-bookcase (plate 139) evolved from the eighteenth-century secretary-desk, but, in contrast to the earlier form, which was a massive, aggressive piece of furniture, the later one tends to have its mass disguised by surface design. The basic form of the Davey secretary-bookcase was found in Hepplewhite's 1788 Guide, the first to mention a "secretary drawer," the main feature of the piece. The Philadelphia example here is typically rectilinear in form, with little in the way of projecting moldings or pilasters. Inlay has replaced the carving of Chippendale styles, and the dimensional ornamentation is replaced by surface patterns of wood veneers polished to a brilliant sheen. In structure, the low-key sophistication is apparent; drawers are hidden behind the doors of the lower section, bookcases behind the upper section, and,

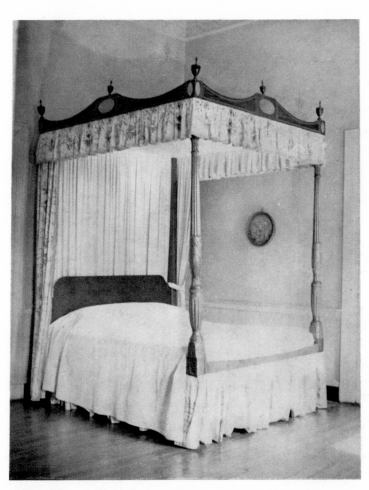

138 High-post bed. 1775–1800. Mahogany, height 108". The Charleston Museum Collection, Charleston, S.C. Joseph Manigault House

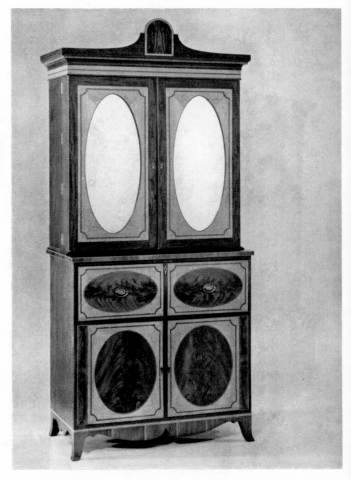

139 John Davey. Secretary, from Philadelphia. c. 1805–10. Satinwood and mahogany veneer, height 95⅞". The Metropolitan Museum of Art, New York. Fletcher Fund, Rogers Fund; Gift of Mrs. Russell Sage; the Sylmaris Collection, Gift of George Coe Graves, 1962

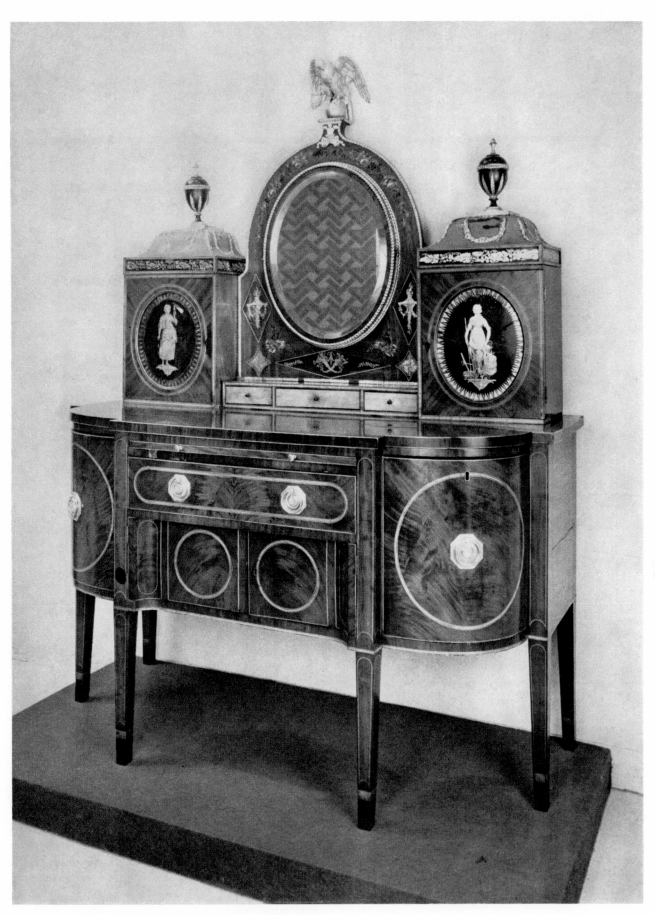

140 Lady's writing desk-dressing table, from Baltimore. c. 1800.
      Mahogany and satinwood, width 54″. Maryland Historical Society, Baltimore

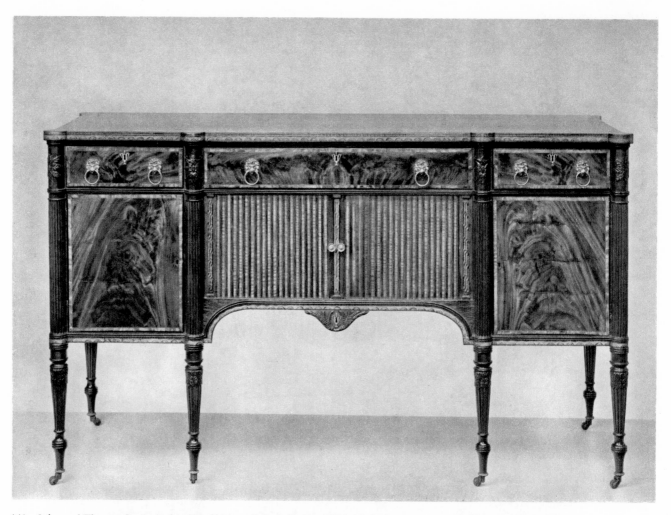

141 John and Thomas Seymour (attrib.). Sideboard, from Boston. 1800–10. Mahogany with veneer work, height 41⅞".
The Metropolitan Museum of Art, New York. Gift of the family of Mr. and Mrs. Andrew Varick Stout, in their memory, 1965

most important in this era, the desk is hidden behind the false center drawer. The drawer front is let down by means of curved hinges and becomes the writing surface. The mirrors not only serve their nominal function but are also a part of the surface decoration, surrounded by veneered shapes echoing those in the base section, as the mirrors in turn echo the shapes of the base panels.

The lady's dressing table (plate 140) is derived from Sheraton's Drawing Book *and provides an interesting comparison with the secretary-bookcase. Both have mahogany as the primary wood, surfaces embellished with inlay, and mirrors as part of the decorative scheme. However, the dressing table is more varied in ornamentation and employs more of the Classical vocabulary: the urns, the swags, and the allegorical figures. It also has inset painted-glass panels, a distinctive Baltimore touch. These ovals are painted dark blue, with figures representing*

Commerce and Industry in their centers. The eagle, urns, and smaller diamond-shaped panels further enrich this ornate version of a typical Federal style form, and illustrate the characteristics of work produced in increasingly prosperous Baltimore at the turn of the century.

The sideboard (plate 141) was manufactured in Boston. It too is mahogany and has veneered panels, but it also has several regional traits. Carving was more common there than in many parts of the country, and legs tended to be more attenuated (cf. plate 140). This sideboard has been attributed to John and Thomas Seymour and has the sliding tambour front typical of their major pieces. The tambour device, made of narrow strips (flattened on the obverse side) glued on a sturdy fabric backing, presented a solid front but could be rolled out of sight. It was useful for desks as well as sideboards, and, when open, revealed interiors painted in the English manner.

(continued from page 112)

MONUMENTAL CLASSICISM— JEFFERSON'S EARLY WORK

Thomas Jefferson's contribution to Early Republican architecture is inestimable. His passion for architecture and his concern for the "correct" expression of American principles in architectural terms led him to take an active, even leading, part in the Classic Revival. Jefferson was a remarkably versatile man—planter, statesman, classical scholar, architect, and gadgeteer. A product of the Age of Reason, he was above all both reasonable and rational, a materialist interested in reality, the present, and utility. He revered Palladio, who made architecture seem so rational and practical, an expression of natural law.

As a gentleman's son, Jefferson had received a rudimentary training in architecture, but the practical need for building on his estate elicited a passion and an avocation. His first serious effort is to be seen in the plans for his home, Monticello, for which an elevation drawing exists (plate 142). The dependence on Palladio is clear. This and his designs for other Virginia houses are a definite departure from the Georgian mode. They were based on Palladio's design of villas for estates in the Veneto, very often working estates, similar to those for which Jefferson designed his houses. The Classical elements of a double-story porch in the correct orders and the Doric frieze were no more important to Jefferson than the plan with its central house, wings, and dependencies spread on the terrain in a commodious way.

All the houses Jefferson actually designed, or even only advised his friends and neighbors about, have this quality of stateliness, rationality, and utility. They were all done after the Revolution, after Jefferson had been Ambassador to France and seen the Roman ruins in Italy.

It was the memory of the Maison Carrée in Nîmes which inspired him to design a Roman temple to house the State Capitol of Virginia (1785–89, plate 143) in Richmond. He sought the aid of the French architect Charles-Louis Clérisseau in drawing up the plans, but the idea and its modification to fit its function and the limitations of American craftsmen were his own. In construction some of the elegance was lost, and Samuel Dobie, who supervised the building and had pretensions to architecture himself, took it upon himself to cut a

142 Thomas Jefferson. Final elevation, first version of Monticello. Before March, 1771. Massachusetts Historical Society, Boston

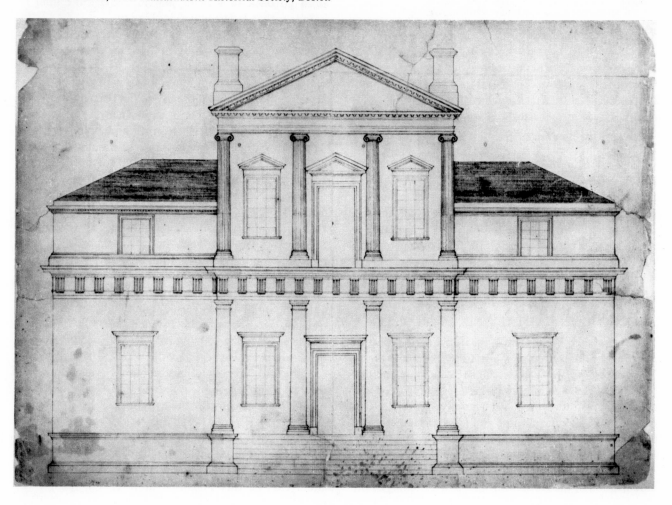

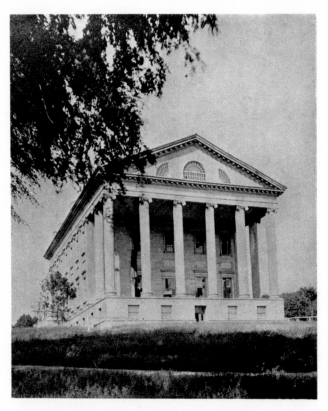

143 Thomas Jefferson. State Capitol, Richmond, Va. 1785–89 (photographed 1865). National Archives, Washington, D.C.

semicircular window in the pediment and to add pilasters between the windows on the sides. Thus the Maison Carrée became an American building. But with all its crudities and provincialism, it must have seemed a building worthy of housing the kind of government Jefferson conceived.

The State Capitol has come in for more criticism than any of Jefferson's other efforts, because it was the first building to use an ancient temple type for a modern purpose. A Classical temple, the repository of an idol, is not, after all, very well adapted to all the functions to which it was eventually put, but the form had ideological significance for Jefferson and his contemporaries, and it helped set the direction in which American architecture was to develop.

THE NATION'S CAPITAL AND LATROBE

Pierre-Charles L'Enfant (1754–1825) had set the tone for a national architecture of Classicism. Through George Washington, he was commissioned to prepare the first capitol of the United States in New York for the presidential inauguration in 1789. The city had offered its City Hall to serve the purpose and L'Enfant transformed it into a cubical mass with an air of Classical simplicity. His Americanization of the ornament presaged a new spirit. He had created the first "American" order, a modification of the Doric with stars in the necking of the

capitals; the Doric frieze had thirteen metopes with a star in each for the original states of the Union; the pediment carried the symbol of the American eagle holding arrows and olive branches in its claws; and decorative plaques over the windows repeated the arrows and branches. From the outset Classicism was the form but Americanism the content.

When the national government was established on the Potomac L'Enfant laid out the plan for the projected new city of Washington, D.C. (plate 144). Starting from scratch, the new governmental buildings erected under the watchful supervision of Thomas Jefferson were to set the Monumental Classical style. Jefferson, recently back from France, hovered over the competitions in 1792 for the Capitol and the President's House. Competitive designs were submitted by many practicing architects and builders, but only Stephen Hallet and William Thornton (plate 145) submitted Monumental Classical conceptions, and curiously similar ones, which eventually led to confusion and recrimination. Thornton got the commission and, perhaps as a diplomatic gesture, Hallet was appointed Superintendent of Construction. Both the Thornton and the Hallet plans show a central section surmounted by a low Roman dome and flanked by symmetrical wings to house the two legislative bodies. Both go back to Roman sources, exactly the kind of grandeur that Jefferson was looking for.

Dr. William Thornton (1759–1828), a West Indian-born English gentleman and physician, was, like Jefferson, a passionate amateur architect. He seems to have understood the need for a new monumentality, going for his design to *Vitruvius Britannicus*, but his plan was more Palladian, even Georgian, than Roman. Thornton and Hallet squabbled with each other and both architects wrangled with the commissioners. Finally, Jefferson appointed Benjamin Latrobe in 1803 to supervise construction of the Capitol.

Benjamin H. Latrobe (1764–1820) was a superbly trained young architect who gave up what promised to be a brilliant career in England to come to the United States in 1796. His professionalism, knowledge, and authority pulled work on the Capitol together and created a monument out of chaos. However, during the occupation of Washington by the British in the War of 1812, the building was gutted by fire and only the outer walls of the wings remained standing.

The second phase of Latrobe's work on the Capitol began in 1815. He repaired the wings, designed a new rotunda and dome as well as new semicircular chambers for the House of Representatives and the Senate, and modified the designs for the eastern and western central facades (plate 146). In all his work on the Capitol, Latrobe utilized a Classical vocabulary, yet his intention was contemporary function and nobility. He produced the first architecture of true grandeur in this country. In later years he was somewhat annoyed that people re-

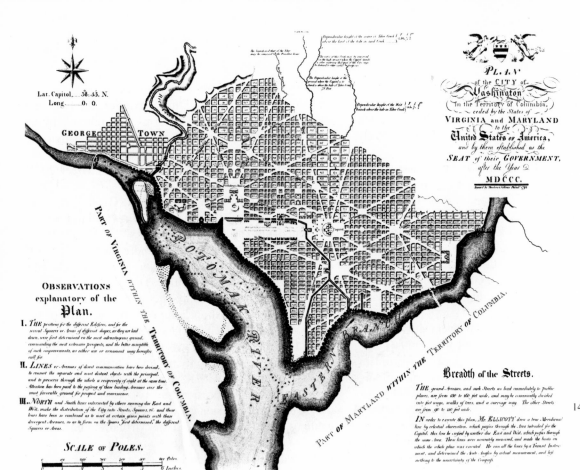

144 Pierre-Charles L'Enfant.
Plan of Washington, D.C.
(as rendered by Andrew
Ellicott). 1792

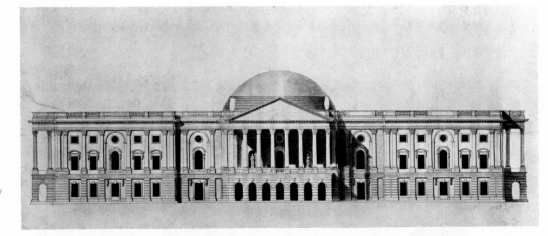

145 William Thornton. Design for
east elevation, U.S. Capitol,
Washington, D.C. 1792. Library
of Congress, Washington, D.C.

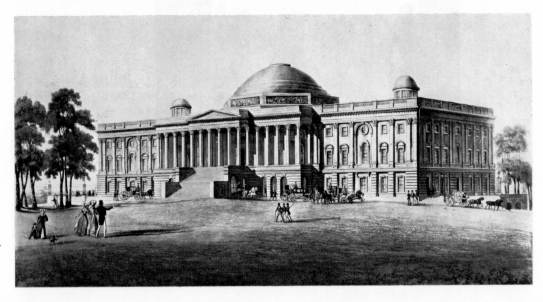

146 Benjamin H. Latrobe. Design
for remodeling U.S. Capitol,
Washington, D.C. 1815. The
New York Public Library.
I. N. Phelps Stokes Collection of
American Historical Prints

membered only his "American orders," the corncob and tobacco capitals (plate 147) he had substituted for the Corinthian acanthus, but they were indications, though minor, of his willingness to use Classical sources freely and with originality.

Compared with the Capitol the White House (1792–1829), designed by the Irishman James Hoban (1762–1831), is something of a disappointment. It is not a Monumental Classical building, although it may have appeared so in the original plan (plate 148). Its only claim to monumentality is in its scale, its white stone, and the porticoes designed by Latrobe in 1807 and constructed in 1824. It is essentially a Georgian building with a heavy dignity rather than the nobility that the Classic Revival was seeking.

Even before Latrobe's major involvement with the Capitol he had executed the Bank of Pennsylvania (1798–1800) in Philadelphia, now destroyed. Latrobe's problem was the design of a public bank, a new kind of building that was certainly unavailable in the repertory of Classical architecture. He seems, at least superficially, to have used the Roman podium form, but the design can also be read less archaeologically as a square central block with a low dome and porticoes at either end. Latrobe had created a central space, ample in scale and dignified in expression, with a coffered dome lit by a simple cupola (plate 149). The flanking cubes contained banking rooms,

and the entire structure was raised above ground level and supported by vaults. On the exterior, the bold and spare massing of geometric forms was relieved by an elegance of proportion and a restrained sensitivity in detail. The Ionic order, possibly borrowed from the Erechtheum, was the first use of a purely Greek order in the United States.

Though Latrobe's preference for the Greek is clear, he could also see that "our religion requires a church wholly different from the [Greek] temples. . . ." Both of the designs he submitted for the Baltimore Cathedral in 1805 accepted the centuries-old tradition of the church. One was Neoclassic, the other Gothic. The disposition of parts was the same in both; only the architectural language was different. The bishop, imbued with the spirit of the time, selected the Neoclassic version, and the building (plate 150), begun in 1806, was finished in 1818, although the portico was erected only in 1863. Latrobe followed a typical church form, with nave and transept, a dome over the crossing, and a portico and two towers at the entrance end; but his signature is seen in the massing of volumes, the low dome, and the virtual elimination of decoration except for the Ionic capitals and the restrained dentilation under the cornice. Yet, as blunt and original a statement as the building is, it is not entirely successful. The onion domes, not his, are no help, but even without them the building does not jell as a unit, and the relation of horizontal and vertical elements is unresolved.

JEFFERSON'S LATER WORK

Monumental Classicism was carried on by Jefferson, Hadfield, Thornton, and younger men. Jefferson matured as an architect during this period, continuing to move from Palladianism and Roman influence toward Monumental Classicism, but his work, despite his originality and intellectual probity, always retained an element of amateurism.

Jefferson redesigned Monticello (plates 65, 142) in 1793 and continued until 1809. He returned to the dome and central plan of Palladio's Villa Rotonda (plate 151), which held a special fascination for him. In 1792, in the competition for the President's house, he submitted anonymously a direct adaptation of it. However, the completed structure of Monticello resembles the Villa Rotonda only in the most general way. Jefferson accepted the local materials of red brick with white trim. The result is actually a freely and imaginatively developed design, which incorporates his conceptions of propriety and dignity, the complex demands of an active existence, and his inveterate addiction to gadgetry. That it is not a completely satisfying building may be due to the fact that it was additive and that the relation of separate elements was never resolved. There is a feeling that the forms were intended for a more monumental structure.

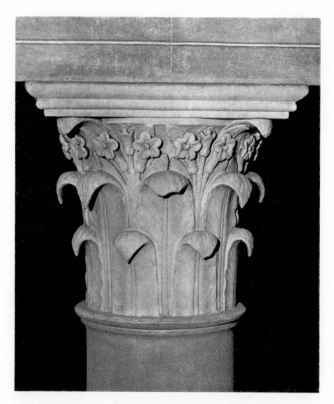

147 Benjamin H. Latrobe. Tobacco capital (carved by Francesco Iardella), U.S. Capitol, Washington, D.C. c. 1815

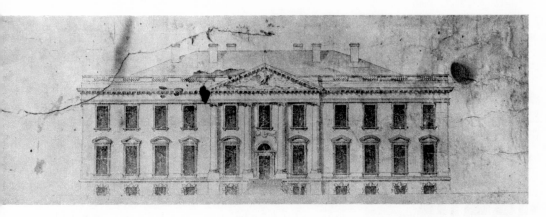

148 James Hoban. Design for an elevation of the White House, Washington, D.C. 1792. Maryland Historical Society, Baltimore

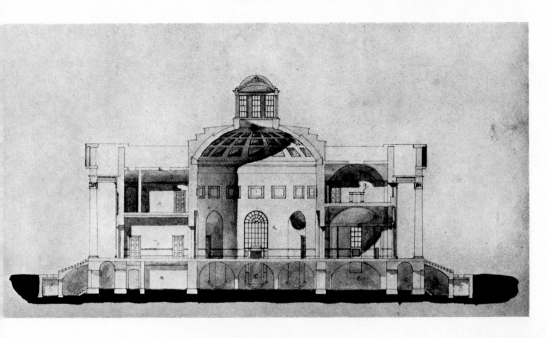

149 Benjamin H. Latrobe. Interior section from east to west, Bank of Pennsylvania, Philadelphia. 1798. Watercolor. The Historical Society of Pennsylvania, Philadelphia

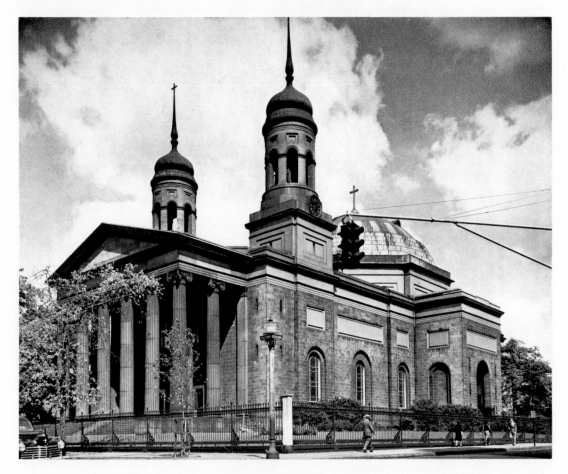

150 Benjamin H. Latrobe. Baltimore Cathedral. 1805–18 (portico 1863)

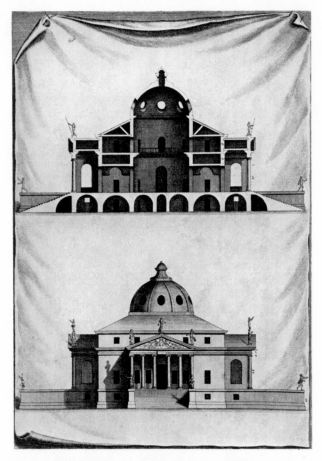

151 Andrea Palladio. Section and elevation, Villa Rotonda, Vicenza, Italy. From Palladio, *I Quattro Libri dell' Architettura*, Leoni edition, London, 1715, Book II, plate 15

The greatest and most successful of Jefferson's architectural efforts is the complex of buildings he designed for the University of Virginia (1817–26) in Charlottesville. In his own probing way he analyzed the aims, resources, and methods of higher education and planned a curriculum to fit them. The design of the campus was based on an "academical village" for an ideal student body of 125, the number of buildings on his division of the university into ten "faculties," the form of the buildings on the theory that architecture could be an instrument of education. The buildings were laid out around a lawn in a U shape. Each building housed a faculty—the living quarters of the professor, the specialized library, and the classroom—all joined by lower dormitories. A running covered colonnade ties together the ten different pavilions built of red brick with white wood trim, the entire procession culminating in the Rotunda (plate 152). The whole, rationally conceived and handsomely landscaped, is undoubtedly the most beautiful campus in the United States.

The individual buildings, as lessons in architecture, were borrowed from a variety of Classical sources; each is a variation on a theme, but all are characterized by the straightforward clarity of the Monumental Classical style. The Rotunda crowned Jefferson's involvement with the Villa Rotonda, but he now moved beyond it to Palladio's own source, the Pantheon. The Rotunda is

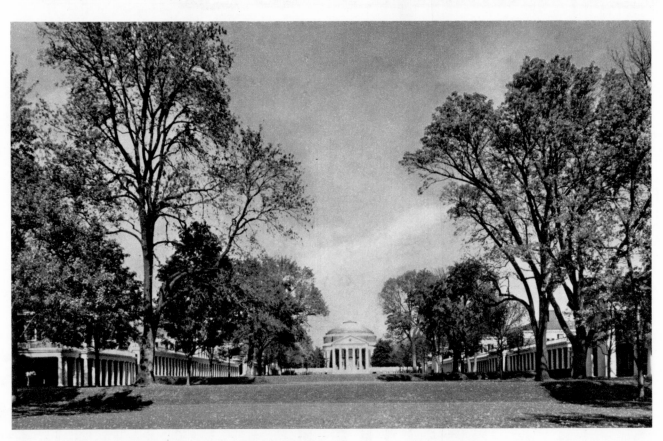

152 Thomas Jefferson. University of Virginia, Charlottesville. 1817–26

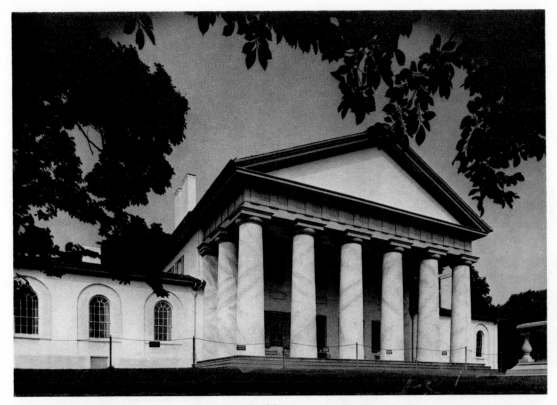

153 George Hadfield. Custis-Lee Mansion, Arlington, Va. Built 1803–04, central block 1817, columns 1820

the badge of Jefferson's pilgrimage to Rome and perhaps his most professional achievement as an architect, but it remains a modest, domesticated, American version of architectural greatness.

FROM MONUMENTAL CLASSICISM TO GREEK REVIVAL

Many of the foreign-born architects who helped form an American architecture in this period never attained success in practice and left little to show for their years here. George Hadfield (1764–1826) was a young architect of great promise. His taste and talent are best seen in the Washington District Court, originally the City Hall (1820–26). One of the finest and most impressive Monumental Classical examples, it has received curiously little attention. It has much the feeling of Latrobe, with its bold composition of big masses, the reduction of decoration to simplified entablature bands, recessed windows in arches, and even the recessed rectangular motif. Hadfield's remodeling of the Lee family mansion, Arlington, Va. (1820, plate 153), also survives. In Arlington the transition from Monumental Classicism to Greek Revival is achieved almost imperceptibly. The unadorned masses of the central block and wings are dominated by a giant portico of "archaic" Doric columns. The portico no longer projects from the house block but now encompasses the whole in a temple form, shifting the roof axis from lateral to frontal and establishing the Greek Revival house type.

Like Hadfield, Maximilien Godefroy (c. 1770–after 1842) had a difficult and abortive career in the United States and left in 1819. His major work was the Unitarian Church (1817–18, plate 154), in Baltimore, a great example of Monumental Classicism, exhibiting all the hallmarks of the style, yet distinguished by unique features. The cubical shape of the building is modified only by the segment of dome that shows on the exterior, the three-arched pedimented loggia of the facade, and the cornice circling the building at the entablature level. The use of a loggia, rather than a projecting portico, and the precise relation of all the parts are reminiscent of Brunelleschi and fifteenth-century Italian Renaissance architecture rather than Roman.

The next generation of architects, nearly all American-born, did their major work during the Greek Revival period. In general, the Greek Revival is distinguishable from Monumental Classicism by (1) a preference for Greek over Roman forms and proportions, (2) the adoption of the Greek temple form, especially in domestic architecture, and (3) the use of the true Doric order. Unfortunately, for purposes of identification, not all these features always occur together, nor is the presence of a single one an adequate criterion for judgment.

Broadly speaking, Monumental Classicism is preponderant and Greek Revival only tentative and sporadic before about 1820, while Greek Revival emerges in strength after that date and dominates until about 1850. There is even some question whether they are not both

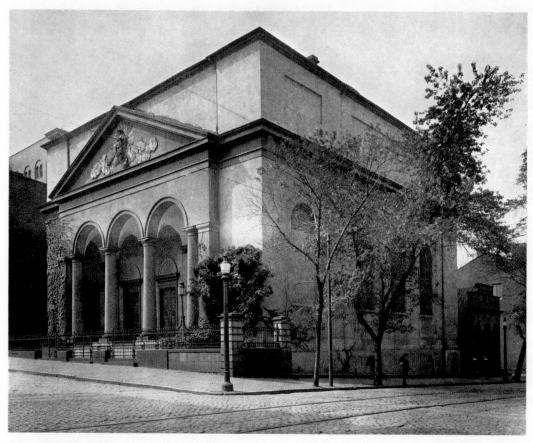

154 Maximilien Godefroy. Unitarian Church
(Christ Church), Baltimore. 1817–18

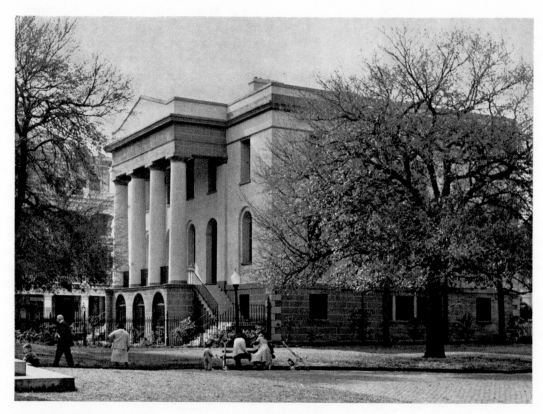

155 Robert Mills. County Records Building ("Fireproof Building"),
Charleston, S.C. 1822–27

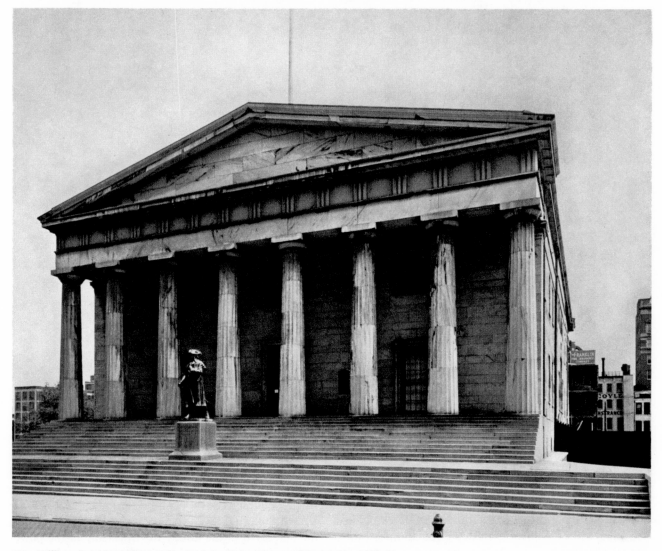

156   William Strickland. Second Bank of the United States, Philadelphia. 1818–24

part of a single continuing and changing style, for architects of both phases had a common concern with
rationality, simplicity, and clarity; with a free adaptation
of the past to the present; and with an open-mindedness
toward new materials and technology.

MILLS AND STRICKLAND

Robert Mills (1781–1855) stands athwart the two periods.
In his intellectual dedication, inherited from Jefferson
and Latrobe, and his aesthetic austerity, he remained
always more a Monumental Classicist than a Greek
Revivalist. Mills and William Strickland (1787–1854)
have always been coupled, for they were the first professionally trained American architects, the major
architects of their generation, and both were students
and assistants of Latrobe and worked out of Philadelphia. Architecturally they had much in common, most
important the acceptance of engineering as an integral

part of American architectural practice. Otherwise they
are two faces to the same coin—Mills serious, practical,
blunt, perhaps even "stodgy"; Strickland adventurous,
inventive, and tasteful. Mills worked for Hoban and
then for two years with Jefferson, who recommended
him to Latrobe; and he assisted Latrobe on the Bank
of Philadelphia and the Baltimore Cathedral. No better
training was available.

Mills's Monumental Classicism can be seen in its
purest form in the County Record Building (1822–27,
plate 155) in Charleston. Compared with the original
elevation rendering it reveals a particular facet of his
artistic personality. The final structure is always more
spare, more forthright, less ingratiating than his meticulous and beautifully detailed drawings. The Classical
quotations and the decorative rhetoric seem to disappear
in the face of the reality of building. The fact that the
structure has always been known in Charleston as the

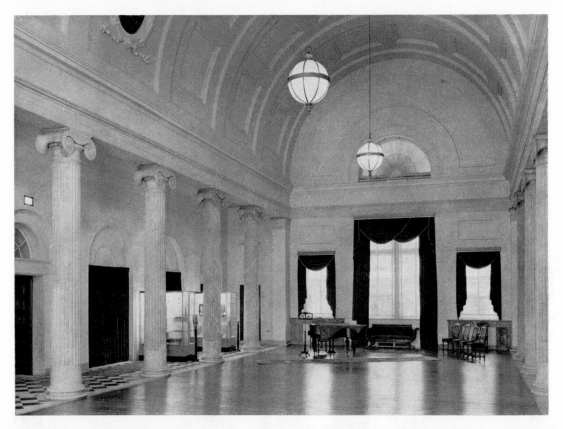

157   William Strickland. The banking room, Second Bank of the United States, Philadelphia. 1818–24

"Fireproof Building" is an indication of Mills's advanced structural thinking. Serviceability was always more important to him than architectural correctness. There is, however, at least in the original design, an obeisance to the growing popularity of the Greek mode.

Unlike Mills, William Strickland found in Monumental Classicism primarily a point of departure. He received his major training from Latrobe from 1803 to about 1805, perhaps even later. Undisciplined and footloose, he left several times and was finally fired. After executing his first independent commission, the

Philadelphia Masonic Hall (1808–11), he drifted out of architecture and did not participate in Monumental Classicism at its height. His return to active practice, when he designed the famous Second Bank of the United States (1818–24, plate 156) in Philadelphia, was the first salvo in the Greek Revival. Only in the power and dignity of the barrel-vaulted central banking room (plate 157), which is curiously oriented on a lateral axis, is anything of the Monumental Classical style evident. The rest is Greek Revival.

(continued on page 130)

DECORATIVE ARTS

In the later years of the Federal period, 1810–25, French influence reached the same level as English, because of a sympathy for the new French Republic and the fact that direct trade between the two nations was made possible. Le style antique, influenced by archaeological discoveries and developed during the Directoire and Consulat periods in France (1795–1804), incorporated not only Classical motifs but other ancient forms as well. When Napoleon returned from Egypt, the Classical vocabulary was supplemented by the exotic Egyptian lotus and sphinx, producing a more international style known as the Empire style.

In England, modification of the French work produced the style known as English Regency, which was transmitted to America through books by Sheraton and others. During the years immediately before and after the War of 1812, the impact of both these styles was most strongly felt and developed in New York, which by then had become this country's style center. Charles Honoré Lannuier (1779–1819), who arrived from France in 1803, produced furniture in "the newest and latest French fashion" and helped set the direction for other cabinetmakers. This curule chair (plate 158), designed by Lannuier or one of his followers, is based on the shape of the folding seats used by the magistrates of ancient Rome. The wood is mahogany (still popular through this period), and the upholstery displays one of the elegantly decorated smooth fabrics favored by Francophile American clients. Carving was more popular than in previous years, and although there is only a small amount on this seat, other pieces bore large carved swans, caryatids, and dolphins.

Duncan Phyfe (1768–1854) is probably America's best-known furniture maker. He was born in Scotland, emigrated to Albany at the end of the Revolutionary War, and moved to New York City in the early nineties. He opened his own shop in 1795 and worked continuously until his retirement in 1847. With a career of over fifty years, his early espousal of the popular English Regency style, and a willingness to adapt to changing tastes, Phyfe earned the description of "The United States Rage." Perhaps most admired for his work up through the twenties, he seems to have disliked the heavier late Empire work, for fewer of his pieces of that period were signed and he described it as "butcher furniture."

The window seat (plate 159) was one of a pair designed

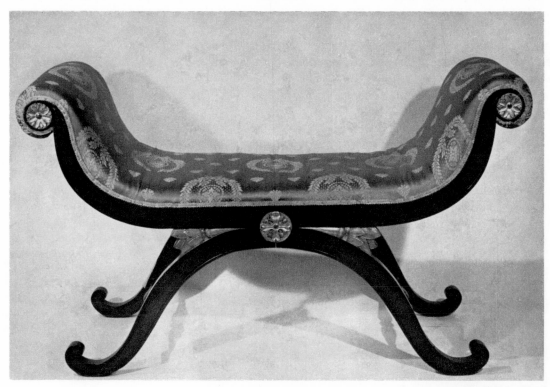

158 Charles Honoré Lannuier (attrib.). Bench, from New York. c. 1815–20. Mahogany with upholstery, length 48″. Albany Institute of History and Art, Albany, N.Y.

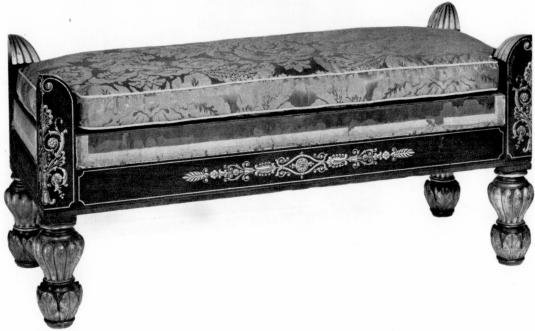

159 Duncan Phyfe. Window seat, from New York. c. 1825. Rosewood veneer upholstered with red damask, width 42½″. The Brooklyn Museum. Gift of Mrs. J. Armory Haskell

during the transitional period from English Regency to the more massive French Restoration style. It is made of rosewood veneers over an ash (or possibly oak) frame, and has applied Greco-Roman gilt ornamentation. The massive upholstered parts and the heavy frame and legs provide a marked contrast to the Federal period pieces and recall the Baroque. The identifying bulbous reeded and carved feet of Duncan Phyfe's style in the mid-twenties were replaced by scroll supports on the armchairs and chaises gondoles of the full-blown Restoration period.

William Hancock (1794–1849) was one of the typical American cabinetmaker-upholsterers who derived their ideas from the established design books. This massive sofa (plate 160) had no direct prototype, but the general form was taken from Sheraton's Cabinet Encyclopaedia of 1805, and the specific shape of the feet can be found on a "Grecian Sofa" in his Cabinet Dictionary. Combining forms as it does, it can only loosely be classified as American Empire. Highly polished mahogany, more extensively carved than the New York seat (plate 158), is combined with opulently upholstered seat, back, and arms. As a final touch, the brass rosettes on the arms are actually pulls which open cylindrical drawers.

Hancock, like a typical American gadgeteer, was evidently proud of the hidden drawers, for throughout the 1820s and 30s he published advertisements illustrating them and had them engraved on his billheads.

At the time that Lannuier was designing Roman-inspired forms (plate 158), specific Greek types were enjoying their own revival. A favorite form was the Greek klismos, well known from numerous ancient vases and shown here in a painted Baltimore version (colorplate 12). The klismos chair always had a rectangular seat, which rested on outflaring front and/or rear legs. The backrest sat squarely atop an extended curving back, and a cushion replaced the traditional side-chair slip seat. The example shown here is slightly Romanized, by virtue of turned rather than saber-shaped front legs, and, following the Baltimore tradition (cf. plate 140), is both painted and extensively decorated. One of nine in a set, each had a different design painted on the tablet, with similar classical paraphernalia decorating the stay rails, side rails, and turned legs.

This form and its sofa counterpart, although more likely in a more purely Grecian form, were popular through the early 1820s, and many households of the prosperous had entire rooms decorated to match the furniture. Benjamin Latrobe designed a set of such furniture for the White House in 1809, only to see all destroyed by the fire in 1814.

Many of the religious groups that developed either homogeneous communities or, in some cases, communistic living experiments, produced distinctive household objects in the later eighteenth and nineteenth centuries, but no others developed so complete an aesthetic as did the American members of the Shakers. They stressed simple directness, antiworldliness, honesty, purity, and unity. Without trying to invent new forms in furniture or household objects, the Shakers strove to create the most functional and essential objects, devoid of applied ornament or unnecessary opulence.

The room shown here is a composite of what was found

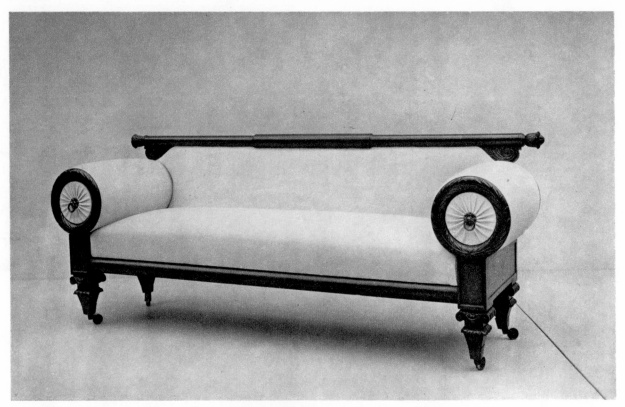

160 William Hancock. Sofa, from Boston. c. 1826-28. Mahogany with upholstery, length 89½". The Metropolitan Museum of Art, New York. Gift of Mrs. William H. Hoppin, 1948

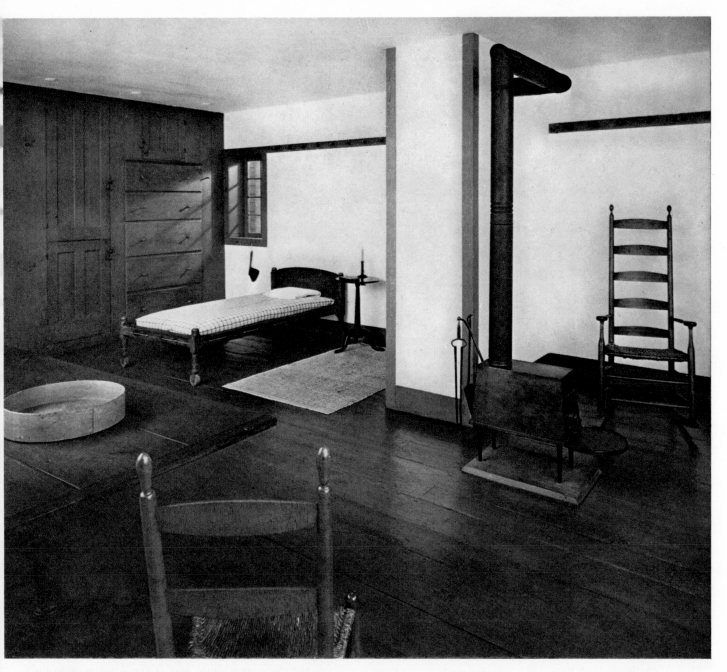

161 Shaker room. 19th century. National Gallery of Art, Washington, D.C. Index of American Design

in many Shaker communities: slat-back rocking chairs, trestle tables, built-in cabinets, and plank floors (plate 161). It is appealing in its austerity to the modern eye but is based on strict laws of the sect. Those laws forbade certain articles and warned against any "superfluously wrought" objects, "odd or fanciful styles of architecture," "beading, mouldings, and cornices." The result was the clean lines and direct forms of the completely utilitarian objects illustrated.

Freestanding furniture such as beds, chairs, or candlestands were designed to be lightweight so that rooms could be easily cleaned and cleared for other uses. The chairs were hung on wall pegs when not in use. Built-in furniture, such as the storage cabinets at the left, were

conceived as essentially part of the structure of the room. They were always flush with walls, and, as all clothing, utensils, and personal objects had to be kept out of sight, a great number were needed in both dwelling and working rooms. All the furniture was, in the early days, either lightly painted or stained in a single color; the use of light stains and varnish, as seen here, reveals the wood grain and is a slightly later development. The most obvious and characteristic emblem of Shaker manufacture is the pine-cone finial at the tops of the chairs, occasionally found on other items as well. Shaker pieces also reflect a unique knowledge and use of varying woods: the built-ins were made of pine, the vertical posts and drawer knobs of hard fruitwoods, and curved pieces of the pliant ash and hickory.

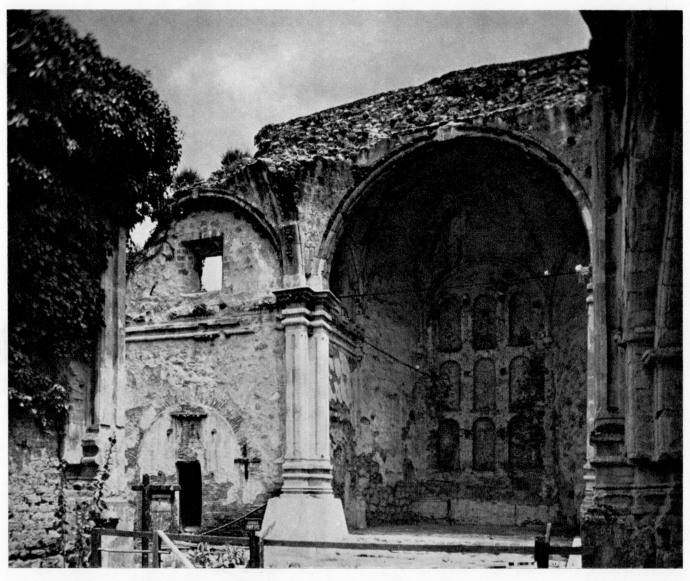

162 Isidoro Aguilar. Decorative carving, San Juan Capistrano, Calif. c. 1797

(continued from page 126)

CALIFORNIA SPANISH COLONIAL

In 1769 Spanish military and missionary forces from Mexico advanced into Alta California. Under the Franciscan Fra Junípero Serra, the first of the California missions was established at San Diego de Alcalá (1769). Eventually there were twenty-one, a day's journey apart, stretching from San Diego to Sonoma.

A California mission complex consisted of a *presidio*, a mission, and a *pueblo*. The *presidio* was a fortified walled enclosure housing the *comandante* and soldiers in offices, storerooms, guardrooms, and dormitories grouped around the four sides of a *plaza*. The mission, also a walled enclosure, was far more extensive, including a church, with sacristy, baptistery, and, usually, a chapel, on one side, dominating the *plaza*, and around the other three sides workshops, storerooms, offices, cells

for the *padre presidente* and friars, kitchen, infirmary, guest rooms, and dormitories for Christian Indians and novitiates. The *pueblo*, outside the wall, was usually a cluster of nondescript adobe or thatched huts.

Missions were self-sufficient communities, largely feudal in character, directed by the friars and dependent on the peonage of the Indian population. During their greatest prosperity (1800–13), under Padre Fermín de Lesuén, the missions were increasingly successful in agriculture, stock raising, and handicraft manufacture. Irrigation was improved, aqueducts were built, and new stone churches were erected. But in 1813 the government turned back some land to the Indians; then, in 1821, after Mexican independence from Spain, came Indian emancipation; and finally, in 1834, the missions were secularized. When the Americans arrived in 1846, the glory of the missions was a thing of the past. Of the original twenty-one, fourteen have been variously preserved, four are in ruins, and three have been "restored."

California mission churches fall somewhere between the provincial splendor of those in Texas and Arizona and the frontier simplicity of New Mexico.

San Carlos Borromeo, Carmel, was founded in 1771 and became the central mission. The present church (1793–97), erected by Lesuén, is in many ways the finest of the mission churches, a bold but sensitive plastic design with a distinctly Moorish flavor. Its two asymmetrical towers flank an arched center section pierced by a beautiful quatrefoil window. The church was badly damaged in the earthquake of 1812 and restored in 1882.

San Juan Capistrano (1797–1806, plate 162), in its ruined state the most legendary and picturesque, was founded in 1776. Built entirely of yellow sandstone with blue-gray sandstone trim by Isidoro Aguilar, master mason of Culiacán, it was roofed with domes over three bays and the nave crossing, and domical vaults over the transept and sanctuary. The exceptional carving of decorative details is probably by Aguilar, who is reputed to have been an Aztec. The church was destroyed in

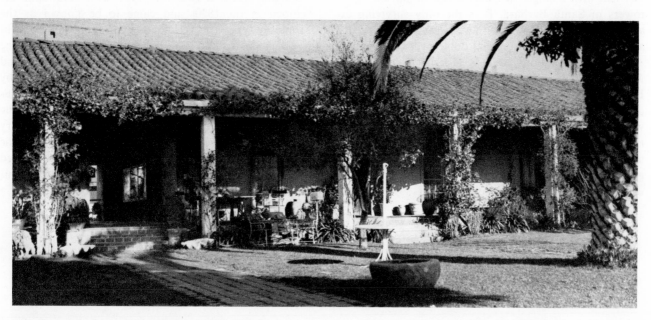

163   Casa de la Guerra, Santa Barbara, Calif. 1819–26

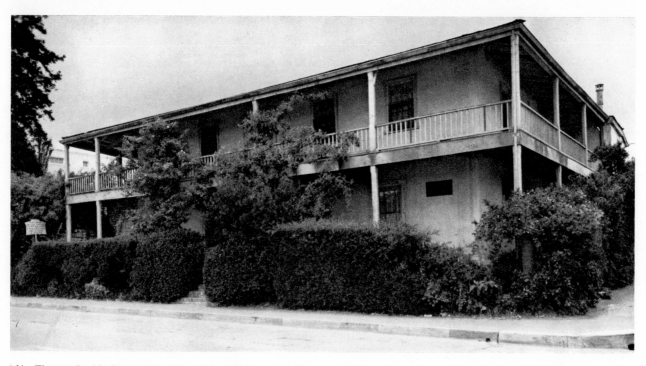

164   Thomas Larkin House, Monterey, Calif. 1834

1812 by the earthquake and never rebuilt.

Santa Barbara (1815–20), founded in 1786 and still functioning as a Franciscan establishment, is the best preserved and maintained of the mission churches. It is built of sandstone, and the facade, outside the walls, is the only symmetrical example among California mission churches. The squat, square towers flank a pilastered Neoclassic temple center said to derive from a Spanish edition of Vitruvius.

San Luis Rey de Francia (1811–15), the largest in size, was founded in 1798. It was built of adobe and brick with a tile roof and molded-brick trim. The facade is asymmetrical with a single *campanario* resembling the squat towers of Santa Barbara. It is the only surviving example of a cruciform plan, with well-developed transepts, and it has a wooden octagonal dome over the crossing.

There were major *presidios* at San Diego (1769), Monterey (1770), San Francisco (1776), and Santa Barbara (1782), but none remains today. With the decline and secularization of the missions, the economy went over to private farming and stock raising. During the golden age of the Mexican *hidalgos* of the 1830s and 1840s, a domestic architecture evolved that was both gracious and informal, adapted to the environment and using local building technology.

The only extant early Spanish domestic architecture in the United States is in California and dates from the short Mexican period and after the American annexation. The *casa de campo* (farm house), including the *hacienda* (farm) and the *rancho* (stock ranch), and the *casa de pueblo* (town house), all were essentially the same one-story, adobe-and-wood structures with rooms on three sides around an open *patio*. Sloping tiled roofs supported by wooden posts or brick piers projected over covered *corredores*, or verandahs, facing the *patio*. An example is the Casa de la Guerra (1819–26), Santa Barbara, a modest but a fine *casa de pueblo* (plate 163).

Farther north a two-story type with verandahs developed in the 1830s and came to be known as the Monterey type. The verandahs were supported by light wooden posts, and the balconies had railings. The ground floor accommodated the kitchen and living and service quarters, and the second floor, with access by exterior staircase, contained the bedrooms. The Thomas Larkin House (1834, plate 164), Monterey, is a classic example, surrounded on three sides by a two-story verandah with a walled patio on the fourth. Only in the twentieth century have American architects recognized the indigenous character and functional aptness of this architecture and begun to adapt it to modern usage.

6
Painting : Icons for a New Nation

American painters of the Early Republican period elude the Neoclassic label. The American public could not easily identify with the Classical heritage in painting: mythology and history, about which they were largely ignorant; and nudity, which offended their religious and moral scruples. For most of them the pictorial arts were still a luxury and a mystery. Those who had the wealth and the desire for art were still almost totally committed to portraiture, the only "practical" art form.

PORTRAITURE

Portraiture during the Early Republican period divides itself into official and private, although the same artists were involved in both. The great demand after the Revolution for portraits of national heroes and statesmen created a body of official portraiture which is sometimes close to the intention of history painting.

Charles Willson Peale (1741–1827) and Gilbert Stuart (1755–1828), the leading portraitists of the time, were not far apart in age and worked contemporaneously. Both had studied in England with West and both returned to America to work. However, Peale's formative years occurred before the Revolution, while Stuart's were spent during and after the war. Naive as Peale's style was before he went abroad, it was committed to the American realism of Copley, and he returned, a good deal more polished technically, to that earlier vision. Stuart, on the other hand, was completely formed by English portrait painting and practiced successfully in London and Dublin before coming home. Peale exemplifies the culture of colonial America, moving into a new era but still rooted in an earlier day, while Stuart speaks of new horizons and a new sophistication. Peale and his contemporaries played out their string before the end of the century and after 1800 the field was left to Stuart and his imitators.

The personality of Charles Willson Peale is so ingratiating and his career so varied and fascinating that his stature as a painter can be lost in the sheer wonder of the man. Apprenticed to a saddler as a child, Peale became

in time harnessmaker, upholsterer, watch- and clock-maker, chaise and sign painter, silversmith, museum curator and lecturer, naturalist, taxidermist, archaeologist, scientist, inventor, dentist, experimental farmer, and, of course, painter in all branches of the art. He devised a set of porcelain false teeth, armatures for stuffed animals, a portable steam bath, a smokeless stove, waxworks, a panorama, and an Eidophusikon (or "moving pictures"); and, in collaboration with Jefferson, a lifelong friend and fellow gadgeteer, he improved the polygraph. As a devoted patriot, he early became in-

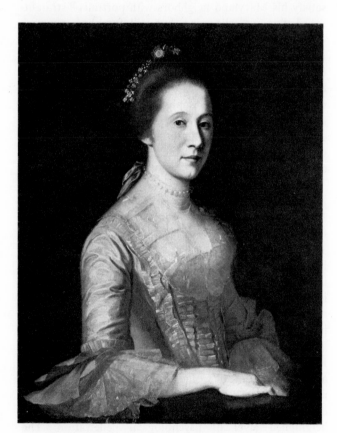

165 Charles Willson Peale. *Mrs. Thomas Harwood*. c. 1771. Oil on canvas, 31 × 24½". The Metropolitan Museum of Art, New York. Morris K. Jesup Fund, 1933

volved in radical politics, and during the Revolution he rose to the rank of captain in the Pennsylvania Militia. At Trenton, Princeton, and Valley Forge, he did miniatures of fellow soldiers and officers, including George Washington.

In 1782 Peale founded the first true museum in the country to house his portraits of Revolutionary heroes, and to these he added examples of natural history in 1786; he learned to preserve specimens, arranged the first natural habitat groups, exhumed and reconstructed a mastodon, and lectured on the exhibits. In 1794 he founded the first artists' society in Philadelphia, the Columbianum, and in 1795 organized in its name the first art exhibition. In 1805 he helped found the Pennsylvania Academy of the Fine Arts and its art school, and, through necessity, became its first professional nude model.

Peale was the best painter in the country between Copley's departure and Stuart's arrival. He tried painting first on his own, found that there was more to it than he had thought, bought *The Handmaid to the Arts* (Robert Dossie, London, 1758), gave John Hesselius a saddle for letting him watch while he painted, and so became a portraitist as well as sign painter. On a trip to Boston he stumbled on Smibert's studio and his paintings. Later he found Copley, who also let him watch while he worked. By now he had learned enough to satisfy his Maryland neighbors with portraits—straightforward, naive, charming, but still fumbling efforts—which could yet impress the local gentry enough to send him abroad to study in 1767. From then on, though he remained devoted to craft, he became an artist rather than an artisan. Two years with West taught him the rudiments of a more sophisticated style, as well as miniature painting, engraving, including mezzotint, and casting in plaster. After his return in 1769 he settled down to painting the prosaic portraits his fellow Americans could understand and would pay for.

Peale's portrait style was rooted in the forthright realism of Copley. His *Mrs. Thomas Harwood* (c. 1771, plate 165) is strikingly close to Copley in its intensity of focus, feeling for material reality, and presence of personality. Though somewhat rigid in pose and less accomplished in handling than a Copley, it is, if anything, more sensuous in its pigment and warmer in feeling and has a greater immediacy of rapport between sitter and painter.

Peale's later serious efforts as a portrait painter, when he was not involved in the business of Washington effigies, the routine recording of the physiognomies of Revolutionary heroes, and the demands of the museum, are a culmination of Colonial portraiture. They reveal a new breadth in composition and sophistication in handling and, despite a recurrent difficulty in drawing, a heightened level of psychological penetration. The double portrait of his sons Raphaelle and Titian, the *Staircase Group* (1795, colorplate 13), was conceived as a

"deception," or *trompe l'oeil*. Set in a door frame with an actual wooden step at the bottom when exhibited at the Columbianum in 1795, it was Peale's supreme effort at the faithful rendition of nature; yet it seems more a genre painting than a portrait. There is, surprisingly, no hesitancy in the conception and manipulation of mass, space, and light, all of which are managed simply and directly and not without sophistication, and the complexities of light and shade are treated with great subtlety. The crisp, clear realism, in its increased sharpness of focus, emphasis on precision of outline, and purity of local color, is surprisingly similar to the French Neoclassicism of the period or perhaps the work of Wright of Derby, the English painter famous for his genre scenes by artificial light.

Throughout his life, even in his prime, Peale was an uneven and often slipshod painter, and one should remember him at his best, as the sympathetic but acute witness to the worth of his Early Republican contemporaries.

William Dunlap, the "American Vasari," rarely missed an opportunity to draw a moral lesson from the lives of his subjects; Ralph Earl (1751–1801) rightfully earned Dunlap's opprobrium so far as drink was concerned, but he certainly did not deserve that mediocre painter's scorn of his art. Earl, despite his shortcomings and unevenness, was a painter of unusual power and remarkable natural gifts. He was born in Worcester County, Mass., and worked in western Connecticut. Leaving America because of his Loyalist sympathies in early 1778, he was active in England until 1785 and, according to his own account, which is open to doubt, studied with Reynolds, West, and Copley. On his return to the United States he was active in Connecticut and New York City. He died in Bolton, Conn., of "intemperance," according to Dunlap.

Earl's paintings before his English period are among the finest examples of the native American tradition stemming from Copley. At this point he must have been largely self-taught, but there is a basic similarity of approach in the realism of his vision and that of Copley and the crude but vigorous images of the Connecticut limners. With all its gaucheries, Earl's *Roger Sherman* (c. 1775, colorplate 14) is a more powerful image than any projected by either Copley or Peale. This staunch and rock-ribbed patriot, a member of Congress from Connecticut and the epitome of the hard-bitten New Englander, sits in his homespuns on a Windsor chair in an absolutely bare space which is yet the corner of a room. Earl has seemingly hacked a form out of solid substance, modeled the head, body, and hands with compulsive bluntness, so that they are insistently real. Yet his realism, unlike Copley's, is concerned not with detail but with bold and generalized forms almost abstract in their simplification. In a fundamental aesthetic sense this is not a naive picture, because the relationship between

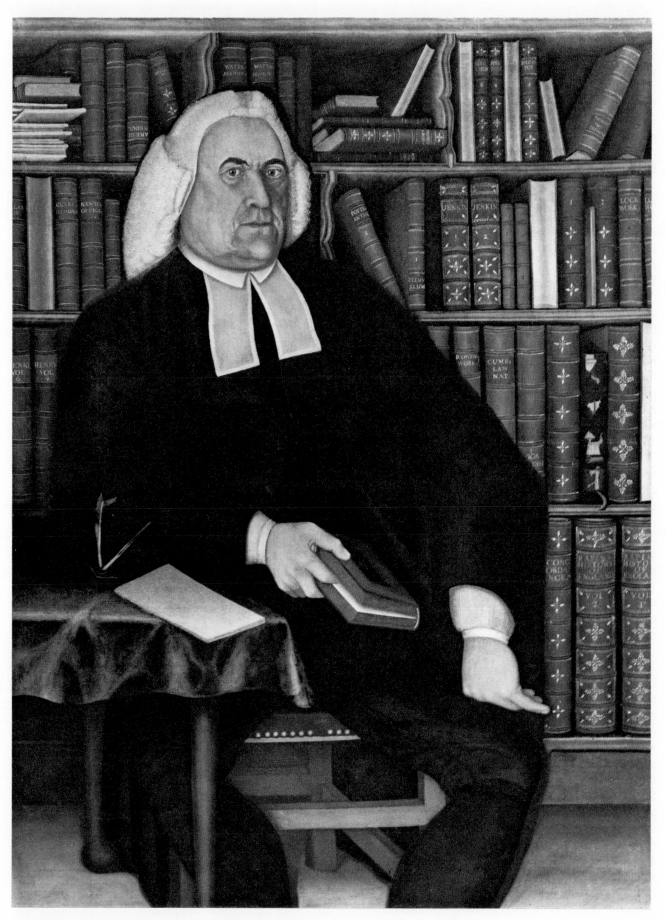

166 Winthrop Chandler (attrib.). *Reverend Ebenezer Devotion*. c. 1770. Oil on canvas,
54½ × 43½″. Devotion House, Brookline Historical Society, Brookline, Mass.

mass and space, interior pattern and frame, light and shade are managed with an unconscious subtlety that is a natural gift. There is also something uncanny in the psychological probity of this portrait.

The English experience upset the naive balance of Earl's art without a compensating advance in sensibility or sophistication, except on the most superficial level. He picked up a bag of social symbols, paraphernalia, and manners which he grafted onto his native style with sometimes dispiriting results.

Earl was the most talented and best trained of an active group of artisan portraitists working in the Connecticut Valley, beginning before the Revolution and continuing into the nineteenth century. All reflect some of the Copley manner in their blunt and even harsh realism. The style is, however, completely lacking in illusionism, depending for its effect on a fanatical concern with fact, a hard but crisp linearity, and a strong feeling for flat color pattern. A typical example is the *Reverend Ebenezer Devotion* (c. 1770, plate 166), attributed to Winthrop Chandler (1747–1790), in which the meticulous rendering of the books overwhelms the silhouette of the tightly drawn figure. A metallic precision in delineation is the hallmark of the Jennys brothers, William and Richard, who, in the incisive and immaculate linearity of their style, created some of the most striking early American portraits (plate 167).

The artisan tradition continued in rural and frontier areas alongside the more sophisticated art of the major cities on the eastern shore. Well into the nineteenth century, even after the spread of photography, it maintained its vitality and its own artistic formulas even while responding to changing fashions. It is something of an artistic curiosity that the artisan level during this period inadvertently produced the closest approximation in the United States of the international Neoclassic style in its clarity of form, restraint in movement and expression, controlled linearity of outline, precision in detail, and clean local color.

Except for Charles Willson Peale, the first group of American painters to study abroad were not very productive or successful. They came home better equipped technically, perhaps, but emotionally less able than their more provincial brethren to face the rigors of American culture. Matthew Pratt (1734–1805) had some modest gifts, including a feeling for color and pigment for its own sake. He spent two and a half years in West's studio, and it is puzzling, considering the quality of some of his portraits, that he should have found it difficult to establish himself in Philadelphia as a portrait painter on his return in 1768. The introspective poetic quality of gentle calm which pervades his most famous picture, *The American School* (1765, plate 168), would presuppose an artist of some sensitivity. Painted and exhibited in England while Pratt was still with West, it represents the latter's paint-

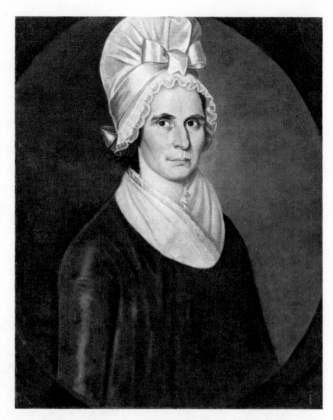

167 William Jennys. *Mrs. William Stoddard Williams.* 1801. Oil on canvas, 29 × 24″. Heritage Foundation, Deerfield, Mass.

ing room. The picture has attained a special niche in the annals of American painting, for it breaks with the hieratic form of the posed portrait, is uniquely complex for Colonial portraiture, and is almost documentary in its depiction of the West studio with a group of young American artists resident at the time.

When Gilbert Stuart returned to New York in late 1792 or early 1793 after eighteen years, he had achieved international renown. It was as something of a returning hero that he moved the next year to Philadelphia, then temporarily the capital of the United States. Philadelphia was the gayest and most cosmopolitan of American cities, and its society had decided leanings toward aristocracy. The Washington administration had been "captured" by the Federalists, by wealthy mercantile and landed interests, and some of its adherents were even talking of monarchy with Washington as king. Stuart's reputation, his sophistication, and the natural elegance of his style were tailor-made for this new and ambitious "nobility." That he was forced by his profession and his own improvidence to serve this pseudoaristocracy must have grated on his intelligence and increased his irascibility. But he gave them what they wanted. When he became secure enough and crotchety enough, he turned away many whom he found overweening, unsympathetic, or uninteresting. Stuart, as has so frequently been said, was a "face painter"; he could or would paint only faces, but at his best, when he found something in the sitter or perhaps in himself, the face reveals all that a face can. He had learned little about portraiture from West. Although he was shrewd enough to borrow from Reynolds and from Gainsborough, he found what he was looking for by returning directly to Van Dyck. However, he belonged to a new generation of English painters who were moving away from the courtliness and artificiality of the older generation toward a more personal style. He must have learned something from Romney's informal and natural manner but is closest to Raeburn, with whom he shares a manner of applying pigment. Although Stuart used a loaded brush, the paint was applied thinly and unmixed, and his touch was very light. The result is a vibrant, coloristic surface that seems to capture the vivacity of living and breathing beings. Stuart saw the face, not the environment, gesture, or costume, as expressive of the man, but he loved the texture of such materials as lace, gold braid, or brass buttons, and painted them with brilliance. His formula called for highlights on forehead, nose, lower lip, and chin, with a sparkle of light in the iris, a glint of moisture in the eye, and sharp but trans-parent touches of shadow under the brows, nose, upper lip, and chin. Out of such limited means, handled with great subtlety, he achieved a palpable reality. Each stroke is an area of color as well as a definition of form.

There is probably no greater portrait in his total oeuvre than the *Mrs. Richard Yates* (c. 1793, colorplate 15), which updates the whole American tradition of realistic portraiture. The old lady is seen with all the unremitting truth of a Copley, but the shrewd and quizzical expression is pure Stuart, transmitted in a momentary flicker of sight. Although he rarely used gesture, here the angularity of movement in her sewing hands reinforces the caustic glint in her glance. The whole is painted with a controlled fluency far beyond anything done so far in the New World.

WASHINGTON PORTRAITS

Stuart's return to the United States to do a portrait of George Washington was a sign of the flourishing business of manufacturing likenesses of a popular hero whose fame extended far beyond the confines of the thirteen states. Washington had become a symbol for libertarians throughout the world, the embodiment of "Roman

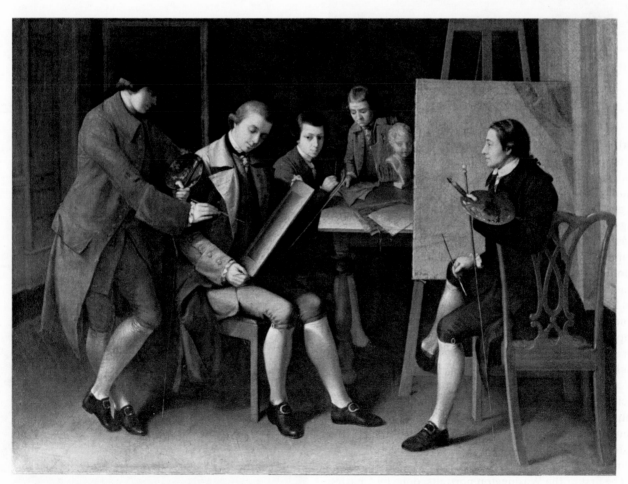

168   Matthew Pratt. *The American School*. 1765. Oil on canvas, 36 × 50¼". The Metropolitan Museum of Art, New York. Gift of Samuel P. Avery, 1897

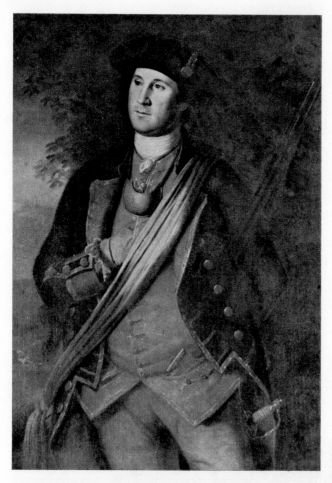

169 Charles Willson Peale. *George Washington*. 1772. Oil on canvas, 60 × 48". Washington and Lee University, Lexington, Va.

Willson Peale, is the so-called "Colonial type" (1772, plate 169), depicting him as a colonel in the Virginia Militia during the French and Indian Wars. The rather wooden characterization of the youthful Washington is perhaps not entirely the result of Peale's artistic limitations, for the subject never seemed at ease in any of his portraits and was not naturally graceful in movement. In spite of its awkwardness, the portrait is solidly painted, colorful, completely honest even to the Colonel's corpulence. Peale's first official commission for a Washington came from the Pennsylvania Council in 1779. The outcome was the *George Washington at Princeton* (1779), in which the Commander-in-Chief is shown standing, legs crossed, leaning on a cannon, with prisoners under guard in the background. As a heroic image it is rather ludicrous; the excessively lanky and disjointed Washington is caught uncertainly between dignity and friendliness. However, this "Continental type" was an immediate and complete success, and Peale made many replicas of it. He also did a somewhat similar full-length representing *Washington at Yorktown* (1784). Both these pictures served as the basis for a Peale industry in Washington portraits. The client could have, according to price, full-, half-, or even bust-length versions; elements were inter-

virtue." European governments and private citizens, American states, cities, organizations, and individuals wanted paintings and prints of him. Aside from the monumental versions of his person in sculpture and paintings, his appearance was immortalized in smaller paintings, miniatures, engravings, and in representations on glass and china, clocks, mirrors, and wall plaques; it was printed on textiles and reproduced in porcelain figurines. Along with the American eagle, his head became the ubiquitous symbol of republican America long before his likeness graced our money, medals, and stamps. With time the authenticity of the likeness became increasingly important, and after his death the image "from life" took on added value. Washington posed only reluctantly, and such life sessions were rare and especially significant. To fill the clamorous demand, artists turned out copies of their originals, and those who had not been granted a sitting simply plagiarized the works of their colleagues. Thus the study of these portraits is more important in a historical than in an artistic sense, and less as portraiture than as an aspect of history painting.

The first of the Washington portraits, done by Charles

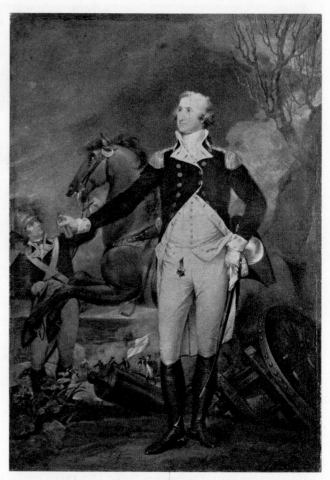

170 John Trumbull. *General George Washington Before the Battle of Trenton*. After 1792. Oil on canvas, 26½ × 18½". The Metropolitan Museum of Art, New York. Bequest of Grace Wilkes, 1922

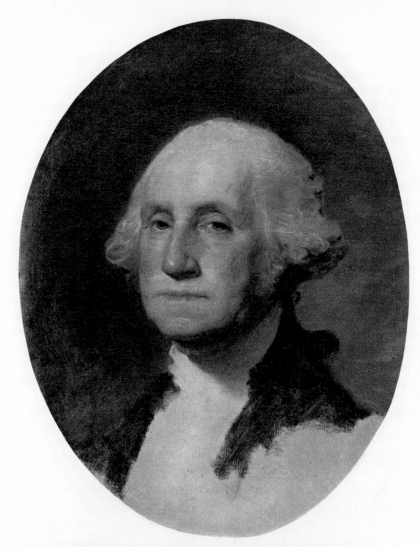

171 Gilbert Stuart. *"Athenaeum" Portrait of George Washington.*
1796. Oil on canvas, 39⅝ × 34½". Boston Athenaeum,
on deposit at the Museum of Fine Arts, Boston

changeable, and backgrounds could be varied to fit particular conditions or preferences. Replicas were produced by Peale himself, his brother James, or with the help of James and his own sons.

In 1787, at the Constitutional Convention, Washington posed for him again, and the bust likeness called the "Convention" portrait was the result, frozen in expression and heavy-handed in execution, the least successful of Peale's Washington repertory but variously copied. In 1795 Peale asked Washington for a last sitting. The request was granted, and Charles turned up with James, Raphaelle, and Rembrandt, all of whom set up their easels and went to work. They were all then officially "life" painters of the great man.

That Peale failed to achieve the heroic image is understandable, since he was by temperament and training ill-equipped to manage grandeur. John Trumbull was by training and avowed intention prepared for the challenge, yet his portraits were as disastrous as Peale's. His first effort at heroic conception, done in England, was based on a Peale bust, since he had not done Washington from life. Engraved and extensively copied, the likeness was not close to commonly accepted examples.

More Romantic in feeling and more accomplished than his first attempts is Trumbull's *George Washington Before the Battle of Trenton* (plate 170), existing in several versions. Here the battle in the background, the denuded tree against a turbulent sky, the shattered cannon on the ground, the dragoon restraining the rearing charger, and the theatrical stance and gesture of the General are all elements that became the stock-in-trade of nineteenth-century Romantic military portraiture, and in that sense the painting is prophetic and interesting. But Trumbull did not manage to convey, as he had hoped, Washington's "military character in the most sublime moment of its exertion." The result is all pose and no action.

It took the antiheroic Stuart to achieve the image that has remained unalterable down to our own time, but it was the person and not the historical symbol that became the icon, for Stuart's own attempts at monumentality also failed. The first sittings, in March, 1795, were something of a fiasco in human terms, although the so-called "Vaughan type," which came out of the sessions, was a creditable picture. Stuart was awed and completely nonplussed by the psychological fortress of Washington. The quality of the man defeated Stuart's natural vivacity of spirit and lightness of touch; he was dissatisfied with the result, although he received immediate orders for thirty-nine copies. Fifteen existing replicas are accepted as from his own hand.

In 1796, Stuart had another chance. According to Stuart's own account, talk about horses and farming stirred the great man into a semblance of animation; at any rate, the result, which pleased Stuart, is the "Athenaeum" portrait (plate 171). He never completed the background of that painting, apparently in order to keep it as a model for copies. It became his potboiler, his "hundred-dollar bill," the price he charged for a replica when he was short of cash, and it is estimated that Stuart himself did some seventy versions. Despite the disfigurement of the mouth due to Washington's new set of false teeth, it is the image that people accepted and still do. In the same year the demand for a statelier and more official portrait eventually led Stuart to attempt what he must have known was beyond his powers. The full-length portrait of Washington in his office was intended for the Mar-

quis of Lansdowne, a famous English Whig, and is thus called the "Lansdowne" portrait. Although competently painted, it is an uninspired and cluttered work, a dismal failure. This did not, however, keep him from executing a number of copies.

Perhaps the finest painting in the Washington iconography, although it is more a historical picture than a portrait, is Thomas Sully's *The Passage of the Delaware* (1819, plate 172). The painting is Romantic without being melodramatic, heroic without pomposity, and, of all the representations of the General in military action, the only one to achieve credibility. In spite of such stock elements as the gnarled tree branch, the rearing horses, and the rather theatrical gestures of the officers, there is a distinct sense of reality in the winter landscape and the action of the foot soldiers. It may not be painted with complete authority throughout; it was, after all, Sully's only effort at monumentality, and Washington seems somewhat remote from the scene, but the composition is original and the strong diagonal movement motivated and compelling.

The culmination of all the Washington worship is ex-

172 Thomas Sully. *The Passage of the Delaware*. 1819. Oil on canvas, 12′2½″ × 17′3″. Museum of Fine Arts, Boston. Gift of the owners of the Old Boston Museum

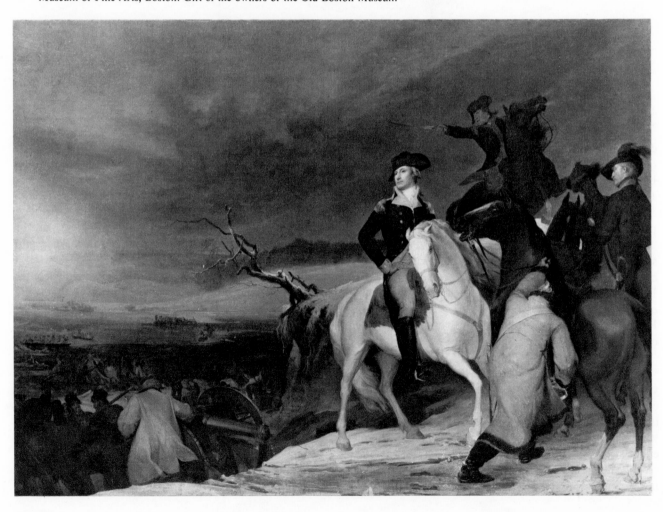

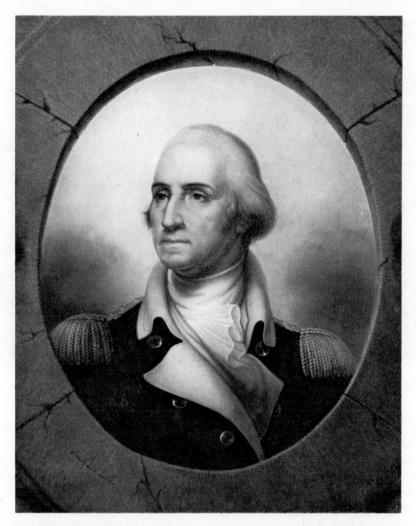

173 Rembrandt Peale. *George Washington* (the "Porthole" portrait). c. 1823.
Oil on canvas, 36¼ × 29⅛". The Metropolitan Museum of Art,
New York. Bequest of Charles Allen Munn, 1924

emplified by the last effort of Rembrandt Peale (1778–1860) to achieve the perfect image, the "Porthole" portrait of about 1823 (plate 173). It is obviously an effort to achieve a deification by consensus—handsomeness, dignity, strength, will, and emotional fire. Set in a painted *trompe-l'oeil* oval frame simulating cracked stone, it presents something of spiritual "deception" in its patent appeal to patriotism and hero worship. Rembrandt spent the last thirty-five years of his life painting replicas and lecturing throughout the country on the true likeness of Washington, eventually billing himself as "the only living painter who ever saw Washington."

HISTORY PAINTING

Unlike the portrait painters, who had only to compete in satisfying a demand, the history painters had to create a demand. They seemed convinced that the nation's taste had matured enough to recognize history painting as the highest aspiration of culture, and that the United States had a special patriotic duty to memorialize the example of its struggle for independence and the rights of man. All they required was financial support, but this did not

materialize, and the grandiose dream of a national historical art vanished.

West and Copley were among the leading European history painters at the end of the eighteenth and beginning of the nineteenth century, and it is really something of a wonder that so few of West's American students caught his enthusiasm. Only among his later students —Trumbull, Allston, and Rembrandt Peale—did West's influence become pronounced. By that time his Classical manner was long forgotten and the Romantic mode was in the ascendancy.

John Trumbull (1756–1843) was particularly equipped to be the painter of the American Revolution. As the son of the Revolutionary governor of Connecticut, he had entrée to the highest circles of American politics and society; he knew Washington, Jefferson, and Adams; he fought in the Revolution as an aide to Washington and Gates; he studied with West and was befriended by David; he had a heroic project and passionate ambition. Yet, suspicious, cantankerous, self-centered, too quick to take umbrage, unforgiving, and eventually bitter, he bickered away his chances at greatness.

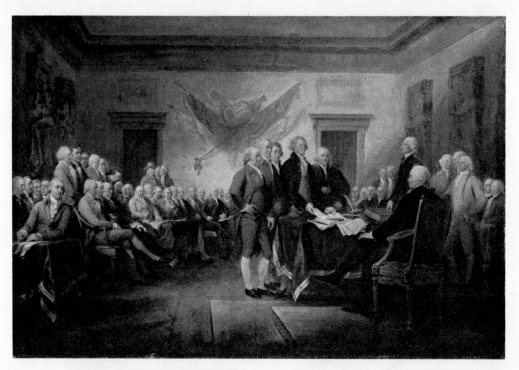

174 John Trumbull. *The Declaration of Independence, July 4, 1776.* 1786–97. Oil on canvas, 21¼ × 31⅛". Yale University Art Gallery, New Haven

He was set on being a painter and while at Harvard took the opportunity to visit Copley for criticism and advice; after graduation he did some painting. He joined the army in 1775 but resigned in a huff in 1777 because he felt he had been slighted in the dating of his promotion to colonel and returned to painting. In 1784 he was in London studying with West.

After an early essay in Classical mythology, Trumbull turned to contemporary history and his project for a history of the American Revolution. He was assisted in the selection of twelve episodes by Adams and Jefferson, who took a continued interest in him and his project. During the next decade he worked in London, Paris, and the United States on sketches for the proposed scenes and portraits of the participants. In 1789 he came back to America hoping to launch a subscription series of engravings after the sketches, but the response proved insufficient and he dropped the project in a mixture of pique and despair, turning his back on art.

At last in 1817 the Congress voted $32,000 as a commission for four of his paintings for the Rotunda of the Capitol. In the same year he was elected president of the American Academy of Fine Arts in New York. For the next decade he was something of a dictator on the American art scene, but his authoritarianism drove the younger painters out of the American Academy. Trumbull spent his last years a rejected and bitter man. In 1831 he gave his paintings to Yale College in return for a life pension.

When Trumbull's paintings for the Rotunda were sent on tour before being put in place, there was a good deal of carping criticism. The literal-minded found fault because some characters who had been absent at the signing of the Declaration of Independence were included and some who had been there were not, but the public had a right to its disappointment, because so much had been expected and the results were dull. The large finished paintings lack the fire and technical brilliance of the earlier sketches, but it may also be that Trumbull was not truly a monumental painter. Unfortunately, for ideological reasons he selected four scenes that were difficult to dramatize, two of which were not among the original sketches. He thus had to supply two new compositions some twenty years after he had laid the project aside, and had to paint two others about thirty years after making the original sketches—*The Declaration of Independence* (1786–97, plate 174) and *The Surrender of Lord Cornwallis at Yorktown* (before 1797). None of the more exciting and dramatically inspired battle scenes was included in the commission, and Congress refused to allow Trumbull to cover the four remaining panels of the Rotunda.

The major source of his style was clearly that of West when his proto-Romanticism was coming to the fore, preceding the Romantic Movement proper by some thirty years. Trumbull went back to the *Death of Wolfe* (colorplate 10) as a starting point for his American history series. The influence of that picture is clearly seen in Trumbull's *Death of General Montgomery in the Attack on Quebec* (1786, colorplate 16). But his sketches have a quality that does not derive from West, a truly light and painterly touch, a delicate vivacity that relates to the Rococo but is put to an entirely different purpose. Seen against these assured and exciting youthful efforts, the rest of his artistic life seems a sad anticlimax.

The life of John Vanderlyn (1775–1852) was artistically

more frustrating and personally even more tragic than that of Trumbull, his archrival. Vanderlyn's earlier life was as favored as his later was clouded. He was born in Kingston, N.Y., the grandson of the Hudson Valley limner Pieter Vanderlyn. A copy Vanderlyn made of a Stuart portrait of Aaron Burr brought him to the attention of that famous and powerful political figure, who eased Vanderlyn's path in the early years, just as Burr's later disgrace made things difficult for the painter who had become so closely identified with him. Burr arranged for him to study with Stuart in Philadelphia for several months before sending him to Paris in 1796 to complete his schooling. Vanderlyn was thus the only American painter of the time to study in France, and, under the tutelage of François-André Vincent, a rival of David, he was trained in the French Neoclassic manner of precise draftsmanship and clear sculptural modeling.

In 1801 he did portraits of Burr and his daughter and, at Burr's suggestion, went to paint several views of Niagara Falls with the hope of marketing engravings of this natural wonder. These studies, among the earliest representations of the falls, are straightforward records except for one in which the dominant form of a stark, dead tree presages the later development of Romantic landscape painting. Vanderlyn was in Rome from 1805 to 1808, during which time he painted his academic

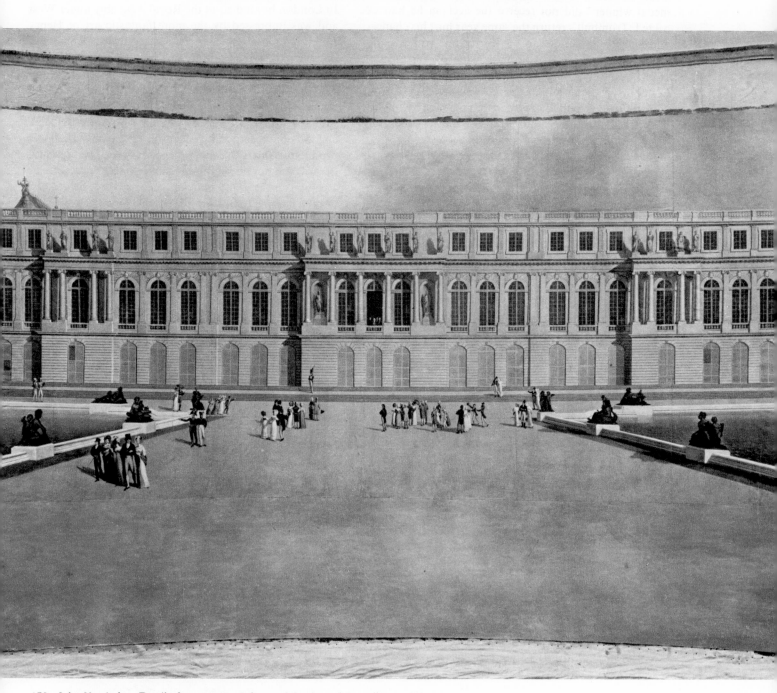

175 John Vanderlyn. Detail of panorama: *Palace and Gardens of Versailles*. c. 1819.
Oil on canvas, 12 × 165'. The Metropolitan Museum of Art, New York.
Gift of the Senate House Association, Kingston, N.Y., 1952

Neoclassic *Marius Among the Ruins of Carthage* (1807), exhibited at the Paris Salon of 1808, and was awarded a gold medal by Napoleon himself. While in Paris, Vanderlyn completed his *Ariadne Asleep on the Island of Naxos* (1812, colorplate 17), unquestionably his finest historical painting. Samuel Isham's apt description is still relevant: "An admirable piece of solid modelling, an academic study from the life, rather devoid of charm, the legs and feet being especially clumsy and inelegant, but executed with a faithfulness and capacity unknown in England." And certainly unknown in America. Not only the standard of technical competence but the nude itself was foreign to American experience.

On his return to the United States in 1815, the "gold-medal winner" did not receive the acclaim he had expected. Trumbull's return the same year hurt his chances, and in 1817 he decided to try his fortune with a panorama based on sketches he had made of Versailles in 1814. Vanderlyn had seen panoramas in Paris and London. The panorama promised well here, since it was planned to have public appeal, combining the excitement of the theater and the cultural tone of the art exhibition. But Vanderlyn's panorama was not a success.

Recently restored to its original condition, this earliest extant American panorama, the only one by a recognized artist of stature, is stylistically unlike any other of Vanderlyn's works; presumably most of the actual painting was done from Vanderlyn's designs by assistants. However, the figures have a verve and authenticity which make their attribution to Vanderlyn likely, and the crisp clarity of the architectural rendering would indicate his close supervision.

He leased a corner of City Hall Park, New York, erected a rotunda with borrowed money, and exhibited in 1819 *The Palace and Gardens of Versailles* (1816–19, plate 175). In adjoining rooms were shown his *Ariadne* and other paintings as well as his copies of old masters. He thought of the exhibition as a first step toward a national museum of art which would also help make his reputation. But the nude *Ariadne* created a minor scandal, and the unfavorable publicity was used to his disadvantage by the Trumbull faction. The city canceled the lease in 1829, leaving Vanderlyn in debt and discouraged. He retired in frustration and bitterness to Kingston, where he spent most of the rest of his life in solitary deterioration.

In 1837 friends with political influence got him a commission from Congress for *The Landing of Columbus* to fill one of the Capitol Rotunda panels, but by that time the task was beyond Vanderlyn's capabilities. He spent two years (1842–44) in Paris supervising the painting of his design, but all the evidence points to its having been carried out by local French painters.

Though Washington Allston (1779–1843) belonged to the generation of history painters, he was also America's first truly Romantic artist. Like Trumbull, he was influenced by West's proto-Romanticism, but, arriving twenty years later, he preferred characteristically Romantic subjects of mystery, foreboding, terror, or poetic reverie. The shift is fundamental, from an outer- to an inner-directed art, from a social to a personal statement, from reality to the imagination. Even his life was a Romantic drama, and his failure was almost as complete as that of Trumbull or Vanderlyn. The body of work that Allston left would indicate that he was something less than the genius his contemporaries thought him to be.

Allston was born to a socially prominent and wealthy South Carolinian family but was educated in New England. At Harvard he tried his hand at writing and painted several themes from a "Gothick" novel of Mrs. Radcliffe. In London he studied at the Royal Academy under West and was impressed by the more fantastic art of Henry Fuseli and John Opie. In 1805 he settled in Rome and became part of the Caffé Greco circle, which included his friends Vanderlyn, Washington Irving, Coleridge, and Thorvaldsen, as well as such famous figures as Keats, Shelley, Turner, Von Humboldt, and Madame de Staël. This must have been heady fare for a young provincial, and Allston absorbed influences like a glutton. His most productive years were divided between London and Bristol, and he was establishing an enviable reputation as a painter in the grand manner when, in 1818, he decided to return home to Boston. There must have been the still-unfulfilled desire to play an important role in the promise that was America in those years after the War of 1812. It was no accident that Trumbull and Vanderlyn returned in 1815, and Allston in 1818, all with the same dream of glory. But the "Athens of America" did not live up to Allston's expectations. Although he was the center of an intellectual coterie whose adulation was untarnished by his lack of productivity, greatness eluded him. The great *Belshazzar's Feast* (1817–43), a painting that he had brought unfinished from England, acted like an incubus rather than an inspiration. The more he worked, the less there was to see, and it was left unfinished at his death. Allston lived in Cambridgeport from 1830 for the rest of his life in financial security, revered as the embodiment of American genius but tragically unfulfilled.

Allston was essentially a derivative and eclectic painter, hoping perhaps for an eventual synthesis, yet achieving only reminiscences of others. His earliest affinities were with the West of *Death on a Pale Horse*, the terrorful fantasies of Fuseli, and the picturesque wildness of Salvator Rosa. In Rome (1805–08) Allston, chameleon-like, reflected the current vogue of Italian Campagna painting practiced by an international group of artists resident there. A turn toward the grand manner of West appears in the work of his second English period (1811–18), when he painted most of his large historical subjects, among which was the *Elijah in the Desert* (1818, colorplate 18). These historical paintings made his reputation, but they are, except for the *Elijah*, among his least in-

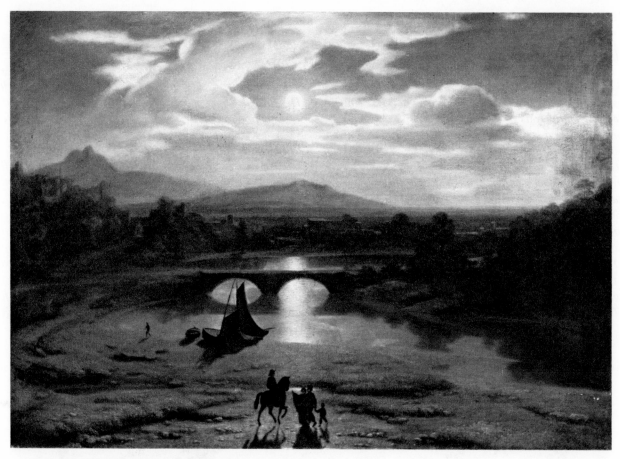

176 Washington Allston. *Moonlit Landscape*. 1819. Oil on canvas, 24 × 35″.
Museum of Fine Arts, Boston. Gift of Dr. W. S. Bigelow

teresting works. The *Elijah* is at least a clear-cut, unadulterated variation on Salvator Rosa, but with a simple power and a harshness of form that is unlike the Italian artist.

On his return to the United States, except for an occasional reversion to the blood and thunder of his earlier Gothicism, he painted gentle Romantic dreams. The best of these, such as the *Moonlit Landscape* (1819, plate 176), were done soon after his return. Allston was important as a symbol, remaining throughout his life an image of excellence and a source of inspiration. He was the first American artist in the modern sense—a man who worked not for material things but for universal values and aesthetic quality. It was an image close to the hearts of the next generation of Romantic artists, and his Romantic landscapes helped open up new vistas in American art.

The failure of history painting was largely one of patronage. Since history painting is a long and laborious process, artists must expect returns commensurate with their investment in time; otherwise, they look elsewhere for support or abandon the form. During the eighteenth century, those who stayed with the genre turned to the public sale of engraved reproductions of paintings as a source of income. This procedure was taken up extensively after midcentury by history painters as an answer to the crisis of backing.

The public exhibition grew out of this search for a new patronage. As early as 1781 Copley, who was trying to establish a reputation, exhibited his *Death of Chatham* in a rented gallery in competition with the annual exhibition of the Royal Academy, an action that made him an estimated profit of five thousand pounds. In some cases the public exhibition and the panorama were combined into a single show, as in Vanderlyn's exhibition. Receipts from attendance and the sale of reproductions, if the exhibition were a success, could replace the more traditional patronage. But the format had to be sold to the public, and this artists and impresarios did with verve, imagination, and acumen. It was West again who hit upon the formula for success. In his old age the great religious sermons he painted and exhibited in London along with explanatory texts made him more money than he had managed as the King's painter. When the Pennsylvania Hospital asked for a contribution in 1816, he sent them his gigantic *Christ Healing the Sick* (c. 1811), which, displayed in a specially constructed building, brought in twenty-five thousand dollars. Recognition that the American public would respond to religious subjects led to a chain reaction that continued for a half-century.

(continued on page 148)

Like English furniture fashions, English taste in fabrics was wholeheartedly embraced in the eighteenth century. Brocades and velvets of Spanish origin, silk and damask from France and Italy, and, most commonly, chintzes from India were all bought through England. The chintzes became so popular that English manufacturers made a vain attempt to produce enough of the material themselves. By midcentury it was not uncommon to find the same imported material used on bedcovers, curtains, and upholstery. With that level of demand, it was only a matter of time till some craftsman decided to become a big fish in a little pond and in 1773 John Hewson, having completed his apprenticeship in England and having discussed the market with Benjamin Franklin, arrived in Philadelphia.

This light and delicate printed bedcover (plate 177) is one of the rare surviving examples of his obvious skill. His handkerchiefs were also much admired, and Martha Washington ordered several for her husband. The few surviving eighteenth-century printed cottons show that the knowledge of dyes seems to have exceeded that of paints and stains used on furniture; except for normal fading, the colors on this bedcover remain fresh, lively, and undimmed by time.

The best-known and most enduring form of needlework was the sampler, which is made even today. It was unique in that, alone among needlework items, the sampler was not a household object of daily use. Rather, the stitchery on a sampler was created for display purposes, but not for amusement; it exhibited the proficiency of the young girl

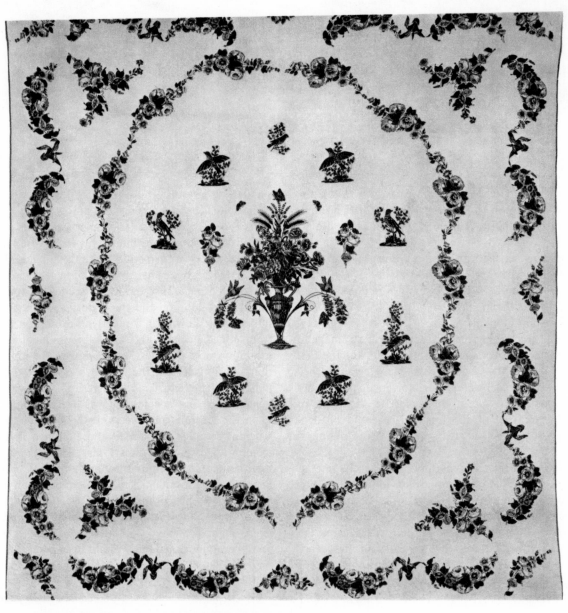

177 John Hewson. Bedspread. 1780–1800. Cotton, 86¼ × 88″.
The Henry Francis du Pont Winterthur Museum, Del.

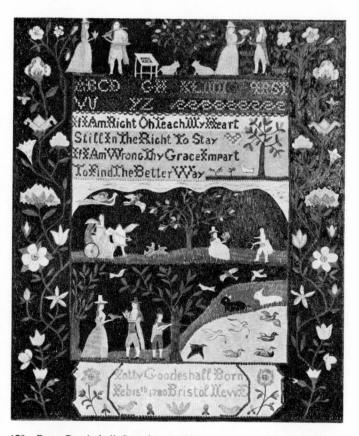

178 Patty Goodeshall. Sampler. c. 1795.
Silk on canvas, $19\frac{1}{2} \times 16\frac{5}{8}''$.
National Gallery of Art, Washington, D.C.

in needlework according to her age and training, preserved samples of various stitches, and served as a practice piece for the letters and numbers needed for marking linens and clothes.

The earliest form of sampler was a long strip of home-woven linen covered with the letters of the alphabet and the numerals embroidered in a variety of stitches. By the end of the seventeenth century, the lettering was surrounded by various displays of flora and fauna, and even human figures had made their appearance. Throughout the eighteenth century samplers became more elaborate, with roman and cursive letters displayed, some offering quotations or Biblical passages. Landscape and other scenes also made their appearance, with Biblical episodes and domestic outdoor views most popular. The inclusion of architectural elements and scenery presented more of an opportunity for display of color and complexity of design. The hunting scene, in a late eighteenth-century work (plate 178), is a fine example of almost all the standard devices of the sampler included on one piece: the alphabet, the pious prayer for guidance, a variety of flowers, three bands of human figures, animals, and birds, and the autobiographical statement at the bottom.

A special kind of needlework, used in America from the late seventeenth century on, was stuffed or corded work,

more recently known as "trapunto." It required two layers of fabric, one fine and closely woven for the top piece, the other of coarse-textured homespun for the backing. The decorative patterns were outlined by stitching through both layers and then were padded by inserting cotton wadding or thick yarn through the coarse mesh of the back fabric. The stuffed areas of the top created sculptured effects, set in relief against the shadowed areas of the stitching. The most popular design elements in trapunto were wreaths, cornucopias, flowers, leaves, and vine tendrils. This exquisite crib coverlet (plate 179) includes both the traditional flowers and leaves and the less commonly found stars and a heart. The areas between the main elements are covered with closely spaced parallel diagonal lines, and the edges are finished with a fine handmade tassel fringe. The use of all-white fabric and stitchery was popular in the early nineteenth century, and examples such as this were called "white work."

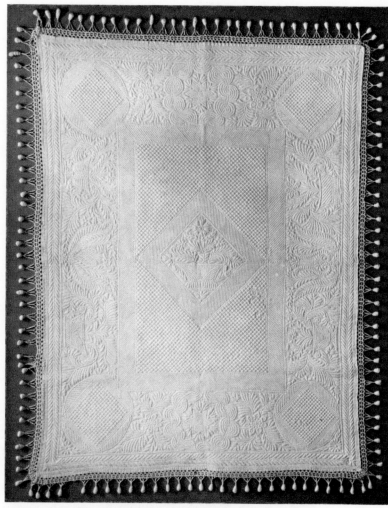

179 Coverlet, from Colbrook, Conn. 1800–20. Cotton with trapunto, 80 × 52". Greenfield Village and the Henry Ford Museum, Dearborn, Mich.

(continued from page 145)

LANDSCAPE, GENRE, AND STILL LIFE

The more intimate and personal forms of painting—landscape, genre, and still life—later so common in American art, were, if anything, even more neglected than history painting. However, the emergence of a tradition of landscape painting was discernible. The first post-Revolutionary interest in landscape appeared in the work of Ralph Earl, who seems to have preferred this form from his beginnings. His *Looking East from Denny Hill* (c. 1800, plate 180) is the first unequivocal landscape painting in America. Despite its obvious provincial shortcomings in composition and drawing, it reveals a combination of realistic observation of the New England countryside and a lyrical mood that presages the Hudson River School.

The native spark smoldered fitfully in a few isolated efforts. Vanderlyn's drawings and paintings of Niagara Falls have been mentioned earlier. Trumbull also did several views of Niagara (c. 1807–08), but they also are more like topographical records for engraving or a panorama.

Once more America was to receive a major impetus from abroad, this time through a group of immigrant English painters and engravers. Though individually unimportant, they brought an English Romantic landscape style which reflected at first the growing influence of Richard Wilson (deriving from Poussin, Claude, and the Dutch seventeenth-century landscapists) and Thomas Gainsborough, whose atmospheric rendering of nature led directly to Turner and Constable. A later group, involved with engravings of topographical views, transformed that art into an expression of more pictorial and Romantic values. In the first wave, in 1795, came Francis Guy (c. 1760–1820), who, despite reported cribbings from other painters, arrived at an original and personal style in his naively conceived and meticulously rendered cityscapes, which are almost genre pictures. His American experience seems to have expunged any memory of the picturesque, the ideal, or the artificial, and we have the sprawling chaos of American urban life seen with literal accuracy and endearing charm. *A Winter Scene in Brooklyn* (1817–20, colorplate 19) presents a Bruegelesque panorama of life. The apparent ingenuousness hides an effective handling of complex formal spatial relationships as well as human incident.

Topographical prints, which had achieved a measure of popularity during the Colonial period, were in even more demand after the Revolution. Again, English artists were instrumental in raising not only the craft but the aesthetic level of such engravings. Philadelphia had become the publishing center of the United States in the post-Revolutionary period, and most of the English engravers were attracted by the opportunities offered. William Russell Birch (1755–1834) was the earliest arrival, in 1794. A new standard of excellence was attained in his *Views of Philadelphia* (1798–1800), consisting of twenty-eight

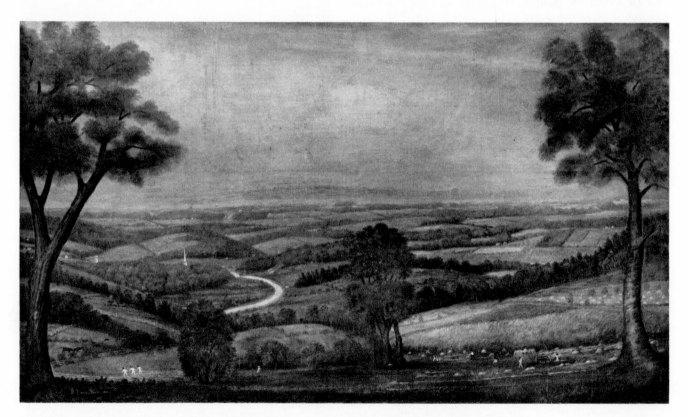

180   Ralph Earl. *Looking East from Denny Hill.* c. 1800. Oil on canvas, 45¾ × 79⅜". Worcester Art Museum

views of the city engraved after his own drawings. His son Thomas (1779–1851) assisted him but later branched out to become the leading marine painter of the period, establishing a genre that remained popular through the century. His most famous paintings, after which engravings were made, were inspired by sea battles of the War of 1812 (plate 181).

Anecdotal painting, which later became so popular in American art, had not as yet found an adequate form of dissemination. When genre art eventually did achieve acceptance, it was through the mass medium of the colored lithograph. The first evidences of it are both sporadic and peripheral, as in signs, illustrations on business cards and handbills, or as subsidiary elements in landscape engravings. The conversation piece moved in the direction of genre by introducing a natural interplay among individuals in a group, and this tendency became more marked in such pictures as Pratt's *American School* and Peale's *Staircase Group*. The lively human elements in Guy's cityscapes, already mentioned, could also easily qualify them as genre pictures. The rare pure genre paintings are, on the whole, minor efforts.

The still life had little currency in the post-Revolutionary period and was held in disdain by artists infected by the grand manner, but still lifes were being painted, and earlier Dutch examples were being offered for sale. The Columbianum exhibition in 1795 listed among its other works five still lifes attributed to Copley, examples by William Birch and James Peale, and five still lifes and two "deceptions" by Raphaelle Peale. Still-life painting was for a while almost a monopoly of the Peale family.

One characteristic aspect of American still-life painting from the outset was a concern with the creation of an illusion of reality, a tendency toward *trompe l'oeil*, or, as the Peales called it, "deception." The type has the sanction of antiquity, for Roman artists had included bits of debris with cast shadows in the designs of mosaic floors. Still life has historically dealt with the realistic rendering of material objects. The very absence of animation or ulterior meaning has permitted the artist to study the structure, surface, texture, color, and illumination of physical bodies for themselves alone and thereby reveal a world of sensuous experience unadulterated by extraneous considerations.

James Peale (1749–1831), more retiring and less gifted and original than his brother, Charles Willson, was active as a miniaturist and portrait painter. He is, however, best known for the still lifes that he continued to produce throughout his life. They follow what might be called the "Peale formula," a group of objects, mostly fruit and vegetables along with bowls and glasses, simply arranged on a tabletop and seen against a dark and undefined background (plate 182). The compositions are far from the elaborate and richly appointed still lifes of the Dutch seventeenth-century painters, closer to the

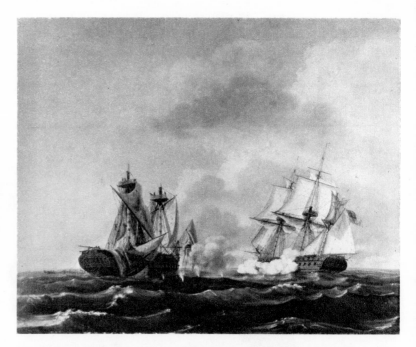

181 Thomas Birch. *Naval Engagement Between the United States and the Macedonian, October 30, 1812.* 1813. Oil on canvas, 28 × 34½". The Historical Society of Pennsylvania, Philadelphia

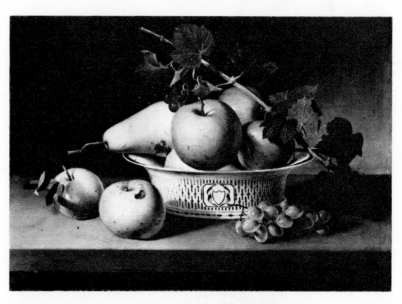

182 James Peale. *Fruits of Autumn.* c. 1827. Oil on canvas, 15½ × 22". Private collection

simpler and more architectonic arrangements of Chardin, although neither so sensuous nor so sophisticated.

Much in the manner of James, but both simpler and more subtle are the still lifes of Raphaelle Peale (1774–1825), the eldest son of Charles Willson. Raphaelle's still lifes are rendered with a crystalline clarity and have an air of dignity one does not expect in inanimate objects. Although his range was narrow and he repeated many objects, each painting is a fresh experience. His most famous work is a picture called *After the Bath* (1823, plate 183), which is ambiguous enough to have been interpreted often as a familiar genre subject, a nude girl behind a sheet hung on a line. It is actually a "deception," a painting or colored print of a nude hidden by a napkin pinned to a tape, the forerunner of the Harnett and Peto *trompe l'oeils* representing tape strips tacked to walls.

But *After the Bath* is more than a prank; it is painted with a true feeling for form and a deep love of the medium. The conception of volume, the rhythmic interplay of shapes, the subtle study of light and texture are masterly. Very few of the more exalted paintings of the period can stand comparison with this unassuming work.

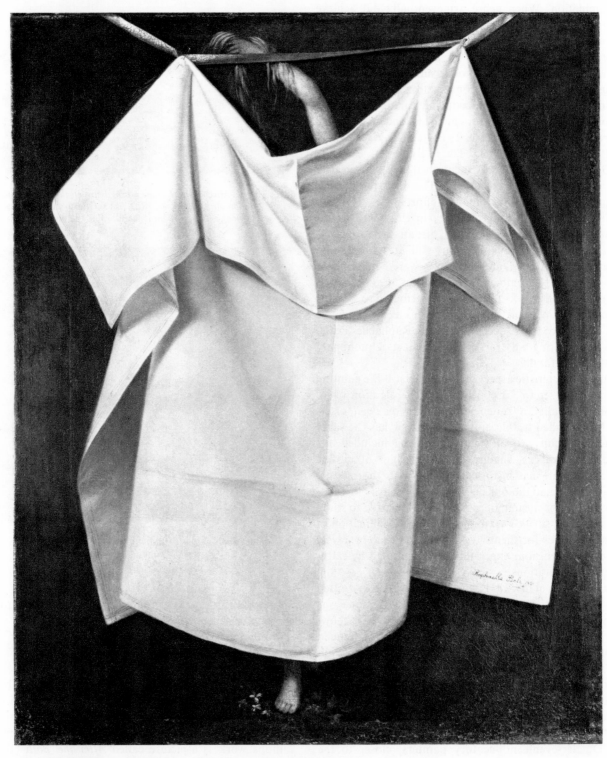

183 Raphaelle Peale. *After the Bath*. 1823. Oil on canvas, 29 × 24".
Nelson Gallery-Atkins Museum, Kansas City, Mo. Nelson Fund

7
Emergence of an American Sculpture

Sculpture had not yet begun to break the bonds of anonymity in artisan production, the limitations of apprenticeship training, or the aesthetic confinement of the craft tradition. Native carvers did create works of artistic merit, but they were unequipped technically and aesthetically to meet the sudden demand for monumental official sculpture that arose with the founding of the new nation. This demand was met first by placing orders abroad and then by attracting European sculptors, beginning in the 1790s. Only in the 1830s did local sculptors begin to replace foreigners as the creators of the heroic images of the new nation. Sculpture, even more than painting, was mobilized to supply patriotic icons, for "imperishable stone" and the visual analogy with Roman bust portraits of Republican heroes made marble the preferred medium. In the first half of the nineteenth century every local politician, rural poet, and soldier seems to have had his physiognomy eternalized; the result was an awesome gallery of forgettable stone faces.

The first major monument of a Revolutionary hero was, naturally, of George Washington, whose face and form were endlessly proliferated in stone and bronze, as they were in painting. In 1784 the Virginia Legislature voted to honor its favorite son with a life-size memorial and, through Thomas Jefferson, offered the commission to Jean-Antoine Houdon (1741–1828), the leading sculptor of France. Accompanied by Franklin, Houdon, a man of strong libertarian sympathies, came to the United States with three assistants in 1785 to observe the President in the flesh. He did a life mask and a terra-cotta bust before returning to Paris, where he finished the work. The statue (plate 184) was installed in the Virginia State House in 1796. The head is probably the finest portrait of Washington, but the figure is more a manikin than a heroic image. Houdon also produced a gallery of other American luminaries.

Among examples of Washington idolatry are a bust portrait by Giuseppe Ceracchi and the ill-fated Canova

monument. In 1815, when North Carolina sought a sculptor to produce a statue of Washington, the Italian Neoclassicist Antonio Canova (1757–1822) was universally recognized as the greatest. Without coming to the United States, Canova used the Ceracchi bust as a model for the head and a Peale drawing for the body; his Washington was contrived in the guise of a seated Roman

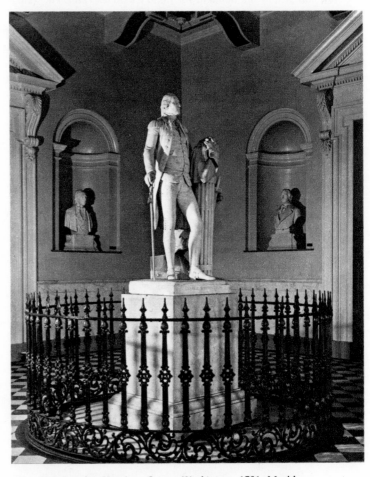

184 Jean-Antoine Houdon. *George Washington*. 1791. Marble, height 6'2" without base. Virginia State House, Richmond

general writing on a tablet in flawless Italian. The monument was installed in the State House in 1821, where it was destroyed when the building burned nine years later.

In the 1790s the transfer of the United States capital to Philadelphia drew sculptors from many countries in Europe. Giuseppe Ceracchi (1751–1802) came to America with the vain hope of finding patronage for a projected $30,000, 100-foot-high monument to Liberty. He was active in Philadelphia artistic circles during his stay, joining Peale and William Rush in the foundation of the Columbianum, and is known to have executed portrait busts of Jefferson and Franklin, but America was not ready for Ceracchi's sculptural dreams of grandeur, and he returned to Europe in 1795.

The construction of the Capitol at Washington in the early 1800s required architectural sculpture, and Latrobe sent to Italy for trained stonecutters. Giuseppe Franzoni (c. 1778–1815) and Giovanni Andrei (1770–1824), who came in 1806, did some allegorical subjects and ornamental carvings on the Capitol building before its burning by the British in 1814 destroyed most of their handiwork. Franzoni is probably best remembered for the famous "corncob" capitals carved for the Capitol. After the War of 1812, reconstruction of the Capitol under Latrobe brought in a new group of Italian sculptors, including Francesco Iardella (1793–1831), who carved the "tobacco" capitals (plate 147).

All the Italian sculptors remained alien to America although they left their indelible traces on the nation's capital. Their Neoclassic vision established aesthetic norms and directed the first generation of American sculptors toward Italy.

(continued on page 154)

DECORATIVE ARTS

By 1790 American shipping had revived the postwar economy, and the demand for luxury articles returned. Joseph Richardson, Jr. (1752–1831), was one of the most important silversmiths in Philadelphia's history and an assayer of the United States Mint from 1795 to 1830. He had trained under his father (his grandfather had been a Philadelphia silversmith as well) and produced excellent work in many styles during his long career. In metalwork, as in other crafts, the artisans employed the Classical vocabulary: the basic urn shape, ovals, decorative swags of foliage. Like other silversmiths, Richardson adopted the Classical fashion in his commissions, and this tea and coffee service (plate 185) is one of his masterpieces. The oval urn form predominates, with alternating fluting and concave sections on all pieces. The variations of form are sophisticated, as is the repetition of basic forms on the finials.

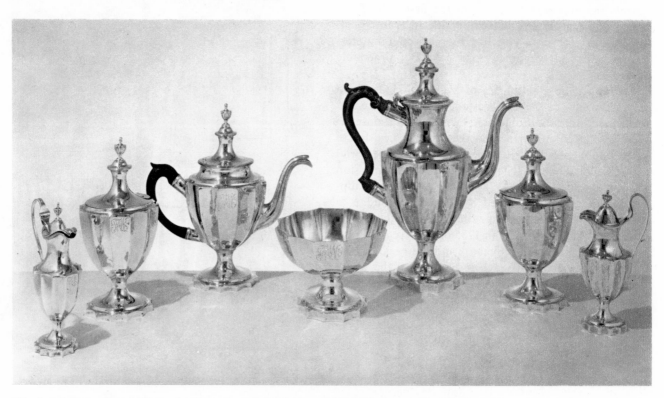

185   Joseph Richardson, Jr. Tea and coffee set, from Philadelphia. c. 1790–1800. Silver, height of teapot 10½".
Philadelphia Museum of Art. Given by Gordon A. Hardwick in memory of Marjory Taylor Hardwick

The practice of presenting silver objects to churches or to individuals was common in the late Colonial and Federal periods, and Paul Revere, Jr., had many commissions for such purposes. The pair of cups shown here (plate 186), ordered for the Church of Christ in Shrewsbury, Mass., follows the canons of the Classical style of the era. Revere created the cups in the shape of the bottom half of the standard urn shape, though with an elongated splayed foot. Simple in design, the cups, by their grace, preserve a static elegance. The high polish on the smooth surface makes the reflection of light an important aesthetic factor. Revere worked in both gold and silver and in his foundry also cast bells, cannon, and other objects. In 1808, at the age of seventy-three, he invented a process for producing rolled sheet copper, a contribution with important industrial applications.

One popular technique brought from Central Europe was enameling of glass, in greatest use at the end of the eighteenth century. Several standard patterns were favored by the German craftsmen: petaled flowers, a bird perched on a stem, or a pair of lovebirds facing each other atop a heart. All these motifs appear on the grouping of flask, mug, and tumbler (plate 187), though they were not produced by the same hand. On all three objects the decoration is carefully placed. The decorative process was to paint the designs with vitrifiable enamels in a selection of bright colors, usually blue, red, white, and yellow, and (rarely) black. The glass would then be fired in a kiln, fusing the enamel permanently to the glass. Many of the designs were standard in German folk tradition and appeared also on ceramics and painted furniture.

Red earthenware continued to be produced by local potters throughout the eighteenth century, but just outside Philadelphia the Pennsylvania-German potters made a unique form of redware known as "sgraffito," or scratched ware. Sgraffito-decorated objects (colorplate 20), such as this dish by Georg Hübener (active 1785–98), were all made by a similar process. The piece, fashioned from red clay, was partially or completely covered by colored liquid clays ("slips") and allowed to dry. Then lines were incised through the slip to expose the red clay under the drawing, and the object was then kiln-fired and cooled. Finally a clear lead glaze was applied and the piece was refired. In this example a large white plate bears splotches of green with the design showing through in the red clay color. The central motif is a pair of doves united at the body to create a single heart, the symbol of love. Flowers surround the center, including two of the stylized tulips traditional among the German Americans. Under the wings of the doves are the designer's initials and above their heads is the date 1786. Also common to the sgraffito form is the circle of lettering around the dish's rim, translating in this case to: "Cath-

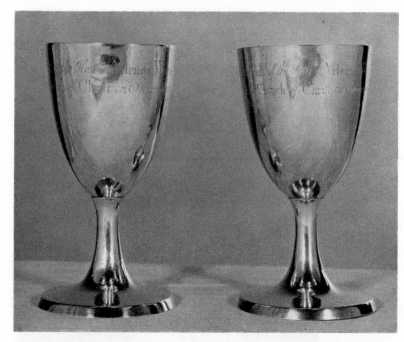

186 Paul Revere, Jr. Presentation cups. 1796. Silver, height 6⅚". First Congregational Church, Shrewsbury, Mass. On permanent loan to the Worcester Art Museum

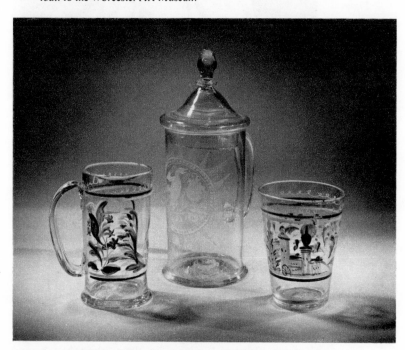

187 Flask, mug, and tumbler of Stiegel type, from Pennsylvania. Late 18th century. Free-blown glass with polychrome enamel, height of mug 5¼". The Toledo Museum of Art, Ohio. Gift of Edward Drummond Libbey, 1917

erine Raeder, her dish, out of earth with understanding the potter makes everything." While Hübener was not alone in this manner of inscription or dating, his few surviving plates provide the most complete documentation and have been helpful in developing a chronology of stylistic developments among the Pennsylvania-German potters.

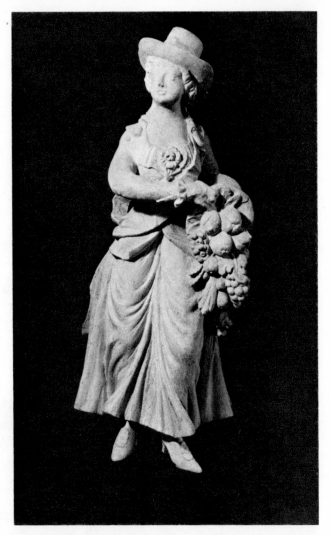

188 John and Simeon Skillin. *Plenty (Pomona)*. 1793. Wood, height 55". Peabody Museum of Salem, Mass.

(continued from page 152)

THE NATIVE TRADITION

Expanding cultural horizons and a growing sophistication were reflected in an increased refinement of the crafts. Reliance was still on pattern books, but the standards in these had risen and they were more current in matters of changing taste. With time, the Neoclassic elements became dominant in them, though a strong Rococo strain continued as a provincial remnant. For artisan carvers such books remained the major source of both sculptural detail and figurative art, almost exclusively limited to ship figureheads and shop signs.

The Skillin brothers, John (1746–1800) and Simeon, Jr. (1756/57–1806), carried the long and illustrious line of New England woodcarvers into the postwar era. Little of their work remains, but carvings attributed to them exhibit a limited technical facility, aesthetic naiveté, and dependence on pattern books. *Plenty* (1793, plate 188), a fairly well-documented work of the Skillins, is said to have been one of four garden figures for Elias Hasket Derby's Salem mansion.

Samuel McIntire (1757–1811), best known as carpenter, contractor, and architect, was also a woodcarver, though most of his work was in architectural and furniture decoration rather than sculpture. There are records of his having produced figureheads and ship carvings. As the bust portrait of *Governor John Winthrop* (1798, plate 189), based on a painted likeness, would indicate, McIntire was not at home in the figurative arts. He is remembered most for his decorative eagles and the medallion bust portraits of Washington, copied from Joseph Wright's profile portrait.

The culmination of New England figurehead carving is to be seen in the one surviving example of the work of Isaac Fowle (act. 1806–1843), nephew and apprentice to Simeon Skillin, Jr., and heir to the Skillin shop: a draped female figure (c. 1820, plate 190) that never crested the waves under a bowsprit, probably serving as Fowle's own shop sign. One can only admire the proud tilt of the chin, the thrust of the strait-laced bosom, and the firm set of the foot and observe with interest the naturalism of the petticoat edge and the elastic ribbing in the shoe. Yet the piece is naive and fumbling in its forms. The "billowing" drapery bunches like hammered sheet iron, the foliated base is ornamentally illiterate, and the figure barely rises above wholesome stolidity.

Only one of the host of woodcarvers rose above the

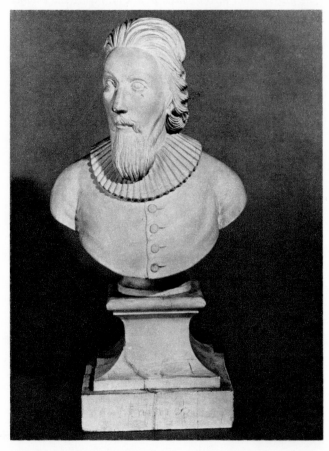

189 Samuel McIntire. *Governor John Winthrop*. 1798. Wood, height 15½". American Antiquarian Society, Worcester, Mass.

artisan level—William Rush (1756–1833) of Philadelphia, whose art was the swan song of the craft. His earliest work was done for the U.S. Navy as well as commercial shipbuilders, and he seems to have been in great demand. For the Navy he supplied ideas, drawings, and even recommendations for other carvers to execute, as in the case of John Skillin, who cut the *Hercules* (c. 1796) for the frigate "Constitution" after a drawing by Rush. In 1808, Rush moved beyond maritime carving with the over-life-size figures of *Comedy* and *Tragedy* for the Chestnut Street Theater. More ambitious and complex than figureheads, they still reveal a dependence on the woodcarving tradition. Rush seems to have been influenced by Charles Taylor's *Artist's Repository or Encyclopedia of the Fine Arts* (London, 1808) for mythological and allegorical themes. His allegories all suffer from the naiveté and provincialism of the source. Only the early *Water Nymph and Bittern* (1809, plate 191) manages to avoid pedantic formulas and retain a freshness of observation. The reality of a living body under the clinging wet drapery has a conviction not to be found in his other ideal figures. The stance may have been suggested by the *Medici Venus* and some details by the *Repository*, but the whole emerges as an original conception—aptly symbolic, both as a fountain group and in the selection of a native American bird.

Rush entered the Washington portrait lists with a life-size wooden figure (1814, plate 192), of which he hoped to sell plaster casts. It is in some ways one of the most satisfying of the monumental representations of Washington, depicting him as relaxed and human, though with great dignity. Unfortunately, the meaningless drapery cuts the figure in two and, with the clutter of iconographic paraphernalia, dissipates its underlying unity.

The major influence on Rush seems to have come from the portraits left behind by Houdon, which exhibit the same attention to naturalistic detail and striving for the expression of personality. Actually Rush was closer to the Rococo spirit, even in his monumental works, than to the Neoclassicism of his time. His most mature and convincing portrait is the symbolic "Pine Knot" *Self-Portrait* (c. 1822, plate 193), in which the forceful head, modeled with assurance, emerges from the bark of a *trompe-l'oeil* pine log.

At this point the native tradition in American sculpture had reached a level of accomplishment in the expression of realism comparable to that achieved by Copley before he left for Europe, though fifty years later. But at its very height this tradition was doomed by a growing sophistication in taste and a new generation of American-born artists who looked toward Europe for training and standards. By 1830 Neoclassicism was firmly established, and woodcarving was relegated to the status of craft.

The need for sculpture, apparent in large government commissions, led native artisans to begin in the 1820s to

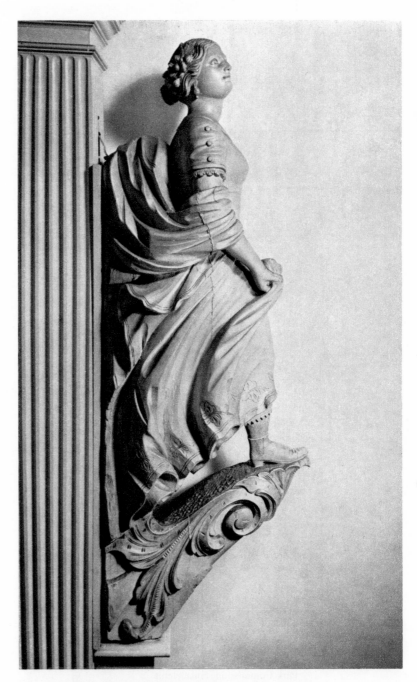

190 Isaac Fowle. *Lady with a Scarf.* c. 1820. Wood, height 74″. The Bostonian Society, Old State House, Boston

work in clay, plaster, and then stone. Also, actual examples of sculpture became more common through the works of immigrant sculptors and the growing collections of casts.

Except for Rush, John Frazee (1790–1852), an artisan stonecutter, was the first American to venture into sculpture as such. Born in Rahway, N.J., of Scottish parentage, he was apprenticed at fourteen to a bricklayer and mason. In 1818 he opened a tombstone business in New York with his brother. The bust of *John Jay* (1831, plate

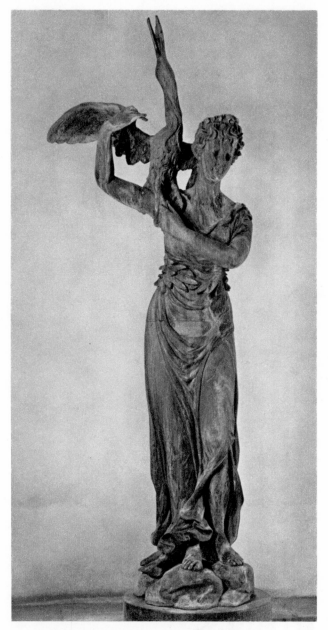

191 William Rush. *Water Nymph and Bittern*. 1809.
Bronze, 91 × 33″. Courtesy the Fairmount
Park Commission, Philadelphia

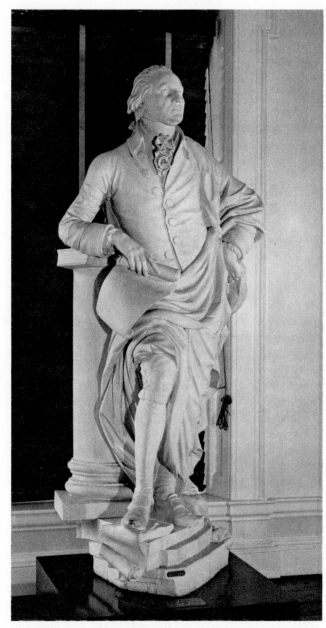

192 William Rush. *George Washington*. 1814. Pine,
life size. Independence National Historical Park
Collection, Philadelphia

194), the first commission given a United States sculptor, reveals a literal realism possibly related to the practice of taking life masks. As the first practicing American sculptor, Frazee received many commissions for portrait busts, but he also continued to produce funerary monuments and copies of busts in plaster and marble. His work remained clumsy, somewhat naive, but always direct, frank, and unpretentious.

Hezekiah Augur (1791–1858) began his sculpture career as a carver of ornamental parts for furniture in New Haven. In 1825 he attracted the attention of Samuel

F. B. Morse, who encouraged him to work in stone. The portrait busts and ideal figures he produced gained him some reputation, but are more interesting as indications of the achievement attainable by a self-taught native artisan than as formal statements. Augur took the step from wood to stone and into the Neoclassic world that Rush never did, but his work still suggests the tradition of woodcarving in its linear cutting, and its formal detail recalls pattern books.

The portraits by John Henri Isaac Browere (1792–1834) belong in a special category, for though their ex-

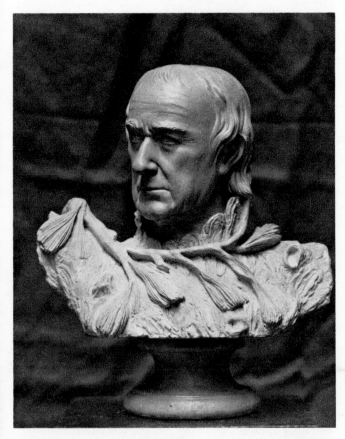

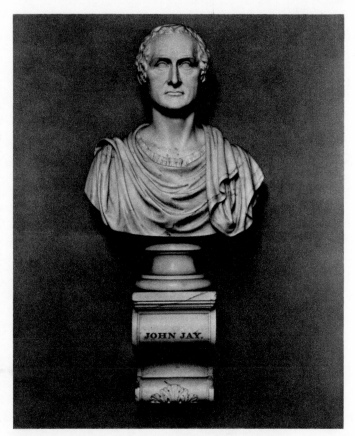

193 William Rush. *Self-Portrait* ("Pine Knot" portrait). c. 1822.
Terra cotta, life size. The Pennsylvania Academy
of the Fine Arts, Philadelphia

194 John Frazee. *John Jay*. 1831. Marble, life size. Supreme
Court Room, U.S. Capitol, Washington, D.C.

treme naturalism is expressive of the taste of the period,
the fact that they were basically life masks made them
suspect as works of art even in their own day. In 1828 he
had made enough life masks of famous men to open his
"Gallery of Busts" in New York. After his death, they
were forgotten until early in this century. Browere's procedure was to incorporate the life mask in a bust portrait
with toga-draped shoulders, thus approximating the
"legitimate" sculptural portraits of the period.

Wax sculpture in America remained essentially a minor
art form, though it was fairly widespread as early as the
eighteenth century. Patience Lowell Wright (1725–1786)
of Bordentown, N.J., America's first female artist,
turned in 1769 to wax portraiture as a means of livelihood
after the death of her husband. Her work was well
received, but in 1772 she left for London, where she
established herself as a successful miniaturist in wax
profile portraits. Her son, Joseph (1756–1793), who returned to the United States in 1782, had studied painting
with West, but most of his work was in wax. A profile
relief bust of Washington as a Roman crowned with a
laurel wreath, done in 1784 in the Neoclassic manner,
has survived (plate 195). The miniaturist wax technique
served Wright well in designing the earliest coins for the
United States Mint.

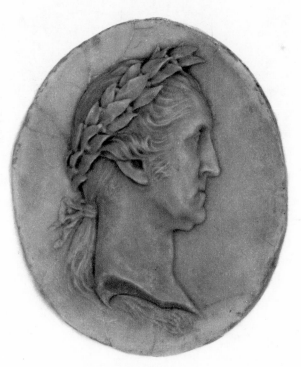

195 Joseph Wright. *George Washington*. c. 1784. Beeswax,
6 × 5″. Henry Francis du Pont Winterthur Museum,
Winterthur, Del.

Emergence of an American Sculpture 157

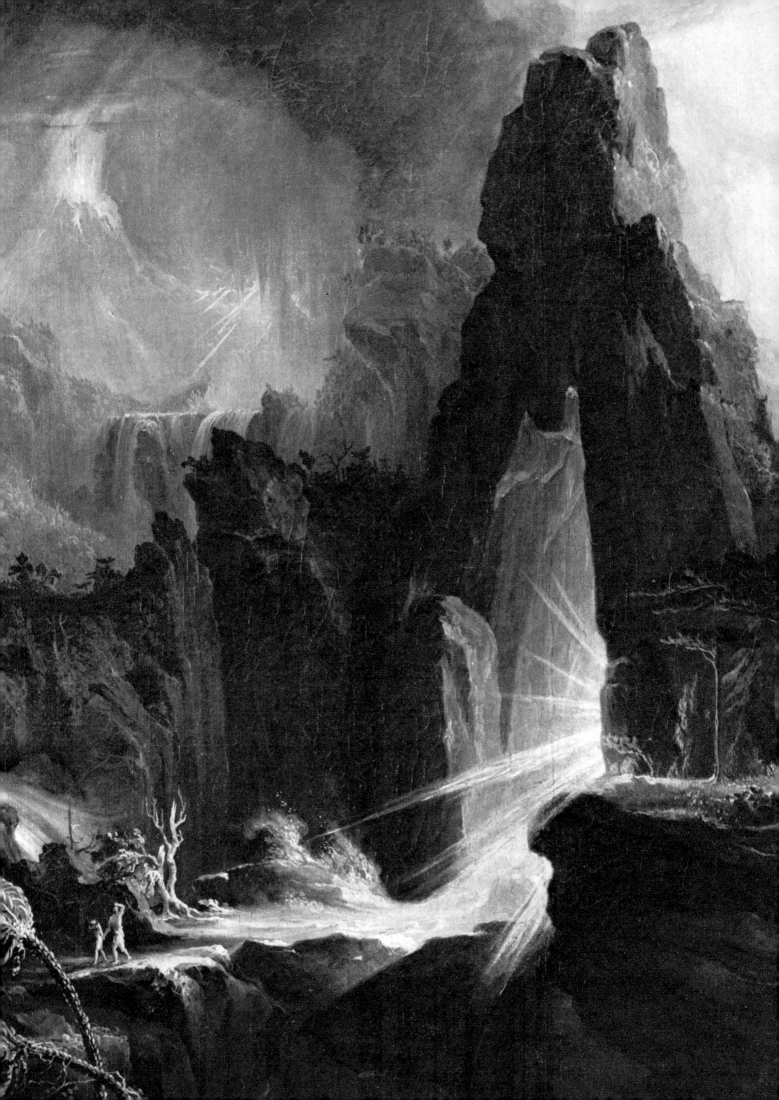

Part 3
THE JACKSONIAN ERA

Although the pieces do not all fit neatly, and one would sometimes prefer 1820 as the terminal date of the Federal period, the election of Andrew Jackson to the presidency in 1828 is usually accepted as the beginning of a new cultural as well as historical era. By the 1820s, all the great Revolutionary figures who had dominated the scene during the Federal period were gone. The stability of the old world had vanished, class distinctions were blurring, and all sorts of new forces were rife under the impact of an expanding economy and technology.

An ever-increasing flow of settlers and speculators moved westward by raft and wagon, and later by steamboat and railroad. As early as Jackson's election, the West had already become a force in American society, demanding recognition of its interests equally with those of the North and the South. The North had almost imperceptibly moved from commerce to industrialization, from artisan production to the factory system, from shipbuilding and trade to textile manufacturing and mining; and the control of economy and politics was passing from the older mercantile aristocracy to the new industrialists and bankers. Industrialism had also affected the South. The development of textile machinery and the invention of the cotton gin lowered the price of cotton and provided the means for satisfying the increasing demand. Cotton now displaced the more balanced plantation economy of an earlier era. And slavery, which had been considered a disappearing evil, suddenly became a necessity. Economic and political leadership slipped from the hands of the humanitarian Jeffersonian agrarians into those of the "slavocracy" of the South Carolina "fire eaters."

The lines of interest were thus drawn and the battle was joined. The prize was the government of the United States. Social and political problems absorbed the American people, and for the first time in its history the United States turned its back on Europe and faced westward.

The election of Jackson as the champion of the common man was made possible by universal manhood suffrage and the use of that new right by a coalition of the West and the new proletarians of the North. Motivated by a social philosophy which combined Jeffersonian agrarianism and frontier egalitarianism, the Jackson administration set out to neutralize the political and economic power of both Northern capitalism and Southern slavocracy. The rule of what its opponents called "mobocracy" established the first popular or mass culture and the distinction between a sophisticated and a popular taste.

This democratization was fostered by the spread of public education, by a great increase in the publishing of books and illustrated periodicals, and in the arts by the mass circulation of prints and plaster statuary, increased exhibitions of art in the major cities, and traveling pictures, statues, and panoramas which penetrated into the hinterland. All this was accompanied by a growth of museums and art organizations in the newer cities, by the ubiquitous "lyceum lectures," and by the art unions, which during their short existence were the most effective means of spreading art among the general public.

In turning its back on Europe and facing westward, America arrived at a new sense of identity, of nationalism, of "manifest destiny," both materially and spiritually. There was not only a growing optimism about the future of American culture but also an increasing insistence that art receive governmental support. Liberal attitudes based on Romantic thought had effectively reversed the older Puritan tenets. Instead of being immoral, art was an uplifting and civilizing experience, leading to virtue, even to God. If public taste was low, then it would be educated, for the health of democracy depended on the practice of virtue and the practice of virtue on the education of citizens. There was also some unconscious agreement between Romantics and know-nothings that the "unspoiled" taste of the common man was inherently superior to that of the "decadent" dilettante.

"Romanticism" is a term overused and misused, but Romanticism itself is a phenomenon that does not lend itself to easy definition or neat packaging. In one of its many aspects it occurs as the dominant form of mid-nineteenth-century American art.

European dominion of the New World went hand in hand with the drive for human dominion over the natural world. This required the belief that man could cope through reason, that everything knowable was manageable, and that the universe was ultimately knowable. This positivist, optimistic, and aggressive attitude helped make the world of today. As against this there arose a doubting, pessimistic, contemplative frame of mind, repelled by materialism, unconvinced of man's perfectibility, and intrigued, saddened, even frightened by the ultimate mystery of life, the universe, and God. Whereas one side believed that the more one knew the closer one came to Truth, the other felt that the more one learned the more tantalizing became the ultimate unanswerable questions. In a cultural sense, these attitudes created an abstract antithesis out of man's natural duality—intellect as against emotion, reason against intuition, objective against subjective, and reality against dream. These became structured responses, styles of art. That they are now identified as Classic and Romantic is in many ways unfortunate, since both terms have other specific meanings in history and language, as well as overtones touching unconscious areas of preference or prejudice. It is perhaps more seriously misleading that the materialist, realist, positivist point of view should have been identified with the Classic, although natural enough, since Greek art in its Classic phase had many features in common with this later materialism, but every subsequent Neoclassic manifestation in style, regardless of its motivation or intention, even if Romantic, could so easily be misread. On the other hand, the common usage of the word "romantic" obscures the serious intent and profound significance of Romanticism as a movement, while its identification with pessimism and retreat from reality ignores its later development as a revolutionary force. For to be against "progress" is not always to be for "reaction"; it depends on what is being defined as progress. And in the nineteenth century, when "Realism" was added to make a triad, the situation became even more confused.

In art the positivist attitude implied logical order, geometric structure, rationality, and clarity. Cultural positivism has usually returned for inspiration to, or attempted a revival of, Classical antiquity. Thus Neoclassicism emphasized restraint: ordered composition, measurable space, local color, and precision of line. Neoclassic painting was perhaps too dependent on Classical sculpture, with its immaculate outline and polished modeling, and especially on bas-relief in its planimetric treatment of space. Romanticism, on the other hand, sought the indefinable and the emotionally expressive. In composition it was intuitive, asymmetrical, and picturesque; in spatial definition naturalistic, fluent, even ambiguous; in color it strove for richness, luminosity, atmosphere, and mood. It was in color and the application of paint that Romanticism expressed itself most completely—in the brushstroke itself implying an immediacy of feeling—rather than in line as a process of conscious control.

When Romanticism as a movement achieved the dominant position in nineteenth-century Europe, its forms evolved in new directions. Its most radical aspect was a new positivism in response to specific historical conditions. The "failure" of the French Revolution was seen as the failure of reason, of the utopian ideals of liberty, equality, and fraternity that had captured men's minds. The revolutionary dream had been transformed into the reality of a new bourgeois society in its most blatant aspects—repressive capitalist consolidation, the worship of Mammon, exploitation, poverty, slums, industrial ugliness, and urban blight. In addition, the democratization of taste had lowered the level of culture to the tawdry and banal. The reaction was a coalescence of aristocratic nostalgia for a departed elegance with the more radical "bohemian" revolt against a culturally restrictive society. Romanticism thus became the expression of a cultured elite, paradoxically the language of both revolt and retreat, positive and negative, optimistic and pessimistic in an infinite variety of permutations. The past became symbolic of the heroic and the ideal in opposition to the commonness and materialism of the present. This attitude, supported by a growing historicity, spawned a series of revival styles in architecture and decoration.

Consonant with this concern with the past is the Romantic preoccupation with time, its inexorability, the mortality of man, the impermanence of his works, and the ultimate negation of all his efforts. In the visual arts, as well as the literary, the ruin was the most satisfying symbol of this poetic rumination on time. The Romantics had a great gift for transforming tragedy into sentiment.

Revulsion against urban existence in a burgeoning industrialism helped inspire the nineteenth-century retreat to nature. This new concept of nature as an emotional or aesthetic experience led to the efflorescence of nature poetry and landscape painting, vacations in the country, travel in search of natural wonders, and English gardens and garden cemeteries. The rejection of contemporary reality led also to fantasy, dreams, and the contrived world of literature. Literature became increasingly important for the visual arts as sensory experience was overlaid with philosophic significance, moral import, and poetic sentiment. Inspired by a growing nationalism, Romantics sought for the origins of "race"—claiming a greater purity for the earlier state—in the ancient sagas, legends, and folk arts of the peoples of Europe.

In architecture the Gothic Revival, which replaced the Greek in both Europe and the United States, reflected the Romantics' rediscovery of the Middle Ages as the antithesis of Classic antiquity—a confrontation of faith and reason, spirituality and materialism, mysticism and reality, Christianity and paganism. The Romantic found in medieval architecture not its complex and logical structure but its sublime mystery, its picturesqueness, its endless world of individual detail. The Gothic presented an image for literature and painting that included, on a more popular level expressed in the "Gothick" novel, the feeling of violence, terror, mystery.

The American taste for the Romantic was fed by the popular English "Gothick" novels, especially those of Mrs. Ann Radcliffe, whose fame was immense. Allston was a devotee of Mrs. Radcliffe's spine chillers. The "blood-pudding school" of literature had its American exponents, culminating in Hawthorne and Poe. In the Romantic tradition, though in different veins, were the good-humored picturesque "folk" tales of Washington Irving and the glamorized versions of the noble savage and frontier life by James Fenimore Cooper. Given the differences among the arts, American Romantic painters covered a similar range of material and strove for similar effects.

In relation to European Romanticism, the American version revealed its provincialism in what can be seen as a regression in artistic standards as well as taste. The earlier Romantics, such as Allston and before him Trumbull and Vanderlyn and later Morse, were more sophisticated artists, European trained and oriented, striving for objectives that were beyond the society to which they had returned. The second generation consisted of painters who had almost all come out of more modest backgrounds, originally trained as craftsmen; others were self-taught or had only the most rudimentary instruction, but the audience to which they were appealing was not aware of such limitations. American art was affected by the leveling influence of democratization and westward expansion and fell prey to its own destiny.

Its destiny was manifest. A continent was before it. The adventure of exploration, conquest, exploitation was a Romantic epic in itself. The American artist was quite ready and happy to express the patriotic sense of his country's future, its wild and magnificent landscape, its beauty and plenty, its adventure, and its common activities. Unfortunately, the art on the whole did not do justice to the reality. There was nothing in it of the sweat and toil, the squalor and brutality, the danger, greed, and passion, the waste and death. American Romantic art did not consciously distort the truth, but it turned its back on the more unpleasant aspects.

There was during this period, perhaps more than at any other time in our history, a rapport between the artist and his public. The dominance of public taste fostered a sentimentalization of the more heroic and profound aspects of Romanticism, and genre and anecdotal art in particular descended to the level of the saccharine and the banal. But this is just as true of the popular anecdotal art of the Victorian era in Europe.

8
Architecture: Eclecticism at Mid-Century

THE GREEK REVIVAL, c. 1820–45

The Greek Revival shared with the earlier Neoclassic movement its basic intentions, aesthetic attitudes, and in some cases even a continuity of personnel. However, the overtones became more complex, reflecting the divergent attitudes emerging in American society. To the abolitionist the Greek Revival signified humanitarianism, and to the slaveholder a rationalization for slavery. The northern industrialist could plan a textile town in which the mansion on the hill and workers' houses were all in the Greek mode. For the freeholder of the frontier it was the mark of civilization. But for all it was unquestionably American building. From the monumental masonry structures of the large cities to the carpentry versions in backwoods settlements, America was committed to Greek forms. The simplicity of the style seemed to lend itself to translation in wood, and even the provincial carpenter could achieve a naive but true dignity. In the hands of the professional the ancient vocabulary was capable of a forthright statement of simple power. And at no other time has the United States matched the level of rational and humane planning for urban living that obtained then.

The significance of the Greek Revival can easily be distorted by too close a focus on its stylistic complexities or by moral or aesthetic judgments about revivalism in general. This was an age of ferment and creativity in all fields, and the American architect especially was confronted with herculean tasks in building for a young nation in a new world. There were no architectural schools in the United States before the Civil War, and the most common route to professionalism was through apprenticeship to other architects, which provided technical competence but limited sources of inspiration or knowledge. Architects, unlike painters and sculptors, seldom traveled abroad and had no firsthand contact with the great monuments of the past except in reproduction. Thus the Greek Revival was a bookish architecture. At the beginning of the century most building, aside from large government contracts, was handled by builders or carpen-

ters who used the standard books or went to architects for plans and drawings. The architect usually furnished the contractor with drawings at a set fee without supervising construction. But by the mid-forties, the larger offices were performing all the functions of the modern architectural firm and were being paid on a percentage basis. During the Greek Revival period the profession of architecture came of age. In 1836 the American Institution of Architects was organized, to be supplanted later by the present American Institute of Architects.

With population growth and urbanization, what were once minor became major problems. For example, prisons and hospitals, mentioned previously as new forms, were now social necessities. Expanding administrative functions, growing cities, and new towns required government buildings of all sorts, from state capitols to post offices and customs houses. Also, the concern with public education led to a proliferation of colleges even in frontier areas, and what were once small town markets became large, permanent buildings.

In domestic building the traditional "country house," in urban as well as rural areas, saw important changes in terms of greater convenience, specialization of function, and new equipment. In the South, with the rise of fortunes based on cotton, sugar, and slavery, the pattern of living approached the seignorial, and architecture responded with complexity of plan, magnificence of scale, and lavishness of decoration. In urban centers the enormous increase in population called for radically new types of housing, planned industrial towns, row houses, hotels. Many of these innovations occurred during the Greek Revival.

Revival architects were also progressive in their utilization of new materials and techniques. Solomon Willard devised the equipment for exploiting his find of local granite. The development of the wooden truss made possible the rapid erection of large-span railroad bridges. The "balloon frame," devised in the 1830s as a result of mass-produced and standardized lumber and cheap nails, revolutionized wooden-house construction. The development of the steam pump, gas lighting, and kitchen, bath, and toilet equipment had its obvious effects. Even central heating and cooling systems had abortive beginnings in those years. The problem of fireproofing became an increasingly important consideration, and architects experimented with advanced methods, including the use of iron.

With all its functional innovations, however, nineteenth-century architecture still remained revivalist. Instead of discovering its forms in its functions, as eventually was done, the nineteenth century found them as analogues by historical example. Revivalism as an aspect of Romanticism was conditioned by two factors: first, a cultural uncertainty in the face of new situations and possibilities; second, the growth of historicity and an increased awareness of the past. To the earlier identification with the past was added a new objective evaluation, which led to a growing catholicity of taste. One could borrow not only from Classical antiquity but from any time or place. Antiquity in itself took on a new cachet.

What the ablest architects had in common was a dedication to a functioning architecture, one which considered requirements, site, cost, technology, materials, and efficiency. The level of building, design, and crafts-

manship was exemplary at least until the 1850s, when expanding industrialism, speculation, and exploitation began to transform objectives and standards.

PHILADELPHIA AND WASHINGTON

Greek Revivalism became the national style by the 1830s, but Philadelphia, which had been at the heart of Monumental Classicism, had moved in that direction ten years earlier. Philadelphia was still the most cosmopolitan city in the country, and it had in Nicholas Biddle—banker, ambassador, and dilettante—a champion of Greece and an arbiter of taste. In *The Port Folio* (1814), he published George Tucker's *On Architecture*, the first defense of the Greek as the ideal form for America, and he was responsible for the competition specifications for Philadelphia's Second Bank of the United States. Strickland's winning design resulted in the first true Greek Revival building in America (plate 156), predating the use of the Doric temple facade in other cities by a decade and the temple form by even more.

Latrobe had quit Philadelphia for Washington in 1807, and Mills departed in 1814. This left Haviland and Strickland in the twenties and thirties as the city's leading architects. Strickland was the most Greek as well as the most graceful of the revival architects, and he used the Greek manner with freedom. The most famous of his Philadelphia buildings, and his masterpiece, is the Merchants' Exchange (1832–34, plate 196), a singularly elegant and imaginative combination of disparate Greek elements. The rectangular block of the building is almost completely devoid of decoration except for the strong horizontals of the cornice and a bold molding over the first story. The large window areas divided into three vertical segments create a sense of spaciousness. The semicircular facade with its *tholos*, or round-temple form, capped by a lantern which is an adaptation of the Choragic Monument of Lysicrates, is open to criticism from both purists and functionalists, but as sheer design it remains a masterly effort. The lower story of alternating large, simple windows and massive plinths serves as a solid base for the airy lightness of the freestanding Corinthian columns supporting a severely plain entablature, which in turn is enlivened by a lacy crown of acroteria.

One of Strickland's pupils, Thomas Ustick Walter (1804–1887), active at first in Philadelphia, is known for Girard College, the most archaeologically Classical of Greek Revival buildings, and for the United States Capitol dome. In his renovation of the Capitol (plate 197) Walter enlarged the Senate and House wings (1851–61) and erected the non-Greek cast-iron dome (1855–65), now its distinguishing characteristic. Unfortunately, his work on the Capitol reflects not only the obvious needs of an expanding nation but the accompanying vulgarization of taste. It is not so much that he used cast iron in imitation of stone—there was no precedent for using this new material in a monumental building in

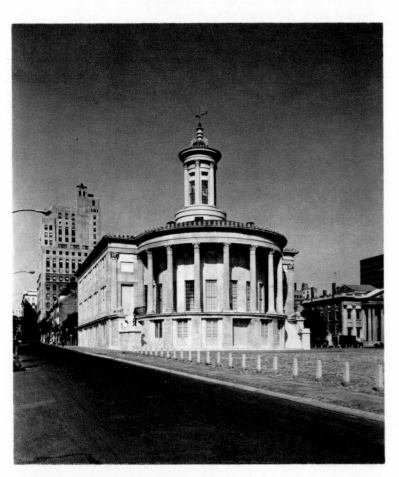

196 William Strickland. Merchants' Exchange, Philadelphia. 1832–34

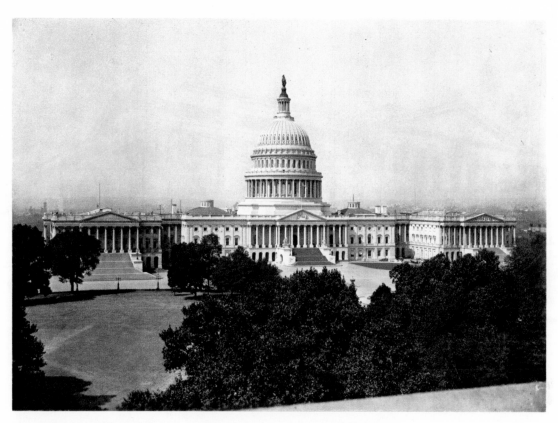

197 Thomas U. Walter. Dome, U.S. Capitol, Washington, D.C. Completed 1865

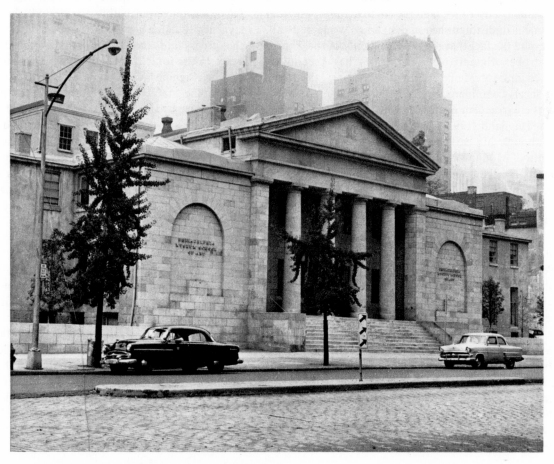

198 John Haviland. Pennsylvania Institute for the Deaf and
Dumb (now Philadelphia College of Art). 1824–25

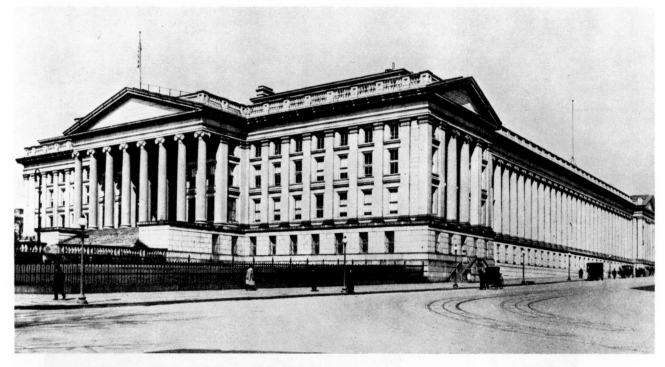

199 Robert Mills. Treasury Building, Washington, D.C. 1836–42

any other way, and a dome on that scale could not have been built in any other material at that time—but that the dome is undistinguished in design and crude in detail. Yet despite the fact that the modest dignity of the Thornton-Latrobe original (plates 145, 146) has been overwhelmed in the great pile of sprawling masonry, the dome, by its sheer scale, manages to unify the whole and dominate its environment in an impressive way.

John Haviland (1792–1852) belongs to the Greek Revival, though his early work reveals the unmistakable influence of Monumental Classicism. Born and trained in England, Haviland went to Philadelphia in 1816 with Hugh Bridport, an artist, to open a school for architectural drawing, and in 1818 Haviland and Bridport published *The Builders' Assistant*, the first American handbook to include plates of the Greek orders. Although Haviland used a Doric portico in the striking facade of the Pennsylvania Institute for the Deaf and Dumb (1824–25, plate 198), now incorporated in the Philadelphia College of Art, the clean cubical block of the wings flanking the recessed porch is reminiscent of Latrobe. Of his later work in the neo-Greek manner in Philadelphia, less is known. He was probably responsible for many of the handsome squares and row houses of old Philadelphia. Like many of the Greek Revivalists, he reflected a growing eclecticism in the use of various styles, including the Gothic (plates 215, 216) and the Egyptian (plate 232).

Mills never became entirely at ease in the Greek Revival. However, his Washington buildings from 1836 to 1842—the Treasury (plate 199), Post Office, and Patent Office—belong well within the period, though they are stylistically much closer to Rome than to Greece. True, the orders are knowledgeably Greek, with a Hellenic grace in the Ionic colonnade of the Treasury, but this is not their significance. The importance of Mills at the time lies in the standards he established for governmental architecture by the integrity, efficiency, and accommodations of his structures. As both engineer and architect, he made no distinction between construction and expression. His masonry and cement vaulting, the basic structural form of these buildings, were intended as efficient and permanent but also as expressive. All the subsequent Classic Revival buildings have not dimmed the dignity, honesty, and power of his designs.

NEW ENGLAND

Three young architects—Parris, Willard, and Rogers—close friends and often collaborators, led Boston architecture from the Adamesque into the Greek Revival. Oddly, all three began as carpenters and came to architecture indirectly. Alexander Parris (1780–1852), of Portland, Me., practiced there from 1801 to 1809. His early work was clearly influenced by Bulfinch, although already distinguished by a striving for greater monumentality. After Portland, Parris spent some time in Richmond, Va., where the presence of Latrobe had a marked effect on his style. His earliest important commission in Boston, the Sears House (1816), now the Somerset Club, was the first glimmer of a new kind of Classicism in that city, but it exhibits no strong break from the Bulfinchian manner in its graceful bows, flat surfaces, and elongated windows. Parris's most important and interesting work was the Quincy Market (1823–26, plate 200), a group of three long, shedlike buildings in Quincy granite, the central one with Doric porticoes on either end and the long line of the mass broken only by a simple central block capped by a shallow dome. There could be nothing more forthright, less archaeological, and yet so Greek Revival in essence than this market. Boston's urban renewal program has brought new life to the Quincy Market.

Solomon Willard (1783–1861) was an unusually talented architect and a man of wide interests, whose importance in the Boston group is not adequately reflected by his few extant works. His discovery of the Quincy granite quarries and his development of machinery to facilitate the cutting and handling of large slabs revolutionized Boston architectural practice and influenced building all over the eastern part of the country. Of Willard's surviving work the obelisk of the Bunker Hill Monument (1825–43) is probably the most familiar.

The most famous and prolific of the Boston group was Isaiah Rogers (1800–1869), whose successful career extended well beyond the Greek Revival. The son of a shipbuilder, Rogers spent the years 1820–21 in Mobile, Ala., where he won an architectural competition, and four years with Willard in Boston before entering independent practice in 1826. Rogers's reputation and the course of his architectural career were set by the success of his first important commission, the Tremont House (1828–29) in Boston, the first truly modern hotel. All the decorative details of the structure were neo-Greek; however, it was most significant in its revolutionary conception and rationality of planning. Everything from basic convenience to the ultimate in creature comforts that technology could then offer was supplied—public rooms ranged along the front on the ground floor; a sumptuous dining room on the same level, serviced from below; one hundred rooms in suite or single along straight corridors with easy access to stairways; and, most spectacular of all, a row of toilets and bathrooms with running water.

Rogers was then commissioned to build New York's Astor House (1832–36), larger, more sumptuous, and technologically more advanced. For the first time water was pumped to a tank on the roof and running water

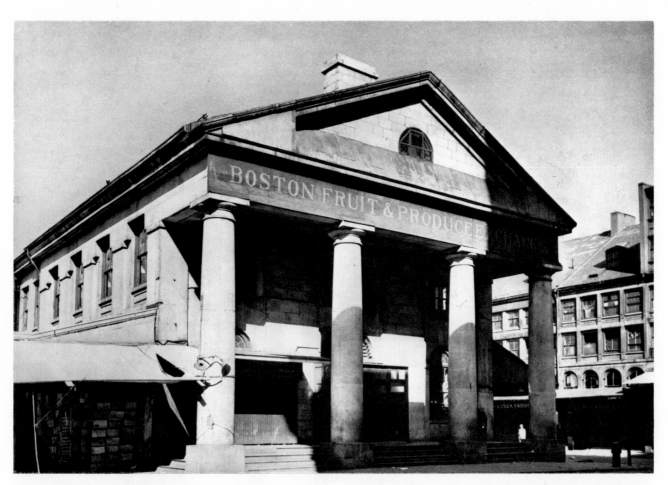

200   Alexander Parris. Quincy Market, Boston. 1823–26

could be supplied to every floor. From 1830 to 1865 he built almost all the major hotels in America. In his earlier years he made important contributions to the repertory of Greek Revival public architecture both in Boston and in New York. In his last years Rogers served as Supervising Architect of the Treasury Department and completed the original Mills Treasury building (plate 199).

Among the many younger architects working in Boston during the Greek Revival, Ammi Burnham Young (1798–1874) was the most noted and successful. He is reputed to have been a student of Parris. His major work was the Boston Customs House (1837–47, plate 201), the culmination of the Greek Revival, in Boston. This splendid old building has been preserved by incorporation as the base of the present Customs House. Built of Quincy granite, it is compact, almost mathematical, in its inevitability of design. In it Young resolved two problems that haunted Greek Revival architects: how to break out of the bonds of the temple form, and how to combine a Roman dome with it. The powerful cadence of the Doric columns and the impeccable interrelationship of the four pedimented facades and the shallow dome make one feel, for once at least, that there really was no problem. During his tenure as Supervising Architect for the Treasury

Department (1852–62) many new post offices and customs houses were built, and government building attained a high level of excellence.

NEW YORK

New York came late to the Greek Revival, in the 1830s. After the opening of the Erie Canal connected the port of New York with the western lands, the city became the leading commercial and cultural center of the Republic. New York's influence on the spread of the Greek Revival derived from two diverse sources. The first was the firm of Town & Davis, the largest architectural office of the time, whose leadership was exerted through the many buildings it designed and the many architects it trained. The second was Minard Lafever's handbooks.

The long and successful partnership of Ithiel Town (1784–1844) and Alexander Jackson Davis allied two quite different personalities and talents—Town, entrepreneur and builder, and Davis, draftsman and designer. The contributions of each are difficult to disentangle. Town seems to have received his training in Boston, probably at Asher Benjamin's school, but his early works were done in New Haven, which he considered his home. He made a fortune as the inventor of the Town truss for

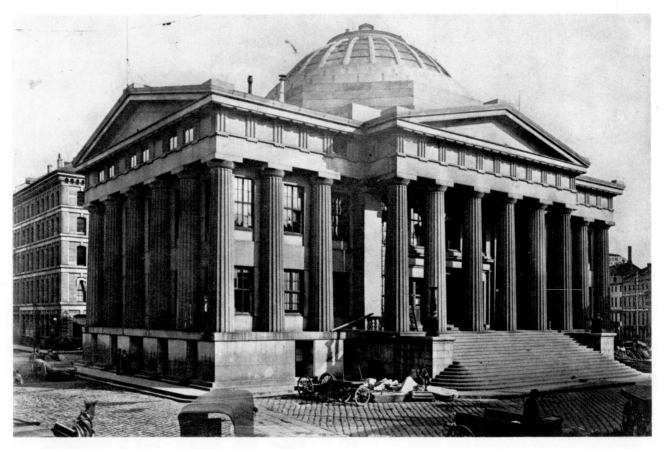

201 Ammi Burnham Young. Customs House, Boston. 1837–47.
Courtesy The Bostonian Society, Old State House, Boston

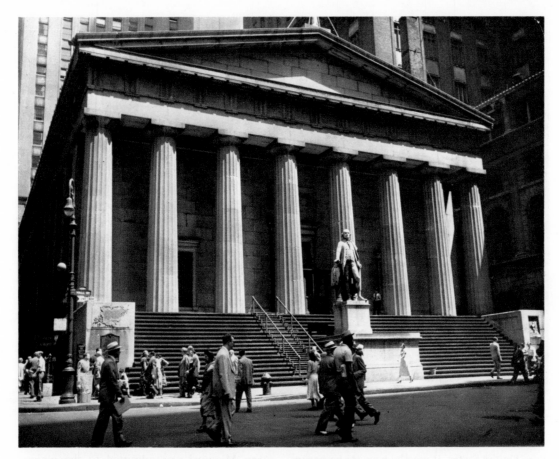

202 Town & Davis with William Ross and John Frazee. Customs House
(later U.S. Sub-Treasury and Federal Hall National Memorial), New York. 1834–42

bridges, traveled widely, and amassed the largest library of books and engravings on art and architecture in the country. In 1826 Town went into practice with Martin Thompson (c. 1786–1877) in New York. Thompson's previous work exhibits a conservative Classicism with an almost Georgian flavor, and the Federal Style was still strong in New York. It may be that the forcefulness of Town's personality and his scholarship were instrumental in breaking its hold. At any rate, by the time Davis was taken into the partnership in 1829, the supremacy of the Greek Revival was assured.

Alexander Jackson Davis (1803–1892) first worked as a topographic draftsman, depicting buildings and landscapes for engravers and lithographers. Even after he was established as an architect, he continued to sell designs and drawings. His study of architecture seems to have been confined to an apprenticeship with Josiah Brady and to a stay in Boston during 1827, where he was, no doubt, influenced by the Classical climate.

Of the various Greek Revival buildings designed by the partners either singly or together, very little now remains in New York: only the Old Customs House (1834–42), a fragment of La Grange (Lafayette) Terrace (1832–33), and perhaps some unidentified commercial buildings. The most important of these is undoubtedly the Customs House, now the Federal Hall National Memorial, on the corner of Wall and Nassau (plate 202). Although Town &

Davis won the competition for the building and the exterior is the Doric temple they planned, the interior is not of their design. The authorities in charge called in a visiting English architect, William Ross, who planned a domed rotunda to be enclosed within the building. John Frazee, the sculptor, who was also a contractor and stonemason, was then employed as architect of the building, supervised its construction, and supplied the detailing and working drawings. The exterior is a faithful adaptation of the Parthenon. Much more impressive are Ross's skylighted, domed rotunda, and the powerful, shallow vaults on stunted Doric supports in the basement.

Town & Davis had an immense practice, extending south to North Carolina and west to Illinois. They designed state capitols for North Carolina, Indiana, and Illinois, and Davis was consultant for that of Ohio. They also built college buildings at Yale, the University of North Carolina, Davidson College, and the Virginia Military Institute. Most of the Town–Davis designs can probably be credited to Davis, and in most of them, before he turned to the Gothic, one can see his predilection for combining a Roman dome with a Greek temple, establishing a type which became almost the hallmark of Greek Revival public building.

Town & Davis exemplify the emerging conception of designer- rather than builder-architect. Minard Lafever (1798–1854) represents the older craftsman or "mechanic"

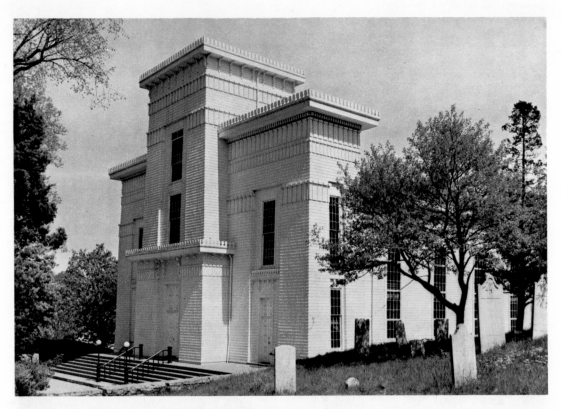

203 Minard Lafever (attrib.). Old Whalers' Church, Sag Harbor, Long Island, N.Y. 1843–44

architect in the United States. It may be because he began as a carpenter in the Finger Lakes area of New York state and understood the needs and limitations of the provincial builder and craftsman that his architectural handbooks had such effect on the Greek Revival vernacular. In New England Asher Benjamin still reigned, but the rest of the country, down to the Gulf States and as far west as the Mississippi, was all Lafever territory, especially in rural and domestic building.

Lafever's career as a practicing architect was overshadowed by the reputations of his more famous colleagues and by the success of his publications; also, fate has dealt harshly with his work, and none of the half-dozen of his extant buildings is in the neo-Greek mode. The most notable Greek Revival structure connected with his name through local tradition is the eccentric, somewhat provincial, yet altogether charming Whalers' Church (1843–44, plate 203) at Sag Harbor, Long Island. This curious effort to wed the Greek to the Egyptian is a remarkably successful excursion into eclecticism. The battering of the sides and the increased scale and vigor of the ornament transmute the essentially Classical elements into a new, powerful, and exceptional statement, but the Whalers' Church remains a sport.

SPREAD OF THE GREEK REVIVAL

One would expect the presence of professional architects in the cities, but architects were also practicing in what were scarcely more than frontier settlements. Talbot Hamlin mentions ten architects by name in St. Louis, a town with a population of under six thousand in 1821,

when Missouri was admitted to the Union, and only about seventeen thousand by 1840. In 1837 the new town of Detroit boasted an architectural drawing school, and six men were listed in the directory as architects. Yet the demand for new buildings was so great that even the designs of local architects, supplemented by those of such national figures as Mills, Strickland, Walter, Rogers, Town & Davis, and others supplied by governmental agencies, were insufficient. Many buildings remain anonymous, the work of builders and contractors depending on the handbooks.

A fruitful development of the Greek Revival occurred in Providence, R.I., where the activities of Russell Warren (1783–1860) and James Bucklin (1801–1890) are especially noteworthy. Warren's earlier efforts, houses for wealthy shipowners of Bristol, R.I., were Adamesque, but his mature work, particularly that done in partnership with Bucklin, reveals a complete acceptance of the newer Greek forms. Among these is the Providence Arcade (1828, plate 204), the only extant example of this newly introduced European type of enclosed shopping center. The Arcade has two facades composed of granite Ionic columns and a very fine skylighted interior with side gallery railings of cast iron. Though academically faulty in the use of the Greek orders, it was noteworthy in its functional innovations and design.

Close to Washington, Baltimore had already attracted many first-rate architects—Latrobe, Godefroy, Mills—who left it a heritage of fine building continued by the Robert Cary Longs, father and son. Richmond had works by Mills and Rogers, and others were added during the height of the Greek Revival. Much of the South remained unresponsive to the new vogue until comparatively late, but Charleston had an unusual efflorescence of the Greek; following a fire in 1838 a spate of Greek temples of increasingly archaeological erudition were erected there.

After the Louisiana Purchase in 1803 the Mississippi waterway tied the Great Lakes to the Gulf of Mexico. In New Orleans the Greek Revival transformed but did not entirely obliterate the Creole heritage. It dates from 1835, when James H. Dakin, a Town & Davis alumnus, joined his brother Charles and the Irish architect James Gallier, who had worked as a draftsman for Town & Davis and been a partner of Lafever for a short time. Separately and in concert the firm of Dakin, Gallier & Dakin did much to change the appearance of New Orleans.

French influence was strong along the Mississippi, and St. Louis, as one of the frontier outposts, was architecturally dependent upon New Orleans, but the city was soon converted into a western station of the Greek Revival by a number of native as well as foreign architects. One of the finest churches of the period is the "old" St. Louis Cathedral (1830–34) by the Edinburgh architect George Morton and the Pennsylvanian Joseph C. Laveille, although it is reminiscent of Monumental Classicism.

The border states of Tennessee and Kentucky were settled before the Revolution by the highland farmers of Virginia and the Carolinas who had followed Daniel Boone through the Cumberland Gap. After the War of 1812 wealthy land and slave owners moved into the valleys and grasslands, while growing cities were populated by people from the North, so that these states remained divided in culture between the South and the North, and in social attitudes among the landed gentry, the soil farmers of the hills, and the new city dwellers. The architecture of the region betrays the cultural strains from which these various people came. In Tennessee the grandiose plantations, built rather late, express the Greek Revival; but there often was a dependence on northern professionals such as Strickland, who was responsible for a number of public buildings in Nashville.

Kentucky was fortunate in the native genius of Gideon Shryock (1802–1880), whose father had sent him to Philadelphia to study with Strickland. His first major work at the age of twenty-five, the Old Capitol (1827–29), Frankfort, was, for a building practically on the frontier, notable both in its use of a refined Ionic temple form and in the competence and clarity with which it was planned (plate 205). Shryock had an independence and a natural grace in design that, in spite of occasional provincialisms, made him one of the truly creative Greek Revival architects.

The Northwest Territory, out of which Ohio, Indiana, Illinois, Michigan, Wisconsin, and Iowa were formed, was settled largely by immigrants from the Northeastern and Middle Atlantic States who brought with them their own local building traditions and their handbooks.

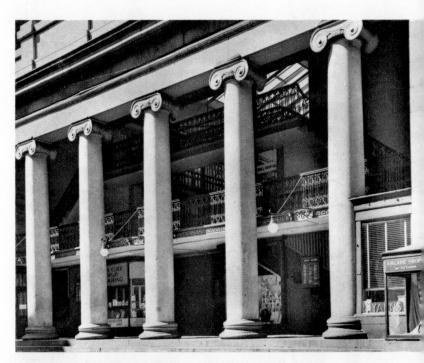

204 Warren & Bucklin. Providence Arcade, Providence, R.I. 1828

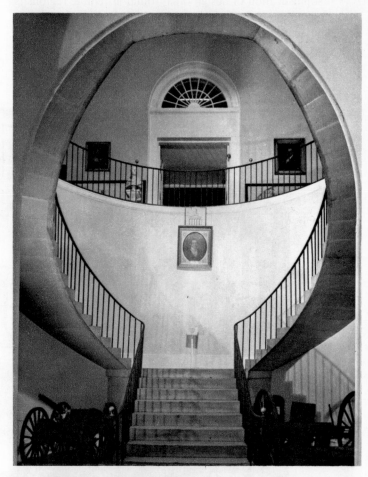

205 Gideon Shryock. Staircase, Old Capitol, Frankfort, Ky. 1827–29

Throughout the country Federal buildings of excellent quality could be found from Stonington, Conn., which had a small Customs House possibly designed by Robert Mills, to San Francisco, where the United States Mint (1869–74), done under the supervision of Alfred B. Mullett, remains as the swan song of Greek Revival public building.

GREEK REVIVAL HOUSES

The vast majority of domestic architecture was still dependent on handbooks for plans and details. Most of these guides were now published and written by Americans and were thus more immediately responsive to local conditions, practices, and tastes. The American authors borrowed freely from European guides and architectural books, but Minard Lafever's three earliest works had the greatest influence on vernacular architecture of the period: *The Young Builder's General Instructor* (1829), tentatively Greek; *The Modern Builder's Guide* (1833), completely Greek and richly inventive; and *The Beauties of Modern Architecture* (1835), the climax of his mature Greek Revival style in beautifully executed plates. The excellence of vernacular craftsmanship during the Greek Revival was due to the competence of its artisans, but the sophistication of design often found in remote regions is traceable to the handbooks.

In urban centers the development of the row house was a major contribution of the Greek Revival period, though it had appeared as early as Bulfinch's Tontine Crescent in 1794. The row house, together with the ubiquitous grid plan, gave American cities their characteristic appearance, at least until the ascendancy of the apartment dwelling. The growth of population in large cities made the free-standing house on its individual plot obsolete. Instead, blocks of contiguous houses were erected by speculative builders to be sold to individual owners. The form is open to obvious criticism. Attached houses on narrow plots permit light and air to enter only from either end. The only practical solution is the basic plan of two rooms to a floor. Furthermore, speculative building can easily lead to a lowering of construction standards, monotony in planning, and a slighting of aesthetic considerations. Urban architecture of this period maintained a high level, perhaps because such houses were built for the affluent and because of the integrity of the architects who designed them. Individual cities produced characteristic types. Boston houses were, as a rule, wider than those in New York or Philadelphia and thus capable of freer internal planning. New York houses usually had higher stoops and consequently a basement floor several steps below street level. In any case, Greek Revival town houses are distinguishable in plan from those of the earlier Federal period mostly in detailing. Only a scattered few are left—fragments of Washington Square in New York, Louisburg Square and streets on Beacon Hill in Boston, Rittenhouse Square in Philadelphia. The most splendid

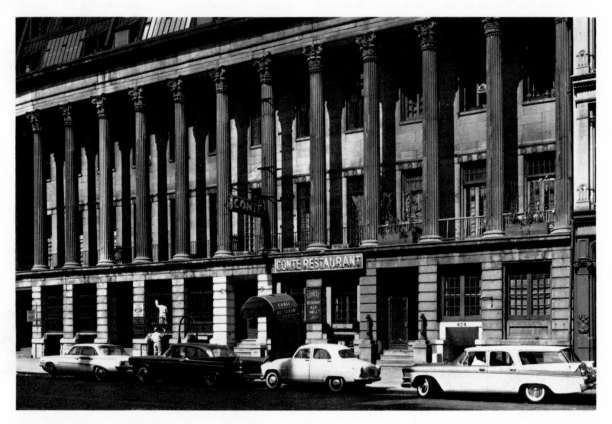

206   Alexander Jackson Davis (attrib.). La Grange Terrace (Lafayette Terrace, Colonnade Row), New York. 1832–33

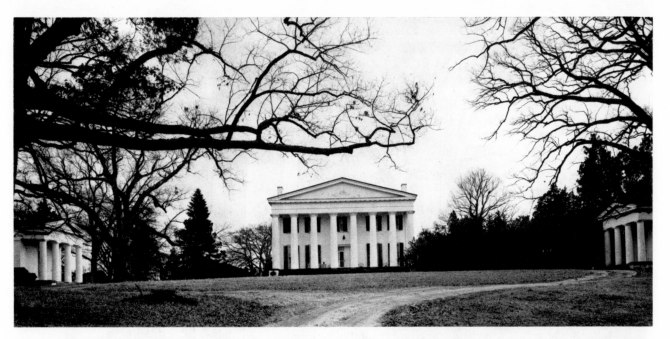

207 Berry Hill, Halifax County, Va. 1835–40

of all was La Grange (Lafayette) Terrace, New York (1832–33), attributed to A. J. Davis, originally nine houses, of which four remain (plate 206). Executed in Westchester marble, the original facade of twenty-eight elegant Corinthian columns two stories high on a rusticated stone base, with each entrance flanked by cast-iron candelabra lamps, could stand comparison with the finest in Europe. Even today, marred by neglect, renovation, and commercial signs, it adds a note of dignity to a drab stretch of urban decline.

The traditional house form had a rich and varied development during the Greek Revival. The pure temple type—a rectangular box with a columnar portico on the short side and a pediment continuous with the low-pitched peaked roof—was an adaptation of the Roman temple form which passed for Greek. The temple type evolved as a series of variations on a theme: the central pedimental block with symmetrical one-story wings, in which the temple form is the dominant element; the two-story-wing type, in which the pedimented roof rising above the mass remains the major axis of the building; and a type in which the portico (sometimes only a pavilion of building height) is added to the house block. The last is often indistinguishable from the Late Georgian houses with giant columnar porticoes or pavilions. These four forms (temple, one-story wings, two-story wings, and portico) were transformed by a series of secondary variations: the substitution of an entablature for the pediment, creating the appearance of a flat-roofed building; recessed instead of projecting porticoes, in which the columns are *in antis;* two-storied porticoes instead of the single giant order; and porticoes on the wings. The free use of such combinations and permutations resulted in a wide repertory of types.

The finest and most imposing of the temple houses is

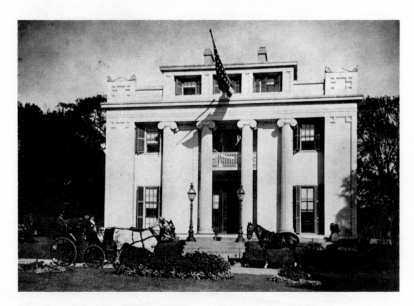

208 Russell Warren. Elmhyrst, Newport, R.I. 1833

Berry Hill (1835–40, plate 207), Halifax County, Va., which stands isolated on a sweeping greensward like a true Greek temple, balanced on either side by a smaller, one-story temple office. Totally different in appearance is the house in which an entablature replaces the pediment. Of this type is the splendid Elmhyrst (1833, plate 208), Newport, R.I., by Russell Warren, in which the four Ionic columns *in antis* form a recessed porch. A variation in the South, as in the A. P. Dearing House (1856) in Athens, Ga., has columns along the front turning the corner and moving partly down both sides in a T shape, producing the appearance of a peripteral colonnade.

Architecturally, the most interesting and pliable was

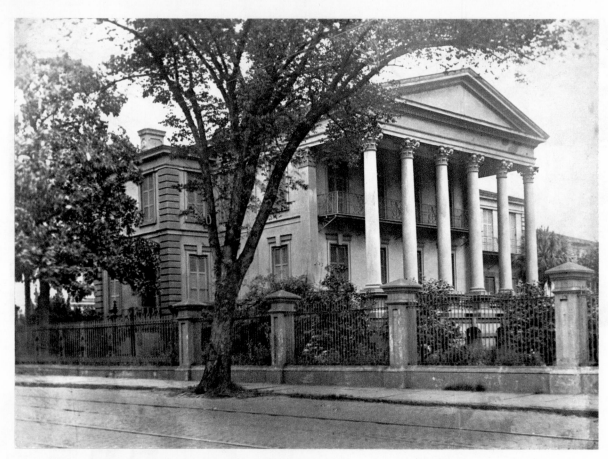

209 Jenkins Mikell House, Charleston, S.C. 1853

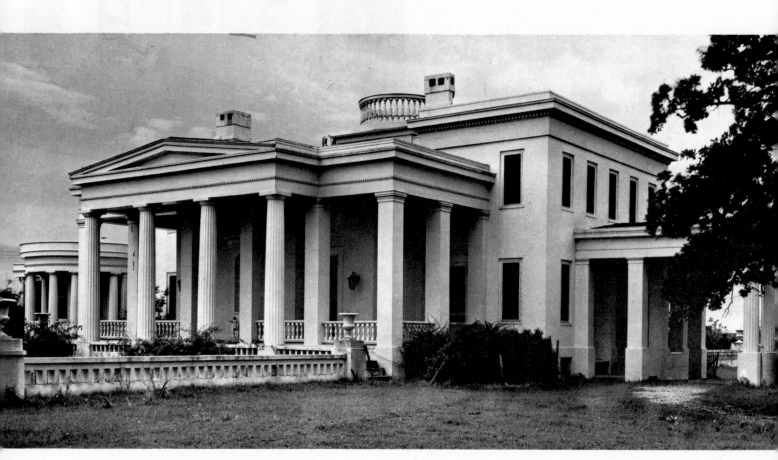

210 Gaineswood, Demopolis, Ala. 1842–c. 1860

the one-story-wing type, in which the interplay of cubical volumes on several levels and crossed axes offered a variety of compositional effects. Many of the finest Greek Revival houses fall within this category. Some were the results of renovation in an effort to give a "modern" Greek look to older structures, such as Arlington (plate 153). Of the two-story-wing type, the Jenkins Mikell House (1853, plate 209), Charleston, is one of the most imposing, with a giant Corinthian colonnade raised on a balustered base. By far the most popular in its varied forms all over the country was the portico type, which includes some of the most sumptuous of the great southern plantations. Several plantations of this period could match Gaineswood (1842–c. 1860, plate 210), Demopolis, Ala., in scale and lavishness, but none surpassed it in aesthetic refinement and originality of conception. The free use of Doric detail in a complex pattern of cubical masses, columns, and piers may seem overwrought in a photograph, but the plan is clear and logical. The imaginative use of balusters and urns and the delightful conceit of a Doric pergola seem much too informed for its reputed amateur architect, General Nathan Bryan Whitfield, the owner.

To the common temple type and its variations, the South added a two-facade form with colonnades on front and rear and a central form with a peripteral colonnade. The latter seems to derive from an indigenous Creole tradition of building. The Hispano-American house type with projecting eaves forming a veranda on all four sides was common in the West Indies and may have come to the continent from there. The Greek Revival peripteral house, with its giant colonnade and cast-iron balconies, survives in notable examples such as Dunleith (c. 1848, plate 211), near Natchez, Miss.

Inventiveness and freedom are to be seen even on the frontier vernacular level. The small, wooden James McAllister House (1839, plate 212), Tecumseh, Mich., is characteristic of a type Hamlin has localized in Michigan and called the "basilica." The pedimented long central "nave" block, with a recessed porch formed by two slender Doric columns *in antis*, rises clearly above the side wings, which project to the portico line. The result is a structure of the utmost simplicity but distinguished by its rationality and unwavering clarity.

Much of Greek Revival architecture was simply keeping up with the latest fashion, dressing buildings with the current symbols of status and refinement, but at its best it produced building of a high order: functional, inventive, refined, and skillful in execution.

ECLECTICISM

By the mid-forties the fabric of the Greek Revival was becoming noticeably threadbare, even in the very sumptuousness of certain plantation houses prior to the Civil War. John Andrews's Belle Grove (1857), near White Castle, La., had seventy-five rooms. Though still Classical

in inspiration, it reflected a growing eclecticism. This monumental pastiche of giant porticoes, extruding semicircular and cubical three-story bays and a two-story wing, was almost Baroque in feeling. Upriver, near Natchez, Miss., was Longwood, a Moorish fantasy begun in 1860 and never finished because of the Civil War. This octagonal extravaganza, which boasted a five-story central rotunda capped by a sixteen-sided cupola and an onion dome, was one of the last and most prodigal of southern antebellum plantation houses and

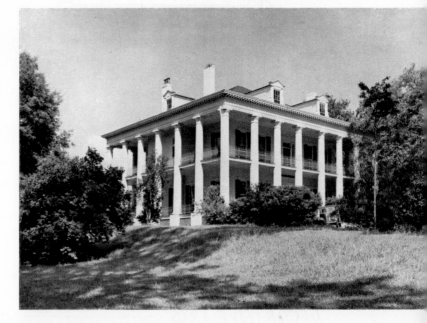

211 Dunleith, Natchez, Miss. c. 1848

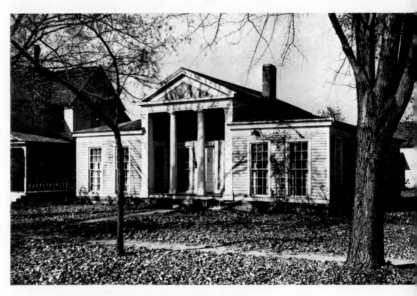

212 James McAllister (Adrian V. Yawger) House, Tecumseh, Mich. 1839

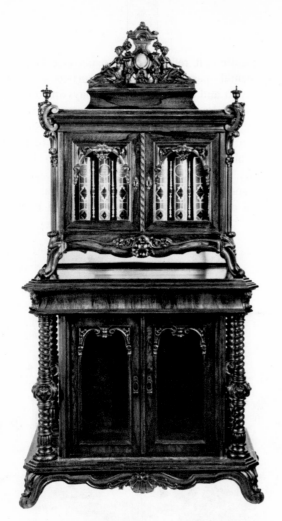

213 Thomas Brooks. Cabinet-bookcase. 1850.
Rosewood, height 72″. The Museum of the
City of New York. Gift of Arthur S. Vernay

DECORATIVE ARTS

During the twenty or so years on both sides of the mid-nineteenth century many revival styles flourished in furniture, often combined in one piece. A tall rosewood bookcase (plate 213) clearly illustrates a confusion rather than a blending of styles. Actually it is two bookcases, one atop the other. The curved legs, French scroll feet, and carved aprons are obviously derived from the Rococo; the pairs of twisted columns on the lower case are based on Baroque forms; the elaborately carved pediment can be traced to the Renaissance; and the arched cresting and symbolic seated goddesses are sixteenth-century reminiscences, as is the central dedicatory cartouche.

This case, with a specially bound set of Audubon's Birds of America, *was presented by a group of New York firemen to the celebrated singer Jenny Lind, the "Swedish Nightingale." The label "Brooks Cabinet Warehouse," which appears on the case, is that of the firm of Thomas Brooks (1811–1887), a Brooklyn cabinetmaker, who was active, alone or with various partners, in the area for many years and exhibited in the New York Crystal Palace in 1857.*

indicative of the demise of the Greek Revival.

Now the very proliferation of Classical forms in architecture led to public surfeit with columns, plain walls, sharp edges, and white paint, and the Romantic preference for variety and the picturesque increasingly found the Classic style unexpressive. In opening the past to investigation, the Greek Revival made change and, eventually, eclecticism inevitable. The primacy of utility in architecture was preached by architects from the Classicist Latrobe to the eclectic Downing, but function was neatly fitted into one or another historical style, or even a commingling of several.

Different modes were acceptable at the same time, and individual architects designed simultaneously in a variety of styles. The touchstone was appropriateness, not only functional but also symbolical. One can even discern a morphological pattern, although it was not rigidly adhered to: the Gothic especially but other medieval forms also were used for ecclesiastical buildings; prisons were castellated; armories were Romanesque; the Egyptian was linked with death; Oriental forms were employed for exotic or ornamental effects. Within this general picture of eclecticism one can note the growing and waning popularity of various styles—Italian Villa, Gothic, Romanesque, and, after the Civil War, the Second Empire—but none of them ever approached the earlier dominance of the Classic.

THE GOTHIC REVIVAL

Of all the post-Classic revivals, the Gothic was the most widespread and influential. In English history the Renaissance had come late, and the Gothic had survived almost into the eighteenth century. Even great post-Renaissance English architects, including Wren, Vanbrugh, Kent, and Hawksmoor, were called upon to design in the Gothic manner, usually for ecclesiastical or related structures. These, however, were more survivals than revivals. Perhaps the earliest evidence of a Gothic revival occurred at the height of the Georgian with the publication of *Gothic Architecture, Improved by Rules and Proportions* by the brothers Batty and Thomas Langley in 1742. From then on it became common practice to introduce Gothic ornamental "fabricks," such as mock medieval ruins, into English gardens for Romantic effect. Eventually houses in imitation of the Gothic style, such as Horace Walpole's Strawberry Hill and its various later progeny, became popular as a more or less playful conceit. The growth of taste for the "Gothick" eventually led to an increased awareness of England's medieval heritage and to archaeological study and restoration. Beginning with the first issue of Grose's *Antiquities of England and Wales* in 1773, the constant flow of literature on medieval architecture reveals a growing interest and sophistication. In England, the "Gothick" phase continued down to about 1820.

America's cultural lag in this case was about twenty

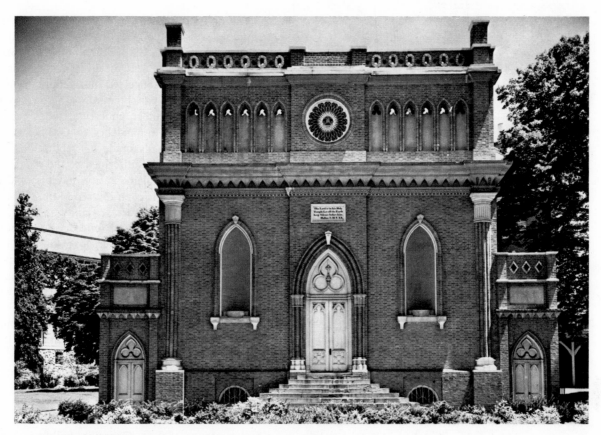

214 Maximilien Godefroy. Chapel of St. Mary's Seminary, Baltimore. 1807

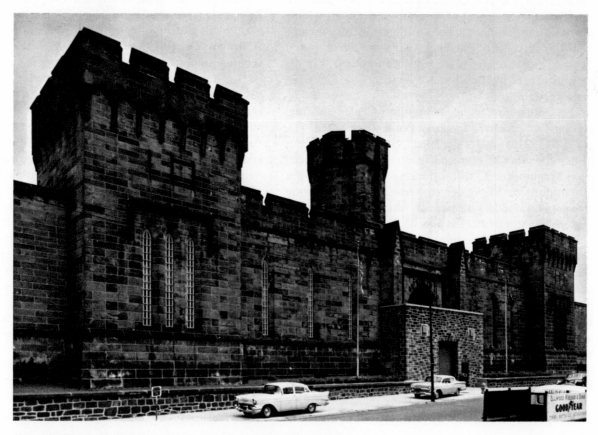

215 John Haviland. Eastern Penitentiary, Philadelphia. 1821–37

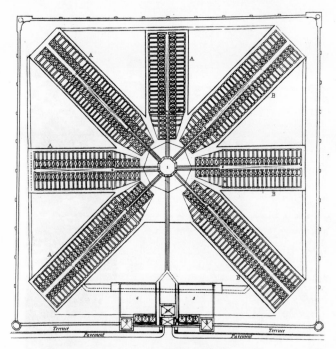

216 John Haviland. Plan, Eastern Penitentiary, Philadelphia. 1821–37. The Historical Society of Pennsylvania, Philadelphia

years, and the "Gothick" phase here had little importance and less quality. After 1800 the Gothic became more common, especially for church buildings, and most leading Neoclassic architects were involved. Since Latrobe's alternate design for the Baltimore Cathedral was not accepted, the first Gothic Revival church in America was Godefroy's Chapel of St. Mary's Seminary (1807, plate 214), in Baltimore. Then in rapid succession came Gothic churches by Bulfinch, Mangin, Greene, and Town. They were, from the evidence available, Gothic only in decorative detail and essentially still Georgian in conception.

The Gothic also found its way into secular building. Haviland's epochal Eastern Penitentiary (1821–37, plates 215, 216) was "castellated" Gothic in detail, but in its rationality of plan and spareness of form derived from Monumental Classical thinking. The selection of a brutal, dungeon-like design to house a penal institution reveals a symbolic intention at variance with the enlightened conception of the plan.

For America architectural books, rather than actual Gothic Revival buildings, eventually had a telling effect. The publications of Augustus W. N. Pugin were crucial in the transformation of the neo-Gothic from a picturesque minor mode into a programmatic style of Christian architecture. Pugin argued that only a Gothic architecture could lead people into Christian ways and beliefs and inspire them to moral behavior. The neo-Gothic was thus provided with a rationale as principled as that of the Neoclassic, and the Romantic taste for the picturesque joined with Christian piety to establish the Gothic in public favor.

The first and prototype of the full-fledged neo-Gothic churches was New York's third Trinity Church (1839–46, plate 217), by Richard Upjohn (1802–1878). It is also the first to look like a medieval building. Related to the Pugin ideal, it was conceived outside and inside as a Perpendicular English parish church. Upjohn was an honest and competent architect, underrated today because of the very conservatism and fidelity to Gothic Revival principles which originally made his reputation. As a dedicated churchman, he subscribed to the Anglican reform program and its implementation in Episcopal circles in the United States. He even refused to build in the Gothic style for nonconformist sects. Trinity, more than most of his output, reveals a visual reticence in its purely symmetrical plan and axial tower, a scholastic regularity in the repetition of elements, and a bareness, almost timidity, in ornamental detail. The interior, though structurally false, is aesthetically coherent. On the whole, it is an informed version of the Perpendicular.

Born in England, Upjohn worked as a cabinetmaker before coming to the United States in 1829. In 1833 he undertook his first architectural commission (now the Symphony House, Bangor, Me.), reminiscent of Bulfinch though indicating an awareness of the neo-Greek. Upjohn also designed Oaklands (1835–36) for R. H. Gardiner, Gardiner, Me., in the Gothic style but less a Tudor manor than a Georgian building. These early experiences presaged Upjohn's later eclecticism. Though he became the most famous designer of Gothic Revival churches, his oeuvre includes examples of the Italian Villa, Romanesque, Early Christian, and Renaissance styles.

Upjohn's larger Gothic churches were as imposing and authentic as any of the time, though on the whole not very ingratiating. He is often seen to better advantage in his small rural churches. As a missionary activity, he designed without fee one church a year for a poor parish, and the demand for his services became so great that he published a series of low-cost designs and instructions in *Upjohns' Rural Architecture* (1852), which inspired many small Gothic Revival churches. Perhaps the most interesting of these were the board-and-batten churches, of which his Trinity Church (1854, plate 218), Warsaw, N.Y., is typical. Board-and-batten construction was an indigenous form of carpentry sheathing in which boards were laid vertically and the joints covered by thin slats, or battens. Aside from being a simple and cheap method of building, the stripping had the aesthetic effect of enlivening the surface, emphasizing the vertical so dear to Gothic Revival taste.

Minard Lafever turned from the Neoclassic and designed a series of churches in the Gothic Revival style. Of all his ecclesiastical work in Manhattan, Brooklyn, and upstate New York only a handful remains. Among those in the Gothic manner, all in Brooklyn, is the Church of the Saviour, now the First Unitarian Church (1842–44, plate 219), on Pierrepont Street, in Collegiate Gothic.

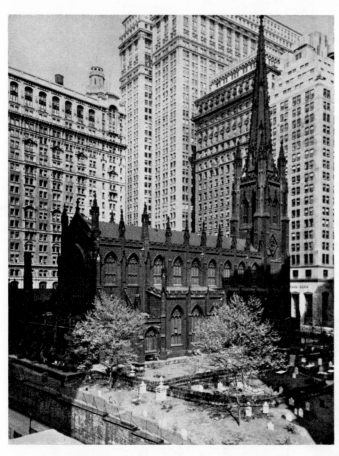

217 Richard Upjohn. Trinity Church, New York. 1839–46

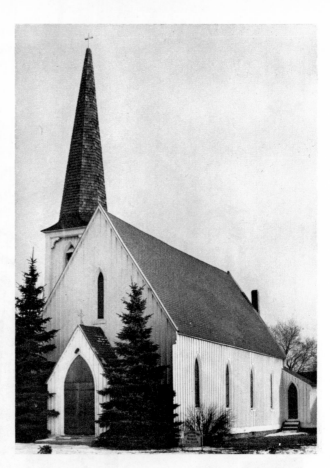

218 Richard Upjohn. Trinity Church, Warsaw, N.Y. 1854

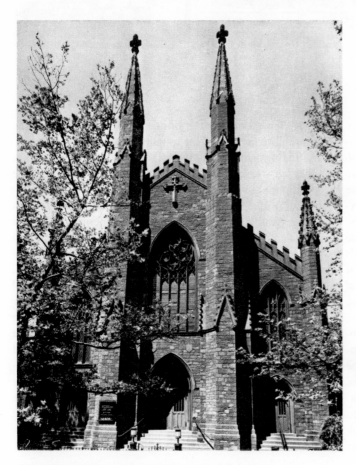

219 Minard Lafever. First Unitarian Church (Church of the Saviour), Brooklyn, N.Y. 1842–44

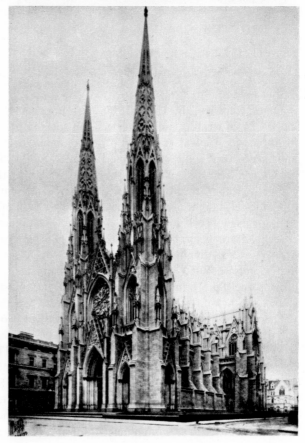

220 James Renwick. St. Patrick's Cathedral, New York. 1853–88

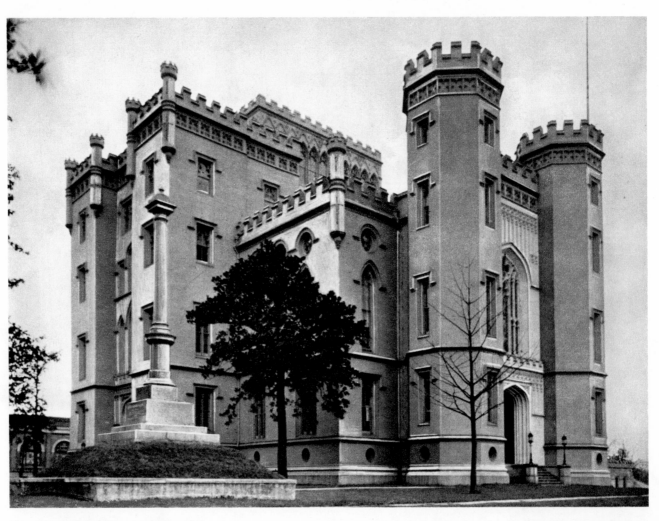

221   Old Capitol, Baton Rouge, La. 1847

James Renwick, Jr. (1818–1895), was born in New York City of wealthy, well-educated, and socially prominent parents. He was graduated from Columbia in 1836 and turned to the study of engineering and architecture on his own. In 1843, Renwick submitted a plan in the competition for Grace Church, and, at the age of twenty-four, the self-taught architect was awarded the commission for New York's wealthiest and most fashionable church. Grace Church was an adaptation of Upjohn's Trinity, except that Renwick had retained the transept that Upjohn omitted and used white marble instead of brownstone. Like Trinity, Grace Church still had plaster vaults.

The climax of Renwick's ecclesiastical work was probably the most important church commission of the century—St. Patrick's Cathedral, New York, in 1853. The cornerstone was laid in 1858, the Cathedral was opened in 1879, and the spires were completed in 1888. St. Patrick's (plate 220) was the first church in the United States to embody clearly the influence of the French Gothic. Renwick was disappointed that the plan was

reduced in execution: the stone vaults became plaster, the flying buttresses intended to support them were omitted, and the projected ambulatory with radiating chapels was squeezed. Nevertheless, in its interior, one does feel the soaring majesty of the Gothic.

The Gothic Revival also found popular acceptance in college building. It was then that the American collegiate identification with the architecture of the ancient English universities, Oxford and Cambridge, first emerged. Neo-Gothic campus buildings were designed by A. J. Davis, Austin, Renwick, and others. Otherwise, the ecclesiastical character of the Gothic inhibited its employment for secular building. Of all the state houses erected during the first half of the century, only Louisiana's in Baton Rouge (1847, plate 221) was neo-Gothic. The political and psychological identification of the Neoclassic with government was too strong to be affected by the new fashion. Only isolated examples of other secular types were done in the Gothic style. It was never as adaptable as the Neoclassic to contemporary building and never produced monuments of comparable interest or important

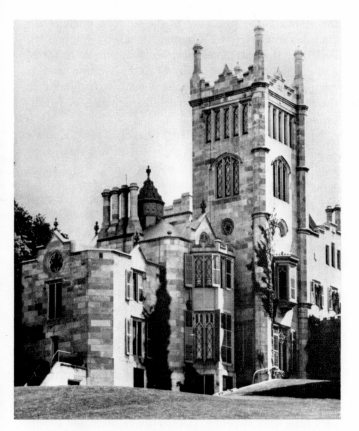

222 Alexander Jackson Davis. Lyndhurst, Tarrytown, N.Y. 1838 (remodeled 1864)

Sometimes the architect followed through with interior furnishings to complement his building design. Alexander Jackson Davis, for example, notes in his diary "fifty designs for furniture" to be used at Lyndhurst (plate 222). His wheelback chair (plate 223) does not reflect actual Gothic furniture; instead it uses Gothic motifs decoratively. The architect has adapted for the chair back the form of a rose window, one of the most spectacular and well known of Gothic forms. The chair is a beautifully balanced and executed design, equal in both originality and quality to the best work in England. Of course, the furniture at Lyndhurst was built by craftsmen to Davis's design. We know that Davis and his sometime partner, A. J. Downing, used the services of several New York firms, one of which, Burns and Trainque, is known to have done other furniture for the house. Perhaps they were the cabinetmakers who produced this fine work in carved oak.

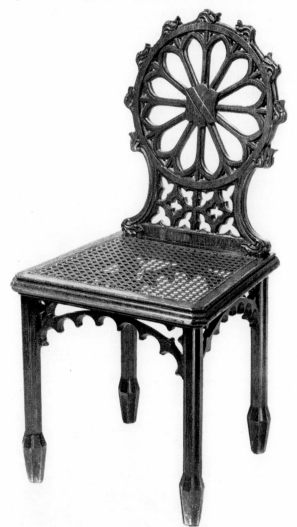

223 Alexander Jackson Davis. Wheelback chair. c. 1841. Oak, height 37¼". Lyndhurst, Tarrytown, N.Y. National Trust for Historic Preservation

structural innovations. One looks to the vernacular reduction of Gothic forms to the techniques of carpentry, or the picturesque inventions of the Romantic cottage, for the original contributions of American neo-Gothic architecture.

GOTHIC REVIVAL HOUSES

Because of the difficulties of carving elaborate decorative details in stone, the Gothic was used most frequently in modest wooden houses, but some impressive mansions were built in the style. A. J. Davis was the leading exponent of this aspect of the domestic Gothic, and his Glen Ellen (1832), the Robert Gilmor, Jr., house, near Baltimore, was probably the first of the Gothic Revival houses. It was the earliest American reflection of the Scottish baronial style, which had started with Abbotsford (1816), built for Sir Walter Scott, and had soon become a vogue in England. Lyndhurst (plate 222), erected in 1838 in Tarrytown, N.Y., was to become much more imposing after the renovation begun in 1864, but it was already picturesque in plan and elevation. Its peaked roofs, turrets, finials, crockets, and tracery windows were the recognizable signs of the Gothic Revival, but more important were the freedom of plan and the complex interrelationship between solid and void forms.

Davis designed many stone mansions in the Gothic mode, but more charming are his wooden cottages, such as the William Rotch House (1845, plate 224), in New Bedford, Mass. Though exceptional in quality, they are standard examples of the rural cottage style in their picturesqueness of composition, steeply pitched roofs, extended eaves with verge- or bargeboards of elaborate scrollwork, trellised verandas, bay windows, and clustered chimneys. Upjohn rarely used the Gothic for domestic building, but Kingscote (1841, plate 225), one of the earliest of Newport's palatial cottages, is Tudor Gothic in style, complex in plan, and entirely picturesque in composition.

ROUND-ARCHED STYLES: ROMANESQUE AND RENAISSANCE

Taken together, the "round-arched" styles—the Romanesque and the Italian Villa—were more numerous than the "pointed," or Gothic, examples. Variously and loosely described at the time as Byzantine, Norman, or Lombard, the Romanesque was reserved almost exclusively for monumental building, while the Italian Villa appeared mainly in domestic architecture. Upjohn adapted round-arched styles for churches of denominations other than Episcopal. Nonconformist sects consciously avoided the Gothic for symbolic reasons. Also,

the Romanesque lent itself to the simpler, boxlike hall churches preferred by Congregationalists, Methodists, Presbyterians, and Unitarians. The simplicity of its forms and decoration, the regularity of its fenestration, and its adaptability to brick construction made it preferable to the Gothic for utilitarian structures, schools, and institutions.

Upjohn's Bowdoin College Chapel (1845–55, plate 226), Brunswick, Me., was designed in a clearly Germanic vein. German cultural influence was strong in the United States during this period, and the Germans, in search of a national revival style, had rediscovered their own great Romanesque tradition. This *Rundbogenstil* had its effect on American architecture through publications and through the arrival in this country of Austro-German architects such as Leopold Eidlitz, Otto Blesch, Alexander Saelzer, and Paul Schulze.

Church building in the Romanesque Revival style was popular from the late forties until after the Civil War, with characteristic examples in New York City, New England, St. Louis, and Columbus, Ohio.

The first monumental use of the Romanesque style in a public building was in the Smithsonian Institution (1847–55, plate 227), Washington, D.C. The rich exterior effect was achieved by the massing of elements with very little carved detail. Despite its eight major towers

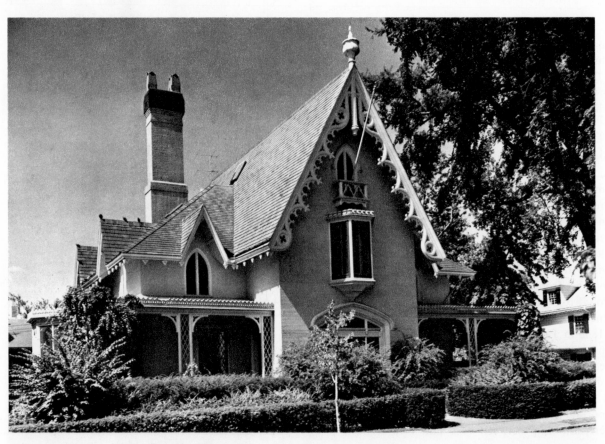

224   Alexander Jackson Davis. William Rotch House, New Bedford, Mass. 1845

and many chimneys of various shapes and sizes, the Smithsonian was designed to be flexible and cheap. The plan, with its museum and galleries, lecture halls, laboratories, and library, was considered prior to the style of the elevation. Careful attention was given to lighting, access, public and private circulation, and fireproofing. The plan is actually symmetrical and the irregular, picturesque appearance quite dependent on the placement of the towers, which also served for forge and furnace flues, freight elevators, and stairways.

Although secular buildings in the round-arched style were fairly numerous, few remain today. Within the style the distinction between the various aspects of the Romanesque and the less prevalent Renaissance Revival is often obscured. The neo-Renaissance mode (often called "Barryesque" after Sir Charles Barry, who led the revival in England) was introduced in this country by the immigrant Scottish architect, John Notman (1810–1865), who did the first Italian Villa houses. His Philadelphia Athenaeum (1845–47) was the first and the purest of the early Renaissance Revival *palazzi*, which were popularized later in the century by McKim, Mead & White. This style was a success in earlier New York commercial buildings by Upjohn. The many post-office and customs-house buildings designed under Ammi B. Young also reveal the change in taste from Neoclassic to Italianate.

THE ITALIAN VILLA

The most revealing indication that the picturesque attitude was more important to eclecticism than any particular historical style was the cohabitation of the medieval Gothic and the Renaissance Italian Villa in domestic architectural bliss. There was no significant difference in either plan or formal disposition but merely a variation in detail, and architects moved with ease from one manner to the other. The Italian Villa was inspired by the rural and peasant architecture of Italy that appeared in the landscapes of Poussin and Claude and was presented to American architects through books such as "the Bible of the Villa style," J. C. Loudon's *An Encyclopedia of Cottage, Farm and Villa Architecture, and Furniture* (1833). After Downing's *Cottage Residences* (1842), all American pattern books included the Italian, or "Tuscan," Villa, and it became a popular form in vernacular building as well as in more palatial houses individually designed by architects.

The larger houses were usually built of stone or of brick surfaced with stucco, and the flat-walled, simple volumes produced a stateliness and formality entirely different from the rusticity and ornamentation of the neo-Gothic. Picturesqueness was achieved by an asymmetrical disposition of horizontal and vertical masses on varying axes and by the exaggeration in scale of Classical ornament around window and door frames and in the heavy eaves brackets. The most obvious feature was the

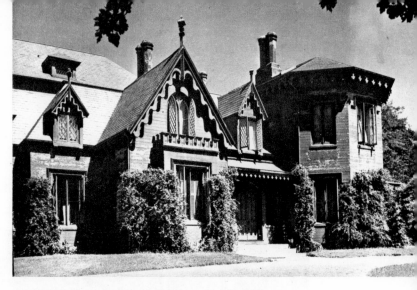

225   Richard Upjohn. Kingscote, Newport, R.I. 1838

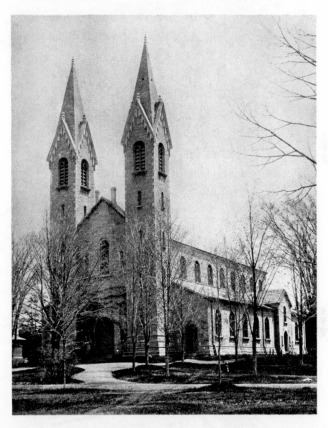

226   Richard Upjohn. Bowdoin College Chapel, Brunswick, Me. 1845–55

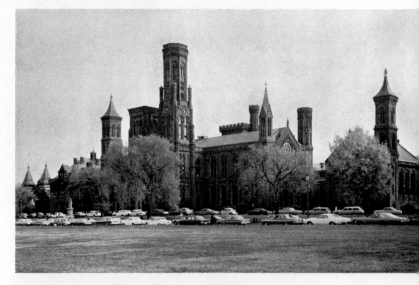

227   James Renwick. The Smithsonian Institution, Washington, D.C. 1847–55

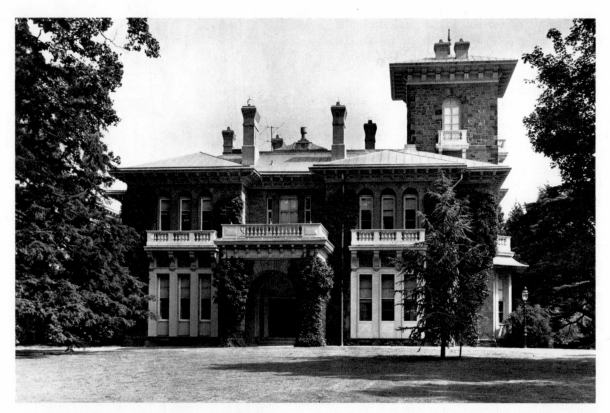

228 John Notman. Prospect, Princeton, N.J. 1849

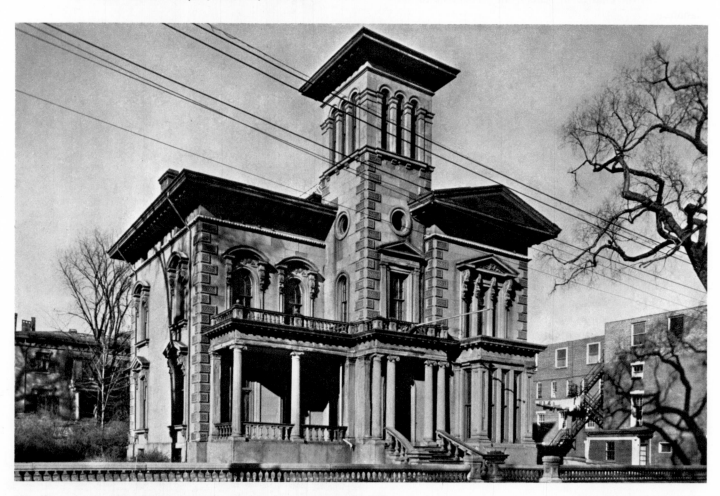

229 Henry Austin. Morse-Libby House (Victoria Mansion), Portland, Me. 1859

square tower, rising off-center above the other, largely horizontal elements and capped by a roof that was almost flat and boldly extended. Characteristic also were round-headed or rectangular windows in groups of two or three and roundheaded double doors or windows enclosed by arches. Interior moldings and ornaments were Classical, large-scaled, and entirely different from the filigree of neo-Gothic decoration.

John Notman's Bishop Doane House (1837, destroyed), Burlington, N.J., is generally considered the earliest of the Italian Villas in America. His Prospect (1849, plate 228), Princeton, N.J., is a large, picturesque composition with a fine square tower. Most of Davis's Italian Villas date from the fifties, when the style reached its height, and though he did distinguished work, this mode seemed to restrict the more inventive side of his artistic personality.

Henry Austin (1804–1891) did his most vigorous work in the two decades before the war in the Italian Villa style. As a protégé of Ithiel Town, Austin had grown out of the Neoclassic into the eclectic and had tried a variety of modes, but he seems to have found the Italian Villa most congenial. His Victoria Mansion, the Morse-Libby House (1859, plate 229), Portland, Me., perhaps the best-known of all the Italian Villas, is an excellent example of the lavish, stately town houses of the period. The asymmetrical composition of vertical tower and irregular horizontal masses, accented by boldly projecting eaves and enriched by vigorous ornament, forecasts the overwrought eclecticism of the postwar period.

(continued on page 186)

DECORATIVE ARTS

By the beginning of the Civil War increased knowledge of mechanized processes had fostered new furniture manufacturing centers in the Midwest. Locations on rivers were essential both for transportation routes and for power sources. Cincinnati was one of the new manufacturing cities, and by 1860 the firm of Mitchell & Rammelsberg was one of the largest furniture makers in the country. The company was typical of furniture manufacturing at the time in that it produced a series of lines, from inexpensive to costly, in a variety of finishes, and in many different styles.

The dressing bureau (plate 230) is over 8 feet tall and is obviously designed for a high-ceilinged room. Its ample size is accentuated by the sweep of the scrolls out from the pediment, and the whole image is one of opulence. The solid base, the weighty pediment, the panels surrounded by moldings, and the cartouche are all mainstream factory-made elements of the Renaissance Revival, but the naturalistic carved flowers and leaves on both sides of the mirror and the scrolls of the candle-stand supports reflect Rococo designs of a century earlier. The mixture of styles results in a handsome piece, illustrating that factory-produced furniture can be of the highest quality.

In the early 1840s a new type of English pottery (named for the Marquis of Rockingham), became popular throughout the United States, though its beginnings are closely identified with the potteries at Bennington, Vt. The Norton Company, in business at Bennington since 1793, produced many forms of ceramics but concentrated on stoneware until the advent of the Rockingham craze. This pitcher (colorplate 21) was one of the basic Rockingham shapes and is typical in coloration and design. The form was made from a light-colored clay and glazed with a particular brown glaze containing certain metal oxides. The amount of the glaze, the points of application, and the heat and number of times the object was fired all determined the exact colora-

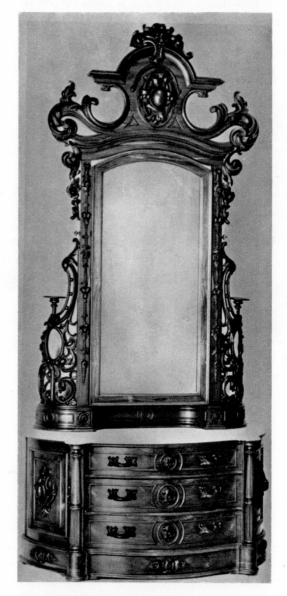

230 Mitchell & Rammelsberg. Bureau, from Cincinnati. c. 1865. Rosewood with marble top, height 9'6". Newark Museum, Newark, N. J. Gift of Grace Trusdell, 1926

tion, and the variations are unlimited. The hound-shaped handle was developed at a rival pottery in 1843 but was in use at Bennington only a year later. Many pottery pitchers were decorated with geometric designs, but the prized ones usually embodied a face as the primary form or featured a scene in relief. Popular subjects included genre scenes

of hunting, fire-fighting, and steamboats or, usually in conjunction with the hound handle, as in colorplate 21, a display of game. By the time the craze subsided in the 1870s, Rockingham ware was used for such objects as tableware, picture frames, cuspidors, and statuettes in a variety of animal and human forms.

(continued from page 185)

DOWNING AND THE COTTAGE

Mid-century "house pattern books" included complete designs with plan, elevation, and landscaping, thus differing from the earlier "builders' guides," which were primarily concerned with building instructions and ornamental details. The pattern books were intended for the general public and dealt with questions of taste rather than problems of construction.

The picturesque cottage had its most persuasive advo-

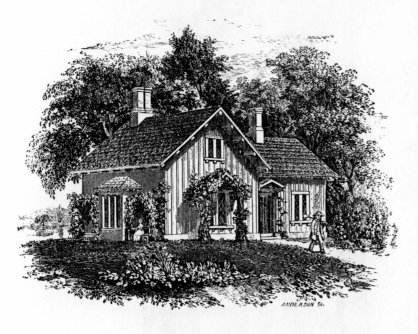

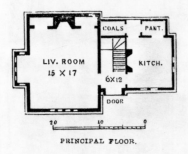

PRINCIPAL FLOOR.

231 Small bracketed cottage. From A. J. Downing, *The Architecture of Country Houses*, D. Appleton, New York, 1850, fig. 9

cate in Andrew Jackson Downing (1815–1852). His books, beginning in 1841, swept the field. A proselytizer rather than an originator, he published the designs of others as well as his own, especially those of Davis, with whom he worked in close collaboration. Downing began his professional life in landscape gardening, subsequently shifting his emphasis to architecture. *Cottage Residences* (1842) was the most popular and influential of his publications, followed by *The Architecture of Country Houses* (1850). Downing soon had many followers and competitors, but it was he who most effectively answered the Romantic urge for picturesqueness, the American concern with economy and efficiency, the pietistic need for moral sanctions, and the middle-class striving for taste and refinement.

Three principles underlay Downing's approach to domestic architecture—"Fitness or Usefulness," "Expression of Purpose," and "Expression of Style." Under "Fitness," he considered the plan for convenience in room arrangement; the orientation of the house in nature for picturesque appearance and view; its adaptation for family needs, maximum economy, and efficiency, including sanitary conveniences and labor-saving devices; and the selection of proper materials. "Expression of Purpose" had the specific meaning for Downing of "truthfulness": the house must express the notion of home, and the home was understood to be the basis of a moral society. However, Downing listed as the most expressive elements chimneys, windows, and porches—essentially the features that created exterior picturesqueness. By an act of legerdemain, taste had become an expression of morality. His antipathy to the white paint of the Greek Revival was not that it hid the "truthful" character of material, but that it clashed with nature, was therefore not picturesque. As for "Expression of Style," history could offer many appropriate faces—"Rural Gothic," "Italian," "Swiss," "Flemish," "Roman"—each appropriate to a particular image except for the Greek, which he dismissed as a "false taste" for "ambitious display." Houses should imitate not the monumental aspects of historical styles but their humbler features. Thus good taste was modest taste; and again Romanticism had been domesticated.

Downing's theories were a curious mixture of realism and Romanticism, but he made Romanticism a viable mode for suburbia and changed the character of the American house from the formal symmetry of the

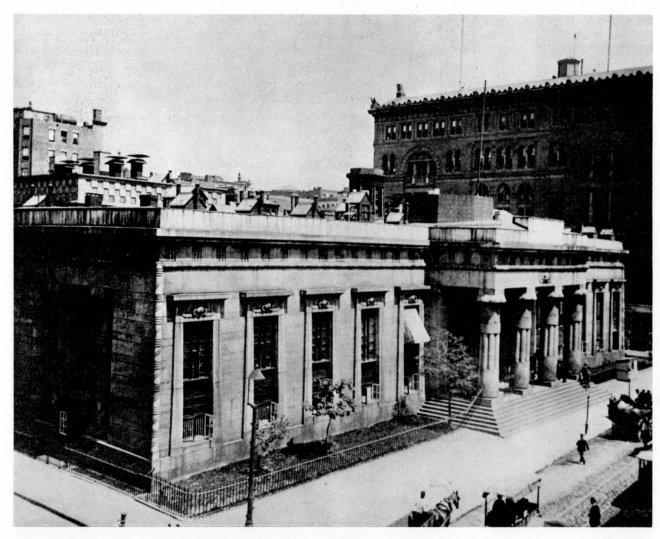

232   John Haviland. New York Halls of Justice ("The Tombs"), New York. 1835–38

Neoclassic period to the freer planning, greater variety, more inventive use of materials, and closer relationship to nature of the Romantic cottage. His own published plans were simple, rational, efficient, and economical. He disposed rooms asymmetrically, but they were still essentially within the confines of the rectangle. The apparent spread outward and the variety of room shape were achieved by comparatively small excrescences: bay windows, verandas, and balconies.

Downing's major contributions, aside from his importance as a propagandist, were his bracketed board-and-batten houses (plate 231). Davis had published board-and-batten house designs, one with brackets, as early as his *Rural Residences* (1837), but Downing made these elements his own and finally arrived at a style that expressed both materials and structure. Here at last the skeleton frame of the building was clearly expressed on the exterior. Downing's Romantic idealism also had a profound effect on environmental thinking. He saw beyond

the problems of the individual house to those of the suburban development and eventually of urbanism. A year before his death, he submitted to President Millard Fillmore a plan for the Romantic "ruralization" of Washington, D.C., and his influence on his protégé, Calvert Vaux, helped form the conception of New York City's Central Park by Olmsted and Vaux, a plan that became the model for city parks throughout the country.

EXOTIC STYLES

Among the less pervasive revival styles that added spice to the cuisine of the picturesque was the Egyptian. Egypt, the scene of Biblical history and Napoleonic adventure, had a Romantic aura. The Egyptianizing elements of the Empire style had already infiltrated the Neoclassic, especially in furniture and interior decor, but it comes as a surprise to find more than sixty buildings in Egyptian style listed by Frank Roos, Jr., as existing in the United States before the Civil War. On the whole, however, the appropriateness of the style was considered limited. It was favored for memorial monuments and, because of its association with death, for tombs and cemetery gateways, but there was no real archaeological understanding of the style nor any consistent use of its elements.

The first evidence of Egyptian influence occurred in the Baltimore Battle Monument (1815–25), a Roman fasces column rising on an Egyptian-style base, designed by Godefroy. Willard introduced the popular obelisk form in the Bunker Hill Monument (1825–43), Charlestown, Mass. And Mills eventually dwarfed Willard's effort in the colossal Washington Monument.

Of the more conventional buildings in the Egyptian style, "The Tombs," officially the New York Halls of Justice (1835–38, plate 232), by John Haviland, is probably the most famous. Here the overtones of ancient law and the death penalty must have played some role in the selection of the style as appropriate for a prison.

There are a few church buildings in this style, notably the Sag Harbor Whalers' Church (plate 203), in which the Egyptian is fused with the Classic and translated into wood in an entirely original manner.

Islamic and Chinese modes in England were more fad than revival, purely exotic and generally playful rather than serious, but Oriental forms soon found their way into American pattern books of the time. Oriental designs had been recommended for garden "fabricks" even in the Georgian period, but after the Civil War such structures became common for pleasure buildings. The iron-and-glass Crystal Palace (1853–54, plate 233) in New York, designed by George Carstenson and Charles Gildemeister, differed from the London original in the addition of Islamic corner minarets and a somewhat Oriental dome.

In commercial architecture the use of Oriental forms was neither widespread nor noteworthy. However, synagogue architecture was one area in which they seemed appropriate. The Romantic spirit had led other sects back to their ancient architectural forms, and Jewish communities were motivated by the same search for identity. There were no ancient synagogues to serve as models, however, and the Bible gives no clue as to the architectural style of Solomon's Temple. Strickland had used the Egyptian style as early as 1822 for the Mikveh-Israel Synagogue (1822–25), Philadelphia, perhaps the earliest attempt to find an appropriate style through identification with the Orient. Other architects turned to the Islamic, which may not seem apt from our point of view but appears to have satisfied people then. The Isaac M. Wise Temple, B'nai Yeshurun (1865–66), Cincinnati, by James K. Wilson, in its effort to be archaeologically accurate, included two minarets.

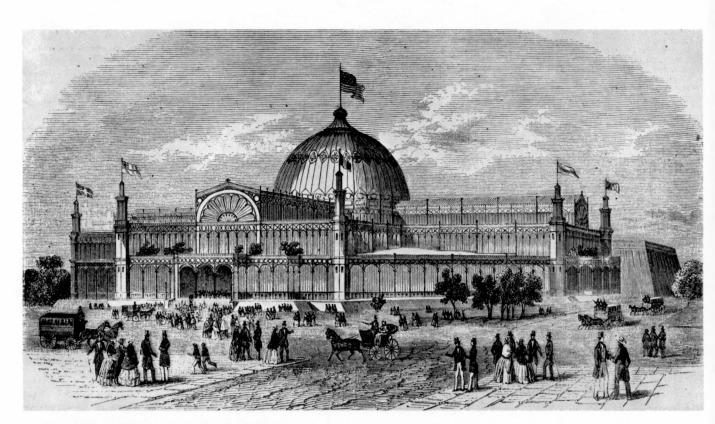

233 George Carstenson and Charles Gildemeister.
Crystal Palace, New York. 1853–54

European interest in *chinoiserie* was a fashion of long standing, though in its inception essentially a courtly taste. The publication of *Designs of Chinese Buildings, Furniture, Dresses, Machines, and Utensils* in 1757 by Sir William Chambers was instrumental in popularizing Chinese forms in England and America. The Georgian Miles Brewton House (plate 68), Charleston, had interior details in the Chinese style, and American furniture faithfully copied "Chinese" Chippendale furniture (plate 77). Although American trade with China in the nineteenth century created an interest in Chinese *objets d'art* and pattern books included designs of "Chinese" villas and houses, the style had little architectural currency.

(continued on page 190)

DECORATIVE ARTS

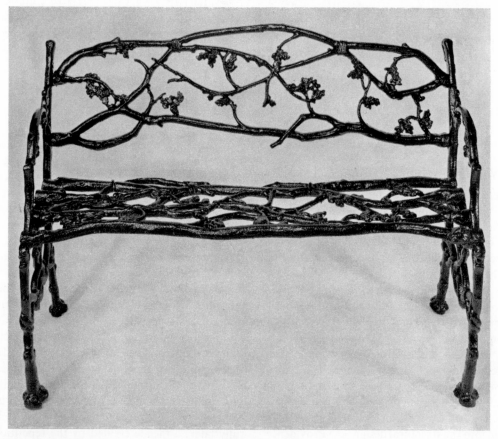

234 Settee. c. 1860–75. Cast iron, length 48″. The Metropolitan Museum of Art, New York. Edgar J. Kaufmann Charitable Fund, 1957

The effect of the Industrial Revolution on furniture making was to introduce mass-production techniques in place of hand labor. In England furniture was being made of cast iron before 1820, and the first set of designs to suggest cast iron for "fashionable furniture" was produced in 1823. The impact was slower here, but by the 1850s cast-iron fountains, umbrella stands, and even tables, chairs, and beds were in use throughout the United States.

The cast-iron settee (plate 234) might have been manufactured in New York, but, as it is unsigned and such pieces were so common, its place of origin cannot be certi-fied. Dating, too, is difficult, because such manufactured furniture, seldom made to order, could remain in stock for many years before being sold or could be continuously made. A four-foot settee such as this was advertised in 1857 and was still available, through a different manufacturer, in the early 1890s. The interest in nature that permeates Romantic art is manifest on this settee in the display of gnarled vegetal forms. This rusticity is part of the overall Romantic yearning which appeared in Gothic mansions as well as picturesque cottages. The heyday of interior cast-iron furniture was comparatively brief.

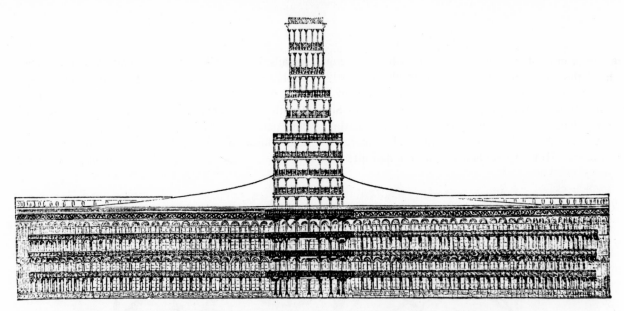

235 James Bogardus. Project for New York Industrial Palace, World's Fair of 1853. From B. Silliman and C. R. Goodrich, eds., *The World of Science, Art and Industry, Illustrated from Examples in The New York Exhibition, 1853–54*, G. P. Putnam, New York, 1854

(continued from page 189)

THE "EARLY IRON AGE"

The development of cast and wrought iron as a building material was a major contribution of the Industrial Revolution, but the evolution of iron construction in what Hitchcock has called the "Early Iron Age" was centered in England, technologically the most advanced country at the time. The American industrial plant was not capable until the 1850s of contributing to this historic process: to that point American ingenuity had revealed itself in the development of the wood balloon frame, which supplanted the heavier mortise-and-tenon-jointed carpentry of an earlier period. Cast-iron columns and, later, beams were increasingly used in large factories and mills in the United States to reinforce the load-bearing function of masonry and wood, but such elements were not generally visible. Only a few early examples attempted openly to integrate iron into the structural design: the Providence Arcade (1828, plate 204), for instance, had stairs, balconies, and balustrades of iron and a roof of iron and glass. In the fifties Ammi Young began to incorporate iron features in his government buildings.

One major American contribution to iron architecture was the exploitation of the cast-iron building. James Bogardus (1800–1874), inventor and manufacturer of machinery, is usually credited with the development of this type of construction, although he may not have invented it. At any rate, his activity in building such structures and the publication of *Cast Iron Buildings* (1856), under his name though ghostwritten, helped spread the system of prefabricated building throughout the country. Bogardus, who called for self-supporting exterior walls composed of prefabricated columns and beams, was perhaps indebted to an iron building fabricated in 1839 by the Scottish engineer, Sir William Fairbairn, for re-erection in Turkey. In 1848, in New York, Bogardus began a four-story building with a cast-iron facade to house his own factory on Centre Street, and completed two others there before it was finished in the following year. His "Cast Iron Building" (1848) for E. H. Laing at Washington and Murray Streets, dismantled in 1971, was erected in two months.

The ease with which the most elaborate and expensive carving could be duplicated in iron casting led to meaningless and often tasteless display and, at the same time, inhibited any search for new and more appropriate decorative forms deriving from the material. Nevertheless, by relieving the wall of its load-bearing function, the first step toward iron-skeleton construction had been taken. The lightness of the iron members also opened the way for the wall surface to become a glass curtain. And finally, the modular character of prefabricated parts introduced an aesthetic element which would be understood more fully later: a facade created by the repetition of a given module.

Bogardus's most radical conception (which might have changed or accelerated the development of American architecture had it been executed) was his design for the New York World's Fair of 1853 (plate 235). He proposed an immense circular hall 1,200 feet in diameter and 60 feet high of standardized iron elements that could be reused after dismantling. The 300-foot central tower with an elevator was to serve both as an observatory and as the support for the suspended catenary-curved roof of sheet iron. This amazingly visionary yet practical plan was passed over for a copy of London's Crystal Palace (plate 233).

Bogardus prefabricated many cast-iron buildings for other parts of the country. Other iron foundries followed his lead and from about 1850 to 1880 produced various cast-iron buildings that were once to be found in cities throughout the nation. Noteworthy among the New York examples is the Haughwout Building (1857, plate 236) at Broadway and Broome Street.

The arguments for the superiority of iron as a building material included the belief that it was fire-resistant. However, iron and glass will melt under intense heat, and after a series of disastrous experiences Europeans became somewhat disillusioned with iron. This fact was brought home to Americans by the great fires in Boston and Chicago in the seventies.

Some of the earliest and most radical developments in iron construction occurred in bridge building, which involved engineering rather than architectural skills. Beginning with the Coalbrookdale Bridge over the Severn in 1777 by Abraham Darby, the history of the iron bridge in England and France is a series of brilliant engineering feats, though the bridges themselves were often bedecked with eclectic ornament. A new direction was indicated by Thomas Telford's Menai Bridge (1819–24), the first great suspension bridge, and still the longest of the type in the British Isles. The principle was not new, but the substitution of iron chain for rope made it feasible for modern use. (James Finley had built several suspension bridges with iron chain in America, the first in 1801.)

The Menai Bridge was hardly completed when Marc Séguin began a span over the Rhone which introduced the wire rope. But it was John Augustus Roebling (1806–1869) in the United States, whose career spanned the years from the "Early Iron Age" to the "Age of Steel," who brought the suspension bridge to magnificent maturity. Born in Germany, Roebling migrated in 1831 to

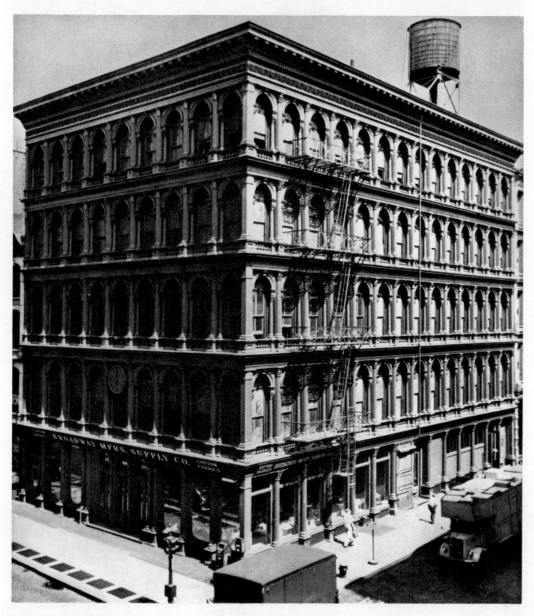

236 Haughwout Building, New York. 1857

Pennsylvania, the center of the iron and coal industries. While working on the Pennsylvania Canal, he developed a wire rope for hauling barges over mountain portages and in 1841 devised a machine for spinning the cable; shortly afterward he improved the cable by binding the steel wires in parallel strands. The first of his suspension structures was an aqueduct for the Pennsylvania Canal (1844–45), followed by a bridge at Pittsburgh (1845–46).

The Brooklyn Bridge (plate 237), his crowning achievement, and even today the paradigm of all suspension bridges, was begun in 1869. Roebling was an engineer and not an architectural designer; the masonry towers of his bridges show a need to acknowledge some reverence for the architectural forms of the past, but the sweep of roadbed and cable is pure engineering, creating a new form which has its own unquestioned aesthetic grandeur.

237 John Augustus Roebling. Brooklyn Bridge. Begun 1869

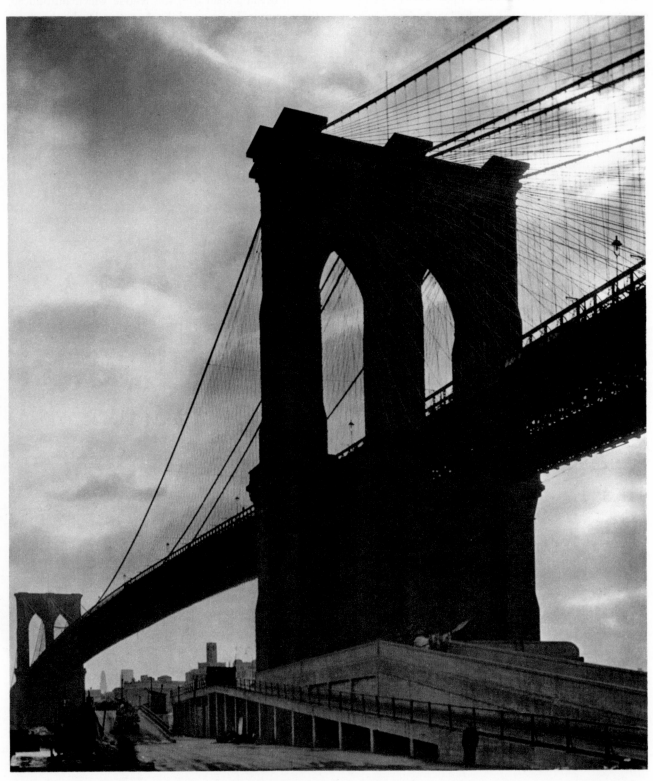

9
Painting for the Public

By and large, painting was appreciated for its literal naturalism and its subject matter, for the memories or sentiments it evoked, for the stories it told or the morals it drew, rather than for its more purely artistic qualities. Though the opportunity for a broader and more satisfying expression was afforded the artists of this generation, popular levels of taste often limited their achievements. The most important artistic developments during the period were the rise to dominance of landscape painting and the increasing interest in genre fed by their reproduction in color lithography. On the popular level the mass production of prints and the expanding use of illustrations in periodicals were influential developments.

ROMANTIC LANDSCAPE AND
THE HUDSON RIVER SCHOOL

Although landscape painting was influenced by popular taste, it was essentially expressive of a higher level of culture and had become the major vehicle for noble sentiment and ideal beauty. Reverence for nature being an important aspect of Romantic expression, the American landscape was in itself a Romantic experience.

The painters who established the tradition of a national landscape art emerged in the 1820s and became known, though they were never an organized group, as the Hudson River School. They were localized in the Hudson Valley, the Berkshires, the Adirondacks, and the White Mountains. Although they sketched out of doors, all except Asher B. Durand painted in their studios, so that many of their pictures are not actual records of specific locales but ideally organized compositions.

Romantic landscape painting may be divided into two major traditions—that of the sublime, the wild and terrorful *(terribilità)* exemplified in the landscapes of Salvator Rosa; and the lyrical, more domesticated landscapes of Claude Lorrain. The distant view, the immense vista, and a general grandeur of scale were common to both. Not until later, with the rise of the Barbizon School in France, did a more intimate conception of nature become prevalent. The American landscape in its primordial state

and large scale lent itself naturally to the first. Yet, except for the fantastic imagination of Thomas Cole, the Hudson River School avoided *terribilità*.

The inception of the school is usually ascribed to the first exhibition of Cole's landscapes in New York in 1825. Both Thomas Doughty and Cole were active in Philadelphia before they exhibited in New York. Thomas Doughty (1793–1856), born in Philadelphia, had left the leather business there in 1820 to become a landscape painter after only some limited independent experiments with oils and a few lessons in drawing. Yet he was mentioned the following year by the well-known Baltimore patron Robert Gilmor, Jr., as having painted two views of his "country seat"; in 1823 he exhibited eight paintings at the Pennsylvania Academy of the Fine Arts. In 1826 Doughty showed two landscapes at the first exhibition of the National Academy of Design, and they were highly praised. Two years later Asher B. Durand exhibited his first landscape, and with his addition to the roster the Hudson River School was launched.

Of the three, who dominated the early development of the school, Doughty was the most limited as a painter, and his work reveals many shortcomings—pedestrian composition, monotony of color, and a niggling detail which led to the derogation "leaf painters." Still, Doughty was capable of poetic statements that could have come only from a deep love of nature. *In Nature's Wonderland* (1835, plate 238) is typical of his unassuming art: sublimity reduced to a minor note by the almost tentative character of the composition; the stock figure of the Romantic wanderer dwarfed by the wilderness; and the fussiness of the brushwork which contradicts the immensity of the natural vista. Yet the glow of light and the sense of silence create a mood.

By far the most interesting painter of the group was Thomas Cole (1801–1848). In his grandeur of conception, imaginative fantasy, moral passion—even obsessive religiosity—he is closer to the turbulent heart of Romanticism than any of his contemporaries. Born in England, Cole worked as a wood engraver in Liverpool

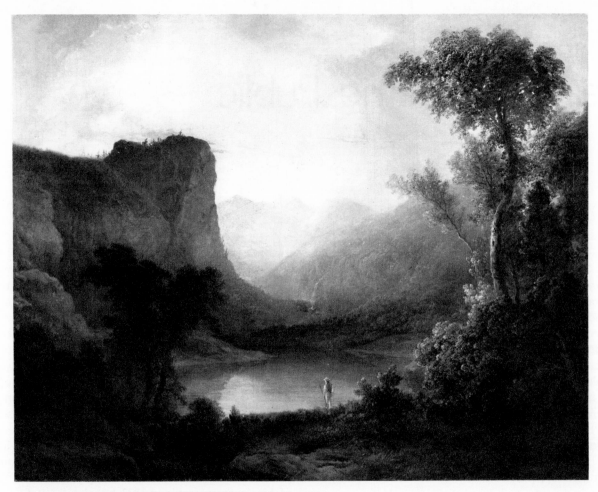

238 Thomas Doughty. *In Nature's Wonderland.* 1835. Oil on canvas,
24¼ × 30″. The Detroit Institute of Arts

before he went to Philadelphia. There he studied drawing
at the Pennsylvania Academy, where he was much taken
by the landscapes of Birch and Doughty. In 1824 he
showed his first landscape at the Academy and in the
following year had his first recognition in New York.

The results of a trip up the Hudson in 1825 made his
immediate reputation. Most of his inspiration and the-
matic material came from the Hudson Valley around
Catskill, but he did go on sketching trips through the
White Mountains, to Maine, and to Niagara Falls. In
1836 he settled in the town of Catskill, where he worked
for the rest of his life. His earlier works are much like
Doughty's, rather straightforward glorifications of the
American wilderness, but some reveal a dramatic flair
and Romantic passion going far beyond Doughty or
any of the later Hudson River School painters. Also,
they are painted with a nervous calligraphy that infuses
them with a sense of the supernatural. Before he began
polishing his pictures to the level of banality, Cole was a
painterly as well as a pictorial Romantic, who expressed
with his brush the breath of experience, sensuous or
spiritual.

Cole had obviously absorbed the *terribilità* of Rosa

at second hand before he went abroad. His *Expulsion
from the Garden of Eden* (1828, plate 239), based on an
engraving by John Martin illustrating *Paradise Lost*,
indicates a susceptibility to the apocalyptic vision which
later became the hallmark of his art. Nature itself becomes the protagonist in a religious revelation, and the
incident of the Expulsion is lost in the vastness of God's
creation.

Cole visited England in 1829 and then traveled in
France and Italy. However, in his allegiance to America
and American scenery he deprecated his European experience as well as European art. He considered himself a
better painter than any of his English contemporaries,
found contemporary French painting "too bloody or too
voluptuous," and in Italy sketched from nature instead of
copying the old masters. Yet after the trip abroad his
paintings reveal a greater monumentality of conception
and scale, a preoccupation with moral sentiment, and a
new concern with the past and Romantic attitudes toward
the passage of time.

Immediately after his return he received the first of
many commissions, the series of five pictures called *The
Course of Empire* (1833–36, colorplate 22), executed for

Luman Reed, the New York patron of American art. This was followed by other series dealing with the same theme: *The Departure* and *The Return* (1837), for William P. Van Rensselaer of Albany; *Past* and *Present* (1838), for P. G. Stuyvesant; and *The Voyage of Life* (1839, plate 240) for Samuel Ward. Cole's deep involvement with these ideas derives from his reading of *Les Ruines; ou, Méditation sur les révolutions des empires* (1791) by the Comte de Volney, which did so much to popularize moral speculations on the death of civilizations.

In *The Course of Empire*, which may have been influenced by Turner's *Building of Carthage*, Cole describes the rise and fall of empires in symbolic terms from the Romantic wildness of the "savage state," to the Classical serenity of the "Arcadian or pastoral state," the splendor of "empire," the cataclysm of "destruction," and the silence of "desolation." At this point philosophic and literary elements have relegated nature and art to secondary roles, and from here on Cole's work is hopelessly riven. He was convinced that what made a work of art great was the sublimity of its theme, an aesthetic fallacy that can be overcome only by supreme artistic ability,

and Cole's equipment was inadequate. His allegorical works lack spontaneity of observation, smacking of studio contrivance. They are cluttered with literary detail and overpolished in execution.

Cole lost much in his search for moral and religious significance. The sketch for *Old Age* (1839, plate 240) in the *Voyage of Life* series, in its broad handling, vibrant touch, and evocation of a momentous vision, is convincing, whereas the puerile elaboration of the finished painting is cloying in its sentimental piety, except for the "surrealist" phantasmagoria of the palace of heaven. This sequence was the ultimate in his allegorical sermons, and the engraved version was the most successful set of religious prints to circulate in the United States. To modern eyes the mixture of fertility of imagination in detail and excruciating philosophic banality results in one of the more ludicrous comments on the destiny of man.

Much of the revival of interest in Cole is a condescending appreciation of the naive imagination of his allegories, so prophetic of Surrealist hallucinations, in preference to his more lasting contributions to landscape painting.

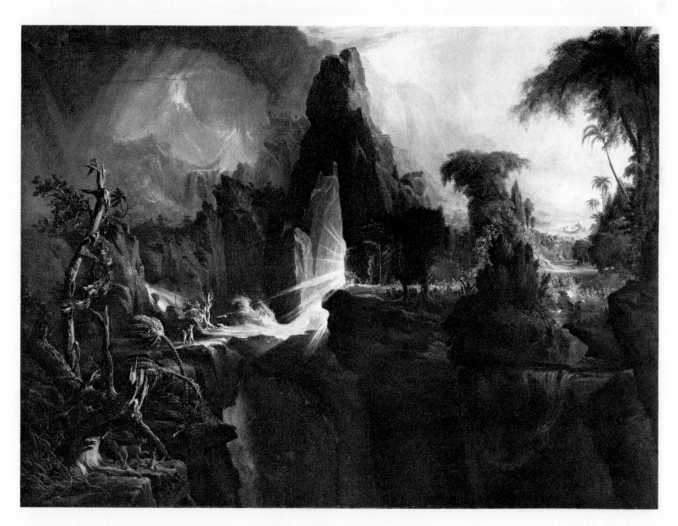

239 Thomas Cole. *Expulsion from the Garden of Eden.* 1828. Oil on canvas, 39 × 54".
Museum of Fine Arts, Boston. M. and M. Karolik Collection

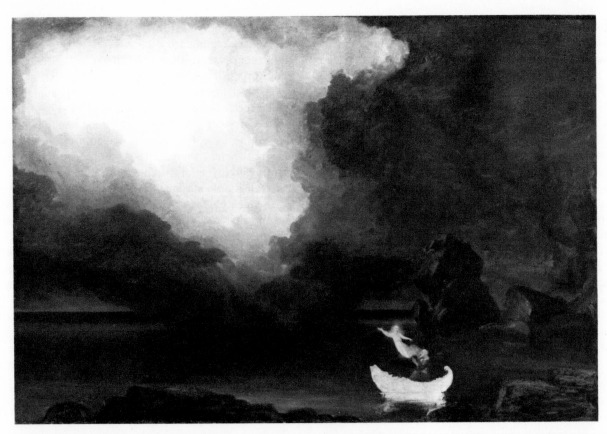

240 Thomas Cole. Sketch for *The Voyage of Life: Old Age*. 1839. Oil on canvas, 25 × 39".
Collection Roy R. Neuberger, New York

But even while he was involved with subject pictures, he could produce so topographically accurate and almost unromantic a vista as *The Oxbow* (1836). And as late as 1846 he could paint *The Mountain Ford*, a paean to the American wilderness and a recapitulation of his own landscape vocabulary.

When Asher B. Durand (1796–1886) exhibited his first landscape at the National Academy of Design, he was already over thirty and acknowledged as the leading engraver in the United States. Not until he was almost forty did he turn to painting as an occupation. Durand had been born in Jefferson Village (now Maplewood), N.J., and was apprenticed at sixteen to Peter Maverick of Newark, whose partner he became in 1817. When John Trumbull, in 1820, requested that Durand engrave his *Declaration of Independence*, Maverick in jealousy dissolved the partnership, but Durand on his own became successful with his engravings of Vanderlyn's *Ariadne* and Allston's *Spalatro*, with illustrations, and of portraits and early Hudson River landscapes.

Luman Reed, who commissioned him to paint a portrait of President Jackson and then all Jackson's predecessors in office, encouraged him to give up engraving for painting. Durand worked first as a portraitist and even tried his hand at genre but, under the guidance of Cole, found his real vocation in landscape painting. Although much influenced by Cole, Durand was an artist of the lyrical rather than of the sublime; like Claude, he sought the picturesque and poetic aspects of nature, rather than its wildness and passion, but, unlike Claude's, his landscapes usually lack the mythic details and nostalgic overtones.

Perhaps his greatest and most characteristic painting, *Summer Afternoon* (1865, plate 241), sums up both his dependence on Claude and his own particular talent. Painted rather late in his career, it indicates a turn to the more intimate landscapes of the Dutch. There is still the Claudian picturesqueness of composition. Behind the intimacy of the foreground stretches the limitless vista, and the scene is enveloped in a silvery light. But overtones of mythology or time have been replaced by contented cows in a rustic setting.

In breaking the barrier of distance and ideality, Durand moved away from the Romantic to the realistic landscape of the immediate and the common. In *The Beeches* (1845, colorplate 23) the vista becomes but a distant backdrop, and the focus is on the literal transcription of the great beeches in the foreground. The fact that he painted directly from nature must have played a significant role in this vision. In the picturesque composition and the poetic subject of shepherd and flock receding into the distance, the painting remains essentially Romantic, but Durand had taken a significant step toward the realistic landscape that the next generation would exploit.

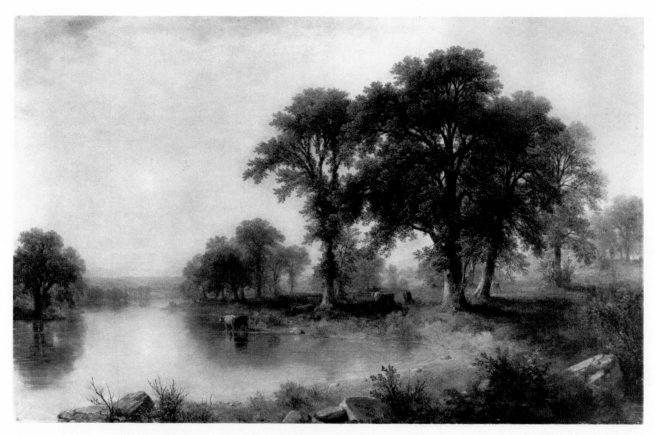

241 Asher B. Durand. *Summer Afternoon.* 1865. Oil on canvas, 22 × 35".
The Metropolitan Museum of Art, New York. Bequest of Maria De Witt Jesup, 1915

Samuel F. B. Morse (1791–1872) belonged to both the Federal Period and the Jacksonian Era. He was perhaps the finest artist of his generation and certain individual pictures are among the best and most interesting of the period, but he produced no lasting image of himself as an artistic personality. Even during his lifetime his artistic stature was lost in his fame as the inventor of the telegraph.

Before graduation from Yale in 1810 he had dabbled in painting and produced a few miniatures. In 1811 he went with Allston to study art in England. In four years with West, but more strongly under the influence of Allston, he absorbed the passion for the "ideal" and the painting of history. In 1821 he was in Washington, working on his lone major effort at history painting in this country, the gigantic *Old House of Representatives* (1822), which he vainly hoped would make his reputation and fortune. It was a unique picture in many ways, not the least of which was its completely un-Romantic handling of a contemporary historical theme. Then in 1825 he was commissioned by New York City to portray Lafayette. The resulting full-length work, in its heroic conception, emotional fire, and spirited handling, is the finest Romantic portrait of the period. With such achievements it is almost incredible that Morse should not have gone on to a brilliant career, but he was sometimes close to starvation.

Morse became involved with invention, and later with the daguerreotype; by 1837 he had abandoned painting forever. Although he belonged to the generation of the early Hudson River School painters, he differed from them in training and inclination. Nevertheless, he produced several landscapes which belong within the general scope of the school and bear comparison with it. They project a realistic observation of American scenery, a flat vernacular statement of fact.

Curiously enough, Morse succumbed to Romantic jargon during his second stay abroad (1829–32), perhaps through the German landscapists he met in Rome, for his *Chapel of the Virgin at Subiaco* (1830–31, colorplate 24) is hardly American in either subject or treatment. A handsome picture, painted with an assurance that his American contemporaries rarely achieved, it belongs within contemporary European Romantic landscape painting in its touristic stereotypes of the picturesque, allusions to the past, and overtones of nostalgia.

The Romantic landscape tradition was carried well past the middle of the century by a middle generation between Doughty, Cole, and Durand and the later one of Church, Bierstadt, and Moran, which finally shifted the emphasis from the East to the newly opened West. This middle generation of John W. Casilear (1811–1893), Jasper F. Cropsey (1823–1900), John F. Kensett, and Thomas W. Whittredge was closely tied to the earlier

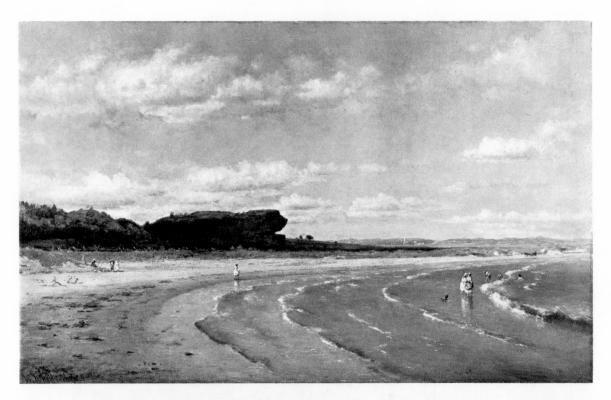

242 Thomas Worthington Whittredge. *Third Beach, Newport*. c. 1870–80.
Oil on canvas, $30\frac{1}{2} \times 50\frac{1}{4}''$. Walker Art Center, Minneapolis

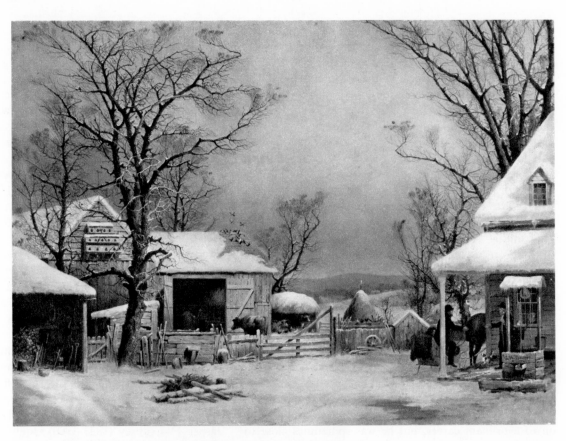

243 George Henry Durrie. *Farmyard in Winter*. 1862. Oil on canvas,
26 × 36″. The New-York Historical Society

group. However, little of Cole's Gothicism was passed on to them; they were all Durand disciples.

LUMINISM

Although Kensett and Whittredge began their careers as Hudson River School men, they converted Durand's idyllic Romanticism into a poetry of the commonplace. There is a recognizable quality in their light that is neither traditional nor European, a light that seems peculiarly North American; it has led some American art historians to postulate a school of "luminism," somewhere between the Romanticism of the Hudson River School and the realism of French Impressionism. If "luminism" is defined in the broadest sense as a new interest in the element of light, in the phenomenal character of a particular light rather than the generalized poetry of light, then it would include much of the work of Kensett and Whittredge, the seascapes of Salmon and Lane, the eccentric Heade, and the sparkling early sketches of Church and Bierstadt. The emergence of this tendency in the fifties calls attention to the cultural change in American society in the decade before the Civil War.

Only recently have the reputations of Kensett and Whittredge increased. Perhaps our own taste in landscape, formed by Impressionism, values their unassuming naturalism and laconic delight in the sensuous. It is difficult to say how much effect the camera had, but their paintings reveal a new interest in the momentary and the particular. Yet they continued to paint in their studios from sketches rather than directly out of doors.

John F. Kensett (1816–1872) began as an engraver, a training which is visible in some of his landscapes. In 1840 he accompanied Durand to Europe and worked there for eight years. On his return Kensett showed little influence from European sources. He found his subjects in the well-worn areas of the Hudson River School but extended the repertory to include the New England coast and the unromantic terrain of Long Island. He even traveled to the upper Mississippi and the mountains of the West. He always painted thinly and with a muted palette, but the sensitive and cool tonal relationships and the immaculate definition of the smallest areas re-create restrained yet personal moments of visual experience. More than any other artist of the school, Kensett reacted to the specific character of a site, as in the prosaic naturalism of *The Shrewsbury River* (1859, colorplate 25). His coastal scenes, in which Romanticism is replaced by a straightforward record of land, sea, and sky in a particular light and atmosphere, are Impressionist paintings but for their lack of high-keyed and broken color.

Thomas Worthington Whittredge (1820–1910) went from a backwoods farm in Ohio to Cincinnati, where he first worked as a house and sign painter and then as a portraitist. His love of nature seems to have led him to landscape painting, and in 1849, with the backing of Nicholas Longworth and other patrons, he left for Eu-

rope, where he remained for ten years. In Düsseldorf he met Emanuel Leutze, and incidentally posed for the figure of General Washington in Leutze's famous *Washington Crossing the Delaware* (plate 255). However, that German hotbed of fanatical detail and polish had no more effect on his art than his European experiences elsewhere.

Whittredge stemmed from Durand's intimate and lyrical phase, but his handling of paint was more fluent and his vision was more informal than that of either Durand or Kensett. His landscapes are broad, gentle, and pastoral, with an emphasis on the horizontal, on openness and quietude. In his later work the real break with Hudson River School Romanticism occurs: his *Third Beach, Newport* (c. 1870–80, plate 242), like a Kensett in its acceptance of the undistinguished coastal landscape, depends entirely on the sweep of beach, sea, and sky almost disappearing in the summer haze.

Quite apart from the central stream of Romantic landscape painting were seascape painters such as Robert Salmon (c. 1775–c. 1850) and Fitz Hugh Lane. Their precise, factual depiction of boats, harbor installations, and shipping activities stemmed from the English tradition of topographical description. The placidity, stereometry of form, geometric precision of detail, conventional rendering, and limpid light may well derive from Canaletto. It is a stylized naturalism based on acute observation of reality but expressed with an artisan's repetition of formula which, when well done, has a charm that transcends its props.

Fitz Hugh Lane (1804–1865), of Gloucester, worked for some twenty years in Boston as a lithographer, rendering views of towns and buildings. Returning to Gloucester after 1847, he spent the rest of his life as a marine painter, retaining an artisan's respect for precision and literal transcription. Lane's thin pigment adds something in openness of space, increased clarity of light, and spidery elegance of detail (colorplate 26).

The landscapes of Martin J. Heade (1819–1904) do not fit neatly into the categories of the period. He shared with most of the "luminists" a preference for the horizontal canvas and an interest in light, though his was unusually dramatic. His art is something of a reversion to the mystery and terror of Allston. In *Approaching Storm: Beach near Newport* (c. 1860, colorplate 27) the lowering darkness of the sky turns the sea into an eerie sheet of phosphorescence and the deserted shore into a lunar landscape. The hint of naiveté with which the waves seem almost embroidered on the surface of the painting and the primness of the ghostly white sails add to the unearthly and "surrealist" sense of mystery. The affinities of Heade's landscapes to Surrealism (or to Magic Realism), along with the naive elements in his technique, make them appealing to modern tastes, but they must be seen also as sincere efforts to capture observed phenomena of nature and quality of space.

Born in Lumberville, Pa., Heade spent some years in

Europe (c. 1837–40) and after his return worked as a portrait painter. In 1863–64 he went to Brazil with an amateur naturalist to do studies for a book on the hummingbirds of South America. The subsequent meticulously detailed paintings of birds and plants in high-keyed, almost lurid colors, aside from their scientific importance and accuracy, have been admired for their technical accomplishment as well as the very Victorian taste in subject and execution for which they were once execrated.

George Henry Durrie (1820–1863), who made his reputation as a Currier & Ives artist, has suffered too long for this popularity. Although not one of the more important Romantic landscapists, he did, unconsciously perhaps, strike the dead level of American popular taste in landscape. Durrie did what no other Hudson River painter had: he transformed landscape into anecdote and in that process humanized it (plate 243). His capacities as an artist could not transcend that commonness of subject from which one can move to universality as well as to banality. Though he composed well and compactly in an academic sense, his forms tend to softness, and his drawing is pedestrian. His color, charming in the snow scenes, lacks the sensuous acuity and personal comment of the "luminists."

THE EPIC LANDSCAPE

In contrast to members of Durand's circle, the somewhat younger, though approximately contemporary, Frederic E. Church and Albert Bierstadt converted the transcendentalism of Cole into a grandiloquent expression of "manifest destiny." They arrived at a style both popular and epic that seemed to fulfill the dream of an indigenous American art.

No earlier painter in American history was so successful as Frederic E. Church (1826–1900). He was hailed as America's leading artist and, in England, as the supreme landscape painter of his time, the heir to Turner. Church's earliest works reveal a strong dependence on Cole, but by 1849 he had almost imperceptibly moved over into the Durand camp. He still retained a feeling for ideality and spatial grandeur, but his horizontal canvases were more bucolic and the handling of light descriptive rather than emotive, much in the manner of the "luminists." After trips to Ecuador in 1853 and in 1857, motivated by his reading of the great German naturalist, Alexander von Humboldt, Church's interests turned from the lyric to the epic, which was henceforth to be his hallmark. He was also much influenced by Turner, whose work he absorbed through engravings, and by the writings of Ruskin.

The New World was for Church the great arena of a cosmic drama and American destiny the fulfillment of a universal plan. A turgid iconography expounded in elaborate brochures accompanied his epic landscapes, exhibited with great showmanship before awestruck multitudes who were as impressed by scenery as by art. The first in the series—*Niagara* (1857)—though an unqualified public success, was aesthetically ambiguous. In *The Heart of the Andes* (1859, plate 244), however, he achieved a coherent artistic vision that combined the spiritual and the scientific, the infinite and the particular, the distant and the immediate. It was a carefully planned composition based on numerous on-the-spot drawings and oil sketches. To achieve the illusion of reality, the artist employed a series of devices minimizing all evidence of the act of painting, establishing a panoramic vision, combining various perspectives, drawing the spectator into the foreground and by elevation transforming him into a disembodied, mobile eye. Church even advised that spectators examine the landscape through binoculars or a tube, in effect destroying it as a picture. *The Heart of the Andes* is a tour de force of spatial illusion, staggering in scale and detail. Yet, with all its novelty and exoticism, it still recalls the Romantic landscape. *Cotopaxi* (1862, colorplate 28), on the other hand, finally captures the dramatic grandeur of New World nature. The conception is more titanic, the composition more imaginative, and the painting, now clearly Turnerian, more evocative.

After the Civil War, Church's cosmology slipped into the realm of the mystical; the striving for immensity became excessive, the influence of Turner more pronounced, the whole overtheatrical. In 1867–69 he visited Europe and the Near East, but the fruits of that sojourn were all rather disappointingly pedantic, though his powers as a painter had not really diminished. His New World grandiosity simply overwhelmed the human scale of the Old World, and he was forced to fall back on spectacular effects and Romantic clichés.

After almost a century there has been a recent revival of interest sparked by a reevaluation of Church's many oil sketches, which reveal a startlingly fresh eye, a directness of observation, and a spontaneity and fluency in recording impressions—most of which were lost in the translation into cosmic rhetoric.

Church had never visited or painted the heroic landscape of the American West. It was Albert Bierstadt (1830–1902), born in Germany, who became the popular painter of the last frontier. Bierstadt had come as a child to New Bedford, Mass., in 1832, but a growing interest in painting led him back to Düsseldorf and to Rome. After his return to the United States in 1857, he painted in the White Mountains and in 1859 accompanied a government-sponsored expedition to map a trail across the Rocky Mountains to California. His portfolio of sketches served as the basis for those gigantic reconstructions of western scenery which made his immediate reputation.

Both Bierstadt and Church were explorer-artists who understood the appeal of their exotic subjects, and they shared a consciousness of public taste and the showmanship to exploit their work. They had in common also a

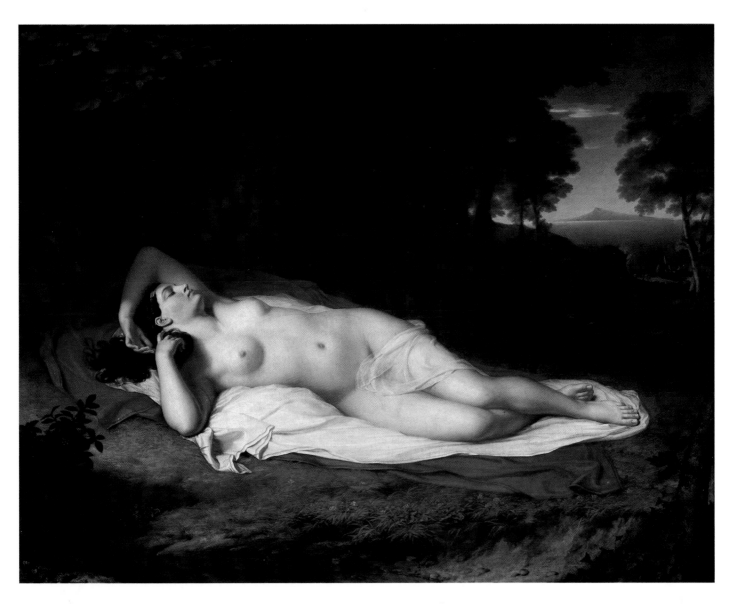

17   John Vanderlyn. *Ariadne Asleep on the Island of Naxos*. 1812. Oil on canvas, 68 × 87″.
The Pennsylvania Academy of the Fine Arts, Philadelphia

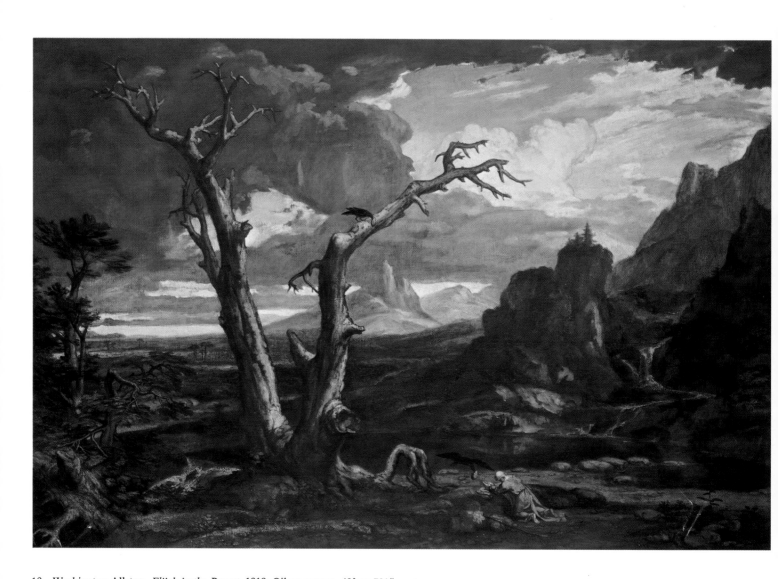

18　Washington Allston. *Elijah in the Desert*. 1818. Oil on canvas, $48\frac{3}{4} \times 72\frac{1}{2}''$.
Museum of Fine Arts, Boston. Gift of Mrs. Samuel Hooper and Alice Hooper

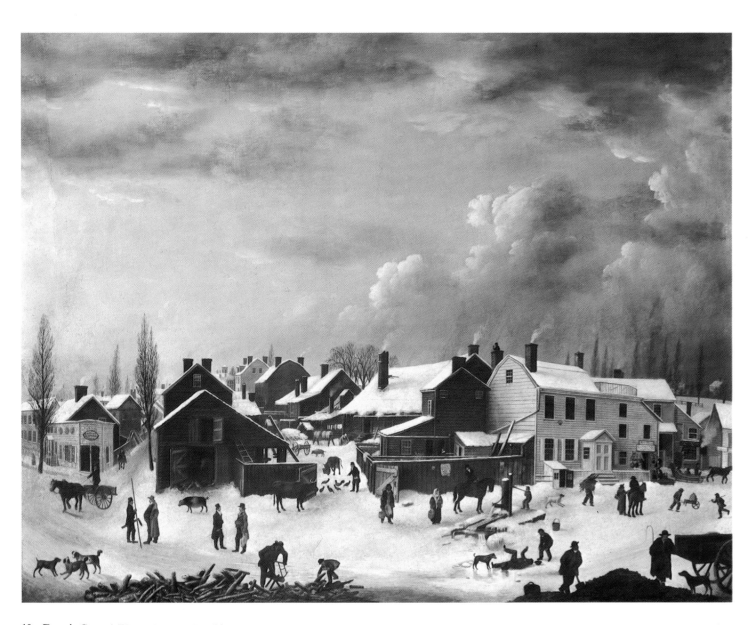

19   Francis Guy. *A Winter Scene in Brooklyn.* 1817–20. Oil on canvas, 58¾ × 75".
The Brooklyn Museum

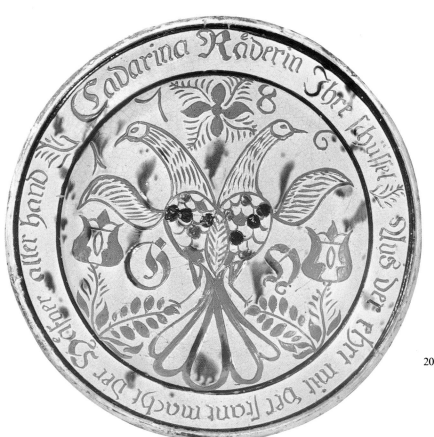

20 Georg Hübener. Dish, from Montgomery County, Pa.
1786. Red clay with lead glaze and sgraffito decoration,
diameter $12\frac{1}{4}''$. Philadelphia Museum of Art.
Gift of John T. Morris

21 Rockingham pitcher, from Bennington, Vt. 1844.
Clay with brown glaze, height $8\frac{1}{2}''$.
National Gallery of Art, Washington, D.C.
Index of American Design

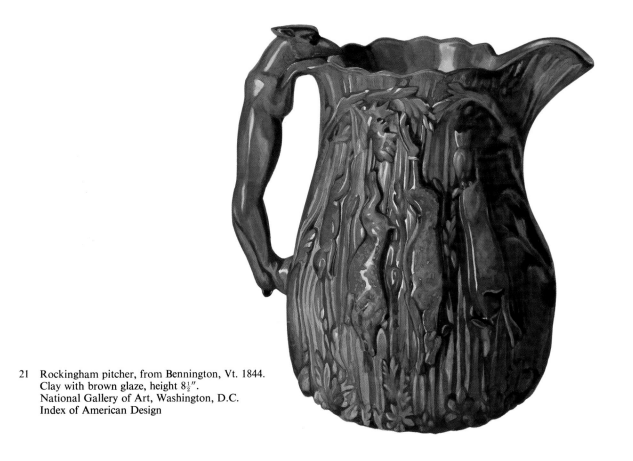

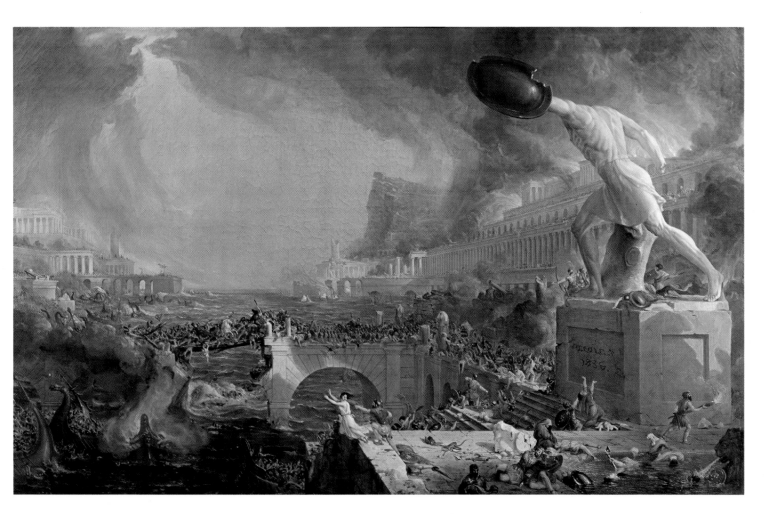

22   Thomas Cole. *The Course of Empire: Destruction*. 1833–36. Oil on canvas, 39 × 61″.
The New-York Historical Society

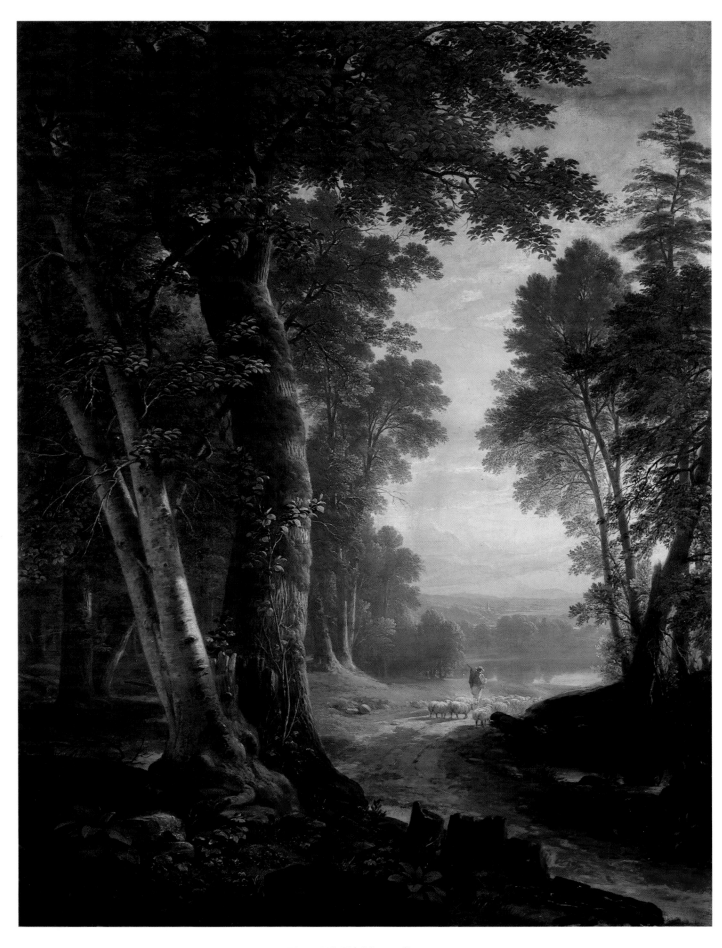

23 Asher B. Durand. *The Beeches*. 1845. Oil on canvas, $60\frac{3}{8} \times 48\frac{1}{8}''$. The Metropolitan
Museum of Art, New York. Bequest of Maria De Witt Jesup, 1915

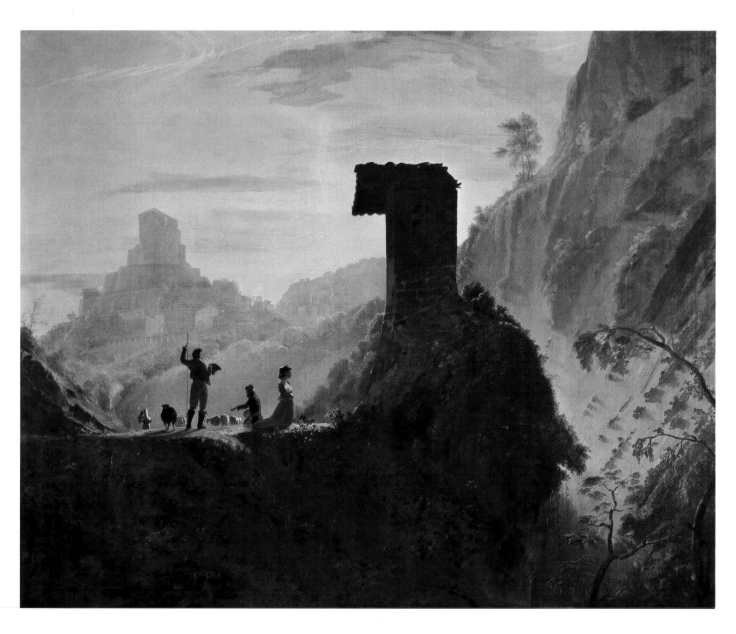

24   Samuel F. B. Morse. *Chapel of the Virgin at Subiaco*. 1830–31.
Oil on canvas, 30 × 37″. Worcester Art Museum

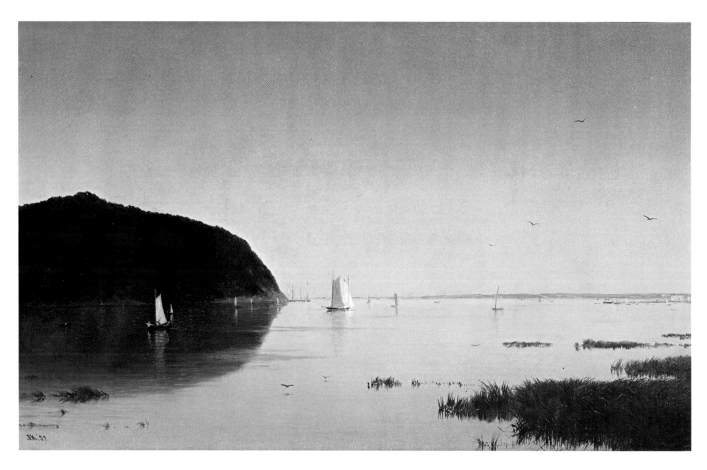

25 John F. Kensett. *The Shrewsbury River*. 1859. Oil on canvas, 18 × 30″.
The New-York Historical Society

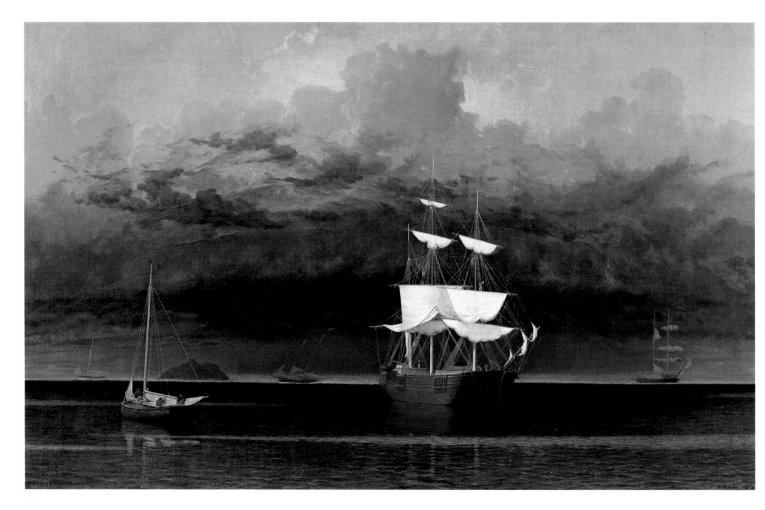

26 Fitz Hugh Lane. *Schooners Before Approaching Storm*. 1860. Oil on canvas, 23½ × 28″.
Private collection, New York

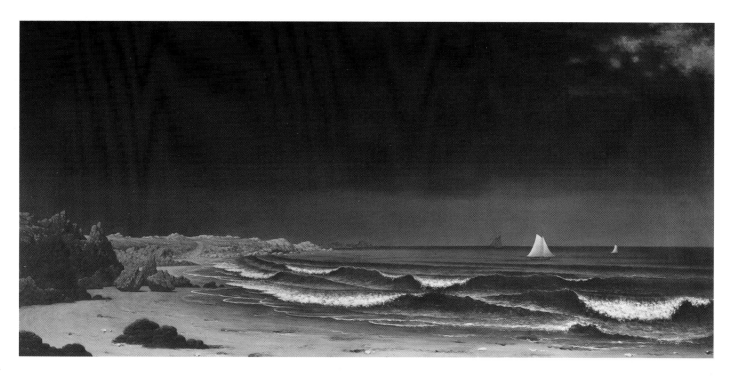

27 Martin J. Heade. *Approaching Storm: Beach near Newport*. c. 1860. Oil on canvas, 28 × 58¼″.
Museum of Fine Arts, Boston. M. and M. Karolik Collection

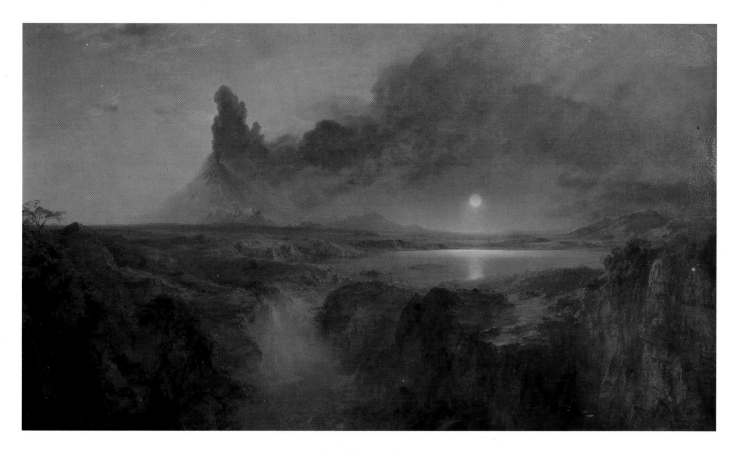

28 Frederic E. Church. *Cotopaxi*. 1862. Oil on canvas, 48 × 85″. Collection John Astor, New York

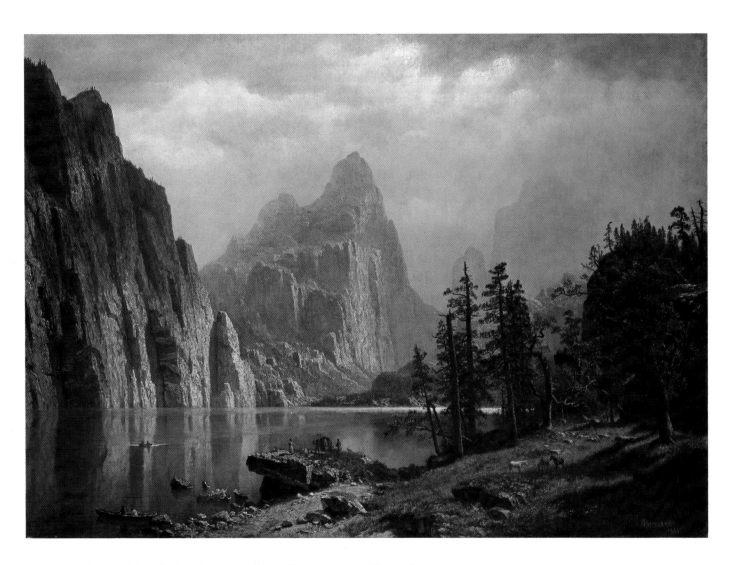

29 Albert Bierstadt. *Merced River, Yosemite Valley.* 1866. Oil on canvas, 36 × 50″.
The Metropolitan Museum of Art, New York. Gift of the sons of William Paton, 1909

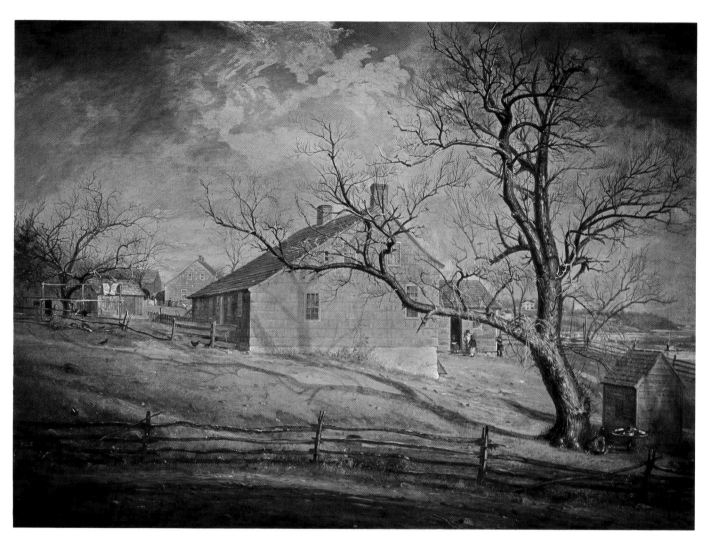

30 William Sidney Mount. *Long Island Farmhouses*. 1854–59. Oil on canvas, $21\frac{7}{8} \times 29\frac{7}{8}''$.
The Metropolitan Museum of Art, New York

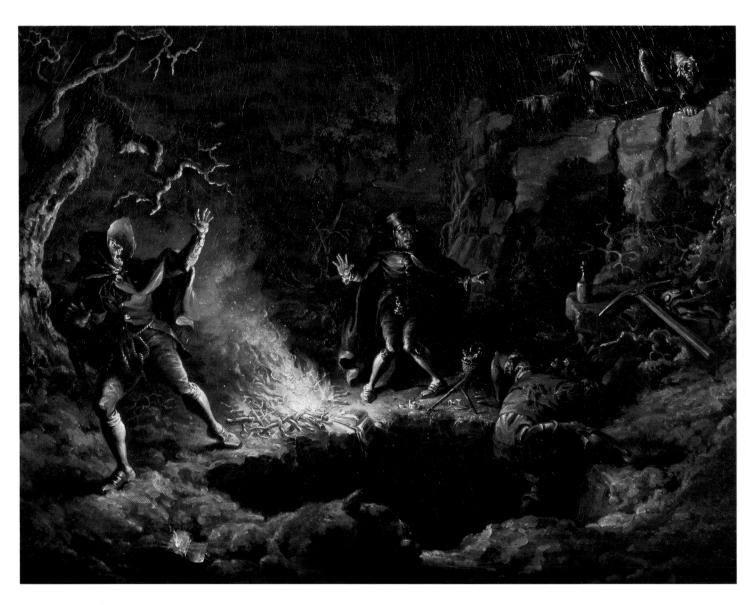

31 John Quidor. *The Money Diggers*. 1832. Oil on canvas, $16\frac{3}{4} \times 21\frac{1}{2}''$.
The Brooklyn Museum. Gift of Mr. and Mrs. A. Bradley Martin

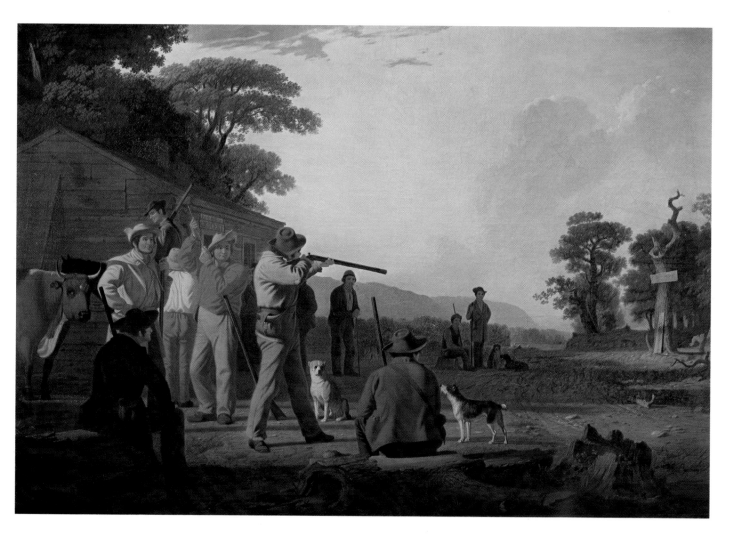

32　George Caleb Bingham. *Shooting for the Beef*. 1850. Oil on canvas, $33\frac{1}{2} \times 49\frac{1}{4}''$.
The Brooklyn Museum

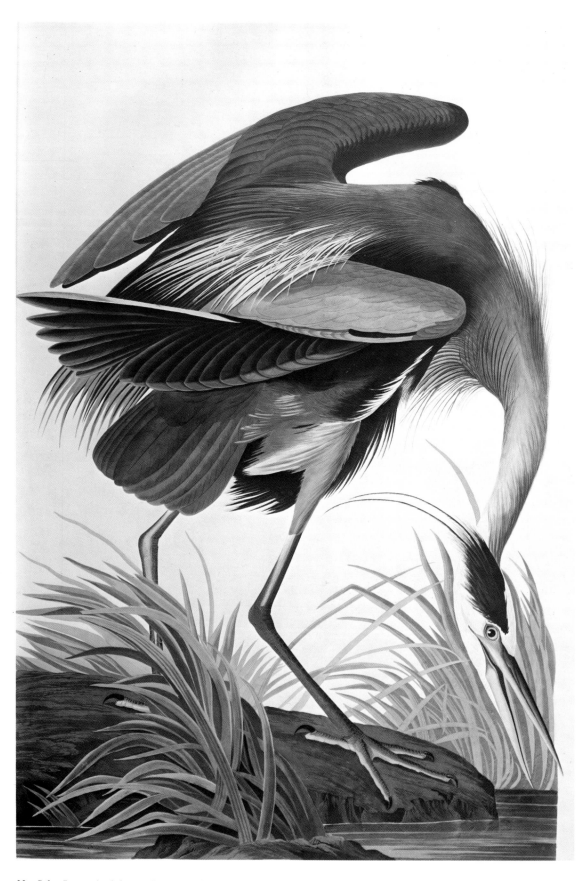

33 John James Audubon. *The Great Blue Heron.* 1821.
Engraving after watercolor, 36 × 25⅜″

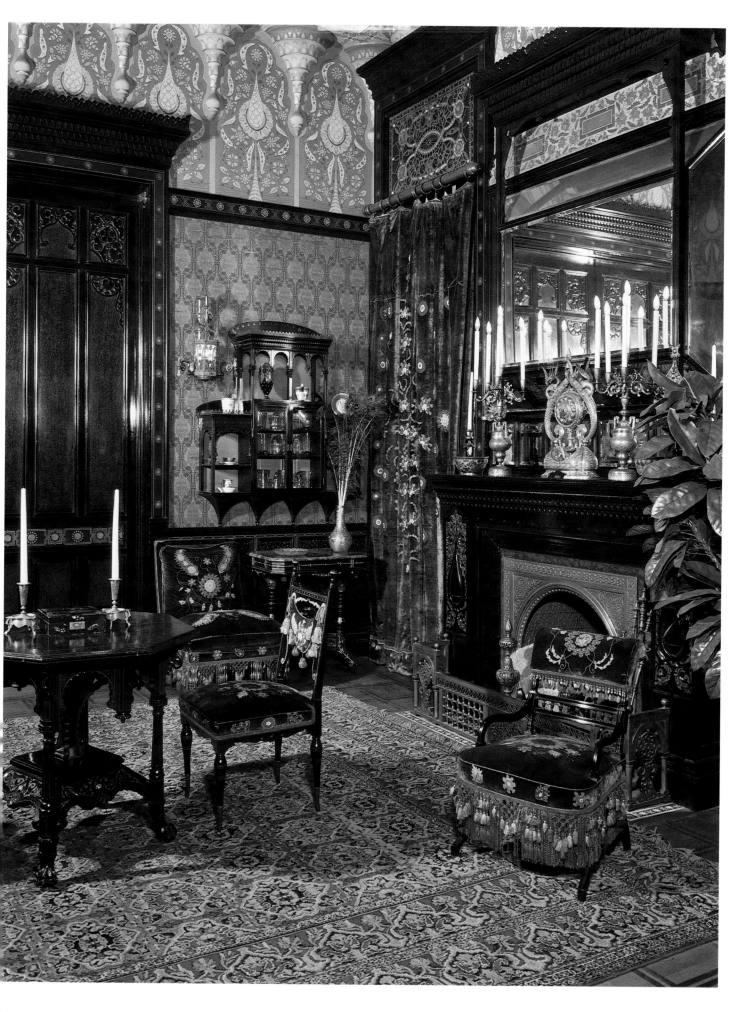

34 Smoking room, from the John D. Rockefeller House, New York. Built 1860.
Reconstructed in the Brooklyn Museum

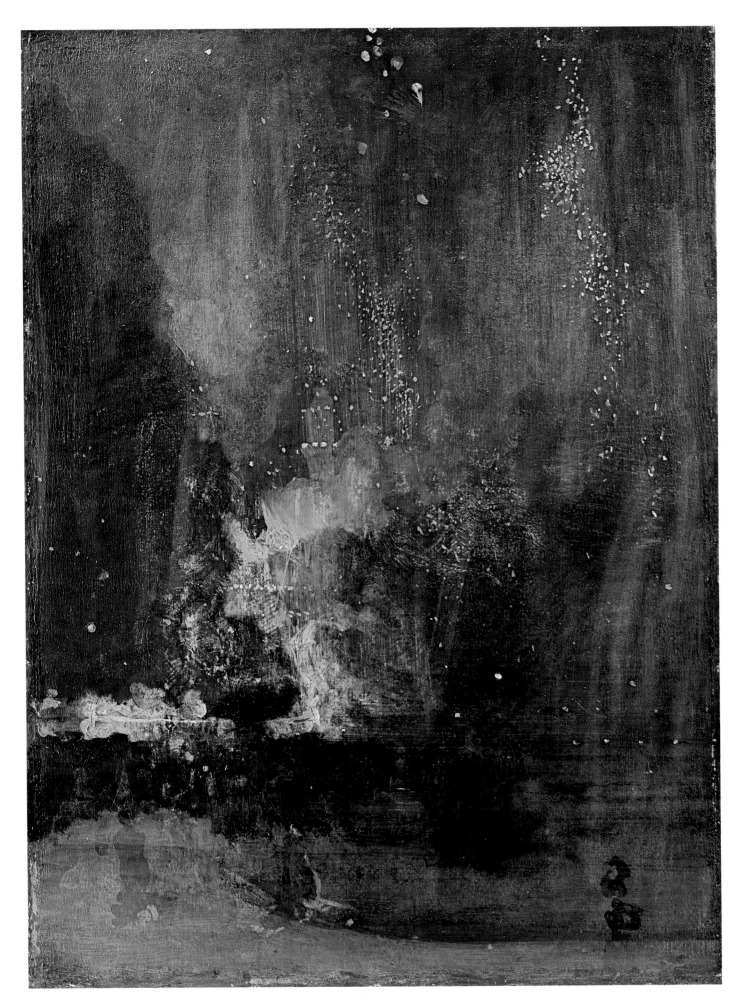

35   James A. McNeill Whistler. *Nocturne in Black and Gold: The Falling Rocket*.
c. 1875. Oil on panel, 24¾ × 18⅜″. The Detroit Institute of Arts

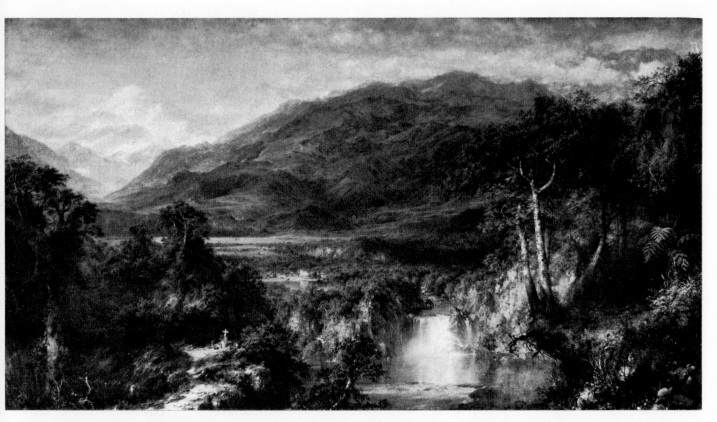

244 Frederic E. Church. *The Heart of the Andes.* 1859. Oil on canvas, 5'6⅛" × 9'11¼".
The Metropolitan Museum of Art, New York. Bequest of Mrs. David Dows, 1909

predilection for the epic vision, the panoramic view, and the outsized canvas. However, Bierstadt had no pretensions to profundity. He was a popular picture maker who had discovered that he could package the sublime for common consumption. Paradoxically, Bierstadt was technically both more sophisticated and less skillful than Church. Whereas Church with provincial fanaticism had attained a kind of perfection in rendering natural data, Bierstadt had absorbed the Düsseldorf formula, which he used without much question. He painted more broadly than Church or than the Hudson River School painters in general. His epic landscapes are best not in detail but in the long view, in their panoramic sweep and theatrical effects—exactly those elements for which he has been criticized. However, such paintings as the *Merced River, Yosemite Valley* (1866, colorplate 29) attempt to match the spectacular aspects of the western landscape, and, despite the sentimental touches of an idyllic Indian encampment, they manage to achieve a certain grandeur.

Bierstadt had a strong sense of composition, but his drawing was erratic and undistinguished. With time his technique became more slovenly, his color disturbingly out of key; and, as he strove increasingly for narrative interest by introducing figures and animals, he fell into bathos. After his great popular appeal and unprecedented success, his fortunes declined. There has been some recent revival of interest in Bierstadt's oil sketches and smaller paintings. Executed directly with a light and

fluent touch, lively in color and luminous in tone, such sketches in their freshness are closer to the work of the "luminists" than to the ponderous epics that brought him fame.

Thomas Moran (1837–1926), born in England, spent a long active life in a production of western landscape paintings that was both prodigious and erratic. He signed on as official artist with a government expedition to Yellowstone in 1870. The watercolor sketches done then served as the basis for the chromolithographic illustrations of the expedition report published in 1876, and they established his reputation as a delineator of western landscape. He later accompanied another government expedition to Colorado. Two large paintings bought by Congress for $10,000 each—*The Grand Canyon of the Yellowstone* and *The Chasm of the Colorado*—are said to have been instrumental in establishing the national park system.

INNESS AND THE NEW LANDSCAPE

While George Inness (1825–1894) owed his beginnings to the Hudson River School and was a contemporary of its second generation, he stands somewhat apart from the traditional schoolmen, the "luminists," and the epic painters. He was a pivotal figure in the development of nineteenth-century landscape painting, straddling two eras. His career can be divided into an early period running through the 1860s, in which he adapted the Hudson River style to his own artistic compulsions, aligning it with the mainstream of European landscape painting; and a late style, after his return from Europe in 1875, when he arrived at the poetic impressionism for which he became famous.

Inness was born near Newburgh, N.Y., of a well-to-do merchant family. From the start, he showed himself a person of independent mind and an unusual temperament, in part perhaps due to his affliction with epilepsy. In 1847 a patron enabled him to make the first of many European trips, and these experiences helped form his early mature style. Of all the American landscapists who traveled abroad, only Inness was so open to the art he encountered: first, the Romantic tradition of Claude, Poussin, and the Dutch, but then also more recent masters such as Constable and Turner, and his own contemporaries, Corot and the Barbizon School, and, finally, Delacroix.

His earliest works were thin and tentative lyrical scenes in the manner of Durand, but in time he worked his way through his borrowings to what was essentially his own vision—naturalistic but poetic, atmospheric rather than linear, coloristic instead of tonal, panoramic yet not heroic, unpicturesque in composition, and painterly in touch. Inness settled in Medfield in 1859 and during the next decade painted the intimate landscape of eastern Massachusetts in the major canvases of his first style, to some his finest. Although he always thought of himself as self-taught, he had clearly absorbed the Barbizon manner. The earliest example of this style, *Delaware Water Gap* (1861, plate 245), retains the grand sweep of the Hudson River School, but, except for the rainbow, the scene has lost the Romantic overtones, and surface detail has given way to a painterly breadth of touch. Inness's commitment to nature was reinforced by his deeply religious feelings. For him landscape painting was the expression of the totality of an emotion rather than physical detail. His later work is discussed in Chapter 12.

(continued on page 219)

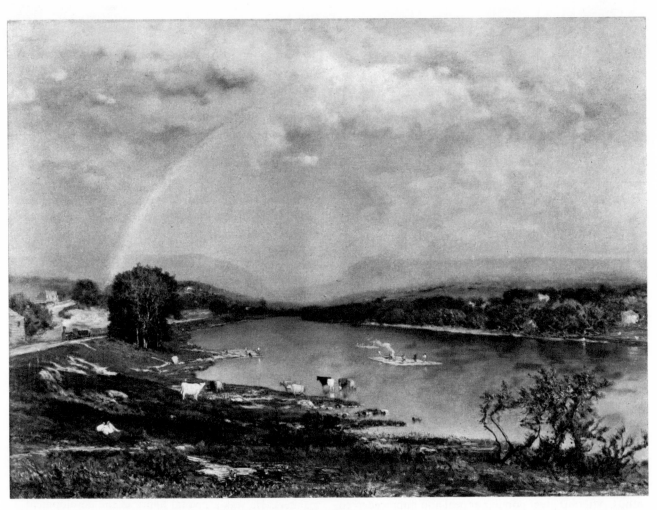

245   George Inness. *Delaware Water Gap*. 1861. Oil on canvas, 36 × 50¼".
The Metropolitan Museum of Art, New York. Morris K. Jesup Fund, 1932

Throughout the Colonial period domestic weaving of cloth was a necessity. Different types of weaving depended on two factors, the complexity of the loom and the patterns from which to create a design. While anyone could eventually buy a complex multiharness loom, great skill was required to transform one of the patterns, called "drafts," into a completed product. The drafts were brought by immigrants from major centers of a weaving tradition in northern Europe and were handed down from generation to generation in this country. Modified by local necessity and custom, they achieved a unique American flavor by the early nineteenth century. At that time, division of labor was sufficiently strong for the establishment of professional weavers, usually of German or Scottish extraction. Coverlets were made at home or in the shops of professionals in a variety of techniques. There were simple overshot weaves, double weaves, and Jacquard weaves. The overshot was the most common and was found wherever Americans lived; the Jacquard type was the most difficult and was produced on hand-operated looms with a special attachment. Highly advanced examples of Jacquard weaving were made as early as 1820 in New York, and the type soon spread through the Midwest. The designs were known for their displays of flowers and leaves and particularly for their borders of patriotic emblems. The example made for Betsy Farmer by J. Cunningham (plate 246) includes an equestrian George Washington with a border of eagles, stars, and patriotic mottoes. As in many of these custom-made coverlets, not only are the weaver's and the customer's names presented, but the location and date as well.

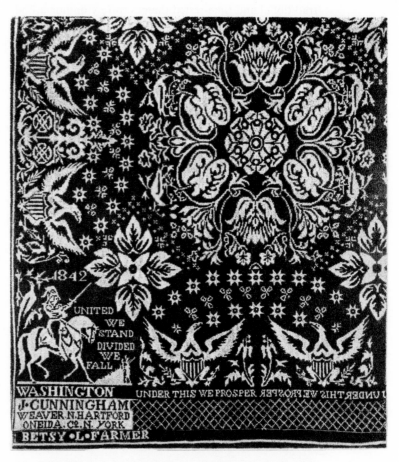

246 J. Cunningham. Coverlet in Jacquard weave, from New York state (detail). 1842. Wool and linen, 94 × 78″. National Gallery of Art, Washington, D.C. Index of American Design

(continued from page 218)

GENRE PAINTING

Genre painting came into prominence during the Jacksonian Era as an expression of popular taste. Its appeal depends entirely on the viewer's recognition of ordinary life experience and an appreciation of the artist's skill in reproducing reality. Genre might not have developed so rapidly and spread so widely had it not been for the phenomenal growth of publication and illustration in a multitude of magazines. Among the visual material might be reproductions of well-known paintings, of paintings especially commissioned and accompanied by "critical" reviews, or illustrations of the literary offerings. In such publications many of the genre painters made their reputations and found an important source of revenue.

Increased circulation of magazines and prints made the older forms of copper engraving obsolete. Steel engraving, wood engraving, and lithography became the mediums of mass reproduction in periodicals or as single sheets. The most characteristic popular art form of the period was the hand-colored lithograph circulated in the thousands by many firms. The most notable of these was Currier & Ives, which commissioned genre subjects from many well-known artists and over a span of fifty years issued some seven thousand prints. Although they vary greatly in quality and at best are not memorable as art, they present a picture of American life in its variety, excitement, and color that the fine arts of the period generally fail to do.

Genre has usually been considered a minor form of aesthetic expression, probably because it has been associated with lower levels of taste and pejoratively with the "middle class." But genre and anecdotal art are capable of serious achievement, as witness Bruegel, Caravaggio, Rembrandt, Vermeer, Hogarth, Goya, Daumier, and Degas. They require the same artistic attitudes and skills as does history painting, except that the latter deals with the heroic. The basic requirements of figure painting are as necessary for both, and the iconography of one may be as complex as the other. But the genre painter has no traditional and time-tested themes to rely on nor a body of previous artistic examples in interpretation of such themes to emulate. His story is the product of his own observation of life.

Although genre and anecdotal art are sometimes inextricably related, genre is more concerned with man's common social relations and activities in a general sense, whereas anecdotal art has an additional narrative element which makes a humorous, moral, or philosophical point. The latter is also often confused with illustration, but illustration depicts a fragment of a literary sequence and is usually incomprehensible without knowledge of the context, whereas anecdotal art is self-contained.

Of all the American genre painters of the period William Sidney Mount (1807–1868) approached most closely Emerson's credo: "Give me insight into to-day, and you may have the antique and future worlds. . . . The meal in the firkin; the milk in the pan; the ballad in the street; the news of the boat; the glance of the eye; the form and gait of the body. . . ." The eternal relevance of the present and the lowly is expressed more simply and less romantically by Mount's image of a genial, unhurried, uncomplicated rural existence.

Mount was born and lived most of his life on Long Island in the kind of environment he depicted so well. He worked at first in New York City and attended the first

classes in drawing organized by the new National Academy of Design in 1826. Illness forced him to return to Long Island, where in 1830 he suddenly turned from portraits and religious painting to genre. The modesty of his work has perhaps obscured the fact that Mount practically alone created the form and character of a native American genre painting. Except for occasional genre pictures, David Claypoole Johnston (1799–1865) was his only predecessor in the field, and he was a satirist in the Cruikshank vein. Mount's connection is more with the tradition of English sentimental genre exemplified by Morland and Wilkie, the popular prints of whose works he could easily have seen. It is interesting that Allston advised Mount to study Ostade and Jan Steen, for it was this Dutch and Flemish genre painting out of which the English school derived.

Mount's style, in its thin glazes, transparent shadows, loaded lights; and limited color range, is reminiscent of Rubens's oil sketches. His technique developed from tight handling and overattentiveness to detail to a much broader and freer treatment without loss of precision. In content he moved from the anecdotal to genre, from the sentimental to the realistic, from genial humor to poetic introspection. In all his works a careful attention to detail was necessary, because Mount was a storyteller and expected his audience to pick up the clues.

News from California (1850, plate 247) is characteristic of Mount's maturer work, in which the anecdotal elements are part of a vignette of life rather than a short story. He sets the scene in the post office, the village's social hub as well as its contact with the outer world. The theme is the reaction to the Gold Rush, seen in terms of a single symbolic human incident. The posters on the wall offering enticements and passage establish the significance of the news being read out. As always, Mount's selection of actors is not haphazard, and the psychological expression of each is carefully studied, for he intends a cross section of reaction. The focal point is the gentleman reading aloud, who by his affluence and superior smile dissociates himself from the common fever. The young couple reacts to the promise of adventure and wealth. But, as frequently with Mount, the minor characters are more interesting than the major. In this case they are the three excluded from the ultimate adventure—the small boy in wide-eyed ecstasy, the old man in hopeless regret, and the black in resignation.

Mount's treatment of blacks is unusual for the time in its awareness of the social problem. By the very nature of his art anything but an implied comment would have disturbed the harmony of his ideal rural world. But though that comment is unobtrusive and personal rather than political, he represents blacks as human beings and with dignity. The heroic stature of the black woman in *Eel Spearing at Setauket* (1845, plate 248) discloses his emotional involvement. Here anecdote has been reduced in favor of mood, and the material grain of things to the

247 William Sidney Mount. *News from California.* 1850. Oil on canvas, 21¼ × 20¼". The Suffolk Museum and Carriage House, Stony Brook, N.Y. Melville Collection

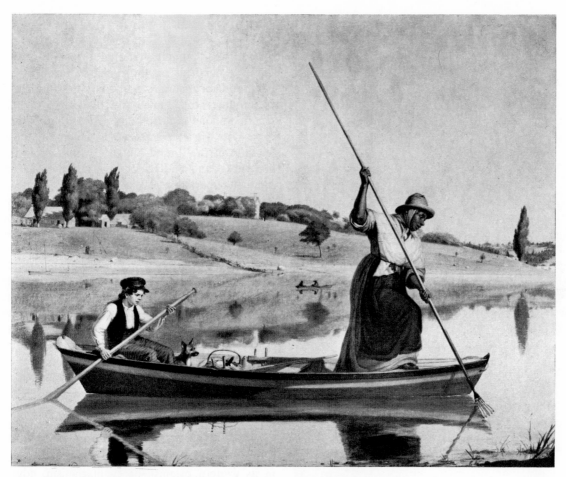

248 William Sidney Mount. *Eel Spearing at Setauket*. 1845. Oil on canvas, 33¼ × 40¼″. New York State Historical Association, Cooperstown

less tangible aspects of nature—light, atmosphere, and even heat and stillness.

By the time he painted the *Long Island Farmhouses* (1854–59, colorplate 30), the physical world has taken the center of the stage; the nondescript landscape tells the story in its homely but sturdy houses aged by time and weather. The neighborly tree casts its delicate shadows on the house and the debris of living spills onto the land. All is enveloped in luminous golden tones. The anecdotal note of children at play is included almost as an afterthought and is hardly discernible.

Richard Caton Woodville (1825–1855) represents a somewhat different stylistic phase of American genre painting. He resembles Mount in his affably amused attitude toward life, but his manner identifies him with Düsseldorf, the world center for sentimental genre, and anecdotal painting. Middle-class taste had so perverted this bastion of academicism that the ideal was equated with Victorian morality and the sublime with painstaking detail.

Woodville was a talented painter, and his limited output can stand comparison with the best examples of the school. He spent most of his active career in Europe painting scenes of American life, which he sent back home for exhibition. Although meticulously accurate in the observation of manners and details of costume, as were all

the Düsseldorfians, Woodville's works lack specific American flavor. They remain too obviously staged studio dramas. In technical proficiency Woodville probably surpassed any of the other American genre artists of his time. His canvases are carefully worked in gradations of tonality, harmony of color, and rich impasto, but his addiction to the surface of the object often denies the importance of the picture's psychological content. His simplest painting remains his finest, *Politics in an Oyster House* (1848, plate 249), in which the limited and clearly defined cubical space contains the physical as well as the emotional interrelationship of the figures. Both the ambience and the types are well observed and rendered with restraint, although there is some self-consciousness about the gestures and expressions. Woodville had the ability to manage a large number of figures in a coherent light and atmosphere within a rational space, no mean achievement for an American painter.

David Gilmour Blythe (1815–1865) was both provincial and unique. He was born near the frontier town of East Liverpool, Ohio, and was active in Pittsburgh, where he seems to have learned portrait painting. The premature death of his wife may be what led him to drink and general bitterness. He struck back at the world crudely but honestly, with a harshness foreign to the art of his time. Had Blythe had the technical equipment, he might

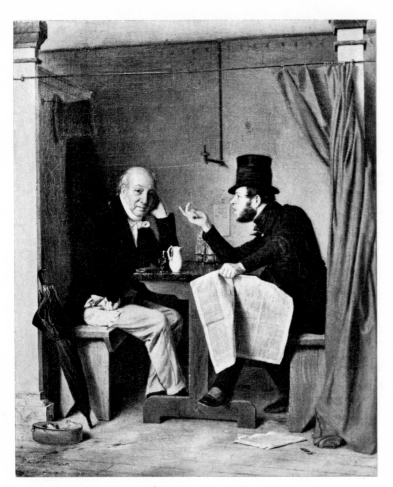

249 Richard Caton Woodville. *Politics in an Oyster House*. 1848.
Oil on canvas, 16 × 13". Walters Art Gallery, Baltimore

a text. Quidor simply preferred to take his themes from literature, and his paintings can stand on their own as anecdotal or genre scenes. He transformed Irving's picturesque "folk" tales into burlesques of "Gothick" terror, walking a narrow line between prank and nightmare. *The Money Diggers* (1832, colorplate 31) is a tableau out of the Grand Guignol, with twisted trees, jagged rocks, and batlike forms, all seen in an eerie firelight. A remarkable play of contrasts is created by brilliant flickering highlights and mysteriously threatening shadows. The robbers are swept into a spasm of action by a ludicrous terror, their grotesque forms galvanized in the lurid light. As a painting, it is a notable achievement, knowingly composed, with all the dynamic action of the figures and writhing shapes of the landscape contained in a unified complex in depth as well as on the picture surface. Though little appreciated, Quidor was one of the most sophisticated painters of the period, carrying on the Allston tradition of solid underpainting and subtle overglazing to create three-dimensional form in light and atmosphere, to which he added his own surface obbligato of "expressionist" brushwork and lively color. The earthy genre types and the luminosity of his paint suggest some firsthand contact with Dutch and Flemish painting.

George Caleb Bingham (1811–1879), more than any other artist of the era, expressed Jacksonian democracy in its western origins—its egalitarianism, adventurousness, and roistering vitality—even though his earliest genre scenes date from after the heyday of "Old Hickory's" power. He recorded the commonplace life of the frontier as he saw it, but in his heroic treatment of the ordinary and his desire to depict the "social and political characteristics" of that society, he was as much a painter of history as of genre.

Bingham was born in Augusta County, Va., but was taken as a boy to Franklin, the major town in Missouri west of St. Louis, in 1819. Forced to help support the family after his father's death in 1823, Bingham first worked as a farmhand and was then apprenticed to a cabinetmaker in Boonville. He was drawn to art at an early age and, although he was interested in theology and law, turned to portrait painting in 1830. His first contact with a sophisticated level of art came in 1838, when he spent three months in Philadelphia studying pictures at the Pennsylvania Academy. It may have been there that he saw his first genre paintings. However, he was soon back in Missouri, executing portraits, becoming involved in politics, and painting political banners. With the election of William Henry Harrison, for whom he had campaigned, Bingham moved to Washington in 1840 and for four years worked as a portrait painter with only moderate success. During the years before his departure for Düsseldorf in 1856, he completed most of his significant genre paintings. His themes dealt mainly with life on the river and, later, the political scene. His was, like Mount's bucolic view of eastern life, a pleasant and sunny version

have been a major figure in American art. From the evidence of his paintings he would seem to have been largely self-taught, for his drawing is ungainly and distorted, his modeling pasty, his brushwork unsure. Yet his paintings exude a remarkable vigor, his exaggerations are descriptively and emotionally effective, and his very deficiencies seem to add an artistic dimension to the grossness of his people and the seaminess of their environment.

Blythe and Quidor were the only genre artists of their time in whose work "Gothick" distortion of form was employed to heighten expression and, in that sense, were closer to Romantic emotionalism than to Victorian moderation. John Quidor (1801–1881) has left a body of work unique in its evocation of the macabre. He had little or no recognition and eked out a living as a painter of signs, banners, fire buckets, and panels for coaches and fire engines. He was not just an artisan, but his was an unpopular kind of art, and he remained on the periphery of the New York art world.

Except for occasional religious paintings, the majority of Quidor's work was in illustration, and most of that was based on Washington Irving's tales of Dutch New York. But the pictures are not illustrations as accompaniment to

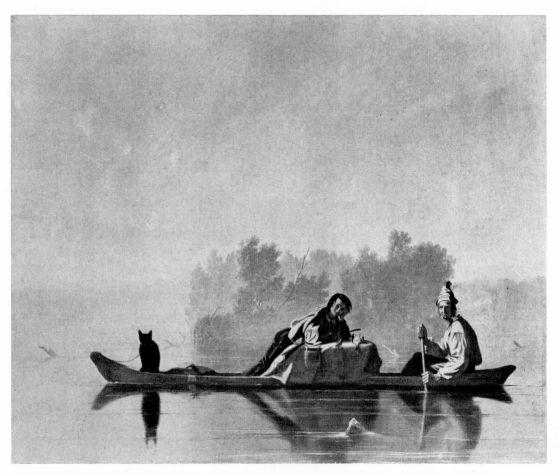

250 George Caleb Bingham. *Fur Traders Descending the Missouri*. c. 1845. Oil on canvas, 29 × 36½″.
The Metropolitan Museum of Art, New York. Morris K. Jesup Fund, 1933

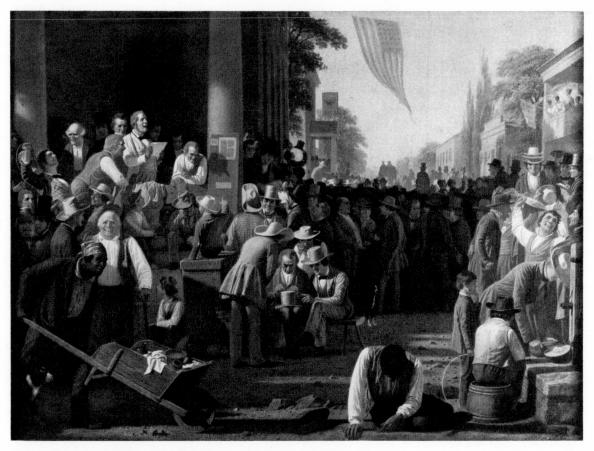

251 George Caleb Bingham. *The Verdict of the People*. 1854–55. Oil on canvas,
46 × 65″. The Boatmen's National Bank of St. Louis

of western existence. In *Fur Traders Descending the Missouri* (c. 1845, plate 250) two men in a dugout canoe drift downriver in the early morning haze; in *Shooting for the Beef* (1850, colorplate 32) a group of frontiersmen engage in a contest in rifle marksmanship.

Bingham learned to compose in the grand manner, using broad horizontal bands of space within which figures are solidly modeled and precisely placed and groups are arranged in stable pyramidal shapes. Every element is clearly defined and simplified. There is a strong sense of Classical order, reminiscent of Poussin, and an obvious dependence on a rudimentary geometric structure in which sharp-edged planks or slender poles and rifles play an insistent role. In his earliest paintings, such as *Fur Traders*, Bingham rather baldly centered his subject, leaving a border of space around the edges. In spite of its crude, hot color and oversharp contrasts of light and shade in the figures, it remains one of his most satisfying efforts. The evocation of lyrical mood, the sheer loveliness of the river in a roseate haze, the delight in the sensuous aspects of the physical world were never again quite equaled in his work.

Eventually Bingham gave up the centralized for a more fluent diagonal form in which a large foreground shape at one side balanced a small distant shape on the other, creating a plunging recession into space. *Shooting for the Beef* is composed in this manner. The low-eye-level view produces a composition of foreground figures in monumental scale contrasted with small background figures, and the powerful three-dimensional form of the seated figure in the central foreground acts as a spatial barrier. The whole is tied together with striking geometric lucidity.

The election series, comprising the *County Election, Stump Speaking, Verdict of the People* (1854–55, plate 251), and perhaps *Canvassing for a Vote*, occupied most of Bingham's artistic efforts for five years. It is an expression of his faith in the democratic process at its grass roots. He avoided any serious consideration of issues and, instead, recorded with good-humored raillery the human aspect of the political process. All types and social classes are included, except for women, for Bingham's was a man's world. All kinds of psychological responses are probed. By this time he had attained a remarkable level of competence in handling large numbers of figures in composition. There is an unfaltering rationality in the way he organized the smaller elements into larger units and interrelated all in a coherent plan. But the final image is synthetic, each object an independent entity coexisting among equals, for Bingham's vision was not sophisticated enough to translate the visual world into a unified experience of mass, space, light, and atmosphere.

In Düsseldorf he identified wholeheartedly with its academic naturalism, seeing in it the reflection of his own aims and principles, but the technical subtleties he absorbed seem to have disturbed the cohesive force of his vision. Bingham had been moving away from his original inspiration even before he went abroad, and Düsseldorf merely reinforced the faults of his style. His later years were devoted to politics and portrait painting, and though he remained a public figure, his achievements were soon forgotten.

THE WEST

The opening of the West had all the ingredients of a Romantic saga—primeval nature, an exotic aboriginal population, and adventure in the unknown. From the very beginning the New World had a fascination for the scientific student as well as the Romantic dreamer, and there was a sense that the inevitable wave of civilization would destroy what had remained untouched for millenniums. Audubon felt that way about his birds, Catlin about his Indians, and even Bingham about the frontier life he loved so well. Intrepid artists—in some cases artists only by necessity—have left an invaluable record of a vanished world, although little of it is of enduring aesthetic value. This is, of course, not true of the work of John James Audubon (1785–1851), whose studies of American birds are inestimable records and artistic masterpieces at the same time.

Audubon, the illegitimate son of a French sea captain and a chambermaid, was born in what is now Haiti. At four he went to France to live with his father in Nantes, where he received his education and his interest in nature was first encouraged. In 1803, to avoid conscription in Napoleon's armies, Audubon came to the United States, and by 1808 he had married and moved to the frontier in Kentucky. From his arrival in this country he had observed and drawn birds, and this passionate avocation was fired in 1810 when the Scottish immigrant artist Alexander Wilson (1766–1813) walked into Audubon's store in Louisville, seeking subscriptions for his *American Ornithology* (1808–13). Not until 1820, however, did Audubon set out down the Mississippi on a flatboat to record the birds of the New World for his own projected publication. His scientific training was acquired mostly on his own; as he said, he was not a "learned" naturalist but a practical one.

For the next six years New Orleans was the base of Audubon's operations. His wife taught school to support the family while he contributed by doing chalk portraits and teaching drawing, French, music, dancing, and fencing. In 1824 he visited Philadelphia, hoping to find support for his publication, but without success. After another year and a half of intensive labor, Audubon left for Europe, where his drawings and stories of personal experience in the wilderness captivated the English, Scottish, and French. Acting as his own publisher and salesman, he managed to keep just ahead of the creditors while, for twelve years, he and his family worked out of London. There the engravers Robert Havell and Robert Havell, Jr., reproduced his drawings in their original size on copper plates by a combination of etching, aquatint, and other processes. The prints were then colored by hand.

The four elephant folio volumes of 435 colorplates were issued between 1827 and 1838 under the title *The Birds of America*; the accompanying text, *Ornithological Biography* (1831–39), in five volumes, was published in Edinburgh. The publication was deservedly successful. Audubon had devised a method of wiring a recently shot bird into a lifelike position and placing it before a background ruled off in small squares. He depicted his birds in action, flying or swimming, scratching a wing, attacking prey, warding off enemies, or feeding their young, all seen from eye level. Assistants, among them his sons, usually painted in the background of appropriate branches or terrain. The necessities of scientific accuracy and the restrictions of the format often led to brilliant formal solutions. *The Great Blue Heron* (1821, colorplate 33) is a case in point. The spindly creature is contorted to fill the prescribed space with an elastic but awkward grace that is both true to the species and exciting as pure design. In the flattening of form, emphasis on silhouette, and relationship of shape to frame, there is a striking resemblance to Japanese painted screens. One can find similarities also in the acuteness of observation and precision in detail, the hard elegance of line, and the delicacy of color. Audubon used watercolor, pastel, ink, oil, egg white, and even scratching on the surface to simulate textures with an exquisite fidelity to nature.

Audubon later embarked on a project of depicting the mammals of America. In 1843 he traveled up the Missouri gathering specimens, but when his sight failed in 1846, it was left to his son, John Woodhouse, to complete *The Viviparous Quadrupeds of North America* (1845–48).

Before the nineteenth century the American attitude toward the Indian had been unequivocal—the only good one was a dead one. By 1830 the Indians, exterminated or driven beyond the Mississippi, no longer posed an immediate obstacle or threat. They could even be thought of in Romantic terms, as examples of natural man, even as heroic and tragically doomed. Their exoticism in appearance and mode of existence added to the Romantic interest, and there was some anthropological and ethnographic interest in their customs.

George Catlin (1796–1872) became and has remained identified in the public mind as *the* Indian painter through his years of devoted study, the authenticity of his observations, the great body of his production, and most of all his publications and the impassioned espousal of the Indian cause in his traveling show of art and life. Born in Wilkes-Barre, Pa., Catlin practiced law before turning to miniature and portrait painting in 1821, after which he plied that trade for almost a decade. He had been captivated by the sight of a group of Indians in full regalia in the streets of Philadelphia, and by 1830 he was in St. Louis doing portraits of Indians. Two years later he

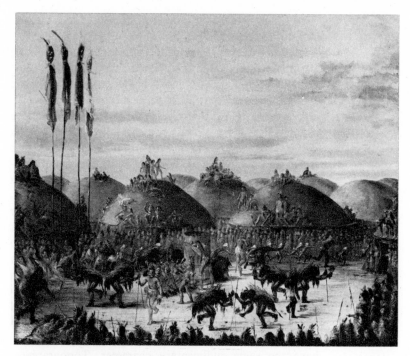

252 George Catlin. *Bull Dance*. c. 1832–36. Oil on canvas, 22⅝ × 27⅝". National Collection of Fine Arts, Smithsonian Institution, Washington, D.C.

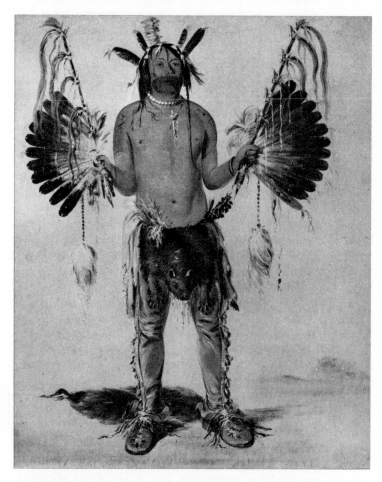

253 George Catlin. *Old Bear*. 1832. Oil on canvas, 29 × 24". National Collection of Fine Arts, Smithsonian Institution, Washington, D.C.

started out with an American Fur Company party taking the first steamboat up the Missouri 2,000 miles to Fort Union. Catlin spent almost eight years among the Indians, was the first artist to penetrate the Far West, and amassed close to six hundred paintings, which he assembled as his traveling "Indian Gallery." His *Letters and Notes of the Manners, Customs, and Condition of the North American Indians* (1841) went through many editions and, aside from its ethnographic value, became a source book for artists who had never seen a live Indian.

His lack of training may actually have been a boon, for a sophisticated artist might have found the conditions under which he had to work too difficult, and those who came later and were trained could not help seeing in set formal patterns. Despite his shortcomings he had an artist's eye for the dramatic sight or moment, for composition, pattern, and linear movement. His scenes of Indian life (plate 252), though often not much more than shorthand notations, are full of vivacity. His landscapes have the same rudimentary character. Topographical rather than Romantic, they record the most spectacular scenery with laconic spareness. Catlin's basic manner is staining the canvas with a minimum of pigment. His miserliness with paint may have been dictated by his insistence on painting on the spot and the necessity of carrying a minimum of equipment. Catlin worked directly and very rapidly, and in his pictures there is practically no drawing in the sense of delineation of form. In completing his paintings, Catlin did not rework them but added detail to the original sketch, thus retaining a freshness of execution and immediacy of observation. Perhaps the most effective of his works are his portraits, in which he often captured in the simplest terms the native pride and common humanity of his Indian subjects underneath their exotic trappings (plate 253). Catlin's "Indian Gallery" was acquired by the Smithsonian Institution only in 1879, after his death.

Seth Eastman (1808–1875) stumbled onto an interest in Indians through his career as an army officer in Indian country. As with Catlin, his training was limited and his technical equipment hardly superior. His paintings and the illustrations for his wife's *American Aboriginal Portfolio* (1853) and Henry R. Schoolcraft's *Information Respecting the History, Condition, and Prospects of the Indian Tribes of the United States* (1851–57) were based in part on his sketches made among the Sioux and Chippewas.

For the Swiss artist Charles (Karl) Bodmer (1809–1893) the Indians were only an incident in a long life of artistic activity. He came to America with the Prussian officer and naturalist Maximilian, Prince of Wied-Neuwied, in 1832. They made their way to Fort Union and beyond to Fort McKenzie. By the end of 1834 they were back in Europe preparing the publication of Maximilian's *Reise in das innere Nord-Amerika . . .* (1839–41); Bodmer executed the watercolors and many of the eighty-one handsome colored aquatints that were made from them.

He had been solidly trained in Zurich and Paris and his observations were accurate enough, but his formal experience colored his vision, and his Indians are actors in a fascinating theatrical performance.

Alfred Jacob Miller (1810–1874) was equally well schooled. He might have persisted as a modest portraitist had he not met an adventurous Scotsman with a wild dream of decorating his family castle with paintings of Indians. In 1837 Miller accompanied Captain William Drummond Stewart to the Rockies and made watercolor sketches of landscapes and Indian life. After two years in Scotland (1840–42) completing a series of large oil paintings for Stewart, Miller returned to portrait painting but continued to reproduce Indian paintings from his original sketches on demand. The paintings are of little consequence, but the small watercolor sketches of that one summer are aesthetically perhaps the most satisfying works in the genre.

John Mix Stanley (1814–1872) had a long and varied career as a documenter of Indian life. He made his first foray into Indian country in 1838. His studies of life among the Creeks, Seminoles, Cherokees, Choctaws, Blackfeet, and Apaches were exhibited in the East, but of the 152 pictures of forty-three different tribes deposited at the Smithsonian all but five were destroyed by fire. Stanley was also a photographer, and much of his work was based on camera records.

Charles (Karl) Wimar (1828–1862), the last of the Indian painters, went to St. Louis from the Rhineland in 1843. Bitten by the Indian bug at an early age, Wimar dedicated his short life to the immortalization of a vanishing race and a childhood dream. He made his initial trip into Indian country in 1849. He went to study at Düsseldorf in 1852, returning to St. Louis in 1856. Although profoundly involved with the Indians and a serious student of their ways, he came too late to see them with the objectivity of some of his predecessors. They appeared to him through a veil of Romantic sentiment and a frame of Düsseldorfian pedantry.

HISTORY PAINTING

Although the ideological basis for government-supported historical painting was strong during the Jacksonian Era, its development was limited. Congress seemed to have washed its hands of art patronage after the negative reception of Trumbull's murals, but pressure continued for completing the remaining four panels of the Rotunda. After much maneuvering by politicians and artists, the assignment was made to John Vanderlyn, Robert W. Weir, John G. Chapman, and Henry Inman. They were all essentially easel painters—Inman even something of a miniaturist—and the paintings were not conceived as heroic compositions. Inman, perhaps fortunately, never got beyond a sketch for the *Emigration of Daniel Boone to Kentucky* before his death, and subsequent politicking for this commission turned up an unknown

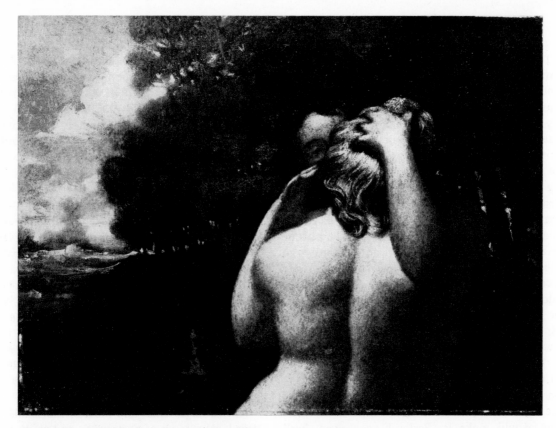

254 William Page. *Cupid and Psyche*. 1843. Oil on canvas, 10¾ × 14¾".
Private collection. Courtesy Kennedy Galleries, Inc., New York

Midwestern candidate, William H. Powell. But the Rotunda area was now at least filled, by Vanderlyn's *Landing of Columbus* (1842–44), Weir's *Embarkation of the Pilgrims* (1837–40), Chapman's *Baptism of Pocahontas* (1837–42), and Powell's *Discovery of the Mississippi River by De Soto* (1848–53).

Aside from Allston, whose last years were sterile, and the handful who painted pictures for the Capitol, very few artists were concerned with history painting during the middle of the century. Of these the most interesting was William Page (1811–1885), a complex and often paradoxical figure. He fascinated and repelled his contemporaries, was equally revered and denounced, and achieved at the time more of a reputation than his work merited but eventually even less recognition than it deserved. Page was the one true heir to Allston's romantic transcendentalism, more concerned with the "soul" of art than with its material character, yet the most sensuous painter of his generation, a poetic mystic, and an inveterate experimenter in the techniques of painting. He is remembered today for only a handful of pictures that have escaped the consequences of his eccentric technical procedures.

Born in Albany, Page went to New York while still a child, became a student of Morse and was in the first drawing class of the National Academy, winning a silver medal in 1827. However, he decided to study for the ministry and returned to art as a portrait painter only in 1831. After several years in New York and Boston, he

left for Europe in 1850. For ten years Page was an important figure in the English-speaking art circles of Florence and Rome.

Page developed a complex method of underpainting and successive layers of glazing that produced a textural richness and coloristic glow unique in its time. The most striking of his historical pictures is *Cupid and Psyche* (1843, plate 254), one of the few works of the period in which Romantic sentiment is expressed with poetic intensity in painterly rather than literary terms. This is the first painting in America in which nudity is seen not through a veil of conventional allusion but as a freshly observed experience. Yet it remains an idealized and lyrical statement of sexuality, not a realistic one. Page was the most sophisticated painter of his generation, and it is only recently that those qualities which his contemporaries vaguely sensed have been recognized and his stature as an artist has been reexamined. A good deal of his activity was directed toward portrait painting, much of which has stood up better than his imaginative painting because it was less experimental. His portraits are among the finest and least conventional of the time.

Other history painters of the period, such as Daniel Huntington (1816–1906) and Henry Peters Gray (1819–1877), were similarly involved with a search for ideal beauty in the art of the past, and in their day their paintings passed for elevated and refined taste. In 1849 the Art Union paid its highest price for Gray's *Wages of War* and the following year exhibited a Huntington retrospective of 130 paintings, an honor never before tendered a living American artist.

Emanuel Leutze (1816–1868) exemplifies a more contemporary kind of history painting, which strove not for the lofty ideal and the old-master manner, but for a particularization of history through naturalism of detail and modernity of technique. Perhaps the major center of this kind of Victorian, middle-class, anecdotalized history painting was Düsseldorf, where Leutze studied, taught, and spent most of his active life. He was born in Württemberg, Germany, was taken to Fredericksburg, Va., as a child, and in 1841 went to Düsseldorf. There he became a paterfamilias to the many American students who gravitated to the city after 1849, when Americans were introduced to German painting with the opening of the Düsseldorf Gallery in New York. Leutze painted his famous *Washington Crossing the Delaware*, now destroyed, and also a larger version in 1851 (plate 255), which was brought to America for exhibition and engraved. Instantaneously successful, it has remained an integral part of American mythology. It exists uneasily between nobility and banality, neither so heroic as patriotic sentiment would see it nor so insipid as aesthetic judgment would make it. Seriously conceived, well composed, and painted with broadness and spirit, it does not fail as image or as illustration but only in the most profound aesthetic sense as a work of art.

In 1859 Leutze settled permanently in the United States, and Congress, shortly after, commissioned him to paint *Westward the Course of Empire Takes Its Way* for the new Capitol extension. A picture with no redeeming features, completely disorganized in composition, slipshod in execution, and garish in color, *Westward* lacks even the popular imagery of the *Crossing*.

THE DECLINE OF PORTRAITURE

Until the Civil War portraiture remained the most stable source of income for the majority of artists. Even photography, at first, had little effect on the portrait market. But, as a taste for a more varied range of subject painting developed, fewer artists of stature turned to portraiture. The result was a proliferation of routine, almost indistinguishable likenesses with neither character nor artistic interest. Eventually the influence of the camera produced a mechanical repetition of pose, expression, and finish, so that the painted portrait looked like the tinted photograph which was originally intended to imitate the painted portrait.

All the larger cities and most of the smaller ones had their local coteries of portraitists, and many of the lesser centers were also serviced by well-known painters who visited the South in season or itinerants who followed the

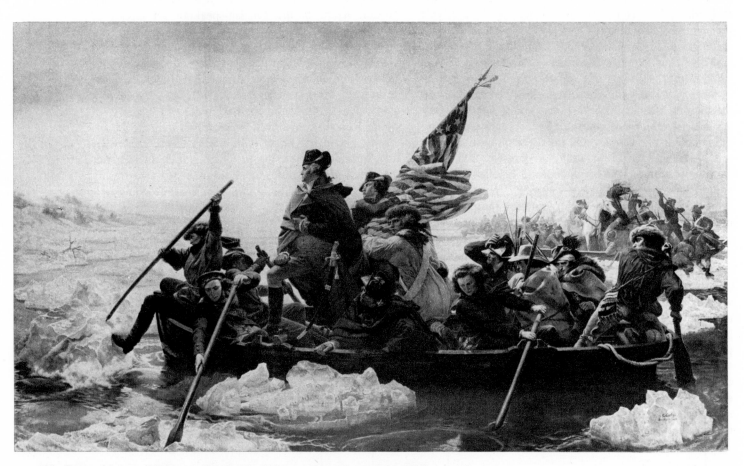

255 Emanuel Leutze. *Washington Crossing the Delaware*. 1851. Oil on canvas, 12′5″ × 21′3″. The Metropolitan Museum of Art, New York. Gift of John S. Kennedy, 1897

settlers to the western frontier. Thomas Sully (1783–1872), undoubtedly the best portrait painter of his generation, was active most of his long life in Philadelphia. He produced about two thousand portraits and five hundred "fancy" pictures. Too many of these were potboilers, but enough of them have quality to raise him above the ruck of journeymen face painters. His best, and most are relatively early, exhibit a fairly solid technical ability, a native elegance, a lightness of touch, and a Romantic sense of mood which is both pensive and sweet, although the sweetness with time became rather sentimental.

In 1807 in Boston Sully was befriended by Stuart, who permitted him to watch as he painted and offered him some criticism and whose influence is strong in his early career. Sully is the only portrait painter who retained something of Stuart's fluency of manner and elegance of touch, qualities reinforced by a trip to England in 1809, when he was impressed by the Romantic virtuosity of Sir Thomas Lawrence. In 1810 he settled in Philadelphia, where he remained, except for professional visits to other cities and a second trip to England in 1837–38, during which he painted his famous *Queen Victoria*. The oil sketch for this portrait (1838, plate 256), painted from life, has a light and airy elegance that is lost in the full-scale version.

In comparison with Sully, his contemporaries were as pedestrian as their sitters were middle class. Aristocratic airs and psychological vitality had given way to the staidly sober and the conventionally pretty. John Wesley Jarvis (1780–1840) painted hard, precise portraits with solid competence and only rare flashes of inspiration. He was essentially a face painter and often collaborated with others in turning out a finished product—from 1802 to 1810 with Joseph Wood (c. 1778–1830) and later with Henry Inman, who served as an apprentice from 1814 to 1822. Such partnerships were common, indicating the routine factory production of portraits to meet the demand.

Aside from John Neagle (1796–1865), who was influenced by his father-in-law, Thomas Sully, and falls between the two generations, the succeeding group of portrait painters turned from the loose brushwork of the Stuart-Lawrence tradition to a tighter, more polished style, presaging the photographic vision of the mid-century. Chester Harding (1792–1866), in age at least, stands between the two generations, but since his introduction

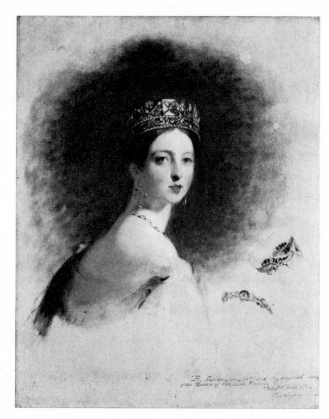

256 Thomas Sully. *Queen Victoria*. 1838. Oil on canvas, 36 × 28¼″. The Metropolitan Museum of Art, New York. Bequest of Francis T. S. Darley, 1914

to painting was belated, he is identified with the younger men. Over a thousand portraits bear witness to his industry, though they rarely rise above the level of the flattering yet faithful likeness. Henry Inman (1801–1846) was generally considered the best portrait painter of his day, but his sentimentalized, prettified, and highly polished pictures now have minor interest as records of the questionable taste of another era.

Toward the end of the period, when portrait painting as a profession declined sharply, the most successful practitioner was George Peter Alexander Healy (1813–1894), who achieved an international reputation and painted many outstanding personalities, from Lincoln to King Louis-Philippe. Though lacking in inspiration, he was a competent craftsman, capable of handling a full-length figure in space with dignity and often with some power—in short, a respectable painter for a society wholeheartedly devoted to respectability.

10
Images in Marble and Bronze

The efflorescence of American sculpture during the Jacksonian Era is one of the strangest chapters in American art. In 1815 North Carolina could find no native sculptor equipped to execute a monumental statue of Washington. Yet scarcely more than six months after the destruction of the Canova *Washington*, Horatio Greenough was commissioned to do one for the Rotunda of the Capitol, and by the mid-thirties three leading sculptors, Greenough, Crawford, and Powers, the first of a long list of expatriates, were working in Italy.

Why this sudden interest in an art that had so long been ignored? Why such high prices and ready approval when commissions for painting were so restricted? Greenough received $20,000 for his *Washington*, Crawford $53,000 for his work on a Washington monument in Richmond, and Mills $50,000 for one in the capital. Was it because sculpture appeared more tangible and permanent than painting, or, like architecture, more official? On a cultural level, sculpture, especially in white marble, was closer to the dominant Neoclassic taste. It was also more clearly an expression of America's political identification with the Classical past than was the more private and personal Romanticism of painting.

The dilemma of American culture, the accommodation of the common with the ideal, is nowhere more pronounced than in sculpture. Riven by the extremes of a provincial and plebeian naturalism and an aristocratic Classical idealization, by an artisan aptitude and the loftiest of aesthetic theories, it often found reconciliation in a delusive sentimentality. If, in the few years it took to learn the rudiments of his craft, a country boy or urban artisan became an international figure in art, how could he distinguish between mechanics and aesthetics? It is not accidental that while their contemporaries were inventing the cotton gin, the apple parer, and the bridge truss so many American sculptors developed mechanical devices for executing statuary.

Within the Neoclassic mode, sculptors who remained in the United States were in general more naturalistic and less stereotyped than their compatriots working in Rome or Florence, because they were farther removed from the Neoclassic source and they did their own carving. The expatriates chose Italy not only because it was the home of Classicism and fine Carrara marble was cheap but because expert stonecutters could be hired at a pittance. Many created little more than the original clay model, which was then cast in plaster, pointed up, and cut by Italian craftsmen. What the artists did not realize is that the high level of available craftsmanship reduced all their works to the same polished inanity.

EXPATRIATES, FIRST GENERATION

Horatio Greenough (1805–1852), the first to settle in Italy, was a proper Bostonian, educated at Harvard, a friend of Emerson and a disciple of Allston, a handsome man and a brilliant conversationalist. He moved with grace in the highest social and intellectual circles at home and abroad. His early training in sculpture was rudimentary, mostly technical. In 1825 he left for Rome, where he produced a number of portrait busts and his first ideal piece, *Abel* (1826), which was praised by Allston. Forced to return home for his health, he spent a year seeking portrait commissions in Boston, Baltimore, and Washington, where his connections led to portraits of President John Quincy Adams and Chief Justice John Marshall. Then he went back to Italy in 1828 to have his plasters done in marble and settled in Florence amid the growing American colony. He met James Fenimore Cooper, who, intent on fostering the cultural elevation of the United States, commissioned him to execute a group based on the singing *putti* of Raphael's *Madonna del Baldacchino*. The *Chanting Cherubs* (1828–30, now lost) was the first major work in marble by an American. Its reception was mixed and disturbing. The American public reacted with such shock to the nudity of the infants that they had to be draped and was disappointed that they did not actually sing.

Nevertheless, the *Chanting Cherubs* established Greenough as the premier American sculptor. In 1832 he was commissioned by Congress to execute a statue of Washington for the Rotunda. The finished marble (plate 257) was set in place in 1841. Based on the *Olympian Zeus* of Phidias, the heroic figure of Washington is nude to the waist, drapery covering the legs and hanging over the right upper arm. However informed Greenough's rationale, it should have been obvious that the American public would not accept its mythic hero partially wrapped in a sheet, regardless of his imposing mien. In a more profound sense the work fails because the insistent naturalism of the head, based on the Houdon portrait as specified in the contract, contradicts the almost abstract nobility of the rest of the figure. It *is* an imposing figure, canonical in proportion, simple and majestic in its mass, but

Greenough misjudged the harshness of the light in the Rotunda and asked to have the statue moved outdoors, with disastrous results. In the expanse of the Capitol grounds it lost its scale, was soiled by weather and pigeons, and collected puddles in the lap.

On balance, Greenough's sculpture remains unimaginative in its naturalism and pedantic in its Classicism. He might have done better in some other field, for he had a first-rate intelligence, and his theoretical writings on art (*The Travels, Observations and Experiences of a Yankee Stonecutter*, under the pseudonym of Horace Bender) are more important contributions than his sculpture. Greenough's proposition of the fundamental

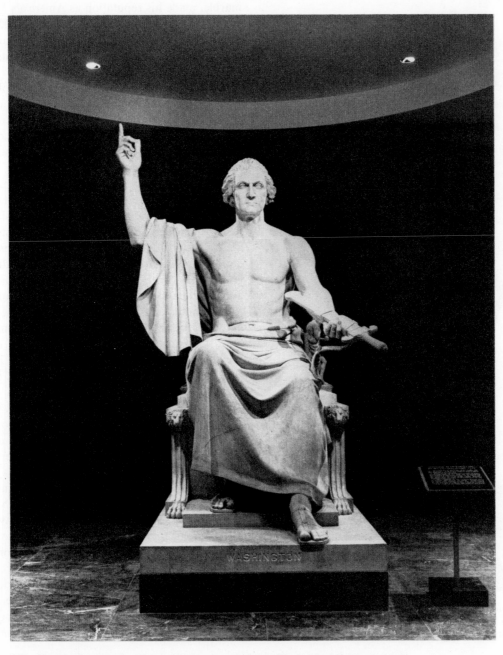

257   Horatio Greenough. *George Washington.* 1840. Marble, height 12′. Museum of Science and Technology, Smithsonian Institution, Washington, D.C.

significance of *function* in the creation of form, though little noted at the time, is one of the most generative aesthetic statements of the nineteenth century.

Greenough was joined in Italy by Thomas Crawford (1811/13–1857) in 1835 and Hiram Powers (1805–1873) in 1837. Powers, out of the Middle West and with a mechanic's background, was to become America's most famous sculptor. He had taken up sculpture as a hobby and received basic instruction in modeling and casting. His earliest sculptural efforts interested Nicholas Longworth, the patriotic Maecenas of Cincinnati artists, and in 1834 Longworth supplied the backing for a move to Washington, where Powers was an instant success with his *Andrew Jackson* (c. 1835, plate 258). In spite of its Neoclassic toga, the bust is realistic without being literal, revealing a search for personality, and achieving a simple

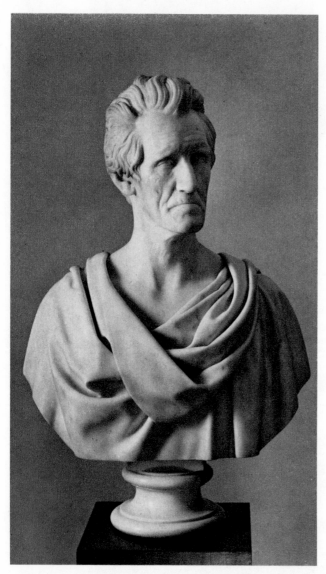

258 Hiram Powers. *Andrew Jackson*. c. 1835. Marble, height 34½″. The Metropolitan Museum of Art, New York. Gift of Mrs. Frances V. Nash, 1894

dignity. Thereafter Powers modeled likenesses of various famous American personages until he moved to Florence in 1837 to have the portraits cut in stone and remained there the rest of his life.

Before long Powers emerged as one of the leading portraitists of the time and is said to have produced some one hundred fifty busts, commanding as much as $1,000 for a marble. His Italianate style was obviously affected by Greenough and Neoclassicism, but the portraits are also imbued with a Romantic spirit, characterized by Wayne Craven as "Byronic." For a sculptor, as for a painter of that period, portraiture was considered an inferior occupation, except in a monument.

Despite meager training in anatomy, Powers began to work on ideal figures as early as 1838, and *The Greek Slave* (plate 259), the first of his figures to be carved in marble, made his reputation as America's Michelangelo. It was bought by an English lord for $4,000, six copies went at the same price, a smaller replica also sold well, and *The Greek Slave* grossed $23,000 on its tour of the United States. The fabulous success of this routine adaptation of the *Medici Venus* was a triumph of shrewd Yankee merchandising, which included an advance man, promotional literature, and the proper clerical endorsements. Represented as a pathetic captive of the infidel Turks, the chained girl in her nudity became a symbol of inviolable Christian virtue. Without the libretto she remains an ungainly and bloodless manikin.

Powers's growing international reputation finally brought him monumental portrait commissions for over-life-size marbles of Calhoun, Daniel Webster, Franklin, and Jefferson. Embalmed in the encomiums of an international reputation, he continued to produce portraits and echoes of his ideal sculpture long past their time, and the glamour of his name was faded before his death.

If "manifest destiny" demanded an American culture hero, it found Thomas Crawford personally, though hardly artistically, a more fitting object of idolatry than even Hiram Powers. Personable, talented, happily married, surrounded by influential friends, Crawford was more successful in his short career than any other American sculptor of the time. He was compared with Phidias, and nominated to inherit the mantle of Canova and Thorwaldsen. It was Robert Launitz, a student of Thorwaldsen, who sent Crawford in 1835 with a letter of introduction to Thorwaldsen, who accepted him as a student. The first American sculptor to settle in Rome, Crawford became the most dedicated of American Neoclassicists. His first works were portraits ordered by traveling Americans, among them that of *Charles Sumner* (1839, plate 260), the brilliant orator and later senator from Massachusetts. The polished elegance of its Byronic Neoclassicism is typical of his portraits of that period and those of Greenough and Powers at the same time.

Like his compatriots, Crawford was soon immersed in ideal themes and in 1839 began the *Orpheus and Cer-*

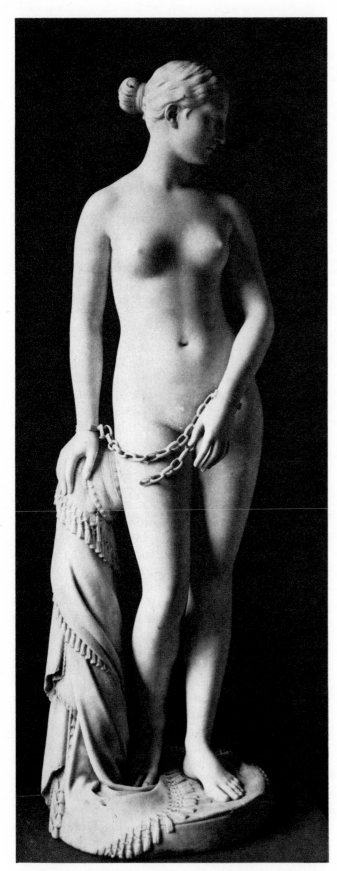

259 Hiram Powers. *The Greek Slave.* 1847. Marble, height 65½″. The Newark Museum, Newark, N.J.

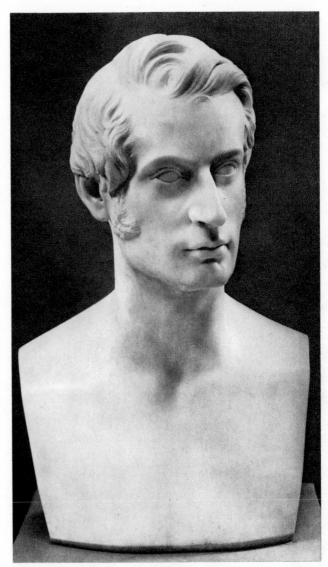

260 Thomas Crawford. *Charles Sumner.* 1839. Marble, height 27″. Museum of Fine Arts, Boston. Bequest of Charles Sumner

berus (plate 261), which was to make his reputation. Carved in stone in 1843, it was exhibited in Boston in 1844 and received with rapturous enthusiasm. Its accompanying scenario—with ill-starred lovers, death, resurrection, grief, mystery, and beauty—had an iconographic description of every detail, gesture, and implied emotion. It was the first nude male statue, though fig-leafed, to be shown in the United States, but clothed in such piety that it could hardly offend. In fact, it is a rather pedestrian variation on the *Apollo Belvedere*—Neoclassic, saccharine, and banal.

Crawford received no important commissions until he won the competition for a *Washington Monument* in Richmond in 1849. Then followed an avalanche of commissions, including the Senate pediment and portal sculptures, the *Armed Freedom* that tops the dome of the Capitol, and the bronze doors of both the Senate and

Images in Marble and Bronze 233

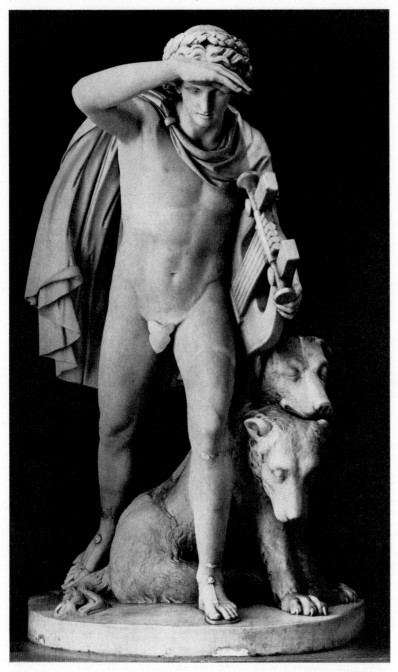

261 Thomas Crawford. *Orpheus and Cerberus*. 1843. Marble, height 67½".
Museum of Fine Arts, Boston, on loan from Boston Athenaeum

the House of Representatives. His remaining years were spent in feverish activity, preparing sketches and models, executing figures in clay, supervising their casting or carving in stone. Much of his work was unfinished at his death, some to be completed by other sculptors.

Whatever the shortcomings of the first generation of expatriate sculptors, they gave America its first international recognition in the field and solidified the dominance of Neoclassicism. All had come to the style late in its history and thus projected it beyond its normal course in the United States. Though they set a level of academic

training and professional practice in sculpture, the dead hand of tradition managed to stultify the development of American sculpture for almost half a century.

EXPATRIATES, SECOND GENERATION

The second-generation Neoclassicists who worked in Italy in the forties and fifties were essentially academic eclectics who mixed modes without the slightest unease, blindly and happily convinced that they were working in the purest vein of Classical principles. Their art was Victorian in its pseudocultural pretensions, its literal naturalism, its ideality, and its Romantic penchant for the mysterious and the exotic, along with a puerility of imagination, emotional triviality, and pious sentiment. Unlike their predecessors, who had come to discover an art form, the second generation removed themselves from their native land without cutting their cultural ties. They ignored the problems of America, though their handiwork peopled its parlors.

During the forties Florence continued as the American expatriate center. The Cincinnatian Shobal Vail Clevenger (1812–1843), aided by Nicholas Longworth, arrived there in 1840. However, his reputation rests on his portrait heads, most of which were done before he went abroad. Doggedly realistic and without pretense, they are strong and simple characterizations of personality with an almost Roman Republican austerity. In his naturalism he was more American than Neoclassic.

Henry Kirke Brown (1814–1886) belongs with the American-oriented sculptors of the period, but he was for a short time an expatriate and a convert to Neoclassicism. Brown began his artistic career as a portrait painter in Boston, then in Cincinnati joined the group patronized by Longworth. His friendship with Clevenger led to an interest in sculpture, and he abandoned the brush for the chisel. In Florence he cut his own busts in stone, which was unusual, and, to signalize his loyalty to American art, began the *Indian Boy* (1843), which he maintained had "as much historical interest and poetry as an Apollo or Bacchus." After moving to Rome, he was converted to the antique and to ideality. In 1846 William Cullen Bryant, sitting for his portrait, persuaded the sculptor to return to America and lend his genius to further its cultural destiny.

At the end of the 1850s Florence ceased to be the hub of American Neoclassicism. Rome became the stronghold, remaining so almost to the end of the century, by which time the style was dead.

Richard Saltonstall Greenough (1819–1904) had been in Florence in 1837 to visit his older brother, Horatio. In the following decade, he gained a modest reputation as a portrait sculptor and decided to go to Rome, where he became a mainstay of the American circle from 1848 to 1853, and again from the mid-1870s to his death. Greenough's portraits are typically Victorian in their mix of idealism, naturalism, and mindless detail. He also turned out his quota of Classical themes. In 1853 he returned home as Boston's most eminent sculptor to execute the $20,000 commission for a statue of *Benjamin Franklin* (plate 262). Completed in 1855, it was cast in bronze and erected in front of Boston's City Hall the next year. The *Franklin* is naturalistic and humane, the benign head in deep thought, the rotund torso balanced on chunky legs; and, though the detail is fussy, the figure has a homely dignity. Greenough settled in Paris in 1856, but his work there was not appreciably different from that of the Americans in Rome. By the time he returned to Rome, Victorian Classicism was moribund, but he continued to work within the limits of his earlier experience, unaware that in the *Circe* (1882, plate 263) he had produced a caricature of all that Victorian sculpture had been.

Out of the same milieu as the Greenoughs came William Wetmore Story (1819–1895). As the son of an Associate Justice of the Supreme Court, he was destined for the legal profession upon graduation from Harvard. Though he showed an early interest in the arts, he was surprised, after the death of his father in 1845, to be asked by the memorial committee to execute the portrait statue for the monument. To fulfill the assignment, he traveled in Europe, worked on the model in Rome in 1848–49, and settled there in 1851. The completed *Justice Joseph Story* (1853) is hardly a memorable work, and although he

263 Richard Saltonstall Greenough. *Circe*. 1882. Marble, height 54½". The Metropolitan Museum of Art, New York. Gift of Misses Alice and Evelyn Blogler and Mrs. W. P. Thompson, 1904

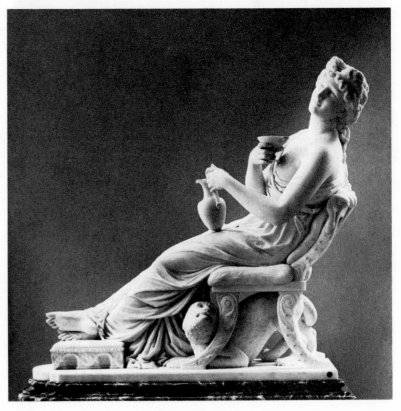

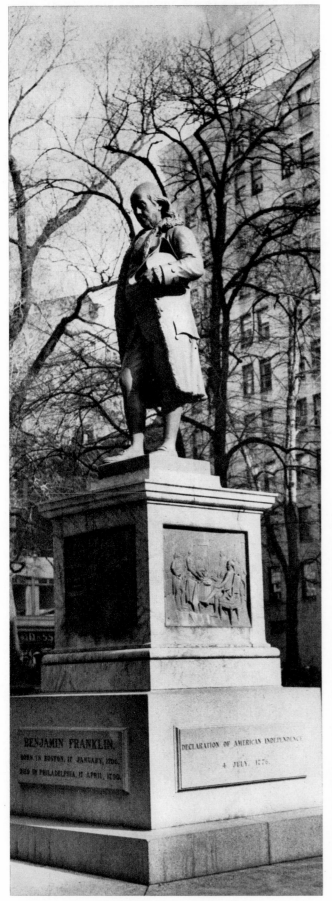

262 Richard Saltonstall Greenough. *Benjamin Franklin*. 1855. Bronze, life size. City Hall, Boston

Images in Marble and Bronze 235

several figures which are among his finest efforts. After the war, Rogers was one of the busiest of war-memorial designers, executing colossal sculptural confections for Cincinnati, Providence, and Detroit.

The most dedicated to the Classic tradition among the second generation was William Rinehart (1825–1874), who had begun his career as a stonecutter in Baltimore. His earliest works brought him the support of William T. Walters, the wealthy collector who made it possible for Rinehart to go to Italy and remained his patron. One of his most popular works was the *Sleeping Children* (1859–60) for Greenmount Cemetery, Baltimore, of which he did some twenty versions (plate 265). The maudlin sentiment aroused by plump and helpless babes carved in stone was one of the common emotional excesses of the period satisfied by a host of Victorian sculptors.

No account of American sculpture in Italy would be complete without mention of the women sculptors who were part of the circle in Rome, perhaps reflecting the movement toward the emancipation of women in the early nineteenth century. During the fifties Rome saw the arrival of Harriet Hosmer (1830–1908), Margaret Foley (c. 1820–1877), Louisa Lander (1826–1923), and Emma Stebbins (1815–1882) and, in the next decade, of Edmonia Lewis (1845–?) and Anne Whitney (1821–1915). None was any better or worse than the general run of male academic eclectics, and they produced their quota of undistinguished ideal figures, monuments, and bust portraits.

(continued on page 240)

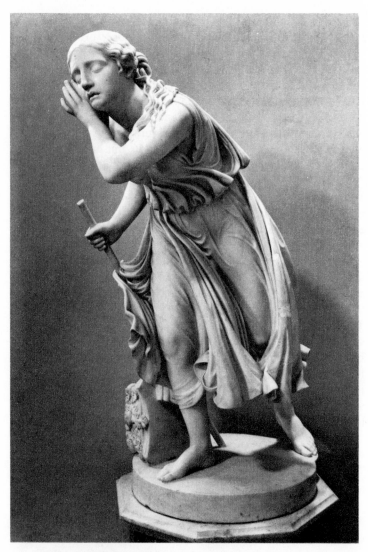

264   Randolph Rogers. *Nydia.* 1859. Marble, height 55".
The Metropolitan Museum of Art, New York.
Gift of James Douglas, 1899

later achieved an enviable reputation, he was never more than competent as a sculptor.

In the vein of bathos *Nydia* (1859, plate 264) by Randolph Rogers was probably supreme in the number of copies purveyed in its day. He had adapted it from the Hellenistic *Old Market Woman* in the Vatican, but the sentiment was consonant with the purple prose of Bulwer-Lytton's *The Last Days of Pompeii*, from which it derived. Rogers (1825–1892) was one of the most successful sculptors of his generation. In 1855 he was commissioned to execute the bronze doors of the Capitol Rotunda. Based on the Ghiberti "Gates of Paradise," the "Columbus" doors are among the first indications of an interest in the Renaissance that continued in Rogers's later monuments. In 1857 he was asked to complete Crawford's unfinished *Washington Monument* in Richmond, which occupied him in part through the Civil War. Rogers had the Crawford plasters cast and executed

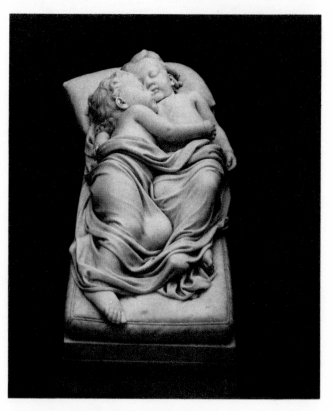

265   William H. Rinehart. *Sleeping Children.* 1868.
Marble, height 17", width 20", length 34".
The Maryland Institute, Baltimore

Much of the history of early American glass is bound up with the entrepreneurs who founded the glass-blowing factories, for almost no glassblowers worked alone. Since neither Stiegel nor Wistar marked his wares, the first that can be firmly attributed are the engraved presentation pieces made by the firm of John Frederick Amelung at New Bremen, Md., from 1785 to 1795. Amelung, another German manufacturer establishing a fledgling glass industry in this country, arrived with the support of investors back in Bremen, Germany, and additional financial backing from interested Maryland residents. Some magnificent pieces were created at the same time that routine window and bottle glass was being made, but the problems of inadequate funding and foreign competition drove him to financial ruin. The works on which Amelung's reputation rests are the comparatively large presentation goblets called "pokals" and several engraved tumblers and sugar bowls. The most famous of these objects is the Bremen Pokal (plate 266), a piece Amelung sent back to Bremen to indicate the type of work he was doing for his financial backers. The pokal is urn-shaped, with a slightly splayed foot and a series of knobs on the stem. The cover is a flattened dome with a knob repeating the bottom of the stem in reverse. The shape is basically Classical, though the light tends to diffuse and temper the feeling of solidity inherent in the form. The engraving is Old World in its imagery and Rococo in style, focusing on a wreath and crown in an elaborate coat of arms. In spite of the excellence of the form and the quality of the engraving, the affluent still preferred the European import, and domestic glassware of the elegance of Amelung's was not seen again for another generation.

During the five years from the start of the Jeffersonian shipping embargo to the end of the War of 1812, American glass manufacturers finally had some relief from the pressure of cheap and fashionable foreign imports, and many of the newer firms prospered. After the war, however, British glass was literally dumped on the American market, below cost, as dealers attempted to regain their competitive edge. At the very moment that the second-generation American glass industry seemed headed for the same oblivion as the first, new technical advances put the infant industry on a sounder basis. The New England Glass Company of East Cambridge, Mass., began using the abundant coal of West Virginia and Pennsylvania instead of local wood to fire their furnaces. A second innovation by this firm was the setting up of a factory to refine the lead needed for fine flint glass. The sugar bowl (plate 267) was a product of those innovations and illustrates the newfound ability of the blower to produce bubble- and impurity-free glass of the highest quality. The swirled ribbing is derived from gadrooning on New England silver a century earlier. The

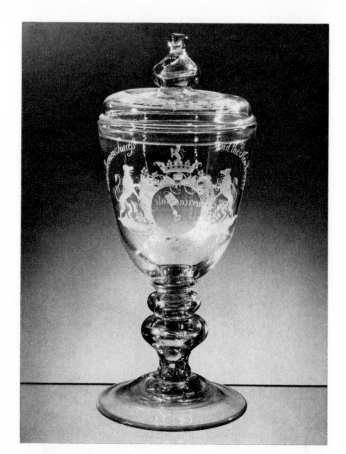

266　New Bremen Glass Manufactory, New Bremen, Md. Goblet with cover ("The Bremen Pokal"). 1788. Free-blown, engraved colorless glass, height 11¼". The Metropolitan Museum of Art, New York. Rogers Fund, 1928

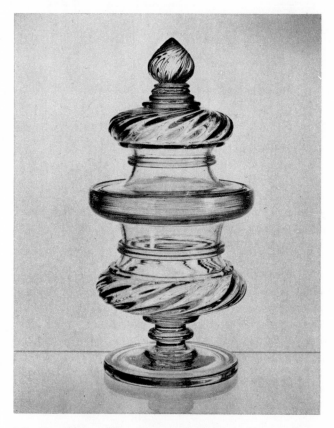

267　New England Glass Company. Sugar bowl with cover, from Massachusetts. c. 1820. Free-blown colorless glass with mold-blown ribbing, height 9¾". The Toledo Museum of Art, Ohio. Gift of Edward Drummond Libbey

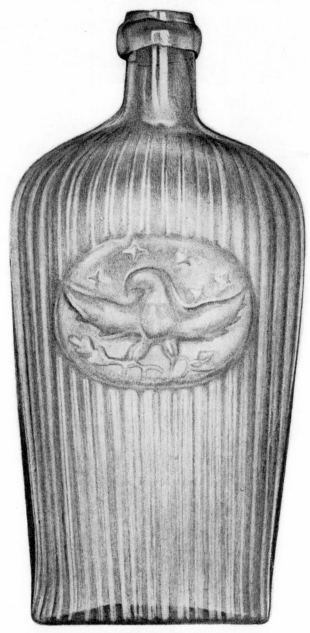

268 Pint flask, watercolor rendering by Orville
A. Carroll. 1845–50. Ribbed molded glass.
National Gallery of Art, Washington, D.C.
Index of American Design

patriotic symbols or historic subjects was popular. Both sides were usually decorated, and certain combinations were commonly paired. No matter what famous general was being honored by profile on one side of a flask, George Washington was bound to be on the other. The American eagle probably appears more often than any other symbol (plate 268). The ribbed flask is unusual in that the symbol occupies only part of the bottle face, with the ribbing being the dominant motif.

The process for making pressed glass was an extremely important development in the effort to make glass manufacturing less expensive. The new technique entirely removed the need for the glassblower by mechanically dropping the

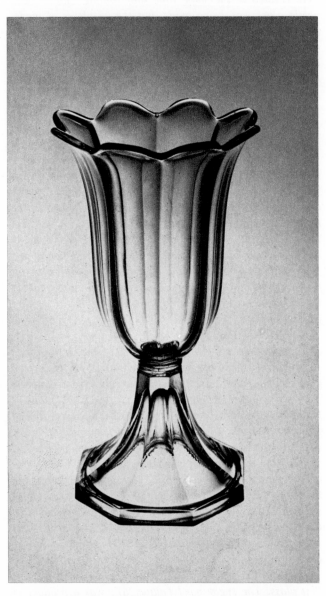

269 Boston & Sandwich Glass Company, Sandwich, Mass.
Vase. 1850–60. Greenish-yellow pressed glass, height 9¾".
Museum of Art, Rhode Island School of Design, Providence.
Gift of Priscilla H. Leonard, in memory of her uncle
Edward E. Leonard

finial is not unlike those often found on Queen Anne furniture, and the outline of the bowl certainly has affinity with the Queen Anne curvilinear form.

The first pocket bottles, or flasks, appeared in the early nineteenth century and were commonly made in full-size molds. The advantages of the mold are three: fewer skilled workmen were needed than for free-blown work; each man could turn out a greater quantity of work; and the standard capacity of the bottle could be guaranteed. The size of such bottles could vary from multigallon "carboys" to half-ounce perfume bottles, but the pint was the most widely used size for the flask. Decoration of the flask with

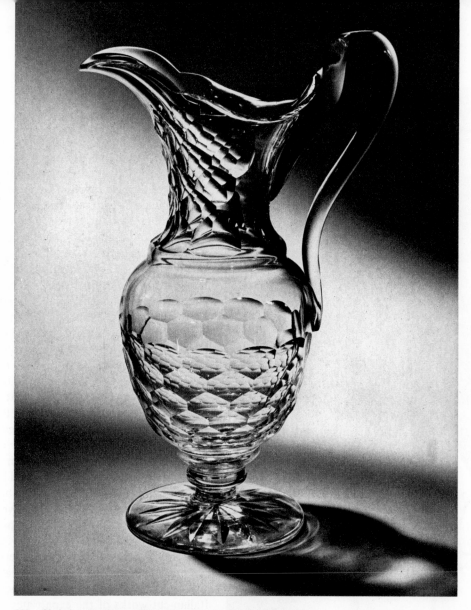

270　Christian Dorflinger Flint Glass Works, Long Island. Ewer.
c. 1852–63. Free-blown and cut glass, height c. 12¼″.
The Corning Museum of Glass, Corning, N.Y.

gather of hot glass into a heated metal mold and using a plunger to force the glass into the extremities of the mold. Because the mechanical plunger could drive the glass with much greater force than a glassblower's breath, stronger, more detailed patterns were created. Moldmaking became a separate business, and the glass firms bought their molds rather than make their own, often with the result that several firms produced particular forms from the same sort of mold. Also, successful designs were immediately copied by competitors, so that it is risky to venture an attribution to a particular firm without corroborative evidence. The popular tulip-shaped vase (plate 269) was issued by several major glass companies after having first achieved popularity as a ceramic vase from the Bennington Pottery Company. Obviously the days of the local glassblower, as the source of everyday tableware, were numbered, and the new manufacturers were able to create new designs suited to the pressed-glass technique.

Cut glass, derived from Europe, was being made in limited quantities in this country in the first decade of the nineteenth century. Cutting required a strong lead glass of high quality that was much more expensive than the glass used for pressing, and the number of handwork steps necessary to obtain the desired effect of light reflection added to the cost. Thus only the more well-to-do could afford much glassware of the lead (flint) variety. Among other firms, Christian Dorflinger's produced such works as this ewer (plate 270), which was clearly an item for ostentatious display, being cut and engraved on an already expensive blown-glass body. The form is a combination of Rococo revival with a bit of the Renaissance in the basic shape of the body and was probably directly influenced by similar objects in silver. The combination of shallow and deep cutting is uniquely contemporary American in design. For technical achievement and exquisite handwork Dorflinger won prize after prize in world's-fair competitions.

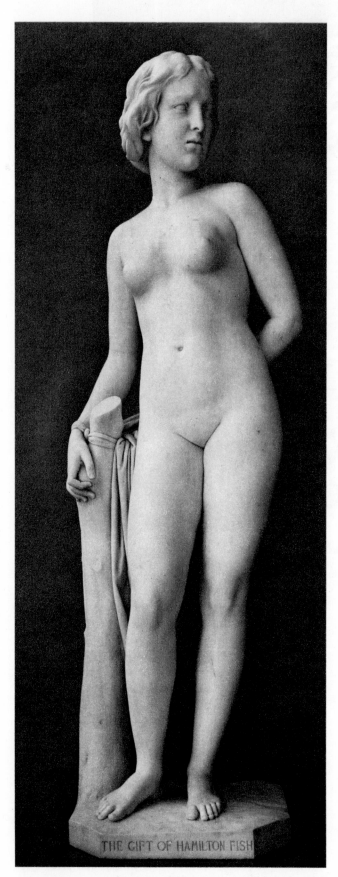

271 Erastus Dow Palmer. *The White Captive*. 1859. Marble,
height 66". The Metropolitan Museum of Art, New York.
Gift of the Honorable Hamilton Fish, 1894

(continued from page 236)

THE NATIVE SCHOOL

Except for William Rimmer, who received little recognition in his lifetime, Erastus Dow Palmer (1817–1904) was the only native sculptor to concern himself primarily with ideal themes. Inspired by a cameo portrait, Palmer taught himself to carve shell and was fairly successful until failing eyesight forced him to work on a larger scale. He found almost instant acceptance with his first ideal bust, an *Infant Ceres* (1849), a portrait of one of his daughters. His *White Captive* (1859, plate 271), the finest of the mid-century ideal nude female figures, in its simplicity, proportions, and graceful *contrapposto*, is close to a Classic canon (if not the *Medici* or *Melian*, then the late Hellenistic *Cyrenean Venus*), with its softly rounded, stockily proportioned, youthful configuration. Palmer more nearly approached the Classic perhaps because he did go back to nature and redistilled an essence. The one un-Classical element in the statue is the head, which is typically Victorian. Rare for America at that time, the marble indicates a restrained response to the calls of the flesh. But *The White Captive* was saddled with a script to match any Victorian morality screed: an American maid, captured and bound by "savage" Indians, is sustained in face of the "grinning brutes" by her Christianity. Still, the lovely, introspective figure manages to rise above forgotten literary allusions.

Palmer's Albany studio was an efficient production unit, employing American stonecutters, some who became sculptors on their own. This may have something to do with the difference in texture of Palmer's marbles from the Italian-cut works of the expatriates.

The most original sculptor of the mid-century, William Rimmer (1816–1879), was an enigmatic personality who belongs to the tragic band of aborted talents that dot the pages of American art like reproaches. Barely a half-dozen of his sculptures are extant, just enough to make the works of his contemporaries pale into insignificance. Rimmer lived with the unsubstantiated belief that he was the son of the lost Dauphin. His father, a cobbler who died a drunkard, seems to have been a cultured man who raised his family in the legend of their royal descent, setting the psychological conditions which made it impossible for the son to adjust to his environment. Both father and son eked out a living, moving from Liverpool, where William was born, to Canada, to Maine, to Boston.

At about fourteen the young Rimmer carved a statuette in gypsum, called *Despair* (c. 1830, plate 272), unique in American sculpture of the period and unbelievable for someone so young. It is possibly the first nude figure done in the United States and, despite some awkwardness, a direct expression of emotion without the paraphernalia of Neoclassic allegory. The sense of terror, pain, and hopelessness expressed in this small figure must have come out of some deep recess of the boy's arranged to have it cast in bronze in 1906. The *Gladiator* is not only a consummate display of anatomical knowledge but also the representation of a being wracked by pain. The Neoclassic reminiscences, also present in Rimmer's drawings, are closer to the Romantic fire of Blake and Fuseli than to the elegant ideality of Canova and Thorwaldsen.

Isolated and unappreciated, Rimmer was a sculptor of Romantic agony in a garden of conventional beauty. His late small bronzes (1871) of *The Dying Centaur* and the *Fighting Lions* most clearly reflect the artistic purpose and the nature of the man.

In the early 1860s Rimmer began to lecture on anatomy in Boston and from 1864 ran his own school. He was

273 William Rimmer. *The Falling Gladiator*. 1861.
Bronze, height 63″. Museum of Fine Arts, Boston.
Gift of Miss Caroline Hunt Rimmer,
Mrs. Adelaide R. Durham, various subscribers

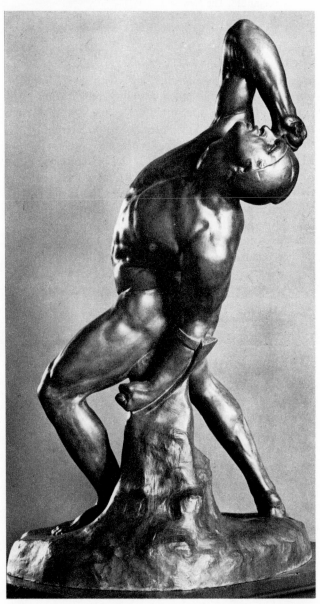

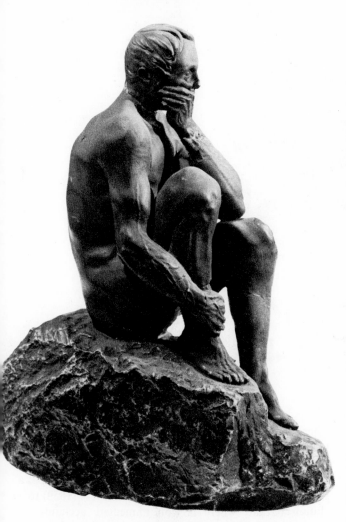

272 William Rimmer. *Despair*. c. 1830. Gypsum, height 10″.
Museum of Fine Arts, Boston.
Gift of Mrs. Henry Simonds

being and was to remain the essence of his life and work.

One might expect a brilliant career from such beginnings, but Rimmer abandoned sculpture for some thirty years, doing sign and scenery painting, pictures for Catholic churches, and portraits at $5 to $20 each. After marriage, he earned his living as a cobbler, with an occasional portrait thrown in. Then, through the friendship of a local doctor, he acquired enough knowledge to practice medicine. During this period there is mention of only one work, a portrait of his daughter, cut directly in stone.

In 1858, at forty-two, Rimmer was influenced to return to sculpture by the wealthy Bostonian patron of the arts, Stephen H. Perkins. His first mature work, as a tribute to Perkins, was a *St. Stephen* (1860), carved directly in granite. Exhibited in Boston, it found no buyer. But Perkins advanced Rimmer the money to begin the life-size *Falling Gladiator* (1861, plate 273). The *Gladiator* was not taken seriously by Bostonians, but Perkins persevered and, in 1862, took a cast with him to Europe, where it received good notices. Though it helped spread Rimmer's reputation, it was buried in the storeroom of the Cooper Union Museum until Daniel Chester French

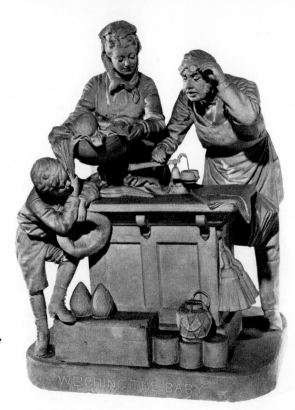

274 John Rogers. *Weighing the Baby*. 1876. Plaster, height 21". The New-York Historical Society

apparently a brilliant teacher, and, with the publication of *Elements of Design* (1864), his fame spread. Peter Cooper offered him the directorship of the School of Design for Women in New York, and he served successfully in that capacity until 1870. Back in Boston, he returned to lecturing on anatomy. In 1877 his monumental *Art Anatomy* was published. In all, Rimmer received only two public commissions, the *Alexander Hamilton* in 1864, now on Commonwealth Avenue, Boston, and *Faith* (1875) for the Plymouth Monument, which was garbled in the cutting. After his death, Boston had a twinge of conscience, held an exhibition of his work at the Museum of Fine Arts, and then forgot him. It is clear in hindsight that Rimmer's art belongs to the mainstream of European mid-century naturalistic sculpture, rather than to the academic Neoclassicism of Rome.

The "Rogers Groups," so popular in the United States during the second half of the nineteenth century, were the sole province of John Rogers (1829–1904) and a uniquely American phenomenon—a successful union of art, industry, and commerce. These parlor ornaments reproduced in plaster and priced from $3 to $25 sold some eighty thousand copies during the life of the company Rogers established. Considering their popularity, it is surprising that they had no competition, for as counterparts of genre painting reproduced in Currier & Ives prints, they appealed to a plebeian taste, while sharing with all Victorian art a predilection for the literary, the morally didactic, and the sentimental.

Rogers came of a cultured New England family in financial decline. He studied "practical subjects" in high school and worked as a machinist, puttering all the while at modeling clay figure groups that pleased his friends.

Then in 1858 he went to study in Paris and Rome. From the beginning this level-headed Yankee knew that neither Italy nor the art being produced there was for him, though he could learn from it. After his return, he sent a small genre group called *The Checker Players* (1859) to a church bazaar, where it won immediate acclaim. He followed it with *The Slave Auction* (1859), a topical subject of potential appeal. Wasting no time, he opened a studio in New York and began producing plaster casts of *The Slave Auction* from gelatin molds. When shops refused to handle the group for fear of offending prosouthern customers, he arranged to peddle them in the streets. After the war he turned to a good-humored kind of genre, a three-dimensional equivalent of the paintings of Mount and Bingham, along with occasional social themes and subjects from literary sources.

Whatever the topic, the groups were essentially the same—anecdotal accounts rich in detail, local color, and human interest. Rogers was a natural storyteller and a skillful craftsman. His observations became more acute and his handling more assured; his control of the medium improved rapidly, and he attained a remarkable descriptive facility. He never attained the heroic, but in the finest of the genre groups, such as *Weighing the Baby* (1876, plate 274), he re-created rural life with warmth, nostalgia, and genial humor. He had a strong plastic sense and emphasized the underlying structure of a form even when it was overladen with detail. He managed also to hold the action to a definable architectonic unit with a surprisingly complex interrelationship between volume and void. In addition, Rogers was an excellent portraitist.

(continued on page 243)

The first important production of porcelain in this country was undertaken at the Tucker Porcelain Company of Philadelphia, opened in 1826 by William C. Tucker. His aim was to produce tableware able to compete with fashionable European models yet sufficiently modified in design for a broad appeal to American taste, though his output included occasionally extremely elaborate Empire style vases and pitchers. The Tucker products were well received, and in 1827 the owner was awarded a medal by the Franklin Institute for "the best porcelain made in Pennsylvania." William Tucker died in 1832, and under the subsequent management of Thomas Tucker a classical simplicity

typified much of the firm's production. This coffee service (plate 275), designed for Thomas's bride in 1838, reflects Tucker taste of the time. The only decoration is a wide gold line around foot and rim, the script initials, and the laurel-leaf swag. The design of the individual pieces is not based on specific Classical prototypes but rather presents the style in a more restrained fashion than did European models of that era. In spite of the quality of such work, the firm could not overcome the snob appeal of European-made porcelain, nor could it compete in price with earthenware and stoneware producers; Tucker closed its doors in 1838.

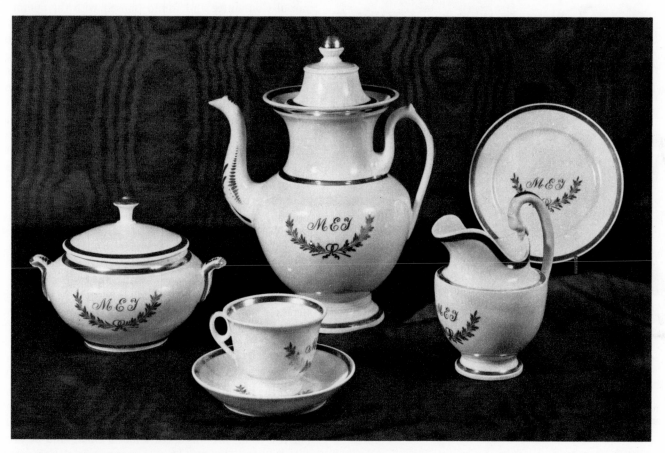

275 Tucker Porcelain Company, Philadelphia. Coffee service. 1835–38. Porcelain, height of pot 8⅞″. The Metropolitan Museum of Art, New York. Rogers Fund, 1963

(continued from page 242)

The specialists in the field of commissioned monuments were Henry Kirke Brown, Clark Mills, and Thomas Ball. The scale of such monuments, and especially the exigencies of the equestrian statue, inevitably led to the replacement of stone by bronze as the preferred material. The effect of the change freed the sculptor from the ubiquitous stonecutter and allowed him to express himself directly (not always an advantage), and cut the tie with the white marble of antiquity and all it symbolized, signaling a

search for new directions. The struggles of these first "bronze-age" sculptors with the medium were direct, practical, almost technological, and unpretentious.

When Henry Kirke Brown returned after four years in Italy, he was eager to revert to the American subject. For the next several years he immersed himself in the Indian theme, sketching Indian settlements and working on sculptures from the studies. One of these, the *Aboriginal Hunter* (1846), distributed by the American Art Union, was extremely successful. The bronze statuettes, produced

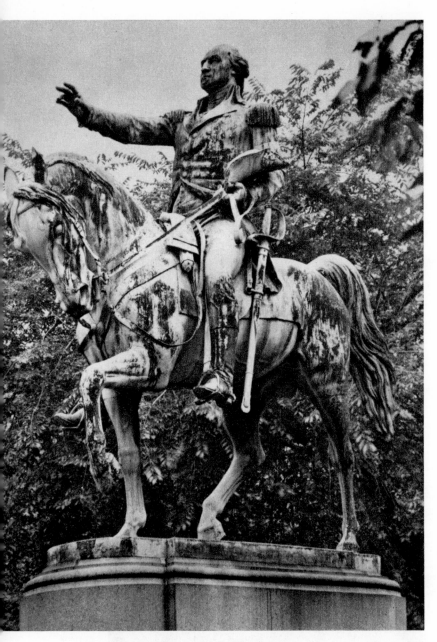

276 Henry Kirke Brown. *George Washington*. 1853–56. Bronze, height 13½'. Union Square, New York

which he must have known, but is even closer to the vigor of Verrocchio's *Colleoni* in Venice. There is a nice balance between the calm, imperious Washington in his regimentals and the stride of the spirited stallion. This was the high point of Brown's career, combining a routine naturalism with an emotional verve in a way which he never managed again.

Clark Mills (1815–1883) was self-taught as a sculptor. In Charleston he learned to be an ornamental plasterer and in the early forties began to do life masks, for which he developed a new procedure. He adapted the masks into portrait busts and soon had many customers. Though rather crude, his work attracted some attention. Mills happened to meet the chairman of the Jackson Memorial Committee and found himself with the commission to execute an equestrian statue of General Jackson (1848–52). He had certainly never seen an equestrian statue and scarcely any full-length figures and had never done anything but a bust portrait. However, he decided on a rearing horse, both forelegs off the ground, a conception that had few successful precedents anywhere. In view of Mills's training, the execution and casting of the *Jackson* was no small achievement. He built his own foundry; learned to cast bronze; and, in spite of some disasters, including having to cast the horse six times before he got an acceptable result, managed to complete the group late in 1852. It was erected in Lafayette Square, opposite the White House, and the public and press were ecstatic. Congress voted him an unheard-of $20,000 bonus and almost immediately appropriated $50,000 for the long-deferred equestrian statue of Washington, for which Mills was awarded the commission.

He built a larger studio and foundry to handle his increased activities, including orders for replicas of the *Jackson* monument. Though a gale destroyed his studio and the foundry burned, he completed the *Washington* and the colossal Crawford *Armed Freedom*, which was placed atop the new Capitol dome in December, 1863. But at the height of his phenomenal success, government support ceased, apparently because he was suspected of dishonest practices in handling the metal assigned to him. The rest of his life was spent under a cloud, and he produced little. The *Washington*, erected in Washington Circle in 1860, is a timid and lackluster affair. The *Jackson*, with all its almost archaic awkwardness, is a daring conception; it captures a great deal of Jackson's challenging spirit and personality.

Slightly younger than Brown and Mills, Thomas Ball (1819–1911) came to sculpture late, after an indifferent career as a painter, so that most of his monument sculpture postdates the Civil War. He turned to sculpture with the aid of John C. King, a Boston sculptor. Three years (1854–57) in Florence, executing portraits and experimenting with ideal themes, left him apparently untouched by Neoclassicism. In Boston again, he began an equestrian *Washington*. Like Mills, Ball had never done a life-

in his own studio foundry, were among the first cast in this country.

By 1850 Brown's Brooklyn studio was busy with a series of monumental projects, among them the colossal equestrian *Washington* (1853–56, plate 276) for New York. Brown's *Washington* had been recently preceded by two other commissions for equestrian monuments, the *Jackson* of Clark Mills in 1848, and the Crawford *Washington* for Richmond in 1849. Brown had seen the *Jackson* in process when he began the plaster model of his 14-foot-high horse and rider. Aesthetically, the Brown *Washington* is the finest equestrian statue of that period; it has something of the grandeur of the *Marcus Aurelius* in Rome, size figure before he undertook the colossal equestrian monument. Devising his own armature on a turntable, and his own procedures, he completed the plaster of the 16-foot group in 1861, but, with the war, bronze was needed for cannons, and it was not until 1869 that it was cast and erected in the Boston Public Gardens. It has a clean look, a calm dignity, and is altogether the finest of his monuments, though it lacks the bravura of the Mills *Jackson* or the verve of the Brown *Washington*.

In contrast to the expatriates, who were concerned with aesthetic theory, the first generation of native monument makers was essentially pragmatic, and though they may have thought of themselves as artists, acted more like entrepreneurs, manufacturers, or engineers. They did not think of themselves as superior to the public; they were interested not in raising its aesthetic quotient but in giving it what it wanted.

PORTRAITURE

Most sculptors depended on bust portraits for a living, and there seems to have been an inexhaustible number of insignificant people eager to have their likenesses in plaster or stone. A gallery of nineteenth-century portrait busts can be one of the more numbing experiences in art. All seem to come from the same hand, the same eye, the same brain. One can scarcely differentiate between the native and the expatriate, except that the works of the latter, cut by Italian craftsmen, have a softer and more polished surface, while those of the former, often cut by local workmen, are somewhat harsher, more insistent on detail, and more photographic.

It was common practice for portraitists to take their plaster busts to be carved in marble in Italy, and some, like Joel Tanner Hart (1810–1877) and John Adams Jackson (1825–1879), stayed there to do portraits of visiting Americans.

At home the native sculptors were also busy supplying the demand. There was an unusual concentration of sculptural activity in Cincinnati and Boston. Bostonians seem to have had a special affinity for the marmorean art, and the American colonies in Florence and Rome were almost Boston outposts.

The South, continuing provincial in matters of art, had few of its own sculptors, depending on itinerants. Alexander Galt (1827–1863), who spent many years in Florence, became *the* sculptor of the Confederacy. Washington, D.C., naturally attracted many portraitists to do busts of political personalities.

In the Middle West, Thomas Dow Jones (1811–1881) continued the tradition in Cincinnati; James Wilson Alexander MacDonald (1824–1908) was active in St. Louis before the war; and Leonard Wells Volk (1828–1895),

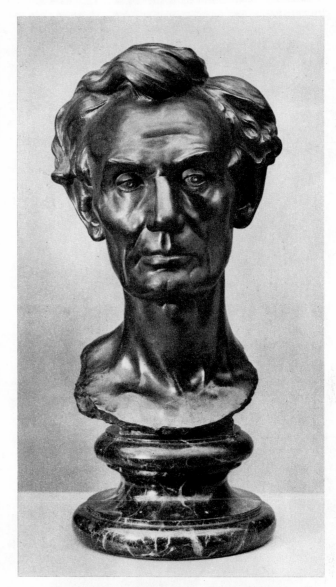

277 Leonard Wells Volk. *Abraham Lincoln*. 1860 (cast 1914 from model of 1860 from a life mask of 1860). Bronze, life size. The Metropolitan Museum of Art, New York. Gift of Theodore B. Starr, 1914

who began his career in St. Louis and spent several years in Rome, became the leading sculptor in Chicago. He is probably best remembered for his portrait bust of Abraham Lincoln (plate 277), done in 1860; the pre-bearded likeness, used so frequently by subsequent delineators, has become the accepted image of the youthful Lincoln. Though based on the life mask Volk made at the time, it is one of the first evidences of a break from the dryness of academic eclecticism and literal naturalism, presaging the style that was to become dominant in the next generation.

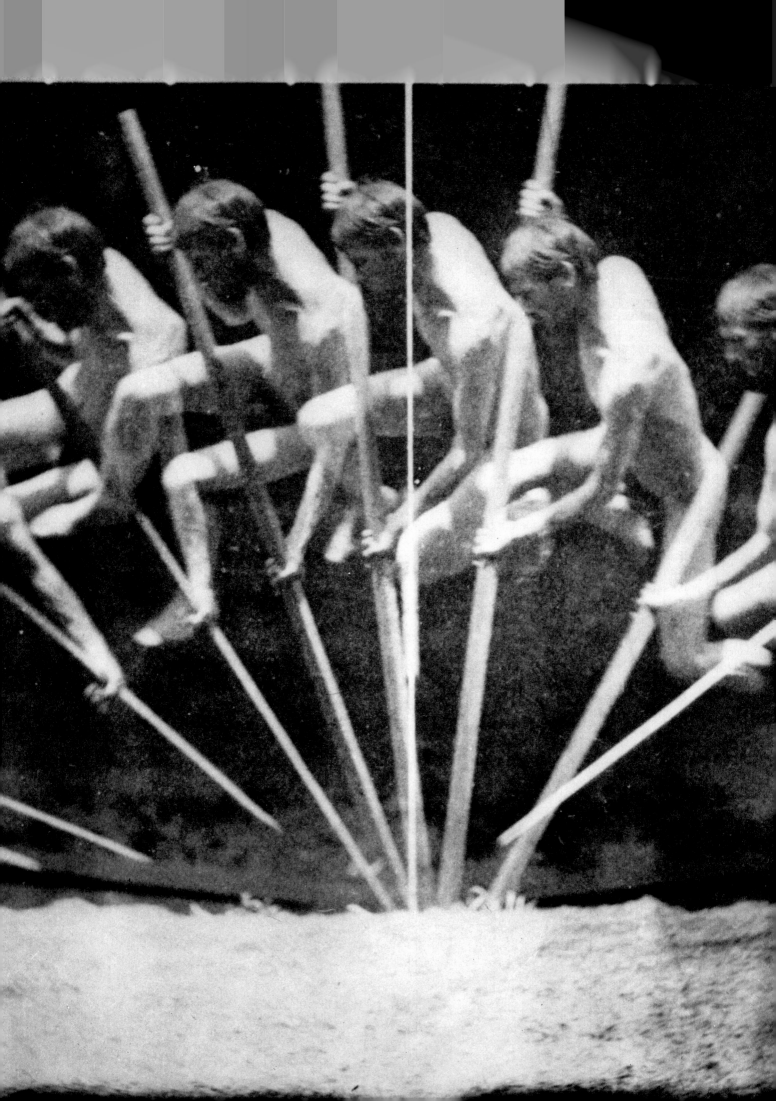

Part 4
CIVIL WAR TO 1900
Reconstruction and Expansion

The changes that followed the Civil War transformed the very nature of American society by the turn of the century. In 1860 the United States was still largely agricultural, but by 1900 the nation had become the leading industrial power in the world. Twelve new states had been added to the union; the population had increased from about 30 million to about 76 million, of whom 15 million were immigrants; the land mass was consolidated; and unprecedented natural resources were available for development.

Even before the Civil War, the American capitalist had become aware that commerce offered less wealth than did production and had begun to move from mercantile to industrial capitalism. After the war new industries expanded eventually into giant corporate bodies and trusts. Cities grew as the flood of workers from rural America and Europe migrated to industrial areas to form a new proletariat. The need to feed an ever-increasing industrial population led to the cultivation of large tracts of land and a growth of industries to supply farm machinery and to process and package products. Industrial, agricultural, and commercial complexes were tied together by new canals, new roads, and an ever-expanding railroad system.

However, America's physical expansion posed new problems—equitable distribution of wealth; control of the power inherent in capital; adjustment of political democracy to an undemocratic economy; recurrent depressions; unemployment and labor strife; urban blight; declining farm income with increasing agricultural production; despoliation of natural resources; assimilation of immigrants; accommodation of political institutions to new demands; and foreign policy. Such problems are still with us.

Peddling of influence, contracts, and jobs; bribery and fraud; waste at public expense; thievery of public lands, resources, and funds—all were common in government at all levels. The industrial and financial North harvested the major fruits of victory; the agricultural West was thrown a bone; the prostrate South was stripped of economic and political power. Almost limitless financial power was centered in the New York banks, and class distinctions were now entirely based on wealth. The road to social and cultural standing was the assumption of European aristocratic trappings. During the "Gilded Age," American millionaires began to emulate the manner and scale of princely existence, building fake palaces and forming "old master" collections.

In an even more profound sense culture had been affected by the phenomenal growth of America into a pluralistic society. In different parts of the country people of different ethnic origins, engaged in different occupations, lived, acted, and thought differently, and it had become difficult to define an American destiny equally meaningful for all. The tasteless extravagance of the *nouveau riche* was matched by a "know-nothing" anti-intellectualism of the rural masses, who saw in culture the evils of cities, the effeteness of the arts, and the decadence of wealth. In this environment the status of the American artist deteriorated. In addition, bread-and-butter portraiture had finally been undermined by photography. The distinction between "fine" and "popular" art became sharper as class interests and tastes diverged. Popular art became increasingly anecdotal and sentimental, and the fine arts took on the guise of gentility. American society found adequate expression perhaps only in its architecture: the artless nature of industrial construction, the flamboyant eclecticism in commercial building, and finally the genius of the Chicago School. Few voices were attuned to the raucous sounds of industrial expansion. Much of the art of the time was a false facade behind which the harsh realities of life were hidden.

11
Architecture: The Battle of Styles

The architecture of the nineteenth century as a whole, and of the second half specifically, has commonly been described as an epic struggle between the forces of reaction expressed in eclecticism and those of progress embodied in functionalism. However, it was an exuberantly productive era, fascinating in its failures as well as in its successes. What was once seen as a single undeviating line of development from Darby's iron bridge over the Severn to the International Style now seems too simplistic. Recent historians have rediscovered aspects of eclecticism which had either an important influence on the mainstream or aesthetic validity in their own right. The separation between architect and engineer in the latter half of the century was real, but architects were not blind to advances in technology. Many had engineering training, some even made important contributions to building technology, and every large architectural firm had its engineer. However, the gap between the purely utilitarian construction of bridges, railroads, canals, dams, or factories and that of traditional structures such as public buildings and dwellings had become irreconcilable. Architecture and engineering had become distinct and specialized professions.

It was in the gray area between engineering and architecture that aesthetic confusion occurred. The problem showed itself clearly in the railroad station, where the train shed was entrusted to the engineer and the station building itself to the architect. Commercial architecture in general teetered between utility and public presence. To be profitable the commercial building had to be serviceable and economical, but it often had to appeal to aesthetic taste as well. Ornateness was directly related to the status consciousness of the client.

Building activity fell off with the financial depression of 1857, and the decline naturally continued through the Civil War, but the postwar boom fostered public and private building on an unprecedented scale. The period is characterized not only by a new level of extravagance but also by an uninhibited and often misguided mingling of elements from various historical sources. The result was at times a provincial pastiche, labeled aptly enough the "General Grant Style," since its life span coincided with the General's term as President (1869–77).

From the end of the Civil War to the Philadelphia Centennial Exhibition in 1876, American taste accepted with equanimity two distinct revival styles, the Victorian Gothic and the French Second Empire. On the face of it, no two modes could be more disparate: the one medieval, towered, pointed-arched, asymmetrical, and polychromed; the other Classical-oriented, mansard-roofed, round-arched, symmetrical, ordered, and, at least in its origins, essentially monochromatic. Yet, somehow the two were converted to a common aggressively plastic picturesqueness expressive of the brash adventurism of the period itself. Churches, schools, libraries, and museums were normally Gothic, while governmental and commercial buildings, or anything intended to appear palatial or luxurious, were more frequently Second Empire.

(continued on page 250)

DECORATIVE ARTS

The Centennial Exhibition in Philadelphia in 1876 introduced several conflicting trends in decoration, from the revival of our colonial heritage to exotic Eastern modes. Various decorators and designers began then to mingle Moorish, East Indian, and Japanese elements, not always distinguishing among the styles they were incorporating. Interest in the Near East was evident in the use of cushions and divans, inlaid tables, brass objects of all kinds, and decorative screens. Many clients had special corners treated in exotic manners, and some even had entire Moorish rooms. The finest such room (colorplate 34) was designed for Arabella Worsham and later owned by John D. Rockefeller. Here divans, cushions, and the rich Oriental rug are almost subordinated to the lavish overall decorative scheme. The woodwork is covered with both deep carving and polychromed ornament taken from Moorish models. The furniture is attributed to George Schastey, who was known for such work and had been one of the "hits" of the Centennial Exhibition. The cabinets and other pieces are carved even more elaborately than the woodwork, and inlay is incorporated throughout. Custom work of such quality was obviously not available to all, but much of the manufactured furniture was designed to satisfy a similar taste.

(continued from page 249)

THE SECOND EMPIRE

The American version of the Second Empire, perhaps because it derived from engraved illustrations, remained somewhat dry, hard, and almost austere, its basic exuberance expressed in an elaboration of elements rather than lushness of surface. While the vogue in the sixties was reinforced by the popularity of Napoleon III and the Empress Eugénie, the architectural influence came not directly from France but through England. However, prefigurations of the mode had appeared in the United States before the war. The most characteristic feature, the mansard roof, named after the seventeenth-century French architect Jules Hardouin-Mansart, occurs as early as the fifties in isolated examples which seem almost a logical outgrowth of the Italian Villa style rather than a new importation.

James Renwick, whose early work had been in medieval revival modes, tried his hand at the Second Empire style in several buildings indicative of an awareness of the new manner. In 1859 he designed a Second Empire building to house the Corcoran Gallery, now the Renwick Gallery (plate 278), Washington, D.C. It was executed in red brick with brownstone trim, and although it was obviously a monumental effort, the result was still a somewhat muddled and provincial reflection of Napoleon III's extension of the Louvre in Paris.

Most Federal building during the General Grant era was in the Second Empire manner. The old State, War,

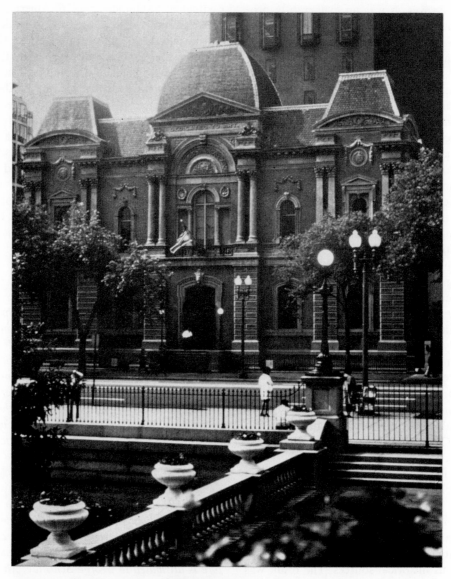

278 James Renwick. The Renwick Gallery (formerly Corcoran Gallery), Washington, D.C. 1859

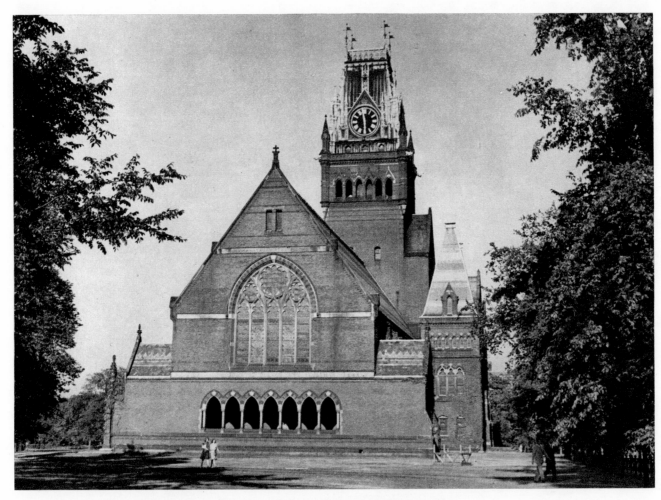

279 Ware & Van Brunt. Memorial Hall, Harvard University, Cambridge, Mass. 1870–78

and Navy Department Building (1871–88), now the Executive Office Building, in Washington, D.C., remains one of the prime examples of the style. It has served for so long as a model of bad taste that modern eyes can scarcely see it in its own terms, as a coherent, insistently plastic mass with a distinct personality. The Philadelphia City Hall (1871–81), designed by John McArthur, Jr., has been equally denigrated, perhaps because of the ungainly, out-of-scale tower capped by a gilded statue of William Penn, which was added more than a decade after the building was finished.

The Second Empire style was short-lived. Certainly not many buildings in the style postdate the panic of 1873. Although it was never a major manner in American architecture, two of the earliest skyscrapers in New York City, George Post's Western Union Building (1873–75) and Richard M. Hunt's Tribune Building (1873–75), both sported mansard roofs.

For urban houses the style became common in the late 1850s and remained popular through the mid-1870s, but it had perhaps its most successful and telling effect in suburban domestic architecture, where its sculptural qualities pleased the picturesque taste of the times. It

was freely substituted for, and even combined with, the earlier pointed Gothic or flat Italian Villa roofs.

The great resort hotels of the period were among the most original confections of Second Empire style. Splendid hostelries of gargantuan proportions were built in the Catskills, Saratoga, Newport, and Atlantic City. Nothing else quite exemplified the social pretensions and essential instability of the General Grant era as did those giant tinderbox fantasies. Economics, time, and fire doomed the delightful dinosaurs to extinction. Only a few crumbling relics can still be seen in such places as Cape May, N.J., and Block Island, R.I.

VICTORIAN GOTHIC

The Gothic Revival continued into the postwar era, although its character was radically altered. The newer, so-called "Victorian Gothic" was the achievement of a new generation influenced by John Ruskin's *Seven Lamps of Architecture*, lauding the English Gothic, and his *Stones of Venice*, in which he shifted allegiance to the Italians. The style, like the Second Empire, was short-lived; absorbed eventually by the Romanesque, it produced few notable monuments.

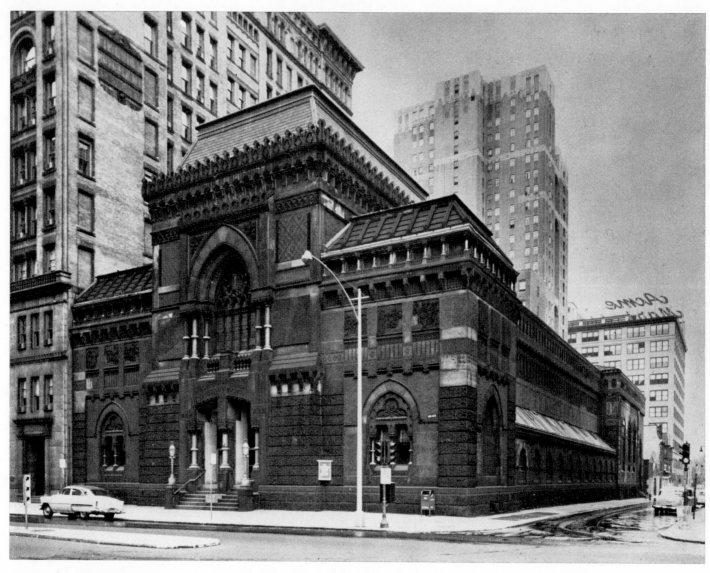

280 Frank Furness. The Pennsylvania Academy of the Fine Arts, Philadelphia. 1872–76

However, a new level of Romantic imaginativeness appeared in the Victorian phase. By emphasizing craft more than structure, Ruskin opened up a range of decorative possibilities. Every inch of the surface became expressive through color, texture, and ornament, producing an often indigestible richness. Victorian Gothic was less a revival style than an imaginative pseudo-Gothic manner in which medieval details were manipulated for picturesque effects. It had no first-rate practitioners, except for Richardson, who converted it to Romanesque, and Frank Furness, who made of it an idiosyncratic personal style. It lent itself most readily to ecclesiastical architecture, as exemplified by Ware & Van Brunt's apogee of the style, Memorial Hall (1870–78, plate 279), Harvard University, a building that is too large to be charming, and not good enough to be important. It was long singled out as a prime example of bad taste, chiefly because the style was out of fashion. It runs the Ruskinian gamut, from plain walls to filigreed spires, banded courses, polychromed tiles, richly textured and vari-colored masonry, through an extensive repertory of window, roof, and finial forms.

Ruskin's identification with the style may have influenced its use for art museums, as in the old Boston Museum of Fine Arts (1876–78), by John H. Sturgis and Charles Brigham, and the still extant wing of The Metropolitan Museum of Art (1878–80) by Calvert Vaux and J. Wray Mould. Academic institutions continued the preference for the Gothic.

Frank Furness (1839–1912) fits somewhere within the Victorian Gothic but not comfortably. An architect of brutal power and perverse originality, he seemed for a long time the epitome of General Grant vulgarity. His first important commission, the new Pennsylvania Academy of the Fine Arts (1872–76, plate 280), planned for the Centennial Exhibition, was a Ruskin-inspired mélange of materials and textures—rusticated brownstone, dressed sandstone, pink granite columns, red and black brick. In the 1880s Furness designed several banks in Philadelphia. His major commission in the 1890s was the massive en-

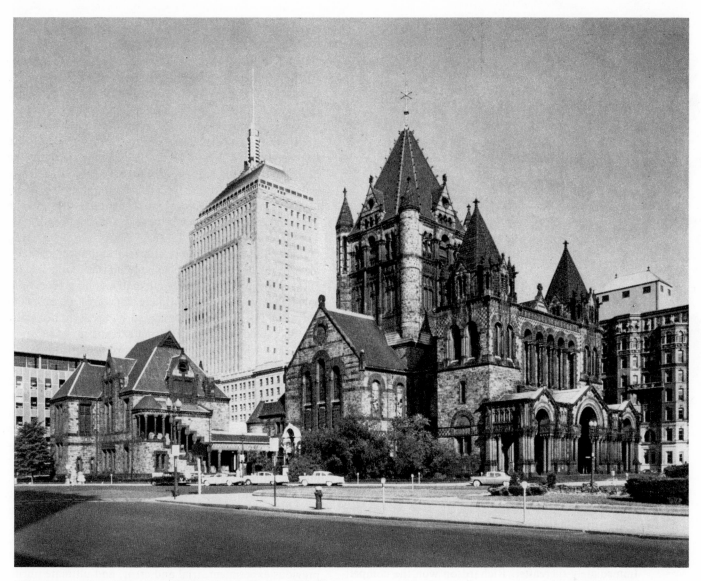

281 Henry Hobson Richardson. Trinity Church, Boston. 1872–77

largement of the Broad Street Station (1892–93), now destroyed, which contained the largest single-span train shed in the world. At his best he was frank, programmatically irreverent toward tradition but never ignorant, searching for a new style that would match and transcend the past.

In domestic architecture the Victorian Gothic influence was felt in the continuing picturesqueness of vernacular wooden building, achieving its culmination in the indigenous development called the Stick Style.

RICHARDSON AND
THE ROMANESQUE

No American architect ever dominated the age in which he lived so completely as did Henry Hobson Richardson (1838–1886). Louis Sullivan's masterpieces said more to the future than to his own time, and Frank Lloyd Wright's influence both here and abroad was as an individual rather than as the center of a movement. Richardson made a style which became that of his time. It has been called the Romanesque Revival, though it could perhaps more accurately be called "Richardsonian." He was ideally equipped to express the vigor, materialism, ruthlessness, and pretension of his time, yet he did not accept its standards. His clients responded by accepting his image of them; "robber barons" were happy to become "merchant princes." The hallmark of his style was quality —in design, materials, and workmanship—and quality symbolized money, security, and status.

Richardson created a monumental architectural style and played a major role in the transformation of domestic building, but in one respect he must be considered retardataire: he avoided the technological challenges of his age, continuing to build in an older tradition. Yet before his death he left to the next generation, in his Marshall Field Wholesale Store, a standard for commercial building which conditioned the development of the skyscraper in Chicago.

Richardson attended the University of Louisiana and then Harvard before going to Paris in 1859 to study ar-

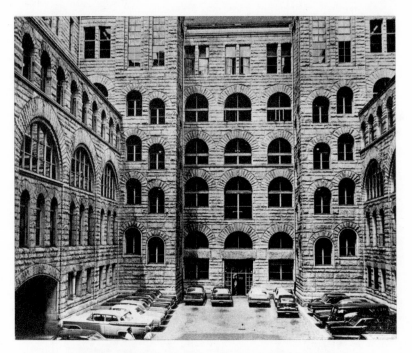

282 Henry Hobson Richardson. Courthouse courtyard,
Allegheny County Buildings, Pittsburgh. 1884–88

chitecture at the École des Beaux-Arts. When he settled
in New York in 1865, he was a soundly trained professional steeped in the French academic system. His first
mature work and his first Romanesquoid building was
the Brattle Square Church (1870–72), now the First
Baptist Church, Boston.

Immediately thereafter, Richardson won the competition for Trinity Church (1872–77, plate 281), Boston,
which established his reputation. Because of the truncated
triangular plot on Copley Square, Trinity had to be built
on a central plan. Richardson designed a building in the
round that offered a variety of picturesque views. The
pink granite in random ashlar with brownstone trim
reveals the Victorian Gothic bias, but, as the work proceeded, Richardson, never a drafting-room architect,
showed a growing interest in archaeological accuracy and
in the French Romanesque, evident in the detailing and
polychrome decoration of the apse. The central tower,
borrowed from the Old Cathedral of Salamanca by Stanford White, then working for Richardson, is perhaps too
pedantic in detail and somewhat flamboyant in comparison with the rest, but its richness carries the simpler lower
masses to a soaring climax.

The Allegheny County Buildings (1884–88), Pittsburgh,
were Richardson's outstanding government project, just
as Trinity was "his" church. They make use of a rather
unpleasant, light-gray, rusticated granite, coloristically
cold and neutral. The major courthouse facade, with its
huge central tower, is commonplace in conception and
mechanical in detailing, but Richardson's genius comes

through in the impressive massing of geometric volumes;
in the compelling rhythms of the fenestration in the
quadrangular interior court (plate 282); and in the primitive power of the masonry itself.

One of Richardson's important functional contributions was in the development of the library; he designed
five between 1877 and 1883. He examined freshly the
needs of the small public library in terms of storage,
service, and circulation; the picturesque grouping of exterior volumes and window bands expresses directly the
necessary disposition of interior spaces and lighting needs.
The Crane Memorial Library (1880–83, plate 283),
Quincy, Mass., is his most coherent and succinct statement in the library form. The building is a simple rectangular mass under a broad and gently sloping tiled roof,
enlivened by the softly swelling curves of three eyelid
dormers. The facade is dominated by an asymmetrically
placed gabled pavilion enclosing a band of small inter-
laced-arch windows above the massive void of the Syrian
entrance arch, which is flanked by a small stair turret.

Richardson's last major opus, the Marshall Field
Wholesale Store (1885–87, plate 284), Chicago, was historically his most important building, for it came at a
time when Romantic eclecticism was frittering away its
energies in elaborations on antiquated ideas and a younger generation of technologically oriented builders was
floundering without aesthetic direction. Undoubtedly,
the projection of his personality on the Chicago scene
was a catalytic element in the emergence of a modern
American architecture,

Richardson had already done a good deal of commercial work, and the Marshall Field Store was the result of
previous experiment, trial and error, and ultimate purifi-
cation. His Cheney Block (1875–76), now the Brown-
Thompson Store, in Hartford, Conn., shows an unusual

283 Henry Hobson Richardson. Crane Memorial
Library, Quincy, Mass. 1880–83

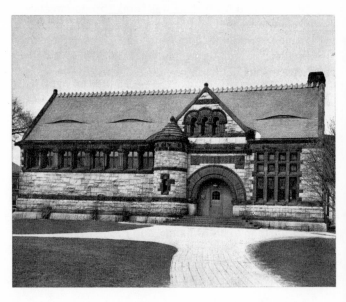

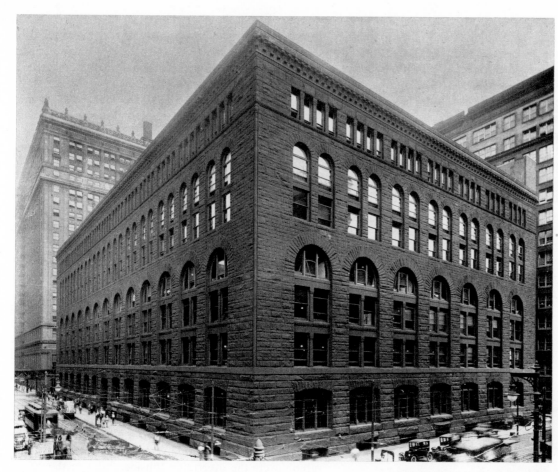

284 Henry Hobson Richardson.
Marshall Field Wholesale
Store, Chicago. 1885–87

balance between Romantic eclecticism and functional necessity, and in design and boldness of execution is hardly a breath away from the Marshall Field Store, but it remains revivalist.

In the Marshall Field Store revivalism was almost completely expunged. The round arches and rusticated masonry seen in the context of a square block capped by a flat cornice are not so much Romanesque as reminiscent of Florentine Renaissance palaces or, perhaps, simply of fundamental masonry forms inherited from the Romans and applied to a contemporary function with frankness and clarity. Richardson used iron columns as interior supports but self-bearing masonry for the exterior walls. It was his taste that insisted on the subtle modulation in proportion, rhythm, and texture, the changing forms and cadences of the windows, the all but imperceptible gradation in masonry courses and rustication, the variations in horizontal and vertical spacing. The exterior of the Marshall Field Store was the embodiment of an artistic personality working at the limits of capacity with honesty toward materials. Its destruction to make way for a parking lot was an act of cultural vandalism.

Richardson's style never led to a Romanesque revival in the sense of a return to historical sources. What re-

mained for a short span was an imitation of his Romantic picturesqueness. He had many followers: men who had worked intimately with him, like McKim and White; independent figures unsettled by the force of his vision, like Sullivan and Root; or the many western architects who may have seen his work only in magazines.

THE RISE OF THE SKYSCRAPER AND THE CHICAGO SCHOOL

When Louis Sullivan spoke of an office building as "a proud and soaring thing," he was looking beyond utility to the symbolism of the skyscraper as an expression of the modern world. The skyscraper is the major contribution of nineteenth-century America to the architectural repertory, and it took on an autonomous character only when the commercial building was forced skyward by post-Civil War population concentration and increased real estate values.

After the Civil War, buildings in the larger cities were not more than four or five stories in height, because clients were reluctant to rent space above the comfortable limit of human vertical mobility. The answer was the elevator. In 1857 the Haughwout Store in New York introduced for the first time in an urban edifice the passenger elevator developed by Elisha G. Otis. The Equitable Life Assurance Building (1868–70), New York, designed by Gilman & Kendall with George B. Post as engineer, was the first office building planned with an elevator; it contained five stories, was 130 feet high, and was an immediate financial success. It soon had competitors. The "elevator building," the first designation of the tall building, thus had its inception in New York. In spite of the panic of 1873, two major elevator buildings were begun in that year: the Tribune Building (1873–75), by Richard M. Hunt, and the Western Union Building (1873–75) by George B. Post. The early tall buildings were generally erected in what might be called "mixed media": exterior self-bearing and partially floor-bearing masonry walls and interior construction of combined wrought and cast iron and masonry, usually brick. With variations, this remained the basic method of skyscraper construction in New York until about 1890.

285   William Le Baron Jenney. Home Insurance Building, Chicago. 1883–85

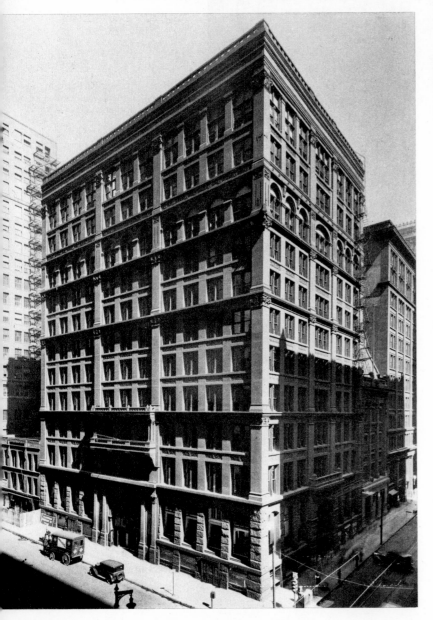

Apart from technological problems, the skyscraper had to be adjusted to an environment of traditional architecture in the city's center, and the increase in scale imposed new problems. A French château did not adapt convincingly to a ten-story office building. Eclecticism became ludicrous when mansard roofs and dormer windows were perched on palisades of masonry and glass. New York had little to do with either the technological or the aesthetic evolution, perhaps because its established architects were committed to eclecticism or because its clients were primarily concerned with the expression of wealth and status.

In retrospect Chicago seems to have been particularly fitted for skyscraper development. In forty years it had grown from a frontier village to become the teeming center of a voracious Western economic expansion. The ugly commercial encampment of industrial installations and flimsy slum dwellings was almost demolished overnight by the great fire of 1871. Chicago's architects had an unprecedented opportunity to build from scratch, and for the next two decades a building boom created the developed form of the skyscraper and the so-called "Chicago Style."

The Chicago School in its heyday produced almost exclusively commercial structures—office buildings, warehouses, stores, factories, hotels, and apartment houses—erected mainly in the constricted area of the Loop. The economic pressures to build vertically, inexpensively, and rapidly were the overriding considerations in the "functional" direction that the Chicago School took. New York architects achieved verticality by mechanical refinements in existing technology; Chicago moved toward the rationalization and transformation of the process itself.

The intimate connection among its architects must have had something to do with the rapid evolution of the skyscraper in Chicago. The story began with Major William LeBaron Jenney (1832–1907), who was the *paterfamilias* of the group and the first to arrive at iron skeletal construction. Jenney was an engineer with little pretension to architecture, which he left mostly to younger members of his firm.

Louis Henri Sullivan (1856–1924) was the greatest architect, the leading theoretician and propagandist, and the most interesting personality of the Chicago School. Born in Boston, he studied architecture and engineering at M.I.T. and the École des Beaux-Arts and came away with a contempt for architectural schooling and eclecticism and a great respect for engineering. He was the only one of the Chicago group who had formal architectural training. After his arrival in Chicago in 1875, he held a variety of architectural jobs before joining Adler in 1879 and becoming a full partner in 1881. From the beginning, Sullivan was the designer and Adler the engineer and businessman of the firm. Dankmar Adler (1844–1900), born in Lengsfeld, Germany, was a

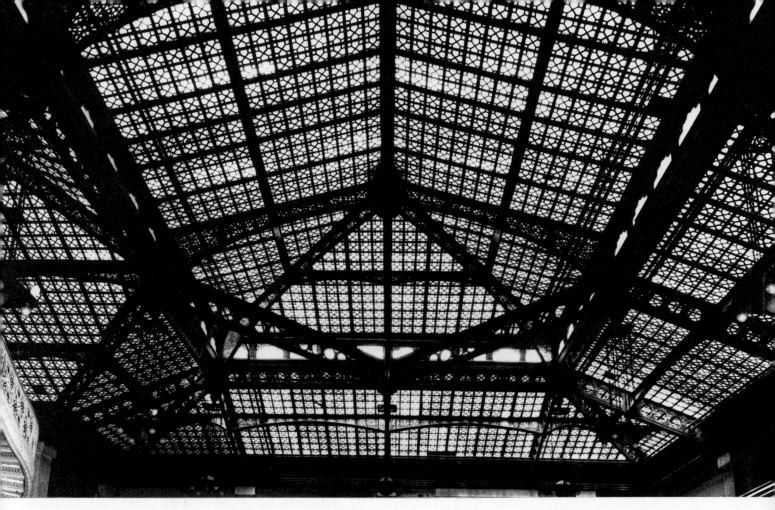

286 Burnham & Root. Interior court, The Rookery, Chicago. 1885–86

brilliant engineer, and whatever structural innovations the firm contributed were undoubtedly due to him, but the firm of Adler & Sullivan was more important to the stylistic than to the technical development of the Chicago School.

Sullivan's architectural evolution was somewhat apart from the mainstream of the Chicago School, though he designed some of its major monuments. In his early work (c. 1880–85) he contributed directly to the evolution of the glass cage, which became the trademark of Chicago. His early facades, though wide-ranging in decorative detail, were the most coherently organized and consistently open. In 1884, in the Ryerson Building, Sullivan first introduced the bay window, which became one of the features of the Chicago School; and in the same year his Troescher Building made the most complete early statement of the glass cage. The ingredients of his later work were already apparent.

The key monument in the technological evolution of the skyscraper was Jenney's Home Insurance Building (1883–85, plate 285), the first completely metal-framed building. The nine-story metal cage (two stories were added in 1891) was of iron for the first six and steel for the remainder, but, unfortunately, the ornamental skin did not live up to the revolutionary character of the skeleton. The Home Insurance Building had no immediate

effect and was absorbed rather haltingly into Chicago building practice.

For instance, The Rookery (1885–86), by Burnham & Root, was of traditional masonry construction on the exterior, but it had a complete iron-skeleton system in the interior court (plate 286). Lit through a glass skylight (with ornamental detailing added by Frank Lloyd Wright in 1905), the court of The Rookery remains one of the finest examples of a feature which became common in early skyscraper design. John Wellborn Root (1850–1891), who was responsible for The Rookery, worked first with Renwick. In Chicago he met Daniel Burnham, with whom he formed a partnership in 1873. Root, the designer of the firm, had a brilliant but short career; Daniel Hudson Burnham (1846–1912), the organizer and "impresario," though now generally underrated, had a long and influential one.

In 1886, the comparatively new firm of Holabird & Roche designed the Tacoma Building (plate 287), which finally arrived at the glass cage as the expression of skeletal construction. The completely rationalized metal structure contained many engineering innovations, including the stabilization of the subsoil by pumped concrete and the first use of rivets instead of bolts to tie the frame together. The Tacoma Building also expressed clearly for the first time the interior skeleton and trans-

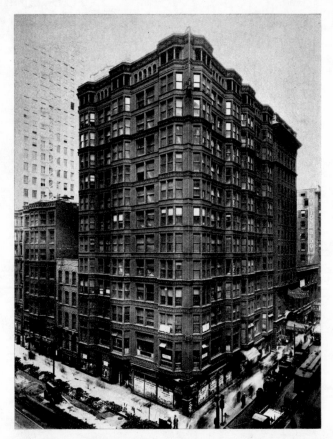

287 Holabird & Roche. Tacoma Building, Chicago. 1886–89

formed the exterior wall into a curtain of glass.

The Rand McNally (1888–90) was the first by Burnham & Root to have a complete skeletal frame and their first in which the frame was entirely of steel, but the exterior was disappointing in its fussiness. In contrast, the Monadnock (1889–91) is an example of formal purity with absolute simplicity of design, but is essentially a replica of the steel-skeleton type in masonry. The building exists today in excellent condition. Interior loads are supported by iron columns, but the brick bearing walls rest on a ground floor of stone. Logical in plan, beautifully executed, and memorable for its simplicity and power, the Monadnock Building still remains a paradox, an architectural tour de force in which an avant-garde form camouflages a traditional structure.

On the other hand, the Reliance Building (1893–95, plate 288) seems to belong, except for its oriel windows, more to the twentieth than the nineteenth century and is considered by many to be the masterpiece of the Chicago School and its most germinal building. Charles B. Atwood, Burnham's assistant after Root's death, is credited with the design. The basic concept derives directly from the Tacoma Building. The oriel bays, the neutral cage, and the dominance of glass are all refined to emphasize the lightness of construction and openness of surface. The transparent-skinned effect of the Reliance Building has hardly been surpassed, except through the present-day illusionistic use of glass for horizontal bands.

A few years earlier Adler & Sullivan were engaged in a project for St. Louis, the Wainwright Building (1890–91, plate 289), which was destined to establish the dominant skyscraper mode in America until well into the twentieth century. In this building Sullivan arrived at a personal synthesis and opened a different avenue of skyscraper design. The skeletal structure takes a columnar form with base, shaft, and capital, which Sullivan explained in retrospect as best expressing the function of the skyscraper. The first two floors (the base) are designed to accommodate stores and public offices; above, the shaft contains a series of identical floors with modular office units; and topping the whole is the capital, which hides the terminus or return of the utilities complex originating in the basement. So far the form expressed the utilitarian and structural function of the building, but Sullivan's conception—"form follows function"—included another ingredient, the "emotional" expression of the building's nature, or social function. The Wainwright rises from a simple, wide-windowed base of red granite and brown sandstone, straight up through red-brick piers with recessed decorated spandrel panels of red terra cotta, to a luxuriant top-story frieze, ending in a bold cornice. However, in order to achieve a sense of organic unity, verticality, and cubical mass, he was forced to belie the skeletal structure. There is no structural reason for the emphasis on the corner piers, for the introduction of alternate piers containing no metal bearing members, nor for the cornice and frieze with its bull's-eye windows. By emphasizing verticality and mass, Sullivan introduced a stylistic counterpoise to the emergent Chicago concept of cage and openness.

It is one of the accidents of history that Sullivan's skyscraper style was not better represented in Chicago. His masterly Guaranty Building (1894–95), now the Prudential, was built in Buffalo. It is almost a twin of the Wainwright, but it appears lighter because the entire skin is of terra cotta and the corner piers are greatly reduced, and more vertically accented because the piers are spaced more closely.

More expressive of skeletal construction and more central to the Chicago School than either Sullivan's vertical shaft or the oriel type was the neutral cage. The cage form was inherent in the nature of commercial buildings, already discernible in the early Boston granite warehouses and in the cast-iron buildings of Bogardus. The reduction in weight achieved by metal framing allowed increased height, the reduction of wall surface permitted more glass area and thus better lighting, and the reduction in structural elements made for greater flexibility in the use of interior space, while the lower cost and speedier construction were decided economic advantages.

The cage type achieved jewel-like perfection in a series of small buildings erected at the turn of the century. The Gage Group (1898–99, plate 290) consists of three

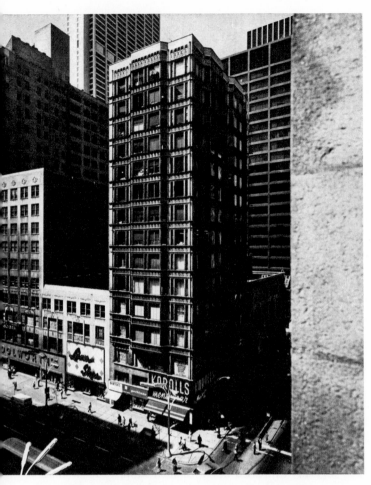

288 Burnham & Root. Reliance Building, Chicago. 1893–95

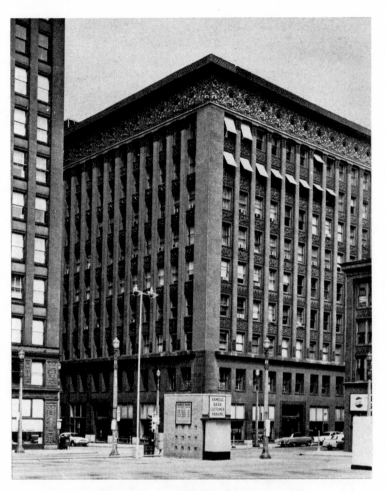

289 Adler & Sullivan. Wainwright Building, St. Louis. 1890–91

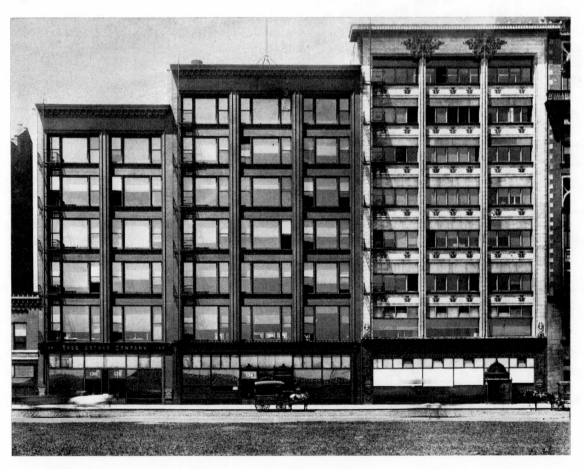

290 Holabird & Roche and Louis Sullivan. Gage Group, Chicago. 1898–99

attached buildings, two adjacent and identical in design by Holabird & Roche, one of two bays and six stories and the other three bays and seven stories; and the third by Sullivan, of three bays and eight stories, with four added in 1902 by Holabird & Roche without altering its character. The exquisite ensemble is hardly matched for airy grace and elegance. The proportions vary slightly and show subtle refinements: Holabird & Roche's somewhat sturdier and more vertical, Sullivan's lighter and more horizontal. Holabird & Roche here produced frank examples of an architecture of steel and glass. Sullivan's facade may appear fussier, but the proportions and the delicacy in detailing are superior. He achieved greater lightness and horizontality by devising a new kind of window with a band of translucent glass above clusters of narrow vertical panes. Certainly his cornice is a more

291   Louis Sullivan. Carson, Pirie, Scott Store, Chicago.
      1899 (extended 1903–4, 1906)

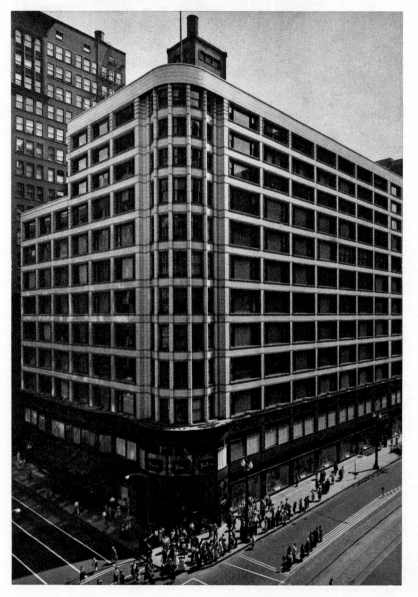

fitting climax. Only in the ornament does the purity of intention seem contradicted. The small decorative elements in the horizontal bands are questionable, but the elaboration of the ground-floor framing and the floral explosions above the vertical piers are Sullivan at his exuberant best.

The Carson, Pirie, Scott Store (plate 291) is Sullivan's last major work and his masterpiece. The nine-story, three-bay unit on Madison Street just off State was erected in 1899. In 1903–04 Sullivan added a larger section twelve stories high, with three bays on Madison and seven on State. D. H. Burnham & Co. completed the State Street block in 1906 with the addition of five bays. The only break in the cagelike block is the round section that turns the corner. Here Sullivan contrasted a vertical accent with the pronounced horizontality of the rest. The two lower floors are treated as a unit, with large display windows framed in lavish metal decoration. Above, the walls rise sheer and unadorned for nine stories. Unfortunately, the tenth floor has been remodeled and the original cornice replaced by an ungainly parapet. The entire building above the second floor is sheathed in thin terra-cotta tile, the windows are cleanly recessed and delicately framed, and the only ornament is a continuous reticent banding at windowsill and lintel, emphasizing the horizontal. The metal frame is nowhere else more logically expressed nor with such sophistication in scale, proportion, and nuance.

Aside from a mania for height, New York's main contribution to the skyscraper was the development of the tower as opposed to the Chicago flat-topped block or shaft. Even the earliest tall buildings in New York tended toward elaboration of terminal elements, and the spire eventually became characteristic of the New York skyline and symbolic of the skyscraper itself.

THE COLUMBIAN EXPOSITION AND "IMPERIAL CLASSICISM"

The World Columbian Exposition of 1893 in Chicago was a symbol of America's entry into the mainstream of international culture, parallel to that in economics and politics. Siegfried Giedion has called it the manifestation of "mercantile classicism," and James Fitch labeled its products "imperial symbols." Its false facades can also be seen as symbols of self-deception. This whipped-cream architecture hid crises of unprecedented scale—financial panic, class warfare, and urban degradation. It was a time of depression, unemployment, and the march on Washington by Coxey's Army. It was also a time of struggle between labor and capital, the Haymarket bombing, the Homestead massacre, and the Pullman strike. Cities were strangling in civic corruption, their poor sunk in filth and disease. The World's Fair and "mercantile classicism" in general did not advertise such difficulties. Columns and cupolas, cupids and cornucopias were expected to hide the crude facts of reality.

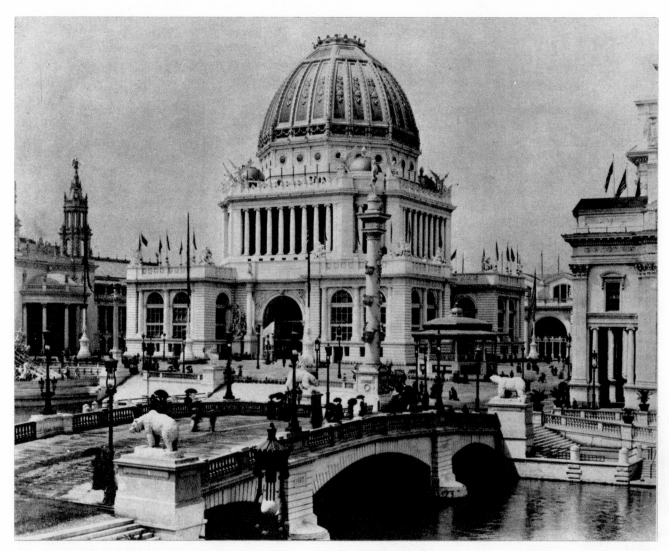

292 Richard M. Hunt. Administration Building, Columbian Exposition, Chicago. 1893.
Courtesy Chicago Historical Society

The stylistic choice of "Classicism" was predictable, for the Beaux-Arts manner, as an outgrowth of the Second Empire, had become the international fashion and practically *de rigueur* for world's fairs. The Columbian Exposition was approached by its architects and artists with more than ordinary seriousness. It was the first time that a group of American artists—architects, sculptors, and painters—had been called together to plan something. They conceived with rationality and grandeur, and the result, despite the plaster confections, was a vision of order and amplitude, culture and cleanliness to stand against the reality of urban boom and blight. The "city beautiful" was to have some effect in the next century, in zoning regulations and in formal planning for civic centers.

The basic plan of the Fair was the work of the great landscape architect Frederick Law Olmsted and his young partner, Henry Codman, who converted the marshy wasteland of Jackson Park along the lake front into a complex of lagoons, canals, ponds, islands, and piers. The major buildings were sited around a formal axis of lagoon and canal. Those awarded to the "visitors" were to be in the "Classical" style, white, naturally, and with a common cornice line. This portion of the Fair, which gave it the name "The White City," included Richard M. Hunt's conglomerate Administration Building (plate 292), McKim, Mead & White's Agricultural Building with a Pantheon dome, Van Brunt & Howe's Electricity Building, George B. Post's Manufacturers and Liberal Arts Building, and Peabody & Stearns's Machinery Hall, called the largest building in the world. At one end of the lagoon was Charles Atwood's Fine Arts Palace, with a facade literally copied from a Prix de Rome project. All these were "Classical" only in the broadest Beaux-Arts sense, a free adaptation of Renaissance and Baroque, Italian, French, and Spanish models.

In other sections of the Fair architectural styles were more varied. Notable among these buildings was the famous Sullivan Transportation Building, a simple, shedlike, arcaded structure, with its "Golden Door" sparkling in colorful, Orientally inspired Art Nouveau decoration. It was no less a structural lie than any of the Beaux-Arts examples.

(continued on page 262)

DECORATIVE ARTS

The Beaux-Arts tradition in architecture had its counterpart in metalwork. At the time of the Columbian Exposition of 1893, in Chicago, this gold presentation vase (plate 293) was designed in the Beaux-Arts style. The inspiration of the form is Classical, and the high-relief figures of body and base are indebted to Rome. In honor of Edward Adams, president of the American Cotton Oil Company, who was credited with saving the firm from bankruptcy, the vase pays tribute not only in the figures on the body but also in the addition of pearls and other gemstones to the already royal gift of gold. The symbols of cotton, the United States, and Mr. Adams's labors are blatant, and the obvious cost of the piece typifies the spirit of the age.

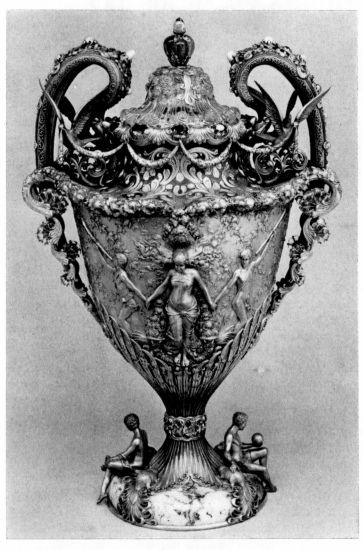

293 Paulding Farnham (for Tiffany & Co.). Vase. 1893–95.
Gold, height 19¼″. The Metropolitan Museum of Art, New York

(continued from page 261)

DOMESTIC ARCHITECTURE: STICK AND SHINGLE

After the Civil War the private house, for the middle and upper classes, had a spectacular architectural development from Richardson through Wright, and the vernacular of wooden building underwent a transformation and efflorescence in the so-called "Stick" and "Shingle" styles. Both grew out of revivalism but evolved as original and indigenous forms.

Richard Morris Hunt (1827–1895), who was most famous for his later palatial buildings, played an important role in the development of the Stick Style. According to Vincent Scully, who invented the term "Stick Style" and has written extensively about it, Hunt's wooden cottages, with their open interiors and their skeletal treatment of exteriors, were his best and most "American" works. Scully feels that they were rooted in the Romantic "rustic" architecture of Europe. He views Hunt's masterpiece in the style, the J. N. A. Griswold House (1862–63, plate 294), now the Art Association, Newport, R.I., as a combination of medieval half-timber, French rustic, and American framing. One might add Swiss chalet to this catalogue. The result is a new and fascinating kind of domestic architecture: rich in spatial relationships, juxtaposing void and solid, vertical and horizontal; proliferating shapes, textures, and carpentry forms.

Probably no single locale has so great a collection of fine Stick Style houses as Newport, which became the summer showplace of the rich in the postwar era. It is perhaps in its final phase that the style is best remembered —the matchstick fantasies of piled gables, spindly turrets, peek-a-boo dormers, and trellised porches, most specimens of which have fallen victim to fire, decay, economy, and changing taste. The Stick Style was fairly short-lived, extending not much beyond the early 1870s, and it had little effect on other American architecture. However, it prepared the way for the Shingle Style and offered a welcome interlude of imaginative improvisation.

In some basic aspects the Shingle Style was inspired by the English Queen Anne. Beginning in the 1860s, Richard Norman Shaw led a revolt of young English architects against the tyranny of the High Victorian Gothic and substituted the more modest Elizabethan cottage. Important features of the Queen Anne, or the "Shavian," style were the picturesque massing of exterior antiquarian elements, the domestic scale, the free plan, and the radical innovation that Hitchcock has described as the "agglutinative" interior, in which the rooms cluster around a central hall with an elaborate staircase derived from the medieval great hall.

Richardson in the United States seems to have arrived at a comparable point at approximately the same time. His houses of the late sixties and early seventies were in

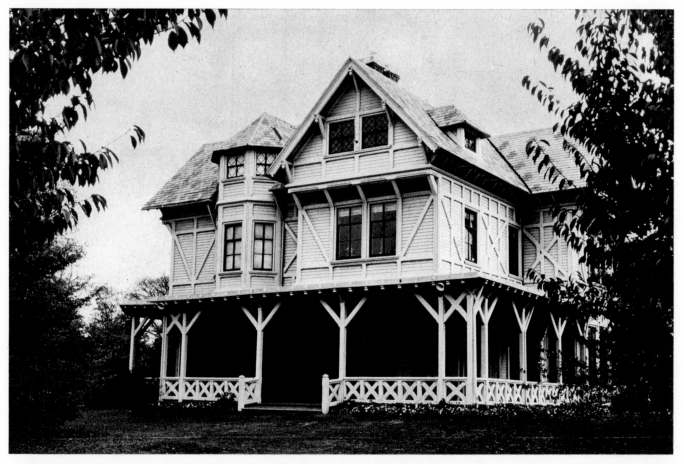

294 Richard M. Hunt. J.N.A. Griswold House (now Art Association), Newport, R.I. 1862–63

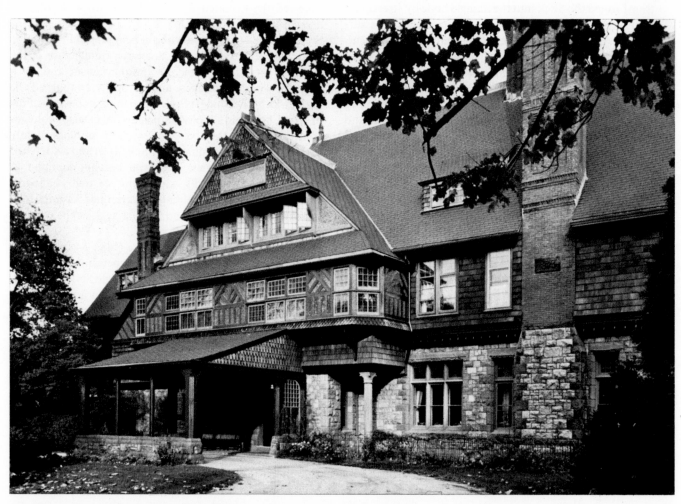

295 Henry Hobson Richardson. William Watts Sherman House, Newport, R.I. 1874–76

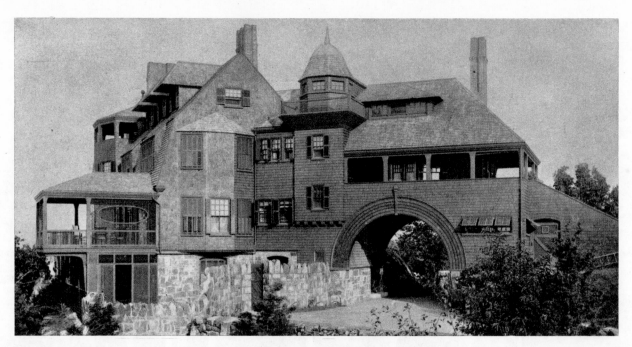

296 Peabody & Stearns. Kragsyde (G. N. Black House), Manchester-by-the-Sea, Mass. 1882–84.
From G. W. Sheldon, *Artistic Country Seats*, D. Appleton, New York, 1886–87, Vol. I

the Stick Style, but a house project (c. 1870) shows the first evidence of a Shavian type of hall, and in the F. W. Andrews House (1872–73), Newport, R.I., no longer extant, his interior plan was freer than that of any English models, and the porches around the central mass were certainly un-English. Almost at once, in the William Watts Sherman House (1874–76, plate 295), Newport, though still referring to the Queen Anne, Richardson transformed the Stick into the Shingle Style by stretching, as it were, a skin over the structural elements. The surface was swept clean, freeing it for textural enrichment, and the building masses were simplified. Much of the decoration and detailing is due to Stanford White, who also enlarged the house in 1881; later it was further expanded. The exterior is an Americanized adaptation of a Shavian manor house, with a lower story of granite and brownstone and an upper of cut shingles, grouped and banded casement windows, and half-timber with decorated plaster on the gable front. But the highly articulated interior volumes of the hall-staircase-fireplace complex are Richardson's major contribution to the Shingle Style and the architecture of the detached house.

The new style answered a deep-felt cultural need. It was natural for Americans to turn from the ugliness of industrial society and political corruption to the nostalgic vision of a rural and virtuous colonial past. This interest was reinforced by the Philadelphia Centennial Exposition, which fostered a recapitulation of American history and a reassessment of the American ethos. Prototype Colonial buildings were obviously compatible with the emerging Shingle Style in such features as the central stack, extrudent plan, and clapboard or shingle exterior surfaces. The revival of shingles for sheathing may have been motivated by either of two factors: The shingle was a rustic material and might imply a kind of Romantic

humbleness. Also, it acted as a scale in a continuous skin that could undulate, as opposed to the linearity and mechanical precision of a clapboard surface.

There is a span when Queen Anne, Colonial revivalism, and Shingle Style all seem to coalesce. One group of American architects assimilated the antiquarian picturesqueness of the Shavian Queen Anne manner without understanding its more radical aspects. Another group followed the Colonial strand. Still a third group finally arrived at a synthesis that is, properly speaking, the Shingle Style—American without being revivalist.

Richardson, returning to domestic architecture in the eighties, turned his back on antiquarianism and, in a series of wooden cottages, unequivocally established the hallmarks of the Shingle Style: interior openness and flow of space, bold and simple composition of exterior volumes contrasting with the sheltering voids of porches, lightly scaled woodwork recalling the Stick Style, and a stretched skin of rough shingles. The type became common in resort towns, especially along the eastern seaboard, where its informal, rambling picturesqueness implied a closeness to soil and sea and harked back to the colonial past.

Kragsyde, the G. N. Black House (1882–84, plate 296), in Manchester-by-the-Sea, Mass., is perhaps the masterpiece of Peabody & Stearns in the Shingle Style, a sprawling complex of varied shingled shapes on a rough stone base, cleverly composed, but rather fussy. The most radical of the younger men working in the style was Bruce Price, voracious in borrowing and exuberant in invention. In the smaller cottages he built for Tuxedo Park, N.Y., Price adapted the open, organic planning of the Shingle Style to a more compact design, emphasizing the geometric order of the elements disposed on a cross axis around a central fireplace.

The firm of McKim, Mead & White contributed greatly to the flowering of the Shingle Style in the early eighties, when it built summer cottages, mostly at Newport, for social-register clients. Stanford White had been in on the style as an assistant to Richardson, and in his new association he produced some of the most exquisite interiors in American architecture. Charles F. McKim had been with Richardson before White but turned to the Shingle Style only at the end of the decade. The Newport Casino (1879–81, plate 297) was the first major work of the firm in the style and one of three important club-houses designed by them. The facade is a rather unprepossessing symmetrical block, essentially reticent, Colonial in flavor. For modern taste, the most exciting aspect of the building is in the piazzas surrounding the court, undoubtedly designed by White. One sees a confection of spatial grace and airy lightness, combining a memory of the spindly Stick Style with the geometric purity of Japanese woodwork—a tour de force in the manipulation of exterior space through wall-less structural elements and latticed screens.

The firm was much more successful in smaller cottages than in the more palatial Shingle Style houses, demonstrating that it is impossible to achieve monumentality out of the rustic or to maintain domesticity in the face of the grandiose. Modest houses such as the Isaac Bell House, Newport, R.I. (1882–83, plate 298), are among the most satisfying in the genre. This has an incomparable lightness of treatment both inside and out, a marvelous fluidity of spatial relations, and an unfaltering sense of

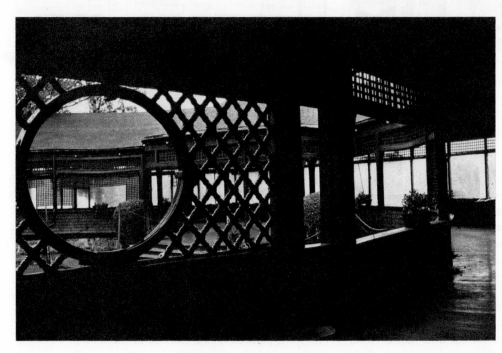

297 McKim, Mead & White.
Interior court, Casino,
Newport, R.I. 1879–81

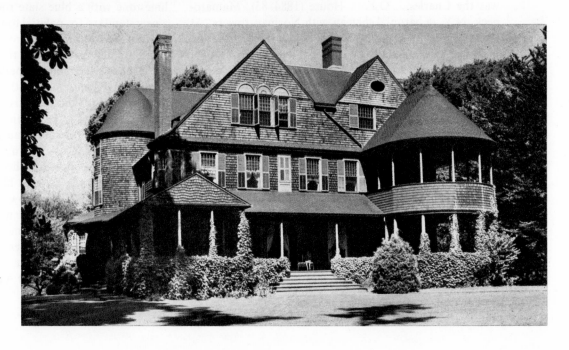

298 McKim, Mead & White.
Isaac Bell House,
Newport, R.I. 1882–83

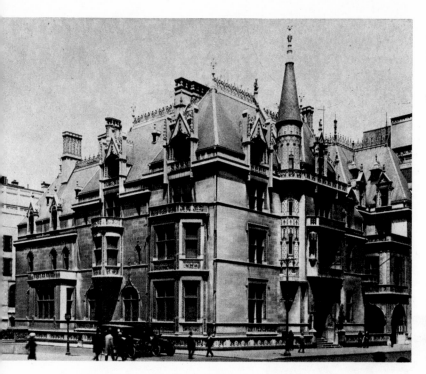

299 Richard M. Hunt. William K. Vanderbilt
Residence, New York. 1879–81

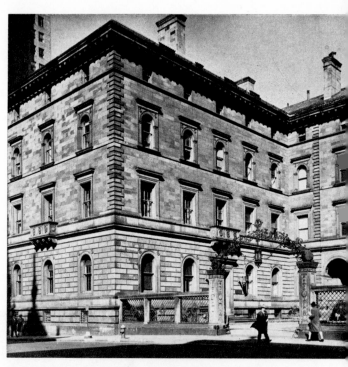

300 McKim, Mead & White. Henry Villard
Houses, New York. 1883–85

scale and proportion. The presence of Stanford White
is strongly felt, particularly in the elegant Japanese-
inspired interiors.

The Shingle Style house was introduced to Chicago
in the mid-eighties, and eastern architects were building
it as far west as Colorado Springs and Pasadena. However, the style had become passé by 1885, submerged by
the Colonial and Classical reactions.

CLASSICAL REACTION
AND ACADEMIC ECLECTICISM

As the practice of McKim, Mead & White increased in
the mid-1880s, the demands of their clients for more
palatial homes led to a more formal and monumental
manner. Their first break from the modest Shingle Style
was the Charles J. Osborn House (1884–85), Mamaroneck, N.Y., a baronial château with Norman towers. At
the same time the Charles T. Cook House (1885), Elberon,
N.J., was still essentially a cottage, but with an overlay of
Colonial Georgian elements. And the new Classical
reaction became evident in two Newport houses: the H.A.
C. Taylor House (1885–86), in the Georgian style; and the
Commodore William Edgar House (1885–86), in the
Adam style.

Perhaps the dynamics of revivalism eventually had to
arrive at academic eclecticism—the scholastic codification of historical styles. By this time most architects were
college graduates, and many had studied abroad at the
École des Beaux-Arts. Formal training was further
advanced by the establishment of architectural curricula
at the Massachusetts Institute of Technology in 1866,
followed by Illinois (1870), Cornell (1871), Columbia
(1881), and Harvard (1890).

It is ironic that just when the basic environmental
problems of the nineteenth century were reaching the
point of crisis, when an explosively expanding industrial
and urban society was fumbling for viable forms, architecture should have become so committed to fashion.
Between 1879 and the financial crisis in 1893 the magnificent palaces of America's moneyed peerage arose—in
New York along Fifth Avenue between 50th and 79th
Streets, called "Millionaires' Row"; and in Newport,
R.I., where they summered. Some of the most powerful
of the new millionaires before 1880 were satisfied with
brownstones by speculative builders. But when Richard
M. Hunt built the William K. Vanderbilt Residence
(1879–81, plate 299) as a château in the style of François
I at a cost of $3 million, the four-story mansion of gray
limestone with a blue slate roof and copper cresting set
a new standard for palatial town houses.

Hunt was the most thoroughly trained and sophisticated architect working in the United States. Steeped in
the Beaux-Arts tradition, he was eminently equipped to
furnish his clients with authentic versions of European
aristocratic architecture. His own preference was for the
style of François I, best seen in the châteaux of the Loire
Valley. The Vanderbilt mansion was princely in every
respect, revealing its cost in scale, materials, craftsmanship, and taste. It established Hunt as the architect of
"Society" and the style as his, and it found immediate
imitation. The château, however, was not really a town
house. It needed space in which to expand. Given the
opportunity, Hunt built some of the grandest palaces for
the new peerage, among them Ochre Court (1888–91) for
Ogden Goelet, in Newport, and Biltmore (1890–95) for
George W. Vanderbilt, near Asheville, N.C.

Imperial eclecticism found its chief expression in the hieratic and monumental styles of the Italian Renaissance and Beaux-Arts Classicism. McKim, Mead & White in the Henry Villard Houses (1883–85, plate 300) derived their design from the Cancelleria in Rome. The large brownstone complex, disposed around a three-sided court and occupying an entire block, is impressive in its simple, declarative monumentality. Perhaps the serious stateliness of the style or its symbolic reference to the mercantile nobility of the Renaissance made it seem close to the image of imperial power and to the American Classical tradition. The Italian Renaissance style reached its climax in two great Newport mansions built at the same time (1892–95) for the Vanderbilts by Hunt. The "Marble House" was a grandiose, though pedantic, neo-Palladian palace. The Breakers (plate 301), equally Palladian and much like the late Renaissance palaces of Genoese merchant princes, suffers from gigantism and scholasticism, as if Hunt had lost his sense of scale and ended in bombast.

McKim, Mead & White achieved their major work, and the prime monument in the neo-Renaissance style during the late nineteenth century, with the Boston Public Library (1887–98, plate 302), their first commission for a large public building. The project was challenging, for the Library, on Copley Square, was to face the great Richardson Trinity (plate 281), on which both McKim and White had worked. It took courage to counterpoise so positive, simple, and intellectually deliberate a structure against the picturesque mass and sensuous texture of Trinity. The long, flat facade, Italianate and Classical, is unusually reticent, although not so austere as the Biblio-

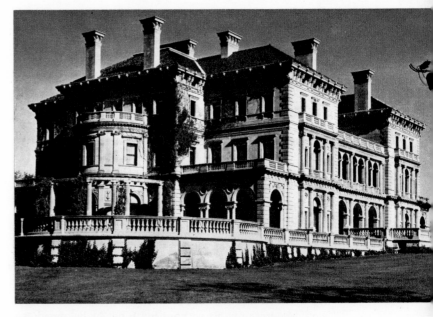

301 Richard M. Hunt. The Breakers, Newport, R.I. 1892–95

thèque Sainte-Geneviève (1843–50), Paris, which may have inspired it. In both the composition is repetitive rather than symmetrical in conception. The center of the Boston Library facade is emphasized by a three-arched loggia with sculptured panels above. McKim, Mead & White insisted on the finest materials and craftsmanship and hired the best artists available as collaborators. Saint-Gaudens, French, and MacMonnies did the sculpture; and Puvis de Chavannes, the most highly regarded

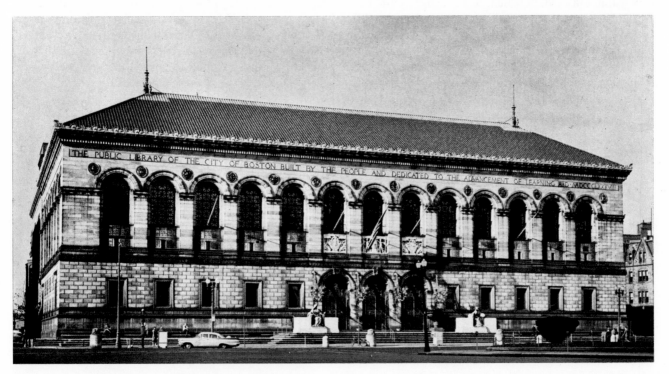

302 McKim, Mead & White. Public Library, Boston. 1887–98

French mural painter, Sargent, and Abbey were commissioned to decorate the interior.

The Library established McKim, Mead & White as the leading architectural firm in the nation and, to accommodate the demands on their services, they became the first "corporate" architectural office. The partners could not manage even the design, so that the "office" took over the bulk of routine commissions, and anonymous production became the normal practice. Most of the enormous output was in the "imperial Classic" mode, and rather dull. The Low Library at Columbia University (1895–98) is one of the firm's most successful ventures in imperial grandeur, a neo-Roman domed mass derived from the Pantheon.

THE EARLY WRIGHT

Frank Lloyd Wright (1869–1959) has often been described, rightly or wrongly, as the greatest architect of the twentieth century (and twentieth-century architecture would be unthinkable without him), but he belonged essentially to the nineteenth. His individualism, moral conviction, and unorthodoxy (characteristics of nineteenth-century New England) were absorbed in the vigorous intellectual climate of his family, and later through Emerson, Thoreau, and Whitman via the rhapsodic prose of Louis Sullivan. He was deeply attached to the frontier, and he felt that "the real American spirit . . . lies in the West and the Middle West." Perhaps this identification with the West and with the past was responsible for his anti-urbanism. Although he produced some masterpieces of urban architecture, he will be remembered more for his revolutionary transformation of the private dwelling. He was committed to an "organic" architecture that grew from within outward, in which, as in medieval architecture (and here his, as well as Sullivan's, dependence on William Morris is clear), form is a response to function. In his project for a house in a prairie town (1900, plate 303), he finally broke open the "box" that had enclosed domestic architecture. From Downing through Richardson to Wright, the free plan evolved into its twentieth-century incarnation, in which interior and exterior were interpenetrating and walls were screens and not barriers.

In 1885 Wright went to work as an apprentice to a local contractor-builder and soon after began attending classes in engineering at the University of Wisconsin. After two years he left for Chicago. In 1887 he was hired by Sullivan, and in 1888 he was given responsibility for the domestic work of the firm. One of the earliest of his houses, his own (1890), in Oak Park, though an unpretentious shingled cottage on the exterior, introduced what were to become benchmarks of his style—rooms merging within a continuous space and a "utility core" that was at the heart of his later radial plans. In the Winslow House (1893) in River Forest, Ill., Wright's first independent commission after breaking with Sullivan, he projected a new kind of nonhistorical, modern Classicism unlike the revivalism of McKim, Mead & White. The house has an abstract formalism in composition, immaculate sharp-edged flat surfaces into which windows are punched, an emphasis on the horizontal through banding and boldly projecting eaves, an elegance of proportion, and a preference for the Classical square window.

Toward the end of the century Wright had fought his way out of formalism and symmetry to a freer and original expression. The important ingredients of his "prairie" style are apparent in the project for the River Forest Golf Club (1898–1901): the intimate relationship between building and site; the open, fluid, self-generating plan; the horizontality and spaciousness; the floating roof planes; the natural materials; the banded fenestration. The Japanese flavor, stemming from his contact with Japanese architecture at the Columbian Exposition, is very strong. Though the mingling of "Tudor" and Japanese elements is rather curious, the plan and composition of volumes are already Wrightian. It was not accidental that by 1900 Wright should have gathered together all the strands in the evolution of the "cottage" and woven them into the fabric of a modern house.

303 Frank Lloyd Wright. Design for Prairie House. *The Ladies' Home Journal*, XVIII, No. 3, February, 1901

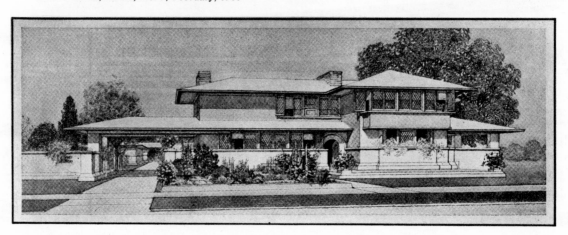

12
Painting: The Gilded Age

The effect of the Civil War on culture was not cataclysmic. The euphoria generated by peace, the preservation of the Union, and, in the North, victory, fostered the illusion of national continuity. In a cultural sense, 1876 was more significant as a date than 1865, because it saw the end of the Grant administration and the opening of the Centennial Exposition in Philadelphia. The Exposition serves as a key to the next period, for the great Corliss engine that dominated Machinery Hall, symbolizing America's technological advances, proved more impressive than a century of American art displayed in a thousand works.

So, after a long reign of nationalist isolation, the arts turned again to Europe. Artists were going abroad to study at an earlier age, and Paris and Munich became new meccas for American students. Entrance to the École des Beaux-Arts was competitive and difficult, but professors did accept nonmatriculated students in their ateliers; however, such students did not undergo the rigorous academic training of the Beaux-Arts curriculum. One might also study with an independent master or enroll in the Académie Julian, specifically organized to accommodate the hordes of foreign students. Here, though space was at a premium, one could work at will and receive criticism from Beaux-Arts masters hired to perform that function. The majority collected a particular bag of tricks, assumed the artist's mien, and came home. Many who could not make what they had learned fit their native environment found it more congenial to live and paint abroad. Undigested borrowings from various European sources gave American painting of the late nineteenth century an air of eclecticism.

Artists returning from study abroad found no ready buyers, for the majority of *nouveau riche* collectors bought the fashion of the period, from Bouguereau to Meissonier or even Corot, rather than their American echoes. Very few knew about the avant-garde artists who were to become the great masters of the period. Wiser collectors began to invest in the old masters, and the collections of J.P. Morgan, Henry Walters, Benjamin Altman, Isabella

Stewart Gardner, John G. Johnson, and Henry G. Marquand were begun, and Mary Cassatt advised her wealthy friends to buy the Impressionists.

Art activity expanded greatly in the postwar period, as witness the establishment of museums, art institutions, and art schools and the increase in the number of collectors, dealers, and artists. Taste was wide enough, or perhaps confused enough, to accept a broader range of expression than previously. One can isolate two main currents in post-Civil War painting, Realism and Romanticism, with Realism dominant in importance. The new visual Realism grew out of the literalism of the Hudson River School and the popular art of the genre painters; the new Romanticism transformed the transcendental philosophy of the Hudson River School into the personal expression of poetic feeling.

THE EXPATRIATES:
WHISTLER, CASSATT, SARGENT

Since it was common for American artists to study, travel, and even live abroad as far back as the eighteenth century, it is rather curious for historians to have singled out Whistler, Cassatt, and Sargent as *the* expatriates. But except for Copley and West, who were colonials, and the sculptors who worked in Europe largely for reasons of craft, the earlier expatriates were inconsequential as artists. These three are a big chunk of American (or non-American) art, so that they are usually honored for their international eminence and slighted for their purported irrelevance to American art and life. In fact, all three thought of themselves as American and had more pertinence for American art than is commonly thought.

The expatriation of James Abbott McNeill Whistler (1834–1903) began when he was taken at the age of nine to St. Petersburg to join his father, who was supervising the building of the railroad to Moscow. His early years in Russia and later visits to his half-sister in England did not prepare him for life in Pomfret, Conn., to which the family moved in 1849. He spent three years at West Point and, after a short stint in the U.S. Coast and Geo-

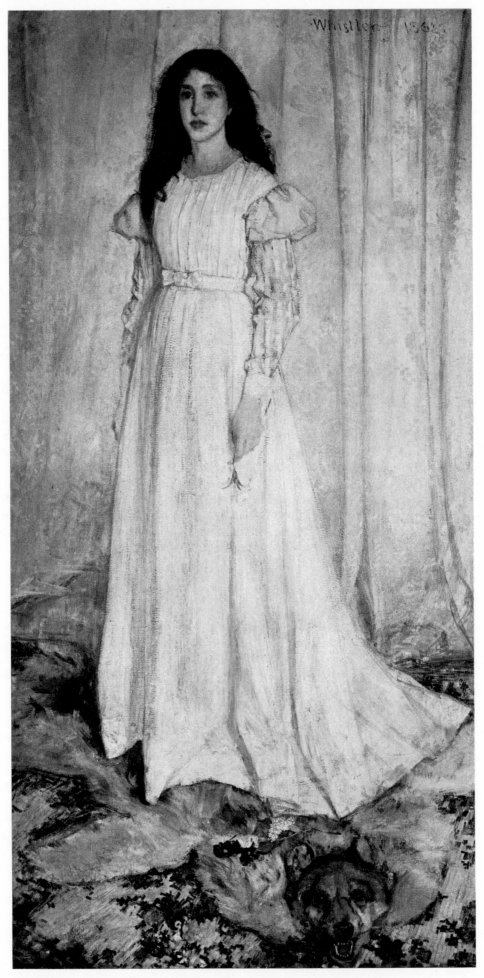

304 James A. McNeill Whistler. *The White Girl*. 1862. Oil on canvas, $84\frac{1}{2} \times 42\frac{1}{2}''$.
National Gallery of Art, Washington, D.C. Harris Whittemore Collection

detic Survey, where he learned engraving, went to Europe in 1855, never to return.

In Paris, Whistler entered the studio of Charles-Gabriel Gleyre, and in 1858 he published the first of his etchings, the *French Set*. He had made many friends, including Fantin-Latour, who introduced him to Courbet, the leader of the Realist movement. Whistler's earliest mature efforts show a strong influence from Courbet. He had already made his mark among his peers when he moved to London, where he lived for the rest of his life. In Wapping-on-Thames, he did a series of paintings of life on the river and began the *Thames Set*, which established his reputation as an etcher.

In 1863 *The White Girl* (1862, plate 304) was exhibited at the famous Salon des Refusés, where, along with Manet's *Le Déjeuner sur l'Herbe*, it was the butt of ridicule. On the other hand, it brought him the praise of avant-garde critics and artists. At this time he was equally accepted by the Courbet entourage and by the younger Realists led by Manet in Paris and the Pre-Raphaelites around Dante Gabriel Rossetti in London—often acting as a kind of ambassador between the two.

Also during the early 1860s Whistler became interested in Japanese prints and porcelain. *The White Girl* and subsequent paintings placed him on the threshold of Impressionism, but a trend away from the main direction of Realism soon became evident. His early preoccupation with Oriental art parallels that of the Impressionists and is expressed more in exotic paraphernalia than in an adaptation of design principles. With the Peacock Room, the fateful project he executed for the London home of Frederick R. Leyland in 1876–77, he entered a new and decorative phase of *japonaiserie*, revealing a flair for interior decoration, in which he became a seminal figure. Those years also saw a turn toward the subjective, tonal impressionism that was to typify his style. Instead of the more objective recording of nature in dazzling sunlight which occupied the French Impressionists, Whistler sought the evanescent, crepuscular moments in which mist shrouded the ugly banks of the industrialized Thames and created a mood of gentle mystery.

In the late sixties Whistler was torn between fidelity to nature and internal aesthetic order. In 1867 he renounced Courbet and "that damned Realism" and cried, "If only I had been a pupil of Ingres!" The next years saw only slight and tentative experiments in composition and color, involving friezes of women in a mixture of Greek and Japanese details. When he began to paint seriously again in the early seventies, he had arrived at his mature style. In the next fifteen years he painted his most famous portraits, beginning with the *Portrait of the Artist's Mother* (1871) and followed almost immediately by the *Thomas Carlyle* (1872–73, plate 305). In them, he stated a new credo: that aesthetics takes precedence over reality. It was also then that he began to retitle pictures,

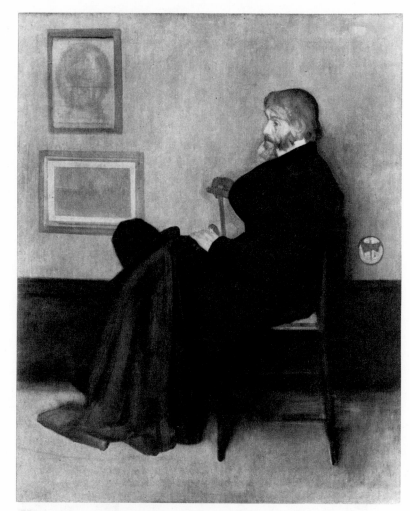

305 James A. McNeill Whistler. *Arrangement in Gray and Black, No. 2: Thomas Carlyle*. 1872–73. Oil on canvas, 67⅜ × 56½". Glasgow Art Gallery and Museum

without reference to subject, as "symphony," "arrangement," "nocturne," "harmony," in accordance with musical practice. Physical reality was subordinated to a compositional format emphasizing flatness, silhouette, rectilinear spatial balance, and tonal harmony, much of which is derivative from Japanese art. It is difficult to approach the *Mother* freshly, since it has been so overexposed; but in spite of some feebleness in drawing, Whistler's most obvious failing, it is an exquisitely composed picture. The more moving portrait of Carlyle, seated in pathetic grandeur, is handled with greater assurance and less sensitivity to formal relationships. Restrained as both portraits are in statement, their revolutionary aesthetic significance was appreciated only later in the century.

After years of ridicule and neglect Whistler was in demand for portraits, had commissions for decorations, and his works were beginning to sell. Then, in a series of catastrophes, his world crumbled. His altercation with Leyland over the decoration of the Peacock Room led to a rupture in relationship, reduction of fee, and bitterness. One of his finest "moonlights," *Nocturne in Black and Gold: The Falling Rocket* (c. 1875, colorplate 35), was singled out for derision by John Ruskin, who attacked Whistler viciously for asking "two hundred guineas for flinging a pot of paint in the public's face." Whistler's suit for libel became a *cause célèbre*, and though he technically won the case with the judgment of a farthing, press and public reactions were unfavorable. The trial expenses forced him into bankruptcy and the loss of his new home, in itself an important aesthetic monument of the period.

Whistler left for Venice in 1880 to do a series of etchings commissioned by the Fine Art Society. From then on his energies were directed largely to etching, lithography, pastel, and watercolor, which in scale and intimacy lent themselves more readily to the nuances and ephemeral effects he sought. In the early 1880s, regaining some of his patronage, he executed the last of his important portraits. Ironically, as his production decreased, recognition and honors accumulated.

Whistler's lasting significance was anti-Realist in his espousal of aestheticism and art for art's sake. His "Ten O'Clock" lecture of 1885, repeated many times, published, and translated into French by Mallarmé, was the manifesto for a new movement that motivated Postimpressionism, Symbolism, Art Nouveau, aestheticism, and much of twentieth-century art. Whistler has still not received his due, perhaps because his achievement never equaled his promise, or because, in leaving Paris, he became peripheral to the vital center. He had talent, intelligence, wit, shrewdness, superb taste, and great perspicacity, but his art suffered from fundamental weaknesses in training, lack of discipline, and an unwillingness to deal with his deficiencies, for he was arrogant, self-indulgent, cantankerous, and pretentious. Yet perhaps no artist of his generation outside the mainstream of French painting had so great an impact.

In contrast, the career of Mary Cassatt (1844–1926) was modest and her influence negligible, though her effect on American taste through the important collectors she advised was profound. Born in Allegheny City, Pa., to parents of wealth and culture, she studied briefly at the Pennsylvania Academy and then in Parma and settled in Paris in 1873. Like many progressive painters of the time, she was "self-taught" in museums rather than academies, traveling extensively, and, like most of them, she returned to the visual realism of Hals, Velázquez, and Rubens, as her earliest works attest. However, her palette was already becoming lighter before she met Degas, who invited her to join the Impressionist group in 1877. From then on his influence was obvious in her work. From Degas she borrowed liberally: his momentary vision, though she never achieved his spontaneity; his compositional devices; his color range and texture; even his subjects. But with it all she remained herself. Aside from being somewhat more heavy-handed, she tended also toward greater three-dimensionality and sweetness of expression. In her pastels she more nearly approached his lightness of touch and grace in movement.

In 1890 Cassatt and Degas visited the exhibition of Japanese prints at the École des Beaux-Arts and were deeply impressed. The Japanese influence is most marked in the series of ten color prints executed by Cassatt in 1891, in which she successfully adapted Japanese stylistic elements to Western subject matter. The Japanese emphasis on line, flat pattern, and compositional arrangement was more fully assimilated in such paintings as *The Bath* (1892, plate 306), in which Impressionism, Japanese art, and her own warmth of sentiment coalesce. She seems to have settled on the woman-and-child theme

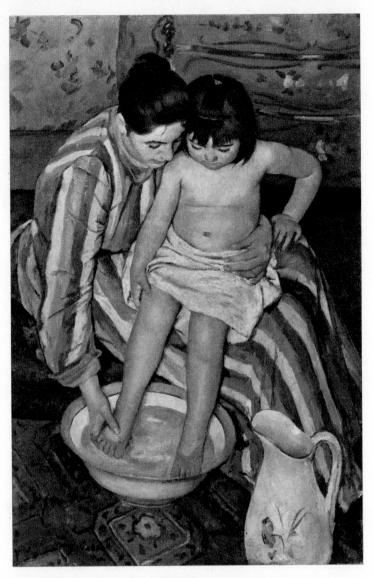

306   Mary Cassatt. *The Bath*. 1892. Oil on canvas, 39½ × 26″
The Art Institute of Chicago. Robert A. Walker Fund

as her personal subject, treating it with a tenderness that is foreign to the Impressionist mode. Though she was not a major artist, her reputation has suffered unduly by comparison with the work of more gifted Impressionists.

Of the three expatriates, John Singer Sargent (1856–1925) has probably sustained the greatest decline in esteem. A leading society portraitist of his time, he was subsequently dismissed as superficial and facile and denigrated for the very gift that made his reputation. Sargent was born in Florence to American parents, and his early years were spent in leisurely travel through Europe. He studied in Rome and in Florence before entering the studio of Carolus-Duran in Paris at eighteen. Carolus-Duran was a solid painter, inspired by the same sources of visual realism that influenced Manet, and Sargent received a thorough technical grounding. His earliest works were slick rather than original, but after a trip to Spain and Holland in 1879–80 and a serious study of Velázquez and Hals, his style gelled suddenly into precocious maturity.

Within the mainstream of visual Realism, he continued the English, rather than the French, tradition of portraiture both in its painterly virtuosity and in its occasional courtly vapidity. Characteristic is the *Daughters of Edward Darley Boit* (1882, colorplate 36), perhaps his closest brush with greatness. Daring in conception and composition, lucid in the handling of light and space, capturing the vibrancy of the children, it nevertheless fails to move one deeply, perhaps because the recording eye chose chic over aesthetic probity. In contrast, perhaps his most famous portrait, *Madame X* (1884, plate 307), is in the French vein of Carolus-Duran, classical in pose and solidly painted. This likeness of Mme. Pierre Gautreau, a society beauty, mingles a flair for style and social elegance in the sheer *élan* of the figure with an unexpected fidelity to physical reality. Mme. Gautreau and her family were ostensibly outraged by the shocking décolleté, but they may have been equally upset by the hint of vulgarity that Sargent, perhaps unconsciously, revealed. Annoyed by the resultant hubbub, he left the French art scene and shortly afterward settled in London. He was before long an internationally famous portraitist.

His mature portrait style was fluent, elegant, and dramatic, expressed in elongated forms and bravura brushwork. Frozen into a position of success and affluence, he avoided challenges and problems, and there was no further development in his style. His willingness to please led to a succession of glossy, empty symbols of social position turned out with technical dispatch. Contemporary taste seems to value Sargent's watercolor sketches over his formal portraits. They were at first travel notes, but he turned to watercolor painting more seriously about 1910. His watercolors have an uncanny visual accuracy and a technical brilliance that are almost unequaled, yet they reveal that Sagrent had very little to say. His manner

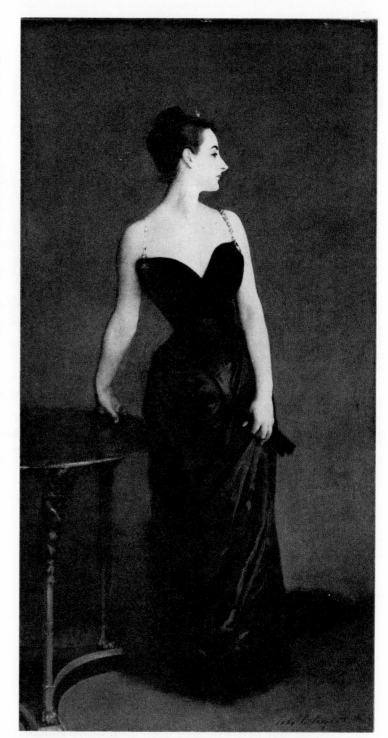

307 John Singer Sargent. *Madame X (Mme. Pierre Gautreau)*. 1884. Oil on canvas, 82⅛ × 43¼". The Metropolitan Museum of Art, New York. Arthur H. Hearn Fund, 1916

spawned a school of American society portraitists, which included J. Carroll Beckwith, John W. Alexander, Irving R. Wiles, and Cecilia Beaux and found an echo even in Robert Henri.

NATIVE REALISM: HOMER, EAKINS, JOHNSON

Although Winslow Homer (1836–1910) was a contemporary of Whistler, there could hardly be a sharper contrast

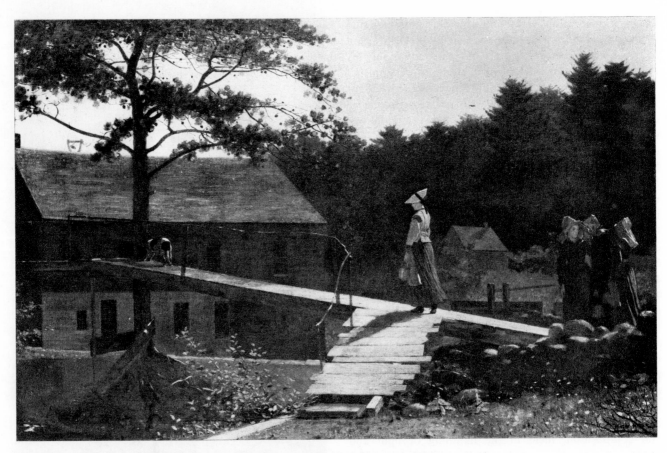

308 Winslow Homer. *The Morning Bell*. 1866. Oil on canvas, 24 × 38¼″. Yale University
Art Gallery, New Haven, Conn. Bequest of Stephen C. Clark

in both personality and relation to American art than between the Yankee recluse and the cosmopolitan aesthete.
Yet their art had some common interests. Though Whistler became part of an international "new movement" in
art, and Homer was the culmination of an older native
school of genre painting, Homer's work was neither so
local or naive as it may appear at first glance. He was
successful from the outset, recognized as the most "American" of American artists.

Homer was born to an old, middle-class New England
family and spent his youth in fairly rural surroundings,
which may have had some effect on his later attitudes
toward life and art. A decline in family fortunes forced
him at nineteen to accept an apprenticeship with a Boston
lithography firm. In 1857 he began contributing illustrations to *Ballou's Pictorial* in Boston and the new *Harper's
Weekly* in New York—chiefly genre scenes based on
the fashionable world of Boston or on New England rural
life. Like Mount before him, he recognized the popular
interest in rural nostalgia and depicted the pleasant rather
than the onerous features of farm life. Within a short
time he had established himself as the country's leading
illustrator. In 1859 he moved to New York and continued
free-lancing, producing genre scenes of New York life.

During the Civil War Homer did scenes of the conflict,

many done on the spot but most executed in his studio in
New York. He had little to report of the fighting; his concern was with the life of the soldier in leisure and boredom, jovial rather than serious. Homer kept a tight rein
on sentimentality, but he satisfied the emotional needs of
civilians at home. His is the most complete artist's
record we have of wartime activity, though he could not
match the documentation provided by photographers
such as Mathew Brady.

After the war Homer turned seriously to painting. He
had studied drawing in Brooklyn and at the National
Academy and had taken a few painting lessons from a
little-known French painter, Frédéric Rondel, but he was
largely self-taught. His painting technique remained simple, the paint applied directly and opaque, comparable to
the manner of Impressionism. In other respects he was no
novice; he came to painting with the ability to tell a story,
compose a scene with many figures, capture a gesture,
characterize an individual, suggest movement, describe
light, and define mass in space. He also had a remarkable
eye and feeling for design. His earliest paintings show
some hesitancy in handling but a strong sense of reality
and a remarkable feeling for light. In *The Morning Bell*
(1866, plate 308) and *Croquet Scene* (1866), the masterpieces of his early years, the sensuous feeling for light and

color, the appearance of things in a particular light at a precise time, create the illusion that one could hear the sounds and smell the aromas of that instant. But Homer also saw things freshly and in a conformation of pattern that was completely his own. His sense of design makes one think of Japanese prints, as in the cant of the wooden bridge that cuts a dominant diagonal through *The Morning Bell*.

Late in 1866 Homer went to Paris, where two of his paintings were being exhibited. On his return, he took up illustration again and continued painting summer-resort and rural genre scenes in the White Mountains, Long Branch, N.J., the Adirondacks, and Gloucester. In these pictures of the seventies he came closest to the Impressionists' attitude and aesthetic, sharing with them themes of pleasant holiday activities—bathing, boating, picnicking, and riding. He continued also the native genre tradition of nostalgia for childhood in a rural setting. In all the post-Paris paintings, the color is higher in key, perhaps because the French experience led to an increased interest in the phenomena of light.

Homer took to serious painting in watercolor during the summer of 1873 in Gloucester, inspired perhaps by an exhibition of English watercolors, and suddenly found a perfect vehicle for his naturalism. He found the medium so congenial that he used it thereafter to sketch from nature, and many of his oils are derived from such sketches, but his oils became more studied as his watercolors absorbed his instinctual response to nature. His control of the medium grew prodigiously from the tentative linearity of the first Gloucester sheets to the Ten Pound Island, Gloucester, watercolors of 1880, in which the translucent washes began to sing through the spidery lines of his drawing (colorplate 37).

In 1875 Homer revisited Petersburg, Va., and in the next two years did a series of paintings on black themes, in which he did not always skirt sentimentality, for, with all his reticence, he was obviously moved by the people's condition and humanity. In 1876, at the age of forty, Homer was a successful artist, well represented at the Centennial Exposition, his pictures selling at modest prices; yet the critical response to his work was ambivalent. In 1881 he went to England, where for two years near Tynemouth on the North Sea he painted the life of the fisherfolk and especially their women. The watercolors and oils that he finished after his return are a complete departure from his earlier work. A new heroic element had entered his art in the majestic figures of these

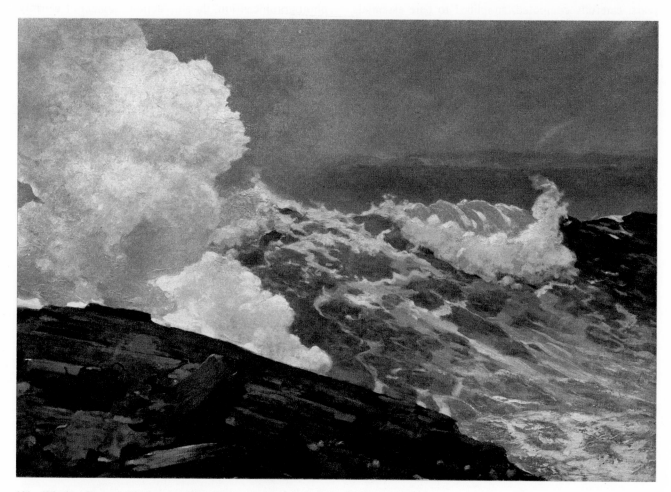

309　Winslow Homer. *Northeaster*. 1895. Oil on canvas, 34⅜ × 50¼″. The Metropolitan Museum of Art, New York. Gift of George A. Hearn, 1910

hardy women, enveloped in the gray light and rain-filled air. Influenced perhaps by English watercolors, his became more finished and three-dimensional and lost their freshness, sparkle, and transparency. Yet these English scenes earned him the greatest acclaim and financial awards he had yet received. After his return, he moved to the rocky, sea-battered coast of Maine, where he spent the rest of his life in increasing isolation. In the following years his pictures of men and the sea won him recognition as America's leading painter. In them, the endless struggle of the Banks fishermen against an implacable ocean transformed the genre subject into a new kind of adventure picture with all the heroicism of history painting.

Homer's regained naturalism was fostered by his watercolors of those years, through the new and brilliant color of his Caribbean sketches, begun in 1884 with a visit to the Bahamas and Cuba and continued, almost to the end of his life; and the more somber but equally brilliant studies of the north woods. In these he achieved an unequaled mastery of the medium.

Beginning in the early nineties, as he became more immured at Prout's Neck, Me., during the winters, his interest in the sea continued to grow until man seemed to recede and the battle of the elements became the drama. These scenes were painstakingly studied over years, carefully composed, simplified to bare essentials, and painted with broadness and a surface fluency more like Sargent's than his own. Paintings such as *Northeaster* (1895, plate 309) have an elemental power and simplicity that none of his earlier work had, but they have lost much of the naturalistic detail that made the latter so immediate and revealing.

When Thomas Eakins (1844–1916) came home from his studies in Europe, he was optimistic about his future, ready to settle down and paint. After some success, at least in esteem, the cultural milieu of Philadelphia began to close in on him, and, almost before he could understand the situation, he was forced into bitter isolation. Perhaps no other city would have been more hospitable, for he was something of a radical artist for his time. Though he was heroic in maintaining his integrity in a hostile environment and fortunate in the financial support of his father, his art could not but be affected by the attrition of neglect.

The only son of a close-knit family, Eakins was an excellent student and artistically gifted. He enrolled in 1861 at the Pennsylvania Academy and took anatomy courses at the Jefferson Medical College. In 1866 he went to Paris, was admitted to the École des Beaux-Arts, and became a student of Jean-Léon Gérôme. These years were fateful for Eakins, for Beaux-Arts training, and that of Gérôme in particular, was founded on drawing, the painstaking delineation of form, as the basis of painting. His own rational, scientific, and mechanical predilections were reinforced by this discipline and he proved an apt pupil, but he learned little about painting.

Eakins must have sensed that his training was incomplete, and when he discovered Velázquez and Ribera on a visit to Spain in 1869, he knew he had found his course and remained to study for six months. Within a year or so his style was formed, not to change substantially for the rest of his life. It was really two styles: one, original, American, and in the direct line of "luminism," which he used in his outdoor sporting pictures; and the other, confined to his indoor genre pictures and portraits, more traditional and charged with emotional empathy, closer to Rembrandt than Velázquez, and to the Munich School than to Courbet or Manet.

Eakins had a deep interest in outdoor life, and many of his early paintings deal with rowing, sailing, and bird hunting. As a Realist with strong scientific preoccupations, he had always to prove that what he saw was true—hence the preliminary perspective and anatomical studies and the dependence on photographic evidence to reinforce visual experience. *Max Schmitt in a Single Scull* (1871, colorplate 38) is a striking innovation in the history of Realism as well as American genre painting. It projects a new kind of vision, photographic in inspiration or influence, concerned with objective recording without reference to theory, memory, or sentiment. Except for Degas, Eakins was the first to grapple with the aesthetic of photographic vision, the stop-action moment of eternity. The *Max Schmitt* is modern in the unquestioning acceptance of the mechanical elegance of the bridges, American in its cool, limpid light. But the contradiction between the sharp focus of studied detail and the immediate impression of visual experience creates an aesthetic ambivalence—a kind of frozen animation—and a poetic quietude.

Eakins's early interior subjects were essentially genre paintings and in most cases also portraits of family members and friends. They are, on the whole, dark and somber in tonality, rather brooding in character, simple and fairly formal in composition, and akin to mid-century Realist painting in Europe. But he was not entirely satisfied with commonplace genre subjects. He was driven by an image of "bigness" in art—the epic, the profound, the timeless—which he sought, like Courbet, in the reality of contemporary life. *The Gross Clinic* (1875, plate 310) is his first and most successful effort to find a heroic realism in his time and make it stand up against the monumental art of the past. Like Rembrandt's *Anatomy Lesson,* which obviously inspired it, it is a group portrait, representing Dr. Samuel David Gross performing an operation and lecturing to students at the Jefferson Medical College. Eakins could never understand why the painting was socially unacceptable, but it had created a scandal when first exhibited, been rejected at the Centennial, although five of his works were shown, and finally hung in the medical section. Regardless of the quality of the painting, it was the uncompromising truth of a few square inches of blood that was repellent. The picture itself is Eakins's

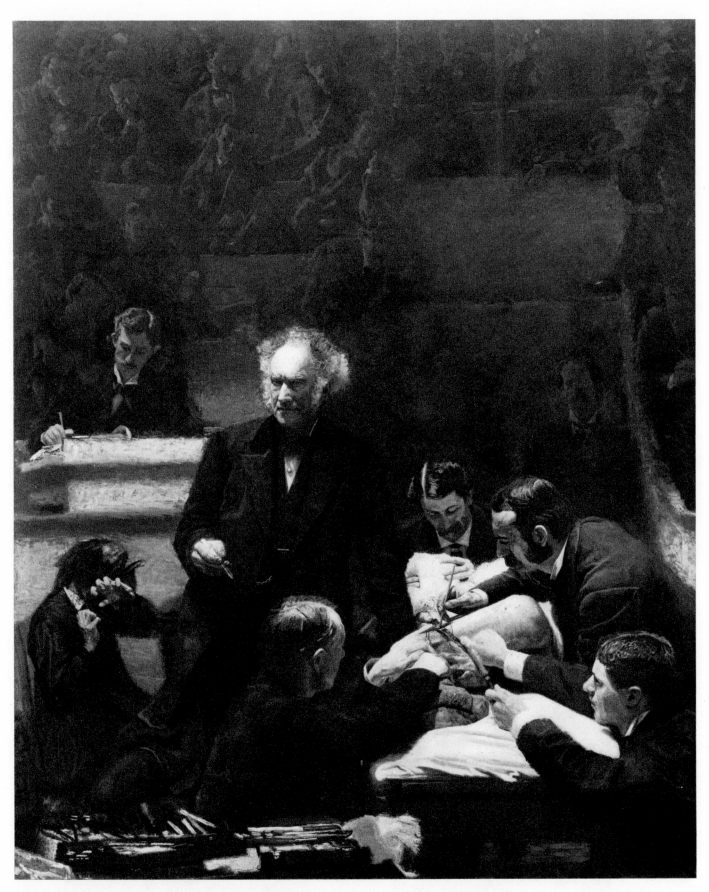

310 Thomas Eakins. *The Gross Clinic*. 1875. Oil on canvas,
96 × 78″. Jefferson Medical College of Philadelphia

most impressive work. Dr. Gross is probably the most compelling single figure in American painting. The leonine head, Rembrandtesque in its depth of character and humanity, and the bloody hand, cruelly factual, dominate the composition and establish a dramatic tension that even the distraction of the operation itself—cluttered, overlighted, and routinely painted—and the hovering wraiths of students cannot destroy. It is history painting of the first order, rather than genre.

On the other hand, in *William Rush Carving His Allegorical Figure of the Schuylkill River* (1877, plate 311) Eakins transformed a history subject into a genre painting. The story of the early Philadelphia sculptor who sought a model to pose nude for him had special meaning for Eakins, and he used it later as an image of his own struggle against puritanism. In all his work there is no more sensuous painting than that of the buxom nude and her clothes scattered on the chair. The frankness of the naked (a word he preferred to "nude") model is far removed from the erotic ideality of Gérôme and completely new to American painting. Still in his thirties, Eakins had established himself as the greatest painter in the United States, although hardly anyone knew it, least of all the art world of Philadelphia. Almost his only income came from teaching. In 1876 he took over the life classes at the

Academy and reorganized the antiquated curriculum around the study of the nude and anatomy. He was appointed director of the school in 1882, but his radical methods aroused opposition, and the display of a completely nude male model in a mixed class led to his dismissal in 1886.

During this time Eakins continued to paint genre pictures and even one pure landscape and some "Arcadian" studies, his only excursions into mythology. His dismissal from the Academy school seems to have driven him further into himself. He abandoned the painting of the life around him to express his own melancholy introspection. From 1884 on, his major work was in portraiture. Though these portraits express his courage and humanity, they are rather conservative, and quite a few seem unfinished. Some, especially in his later years, seem to have been done largely from photographs. *The Agnew Clinic* (1889) was originally commissioned as an individual portrait but Eakins requested permission to paint a huge canvas at no increase in the price of $750, the largest fee he ever received. As a pendant to *The Gross Clinic*, it reflects changes in medical practice as well as in Eakins's art. The antiseptic dress of the participants is reinforced by the cold white glare of the illumination, and the daring composition isolates the doctor in profile from the attending

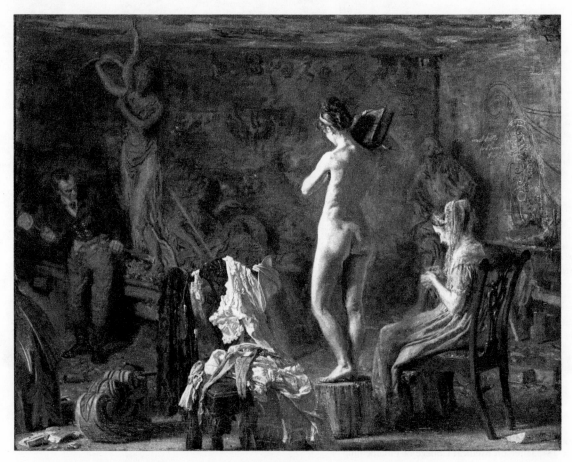

311   Thomas Eakins. *William Rush Carving His Allegorical Figure of the Schuylkill River.*
1877. Oil on canvas, 20⅛ × 26½". Philadelphia Museum of Art.
Gift of Mrs. Thomas Eakins and Miss Mary A. Williams

figures. Although painted with vigor, the tableau is neither cohesive nor compelling, and the frieze of shadowy observers forms a spaceless backdrop. Only the brilliant portrait of Dr. Agnew comes across with conviction.

The smaller and the less formal portraits are often more satisfying, perhaps because Eakins allowed the innate warmth of his nature to show through, as in the pensive *Miss Amelia C. Van Buren* (1889–91, plate 312), painted with a wonderful feeling for weight and texture, luminous in the ivory skin tonalities. Such portraits are documents of emotional involvement, psychological probing, and affection.

Only late in life did Eakins receive recognition in honors, awards, and critical appreciation. Perhaps more tragic than neglect was his own failure to fulfill his potential. No artist was better equipped to meet the challenges of a changing world. As a Realist he had all of turbulent, colorful, brutal, ugly America to paint. But his art was bent from its original inclination, and it took dogged courage to keep it alive and fruitful.

The long career of (Jonathan) Eastman Johnson (1824–1906) encompassed the transition from pre- to postwar American painting. Johnson went to Boston from rural Maine at sixteen to learn lithography and after two years returned home as a crayon portraitist, practicing also in Boston, Cambridge, and Washington, then going to Düsseldorf. Dissatisfied, he visited London, moved to The Hague to paint portraits and study the great Dutch masters, and went on to Paris, where he seems to have worked with Couture.

When Johnson returned to the United States, he painted Indians and frontier life around Lake Superior, worked as a portraitist in Cincinnati and Washington, and finally settled in New York City by 1858. In the next two decades he was largely occupied with genre themes, many of which were issued as prints. Johnson belongs among the mid-century sentimental genre artists catering to popular taste, and he shares their obvious faults. But he was a better painter, and could move beyond their limitations into the realm of emotion and also share the objective naturalism of Homer and Eakins. In the 1870s he produced a series of paintings in Nantucket which he thought of as "finished sketches," approximating the straightforward naturalism of Homer, who may have influenced him. *In the Fields* (1875–80, plate 313) has the same directness of observation and shorthand notation of physical fact with a somewhat more sensuous feeling for pigment. These small sketches are both a summation of "luminist" tradition and precursors of Impressionism.

After 1880 Johnson turned from genre to portrait painting. At times he achieved a psychological penetration and painterly richness worthy of the finest of Eakins's portraits. The memory of Rembrandt comes through strongly in the deep, warm shadows, the somber opulence of color, the solid modeling of form.

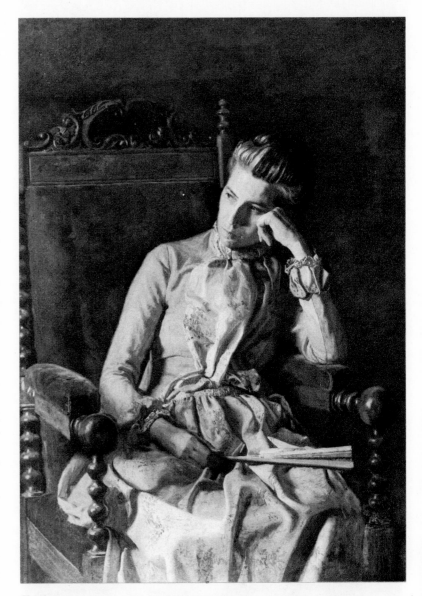

312 Thomas Eakins. *Miss Amelia C. Van Buren.* 1889–91. Oil on canvas, 45 × 32″. The Phillips Collection, Washington, D.C.

THE MUNICH SCHOOL: DUVENECK AND CHASE

In the 1870s American art students, many from the Middle West and with German backgrounds, were attracted to Munich, which was even considered by some to be the "art capital" of Europe. In 1869 the first international art exhibition held in Munich presented an array of foreign art, including even Manet, and many young Munich painters and students were greatly impressed by Courbet, whose visit helped galvanize the Realistic circle around Wilhelm Leibl (1844–1900). Leibl, like Manet, sought the sources of Realism in Spanish painting and Velázquez, but he was even more profoundly influenced by Hals, Rubens, and Brouwer. The choice of commonplace subjects, loose and spirited brushwork, and dark, limited tonal range became the hallmarks of the Munich School.

Frank Duveneck (1848–1919), of German extraction, was born in Covington, Ky., and while still a boy had

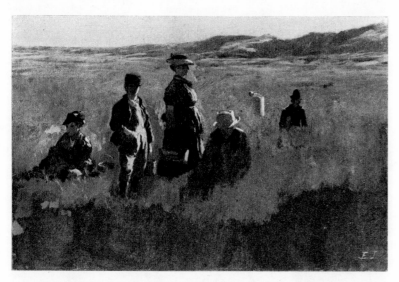

313 Eastman Johnson. *In the Fields*. 1875–80. Oil on board, 17¾ × 27½".
The Detroit Institute of Arts. The Dexter M. Ferry, Jr., Fund

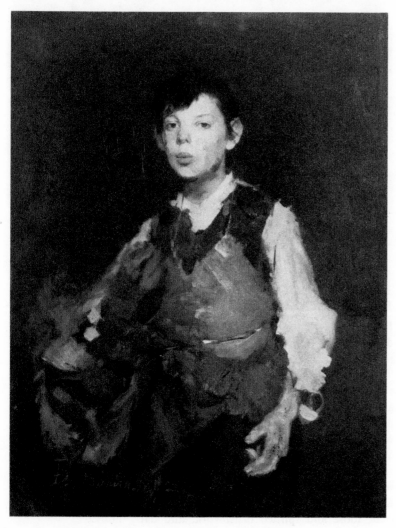

314 Frank Duveneck. *Whistling Boy*. 1872. Oil on canvas,
28 × 21½". Cincinnati Art Museum

begun to work at painting and decorating for churches. In 1870 he left to study in Munich, where he soon came under the influence of the Leibl Kreis and intensified their fluent brushwork and dark tonality into a personal style. Duveneck worked rapidly and wetly from dark underpainting into light with broad, squarish brushstrokes, defining form vigorously. His color range was restricted and conceived tonally, the pigment applied with a decided impasto. In the Hals-like *Whistling Boy* (1872, plate 314) Duveneck's style is already set, confident, fluent, expansive, capturing the moment and suggesting through bold surface planes the underlying structure.

After three years in Munich, Duveneck worked for a while in the Middle West. He showed five paintings at the Boston Arts Club in 1875, and, when he received the critical accolade of William Morris Hunt, became an overnight sensation, appreciated for his combination of old-master appearance with a modern European manner. Then he returned to Munich and set up his own school, attracting many American students who came to be known as the "Duveneck Boys." Duveneck taught a formula for capturing the appearance of reality in purely painterly terms. Yet, with all his gifts, he really had little to say.

William Merritt Chase (1849–1916), who proved a greater force in American painting of that period, also came from the Middle West. After a short stint at the National Academy of Design in New York, he set up as a painter in St. Louis and before long found patrons willing to finance his study in Munich. A gifted and facile student, Chase learned the Munich manner so well that he was offered a teaching position, but he returned instead to the United States to begin his career as the most popular and influential teacher of the period.

Chase became the image of the successful artist—gregarious, socially polished, and politically adept. He dressed elegantly, kept a white wolfhound, and had a black servant who wore a robe and a red fez. He served for ten years as president of the Society of American Artists, was a member of the prestigious "Ten," was elected to all the artistic societies, and received countless honors and awards. He soon dropped the murky palette of the Munich School but retained its slashing brushwork and animated surface. He absorbed influences like a sponge, but he achieved an eclecticism all his own, superficial perhaps, yet light, airy, brilliant, and curiously honest in his response to the visual world.

His qualities as a painter are most apparent in his genre scenes and landscapes. The Shinnecock paintings of the nineties, bathed in an all-pervading light, reducing form to color (e.g., *Shinnecock, Long Island*, c. 1895; colorplate 39), reveal his strength in the direct and sensuous response to visual data, his growing interest in sunlight, and a consequent heightening of palette until it was substantially Impressionist in range.

(continued on page 282)

During the height of Victorian fashion the lap quilt (plate 315), a descendant of earlier patchwork quilts, was used in the living room or parlor, rather than the bedroom. Since it was meant to be seen, the patches were made of silk, satin, and velvet, embroidered with silk thread. Only on the back were cotton chintz and cotton thread used. Given the Victorian obsession with nostalgia and sentiment, it is not surprising that the patches were cut from old wedding dresses, cravats, evening gowns, and other mementoes of the family of the creator. The term "crazy quilt" was used when the patches were of random size and shape. The pieces were sewn onto cotton squares, and the squares were then sewn together; the embroidery in silk thread was reserved for outlining the patches and for the flowers, plants, and animals delineated on the patches.

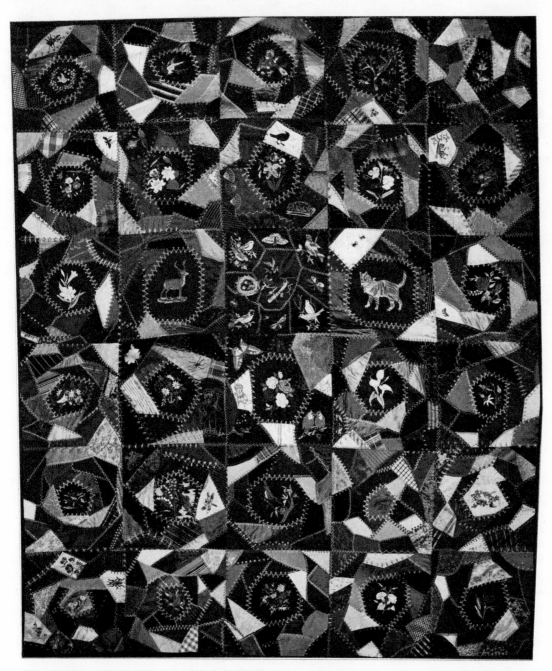

315 Catherine Ziegler Hicks. Lap quilt. c. 1876. Patchwork with embroidery, c. 78 × 65". Philadelphia Museum of Art. Gift of Ralph T. K. Cornwell in memory of his mother, Amy Josephine Kline Cornwell

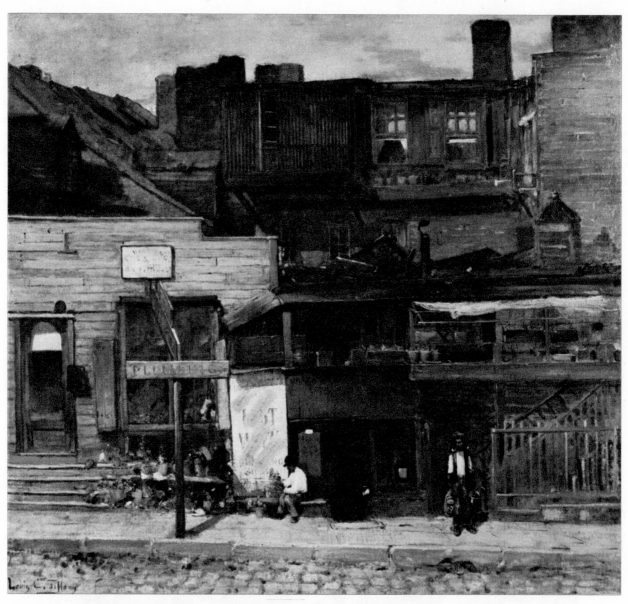

316 Louis Comfort Tiffany. *Duane Street, New York*. c. 1878. Oil on canvas,
27 × 30". The Brooklyn Museum. Dick S. Ramsay Fund

(*continued from page 280*)

GENRE, STILL LIFE, AND TROMPE L'OEIL

In the 1880s both Homer and Eakins turned from genre painting in response to a general evolution away from the literary to the visual, but well-known painters sometimes did genre scenes just as they did portrait, landscape, or still-life paintings. Much of the work of the American Impressionists deals with scenes of everyday life, and so does that of many Romantic artists of the period. The whole genteel tradition at the end of the century is also largely concerned with human activity, though within a new upper-class frame.

On the other hand, the increase in popular periodicals and the advance in reproductive techniques fostered anecdotal art and illustration. A number of artists continued in the prewar tradition of Mount and Bingham, and of Woodville and the Düsseldorf manner. One of these, Thomas Waterman Wood (1823–1903), born in Montpelier, Vt., made his reputation on New England rural scenes. A more accomplished painter of rural scenes was John Whetton Ehninger (1827–1889), who was born in New York City, graduated from Columbia College, and studied in Düsseldorf with Leutze and later in Paris with Couture. He was a successful illustrator but also painted genre subjects with polished competence and a foreign cast.

By far the most popular genre painter of the period was British-born John George Brown (1831–1913), whose sentimental, sad-eyed bootblacks and newsboys made his name a byword and produced an income in the neighborhood of $40,000 a year. Brown brought with him the highly polished, anecdotal style of English Victorian academic genre painting, but his early efforts in this country show a marked influence from Homer's rural genre scenes, though in a more sentimental vein. A departure is his *Longshoremen's Noon* (1879), depicting a group of workers in what appears to be a political discussion during their lunch hour. It is one of the few paintings of the time to recognize the existence of an industrial working class, with its "labor problem."

Thomas Hovenden (1840–1895) was born in Ireland and came to the United States in 1863. A well-trained academic genre painter with a style that retained its European flavor, he was closer to Woodville than to Mount or Homer.

The Civil War offered an opportunity for reportage and genre painting that was exploited by such artists as Homer and Johnson, but most of the work produced does not equal the camera records, and the genre pictures are mostly trivial. Westward expansion after the war led to a renewed interest in frontier life. Magazines carried illustrations dealing with the migration of settlers, the building of railroads, life on the plains, Indian wars, and the new American mythical hero—the cowboy. Little of this material found its way into painting.

Among the most famous of the artists of the West were Frederic Remington (1861–1909), Charles Marion Russell (1864–1926), and Charles Schreyvogel (1861–1912), all of whom achieved their greatest renown after the turn of the century. Remington and Russell were primarily illustrators and depicted contemporary life on the range. Schreyvogel worked entirely for reproduction and was in a sense a historical painter dealing with military life and Indian wars of the past. All three also treated similar subjects in sculpture. Of those who recorded the roistering life of California from the Gold Rush to the San Francisco earthquake only Charles Christian Nahl (1818–1897) is worthy of mention. German-born and -trained, he went to New York in 1849 and soon after made his way to San Francisco, where he worked as a portrait painter. His genre scenes of mining-camp life capture something of the rough masculine violence and humor, except that they seem to have been seen through the eyes of a Düsseldorfian.

In retrospect, the popular genre painters and illustrators said little that was profoundly revealing about American life in the late nineteenth century. For exceptional work one has to look to non-genre painters or an occasional artist such as Louis Comfort Tiffany (1848–1933), better known for his work in stained glass and as America's foremost Art Nouveau designer. Most of his paintings, small oil sketches, deal with exotic subjects. *Duane Street, New York* (c. 1878, plate 316), is a view of slum life rare for that time and painted with freshness and verve.

(continued on page 284)

DECORATIVE ARTS

Louis C. Tiffany was the major disseminator of the Art Nouveau style in American decoration. Flowing curves based on natural forms are characteristic of the style, incorporating elements from plant life as well as motifs inspired by flames, smoke, and waves. Exaggerated human elements, such as the long, flowing hair of a young woman, and certain animal forms, such as butterflies, snakes, and peacocks, were often represented. The hand mirror (plate 317) includes an enamel peacock on the back and another one of silver (with sapphire eye) forming the entire handle. Delicate, and even erotic, this kind of personal and intimate object became identified with Art Nouveau, and the artist's fantasy was given free reign by Tiffany and his firm.

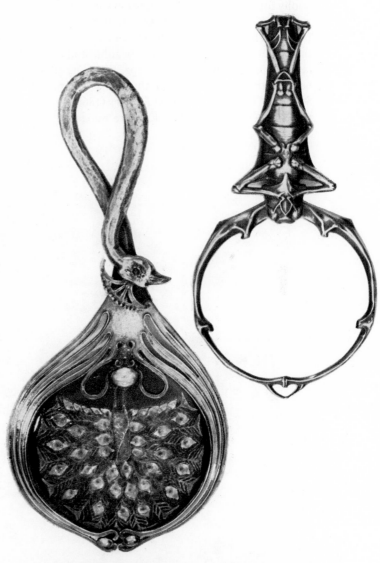

317 Louis Comfort Tiffany. Hand mirror. c. 1900. Silver, enamel, and sapphires, length 10¼". The Museum of Modern Art, New York. Gift of Joseph H. Heil

(continued from page 283)

Little of the dramatic impact of industrial development in the late nineteenth century is reflected in art. Neither the industrial plant nor the role of labor seemed picturesque or heroic enough. One finds only scattered references to labor and usually inferentially, as in Brown's *Longshoremen's Noon*. Much more impressive is *Steelworkers—Noontime* (c. 1882, plate 318) by Thomas P. Anshutz (1851–1912), pupil and assistant of Eakins at the Pennsylvania Academy and the artistic bridge between nineteenth-century Realism and the Ashcan School. However, neither painting deals with what might be labor's heroic implications. The Anshutz conveys a physical sturdiness which borders on the heroic without destroying the immediacy of the prosaic. Though it suffers from a too obvious posing of figures and a sometimes niggling concern with detail, the quality of the light modeling the bodily forms imparts to it an uncanny sense of reality.

Rare in American art are the industrial themes of John F. Weir (1841–1926), the elder brother of J. Alden and the son of Robert W. (1803–1889). John studied with his father and later briefly in Europe, returning in 1869 to become the first director of the newly organized Yale School of Fine Arts. *The Gun Foundry* (1866) and *Forging the Shaft* (1877, colorplate 40) were remarkable for the time at which they were executed. Weir caught the drama of the industrial scene in the titanic scale of the foundry and its apparatus and the belching furnace fire illuminating in sharp chiaroscuro the action of the dwarfed workmen.

Still-life painting found limited acceptance in the latter part of the century, appealing neither to the sophisticated taste for the aesthetic nor to the popular taste for the anecdotal. Yet in the postwar period there was a remarkable efflorescence of *trompe-l'oeil* still-life painting by William Michael Harnett, John Frederick Peto, John Haberle, and a host of lesser-known artists.

The most successful of the group was the Irish-born William Michael Harnett (1848–1892), who worked for a decade in Philadelphia and New York as an engraver on silverware while attending classes at the Pennsylvania Academy and later at Cooper Union and the National Academy before becoming a painter. His earliest exhibited works, still lifes rather than *trompe l'oeil*, are in the tradition of the Peales. In Philadelphia, at least, the still-life form was still alive in the work of surviving members of the Peale family and in a more elaborate manner in that of John F. Francis (1808–1886).

Harnett's dependence on the Peales is apparent in the borrowing of their simple grouping of fruit, vegetables,

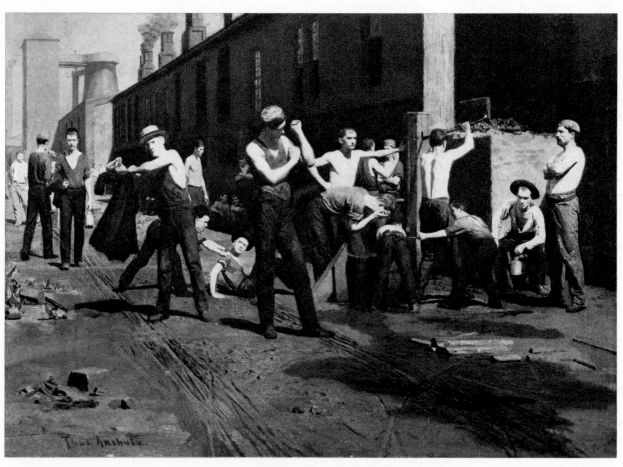

318 Thomas P. Anshutz. *Steelworkers—Noontime.* c. 1882. Oil on canvas, 17 × 24".
Private collection. Courtesy Kennedy Galleries, Inc., New York

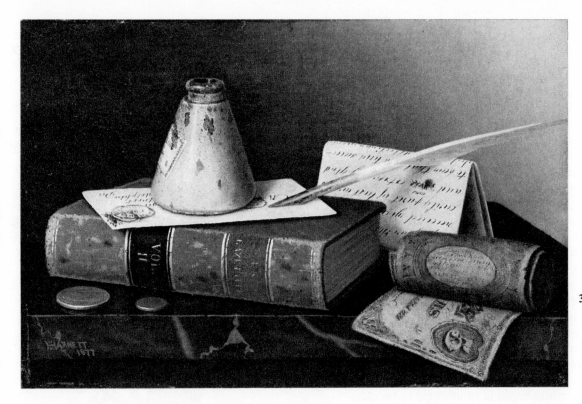

319 William Michael Harnett.
Still Life—Writing Table.
1877. Oil on canvas, 8 × 12″.
Philadelphia Museum of Art.
The Alex Simpson, Jr.,
Collection

and other objects on a horizontal shelf-table against an undefined and usually dark background. These are traditional still lifes, but the impulse to intensify the palpability of the real is visible in the elements overhanging or projecting beyond the ledge and in the rather naive application of pigment in relief to such details as nail heads. Harnett may also have derived from Raphaelle Peale the conception of the currency picture. Harnett's *Five Dollar Bill* (1877) was the first of a series and the first of his purely *trompe-l'oeil* pictures. He may have discovered then that deception is effective in direct ratio to flatness, and the greater the depth, the less convincing the illusion.

Harnett developed several iconographic types that became particularly his own. The *memento mori* still lifes were traditional, but the "smoker" (mug and pipe or cigar box and pipes), writing-table, and book paintings were personal themes that he repeated in endless variations. The story element in Harnett is fundamental, though not always in an anecdotal sense. His still lifes are almost genre pictures. The objects he selected so carefully and repeated so frequently were the *dramatis personae* in compositions which were the expression of a desire to immortalize the simple joys of a humble world, to monumentalize the commonplace. His preference was for ordinary objects, but they become projections of a human being who has left them temporarily. The *Still Life—Writing Table* (1877, plate 319) has as many references to the world beyond as does a Vermeer genre scene of a woman writing or reading a letter, and basically the same expressive intentions.

Harnett was much concerned with nostalgia and the pathos of the discarded, as in *Job Lot—Cheap* (1878),

where a pile of secondhand books reflects the human tragedy of the used, the obsolescent, the unwanted. He tells his story by implication (though his titles are rather obvious), through the objects. He convinces us not through form alone but through the nature of material, contrasting the warmth of leather and the coldness of metal, the lightness of paper and the heaviness of marble, the softness of fruit and the hardness of wood, the sparkle of salt glaze and the glow of ivory.

Most of the *trompe-l'oeil* themes originated with Harnett, but the "rack picture," a webbing of tapes tacked to a vertical surface and holding letters, postcards, tickets, and so on, appears to have been done slightly earlier and with greater frequency by John Frederick Peto (1854–1907), a fellow Philadelphian and admirer of Harnett. For some time after the rediscovery of Harnett in the 1930s, many of Peto's paintings with forged signatures passed for Harnett's, and only through the sleuthing of Alfred Frankenstein has the forgotten life's work of Peto been reconstructed. Peto was listed as a painter in the Philadelphia Academy from 1879 to 1887. He seems to have known Harnett well. Peto eked out a living painting portraits and "office boards" and taking photographs, but eventually he drifted into oblivion. He borrowed from Harnett the smoking, writing-table, book, and money themes, and later the music and hunt subjects, but remained always himself. His recurrent rack picture seems to have grown out of the "office boards" done as decorations for business premises. The type goes back to the seventeenth century, tapes and all, and it offers the *trompe-l'oeil* painter the ideal condition for illusion, for the board or surface is identical with the picture's background and everything else is depicted as existing in front of it. Peto's paintings were more anecdotal and sentimental than Harnett's, as witness *The Poor Man's Store* (1885, plate 320), and stylistically quite different. One might almost say that Peto was not really a *trompe-l'oeil* painter, that he merely used *trompe-l'oeil* subjects, for his handling was never unusually detailed, sharp-edged, or texturally differentiated. The general quality of light dominates his painting and connects him with the "luminists." The feeling for paint is always more pronounced than the illusion of reality, and in that sense Peto is often a more satisfying painter than Harnett. Peto borrowed Harnett's monumental hunt compositions, which he transformed, as in *Still Life with Lanterns* (after 1890, colorplate 41).

When Harnett was ready to go abroad in 1880 he gravitated to Munich. In his four years there, his work took on an unwonted richness of subject and complexity of composition, as well as a broader touch. However, the increased elegance resulted in "fancy" pictures which lack the authenticity of his earlier work. On the other hand, the hunt pictures begun in Munich led to his most notable later productions. They were derived from seventeenth-century game paintings and influenced by contemporary photographic studies. Harnett did four such still

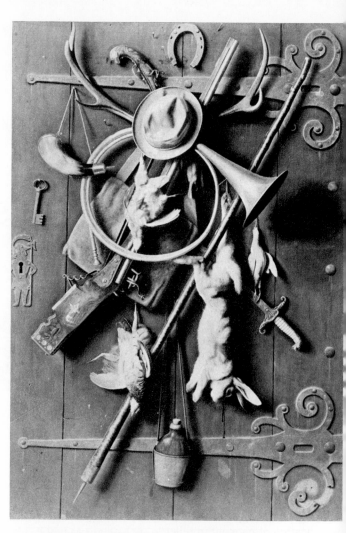

321 William Michael Harnett. *After the Hunt*. 1885.
Oil on canvas, 71 × 48″. The Fine Arts Museums of San Francisco. Mildred Anna Williams Collection

lifes, beginning in 1883. All show a miscellany of game and hunting paraphernalia hanging from an old wooden door with heavy iron hinges and keyhole, and all are life-size, impressive compositions with an unmatched virtuosity in *trompe-l'oeil* effects. The last, *After the Hunt* (1885, plate 321), was painted in Paris and hung for many years in a famous downtown New York saloon, sponsoring imitation in countless hotel lobbies and bars.

After his return to the United States in 1886, his work showed a return to simplicity, to American subject matter, and to Classical order, as opposed to the opulence and Teutonism of the hunt paintings. *Trompe l'oeil* became expressive art, presented with economy, taste, and sincerity. A modest grandeur of conception informs *The Old Violin* (1886), which was reproduced as a chromolithograph and widely copied. Harnett himself redid it several times, as he did so many themes.

John Haberle (1856–1933), in his wry and somewhat raffish manner, exploited the humor inherent in the *trompe-l'oeil* process, trapping the viewer in visual paradoxes. In *The Changes of Time* (1888) a satyr-head key-

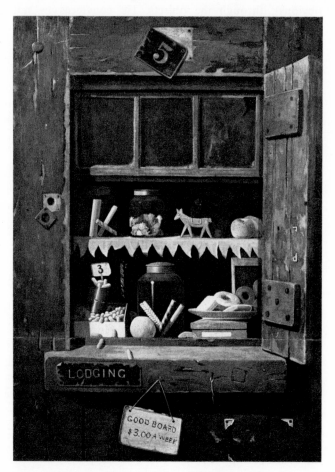

320 John Frederick Peto. *The Poor Man's Store*. 1885.
Oil on canvas, 36 × 25½″. Museum of Fine Arts, Boston. M. and M. Karolik Collection

plate is screwed to both door and frame, so that the lock can never be opened. And in *A Bachelor's Drawer* (1890–94) the contents of the drawer are perversely mounted all over the exterior so that the drawer cannot be opened.

Haberle's flat, linear style, more common to watercolor, militates against illusion, though he worked assiduously to achieve it, using the most difficult objects and trickiest effects to call attention to the effort involved—bills, stamps, coins, newspaper clippings (which are legible and allude always to himself), cracked glass, magnification, photographs, and wood graining. He is interesting iconographically for his use of such vernacular objects as cigarette, greeting, and playing cards and "girlie" pictures. In contrast to Harnett and Peto, he preferred nonaesthetic objects. His art lacks the serious grandeur of Harnett and the sensitive lyricism of Peto, but it offers a waggish imagination.

A host of imitators and plagiarists followed Harnett. The most interesting of these lesser personalities is Jefferson David Chalfant (1857–1931), who, though beholden to Harnett, plagiarized with taste and beautiful craftsmanship. He tended to strip down Harnett's compositions and focus on the basic elements, rendering them with luminous intensity.

THE NEW ROMANTICISM

The Romantic strain in American painting continued after the Civil War, though its character was altered, and, if it appeared less American than Realism, it seemed also more artistic.

It was William Morris Hunt (1824–1879) who was most influential in changing American preferences. Having studied and lived with Millet at Barbizon, he returned to Newport and Boston with paintings by his revered master, as well as Corot, Rousseau, and Daubigny, to spread the new gospel. When he settled in Newport in 1855, he was somewhat oversophisticated for painting portraits of local worthies or summer residents. His search for the ephemeral essence may have been an unconscious accommodation to his lack of discipline and his limitations as an artist. He could both admit a weakness in anatomy and decline to correct it for fear of failing to recapture the essence of a painting. But he had no such timidity when it came to theorizing or teaching, and he profoundly affected his students.

An attractive, gregarious gentleman of wit, with an aura of genius, he was the more irresistible for being well-born and married to a Boston heiress. His effect on taste

322 William Morris Hunt. *The Flight of Night*. 1878. Oil and chalk on canvas, 62 × 99″. The Pennsylvania Academy of the Fine Arts, Philadelphia

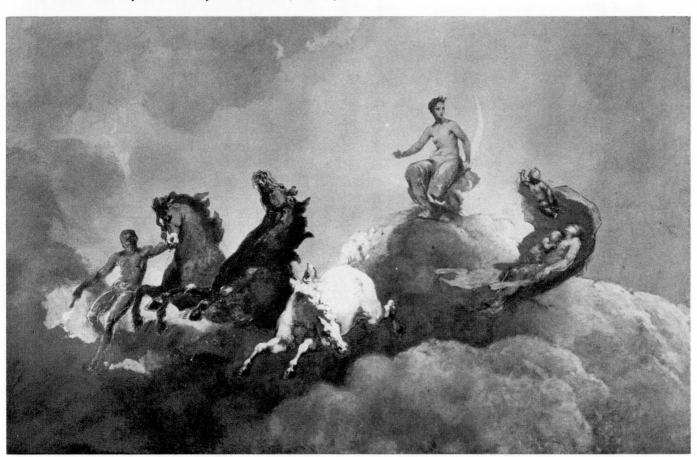

was undeniable. Bostonians bought Barbizon paintings before the French did, and even the Impressionists had a friendlier reception in the 1880s in Boston than in Paris.

As an artist Hunt offered more promise than achievement, although it must be remembered that most of his work was destroyed by fire in 1872. Many of his female figure pieces are reminiscent of Corot in composition and gentle lyricism. Like Inness, Hunt made much of suggestion, of the stimulation of imagination by the undefined, as if resolution would destroy the poetic illusion. His portraits, however, are forthright and vigorous.

Hunt is probably best remembered for the ill-fated mural decorations for the New York State Capitol at Albany, executed in two months in 1878. The compositions for the two huge lunettes reflect something of nineteenth-century French academic mural painting—bombastic, but with the breadth and fluency of a grander tradition. Hunt was not equipped to handle the heroic on such a scale, though the preparatory oil sketches (1878, plate 322) reveal, despite flabbiness in composition and drawing, a feeling for dramatic movement and heroic poetry new in American mural painting. Unfortunately, the oil paint applied directly to the stone surface soon deteriorated. Hunt suffered a general depression which

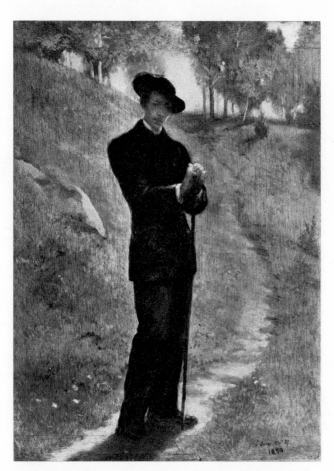

323 John La Farge. *Portrait of the Artist*. 1859. Oil on wood, 16 × 11½". The Metropolitan Museum of Art, New York. Samuel D. Lee Fund, 1934

ended in what was evidently suicide by drowning several months later.

Hunt's emphasis on poetic sentiment influenced a generation of Romantic figure painters. George Fuller (1822–1884) found a brooding mystery in the people and landscape of New England, transforming the ordinary into an idyll of some distant time and place. Robert Loftin Newman (1827–1912) might achieve a luminous color passage or the suggestion of a moving compositional relationship, but he rarely carried his ideas to completion.

John La Farge (1835–1910) was much like Hunt—upper-class, well educated, cosmopolitan. Both were highly intellectual, and both were brilliant talkers. They even had in common a streak of dilettantism, which La Farge, at least, overcame to emerge as the major artist-entrepreneur of his time. The most cultured and sophisticated artist working in the United States in the late nineteenth century, he had an immense potential for achievement and influence; yet he is hardly mentioned today. Stylistically, La Farge stands somewhere between the Romanticism of Hunt and the Realism of Whistler, but instead of resolving the conflict, he led Romantic Realism up the high road to the academic fatuities of "imperial Classicism."

Born in New York City into a family of French émigrés, the young La Farge went abroad in 1856 and in Paris stayed with his relatives, the Saint-Victors. The brilliant *feuilletoniste* Paul de Saint-Victor introduced him to Gautier, Baudelaire, Flaubert, Sainte-Beuve, Gavarni, and Chassériau. The greatest influence on La Farge was Chassériau, whose attempt to find a common ground for Classicism and Romanticism must have attracted the young man.

After a stopover in England, where he was impressed by the Pre-Raphaelite effort to express a Romantic idea in naturalistic terms, La Farge returned home. In 1859 he spent the year at Newport with William Morris Hunt, painting seriously for the first time. La Farge's *Portrait of the Artist* (1859, plate 323) is Huntian in the simplified silhouette, luminous haze enveloping form, and general Romantic feeling. During the next decade La Farge became involved in the study of optics and, paralleling the development of Impressionism, set himself the problem of painting the "commonplace" aspects of nature in "the exact time of day and circumstances of light." Also at this time he discovered Japanese art; he was among the first Western artists who understood and wrote about its aesthetic significance.

La Farge's modest, searching efforts of the sixties—landscapes, flower pieces, and still lifes—were realistic, carefully painted, and rich in color. In the seventies he began to seek a viable contemporary mode for the religious themes and monumental decorations which were to make his reputation. In 1876 Richardson called on him to decorate the interior of Trinity Church, Boston. By this time La Farge had become interested in stained

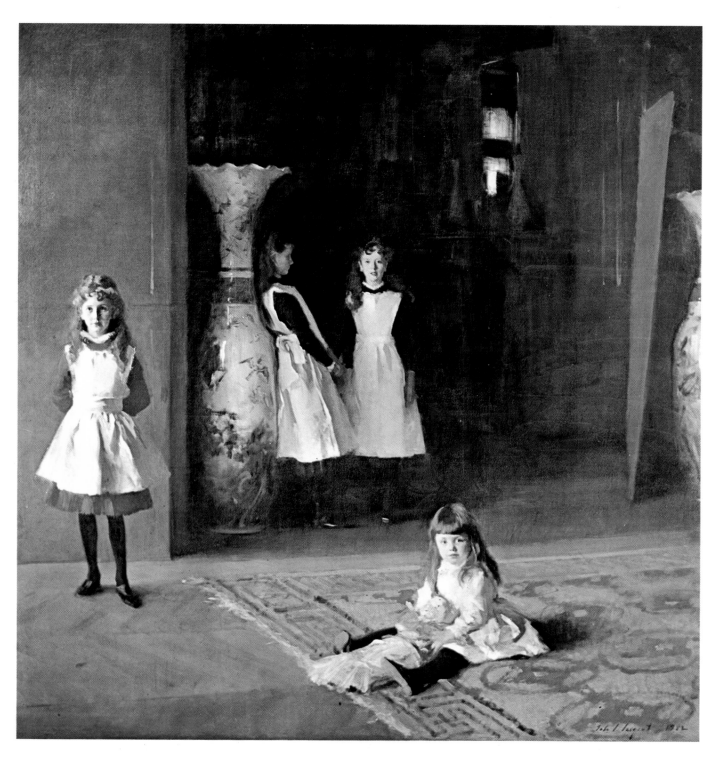

36 John Singer Sargent. *Daughters of Edward Darley Boit.* 1882. Oil on canvas, 87″ square.
Museum of Fine Arts, Boston. Gift of Mary Louisa Boit, Florence D. Boit,
Jane Hubbard Boit, and Julia Overing Boit, in memory of their father

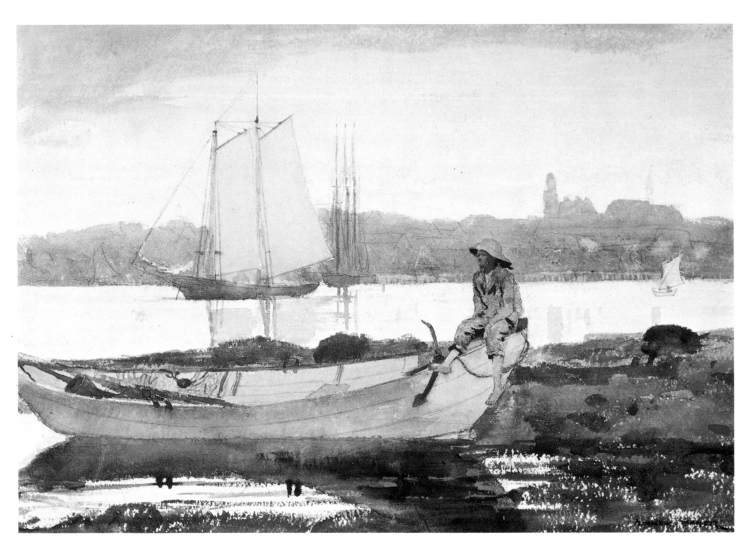

37   Winslow Homer. *Gloucester Harbor and Dory*. 1880. Watercolor, 9 × 13¼″.
Fogg Art Museum, Harvard University, Cambridge, Mass.

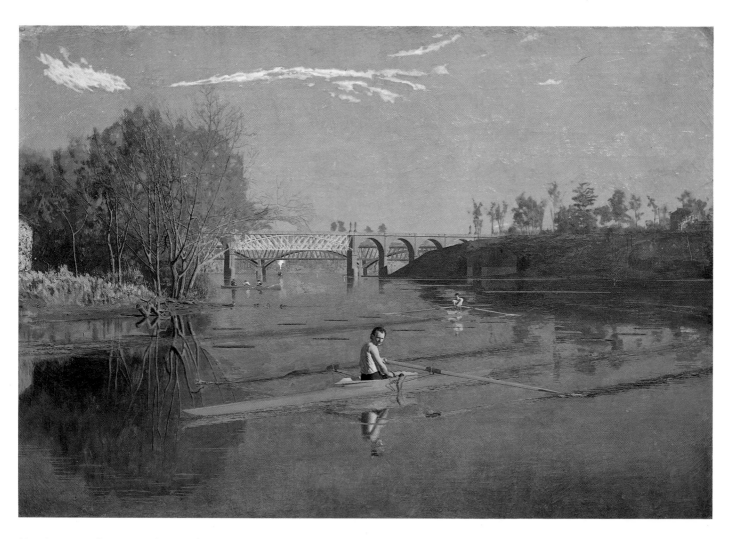

38   Thomas Eakins. *Max Schmitt in a Single Scull*. 1871. Oil on canvas, $32\frac{1}{4} \times 46\frac{1}{4}''$. The Metropolitan
Museum of Art, New York. Alfred N. Punnett Fund and gift of George D. Pratt, 1934

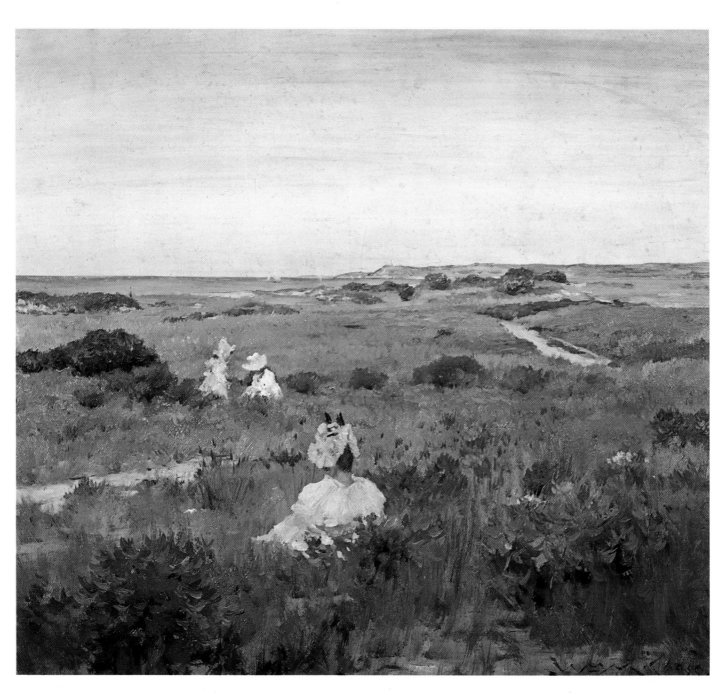

39 William Merritt Chase. *Landscape: Shinnecock, Long Island.* c. 1895. Oil on panel, $14\frac{1}{4} \times 16''$.
The Art Museum, Princeton University, Princeton, N.J.

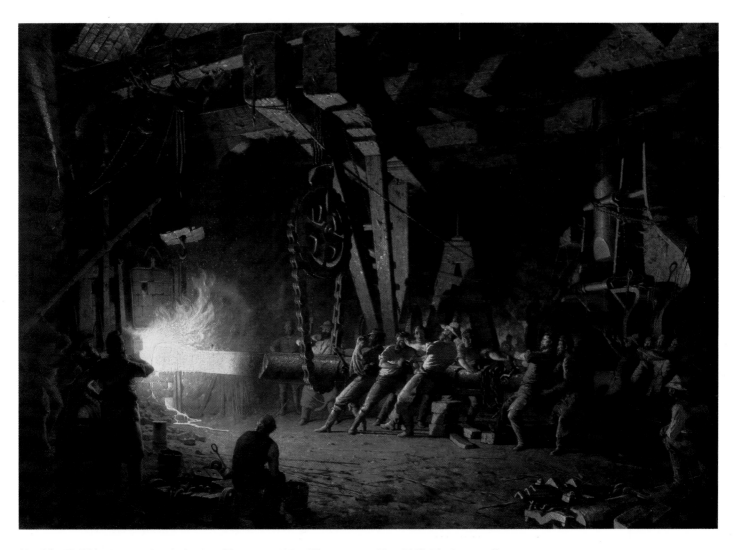

40　John F. Weir. *Forging the Shaft: A Welding Heat*. 1877. Oil on canvas, 52 × 73¼″. The Metropolitan
Museum of Art, New York. Gift of Lyman G. Bloomingdale, 1901

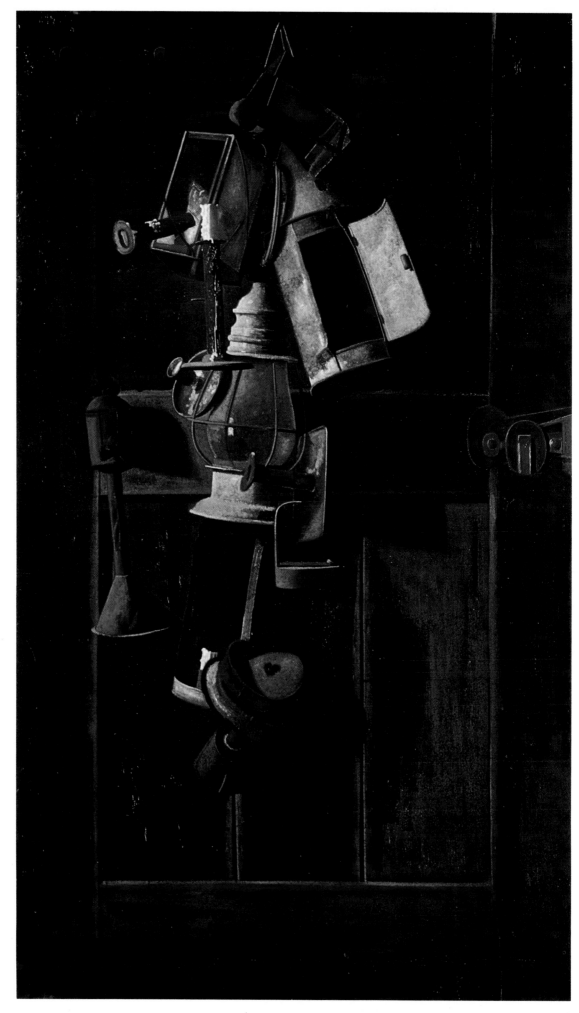

41 John Frederick Peto. *Still Life with Lanterns*. After 1890. Oil on canvas, 50 × 30″.
The Brooklyn Museum. Dick S. Ramsay Fund

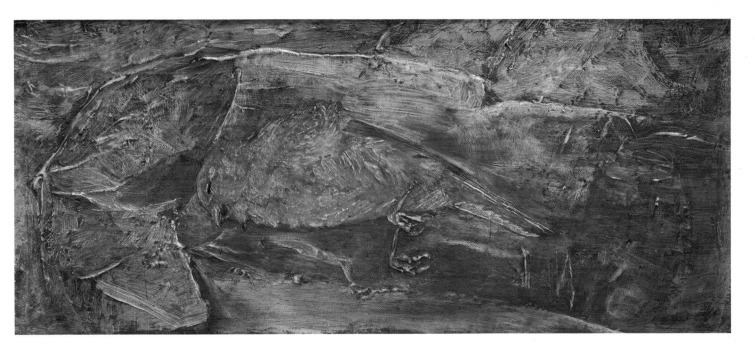

42 Albert Pinkham Ryder. *The Dead Bird*. 1890–1900. Oil on wood, $4\frac{1}{4} \times 9\frac{7}{8}''$.
The Phillips Collection, Washington, D.C.

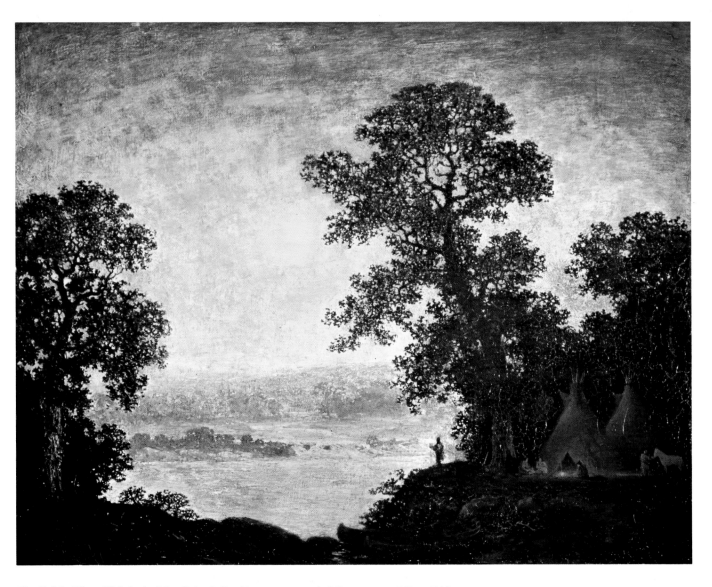

43 Ralph Albert Blakelock. *Moonlight, Indian Encampment*. n.d. Oil on canvas, $26\frac{1}{2} \times 33\frac{3}{4}''$.
National Collection of Fine Arts, Smithsonian Institution, Washington, D.C.

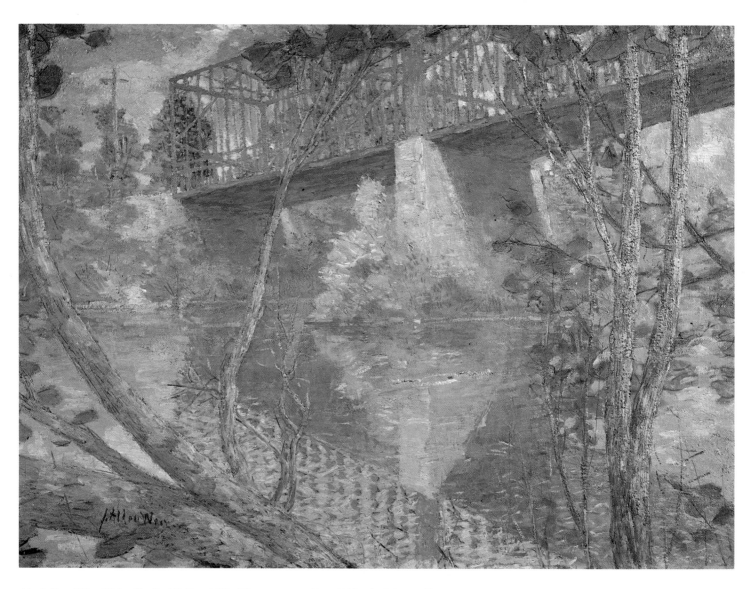

44　Julian Alden Weir. *The Red Bridge*. 1895. Oil on canvas, $24\frac{1}{4} \times 33\frac{3}{4}''$. The Metropolitan Museum of Art, New York. Gift of Mrs. John A. Rutherford

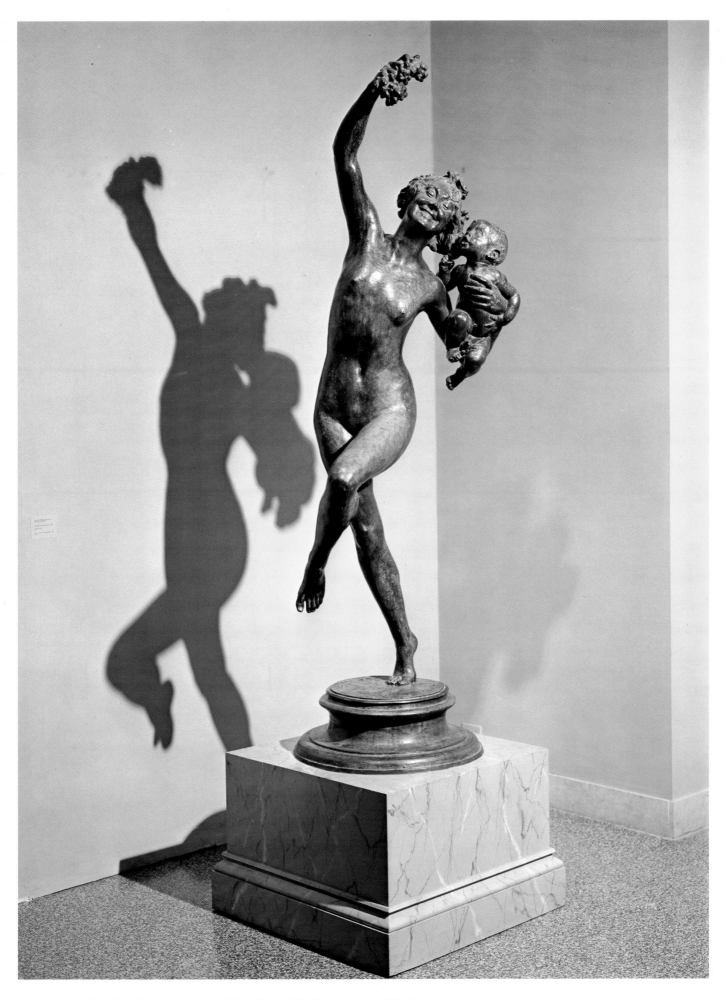

45 Frederick MacMonnies. *Bacchante and Infant Faun*. 1893. Bronze, height 83″. The Metropolitan
Museum of Art, New York. Gift of Charles Follen McKim

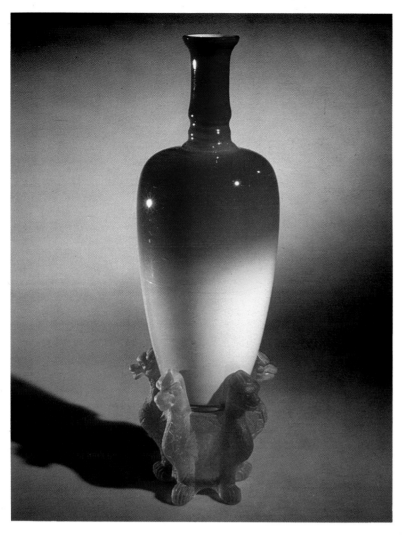

46 Hobbs, Brockunier & Company. "The Morgan Vase," from
Wheeling, W.Va. c. 1886. Peach-blow glass with
pressed amber stand, height (with stand) c. 10″.
The Corning Museum of Glass, Corning, N.Y.

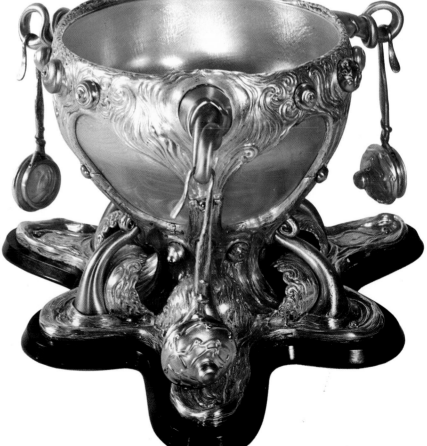

47 Louis Comfort Tiffany. Punch bowl made for the
Paris Exposition of 1900.
Favrile glass mounted in gilded silver, height $14\frac{1}{4}$″.
Virginia Museum of Fine Arts, Richmond

298

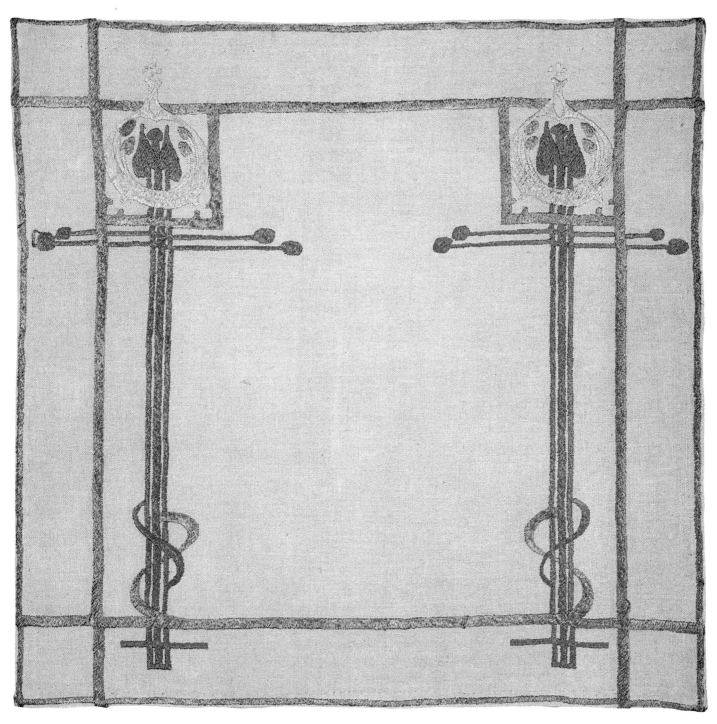

48   George Grant Elmslie. Table cover. 1910. Embroidered silk on linen,
    $21\frac{1}{2} \times 20\frac{1}{2}''$. Collection David and Patricia Gebhard, Santa Barbara, Calif.

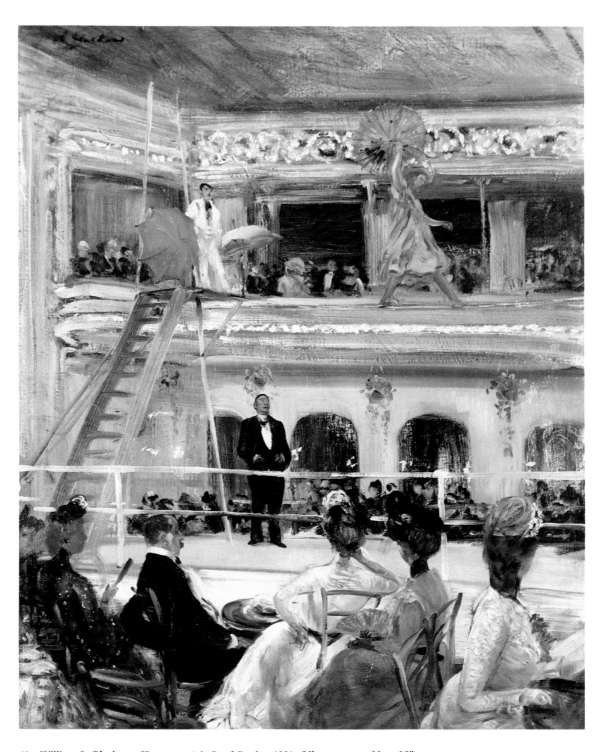

49 William J. Glackens. *Hammerstein's Roof Garden*. 1901. Oil on canvas, 30 × 25″.
Whitney Museum of American Art, New York

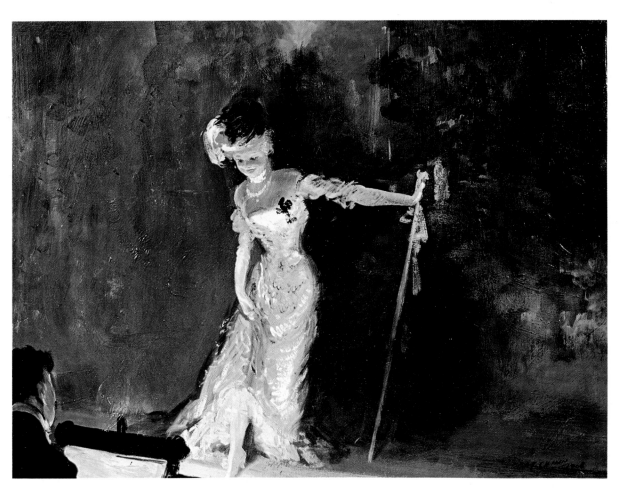

50   Everett Shinn. *Revue*. 1908. Oil on canvas, 18 × 24″.
Whitney Museum of American Art, New York

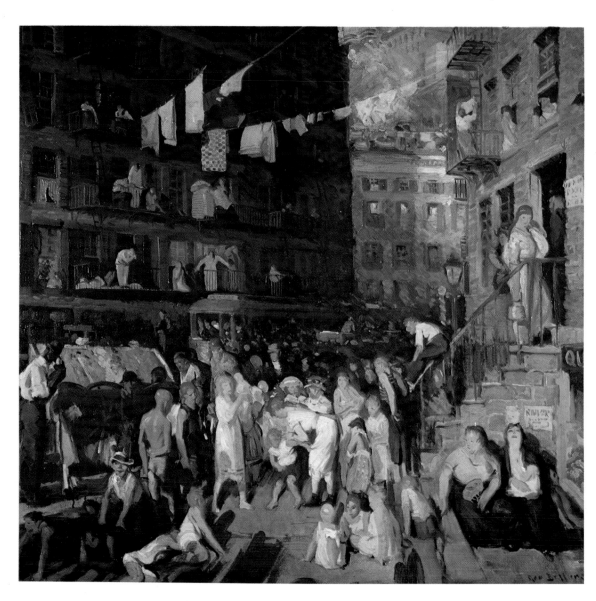

51　George Bellows. *Cliff Dwellers*. 1913. Oil on canvas, $39\frac{1}{2} \times 41\frac{1}{2}''$.
Los Angeles County Museum of Art

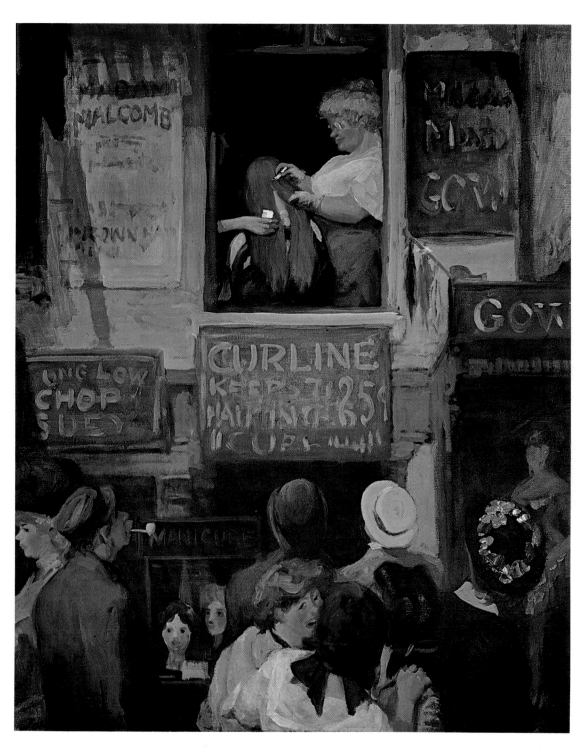

52   John Sloan. *Hairdresser's Window*. 1907. Oil on canvas, $31\frac{7}{8} \times 26''$.
Wadsworth Atheneum, Hartford, Conn.
The Ella Gallup Sumner and Mary Catlin Sumner Collection

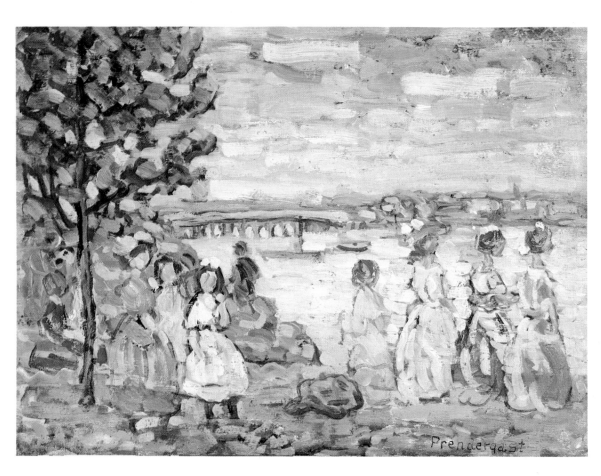

53 Maurice Prendergast. *Evening Walk*. 1917–20. Oil on panel, 15 × 24″.
Private collection, New York

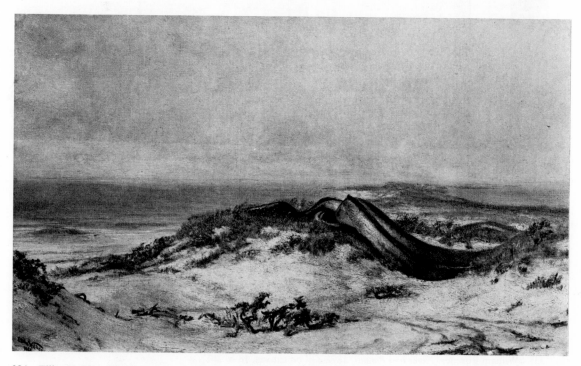

324 Elihu Vedder. *The Lair of the Sea Serpent*. 1864. Oil on canvas, 21 × 36".
Museum of Fine Arts, Boston. Bequest of Thomas G. Appleton

glass but had no real experience in large-scale interior decoration. However, within four months, he designed and completed with ten to fifteen assistants the painting of the immense interior. Despite its obvious aesthetic weaknesses and subsequent emasculation of the scheme by renovations, it remains a rich and coherent conception, the model for many later church interiors.

Trinity made La Farge the premier interior designer and mural painter in America, and with his activities in stained glass he had more work than he could handle. But even the finest of his painted decorations reveal both the strength and the weakness of his academic eclecticism, and he arrived at a Neoclassicism that paralleled the architectural "imperial Classicism" of Richard M. Hunt. La Farge's major energies during his maturity were directed toward the revival of stained glass. He set to work from the ground up, manufacturing the glass, developing new kinds, such as the famous "opaline," and devising new techniques. He was responsible for several thousand windows in churches and dwellings. Technically, at least, he reconstituted the craft, but it took the genius of Louis C. Tiffany to transform that tradition into a resplendent expression of the international Art Nouveau style.

La Farge's interest in Pre-Raphaelitism was exceptional, for the movement had only a limited influence in America. It is most evident in his black-and-white illustrations for books and especially for *The Riverside Magazine*, done in 1866. The literary themes, laced with mystery and terror, were executed in the sinuous line

and with the decorative disposition of form of the Pre-Raphaelites.

The chief example of the Pre-Raphaelite influence is Elihu Vedder (1836–1923), a friend and admirer of La Farge. After studying briefly in Paris, Vedder worked in Italy until his return to the United States in 1861 and earned his living at a variety of hack jobs. Meanwhile, he began work on his strangely imaginative pictures. They are not profound, having the quality of illustration, yet there is an air of mystery about Vedder's imagery that transcends both the triteness of subject and the almost naive academicism of style. *The Lair of the Sea Serpent* (1864, plate 324) is memorable even if one knows that the model was a dead eel washed up on the Long Island shore. The very ambivalence of the blowup creates a Romantic or surreal image.

Vedder is best remembered for his illustrations for *The Rubaiyat of Omar Khayyam*, published in 1884, in which the gentle Romantic melancholy of the drawings echoes Edward Fitzgerald's transformation of the medieval Persian original. The illustrations are strikingly pre-Raphaelite in imagery, linear pattern, and decorative arrangement.

The brooding mood in Vedder's most imaginative work belied his sunny disposition. In contrast, William Rimmer (1816–1879) seems to have expressed all his frustration and bitterness in his art. Better known as a sculptor and teacher of anatomy, he was also a painter, though few of his paintings have survived. Most of those we know have not weathered time very well, since he was an amateur in

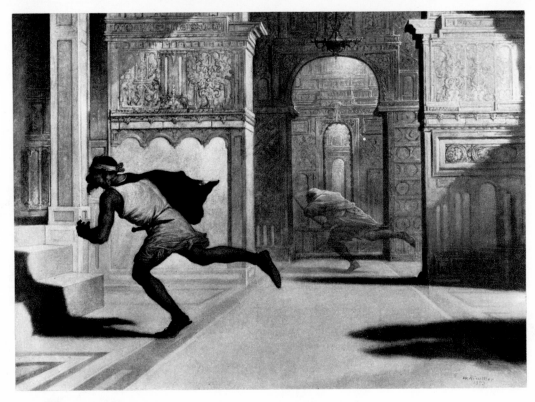

325　William Rimmer. *Flight and Pursuit*. 1872. Oil on canvas, 18 × 26¼″.
Museum of Fine Arts, Boston. Bequest of Miss Edith Nichols

paint as he was in sculpture. But his brain teemed with mystical visions and nightmarish fantasies. One of the most haunting imaginative paintings of the century is Rimmer's *Flight and Pursuit* (1872, plate 325). The panicked flight of an assassin/victim, man/conscience, good/evil down the endless corridors of the mind/time is a nightmare that probes the depths of Rimmer's own troubled spirit and beyond to the unconscious of man.

Albert Pinkham Ryder (1847–1917) was the most original Romantic painter of the century. His art is the culmination of a tendency that began with Allston and came down through Page, Hunt, and, to a certain extent, La Farge. These artists sought the spiritual essence rather than the physical description of reality or a dream. They were heirs to the Venetian tradition of luminous, translucent, sensuous color, conveying a meaning independent of its context. Their emphasis was on the direct communication of emotion or mood instead of story or idea, thus differing from the literary stream that includes Cole, Quidor, Vedder, Rimmer, and, again to some extent, La Farge.

Ryder seems out of place in nineteenth-century America, but even though he may have presaged subsequent artistic movements and inspired later artists, he belonged to his own time and place. He was a product of the new forces in American art brought back from Europe by the younger men. In the art scene of the time one discerns a grouping of "tonal" painters with a preference for the lower registers, crepuscular effects, and a brooding sadness. Among them were Hunt and his circle, the early La Farge, Ryder, Blakelock, Inness and some of his disciples.

Tangential but relevant are the nocturnes of Whistler. Ryder does not stand isolated, though his art is obstinately his own.

Ryder was the only artist of his time on whom the external world had no hold. Solitude, asceticism, irresponsibility were the preconditions of his freedom to live completely and intensely with and for his art. He was not really a recluse, for he had close friends in the art world, was a founder of the Society of American Artists, and showed at their annual exhibitions. Although he did not sell widely, he had a few loyal patrons, and at a sale in 1899 his pictures brought prices only slightly lower than those of Inness and Homer.

In a small walk-up tenement on 15th Street, New York, amid the clutter of years, he worked and reworked the small magical canvases that embodied his dreams. Heedless of chemistry or craft, he laid on layer after layer of cheap pigment mixed with varnish, sometimes using alcohol as a solvent, and varnished the surface after each session until the paint stood out in undulating relief. He might carry an image in his mind for years before committing it to canvas; the painting remained in flux as he worked; forms were altered, moved, or expunged; accidents of color led to new explorations; and the canvas could be put aside indefinitely. Any Ryder painting contains below the outer skin a sequence of other paintings. The long maturation period produced the irreducible images, the translucent lacquered surfaces, the gemlike color, but it also led to a darkening and cracking of the pigment, so that the original intention has been irretrievably lost. Because of his working method, dating his pictures is difficult, but a general chronology has been established on available evidence: the earliest works were done in the 1870s; the most productive period was about 1880 to 1900; after that he mainly reworked older pictures.

Ryder was born in New Bedford, Mass., when it was a whaling port. His sight was impaired in childhood by a faulty vaccination. When the family moved to New York City in 1870, he attended the National Academy school, but he was essentially self-taught. He never studied abroad, though he visited Europe several times. What he thought about the art he saw, he kept to himself.

From his earliest works Ryder seems to have known what he was after. There was little change in his style; yet there is a great variety within a limited range. The pastoral scenes, which are closest to observed reality, seem to be the earliest. In these Ryder is not concerned with truth to nature but with transforming his memory of it into pigment.

The works of his maturity fall into fairly distinct categories: those inspired by literary themes from Shake-

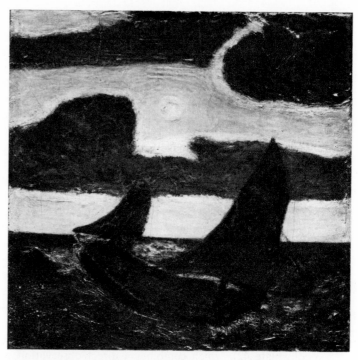

326 Albert Pinkham Ryder. *Moonlight Marine.* 1870–90. Oil on wood, 11⅜ × 12″. The Metropolitan Museum of Art, New York. Samuel D. Lee Fund

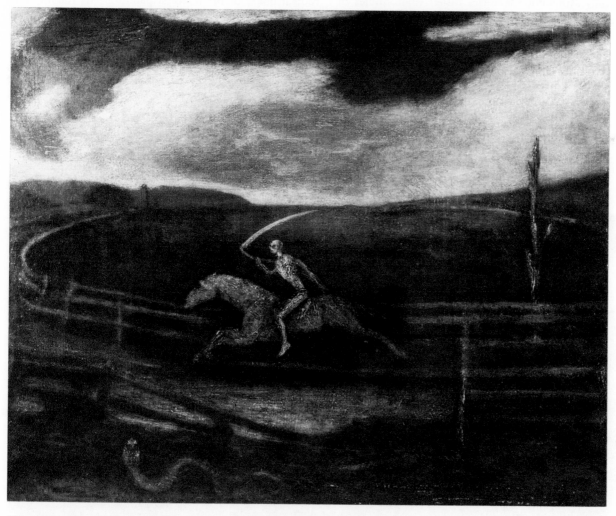

327 Albert Pinkham Ryder. *The Race Track (Death on a Pale Horse).* 1890–1910. Oil on canvas, 28¼ × 35¼″. The Cleveland Museum of Art. Purchase, J. H. Wade Fund

speare, the Bible, and Wagnerian operas; and marine subjects. It is often said that all Ryder's marines are versions of the same picture—the silhouette of a little sailboat bobbing on the vast sea glowing green out of blackness, the hulking cloud phantoms against the sky, the silver moonlight bathing the world in phosphorescence. These features have become clichés for both the public and the forger. Slightly more than 150 authentic Ryders are extant, and there are possibly five times that many fakes. But such examples as the *Moonlight Marine* (1870–90, plate 326) have an indescribable surface richness, a depth and luminosity of color, a tightness of organization, an inner conviction.

After 1900 Ryder's creative energies seem to have diminished, but there are notable late paintings such as *The Race Track (Death on a Pale Horse,* 1890–1910, plate 327), a somewhat naive though starkly compelling metaphor. The only work that seems to have been painted from nature is the small and poignant *Dead Bird* (1890–1900, colorplate 42), which combines a direct observation of fact with a mystical empathy for the pitiable little corpse on a crumpled piece of paper.

Ralph Albert Blakelock (1847–1919) could be included among the landscapists except that his woodland scenes were really Romantic memories rather than studies of nature. His repertory was even more limited than Ryder's —dark foreground trees silhouetted in a fretwork of leaves against a sunset or moonlit sky, often with an encampment of Indians around a glowing fire. The arabesque of foliage, the sparkle of light through the dark mass, the small firelit figures create a shimmering surface. Working with small touches of pigment, he built up his paint to a heavy impasto and polished the surface with pumice before applying the final layer of color.

Blakelock attended Cooper Union, but was essentially self-taught. From 1869 to 1872 he traveled through the West making sketches, and the memory of Indian encampments later appeared in many of his paintings (colorplate 43). He was burdened by a large family and was forced to sell his pictures to unscrupulous dealers who took outrageous advantage of his need. He broke under the strain of a precarious existence in 1899 and was committed to an asylum, where he spent seventeen years in a kind of euphoric oblivion. The forgery of Blakelock paintings began while he was still alive, and the problem of authenticating his works is probably greater than for Ryder.

The shift in taste during the last quarter of the century is manifest in the later work of George Inness and, following him, two younger landscape painters, Alexander Wyant and Homer Martin, who made the transition from the Hudson River School to a new poetic tonalism. Inness had broken from the older tradition, and after his return from abroad in 1875, his art passed into a more radical phase of broad tonal painting. His Italian landscapes had added a picturesqueness foreign to his earlier American scenes. Assurance and a self-conscious aestheticism mark *The Monk* (1873, plate 328), a picture of striking Romantic effects in composition and light.

However, by the 1880s his style had become more

328 George Inness. *The Monk.* 1873. Oil on canvas, 39½ × 64".
Addison Gallery of American Art, Phillips Academy, Andover, Mass.

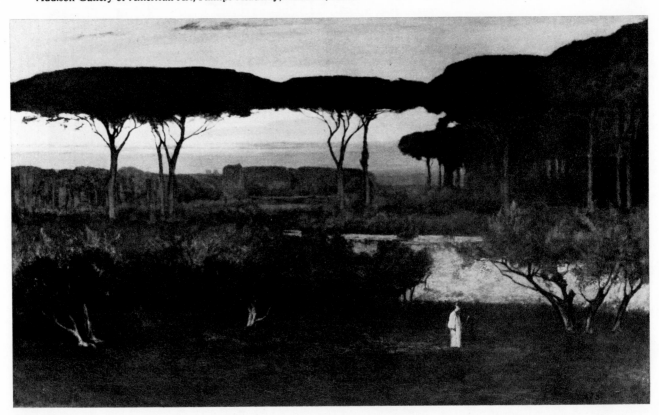

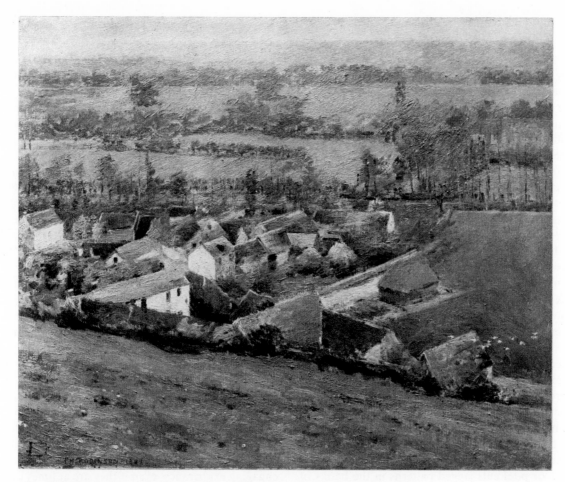

329 Theodore Robinson. *Bird's-Eye View—Giverny*. 1889. Oil on canvas, 26 × 32¼″.
The Metropolitan Museum of Art, New York. Gift of George A. Hearn, 1910

intimate, his brushwork more cursory, as he sought to capture the vagaries of transient light. His late works have a remarkable affinity with the late silvery woodland idylls of Corot and with Whistler's nocturnes. This phase was Impressionism of a sort, though it eschewed the clarity of bright sunlight and the tyranny of fact, seeking instead a poetic reverie expressed in evanescent forms and subtle tonalities. Inness was a prodigious worker, though erratic; he poured out "impressions" from memory. Too often they are only suggestions, touches of color that do not coalesce into forms, shapes that dissolve. After a decline, Inness's reputation is undergoing a readjustment and there is a growing recognition of the more enduring quality of his earlier, more solidly painted landscapes.

Alexander Helwig Wyant (1836–1892) painted his early landscapes in the detailed naturalism of the Hudson River School, though his panoramic effects indicate a kinship with Church and Bierstadt. Later his style became more personal, smaller in scale, and akin to the Barbizon School, reflecting especially Corot and Rousseau.

Homer Dodge Martin (1836–1897) studied briefly at the National Academy. His early landscapes of the White Mountains, the Adirondacks, and the North Carolina Smokies are similar to the earlier works of Kensett—thinly painted, dry, and studiously detailed.

However, he went abroad and was profoundly influenced by Impressionism. Even after his return, he continued to paint recollections of the French landscape. Martin never accepted the Impressionists' technique of broken color or the scientific study of light, but he incorporated into his own Romantic lyricism their higher-keyed palette and airiness. Despite his timid stab at Impressionism and the personal poeticism of Inness, the American Romantic landscapists were essentially retardataire.

THE AMERICAN IMPRESSIONISTS AND "THE TEN"

The "luminism" of Kensett, Whittredge, and Heade, and the outdoor paintings of Eakins, Eastman Johnson, and Homer had independently come within a breath of Impressionism. Sargent in his watercolors and Chase in his Long Island landscapes had shown an awareness of Impressionism. But it was a new generation of American painters in France during the 1880s who finally reacted directly to Impressionism—Theodore Robinson, John Twachtman, Alden Weir, and Childe Hassam.

Except for Mary Cassatt, Theodore Robinson (1852–1896) was the closest of all to the French. He studied briefly in Chicago and New York and then in Paris, where he worked with Carolus-Duran and Gérôme. In 1888 he met Monet, settled in Giverny, and worked with the French master until his return to the United States. Robinson, like Mary Cassatt, was more concerned with three-dimensional form than the French Impressionists, who were intent upon the dissolution of form in light. He did loosen up eventually; his touch became surer, though never bold, and his color more sonorous, but he preferred muted, pearly tonalities that conveyed a gentle, poetic tone, as in *Bird's-Eye View—Giverny* (1889, plate 329), which is quite close to the work of Pissarro and Sisley. On the other hand, the finest of his American landscapes suggest an acclimatization to the native scene and a use of light recalling the "luminist" tradition.

John Henry Twachtman (1853–1902) arrived at Impressionism in a more circuitous fashion. He studied in Cincinnati at the Ohio Mechanics Institute and with Duveneck. After shuttling between Europe and the United States, Twachtman came home in 1886, painting in the Barbizon manner, though his palette had been lightened by his contact with Impressionism. Not until 1888, when he moved to Greenwich, Conn., did his style become clearly Impressionist although far from orthodox. His preference for winter landscapes was unique, and his preoccupation with light on snow led to subtle variations within a narrow color range, at times, through overrefinement, to a haze of white pigment that is rather leaden. He flattened the picture decisively, so that the dark water of a brook or pool cuts jagged patterns in the banks of snow shimmering in the cold winter sun. Despite his faithfulness to visual experience, the result is sometimes strangely un-Impressionistic in its strong rhythmic forms and lyrical strivings.

Julian Alden Weir (1852–1919) had neither the grace of Robinson nor the originality and singleness of purpose of Twachtman. He grafted a sparkling skin of Impressionism on an essentially conservative vision, producing pleasant but pedestrian pictures. In *The Red Bridge* (1895, colorplate 44) he even achieved an unexpected freshness of observation and originality of composition, but too often his routine application of fragmented color produced a mess of chalky pigment.

The most talented of the group was the somewhat younger Frederick Childe Hassam (1859–1935). He attended the Boston Art Club and the Lowell Institute, was apprenticed to an engraver, and became an illustrator, an occupation he continued even after he was a successful painter. He went abroad first in 1883. A receptive student and facile craftsman, he brought back a proto-Impressionist style of tonal painting that was a bit slick yet perceptive. His many urban scenes of the 1880s were an innovation in American painting. Somber in hue but sprightly in execution, they project a romantic view of city life in the haze of snow, rain, or twilight that forecast the Ashcan School. Characteristic is *Rainy Day, Boston* (1885, plate 330).

A stay in Paris from 1885 to 1888 resulted in Hassam's conversion to Impressionism. He came close to the central manner of the French—high-keyed pure color, clearly differentiated brushstrokes, dissolution of form, and a holiday mood. His city- and landscapes have an engaging exuberance, even if they are at times brassy and superficial.

An entire generation of painters born about 1860 were influenced by Impressionism or remained faithful to it into the twentieth century. One with real talent was Maurice Prendergast (1859–1924), who patiently worked out his own solutions somewhat later.

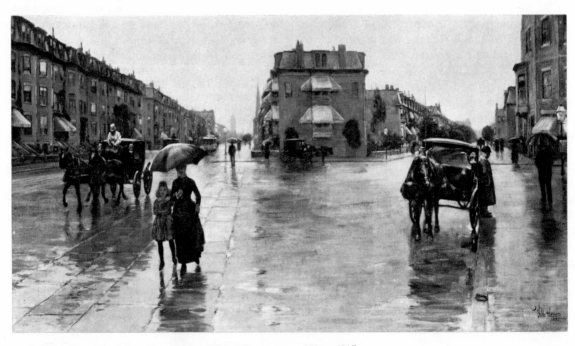

330 Childe Hassam. *Rainy Day, Boston.* 1885. Oil on canvas, 26¼ × 48¼".
The Toledo Museum of Art, Ohio. Gift of Florence Scott Libbey, 1956

Prompted by Twachtman, a group of successful and congenial New York and Boston artists joined in an informal alliance called "The Ten" and exhibited jointly in 1898—Frank W. Benson (1862–1951), Joseph De Camp (1858–1923), Thomas W. Dewing (1851–1938), Childe Hassam, Willard L. Metcalf (1858–1925), Robert Reid (1862–1929), Edward E. Simmons (1852–1931), Edmund C. Tarbell (1862–1938), John W. Twachtman, and J. Alden Weir (with the addition after Twachtman's death of William M. Chase). The binding tie was some connection with Impressionism, but, except for Hassam, they also shared a poetic gentility. Benson, De Camp, and especially Tarbell depicted a world of elegance, with porcelain ladies at tea in the filtered illumination of curtained interiors or in the dappled light of their gardens. The haunting poetry of Dewing's art differs from the gentle decorum more characteristic of "The Ten" in its air of brooding melancholy, almost foreboding.

DECORATIVE ARTS

In the 1870s, a group of young women, impressed with the Oriental ceramics and the French underglaze ware at the Centennial Exhibition in Philadelphia, formed a Woman's Pottery Club to paint chinaware and produce what became known as "Cincinnati Limoges." In 1880 Maria Longworth Nichols, a wealthy young matron, established a private pottery named "Rookwood" (after the family estate) which experimented with glaze techniques and served as a distributor and commercial kiln for the women amateurs. Eventually the firm became independent of the amateurs, and, after solidifying a style and winning a gold medal at the World's Fair in Paris in 1889, Mrs. Nichols turned the business over to her professional staff. The basket (plate 331) by Maria Nichols combines many of the elements of early art pottery. The shape is almost free-form, with lions' heads serving as feet. The decoration includes both overglazes and underglazes in a Japanese spider motif. The spiders and web were painted on before the piece was fired; then the gilt work was applied. This sort of pottery was as popular as art glass and was widely copied with the same motifs, primarily in the already established glassmaking centers of Steubenville and Zanesville, Ohio.

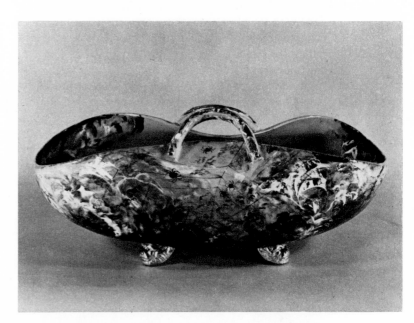

331 Maria Longworth Nichols (for Rookwood Pottery). Basket. 1882. Ceramic, length 20″. The Cincinnati Art Museum. Gift of Mrs. Roy D. Kercheval

ACADEMIC AND MURAL PAINTING

Academic painting at the end of the nineteenth century was a rather loose amalgam of acceptable styles. The National Academy of Design was dominated by American-oriented artists who felt threatened by the work of young men trained in Munich or Paris. In 1877 a revolt among younger artists and some sympathetic academicians led to the formation of the Society of American Artists, which included La Farge and Inness as well as Saint-Gaudens and Ryder. Though the "new movement" seemed a threat for a while, the two "academies" learned to live amicably together until their quiet merger in 1906. "Academic" included almost anything from the exoticism of Robert F. Blum (1857–1903) to the agrarian sagas of Horatio Walker (1858–1938). In its ranks were the Romantic idealists Abbott Thayer (1849–1921) and George De Forest Brush (1855–1941), who exalted American womanhood into an image of milk-fed divinity and motherhood into cloying treacle. Only a handful of these artists deserve a second look. Cecilia Beaux (1863–1942) was a very accomplished and vigorous portraitist in the manner of Sargent; Robert W. Vonnoh (1858–1933) painted solid and sober portraits in the French Realist tradition; and Robert Blum is worth reexamination for the brilliance of his technique.

The exceptional growth of mural painting in the last decades of the century may have been a response to the demands of "imperial Classicism" in architecture, where the scale of building and the blank surfaces of wall, ceiling, and dome called for decoration. In 1876 La Farge's interior decor of Trinity Church initiated an era of architectural decoration in which architects were to play a major role. By the 1880s, churches, hotels, and the new palatial clubs were employing artists to embellish their interiors. Mural painting, stained-glass windows, and sculptural ornamentation became common in such projects and in theaters, banks, and the mansions of the merchant princes. It did not matter that American painters had no training or tradition in mural techniques (except for the nucleus trained under La Farge at Trinity Church). They found a ready-made formula in the Beaux-Arts style of the French academicians, as the architects had before them. The flourishing activity drew together architect, painter, and sculptor in a dream of Renaissance creativity, culminating in the Columbian Exposition. These latter efforts at "imperial Classic" grandeur are gone with the plaster structures they graced, but acres of comparable mural painting still cover the walls of public buildings. It is difficult to be certain that all of it is as worthless as it would seem.

Aside from the Chicago Fair, the greatest mural bonanza was the decoration of the new Library of Congress, completed in the late 1890s, which employed most of the better-known muralists of the time and established the principle of providing art for Federal buildings. The most impressive project was the decoration of the new Boston Public Library by the Frenchman Puvis de Chavannes, and by Sargent and Abbey. Puvis painted his canvases without having seen the interior for which they were intended. The pale, wispy allegorical figures are not up to his usual standard and, in any case, are not American painting.

Edwin Austin Abbey (1852–1911), one of America's most popular illustrators, delighted a vast public with his historical and literary subjects. In the Delivery Room he painted the *Quest for the Holy Grail* in a colorful panoply of costumed character actors. The detail is too insistent for the dramatic action, but the whole has illustrative interest and decorative charm.

Despite their shortcomings, the Sargent murals, unfortunately crowded in a narrow gallery over a staircase, are the most interesting. Selecting the Judeo-Christian religion as subject, he wrestled with the presentation for more than twenty-five years. Nothing in his background prepared him for the task, and he fell back on art-historical precedent, fitting the style to the theme with scholarly preciseness, from the neo-Baroque theatricality of *The Prophets* to the hieratic symbolism of the pseudo-Byzantine *Doctrine of the Trinity*. The disparity of modes does not make for coherence, and the flat, abstract, medieval forms of the *Trinity* lunette and frieze are anachronistically modeled in the spirit of Pre-Raphaelite updating of antiquity. Still the murals reveal Sargent's remarkable gifts.

One may regret the opportunity lost by American mural painters when they resorted, as they so often did, to an endless repetition of buxom female allegorical figures in classical drapery personifying anything from the Trinity to the Telephone; but the Europeans were no more successful in finding an official voice.

13
Sculpture: Mostly Monumental

Sculpture after the Civil War paralleled the evolution of painting, with the emergence of a new Realism and the discovery of Paris as a new influence, but its public character conditioned its development in ways that did not affect painting. Monuments, official portraits, and architectural sculpture are commissioned, paid for, and judged as establishment taste, and the sculptor's function depends on public acceptance. Sculpture was, therefore, more conservative and rhetorical, less adventurous and idiosyncratic.

The response to the Civil War as an expression of individual or public sentiment was more pronounced in sculpture than in painting, and the prevailing attitude was pro-North and antislavery. In the North such sentiments were institutionalized into civic monuments. Every hamlet had its war memorial in permanent stone, bronze, or cast iron, all of which kept a horde of sculptors lucratively busy. The defeated South, steeped in rancor and burdened with the demands of reconstruction, could not freely participate in this orgy of plastic commemoration. Still, for a while, at least, the erection of statues of southern Revolutionary War heroes affirmed the southern heritage.

The assassination of Lincoln had created a martyr whose image could serve as a symbolic reference to the idealism that had motivated the conflict, and, with time, monuments to his memory began to rival in number even those to Washington.

As in painting, postwar sculpture was for some time dominated by an older generation of established artists, both expatriate academic Neoclassicists and the native monument makers. The Neoclassicists prevailed at the Centennial Exposition, but they were playing out their string on reputation.

Edmonia Lewis (1845–?) created quite a sensation in Rome. Born of a Chippewa mother and a black father, she graduated from Oberlin College and made her way to Boston and to William Lloyd Garrison, who helped launch her on a sculpture career. Following her early success with Civil War subjects, she turned in Rome to Indian and Biblical themes. Her greatest triumph came with the *Death of Cleopatra*, exhibited at the Centennial, a typical Victorian literary subject but with an element of the macabre in the depiction of the effect of death on beauty. Then she simply disappeared from the scene.

Of the old-guard monument sculptors, Thomas Ball continued to work as an expatriate in Florence, but his style was tied to the naturalism of the native school rather than to the Neoclassic tradition. His most famous work of the postwar years was the *Emancipation Group* (1874, plate 332). More than any Lincoln memorial of the time it captured the imagination of the public in its mixture of naturalism and sentimentality.

(continued on page 315)

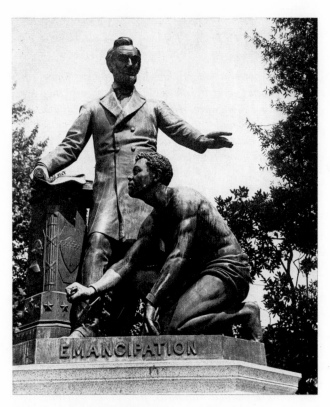

332 Thomas Ball. *Emancipation Group.* 1874. Bronze, heroic size. Washington, D.C.

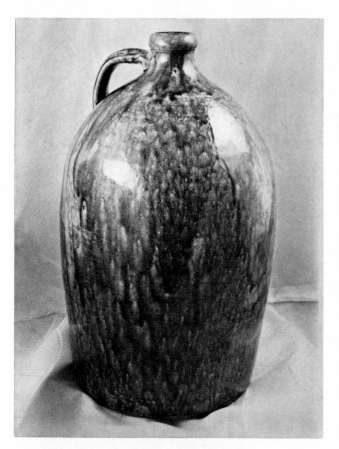

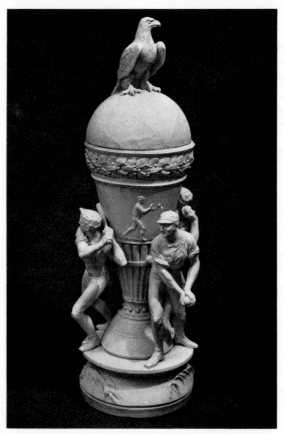

333 Meader Pottery, Cleveland, Ga. Jug. c. 1880.
Stoneware, height 17″.
Florida State Museum, Gainesville

334 Isaac Broome (Ott & Brewer Co., Trenton, N.J.).
Baseball vase. 1876. Parian porcelain bisque,
height 32″. New Jersey State Museum, Trenton.
The Brewer Collection

DECORATIVE ARTS

American potters had produced earthenware since early colonial times, and by the eighteenth century they were also making stoneware. This alternate form of domestic crockery was made of gray clays that, when kiln-fired, produced a hard, shiny surface. Unlike the red earthenware, it was nonporous and thus well suited for food storage. The vessels were usually salt-glazed by a simple process of attacking the glaze with salt during the firing. The result is a tough, pitted surface. The jug shown (plate 333) was thrown in Georgia, where, as in much of the Southeast, quantities of suitable clay existed. Its dating, well into the nineteenth century, is supported by the shape, showing the transition from the earlier ovoid form to the later flat-topped vessel. As with almost all stoneware produced after 1800, the inside of the jug is sealed with the dark brown glaze known as "Albany slip" in the North, but referred to as "tobacco spit" in the area where the Meader Pottery existed from 1830 to 1900. Although this piece is simply formed and undecorated, many of the stoneware jugs, crocks, and jars had either incised line decoration or were painted with birds, flowers, or patriotic symbols like those found on mid-nineteenth-century American molded glass or in folk paintings. Stoneware is still being

made, and the 1960s saw some revival of interest in the medium, now used extensively for everyday tableware.

One of the most successful of mass-produced ceramics in the nineteenth century was "Parian ware," a white stoneware named for the fine marble from the Greek island of Paros. Figurines and busts of famous historic figures were fabricated for popular consumption, and by 1876 almost every home could boast of some Parian objects. It is often impossible to differentiate between the best of American Parian ware and that of France or England, but the subject of this example (plate 334) leaves no doubt as to its origin. Designed for display at the Philadelphia Centennial Exhibition of 1876, the baseball vase celebrates an already popular pastime. The imagery is a mixture of Classical and American patriotic: the conical form is based on the Roman fasces, although baseball bats are substituted for the bundle of rods and a buckled belt for the leather thong; the top of the cone is a half baseball; the eagle symbolizes both ancient Rome and the United States; and the Classical frieze is composed of baseball players in low relief. The mixed imagery represents a standard American Victorian attitude toward symbolism.

(continued from page 313)

REALISM

A transitional generation of monument makers, most of whom were born in the 1830s and came on the scene after the war, carried on the earlier naturalist tradition. Anne Whitney (1821–1915), who had gone to Rome in 1867, returned to Boston in 1871 and soon afterward received from Massachusetts the commission for a *Samuel Adams*. Cut in marble in Florence in 1875, it established her as one of New England's leading sculptors, and in the following years she executed portrait statues and busts of many worthies, including personalities in the women's rights movement. She maintained a straightforward naturalism in the manner of Thomas Ball.

Launt Thompson (1833–1894), born in Ireland and raised in Albany, N.Y., received his training in the studio of Erastus Palmer. He quickly established himself with a series of ideal sculptures. After two years in Rome following the war, Thompson returned to an active career in portraiture and monumental statuary. His work of those years reflects a growing tendency in American sculpture away from prewar literalism to a more vivid sense of reality. Others of this period include George Edwin Bissell (1839–1920), Franklin Simmons (1839–1913), and Martin Milmore (1844–1883), all monument makers. Much of their work is typical of the practically anonymous monuments that crowded the cemeteries and dotted the urban landscape of the late nineteenth century.

John Quincy Adams Ward (1830–1910) stands with one foot in antebellum provincial America and the other in a new world of industrial and imperial expansion. It is the measure of his stature as an artist that he could carry the integrity of the native tradition he inherited from Henry Kirke Brown over into a more sophisticated milieu. He converted a naive naturalism into a heroic Realism, expressing some aspects of the American character more profoundly than any other nineteenth-century sculptor. Suspicious of imaginative projection or allegory, he was at his best in making the simple and the obvious memorable. Ward served as an assistant to Brown during the years of the *Washington* project, taking an active role. It was not until 1864 that he made his reputation with the *Indian Hunter* (plate 335), a statuette based on a sketch he may have done while still in Brown's studio, but he spent several months among the Indians before revising the composition. The result was a huge success, and he was commissioned to do a larger version for Central Park. The statuette is carefully, compactly, almost academically composed, but the concentrated tautness in the movement of the man and dog is emotionally compelling and new to American sculpture. In the mainstream of European male nude figure sculpture, it is not an echo or a pastiche, but an original conception on its own terms.

From then on Ward was caught up in the national passion for monuments. He executed war memorials, portrait statues, equestrian groups, allegorical figures, and architectural decorations with great success, became quite wealthy, and was elected president of the National Academy of Design in 1873 and first president of the National Sculpture Society in 1893.

Much of what he did is competent pomp, but everything he produced has a sense of scale and dignity. He was not particularly good at historical subjects. Ward's real strength was in the present and the real, best seen in his *Horace Greeley* (1890) and the *Henry Ward Beecher* (1891). The *Greeley* is an antimonument monument, an attempt to realize an informal personality and pose within the limitations of a memorial. In contrast, the *Beecher* was intended as heroic, with the figure of the preacher conceived as a monolithic bulk on wide-planted legs and capped by an arrogant leonine head. The intimacy and warmth of the preliminary study (plate 336) was transmuted in the monument in Borough Hall Square, Brooklyn, into public stance and intellectual power. The detail

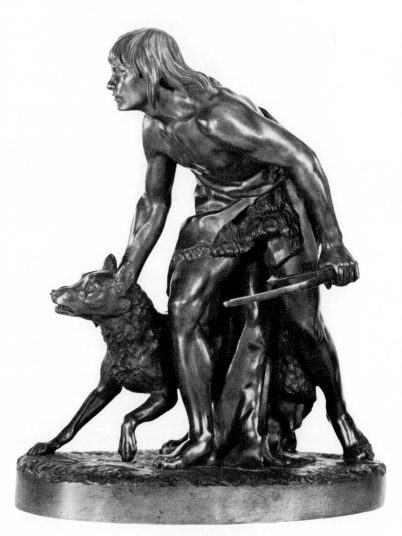

335 John Quincy Adams Ward. *Indian Hunter*. 1864. Bronze, height 16″. The New-York Historical Society

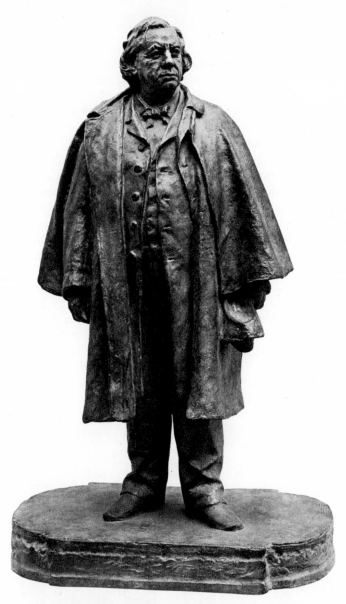

336 John Quincy Adams Ward. *Henry Ward Beecher*. 1891. Bronze, height 14½". The Metropolitan Museum of Art, New York. Rogers Fund, 1917

of dress was played down, focusing attention on the rugged and time-battered face.

Ward worked to the very end in his eightieth year, leaving a formidable array of public monuments from Vermont to South Carolina. He had carried the native tradition of Realism about as far as it could go before it was overwhelmed by Beaux-Arts internationalism.

BEAUX-ARTS—THE FIRST PHASE

Three young sculptors, Olin Levi Warner, Augustus Saint-Gaudens, and Daniel Chester French, were to lead American sculpture back to Europe and on to new heights of international recognition. Saint-Gaudens and Warner turned to Paris in the late 1860s and established it as the spiritual home of American sculptors for more than half a century. Both enrolled in the École des Beaux-Arts, the bastion of French academicism.

Saint-Gaudens and French were the legitimate artistic

heirs to Quincy Ward's Realism, and Saint-Gaudens never entirely forgot that heritage, though both succumbed in different degrees to the insipid ideality of the Beaux-Arts style. Augustus Saint-Gaudens (1848–1907) was born in Dublin and brought to the United States as a child, learned the craft of cameo cutting, and studied art at Cooper Union and the National Academy of Design. In 1867 he was admitted to the École des Beaux-Arts in the atelier of Jouffroy, one of the most celebrated of academicians. After interludes in Rome, in New York, and Rome again, he came back to America in 1875, with his underlying Realism hardly visible under layers of French surface vivacity, Renaissance elegance, and a dedication to ideality—all marketable qualities in a *nouveau-riche* culture.

Saint-Gaudens had several pieces in the Centennial and was thought of as one of the most promising men of the "new movement." He had come to know Stanford White, McKim, and La Farge, men of great power in aesthetic matters, and their conviction that Saint-Gaudens was America's greatest sculptor helped to establish him as such. In subsequent years he was to work on many ventures with them.

When he returned to Paris in 1877, he had a series of important commissions to fill. The major project was the bronze Admiral David Glasgow Farragut monument (1878–81, plate 337). This work projected Ward's Realism into a new age so aptly that it unquestionably influenced Ward's own later *Beecher*. The figure itself is deceptively simple, the body encased in the most unheroic of costumes, the massive head topped by a ridiculous naval cap, yet what comes through is the commanding presence of a seaman, feet planted firmly apart on a rolling deck, eyes fixed on the distance. Only one flap of the coat answers to the breeze; the rest is adamant physical and mental resolution. Except for Ward's *Beecher*, the *Farragut* is the high point of Realist sculpture in nineteenth-century America. The base, designed by Stanford White, seems almost a stylistic contradiction. The exedra shape and the low relief carving reflect White's brilliant decorative sense. The faintly Pre-Raphaelite allegorical figures reveal Saint-Gaudens's concern with instant ideality, but the Art Nouveau handling of masses, sharp definition of edges, slightly eccentric forms, and intricate rhythmic linear patterns of drapery and waves are certainly White's. The elegance and abstraction of the pedestal serve as a foil to the rugged reality of the figure.

In 1881 Saint-Gaudens settled in New York. He was active in the decoration of the Vanderbilt and Villard Houses, including a series of relief medallions. From his early cameo-cutting days, he had shown a preference for relief carving and, over the years, had used that form with sensitivity, decorative flair, and a decided pseudo-Renaissance flavor. He was also increasingly occupied with major commissions, including the standing *Abraham Lincoln* (1887) for Chicago's Lincoln Park.

Perhaps his most famous work is the Adams Memorial (1886–91, plate 338), commissioned by Henry Adams in memory of his wife. A radical departure in funerary monuments, it consists of a shrouded figure in bronze, seated on a rough boulder and backed by a granite plinth of Classical design. The brooding figure is susceptible of a variety of interpretations from the banal to the profound —and, in its day, from sacrilege to universal truth. Aside from its philosophic intentions, it is a handsome sculptural form with a richly worked surface, and it is a pity that the ideal figure under that magnificent drapery is rather commonplace.

Saint-Gaudens had been working on the Robert Gould Shaw Memorial since 1884, and it was not finished until twelve years later. Its heroic relief form was another in-

novation in American memorial sculpture. It is not a revivalist work, except for the incongruous intrusion of Victory personified in a realistic conception. Saint-Gaudens successfully conveyed the heroic dedication of the anonymous, yet individualized, black troops and of the modest leader, who, ramrod straight on a mettlesome horse, seems so vulnerable in his historic mission.

The more flamboyant and intentionally heroic *General William Tecumseh Sherman* (1897–1903), in Central Park, New York, was his last major monument. Both as a portrait and as an equestrian statue, it is a brilliant performance. The lean, surging animal and the alertly poised rider make a dynamic group. But though he thought that his Americanized Nike leading Sherman was "the grandest 'Victory' anybody ever made," she is

337 Augustus Saint-Gaudens. *Admiral David Glasgow Farragut.* 1878–81. Bronze and stone, heroic size. Madison Square Park, New York

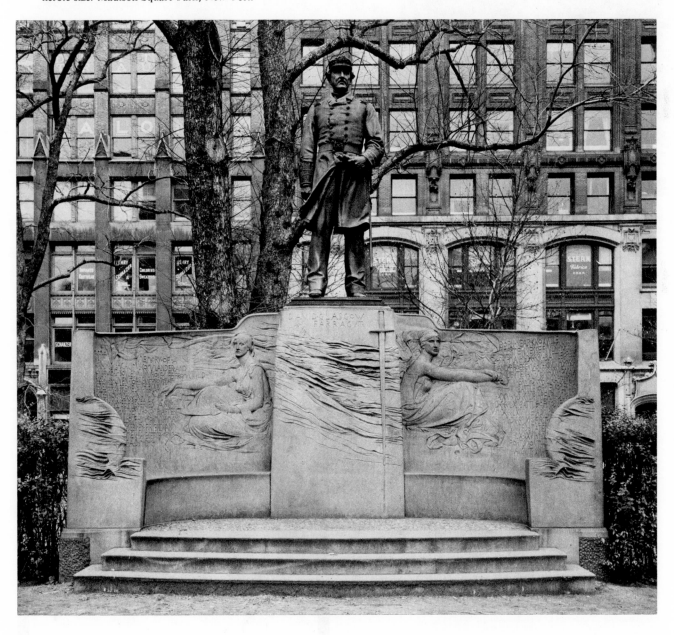

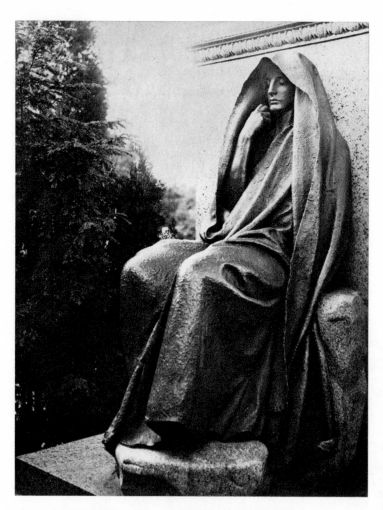

338 Augustus Saint-Gaudens. Adams Memorial. 1886–91. Bronze, height 70″. Rock Creek Cemetery, Washington, D.C.

The transition to the second phase of the Beaux-Arts style is best exemplified by the career of Daniel Chester French (1850–1931), who was raised in Cambridge and then Concord, Mass. One of his earliest works was called *Joe's Farewell* (1871), a literary genre piece based on an incident in Dickens's *Barnaby Rudge*. The statuette was mass-produced and won him local acclaim, an indication of the innate feeling for the popular that was to inform all his art. French studied drawing with William Morris Hunt, heard Rimmer lecture on anatomy, and worked briefly with Quincy Ward. Local favor led to a commission for a monument commemorating the centennial of the Battle of Concord. The famous *Minute Man* (1873–74, plate 339) was cast in bronze and erected at the bridge in Concord in 1875; a bronze replica exhibited at the Centennial the following year helped establish his reputa-

distracting, too real to be ideal and too ideal for the reality of the horse and rider.

Saint-Gaudens enriched as well as compromised the American Realist tradition. French training gave his work a new sensuousness and sophistication, but his penchant for the ideal led American sculpture once again into a period of intellectual vapidity.

Olin Levi Warner (1844–1896) was never so successful or influential as Saint-Gaudens. He entered the Beaux-Arts shortly after Saint-Gaudens and studied with Jouffroy and then with Carpeaux. At the Centennial he gained some recognition and slowly built a reputation with his delicate portrait medallions and graceful statuettes, which could pass for the work of any French student of Jouffroy.

Warner began to receive monumental commissions, and by 1893 he was at work on projects for the Columbian Exposition. Having finally achieved national recognition, he was awarded the commission for the bronze doors of the new Library of Congress building, but he completed only one before his death. His was essentially a minor talent best seen in the gemlike perfection of the medallion portraits of Indian chiefs done during his

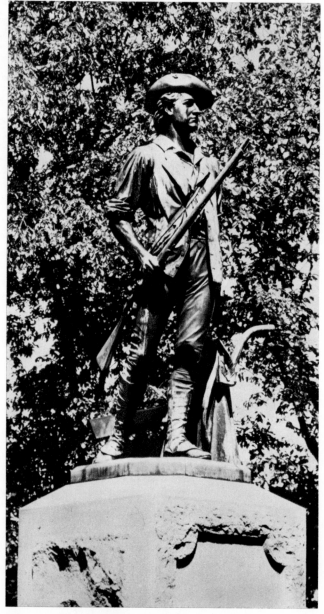

339 Daniel Chester French. *Minute Man*. 1873–74. Bronze, heroic size. Concord, Mass.

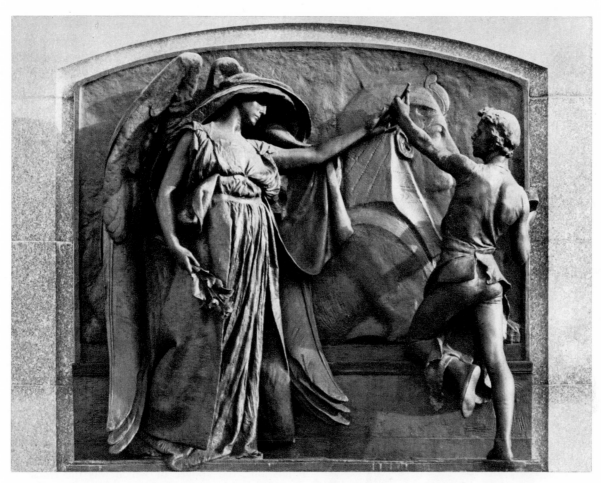

340 Daniel Chester French. *The Angel of Death and the Sculptor*. 1891–92.
Bronze, height 92". Forest Hills Cemetery, Roxbury, Mass.

tion. The sculpture transforms a Classical model (said to
have been a cast of the *Apollo Belvedere*) through naturalistic detail into a popular, patriotic, and palpably American image. Despite a thinness in modeling and a certain
lack of sophistication, the figure has an undeniable verve
and directness, and the composition is managed with
competence.

In the next decade, settled in Washington, he executed
many portraits and commissions for allegorical statuary in new public buildings of the post-Centennial
period. By 1886 French was in Paris to execute a statue of
General Lewis Cass, destined for Statuary Hall, and while
there worked in the studio of Mercié. French became *the*
sculptor of "imperial Classicism." Well into the twentieth
century, his studio produced a staggering sequence of
monuments and architectural decoration. The amalgam
of exalted sentiment expressed in allegorical generality,
ample though vapid Neoclassic forms, and ingratiating
naturalistic detail produced a pseudo-heroic style to
match the pomposities of "imperial Classical" architecture. None of his works is more characteristic than *The
Angel of Death and the Sculptor* (1891–92, plate 340), a
memorial to Martin Milmore. The matronly angel,
swathed in voluminous drapery and sporting a set of
oversized wings, is a typical, all-purpose Beaux-Arts prop
that falls short of the tragic.

BEAUX-ARTS—THE SECOND PHASE

While some of the older men moved into the second
phase of the Beaux-Arts style, the majority of late nineteenth-century sculptors had just begun their careers
before 1900. The two most interesting artists of this
second generation reflect two different facets of French
influence. Frederick MacMonnies was the culmination
of the neo-Rococo phase of Beaux-Arts tradition and
George Grey Barnard the harbinger of a new influence
on the international scene, that of Rodin.

Born in Brooklyn, Frederick William MacMonnies
(1863–1937) entered the Saint-Gaudens studio as a helper
in 1881, was then a student, and later an assistant. He
also attended the National Academy of Design and the
Art Students League and, in 1884, went to Paris to study
with Mercié and with Falguière, whose assistant he became, absorbing the spiritual vivacity and the Impressionist surface that were the hallmarks of that master's style.

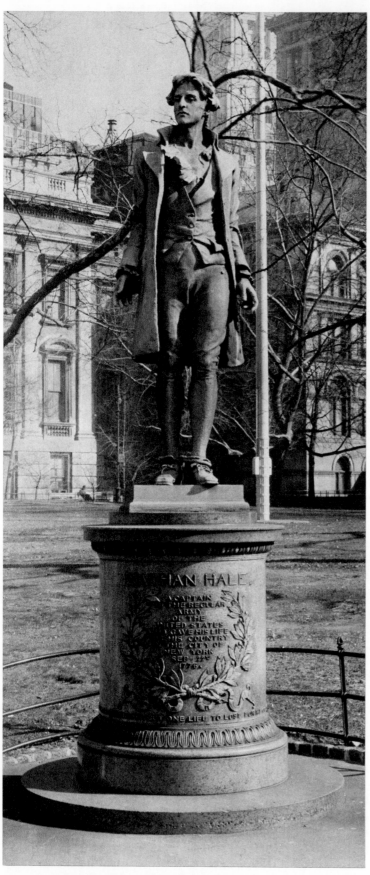

341 Frederick MacMonnies. *Nathan Hale*. 1890. Bronze, heroic size. City Hall Park, New York

From MacMonnies's Paris studio in the next decade came an incredible range of projects. He established himself on a par with Saint-Gaudens and French, while adding a new lightness to the fabric of American sculpture. In 1890 he was at work on major commissions, including the *Nathan Hale* (plate 341) for City Hall Park, New York. In its basic naturalism it recalls French's *Minute Man* and has a similar alertness and sense of vitality, but it is more theatrical and less convincing, almost feminine in mien, perhaps reflecting the neo-Rococo.

With the *Bacchante and Infant Faun* (1893, colorplate 45), America was faced once again with the problem of nudity in art, and this time in unequivocal terms. A frankly sensuous, gamboling nude female, in spite of its Beaux-Arts elegance and idealization, it was seen as wanton. Ostensibly it was her "drunken indecency" that impelled the Women's Christian Temperance Union to join with Harvard's artistic arbiter, Charles Eliot Norton, to expel it from the new Boston Public Library. Charles McKim, who received it as a gift from the sculptor, then gave it to The Metropolitan Museum of Art. The public scandal did not hurt MacMonnies's artistic standing, but his reputation as the *enfant terrible* of American sculpture followed him through his career.

Although MacMonnies's Columbian Fountain at the Chicago Fair, the centerpiece of the lagoon, bordered on the absurd, it was proof that he could handle Beaux-Arts pomposity with aplomb. He had his spate of public commissions, the apogee of which was the *Horse Tamers* (c. 1900), a spectacular group of rearing animals and restraining male nudes, now in Prospect Park Plaza, Brooklyn. The surging mass is a demonstration of Beaux-Arts skill and bravura modeling.

George Grey Barnard (1863–1938) stands somewhat apart from these Beaux-Arts sculptors, but he shares with them a dedication to a monumental, allegorical, idealized art. Like Rodin, he had an aura of radicalism that was unsettling to his contemporaries. For a time, at least, it seemed that his genius could not be contained by the formulas of academic sculpture. He had studied at the Chicago Art Institute, where he was inspired by the Michelangelo casts. By 1883 he had saved enough money to attend the École des Beaux-Arts, but his major influence was Rodin, whose source was also Michelangelo. Barnard spent almost a decade in Paris in poverty, virtual isolation, and struggle to achieve a personal style and to find a means of expressing humanity's most profound emotions. In 1886 Alfred Corning Clark saw the *Crouching Boy* (c. 1884) in Barnard's studio, paid for its execution in marble, and became his major support.

In 1888 Barnard began work on what he called "the group," which, beginning with a quotation from a poem of Victor Hugo, "Je sens deux hommes en moi," is now entitled *Struggle of the Two Natures in Man* (plate 342). The gigantic tableau took six years from clay to marble, and Barnard did the cutting himself, except for the preliminary roughing from the plaster. In 1894, when the *Two Natures* was exhibited at the Salon, along with five others of his pieces, Barnard was an overnight sensation. Though reminiscent of Michelangelo and Rodin, the work had an air of originality, of a personal involvement, and it was executed with consummate skill and with a broadness that appeared modern. The theme seemed to transcend the allegorical clichés of the Beaux-Arts repertory and to reach into the wells of human memory for some profound psychic insight into heroic form.

In 1896 Barnard had a disappointing exhibition in New York. The American art world was less ready than the French for innovations. Thereafter he worked on a series of individual pieces. In 1902 he undertook the mammoth project for the Capitol at Harrisburg, Pa., which absorbed him until its completion, on a much reduced scale, in 1910 and was an unfortunate anticlimax to an earlier career of bright promise.

Among the many other sculptors of that generation trained at the École was Herbert Adams (1858–1945), who developed an individual and mannered portrait style derived from Italian Renaissance polychrome busts, but he, too, was caught up in the passion for monumental sculpture. Paul Wayland Bartlett (1865–1925) was taken to Paris as a child and had a thorough training in art, in-

cluding study with Frémiet, the *animalier*, at the Jardin des Plantes. He later executed many imaginary portrait statues in a typical Beaux-Arts popular genre style.

The Columbian Exposition put the final cachet on Beaux-Arts sculpture, which, in the mid-eighties, became the handmaiden of "imperial Classical" architecture. Even European sculptors such as Karl Bitter and Isadore Konti from Vienna, Philip Martiny from Strasbourg, and John Massey Rhind from Edinburgh, all trained in the international Beaux-Arts tradition, were attracted to supplement the roster of American sculptors working on public projects. And the sequence of later international expositions—the Pan-American in Buffalo in 1901, the Louisiana Purchase in St. Louis in 1904, and the Panama-Pacific in San Francisco in 1915—provided support for a generation of American and European Beaux-Arts sculptors. The Beaux-Arts-dominated National Sculptors Society, formed in 1893, established a virtual monopoly in the field that persisted well into the twentieth century. The sculptures produced had the common characteristics of the Beaux-Arts style—monumental scale, idealized conception, and generalized iconography. Within this framework it is difficult to single out what was specifically American or noteworthy.

(continued on page 322)

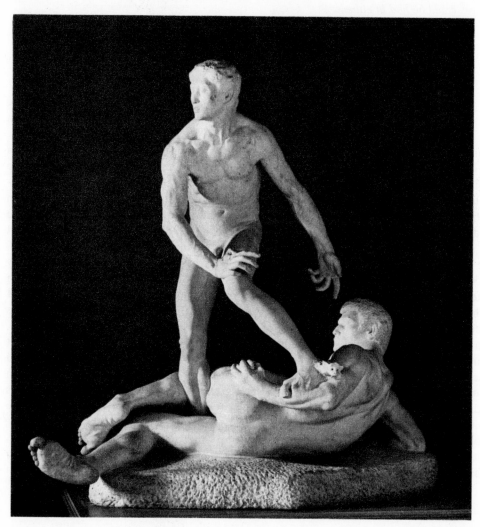

342 George Grey Barnard. *Struggle of the Two Natures in Man.* Completed 1894. Marble, 8′5½″ × 8′3″. The Metropolitan Museum of Art, New York. Gift of Alfred Corning Clark, 1896

Sculpture: Mostly Monumental 321

When a famous early Chinese porcelain vase owned by Mary Morgan was sold at auction for the then high price of $18,000, the attendant publicity led to considerable imitation in glass of the type and colors and, as in colorplate 46, known as "The Morgan Vase," of the actual vase and base. Its main appeal was the delicate blending of the colors graduated from red to yellow. This effect was copied by several companies in addition to Hobbs, Brockanier, & Co., under varying trade names: Amberina, Coral, Rose Amber, and Peachblow. In each a particular chemical formula produced the yellow or gold of the vase which, when reheated, turned a rich shade of red. By carefully controlling the reheating process, a subtle gradation of color was made possible. Other multicolor glass being made in the last quarter of the century often had several forms of decoration. All can be called "art glass." It was usually handmade and expensive, and was often quite ornate. Victorian taste favored some rather elaborate applied decoration and was eclectic in the appropriation of shapes and designs from other cultures. The company that produced "The Morgan Vase" imitation also produced several other forms in the same colors, including a large pitcher in the shape of a Near Eastern ewer and a small one in Classical form. Any of the pieces could be had in either glossy or matte finish.

Louis C. Tiffany, as a major designer of leaded glass, further enhanced his reputation as a general designer and decorator. At the Exposition Universelle in Paris, in 1900, this Art Nouveau punch bowl (colorplate 47), designed for the exhibition, was clearly the hit of the show. The United States Commission, which reported on the Exposition in the third American Art Annual, described it: "The glass is encased in a frame of chased and wrought golden metal, the design of the base suggesting the effect of breaking waves, while from their foaming crests spring six arms of peacock-hued Favrile glass; they in turn support the uprights of the frame, becoming a richly ornamental band at the top. Three of the supports end in quaintly twisted finials of lustre glass from which hang ladles of metal and iridescent glass."

The colors are particularly rich on both the bowl and the mount, going far beyond the color gradations illustrated in such art-glass forms as "The Morgan Vase" (colorplate 46), and the subtle iridescence of the bowl contrasts with the boldness of the silvered bronze. A bravura demonstration of the extremes of Tiffany's potential, it indicates the extravagance then still enjoyed in American decorative arts.

(continued from page 321)

THE "WILD WEST"

Toward the end of the century there was a growing awareness that the West was rapidly becoming "civilized." At the Columbian Exposition much of the statuary was concerned with the denizens, both human and animal, of the wilderness. The sculptors whose themes were Indians, pioneers, cowboys, and animals formed a more or less cohesive group, and a surprising number came from the West. What may have set this group somewhat apart from the *fin-de-siècle* Beaux-Arts men, though many came out of the same French ateliers, was that they were recapitulating in their art, not the acceptable formulas of the studio, but a life they had actually known.

The theme of the Indian as a symbol of our vanished past continued in isolated instances after the Centennial among sculptors who had studied in Paris. John J. Boyle (1851–1917) was an Eakins pupil at the Pennsylvania Academy and in 1877 entered the École des Beaux-Arts. After his return to Philadelphia in 1880, he was commissioned to do a number of monumental Indian groups. Paul Bartlett made his debut with an Indian subject. The *Bear Tamer* (1887, plate 343), his first major effort, is a charming genre scene, full of spirited action, naturalistic detail, and a lush handling of material. Bartlett's Indian is an exoticism, however, rather than a serious subject.

Cyrus Edwin Dallin (1861–1944), the first American sculptor to dedicate himself to the Indian theme, grew up near Salt Lake City among the Utes and retained a lifelong affection for Indians. In 1880 he went to Boston to study and two years later opened his own studio, where he produced his earliest Indian subjects. In 1888 he went to Paris and worked with Chapu at the Académie Julian. The arrival in Paris of Buffalo Bill's Wild West Show stirred memories of his early experience, and he began the first of four monumental equestrian groups, *A Signal of Peace* (1889–90, plate 344). Dallin's cycle is the epic of a race fated for extinction, from racial nobility, through the premonition of doom and the struggle against injustice, to tragic defeat. The conception is heroic and Romantic, the treatment broad and in the older tradition of native Realism, the detail ethnically accurate. Dallin's remain the most monumental and mythic images of the vanishing Indian.

Hermon Atkins MacNeil (1866–1947), an easterner, was trained in Paris at the Académie Julian under Chapu and at the École under Falguière. He went to Chicago in

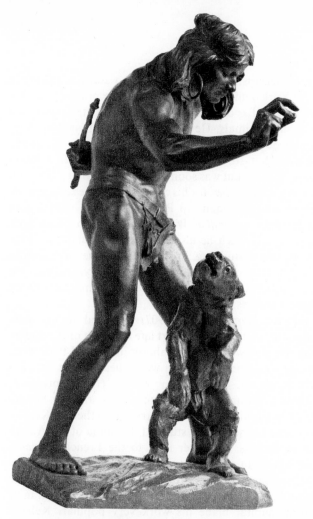

343 Paul Wayland Bartlett. *The Bear Tamer*. 1887. Bronze, height 68½". Corcoran Gallery of Art, Washington, D.C. Gift of Mrs. Paul Wayland Bartlett

Louis Fair he executed four large groups dealing with western life. Solon Borglum's modeling, in the *animalier* tradition, was full of movement and sparkle; the treatment of subject was melodramatic.

Most of the sculpture of John Gutzon Borglum (1871–1941) belongs in the twentieth century. He is best known for his colossal mountainside monuments, but his earliest sculpture was of western subjects. He studied painting first in San Francisco and Paris, and then sculpture with Mercié. His *Indian Scouts* was exhibited at the Chicago Fair, and the most famous of his early works, *The Mares of Diomedes* (1904), at the St. Louis Exposition. In the latter, the surging action and impressionistic detail of the stampeding mustangs in mythological guise reflect the French *animalier* manner of Barye and Frémiet, rather than his later allegiance to the heroic breadth of Rodin and Barnard.

1891 to assist Philip Martiny on the Agricultural Building and did some work on his own on the Electricity Building. While there, he seems to have discovered the Indian—in art as well as in Buffalo Bill's Wild West Show. He went to live among the Pueblo Indians and utilized that experience in four reliefs for the Marquette Building in Chicago. Then, in 1896 in Rome, he began working on a series of sculptures that established his reputation in the Indian field. He was awarded a medal at the Paris Exposition of 1900 and received commissions for the Pan-American Exposition. MacNeil continued to work on Indian themes until 1910, when he turned to the broader field of monumental and architectural sculpture.

Solon Hannibal Borglum (1868–1922) and his brother, Gutzon, were raised in Indian country, and most of Solon's work was concerned with western themes. At the Cincinnati Art School he won a scholarship in 1897 to study in Paris, where he worked under Frémiet and Puech. The sculptures of the next two years were spirited studies of horses with an occasional figure. He achieved his first recognition at the Paris Exposition of 1900, where he was awarded a silver medal for a series of three statuettes. An extensive collection of his small bronzes was shown at the Pan-American Exposition. For the St.

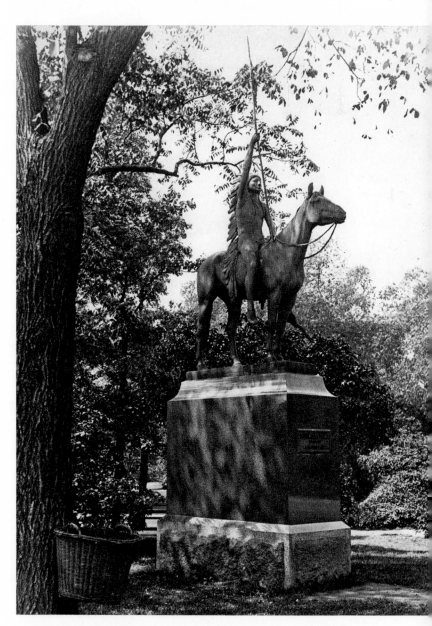

344 Cyrus Edwin Dallin. *A Signal of Peace*. 1889–90. Bronze, life size. Lincoln Park, Chicago. Courtesy Chicago Historical Society

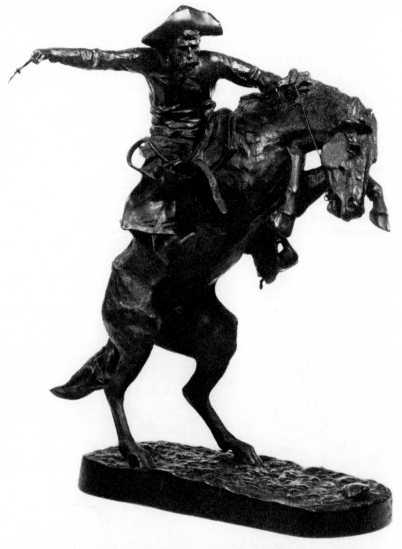

345 Frederic Remington. *The Bronco Buster*. 1895. Bronze, height 23".
National Cowboy Hall of Fame, Oklahoma City, Okla.

Frederic Remington (1861–1909), the most famous illustrator of the West, turned to sculpture in 1895 with *The Bronco Buster* (plate 345), and before his death executed fifteen statuettes of cowboys, Indians, and Army troopers that were reproduced in large numbers and increased his already enormous popularity. Like his paintings and illustrations, they are shrewd, sharply observed, accurate, theatrical accounts of a romantic past. Remington very consciously exploited his own experience to create and maintain a myth. Considering his lack of formal training in the medium, he did this with unusual verve and skill, though the modeling is often literal and meager.

Alexander Phimister Proctor (1862–1950) covered the gamut of themes, ranging in scale from statuette to monument. His youthful experiences were of frontier life and

the wilderness. In 1891 he moved to study sculpture in New York and began to work on decorations for the Columbian Exposition, for which he executed more than thirty-five animals. He also did two of the major sculptural groups at the Fair, the equestrian *Indian Scout* and *Cowboy* that stood above the main basin. He went to study in Paris, but was soon called back by Saint-Gaudens to execute the horses for his equestrian statues of Generals Logan and Sherman. In Paris in 1900 he won a gold medal with his *Indian Warrior* at the Exposition Universelle, for which he also executed the quadriga of the United States Building. Proctor became the most famous monumental animal sculptor in the country, and over the next half-century he executed a host of monuments on frontier themes.

Edward Kemeys (1843–1907) belonged to an older generation, but he came to art late and then only accidentally. He was working as a laborer in Central Park when he saw someone modeling a wolf's head at the zoo. His first sculpture, *Hudson Bay Wolves* (1871), produced without schooling, was an instant success and was bought for Philadelphia's Fairmount Park. From then on Kemeys dedicated himself to the study of the fauna of the American wilderness. He never took to the French *animalier* tradition, retaining always a rather naive and direct Realism based on his naturalist interests. An ability to capture the character and personality of the animal in its natural habitat made his work very popular. Kemeys executed many of the animal decorations at the Chicago Fair and was well represented in the fine arts section. The pair of bronze lions in front of the Chicago Art Institute also date from this period. Edward Clark Potter (1857–1923), the horse sculptor, was best known for his collaboration with Daniel Chester French on a series of equestrian monuments. He did several on his own and was also responsible for the supercilious lions in front of the New York Public Library. This tradition of animal sculpture was carried into the twentieth century by Frederick G. R. Roth (1872–1944), trained in Vienna and Berlin; Herbert Haseltine (1877–1962), in Munich, Rome, and Paris; and Anna Vaughn Hyatt Huntington (1876–1973), entirely in the United States.

The complacency in which American sculpture was bathed at the turn of the century is reflected in *The History of American Sculpture* (1903) by Lorado Taft. This publication deserves credit as the first attempt at a survey of American sculpture, but it is now more interesting as an indication of the taste of a practicing Beaux-Arts sculptor. It reveals a too easy acceptance of academic standards—lofty sentiment, idealized form, and technical skill—and of success as measured in public commissions, academic awards, and financial rewards. There is no sign of questioning, no awareness of the winds of change stirring abroad.

14
Photography: The Birth of a New Art

Photography, the first visual medium derived directly from the scientific revolution, has been used during its short life for factual statement, for persuasion, for entertainment, and for personal artistic expression.

The enthusiastic acceptance of the new medium in this country in 1839 suggests that Americans in particular were eager for a graphic means of depicting the real world with surpassing naturalism. Before long photography began to affect the older arts both directly and in less obvious ways. It provided artists with information about phenomena previously inaccurately seen, such as the gait of man and beast and the shape of cloth in motion. It made possible verisimilitude in portraiture, landscape, and graphic illustration, especially after the invention of projection enlarging devices. More important, the visual appearance of the photograph—its registration of light and shadow and its focus upon a specific portion of the visual spectrum—began to suggest fresh ways of handling volume and composition in painting and graphic art. Finally, the photograph, unencumbered by traditional ideas of appropriate subject matter, suggested new visual themes.

Initially, however, photographers turned to the older arts for ideas about form and content. Their portraiture in particular derived its poses and lighting from popularly accepted styles in painting. Landscape, too, was frequently photographed with an awareness of painted precedents. Throughout its history, photography has had two aspects. One has been to emphasize the aesthetic nature of the medium, resulting in a close stylistic affinity with painting. The other has been to assert the more scientific role of photography as social document, visual record, and tool of communication. Over the years photography has won its own domain and filtered back to the more traditional arts.

THE UNIQUE IMAGE: DAGUERREOTYPE

The painter and inventor, Samuel F. B. Morse, visiting Paris in 1839, was one of the first Americans to become acquainted with the daguerreotype, a pictorial image named after its founder, J. L. M. Daguerre. The process enabled a laterally reversed image of an illuminated portion of the visible world to be transferred in monochrome through an optical element (the lens), enclosed in a darkened chamber (the camera), onto a chemically treated plate (the film). This image was made more visible and permanent through the use of chemical agents (developing and fixing). The process, unlike one on paper being developed in England at the same time, created a unique image in which both the negative and the positive were incorporated in the same picture.

When Morse returned to New York, his enthusiasm for the new picture-making process helped pave the way for widespread acceptance. However, when instructions arrived in the United States shortly after the Paris announcement, it was evident that the long exposure required to produce the image would make portraiture difficult if not impossible. In association with an eminent chemist, Dr. John Draper, Morse experimented with making portraits and devoted himself to teaching the process to others. By the summer of 1840, Dr. Draper and others in Philadelphia, Boston, and New York had shortened exposure time so that portraiture became commercially feasible. The success that Europeans thought was due to the "brighter American sun" was more likely the result of ingenuity and the absence of franchise restrictions. Lenses, plates, and camera apparatus were refined, and the studios in which exposures were made were enclosed in glass to illuminate the sitter with as much light as possible. From 1840 to 1860, as daguerreotype portraiture became a thriving industry, artists frequently left unsuccessful careers in the traditional arts to become operators, casemakers, and colorists.

A wide range of craftsmanship and aesthetic quality characterized daguerreotypes as a result of their commercial nature. Nearly all early portraits still engender admiration for the fineness of the image, but relatively few are outstanding examples of the artistry and the

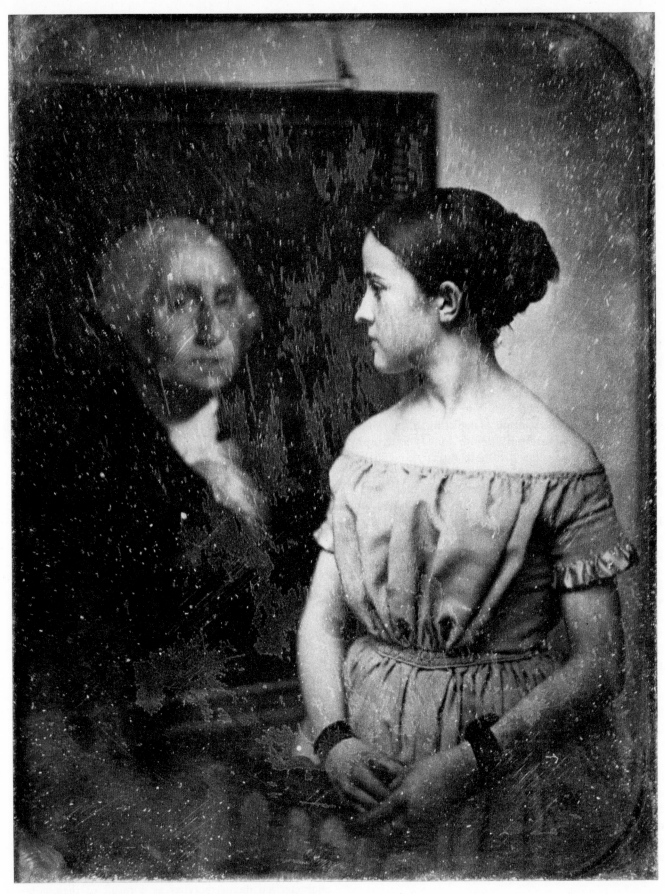

346   Southworth & Hawes. *Unidentified Child.* n.d. Daguerreotype,
      whole plate. The Metropolitan Museum of Art, New York.
      Gift of I. N. Phelps Stokes, Edward S. Hawes, Alice Mary Hawes,
      Marian Augusta Hawes, 1937

psychological probity of which the medium was capable. The best portraits of the time were produced by Albert Sands Southworth (1811–1894) and Josiah Johnson Hawes (1808–1901), whose productive partnership, Southworth & Hawes, began in Boston in 1843 and lasted until 1862. Like many others, both had received training in the medium, Southworth with Morse himself. In addition to achieving a likeness, which was naturally enough the aim of all early portraiture, the Southworth & Hawes image combined exactitude of appearance with the expression of character, creating a strong sense of psychological presence. The sitter was represented as he or she "ought to be" (in Southworth's words)—idealized so that outstanding traits were seen through pose, lighting, and background. By constantly varying these elements in their 1,500 extant daguerreotypes, they created unusually sensitive images of the famous and the unknown, such as *Unidentified Child* (plate 346).

Mathew Brady (1823–1896) was another who began a career of exceptional merit, possibly after studying painting with William Page and daguerreotyping with Morse. After 1844 he opened portrait studios in New York and in Washington, attracting the famous and powerful. Brady conceived of his clientele as a *Gallery of Illustrious Men* (published in lithograph in 1850) and concentrated on political figures. Lincoln is said to have attributed his election success to the Brady portrait made of him on the day of his Cooper Union speech in 1860. Brady's daguerreotypes, such as that of *John C. Fremont* (plate 347), have a straightforward quality derived from simplicity of pose, lighting, and background. As was common at the time, Brady supervised the pose and lighting, while operators made the actual exposures. Other fine daguerreotypists of the period were Edward Anthony, John Plumbe, and Marcus Root.

Finely detailed as they were, daguerreotype portraits fell short of the ultimate reality because they lacked color. Therefore it was common practice to employ artists to hand-color portions of the image on the plate to impart greater naturalism. During their period of popularity, daguerreotypists continually experimented to capture natural colors as well as tonal values but met with little success. The only recorded color daguerreotype, made in 1851, resulted from a combination of factors which the inventor, Levi Hill, was unable to repeat. Color did not become completely practical until the twentieth century.

Although genre painting was at the height of its popularity in the 1840s, most daguerreotypists were content to produce straightforward portraits without trying to tell a story. Exceptions were Alexander Hesler (1823–1895) and George N. Barnard (1819–1902), who wished to emulate the popular themes in painting. However, technical limitations made recording actual events very difficult (Barnard's view of a fire at Oswego being a fortuitous exception), so that simple genre scenes were

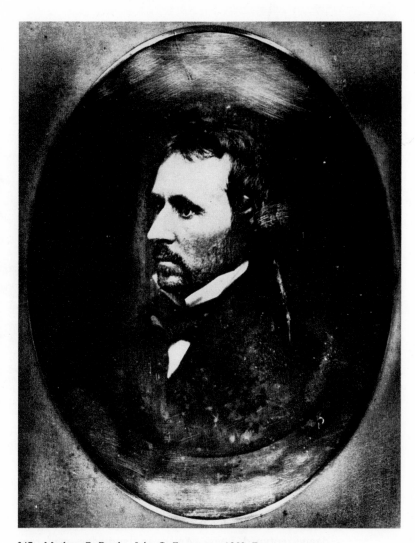

347 Mathew B. Brady. *John C. Fremont*. c. 1850. Daguerreotype, Imperial plate. Oakland Museum, Oakland, Calif.

restaged and exposed within the studio. After the adoption of paper prints, genre subjects became very popular.

Because the daguerreotype arrived in the United States during a period of territorial expansion, landscape imagery was sought by politicians, travelers, and explorers, as well as by artists who wished to paint the native scenery. Morse was particularly influential with the artists when in his role as President of the National Academy of Design he urged acceptance of the daguerreotype as a facsimile of nature itself, a force that would enrich rather than compete with painting. As early as 1840 full-plate images ($6\frac{1}{2} \times 8\frac{1}{2}$ inches) of New England landscapes were made by Samuel Bemis and Anson Clark. In the following year daguerreotypes were taken to record explorations in the Yucatan and in a boundary dispute in the Northeast, although not with complete success. By the 1850s there were daguerreotype images of natural wonders such as Niagara Falls. Daguerreotypists operated with uneven success on a number of western expeditions, including one led by

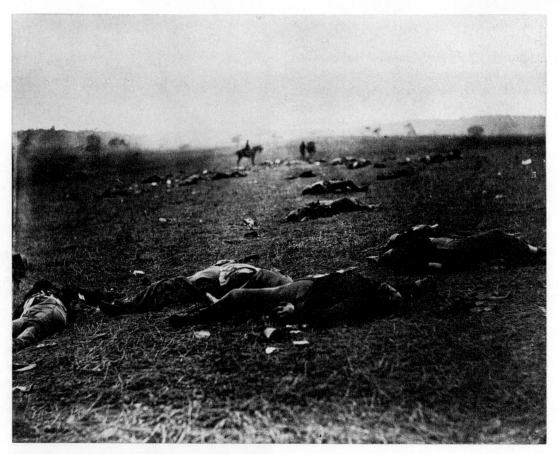

348 Alexander Gardner and Timothy O'Sullivan. *A Harvest of Death.*
1863. Wet plate, albumen. The New York Public Library

Fremont, who retained Simon Carvalho to provide a visual record of the Rocky Mountains in 1853. In its daguerreotyped image American landscape was represented either as transcendental experience, similar to that evoked by Hudson River and "luminist" painters, or as mundane document. This dichotomy continued to characterize photography long after the daguerreotype had been supplanted by glass negative and paper print.

Whether in reaction to the small size of the plate, relative to the painter's canvas, or from a desire to capitalize on the popularity of the painted panorama during the mid-nineteenth century, landscape daguerreotypists sometimes took a number of contiguous views. Displayed together, these constituted a panorama. Although none have survived, John Wesley Jones is said to have made 1,500 daguerreotypes on which he based his painted pantoscope of California. The panorama enabled daguerreotypists to capture the breadth and extent of American scenery, as William Shew did in a five-plate panorama of the San Francisco harbor in 1852.

MULTIPLYING THE IMAGE

The negative-positive process known as photography provides an image in reverse tonal scale and lateral position on a transparent substance called "film" (first paper; later glass and cellulose). When this image is transferred to another support (usually paper), it returns to normal tonal relationship and position. The process was announced in England by William Henry Fox Talbot at the same time as the daguerreotype. Although the Langenheim brothers of Phildelphia attempted to popularize it, Americans were slow at first in accepting the paper process, partly because the finer detail of the daguerreotype appealed to the commercially oriented portrait industry and to the native preference for visual naturalism. Also, the value of duplication was not immediately realized. Paper photography became more acceptable in the United States after 1851, when the collodion process (developed in England by Frederick Scott Archer) made possible a more finely detailed grainless negative on glass. The first application was as a surrogate daguerreotype, called "ambrotype," in which the negative on glass reversed itself into a positive when backed with black paint or fabric. After short-lived popularity, the ambrotype was supplanted by another nonduplicable process, the tintype, which, being light and less destructible, filled the portrait needs of Civil War soldiery and their families.

ON THE SPOT, 1860–90

More than most pictorial instrumentalities, the photograph directly reflects changing conditions of national

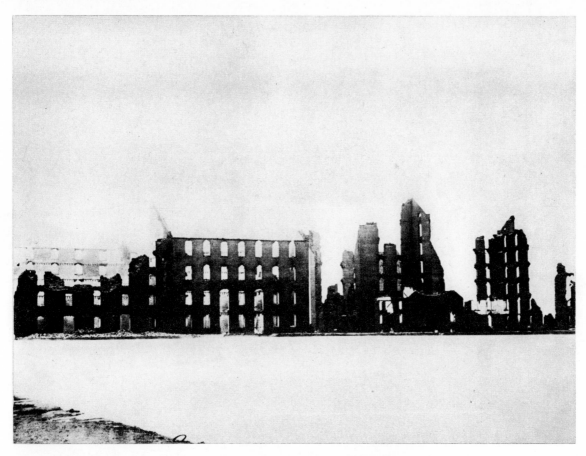

349 Alexander Gardner or unknown Brady photographer. *The Ruins of Richmond*. 1865.
Wet plate, albumen. International Museum of Photography at George Eastman House, Rochester, N.Y.

life. In 1860 photographers, using glass negatives to produce regular paper prints and stereographs (see below), were eager to record the struggle between the Union and the Confederacy and to accompany westward expeditions searching for areas for mining and land development. Shortly afterward they were ready to document the recreational activities made possible by recently acquired affluence and leisure.

The negative-positive process made on-the-spot photography possible, and the Civil War afforded American photographers the first full-scale opportunity to take the camera out of the studio and onto the field. The project to document the conflict, called "Brady's Photographic Corps," was organized by Mathew Brady, the renowned portraitist. To a large extent he financed the supplies and obtained the operators, although not all remained in his employ. Brady conceived of a mobile horse-drawn darkroom, which was necessary because collodion glass plates had to be sensitized just prior to exposure—hence the term "wet-plate"—and developed shortly thereafter. In addition, photographers had to transport cameras and tripods; glass plates of various sizes; chemicals necessary to coat, develop, and fix the negative; as well as paraphernalia for weighing, mixing, and storing. This cumbersome technology was used throughout the Civil War and for the later western expeditions, on which portable tent darkrooms replaced mobile wagons.

Eventually more than three hundred photographers provided visual material for the Union Army alone, but the superior work of several of Brady's men—Alexander Gardner (1821–1882), Timothy O'Sullivan (1840–1882), and George N. Barnard—resulted in hundreds of exceptionally vivid images. For the first time nonparticipants could see the reality of war—the boredom of much of army life and the unheroic nature of death on the field—in images such as *A Harvest of Death* (plate 348) and *Ruins of Richmond* (plate 349). These images were exhibited at Sanitary Commission Fairs, sold in stereograph sets, and published with photographic prints pasted into the text, as in Gardner's *Sketchbook of the Civil War* and Barnard's *Photographic Views of Sherman's Campaign*. By the end of the war illustrators were copying and tracing over photographs in an effort to provide the realistic incident and detail demanded by readers of the illustrated press. Painters too, Winslow Homer among them, appear to have been influenced by the camera's framing of a scene and the pattern of sunlight and shadow registered on the photographic print.

Even before the Civil War had ended, expeditionary photographers achieved success with the collodion

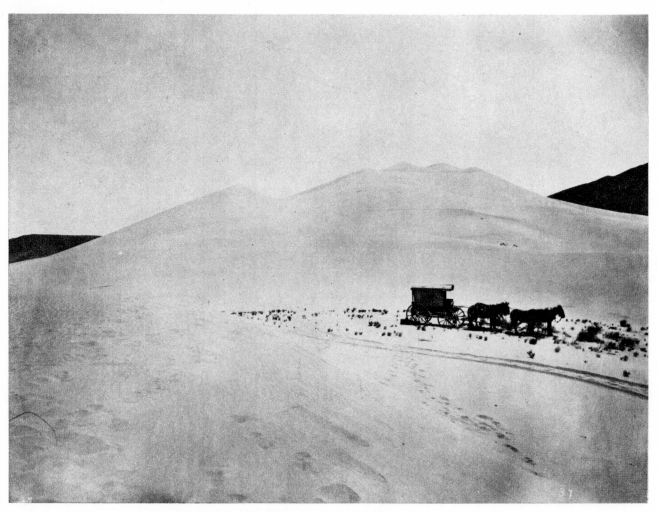

350 Timothy O'Sullivan. *Desert Sand Hills near Carson Sink, Nev.* 1868. Wet plate, 8 × 10″.
International Museum of Photography at George Eastman House, Rochester, N.Y.

process. After 1864 factual photographic records (geographic, archaeological, and ethnic) expressed the essence of the western wilderness. During the sixties and seventies expeditionary photography required considerable planning and financial outlay and had to be backed by Federal agencies such as the United States Geological Survey, or by railroad companies aiming to draw settlers to the West. The unwieldy equipment, with cameras and plates sometimes measuring as much as 22 × 25 inches, was difficult to transport through mountainous terrain and river gorges. Extremes of temperature might adversely affect the negative material, or the entire outfit might be lost when the pack animal lost its footing. Despite the arduousness of the enterprise, Timothy O'Sullivan and Carleton E. Watkins (1829–1916) were able to dramatize the vast and pristine silence of the West in *Desert Sand Hills Near Carson Sink* (plate 350) and *Cathedral Rock, Yosemite* (plate 351). Others equally active in western landscape photography were William Henry Jackson (1843–1942), Eadweard Muybridge (1830–1904), and Andrew Joseph Russell (1831–1876).

In effect, the novelty of the undertaking forced all these photographers to create their own aesthetic, even when they were aware of traditional landscape art. Others, such as Charles R. Savage and Will Soule (1836–1908), became studio photographers on the frontier and presented Indian sitters as proud and confident tribesmen against painted studio backdrops, as in Soule's *Brave in War Dress* (plate 352).

From 1868 to the closing of the frontier, the photograph was a major adjunct of American national policy, providing the "truthful witness" to the lands and resources available for development. In 1870 the United States Navy included O'Sullivan on a mission to Panama to investigate suitable routes for a proposed canal. Muybridge photographed in Alaska in 1868 and for coffee-growing interests in Central America in 1875. The prints from the collodion negatives taken on expeditions were made on silver chloride paper (called "salt prints"), often albumenized to create a glossier surface. They ranged in size from stereographs (see below) to single prints from 5 × 8 inches up to 22 × 25 inches. Photographic prints were sold by firms such as Lawrence & Houseworth in San Francisco, displayed in galleries such as the famous Goupil's and at expositions, in the United States and abroad, including the Philadelphia Centennial. In addition, photographs were mounted and bound in albums to demonstrate to Congress and special interest groups the need for such actions as additional expedition financing or setting aside public park land.

During the heyday of the collodion process, landscape photographers often worked directly with artists. John Dunmore and George Critcherson accompanied painter William Bradford on his 1869 expedition to the Arctic Circle, providing the material for that artist's famous Arctic canvases and illustrated lectures. When Frederic Church visited the Near East in 1868, he too was accompanied by a photographer who made exposures of the subjects that the artist sketched. After the dry plate (see below) became practicable, both amateurs and professionals found landscape photography easier; and painters, among them Thomas Eakins, made their own landscape views as studies for paintings.

The stereograph, demonstrated first in England and then perfected in France, is a photographic image which creates the illusion of three-dimensionality. Actually it consists of two images of the same subject, taken with a camera with two lenses placed approximately $2\frac{1}{2}$ inches apart horizontally (or less frequently by two cameras so placed). After printing, the two positives are pasted together side by side on a 3 × 8-inch card, which is inserted into a special viewer comprising two eyeholes and a special device for adjusting the distance of the card from the eye so that the two images merge into a single picture. The viewer then seems to experience the presence of the depth dimension.

By 1860 stereography had become so popular in America that Oliver Wendell Holmes, one of photography's early enthusiasts, estimated that he had seen over 100,000 stereograph views and had himself invented an inexpensive viewing device to make this activity even more accessible. Middle-class folk, travelers seeking souvenirs as well as wishful stay-at-homes, provided an avid public for stereograph imagery of vacation pleasures. A category of photographic imagery in which domestic scenes and popular jokes were reenacted and photographed in the studio, as in *The Haunted Lane* (plate 353), satisfied the taste for genre subjects previously accommodated by paintings. Other subjects included flowers, spiritualist scenes involving photographic tricks, and scenery. While such images are fascinating indicators of the level of popular taste, few can be considered aesthetically significant.

Even before the Civil War portrait photography had undergone considerable commercial expansion as a result of the duplicable process. The public was provided

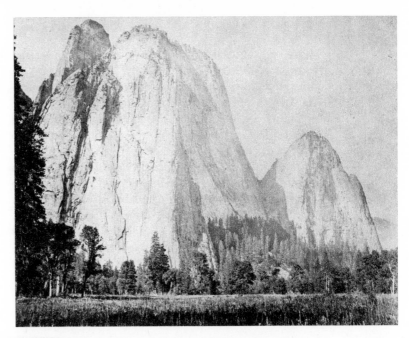

351 Carleton E. Watkins. *Cathedral Rock, Yosemite.* c. 1866.
Wet plate, mammoth plate. The Metropolitan Museum of Art, New York.
Whittelsey Fund, 1922

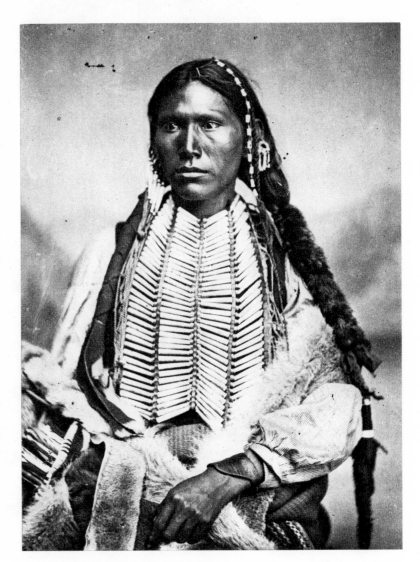

352 Will Soule. *Brave in War Dress.* 1870–75.
Los Angeles County Museum

with a greater selection of views, mounts, and sizes, from *carte-de-visite* (approximately 2¼ × 3½ inches) to Imperial (approximately 9 × 12 inches) and even life-size, but the product itself was characterized by little originality or competence. As a result, professional societies and publications in the seventies aimed to improve the quality of the studio portrait. In addition to technical information, magazines featured articles on lighting, placement, and costume and ran series on aesthetics in which the great painted portraits of the past were held up as models. Nevertheless, even the most popular works—portraits of society and theatrical personages—demonstrate little psychological or aesthetic sensibility. In fact, the finest portraits of the period

were the work of an amateur, the painter Thomas Eakins, who used the camera in *Amelia Van Buren and Cat* (plate 354) to explore modeling and expression rather than to delineate outward appearance.

One of the era's most dramatic photographic events concerned the effort to capture an instant of motion on film. In 1872 the California landscapist Muybridge became associated with ex-Governor Stanford in a project to record the position of a racehorse's feet in motion. Muybridge's qualified success in producing an image of the horse, Occident, trotting at the rate of thirty-six feet per second, led Stanford to underwrite further limited efforts, in 1878 resulting in the first scientific analysis of a horse's gait. In 1884 Muybridge moved

353 L. M. Melander & Bro. *The Haunted Lane.* 1876–89. Library of Congress, Washington, D.C.

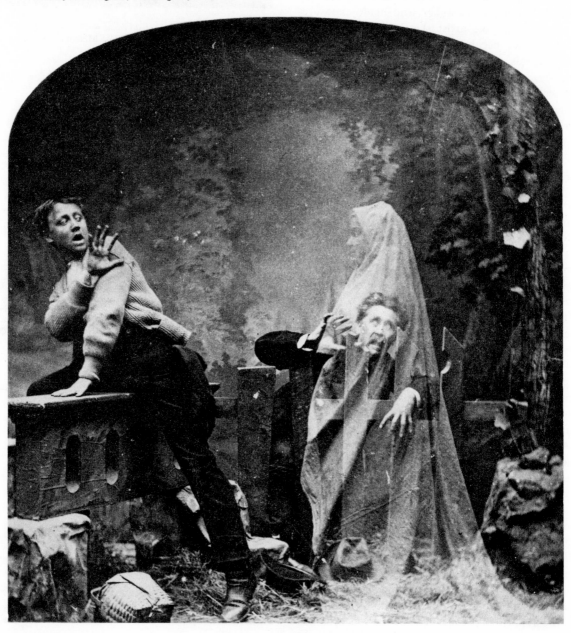

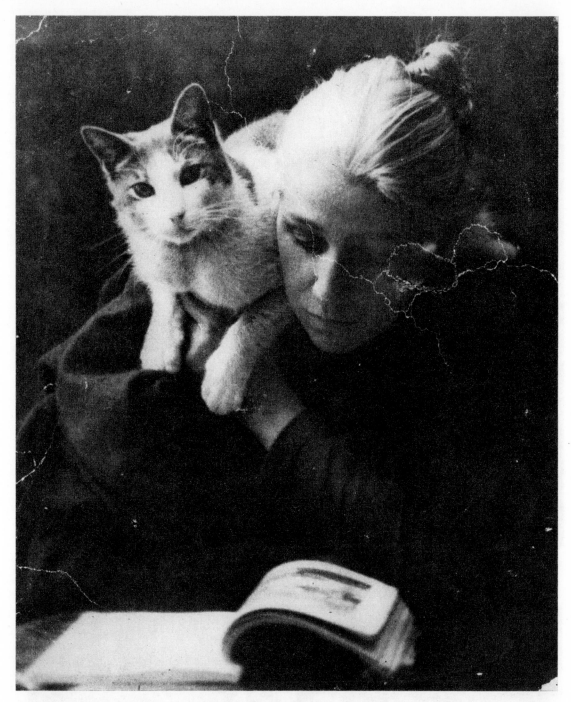

354 Thomas Eakins. *Amelia Van Buren and Cat*. c. 1891. Platinum print, 6¾ × 8″.
The Metropolitan Museum of Art, New York. David Hunter McAlpin Fund, 1943

the experiments to the University of Pennsylvania. There he used a battery of cameras with electrically operated shutters placed at regular intervals to capture successive phases of a variety of animal and human motion, as in *Figure Hopping* (plate 355), which he published in 1887 and 1901. In addition, he perfected a device based on a child's toy which he called a "zoopraxiscope" or a "zoogyroscope"; it projected consecutive still images in rapid succession on a screen to simulate actual movement. Although Eakins had worked briefly with Muybridge at the University of Pennsylvania, his contribution to the study of motion was similar to that of the

French physiologist Marey, in that the consecutive stages of an action were visible on the same negative, as in *Pole Vaulter* (plate 356).

The great range and flexibility of modern photography were not possible until the dry plate was substituted for the wet collodion negative. Because wet-plate technology was so unwieldy, experiments had been under way as early as the sixties to produce a collodio-bromide film that could be purchased, stored, and used when needed. By 1878 success was achieved after gelatin had been substituted for collodion by the Englishman Dr. Richard Leach Maddox. Further improvements in the negative

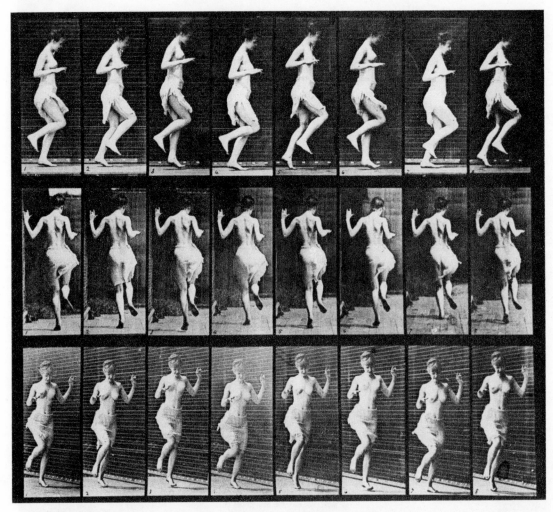

355   Eadweard Muybridge. *Figure Hopping.* c. 1887. The Cooper-Hewitt Museum,
The Smithsonian Institution's National Museum of Design, New York

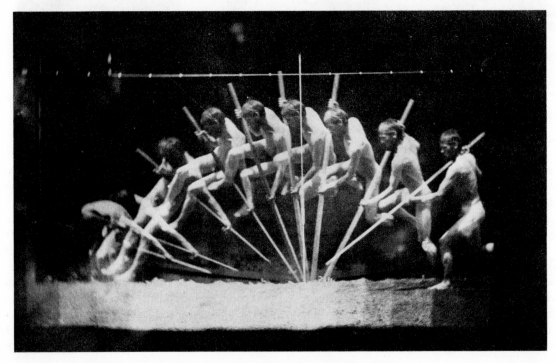

356   Thomas Eakins. *Pole Vaulter (George Reynolds).* 1884. Wet plate, $3\frac{5}{8} \times 4\frac{3}{4}''$.
The Metropolitan Museum of Art, New York. Gift of Charles Bregler, 1941

material were made by Charles H. Bennett.

During the decade following the appearance of dry plates, other technological advances also made photography easier for the professional and more accessible to the amateur. Numerous small cameras intended for making quick, simple exposures (snapshots) were marketed. The most notable was the Kodak, first manufactured in 1888 by George Eastman. Designed to be used with roll film, another invention of the period, the camera was loaded at the factory with film for 100 exposures and was returned there for processing. Afterward, negatives, prints, and a freshly loaded camera were returned to the sender. From 1889 on, Eastman substituted Hannibal Goodwin's earlier invention of transparent roll film for his own paper-backed type (and incidentally involved himself in a protracted lawsuit over patent rights). This film allowed the negative to be processed at home, increasing the appeal to amateurs even further. Standardization of the developing process and improvement in the color sensitivity of film were accompanied by the manufacture of sharper lenses and faster shutters, more manageable enlargers, and gelatin-bromide papers that did not require sensitizing by the photographer. In addition to providing the public with a pictorial hobby, these developments, along with concurrent ones in photomechanical reproduction, enlarged the use of photography for scientific and journalistic purposes. At the same time, they caused serious photographers to reevaluate the role of their medium in the arts.

The photographic image offered the nineteenth-century artist a new way of seeing, as well as providing previously unavailable information, and artists reacted to the medium in varying ways. Eakins's interest in photography was singularly creative and honest, but western painters such as Russell and Remington also acknowledged the aid of photography in their work. Some artists, among them John George Brown, used photographs frequently but less openly, while others painted over photographic images enlarged, developed, and fixed upon canvas or paper. Portrait artists especially benefited from this procedure.

By the eighties, photographers could record a wide range of real-life activities, instead of requiring studio reenactments of genre scenes, but on close examination it became obvious that the photograph did not represent actuality in the same way that the painter had traditionally perceived it. For one thing, the photographer often selected moments that were casual and unimportant—merely part of a larger continuum of time and space—whereas the painter traditionally chose to depict an event of significance. Depending on the way the scene was composed and framed, and the nature of the gesture and expression captured, the photograph might suggest both what had already happened and what was about to transpire. It substituted a sense of the fluidity of time for the discrete and eternalized moment that had been the focus of pictorial art. In addition, the photograph often demonstrated the illogicality of appearances and the strange conjunction of forms that exist in actuality but rarely in the painted image. As painters became aware of the new vision and began to integrate its message into their work, it became evident that henceforth the relationship between photography and the older medium would be symbiotic rather than hierarchical.

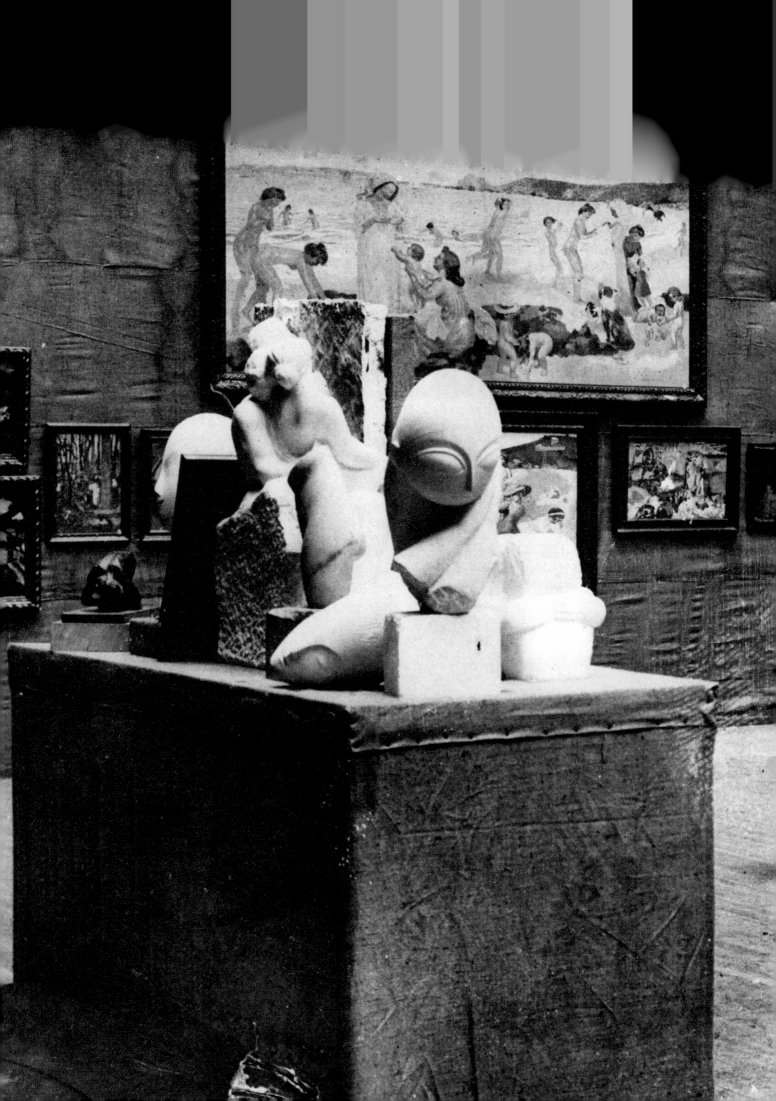

Part 5
TURN OF THE CENTURY
TO WORLD WAR I

The general historical consensus is that in the United States the period from about 1890 to 1910, or from the financial panic of 1893 to the outbreak of World War I, was transitional. Much in the earlier decade presaged the twentieth century, while much in the later retained the character of the nineteenth. The 1890s, especially, witnessed the culmination of economic and social developments that were the fulfillment, in a sense, of the dream of American destiny. On the other hand, that last decade of the century saw also the exacerbation of economic, social, political, and regional antagonism attendant on the country's phenomenal growth. By the end of the century industrial capitalism had reached monopolistic consolidation in almost all areas of the economy. After the crash of 1893, this consolidation was intensified through the growing power of finance capital, preparing the way for the economy of the twentieth century.

Growth itself is not progress, and at the turn of the century the seams of the American polity were splitting. Everything had grown too rapidly and inequities were everywhere—in wealth, opportunity, status, and power. There was a dawning awareness of the prodigal squandering of natural resources, of the human cost in industrial expansion, of the subversion of government for private ends.

American culture during these decades was insular, narrow-minded, self-satisfied, subject to a provincial complacency that was the result of old ignorance and new wealth. American art had become essentially conservative. The National Academy of Design was still dominated by pseudo-Classicism. Artistically, the "academy" was an agglomeration of many tendencies. In painting it included disciples of the Barbizon School, slick portraitists in the tradition of Sargent and Chase, remnants even

of the Düsseldorf genre school, the brush wizards of Munich, the bastard style of academic painting, Impressionists, and various eclectic combinations and permutations of all these tendencies. In sculpture one found a provincial literal Realism, French academic elegance, or the beginnings of a Rodinesque grandeur.

Organizationally, the Academy was a great brake upon American art, its self-perpetuating membership contriving to stifle nonconformism through a rigid system of election of members, and the market for American art had become limited. Dealers were handling either old masters or recognized academicians. The new museums and the great American collections then being formed were not primarily interested in American art. Also, American artists had no *salon des refusés*. There was scarcely a hint of the twentieth century in American painting of the last decade of the nineteenth. It took the Realism of the Ashcan School (though stylistically rooted in the nineteenth century) to shepherd the twentieth century through its contemporary urban focus. Not until the second decade did American artists begin to come to terms with modernism, the dominant stream in the art of the twentieth century.

Only in architecture, where the connections with economic and technological developments are more obvious, did the break from nineteenth-century attitudes surface in the 1890s. America looked forward to the new century with unwitting optimism, to a new and more inclusive American destiny.

The year 1900, as a century marker, had more than the normal psychological impact of an epochal date. It heralded the twentieth century, which was from the start identified with modernity.

15
Pioneers of Modern Architecture

Less inhibited than Europe by the weight of a long historical tradition and an established professional body, American architects responded with greater alacrity to the development of new, specialized building archetypes. The two special achievements of American architecture up to 1900, the skyscraper and the almost universal individual dwelling, have given a particularly varied density and texture to the modern American city, in contrast to the European metropolis, which tends to be built over at a much more even rate, whether the land is used for commercial, industrial, or residential purposes.

Thanks to this clear differentiation of building types, the beginnings of modern architecture are especially rich in the United States, and the split between the new modes and the more conventional, historicizing styles is unmistakable. Innovations in design in the early twentieth century were largely confined to commercial, industrial, and residential projects, while traditional solutions tended, until after World War II, to be the norm in civic and monumental schemes. Historically, a sharp distinction is usually maintained between solitary individualists such as Louis Sullivan and Frank Lloyd Wright and the traditional architectural establishment, represented by the large offices of McKim, Mead & White, Daniel H. Burnham, and Cass Gilbert. Yet the works of these two divergent groups sprang from many of the same sources.

The patriarchal figure for American architects of the early twentieth century was Richardson (see Chapter 11). Out of his prosaic ordering of masonry masses and round-arched windows and entrances, two lines may be traced. His sparse forms and relative freedom from historical prototypes, especially in his later works, and his reliance upon the straightforward expressive effect of a material such as rough, quarry-faced ashlar pointed the way toward the work of Sullivan and Wright in Chicago. Similarly, his timbered, shingled houses established a tradition that would be developed in personal, idiosyncratic ways by Bernard Maybeck (1862–1957) and

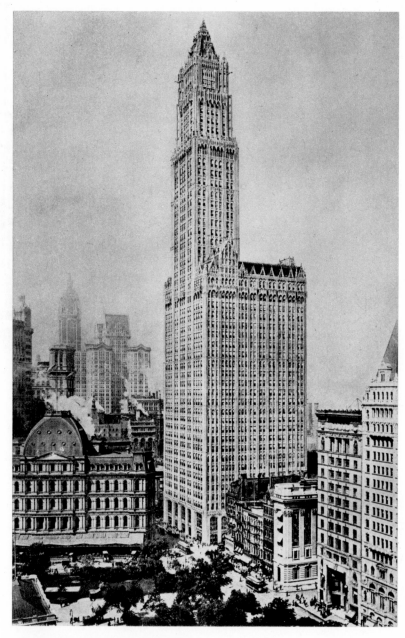

357 Cass Gilbert. Woolworth Building, New York. 1913

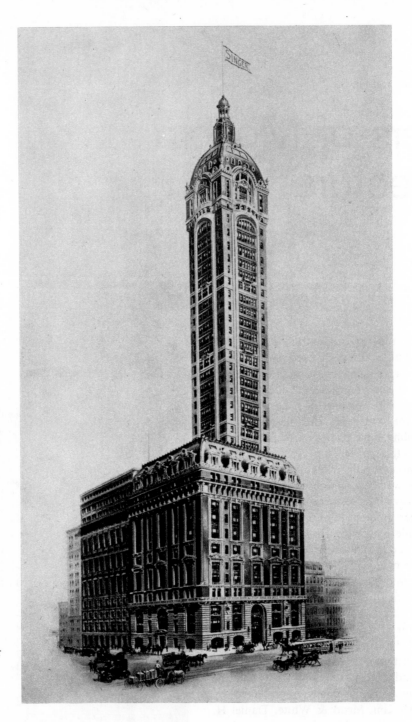

358 Ernest Flagg. Second Singer
Building, New York.
1906–8 (demolished)

Charles and Henry Greene (1868–1957 and 1870–1956, respectively) on the West Coast after 1900. Richardson's double legacy to twentieth-century American architecture created a dichotomy that would last for nearly fifty years.

No organized group dominated avant-garde architecture during the first decade of the century, though it is reasonable to link the followers and disciples of Sullivan and of Wright into a Prairie School. Nor did the new architecture ever achieve a group manifestation; the numerous World's Fairs of the period in St. Louis, San Francisco, and San Diego were dominated by the establishment and given over to vast, seductive panoramas of

academic design with considerable pictorial effect in their own terms but of limited functional integration. The work of Sullivan, as the most distinctive of the Chicago skyscraper architects, had a wide geographical distribution, despite the relatively small number of buildings that constituted his active career, but it did not ensure anything like the wide influence on subsequent commercial design realized by Richardson in the previous generation.

In contrast to the relatively free designs characteristic of the Chicago School before 1900, numerous academic and historicizing skyscrapers were built, and, to the regret of many, this conservative mode of dressing up a com-

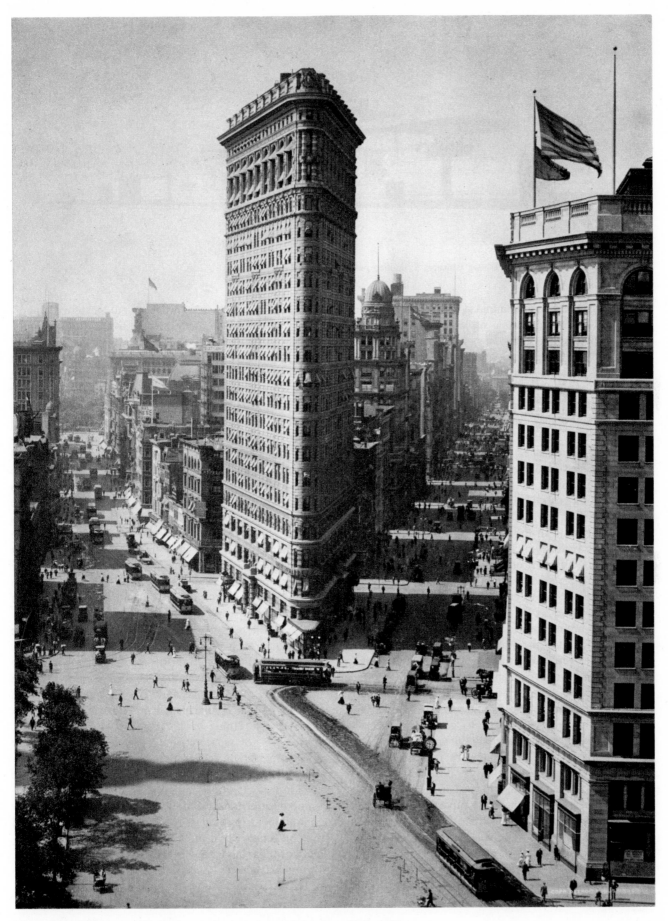

359 D. H. Burnham and Co. Flatiron (formerly Fuller) Building, New York. 1902

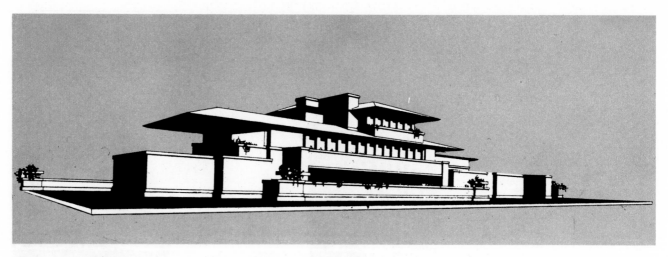

360 Frank Lloyd Wright. Robie House, Chicago. Simplified perspective. 1909

mercial design tended to dominate the work of the generation after 1900. A remarkable success in the employment of historical forms in a colossus of modern construction is the soaring Gothic-clad Woolworth Building, New York (1913, plate 357), the work of Cass Gilbert (1859–1934), and for many years the world's tallest office building. Somewhat apart from the main line of independent or traditional skyscraper design is the second Singer Building, New York (1906–8, plate 358), by Ernest Flagg (1857–1947), demolished, as were so many fine landmarks of the period, in the 1960s. Another impressive, but more durable, effort to adapt historical motifs to the tallest building of *its* day is the Flatiron (formerly Fuller) Building, New York (1902, plate 359), by D. H. Burnham & Company. In these three New York skyscrapers a solution to vertical unity was sought through the use of a tall, attenuated shaft of relative simplicity, regularity, and continuity, placed on an elaborate base designed to relate to the street and capped with a distinctive spire, dome, or cornice.

Domestic architecture of the early twentieth century has been, for the historian, almost completely dominated by the overpowering figure of Frank Lloyd Wright. Wright's houses and occasional public buildings of the pre–World War I period had at least a momentary influence upon the group of architects in the Middle West known as the Prairie School. His greatest impact was destined to be upon the emerging European avant-garde, many of whom would ultimately be recognized as the masters of the International Style. Probably no other artist has had so seminal an influence on his peers abroad.

Although Wright was the most important of Sullivan's disciples, his work is mainly domestic, a field that interested Sullivan only slightly. The growing specialization of building genres—a phenomenon that certainly abetted Sullivan in the rapid perfection of his style of office building—was even more important to Wright. One can argue that Wright's ambitions as an architect of

monuments were hardly well served by actual opportunity, yet he was uniquely devoted to the problem of the individual residence throughout his life. The essence of his style is its domesticity; thus it seems improbable that he could have thrived initially except as an architect working in the suburbs of a large American city about 1900, with its regular demand for private dwellings.

Wright's early practice ranged from the modest cottage and the suburban family dwelling to an occasional mansion with requisite carriage house, conservatory, and garden. All seem to have been designed to moderate scale; even the most elaborate do not impose themselves as ostentatious or monumental. Ideally the "Prairie House" (a name adopted by Wright for his work of this period) should sit flat upon the ground, shunning the dank subterranean cellar. Its formal characteristics should emphasize the predominant horizontals of the site (often a tight, narrow plot in the subdivisions of Chicago or Oak Park), and the low-pitched, wide-flaring roof should further stress the ground-hugging effect. By now many of these features have been bowdlerized in the ubiquitous ranch house of present-day subdivisions.

The subsidiary exterior forms of the Prairie House tend to emphasize a layered effect, and in many cases the interlocking of horizontal and vertical elements results in a breakup of the boxlike nature of the basic mass, notably in the Robie House (1909, plate 360). In the interior, spaces are not separated but flow together; the major division is usually accomplished with a large fireplace—the symbolic, functional, and structural core of the home—with distinct spaces radiating from this center. Conventional individual windows are frequently replaced by continuous strips of glass rectangles or squares separated only by simple wood mullions. Working within this original formula, and taking heed of each client's need, Wright was able to conceive of a seemingly infinite number of variations.

(continued on page 344)

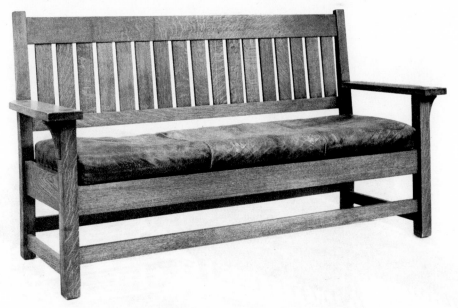

361 Gustav Stickley. Settle. c. 1909. Oak with leather cushions, width 71¼".
The Art Institute of Chicago. Gift of Mr. and Mrs. John E. Evans, Jr.

DECORATIVE ARTS

One of the most important and far-reaching American manifestations of the Arts and Crafts Movement was the creation of a simple and almost completely unadorned line of furniture called "Craftsman." Gustav Stickley, who was influenced by the writings of Ruskin and the work of the English designer Voysey, established workshops in 1898 at Eastwood, N.Y. In 1901 the monthly periodical Craftsman was launched to spread the aesthetic of its founder. At the height of his popularity Stickley explained his ideas in The Furniture Styles (1909). The movable settle (plate 361), like his chairs, bookcases, and tables, is quite severe in its squared-off and obviously joined construction. The wood was cut to emphasize the grain as the only form of ornament, whether used alone or combined with leather cushions. A catalog item, the settle first appeared in 1909 and sold for fifty dollars. Imitators using cheaper wood or veneers were able to sell for less. The Craftsman ideal has found new support in the work of independent craftsmen since the 1960s.

Frank Lloyd Wright's early furniture was always designed for specific locations. He often used built-in furniture to control the whole interior scheme, but, failing that, he created sets of movable pieces. Most of his work was in oak, and the armchair (plate 362) reflects his interest in the potential of the grain. The contrast of carved forms with the severity of the verticals differs from Stickley's uniform rectilinear quality. The Darwin R. Martin house, in Buffalo, N.Y., designed and furnished by Wright, was one of his early masterpieces. The chairs from that house retain the vigor and exciting quality of Wright's early mature creative period.

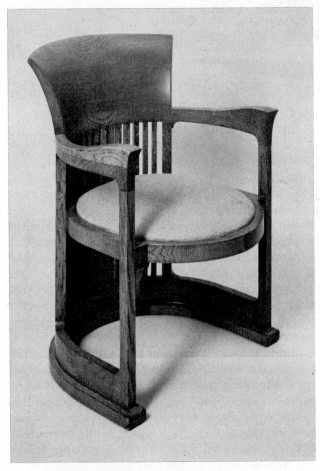

362 Frank Lloyd Wright. Armchair. 1904. Oak, height 32".
Albright-Knox Art Gallery, Buffalo, N.Y.
Gift of Darwin R. Martin

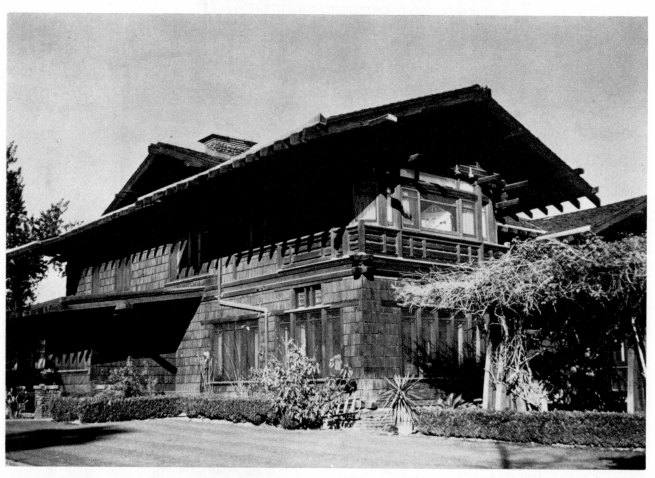

363 Greene & Greene. Blacker House, Pasadena, Calif. 1907

(continued from page 342)

Parallel to Wright's efforts are the houses of Charles and Henry Greene, whose practice was centered about the Los Angeles suburb of Pasadena. Independent, yet related to the tradition of nineteenth-century domestic architecture in wood (as was Wright), their works, such as the Blacker House (1907, plate 363), are elaborate, elegant treatises in timber construction, but their manner lacked the creative cutting edge that would lift Wright's work beyond its local milieu. The brothers enjoyed a considerable success in the first decade of the century, then slipped from favor.

Much the same pattern is to be found in the career of another, but very different, architect practicing in southern California at that time: Irving Gill (1870–1936). A native of central New York state, Gill worked from 1890 to 1892 with Adler & Sullivan in Chicago (where he would have met Wright), and then moved to the West Coast. Characteristic of his style is the Walter Dodge House, Los Angeles (1915–16, plate 364), another casualty of the 1960s. Gill, interested in concrete from an early date, offers in his work parallels to both the reductive, pale-surfaced buildings of Adolf Loos in Austria and the Hispano-American Colonial revival that pervaded the

Southwest during the early twentieth century. His crisp geometries, with their flat roofs, rectangular windows, round-arched openings, and stuccoed surfaces, are basically a simplification of an indigenous revival movement.

The buildings of Bernard Maybeck represent a corollary to the work of the Greenes and Gill. Maybeck had been trained in Paris at the École des Beaux-Arts, as had Richardson and Sullivan before him, but his response to that education was capricious. His First Church of Christ, Scientist, Berkeley (1909–11, plate 365), was a richly ornamented fantasia on several medieval and Gothic themes. Columns in cast concrete are juxtaposed to wooden posts and beams, and the rich timbered finish of the interior can be contrasted on the exterior to the overlapping eaves sheltering walls of asbestos siding and windows of rectangular industrial-metal sash. A curious mixture, altogether characteristic of Maybeck's puckish temperament. The lush, autumnal Classicism of his Palace of Fine Arts (plate 366), a plaster-and-wood creation for the 1915 Panama-Pacific Exposition in San Francisco more closely reflects his Beaux-Arts training, yet at the same time demonstrates the picturesque nature of his talent. (The building survived, dilapidated, until its re-

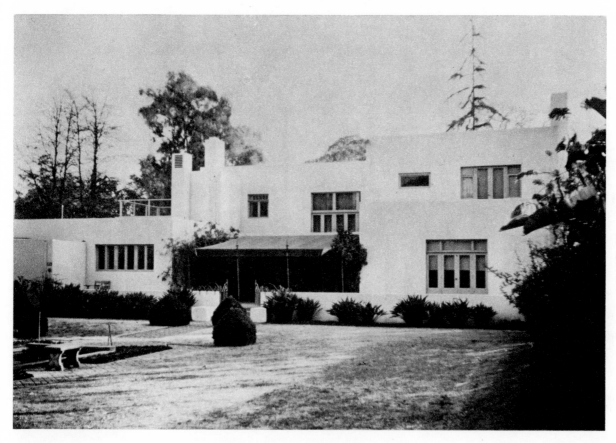

364 Irving Gill. Walter Dodge House, Los Angeles. 1915–16 (demolished)

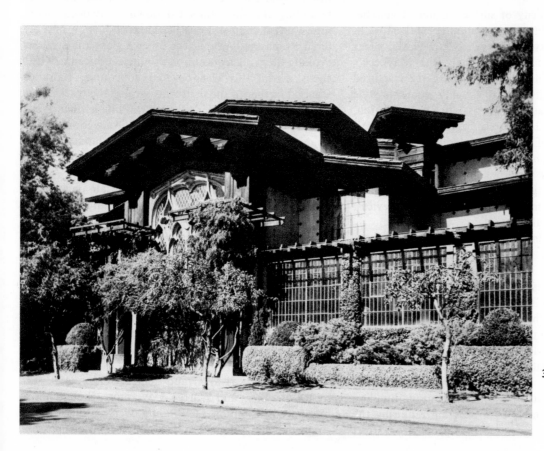

365 Bernard Maybeck.
First Church of Christ,
Scientist, Berkeley, Calif.
1909–11

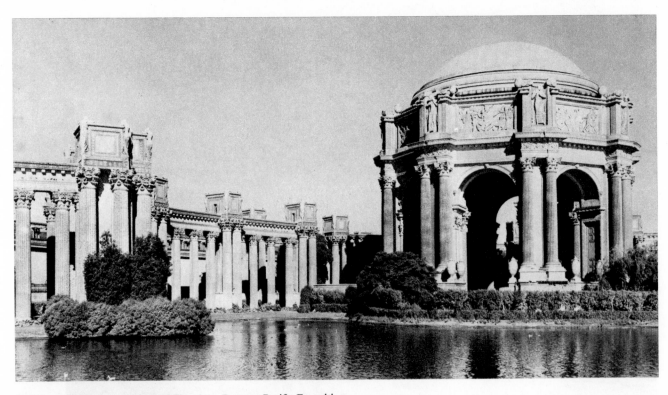

366 Bernard Maybeck. Palace of Fine Arts, Panama-Pacific Exposition,
San Francisco. 1915 (since replaced with replica)

placement by a stiff, cold copy in permanent materials in the 1960s.)

A contrasting simplicity of surface, if not of volume, can be seen in Wright's earliest monumental effort in poured concrete, Unity Church, Oak Park (1906, plates 367, 368), which compares interestingly with Maybeck's slightly later church in Berkeley. In part, the fractured cubic forms are an offshoot of Wright's domestic style of that decade, but mass is more assertive in his church, the height of the building barely balanced by the horizontal slabs of the roof cornice. The main meeting room, almost biaxially symmetrical and nearly entirely illuminated by clerestory windows, produces a space and volume radical in its geometric abstraction yet rigidly Classic in its use of time-hallowed compositional devices, notably the ideal central plan.

Public monuments in the early twentieth century can be exemplified by the great generation of railroad terminals, some of which have already followed their nineteenth-century predecessors to demolition. New York's Pennsylvania Station (1906–10, plates 369, 370), by McKim, Mead & White, was appreciated fully only after its destruction in the 1960s. Frequently ridiculed in its lifetime as a somewhat implausible adaptation of the design of a Roman bath to a modern train depot (and entry to a metropolis), it is admired now for almost the very same reason: that this particular antique building type was indeed adaptable to a program requiring the smooth movement of large numbers of people from street to railroad car under often unfavorable weather conditions. From major entrances on each of the four streets bounding the site, stairs led down to two enormous, high-vaulted rooms, one a literal reproduction of a coffered Roman groin vault, the other a glass-and-steel hall evoking the modern tradition of nineteenth-century train sheds. From this glass-covered concourse, stairs descended farther to the platforms serving the tracks. Penn Station was New York's gateway to Philadelphia, Washington, Chicago, and distant points. As a low, ground-hugging mass, dominated by long colonnades on its main facade, it formed a superb contrast to the verticality of the commercial architecture around it.

Academic Classicism, often inappropriate or awkward when applied to many contemporary situations, provided a workable matrix for programs requiring movement of crowds or the interconnection of a variety of functional elements. Significantly, this type of axial planning with graduated masses was employed by Wright in the design of the Imperial Hotel, Tokyo (1915–22, plate 371), even though the proportions and style of the building grew out of his distinctively low-slung, horizontally disposed Prairie Style, aesthetically a world removed from the sedate mixture of columns, arches, and vaults of Penn Station.

Penn Station's rival, Grand Central Station (1903–13), by Reed & Stem and Warren & Wetmore, though not so original an invention as Wright's overseas masterpiece, suggested that progress and development were possible

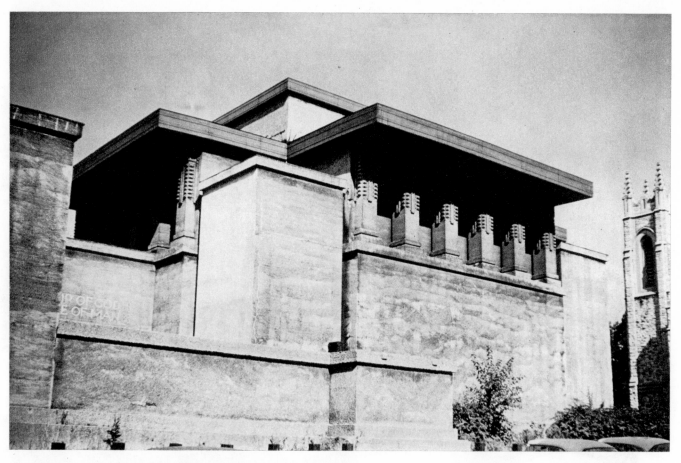

367 Frank Lloyd Wright. Unity Church, Oak Park, Ill. 1906

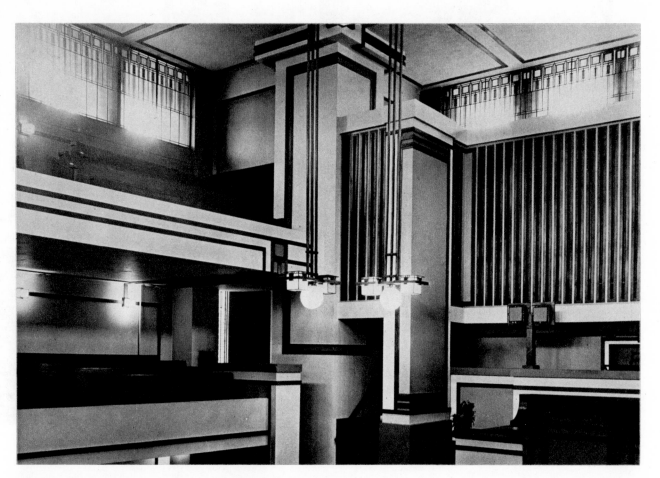

368 Frank Lloyd Wright. Unity Church, Oak Park, Ill. Interior. 1906

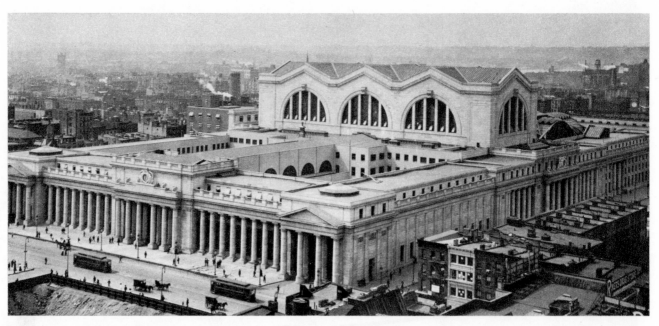

369 McKim, Mead & White. Pennsylvania Station, New York. 1906–10 (demolished)

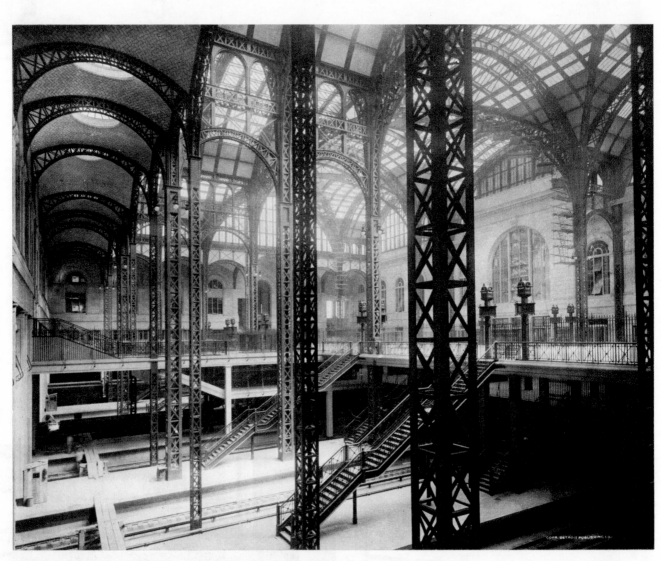

370 McKim, Mead & White. Pennsylvania Station, New York, original disposition,
showing platform and tracks. 1906–10 (demolished)

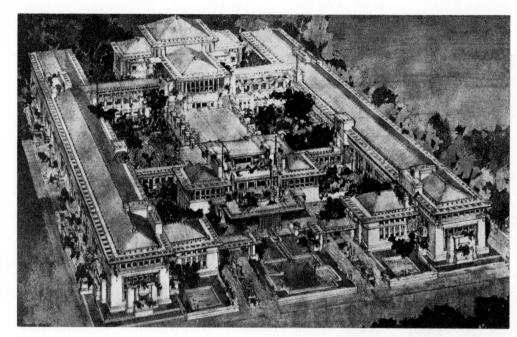

371 Frank Lloyd Wright.
Imperial Hotel, Tokyo.
Exterior perspective.
1915–22 (demolished)

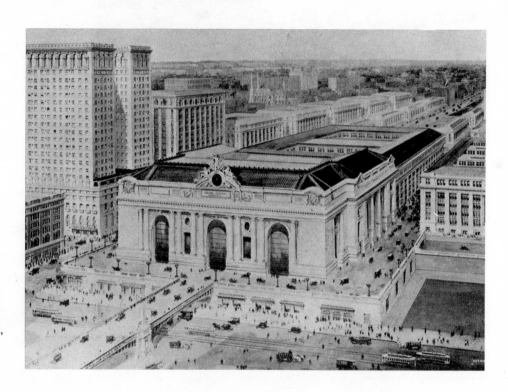

372 Reed & Stem; Warren & Wetmore.
Project for Grand Central Terminal,
New York. 1903–13

even within the confines of massive, Roman-inspired elevations (plate 372). Ramps link the street to upper- and lower-level concourses, facilitating movement especially for arriving passengers going up to the street. The covering of the track level north of the station made possible the development of Park Avenue, and led the designers to carry the avenue around and through the upper parts of the building and across Forty-second Street, on the south side, by a bridge. The separation and interconnection of rail, vehicular, and pedestrian traffic were treated here in a way that predicts the Futurist projects of Sant'Elia in Italy and, ultimately, certain aspects of Le Corbusier's Ville Radieuse projects of the 1920s.

Each in its own way, Grand Central and the Imperial Hotel provide a much too optimistic indication of the further possibilities of traditional architecture at the beginning of the century. The popularity of Wright, Greene & Greene, Maybeck, and Gill waned drastically about 1910; of the entire group, only Wright had the strength, genius, and good fortune to persevere until another rotation in the cycle of taste brought him and his work back into favor in the thirties.

Even Sullivan, who lived and continued his practice in fairly straitened circumstances until 1924, had little work

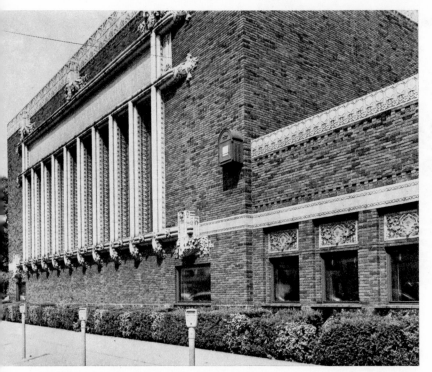

to do save for a handful of small banks in Middle Western towns of modest size (plate 373). Much of his time and energy during the last quarter-century of what would ultimately be a tragic, half-wasted career was devoted to the publication of *Kindergarten Chats* and *The Autobiography of an Idea*. Of his pupils, Purcell & Elmslie were the most successful. This partnership was responsible for one of the few truly great Prairie Houses not by Wright: the sentinel-like Bradley House, Woods Hole, Mass. (1912, plate 374), its main body raised upon a contracted basement to command the view of the ocean. The relative failure and invisibility of Sullivan's legacy become even more ironic when measured against the scholarly expertise of a contemporary monumental shrine, Henry Bacon's suave, knowledgeable Lincoln Memorial (1917). For all its outward virtues, the structure is a frigid accomplishment, only superficially in accord with the progressive spirit of an earlier Neoclassicism in the national capital.

373 Louis Sullivan. People's Savings and Loan
    Association Bank, Sidney, Ohio. 1917–18

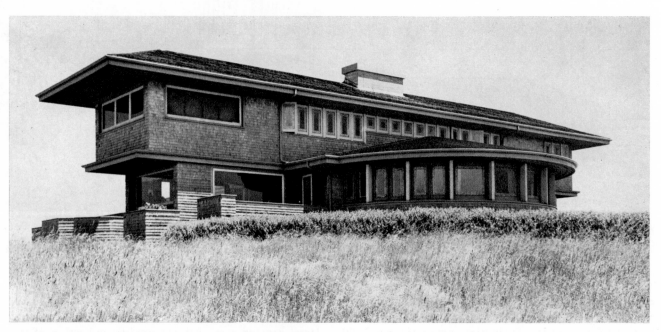

374 Purcell & Elmslie. Bradley House, Woods Hole, Mass. 1912

16
Painting: The Opening Skirmishes

Within a very short time after the turn of the century the conflicts and inequities brought about by America's heady industrial growth were to be expressed in an art and a literature of protest under the aegis of naturalism. But momentarily the whole motive for the new era of the twentieth century—a growing sentiment for radical reform—was lost in a wave of business confidence. Until the emergence of muckraking agitation under Theodore Roosevelt, the nation was in a self-congratulatory mood. It was the era of the Gibson Girl in popular art and of adventure fiction and historical confectionery in the novel. The very real and present terrors of the economic struggle set forth in the Realist novels of Frank Norris, Stephen Crane, and Theodore Dreiser were brushed aside as the century of hope breathed its last and the Gilded Age enjoyed a final flourish.

Dreiser's *Sister Carrie*, published in 1900, was immediately suppressed as too sordid and "pornographic" because it honestly described the compromising relationships which economic circumstances forced upon a woman of the new urban proletariat. While Dreiser was being spurned, popular taste continued to endorse Horatio Alger's gratifying fables of success and such romantic delectations as Charles Major's *When Knighthood Was in Flower* (1898). The literate turned to *The Century* and other such periodicals, whose editors took care never to sully their pages with the more unpleasant facts of contemporary existence. In the hands of *The Century's* long-time editor, Richard Watson Gilder, the genteel tradition was safe. He had the dubious distinction of rejecting Stephen Crane's early venture in realism, *Maggie* (1893), and he once even confessed that he had edited the indelicacies out of *Huckleberry Finn*.

After 1900, however, there were clear stirrings of revolt against such absurd prudishness and against the escapist fantasies and corrupt values of the Gilded Age. Actually, as early as 1886, the novelist and critic William Dean Howells had pleaded for a specifically American and "democratic art" capable of dealing with the urban casualties of industrialization in a more humane spirit.

He called for an end to the charade of the genteel tradition and proposed in its place an art that would "front the everyday world and catch the charm of its work-worn, careworn, brave, kindly face."

A CHALLENGE TO GENTILITY: HENRI AND THE EIGHT

In Theodore Roosevelt's second term (1904–08) a new spirit of insurgence seized the American imagination as national interest focused on reform. Writers took up the cause of the common man against organized corporate power and abuses of privilege. Painters awoke to the teeming life of the streets and found a new sympathy for the oppressed humanity of our industrial centers. It was characteristic that, in the period of "exposé" journalism and the "exposé" fiction of the naturalists, progressive painting should be in the hands of a group of newspaper-trained artist-journalists. There was a certain naive romanticism and boyish opportunism in the manner in which these new painters, and even such new writers as Jack London, assumed their reformist postures. The Rooseveltian appetite for life, which helped free them from a stagnant past, was refreshing and salutary. But it was shallow, too, and reportorial realism did not offer the most durable basis for a new art.

The new movement in painting was not directly concerned with radical politics or the class struggle, as was literature, and on the whole it substituted a more tolerant, even hedonistic, spirit for the moral indignation of the naturalist writers. Although later identified with the New York scene, it first centered around Philadelphia, and many of its participants had studied at the Pennsylvania Academy with Thomas Anschutz, the pupil of Thomas Eakins.

The first group of American artists to advocate a new kind of "democratic art" and to explore the everyday life of ordinary people in large cities came to be known as "The Eight," or, loosely, in a reference to their humble content, "The Ashcan School." Led by Robert Henri (1865–1929), they shared a passionate conviction that

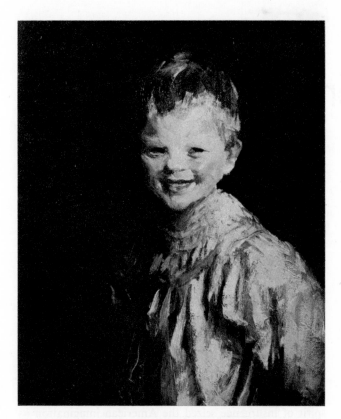

375 Robert Henri. *Laughing Child*. 1907. Oil on canvas, 24 × 20″.
Whitney Museum of American Art, New York

for the viability of human emotions. "Because we are
saturated with life, because we are human," as he was
quoted in *The Art Spirit* (1923), "our strongest motive is
Life, humanity; and the stronger the motive back of a
line, the stronger, and therefore more beautiful, the line
will be. . . . It isn't the subject that counts but what
you feel about it."

Henri had studied for two years at the Pennsylvania
Academy under Anschutz and then, in 1888, entered a
conventional Beaux-Arts studio in Paris. The academic
productions there seemed sterile and unpromising, but,
in common with most French students, he was at a loss
to understand late Impressionism and totally unaware of
Postimpressionist painting. In the late 1880s and the
nineties, the works of Cézanne, Van Gogh, and Gauguin
were known only to a small, select circle in Paris. It took
the great private and salon retrospectives of Van Gogh
in 1901 and 1905, of Gauguin in 1903 and 1906, and of
Cézanne in 1906 and 1907 to offer at first hand the
experience of those major innovations in color and form
which were to inspire Fauvism, Cubism, and Expressionism.

In Manet's early "Spanish" period, in Hals, and in
Velázquez, Henri discovered both a simple pictorial
formula and a picturesque subject matter that he could
assimilate. There was often a certain gypsy quality about
Henri's preferred subjects. The style he finally arrived
at was no more nor less daring than Duveneck's, but
thematically less conventional. Like many other late
nineteenth-century painters, he worked in the vein of
what the art critic Frank Jewett Mather called Manet's
"dark Impressionism."

Laughing Child (plate 375) is a fine example of Henri's
vivacious early manner, as he tried to fuse the activist
American spirit with brilliant Continental brushwork
and to establish an emotional contact with his human
subject. *The Masquerade Dress: Portrait of Mrs. Robert
Henri* (plate 376) shows his art at its best, in lucent paint
passages almost worthy of Manet. His obvious identification with his sitter (in this case his wife) gives the
work a special glow and even an Expressionist exuberance in the handling. Although he could not convey the
vibrant human presence with the technical brilliance or
psychological penetration of Degas or Manet, he was an
excellent observer of the human moment and amply
demonstrated his marvelous sense of paint handling.

While Henri's interest in specifically urban themes—
the lower-class scenes and slums that were beginning to
engage social reformers—was sincere, both he and his
colleagues painted what they saw more in the spirit of
good-natured reporting than social protest. Their choices
of subjects and sense of urban enjoyment evoke French
Impressionism in mood. On the other hand, Henri,
though he owed an obvious debt to Manet, offered little
hint of those optical and plastic "sensations" at the core
of French Impressionism. Nor was he aware of those

painting must reflect the artist's involvement with life as
it is lived, rather than with some polite and unreal pictorial surrogate. Although their paintings represented
an abrupt departure from contemporary academicism,
the new direction of The Eight lay more in content and
viewpoint than in style. No more advanced than pre-
Impressionist French painting, their formally unsophis-
ticated pictures did not change the course of American
art, but they did rebel against the genteel tradition and
the National Academy by opening up art to contemporary life. Their mild aesthetic revisionism sought
evolutionary, rather than revolutionary, change.

Robert Henri paradoxically tried to compensate for
American cultural inadequacy and impoverished visual
traditions, just as he insisted, with equal intensity, on the
importance of American life and daily experience as fit
subject matter for art. "What is necessary for art in
America," he wrote in 1909, "is first an appreciation of
the great native ideas . . . and then the achievement of
masterly freedom in expressing them." His message, in
the words of John Sloan, who later acknowledged Henri
as his "father in art," was "making pictures from life."
"Life" became the operative word in Henri's vocabulary, the litany of his teaching. It referred not so much to
the artist's recording of an object in the external world as
to the inward sensation of "being alive," enhanced by
the act and exercise of the painting craft. Henri pleaded

dynamic elements in the art of the radical painters in France whose atomization of the world of appearances was to suppress naturalistic illusion altogether in the art of the twentieth-century avant-garde. Henri failed to understand (and later bitterly opposed) abstract art, whether American or European.

When he returned from abroad to teach at the Pennsylvania Academy in Philadelphia in 1891, Henri met the group of young artist-illustrators who had been working for Edward Davis, the art director of the *Philadelphia Press* (and father of Stuart Davis). They were William Glackens, George Luks, Everett Shinn, and John Sloan. Henri imparted to these young disciples a new cosmopolitan spirit; he urged them to travel abroad and to devote themselves to oil painting rather than to illustration, or at least to combine the two vocations. In 1904 he set up a school of his own in New York City's Lincoln Arcade, in a Latin Quarter district on upper Broadway. Gathered there were all the rebels against the genteel tradition, the Philadelphia artists who had followed Henri to New York, and others, such as George Bellows and Glenn O. Coleman, who were to associate themselves with the new Realism.

For the Philadelphia group Henri was a welcome antidote to the academic Beaux-Arts styles and bloodless aestheticism dominating the period, as he redirected their attention to subjects taken from contemporary city life—the rooftops and backyards, Bohemian restaurants, ferryboats, and crowded streets. Following his example, they were innovotive primarily in subject matter rather than in formal structure or style, changing in their attitude not toward painting but toward life. It was a journalists' revolution, initiated by a group of eager young men more at home with the atmosphere of the city room than with Victorian refinement and decorum. As compared with contemporary European developments, their work was not revolutionary, but the "vulgarity" of their subject matter was enough to provoke sharp criticism for a time, at least, until their offenses paled beside the public outrage aroused by the introduction of avant-garde modernism at the Armory Show of 1913.

The Philadelphia painters presented a variety of individual temperaments and styles. Glackens (1870–1938) and Shinn (1873–1953) were the worldlings, drawn to society and the life of fashion, which they rendered in their early work with zest. Glackens had worked in a muted, Whistlerian landscape idiom after a year in Paris during the mid-nineties. Then, with the examples of Henri and of earlier Parisian painting, he began to paint in the "dark Impressionist" manner of Manet. After his apprenticeship with the *Philadelphia Press* and his Paris sojourn, Glackens went to Cuba in 1898, along with George Luks, to cover the Spanish-American War. Upon his return to New York, he began drawing its street scenes with more directness, finding in the push-

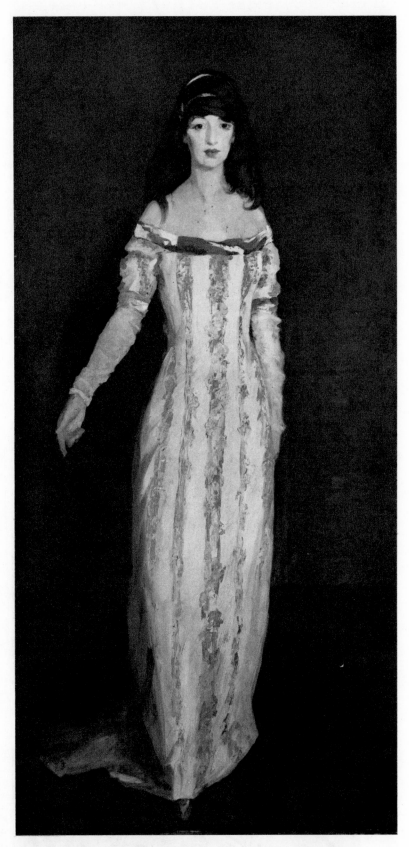

376 Robert Henri. *The Masquerade Dress: Portrait of Mrs. Robert Henri*. 1911. Oil on canvas, 76½ × 36¼". The Metropolitan Museum of Art, New York. Arthur H. Hearn Fund, 1958

carts, crowds, and tenements a stimulating new source of subject matter. Fastidious by nature, he generally left the shabbier aspects of urban life to his fellow Realists, Sloan, Luks, and Bellows. His favorite motifs and haunts were the parks, with their swarming, exuberant children and holiday spirit, and scenes of fashionable life in the shops and restaurants of New York. *Chez Mouquin* (plate 377) depicts a restaurant where he and many of the artists and newspapermen often dined. The man holding the glass is Jim Moore, owner of another favorite cabaret and convivial friend of the Realist painters.

Chez Mouquin belongs to Glackens's first and perhaps best period, when he managed to combine swift portrait studies with his particular kind of genre scene. *Hammerstein's Roof Garden* (colorplate 49), painted somewhat earlier, suggests the blond tonalities, tentative painterliness, and fluent brushwork of the French Impressionist Berthe Morisot. Theater offered the new American Realists vital gestures within a framework of popular entertainment which suited their "democratic"

377 William J. Glackens. *Chez Mouquin*. 1905.
Oil on canvas, 48⅛ × 36¼". The Art Institute of Chicago.
Friends of American Art Collection

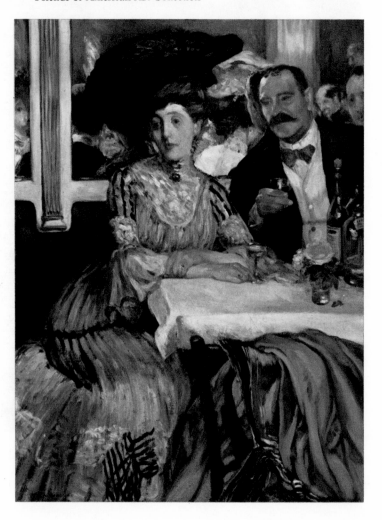

spirit. After 1910, however, the tempo of the Realists' response to life noticeably slackened, and they began to strain after a more distinctive and perhaps artificial "style." In Glackens's work the results were tragic, as he succumbed to a saccharine formula derived from Renoir which seemed indistinguishable from routine magazine illustration.

Something of the same pattern may be discerned in the evolution of Shinn's art. He too submitted to sophisticated European models, applying them in a lively if somewhat derivative fashion to the American scene. As early as 1899 Shinn was capturing vital street scenes in pastel, such as *Sixth Avenue Elevated After Midnight*, with the mixed mood so typical of the Realist group, which viewed the city as both an interesting phenomenon and a source of human energy. However, Degas was his greatest inspiration, and, like the French master, Shinn found his most sympathetic subject matter in the theater's world of illusion. He caught performers in action under the lights or fashionable theatergoers descending from their carriages beside bright marquees, often with an ashcan or disheveled-looking passersby in the background. *London Hippodrome* (plate 378) and *Revue* (colorplate 50) dramatically focus upon the world of the circus and the footlights, much the same democratic world of popular entertainment which engaged the French Impressionists. For both groups, Realists and Impressionists, separated by some thirty years, the acceptance of public spectacle and its accessibility to the emerging *bourgeoisie* became a metaphor for the new stature accorded social pleasure. Shinn lacked, as did all The Eight who were Realists, the fundamental trait of physical sensuality, so that he did not explore the painting medium for its own sake. Silken textures and the kind of well-crafted painting typical of William Merritt Chase and other academics were foreign to him. From pre-Impressionist and Impressionist painting, Shinn and the Realists derived both their social outlook and a superficial reportorial technique, rather than a more profound feeling for the expressive possibilities of the painting medium. Like Glackens, Shinn failed to sustain his early promise, and his more shallow themes exhausted their charm with repetition.

Shinn was the dandy of the Realists, with many friends in the theater and in society. His taste for luxury, in conjunction with the Realism of his art, attracted Theodore Dreiser, and he was said to have been the model for the Realist painter Eugene Witla, corrupted by power in Dreiser's novel *The Genius* (1915). In that novel the artist is a remarkable but credible figure, not only realizing his ambition to create truthful images of the world about him but also achieving his dreams of commercial power as a celebrated publishing potentate. The character embodies a decidedly romantic view of the possible social role of the artist, and in an oblique way, it might explain the American Realist painters' failure to reach more enduring pictorial solutions. So much of their artistic personalities were absorbed by life that they were inhibited from a more serious investigation of the demanding formal problems of art.

Famous for his tall tales and bombast, George Luks (1867–1933) became known as the most colorful figure among the new Realists, and perhaps he best projected the boyish romanticism of the Roosevelt era. He was trained in Paris, Munich, and Düsseldorf, where he joined the cult of the slashing brush, and then returned to study in Philadelphia at the Pennsylvania Academy. He also served as a war correspondent in Cuba and did a prodigious amount of newspaper illustration before his paintings began to sell. Technically, Luks, like Henri, found his inspiration in the direct painting tradition of Manet and Velázquez and particularly in the earthy themes, good humor, and animal spirits of Hals. Luks was attracted to scenes of physical action and conflict, memorably encapsulated in one of his better-known images, *The Wrestlers* (1905, plate 379). He also painted street scenes concentrating on the life of the newly arrived immigrants who were trans-

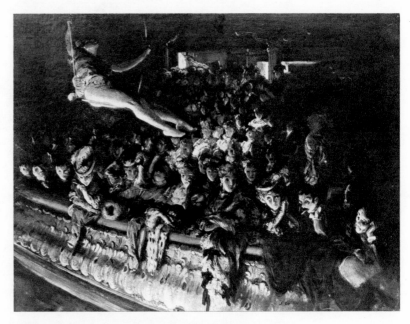

378 Everett Shinn. *London Hippodrome*. 1902. Oil on canvas, 26⅜ × 35¼″. The Art Institute of Chicago.
Gift of the Friends of American Art

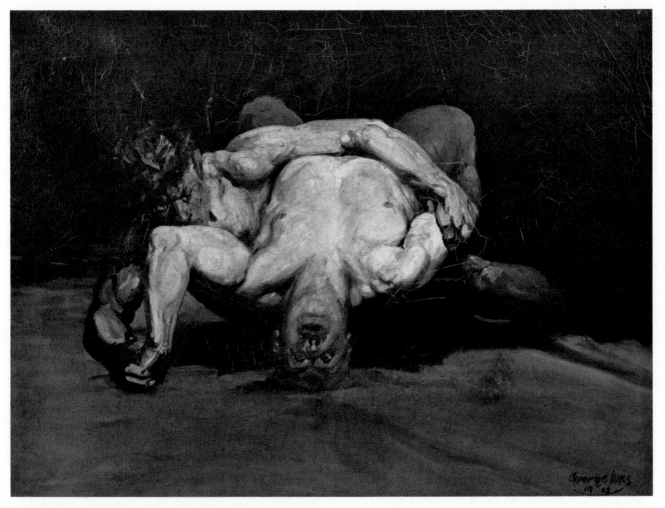

379 George Luks. *The Wrestlers*. 1905. Oil on canvas, 66¼ × 81¼″.
Museum of Fine Arts, Boston. Charles Henry Hayden Fund

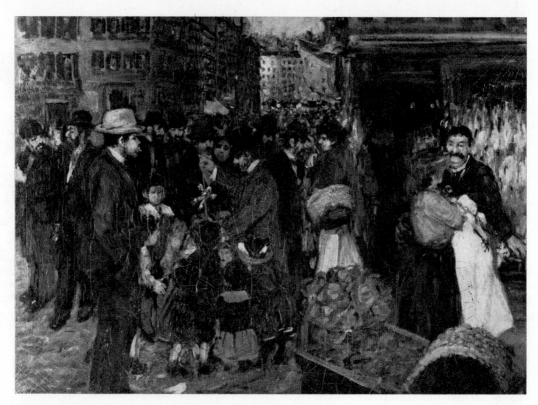

380 George Luks. *Hester Street*. 1905. Oil on canvas, 26 × 35¾″.
The Brooklyn Museum. Dick S. Ramsay Fund

forming the lower East Side into a warm, if shabby, bazaar and bringing new stirrings of cultural ferment. *Hester Street* (1905, plate 380) captures in an emblematic scene the bustling life of the crowded pushcart district, during a period whose human miseries we now view with nostalgia rather than the dismay of contemporary social critics. By comparison, the contemporary urban problems of crime, pollution, physical rot, and general social disintegration have produced a far more ominous and pessimistic social atmosphere.

In their search for vital pictorial styles, the Realists found little enough in their traditional past to consult. Even those artists in whom they had come to recognize distinctive American qualities were of no immediate use to them. Nineteenth-century popular illustration and genre painting, given a variety of individual inflections by Bingham, Mount, and Homer, were hopelessly dated; Eakins's realism, with its passionate scientific concern for form, seemed pedantic; and the crude artisanship and contemplative strain of Ryder's painting scarcely suited the new age of energy. Drawing at least nominally on the European past instead, Luks, Henri, and other Realists fixed on painting idioms of maximum informality to convey in the most direct and elementary way their pleasure in everyday reality. Despite their disclaimers, they also aspired to the European sense of style in art. Though they insisted that art be democratic, and viable in human terms, they were extremely conscious of their artistic posture.

Luks was a supreme egoist capable of the provincial's sublime arrogance. A one-time coal miner and a self-styled pugilist, as well as a bellicose newspaperman with a taste for distant wars, he identified himself with the struggles of the working classes. He also eliminated from his artistic canon almost all European art which did not deal directly with lower-class life. Hals alone, he boasted, was worthy of comparison with his own achievement. In his pronouncements, Luks scorned European style as effete with the strident anti-intellectualism which was to become the hallmark of the American artist-primitive: "The world has but two artists, Frans Hals and little old George Luks." And he would fume when people spoke of painting as an end in itself: "Art—my slats! Guts! Guts! Life! Life! I can paint with a shoestring dipped in pitch and lard."

Although he did not officially exhibit with The Eight, George Bellows (1882–1925) was associated with them as a Realist, and some of his better-known themes resembled those of Luks in their celebration of manly virtue and violent physical combat. Like Luks, he was a rugged athlete and a student of Henri's. In *Stag at Sharkey's* (1909, plate 381) Bellows maximized the moment of physical contact and bloody violence in the prizefight, held before a group of avid spectators. His *Cliff Dwellers* (1913, colorplate 51) is undoubtedly one of the most powerful and richly painted evocations of tenement life in the vital and ramshackle New York slums. He defines his human characters broadly as slovenly but pleasant and good-natured figures, with an earthy, gamin charm. Their energies spill out of the frame, and are matched by an appropriately loose, exuberant brushwork.

Of all the artists who felt Henri's influence, John Sloan (1871–1951) was on the most intimate personal terms with him and perhaps owed most to the older artist. Sloan began to paint seriously in 1897, when he shared a studio with Henri; later he followed Henri to New York. Until Henri introduced him to Forain, Daumier, and Goya, Sloan had been doing intricate newspaper illustration graphics and cartoons inspired by the decorative style of Art Nouveau. From these new and more vital aesthetic hints, and from Henri's own "dark Impressionism," Sloan evolved the pictorial formula of his Realism. It mixed elements of illustration and caricature with a feeling for the painterly means. Like the painting of so many of the other newspaper-trained artists, his work betrays a curious mixture of hackwork and sensibility.

Sloan moved to New York permanently in 1904, continuing his career as illustrator for magazines and newspapers, but finding more time to paint. He had begun to establish links to the new American Realists as early as 1900 with paintings of Philadelphia city life. These retained a certain nineteenth-century flavor of picturesque genre, however, and only after 1904 did he begin systematically to observe the life of the New York streets from a fresh and less sentimental point of view. A tireless stroller and "incorrigible window watcher," in his own words, Sloan came to see the New York slums as a kind of stage set where all sorts of lively, unexpected business was in progress. He became indefatigable in his search for human drama, recording little vignettes of urban life in a diary as well as in his paintings. The lower East Side, the West Side below Fourteenth Street, and the Bowery, which he described as "a maze of living incident," were some of his favorite haunts. The fact that he found vitality and human interest in the seamier pockets of the big city was quite in tune with the spirit of the new Realism, as was his tendency to give human squalor the touch of romance.

In his diary of June 5, 1907, he noted: "Walked up to Henri's studio. On the way saw a humorous sight of interest. A window, low, second story, bleached blond hairdresser bleaching the hair of a client. A small interested crowd about." He reproduced the incident in his vivid *Hairdresser's Window* (1907, colorplate 52), which became a modern version of Hogarth's scenes of eighteenth-century London life, but Sloan recorded his

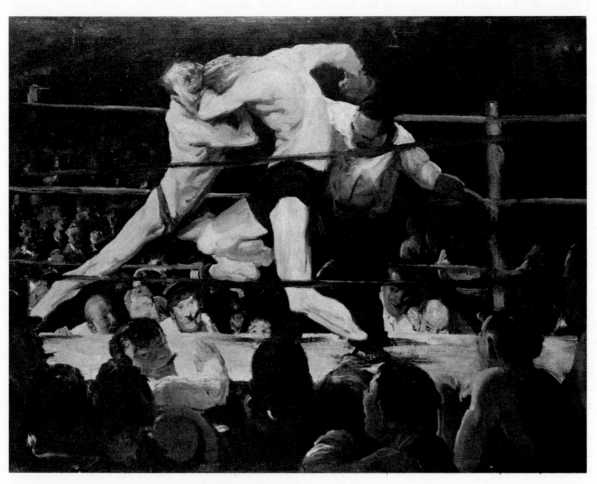

381 George Bellows. *Stag at Sharkey's*. 1909. Oil on canvas, 36¼ × 48¼".
The Cleveland Museum of Art. Hinman B. Hurlbut Collection

observations with a keener eye for the telling detail, even though the characterizations remain caricatures.

Sloan's best pictures register the pulse of urban life in a broad spirit of critical but good-humored Realism, exposing the pretensions of people of both high and low degree with a mixture of satire and sentimental moralizing which has been the hallmark of popular illustration since Daumier. He pointedly ignored the more sordid and grotesque side of New York, the crimes and blatant social miseries which were to preoccupy the urban Realists and Expressionists of a later date.

The literature and art of the Gilded Age had either sentimentalized "the poor" and the derelict as harmless, lovable ruffians or coldly ignored them. Under the new dispensation of social reform, the destitute became a real and pressing problem, enlisting the passionate interest not only of social workers but of artists and writers as well. Stephen Crane stood on his feet most of one night in a blizzard down on the Bowery, observing a breadline for his story "The Men in the Storm," one of the first primitive ventures in American naturalism. In his own way, John Sloan was equally conscientious about immersing himself in the raw American experience and painting lower-class life faithfully. He admitted to the most aroused social concern and committed political interests of any of The Eight. He even joined the Socialist Party in 1910 and was the party's candidate for the New York State Assembly that same year. By 1912 he had become the art editor of the left-wing news journal, *The Masses*.

Despite his political activism and the milder interest of his colleagues in reform, however, Sloan himself felt there was little overt social content in the new Realist paintings. His graphic lampoons of class exploitation were another matter. The sketches of courtroom scenes, labor strikes, and greedy, corpulent capitalists were vivid and moving indictments of social injustice under the American class system. In painting, it was the humane and poetic qualities of his subjects that attracted him, and he viewed and recorded their foibles with a certain amused detachment. He scarcely mingled with the common people or identified with their social despair despite his abortive political career.

Sloan's naturalism was not so coarse-grained as Luks's nor so superficial in its investigation of natural appearances as Shinn's or Glackens's. He was more the careful craftsman, and though a less fluent stylist, he achieved an art of perhaps greater sincerity and depth of feeling. His foreground was the unpromising commonplace: the sidewalks of New York, a gloomy downtown barroom, a woman wearily hanging out wash from a tenement fire escape. But his background often lent a poetic and elusive quality to the dreary prose of everyday life. His frequent theme of a dimly lit interior with a solitary human occupant undoubtedly later inspired certain aspects of romantic realism in the work of Edward Hopper (1882–1967). The difference between Hopper and Sloan in rather similar scenes is that between romantic melancholy in mood, with a sense of human desolation, and an irresistible optimism and human warmth.

In affirming his tenacious and resonant humanism within the atmosphere and limits of a "small," essentially illustrational artistic style, Sloan surpassed even his own modest pretensions. He is remembered as an American Hogarth for his ability to catch common people of gross character. Actually, despite a certain humor and energy in handling, Sloan's people are not very remarkable comic inventions. The artist's rather crude caricatures represented a struggle to conquer his ineptness at vital characterization; often his figurations just miss being routine visual clichés of popular illustration. Sloan did have something urgent to communicate about life, but with pictorial means that were not altogether adequate for the job. He more than compensated, however, by evoking a distinctive romantic atmosphere and mood and by conveying his own sense of innocence and wonder before "the lure of the great cities."

Dreiser's novels, Crane's New York sketches, and Sloan's city paintings are of a piece, linked by the dream and promise of America. They express a wish for some larger individual fulfillment, for a more splendid existence than the crushing real world offered the harried city dweller. Much like Dreiser in his ponderous, labored technique, and Crane in his patently artificial reproductions of lower-class speech, Sloan reveals the strain of forging a romantic idiom around the refractory materials of the new naturalism. He was not sufficiently sophisticated or detached to be able to subdue the brute aspects of existence within a framework of aesthetic hedonism, as the French Realists Degas and Lautrec had done. His message was that of a minor romantic sensibility.

The sense of a failed romanticism perhaps figures in the later atmosphere of discouragement in Hopper's drab American scenes. Despite the positive mood of energy and hope of the Roosevelt era, there was a continuing thread of romance and introspection in American art. Even Ryder's extreme example haunted the most robust and extrovert twentieth-century American Realists. (Oddly enough, Henri felt that Ryder might have made a suitable member of the dominantly Realist group of The Eight. In a diary entry of 1927 he reminisced about "the two men who might have been of the '8' had one of them been younger or the other older. A. P. Ryder and George Bellows.")

Sloan's taste for romantic mystery was expressed by certain almost theatrical devices such as the heightening of chiaroscuro and the suggestive play of his lighting. The nocturnal scene *The Haymarket* (1907, plate 382) has a mystery which blurs and enlarges its literal meaning as

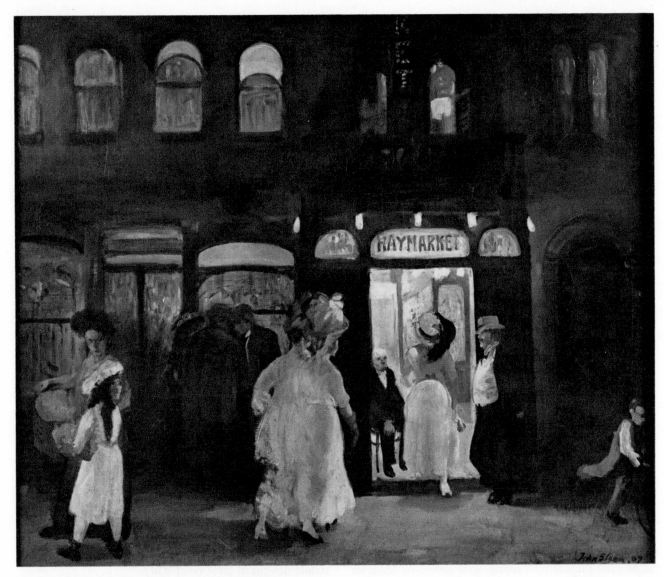

382 John Sloan. *The Haymarket.* 1907. Oil on canvas, 26 × 31⅞".
The Brooklyn Museum. Gift of Mrs. Harry Payne Whitney

a transcription of fact. In one of the city's disreputable districts three dressy ladies emerge from a rich, mahogany darkness into the luminous doorway of a dance hall under the appreciative eye of a sidewalk Lothario; to one side a child rolls a hoop; a mother, carrying wash, tries to distract her little daughter from taking an interest in the scene. One is reminded that Sloan, on one of his many walks, noted a streetwalker gaudily arrayed in a great plumed hat that made her look like "some wild creature of the night."

The rich shadows and the scintillation of light in Sloan's paintings at best create an intensely lyric impression. J. B. Yeats, father of the poet William Butler Yeats and an intimate of Sloan, liked to speak of the artist's "mountain gloom." Sloan's darkling romanticism brought the post-Civil War "Brown Decades" full circle, taking its cue perhaps from their gloomy decor and matching pessimism. When, in later years, Sloan pursued a more brilliant and objective color

scheme in an effort to meet the challenge of the School of Paris, or of an "ultramodernism," as he put it, his art lost its distinctive character.

EXHIBITIONS FOR THE INDEPENDENTS

The Realist group's new departures in mood, subject matter, and social attitude, if not in style and technique, soon aroused the open hostility of the official art world. The challenge of Henri, Luks, Sloan, Glackens, and Shinn to contemporary authority met with increasing rejections of their work by the National Academy and the Society of American Artists. Suppression by these institutions was tantamount to denial of public exposure, since private art galleries were then few in number. When, in 1907, the jury for the National Academy annual (on which Henri, ironically enough, served) voted to exclude entries by several members of his group, Henri withdrew from the exhibition in protest. With Glackens,

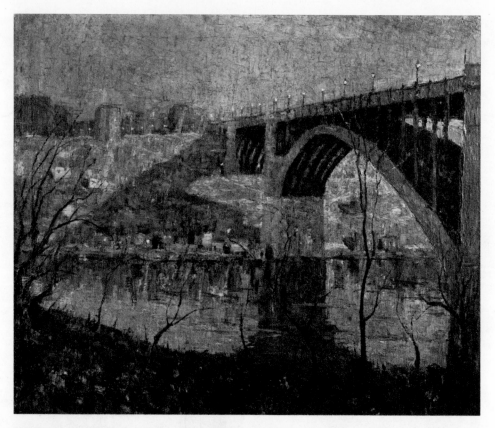

383 Ernest Lawson. *Spring Night, Harlem River.* 1913. Oil on canvas, 25 × 30″.
The Phillips Collection, Washington, D.C.

Sloan and Henri laid plans for a counterexhibition, and thus was born the germ of the first large independents' show of the new century.

The show took place at the Macbeth Gallery in New York in 1908. Henri, Sloan, Luks, Glackens, and Shinn, the original Philadelphia rebels, were joined by Maurice Prendergast, Ernest Lawson, and Arthur B. Davies. These three artists were of a rather different aesthetic character; it was often the case that insurgent manifestations of early modernist art were organized on principles of opposition to establishment values and to oppressive institutions rather than on coherent stylistic grounds. The group immediately became known in the newspapers as the "Eight Independent Painters," or simply "The Eight." Prendergast was an Impressionist who was aware of Cézanne; Lawson also worked in an Impressionist style; and Davies painted allegorical landscapes in a dreamy Pre-Raphaelite manner. While the original core of five Realists and their viewpoints seemed most central to The Eight, the additional trio of painters, whose work was more conservative, did manifestly share their spirit of rebellion against the parochial policies of the academies.

With hindsight today we may find Maurice Prendergast (1859–1924) the most original and modern painter of The Eight. *Evening Walk* (1917–20, colorplate 53) is a curious combination of modern and archaic styles. Its decorative, tapestry-like promenade recalls Puvis de Chavannes as much as Vuillard and the other Nabis. In fact, he was probably the first true American modernist, a painter who understood Cézanne's color theory and general aims before the French master was even known in this country. By the time he joined The Eight, Prendergast had evolved a very personal kind of Postimpressionist style, using enlarged color patches to weave intricate designs of great complexity.

Ernest Lawson (1873–1939) reveals in *Spring Night, Harlem River* (1913, plate 383) a more conventional Impressionist vision, although the subtlety and delicacy of his art transformed the roughly textured paint surfaces and robust style of the French masters into one of lyrical nuance. It is curious that three decades after emerging in Europe, Impressionism was still viewed and welcomed in America as a reinvigoration of our cultural life. Among The Eight, however, it became clear that American Impressionism, and related styles among artists who might be linked sympathetically with them, was destined to deal with urban realities as well as rustic idylls and the more smiling aspects of nature.

Arthur B. Davies (1862–1928) was a particular anomaly among The Eight. His dreamlike, Pre-Raphaelite *Unicorns* (1906, plate 384) seemed more appropriate to a Victorian salon than to the irreverent vernacular Realism of his fellow American artists. He rendered his imaginary Symbolist landscapes in soft and muted tones, inspiring the painter Guy Pène du Bois to describe them as settings "in which attenuated nudes walked in rhythmic strides borrowed from the languor of lovers." Although his style was archaic in its Symbolist mood, it had a certain

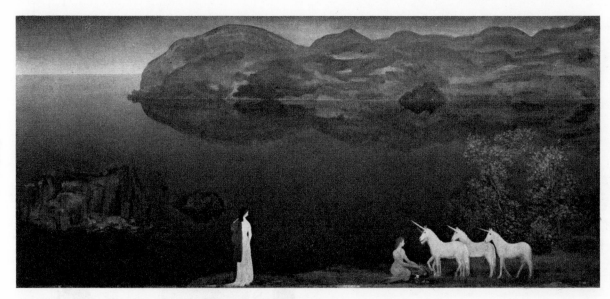

384 Arthur B. Davies. *Unicorns*. 1906. Oil on canvas, 18¼ × 40¼".
The Metropolitan Museum of Art, New York. Bequest of Lillie P. Bliss, 1931

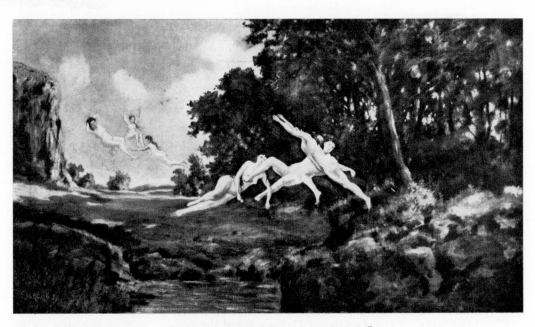

385 Louis Michel Eilshemius. *Afternoon Wind*. 1899. Oil on canvas, 20 × 36".
The Museum of Modern Art, New York. Given anonymously

ingenuousness of fantasy which can be linked to a native tradition of visionary art, exemplified in the hypnotic turn-of-the-century *Afternoon Wind* (1899, plate 385) by Louis M. Eilshemius (1864–1941). A man of the world, Davies was a far more sophisticated connoisseur of current artistic trends than the provincial Henri and his followers. Neither social commentary nor an American chauvinist bias distracted him from acknowledging the importance of European modernism. Although his art was rooted in the past, and he significantly made his first artistic alliance with the generally conservative Realist group, he later became involved in the selection of the stylistically controversial and most advanced American art exhibition, the Armory Show (see below). Afterward he began to fragment his own pictorial forms and reorganized his art to conform to the new values he had discovered in the radical paintings that he had borrowed from Europe for that dramatic international exhibition.

While all these painters had their special interests and attractions, it was the five Realists among The Eight—Henri, Glackens, Luks, Shinn, and Sloan—who most deeply impressed the public at large with their candid,

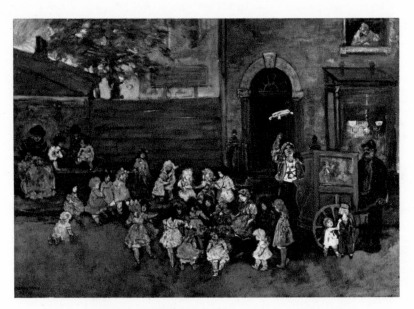

386 Jerome Myers. *The Tambourine*. 1905. Oil on canvas, 22 × 32".
The Phillips Collection, Washington, D.C.

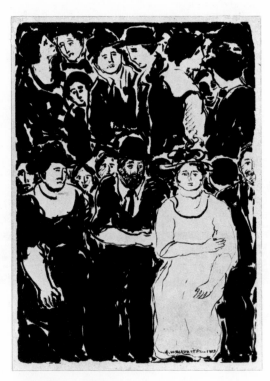

388 Abraham Walkowitz. *East Side Figures*. 1903.
Ink, 10 × 7". Collection Mr. and Mrs.
H. Lawrence Herring, New York

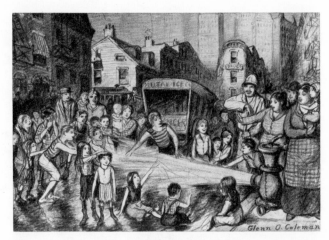

387 Glenn O. Coleman. *Street Bathers*. c. 1906. Crayon,
11 × 15¾". Whitney Museum of American Art, New York

vibrant, and life-oriented paintings. Their Realism won
them such sobriquets in the press as "the revolutionary
black gang," "The Apostles of Ugliness," and the best-
known, "Ashcan School." Soon, in the public image,
other Realists (plates 386, 387) began to be associated
with the new "school"—Jerome Myers (1867–1940),
Eugene Higgins (1874–1958), and Glenn Coleman
(1887–1932), as well as Bellows, whose prizefights in
particular, along with Sloan's saloon scenes and Luks's
street subjects, became emblematic of the Ashcan School.
Even Abraham Walkowitz (1880–1965), who is better
known for his later Cubist cityscapes and rather sentimental figure groups, emulated The Eight's Realism in
his *East Side Figures* (1903, plate 388), evoking the ethnic
vitality of an immigrant neighborhood with a dramatically simple system of graphic signs.

In their first and, as it turned out, last, exhibition as an
organized group, The Eight scored a great success financially, despite some castigation in the press. In fact, Henri
had gone to some lengths to cultivate and educate a few
responsive critics such as James Gibbons Huneker, a
friend of Luks, who gave a generally sympathetic account of the group's intentions and achievement. For
the most part, they were derided by journalists for the
conventional reasons which have commonly brought
Realism under attack: its treatment of vernacular themes,
or, in the words of one reviewer, its "unhealthy nay even
coarse and vulgar point of view." The Realists were also
chastised for their "poor drawing" and "weak technique," another criticism which has often been leveled
at the genre, reflecting a prevailing academic bias. That
the art exhibited was "revolutionary" was another ob-
jection, although, in fact, none of it was, either in style
or subject matter; to no avail did the more sympathetic
critics point out that the styles of The Eight were as much
as three decades out of date as compared with French
innovation. In spite of, or possibly because of, the sniping
of journalists, the public came in droves. The new insurgent spirit could no longer be either contained or
denied and, with so much support in the atmosphere of
political progressivism, it encountered less actual resistance than had been anticipated. "We've made a
success," Sloan wrote in elation after the first sales returns were in. "The sales at the exhibition amount to
near $4,000. Macbeth is pleased as 'Punch'!" Even the
Pennsylvania Academy soon jumped on the bandwagon,
asking for the show and circulating it among eight

cities after the New York exhibition closed.

The amorphous program and heterogeneous styles of The Eight did not promise long collective life, however, and the 1908 grouping was never repeated. As James Thrall Soby has observed, it "consisted of artists who, finding themselves more closely allied in friendship than in belief, formed their title by the anti-doctrinal expedient of counting noses." Perhaps the most salutary result of their loose association was the revival of a languishing tradition of artistic protest. Organized dissent had died with the decay of the Society of American Artists. Now the insurgents laid elaborate plans for bringing new currents of art to the American public. "Eventually the 'men of the rebellion' expect to have a gallery of their own," the *New York Herald* reported in 1907, "where they . . . can show two or three hundred works of art. It is likely, too, that they may ask several English artists to send over their paintings from London to be exhibited with the American group. The whole collection may be shown in turn in several large cities in the United States."

This statement anticipated the huge "Exhibition of Independent Artists" organized in 1910 by the original members of The Eight and such camp followers as Rockwell Kent (1882–1971), Bellows, and Glenn Coleman. Henri reviewed this exhibition for the *Craftsman* in 1910, presenting a lengthy, personal statement of his philosophy of art and including a spirited defense of the artist's "freedom to think and to show what you are thinking about." He found himself supporting a wide range of expression, from Kent's stylized epics of heroic fishermen such as *Toilers of the Sea* (1907, plate 389) to Glackens's nude studies and Sloan's New York street genre scenes, reflecting his "love of the people." Undoubtedly, it was this eclecticism and stylistic *laissez-faire* which made the polyglot Realist, Impressionist, and Symbolist art of The Eight so vulnerable to the more rigorous formal viewpoints of the new modernist Americans then emerging simultaneously in exhibitions at Alfred Stieglitz's Gallery 291. With its courageous precedent of eliminating the academic position of privilege and overcoming restrictive qualifications for entry, the independents' exhibition of 1910 foreshadowed New York's great adventure and discovery of international modern art of a radically different sort at the Sixty-Ninth Regiment Armory in 1913. Overnight the Armory Show made realism seem conservative and dated. Nevertheless, The Eight were the first Americans in this century to revive an insurgent and protestant mood, to attack urban ugliness, and to venture, albeit timidly and with outmoded pictorial means, into the modern mainstream by breaking the hold of the academic past.

(continued on page 366)

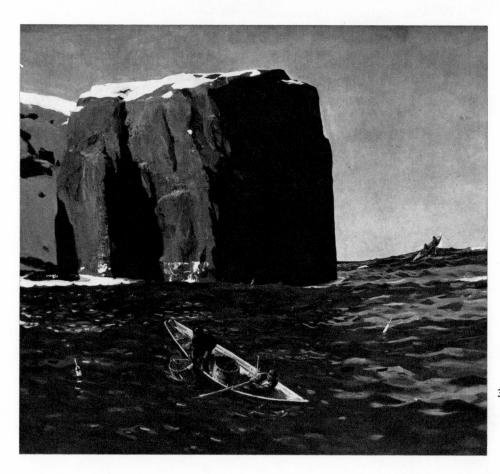

389 Rockwell Kent. *Toilers of the Sea.* 1907. Oil on canvas, 38 × 44″. The New Britain Museum of American Art, New Britain, Conn. Charles F. Smith Fund

What William Morris was to the English Arts and Crafts Movement Elbert Hubbard was, in a more limited and less original fashion, to the American version of the movement. Hubbard, like his mentor, started a bindery, a leather shop, and a furniture factory. As a well-established artistic community, operating under the name Roycroft, Hubbard's East Aurora firm, near Buffalo,

N.Y., soon had an inn, a magazine, and an apprentice system for training in the crafts. Metalwork was a later addition to the community's activities, appearing in the catalog about 1909, the approximate date of this copper smoking set (plate 390). The names of some of the metalworkers are known to us, but the designer of this set is unidentified. It is an interesting blend of simple craft tech-

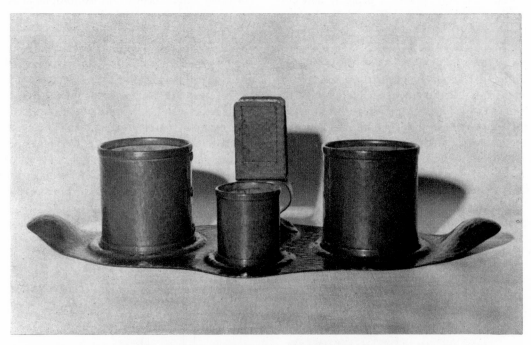

390 Roycroft Copper Shop. Smoking set. c. 1909. Copper, width 14″.
Elbert Hubbard Library Museum, East Aurora, N.Y.

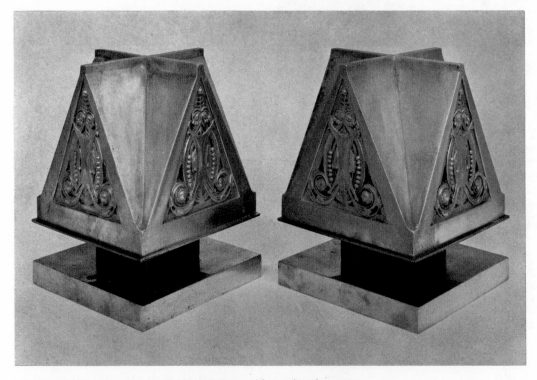

391 George Grant Elmslie. Andirons. 1912. Brass with cast-iron log rests,
height 10½″. The Art Institute of Chicago. Gift of Mrs. George A. Harvey

niques, including the visible joints and roughly hammered surface designs, combined with some Art Nouveau feeling in the design of the base, a combination not at all unusual in Roycroft items. Hubbard was a guiding spirit, neither artist nor designer, who could nonetheless breathe spirit and vitality into an artistic enterprise. He died in the sinking of the Lusitania in 1915.

During the period when the Arts and Crafts Movement flourished (1876–1916) in America, designers such as George Grant Elmslie (1871–1952) and his more famous colleague, Frank Lloyd Wright, were vitally interested in the creation of harmony in all parts of the house: architectural design, furniture, and the entire range of household accessories. Elmslie worked for Louis Sullivan from 1889 until 1909, and it is obvious that, in his designs for furniture, textiles, and metal, he was greatly influenced by both Sullivan and Wright.

The design of the table cover (colorplate 48), which was made for his own house, resembles the slightly later window by Wright (plate 392) in terms of the play between rectangles and squares and in the emphasis on subtle outline. The blue-and-green silk embroidery, executed by Elmslie's wife, is also similar in color to the stained-glass windows of various Prairie School architects and designers. Both the curved lines wrapped about the verticals and the intertwined form above them are traceable to Sullivan. On the andirons (plate 391), the organic ornamentation is more intricate and more aggressive, while at the same time purely geometric form is stronger, perhaps reflecting the solidity required by the purpose of the andirons.

With the same care and sense of total design that Frank Lloyd Wright designed homes and their furnishings, he also created leaded-glass windows for his buildings. One of his best-known integrated designs was for the Avery Coonley Playhouse in Riverside, Ill., which was the setting of this tall, narrow window (plate 392). Whereas many of the earlier Wright windows were abstract versions of natural forms, this one is completely nonrepresentational, perhaps paralleling experiments being undertaken by European painters and anticipating the Art Deco style by about a decade. One interesting detail is the rectilinear design near the lower right, which appears to form the shape of an American flag, the alternating glass and lead creating the thirteen stripes. Wright's skill in balancing color and shape in such windows was masterly, but, unfortunately, interest in that medium was declining at the time. Only after his death did a reappraisal of this work result in a new appreciation and determined effort to save the remaining windows from destruction.

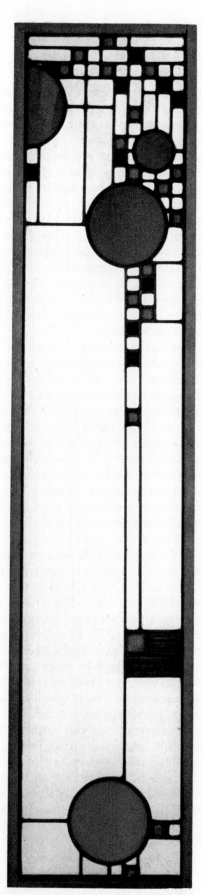

392 Frank Lloyd Wright. Window. 1912. Multicolored leaded glass, 62 × 13⅝". Collection Mr. and Mrs. Walter A. Netsch, Jr., Chicago

(continued from page 363)

STIEGLITZ AND THE MODERNIST CONTROVERSY

The year 1908 saw the Realism of The Eight established, but it also inaugurated Alfred Stieglitz's exhibitions of the radical European moderns. In fact, so important a role did Stieglitz play in introducing the American public to avant-garde European art that he can justly be compared with Gertrude Stein as one of the two crucial figures in establishing European modernism in America. Miss Stein was among the first to admire and buy the paintings of Cézanne, Picasso, and Matisse, when those artists were either unknown or despised in Paris. In New York Stieglitz, with similar acuteness, singled out new talent, crusaded for excellence, and provided a favorable atmosphere for innovation. His efforts, aided by his associate, Edward Steichen, infused new vitality into the fine arts and photography in America in the first two decades of the new century.

This was the memorable year in which the official art world suddenly became aware that the new art posed a threat to traditional values. The growing misgivings with which contemporary authority faced the future were candidly, if inadvertently, expressed by Sir Caspar Purdon Clarke, director of the august Metropolitan Museum. In an interview which (like so many of the more painful dodo observations delivered by conservative opinion) was reprinted in *Camera Work*, Stieglitz's pioneering quarterly journal, Clarke solemnly warned: "There is a state of unrest all over the world in art as in all other things. It is the same in literature, as in music, in painting, and in sculpture. And I dislike unrest."

Sir Purdon could not have chosen a more apt word to describe that new mood which was about to produce so stimulating and fertile an episode in American creative life. Between 1908 and World War I there emerged a group of young artists who were sympathetic to contemporary European art and felt little or no inhibition about experimenting with modern idioms. While the Henri Realists were engaged by urban subject matter in a dated pictorial style, these younger artists for the most part had been studying or working in Paris, where they had begun to establish direct contact with the most emancipated expressions of the aesthetic revolutions of their time. Max Weber and Arthur Burdett Frost, Jr., were among the first foreigners to join Matisse's new painting class, which started in 1907; they were followed later by Arthur B. Carles, Morgan Russell, and Patrick Henry Bruce. At about the same time Alfred Maurer, who took up residence in Paris in 1900 and thus became the first American expatriate painter of the new generation, felt the influence of Matisse and Fauve painting. By 1908 there were enough young American artists of progressive tendency in Paris, including also Steichen and others, to form the New Society of American Artists in Paris, supplanting a more conservative parent organization which had been in existence for some years.

During the period 1900–13, nearly every significant modern American artist traveled to Europe. For most, Paris was a mandatory stop if not their primary destination. Carles, Arthur B. Dove, Marsden Hartley, John Marin, Charles Sheeler, Abraham Walkowitz, and many others lived there for long or short periods of time. In a typical evolution, Walkowitz, for example, began his series of free drawings of Isadora Duncan in Paris about 1906 under the relatively conservative influence of Rodin, but he progressed soon after his return to America to the more radical abstraction of his Cubist *New York* (1917, plate 393). It is interesting to note how often modern painting in this country began with the determination of these pioneers to express their excited response to life in America by utilizing the new vocabulary of line and color that they had discovered in Europe. The Realist Jerome Myers remembered the repatriated Walkowitz as a "John the Baptist" returning from Paris "to preach the gospel in modern art."

The roster of Americans who studied in Europe between 1904 and 1912 includes many other names now familiar to us—Charles Demuth, Stanton Macdonald-Wright, Andrew Dasburg, William and Marguerite Zorach, Thomas Hart Benton, Morton Schamberg, Joseph Stella, Oscar Bluemner, John Covert. There they felt at first hand the impact of abstract art and the influence of such new movements as Fauvism, Cubism, Futurism, Der Blaue Reiter (the Blue Rider), and Orphism. As they began to drift back to America in the years preceding World War I and to exhibit paintings that revealed distinct Continental derivations, the whole center of gravity of the American art world shifted. The insurgent spirit of the Realists survived, but their forms assumed the traits of French modernism. On the eve of the war it seemed that New York was about to become an aesthetic outpost of Paris, and that a new spirit of intellectual adventure might work a permanent transformation on the provincial American cultural scene.

Exciting new beginnings could be seen everywhere, from the fantastic growth of the "little" magazines to new ventures in experimental theater; from the poetry renaissance in Chicago to the emergence of a promising new crop of writers with dedicated patrons and literary hostesses who conducted salons on both sides of the Atlantic. The "new," whether in poetry, prose, the theater, painting, or progressive politics, found widespread support from America's best critical and creative minds. Such new publications as *Seven Arts, Dial, The New Republic, The Little Review, Smart Set,* and *Camera Work* demonstrated the solidarity of the eager champions of the new spirit. Writing and painting were envisioned as part of one great advancing cause whose aim was nothing less than the reconstruction of man and his society. The brilliant, young, social-minded critics who

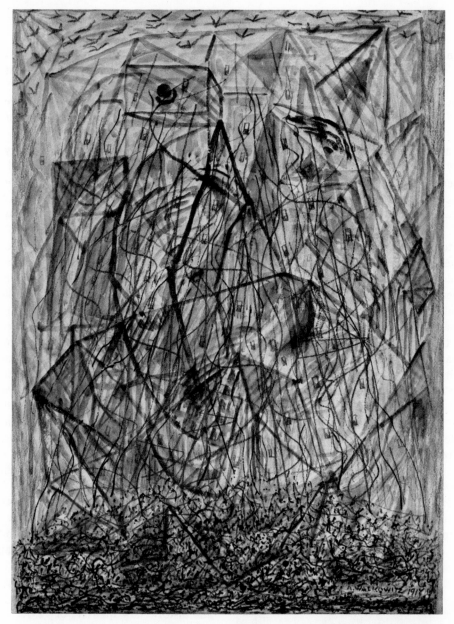

393 Abraham Walkowitz. *New York*. 1917. Watercolor, ink, pencil, 30⅝ × 21¾″. Whitney Museum of American Art, New York. Gift of the artist in memory of Juliana Force

wrote for *Seven Arts* directed a withering fire against entrenched powers in both the art world and the social scene. A spirit of enlightenment, verbalized in the impressionistic language of utopian yearning, invaded criticism. Writing of Postimpressionism, Hutchins Hapgood of the *New York Globe* declared: "It shakes the old foundations and leads to a new life, whether the programs and ideas have permanent validity or not" (*Camera Work*, No. 42, p. 13). James Oppenheim, founder of *Seven Arts*, which, like so many of the brightest hopes and expectations of modernism, expired with the war, anticipated a time when "the lost soul among nations, America, could be regenerated by art."

Out of this atmosphere of high hopes emerged Alfred Stieglitz (1864–1946), an artist with the camera, an art dealer, and the first impresario of modern art in America.

It is customary to date American modernism from the dramatic Armory Show of 1913, an event of unquestionable significance in the history of American taste. Stieglitz, however, had been showing advanced European art, and Americans working under its direct influence, for the five preceding years. In 1910 the most important young American modernists—Dove, Weber, Maurer, Marin, and Hartley—exhibited at "291," Stieglitz's Photo-Secession Gallery, which was at the time "the one place in America where modern art received serious consideration," as Milton Brown has put it in *American Painting from the Armory Show to the Depression*. Stieglitz also played a sheltering, patriarchal role for painters at a time when they desperately needed guidance and support, and gave them a sense of belonging to an active, cosmopolitan art life of exacting standards comparable to those in Europe. Thanks largely to the Stieglitz protectorate, the American artist was freed of his provincial diffidence and a demoralizing sense of isolation. Dove later acknowledged his dealer's critical role for the vulnerable avant-garde American artist. "I do not think," he wrote in 1934, "I could have existed as a painter without that super-encouragement and the battle he has fought day by day for twenty-five years."

Stieglitz represented a new type of personality in the arts. He was a second-generation American of Jewish-German descent whose parents immigrated at the time of the Civil War. After 1900 the massive waves of immigration began to affect the art scene, giving it a more international character and making the port of New York a more cosmopolitan cultural center. In Stieglitz's generation a number of significant artistic personalities of foreign descent contributed to the intermingling of racial and national strains: the painters Stella, Walkowitz, and Weber; the sculptors Jacob Epstein and Gaston Lachaise. As in Paris, with the advent of *émigrés* such as Picasso, Miró, Gris, Modigliani, Soutine, and Chagall, the mainstream of art in twentieth-century New York was enriched by many ethnic and cultural currents which gave new fluidity to the social structure and created a more tolerant intellectual atmosphere.

In 1906 Stieglitz and his friend Steichen (1879–1973), a young painter and photographer, opened the Little Gallery of the Photo-Secession in the three-room attic of a brownstone at 291 Fifth Avenue, New York. The next year Stieglitz began to exhibit art as well as photographs. "The Secession Idea," he explained in *Camera Work*,

"is neither the servant nor the product of a medium. It is a spirit." And Stieglitz promised that his little gallery would remain hospitable to artistic effort in any medium so long as it showed "honesty of aim, honesty of self-expression, honesty of revolt against the autocracy of convention."

Soon the Photo-Secession Gallery exhibitions were dominated by advanced painting and sculpture emanating from Paris. Steichen spent his summers in France and was on familiar terms with many of the new French artists. He now acted as an enthusiastic liaison for Stieglitz. It was he who proposed the first two exhibitions of European moderns: a show of Rodin's watercolors in January, 1908, followed four months later by Matisse drawings. These two exhibitions encountered in the press a stony indifference that might have dampened less ardent spirits. The dean of American newspaper critics, Royal Cortissoz of the *New York Herald*, described the Rodin watercolors as "studio driftwood." The Matisse exhibition, his first in America, excited even more of the patronizing derision that became the customary press response to Stieglitz's shows. However, there were already critics of more modern sympathies active in New York at this time, among them Huneker, who praised the Matisse show in *Camera Work* (July, 1908) for the artist's "agility of line, velocity in notation, and uncompromising attitude in the presence of the human machine." Charles H. Caffin, also in *Camera Work* (January, 1909), showed an awareness of Matisse's actual intentions, based on his own interview with the artist.

After the Matisse show the Photo-Secession Gallery found itself in financial difficulties and was forced to abandon its quarters, but Stieglitz enlisted additional support and, in the fall of 1908, reopened his gallery in different rooms at the same address, 291 Fifth Avenue. The historic new quarters of "291," as the gallery came to be known, inaugurated a more intensive phase of exhibiting activities. The vital statistics of Stieglitz's shows comprise an imposing survey of early modernism. They reveal, too, the growing participation of Americans in the new movements. In 1909 he gave Maurer, Hartley, and Marin their first one-man shows in this country. The critics were particularly shocked by the exhibition of Alfred H. Maurer (1868–1932). After a period of loosely brushed landscapes, vaguely Fauve in inspiration, he had come under the influence of Cubism and developed his characteristic elongated, large-eyed figure painting, often of paired heads, derived in part from Modigliani, Cézanne, and Picasso. He also painted still life on overlapped planes in a Cubist manner which continued in subsequent years through such works of the thirties as *Still Life with Doily* (plate 394).

The large independents' exhibition organized in 1910 by the New York Realists, excluding the Stieglitz artists, was countered by "291" with a group show, "Younger American Painters," which included Maurer, Hartley,

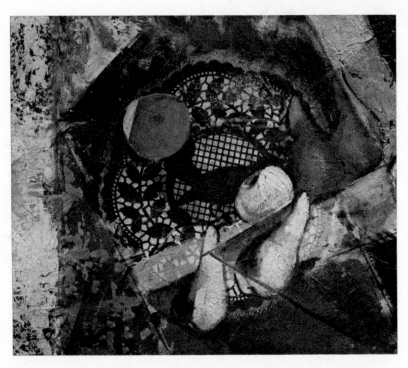

394 Alfred H. Maurer. *Still Life with Doily.* c. 1930–31. Oil on pressed board, 18 × 21¼". Brandeis University Art Collection, Rose Art Museum, Waltham, Mass. Gift of Mr. and Mrs. Ben Heller

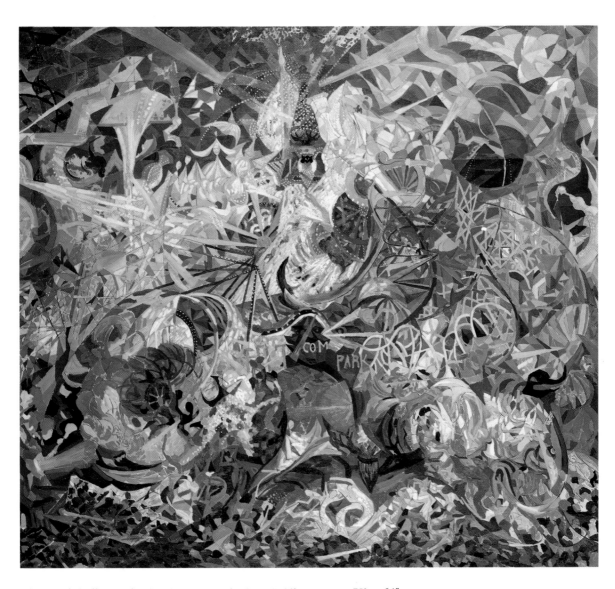

54 Joseph Stella. *Battle of Lights, Coney Island.* 1914. Oil on canvas, $75\frac{3}{4} \times 84''$.
Yale University Art Gallery,
New Haven, Conn. Gift of Collection Société Anonyme

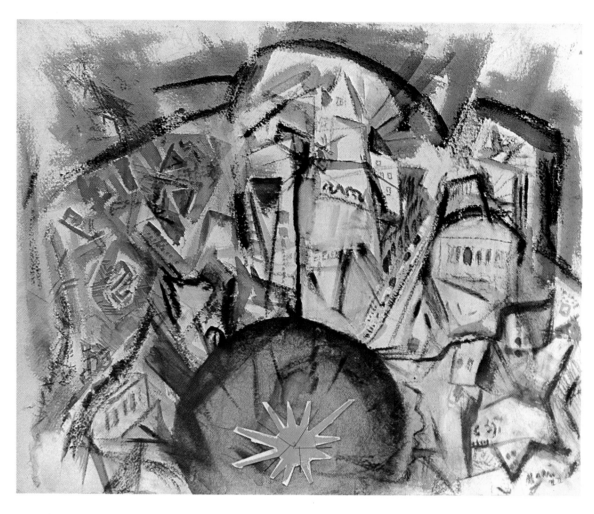

55 John Marin. *Lower Manhattan* (*Composing Derived from Top of the Woolworth*). 1922.
Watercolor and collage on paper, $21\frac{5}{8} \times 26\frac{7}{8}''$.
The Museum of Modern Art, New York. Lillie P. Bliss Bequest

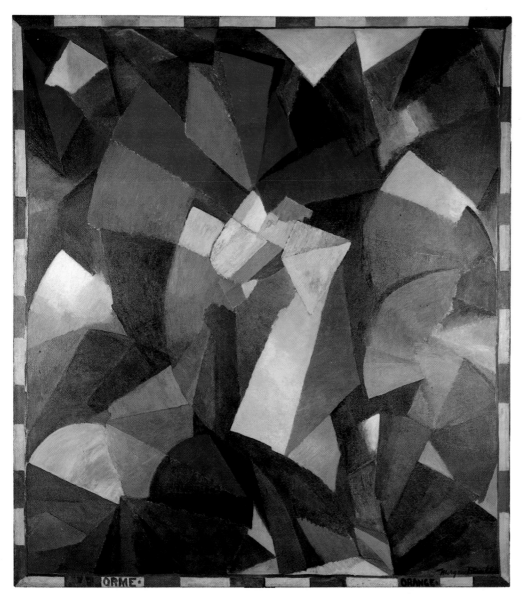

56 Morgan Russell. *Synchromy in Orange: To Form.* 1913–14.
Oil on canvas, 11′3″ × 10′3″. The Albright-Knox Art Gallery,
Buffalo, N.Y. Gift of Seymour H. Knox

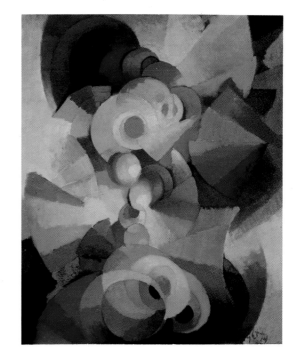

57 Stanton Macdonald-Wright.
"Conception" Synchromy. 1915.
Oil on canvas, 30 × 24″.
Whitney Museum of American Art,
New York

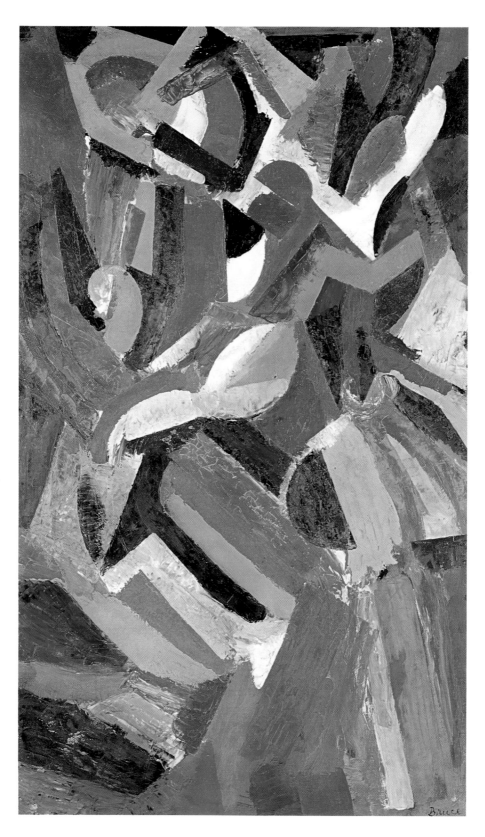

58 Patrick Henry Bruce. *Composition III*. 1916–17. Oil on canvas, $63\frac{1}{4} \times 38''$.
Yale University Art Gallery, New Haven, Conn. Gift of Collection Société Anonyme

59 *Right:* Marcel Duchamp. *The Bride Stripped Bare by Her Bachelors, Even.*
1915–23. Oil and lead wire on glass, $8'1\frac{1}{4}'' \times 5'9\frac{1}{8}''$.
Philadelphia Museum of Art. Louise and Walter Arensberg Collection

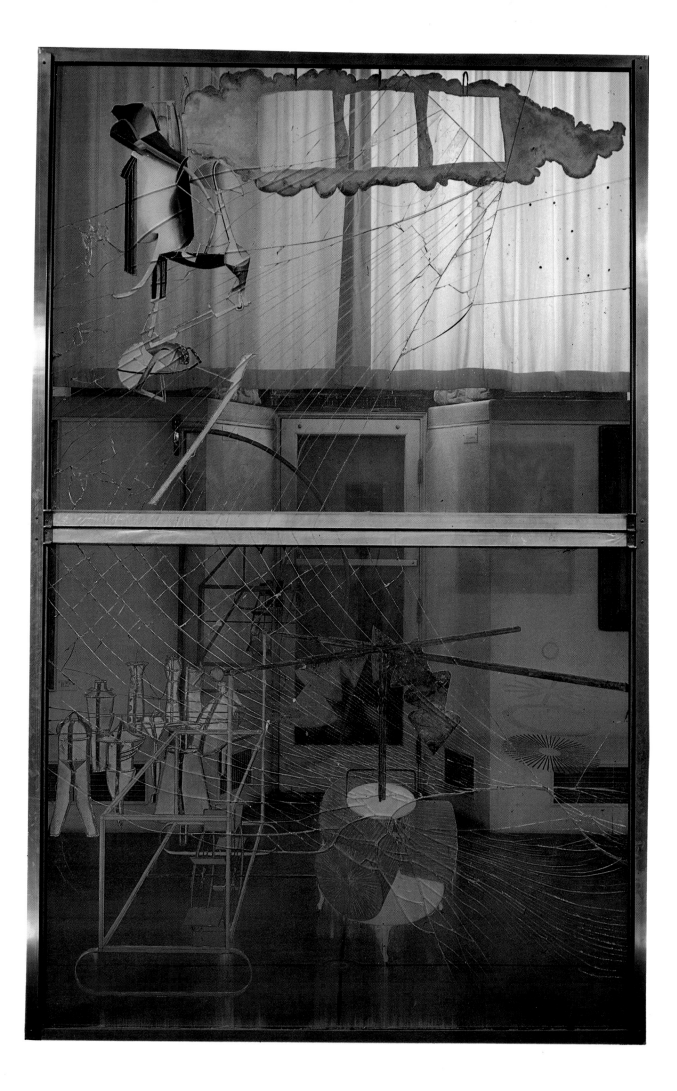

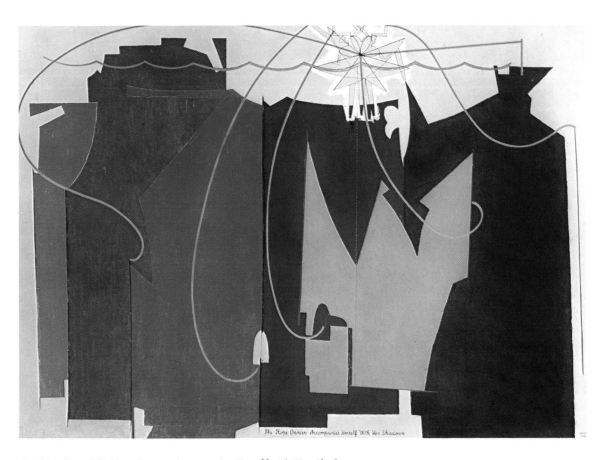

60   Man Ray. *The Rope Dancer Accompanies Herself with Her Shadows.*
1916. Oil on canvas, 52 × 73⅜″. The Museum of Modern Art,
New York. Gift of G. David Thompson

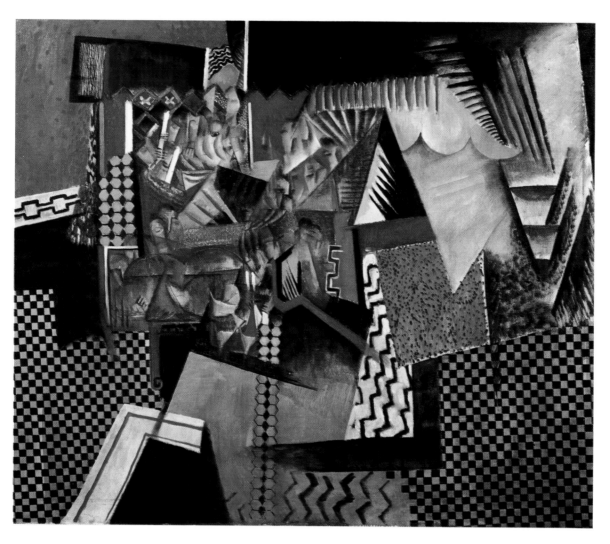

61 Max Weber. *Chinese Restaurant*. 1915. Oil on canvas, 40 × 48″.
Whitney Museum of American Art, New York

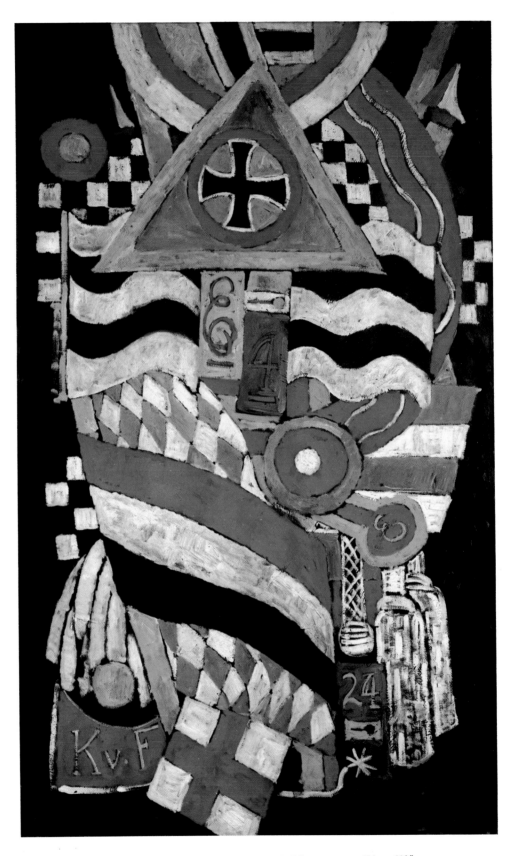

62   Marsden Hartley. *Portrait of a German Officer*. 1914. Oil on canvas, $69\frac{1}{4} \times 41\frac{3}{8}''$.
The Metropolitan Museum of Art, New York. Alfred Stieglitz Collection, 1949

Marin, Dove, Steichen, Weber, and Carles. In a sense this exhibition challenged the Realists' claim as the representatives of progressive tendencies, and made clear the growing distinction between American scene painting and abstract or semiabstract modes. However, both were inspired by the spectacle of urban life. Instead of imitating the studio themes or scenes of Paris, Weber and Stella turned their attention to New York—adopting the subject matter, but not the pictorial manner of the Ashcan School. Max Weber (1881–1961), always a gifted eclectic, experimented with urban imagery of a hallucinatory character, utilizing a Cubist–Futurist vocabulary of shapes and movement. His *Tea* (1911, plate 395) and *Rush Hour, New York* (1915, plate 396) capture the feverish excitement of the city in kaleidoscopic, fragmented forms. For Weber, the modern automated subway and its throngs were as romantic in a mechanized pictorial translation as the picturesque scenes limned by The Eight. Joseph Stella (1880–1946) in his *Battle of Lights, Coney Island* (1914, colorplate 54) exalts the

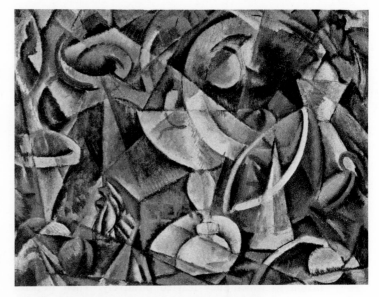

395 Max Weber. *Tea*. 1911. Oil on canvas, 12 × 16".
Private collection

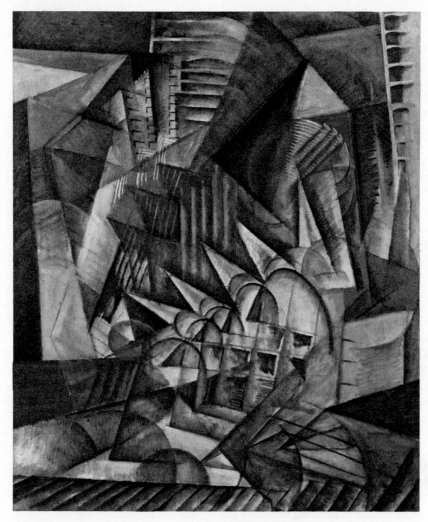

396 Max Weber. *Rush Hour, New York*. 1915. Oil on canvas,
36 × 30". National Gallery of Art, Washington, D.C.
Gift of the Avalon Foundation, 1970

dizzying spectacle of an amusement park at night, and his *Brooklyn Bridge* of 1917–18 converts the modern metropolis into a symbol of speed, vulgar energy, and technological progress. The cult of the modern city, and of New York in particular, at a moment of heady growth and expansion, did much to inspire these landmark paintings of early American modernism.

Like Weber and Maurer, John Marin (1870–1953) took his first inspiration from Fauvism, and he was also deeply impressed by Cézanne's watercolors, but when he returned from abroad, he experienced a profound emotional response to the American scene. *Lower Manhattan (Composing Derived from Top of the Woolworth)* (1922, colorplate 55) pictures the frenetic activity and excitement of New York as a teeming architectural complex of skyscrapers and bridges. Weber, Stella, and Marin all found in the city elements of motion and visual confusion to which they reacted positively. Their hopeful and empathetic visual responses were in tune with the wonder verbalized by William James who wrote in a 1907 letter to his novelist brother Henry: "The first impression of New York. . . is one of repulsion at the clangor, disorder, and permanent earthquake conditions. But this time, installed. . . in the center of the cyclone, I caught the pulse of the machine, took up the rhythm, and vibrated *mit*, and found it simply magnificent. . . ."

From 1910 until 1917, when the war temporarily closed his gallery, Stieglitz scored an impressive number of American firsts with a series of pioneering exhibitions: Cézanne's watercolors; Picasso's watercolors and drawings; Henri Rousseau's paintings; Manolo's and Matisse's sculpture. He also in this period gave Francis Picabia, Constantin Brancusi, and the Americans Walkowitz, Oscar Bluemner, Elie Nadelman, and Georgia O'Keeffe their first significant exhibitions in this country, and he presented the first serious exhibition of children's drawings and of Negro sculpture anywhere in the world. In his succeeding galleries, The Intimate Gallery (1925–29) and An American Place (1929–46), Stieglitz presented such outstanding work as the sculpture of Gaston Lachaise and the paintings of Demuth, and staged regular exhibitions of his "stable" of artists, including Marin, O'Keeffe, Hartley, and Dove. No dealer in America, and few in Europe, had launched so much significant new painting and sculpture in so short a period.

Stieglitz was, of course, a good deal more than a dealer as we understand the term today. He was a creative artist in his own right, and his relations to his American artists were, to say the least, unconventional, with commercial considerations refreshingly absent. He saw himself and his artists as workers in the cause of creative freedom, and "291" took on a symbolic character, often encouraging among its admirers a spirit of almost mystical reverence. He felt an obligation to discern and uphold excellence in art. His incorruptibility, fine discrimination, and even arrogance in deciding to whom the art objects in his care might be sold, without defiling their intention, made him a legendary and rather intimidating figure. In a typical catalog foreword, written for The Forum Exhibition of Modern American Painters in 1916, Stieglitz bluntly expressed his views of the commercial gallery system. At the same time, he disclosed his own objectives in showing art. "I feel," he wrote, "that the system now in vogue of bringing the public into contact with the painting of to-day is basically wrong. The usual exhibition is nothing but a noise maker. . . . It does not do what it is professedly to do: To bring about a closer Life between Expression and Individual."

Since the new art forms were linked to ideal hopes for fundamental social and spiritual change, World War I, with its base economic motives and its destruction of human values, inevitably had a devastating and disillusioning effect. Experimental modernism suffered an enormous decline in prestige after the war. The fact that this decline took a more drastic form in America, and that the movement was riddled with more damaging defections than in Europe, is explained in part by the intensity of the underlying utopian sentiment. All such optimism was dissipated in the mistrustful mood of the postwar period. Perhaps it was even more important, however, that American artists had made only a superficial alliance with the new European styles, and, in the absence of strong abstract traditions of their own, were not yet prepared to surrender all their earlier attitudes. Andrew Dasburg, one of the better abstract American artists of the decade between 1910 and 1920, later speculated as to why so central an impulse as Cubism had not become a dominant force among our eclectic and impressionable artists. He concluded that Americans lack the intellectual integrity to work logically within the limitations inherent in such an idea, preferring instead to gather the best from many sources and to combine a variety of forms. This eclecticism, he implied, operates against the creation of works that possess "the contagious force of Cubism."

For Europeans, representational art had largely exhausted itself by 1910, whereas the radical new concepts built around abstract art promised further progress and invention. Americans, however, retained their attachment to Realism, and it was reinforced by reaction to the war, submerging modern idioms for nearly twenty years, until the mid-forties. Also, America had not yet firmly established its visual traditions and was not ready to provide long-term nurture for new movements and concepts. As Lloyd Goodrich has pointed out, the achievement of early American modernists was in individual expression rather than in basic innovations by movements and schools. Perhaps early American modernism was also encumbered by too much ideological baggage, diverting it from the more essential formal considerations necessary to sustain a collective style. But that, too, was in the American grain.

An important aspect of Stieglitz's influence was his handsomely printed quarterly publication, *Camera Work* (1902–17). In this magazine, which was primarily planned to launch photography as high art (see Chapter 17), appeared also the first sustained, serious criticism of American artistic life and culture, and the first tentative "modern" art criticism. Many of the articles, especially those written by the brilliant Benjamin de Casseres and the Mexican caricaturist and critic Marius de Zayas, may now seem dated by their romantic atmosphere and attachment to the *passé* values of Symbolism, Impressionism, and the decadent bohemianism of the "Mauve Decade," but they represented the apprenticeship to the modern spirit in America.

THE ARMORY SHOW SCANDAL

The competitive feeling between the Realists surrounding Henri and the modernists sponsored by Stieglitz, which had emerged at the time of the 1910 rival exhibitions, later flared into open antagonism. The following year Rockwell Kent proposed to Sloan another indepen-

dents' show, but stipulated that the exhibiting artists agree not to submit paintings to the National Academy exhibition of that year. The proposed show took place, but Sloan, Henri, Glackens, Lawson, and Shinn did not participate, since they refused to abide by Kent's condition. Among those who did agree and exhibited were, ironically enough, the modernists Maurer, Marin, and Hartley.

In 1911, Jerome Myers, Walt Kuhn, and Elmer L. MacRae discussed a more ambitious exhibition. A committee of twenty-five, dominated by the original members of The Eight and calling itself the Association of American Painters and Sculptors, was formed to plan another comprehensive showing of independent artists. For about a year the group tried without success to provide an exhibition hall and money for the venture. At the moment of greatest discouragement Arthur B. Davies, who had a formidable reputation as a fund raiser, agreed to shoulder the main responsibility for the exhibition. Davies almost single-handedly changed the original conception of the show into the great survey of

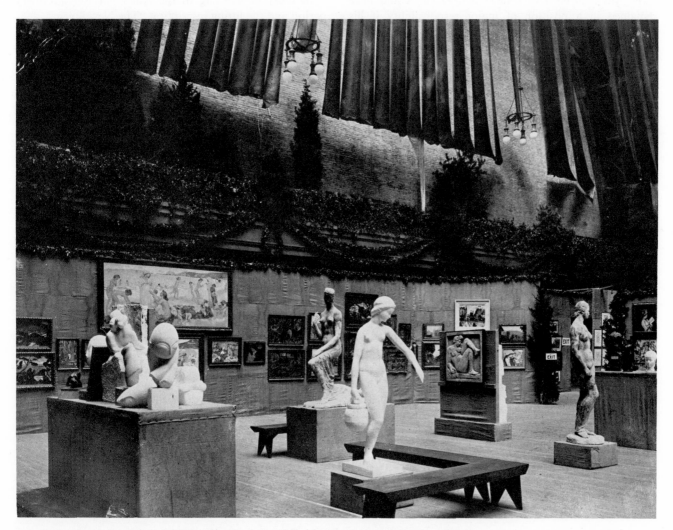

397 "International Exhibition of Modern Art," interior view. Armory Show, New York, 1913

modern European art now known as the Armory Show. The move did not ingratiate him with his more nationalist-minded associates. They were helpless to oppose him in the beginning, however, since he alone held out the promise of adequate financial backing. "Thus it was that I," wrote Jerome Myers later (*Artist in Manhattan*, 1940), describing his appeal to Davies for assistance, "an American art patriot, who painted ashcans and the little people around them, took part in inducing to become the head of our association the one American artist who had little to do with his contemporaries, who had vast influence with the wealthiest women, who painted unicorns and maidens under moonlight."

A number of differing versions of the origins of the Armory Show were written many years after the event by men who admitted to partisanship for either Davies or the forces opposing him within the committee. From the point of view of Guy Pène du Bois, a fellow member and publicist for the group, who later complained that Davies was a "severe, arrogant, implacable" man, the new president deprived the show of its value as a national demonstration by favoring the foreign entries. The new European art did become the public sensation of the show, yet it is hard to believe that Davies could have remained in a position of major responsibility if his behavior had been as biased as it was later remembered, or if the majority of the committee had been in open conflict with him. Only after the exhibition took place, and public reactions were in, did disgruntled members strongly attack the change in policy. There seems little doubt that Davies was the guiding spirit of the show, and that his ideas must have intrigued the committee to a degree, since they did accommodate him. It is also certain that Kuhn, the secretary of the Association, and another painter, Walter Pach, as liaison in Paris, played a fundamental role in making the actual European selections on the spot.

The idea of a comprehensive show of new art tendencies had already occurred to many Europeans outside France. In 1911 the English critic Roger Fry staged, amid public hoots and critical protest, the first Grafton Gallery Postimpressionist exhibition in London. Then, in 1912, a large group of paintings by Van Gogh, Gauguin, Cézanne, and Munch, with others by living moderns, was shown in Cologne in an exhibition called the "Sonderbund." That show precipitated Davies's dream of gathering a large European cross section in America, for he sent the catalog to Kuhn with the note: "I wish we could have a show like this." Kuhn immediately set off for Cologne and contracted to borrow a large group of the paintings. He then proceeded to The Hague, where he saw pictures by Redon and borrowed a roomful for the New York exhibition. In Paris, Kuhn was suddenly overcome by "the magnitude and importance of the whole thing" and cabled Davies, who joined him there.

During the next several weeks Davies and Kuhn

"practically lived in taxicabs," tracking down artists and making arrangements with their dealers for loans. Alfred Maurer introduced them to Ambroise Vollard, the dealer who had exhibited many of the Impressionists and Postimpressionists, and Walter Pach was an invaluable contact with living French artists. In London, they went to see Roger Fry's second modern exhibition at the Grafton Gallery and arranged to borrow from the show. When they returned to America, they left Pach to look after details of packing and shipping.

In New York the group set about trying to arouse enthusiasm for their unprecedented exhibition, which was to be held in the Armory of the New York National Guard's Sixty-Ninth Regiment at Twenty-Sixth Street and Lexington Avenue. Kuhn persuaded Frederick James Gregg of the *New York Sun* to take charge of publicity, along with Guy Pène du Bois, editor of *Arts and Decoration*. At the last minute the great barracks-like hall of the Armory (plate 397) was softened by symbolic swags of evergreen and other decorations financed by the generous Mrs. Gertrude Vanderbilt Whitney. The exhibition opened on Feb. 17, 1913, with a band bravely playing and art students distributing catalogs and badges with the pine-tree flag of the American Revolutionary period and the fitting inscription "The New Spirit."

The Armory Show contained about thirteen hundred pieces of sculpture, paintings, and drawings; it included a large American selection, made by William Glackens, which comprised three-quarters of the whole. Works by most of the celebrated modernists—Picasso, Matisse, Brancusi, Duchamp, Kandinsky, Picabia, Léger, Braque, Rouault, Maillol, Lehmbruck—were represented, as well as a large group of paintings by Cézanne, Redon, Van Gogh, and Gauguin. In fact, Davies's aim was nothing less than to show the evolution of modern art since the Romantic period. To give a proper historical perspective to the revolutionary works of the present, he set them off with pictures by Delacroix, Ingres, Corot, Courbet, and the Impressionists and the Postimpressionists. Despite the absence of the Italian Futurists— Davies tended to misconstrue them as "feeble realists," and they had, anyway, refused to enter unless allowed to exhibit as a group—and a weak German Expressionist section, the exhibition made an impressive representation of the major early modernist currents.

With our advantage of hindsight, we might now quarrel with certain serious omissions, and with the inclusion of nineteenth-century movements beside the work of living artists, in Davies's effort to establish a plausible historical framework for modern art. Nevertheless, the show was an admirably serious effort to demonstrate the logical evolution of modern art over a century of development. As Davies reasonably declared in his "Explanatory Statement," the show was not intended as a polemic: "The Society has embarked on no propaganda. It proposes to enter on no controversy with an institution. Its sole

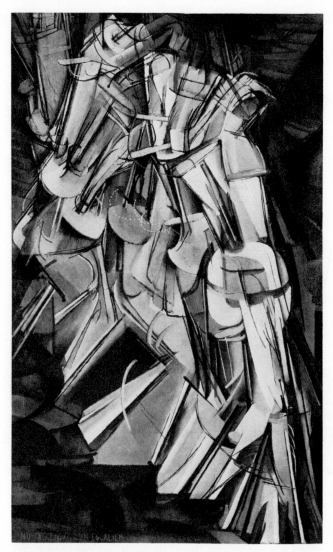

398 Marcel Duchamp. *Nude Descending a Staircase, No. 2.* 1912.
Oil on canvas, 58 × 35". Philadelphia Museum of Art.
The Louise and Walter Arensberg Collection

an equal number were admitted without charge.

Undoubtedly the most intriguing puzzle of the show was *Nude Descending a Staircase, No. 2* (1912, plate 398) by Marcel Duchamp (1887–1968), and it became something of a *cause célèbre*. Julian Street called it an "explosion in a shingle factory"; newspaper cartoonists had a field day lampooning it under such titles as *The Rude Descending the Staircase (Rush Hour at the Subway)* (plate 399), drawing everyday American experiences in pseudo-Cubist style. Amusingly enough, the mock-Cubist styles adopted to poke fun at the new art were a good deal more lively than the intricate Art Nouveau conventions most of the newspaper illustrators normally affected. Written criticism of the show was less lighthearted. Conservative critics, fundamentally and deeply threatened, were hostile and often unscrupulous. Except for the publicists hired to promote the exhibition, the enlightened comments of Henry McBride and Harriet Monroe, the critics who wrote for *Camera Work*, and James Huneker, the reports of the exhibition were uncomprehending and derogatory to the point of hysteria.

The New York Times described the show as "*pathological!*" and singled out the Cubists and Futurists (the latter represented only by Joseph Stella in an ambiguous example of the Italian modernist style) for special abuse, decrying them as "cousins to the anarchists in politics." Royal Cortissoz, pundit of the *New York Herald*, fumed: "This is not a movement and a principle. It is unadulterated cheek." Banner headlines on the order of "Making Insanity Profitable" were characteristic. In an article entitled "Lawless Art," *Art and Progress*,

object is to put the paintings, sculptures, and so on, on exhibition so that the intelligent may judge for themselves, by themselves. . . . "

Overnight, however, the Armory Show became front-page news, the center of heated controversy. The reaction ranged from mock howls of pain to serious threats of violence. A number of public officials urged that the exhibition be closed as a menace to morality, and that the activities of the Association be legally proscribed. The general public joined the chorus of jeers and outrage but also enjoyed the spectacle of scandal in high culture. Judged by the amount of newsprint devoted to it, the exhibition was without precedent; for the first time in American history modern art achieved national notice, if not prestige. Even such an exalted public figure as ex-President Theodore Roosevelt felt impelled to deliver an opinion on modern art in print. The Armory Show became an event not to be missed, although by no means approved. In the three cities where it was shown, New York, Chicago, and Boston, a quarter of a million paid admissions were recorded, and it is estimated that

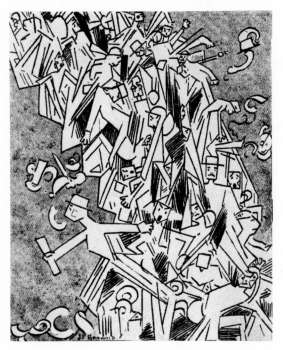

399 J. F. Griswold. *The Rude Descending the Staircase (Rush Hour at the Subway)*. Cartoon.
New York *Evening Sun*, March 20, 1913

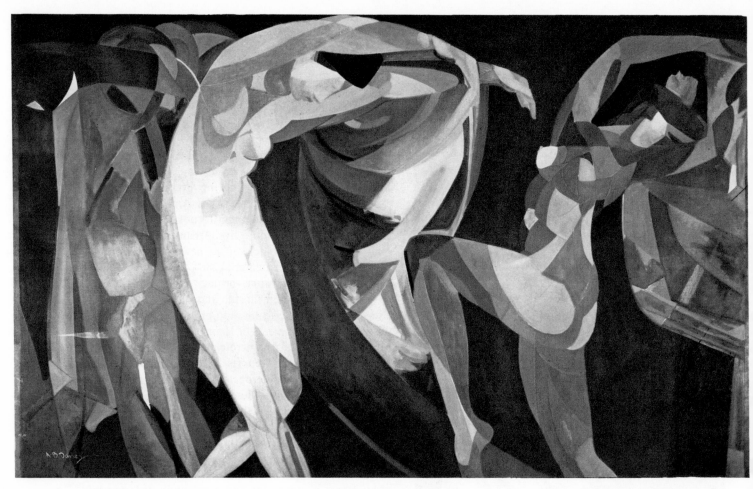

400 Arthur B. Davies. *Dancers.* n.d. Oil on canvas, 7′ × 12′6″. The Detroit Institute of Arts, Detroit, Mich. Gift of Ralph H. Booth

the official magazine of the American Federation of Arts, compared the new European artists to "anarchists, bombthrowers, lunatics, depravers."

At the Art Institute of Chicago, where a selection from the Armory Show was presented after the New York closing, the exhibition provoked incensed responses and even public disorders. The opening coincided with an Illinois morals investigation, and the state vice commission was warned that some of the outlandish new paintings were "immoral and suggestive." The commission's inquiry was inconclusive, and no action was taken, but according to legend, the Chicago underworld, enticed by the prospect of salacious art in high places, visited the show in great numbers. Art students at the Institute were advised by their instructors to shun the exhibition like the plague, or they were conducted through it in the spirit of "crime does not pay." Thus indoctrinated, the students responded by burning Brancusi, Matisse, and Walter Pach in effigy. As a working art critic Harriet Monroe, one of the leaders of the Chicago poetry renaissance and founder of *Poetry* magazine, courageously and reasonably tried to present the case for modern art, but hers was a brave and lonely voice.

Meyer Schapiro has pointed out in his essay on the Armory Show, "Rebellion in Art," that the exhibition posed a more serious threat to traditionalists than it did to the modernists, despite the violent attacks on the latter. If the spokesmen for the status quo were correct in their repeated charges that the new art was produced by lunatics, charlatans, and political subversives, it should have caused them less apprehension, for the public certainly showed no signs of being deluded or corrupted. Yet the conservative critics and artists felt the need to justify themselves. The vehemence of such a generally level-headed critic as Frank Jewett Mather and of the stuffy academician Kenyon Cox indicated how deeply disturbed and defensive they were. Cox warned, in a series of ponderous meditations in *The New York Times*, that the "real meaning" of experimental art was "nothing else than the total destruction of the art of painting." Mather conceded some value to the new directions but feared that art was "left the prey of boisterous and undisciplined personalities."

In subsequent years the enemies of modernism consolidated their position and remained on guard against further erosion of tradition. In time, however, they were unable to present a positive artistic alternative, for even the art that they defended became only a retarded, academic derivative of some form of modernism.

The *succès d'estime* accorded modernism following

the Armory Show was due in great part to the efforts of a handful of discerning patrons, collectors, critics, and dealers who ignored the clamor of dissent. The encouragement of the Stein family in Paris has been mentioned earlier. Under the influence of the Steins, the Cone sisters, of Baltimore, also bought Matisse in his Fauve period and then courageously acquired other modern painters. The advent of Stieglitz and then the Armory Show stimulated the formation of such impressive modern collections as those of John Quinn, Dr. Albert Barnes, Walter Arensberg, Arthur Jerome Eddy, and Lillie P. Bliss. Today they form the nucleus of some of our outstanding museum collections in late nineteenth- and twentieth-century art. Yet it was many years before museums could exert their influence on general standards of taste and elicit public acceptance of the revolutionary art of the twentieth century.

NEW SPONSORS, NEW SHOWS

Established values in the art world itself were thoroughly shaken after the Armory Show. As an index to the change in taste, prices of the Impressionists, Postimpressionists, and twentieth-century European art rose rapidly after 1913, and the market for modern art boomed. Three hundred paintings were purchased directly from the show. John Quinn spent between five and six thousand dollars to form the main body of a superb collection which was later sold at auction. After the show, new galleries sympathetic to modern art, such as the Daniel, the Bourgeois, and the Modern, the last organized by Marius de Zayas with Walter Arensberg's financial support, sprang into existence and implemented the effort that Stieglitz had for many years carried on alone.

Thus, "advanced" painting that no gallery other than "291" would previously have touched now found its way into exhibitions. A case in point was that of the Synchromists. Early in 1914, the Carroll Gallery showed the paintings of Morgan Russell (1886–1953) and Stanton Macdonald-Wright (1890–1973), cofounders of a movement that was one of the most interesting American ventures of the period. They had been in Paris between 1912 and 1913, when Robert Delaunay, with Frank (František) Kupka, had begun loosening up Cubist structure and directing it toward a free, pure-color abstraction; their brilliant chromatic experiments were allied to but independent of Kandinsky's "Improvisations" of these and the immediately preceding years. A few months after Delaunay and Kupka had made these color innovations, in the style that Guillaume Apollinaire later dubbed Orphism, the two young Americans arrived at an almost indistinguishable visual idiom. They later protested in manifestos that they, rather than the Europeans, had originated the brilliant chromatic abstraction.

Whatever the justice of their claim, they worked with enough expressive individuality and verve to make the problem of derivation irrelevant. Russell's *Synchromy in Orange: To Form* (1913–14, colorplate 56) and MacDonald-Wright's *"Conception" Synchromy* (1915, colorplate 57) are characteristic abstract compositions painted in flowing, rhythmic bars and arcs of intense hue. These chromatic exercises employ methods related to musical composition in their balance of dominant color chords against which minor color accents play in endless variations. The analogy with music appeared frequently in the writings of Macdonald-Wright and Russell and of their primary elucidator and champion, Willard Huntington Wright, Stanton's brother. Later they were joined in their small but influential movement by Arthur B. Davies, Patrick Henry Bruce (1880–1937), and Arthur Burdett Frost, Jr., among others.

Bruce and Davies worked in contrasting styles, within the high key and general abstract panoply of Synchromist color. Davies's *Dancers* (plate 400) applies the chromatic formula to a mobile figurative group reduced to overlapping Cubist planes. Bruce worked for a time in a manner close to that of Macdonald-Wright and Russell, as in *Composition III* (colorplate 58). Later he developed a more original and personal style of thickly pigmented color wedges and geometric shapes, often retaining clear references to still-life arrangements, as in *Forms* (1925–26, plate 401).

Although Synchromism petered out with World War I, during its heyday it could boast of perhaps half a dozen American followers, who reached their most notable public success as a homogeneous group when they were shown together with other moderns in the Forum Exhibition in 1916 (see below).

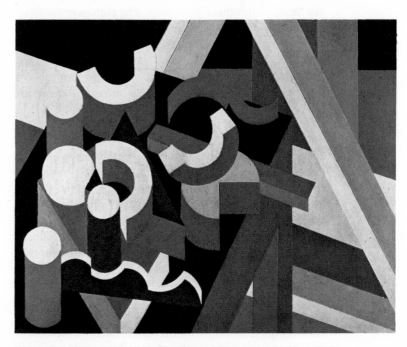

401 Patrick Henry Bruce. *Forms.* 1925–26. Oil on canvas, 28¾ × 35¾". The Corcoran Gallery of Art, Washington, D.C.

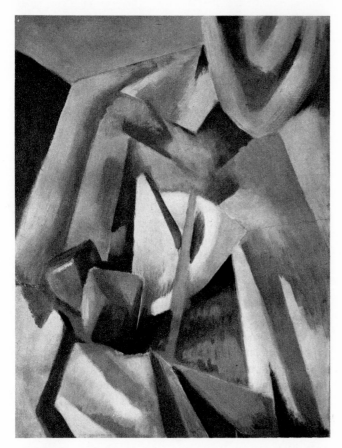

402 Thomas Hart Benton. *Constructivist Still Life, Synchromist Color*. 1917. Oil on paper, 17½ × 13⅝". The Columbus Museum of Art, Columbus, Ohio. Gift of Carl A. Magnuson

Another sign of the more emancipated artistic atmosphere brought about by the Armory Show was Mrs. Gertrude Vanderbilt Whitney's establishment in 1915 of the Friends of the Young Artists, from which grew the Whitney Studio Club three years later. The club gave its artist members individual and group exhibitions; it was the germ of New York City's present Whitney Museum of American Art, which opened in 1931. The Whitney Museum has devoted itself to encouraging contemporary American artists by purchases and interpretive exhibitions.

One of the most adventurous and significant presentations of the new American art following the Armory Show was the Forum Exhibition of Modern American Painters in 1916, organized by Willard Huntington Wright. Wright had been an accomplished literary journalist and the editor of *Smart Set*, thus preceding H. L. Mencken and George Jean Nathan as the director of one of the period's most sophisticated literary publications. Wright returned from Europe in 1915 to write a monthly art chronicle for *Forum* magazine and to contribute art criticism to *Camera Work* and brought out his book, *Modern Painting*, a year after the publication of Arthur Jerome Eddy's *Cubists and Post-Impressionists*, the pioneering American work on modern art. He became a serious and discerning critic, despite his partisanship for Synchromism, which ultimately blinded him to the in-

fluential contribution of Matisse, the Cubists, the Futurists, and other contemporary aesthetic viewpoints. Nevertheless, his rationale for nonobjective expressions was more daring than any that had been advanced, including contributions to *Camera Work*. The show that he induced *Forum* magazine to sponsor proved to be an illuminating demonstration of the meanings and visual resources of American modern art in the period.

In the Forum Exhibition Wright assembled an authoritative show of advanced painting and tried to pursuade the public that it had been hoodwinked into accepting a good deal of spurious art and pseudomodernism. He declared his intention in the catalog foreword "to turn attention for the moment away from European art" and redirect it to native efforts, which had been obscured by the sensation that Duchamp and others had made at the Armory Show. Wright secured as a committee of sponsors an open-minded group of prominent men to certify and help explain the work in the exhibition. They were the critic Christian Brinton, an editor of *Art in America*; Robert Henri; W. H. de B. Nelson, editor of *International Studio*; Alfred Stieglitz; and Dr. John Weichsel, president of the People's Art Guild, an organization that mixed proselytizing for advanced art with social welfare work. Seventeen artists were represented in the show, and each wrote an explanatory note to his work. The participants were Thomas Hart Benton, Oscar Bluemner, Andrew Dasburg, Arthur Dove, George Of, Ben Benn, Marsden Hartley, Stanton Macdonald-Wright, John Marin, Alfred Maurer, Henry McFee, Man Ray, Morgan Russell, Charles Sheeler, Abraham Walkowitz, and Marguerite and William Zorach. Ironically, Thomas Hart Benton (1889–1975), later a bitter enemy of modern art and a leading regionalist, was represented in the exhibition by an abstract, Synchromist composition, *Constructivist Still Life, Synchromist Color* (1917, plate 402), made under Macdonald-Wright's influence. All the artists but Ben Benn and George Of were working under the influence of Cubism, Matisse, or Synchromism, and almost without exception their visual statements stressed formal values rather than representational subject matter. For a number, the work they showed was to remain the most boldly experimental of their careers.

On the defensive after the nightmarish reception of the Armory Show, Wright protested in his catalog foreword, "Not one man represented in this exhibition is either a charlatan or a maniac." With some impatience and in a schoolmasterish tone he exhorted the public to accept work "vouched for by men whose integrity and knowledge of art are beyond question." He continued: "To ridicule the pictures here on view can only be a confession of ignorance. All new excursions into the field of knowledge have been met with ridicule; but despite that ridicule, the new has persisted, in time becoming the old and the accepted."

Wright was perhaps the first American critic with

serious intellectual pretensions to reverse customary art-historical protocol, interpreting the past through the eyes of the present instead of stepping out of his time and measuring the present invidiously as an inevitable decline from traditional artistic achievement. Following the example of Roger Fry and Clive Bell in England, he sought in the art of the past a universal principle of design and formal organization, of "significant form," in the apt phrase coined by Bell, which might provide a universal basis for all aesthetic experience. In the Forum catalog, Wright declared, with a good deal of courage, that the greatest art of the past moves us for exactly the same reasons that abstract art of the present does. He also defended abstraction: "It is neither the subject-matter nor the painter's approximation to nature which makes his work great: it is the inherent aesthetic qualities of order, rhythm, composition and form."

Wright's criticism corresponded in time and temper to a heroic moment in American painting. But not long afterward, undoubtedly because of the cruel erosion of hope and confidence that followed World War I, both criticism and art retreated to safer, more traditional modes of thought and feeling. Wright himself later became obsessed with esoteric color theory and put his aesthetic faith in the color organ. Then he gave up art criticism altogether to become a popular detective-story writer under the pseudonym S. S. Van Dine.

Nationalist feeling aggressively reclaimed its position of dominance soon after the Armory Show. Even as the more progressive American artists received stimulation and encouragement from the exhibition, a strong reaction was building against European leadership. Much was made of the disparaging comparison between American and European artists. The publicist for the Armory Show, Frederick James Gregg, declared that "the vast mass of the American works exhibited represented simply arrested development." William Glackens, depressed by the American section, said: "We have no innovators here. Everything worthwhile in our art is due to the influence of French art. We have not arrived at a national art. . . . Our own art is arid and bloodless." This sense of failure and cultural inferiority, though by no means universal, led to more attacks on the international spirit. Jerome Myers complained bitterly: "Davies had unlocked the door to foreign art and thrown the key away. Our land of opportunity was thrown wide open to foreign art, unrestricted and triumphant."

The crosscurrents and conflicts of the influence of European modernism and a renewed interest in the American scene divided progressive forces in American painting. In 1917 the idea of the independents was revived with the founding of the Society of Independent Artists. The slate of new officers was balanced between moderates and radicals. William Glackens became president; Maurice Prendergast, vice-president; Walter Pach, treasurer; John Covert, secretary; and Walter Arensberg, managing

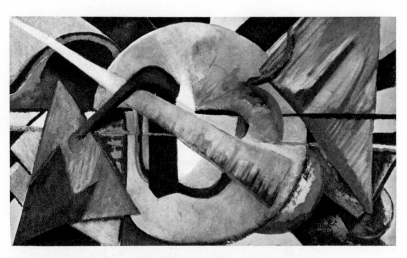

403 Katherine S. Dreier. *Abstract Portrait of Marcel Duchamp.* 1918. Oil on canvas, 18 × 32″. The Museum of Modern Art, New York. Abby Aldrich Rockefeller Fund

director. Taking its slogan from the celebrated French Independents of 1884, "No Jury—No Prizes," the Society held its historic first exhibition with 2,500 works by 1,300 artists. The show was primarily a cross section of American art, much of it mediocre, but it also included the best modern painters in this country and a number of distinguished Europeans.

Opinion as to the importance of the show was strongly divided. Marcel Duchamp ridiculed the publicized "open-mindedness" of the exhibition by submitting an ordinary urinal signed "R. Mutt" and entitled *Fountain,* which was rejected by the scandalized exhibition committee. Henri later complained about the large amount of amateurish work in the show, and he was particularly critical of the radical moderns who took their inspiration from European art. During the war the independents' organization languished, although it continued to hold annual exhibitions. When it renewed activities in the postwar period, the more conservative viewpoint dominated its exhibitions, and the few advanced artists who continued to exhibit shifted to a more realistic interpretation of the American scene.

A legacy of Stieglitz's Gallery 291 was the formation of the Société Anonyme in 1920 by Katherine S. Dreier, Marcel Duchamp, and Man Ray. An itinerant museum and collection of modern painting and sculpture, the Société (or the Museum of Modern Art, as it was first known) bought and circulated new art, with emphasis on nonobjective styles. Its guiding spirit, Katherine Dreier (1877–1952), was an amateur painter (plate 403) who wrote, lectured extensively, and arranged lectures by artists and critics in an effort to promote the understanding of modern art in America. Among the European artists that the Société presented in their first American exhibitions were Schwitters, Campendonk, Klee, Malevich, Miró, Baumeister, and Vantongerloo. The bulk of the Société's fine collection was given in 1941 to the Yale University Art Gallery, where one may still see paintings by some of the neglected and interesting early American moderns: Patrick Henry Bruce, Morton Schamberg, John Covert, and Joseph Stella, as well as Duchamp, Picabia, and the European moderns. It is not too farfetched to consider the opening of the Museum of Modern Art in New York in 1929 as a logical sequel to the pioneering Stieglitz activity, and the educational zeal of "291" has been passed on to other celebrated public collections of modern art.

DADA IN AMERICA

For a short time, Dada received an enthusiastic welcome in America, thanks once again in large part to Stieglitz, and his gallery, and his publication. The New York Dada episode had a strong, shaping influence on American art of the teens and twenties. Only in recent years have the complex and fascinating relations of Marcel Duchamp, Francis Picabia, and Man Ray with American art, through their participation in the Stieglitz and the Arensberg circles, been explored. As the reputations of Duchamp, Dada, and their exegetes rapidly expanded, the longtime and pervasive reluctance to give serious consideration to American Dada began to give way. For decades, the disruptive iconoclasm of the Dada phenomenon seemed contrary to the Americans' faith in order, logic, and reason. Dada's open rebellion and nihilism threatened the *status quo*, and even seemed un-American to many native artists, who viewed it as a form of European lunacy or an affectation.

The first prophetic evidence of the Dada spirit appeared, paradoxically, in *Camera Work*, an unlikely vehicle for Dada iconoclasm, in view of the editor's evangelical faith in modern art. In the issue of April, 1912, De Casseres invoked what was to become, under the pressures of World War I, a familiar litany of revolt: "All great movements begin with the gesture of hate, of irony, of revenge. . . . There is a reevaluation going on in the art of the world today. There is a healthy mockery, a healthy anarchic spirit abroad. . . . No art is perfect until you have smashed it."

Then, in 1913 Picabia arrived in New York to see the Armory Show, where his own work and Marcel Duchamp's *Nude Descending a Staircase* were scandalizing the public. Picabia's contacts with Duchamp in Paris had already made him discontented with the limits of art, even as the Cubists had rather liberally extended those limits. In New York, Picabia made contact immediately with Stieglitz and his gallery, and with Benjamin de Casseres and Maurice de Zayas. The diagrammatic "machine" drawings which he began soon after to contribute to Stieglitz's "291" were the first visual documents in America to announce the Dada spirit. In fact, Picabia himself helped replace *Camera Work* in 1915 with the new publication *291*. For this proto-Dada magazine he did his characteristic mechanical drawings to which were appended provocative titles such as *A Young American Girl in a State of Nudity*. Visual puns vied with *idéogrammes* by Guillaume Apollinaire, typographical experiments, fantastic prose-poem fragments by Stieglitz himself, and other inspirational contributions in free verse to make *291* in its brief year of existence, and in all its twelve numbers, the boldest and most original venture in American publishing. Like the criticism of De Casseres and Zayas, however, *291* exercised a certain restraint in stating the case for the disenchanted modern.

American disillusion never matched the extreme positions of the European Dadaists in their rebellion against modern society and the machine. The bizarre and fantastic forms that Picabia and Duchamp adopted to deprecate and to exorcise the mechanistic environment of modern life, and to challenge the "noble" conventions of the figurative styles of the past, did not gain widespread currency in American art. Perhaps the sentimental attachment of the American to the machine as a creator of material comfort, and his basic optimism about the future, did not permit him to view technology critically. The social violence in European Dada's feigned madness and anarchism was antipathetic to the milder reformist American spirit. Nor were Americans capable of the kind of ingenuity and wit which animated the zany spirit of play so integral to the inventions of Dada art.

In 1915, a year before Dada as such was officially baptized by Tristan Tzara, Jean Arp, Richard Hulsenbeck, and company in Zurich, Marcel Duchamp appeared in New York. Overnight he became a dominant figure in the city's more intellectual art circles, especially the group that assembled regularly in the salon of the collector Walter S. Arensberg. Their nucleus consisted of himself, Picabia, and Man Ray but included among its regular and occasional visitors: Joseph Stella, Marsden Hartley, Albert Gleizes, Jean Crotti, Charles Demuth, Charles Sheeler, Arthur Dove, John Covert, Morton Schamberg, Walter Pach, John Sloan, George Bellows, Isadora Duncan, William Carlos Williams, and Edgar Varèse.

Duchamp was already notorious for his *Nude Descending a Staircase*. Now he began to plan his masterpiece and the *summa* of his ideas, *The Bride Stripped Bare by Her Bachelors, Even* (colorplate 59), a "love machine" which combined erotic obsession with extremely complex and erudite philosophical references. In a window-like structure Duchamp created an elaborate system of machine imagery to symbolize generally the futility of human sexual union. In 1918, while still in New York, Duchamp executed his last painting, *Tu m'*, a sprawling collection of painted shadows of his "readymades" and such real objects as a safety pin and bottle brush in which the immaterial abstract shapes and identifiable objects appear interchangeable. In New York he also produced many of his "readymades," common manufactured objects inten-

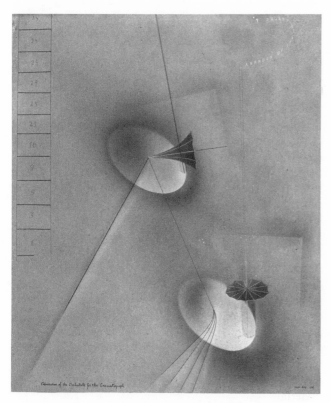

404 Man Ray. *Admiration of the Orchestrelle for the Cinematograph*. 1919. Gouache, wash and ink, and air brush, 26 × 21½″. The Museum of Modern Art, New York. Gift of A. Conger Goodyear

away from painting via collage and its eye-deceiving equivalent in paint, Man Ray took the next step along the road traveled by his friend Duchamp by wholly eliminating brush and traditional paints. From 1917 until the end of the Dada period, about 1922, he was primarily an object maker and an explorer of new mechanical methods of image making, including a new kind of lensless photography (see Chapter 17).

Taking a leaf from Duchamp's provocative and scandalous "readymades," Man Ray affirmed the prerogative of the artist to be completely private and self-referential, recording the most obscure stirrings of the unconscious. His 1921 Dada object, *Gift*, one of a bizarre series made in Paris, is an ordinary flatiron studded with nails to create a menacing image of aggression and potential danger. In photography Man Ray found a peculiarly suitable modern form of representation and image registration. He wrote in his autobiography, *Self-Portrait* (1963): "I could not help thinking that since photography had liberated the modern painter from the drudgery of faithful representation, this field would become the exclusive one of the photograph, helping it to become an art in its own right."

His experiments in painting had involved the search for an automatic mechanical technique related to photography. In 1919 he executed his first "aerographs,"

tionally devoid of aesthetic interest, which in an ironic spirit subverted by the act of choice the very foundations of the artist's function as a creator. Finally, in 1920, Duchamp rejected the role of artist altogether for that of "engineer," and devoted thereafter the major part of his career to chess.

Man Ray (1890–1976) was the first and most important American artist to join the Dada ranks, and his art was decisively influenced by Duchamp. Man Ray had been raised in New York, and his early painting style was more or less Cubist, reflecting the modern art he had seen at the Armory Show. In 1915, in Ridgefield, N.J., he met Marcel Duchamp, beginning a close and lifelong friendship. When Picabia arrived in New York, the three launched the as yet unnamed Dada movement. By 1916, in *The Rope Dancer Accompanies Herself with Her Shadows* (colorplate 60), his work reflected Duchamp's interest in movement and states of change. Painted entirely in oils, the picture is a transposition of ideas that Man Ray had been developing in a series of colored-paper collages influenced by Cubism; it was really a kind of trompe-l'oeil of a collage. The dancer, at the top of the canvas, is a small schematic figure whose legs and skirts are shown simultaneously in different positions. The same Duchampian principle allows the rope to be represented six times, forming lariat-like arabesques that swing out to enclose the "shadows," which are large, flat, abstract color shapes. Having moved

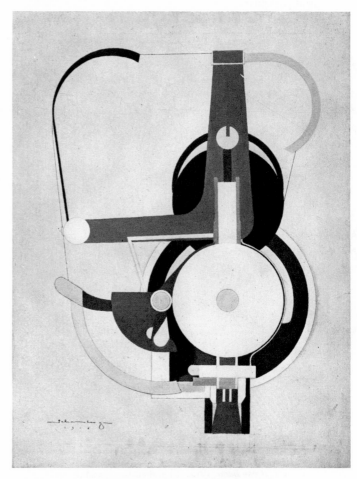

405 Morton L. Schamberg. *Machine*. 1916. Oil on canvas, 30⅛ × 22¾″. Yale University Art Gallery, New Haven, Conn. Gift of Collection Société Anonyme

paintings made with the commercial technique of airbrushing, which is often used in retouching photographs. *Admiration of the Orchestrelle for the Cinematograph* (plate 404) is an example of the intriguing flatness and nonpainterly quality of the "aerographs," which closely resemble photographs. Its title has the punning irony of Duchamp and Picabia, and it creates a veiled erotic situation by the juxtaposition of silhouettes of suggestive machine shapes.

Morton L. Schamberg (1882–1918) was the first American after Man Ray to produce work directly related to Dada. His friend Charles Sheeler had introduced him to Duchamp, Picabia, Man Ray, and the Arensberg circle. Schamberg's paintings (e.g., plate 405) relate in particular to Picabia's machinist style.

THE PRECISIONISTS

Picabia's and Duchamp's machinist imagery and their polemics, Man Ray's mechanical techniques in photography, and Schamberg's explicit visual statements became in the 1920s an important source of the American Precisionist movement. The Precisionists combined "immaculate" surfaces and a Cézannesque and Cubist formal vocabulary with meticulous drawing utilizing geometric angles, curves, and clean lines. Colors were low-keyed, and in general the painters avoided pictorial means that would express an obvious, exuberant sensuality or a prodigal spirit.

Charles Demuth (1883–1935) was the first to elaborate

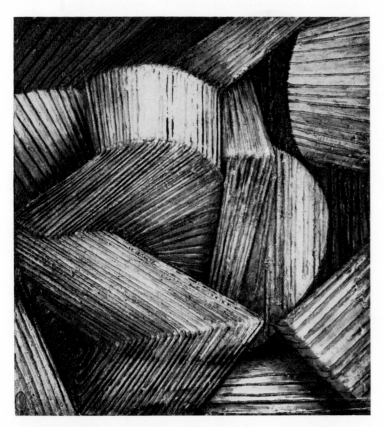

406 John R. Covert. *Brass Band.* 1919. Oil and string on composition board, 26 × 24″. Yale University Art Gallery, New Haven, Conn. Gift of Collection Société Anonyme

the clean sharp edges of the emerging Precisionist techniques around a subject matter of the American industrial landscape, followed by Sheeler and Stella. Demuth rendered in exquisite style architectural and industrial themes: steamships, grain elevators, factories, and towers, as well as domestic architecture in the Pennsylvania Dutch countryside around Lancaster where he lived. Charles Sheeler (1883–1965) adopted his own kind of Cubist realism in the twenties, built around a subject matter similar to Demuth's but rendered in a more meticulously illusionistic rather than an abstract fashion, emulating the sharp-focus precision of the photograph. A less known American, John R. Covert (1882–1960) also experienced the machine aesthetic and the Dada influence obliquely. In *Brass Band* (1919, plate 406) he defines planes and spatial directions by attaching strings directly to the composition board, much as Duchamp had attached wire to the glass surface of *The Bride.*

Probably the strongest Dada reaction was found in visual and verbal puns used in his collages by Arthur G. Dove (1880–1946) and in their provocative foreign materials.

None of the American Precisionists or the abstract artists of the period, however, permitted themselves the open acts of social defiance and aesthetic subversion found in the art and behavior of Duchamp and Picabia. As Man Ray, in an interview with the critic Arturo Schwartz, said just before his death: "The idea of scandal and provoking people, which is one of the principles of Dada, was entirely foreign to the American spirit." The Precisionists' mature pictures were bland, schematic interpretations of the new industrial landscape, objective to a fault and, with some notable exceptions, uncritical in their observations. The American artist could not match the European's aesthetic detachment from his culture. He felt no deep sense of alienation from his own industrial environment. Much of the work of the Precisionists was done after World War I (see Chapter 19).

Joseph Stella (1876–1946), in a more agitated and subjective mood, registered the fresh impact on his senses of the new American dynamism with a note of Futurist stridency. Of one of his paintings of *Brooklyn Bridge* (plate 407) he wrote: "To realize this towering imperative vision, I lived days of anxiety, torture and delight alike, trembling all over with emotion. . . . Upon the swarming darkness of the night, I rung all the bells of alarm with the blaze of electricity scattered in lightnings down the oblique cables, the dynamic pillars of my composition, and to render more pungent the mystery of my metallic apparition, through the green and red glare of the signals I excavated here and there caves as subterranean passages to infernal recesses."

After the brief New York Dada episode, for most American artists modernism became identified once again with the American promise. Just as John Sloan,

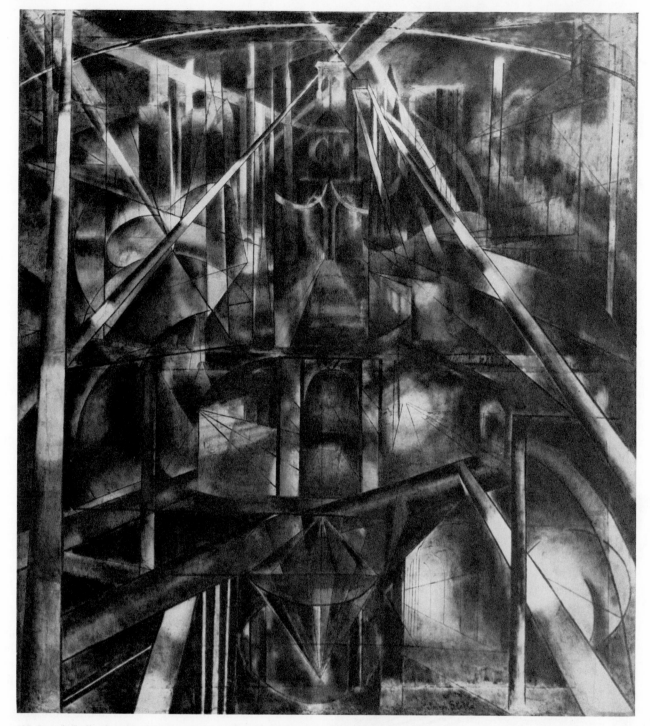

407 Joseph Stella. *Brooklyn Bridge.* 1917–18. Oil on canvas, 84 × 76″. Yale University Art Gallery, New Haven, Conn. Gift of Collection Société Anonyme

Robert Henri, and their associates had captured something of the American dream in their Realism, so the first wave of modernists also approached the formal rigors of modernist styles in a mood of almost naive optimism. They would not brook the limits imposed by Cubism, or inflict on themselves the conditions of working "logically within the limitations inherent in an idea." Dada never had a wide following, nor did it leave a lasting imprint on the art of this country, as it did in Europe.

And Futurism, which canonized the machine and exalted modern life in a programmatic art, was given a more subjective and unsystematized account in Joseph Stella's painting and verbal utterances. The Americans did not yet take the radical step of entirely dissociating art from the world of sight. A gap persisted between abstraction and the painting that clung to naturalist illusion, and with few exceptions, this gap was not decisively closed by the early American modernists.

17
Photography: Document or Art Medium?

After 1890 photographic activity in the United States was characterized by various groups with divergent interests. Serious amateur photographers were eager to distinguish their work from banal snapshots and pretentious hobbyist images on the one hand and from the various types of commercial imagery on the other. They began to regard photography as a creative pursuit and the print as an expressive object, similar to a lithograph or an etching and, like them, susceptible to hand intervention

408 Alfred Stieglitz. *Sun Rays—Paula—Berlin.* 1889?
Chloride, 8 × 10″. The Art Institute of Chicago

in the processing. To some extent their views were influenced by Peter Henry Emerson, whose 1889 book, *Naturalistic Photography*, published in England, was widely read in America. Emerson urged that "pictorial photography," as art photography was then called, begin to display the same styles and standards as other art media.

At that time photography emerged as an adjunct of journalism and social documentation, often producing images with as much expressive content as pictorial works made for personal artistic purposes. However, in the late nineteenth and early twentieth centuries such photographs were regarded as scientific evidence of events or conditions and were not accepted as art because they were not concerned with beauty. Although the dichotomy between art and the document persisted for a long time, today such images are acknowledged to reveal the photographer's sensibilities as much as if they had been made solely for personal expression.

Alfred Stieglitz (1864–1946), an American who had received his photographic education in Germany in the 1880s, was the most persuasive and dynamic figure among those who aimed to improve creative photography in the United States. By 1889 Stieglitz's aesthetic had evolved from a preference for genre subjects to one more photographic in style and content. In *Sun Ray—Paula—Berlin* (plate 408) storytelling is subordinated to the sense of poignant intimacy created by pose, light and shadow, and detail. Shortly after his return to New York in 1890, Stieglitz began to realize further the potential of the medium by photographing city subjects previously considered too vulgar for art.

Between 1893, when he became editor of *American Amateur Photography*, and 1917, Stieglitz was active on many photographic fronts. Through the New York Camera Club and its journal *Camera Notes*, and on exhibition committees and juries, he worked to convince photographers that the medium should develop an appropriate aesthetic. He urged that photographs be judged for originality and feeling in the same way as the other arts, a position endorsed by Charles Caffin in *Photography as a Fine Art.* In 1902, finally unable to impose such standards on camera-club hobbyists, Stieglitz gathered examples from some of the best pictorial photographers and arranged an exhibition at the National Arts Club in New York, launching the Photo-Secession.

The Photo-Secession was both an organization and an idea. Its membership included most of the advanced pictorialists of the time: Frank Eugene (1865–1936), Gertrude Kasebier (1852–1934), Edward Steichen (1879–1973), and Clarence H. White (1871–1925). Later, younger photographers, among them Alvin Langdon Coburn (1882–1966) and Karl Struss (b. 1886) joined. The Secession was not doctrinaire in its approach to photography. Despite Stieglitz's preference for the unmanipulated negative in his own work, Steichen and Eugene, influenced by previous training as painters, did extensive handwork on their images, producing works such as Steichen's *Self-Portrait with Palette and Brush* (plate 409), a pigment print which is almost indistinguishable from a lithograph. Initially most Secessionists considered a soft image desirable in order to distinguish their work from journalistic and commercial photographs, but attitudes toward sharpness began to change about 1910. Because they considered the photograph an art object—to be exhibited—Secessionists were fastidious about processing and printing for permanence, with platinum paper the material of choice. The pronounced attention to processing and materials frequently disposed outsiders to consider the Secessionists and their imagery "precious."

Established Secessionists generally chose to photograph subject matter similar to that of late nineteenth-century painting. Moody landscapes, portraits, genteel genre scenes, and tonal still lifes predominated. Gertrude Kasebier, whose *Evelyn Nesbit* (plate 410) effectively projects the petulant charm of the sitter, was a renowned portraitist when she joined the Secession. *Camera Work* featured her romantic images of maternity in the first issue, and she exhibited with the group until 1912. Clarence White, an amateur from Newark, Ohio, also was well known among salon circles for his images of women and children. Much of his work, with its concentration on lighting and composition, evokes the essence of Victorian gentility in a manner reminiscent of Whistler and Sargent. White, active in the early years of the Secession, was influential in photographic education as well, teaching first at Columbia University and later at his own prestigious Clarence White School of Photography. Although acceptable for study purposes, the nude had always been considered too *risqué* a subject for art photography; now it was photographed out of doors in sylvan settings and inside romantically appointed studios by Annie Brigman (1869–1950), Eugene, Steichen, Stieglitz, and White. In 1907 these last two

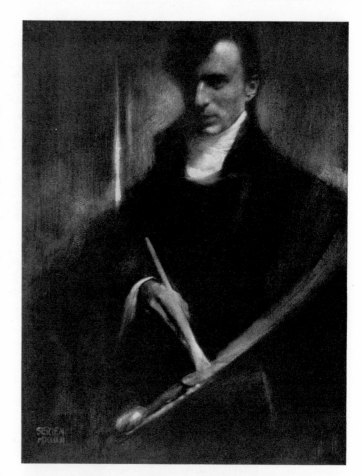

409 Edward Steichen. *Self-Portrait with Palette and Brush.* 1901. Pigment print, 8½ × 6¾".
Reprinted with the permission of Joanna T. Steichen

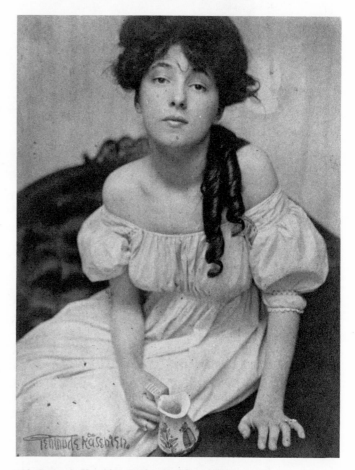

410 Gertrude Kasebier. *Evelyn Nesbit.* c. 1903.
Gelatin silver, 8⅛ × 6⅛". International Museum of Photography at the George Eastman House, Rochester, N.Y.

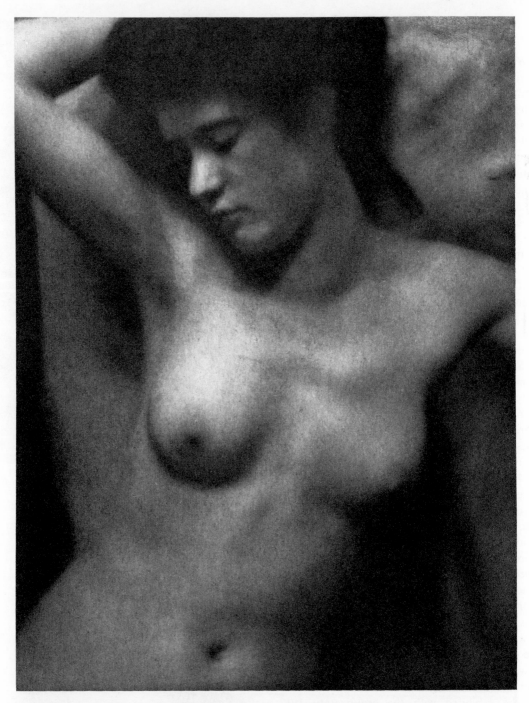

411 Clarence H. White and Alfred Stieglitz. *Torso*. 1907. Platinum, 9½ × 8¼".
On extended loan to The Museum of Modern Art, New York. Estate of Lewis F. White

collaborated on a series of nudes, meant to suggest sensuousness without being explicit, as in *Torso* (plate 411).

As a younger member with boundless energy, Steichen had a strong voice in Secession activities, despite being abroad for long periods. White and Stieglitz first recognized Steichen's ability after the Milwaukee artist had submitted photographs to the Chicago Salon of 1900. In style his work ranged from Whistlerian Impressionism to forceful portraiture. He was one of the first in America to experiment with autochrome color photography (see Chapter 24).

Coburn came to Stieglitz's notice after the young man had exhibited and helped hang the Secessionist show at Pittsburgh's Carnegie Institute in 1904. Despite frequent and long sojourns abroad, where he photographed well-known Britons and experimented with gravure printing, Coburn was greatly inspired by the dynamism of New York City. He claimed that only photography could capture its atmosphere and changeability. About 1911 he became concerned with abstract spatial relationships and sought unusual vantage points and angles from which to photograph the city. In *The Octopus* (plate 412), a view from above Madison Square Park, the delicate tree forms and the strong, sweeping arcs convey both the force and the instability of urban life. Struss, a latecomer to the Secession, expressed similar interests in the city scene at the same time.

In contrast to the more conservative members of the Secession, Stieglitz, Coburn, Struss, and occasionally Steichen avoided common pictorialist subjects for non-narrative imagery of the metropolis. Recognizing the progressive nature of their medium, they responded to what novelist Theodore Dreiser called "the color of a great city," producing images similar in content, although not in style, to the Ashcan works of the New York Realist painters. *The Steerage* (plate 413), a 1907 Stieglitz work that Picasso later found impressive, is a highly structured arrangement of the shapes formed by ship architecture and people, expressive of Stieglitz's yearning for human warmth. For a brief period in 1908 Realist painters and Secession photographers shared enough common vision to exhibit together, but their artistic aims and temperaments diverged soon afterward.

Stieglitz had hoped to eradicate the provinciality of the American response to photography through the medium of the Photo-Secession. In 1903, aided by Steichen, he started to publish *Camera Work*, and two years later, again urged on by Steichen, he opened the gallery known as "291." At first *Camera Work* featured only photography—the work of the Secession and their European counterparts—just as at first "291" exhibited this work exclusively. Between 1912 and 1916, "291" showed no photographs other than Stieglitz's own, an indication of his disappointment with the American photographer's inability to accommodate the new ideas then percolating in European art circles. However, these new visual solutions, seen first in *Camera Work*, at "291," and then in greater measure at the 1913 Armory Show, were of great significance to younger photographers such as Paul Strand and Charles Sheeler, as well as to Stieglitz himself.

In 1915 Paul Strand (1890–1976) began to experiment with a photographic equivalent of Cubism, creating images in which forms and tonal values are independent of recognizable subject matter. Soon he began to integrate the Cubist aesthetic into a more recognizable image, expressive of the rhythm of city life, as in *Viaduct* (plate 414). He began also to use his reflex camera as a "candid" apparatus in order to capture the unposed gesture and natural expression of anonymous individuals. Strand's work, judged at the time as "brutal and direct," was ex-

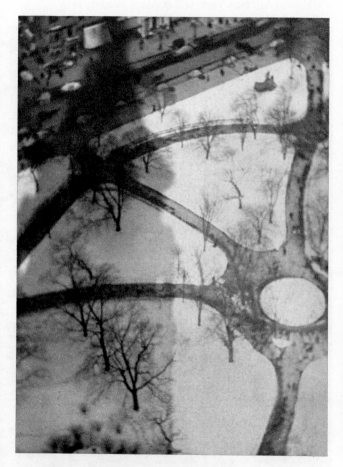

412 Alvin Langdon Coburn. *The Octopus.* 1912.
International Museum of Photography at the
George Eastman House, Rochester, N.Y.

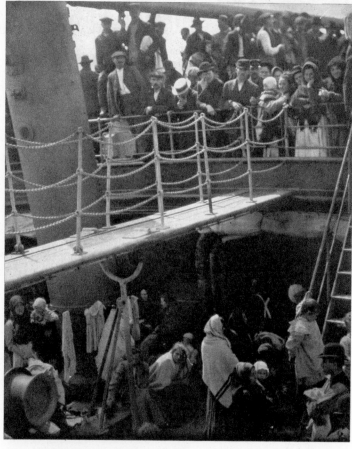

413 Alfred Stieglitz. *The Steerage.* 1907.
Chloride, 4 × 5".
Collection Peter Pollack, New York

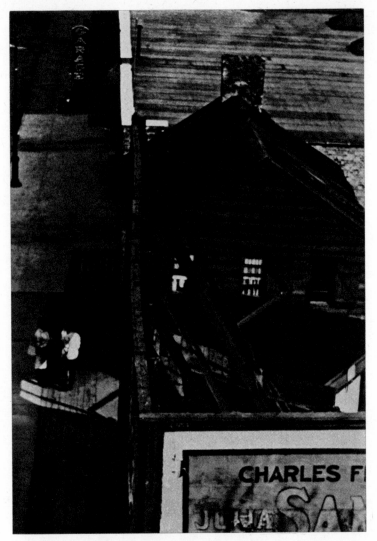

414 Paul Strand. *Viaduct*. 1915/16. Platinum.
©1971 by The Estate of Paul and Hazel Strand

portraits of Georgia O'Keeffe. By 1918 Steichen and Strand were in the Army, and the gallery and publication ceased to exist. Although Stieglitz was to open An Intimate Gallery in 1925 and An American Place in 1929, his influence on the photographic scene was never again so forceful.

With few exceptions, West Coast pictorial photographers were not involved in the Photo-Secession, but their subjects and styles were similar to those of more conservative eastern Secession members. Being far from the centers of avant-garde activity, westerners became aware of trends in art later. In 1921, long after modern art had been shown at the San Francisco Exposition of 1915, the most prominent California pictorialist, Edward Weston (1886–1958), became conscious of the new aesthetic in art and photography. En route to New York (where he visited with Stieglitz and met Strand) he photographed the industrial architecture of the Armco Steel works (plate 416). Unlike Coburn's evocation of restless energy in his 1910 images of Pittsburgh factories, Weston's industrial photographs emphasized the sleek geometry and precision of mechanical forms, a direction that was to become characteristic of much painting and photography of the decade. At about the same time Imogen Cunningham (1883–1976), a Seattle pictorialist

415 Charles Sheeler. *Stairwell No. 70*. 1917. The Museum of Modern Art, New York. Gift of Alfred Stieglitz, 1933

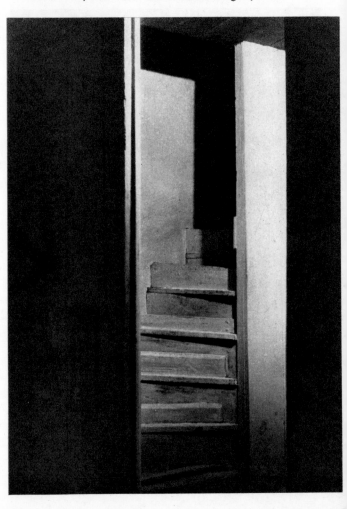

hibited at "291" in 1916; a year later he began his close-up studies of mechanical forms. Stieglitz devoted the two last issues of *Camera Work* to the young photographer, whom he spoke of as the only important American talent since Coburn. Charles Sheeler (1883–1965), a Philadelphia painter who had turned to architectural photography as a means of livelihood, had begun to photograph buildings and interiors such as *Stairwell, No. 70* (plate 415) in 1914. In these, he emphasized uncluttered shape, strong value contrast, and surface texture rather than naturalistic spatial relationships.

For Stieglitz, Steichen, and the Secessionists, American entry into World War I in 1917 was the terminal point of an era that was already disintegrating. White and other Photo-Secessionists, uncomfortable with avant-garde aesthetics, had formed the Pictorial Photographers of America in 1916. Stieglitz had begun to investigate abstract relationships as early as 1915, but his inherent romanticism led him to search for metaphors of feeling in the amorphousness of sky and clouds and in his extended

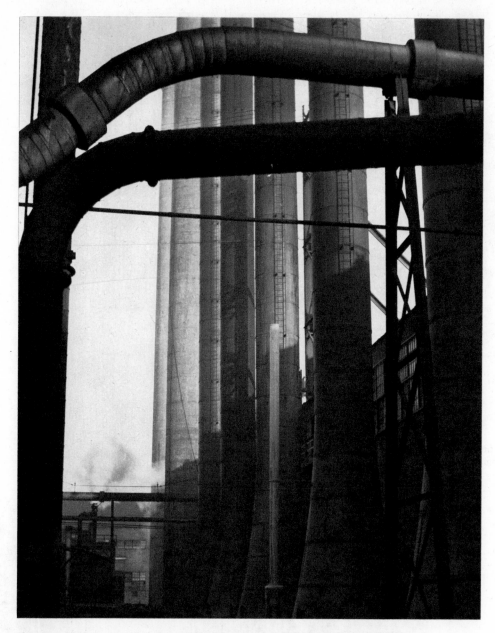

416 Edward Weston. *Armco Steel*. 1922. Courtesy of Cole Weston, Carmel, Calif.

of Pre-Raphaelite persuasion, moved to California and began her sharply patterned portraits and close-up images of organic life.

Shortly before Stieglitz initiated his campaign to elevate pictorial photography, the mechanical reproduction of the photograph in the same operation as printing type became possible. A method of reproducing a photographic image on the printing press had been discovered in 1824, even before the photographic process had been completely realized. Later developments included heliotypes and collotypes—photographs reproduced by the application of lithography—and photogravure and Woodburytypes—reproductions based on intaglio etching methods. Despite their excellent translation of photographic detail and values, the fact that it was necessary to print separately, in some cases trim the borders and insert the reproductions individual-

ly into a book, made these methods costly and time-consuming.

In the 1880s book publishers sought a new method by which photographs could be printed simultaneously with the text, as wood blocks had long been in the periodical press. Using a technique discovered just before the Civil War, illustrators frequently engraved directly over a photograph on a block, translating the continuous gradations of the camera image into lines and dots, a method which suggested that the uniform surface of the photograph might be broken into a mechanical code of dots or lines by rephotographing the image through a screen onto a metal plate and etching the plate. "Halftone," or "photoengraving," as this process was called, made possible much wider use of the photograph as illustration and inaugurated the pervasive use of photography in journalism.

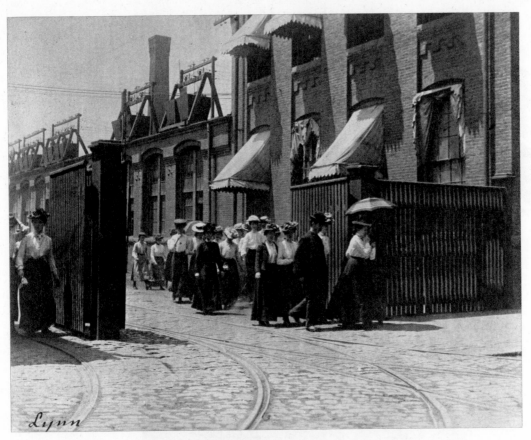

417 Frances Benjamin Johnston. *Shoe Workers, Lynn, Mass.*
1895. Library of Congress, Washington, D.C.

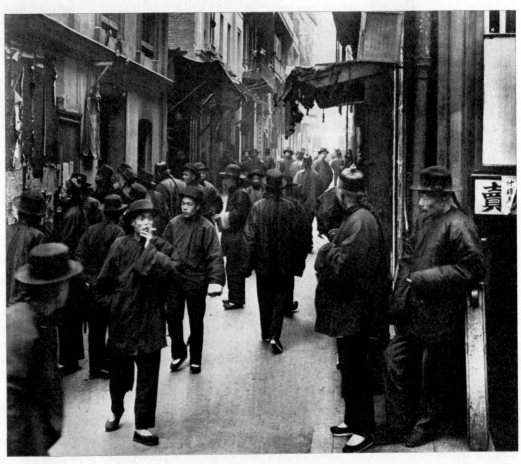

418 Arnold Genthe. *Street of Gamblers.* 1896. International Museum
of Photography at the George Eastman House, Rochester, N.Y.

Photojournalists, recording events to be seen briefly and soon ignored, did not ordinarily concern themselves with either art or personal expression, and in retrospect their images often seem dull and uninspired. In this regard, Frances Benjamin Johnston (1864–1952) and Arnold Genthe (1869–1942) were exceptional. Johnston, a Washington illustrator turned photographer, participated in the salons of the nineties and joined the Photo-Secession in 1904. She demonstrated her expert handling of lighting and composition in images such as *Shoe Workers, Lynn, Mass.* (plate 417), where she invested the scene with a keen sense of the moment of release from toil. Johnston's most famous work, a series of 150 photographs of Hampton Institute, attempted to show the progress of industrial education for American blacks. Genthe worked in San Francisco between 1895 and 1911, when he moved to New York and concentrated on soft-focus portraits of theatrical celebrities. His unposed photographs of urban activity, such as *Street of Gamblers* (plate 418), made in the Chinese quarter in 1896, evoke a sense of mystery, while his earthquake images of a decade later recreate the surreal confusion of that event.

After 1890 photographs made for publications became increasingly focused on social conditions. Industrial progress, which created the urban slum and the sweatshop, had now provided the technology to counter these evils in the camera and the halftone. Photographs, and the print-compatible technology for reproducing them, became undeniable witnesses of the need for social change, a role first assigned them in this country by Jacob A. Riis (1849–1914), the penniless immigrant who became a police reporter for the *New York Tribune* in 1877. Riis's activity brought him into direct contact with the wretched conditions of a slum known as "death's thoroughfare," and he taught himself to photograph in order to provide authorities with irrefutable proof of the degradation caused by miserable living conditions. The photograph *Bandits' Roost* (plate 419), made under his supervision, portrays the fetid milieu with surpassing particularity, despite the fact that Riis was an outsider looking in.

Riis conceived of photographs as useful and had them made into lantern slides for illustrated lectures. They were the basis for illustrations accompanying his magazine articles, which he gathered together and published as *How the Other Half Lives*. This 1890 publication was the first in America to use photographs as documentary illustrations of social conditions and among the first to reproduce a number of them by the halftone process (the remainder were translated into engravings). The success of Riis's enterprise led to the razing of notorious tenements and the construction of a park on the site. However, a greater effect was to insure that photography would thereafter play an important role in illustrating campaigns for social change. After 1900 a number of

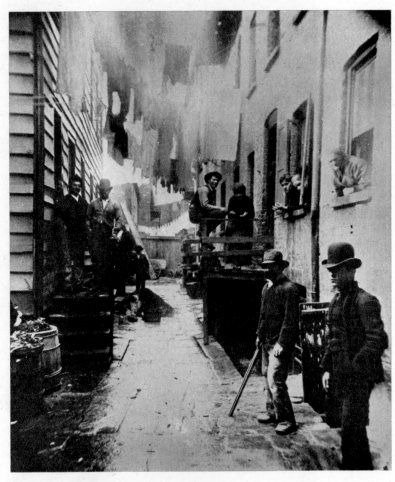

419 Jacob A. Riis and unknown collaborator.
Bandits' Roost. 1888. The Museum of the
City of New York. Jacob A. Riis Collection.
Print by Alexander Allard

photographers, among them Jessie Tarbox Beals, Ralph R. Earle, George Hare, Jr., and Charles Weller, specialized in social photography, but the most significant figure in the field was Lewis W. Hine (1874–1940).

Hine had moved from Wisconsin at the turn of the century to teach at the Ethical Culture School in New York. In 1904, even before he started what may have been the first accredited photography class in a secondary school, he made his first social pictures at Ellis Island in connection with the school's efforts to instill respect for immigrant life. Soon after, joining artist Joseph Stella on a pioneer social investigation, The Pittsburgh Survey, Hine gave up teaching to become, as he called it, "a social photographer." He worked for social organizations and periodicals, mainly The National Child Labor Committee and *The Survey*, supplying photographic and written documentation about child workers in mills, mines, street trades, and on farms. He edited the sequences, planned the organizational publicity, delivered slide lectures, and arranged photographic displays for conventions and expositions. In short, he conceived the matrix for social

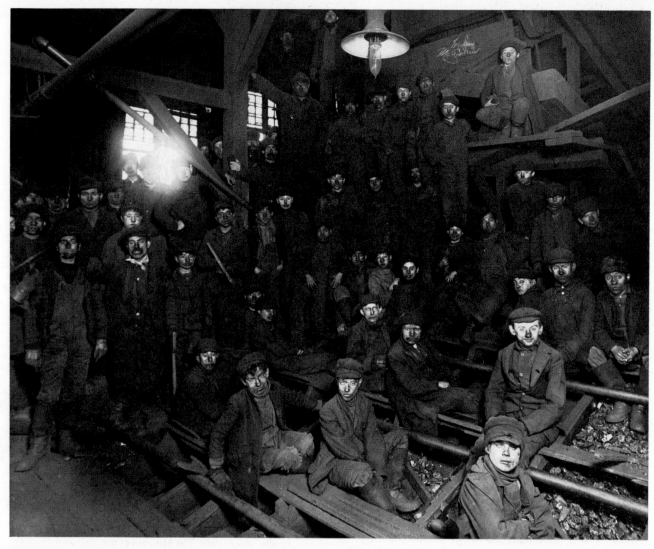

420 Lewis W. Hine. *In a Mine Breaker*. 1911.
Private collection

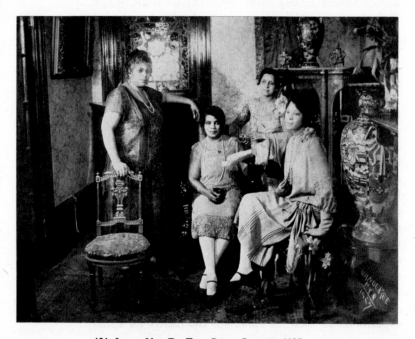

421 James Van DerZee. *Group Portrait*. 1927.
Studio Museum, Harlem, New York

photography which has remained in use up to the present. Although he used cumbersome equipment, he caught the restless quality of life in the street, foreshadowing small-camera practice. His posed compositions such as *In a Mine Breaker* (plate 420) are remarkable not only because they document inequity, but because they express Hine's passionate concern that the human spirit not be warped by social conditions.

Riis and Hine placed their photographs in the journalistic media in order to convince and persuade, in effect creating what has come to be called "documentary photography." Other photographers were also engaged in projects they hoped would influence attitudes, although access to the popular press was not so immediate. Still others created social documents almost without knowing it, because they were moved by some aspect of life around them to do more than make casual snapshots. Leigh Richmond Miner's (1864–1935) photographs of the black community on St. Helena Island in the first decade heroicize the subjects and romanticize their simple existence. A similar approach later informed the work of Doris Ulmann (1884–1934), who photographed southern blacks and Appalachian mountain folk during the early thirties. Darius Kinsey (1871–1945), on the other hand, seems to have approached the loggers of the Pacific Northwest, whose occupation he documented at the turn of the century, with no artistic or sociological preconceptions. The photographs are compelling because the careful composition and craftsmanship re-create the feel of western logging camps. In similar unpretentious fashion, E. J. Bellocq (active c. 1900–1912) photographed women in the red-light district of New Orleans, suggesting the pride and sorrow of their existence, while Charles Currier (1851–1938), a Boston photographer, evoked a sense of New England tranquillity and orderliness in images of interiors. Taken together, James Van DerZee's (b.1886) photographs, of which *Group Portrait* (plate 421) is an example, mirror the aspirations of middle-class blacks in Harlem in the twenties.

The tendency to heroicize seems particularly apparent in photographs of peoples and cultures outside the confines of American industrialized society—groups such as rural blacks, Appalachian mountain folk, and especially American Indians. Although aboriginal culture had been all but destroyed by the time of Wounded Knee in 1890, Indian tribal life had come to symbolize a more humane order of civilization. At this time photographers such as Frank A. Rinehart, F. H. Nowell, and William Dinwiddie started to make extensive records of tribal life for the Bureau of American Ethnology, in some cases projecting forcefully a vanished existence.

Several photographers of Indian life were enthusiasts who were convinced that aboriginal culture offered important insights for contemporary America. The patronage of millionaires Edward S. Harriman and J. P. Morgan enabled Edward S. Curtis (1868–1952), a Seattle photographer, to document Indian culture tribe by tribe, a project that occupied him for thirty years. By carefully controlling composition and lighting, and by producing fine, gold-toned prints, as in *Watching the Dancers* (plate 422), Curtis expressed his respect for the legendary quality of this existence. Adam Clark Vroman (1856–1915) worked among the Hopi between 1894 and 1905. Less sentimental than Curtis's work, his portraits (plate 423) also emphasize the vigor and strength of an ancient people whose extermination he deplored.

Shortly after photography was developed, several European women of means adopted it as a medium of personal expression. However, few in America became actively engaged in photography until the late 1880s. Daguerreotyping and wet-plate technology required commitments of time, as well as freedom from responsibility, that most American women could not afford. By 1890 simplified techniques combined with a greater measure of affluence and leisure induced women to devote them-

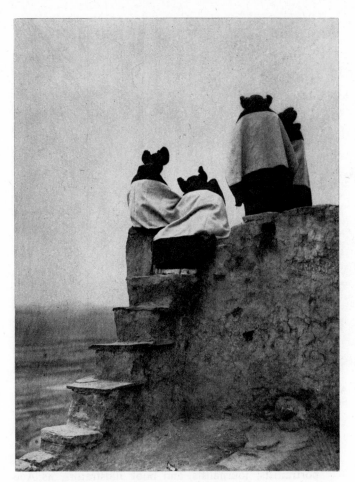

422 Edward S. Curtis. *Watching the Dancers*. n.d. The Pierpont Morgan Library, New York

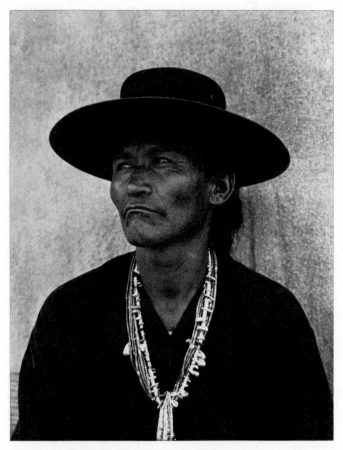

423 Adam Clark Vroman. *Navajo Man Coyote*. 1901. Southwest Museum, Highland Park, Calif.

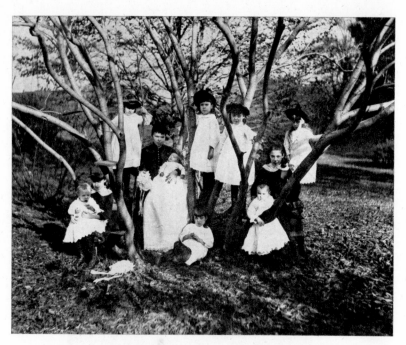

424 Alice Austen. *The Cocroft Children in a Tree.* 1886. The Staten Island Historical Society, N.Y. Alice Austen Collection

selves to photography, both professionally and as amateurs. As already noted, women were renowned as portraitists, journalists, and book illustrators, as Adelaide Hanscom Leeson was for her images for the 1905 edition of *The Rubáiyát of Omar Khayyám*. Women, among them Eva Watson-Schutze, Alice Boughton, Brigman, Kasebier, and Johnston, exhibited at pictorial salons, won prizes at major expositions, served on exhibition juries, and wrote on photography for popular and professional journals. In short, the great flexibility of the medium and the lack of discrimination in training enabled many women to release their creative energies more successfully in photography than in the older visual arts.

Photography also fulfilled a social and psychological role for a number of women of independent character and unconventional inclinations by allowing them to function in a society that frowned on female aggressiveness. Armed with cameras, they were released from the stultifying demands of Victorian existence, although that same existence might provide the substance of their vision. Alice Austen (1866–1952) was one of several (among them Chansonetta Stanley Emmons, Marie Kendall, and Kate Matthews) who created an extensive document—in her case of the leisured life on Staten Island at the end of the nineteenth century. In addition, the camera enabled her to step away from her own milieu and face immigrants and street people in lower Manhattan. Although she was fastidious in composition and technique, Austen's images are seldom impassioned but instead reveal a wry sense of humor, as in *The Cocroft Children in a Tree* (plate 424). Increasingly, as photography enabled enterprising women

to engage in activities without disadvantage or exploitation, their talents and abilities came to be as celebrated as if they were men, witness Margaret Bourke-White, Imogen Cunningham, Dorothea Lange, and Berenice Abbott.

During the 1920s serious photographers became aware of the pronounced industrial character of American society. Machinery and industrial architecture were chosen more frequently as subjects and were formed into sharply delineated and carefully composed close-up images. The attitude to nature changed from romantic appreciation to a more scientific one, in which the camera became a probing instrument for examining the nature of organic life. This approach characterized the work of Strand, who returned to still photography after his Army experience as a medical photographer. His photographs of lathes and camera interiors reveal the elegant geometry of machinery, while his images of rocks and growth divulge the miraculous complexity of their shape and texture. After 1925 Strand's almost hermetic vision was enlarged by experiencing the character and sweep of North American landscape on trips to Maine, Colorado, and the Gaspé.

Sheeler, who had moved to New York in 1919, con-

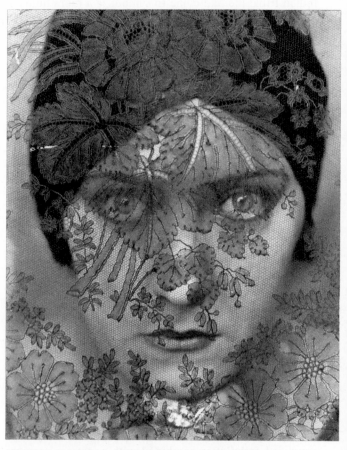

425 Edward Steichen. *Gloria Swanson.* 1924. Reprinted with the permission of Joanna T. Steichen

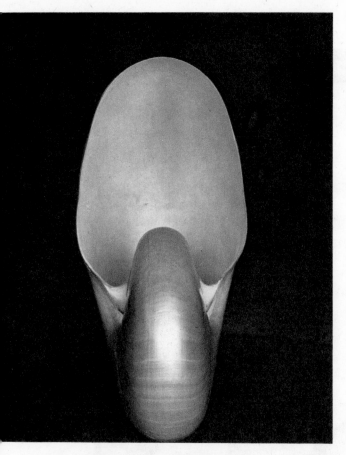

426 Edward Weston. *Chambered Nautilus*. 1927.
Courtesy of Cole Weston, Carmel, Calif.

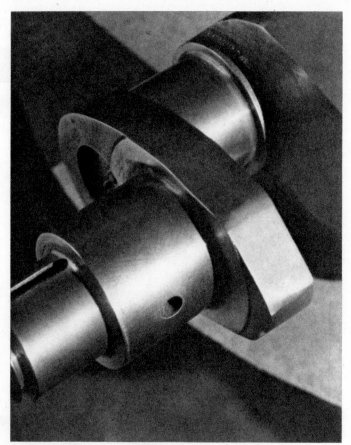

427 Paul Outerbridge. *Crankshaft*. 1923.
The Metropolitan Museum of Art, New York

tinued his interest in architecture, investigating the complex angularity of skyscrapers in lower Manhattan instead of the simple shapes of Pennsylvania barns. Using such images, he and Strand collaborated in 1920 on perhaps the first art film made in America, *Manhatta* (released as *New York the Magnificent*). The clean sharpness of the imagery expressed the spirit embodied in Walt Whitman's "city of the world." Throughout most of the twenties Sheeler's photography, like his painting, was concerned with the scientific functionalism of industry and in 1927 he received a gratifying commission from the Ford Motor Company, which led to his recognition as this country's preeminent photographer of industrial technology.

As a result of Steichen's experiences as airborne photographer during the war, his approach underwent change, also, toward sharper and less romantic images. He developed an interest in dynamic symmetry, a design formula which structured a number of his photographs. After 1923 Steichen concentrated on magazine and advertising commissions, revitalizing these photographically backward areas with his extraordinary technical skill and his talent for decorative design, as seen in *Gloria Swanson* (plate 425).

On the West Coast Cunningham and Weston continued their investigations of organic growth, often divorcing this matter from its context. Cunningham's sharply focused

images directed attention to shape, pattern, and texture with such intensity that, as in Georgia O'Keeffe's painting, these elements seem not to exist in the world of mundane experience. Weston, in Mexico between 1923 and 1927, at first portrayed human expression in similar terms, but soon began to concentrate on isolated objects in such manner that their reality became subsumed in another form. Back in California, he chose easily accessible and common materials—household utensils, vegetables, shells—from which he fashioned striking images. Objects such as *Chambered Nautilus* (plate 426) create tension between the thing itself and abstract design qualities through Weston's fastidious control of lighting and composition. The salient features of the decade—geometric and natural form, close up and in sharp focus—characterized the work of a number of other photographers, including Paul Outerbridge (1896–1959), as in his *Crankshaft* (plate 427), and were summed up in the 1929 *Film und Foto* exhibition, held in Stuttgart, Germany. Organized by Steichen and Weston, who also wrote the catalog, it included all the major figures in American art photography in the twenties, with the exception of Stieglitz and Strand.

Toward the end of the decade new perceptions of industrial power became apparent. The shift in visual emphasis is seen in the output of young photographers, especially Margaret Bourke-White (1904–1971) and

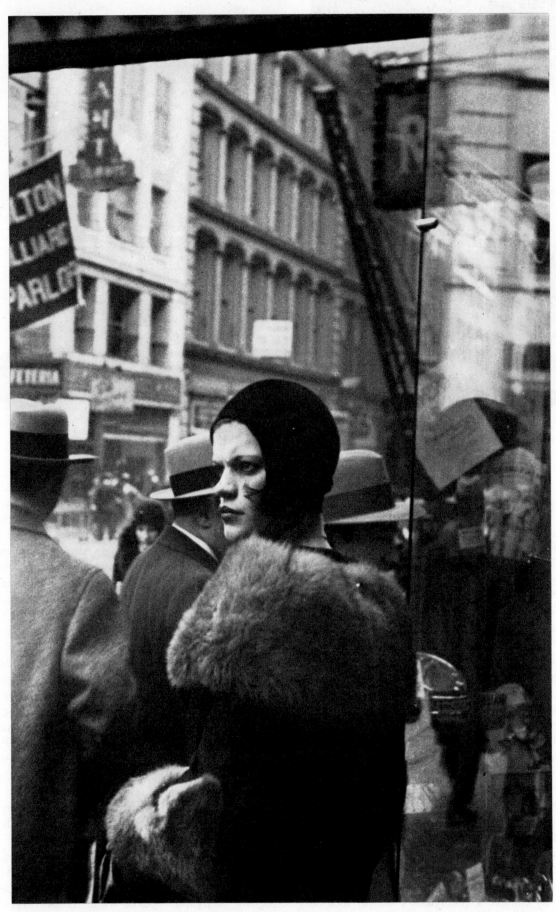

428 Walker Evans. *Girl on Fulton Street*. 1929.
     The Estate of Walker Evans, Bethany, Conn.

Ralph Steiner (b.1899). While still concerned with the machine, their work stresses the energy and tension associated with industrial power, rather than geometric design and rationalism. At the same time, the development of the 35-mm., eye-level camera and faster lenses, shutters, and film speeds changed the nature of photographic imagery. It enabled photographers to discover "the decisive moment"—when unexpected visual congruities reveal significant moods and meanings. In this manner, Walker Evans (1903–1975) captured the tense complexion of urban life in the facial expression, gesture, and window reflections of *Girl on Fulton Street* (plate 428). Evans, who returned to the United States from Paris in 1927, at first worked with a small camera in opposition to what he considered the artistic affectations of Stieglitz and Steichen. His subject matter—billboards, gas stations, Coney Island—reflects his awareness of native culture and points a direction for photography (and the other arts) during the thirties.

From the Stuttgart exhibition it was obvious that, unlike their European counterparts, most Americans were not interested in experimenting with extreme avant-garde imagery. Other than those living in Europe, few made completely abstract images, either with a camera or as photograms, using only the play of light on a sensitized surface. By the twenties, Coburn, who had created *Vortograph* (plate 429) in England in 1917 by photographing through a kaleidoscope, had virtually stopped experimenting. In the mid-twenties, Francis Bruguière (1880–1945), a theatrical photographer who spent considerable time abroad, worked on cut-paper arrangements which he photographed in varied illumination, producing images such as *The Heart Rejoices on Release* (plate 430). Man Ray (1890–1976), who made his home in Paris, was absorbed by photograms, which he called "rayographs." He continued experiments with cameraless images, solarization, and other technical extensions at the same time that he made straight portraits and created surrealist imagery. Before World War II surrealism was of even less interest in this country than abstraction although George Platt Lynes produced some neo-Romantic photographs which appear similar in mood. In Europe, Max Ernst, Hannah Hoch, and John Heartfield were using photomontage and combining graphic and photographic imagery with compelling effect, but this direction held no attraction in America at that time.

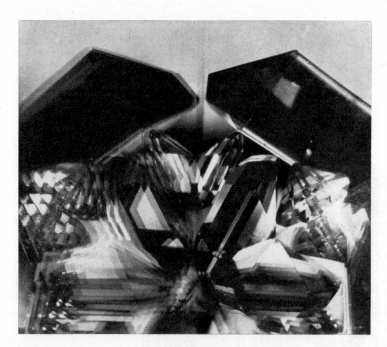

429 Alvin Langdon Coburn. *Vortograph*. 1917. International Museum of Photography at the George Eastman House, Rochester, N.Y.

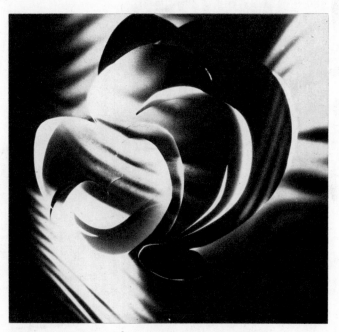

430 Francis Bruguière. *The Heart Rejoices on Release*. c. 1925. International Museum of Photography at the George Eastman House, Rochester, N.Y.

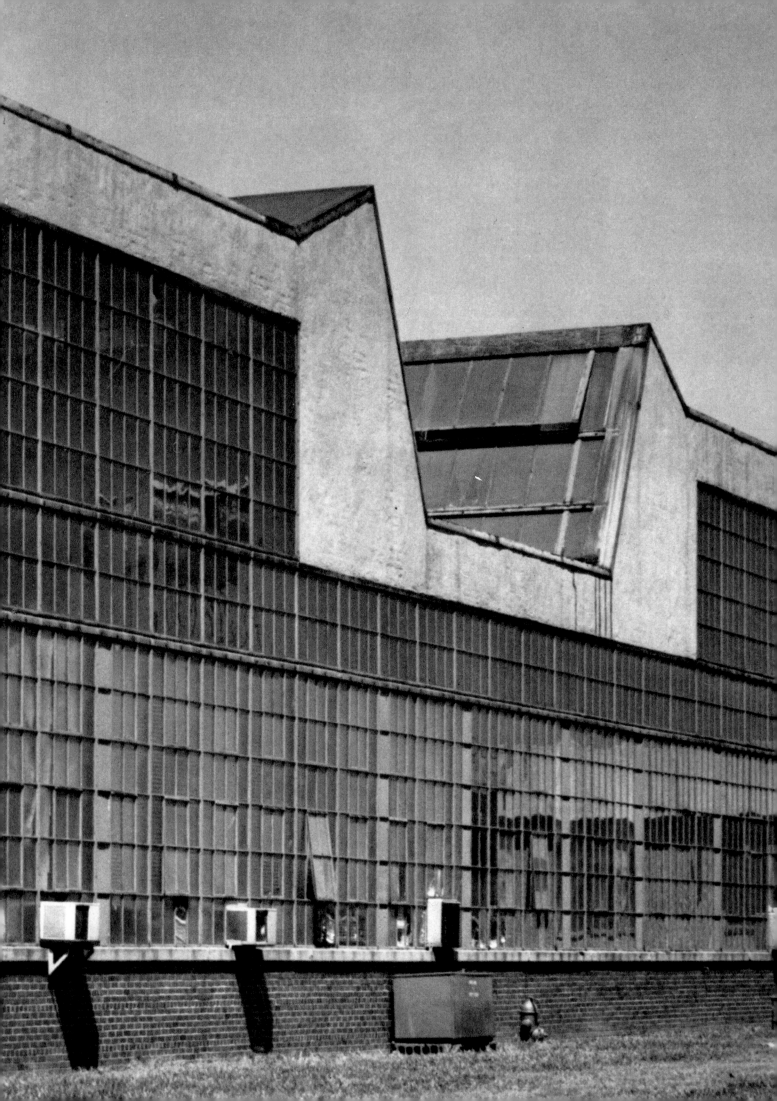

Part 6
BETWEEN WORLD WARS

Architecture in America between the great wars has yet to receive adequate recognition. In the twenties and thirties the activity followed the pioneer innovations in structure and design (both commercial and residential) and preceded the universal acceptance and institutionalization of the modern idiom that finally occurred in the late forties. As a period it is overshadowed in worldwide perspective by the extraordinary achievements of the new architecture in Europe, which came to be known as the International Style. This revolutionary movement was destined to establish, to all intents and purposes, the distinctive vocabulary and syntax of subsequent twentieth-century architecture. Hence this era in American design coincides with, and is largely eclipsed by, the early maturity of the great European innovators—among them, Le Corbusier, Mies van der Rohe, and Gropius—several of whom migrated to the United States toward the end of the period, seeking refuge from political circumstances that made it impossible to continue work in their homelands.

These bellwethers of the "International" architecture advocated a reductive, cubic geometry (its forms largely inspired by the new abstract painting as well as by the early domestic work of Wright), of glass walls and concealed supports that gave a sense of weightlessness and transparency to the structure. This vocabulary made only a sporadic and inconclusive appearance on these shores prior to the arrival of Gropius and Mies van der Rohe in the late 1930s—and even then radical modernism remained a minority movement for another decade.

As for painting, the Armory Show had put the custodians of orthodoxy on the defensive, but the unforeseen attention focused on European innovation at the expense of native art was the signal for a retreat from internationalism. The contagious idealism kindled during the early Stieglitz period was somehow mislaid in the war. The high expectations of one generation were exchanged for the caution and skepticism of another. Randolph Bourne wrote bitterly but prophetically in his war diary in 1917: "The war . . . or American promise. One must choose. . . . For the effect of the war will be to impoverish the American promise."

In the twenties a new mood of disenchantment set in, and the positive and experimental side of modernism no longer served as a summons to action for young American artists. They were no longer concerned with testing themselves by European standards, by the aesthetic criteria of a culture that the war had convinced them was in its decline. Interest in the American scene as a reassuring source of common experience revived, but often with a new addiction to its grotesque aspects. The experimental spirit lost momentum and its collective hold on many artists. Modernism became a shallow affair, a matter of imitative clichés easily mastered and as easily discarded. In the conservative interregnum between 1920 and 1940, the Armory Show, on the whole, lost its powers as a catalyst for artistic change. A few of its converts to modernism remained steadfast, however, and building on a legacy handed on by Stieglitz as well, they courageously fashioned their own distinctive native styles within the broad framework of modernist art in the decade that followed.

Much of the impact of modernist style on taste was felt in the field of decoration, bringing about a transformation in the design of utilitarian objects. In the applied arts a kind of debased currency of modernism flooded the marketplace and made the new forms of art common and welcome. It is still a question, however, whether the basic sentiment of modernity, as an unceasing quest for new freedoms of expression, today disturbs the lay public any less than it did in 1913.

18
Architecture, American Style, 1920–45

In the twenties and thirties American architecture pursued an unsteady course, either employing a variety of historical and traditional modes or, often no more logically, introducing modernistic features without getting to the root of the construction problems and social issues that were the concerns of the new European architecture.

Frank Lloyd Wright, whose earlier Prairie Houses were a crucial formative influence on the new European architects of the 1920s, was frequently sarcastic, or bluntly hostile, when speaking of the early works of the International Style. Subsequently he relented to the point of incorporating some of its effects in later work such as Falling Water of 1936. The only major innovator of 1900 to survive as an active designer, he seemed even more isolated than before—cut off from most of his professional colleagues because of his convictions, and hardly in touch with that handful of others who were separately seeking a path toward architectural reform. Beginning with the Barnsdall (Hollyhock) House, Los Angeles (c. 1917–20, plates 431, 432), Wright opted for a personal reinterpretation of traditional adobe shapes of the Southwest and found inspiration in the generous, massive forms of the pre-Columbian architecture of Central America. The resulting ponderous volumes seem reactionary in view of the equally simple but open, largely transparent geometry then being introduced in Europe. But Wright's California mode, further developed in a series of concrete-block houses, was original; it grew out of his concern with the southern California landscape and its indigenous architecture.

Southern California was the locale of other progressive architects at this time. The young Viennese architect Rudolph M. Schindler (1887–1953), who had been trained at the Vienna Academy by Otto Wagner, was left in charge during Wright's trips to Japan to supervise the construction of the Imperial Hotel. Schindler's own concerns for the architecture of the Southwest (he had been to Taos in 1915) might even have stimulated his employer's interests in native American prototypes. However, Schindler and Wright grew apart by the early

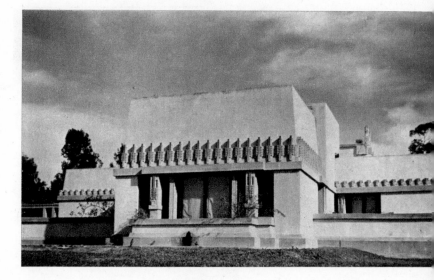

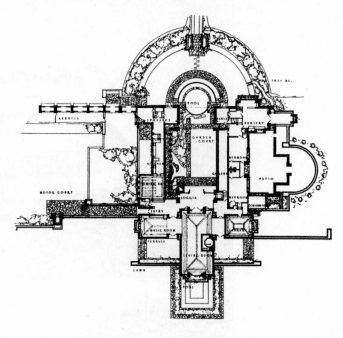

431, 432 Frank Lloyd Wright. Barnsdall (Hollyhock) House, Los Angeles. Exterior and plan. c. 1917–20

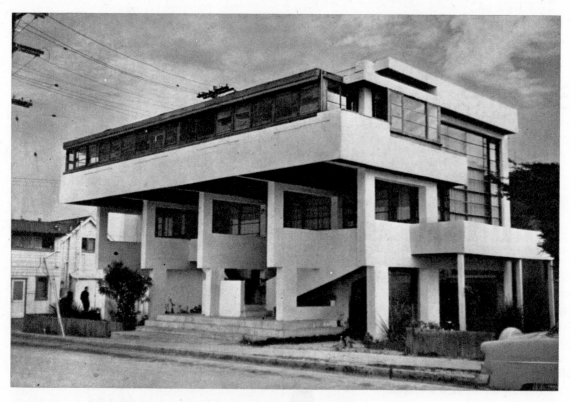

433 Rudolph M. Schindler. Lovell House, Newport Beach, Calif. 1925–26

434 Richard Neutra. Lovell House, Griffith Park, Los Angeles. 1929

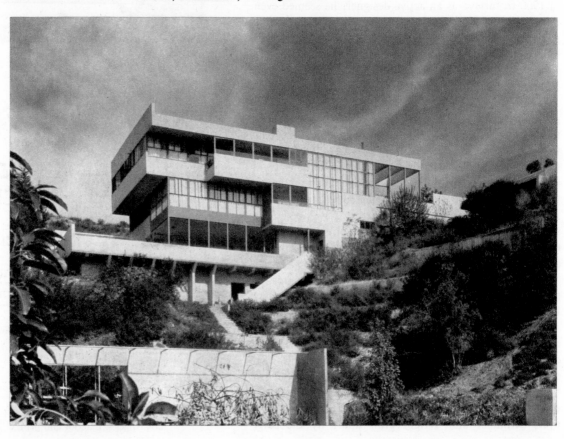

twenties, perhaps with some ill feeling, and each went his separate way; their failure to make a common cause was typical of the time and place.

Schindler's Lovell House, Newport Beach, Calif. (1925–26, plate 433), was the earliest masterpiece of the new International Style on American shores, its openness and structural delicacy the antithesis of Wright's surprisingly ponderous works of the period. Perched within an open concrete frame, and featuring a two-story living room with a floor-to-ceiling glass wall at one end, it was an original transcription of many new characteristics of European architecture: hovering, cantilevered volumes, white stucco or concrete surfaces, and a general aura of functional transparency. Schindler remained alone in his efforts, however, save for the arrival of another Viennese, Richard Neutra (1892–1970), in 1925. They maintained an informal partnership for a brief period and submitted a project for the League of Nations competition in 1926, but their association (apparently also their friendship) was ruptured when Neutra was chosen to build the second Lovell House on the side of a steep ravine in Griffith Park, Los Angeles (1929, plate 434). Neutra displayed an intimate knowledge of International Style aesthetics in his design of a complex, multilevel steel-framed house with large strips and curtains of glass, reproducing the characteristic fragility of the new European mode.

Neutra was kept busy during the thirties with the construction of houses and apartments in and around Los Angeles, and some of his finest, most delicately structured houses date from the late 1940s.

If southern California then seemed the most fertile area of architectural experiment, especially on the domestic level, professional action was still concentrated in the Middle West and East, chiefly in Chicago and New York. The episode in skyscraper design that took place is generally treated in a negative fashion, compared unfavorably either to the works of the early pioneers of 1900 or to the institutionalized modernism of the fifties and sixties. The key event at the beginning of the period was the international competition in 1922 for the Chicago Tribune Tower. It is customary to deplore the winning and executed design in the Gothic mode (plate 435), by John Mead Howells and Raymond M. Hood (1881–1934), and to cite as superior either the second-place design—a more delicately applied Gothic upon an unquestionably finer mass—by the Finnish architect Eliel Saarinen, or the uncompromisingly contemporary idiom of the entry submitted by Walter Gropius and Adolf Meyer. Critics have tended to look not too inquisitively at the 263 entries, featuring the usual mixture of competence, mediocrity, and sheer hokum, thereby overlooking the trend of the jury's preference. The first three designs as well as a number of honorable mentions were slanted toward the Gothic. The remainder of honorable mentions went to mildly modernistic designs that sug-

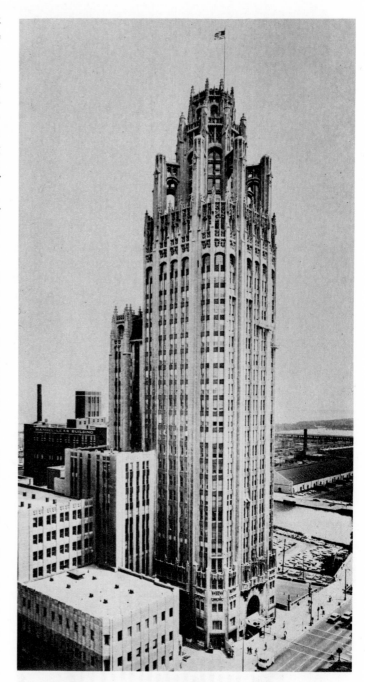

435 John Mead Howells and Raymond Hood. Chicago Tribune Tower. 1922-25

gested a kind of "invisible" Gothic ancestry. Classicizing and Renaissance-inspired projects were passed over almost uniformly.

Interestingly, Wright did not enter the competition; neither he nor Sullivan was among the list of ten invited architects. The buildings that were to grow out of the Tribune Tower competition were devoid of contact with the older Chicago School, and a case can be made for tracing their genealogy back to the New York skyscrapers of the late nineteenth century. (Midwestern tradition seemed momentarily moribund, but its char-

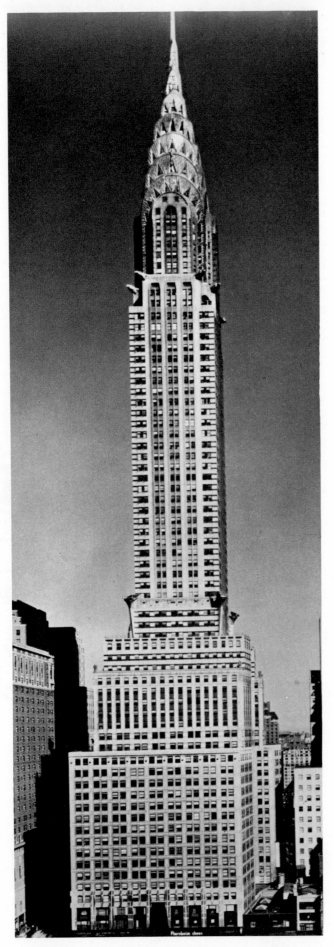

436 William van Alen. Chrysler Building, New York. 1930

acteristics were to reappear a generation later when American architects took up the manner of a German architect, resident for the second half of his working life in Chicago: Mies van der Rohe.)

Although the Tribune Tower as executed was a fairly explicit Gothic design, it was clear from a variety of competition projects that the more thoughtful designers were exploring means of getting beyond the pitfalls of a literally historicizing image. Nonetheless, the obvious appropriateness of Gothic verticality was maintained, and within a decade Hood had designed the New York Daily News Building as a planar shaft with continuous vertical window strips, avoiding literal historical reference but retaining a medieval underlay. Thus the Gothic skyscraper, with its inherent flaws and iconographic illogic, was a progenitor of this modernistic style, which provided in rapid succession in New York the two tallest skyscrapers after the Woolworth: the Chrysler (1930, plate 436), by William van Alen (1,048 feet to the top of its spire); and the Empire State (1931, plate 437), by Shreve, Lamb & Harmon (1,250 feet to the top of the original tower).

The Chrysler and the Empire State were long deprecated by critics and historians who measured stylistic accomplishment largely by European developments, but, partly because of the chic attributed to this bygone era by Pop artists in the 1960s, these buildings have now attained serious status. The highly original spires, functioning as did the Gothic octagon on the Tribune Tower but in a manner more consistent with the main body of the shaft, are seen today as decisive additions to the skyline in a metropolis where the sheer tower with flat deck (or simulation of same) has become the rule. Once ridiculed, the step-back ziggurat silhouette imposed upon so many Manhattan commercial blocks by zoning regulations, and rendered in sublime chiaroscuro in the imaginary projects of Hugh Ferriss (plate 438), one of the most sought-after architectural delineators of the era, currently seems to be a fortuitous virtue of an earlier day. When stylized in the elevations of the various buildings of Rockefeller Center (1931–40, plate 439, by Reinhard & Hofmeister; Corbett, Harrison & Mac-Murray; Hood & Fouilhoux), it can be read as an element of futuristic design, giving the otherwise inert slab a dynamic, forward-moving quality to complement the bland repetitive verticals of the window embrasures. Or, handled in the manner of "industrial design" (the up-to-date packaging of radios, refrigerators, and other appliances), as in Raymond Hood's first McGraw-Hill Building (1931, plate 440), not just the spire but the whole structure becomes an Art Deco artifact. In its emphasis on horizontal rather than vertical window strips, separated by aquamarine tiles, McGraw-Hill seems to be an atypical reflection of European design formulas in a Manhattan skyscraper of the period.

Even more distinctively representative of International

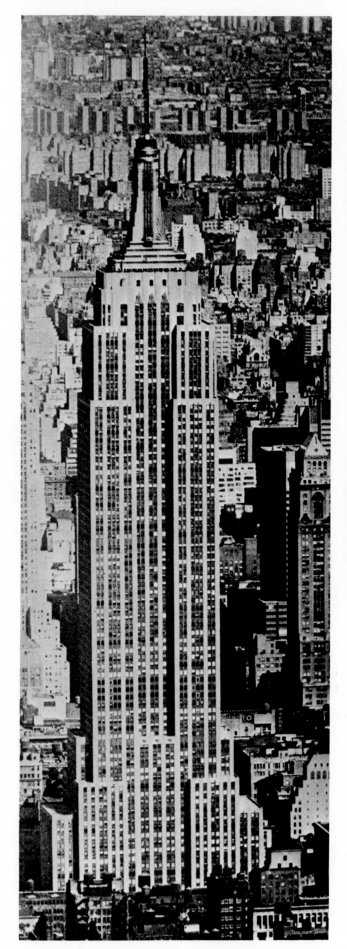

437 Shreve, Lamb & Harmon. Empire State Building,
New York. 1931

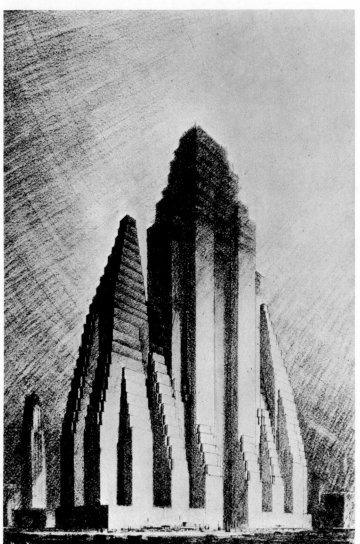

438 Hugh Ferriss. *The effect of zoning on skyscrapers.* 1929

tendencies is the Philadelphia Saving Fund Society
(PSFS) Building (1932, plate 441), by the firm of Howe
& Lescaze. Howe had previously been a partner in a
Philadelphia firm specializing in lush, evocative suburban
houses in a variety of provincial medieval modes, and
his young partner was a recent arrival from Switzerland.
Howe performed a dramatic turnabout with this unique
structure, which is more cosmopolitan than any other
American skyscraper before the late forties. The lower
portion, containing shops and the banking room, is
clearly differentiated from the office tower above; on
certain of its faces the window strips and structural
columns are constructed in an interwoven fashion that
goes deeper than the "industrial design" look of many
buildings of the day. Other features, however, such as the
curving wall just above street level, are reminders of the
characteristic streamlining of the 1930s.

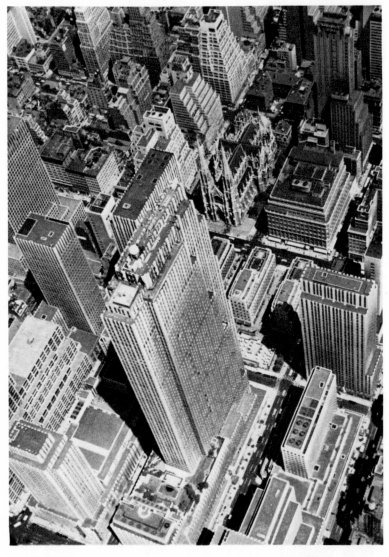

439 Reinhard & Hofmeister; Corbett, Harrison & Macmurray;
Hood & Fouilhoux. Rockefeller Center, New York. 1931–40

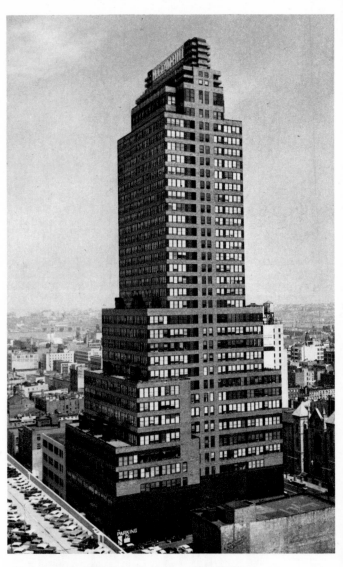

440 Raymond Hood. Former McGraw-Hill Building,
New York. 1931

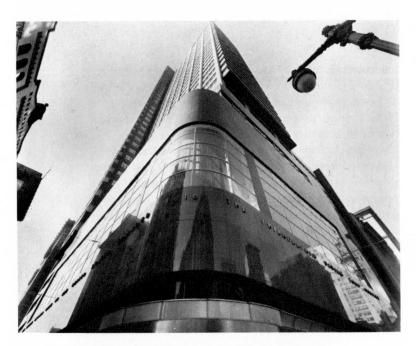

441 George Howe and William Lescaze. Philadelphia Saving
Fund Society (PSFS) Building, Philadelphia. 1932

Industrial design—the adaptation of streamline, tear-drop, airflow forms to factory products, household artifacts, furnishings, shop fronts, not to mention automobile, train, and aircraft design—is one of the most important visual developments of the 1930s. As a movement it seems to have been generated spontaneously in the work of Norman Bel Geddes, Raymond Loewy, Henry Dreyfuss, and Walter Dorwin Teague. Functional as streamlined forms may have been in airplane design of the thirties—in the revolutionary development of the low-wing monoplane—these shapes were primarily decorative insignia when adapted to auto designs such as the Chrysler "Airflow" or Lincoln "Zephyr," or locomotive designs such as the sleek casings (largely unrelated to the inner workings) of the New York Central or Pennsylvania Railroad steam engines of the day. No more functional in the same sense were the wraparound, chrome-trimmed forms of modernistic furniture.

(continued on page 414)

The term "Art Deco" has become associated with the broad interest in overall or "total" design. That is, every aspect of an Art Deco building was treated by the designer: furniture, draperies, and even doorknobs. Modernity for its own sake and an aesthetic of the machine look were the order of the day, often with emphasis on geometric shapes. Sunburst patterns, lightning ziggurats, and, after the opening of King Tutankhamen's tomb in 1923, formalized Egyptian forms were popular ornamental devices. Donald Deskey, the designer of the interior of Radio City Music Hall in New York, commented on the influence of Expo '25, the exhibition of decorative arts in Paris, on the ornamentation of every available surface, and on the influence of the French: Poiret, Lalique, and Sonia Delaunay. Through the 1920s most American manufacturers were still producing machine-made reproductions of period furniture. Radio City Music Hall and its furniture reflect the Art Deco style and the accompanying interest in theme. The women's lounge (plate 442) is only one of the thirty-one smoking rooms and lounges throughout the building that Deskey planned. Themes such as "Men Without Women" or "A History of Cosmetics" were used, with murals by such artists as the young Yasuo Kuniyoshi, and paintings, furniture, and even lighting fixtures were coordinated in color scheme and design. "Machine" shapes predominate on couches, chairs, and tables, and glittering brash colors complement the materials: aluminum, Bakelite, Formica, patent leather, and chrome-plated steel.

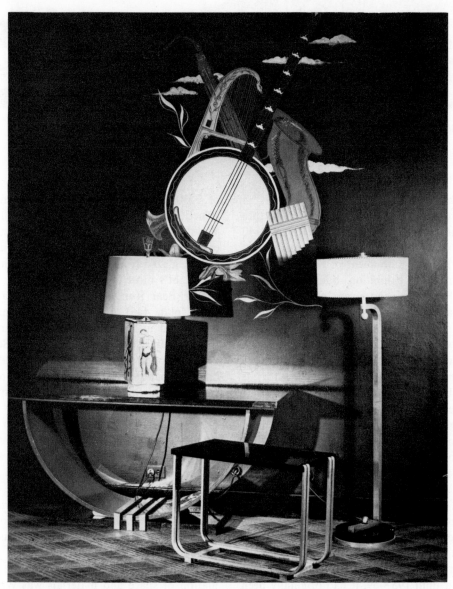

442 Donald Deskey.
Women's lounge,
Radio City Music Hall,
New York. 1932

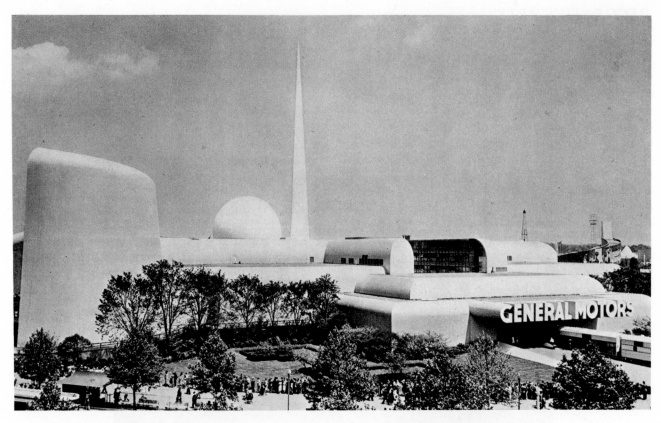

443 New York World's Fair. 1939–40

(continued from page 412)

The impact of the streamline movement in architecture was heaviest at the New York World's Fair of 1939–40 (plate 443), after which its influence was largely spent. In the (temporary) theme monument of the Trylon and Perisphere and in such exhibition buildings as the General Motors Futurama, conceived by Norman Bel Geddes, it found an appropriate vehicle.

Wright's major commercial commission of this period, the Johnson Wax Building, Racine, Wisc. (1936–39, plate 444), comes within a hairbreadth of inclusion in the streamline movement. The stylistic inspiration for its brick and glass-tube sheath is, however, almost certainly the German Expressionist manner of Erich Mendelsohn. The smooth, angle-avoiding surfaces of the building, both inside and out, are quite different from Wright's earlier compositional features, and the circle and its segments became one of the standard design alternatives in his later work. The concept of the Guggenheim Museum, New York (plate 445), with its continuous ramp spiraling around a circular light well, the space literally reproduced in the shape of the exterior, is a logical outgrowth of the fluent spaces and continuous enclosing surfaces of Johnson Wax. Although the museum was not built until 1957–59, it had originally been designed in 1943. Consequently, it is as much an offshoot

of 1930s modernism as it is a contemporary (in construction) of that architectural development after World War II which featured the extensive use of massive concrete forms to create dense volumes, in reaction to the brittle, glazed transparency of the earlier postwar mode.

Wright's most famous house of the period is Falling Water, Bear Run, Pa., built for Edgar Kaufmann, Sr. (1936, plate 446). A house of many balconies, it can be interpreted as a further elaboration and exploration of the tray and shelflike theme of the Schindler and the Neutra Lovell houses. The clear, pale surfaces of the balcony parapets seem to be appropriated from the International Style, but the dynamic interpenetration of volumes and voids could derive either from that source or from Wright's earlier work. Wright himself correctly pointed out the similarity of mass between Falling Water and a house in Oak Park, Ill., built a quarter-century earlier. Characteristically, he followed the main line of American naturalism in siting the house on a ravine above a stream so that the flowing water seems completely integrated in the architect's design. Moreover, the balconies on the downstream side are placed so as to echo the rock ledges over which the stream cascades.

The most remarkable essay of the period in the manipulation of space and materials was Wright's own winter residence and studio, Taliesin West, Scottsdale, Ariz.,

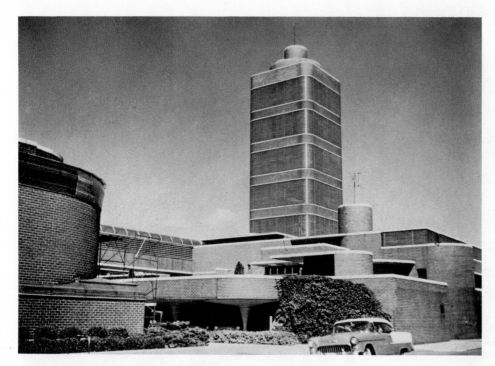

444 Frank Lloyd Wright. Johnson Wax Building, 1936–39, and Research Tower, 1946–49, Racine, Wis.

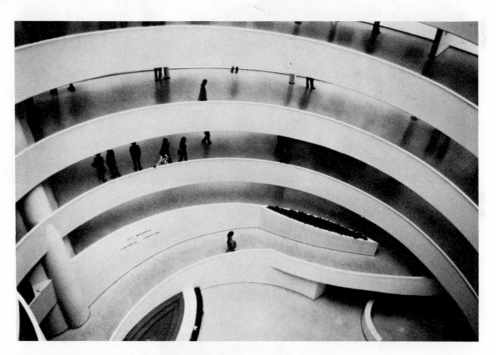

445 Frank Lloyd Wright. The Solomon R. Guggenheim Museum, New York. Interior. Designed 1943; constructed 1957–59

begun in 1938 (plate 447). There he created an oasis in the desert, the raked slope of the roofs and the battered, rough masonry walls echoing the backdrop of the mountains. In plan (plate 448), with its varying intersecting angles, Taliesin West shows another option that Wright introduced into his later domestic work. This desert retreat is the most personal of all Wright's works, a striking contrast to the cosmopolitan mien of Falling Water or Johnson Wax.

In the light of subsequent events, Falling Water, with its integration of several modernist traditions, seems to have signaled a welcome for the arrival of the several distinguished European designers, led by Gropius and Mies van der Rohe, who were to continue and conclude their careers in the New World. Preceding them by a decade was Eliel Saarinen (1873–1950), recipient of second prize in the Tribune Tower competition, who brought a turn-of-the-century romanticism prevalent in

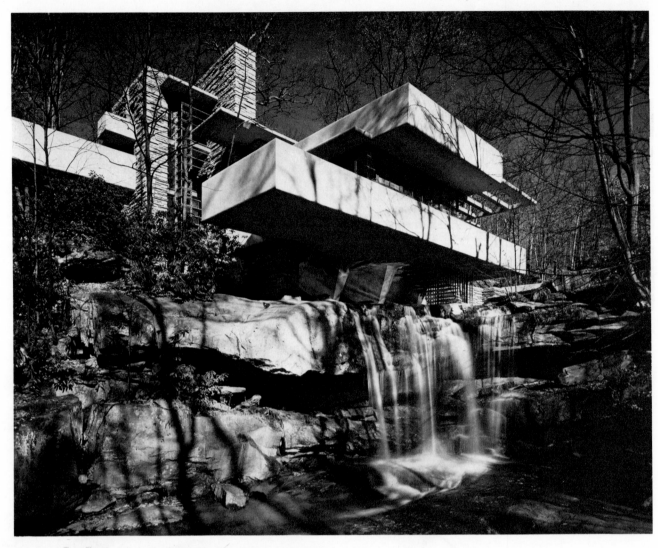

446 Frank Lloyd Wright. Falling Water,
Bear Run, Pa. 1936

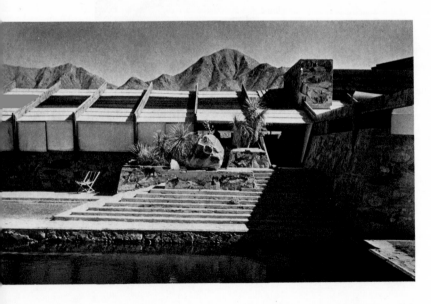

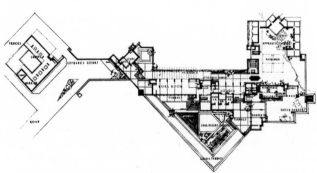

447, 448 Frank Lloyd Wright. Taliesin West, Scottsdale, Ariz.
Exterior and plan. 1938 to date

his native Finland (he had designed the Helsinki depot in 1904) to his work at Cranbrook School, Bloomfield Hills, Mich., beginning in 1925. Although never drawn to the austere purism of the International Style, Saarinen, whose son, Eero (1910–1961), became a prominent architect of the fifties, allowed his designs to take on a simpler, geometric cast toward the end of the thirties. Notable examples are churches at Columbus, Ind. (1940–42, plate 449), and Minneapolis (1949).

Leading architects, as well as mathematicians, physicists, and art historians, were fleeing Germany in the 1930s. In 1937 Walter Gropius (1883–1969) and Marcel Breuer (b. 1902)—who later formed a partnership for a few years—were brought to Harvard to reform the curriculum; among their students who were to become leaders of the profession were Philip Johnson (b. 1906) and Paul Rudolph (b. 1918). That same year László Moholy-Nagy (1895–1946), the versatile Bauhaus designer and teacher, moved to Chicago to teach at the short-lived New Bauhaus. Ludwig Mies van der Rohe (1886–1969) arrived in Chicago in 1938 to take charge of the architectural department at Illinois Institute of Technology (formerly the Armour Institute). The Expressionist architect Erich Mendelsohn (1887–1953) arrived in 1941, after stays in England and Palestine, to settle in San Francisco and teach for a brief period at Berkeley.

Parenthetically, the emergence of a Bay Region school of architects about 1940 should be noted. Rooted in the romantic wood-framed houses of Bernard Maybeck (1862–1957) or Greene & Greene, and represented by architects such as William W. Wurster (b. 1895), this trend, referred to as "organic" by some critics, largely ignored the precise geometries of the International Style in favor of refining and modernizing an indigenous vernacular tradition.

For a short time before America's entrance into World War II, Gropius and Breuer were active as designers of small houses around Boston and Cambridge. In addition to houses for themselves was one for James Ford at Lincoln, Mass. (1939, plate 450). In these works the crisp contours and clear surfaces of Bauhaus styling, originally worked out in concrete and stucco, were transposed into wood-framed houses with flush vertical siding, the whole painted white.

Ludwig Mies van der Rohe's first works in America were altogether different, even though their roots in Europe were identical to those of Gropius, and in the long run Mies was to have a greater impact as a designer upon the future course of architecture. In 1939 he was asked to produce a master plan for Illinois Institute of Technology (plate 451), and over the course of the next decade and a half he built a number of buildings on the site, including a power house, a chapel, several classroom and laboratory structures, and Crown Hall, a vast open glazed space that served as the School of Architecture (plate 452). The timing of this project, its distinctive

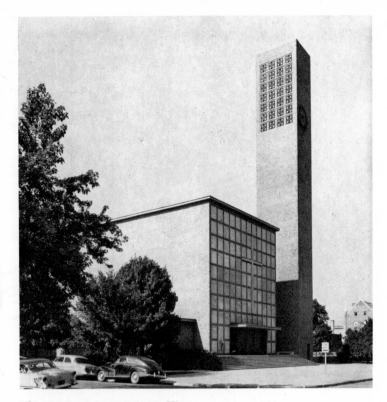

449 Eliel Saarinen and Eero Saarinen. Church of Christ, Columbus, Ind. 1940–42

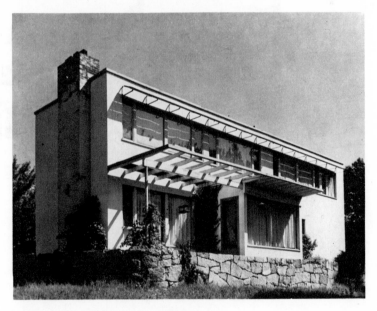

450 Walter Gropius and Marcel Breuer. James Ford House, Lincoln, Mass. 1939

characteristics, and the fact that some of the buildings were actually completed during the war placed Mies conspicuously in the forefront of architectural design, especially in its nondomestic aspect, soon after the end of hostilities. By the early 1950s he was recognized everywhere as the leader of the new American design and the ultimate heir of the Chicago School.

Mies's adaptation and regularization of the International Style saw the elimination of its active, dynamic, irregular aspects. In place of unstable geometries, inter-

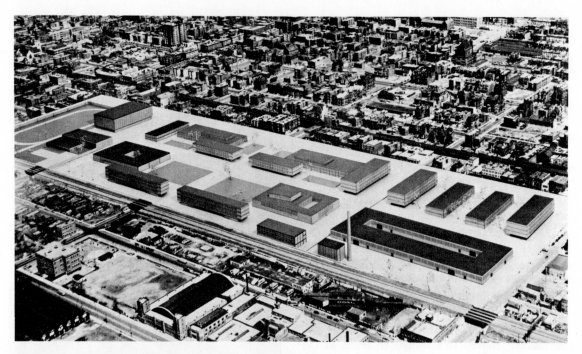

451 Ludwig Mies van der Rohe. Second, definitive scheme for the
Illinois Institute of Technology, Chicago. Aerial view. 1940 (only partially completed)

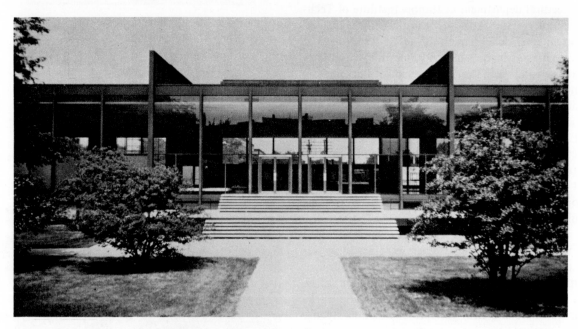

452 Ludwig Mies van der Rohe. Crown Hall (School of Architecture),
Illinois Institute of Technology, Chicago. 1952–56

locking spaces, and narrow, unaccented contours, he chose to design the campus on the basis of a regular, static square module. Working with predominantly low, horizontal masses, he created a bay system of equally expressive vertical supports with precise emphasis at the corners, contrasting with earlier tendencies to avoid a strong statement at the angles. The various rectangular cubes were arranged in an unobtrusive symmetry to form a series of partly enclosed courts, which, open at their angles, provided for an easy, unostentatious spatial flow. Regularity, repetition, linear precision, and structural clarity replaced the unstable elements of flux and even ambiguity characteristic of some of his earlier works in Europe. So neat was Mies's tying up of the International Style's loose ends that it seemed for a time as if he had led modernist architecture into a classicizing solution, in which further development would be based upon certain restricted canons of proportion, or upon the invention of subtle refinements in the balancing of structural and surface tensions.

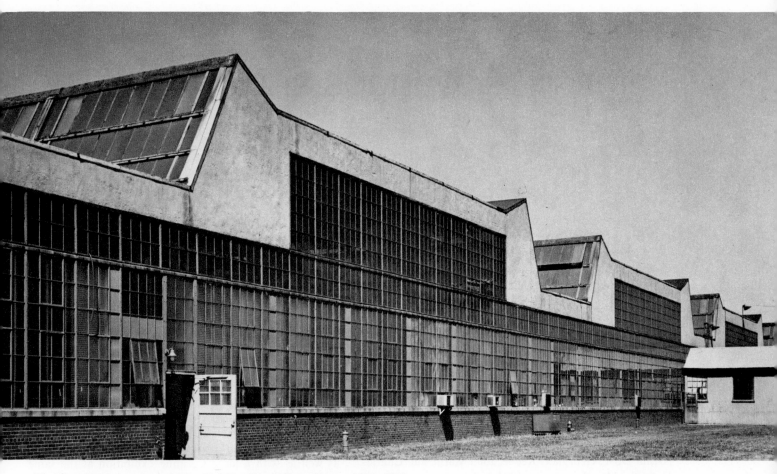

453 Albert Kahn Associates. Dodge Half-Ton Truck Plant, Warren, Mich. 1937

Although Mies's achievement in Americanizing the International Style to a degree undreamed of by a Neutra or a Gropius was largely the result of his own inner evolution, of his search for the best solution, his industrial style of steel, glass, and brick was anticipated in the numerous factories of the 1930s by the Detroit firm of Albert Kahn Associates. Kahn had one of the most typical, wide-ranging practices of any large, comprehensive architectural firm of the day. In 1917 he began the famed River Rouge plant for the Ford Motor Company; he also specialized in neo-Gothic and neo-Georgian mansions for industry executives in nearby Grosse Pointe and other exclusive suburbs; and numerous banks and office buildings, classicizing as well as Gothicizing, in downtown Detroit. Kahn Associates' various factories of the late 1930s, notably those for General Motors and the Chrysler Corporation (plate 453), exhibit a refined precision of architectural detail that is remarkable for the period, and is surely a source for the Miesian

style that would be adapted to downtown skyscrapers by 1950.

The interwar period thus ends with the transfusion of a still evolving European mode into the mainstream of progressive American architecture, which previously had seen this work chiefly in southern California. Equal with—certainly not unrelated to—this phenomenon were Wright's reassertion of his genius and his emphasis upon the organic, nature-oriented, antiurban aspects of his buildings and philosophy—in contrast to the industrial, technological, city-oriented architecture of Mies. These two developments emerged when the indigenous modernism of American commercial design of the twenties and thirties was declining in importance, mainly because of the paucity of building commissions during the Depression. Neither this native commercial style nor its corollary, the streamline industrial design celebrated at the New York World's Fair of 1939–40, survived the period of inactivity caused by World War II.

19
Painting: Advances and Retreats

Even before World War I a number of American artists had begun to develop consistently modern styles from their contact with advanced Parisian painting, at first through study abroad and then at home under Stieglitz's auspices. Their painting spans a long and often contradictory period, from the lusty birth of innovation before the war, through the virtual extinction of the modernist impulse in the late twenties and the thirties, to the emergence of a new generation of abstractionists in the early forties. In the prevailing climate of artistic conservatism after the war, many painters (and sculptors too) succumbed to less demanding representational styles.

The central figures among those who contributed to the first flowering of experimental art on native grounds were Alfred Maurer, Max Weber, Marsden Hartley, Arthur Dove, Georgia O'Keeffe, John Marin, and Charles Demuth. Maurer, who by 1904 had become a welcome visitor in the Paris apartment of Gertrude and Leo Stein, was certainly one of the first Americans to react favorably to the new European art. In 1908 his rather fashionable salon-painting manner, which took its cue from Sargent and from Maurer's American teacher, William Merritt Chase, had begun to change under the influence of Matisse's Fauve painting. Maurer was probably introduced to Matisse's new style through the Steins, who had begun to collect the French artist's work after the Autumn Salon of 1905, where the Fauves had first exhibited together. Max Weber and Patrick Henry Bruce joined Matisse's first painting class as did Arthur Dove, who arrived in Paris in 1907. Dove and Arthur B. Carles both probably became aware of new currents in painting through Maurer.

MAX WEBER

It was perhaps Max Weber (1881–1961) who in the beginning best understood, and conveyed with a sense of passionate conviction, the new European sense of art, in both his paintings and his declarations. Through the first two decades of his art he showed the kind of professionalism in medium and the instinctive grasp of formal principle that had traditionally been associated with art emanating from Paris. If, in retrospect, his career seems marked by eclecticism and a constant shifting of aesthetic ground, he nevertheless provided an example of seriousness in painting that made more consistent talents seem less adventurous or ambitious.

Weber was born in Russia and emigrated to America with his family at the age of ten. His artistic education began at the Pratt Institute in Brooklyn, when he took Arthur Wesley Dow's popular composition course. Dow was a pioneer of the new passion for Oriental art, and his interest in the decorative styles of Japanese art and in a non-naturalistic use of color, as exemplified by Gauguin and the Nabis, made him an enlightened and vital teacher. By 1905 Weber had managed to put aside sufficient funds to go to Paris. His arrival coincided with the public debut of Matisse and the other Fauve painters, as well as with a large Cézanne exhibition at the same celebrated Autumn Salon. By 1908 Cézanne had become the acknowledged inspiration of the early Cubist paintings of Picasso and Braque. That year Weber came directly into contact with the new French painting when he enrolled in Matisse's private *Académie*. He rounded out his catholic but coherent range of artistic influence with the primitive painter Henri Rousseau, whom he had come to know rather intimately before his return to America at the end of the year.

The combined influences of Cézanne, Matisse, Rousseau, and Cubism were to shape Weber's early style. Yet, such influences were little in evidence when he held his first American one-man show early in 1909. In the fall of that year he met Alfred Stieglitz and went to live for a brief period in a room adjoining "291," where he assisted Stieglitz in hanging his shows. In 1910 he was included in "291's" show "Younger American Painters," which provoked the first press attacks on the emerging American vanguard and marked the beginning of a series of bellicose deprecations that greeted Weber's successive exhibitions. At the time, the artist's interests were widening in line with the new aesthetic viewpoints he had absorbed abroad. Perhaps it was Picasso's Negro period that drove him to investigate Mayan and Aztec sculpture, the totems of Pacific Indians, and other examples of primitive art in New York's Museum of Natural History.

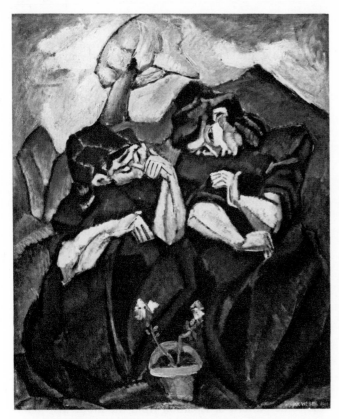

454 Max Weber. *The Geranium*. 1911. Oil on canvas, 39⅞ × 32¼″. The Museum of Modern Art, New York. Acquired through the Lillie P. Bliss Bequest

455 Max Weber. *Beautification*. 1942. Oil on canvas, 36 × 28″. Whereabouts unknown

Weber also began to contribute articles to *Camera Work* on the relevance of primitive cultures to modern sensibility, and with considerable eloquence he set forth his views on the dynamic new spatial concepts underlying the Cubist movement. In an article of July, 1910, entitled "The Fourth Dimension from a Plastic Point of View," he wrote: "In plastic art there is a fourth dimension which may be described as the last consciousness of a great and overwhelming sense of space-magnitude in all directions at the same time." In European art, of course, the ecstatic discovery of the space-time continuum had become a common feature of many theoretical disquisitions on Cubist painting by Apollinaire, Metzinger, and others.

Between 1910 and 1912 Weber experimented with Cubist structure and composed more aggressively in sharply angled, geometric forms (plate 395). *The Geranium* (1911, plate 454) shows a fine understanding of early Cubism; the two compact female forms resemble Picasso's figuration of 1908 and 1909. Weber, however, achieved a distinctive personal variant on the style by synthesizing its formalism with Matisse's brilliant, sensuous palette. In the masks and resigned attitudes of his figures there are elements of caricature and a touch of poetic melancholy which bear the stamp of genuine artistic temperament. The rather tender and wistful characterization of the figures, for all their formalism, may have grown out of Weber's awareness of himself as a Jew, a consciousness of origins which played a large part

in his choice of themes in his later years.

The reactions of critics to Weber's new paintings, hung at "291" in his one-man show of 1911, were surprisingly vicious. One writer compared his forms to "the emanations of someone not in his right mind." Another was aghast at the artist's "brutal, vulgar and unnecessary display of art license." And still another wrote: "Such grotesquerie could only be acquired by long and perverse practice." Weber's melancholy, rather poetic version of Cubism provided one of the favorite whipping boys just prior to the Armory Show.

Weber's paintings of about 1915 presented his own unorthodox translation of current modes. His agitated evocations of New York (cf. plate 396) were concerned as much with emotion as with formal expression. Cubism was his point of departure, but his rapturous response to the pulse and visual brilliance of the city brought him closer to Futurism in a vocabulary of forms that exploited violent, kaleidoscopic effects, even suggesting a mood of apprehension.

In many of the paintings executed between 1915 and 1917, Weber communicated a new sense of release and excitement, even when his formal synthesis was perhaps strained by conflicting elements of movement and decoration. *Chinese Restaurant* (1915, colorplate 61) is one of the more ambitious American paintings in a period notable for boldly experimental work. While today it may be judged an uncertain artistic success because of its stylistic inconsistencies, it is still a convincing demonstration of a vital native assimilation of European aesthetics. On the one hand, the painting seems to be a venture in decorative Cubism, and its rich, ornamental surface and varied patterning can be related to collage. These effects, however, coexist with pockets of fluid, transparent space disclosing glimpses in shallow depth of the multiple images and fragmentary geometric structures derived from Analytical Cubism. On another plane, mobile visual sequences in shifting depth suggest the Futurist effort to capture kinetic sensations. Yet the picture has an undeniable impact, perhaps because it literally re-creates Weber's own impressions of the bizarre decor of his subject. "On entering a Chinese restaurant from the darkness . . . outside," he wrote, "a maze and blaze of light seemed to split into fragments the interior and its contents, the human and the inanimate. For the time being the static became transient and fugitive—oblique planes and contours took on vertical and horizontal positions, and the horizontal became oblique, the light so piercing and luminous, the color so liquid and the light and movement so enchanting! To express this, kaleidoscopic means had to be chosen."

After 1917, responding to the revival of interest in naturalism abroad, Weber began to incorporate more realistic descriptive detail into his painting, with some damaging disunity to his style. Caught in the aesthetic crosscurrents of the early twenties, he emulated Picasso's inflated Neoclassical style. Then he painted landscapes in a manner that combined the palette of Cézanne with a coarser pigment surface and Expressionist vehemence in handling. He became a lapidary of jeweled color and thick, shining paint paste, but much of his

originality and energy were lost, despite his skill in manipulating voluptuous surface.

In the forties, Weber painted more schematically in a thin fluid oil wash, taking his figure style perhaps from Picasso's *Guernica*, and lacing his overworked surfaces with a network of line. His subjects were often Hasidic scholars engaged in argument or moving in fantastic gyrations. He tried to strike a mystical note in themes of prayer and contemplation and in idyllic scenes of women singing, playing instruments, or tending themselves, as in *Beautification* (1942, plate 455), whose mood recalls Biblical scenes perhaps from *The Song of Songs*. His style became classic, representational, and mythic. Weber's late work is related only tenuously in character or quality to the achievement of *The Geranium, Chinese Restaurant*, or even to his Expressionist style of the early twenties.

MARSDEN HARTLEY

The paintings of Marsden Hartley (1887–1943) similarly show the generative powers of the first modern impulses received from Europe, and, with modifications, the same pattern of isolation from the modernist mainstream, compromise, and finally, a lapse into more comfortable personal stereotypes of both style and subject matter. Although he, too, felt the influence of Matisse and the Fauves, at least obliquely, his early work seemed conservative, close in spirit and technique to that of the traditional Italian Impressionist Giovanni Segantini, whose heavy impasto and stitchlike brushstroke Hartley adopted in landscapes of about 1908, when he lived in New York and summered in Maine. Vivid color touches, built up in assertive texture and relief, were used to capture the strength and intimacy of the Maine countryside, which Hartley loved and painted repeatedly throughout his life.

However, after his first one-man show with Stieglitz, the gallery owner managed to find formal values in Hartley's work consonant with the more adventurous painting of his other artists. Stieglitz commented in *Camera Work*: ". . . his interpretation of sky, mountains and woods in brilliant coloring is of a decorative rather than realistic effect." Some of the work exhibited at "291" had become more concentrated formally, unified around a style that suggested both the expressive, rhythmic brushwork of Van Gogh and the somber tonalities of Ryder.

Hartley went abroad in 1912, and there he began to experiment with Cubism. He loosened his Cubist structure, in response to the high-keyed colors and the more inspirational abstract art of Wassily Kandinsky and the members of The Blue Rider (*Der Blaue Reiter*). That same year, at the invitation of Franz Marc, he showed with The Blue Rider in the first German Autumn Salon in Berlin, organized by Herwarth Walden, editor of *Der Sturm* and an important early champion of modern art.

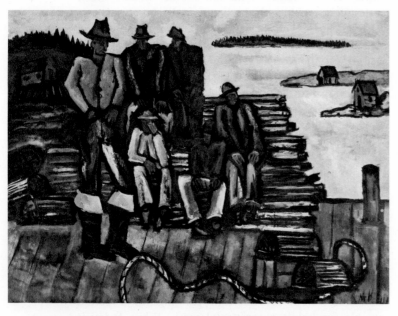

456 Marsden Hartley. *Lobster Fishermen.* 1940–41. Oil on composition board, 29¾ × 40⅞". The Metropolitan Museum of Art, New York. Arthur H. Hearn Fund, 1942

By 1914 Hartley had arrived at a personal synthesis of the emblematic insignia and ornament of decorative Cubism with the fluid movement and intense spectrum colors of Kandinsky's first abstract style. His *Portrait of a German Officer* (1914, colorplate 62) is bold and aggressive, incorporating references to German militarism in such repeated symbols as the military cross within a scheme of strident, primary color set off by irregular areas of flat black. Bright, bold, and deceptively simple, these works prefigure the "Pop" paintings of the 1960s, especially those of Robert Indiana.

The next year Hartley moved toward a new austerity and experimented with flat, slablike arrangements of rectilinear shapes, somewhat Constructivist in spirit. His palette was softened toward pastels and neutral hues, and he employed blander forms, held in subtle tension despite their drastic geometric simplicity. The very few of his paintings remaining from this brief period have an individuality in color and a most interesting balance of elegance with strength. They also indicate an assured grasp of abstract idioms that was soon to atrophy in the equivocal atmosphere of American art. Like Weber, Hartley was able for a short time to establish his integrity as an artist within the radical structural language of European abstraction. He expressed his emotions forcefully and with a distinction that eluded him in later years, when he found a more obviously personal artistic identity and worked with a simplified, decorative pictorial formula.

Following the general tendency of the twenties to return to the object and to nature, Hartley rediscovered Cézanne about 1926, a Cézanne, however, whose vibrancy and tenuousness he hardened into emphatic decoration and an enameled, facile coherence of form. Beginning in 1931 with his *Dogtown* landscapes painted in the vicinity of Gloucester, he worked in his own style of rugged Expressionism. *Lobster Fishermen* (1940–41, plate 456) was painted on the Northeast coast he liked to frequent, between Gloucester and Maine, in the heavily outlined, diagrammatic, and austere style of his later years. It is a work of power and an almost primitive simplicity.

Between 1908 and 1917, before he had resolved his period of experiment and begun to state too succinctly his rather circumscribed artistic personality, Hartley demonstrated his most impressive powers of invention.

ARTHUR DOVE

The performance of Arthur G. Dove (1880–1946) was more consistent, if apparently less ambitious, than either Hartley's or Weber's. Once he had arrived at his own pictorial language of abstraction, he pursued it to its radical conclusions and never recanted. In Europe between 1907 and 1909, Alfred Maurer and Arthur Carles had put Dove in contact with the work of the contem-

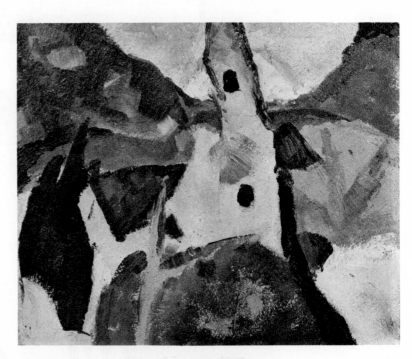

457 Arthur G. Dove. *Abstraction Number 1.* 1910.
Oil on composition board, 9 × 10½".
Courtesy Terry Dintenfass Gallery, New York

porary French vanguard. Back in America in 1910, he painted what was apparently the country's first entirely nonrepresentational painting, *Abstraction Number 1* (plate 457). It coincided in time with the first of Kandinsky's abstract paintings, although Dove's precocious discovery of abstraction now seems to have been fragmentary and perhaps inconclusive, since he did not develop a consistent nonobjective style in the years immediately following. In fact, it became clear that Dove, like Picasso and other modernists, was not interested in completely severing his links with nature, and his later abstraction always retained a condensed but recognizable imagery.

By 1915 Dove had firmly established himself in a painting genre of flowing, amorphous shapes, muted color, and repeated rhythmic accents. After that year his forms were related to the soft color masses of the Synchromists, to Kandinsky, and, more ancestrally, to the organic shapes of Gauguin and Art Nouveau. During his earliest phase, Dove painted in a restrained, monochromatic palette reinforced by sober earth colors. Later he showed a preference for more resonant tonalities but always retained neutrals, tans, and warm blacks as a foil for his intense hues. Like the early Kandinsky of 1910–14, Dove used colors and forms to suggest an attenuation of naturalistic shapes and a diffusion of local colors taken from actual scenes. Although he abstracted his landscape impressions, his organic forms constantly evoked nature, analogically if not more directly. As he said: "I should like to take wind and water and sand as a motif and work with them, but it has to be simplified in most cases

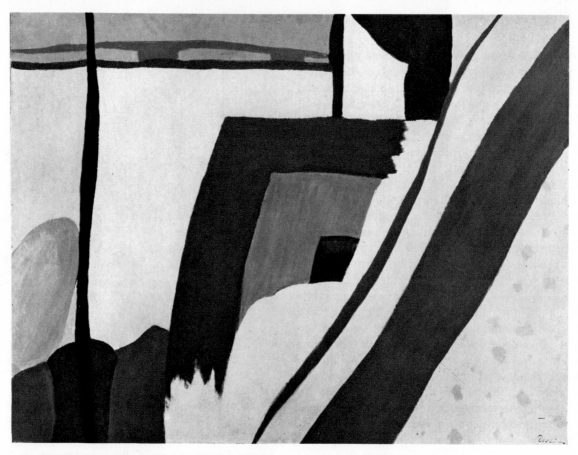

458 Arthur G. Dove. *Sand Barge*. 1930. Oil on composition board,
30 × 40″. The Phillips Collection, Washington, D.C.

to color and force lines and substances just as music has done with sound."

Dove expressed a mood of poetic reverence toward nature, and even his most formal paintings convey a sense of being saturated in landscape color and of some underlying relation to real experience. Both in his earliest abstraction and in later works such as *That Red One* (1944, colorplate 63) his expanding circular shapes, either graduated in concentric bands of diminishing color intensity or sharply contrasted, clearly suggest a symbolic representation of light and a mood of mysticism. In the Forum Exhibition catalog he had stated that his artistic aim was to find visual symbols which espoused the inner stirrings of the self and also represented external nature. "My wish," he wrote, "is to work so unassailably that one could let one's worst instincts go unanalyzed. . . ." This statement is reminiscent of the French artist Odilon Redon, to whose work Dove bears certain spiritual affinities. Redon wrote of his dreaming, Symbolist art: "I intend an irradiation which seizes the spirit and escapes all analysis."

Dove's paintings strike a balance between the fantastic-Symbolist modes of turn-of-the-century art and the more vivid flowing color bands of his contemporaries, the Synchromists. Intellectually, he mistrusted the analytical methods of Cubism and his more intuitive philosophy

of creation is best illuminated by the parallel views of Henri Bergson, whose position was popular in avant-garde circles about 1900. For Bergson it was intuition, rather than rational analysis, that made it possible for the observer to identify empathetically with the inner spirit of the observed object. Like both Marc and Kandinsky, Dove was engaged by a moderate form of pantheism.

Sand Barge (1930, plate 458) is a variant on Dove's radial cores of light, in a key of muted earth colors; its repeated, rectilinear image becomes a visual equivalent of exploding energy, another symbol for nature's rhythms and expansive forces. For the most part, his art was close to the earth, with motifs transformed into fluid patterns and resonant color harmonies.

In another aspect, however, Dove was also an effective ironist. A surprisingly irreverent side of his artistic personality emerged in his collages and assemblages. Between 1924 and 1930 he produced twenty-five of these shallow constructions with attached material objects, which he chose to call "things." According to Georgia O'Keeffe, Dove turned to collage "because it was cheaper than painting and also it amused him. . . ." Undoubtedly, the object–portraits of Picabia and the stunts of American Dada had left their marks on Dove, too, even though he adopted their formal strategies a decade after

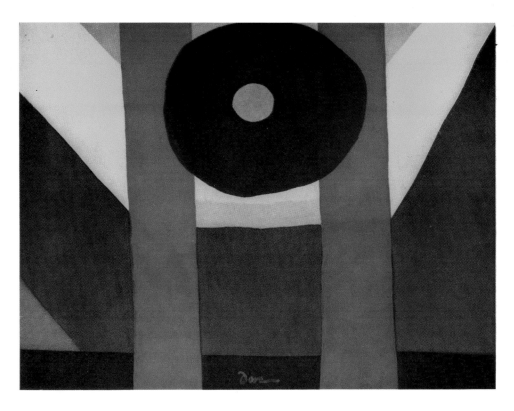

63   Arthur G. Dove. *That Red One*. 1944. Oil on canvas, 27 × 36″.
William H. Lane Foundation, Leominster, Mass.

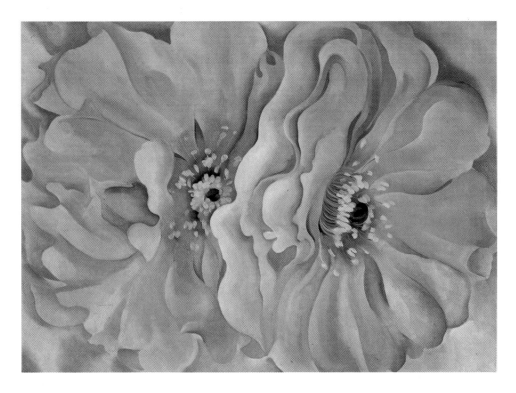

64   Georgia O'Keeffe. *Yellow Cactus Flowers*. 1929. Oil on canvas,
29¾ × 41½″. Fort Worth Art Center,
Fort Worth, Tex. Gift of William E. Scott Foundation

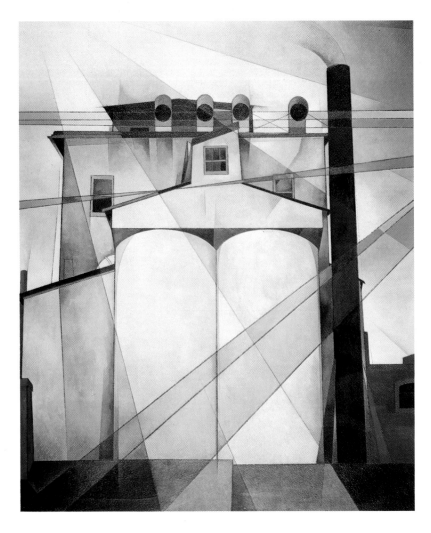

65   Charles Demuth. *My Egypt*. 1927. Oil on composition board,
$35\frac{3}{4} \times 30''$. Whitney Museum of American Art, New York

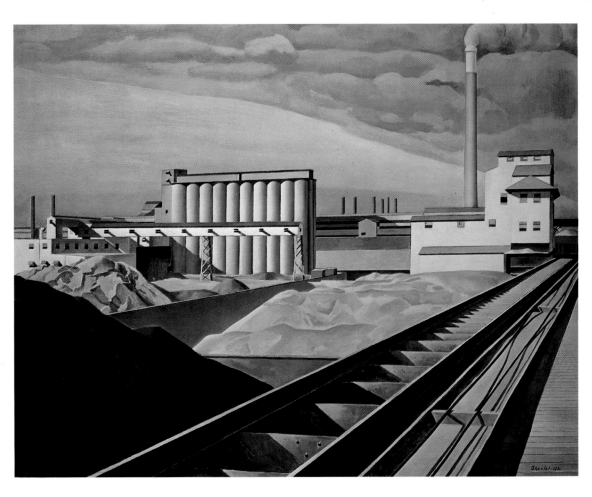

66   Charles Sheeler. *Classic Landscape*. 1931. Oil on canvas, 25 × 32¼″.
Collection Estate of Mrs. Edsel B. Ford

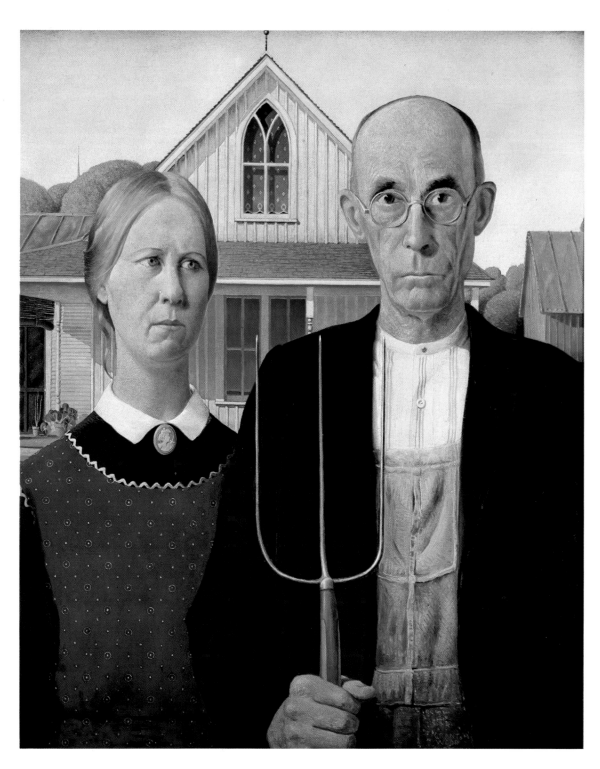

67   Grant Wood. *American Gothic*. 1930. Oil on beaverboard, $29\frac{7}{8} \times 24\frac{7}{8}''$.
The Art Institute of Chicago. Friends of American Art Collection

428

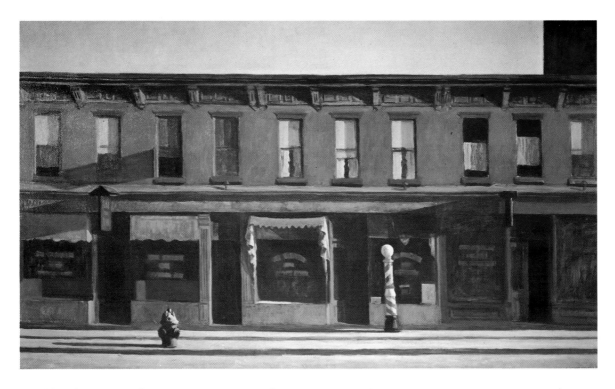

68   Edward Hopper. *Early Sunday Morning*. 1930. Oil on canvas, 35 × 60″.
Whitney Museum of American Art, New York

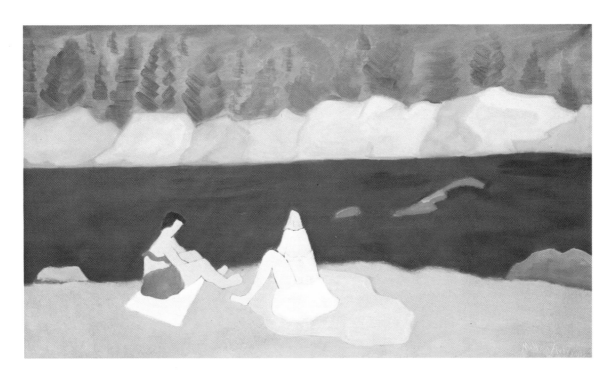

69   Milton Avery. *Swimmers and Sunbathers*. 1945. Oil on canvas, 28 × 48⅛″.
The Metropolitan Museum of Art, New York

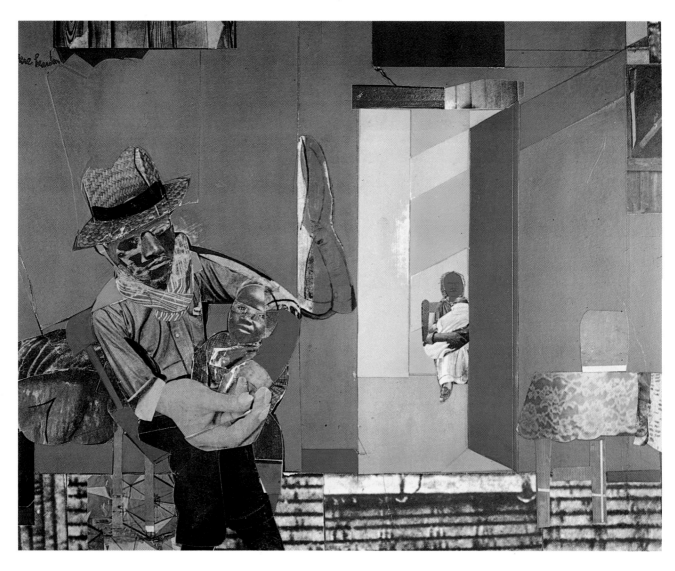

70 Romare Bearden. *Interior*. 1969. Collage, 9 × 11½″.
Cordier & Ekstrom Gallery, New York

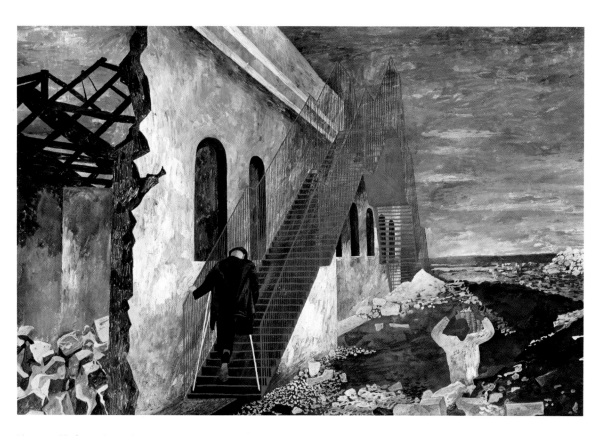

71 Ben Shahn. *The Red Stairway*. 1944. Tempera on Masonite, $16 \times 23\frac{5}{8}''$.
City Art Museum of St. Louis, Mo.

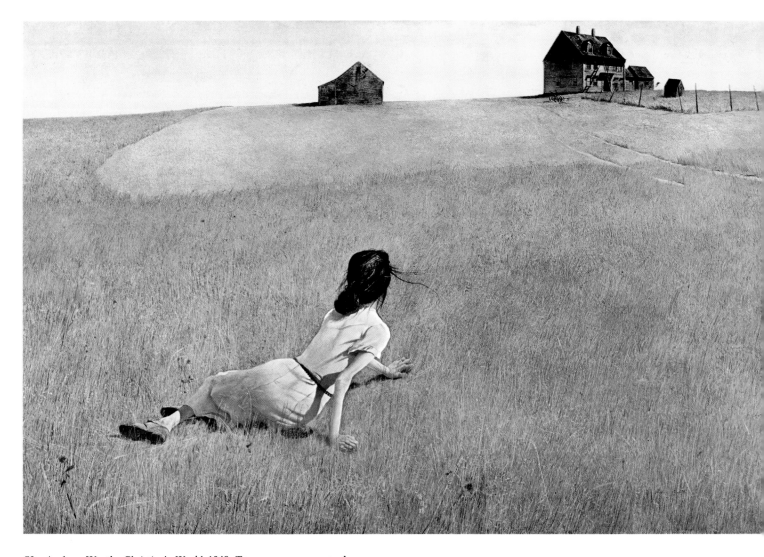

72 Andrew Wyeth. *Christina's World*. 1948. Tempera on gesso panel,
$32\frac{1}{4} \times 47\frac{3}{4}''$. The Museum of Modern Art, New York

Picabia and Duchamp had had their sharpest impact on American art. From Dove's viewpoint Picabia's most memorable "portrait" was that of Stieglitz (1915, plate 459), who was diagrammed as a folding camera with the inscriptions, "Ideal," and "Ici, c'est ici Stieglitz/foi et amour." Dove's *Portrait of Alfred Stieglitz* (1925, plate 460) combined on a sheet of cardboard a camera lens, photographic plate, watch springs, and piece of steel wool to symbolize his dealer. Whatever their ideological content, he transformed his collages into an intimate expressive form. Employing fragments of everyday reality, he evolved a poetry of the commonplace, distinguished by its simplicity, good humor, and grace.

GEORGIA O'KEEFFE

Related to Dove in the organic forms, muted colors, and shifting circular densities and cores of light of her early abstraction, Georgia O'Keeffe (b. 1887) was the solitary woman among Stieglitz's distinguished American modern painters. In the first decade of the new century she had studied first at the Art Institute of Chicago and then, in 1907 and 1908, at the Art Students League in New York, where one of her instructors was William Merritt Chase. A more important influence was Arthur Wesley Dow, whom she encountered in New York at Columbia's Teachers College. Apparently, he stirred her with such ideas as: "Art is decadent when designers and painters lack inventive powers and merely imitate nature or the creation of others. . . . The Japanese know no such divisions as representative or decorative; they conceive of painting as the art of two dimensions; as art in which roundness and nature-imitation are subordinate to the flat relations." Several winters spent in Texas apparently turned her mind to the presence of abstract form and space in the landscape, an insight that fused with Dow's inspired teaching.

She met Stieglitz in 1916 and showed him her experimental watercolors and drawings, which elicited his celebrated remark: "Finally, a woman on paper." Stieglitz exhibited the works at "291" and in 1917 gave O'Keeffe her first individual exhibition. Thereafter, they lived together and were married in 1924.

Her charcoals of this period, such as *Drawing No. 13* (1916, plate 461), distill landscape impressions, as did Dove's work, and similarly move toward a radical form of biomorphic abstraction. Even more original were such watercolors as *Light Coming on the Plains*, in which a sense of boundlessness is achieved by a daring reduction of pictorial means to a simple scheme of symmetrically opposed color stains. These paintings of about 1917 anticipated the color-field painting of the 1950s and 1960s.

In the twenties, perhaps influenced by Stieglitz's photographic series of cloud and landscape fragments, or "Equivalents," O'Keeffe began to isolate her images, often

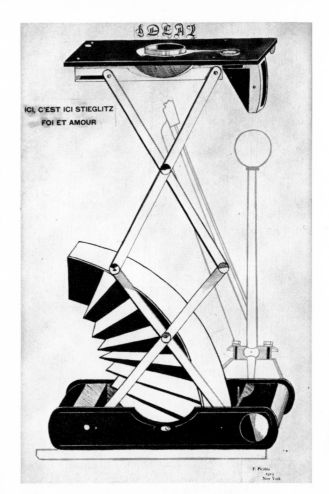

459 Francis Picabia. *Ici, c'est ici Alfred Stieglitz?* 1915. Pen and red and black ink, $29\frac{7}{8} \times 20''$. The Metropolitan Museum of Art, New York. The Alfred Stieglitz Collection, 1949

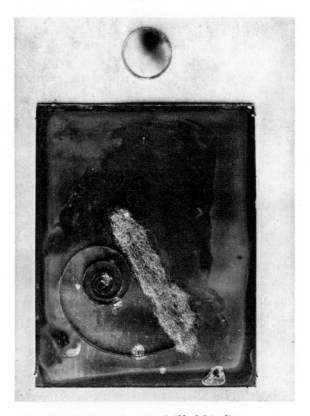

460 Arthur G. Dove. *Portrait of Alfred Stieglitz.* 1925. Collage of camera lens, photographic plate, clock and watch springs, and steel wool on cardboard, $15\frac{7}{8} \times 12\frac{1}{8}''$. The Museum of Modern Art, New York. Edward M. M. Warburg Fund

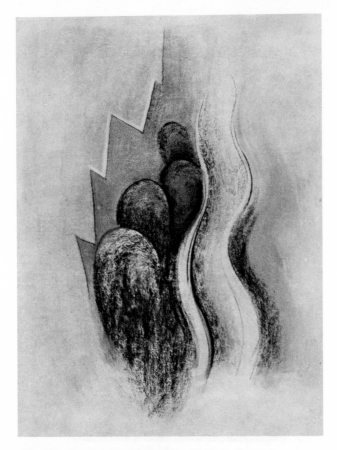

461 Georgia O'Keeffe. *Drawing No. 13*. 1916. Charcoal, 24⅜ × 18½". The Metropolitan Museum of Art, New York. The Alfred Stieglitz Collection

fresh content and significant new forms. She played with ideas of the distinct and the veiled, concentration and diffusion, until these qualities took on the character of statements about the ambiguities of experience itself. Abstraction, in her terms, was not merely an occasion for the exposition of form. She subverted rational ego in favor of a more informal and "open" kind of painting, as Mark Rothko and, in a different fashion, Kenneth Noland were to do much later. Though she accepted the standard aspects of European nonobjective styles, from geometric to biomorphic abstraction, she subtracted something of their explicitness. Her art seems characteristically American in standing aloof from final certainties. Despite their generally intimate scale, and without the force of prevailing influence, the paintings of O'Keeffe and Dove prophesied the attitudes and an imagery of post-World War II color-field painting. They are part of an intelligible continuity of taste and change between two otherwise antithetical generations.

enlarged flowers, as in *Yellow Cactus Flowers* (colorplate 64), and to magnify details until they lost recognizability as representational objects, becoming the same kind of abstract emblem that Dove sought—a microcosm of the universe. Also at that time O'Keeffe went through a stylistic phase of severe, crisp edges; rigorous patterned formality; and austere paint surfaces. These traits delineate the urban landscape in such work as her brilliant *Radiator Building—Night, New York* (1927, plate 462). The sharp-focus, meticulous photographs by Paul Strand and Edward Weston and perhaps also Charles Sheeler's paintings and photographs were influential in her Precisionist work as she reconstructed, with a scrupulous, almost clinical accuracy, the chilling geometries of New York's high-rise buildings.

From the thirties on, she spent her winters in New Mexico, near Santa Fe, and moved there permanently after Stieglitz's death in 1946. There her work became increasingly abstract. Even after her ninetieth birthday, she continues to paint her unique abstract emblems from the same landscape of grandeur and vacancy, in larger scale but always with her characteristic combination of formal power and romantic mystery.

The tradition of biomorphic abstraction was given a very individual inflection by Dove and O'Keeffe. O'Keeffe in particular seemed able to invest abstract painting with

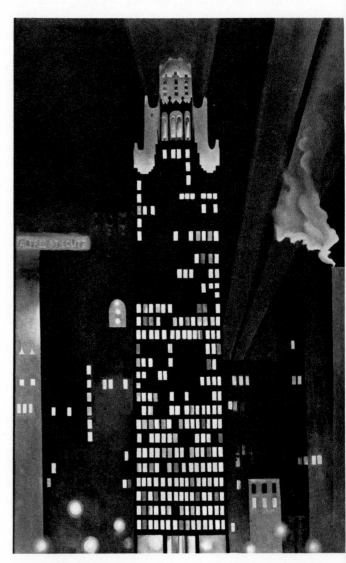

462 Georgia O'Keeffe. *Radiator Building—Night, New York*. 1927. Oil on canvas, 48 × 30". Fisk University, Nashville, Tenn. The Alfred Stieglitz Collection

JOHN MARIN

John Marin (1870–1953) is an artist who does not date, even though he can scarcely be described as an influence on, or a significant forebear of, contemporary art. This may be explained in part by his fierce attachment to values of freedom, traditional traits of American romantic individualism, and in part by his formal invention. The lyrical effusions so often associated with Marin's art and his scintillating mastery of the watercolor medium interest present-day artists less than his expressive graphic structures and paint surfaces. "Drawing," he wrote, "is the path of all movement Great and Small—/Drawing is the path made visible." Late in his life, when Marin had begun to work consistently in oils, he told a biographer that he wished "to give paint a chance to show itself entirely as paint." This insistence on the stubborn, irreducible, material reality of paint later became the heartbeat of artistic creation in America, with the emergence of the "Action" painters after World War II. If Marin still engages the interest of vanguard artists today, it is because he managed to further the destruction of traditional illusionist means with a commitment to abstraction of such depth and persistence as to help generate a fundamental change in American artistic consciousness.

Marin's energy and spontaneity relate him to both the first and the second phases of American modernism. A statement that he made in 1947, renewing his earlier mood of aesthetic experiment, now seems to anticipate the aims of the Abstract Expressionists. "Using paint *as* paint," he said, "is different from using paint to paint a picture. I'm calling my pictures this year 'Movements in Paint' and not movements of boat, sea, or sky, because . . . I am representing paint first of all, and not the motif primarily."

In his undisguised and articulate passion for artistic freedom Marin quite often consciously played the role of the eccentric individualist, adopting the folkloristic image of the shrewd, laconic Yankee who scorns the "highfalutin'," mistrusts intellectualism, affects a picturesque personal style, and resorts to backwoods idiom in language. The paradox of Marin, as of so many American artists, lies in the combination of aggressive native pride carried to the point of gleeful provincialism with an abiding respect for cosmopolitan aesthetics. His art successfully unites these warring impulses.

Marin came to modern art relatively late, and after considerable hesitation. He had apprenticed himself to an architect (a fact that has often been used inconclusively to explain his feeling for pictorial structures), and he actually practiced as an architect before settling on painting. At the age of twenty-eight he entered the Pennsylvania Academy, where he worked under William Merritt Chase and Thomas Anschutz. There Marin met Arthur Carles, who later shared his taste for advanced

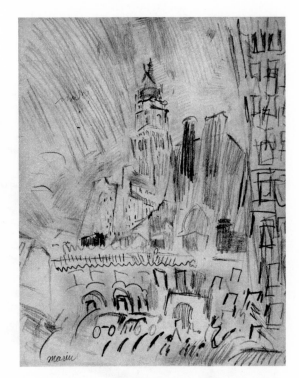

463 John Marin. *Woolworth Building and Vicinity.* 1914. Pencil, 9½ × 7½". Estate of Edith Gregor Halpert

European art and became a close companion in Paris. From 1905 to 1911 Marin lived abroad and made a considerable reputation from his etchings of European monuments, executed in a delicate, atmospheric style which suggests Whistler's tonal refinement and aestheticism. Even in his early European *Wanderjahre*, when he seemed to be compiling a careful notebook on the European past with much emphasis on unspectacular, descriptive detail, his more wayward impulses erupted. The expressive broken lines in his early etching of the Cathedral at Rouen translate his motif in a characteristically soaring image of energy.

By 1908 he had begun to employ fresh color and exercise a new freedom in the watercolor medium, in a loose but intense adaptation of Neo-Impressionist technique. In 1910, at Kufstein in the Austrian Tyrol, Marin executed a series of scenic watercolors in which for the first time he developed a highly personal system of abbreviated marks to communicate his vision of nature with an intensity rarely achieved in so limpid and transparent a medium. With his light touch and economy of means, Marin, like the Zen masters, could project a sense of diaphanous weightlessness along with an elemental vitality.

In 1909 he held his first one-man show at the Stieglitz gallery, and the exhibition enjoyed a considerable *succès d'estime*. Writing in *Camera Work* (July, 1909), the critic Charles Caffin, scenting the abstract bias of Marin's work, wrote: "Consciousness of facts disappears in a spiritualized version of form and color."

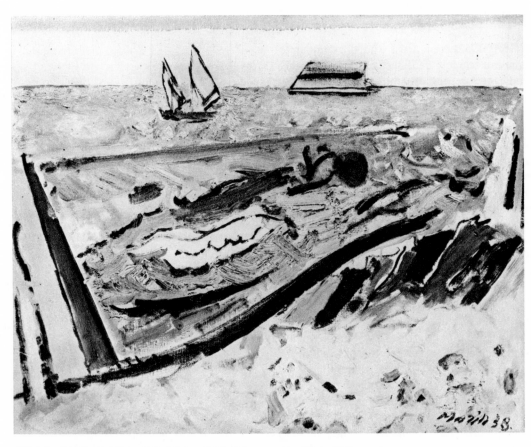

464 John Marin. *Off Cape Split, Maine*. 1938. Oil on canvas, 22½ × 28⅛".
The Metropolitan Museum of Art, New York. George A. Hearn Fund, 1946

Only in 1911 and 1912, however, after he had passed his fortieth birthday, did Marin's modernism decisively announce itself in a dynamic new graphic style, with the first of his etchings of the Woolworth Building and the Brooklyn Bridge. At "291" he had the opportunity in 1911 to see exhibitions of Cézanne's late watercolors and the early Cubist drawings and watercolors of Picasso. His exposure to this work was important in the transition in Marin's style from his still anecdotal European etchings. His new manner synthesized the spontaneous color and the heightened sensations of the Fauves, the formal rigors of Cubism, and, most deeply of all, the structured yet fluid color accents in Cézanne's late watercolors. These influences were ignited by the artist's intense and individual reaction to the dynamism of New York, a New York in the midst of a building boom. Such landmarks as the Manhattan Bridge, the Woolworth Building, and Grand Central Terminal had either just been completed or were in construction. In these structures Marin found a concrete manifestation of the spirit of explosive growth and the romantic promise of America, and his impressions had a fresh impact after a prolonged absence on the Continent. His ability to compose rhythmically and to register his vision with utmost rapidity and brevity is brilliantly demonstrated in his drawing

Woolworth Building and Vicinity (1914, plate 463), and his contemporary etchings of New York's rising skyline. It was Marin's special gift to bring off the evocative, lyrical fragment with little apparent effort or meditation. Echoing the Futurists' kineticism and urban dynamism, he fragmented New York buildings, bridges, and skyline into turbulent and mobile lines and flat color masses. To Stieglitz he wrote in 1913: ". . . the whole city is alive; buildings, people, all are alive; and the more they move me the more I feel them to be alive."

In 1914 Marin began to summer on the Maine coast, which was to become one of his favored painting locales. His first watercolors based on nature there showed more reticence than those he had done from urban motifs. Their delicacy of tone and atmospheric effects, despite the use of broken color, related these works more to his experiments in the Tyrol than to the explosive New York views. About 1919 landscape and city views became unified around an abstract, structural core as Marin began to simplify radically, employing what he described as "frames within frames," a free system of rectilinear compartments whose emphatic outlines prevented his "movements" from sliding off the edges of the picture.

From the twenties until his death Marin continually drew on nature for his motifs. He was fascinated by the rugged contours of the Maine landscape and the sea, but he transposed his impressions into abstract pictorial design. During the early thirties he worked consistently in oils and made the physical viscosity and resistance of the pigment do some of the structural work of his explicit graphic organization. His fluid approach showed a remarkable freedom in a period when the geometric bias of Cubism still dominated abstract and non-figurative idioms. By the late thirties and forties, he depended almost exclusively on a few salient movements, large planes of color, and the expressive potential of the paint itself. His effects were coarser, and his strength lay in his intense, vital surfaces, which more than compensated for the elimination of descriptive interest. In *Off Cape Split, Maine* (1938, plate 464) the effort "to show paint as paint" and the rich impasto of the painted surface command our attention rather than the sketchy image of a ship dancing on the sea. Marin did not wish to free himself from nature completely, and even in this last phase he remained as keenly visual as he was architectural and tactile. There is a residual delicacy of color in his watercolors and in his variety of soft pinks, powder blues, and violets, which have a chromatic refinement comparable to Cézanne's subtle palette.

While Marin's oils today excite interest among contemporary artists, his watercolors were perhaps his most decisive and original contribution. Taking his cue from Cézanne, he learned to use transparent watercolor planes and chromatic accents to create plastic structures, giving the medium a refreshing new vitality and a peculiarly American integrity. At the end of his life Marin surrendered himself to broadly lyrical impulses based merely on rhythmic color phrase, re-evoking the more impetuous and romantic spirit of his youth during the decade between 1910 and 1920.

CHARLES DEMUTH

Another American master of the watercolor medium was Charles Demuth (1883–1935). Like Marin, he adopted Cézanne's method of using delicate touches and dilute washes to create a fine structure of colored planes. For Demuth the limitations of the lighter medium allowed a greater reticence than oils and afforded precise effects and a clarity that seemed to jibe with his own temperament, fastidiousness, and sensibility. He once remarked, with customary insight and modesty: "John Marin and I drew our inspiration from the same source, French modernism. He brought his up in buckets and spilt much along the way. I dipped mine out with a teaspoon, but I never spilled a drop."

Thirteen years Marin's junior, Demuth was far more urbane and reserved in manner, with something of the expatriate dandy about him. His art was as much a matter of intellect, tact, and exquisite style as Marin's was of energy and impetuousness. Demuth was born in Lancaster, Pa., and his painting embodies something

of the clean line and simple formal elegance of Pennsylvania Dutch folk art. Many of his works were inspired directly by the orderly Colonial architecture of his childhood and youth.

Some self-imposed puritanical restraint, in conjunction with delicate health, may have prevented Demuth from realizing the fullest possibilities of his painting. His art is fragile and cold rather than robust, but it shows a perfection of taste, an aristocratic grace, and, at its best, unexpected strength. Demuth's achievement is the more remarkable since, unlike Marin, Weber, Dove, Hartley, Stella, and others, he did not absorb the formal lessons of his expatriate art education and then apply them to the dynamics of the American urban experience. Rather, he used Parisian aesthetics as a shield against a too violent or disruptive native experience, which he approached in a spirit of ironic detachment. He shrank from the spectacle of American progress and technological power and, indeed, from any kind of extravagance, looseness, or excess. There was no identification in his work with the serious sociological problems attending the technological transformation of the country.

In 1905, at the age of twenty-two, Demuth enrolled at the Pennsylvania Academy and, following in the footsteps of Marin, Carles, and Maurer, worked with Thomas

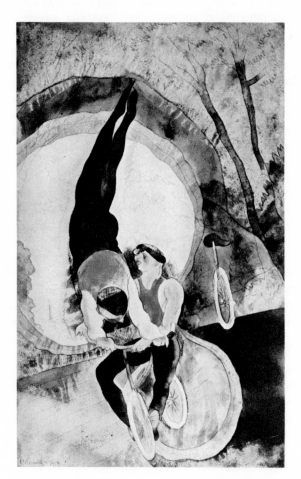

465 Charles Demuth. *Acrobats*. 1919. Watercolor and pencil, 13 × 7⅞". The Museum of Modern Art, New York. Gift of Abby Aldrich Rockefeller

Anschutz. He spent a year in Paris in 1907 and then in 1912 went to Europe again for a two-year period. He may have been aware of the Fauves and the Cubists while abroad, but he showed no direct evidence of the new experimental moods in his art until his return to America. In 1915 he was doing delicate, rather freely handled watercolor landscapes that suggested Marin's influence and fragile flower pieces that recapitulated Rodin's faint color washes. (Rodin had been shown at Stieglitz's gallery in 1908 and again in 1910.) The style and sentiment of these very early paintings were to remain characteristic of Demuth's art.

That same year he began a series of watercolor illustrations for Emile Zola's *Nana*, one of the early, shocking declarations of French naturalism. During the next four years, simply for his own amusement, Demuth illustrated Henry James's *The Turn of the Screw*, Poe's *"The Masque of the Red Death,"* and other writings. These haunted illustrations reveal a lively romantic taste and literary imagination and great deftness in the watercolor medium. Informal and free, their play of delicate stains against sinuous curvilinear contours suggests a certain mild perfume of the romantic decadence. (Demuth admired both Aubrey Beardsley and Toulouse-Lautrec for their graphic styles, aristocratic attenuations, and taste for a picturesque "wickedness.") Most of all, these early watercolors suggest Jules Pascin, in manner and in the mingling of introspective mood and worldliness.

From 1917 to 1919 Demuth carried out a far more ambitious series of watercolors of vaudeville and nightclub performers that passed beyond illustration. The preciosity of his early style, with its thinness and artificial quality, gave way to more decisive composition, forceful color, and a new expressive power, as he pitted himself against action in the real world. Like Toulouse-Lautrec, Demuth was physically incapacitated to a degree, first by lameness and then, after 1920, more seriously by diabetes. The grace and agility of acrobatic and theatrical performers may therefore have had a particular appeal to him. *Acrobats* (1919, plate 465) concentrates directly on the physical agility of his performers, rather than their psychology, and thus permits him better to integrate style and subject. Thin, luminous washes of color, an energetic, disembodied contour, and flowing rhythms connect foreground and background in a sweeping serpentine pattern. The daring composition, with its delicate poise of silhouetted shapes, provides a vivid counterpart to the dexterity and weightlessness of the figures. *Acrobats* reveals a new formal approach reflecting the influence of Dove and O'Keeffe, whom Demuth had encountered through Stieglitz. Yet his art was unique in that it created a tension between a form of "soft" abstraction, with its possible spiritual implications of passivity and mystery, and lively human action.

A complementary style of "hard" geometric abstraction emerged during a trip to Bermuda in 1916. In architectural studies and seascapes Demuth began to use the directional lines, analytical structure, and transparent planes of Cubism. He parted company with his European sources, however, in the effort to create, within architectonic discipline, diaphanous effects of light. He interpreted his motifs as flattened prismatic shapes, extending their edges subtly, attenuating and recomposing them in a crisscross of intersecting diagonals and shafts of light, like a night sky raked by searchlights. This was the method of Lyonel Feininger (1871–1956), the American-born modernist who spent his formative youth and maturity in Germany, and was associated there with The Blue Rider and the Bauhaus. Feininger's art, however, communicates an atmosphere of mystical contemplation, is apparitional in form and inward in mood, suggesting a relationship to northern European modes of feeling.

About 1920 Demuth began to work in tempera and oil as well as in watercolor. Apparently he found these mediums more congenial to his new motifs of the industrial landscape and severely simplified urban architecture, which he painted in a mood of classical austerity identifiable with the emerging Precisionist movement. Each of the Precisionists added an individual inflection to the collective style, and Demuth, in particular, felt the influence of Duchamp and Dada, as he moved away from a literalist respect for utilitarian objects and motifs to more mocking attitudes. *My Egypt* (1927, colorplate 65) equates the American grain elevator with the dehumanizing monumentalism of the Egyptian pyramids. Despite the frequent irony of his titles, Demuth's fascination with machinery and the structures of urbanism was expressed in terms of personal poetry rather than protest. Undoubtedly it was Duchamp's irreverence that led him to question his own attitude toward the values of the "Machine Age."

However, Demuth did not use his art to discredit the principles or methods of traditional illusionist art. To do so would have undermined his own position. In a nation which still identified the machine with the American promise and saw it as a part of the complex story of a people's deliverance from the wilderness, artists did not care to risk those adventurous excursions into the unmarked psychic regions where Dada's disquieting puns and iconoclasm took shape. Demuth is closest to the Dada spirit perhaps in his handsome homage to the poet William Carlos Williams, *I Saw the Figure Five in Gold* (1928, plate 466). The title is taken from the first line of a poem by his friend. The painting reveals a cunning sense of artifice and free association in its symbolism, connecting it both to decorative Cubism and to Duchamp. It mingles visual, auditory, and extrapictorial associations for dramatic purposes, giving the composition an unexpected urgency. The golden number five is repeated and recessed against a red rectilinear shape that throws it back again, like an echo reverberating from a wall, and evokes the drama of the poem, which describes a fire-

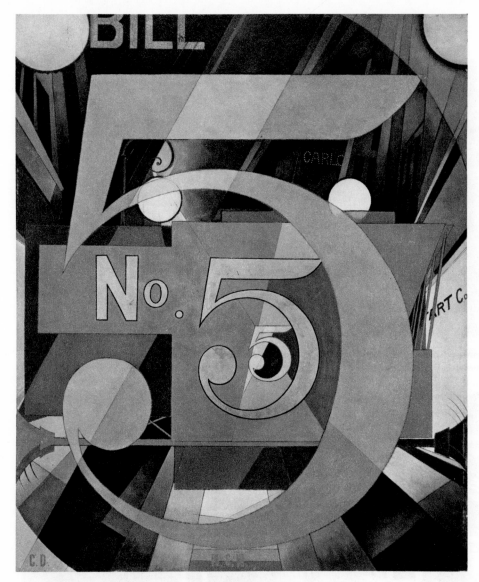

466 Charles Demuth. *I Saw the Figure Five in Gold*. 1928.
Oil on composition board, 36 × 29¾″. The Metropolitan
Museum of Art, New York. The Alfred Stieglitz Collection, 1949

truck answering an alarm. Demuth created an emblem of brilliance and intensity, with a kaleidoscopic effect formally related to the whirling structures of Stella. There is wit in Demuth's condensed allusions, in such references as "Art Co," but there the reminiscences of Dada end. His art has more relation to the bland tectonics of geometric abstraction than to the disruptive psychological strategies and blatant iconoclasm of Dada.

Demuth's delicate color sense was evident in the more realistic watercolors of flowers and still life that preoccupied him in the last decade of his life, but the fanciful quality and freedom of his earlier watercolors had also given way to a colder efficiency and often to a more commonplace literalism, as if in recognition that the mood of aesthetic experiment was passing from the American art scene. He was an artist of restricted sensibility who found it necessary to concentrate all his visual resources at one point, but for continuous creative impulse and for his distinction as a stylist he must stand in the first rank of the pioneers of twentieth-century American art.

SHEELER AND THE LATER PRECISIONISTS

The exponents of geometric form and urban subject matter made up a loose entity in American art about 1920 that was later characterized as "Precisionism." Besides Demuth, they included Charles Sheeler, Preston Dickinson, Niles Spencer, Louis Lozowick, and others, all of whom experimented with a more formal approach to the metropolitan image that had moved Marin, Stella, and Weber to visual statements of an expressive and subjective urgency. Stella's Brooklyn Bridge series and the ensemble, *New York Interpreted*, 1920–22, of which *The Port* (plate 467) formed the first panel, are probably the first bona fide American examples of the familiar European machine aesthetic of the period. Unlike Stella,

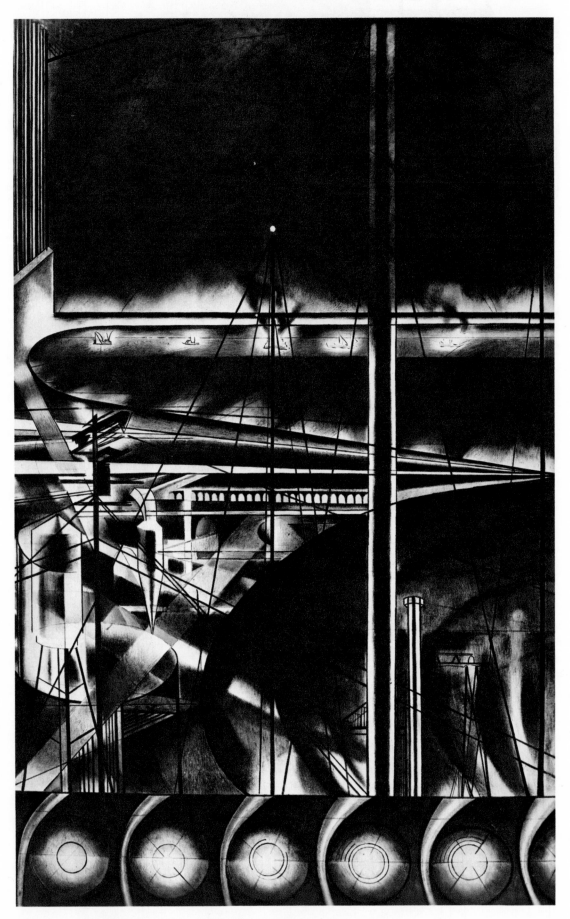

467 Joseph Stella. *The Port,* first panel of *New York Interpreted* series. 1920–22.
Oil on canvas, 88¼ × 54″. The Newark Museum, Newark, N.J.
Felix Fuld Bequest Fund Purchase, 1937

the artists who came forward in the twenties took a more detached and coolly objective view of the romance of the modern city Their chief concern became the formal resolution of their selected motifs in terms of functional perfection like that of machinery. In this regard, the photographic image, with its static shapes, brilliant contrasts of light and dark, sharp-focus precision, and seamless surfaces played an important mediating role.

In a recent study of Charles Sheeler (1883–1965) Martin Friedman has observed that, in addition to his roots in Cubist analytical methods and his taste for the seductions of the machine aesthetic, which he shared with Demuth, Sheeler "represents the clinical extreme of Regionalist art." His formalism and polished photographic precision only heightened the fiction of the American environment as a streamlined and aseptic model of functional perfection, "insulated from the effects of natural erosion." Friedman notes that Sheeler's paintings "radiate an apprehensive and melancholy atmosphere. The rare occasion when a figure intrudes ... only heightens the sense of isolation." Despite his favorable experience of European art in 1909, when he was in Paris briefly with his friend Morton Schamberg, on his return home Sheeler began to transform Cubist formal structure in the direction of Realism, in order to concentrate on native American subjects, both rural and urban. These he ultimately recorded with a new kind of illusionistic clarity in such works as *Classic Landscape* (1931, colorplate 66), which in effect reconstituted the American industrial landscape as a new kind of mythical, if rather sterile, modern Eden.

From a more or less routine but effective adaption of Cubism's transparent planes to architectural phenomena in his early work, Sheeler proceeded to a more tangible and factual art that linked subtle draftsmanship with a remarkable talent as a photographer for isolating and dramatizing motifs in terms of light play on surfaces. *Upper Deck* (1929, plate 468) is related to a Demuth painting of 1921, *Paquebot, Paris*, in its forms and simplified structural analysis. However, Sheeler's visual data are by comparison explicit, even photographic in their palpable reality. He refused to romanticize his facts, but still his dehumanized and frozen barns, factories, machines, and even his domestic interiors managed to project a mood of ideality by the very elimination of evidence of time's passage and the process of chance. The immaculate immobility of his imagery conveys a certain mystery by its magical clarity of visual detail. These pictorial effects were linked to the phenomenon of the New Objectivity in Europe and to the nascent, illusionistic Surrealism that Dali was soon to make one of the most familiar pictorial stereotypes of modern art. At times a softer, more poetic spirit pervades Sheeler's work. In *Architectural Cadences* (1954, plate 469) the play of overlapped planes of tangible shapes and intan-

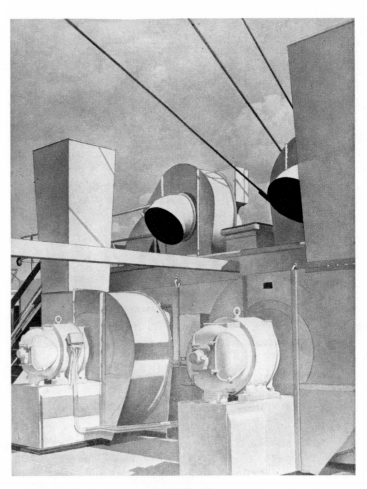

468 Charles Sheeler. *Upper Deck*. 1929. Oil on canvas, 29⅛ × 22⅛". Fogg Art Museum, Harvard University, Cambridge, Mass. Louise E. Bettens Fund Purchase

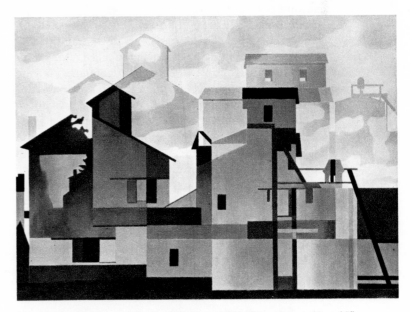

469 Charles Sheeler. *Architectural Cadences*. 1954. Oil on canvas, 25 × 35". Whitney Museum of American Art, New York

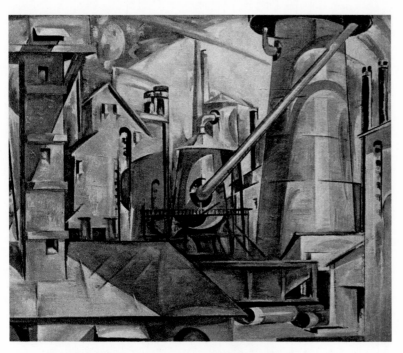

470 Preston Dickinson. *Industry II*. n.d. Oil on canvas, 24¾ × 30″. Whitney Museum of American Art, New York. Gift of Mr. and Mrs. Alan H. Temple

gible shadows creates a complex and ambiguous formal synthesis closer to the refined spirit of Demuth than the matter-of-fact delineation of the commonplace with which Sheeler's art is usually associated.

Sheeler and the later Precisionists, including Preston Dickinson (1891–1930) and Niles Spencer (1893–1953) scrupulously translated the American industrial environment into simple, sharply defined compositions of a machine-like clarity and precision. They also struck an uneasy balance between an ascetic, decorative Cubism and photography. The dry and literalistic tradition has continued in our time in the manner called "Magic, or Sharp-focus, Realism"—a style that combines intense factualism on a photographic model with slick magazine illustrative conventions. The occasional, fugitive touch of fantasy or symbolic overtones in this painting manner does not disguise its kinship with a historical American bias for the disembodied visual fact. Such painting evolves out of a basic puritanism, a mistrust of hedonism, which is at the core of much American artistic sensibility. The denial of the sensuous character of the material means of painting has been one of the identifiable marks of American provincialism and its most damaging limitation, from the journeymen painters of the eighteenth century to Winslow Homer, from Charles Demuth and Charles Sheeler to Ben Shahn and Andrew Wyeth. It may even be one of the hidden reasons for the American predilection for watercolor.

Dickinson treated both natural and industrial landscapes in a more decorative manner than other Preci-

sionists, instead of simplifying them by the elimination of detail. The delicate fragmentation of solid shapes in *Industry II* (n.d., plate 470) is similar to the calligraphic style of the Japanese Ukiyo-e print, which the artist greatly admired. Niles Spencer showed a harmony and warmth of earth colors of unusual richness and resonance within the austerely patterned style of Precisionist wit in *City Walls* (1921, plate 471). By the thirties the idealized cityscapes and polished surfaces and forms of the Precisionist vision were showing serious signs of disruption into the more fanciful, Surrealist-tinged allegories of Peter Blume (b. 1906) and Louis Guglielmi (1906–1956), as the formerly admired urban geometries became a symbol of claustrophobic entrapment.

The original spirit of Precisionist style had grown out of the perhaps unstable but optimistic mood with which the exuberant, even fanatical, Futurists in Italy launched their manifestos, exalting speed, technological progress, and urban dynamism. With the appearance of the so-called "machine aesthetic" in the twenties, crystallized by Le Corbusier's *L'Esprit Nouveau*, and with the success

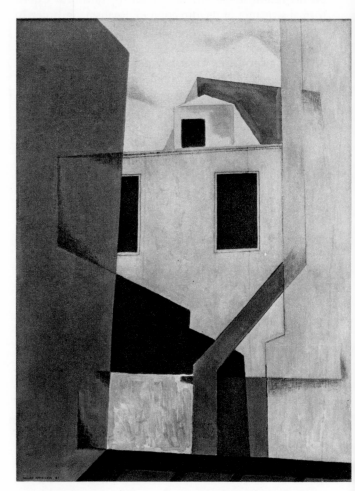

471 Niles Spencer. *City Walls*. 1921. Oil on canvas, 39⅜ × 28¾″. The Museum of Modern Art, New York. Given anonymously

of the Dutch de Stijl group and the Bauhaus, many Americans felt confirmed in their own identification with the utopian promise of machine civilization. In 1927 Louis Lozowick (1892–1973), a pioneer Precisionist whose work is little known, wrote in an essay entitled "The Americanization of Art": "The skyscrapers of New York, the grain elevators of Minneapolis, the steel mills of Pittsburgh, the oil wells of Oklahoma, the copper mines of Butte, the lumber yards of Seattle, give the American cultural epic in its diapason."

Machine-Age paintings were viewed in America and in Europe both as symbols of a new kind of mechanistic beauty and as didactic models for a new industrial society in which the machine could become the rational servant of man. Marcel Duchamp, as a disenchanted European expatriate, urged Demuth in 1921 to return from Paris to New York because "New York is the place—there are modern ideas—Europe is finished." The myths of Ameri-

can technology, power, and social innocence conspired with postbellum fatigue and a sense of the onset of decadence in Europe to discourage the vision of a radical modern art movement of sweeping dimensions in this country. However, such heady expectations were being contested and proven baseless at that very moment by a conservative artistic reaction which submerged abstraction and the mildly Dadaist American currents in a new wave of Realism. Ironically enough, the Precisionists themselves may have to some degree precipitated the decline of avant-garde fortunes in the twenties and thirties, when they sought to apply Cubist methods to indigenous subject matter. The modern American artist of the twenties found himself on the horns of a dilemma: the more deeply he established his personal authenticity by confronting the American experience, the greater the risk to his art of provincial isolation and intellectual stagnation.

(continued on page 444)

DECORATIVE ARTS

Frederick Carder (1864–1963) was trained in England at his family's pottery, studied chemistry and metallurgy, and began designing glass for an English firm. On a visit to the United States to learn manufacturing techniques, he decided to remain in this country and with several other men opened the Steuben Glass Works during the first decade of the twentieth century. He contributed his designing skill to the production of a wide variety of styles, includ-

ing Art Nouveau, Neoclassical, and assorted exotic modes, and invented several new glassmaking techniques. The small bowl (plate 472) exemplifies one of his new processes, intarsia. It is created by melting a colored glass overlay into the clear blown glass of the basic form, permanently encasing the decorative motif. The pattern of stylized chrysanthemums is in dark blue, and the rim and foot are black.

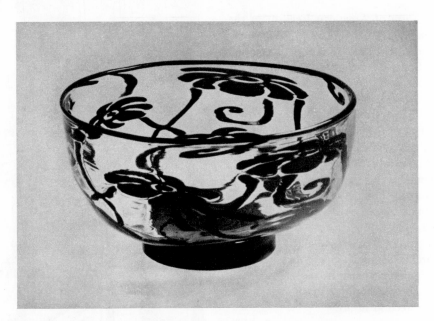

472 Frederick Carder. Bowl, for Steuben Glass, Division of Corning Glass Works. 1930–40. Intarsia glass; clear blown glass with encased blue decoration; height 2¾". Museum of Art, Rhode Island School of Design, Providence. Gift of the Estate of William E. Brigham

(continued from page 443)

REALISM AND THE AMERICAN SCENE

The period between the Great Depression and World War II (i.e., from the Stock Market crash of October, 1929, to the Nazi invasions in Europe in 1939) was one of intense national self-examination for American artists. Many began consciously to turn away from European trends in an effort to establish a more comfortable native posture in art that would express their commitment to political, cultural, and social problems. The turbulent forces of the thirties—the Depression, the rise of Fascism, the threat of World War II, and radical politics—sapped much of the impetus of the prewar avant-garde, and a more socially conscious art emerged to document the American scene.

By the Depression years two quite distinctive developments revived the native tradition of Realism, both growing out of extensions of the Ashcan School. One of these directions focused upon the American scene as a way of life: the city communicating a mood of sullen endurance; the open agricultural lands more optimistically envisioned. Edward Hopper and, to a lesser degree, Charles Burchfield painted the loneliness of anonymous big-city life or the poignancy and frustrations of the small midwestern towns that Sinclair Lewis and Sherwood Anderson had documented in their fiction. For the programmatic Regionalists, led by Thomas Hart Benton and abetted by the chauvinistic writings of the critic Thomas Craven, American history and folklore served as a propagandist weapon of attack on European values and elitist modern art.

The second major form of American Realism in the thirties was a visceral reaction of social protest to the bitter effects of the economic crisis that cast such a pall over American life. Some of the artists had been cartoonists and newspaper journalists, much like their predecessors among The Eight, but with a more radical political bent.

Although the painting of the period as a whole was by no means either exclusively Realist or popular and reflective of social and political ferment, the modern movement was, at least temporarily, submerged by American Scene painting, such as the popular *American Gothic*, by Grant Wood (colorplate 67). The new wave of Realism had begun with the indigenous imagery of the Precisionists; it became more gently nostalgic and sentimental in the hands of Burchfield and Hopper; and it finally took on an Expressionist stridency in the late thirties. Realism in one aspect or another once again became the dominant American direction in art.

BURCHFIELD AND HOPPER

The paintings of Charles Burchfield (1893–1967) and Edward Hopper (1882–1967) provided the first notable evidence of the revival of Realism in a new form often referred to as "American Scene painting." These artists shared none of the exuberance or the reforming zeal of The Eight, however. Their art was cheerless, haunted by romantic nostalgia, even addicted to the grotesque. It began by seeking refuge in the familiar as a rebuke to the conundrums of the modernists, but the reality it set forth was a world of shadows, oppressed by an atmosphere of human desolation. Like some of the American Precisionists who had begun to react negatively to the machine and to the new landscape of power, the Romantic Realists, using different pictorial metaphors, told of the disenchantment and the spiritual vacancy behind the American success story.

These two artists, pictorially, were as limited, average, and undistinguished as the humiliated landscape, the dilapidated and gloomily picturesque architecture, and the drab urban scenes that they made the stock-in-trade of their subject matter. Theirs was an under-

473 Charles Burchfield. *Church Bells Ringing, Rainy Winter Night.* 1917. Watercolor, 30 × 19". The Cleveland Museum of Art. Gift of Louise M. Dunn in memory of Henry G. Keller

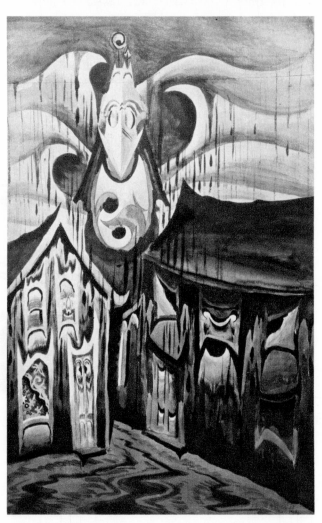

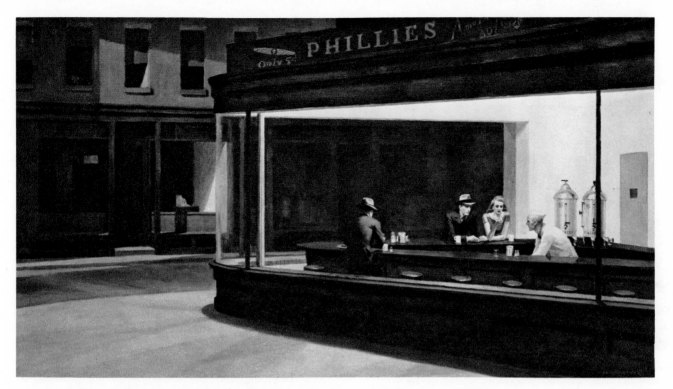

474 Edward Hopper. *Nighthawks*. 1942. Oil on canvas, 30 × 60″.
The Art Institute of Chicago. Friends of American Art Collection

privileged art, disinclined to draw attention to itself;
the least attractive aspects of American life were presented without apology, although with some sense of
mystery. Sinclair Lewis's typical American main street,
"where dullness is made God," establishes the tone for
Hopper's paintings of the national spiritual vacuum and
his visual descriptions of mechanical lives set in stagnant
scenes. Burchfield was an acknowledged admirer of
Sherwood Anderson's writing. Perhaps he was drawn to
the novelist's sentimental lyricism, his fascination with
the ordinary, and his brooding introspection in the face
of the moral rot of small-town existence. Anderson's
description of himself as a writer "whose sympathy went
out to the little frame houses on often mean enough
streets in American towns, to defeated people, often with
thwarted lives" might appropriately be identified with
some facets of Burchfield's artistic personality. In the
small-town backwaters of American life Burchfield found
a symbolic projection of a private ennui that could deepen
into fantasy.

He grew up in Salem, Ohio, went briefly to the Cleveland School of Art, and returned to Salem in 1916. Between that date and his induction into the army in 1918,
he independently arrived at a fanciful symbolic mode of
expression in watercolor that suggests the paintings of
Edvard Munch and the melancholy, introspective mood
of much European art of the turn-of-the-century era.
Back in Salem, Burchfield wrote, he experienced a personal crisis: "A curious depression assailed me, and I
worked constantly to keep it down." *Church Bells Ringing,
Rainy Winter Night* (1917, plate 473) is one of the brilliant
watercolor fantasies that he produced in this troubled

period, turning the familiar landscape of his youth into a
representation of childhood fears and ghostly apparitions.

In 1920 he became interested in painting the evocative
qualities of American vernacular architecture. Once
described by the critic Henry McBride as "songs of hate,"
these pictures owe their mood of desolation as much to
the melancholy subject matter as to Burchfield's attitude
toward it. Many of them were done around Buffalo, N.Y.,
where he moved permanently in 1921 and began to
document the American Scene more objectively than in
his early Symbolist and Expressionist inventions. The
great vacant facades of the homes of the "Awkward Age"
offered a new outlet for his mood of nostalgia. Sometimes
fantasy was given humorous relief by caricature, particularly as he introduced figures into his compositions.
At other times he used the extravagant, peaked architectural relics of Buffalo to create a more somber atmosphere.

At the end of the twenties and through the thirties his
feeling for the weird became further diluted, almost as
if even the grotesque were powerless to deal with the
vulgarity of visual reality in America. Decayed house
fronts, ramshackle factories, and dismal back streets
were set down now with little aesthetic or imaginative
elaboration. The artist seemed to succumb to the enervat-
ing tempo, the gritty ugliness of the life he had chosen
to treat, repeating and ritualizing the scenes with a discouraged objectivity. American materialism seemed to
take its revenge finally by blunting his imagination.

What Burchfield was to domestic wooden architecture
and to the rural or small-town scene, Hopper was to the
drab "modernistic" America of the large cities. In the

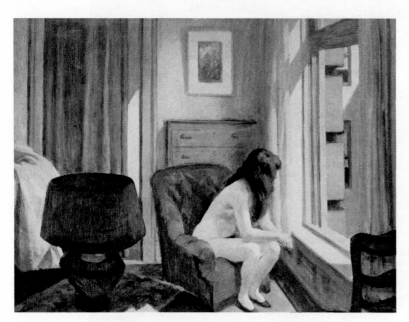

475 Edward Hopper. *Eleven A.M.* 1926. Oil on canvas, 28 × 36".
Hirshhorn Museum and Sculpture Garden,
Smithsonian Institution, Washington, D.C.

inhuman surfaces of urban life—anonymous brick houses, store fronts, cafeterias, neon signs, gas pumps, cinemas, pavements, lampposts, and fire hydrants—he found metaphors for spiritual vacancy and imprisonment. Like Burchfield, he was an artist of American ennui and loneliness; unlike him, Hopper never expressed explicit fantasy or subordinated description of visual phenomena to free invention.

Hopper always managed to extract some beauty from the ugliness and monotony of his stagnant scenes. In *Nighthawks* (1942, plate 474) his motif is nothing more than a deserted street at night with a brightly lit diner, its preoccupied customers sitting torpidly, like Surrealist dummies. A subject he repeatedly painted is the interior of a movie "palace," executed in a manner that vividly summons up the artificial dream world of the cinema. Contrasts in color, value, and degree of definition set apart the amorphous black mass of the spectators in their helpless surrender and the brilliant square of white screen. Vacuity is compounded with inanition in the figure of an inattentive usherette who stands to one side, lost in her own thoughts.

Light plays its part in his work by creating mood and revealing form with utmost clarity. *Early Sunday Morning* (1930, colorplate 68) presents an empty street and building fronts, with no sign of the human presence. Yet the strong patterns of light and shade create a pictorial drama and lend the familiar scene a redeeming poetry and dignity, despite its architectural banality. Hopper's night scenes particularly evoke a romantic atmosphere as no American Realist since John Sloan had done. He was in all probability influenced by various members of

The Eight, whom he knew and for a time imitated in the earlier years of the century, and he later acknowledged his debt to Sloan, praising his ability to render "remarkably the quality of a brooding silent interior in this vast city of ours."

Coming to maturity in a period whose prevailing temper was directed either to reportorial Realism or to experimental abstraction, Hopper set himself against both tendencies and took a long time in working out his own distinctive style. He studied for five years under Robert Henri and Kenneth Hayes Miller and then went to Paris in 1906. On his return Hopper participated in the first exhibition of the Independents in 1910, but did not take part in the early demonstrations of a more radical modernism at Stieglitz's gallery, the Forum Gallery, or in the Armory Show. Discouraged by his own personal struggle to live by art, and alienated by the more radical artistic tendencies, he abandoned painting altogether for etching and commercial illustration from 1915 to 1923.

For an artist whose choice of subject and handling reflected an ingrained puritanism, an austere geometry of compositional structure, the powerful female nudes he occasionally painted seem surprising in their psychological penetration. In *Eleven A. M.* (1926, plate 475), a nude woman stares absently through an apartment window facing the bleakness of another uneventful day, but even the boredom of the scene cannot conceal its sexual tension. The picture is a haunting expression of Hopper's central theme—the vacancy and frustration of modern urban existence.

Unlike most other Realists of his period, Hopper has not been dismissed by modernist artists and critics as a backslider from abstraction. In fact, his reputation has risen dramatically, even among dedicated progressivists, as a remarkable exception to the Realist pattern of subordinating formal qualities to a sentimental subject matter.

THE REGIONALIST MYTH

For Thomas Hart Benton (1889–1975), John Steuart Curry (1897–1946), Grant Wood (1892–1942), and other Regionalist painters, Burchfield's art, in its makeshift, illustrative style and dogged American Scene subject matter, may have supplied the first hint of a violent rebuke to modernism. But these artists replaced Burchfield's despondency with false optimism and interpreted his subject matter as an endorsement of a new jingoism. In some of his midwestern farm scenes, Burchfield had painted a rural America from which pioneer zest had long since vanished, leaving a tedium of endless chores, loneliness, and fears. Benton and Curry assimilated Burchfield's gnarled distortions in form, his ornamental arabesques, but brightened his palette and mood and tried to re-create the heroic saga of the American West.

In the hands of Benton, Curry, and Wood, the Regionalist myth became an effective, if strident, propaganda instrument for repudiating European modernism and its deluded American supporters. The chauvinist boast can be summed up in Benton's words: "A windmill, a junk heap, and a Rotarian have more meaning to me than Notre Dame or the Parthenon." Although Benton developed a rhythmically controlled Expressionist manner in the thirties, he was clearly aware of Renaissance composition and structure, and his paintings recall Tintoretto and Michelangelo. His epic figurative sources, like his brief flirtation with abstract form, lend further irony to his intemperate attacks on European art. He used his energetic, if somewhat mannered, figure style to illustrate cotton fields, folklore, subjects from history, and the myth of the opening of the West, as well as an occasional allegory of urban life in such works as his *City Activities with Subway* (1931, plate 476). Benton's broad caricatural gifts were best suited perhaps for mural painting, and in a series of ambitious murals executed after 1930, beginning with the New York series in the New School for Social Research, he realized his own vigorous conception of America at work and at play on the grand scale. Despite his simplistic cultural viewpoint, his work conveys a sense of power and dynamism no longer easy to dismiss.

In *American Gothic* (1930, colorplate 67) Grant Wood created a minor masterpiece despite its stereotyped, neoprimitive style. Like the Renaissance Flemish painters whom he apparently emulated, Wood's painting profits by its meticulous clarity of detail, stiff poses, and strong design. Although he intended it as a satire on tight-lipped American repression, it became instead the revered symbol of the Middle Western Regionalist program. The figures in the picture are those of Wood's sister and his dentist, and the house is in Iowa.

The Regionalist painters were dismaying, both for their repudiation of modern principles of design and for their nostalgic effort to find hardly credible social panaceas identified with a simpler, more virtuous past. They turned to the Middle West, whose people, folkways, and myths seemed to have a uniquely American and reassuring character. Theirs was an art of the country (plate 477), rather than the grim, industrialized city—an America of hillbillies, folksingers, revival meetings, and, ironically, in the Depression years, prosperous farms with limitless horizons of waving wheat. Despite the sincerity

476 Thomas Hart Benton. *City Activities with Subway.* Mural, 1931. Oil and egg tempera on linen, mounted on reinforced wallboard, 7½′ × 12′. The New School for Social Research, New York

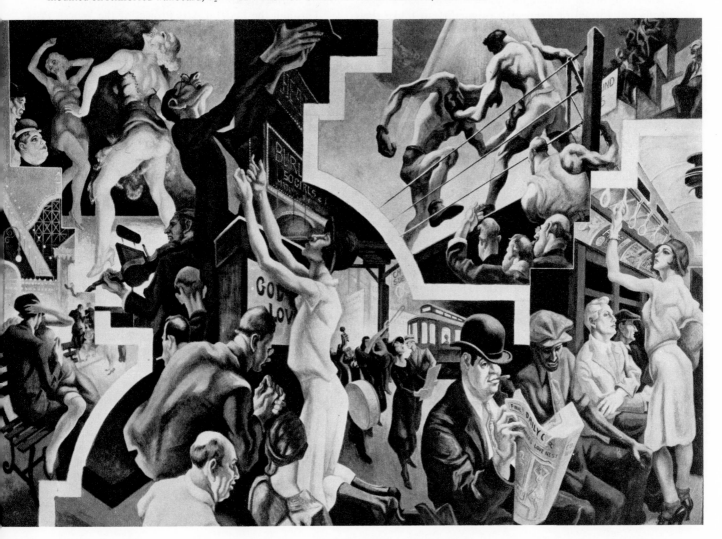

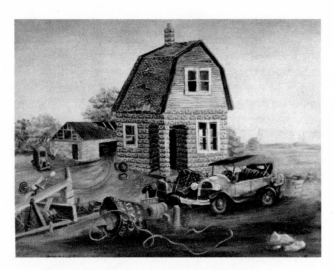

477 Aaron Bohrod. *Landscape near Chicago*. 1934.
Oil on composition board, 24 × 32".
Whitney Museum of American Art, New York

of much of the effort to reach a reconciliation with the American social environment, there were obvious xenophobic and puritanic elements in their often fanatical pursuit of the American heritage. Overreacting to a nationalistic cultural climate, many artists who rode the American Scene bandwagon failed to give their subjects sufficient formal or expressive originality to make their enthusiasms persuasive in pictorial terms. For a brief period in the late thirties a number of artists were attracted to regionalist subjects, but public interest in the movement faded rapidly and by the forties it was largely forgotten.

SOCIAL REALISM AND THE DEPRESSION

Social Realist painting in the thirties and early forties was a product not only of the visual explorations of Burchfield, Hopper, and the Regionalists, but even more directly a reaction to the political and economic crisis of the Depression. That tragic event drove American artists into a new search for their cultural identity, first through themes of social protest in Realism, and then, at least in part from the stimulation supplied by the Federal Art Project, through surprising experiments with Constructivist abstraction. Until the Depression, pictorial and social comment in art had been confined almost exclusively to cartoons appearing in the press and had not been expressed in fine arts even by Socialists such as John Sloan. But the state of economic hopelessness in the early thirties, in conjunction with a government-sponsored art program, now produced an art primarily concerned with social themes. Social content overrode any other objective aesthetic criteria, and radical politics became a source both of imagery and a new idealistic spirit in representational styles, which were often weighted heavily with Marxist clichés. This new art turned its back

with impartial disdain on American Scene painting and modernism.

Fortunately, the most important influence on it was not the sterile academic "Social Realism" of the Soviet Union, but the more vital and inventive monumental styles of the revolutionary Mexican painters Diego Rivera, José Orozco, and David Siqueiros, all of whom executed important murals in the United States. Rivera, the best known and the busiest of them, filled the walls of Mexican public buildings with murals that preached the ideals of social revolution and the evils of capitalism in a style combining decorative elements from Post-impressionism, occasional savage social caricature, and the hieratic compositions of fourteenth-century Italian religious art. In the United States, he made murals for the San Francisco Stock Exchange, the Detroit Institute of Arts, and, in 1933, Rockefeller Center in New York. Because a head of Lenin appeared in this last, the sponsors had the work destroyed. As in the case of Orozco, who painted important murals at Pomona College, at Dartmouth College, and at the New School for Social Research, New York, the nihilism and subversion of Mexican Socialist art were denounced, but not before a considerable impact was felt on the art of social protest that was emerging in the government art programs.

Through the Federal Arts Project of the Works Progress Administration, a process of democratization of the arts, forgotten since before the Civil War, was taken up again, as actors, writers, sculptors, musicians, painters and photographers were able to bring their talents to a public hungry for the arts, while at the same time destitute artists could earn a living during the crisis years. The Federal Art Project lasted from 1934 until World War II brought an end to this unique experiment. During its administration, it employed more than 5,000 artists in almost every state in the Union and adorned a multitude of public buildings with more than a million works of art. Although the program admittedly spawned much mediocre painting, it also produced a considerable amount of aesthetic merit, including a surprising number of monumental abstract murals by such artists as Arshile Gorky and James Brooks.

By the middle thirties, the social-content painters were more dominant than the rival Regionalists, especially in the large cities. Militant radicalism was probably more of a factor in their popularity than artistic style, but the movement did also help to shape the careers of many painters who made significant contributions to American art, among them William Gropper, Robert Gwathmey, Philip Evergood, Jack Levine, and Ben Shahn. From their allegorical WPA murals with pictorial stereotypes derived from a combination of Mexican nationalists and Quattrocento frescoes, these Americans progressed to a more personal expression in their

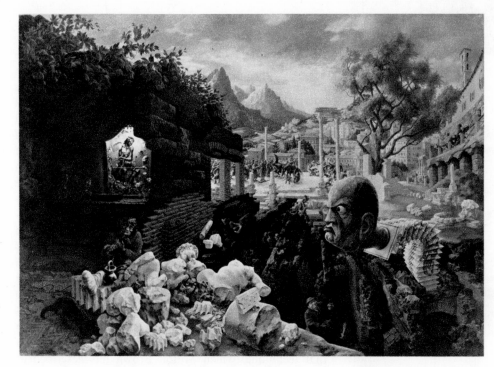

478 Peter Blume. *The Eternal City*. 1937.
Oil on composition board, 34 × 47⅛".
The Museum of Modern Art, New York.
Mrs. Simon Guggenheim Fund

easel paintings. Ultimately they gave a new edge to satire and fantasy in application to social life and imparted stronger moral convictions to art. In some instances another kind of synthesis was achieved in the form of "social Surrealism," an art primarily of personal dream images reacting to the urgencies of the social situation. One example is the bizarre and gruesome depiction of Mussolini and the powerful symbolic attack on Italian Fascism in *The Eternal City* (1937, plate 478) by Peter Blume.

In retrospect the varieties of 1930s Realism are surprising, and they seem even to acquire more visual appeal and personal character with the passage of time. William Gropper (1897–1977) lampooned capitalist bullies who exploited the working man and depicted corrupt or cynical politicians, in the *New Masses*. The removal of social animus permits us better to appreciate his abrupt and powerful simplicities of design and figuration (plate 479).

One of the artists who endured the trials and social tribulations of his time with a more personal kind of vision was Philip Evergood (1901–1973), whose grotesqueries have lost little of their bite. *Lily and the Sparrows* (1939, plate 480) leaves one uncertain whether the lumpy personage is meant to be a deformity or merely an embodiment of boisterous human energy. In any case, the tenement scene of bird-feeding strains credibility, and its exaggeration of anatomy and perspective brings us close to the atmosphere of a troubling dream. A different and more personal romanticism sustains the theatrical

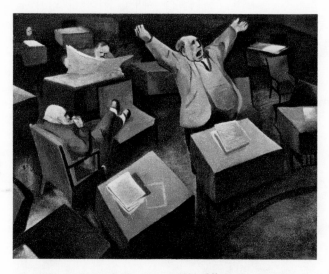

479 William Gropper. *The Senate*. 1935. Oil on canvas,
25⅛ × 33⅛". The Museum of Modern Art,
New York. Gift of A. Conger Goodyear

settings of tumbling figures and studio props in the extravagant but elegantly painted imaginary scenarios of Edwin Dickinson (b. 1891) such as *Composition with Still Life* (1933–37, plate 481). This mild decadence turned into positive melodrama with the studies of visible human deterioration by Ivan le Lorraine Albright (b. 1897).

Other notable Social and Romantic Realists who began to make their reputations in the thirties included Reg-

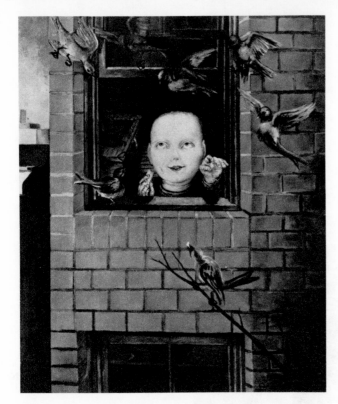

480 Philip Evergood. *Lily and the Sparrows*. 1939.
Oil on composition board, 30 × 24".
Whitney Museum of American Art, New York

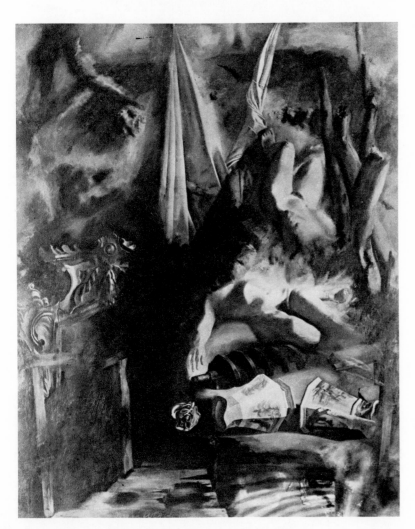

481 Edwin Dickinson. *Composition with Still Life*. 1933–37.
Oil on canvas, 8'1" × 6'5¾". The Museum of Modern Art,
New York. Gift of Mr. and Mrs. Ansley W. Sawyer

inald Marsh; the brothers Raphael, Isaac, and Moses Soyer; Isabel Bishop; and Milton Avery. Marsh (1898–1954) became celebrated for the robust characters he depicted on New York's skid row, a derelict population that he endowed with almost monumental energies, as in *The Bowery* (1930, plate 482), utilizing the visual rhetoric of High Renaissance style. The Soyers developed their touching genre portraits of exhausted shopgirls and absorbed office workers, which like so much Realism of the period dramatize the human cost of the Depression experience. Raphael Soyer's *Office Girls* (1936, plate 483) is a simple and moving statement of the melancholy lives of the brave, although passive, urban proletariat. One detects a remote influence of Degas and Pascin in the choice of subject, the self-absorbed mood, and the sensuous handling of paint surfaces. Isabel Bishop (b. 1902) exemplifies the viable eclecticism of the period in her paintings of common people, whom she posed and painted in thinned oil washes with the unsentimental professionalism and technical skills of an old master. *Waiting* (1938, plate 484) is an example of that technique, which Milton Brown has described as "a method close to Rubens' sketching style, with its transparent shadows and loaded lights."

Milton Avery's *Swimmers and Sunbathers* (1945, colorplate 69) adheres to the formula that he had developed in the thirties: simplified patterns taken from landscape and human forms, with rudimentary outlines and color harmonies revealing his admiration for Matisse. His thinly brushed strokes of pigment, bold chromatic sequences, and increasing scale of shape and overall dimensions were later to have a direct impact on the abstract painting of Adolph Gottlieb and Mark Rothko. Avery was one of the few artists in the 1930s working in a basically figurative style who tried to maintain some significant continuity with European modernism.

The Depression period also encouraged variations on primitive expression, recalling a long folk tradition extending back to the colonial limners. Louis Eilshemius (1864–1941), who had studied academic painting at the Art Students League in New York, later abandoned his training for more naive and fantastic forms of painting under the compulsions of his personal vision. John Kane (1860–1934), after spending his life in the mines and on the railroads of Pennsylvania, painted the American industrial landscape in flattened perspective, with the symmetries of design, emphatic ornament, and childlike delight in extraneous detail that we associate with pictorial primitivism. Another artistic personality within this sphere was Horace Pippin (1888–1956), a self-taught black artist who began to paint only at the age of forty-two. His colors are more vivid and original than those of many primitives, perhaps because of his interest in Matisse, whose work in the Barnes Foundation in Merion, Pa., Pippin had been able to visit from his home in nearby West Chester in the 1930s. Perhaps the most

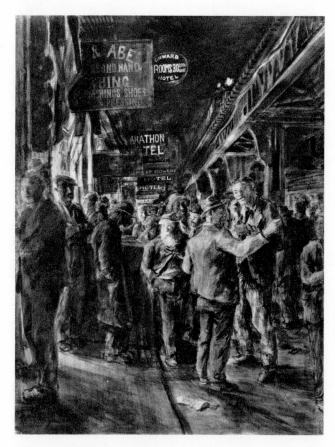

482 Reginald Marsh. *The Bowery*. 1930. Oil on canvas, 48 × 36".
The Metropolitan Museum of Art, New York.
Arthur H. Hearn Fund, 1932

celebrated American primitive was Anna Mary Robertson Moses (1860–1961), known as "Grandma Moses," who began to paint her attractive, childlike farm scenes in 1927, when she was sixty-seven. The idea that nonprofessional painting had validity and even artistic merit comparable to high art forms was advanced in the thirties by exhibitions held at the Newark Museum, Newark, N. J., in 1930 and 1931, and at The Museum of Modern Art, New York, in 1939.

One of the most interesting developments of the 1930s, as the grim realities of the Depression replaced the frivolity of the Jazz Age, was a growing self-consciousness on the part of black artists, for whom the economic crisis provided an occasion for linking themselves to common themes of social protest. Alain Locke, a black advocate of American Scene painting, described the thirties as a time when "American art was rediscovering the Negro." In a sense, both Regionalist and social-protest art gave black imagery a new legitimacy, both as part of the myth of American historical evolution and as a symbol of racial oppression. Curiously, these circumstances permitted the black artist to view himself and his racial subject matter with a new pride, sanctioned by white interests and precedent. Not unreasonably, apart from their attraction to primitivism, the black artists of the twentieth century tended to identify with American Scene painting, rather than with modernism in its European and formally sophisticated examples. However, there were conflicts in this evolution. The historian James A. Porter, in an essay assessing the 1930s, could wish that black artistic

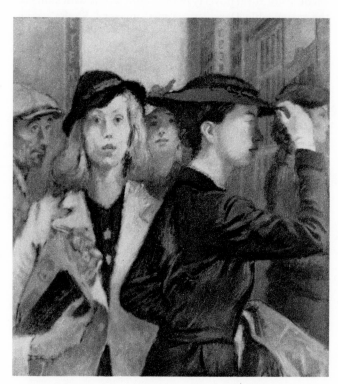

483 Raphael Soyer. *Office Girls*. 1936. Oil on canvas, 26 × 24".
Whitney Museum of American Art, New York

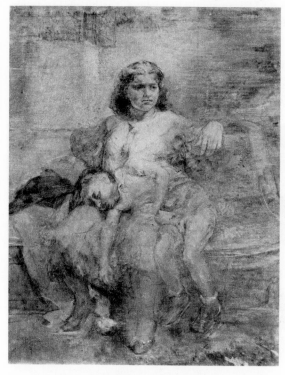

484 Isabel Bishop. *Waiting*. 1938. Oil and tempera on gesso panel, 29 × 22½". The Newark Museum, Newark, N.J. Arthur F. Egner Memorial Committee Purchase, 1944

Painting: Advances and Retreats 451

"efforts at social criticism were more direct and accusatory—less concerned with daydreaming or with symbolistic wishfulness." Yet, one of the best of the emerging black artists, Romare Bearden (b. 1914), courageously identified himself with modernism and deplored the self-pitying character of much stereotyped black art as examples of "timidity" and "mere rehashings" of "hackneyed and uninspired" social themes. Later, in 1946, as black artists became a significant part of the art mainstream, and as ethnic or racial consciousness became increasingly difficult to discern in their art, Bearden wrote: "It would be highly artificial for the Negro artist to attempt a resurrection of African culture in America. . . . Culture is not a biologically inherited phenomenon. . . . Modigliani, Picasso, Epstein and other modern artists studied African sculpture to reinforce their own design concepts. . . . Any Negro artist who cared to [could] do the same. . . . The true artist feels that there is only one art—and it belongs to all mankind."

Bearden did not become well known until the forties, when he exhibited at the Kootz Gallery in New York with the American Abstract Expressionists. He has utilized elements of photographs and collage in Cubist-inspired compositions and extended the basic formula in later works such as *Interior* (1969, colorplate 70). His subject matter is urban black life, but the style is fluent and international, and he shows a consistent development, despite his dependence on a Cubist armature. A discerning critic has described Bearden as one of the few "universal" black artists seeking a balance between the rigorous formal criteria of modern art and race consciousness. David Driskell, in 1975, wrote: "Bearden's artistry is not the Black content of his work, which is often laden with Neo-African symbols; instead it is his ability to express in a catholic sense those humanizing characteristics of blackness that are synonymous with universal man."

Jacob Lawrence (b. 1917) was another of the more significant black artists to emerge during or immediately after the Depression in original styles and work of a decidedly professional character. Though Lawrence affected a neoprimitive style, in fact he used simple silhouettes and a rather naïve imagery related to graphic illustration to create a tough, urban idiom. His paintings are decorative but intensely felt, with a rousing animal vitality to balance familiar themes of social injustice and violence. He probed the problem of race relations in his panel, "One of the largest race riots occurred in East St. Louis," taken from a series of paintings called *The Migration of the Negro* (1940–41, plate 485). The hatchet-like forms echo the violence of theme and recall a similar scene of mayhem in a deliberately constricted but explosive composition, Goya's *The Third of May, 1808*, which visually castigated the Napoleonic persecutions and civilian atrocities. Lawrence's painting proved sadly prophetic of the eruption of racial tensions in later years.

SHAHN AND WYETH

Ben Shahn (1898–1969) was one of the more prolific WPA muralists, and a rare one, whose spirit of social commitment was enriched both by humane values and a cognizance of the importance of modern abstraction. His edgy, nervous line and sense of a condensed, cartographic space derived probably from Paul Klee, as did a poster-like flatness and chromatic brilliance in his art. He was a photographer, like many artists of his generation, and close particularly to Walker Evans, whose documentary accounts of rural poverty in the South left us with some of the memorable Depression years' imagery. Shahn's own pictorial efforts combine the haunting images and parables of social oppression with the elliptical devices of modernism.

Shahn grew up in an atmosphere of left-wing radicalism. Many of his early projects in the 1930s took the form of social polemic and caricature. In fact, he first came to public attention with the twenty-three gouaches he painted in 1931–32 dealing with the trial and execution of Nicola Sacco and Bartolomeo Vanzetti, two Italian immigrants convicted of a murder that it is now argued they did not commit. *The Passion of Sacco and Vanzetti* (plate 486), showing the victims of antiradical hysteria and their elegant judges, who were Boston Brahmins, is a bitter and still affecting satire on social hypocrisy and injustice.

As Shahn developed in the late 1930s and early 1940s, he began to move from a public art of direct social criticism to a more personal statement that portrayed the individual in terms of private emotional experience. Elegiac poetic content replaced satire. He painted the old and homeless marooned on a park bench; children carried away by the excitement of play; or lovers in a park, im-

485 Jacob Lawrence. "One of the largest race riots occurred in East St. Louis," from the series *The Migration of the Negro*, 1940–41. Tempera on board, 12 × 18″. The Museum of Modern Art, New York. Gift of Mrs. David M. Levy

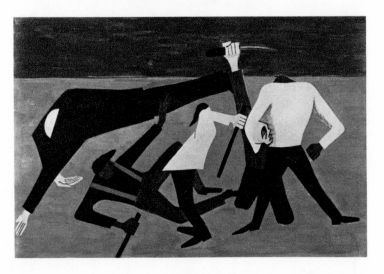

prisoned by a network of fence railing and their own dreams. The figures are reduced to expressive silhouettes pressed into the maze of urban building patterns, eloquent images of loneliness in a style that was hard-boiled and sensitive by turns. *The Red Stairway* (1944, colorplate 71) registers a poignant commentary on the subject of human abandonment and man's cruelty to man.

Shahn most often used tempera, obtaining effects of dry incandescence with a metallic luster. His surfaces, his colors, his expressive language of image and symbol progressively reflected the influence of Klee; yet the nervous pulse of his work and its commercial-art blatancy are unmistakably native. Drawing on a sophisticated, semi-abstract idiom, Shahn portrayed the American scene with interpretive imagination. He was often a lyricist and always a fine reporter.

Shahn's magical Realism became in later years a formative influence on many younger contemporaries, one of the most notable being Andrew Wyeth (b. 1917), son of the celebrated illustrator N. C. Wyeth. Andrew Wyeth, beginning in the late 1930s, worked in both watercolor and tempera, and in certain works he shared something of Shahn's precision of flat detail and sense of human solitariness. In Wyeth's case, however, the theme of loneliness was linked to nature and the vast outdoors, particularly at his rural home in Chadds Ford, Pa., and in Maine, where he spends his summers.

Despite a more modern note of psychological anguish, Wyeth also shows clear affinities with the Regionalists who turned away from the "corruption" of urban life to celebrate the homespun virtues of the frontier and the country. His style owes a considerable debt to his brother-in-law, Peter Hurd (b. 1904), who became known for the spare simplicity of his arid Southwest landscape paintings; Hurd was also earlier in using the meticulous tempera technique for which Wyeth is so well known. However, by comparison, Wyeth is an almost clinically direct, Realist reporter. He seems, in fact, to strive frankly for the verisimilitude of the photograph. The sense of spiritual malaise in the American scene that both Shahn and Hopper underlined has also become his major theme. He sometimes approaches Shahn's manner of expressing fantasy by setting a figure starkly against an intricately embroidered, microscopically exact expanse of nature—a nature haunted by somber forces.

The first painting to bring Wyeth fame was *Christina's World* (1948, colorplate 72). In it a Maine neighbor, crippled by paralysis, reaches tensely and awkwardly toward farmhouses looming almost symbolically on the brow of a hill like some unattainable goal. The fine, grassy field is a magical tracery of abstract writing, reminiscent both of Shahn and of Mark Tobey and underlining the essential eclecticism of Wyeth's pictorial manner. The mood of despair and the colors—the arid brown of the landscape and the chemical pink of the girl's dress—verge on Surrealist intensity, but the parable of

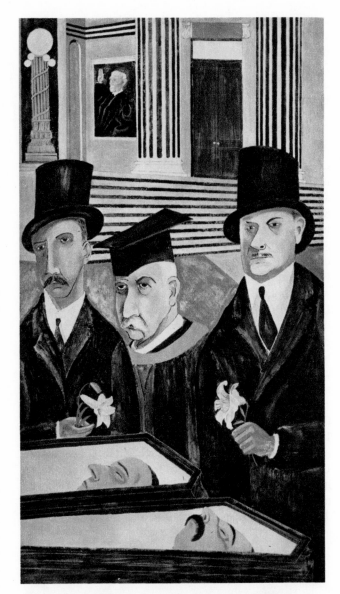

486 Ben Shahn. *The Passion of Sacco and Vanzetti*, from the series of 23 paintings. 1931–32. Tempera on canvas, $84\frac{1}{2} \times 48''$. Whitney Museum of American Art, New York. Gift of Edith and Milton Lowenthal in memory of Juliana Force

entrapment and frustration seems obvious and contrived.

What most appeals to the public, one must conclude, apart from Wyeth's conspicuous virtuosity, is the artist's banality of imagination and lack of pictorial ambition. He comfortably fits the commonsense ethos and non-heroic mood of today's popular culture, despite his occasional lapses into gloomy introspection. The veteran of World War I, shabby but proud in his military jacket with his medals; the young boy dreaming of heroic exploits on the battlefield and wearing a borrowed airman's jacket too large for him; the affectionately but patronizingly portrayed blacks around Chadds Ford, from charming pickaninnies to wizened grandpas; the wine-sodden drifter—these are all apparently actual people who have surrounded Wyeth at his farm. It would be tempting to invest them with the power of myth, but they refuse to function symbolically in a larger dimension. They are quickly grasped and soon forgotten, the more so today because the imagery seems dated.

EXPRESSIONISM AND FANTASY

Along with Social Realism and Romantic Realism, the dominating tendency of the 1940s was Expressionism. It is still practiced by a few distinguished American artists, although today it has generally merged with abstraction. Strong subjective feeling, brilliant color, and violent handling became for a time identifying trademarks of American painting, particularly when combined with either social protest or strong personal fantasy. One of the most individual Expressionist painters of the forties was Hyman Bloom (b. 1913). Russian-born, trained in Boston, Bloom was influenced by the blazing color and distortions of Chaim Soutine and El Greco. He evolved a personal imagery of cantors, rabbis, and synagogue interiors of an extraordinary vividness, with stupendous color effects, rich visual sensations, and a mood of deep and sincere emotion.

Jack Levine (b. 1915) was Bloom's fellow student at the Boston Museum School and two years his senior. Like Bloom, he owed a technical debt to Soutine and to other European Expressionists such as Georges Rouault. Unlike Bloom's, his art is worldly and satirical and takes its stand as an indictment of the avarice of the rich, the miscarriage of justice, the squalor of official public life. *The Feast of Pure Reason* (1937, plate 487), one of his

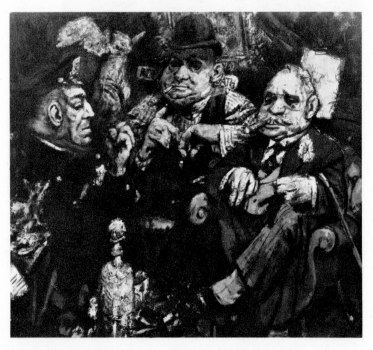

487 Jack Levine. *The Feast of Pure Reason*. 1937. Oil on canvas, 42 × 48″. The Museum of Modern Art, New York. On extended loan from the United States WPA Art Program

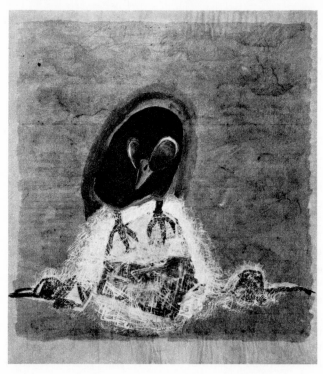

488 Morris Graves. *Blind Bird*. 1940. Gouache, 30⅛ × 27″. The Museum of Modern Art, New York. Purchase

first visual diatribes against self-serving officials and the conspiracy of political bosses, police, and business, is a native parable of urban corruption painted with surprising maturity for the WPA Art Program at the age of twenty-two.

Though the style approaches caricature, it also recalls Rouault's rich jeweled pigmentation and sense of moral outrage. Levine is essentially a Realist reporter. Even his most diffusely painted and violent distortions cannot dislodge a certain literalism. Today his inflamed social conscience and satirical themes seem remote from the dominant artistic preoccupations. His palette has lightened, and his pictorial effects have become elaborately illusionist; he paints now in thin washes, creating a fine filament of form and atmosphere in an effort to give his subjects a quality of mystery. His subject matter of Biblical figures and myth and their archaic, old-master handling seem designed to fulfill his earliest stated ambition, "to bring the great tradition up to date."

European Expressionism shaped the work of many other artists who depicted the American scene at an even higher pitch of emotional violence and grisly fantasy. A combination of apocalyptic social vision and personal fantasy has been mentioned earlier as "social Surrealism." In 1938 a review of the first one-man show of Louis Guglielmi called one of his paintings, which protested against the Sacco-Vanzetti affair, "a social document shrouded in the language of Surrealism." His visual symbolism and paintings by Peter Blume of 1934 were exceptional examples of the style in the period. Curiously, Blume's modified Surrealist art predated by two years the influential exhibition in New York at The

Museum of Modern Art, "Fantastic Art, Dada and Surrealism," which played a major role in introducing American artists and the public to Surrealism. The creative principle of automatism in that art was to have a profound effect during the 1940s on the pictorial methods of the Abstract Expressionists, but the more academic and *trompe-l'oeil* Surrealist painting typified by Salvador Dali first influenced American art in the 1930s, though without making serious changes in artistic traditions. A romantic and introspective vision has been more generally characteristic of American expressions of fantasy than the illusionistic devices of Surrealism. (See also Chapter 22.)

Mysticism is one of the sources of the American artistic imagination, as in the case of Morris Graves (b. 1910). His *Blind Bird* (1940, plate 488) is the product of intense personal vision and deep religious feeling. The small, passionate utterance recalls the narrow and confined but powerful sensibility of Ryder and the poems of Emily Dickinson. In Graves a new kind of American Regionalism is represented, associated with the Pacific Northwest. He traveled briefly in Europe and Japan but otherwise has spent his life in Seattle. Like his neighbor and mentor, Mark Tobey (1890–1976), he was strongly drawn to Oriental philosophy and to Zen painting, particularly to *sumi* painting, with its spontaneous, abstract signs. Tobey became known for his "white writing," a delicate, automatic, nonrepresentational script that is probably indebted as much to Paul Klee as to the art of the East. Graves's art is, by contrast, imagistic and particularized, though it has been somewhat influenced by the otherworldly atmosphere and many of the devices of Tobey's style. Graves made a tender poetry from such images as a pine tree tremulously holding a full moon in its branches, or tiny birds and snakes, images which seem to be secreted rather than painted on the canvas or paper. His art is rapt, visionary, hypnotic. In recent years his mysticism has sometimes raised a communication problem for all but the rare, indoctrinated religious spirit like himself. His technique so closely imitates that of the East, even to the use of scrolls and the cultivation of an archaic patina, that his art has often seemed little more than a replica of ancient Chinese or Korean painting.

Following a more challenging and vital artistic evolution, Mark Tobey came to represent the unusual case of an American abstract painter who received warmer appreciation in Europe than at home. He was almost certainly the first American artist, preceding even Jackson Pollock, to adopt a tangled, linear nonobjective style, but he was quite justly never credited with the invention of the "allover" painting, as it was understood in the New York school (see Chapter 22). His "white-writing" technique, adopted in the 1930s, seemed to be more akin to Japanese calligraphy than to Western abstraction, and his art always remained a metaphor for the cosmology of religious ideas that he discovered

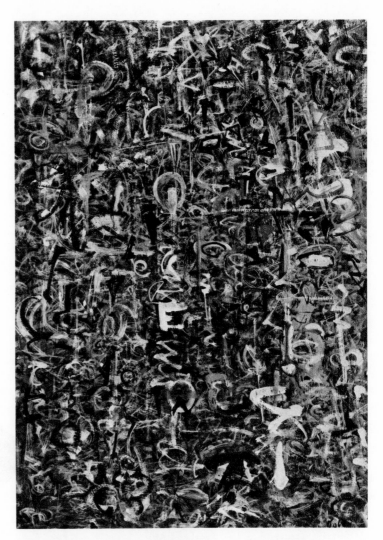

489 Mark Tobey. *Tundra*. 1944. Tempera on board, 24 × 16½".
Neuberger Museum, Purchase, N.Y.
Gift of Roy R. Neuberger

in his Eastern travels. Because of this inspiration for his unique and delicately lyrical art (plate 489), native critics have never assigned him a major role in the development of American Abstract Expressionist art.

RESURGENCE OF ABSTRACTION

Recent research and historical exhibitions have made it clear that the Great Depression did not propel all artists into a narrow set of options limited to social-protest statements, Regionalist American Scene revivals, or escapist art of personal fantasy. Geometric abstraction continued to thrive in this period under the influence and prodding of European abstractionists who came here and with the formation of native groups who espoused the still vital traditions of Russian Constructivism and Dutch de Stijl painting. In Europe abstract painting had never gone into an eclipse, and it reached artists in the United States first by way of exhibitions and publications and then in the person of a distinguished émigré generation. Josef Albers joined the Black Mountain College faculty in 1933, having fled Hitler's oppression of intellectuals. The teachings of Albers became widely influential, spreading his theories of color and the general principles of geometric abstraction, particularly in Op Art of the 1960s. Other prominent Europeans also came to teach. Hans Hofmann came in 1936, bringing a more Expressionist and intuitive art, which became a powerful force in the 1940s. Another major artist from Germany's Bauhaus, László Moholy-Nagy, arrived in 1937 to establish the Chicago Bauhaus. Fritz Glarner came in 1937, and Piet Mondrian, who was well known and had distinguished disciples, in 1940.

Sam Hélion, a leader of *Abstraction-Creation* in France, was a familiar name to New Yorkers who kept in touch with vanguard European directions. He was a frequent visitor between 1934 and 1943, when he had almost annual one-man shows in New York galleries. He also advised the collector and painter A. E. Gallatin, and was probably responsible for some of the most important acquisitions of Gallatin's "Museum of Living Art," then housed at New York University.

In the late 1930s there was a growing resolution of a sense of crisis in abstract art internationally and a general resurgence of nonobjective expressions under the aegis of such European groups in Paris as *Abstraction-Creation* and *Art Concret* and in London, *The Circle and the Square*. A number of young American abstractionists maintained informal relations with these groups, and some even showed with them. In America, arguments about art theory in such journals as *Art Front* between advocates of social-protest art and abstraction suggest a widening debate on the relation of

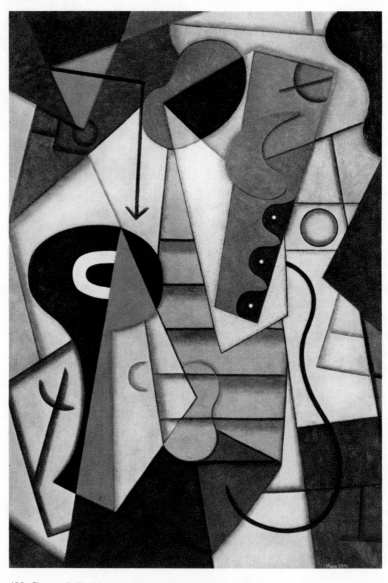

490 George L.K. Morris. *Nautical Composition*. 1937–42.
Oil on canvas, 51 × 35″. Whitney Museum of American Art, New York

abstract art to the outside world and to radical politics.

By 1936 the resurgence of abstraction was strong enough to lead to the founding of the American Abstract Artists organization. The original group included Rosalind Bengelsdorf, Byron Browne, Albert Swinden, Ibram Lassaw (at whose studio they first met), Burgoyne Diller, Balcomb Greene, Gertrude Greene, and Harry Holtzman. Artists who later participated in meetings or joint exhibitions were Josef Albers, Ilya Bolotowsky, Werner Drewes, Stuart Davis, Arshile Gorky, Carl Holty, Willem de Kooning, Alice Mason, George L. K. Morris, Charles Shaw, and Theodore Roszak. The group's aesthetic position was open-ended enough to include a wide range of abstract styles, with geometric/constructivist, neoplastic, Cubist, Expressionist, and biomorphic elements. Of considerable interest in themselves, these developments, and the artists who participated in them in early maturity, created the basis for the flowering of American art in the form of Abstract Expressionism during the 1940s.

In recent years a number of scholars and critics have concluded that the more sophisticated formal art which emerged under A.A.A. auspices represents aesthetic productions of higher quality than the socially conscious or Regionalist art of the period. On the surface, abstract art seemed entirely divorced from social currents in a politically divided and turbulent period. Actually, such artists as Stuart Davis and Balcombe Greene, who wrote regularly in the Artists' Union radical journal *Art Front*, concerned themselves as passionately with contemporary issues as with "pure" art. Their published rationalizations of abstraction were characteristic of the thirties, too, for it was their declared aim to affirm a revolutionary morality as persuasive as that of the Social Realists, not through a specific political commitment, but rather through the intrinsic involvement and values of the art activity itself. It is not difficult to find a connection here to the transvaluation process in the criticism of Harold Rosenberg, who began to write in *Art Front* in the thirties as a Marxist spokesman but by 1951 had invented the Existentialist concept of creativity embodied in his epithet, "Action Painting."

Most of the A.A.A artists worked in precise, sharp-edged rectilinear shapes with geometric curves, and in flat color areas, a group style recognizable in *Nautical Composition* (1937–42, plate 490) by George L. K. Morris (b. 1905). There were also some unusual combinations of biomorphic shapes with geometric purity in the fascinating collages and paintings of Ad Reinhardt (1913–1967) in the period when he belonged to the American Abstract Artists group and showed in their company such work as *Untitled* (1940, plate 491). Although biomorphic abstraction continued to flourish and had at least one important disciple in Arshile Gorky (1905–1948), geometric abstraction appealed to a much larger segment of the avant-garde, possibly because of the common Ameri-

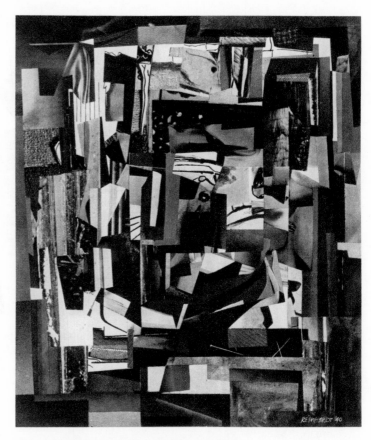

491 Ad Reinhardt. *Untitled*. 1940. Paper collage, 15¼ × 13". Whereabouts unknown

can sympathy for machine forms and also, surely, in reaction to the emotionalism and violence of urban Expressionist art.

In his work of the early 1930s Gorky set himself the ambitious goal of fusing Picasso's Synthetic Cubism with a Surrealist atmosphere of metamorphic form and biomorphism. His eclecticism represented the first serious effort, later characteristic of the entire forties generation, to master and synthesize two disparate traditions—the flatness and geometry of Cubist structure with the fluidity and improvisatory energy of automatic Surrealism. Parts of Gorky's impressive WPA mural for Newark Airport, recently rediscovered, were semiabstract. Entitled *Aviation, Evolution of Forms under Aerodynamic Limitations* (1935–36, plate 492), it was made up of composites of abstract but recognizable airplane parts and symbols of flight.

Just before this period Gorky had made portraits of supreme elegance, such as *The Artist and His Mother* (1926–29, colorplate 73), which exhibits a variety of influences from Picasso and Joan Miró to Ingres and Cézanne. It anticipates his more radical 1940s abstractions in its disembodied contour lines, loosely painted areas, and the thin bright color masses that detach themselves as organic shapes. The growing influence of Miró

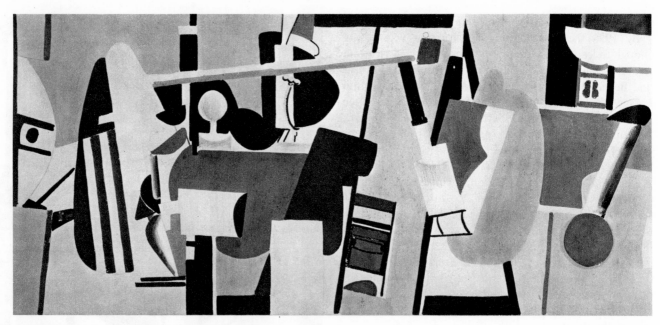

492 Arshile Gorky. Study for a mural for the Administration Building, Newark Airport, Newark, N.J. 1935–36. Gouache, $13\frac{5}{8} \times 29\frac{7}{8}''$. Estate of Arshile Gorky

and of Matta's more poetic and spontaneous abstraction became evident at the end of the 1930s and in the early 1940s.

Somewhere between Gorky's biomorphic style and a more Precisionist abstraction, marked by sharp formal delineations and hard, flat colors and derived from Léger, Hélion, and Synthetic Cubism, stood the art of Stuart Davis (1894–1964), perhaps America's most influential painter in the transitional 1930s. For the younger abstract artists he was something of a cultural hero, in that he had persisted in his semiabstract and unapologetically international art almost since the period of the Armory Show, despite considerable public hostility to modernism and the shift in America to a mood of cultural isolationism. Davis's art stands as a major link between America's first phase of advanced art and contemporary experiment. While his expression is not directly related in style or aims to present-day abstraction, in the 1930s it provided a point of support for young artists who were beginning to move toward abstraction. David Smith, the sculptor, found stimulation in Davis's liberal viewpoint on the WPA art project, and some of the more geometric abstractions by Arshile Gorky in the same era bear a resemblance to Davis's work of about 1927–30, as do many of the paintings of the members of the American Abstract Artists group.

Davis dates from the period of the first Realists, The Eight, many of whom he came to know as a boy in Philadelphia, where his father was art director of the *Philadelphia Press*, for which Shinn, Luks, Henri, and Sloan worked as artist-journalists. In 1910 Davis began to study painting in New York with Robert Henri. After

working with him for three years, Davis was painting in a manner of simplified Realism. Soon after leaving school he joined other artists of the new Realist camp as an illustrator for *The Masses*. In 1916, with four other artists, he withdrew from the magazine over policy differences. At the time of the rupture Art Young, the art director of *The Masses* and victor in the ideological scuffle, issued a statement in the *New York Sun* of April 8. "The five dissenting artists want to run pictures of ash cans and girls hitching up their skirts in Horatio Street—regardless of ideas—and without title."

The break with *The Masses* apparently confirmed Davis's growing doubts about Realism and descriptive subject matter already stirred by the Armory Show, which, in later years, he described as "the greatest single influence I have experienced in my work." In 1920 Davis moved toward a more uncompromising nonrepresentational art, using "a conceptual instead of an optical perspective." The following year he was executing such works as *Lucky Strike* (plate 493), his own painted version of the Cubists' *papiers collés*. In 1927 he began the first of a series of abstract variations in the spirit of decorative Cubism, based on the motif of an eggbeater, an electric fan, and a rubber glove. In these paintings Davis drastically simplified his forms, eliminating all but the most schematic descriptive content and reducing that to a system of flat planes and geometric shapes. "I felt," he was later to say, "that a subject had its emotional reality fundamentally through our awareness of such planes and their spatial relationships." The next year he went to Paris, where he found his radical experimental mood confirmed. Returning in 1929, he was immediately depressed by the "gigantism" and inhumanity of New York City, but was convinced that, as an American artist, he needed its "impersonal dynamics."

During the thirties and forties, Davis's style became more abstract but denser in its linear detail, full of cadenced movement and restless surface activity. Even so, he still depended on locale, introducing a cursive script of lettering fragments taken from signs and glimpses of characteristic American shop fronts, houses, or streets. Despite his debt to decorative Cubism, and perhaps most of all to Léger (whom he once described as "the most American painter painting today"), Davis managed to maintain a distinctly native inflection, a special lightness, and an altogether personal, whimsical humor. He remained his own man—inventive, positive, with a feeling for the tangible realities of the American environment. If his painting sometimes seemed too close to the spirit of the poster and merely a form of graceful decoration, he also showed an impressive structural color sense. "I think of color," he said, "as an interval of space—not as red or blue. People used to think of color and form as two things. I think of them as the same thing. . . . Color in a painting represents different positions in space."

Partial to jazz and other popular art forms, Davis sought to inject brisk new rhythms and an irreverent gaiety into abstract painting. Some of his irregular silhouettes and his bright color seem to have anticipated the playful *Jazz* cutouts of Matisse's last years. Unlike Matisse, Davis used his scraps of words to give an abrasive, contemporary quality to his fragmented, collage-like painting, the shock of a suddenly evoked reality in the midst of an abstract pictorial scheme. In *Visa* (1951, colorplate 74) a spark-plug brand name, "Champion," and the phrase, "The Amazing Continuity," seem to suggest some mystical sense of unity, all playing against an optically jarring, energized color scheme. He used words in his pictures, as he said, "because they are a part of an urban subject matter." The content of one of his phrases he described as being "as real as any shape of a face or a tree. . . ." Davis evolved an abstract visual language that was also a sensitive recorder of real impressions—a modest language, perhaps, but passionate, unmistakably American, and decisively his own. To the generation of artists who drew on the American scene, his work must have posed a challenge, for it provided

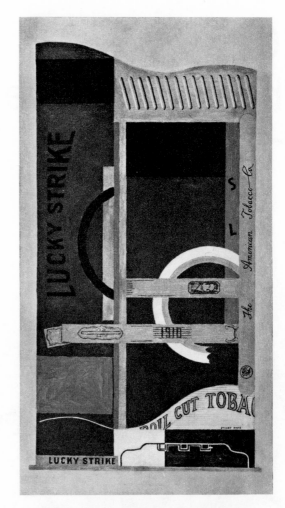

493 Stuart Davis. *Lucky Strike*. 1921. Oil on canvas, 33¼ × 18″. The Museum of Modern Art, New York. Gift of The American Tobacco Company, Inc.

more refreshing answers in the quest for a native art than the various styles of Romantic Realism offered. He set forth a high standard of taste, if not a direct incentive for further experiment. Throughout the period of antimodern reaction Davis painted according to aesthetic principles more exacting than those of most of his contemporaries. The generation of abstract artists after World War II was to find solace and encouragement in his simple statement: "The act of painting is not a duplication of experience, but the extension of experience on the plane of formal invention."

20
Photography: Developments of the Depression

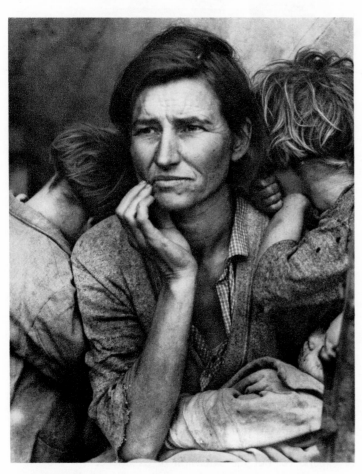

494 Dorothea Lange. *Migrant Mother, California.* 1936.
Library of Congress, Washington, D.C.

From the 1930s on, photographic expression continued to reflect many of the same currents as the other visual arts. In response to the Depression, photographers began to focus on the effects of the national tragedy at the same time that painters were turning to the American urban and rural scene. Photographs made under the auspices of government and private agencies were shown in nonart contexts, achieving their effect through size, arrange-

ment, and quantity, as well as subject matter. Today, while some of these images are merely records, others, such as Dorothea Lange's *Migrant Mother* (plate 494) seem to epitomize their time.

In 1934, when forty-five million people were, as Franklin D. Roosevelt said, "ill-clothed, ill-housed and ill-fed," an unprecedented photographic project was devised by Roy E. Stryker for the Department of Agriculture. Stryker, who had become aware of the impact of photographs when selecting images for a textbook on economic conditions in 1925, secured the services of Walker Evans, Dorothea Lange (1895–1968), Carl Mydans, Arthur Rothstein (b. 1915), and the painter Ben Shahn. Under the auspices of the Farm Security Administration, these photographers, and later others, were assigned to photograph a variety of conditions in small towns, on farms, and in resettlement camps in order to demonstrate the need for Federal assistance for the rural poor. The document that emerged (now housed in the Library of Congress) brought to life the economic and social disaster and made images available to audiences not ordinarily reached by the visual arts.

With a single exception, FSA photographers used small, fast equipment that enabled them to record fleeting expressions, such as the anxiety in Shahn's *Family of Rehabilitation Clients* (plate 495) and the wistfulness of Rothstein's *Girl at Gee's Bend* (plate 496). Lange's work, continuing a direction she had begun in 1931, when she photographed agricultural workers in California, is characterized by terse understatement as she projects specific emotions through her choice of telling expression, gesture, or landscape configuration. After World War II, Lange continued working in the United States, Egypt, and the Far East in order to reveal, as she put it, "the values and purposes of our complex world."

Evans, already known for photographs of New York and New England architecture, was unique among FSA photographers in that he used an 8 × 10 camera and was fastidious about selection and composition. His images evoke the pride and pathos of life in the rural South,

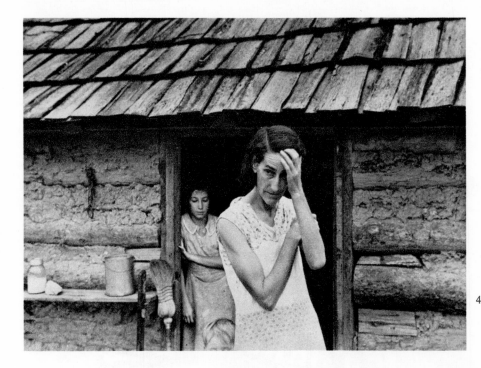

495 Ben Shahn. *Family of Rehabilitation Clients, Boone County, Ark.* 1935. Library of Congress, Washington, D.C.

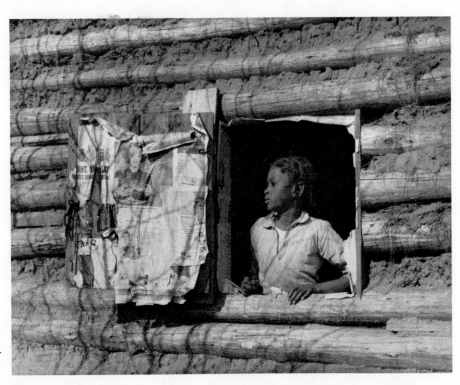

496 Arthur Rothstein. *Girl at Gee's Bend, Ala.* 1937. Library of Congress, Washington, D.C.

often through artifact and architecture. In 1936 Evans joined James Agee, a writer for *Fortune* magazine, to work on an independent project, eventually published as *Let Us Now Praise Famous Men.* In this work text and image form a poetic re-creation of southern sharecropping life. From 1945 until he joined the faculty of Yale University twenty years later, Evans was on the staff of *Fortune.* Although documentary photography usually required sources beyond the means of the individual, several photographers were able to work in the documentary mode and secure publishers for their work. Foremost among them was Margaret Bourke-White, whose images of rural southern tenant farmers were published, with text by Erskine Caldwell, in 1937 as *You Have Seen Their Faces,* one of the first photographic essays available in soft cover.

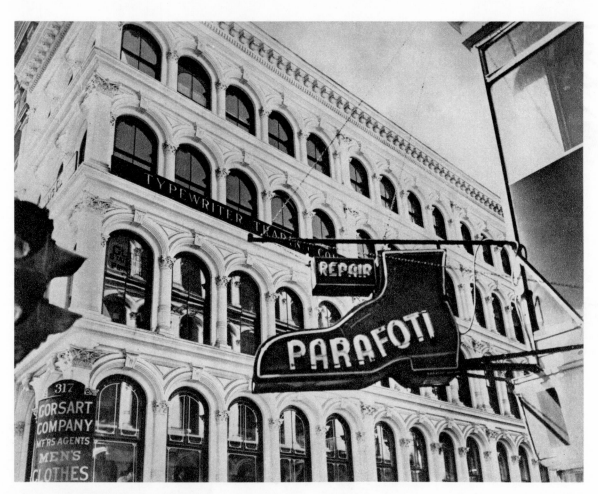

497 Berenice Abbott. *Facade of 317 Broadway*. 1939.
Private collection

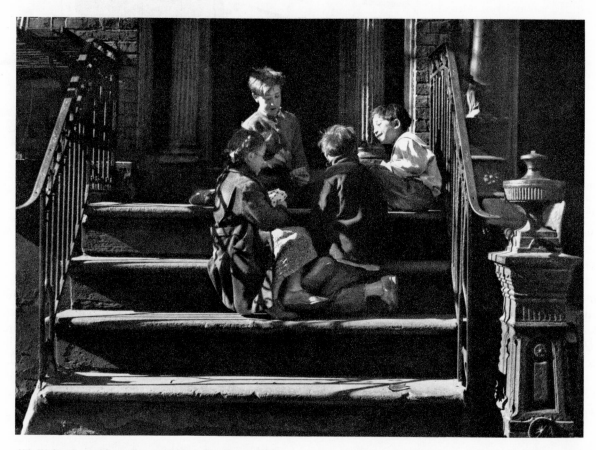

498 Walter Rosenblum. *Gypsy Children, Pitt Street*. 1938.
Collection the photographer

The Works Progress Administration, another agency of the Depression era, authorized photographic documentation of urban life under the direction of the Federal Art Project. The best-known and most complete urban document was begun independently by Berenice Abbott (b. 1898), who had returned to New York in 1929 after establishing herself as a portraitist of artistic and literary personalities in Paris. Her images, entitled *Changing New York* when they were exhibited and published under the auspices of the New York City Federal Art Project in 1937, suggest the dramatic quality of the physical city (plate 497), without emphasizing social conditions or human needs.

As subject matter, the city continued to inspire a wide variety of approaches in photography, whether commissioned by organizations or created by individuals. In 1931 the Empire State Building Corporation retained Lewis Hine to document the construction of the world's tallest skyscraper, a project he fulfilled with imagination and daring. Photographers in the Photo League, a New-York-based organization that existed from 1936 until 1951, concerned themselves mainly with the urban social scene. Among those involved were Sid Grossman, Sol Libsholm, and Morris Engel, whose work conveys the corroding bitterness of the time. Warmth and camaraderie, another aspect of the period, are expressed in Walter Rosenblum's (b. 1919) *Gypsy Children on Pitt Street* (plate 498). Following World War II, the League ran a successful school and gallery and numbered among its members many of America's renowned photographers until it became a victim of the political repression of the fifties. Among the individuals who found visual excitement and drama in the city were Arthur Fellig (1899–1968), who, as Weegee, published his photographs in *Naked City* (1945); Andreas Feininger (b. 1906), who captured the liveliness of dense crowds and even denser structures in *Fifth Avenue, New York* (plate 499); and Helen Levitt (b. 1918), for whom the street life of children had special appeal.

During the thirties the documentary film seemed to offer some photographers the most direct form for communicating their concern with social and political ideas. Paul Strand, after spending the early thirties in New Mexico photographing landscape and indigenous architecture, was invited by the Mexican government to produce a documentary film, *The Wave*, on the struggle of fishermen near Vera Cruz to obtain decent pay. After Strand returned to the United States in 1935, he continued to work in this medium, filming Pare Lorentz's *Plough That Broke the Plains* with Ralph Steiner and Leo

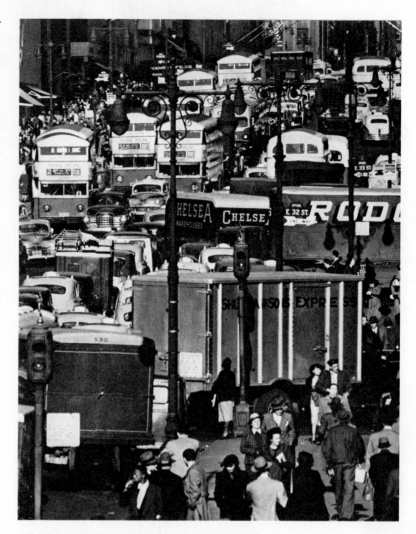

499 Andreas Feininger. *Fifth Avenue, New York*. 1948. Collection the photographer

Hurwitz. Also with Hurwitz and others, Strand organized Frontier Films in order to make socially oriented documentaries, the best-known of which is *Native Land*. Steiner, who had been making short art and documentary films since the twenties, continued working with Lorentz and photographed *The City* with Willard Van Dyke. When Strand returned to still photography about 1945, his experiences with film led him to conceive of the book format as a means of presenting a sequential yet integrated visual experience. Between 1950 and 1976 he produced seven books in which photographs constitute with the text an anthology of existence in a specific time and place.

Part 7
THE POSTWAR DECADES:
Painting Steals the Show

At the beginning of the postwar period, most of the younger American architects preferred to remain in the shadows of the almost legendary heroes of the original modern struggle: Le Corbusier, Wright, Gropius, Mies. Only slowly did they seek a place of their own, and frequently their work suggests that they were not completely prepared for the responsibility or that they were intimidated by their devotion to a group of ideals and a handful of prophets. Their education, whether classical or modernist, and their early experience, primarily in domestic construction, left them with little or no experience to cope with the scale of operation of the post-1950 urban and suburban building boom, its manipulative speculation, its use and misuse of Federal and other government grants, and the galloping inflation of construction costs. The idealism of these young architects was swept up by the dizzying success of modernism's adoption by all the institutions of power, and by the subsequent realization that, despite their efforts to create and propagate a new architecture, they were merely being asked to design the emperor's new clothes.

Appropriately, Chicago designers hewed to the Miesian paradigm longer and more faithfully than architects elsewhere, with the result that, while several historic structures in the Loop have been lost, they have generally been replaced by recent works of respectable design in an idiom fitting the historical tradition of the neighborhood.

Toward the end of the fifties, the omnipresent shadows of the giants began to wane; Gropius and Mies remained active until their deaths in 1969, but Gropius played less and less of a role in his firm, The Architects' Collaborative (TAC), and Mies was partly forgotten, chiefly because he stubbornly refused to change. Only the influence of Le Corbusier seemed to last into the 1960s, thanks to the construction of his Carpenter Center for Harvard University, completed in 1964.

American painting, on the other hand, entered the postwar period with a slew of artists who were just reaching their creative majority. Infused with a new energy that was partly derived from the stimuli of European artists who had spent the war years in New York, painting in America acquired new strength, also partly as a consequence of its own inner growth, a natural process of maturation which allowed it to shuck its affected provinciality and its feelings of inferiority to contemporary European movements.

In sculpture a reaction had taken place about the turn of the century, as it had in painting, against the academic sterility of the still popular Beaux-Arts tradition, but until World War II modern American sculpture showed less energy and less sense of adventure than painting. Even the following decade produced only a handful of distinctly individual sculptors.

21
Postwar Architecture, 1945–60

The triumph of the modern architectural idiom, if admittedly often only on a formalist level, was accomplished initially through a takeover of the architectural schools, swiftly executed coups d'état that met little resistance and were frequently abetted by sympathetic university administrators. Secondly, beginning in 1950–52 with Lever House, New York, large commercial enterprises opted for a "contemporary" image for their corporate headquarters, meaning in this case the Miesian reduction and codification of the International Style's steel-and-glass formula. There was no turning back from this step; it was uniformly followed by commerce, banking, industry, and other normally conservative institutions. Even the Federal government, though still capable as late as the 1960s of follies such as the Rayburn Office Building, Washington, D.C., looked to freshen its image by means of contemporary design and secured Mies to design Chicago's new Federal Center. However, the latent cynicism, speculative interests, and self-serving nature of this broadened patronage soon exacted a frightening toll in the rapidity with which modern design, even in expert hands, turned into an opportunistic cliché. Consequently, no sooner had it achieved worldly success than the new architecture found itself face to face with a crisis that can only be called inflationary and that, before 1960, demanded a reexamination of methods and goals. Beginning in the late fifties, and with varying degrees of success, numerous architects sought to design or to rationalize themselves out of the bind produced by slick, pared-down contemporary commercial design.

But this is to get ahead of the story. The domestic designs of the forties, relatively small in number as well as modest in size, illustrate the diversity of choice available within the modern idiom. Probably the most widely admired domestic architect at that time on the East Coast was Marcel Breuer, who further developed the type of frame dwelling that he and Gropius had introduced upon their arrival in the late thirties. In the Geller House, Lawrence, Long Island (1946, plate 500), he employed a reverse pitch, or "butterfly," roof, breaking with the flat roof (or deck) tradition of the earlier International Style. The vertical wood siding, instead of being painted white,

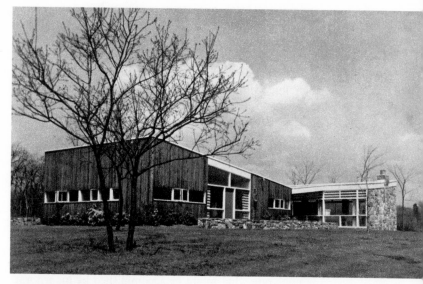

500 Marcel Breuer. Geller House,
Lawrence, Long Island, N.Y. 1946

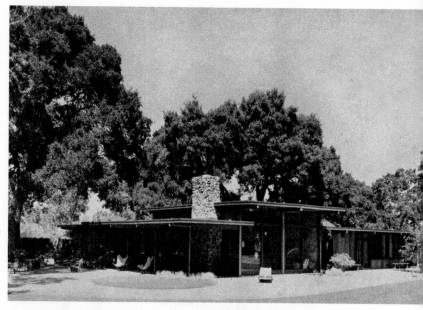

501 William W. Wurster. Schuman House,
Woodside, Calif. 1949

was stained a dark hue (this feature had first appeared in a Gropius-Breuer house of 1940 but became commonplace only after the war), and this natural surface was played off against a rough fieldstone fireplace wall. Although devices such as ribbon windows and floor-to-ceiling glass panels were preserved from the old modernist tradition, the crystalline geometric image was muted, replaced by a somewhat grudging picturesque effect.

Another type of natural-finished house is represented by the San Francisco Bay Region mode of William W. Wurster (b. 1895). In Wurster's work plainness becomes a virtue, structure and massing are kept simple, and structural components themselves are reduced and expressively underplayed (plate 501). In its own way, his appropriately homely architecture is as reductive as that of earlier European modernists, though his style (or lack of it) is a world removed from their clear, machine-inspired finishes.

California is a land of contrasts, no less in architecture than in any other field of activity. Thus it is scarcely surprising to find there both the most naturalistic, rough-finished houses outside the work of Wright and the most industrially oriented dwelling of the period. Charles Eames (1907–1978) provides with his own house in Santa Monica (1949, plate 502) a stark clarity and a regular geometry that differ strikingly from the rather shapeless, almost awkward massing of Bay Region work. The metal columnar supports are of extreme thinness, giving the whole an exaggerated linearity, although Eames's linearity creates an effect unlike that of Breuer. Eames's house was built of off-the-shelf industrial components to demonstrate what might be accomplished by incorporating a selection of factory-produced elements in a custom-designed house—an experiment that, curiously, had no sequel. *(continued on page 469)*

DECORATIVE ARTS

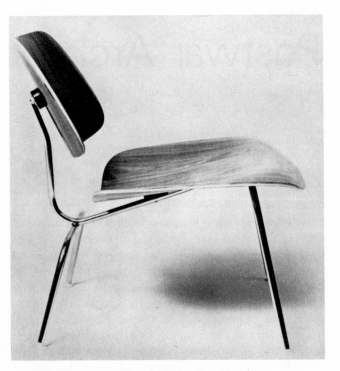

503 Charles Eames for Herman Miller, Inc., New York. LCM chair. 1946. Molded plywood, height 27⅜"

Comfortable, flexible, and well-constructed mass-produced furniture, often the creation of the industrial designer, was introduced to the public at the World's Fair of 1933 in Chicago, and by the end of the thirties, the firm of Herman Miller, Inc., was identified as a pioneer in encouraging the innovative creations of such designers as Charles Eames. After collaborating with the Finnish-born architect Eero Saarinen on a prize-winning design for a molded plywood chair that proved too expensive to manufacture, Eames moved to California and designed movie sets in Hollywood. He kept on experimenting with the molding process in his spare time, determined to create furniture that could be produced at a reasonable cost. In 1946 he succeeded with a chair (plate 503) which was shown in a one-man exhibition of his plywood furniture at The Museum of Modern Art, New York. The molded plywood back is joined with a frame of either plywood or metal to a plywood seat. Shock mounts of rubber at the joinings produce resiliency and make the chair quite comfortable. The grain of the wood, as in the earlier furniture of Stickley and Wright, is visibly an important decorative element, as is the complexity of the flowing, unconventional forms of both back and seat. Later, Eames and other designers were to use such new materials as Fiberglas and chrome-plated tubing to continue the evolution of furniture through modern technology.

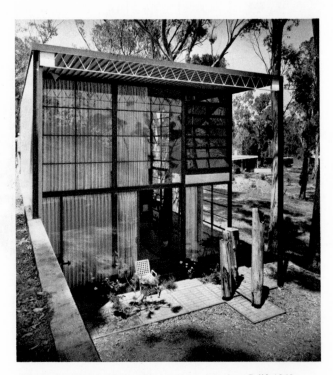

502 Charles Eames. Eames House, Santa Monica, Calif. 1949

(continued from page 468)

Ludwig Mies van der Rohe's Farnsworth House, Plano, Ill. (plate 504), designed in 1946 but not completed until 1951, was at the time widely discussed—but generally as a *building* rather than as a *house*. Perhaps the most perfect, temple-like design in the history of recent architecture, with its regular procession of white steel columns holding a rectangular glass cube above the site, it was a fascinating concept, suggestive of a new world of remote, imperturbable autonomy. As one of the most beautiful art objects of the twentieth century, thanks to the determination of the architect to apply his universal system (irrespective of incidental considerations), and the willingness of the client to accept the architect's role as benevolent autocrat, the Farnsworth House is somewhat inconsequential on a functional level. It was a historic monument almost from the very moment of inception of the design; and notwithstanding its worthy successors, chiefly from the hand of Philip Johnson (b. 1906), the vision of a form so ideal and esoteric could have little positive effect on contemporary domestic design. Nonetheless, in the fifties and sixties functionally appropriate fragments of this impeccable vision appeared in entrance lobbies of office buildings throughout the country.

Johnson's own house at New Canaan, Conn. (1947–49, plate 505), is almost too candidly based upon the Miesian paradigm, despite important differences of detail, and after the passage of thirty years it has become but one of several components in a varied architectural landscape, including a guest house virtually devoid of windows, an underground art gallery, and a miniature pavilion in an artificial lake. These components, forming a single country estate and striking in themselves, nonetheless lack many circumstantial elements of customary domestic architecture and thus deprive the whole and the parts of a sense of reality. Johnson's, like Mies's house, represents an eccentric, speculative strain in twentieth-century architecture, an important and characteristic factor in an idiom that often is erroneously thought to be inevitably practical and down-to-earth.

Also eccentric, and in other ways equally determined to explore alternative modes of domestic design, is the Dome Desert House, Cave Creek, near Phoenix, Ariz. (1950, plate 506), by Paolo Soleri (b. 1919) and Mark Mills. It is an effort to come to grips with the special requirements for survival in a desert environment. Johnson's house is, in effect, a greenhouse turned inside out, with the plants outside and the people inside, sheltered from the elements and able to watch but not participate in the ebb and flow of the seasons. The dome of the Soleri and Mills house is partly opaque and can be rotated to protect against the sun or partly rolled back to take advantage of the breeze. The main body of the house is below the level of the desert to insulate against excessive heat or cold. The basic attitude of the Dome House is at odds with that of the Glass House. The Glass House is hypercivilized, a means of shelter from the environment, providing for visual but not actual contact with surrounding nature, while the Dome House indicates a more direct, primitive, tactile contact with site and climate, momentary changes in weather requiring a definite

504 Ludwig Mies van der Rohe. Farnsworth House, Plano, Ill.
   Designed 1946; completed 1951

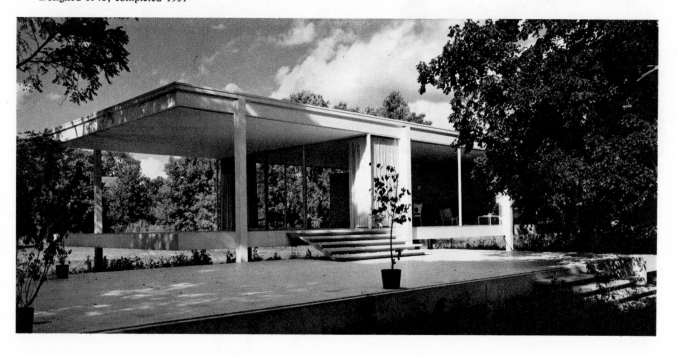

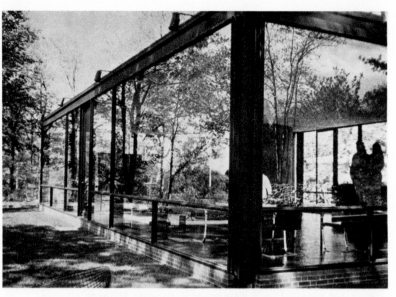

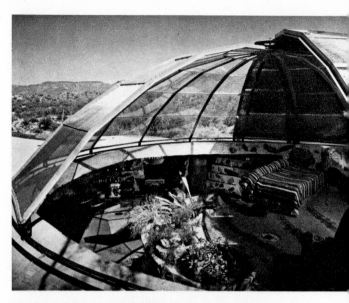

505 Philip Johnson. Glass House, New Canaan, Conn. 1947–49

506 Paolo Soleri and Mark Mills. Dome Desert House, Cave Creek, Ariz. 1950

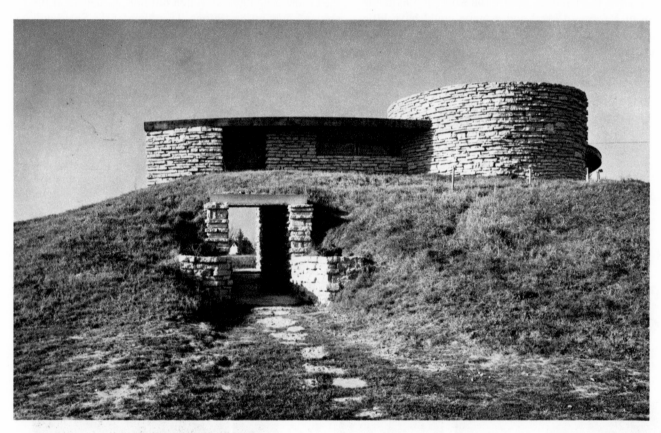

507 Frank Lloyd Wright. Second Herbert Jacobs House, Middleton, Wis. Exterior and plan. 1948

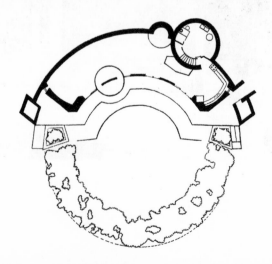

response from the occupant. Thus the ongoing contemporary architectural polemic: one extreme reaching for a greater refinement and calculation of design, the other seeking ways that seem almost primitivistic in their effort to restore unimpeded contact between man and the environment. It is the modern version of a persistent schism in American intellectual life: the pull between town and country, between the urban and rural (with the suburbs forming a limbo that may yet submerge both).

In the areas between these two poles, other types of contemporary domestic design were possible. The indefatigable Wright never lacked for new images in his later work, such as the second Herbert Jacobs House, Middleton, Wis. (1948, plate 507). The plan is based on a large segment of a circle together with several small ones. Incorporated into the hillside by an artificial mound, the house is archaizing in much the same way as is the Soleri-Mills Desert House. Other advanced domestic work of the forties and early fifties has a leaner look than Wright's bountiful approach to form permitted.

This quality of brittleness, then typifying the most diverse trends in domestic architecture, also influenced large-scale commercial and institutional work at the beginning of the fifties, but with limited success. The resulting urban structures lacked the very diversity and sense of exploration apparent in houses. There seemed to be few possibilities, and these were chiefly based upon the Miesian system, which offered the virtue of structural clarity and a certain nobility of proportion that was often absent in the work of followers. The sole available alternative to the studied formality and industrial simplicity of Mies's glazed prism for urban-scaled buildings was the brick-clad, conventionally fenestrated Baker House Dormitory for M.I.T., Cambridge, Mass. (1947–49, plate 508), by the Finnish architect Alvar Aalto (1898–1976). The noteworthy features of this structure are the undulating façade along the Charles River and the external articulation of the staircases on the opposite façade. These two devices were unusual responses to program and site, and thus did not seem to allow of general application. A building such as Baker House could not provide a necessary formula as did the Miesian system, a basic formula which a large, impersonal firm would need in order to function. It was this sort of pressure a half-century earlier that had led McKim, Mead & White to adopt a simplified Roman classicism with its system-determined repertory of forms. The corporate-design offices of mid-century were only responding similarly to the need to standardize quality in the face of rising quantitative demand.

Lever House, New York (1950–52, plate 509), was the first popular success from the firm of Skidmore, Owings & Merrill. More than Mies himself, it was responsible for popularizing his distinctive, reductive solution. They even simplified his glass-and-steel vocabulary, and toward the end of the decade they modified the grid façades of their

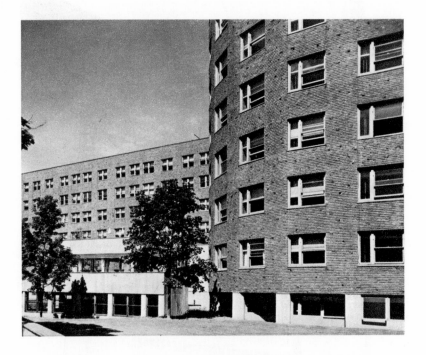

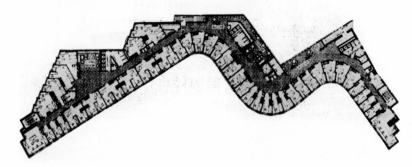

508 Alvar Aalto. Baker House Dormitory, Massachusetts Institute of Technology, Cambridge, Mass. Exterior and plan. 1947–49

slablike towers with various devices, never relenting in the ordered repetition of standard elements, never sacrificing to a momentary decorative whim. Other large firms, such as Harrison & Abramovitz, have evidenced nothing approaching the corporate homogeneity of Skidmore, Owings & Merrill, and the smaller, more individualized offices of a Philip Johnson or an Eero Saarinen seem nothing if not capricious by comparison.

New York's Seagram Building (1955–58, plate 510), in which Johnson collaborated with Mies, was the paragon of postwar skyscraper design. A sheer, bronze-clad tower, it takes up but half the site and faces an open plaza on Park Avenue, diagonally across the avenue from Lever House; it is supported in back by a cluster of lower blocks. The plaza is a podium raised above the street grade, leading to the elegantly proportioned glass-walled lobby (on the same level), where the elevator enclosures form discrete, freestanding solid masses. In their geometry, Miesian skyscrapers almost invariably

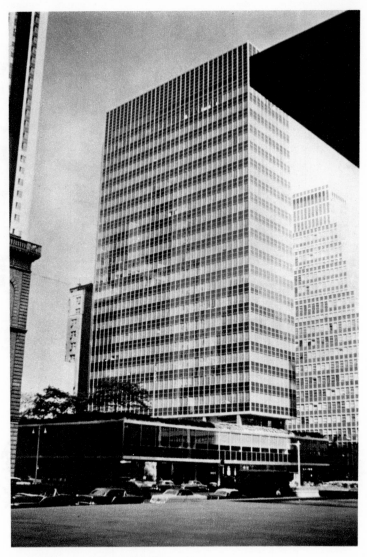

509 Skidmore, Owings & Merrill.
Lever House, New York. 1950–52

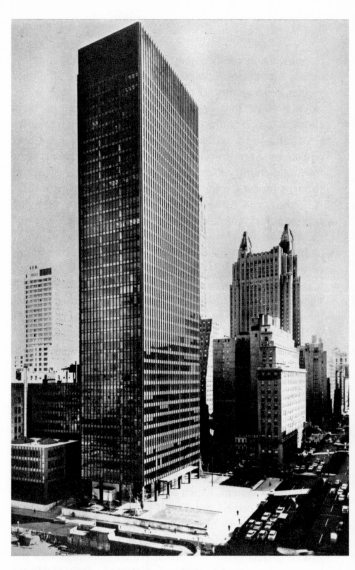

510 Ludwig Mies van der Rohe and Philip Johnson.
Seagram Building, New York. 1955–58

avoid the step-back outline topped by slender towers or pinnacles, characteristic features of the 1920s which were ridiculed by fashionable mid-century taste. These up-ended rectangular cubes, with pronouncedly gridlike envelopes and carefully expressed structural frames, recall instead the earlier office buildings of the first Chicago School.

The great drawback of this pristine, formalist mode is its lack of urban sociability. Cubic glass towers preserve an almost surrealistic newness, even after decades, which makes their neighbors look unnecessarily tawdry by comparison. Moreover, these mid-century skyscrapers are often placed in windswept plazas or on raised podiums, thus visually separating their entry from the street. This is in opposition to buildings of the thirties such as Rockefeller Center, where the entrances are closely related to the space of the street.

It was inevitable that architects would become restless with this exacting, restrictive mode (and not because of its functional drawbacks), and although Mies himself never abandoned it, the late fifties saw many deviant gestures toward what might generally be called enrichment. It is at this juncture that a cryptic academicism begins to cloud the image of contemporary design. In the name of variety, individuality, humanization, or a host of other banal slogans, designers began to deck out their basic cubic forms—and often to confuse them as well—with all manner of grilles, fins, screens, shadow devices, some no more substantial than the annually changing chrome ornamentation of automobiles. Edward Durell Stone (1902–1978) was among the earliest in this genre (United States Embassy, New Delhi, 1957–59, plate 511) and initially won high praise, although the luster of this style paled quickly in the eyes of other architects and critics.

From the late 1950s onward, Philip Johnson has several times attempted to convert the latent classicism of Mies's modular steel-frame mode into a more formally monumental architecture, feeling, with justification, that this genre generally had eluded satisfactory solutions since the demise of the academic Classicism successfully practiced by McKim, Mead & White as recently as the early twentieth century. Works such as the illusionistically vaulted Port Chester Synagogue, N. Y. (1956, plate 512), remain, however, tentative, historicizing works that had no important issue. The whole effort to establish a contemporary monumentality was discredited by the three ill-proportioned, faultily coordinated façades of Lincoln Center, New York (1957–66, plate 513), individually the works of Johnson, Wallace K. Harrison (b. 1895), and Max Abramovitz (b. 1908). Here the architects seemed

to have been dreaming of re-creating an eighteenth-century classical square with harmonious façades. Alas, the competitive atmosphere of mid-century modernism was inhospitable to the kind of spontaneous cooperation and instinctive tradition of mutual consideration necessary for the success of so ambitious a project in urban design. Even worse, Lincoln Center seems irrelevant to the familiar grid plan of New York, as the buildings antagonistically turn their backs on the streets and avenues—an instructive contrast to the design of Rockefeller Center, where a conglomeration of newly styled buildings

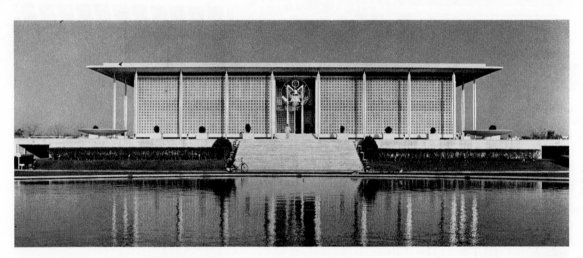

511 Edward Durell Stone. United States Embassy, New Delhi. 1957–59

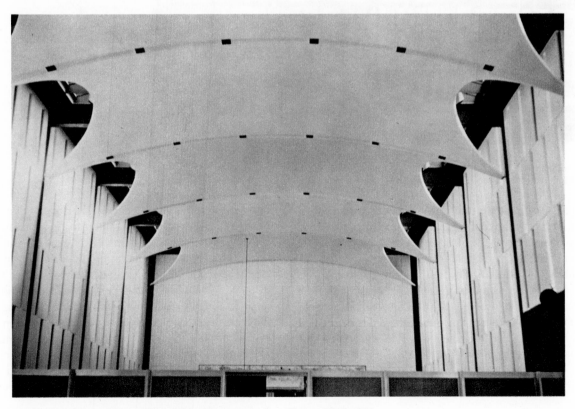

512 Philip Johnson. Kneses Tifereth Israel Synagogue, Port Chester, N.Y. 1956

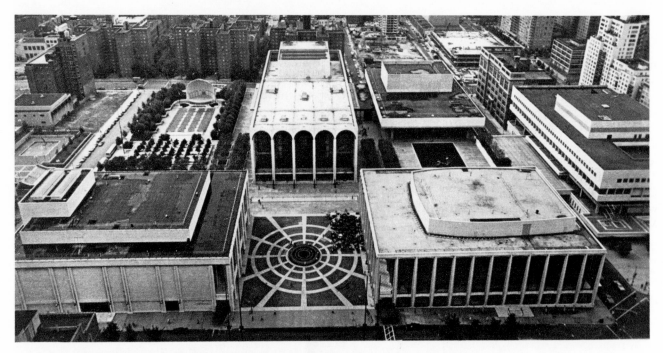

513 Lincoln Center, New York. *Left to right:* New York State Theater, 1964, by Philip Johnson; Metropolitan Opera House, 1966, by Wallace K. Harrison; Vivian Beaumont Theater, 1965, by Eero Saarinen; Philharmonic Hall, 1962, by Max Abramovitz

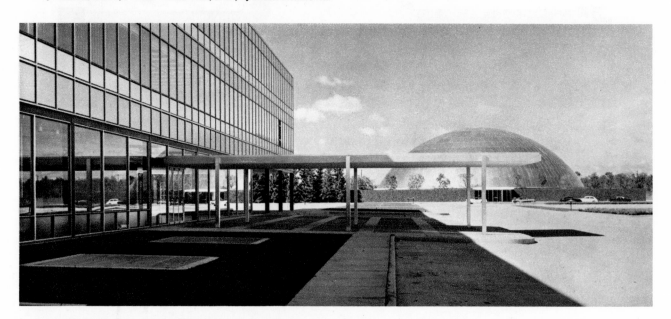

514 Eero Saarinen. General Motors Technical Center, Warren, Mich. Styling Administration Building (*left*) and Styling Auditorium (*right*). 1948–56

was made to fit comfortably into the midtown grid of streets, to contribute to its character rather than oppose it.

Eero Saarinen was the most restless of architects active in this period, and though his quest was sincere, his work is remarkably uneven. The ambivalent quality in his design is certainly as much, if not more, a product of the times as of his own insecurity. Not an intellectual designer on the order of Johnson, nor out of the old functionalist tradition like Breuer, Saarinen was a skillful creator of pictorial and spatial effects. He began as a partner of his father, Eliel. Unlike Johnson, who had been trained at Harvard under Gropius and Breuer and had an even

longer standing commitment to the International Style through his work as author and critic, Saarinen had been trained in the traditional mode at Yale in the 1930s. Thus, like most of his generation, he was predisposed to adopt the pictorial aspects of modernism rather than its formal or functional purity and intellectual discipline. Eero Saarinen's first major independent achievement was the General Motors Technical Center, Warren, Mich. (1948–56, plate 514), a grouping of low rectangular buildings around an enormous lagoon, superficially in the style of Mies. Saarinen did not make use of a regular module to create a rhythmically proportioned uniform pattern for his façades; instead he resorted to a variety of colors and patterns to create a pictorial effect.

Saarinen went from one commission to another without leaving behind a particular, personal impression. His defense was that he was looking for an individual style to fit each job, a justification which had the ring of logic. Each building tended to be a new beginning, with all the awkwardness and unresolved details that such a wasteful process implied. Each tended to be, above all else, a graphic, emotion-packed, or somehow "relevant" communicating image. The TWA Terminal at Kennedy Airport, New York (1956–62, plate 515), is a familiar and largely successful instance. Saarinen wished to provide an emblematic design that would stand out in the midst of the banal, low-voltage, pseudo-Miesian design of the other terminal buildings at Kennedy, two of them by Skidmore, Owings & Merrill. He wanted something that expressed flight, and he found it in a sketch by the German Expressionist Erich Mendelsohn: a broad, soaring concrete shell roof (soaring, that is, as high as was permitted by the airport control tower's need for an unobstructed view of the runways). To the engineers was left the problem of making the beast stand, once Saarinen and his staff had created a distinctive exterior image and a provocative, expressive series of flowing spaces on the interior.

Of the architects of the fifties and early sixties, only one managed to rise above the parochial diversity and rash of transient solutions: Louis I. Kahn (1901–1974). An older figure on the scene, he had been trained in the academic tradition at the University of Pennsylvania in the 1920s. Ill at ease with various manifestations of modernism, he nonetheless came under the aegis of George Howe (1886–1955) and, after the lean years of the Depression, became his partner by 1941. Kahn's reputation was established first among his students at Yale and at Pennsylvania, and his speculative projects were published in the early fifties in the Yale student magazine, *Perspecta*. Almost as a byproduct of his years of teaching at Yale was the design of his first major building, the university art gallery (1951–54, plate 516). Outwardly Miesian in its severe glass-and-brick cube, as any up-to-date building of the period was expected to be, it offered on the interior a number of novel, unclassifiable features. The tetrahedral web structure of the concrete ceiling slab was his first, tentative effort to split away from the ubiquitous planar surfaces customary in contemporary practice. Kahn, in fact, remained a somewhat alienated, unfulfilled designer until the climate of changing taste in the late 1950s gave him the courage to break cleanly with just about every formal and syntactic cliché, especially the Miesian package. In his speculative projects he toyed with unusually shaped, diagonally braced skyscrapers or bulky cylindrical towers whose mass was a world removed from the lean, hungry look of most contemporary work (plate 517). His plans were formal, even

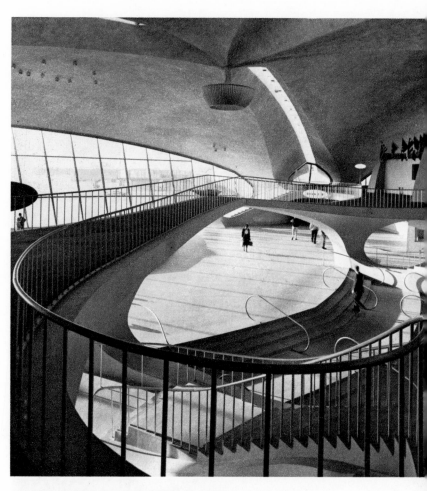

515 Eero Saarinen. Interior of TWA Terminal, John F. Kennedy International Airport, New York. 1956–62

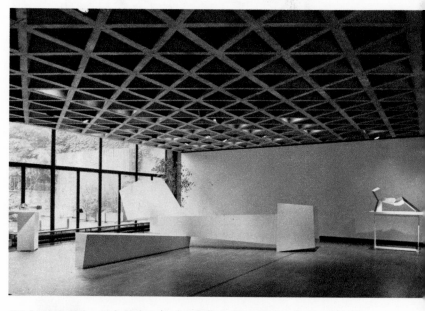

516 Louis I. Kahn. Yale University Art Gallery, New Haven, Conn. 1951–54. Interior, showing installation of exhibition of *James Rosati Sculpture*, 1970

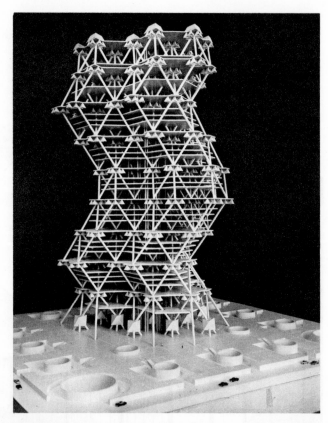

517 Louis I. Kahn. Model for skyscraper. c. 1956

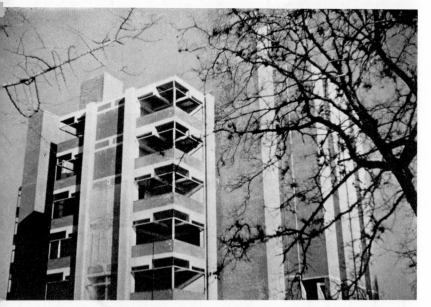

518 Louis I. Kahn. Richards Medical Research Building, University of Pennsylvania, Philadelphia. View of tower under construction, showing concrete frame later hidden by glass. 1957–60

Beaux-Arts classic in their inspiration, with separate, distinct spaces arranged in progressive sequences—the antithesis of the open plan and flowing spaces hallowed by decades of use in twentieth-century architecture.

Kahn's breakthrough came with the design and construction of the Richards Medical Research Building, University of Pennsylvania, Philadelphia (the first portion of which was constructed in 1957–60). A conglomerate mass of concrete, brick, and glass towers, of an unusually accentuated vertical bulk, it was based on a novel construction system of precast concrete ceiling-and-floor members (plate 518). Kahn's way of handling strong, simple, palpable masses (as opposed to tidy, linear, and planar forms of conventional modernism), was continued in his Unitarian Church, Rochester, N. Y. (1959–62), and in the dormitories for Bryn Mawr College, Bryn Mawr, Pa. (1961–65). Not since the early works of Frank Lloyd Wright, such as his Unity Church, Oak Park, had a progressive architect handled tactile, solid-seeming volumes with such assurance.

In 1959 Frank Lloyd Wright died at the age of ninety-two. Although he had been active until the end and was respected and admired by the entire profession, his designs had a steeply decreasing rate of influence—and this despite the public's notion of modern architecture, which then was largely derived from news and magazine reports of his final works, including the posthumous completion of the Guggenheim Museum. The active role of the "heroic" generation and the aura cast by their continuing presence were beginning to taper off.

Consequently, in postwar architecture there is nothing approaching the grand gesture of Abstract Expressionism in painting, no sense of having created a special epoch, one apart, yet descended, from earlier endeavors. Only Louis Kahn can be mentioned alongside the painters of the time. The painters had, in effect, freed themselves from their own insecurities concerning the "superiority" of Europe, while their contemporaries, the architects, were still carrying the freight of a modernism exported from Europe. For better *and* worse, they had become the proponents of a contrived, somewhat denatured reinterpretation of an earlier heroic age, whose encounters had taken place several thousand miles away. Thus American architects had, over two generations, been doubly deprived: cultural isolationism had kept them from participating in the early achievements of the International Style during the twenties and thirties, and in their belated effort to catch up, they had no means of sharing in anything akin to the excitement generated by the new American painting of the forties and fifties.

22
Abstract Expressionism: The Heroic Generation

The first painting movement to bring American artists worldwide notice after World War II was Abstract Expressionism, or, in the epithet coined in 1951 by the late critic Harold Rosenberg, "Action Painting." These terms describe a loose association of artists guided by common aims who emerged when the school of Paris appeared to be bereft of new ideas and dying of its own highly praised skill. For the moment it seemed even as if the main impulses of French modernism had been expatriated and driven underground in New York. The budding American vanguard drew support and inspiration in its complex beginnings from contact during the war years with a number of foreign artists and intellectuals. Fernand Léger, Yves Tanguy, Piet Mondrian, André Breton, Max Ernst, and Roberto Matta Echaurren, among others, maintained warm and influential relationships with many of the younger Americans and bridged the intimidating distance between American provincialism and the European avant-garde. A number of these visitors showed at Peggy Guggenheim's Art of This Century Gallery in New York, and there also, between 1943 and 1946, the pioneer American Abstract Expressionists—Jackson Pollock, Mark Rothko, Clyfford Still, Hans Hofmann, Robert Motherwell, and William Baziotes—had their first one-man shows. The movement that they represented grew quickly to dominance. By the mid-fifties it had achieved international recognition and brought the beginnings of affluence to many of its artists. Today those exciting years are looked back upon as a golden age in modern American art.

SURREALIST LINKS

The Surrealist group particularly became an important catalyst in enabling the young American artists to express in pictorial form, with immediacy, a postwar sense of profound personal crisis. The moods and the Existentialist concerns of the new generation found an eloquent spokesman in Robert Motherwell (b. 1915). "The need," he said, "is for felt experience—intense, immediate, direct, subtle, unified, warm, vivid, rhythmic." Many painters began to concentrate on the act of painting itself, on the principle that if the artist emptied his mind of preconceptions and applied pigment with a maximum of spontaneity, the images he made would be an expression of the deepest levels of his being. Like the poet and high priest of Surrealism, André Breton, who was in America at the time, the painters took their cues from the "automatist" strategy of the Surrealists, which in turn exploited the methods and free associations of modern psychoanalysis in order to release personal fantasies. Breton directly encouraged Arshile Gorky and made contact with many other Americans, including Motherwell. It was Motherwell who substituted the phrase "plastic automatism" for Breton's "psychic automatism," as defined in the First Surrealist Manifesto. He thus established an important distinction between the Surrealist art of subconscious imagery and the procedures and goals of the young Americans who sought a more direct physical involvement with the "act of painting."

POLLOCK AND GORKY

The first one-man show of Jackson Pollock (1912–1956), held in 1943 at Peggy Guggenheim's gallery, became symbolic of the new approach. In retrospect, it was a visual manifesto for a different kind of abstract painting, but at first Pollock's work was mistakenly identified too closely with that of the European Surrealists who exhibited at the same gallery. In fact, his rather narrow and violent painting did reveal obvious relationships to automatism. The somewhat ominous, if not altogether explicit, animal imagery of *The She-Wolf* (1943, colorplate 75) is a measure of his struggle both with Surrealist fantasy and with the monstrous creatures of Picasso's *Guernica* period. One of a number of works with allegorical titles, the painting reflects Pollock's effort to fuse myth and the unconscious in a fresh pictorial style, mingling figurative and abstract elements with an all-over cursive "writing" in paint and emphasizing the drama of the painting "act" by the vehemence of his handling.

By 1947 Pollock had eliminated recognizable allusions

to mythic subject matter from his work and begun to pour and spray paint on canvas in repeated rhythmic gestures. He used the technique of automatism to get his picture started but, unlike the Surrealists, did not expect the method to yield cosmic truths or to reveal the unconscious mind. He made his vast paintings by spilling liquid paint on unstretched canvases laid flat on the floor; "this way," as he said, "I can walk around it, work from the four sides and literally be *in* the painting." The forms that resulted were determined by his own actions and decisions as an artist working with the exigencies of the moment. Like the process of living, the painting act was conceived as open-ended; chance, risk, physical actions, and gesture all played their part as both content and form of the finished work. The increasing velocity with which he painted resulted in the "all-over" composition of *Number One* (1950), which consists of unending networks of lines folding in on each other, with the effect of energized space and a perpetual flux of motion. Described by the critic Clement Greenberg as a "huge baroque scrawl in aluminum, black, white, madder, and blue," the violent drawings on the surface and the excited application of paint make the susceptible viewer experience the painting act itself.

In recent years, however, the optical character of Pollock's "field" paintings, rather than their gestural violence, has attracted critical attention and become the influential factor for other artists. *Number One, Autumn Rhythm,* and other monumental canvases of about 1950 (cf. plate 519) are no longer understood simply as cathartic or expressionist outbursts. Instead they are appreciated for the environmental scale and the visual dynamics which erase the boundaries between the work of art and the space the audience occupies, and they are linked historically with the late water landscapes of Monet and forward in time with the color-field paintings that matured in the 1960s (see Chapter 26).

Another indication of the American transformation of Surrealist sources was the exquisite art of Arshile Gorky. (See also Chapter 19.) He openly acknowledged his attachment to the most talented of the younger Surrealists, the Chilean Matta, who became a familiar figure in New York during the war years. Matta used translucent washes to create an illusion of fluid forms dissolving in an infinite spatial depth. He called his landscapes psychological morphologies and "inscapes," and he created them by spilling thin films of paint on canvas, spreading them with rags, and then using the brush to define smaller areas and

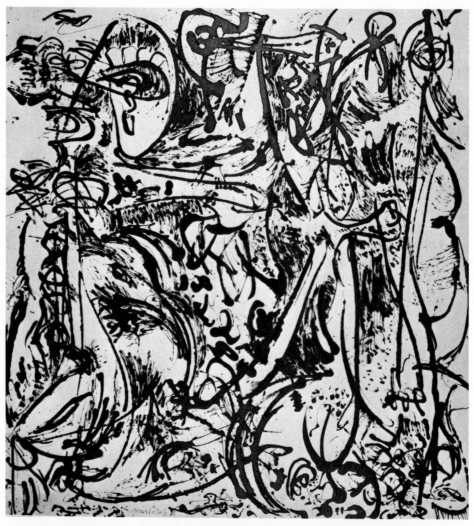

519 Jackson Pollock. *Echo (Number 25)*. 1951. Enamel paint on canvas, $91\frac{7}{8} \times 86''$. The Museum of Modern Art, New York. Acquired through the Lillie P. Bliss Bequest and the Mr. and Mrs. David Rockefeller Fund

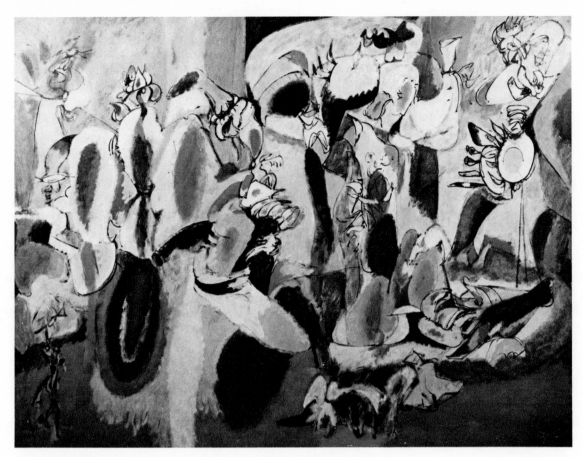

520 Arshile Gorky. *The Liver Is the Cock's Comb*. 1944. Oil on canvas, 72 × 98″.
The Albright-Knox Art Gallery, Buffalo, N.Y. Gift of Seymour H. Knox

shapes. Accidents of spilling suggested definition and meanings, and thus upheld the improvisational and random bias of the formal Surrealists.

For Gorky, Matta's fantastic interior landscapes were clearly of more interest for their fluid morphologies of form than for their theatrical effects, which often seemed too reminiscent of the meticulously painted pictorial illusions of Dali and Tanguy. Gorky assimilated the atmosphere of Matta's veiled eroticism but turned his own sensuality to a different account. He transformed Matta's spatial theater into abstract and anti-illusionistic shapes which had their impact principally through paint marks and material surface. In 1944, only three years before his tragic death by suicide, Gorky was able to throw off the more obvious Surrealist influences and create a more personally identifiable and authentic imagery. That year, working from drawings made in Virginia the preceding summer, he produced a series of paintings with a new richness of form, sensuous color, and freedom of handling.

In *The Liver Is the Cock's Comb* (1944, plate 520) the characteristic Surrealist ambiguity of shape and the emphasis on spontaneity fostered by automatist techniques are still pronounced but are assimilated to a highly personal style. Mixed references to botanical elements and to male and female genitalia are the only recognizable

forms to emerge from an anarchistic swarm of linear overwriting and color spotting. The vaguely erotic mood is perhaps the most important aspect of Gorky's continuing attachment to Surrealism, but the element of pictorial improvisation also evokes Kandinsky and, more significantly, links this work to the pictorial methods of such emerging Abstract Expressionists as Pollock, Hans Hofmann, and Willem de Kooning, who also gave surface, material pigment, and brushstroke a wider role at the expense of traditional illusionism.

By 1947 most of the European Surrealists had returned to France, and their influence was on the wane in the face of a strongly independent American accomplishment. Pollock's "drip" style was symbolic of the change and helped establish the new-found authority of the American avant-garde. Existentialist engagement, and self-definition in the act of painting, had replaced the Surrealist commitment to dream and the unconscious.

AN EXISTENTIALIST HERO: DE KOONING

Perhaps the most obvious Existentialist among the "Action Painters" was Willem de Kooning (b. 1904), who shared the leadership of the American avant-garde with Pollock and was to have even more influence upon the younger artists. De Kooning's first individually identifiable forms, such as those of his well-known *Pink Angels* (1945), are a condensation of opposing, curved pelvic silhouettes, or imaginary anatomies in flattened emblematic form, derivative of the fluid shapes used by Picasso and Miró in the early 1930s. De Kooning's content was not essentially fantastic, however, and it is only a short step in his art from images rooted in the Surrealist imagination to the fragmented and freely registered color shapes of his mature painting.

After 1942 de Kooning's style was a fusion of Cubist structure, Expressionist handling, and Surrealist automatism. About 1948 the elements of violence and erotic fantasy were subdued and incorporated within a larger presence, and, as in the case of Pollock, a clearer formal intention dominated his work—the autonomy of the painting act itself. The important painting *Excavation* (1950, plate 521) was first seen in the 1950 Venice Biennale, and it won first prize in 1951 at the Chicago Art Institute Annual. The teeming composition is representative of his complex and dense style, with its suggestions of both human anatomy and the life of the city. Primarily, it is an embodiment of de Kooning's anxious and restless viewpoint. Space is articulated by accelerating and fragmenting form. The mobile and organic shapes are ceaselessly shifting, with the dominant images and their backgrounds constantly interchanged. As one critic described

it, "Parts do not exist. . . . It is impossible to tell what is on top of what." With the intense fluctuation of foreground and background planes, the painting becomes ambiguous and fluid. The activism of the atomized surface links the work with Jackson Pollock's open drip paintings.

De Kooning's imposing reputation was based on a unique stylistic synthesis of paradoxical elements. With brilliance and éclat he managed to combine qualities of personal intensity and plastic finesse, a furiously muscular brushwork and refined abstract calligraphy, traditional figuration with a tensely structured, depthless space. For a new generation of American artists intent on self-definition through painting, he came to represent the essence of their sense of commitment in the search for contemporary authenticity. Overnight he attained the status of Existentialist hero, one who risked everything willingly in the "act" of painting and boldly enacted his personal drama through the creative process. The speed with which he executed his paintings, the hot improvisational rush of his images, and even his messy, overworked surfaces fused time, gesture, and event in a new unified pictorial structure.

For de Kooning, art and life were to be conquered dangerously, each by means of the other. His painting

521 Willem de Kooning. *Excavation.* 1950. Oil on canvas, 6′ 8⅛″ × 8′ 4⅛″. The Art Institute of Chicago. Gift of Mr. Edgar Kaufmann, Jr., and Mr. and Mrs. Noah Goldowsky

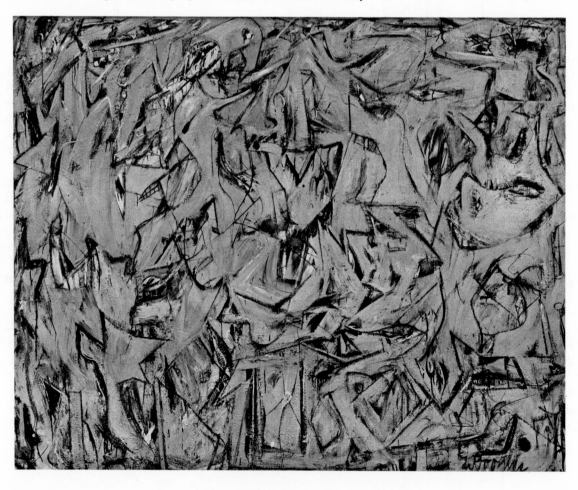

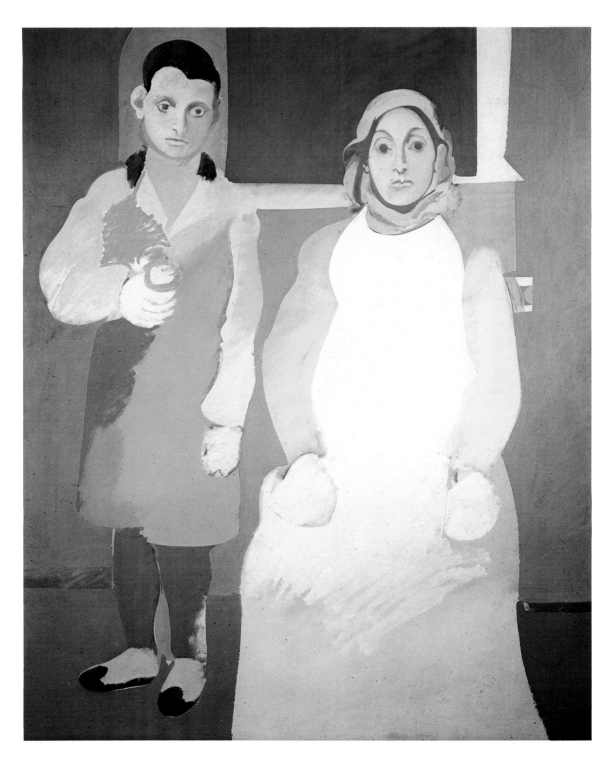

73 Arshile Gorky. *The Artist and His Mother*. 1926–29. Oil on canvas, 60 × 50″.
Whitney Museum of American Art, New York. Gift of Julien Levy
for Maro and Natasha Gorky in memory of their father

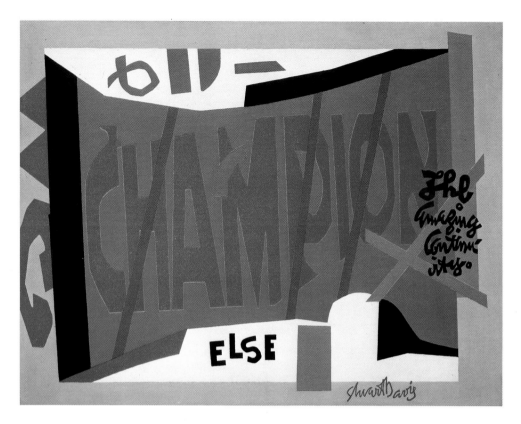

74 Stuart Davis. *Visa*. 1951. Oil on canvas, 40 × 52″. The Museum of Modern Art, New York. Gift of Mrs. Gertrud A. Mellon

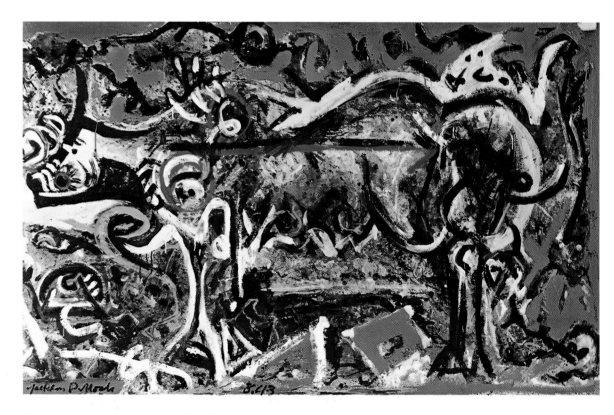

75 Jackson Pollock. *The She-Wolf*. 1943. Oil on canvas, $41\frac{7}{8} \times 67″$. The Museum of Modern Art, New York. Purchase

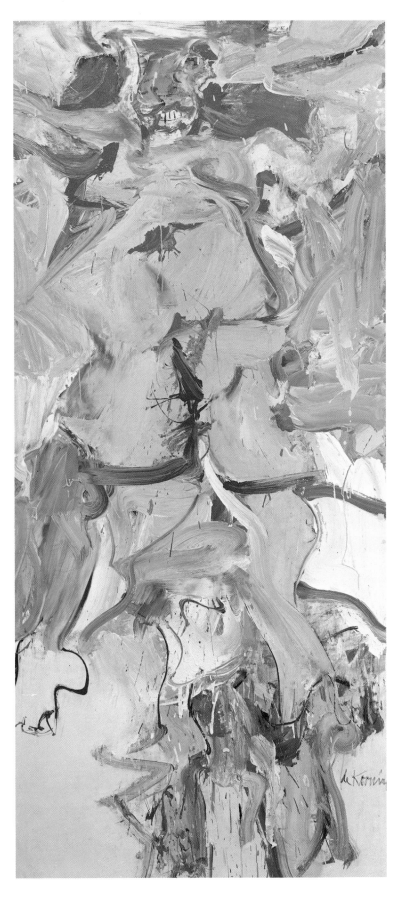

76 Willem de Kooning. *Woman, Sag Harbor*. 1964. Oil on wood, 80 × 36″.
Smithsonian Institution, Washington, D.C.,
Hirshhorn Museum and Sculpture Garden

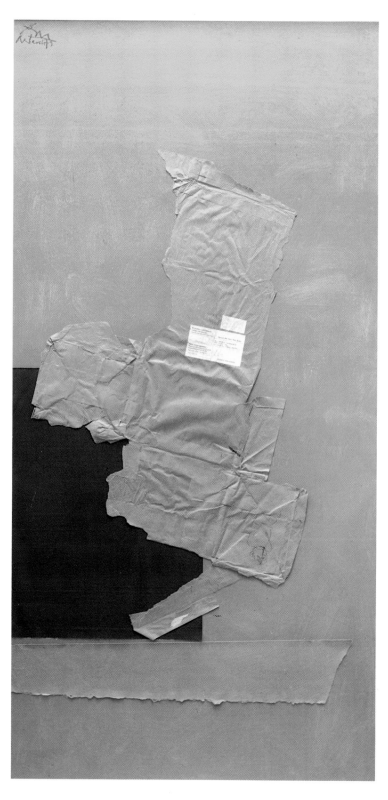

77   Robert Motherwell. *In Memoriam: Wittenborn Collage*. 1975.
      Collage and acrylic on canvas board, 72 × 36″.
      Collection the artist

78 Barnett Newman. *Vir Heroicus Sublimis.* 1950–51. Oil on canvas, 8′ × 17′10″.
The Museum of Modern Art, New York. Gift of Mr. and Mrs. Ben Heller

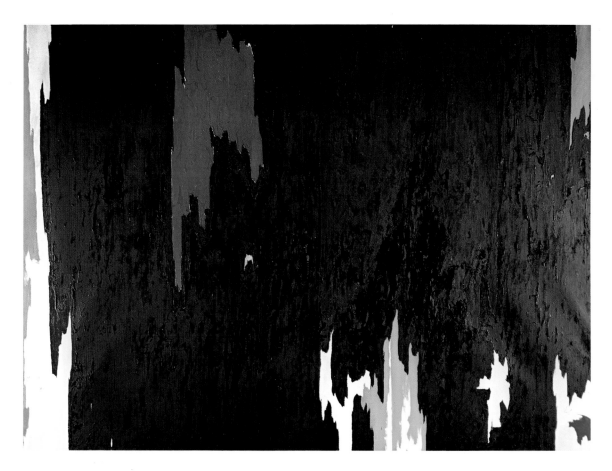

79 Clyfford Still. *Untitled.* 1957. Oil on canvas, 9′4″ × 12′10″.
Whitney Museum of American Art, New York.
Gift of the Friends of the Whitney Museum of American Art

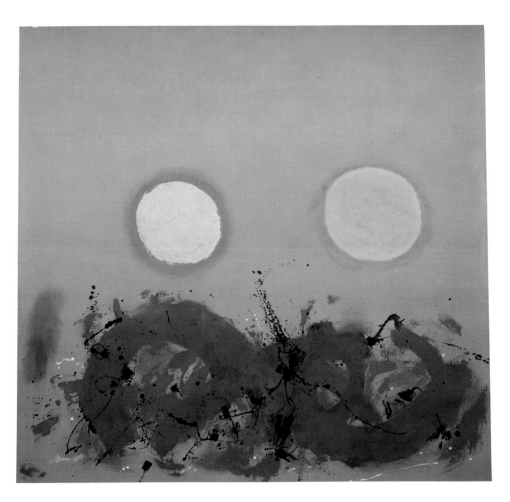

80 Adolph Gottlieb. *Duet*. 1962. Oil on canvas, 84 × 90″.
The High Museum, Atlanta, Ga.

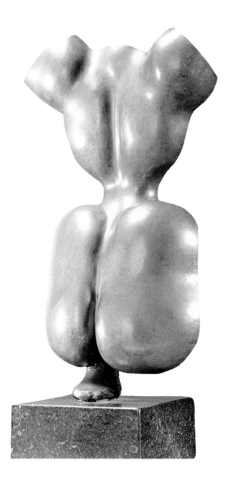

81 Gaston Lachaise. *Torso*. 1930.
Bronze, height 11½″. Whitney
Museum of American Art, New York

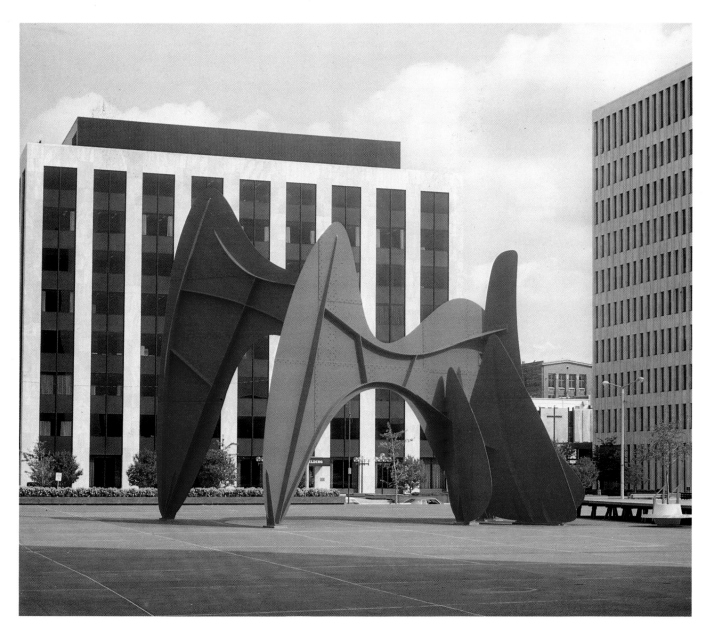

82　Alexander Calder. *La Grande Vitesse*. 1969. Stabile.
Vandenberg Plaza, Grand Rapids, Mich.

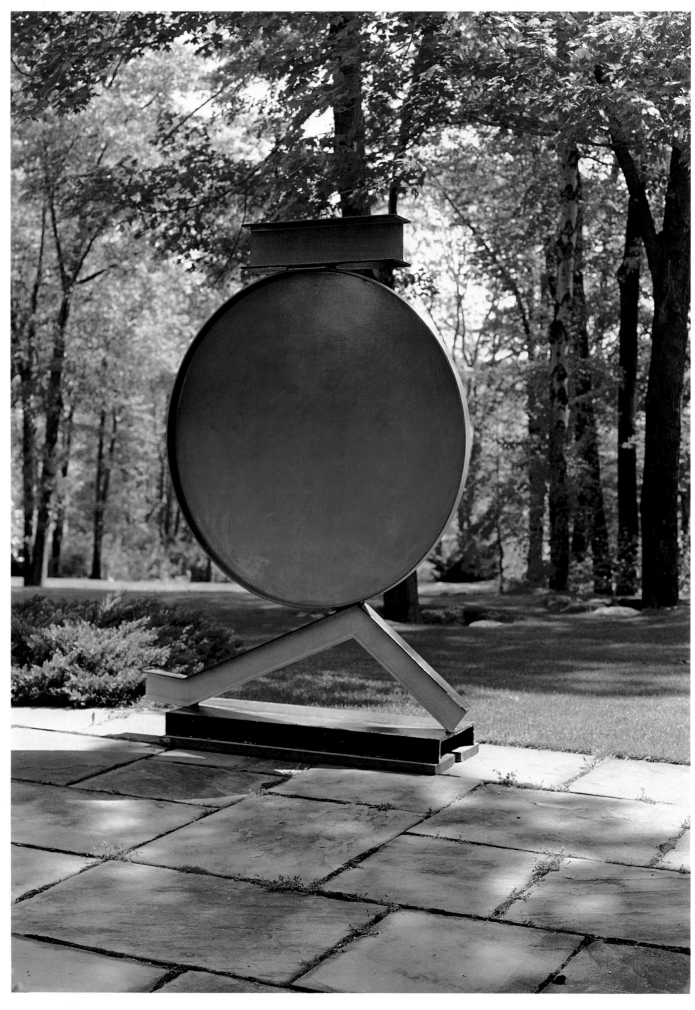

83 David Smith. *Bec-Dida Day*. 1963. Polychromed steel, $90\frac{7}{8} \times 65\frac{1}{4} \times 18''$. Private collection, Greenwich, Conn.

became the potent antidote to lifeless abstraction and any rigid formal principle. "Art never seems to make me peaceful or pure," he once wrote. "I do not think of inside or outside—or of art in general—as a situation of comfort. . . . Some painters, including myself, are too nervous to find out where they ought to sit. They do not want to 'sit in style.' Rather, they have found that painting . . . any style of painting . . . to be painting at all . . . is a way of living today. That is where the form lies."

It was in this context that he invented his most famous image series, *Woman* (e.g., *Woman, Sag Harbor*, 1964, colorplate 76). Even a solidly academic artistic education in Holland and the mandarin influences of Arshile Gorky did not prevent him from returning to an early obsession with this cult image. The series scandalized the more rigidly nonobjective American vanguard artists, who viewed it as a surrender to a pallid neohumanism. In fact, it was just the opposite, an assertion of individual freedom, cognizant of relevant aspects of American popular culture and the urban environment. In recent years the trapped energies of de Kooning's claustrophobic spaces have escaped into a more controlled and calm external environment. The *Woman* image as continued today includes elements of both comedy and lyricism in her latest metamorphosis as landscape. Many of the familiar color contrasts of virulent pinks and yellows set against electric blues and greens are still in evidence, but they no longer contain the old bite of aggression. The mood of his painting is pastoral and even tender, identifying the torn and dismembered human figure with the vast expanses and openness of nature. His paintings now seem bathed in the pristine light of the gentle Long Island seaside, where he has his current studio, reminding one in mood, luminosity, and even configuration of Dutch landscapes. The sense of personal crisis and desperation which linked de Kooning's earlier paintings with the philosophical concept of alienation has dissolved in the vast reaches of sky, the brilliant light and soothing horizontals of a benevolent marine environment.

In the late 1940s and the early 1950s, de Kooning became the acknowledged leader of American progressive painting, providing a dictionary of vital pictorial ideas and a departure for new explorations. Pollock's direct influence was negligible until color-field painting came into vogue. In the interval de Kooning's painterliness, with its aggressive incorporation of traditional figuration and its equally compelling abstract invention, decisively affected younger artists.

GESTURE PAINTERS

If any artist deserved Harold Rosenberg's epithet of "Action Painter," it was Franz Kline (1910–1962), who translated gesture into a lattice of broad black bands, like the enlarged strokes of a housepainter's brush. At

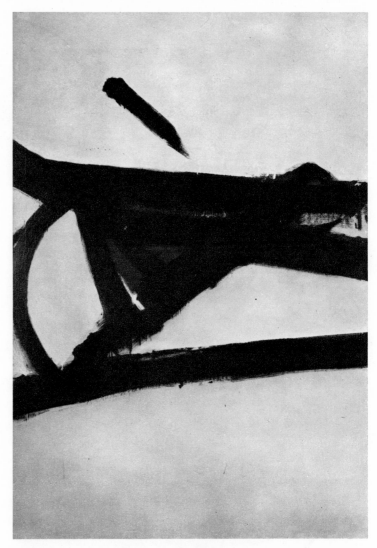

522 Franz Kline. *Accent Grave*. 1955. Oil on canvas, 75¼ × 51¾". Cleveland Museum of Art

its best, in paintings such as *Accent Grave* (1955, plate 522), Kline's work conveys a sense of tensely controlled excitement with the act of painting. The negligent edges of shape, the changes, revisions, and overpainting give us the impression that the artist is directly engaged by the creative process.

Prior to 1949 Kline had painted figurative works which alternately reflected the moods of the bustling metropolis of New York or the serenity of his native Pennsylvania. About 1950 he began to work under de Kooning's influence. It was then that he eliminated color from his art and began to create monumental compositions built up in powerful linear structures. Later his brushstrokes became broader and swifter. Although his paintings were entirely abstract after 1951, they still reflected the pattern of the urban landscape. In scale they evoked the ample loft spaces of both artists in downtown New York and a form of mural painting identified with the wall rather than with intimate easel production. In his first one-man show, in 1951, Kline demonstrated something of de

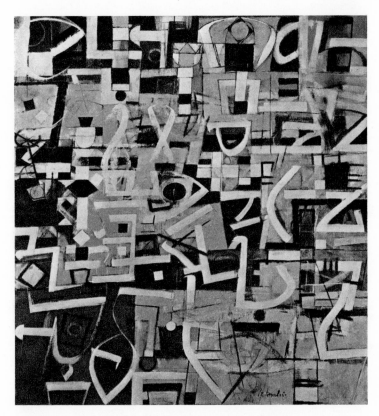

523 Bradley Walker Tomlin. *Number 20*. 1949. Oil on canvas,
7' 2" × 6' 8¼". The Museum of Modern Art,
New York. Gift of Philip C. Johnson

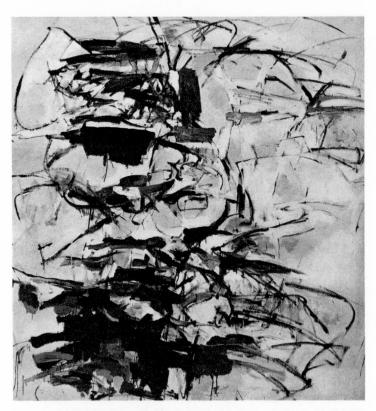

524 Joan Mitchell. *Mont St. Hilaire*. 1957.
Oil on canvas, 80 × 76".
The Lannan Foundation, Palm Beach, Fla.

Kooning's vigorous decisiveness within an essentially equivocal expressive language—a drastic simplification of image and the reduction of his palette to black and white.

Because Kline's stark black ciphers were obviously the direct translation of movement and the energies of bodily action, his art came to express perfectly the idea of gesture as a value system in painting. That such a heroically reduced visual rhetoric could communicate with authority and encompass complex meanings in the interplay of forms has been one of the enduring revelations of Action Painting. Observers have often tried to relate Kline's forms to oriental art, seeing them as gigantic enlargements of ideograms, but the resemblance is misleading. As Kline said, "People sometimes think I take a white canvas and paint a black sign on it, but this is not true. I paint the white as well as the black, and the white is just as important."

The powerfully condensed *Accent Grave* was shown in the Museum of Modern Art's influential 1958–59 exhibition entitled "The New American Painting," which circulated abroad and confirmed the importance of American Abstract Expressionsim for European audiences and artists. The painting is an excellent example of Kline's grand black-and-white paint configurations, which represent a new kind of pictorial dynamism. He coordinated ambiguities in spatial depth and formal character, as calligraphic marks with a constructivist network of skewed but structurally taut signs. The mat and shiny, opaque and transparent handling gives an impression of different velocities, and the forms meet with force as they assault the perimeters of the canvas.

Many of the other Action Painters in the Kline and de Kooning tradition of excited paint marks and energetic handling were clustered together by critics as "gesture" painters, in opposition to a markedly different style of color-field, or chromatic, abstraction, which was emerging simultaneously in the fifties in New York. Bradley Walker Tomlin (1899–1953; plate 523), Lee Krasner (Jackson Pollock's widow, b. 1908), Conrad Marca-Relli (b. 1913), James Brooks (b. 1906), Esteban Vicente (b. 1906), and Jack Tworkov (b. 1900) were among the more distinguished older generation of gestural artists.

Richard Diebenkorn (b. 1922) and two women in the younger generation, Grace Hartigan (b. 1922) and Joan Mitchell (b. 1926), consolidated the discoveries of the Action Painters with distinctive personalizations of idiom, either in the direction of Realism in the case of both Hartigan and Diebenkorn, or toward an ambitious "all-over" field painting in Mitchell's monumental canvases (plate 524). In the 1960s, Diebenkorn emerged as an artist of considerable formal power and sensuous charm with his *Ocean Park* series (plate 525), which retained a landscape atmosphere despite their abstract structure.

There was considerable diversity in approach and

temperament even among the pioneering band of gesture painters. Philip Guston (b. 1912) brought to the style a searching intellect and probing brush. His loaded and slow-moving brushstroke suspends and visibly prolongs the painting gesture in *The Day* (1964, plate 526), creating strongly felt metaphors for doubt and certainty, chaos and order, disquiet and calm, through sensitive elaboration of layered paint. Even in his recent figurative work, with wayward suggestions of cartoon figures from the comic strip Krazy Kat, and allusions to still life, Guston uses his art as a vehicle for self-revelation. The glow of the pigment and the shimmering brush mark are seen as a record of psychic activity, and even personal anguish.

HOFMANN

Hans Hofmann (1880–1966) has, retrospectively, occupied an increasingly important place in the front ranks of the Abstract Expressionist gestural painters. Because he took a lifelong interest in art education and his influence as a teacher was immense, he has sometimes been considered academic and his original achievement underestimated. Actually, he could with some justice claim priorities in exploring the freer modes of Action Painting. As early as 1940, in his innovative painting *Spring*, he used the technique of dripping and spraying paint on the canvas surface, a method that Pollock later appropriated. In his conversations, Hofmann distinguished between traditional concepts of fixed form and the idea of mobile form, which might serve a process of continuous transformation and spatial movement. In his work, paint stroke, mark, and drip instantly registered as coherent and intelligible form when they encountered the canvas surface. This was the generic painting style that revolutionized American art in the late 1940s.

Fairy Tale (plate 527) was shown at Hofmann's first one-man exhibition, at Peggy Guggenheim's gallery in 1944. It is closely related to Pollock's *She-Wolf* (colorplate 75) in its totemic content and its combination of automatism, cursive line, and thick impasto. The colors are conceived as an adjunct to linear form, filling the areas between freely moving, disembodied contours.

For a brief time in the early forties, Hofmann seemed close to the spirit of the Surrealists, as he elaborated an imagery of fantastic creatures and incorporated mythic content and biomorphic form in his organic compositions. Throughout most of his career, however, he attempted to merge a compact Cubist structure with Expressionist color in a grand pictorial synthesis. He loosened Cubist design by opening its closed planes and using color itself to determine structure. His work became increasingly free, and in the late 1950s he began to place isolated color planes of a distinct rectangular shape against a ground of agitated brushstrokes. *The Golden Wall* (1961,

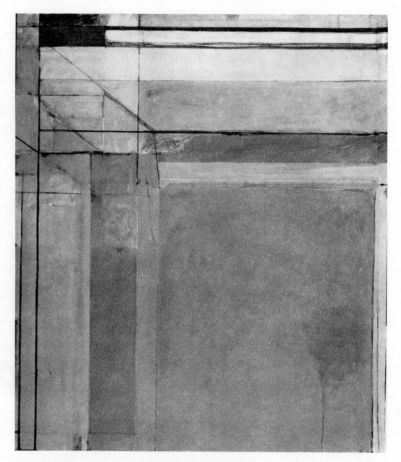

525 Richard Diebenkorn. *Ocean Park, No. 79.* 1975. Oil on canvas, 93 × 81″. Private collection

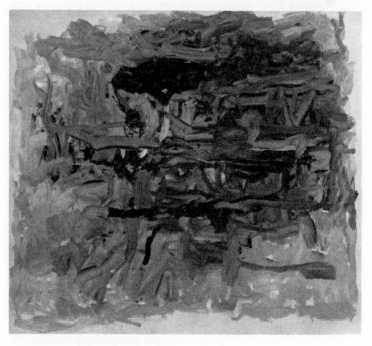

526 Philip Guston. *The Day.* 1964. Oil on canvas, 77 × 79½″. Collection the artist

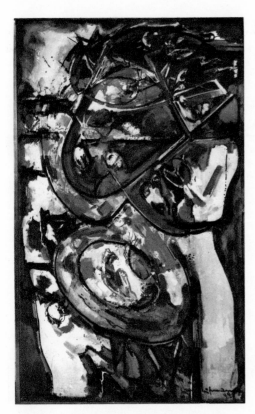

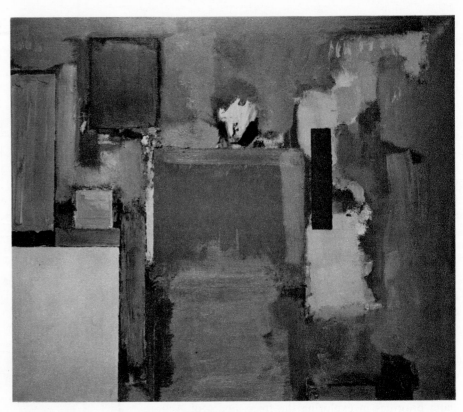

527 Hans Hofmann. *Fairy Tale*. 1944. Oil on plywood, 60 × 36″. Estate of the artist

528 Hans Hofmann. *The Golden Wall*. 1961. Oil on canvas, 60 × 72″. The Art Institute of Chicago

plate 528) is an example of this type of composition, consisting of an ensemble of vigorously brushed and high-keyed color planes. Such compositions realized superbly Hofmann's lifelong ambition to create his synthesis of Cubist architecture and Fauvist chromatics in an original, nonobjective style.

MOTHERWELL

Robert Motherwell, whose writings have been mentioned earlier, helped set the high and serious intellectual tone of the Action Painting movement. Working under the mixed influence of Picasso, Matisse, and Kurt Schwitters, he made an eloquent personal vehicle of the collage. His black-and-white "Elegies to the Spanish Republic," beginning in the late 1940s, are among his most durable and memorable series of major quality. He has now completed more than a hundred of these stark paintings of large horizontal format, which he characterizes as "general metaphors for life and death and their interrelation." Dedicated to the ordeal of Republican Spain, they were probably decisive in the formation of Kline's more specialized manner.

Motherwell provides an interesting exception to the either/or pattern of gestural and nongestural field painting among the Abstract Expressionists. Over the past decade he has visually associated himself with the color-field paintings of Barnett Newman and Mark Rothko to a surprising degree, rather than with the more emotive, gestural style of Abstract Expressionism, to which he originally gave such strong impetus. He can legitimately be placed in the broad and eclectic tendency of field painting, in relation to his *Open* series as well as to some of his monumental collages, which work against a mono-chrome color ground and read as a single image. Even the reductive color planes of *Open No. 37 in Orange* (1969, plate 529), with their elementary linear configuration, retain personal and symbolic meanings, however. The artist does not intend these large color fields as merely formalist play or direct sensuous expression. He means them to contain a visual statement about the idea of "openness in philosophical and historical terms."

Throughout his career, Motherwell's acute intellect and historical sensibilities have impelled him to identify his paintings with feeling and with events, under the literary influence of French Surrealism and the Symbolist poets and through contact with Picasso and Miró. From his Spanish Elegy series to his *Je t'aime* paintings and collages, celebrating moments in his personal life, he has regarded his painting as a form of confession as well as a plastic expression within the modernist mainstream. For Motherwell the collage became both a form of personal catharsis and playful invention. Such recent collages as *Wittenborn Collage* (1975, colorplate 77) have a new impressiveness of scale, resembling his large *Open* painting series. Over the years, his collages have invited comparison with the great Cubist works of Picasso and Braque and with Matisse's cutouts.

COLOR-FIELD PAINTERS

By the late 1940s the charged expressive brushwork of the gesture painters and their vehement emotionalism had significantly given way to greater breadth, refinement, and objectivity. Pollock's open drip paintings absorbed pictorial incident and detail into a uniform field of accents. Disrupting image fragments and points of psychological stress and violence in paint handling were subordinated to the overall effect of the painting. As the entire painted rectangle became more uniformly accented, it achieved a single-image effect, arranging itself in the eye of the viewer as a consistent and unified optical texture. This development bore with it a drastic increase in scale and thereby in impressiveness.

The same intuition of an expansive and uniform pictorial field, and a more monolithic pictorial order, was already embodied in the radical painting styles of Barnett Newman (1905–1970), Clyfford Still (b. 1904), and Mark Rothko (1903–1970). Their art, by the late 1940s, operated on a set of assumptions opposed to gestural Action Painting. Whereas Pollock and de Kooning achieved spatial envelopment by dismantling form and setting it in motion, the more quietist abstract artists gained an equal-ly potent expansive force by the deceleration of small variegated shapes into dominant islands, zones, and finally boundless fields of intense, homogeneous color. In place of the hand's motor activity, color sensation and optical ambiguity expressed qualities of change, playing on the dynamics of perception. The chromatic abstractionists, Newman, Still, and Rothko, created great unvaried expanses of usually bright hue in unbroken "color fields," rather than by stressing sequential linear detail, agitated surface, and formal diversity. Their large canvases were intended to subdue the spectator's ego and to create a sense of tranquil awe.

The artists of this tendency stated their aims clearly in publications of the period, notable among them *The Tiger's Eye*. Rothko's awesome scale and unrelieved color sensation, for example, were meant to assert the boundlessness and the mystery of being, in keeping with Edmund Burke's concept of "the sublime" in art. The critic Robert Rosenblum later aptly characterized this novel art as "the abstract sublime" and linked it to Romantic landscape painting of the nineteenth century.

The pursuit of ultimate transcendental truths, rather than Existentialist values, by the color-field painters had in its background an earlier phase of flirtation with Surrealism and "myth" which paralleled the intellectual development of the gestural painters. Rothko, Still, Newman, and Adolph Gottlieb (1903–1974), among the color-field painters, tapped eccentric sources of the collective unconscious in Jungian terms, to liberate themselves

529 Robert Motherwell. *Open No. 37 in Orange.* 1969. Polymer paint and charcoal on canvas, 6′ 4″ × 9′ 6″. Private collection

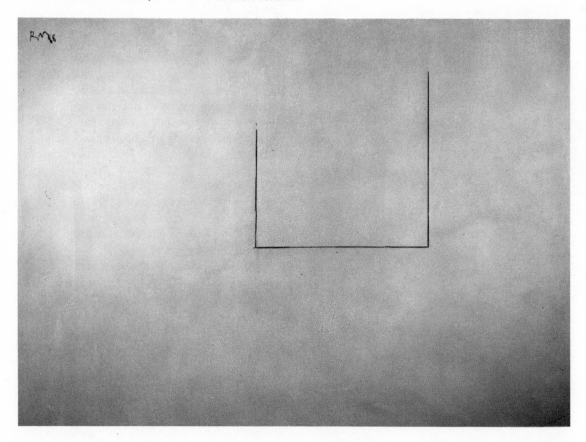

from the sterile academicism of purist abstraction and from the oppression of dominant Social Realist painting of the post-Depression period. It is difficult to remember that "subject matter," rather than worn-out forms of modernist abstraction, was the beacon guiding the emerging art of the early forties. Ancient myths and primitive art were thought to reveal universal symbols of the unconscious mind. Only later did the concept of myth and the creative unconscious fuse with a new conception of the painting act itself. Gottlieb and Rothko declared their intention to create, through myth-inspired paintings and a more fanciful imagery, a "tragic and timeless art." In a widely noted letter of 1943 written to *The New York Times*, the two artists, assisted anonymously by Barnett Newman, declared: "To us, art is an adventure into an unknown world . . . of the imagination which is fancy-free and violently opposed to common sense. . . . It is a widely accepted notion among painters that it does not matter what one paints as long as it is well painted. This is the essence of academicism. There is no such thing as a good painting about nothing. We assert that the subject is crucial."

As early as 1941, William Baziotes (1912–1963) began to utilize the Surrealists' automatic techniques to paint biomorphic abstractions with a mythic content. Influenced most strongly by Miró, he painted rather fearsome creatures from mythology, stressing the primacy of subject matter and apparently thinking of his paintings as "mirrors" that reflected the more bizarre and demonic side of the unconscious. Baziotes created in paint dreamlike, archetypal forms to represent interior states. Increasingly, however, he emphasized pictorial process rather than personal fantasy and symbolism in his painting. About 1946 he reduced the number of his shapes and enlarged them. To preserve a sense of spontaneity, he applied color freely on the canvas; the edges of his color forms are crudely drawn, broken, or blurred. Fascinated by underwater life, as were Rothko and Gottlieb also, Baziotes painted forms resembling biological life at elementary levels, and favored greens, blues, and purples—colors which evoked a sense of watery depths in a changing light. His *Dwarf* (1947, plate 530) floats on an indeterminate ground, toylike and only vaguely menacing in its deformations. The image, unlike the menacing creatures of the Surrealist imagination, conveys a sense of relative calm and introspection.

About 1942 Barnett Newman began to abandon mythic figurations for abstract emblems. In the art of aboriginal people he discovered the powers of simple abstraction. As he wrote, in an introduction to an exhibition of the paintings of the Northwest Coast Indians in 1946, ". . . the dominant aesthetic tradition was abstract. They depicted their mythological gods and totemic monsters in abstract symbols, using organic shapes, without regard to the contours of appearance." The conflicting urges to be both primitive and modern, abstract and symbolic, had fused. In Newman's painting the turning point came in 1948, with *Onement I*, the first of a series. With its undifferentiated background of uneven densities and its thickly painted center stripe, a new kind of symmetrically disposed, meditative pictorial icon emerged. Some of the significant changes are vividly experienced in the immense red color field of Newman's *Vir Heroicus Sublimis* (1950–51, colorplate 78). This colossal painting deals with pictorial decorum in a new way. The familiar agitated spatial movement, flux, and calligraphic signs of Abstract Expressionist painting have been replaced, and grandly solemnized, by a complex pulsation of high-keyed color over a pictorial field of vast expanse, divided by five fine vertical bands. The fragile and oscillating stripes play tricks on the eye and the mind by their alternate compliance and aggression. They range in visibility from strident vividness to a subliminal subtlety that produces wavering afterimages, subverting the idea of geometric partition of space and replacing Cubist compositional strategy with a single-image, or field, Gestalt. Newman's sources, like Pollock's, are momentary and, despite his repeating optical stripe and geometric structure, take account of the spectator's psychological absorption in the large expanse of color form and the effort required to perceive the work as a stable totality.

Some of the most original aspects of Newman's work, paintings of radical format and a rare group of geometric sculptures (see Chapter 23), were scarcely noted in the fifties but heralded a change for artists of the next decade. His painting *The Wild*, of 1950, was a length of stretched canvas with a stripe of scarcely modulated color eight feet high and an inch and one-half wide—one of his famous painted lines translated into a three-dimensional object.

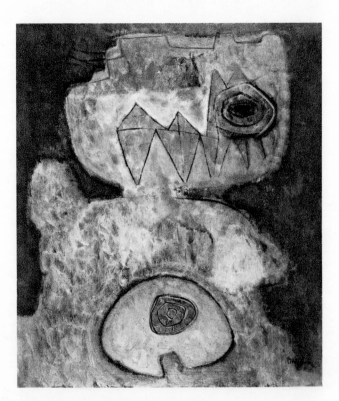

530 William Baziotes. *Dwarf*. 1947. Oil on canvas, 42 × 36⅛". The Museum of Modern Art, New York. A. Conger Goodyear Fund

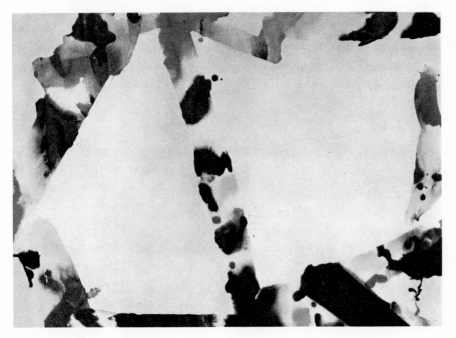

531 Sam Francis. *Untitled*. 1969.
Acrylic on paper, 31 × 43".
André Emmerich Gallery, New York

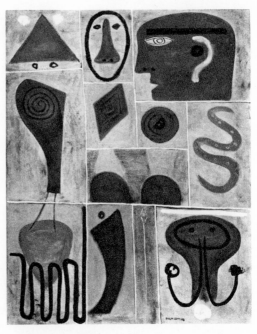

532 Adolph Gottlieb. *Voyager's Return*. 1946.
Oil on canvas, 37⅞ × 29⅞". The Museum
of Modern Art, New York. Gift of
Mr. and Mrs. Roy R. Neuberger

It also became a direct forebear of the shaped canvases and "deductive" structures of Frank Stella in the 1960s (see Chapter 26).

Clyfford Still's monumental areas of homogeneous hue, whether bright or somber, and his determination to dispense with Cubist structuring and linearity (cf. colorplate 79), helped to define the tendency that the critic Clement Greenberg later termed "Post-Painterly Abstraction." Some younger artists seemed able to combine both gestural and color-field abstraction. The dripped, liquid paint applications of Sam Francis (b. 1923) owed something to the controlled accidents of Pollock's open drip technique; but, in his early style, when Francis massed his congested and dribbled kidney shapes in consistent curtains of luminous darkness, relieved by the marginal activity of brilliant touches, his main debt was clearly to Still (plate 531).

Adolph Gottlieb adopted a system of pictographs within an abstract grid as a mode of probing the human psyche; these served to evoke mystery and to create a new vocabulary of signs of a personal character (cf. plate 532). His early pictographs were based, as he said, upon "introspection, free association, and automatism" and were Surrealistic in conception and execution. The later *Burst* series, by contrast, was built on a simplified arrangement of one or two primary shapes opposed to one another in a field of saturated color. The images in the *Bursts* have been identified as metaphors for the sun and earth, but Gottlieb usually insisted that he did not allude directly to nature. His compositions focused primarily on the ambiguous, yet strong, relationship between forms. In *Duet* (1962, colorplate 80), the main contrast exists in the dis-

parity between two clearly delineated disks and the coiling linear cluster below. The latter suggests the gestural mode and the randomness of Action Painting. The glowing color disks above have a muffled radiance which evokes the optical pulsations of Rothko.

Mark Rothko is best known for the soft and luminous rectangular compositions of blocky form that he began to paint in the 1950s. These compositions were rendered in a variety of chromatic combinations, ranging from dark and somber monochromes to pulsating fields of subliminal brightness. However, in his earlier work, about 1942, Rothko adopted the Surrealist technique of automatism, combining human, animal, and plant forms into inventive biomorphs, somewhat similar to Gorky's hybrids and Baziotes' suggestive symbols. *Slow Swirl by the Edge of the Sea* (1944, plate 533) floats on a background of diffuse patches of color, a group of creature-like shapes thinly painted in oil and freely brushed. Soon afterward, Rothko abandoned his ideographic symbols and automatist calligraphy to paint washes of bright color with no image suggestions whatever. The change of heart was perhaps rationalized by his romantic theories of the "sublime," within which context any references to finite nature and specific forms might be considered a constraint.

In his magnificent color-field paintings from the fifties onward, Rothko created simple configurations of two or three stacked rectangles of softly luminous colors. These works invited the spectator into a quiet and controlled space, encouraging a mood of reverie and exaltation. Their thin sheets of veiled color struck the same sustained note of even-burning intensity as the color fields of

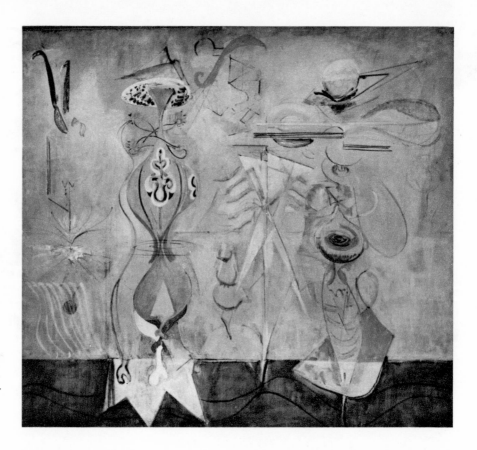

533 Mark Rothko. *Slow Swirl by the Edge of the Sea*. 1944. Oil on canvas, 6′ 3″ × 7′ ½″. Estate of the artist

Newman and Still, but Rothko's surfaces made more concessions to a traditional sensuousness transmitted to him through Matisse and Milton Avery. The boundaries separating Rothko's sparse color forms and their grounds are left deliberately hazy to allow room for expansion and for subtle internal relationships which generate vague suggestions of new metamorphic life within a structure of utmost simplicity. His colors run toward intolerable brightness or dark hues of subliminal refinement. His art is unapologetically emotional and impressionistic, unlike the conceptualism and intellectual programs that came to dominate art during the sixties. Within a generally moderate scale between the intimate easel convention and mural painting, his work conveys a grandeur and moral force unique in American art.

Although Rothko's intensely personal, poetic idiom today seems remote from current modes, which have shifted emphasis toward impersonality and anonymous fabrication, his technique of using paint as a dye, dissolving its paste in thin washes and sometimes leaving the canvas weave exposed and aesthetically active, profoundly influenced a significant new direction of abstract painting. Pollock, in his black paintings on unsized canvas, and Hofmann, too, had soaked liquid or thinned paint medium into unsized canvas, minimizing the pressures of the hand.

Helen Frankenthaler (b. 1928) was undoubtedly aware of these examples in the early 1950s, when she began to work consistently with diluted solutions that gave a new kind of luminosity to her colors. Indeed, she and a num-

ber of other artists of the 1960s and thereafter, whom Clement Greenberg linked in a style of "Post-Painterly Abstraction," significantly transformed and metamorphosed their Abstract Expressionist inheritance (see Chapter 26).

Another development of the fifties that also came to play an influential role in the next decade was the reduction of chromatic expression to monochromes and a rigid geometric formula in the black canvases of Ad Reinhardt (1913–1967). His segmented compositional grids are so dark and even in emphasis that distinctions of form and color require the most intense scrutiny. The almost imperceptible movement that the eye is allowed from one constellation of geometric shapes to another, and the shifts from faint color to none, reconstitute in quintessential expressive form certain ideas of change and stability, activity and quiescence, that lie at the heart of much innovative contemporary expression. Reinhardt's reductive means and the severity of his impassive icons, with their painstakingly worked surfaces, are the most extreme example of purity in contemporary American painting. In their context of renunciation and austerity the faint tremors of personal sensibility, as they can be discerned under proper light conditions, register with added force and poignancy.

More than any other artist of his generation, Reinhardt has proven prophetic of the "cool" Minimal abstract painting and sculpture of the 1960s. His tireless insistence —both in his art and in his inspired "art dogmas"—on a scheme of values congenial to the Eastern mind, admiring vacuity, repetition, refinement, and inaction, confirms the radical nonobjective painting and reductivist sculpture of today. The wonder is that Reinhardt was able to adhere steadfastly to his ascetic principles, to uphold his personal orthodoxy against the taste of the times, which strongly favored a drama of personal crisis and emotional release. After operating more or less underground during the fifties, Reinhardt's standardized and highly disciplined academic abstraction emerged to sanction the explorations of a generation who reacted decisively against the subjective storm and stress of the Action Painters.

His black paintings (plate 534), made after 1954, with their subliminal visibility and uniform design, are even less "interesting" or engaging by way of surface detail or pictorial dynamics than those of Barnett Newman.

While the "crisis" aesthetic of de Kooning, with his hyperactive, seething surfaces, seems diametrically opposed to Reinhardt's quietism, these antipodal artists can be related by the very extremes to which they pushed their art. Both alternately tested either the Expressionist or the doctrinaire abstract modes they inherited and redefined them in valid contemporary terms—de Kooning by his wide inclusions of historic styles and fragmentary human subject matter, and Reinhardt, inversely, by sharply restricting his pictorial means in an uncompromising purist abstraction. But at some far point their contradictions meet. De Kooning, and Pollock, too, sacrificed "personality" to the working process through grand and wasteful expenditures of energy, while Reinhardt suppressed the sense of ego by expunging the signs of individual authorship. Both expressions, representing the polarities of American painting of the 1950s, are viable and universal, and they remain as applicable to the historic art process as the ancient dualisms of romantic and classic.

The division among the Abstract Expressionists between an art of energy and impassivity, of impulse and color sensation, was recognized and acknowledged as early as 1950 by various critics, including Meyer Schapiro, who later lectured on the new painters in 1956 in London. His remarks were published in a revealing article in *The Listener*. There he contrasted Pollock's restless complexity and the relatively inert and bare painting of Rothko, Still, and Newman. As Schapiro wrote: "Each seeks an absolute in which the receptive viewer can lose himself, the one in compulsive movement, the other in all-pervading, as if internalized, sensation of a dominant color. The result in both is a painted world with a powerful immediate impact." The influence of the less dramatic, obviously less "Existential" painters, Rothko, Still, and Newman, was limited until the early 1960s by the widespread impact of de Kooning on younger American artists. Only when the momentum of Action Painting began to exhaust itself did the search begin for a different set of antecedents in the art of the pioneering Abstract Expressionists.

Historical accounts of this period of discovery and consolidation cannot today be viewed as settled or definitive. Many aspects of the crucial episode in American art after World War II are still disputed, as the spate of letters from the surviving Action Painters contesting claims and priorities that have been published in recent years in art journals makes abundantly clear. The example of intellectual adventure and moral courage put forth by these artists has persisted, even though their crisis rhetoric may now be discounted as inappropriate to our condition.

534 Ad Reinhardt. Installation view, "The Black Square Room," The Jewish Museum, New York. 1966–67

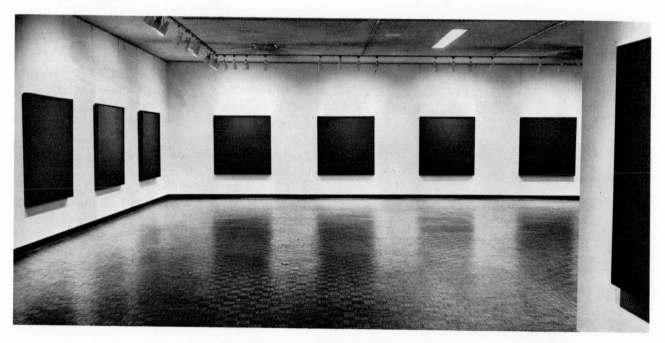

23
Sculpture in Transition: 1900 to the Present

Although it is generally true that a relatively small number of good sculptors exist even in periods of abundant creativity, the first four decades of the twentieth century exhibited an unusual scarcity of first-rate sculptural talent, at least by comparison with painting. As the extravagance of the Beaux-Arts style, which had shaped so many impressive public and private structures, waned on the eve of World War I, no comparable impact on American sculpture could be discerned from the modernism of Europe.

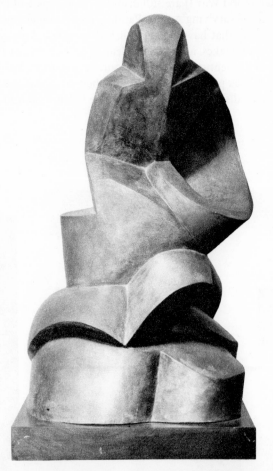

535 Max Weber. *Spiral Rhythm*. 1915. Bronze, height 24½". Hirshhorn Museum and Sculpture Garden, Smithsonian Institution, Washington, D.C.

Max Weber was one of the few Americans of the early decades to attempt sculptural abstraction. His *Spiral Rhythm* (1915, plate 535) reveals a spirit equidistant from the Futurist dynamics of Umberto Boccioni and the more solid geometric volume typical of Cubist sculpture.

THE EARLY DECADES

The Realism of the Ashcan group in painting found a parallel in sculpture with the appearance of a group of genre sculptors in the early years of the century. In response perhaps to the social zeal of the naturalist writers and to a general reforming impulse, the Swedish sculptor Charles Haag (1867–1934) began to model groups of strikers in heroic attitudes shortly after he settled in America in 1903. His Impressionistic surfaces derived from Rodin; his vigorous handling and undisguised working-class sympathies were shared by Mahonri Young (1877–1957), who was doing energetic bronzes of laborers and stevedores in the same period. Later Young, like Luks and Bellows, turned to prizefighter subjects and became celebrated for the muscular vigor of his athletes in action (plate 536).

Like painting, sculpture passed through a period of moderate experimentation up to the twenties, but by the thirties it was dominated by realistic sentiment and expressionist mannerism once more. The tenacity of representational modes of sculpture in America paralleled the painting situation. Only a few authentic pioneers in modern American sculpture were affected by radical European art forms, and without exception they gave their Continental sources a more stylized and decorative character.

Elie Nadelman (1885–1946), for example, who came to America from Poland in 1914, had experienced at first hand the influence of the Munich Jugendstil and the school of Paris. Between 1907 and 1914, after contact with Paris Cubism, he worked in a more analytical spirit, reducing his figures to a regularized system of curved volumes and their logical spatial echoes. Nonetheless,

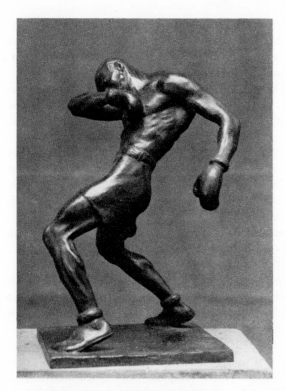

536 Mahonri Young. *Middleweight (Enzo Fiermonte)*. c. 1929. Bronze, height 27".
Whereabouts unknown

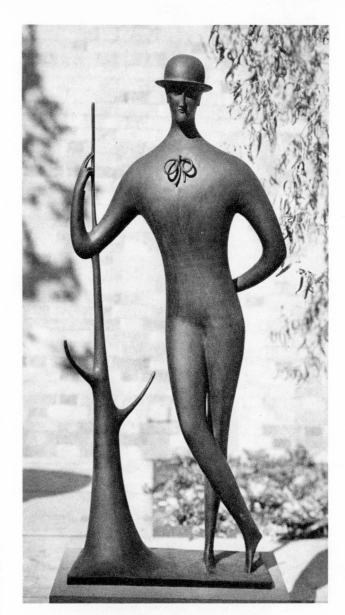

537 Elie Nadelman. *Man in the Open Air*. c. 1915.
Bronze, height 54½". The Museum of Modern Art,
New York. Gift of William S. Paley

he retained a certain tapered elegance of form and never overcame the quality of mannered refinement in his work. Essentially his style stems from Art Nouveau, despite an apparent commitment to the scrupulous streamlining and drastic geometric simplifications of more recent forms. Nadelman's arbitrary, stylized grace was eminently suitable, however, for the modish and witty statuettes and figures which became his stock-in-trade after he settled in America at the age of thirty-two. With his American wife, he was among the first to appreciate and collect American folk art, the cleanly incised forms and iconic character of which obviously contributed to his own mannered formula. In *Man in the Open Air* (plate 537) the fashionable bowler hat of his figure and the detail of a string bow tie conspire to create an effect of both gravity and humor, savoir-faire and classical *contrapposto*, in a dandified image that is a model of patrician poise and yet hauntingly suggests an archaic Greek torso.

Nadelman was only one of a number of European sculptors who settled in America after forming their mature style and enriched our cultural heritage. Among them were Alexander Archipenko (1887–1964), Carl Milles (1875–1955), and Ivan Mestrovič (1883–1962), with their semi-abstract, figural pieces; the Constructivist Naum Gabo (1890–1977), with his geometric abstractions utilizing new sculptural materials; Jacques Lipchitz (1891–1973), both a Cubist and a Symbolist-

figural sculptor. Their influence actually preceded their gaining American nationality but continued after they became residents and citizens.

Nadelman's influence in the direction of increasingly simplified form and linear emphasis was felt in particular by Gaston Lachaise (1882–1935). Lachaise is another sculptor whose national identity was at best uncertain but who was assuredly one of the pioneers of modern sculpture in America. Parisian by birth, he came to the United States in 1906, having already studied at the Académie Nationale des Beaux-Arts, exhibited frequently at the Salon des Artistes Françaises, and worked for René Lalique, the designer of Art Nouveau jewelry and glass objects. In America Lachaise was first an assistant to the academician Henry Hudson Kitson and then to Paul Manship. In 1913 he showed the first signs

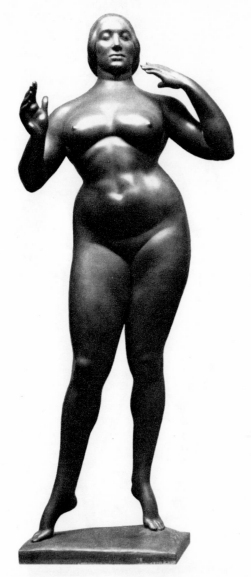

538 Gaston Lachaise. *Standing Woman.*
1912–27. Bronze, height 70″. Whitney
Museum of American Art, New York

ing thighs, and powerful legs. In other works of his maturity he carried the exaggeration of the female's sensual endowments to a point of abstraction, as in the *Torso* (1930, colorplate 81).

The stylish refinement that is acceptable in phases of Lachaise's work and lies at the heart of much of Nadelman's became a distractingly shallow feature in the work of America's probably most famous native-born sculptor of the period, Paul Manship (1885–1966). Many of his sculptures have classical subjects, but their interpretation is modern, or modernistic, perhaps, with an emphasis on linear grace and simplicity (plate 539). Returning in 1912 from a three-year sojourn at the American Academy in Rome, Manship soon began to show in his work the elegance of shape, clarity of outline, and streamlined decorative stylization of hair and drapery which became identified popularly with a facile kind of modernism, even though he made continual formal overtures to archaic Greek sculpture as well. With his first exhibition, in 1913, his success was immediate. His audience liked his work for its craftsmanship and simple lyricism, despite its semi-abstract character. Actually, his sculpture was much like Lachaise's early work and bore a relationship to Art Nouveau, particularly to the glass figurines of Gallé and to the lamps of Louis Comfort Tiffany. Albert Gallatin, an amateur painter and later a noted collector of abstract art, introduced Manship's early exhibitions. He commented improbably on the "fire and vigor" of the sculpture, asserting that it struck "a purely modern note." The exuberance and apparent spontaneity of Manship's pieces, which now seem strained and academic at heart,

of his own distinct style, characterized by fluent articulation of surface, massive yet weightless volume, and masterly control of rhythmic movement. In the 1920s and thirties Lachaise's female figures grew more distorted and expansive, eventually resembling grotesquely swollen prehistoric fertility sculpture. Lachaise also preserved something of the sinuous, flowing line of Art Nouveau, but the subtle interplay and resolution of masses in motion gave his sculpture more expressive power than that of Elie Nadelman. Although primarily a modeler, he was also adept at direct carving, a method that had gone out of style in the first years of the century. He sought, as he said, to express "the glorification of the human being, of the human body, of the human spirit." With consummate craftsmanship, he fashioned figures of gargantuan voluptuousness, earthy and swelling with opulent curves. The surging contours of *Standing Woman* (plate 538) deftly control the design motif formed by the ample breasts, heart-shaped stomach, wasp waist, swell-

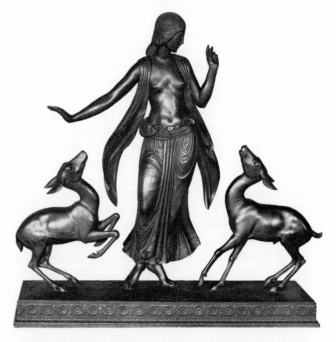

539 Paul Manship. *Dancer and Gazelles.* 1916. Bronze, height 32¼″. National Collection of Fine Arts, Smithsonian Institution, Washington, D.C. Bequest of the artist

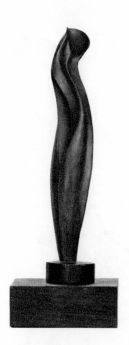

540 Robert Laurent.
The Flame. c. 1917.
Wood, height 18″.
Whitney Museum
of American Art,
New York.
Gift of Bartlett Arkell

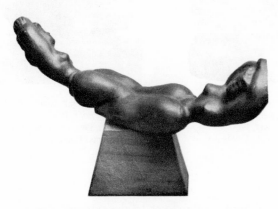

541 Chaim Gross. *Performers.* 1944. Bronze, length 19″.
Hirshhorn Museum and Sculpture Garden,
Smithsonian Institution, Washington, D.C.

The dominant avant-garde painting movement of the 1920s, Precisionism, did not number many sculptors among its direct practitioners, although Morton Schamberg's isolated image *God* (c. 1918, plate 542) combined Precisionist taste for machine-age imagery, in this instance plumbing, with Duchampian irony. Undoubtedly, the most considerable talent among the early sculptors who employed geometric forms related to a machine aesthetic was John Storrs (1885–1956), who in the early years of his career had participated in the experiments of the Cubists. A young man of considerable financial means, Storrs traveled extensively abroad and studied in Europe. After working in Rodin's atelier, he became involved with the more avant-garde sculptors who began to challenge traditional styles and techniques. By World War I he was making his own quite respectable Cubist sculpture, and by the 1920s he had undertaken an experiment probably unique in America of creating entirely nonobjective sculptures (plate 543). He slipped into obscurity for years, until an exhibition in 1965 stirred new interest in his work, but he was a figure of some consequence nonetheless. His simplified shafts of stone and metal of the 1920s are heralds of the same romance with machine technology, and particularly with the new skyscrapers, which enchanted such Precisionists as Demuth and Sheeler and became a stylistic feature of Art Deco in both architecture and applied design. Yet even his most graceful sculptures remain rooted in Cubist structure and theory and cannot be understood solely as ornamental objects. From 1915 until the early thirties, he was the only American to keep alive the possibilities of an abstract sculpture.

briefly gave him an undeserved reputation as an authentic American pioneer in modern sculpture.

Born in Brittany, Robert Laurent (1890–1970) came to America from France during the war years. After studying in Paris during the Cubist period, he had his first one-man show at the Daniel Gallery, New York, in 1915. He worked most successfully in wood, emphasizing both abstract form and the graining and textures of the material (plate 540). He was another of the early prophets of a new kind of sculptural form in this country, introducing reductive abstraction with respect for the medium of wood.

Probably the finest woodcarver in America, however, was Chaim Gross (b. 1904), from Austria-Hungary, who came to this country in 1921. His spiraling, acrobatic forms with their interlocking limbs (plate 541) forecast a new concern with more intricate spatial relationships which became an important aspect of American sculpture in the thirties and thereafter.

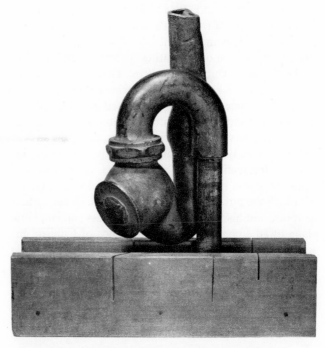

542 Morton L. Schamberg (assisted in the construction by Elsa von Freytag Loringhoven). *God.* c. 1918. Miter box and plumbing trap, height 10½″. Philadelphia Museum of Art. The Louise and Walter Arensberg Collection

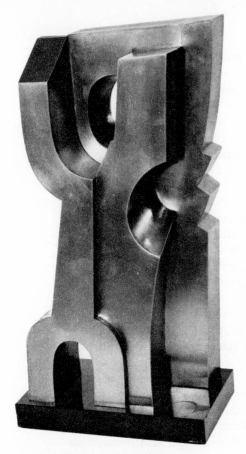

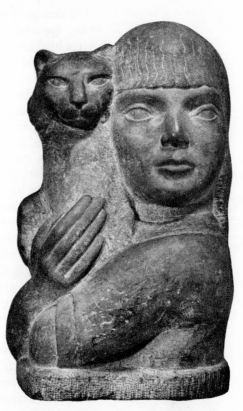

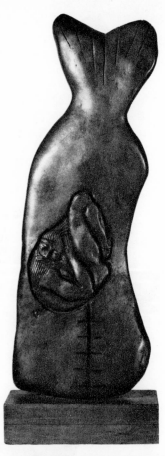

543 John Storrs. *Composition Around Two Voids*. 1932. Stainless steel, height 20″. Whitney Museum of American Art, New York. Gift of Monique Storrs Booz

544 William Zorach. *Child with Cat*. 1926. Tennessee marble, height 18″. The Museum of Modern Art, New York. Gift of Mr. and Mrs. Sam A. Lewisohn

545 John B. Flannagan. *Jonah and the Whale*. 1937. Bronze, height 29½″. The Minneapolis Institute of Arts. Purchase Martha T. Wallace Fund

Like Storrs, William Zorach (1887–1966) was greatly influenced by Cubism and other European avant-garde movements. He was also drawn to direct carving, which for him became tantamount to expressing a new candor about the nature of the artist's materials and a part of his search for simple monumentality. Zorach, and his wife Marguerite, had shown paintings influenced by Fauvism in the Forum Exhibition of 1916. That year, however, Zorach turned to sculpture as his principal medium, employing a geometric stylization related to Cubism. His forms underwent a drastic simplification and bent to the rule of the curve and the right angle, but Zorach was never completely a Cubist or Constructivist sculptor; his aim was the realization of an idealized yet consistently representational imagery, with solidly enclosed volumes. Although the powerful formal organization of his earliest sculpture and his feeling for simplified mass and emphatic plane owed something to the experience of Cubism, his critics have more often related these elements in his style to the modern classicism of Aristide Maillol.

In the late twenties Zorach began to employ cramped compact forms (plate 544). Pressed into unity by the sculptor's forceful will, or deliberately imprisoned by the too narrow confines of his stone blocks, these constricted,

angular forms were closer to the spirit of Romanesque relief than they were to the fluent grace and breadth of Maillol. Like many other American artists of the period, Zorach seemed to be moving toward Expressionist distortion.

A controlled Expressionism was also the basis of the style of one of the most interesting stonecarvers who emerged in the 1930s, John B. Flannagan (1895–1942). Flannagan's earlier work had been Gothic images of suffering, attenuated, freestanding figures in wood handled like bas-relief, with affinities to both German Expressionism and primitive Christian art. In the next decade his style broadened, and became more ample and rounded; in place of Expressionist torment, he substituted an effective and personal formal motif: a winding, circular, or spiral movement which conveyed a feeling of both enclosure and growth. His subjects were almost exclusively drawn from the animal and insect kingdoms, although he executed a number of sensitive portraits and figure compositions. Flannagan's forms emerged from their stones as a chick from its egg, or they were shown in cross-section, usually within a womblike enclosure (plate 545). The cyclical movement of emergence and return to the source made a modest but convincing allegory of birth and death. Flannagan's characterization of animal life was sometimes poignant and often humorous; it was invariably acute in its observation.

After the early 1930s a younger generation of Americans began to move in experimental directions which were to fulfill the promise held out for sculpture by the methods of Cubism and Constructivism. A number of the American Abstract Artists group, formed in 1937, were sculptors who had begun to explore a new kind of Precisionist abstraction, generally under the influence of Mondrian and Constructivist sculpture. Burgoyne Diller (1906–1965) made three-dimensional painted wooden reliefs, expressing in flat, primary tones and in black and white the sense of order and structure in solids and voids that mark Mondrian's art (plate 546). José de Rivera (b. 1904) worked in stainless steel and metal with purist, extremely simplified forms, which were the machine-related counterpart of Brancusi's idealized forms (plate 547). Other aspects of geometric style (e.g., plate 548) appeared in perhaps more isolated works of some distinction by Sidney Gordin (b. 1918), Richard Lippold (b.

1915), and Theodore Roszak (b. 1907), who moved on to Expressionist sculpture in the forties.

CALDER

In terms of innovative sculpture of the machine age, Alexander Calder (1898–1976) was clearly the most significant single figure and the important link between American abstract art of the thirties and postwar sculpture. During the socially discouraging years of the Depression, he was one of the few Americans of stature to uphold the experimental spirit in sculpture. By 1932 he had produced

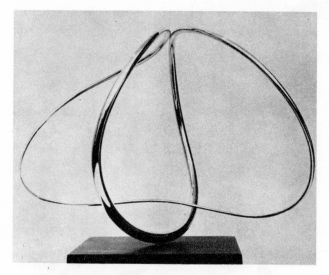

547 José de Rivera. *Construction No. 103*. 1967. Bronze, height 9¼". Collection Mr. and Mrs. Lionel R. Bauman, New York

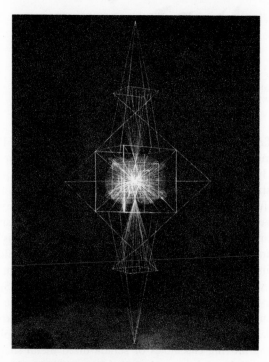

548 Richard Lippold. *Variation Number 7: Full Moon.* 1949–50. Brass rods, nickel-chromium, and stainless-steel wire, height 10'. The Museum of Modern Art, New York. Mrs. Simon Guggenheim Fund

546 Burgoyne Diller. *Color Structure No. 2*. 1963. Formica on wood, 72¼ × 48 × 17". Collection Noah Goldowsky Gallery and R. Bellamy, New York

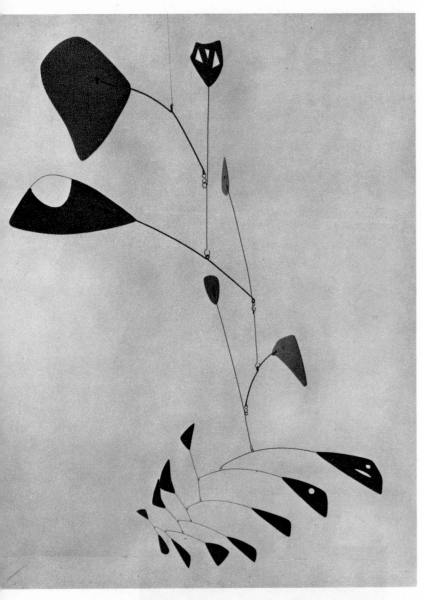

549 Alexander Calder. *Black Mobile with Hole.* 1954.
Painted steel with metal rods, 88 × 102".
Collection Mr. and Mrs. Jean Davidson, Sacramento, Calif.

his first motorized, freestanding sculptures, and by 1934 he had done a series of suspended mobiles with all the wit and lyrical invention which characterized his subsequent constructions. His special gifts were a wry humor, a playful fantasy, and a wonderfully resourceful inventiveness. Most important, too, was Calder's sensitive commitment to metals. The basic conception of his art became, as he put it, "the idea of detached bodies floating in space, of different sizes and densities . . . some at rest while others move in peculiar manners. . . . Symmetry and order do not make a composition. It is the apparent accident to regularity which makes or mars a work." Calder's organized formal accidents, taking place among moving ensembles of standardized metal shapes, which in themselves would have given supreme pleasure

to the most austere modern engineer, took the sting out of mechanization. Using almost uniform shapes, if not sizes, cut out of sheet steel, Calder gave to modern machine civilization a new lyricism in a novel form of artistic expression.

His deceptively simple and irresistible constructions have sometimes been described disapprovingly, in our solemn age, as aesthetic playthings. Neither Klee nor Miró would have considered the term a reproach. Calder, indeed, won his first recognition as a maker of animated toys; his famous miniature circus, with its expressive wire-and-wood figures of big-top performers, delighted Miró and attracted the enthusiastic interest of a wide circle of international artists in Paris between 1927 and 1930.

During the thirties Calder continued his work in three-dimensional construction, living in Paris most of the year, with occasional visits to America. Direct contacts with Mondrian and Miró were important factors in the evolution of his style. By 1932 he had put aside his representational sculpture in wire for the first ventures in those freestanding motor-driven structures, "stabiles," and somewhat later, the wind-propelled "mobiles" (plate 549) on which his major reputation is based.

It is impossible now to think of Calder's inventions apart from the American experience, even as we grant that he was the most international and urbane of our modern masters. His flower-like constructions often seem a witty and tactful commentary on the national passion for mechanical gadgets. The mobile brings mechanism into contact with a world of tenuous natural growth and achieves an organic-aesthetic life of its own. Its exquisite movements and endlessly varied spatial configurations seem to obey rhythmic principles which we associate with nature.

Until the 1960s, Calder seemed to be moving, with no diminution of invention or ingenuity, along the established paths he had laid out for himself in Paris some thirty years before. In the decade before his death, however, his magnificent stabiles became environmental in scale and must rank among the most impressive monumental sculpture in metal of the century (colorplate 82). Ideally, these imposing, yet buoyant forms should be experienced as part of the landscape, and they are, in fact, large enough to provide shelter or to be walked through and under. The enlargement of their swelling, Miróesque shapes, invariably painted either black or a sizzling orange-red, and the emphasis on their welding seams and rivets contribute to an intensified presence and formal power. Because the curving and angled forms are sheer and elegant, they can be associated with the work of contemporary Minimalist sculptors, who also use biomorphic or geometric shapes on a vast scale to achieve contradictory effects of antigravitational lightness and an illusionist play of sensuous surface.

(continued on page 506)

During the 1930s some effort to involve potters and other handcraftsmen was made by the WPA, but it was only the arrival of European émigrés and the opening of several important crafts-oriented art schools that reactivated American applied arts during that era. Among the new arrivals were Gertrud and Otto Natzler from Vienna, who had no formal instruction in ceramics when they began to work here in 1933. By the time they settled in Los Angeles in 1939, they had evolved a collaboration that was to place them among the foremost of ceramists. Otto Natzler (b. 1908) had become an expert on glazes, eventually developing about 2,500 different formulas, and Gertrud Natzler (1908–1971) created exceptionally classical and handsome shapes to which the glazes were applied. The illustrated bowl (plate 550) shows one of their more famous glazes, called "crater." The surface is pitted in an overall design against subtly colored bands which run horizontally around the inverted bell shape.

After 1950 or so, a new image was being forged for the craftsman. No longer the product of an apprenticeship or factory system, but often trained in an art school or university emphasizing exposure to all two- and three-dimensional mediums, the craftsman often approaches his medium in the manner of a "fine" artist. Peter Voulkos (b. 1924), the creator of the ceramic pot in plate 551, turned from traditional wheel-thrown pottery to hand-built forms. Although this piece is technically a pot, Voulkos was interested in the expressive qualities of the clay, as manipulated by the artist. Abandoning the symmetry permitted by the wheel, he has emphasized the sculptural value of the parts of this form: neck, elongated rim, and body joined together. He often uses contemporary painting materials instead of traditional glazes, upsetting the distinctions among painter, ceramist, and sculptor, as the artists in other mediums have done in the past two or three decades. These factors indicate that craft techniques—metalworking, glassblowing, weaving—have been absorbed into the fine arts.

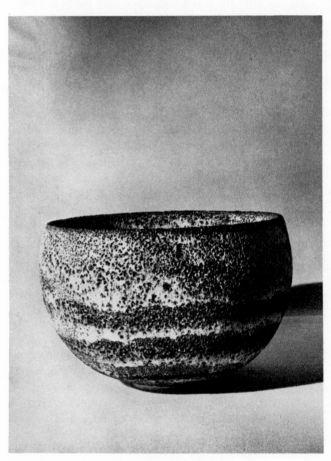

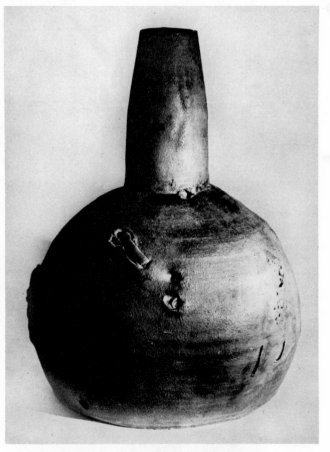

550 Gertrud and Otto Natzler. Bowl. 1956.
Gray earthenware with "crater" glaze, height 8⅝".
Everson Museum of Art, Syracuse, N.Y.

551 Peter Voulkos. Vase, *Aratsa*. 1968. Stoneware, with iron-copper slip and clear glaze, 26¼ × 19½ × 19". Herbert F. Johnson Museum of Art, Cornell University, Ithaca, N.Y. Gift of S. C. Johnson and Son, Inc.

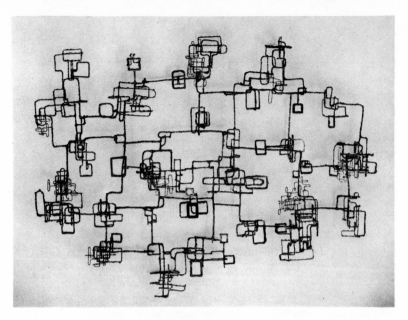

552 Ibram Lassaw. *Clouds of Magellan.* 1952.
Welded bronze and steel, 52 × 70 × 18″.
Private collection

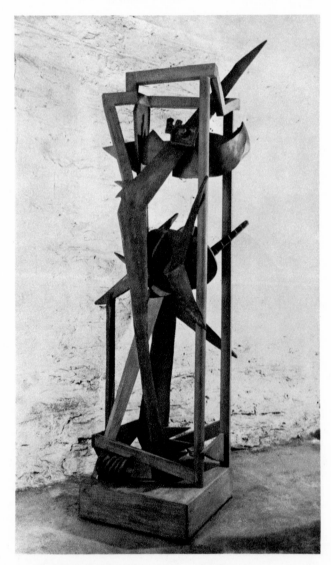

553 Seymour Lipton. *Imprisoned Figure.* 1948.
Wood and sheet lead, height 84¾″. The Museum
of Modern Art, New York. Gift of the artist

(continued from page 504)

POSTWAR INNOVATIONS

The period after World War II produced a major breakthrough in American sculptural innovation and at least one major figure, David Smith, who towered above his contemporaries. Sculpture shared with Action Painting many of its seminal insights, but by the early sixties the changes in sculptural idioms were so profound as to involve radical redefinition of the medium itself. Assemblage, "junk sculpture," and new types of geometric structures using reductive form to create visual ambiguity have led to fresh artistic alignments, blurring the traditional distinctions between painter and sculptor. As a result, the visual ideas treated by painting and sculpture today seem surprisingly interdependent, as they were in the Baroque age, another period marked by an extraordinary surge of energy and invention that transgressed the integrity of individual mediums and brought them into a new synthesis. The emergence of sculpture as a primary, even dominant, force has distinguished the position of American art during the last two decades.

Shortly after the war an idiom of fluid metal construction appeared as the major tendency in advanced American sculpture. Freely adapting from Surrealism its addiction to accident, welder-sculptors built forms in a variety of techniques that combined improvisation with new kinds of surfaces and with the formal ideals of modern Constructivism. Many of the first ventures were fantasy-ridden and aggressive in handling, despite a fundamental concern with the expressive potential of the medium.

The new work was not all exasperation or strident feeling, however, and allowed for a variety of moods, from dramatic emotionalism to quietism. The first metal sculptures of Ibram Lassaw (b. 1913) in the early 1950s were intricate cage constructions which delicately fused grids in three dimensions to create an atmosphere of luminous serenity (plate 552). Seymour Lipton (b. 1903) established an unexpected relationship between the organic forms of nature, which dramatized the life processes, and the revealed dynamics of the creative act (plate 553). Herbert Ferber (b. 1906) created a thorny and barbed but spatially liberated imagery (plate 554). David Hare (b. 1917) by using hybrid forms made overt references to Dadaist discontinuities and to the pull of primitive cultures (plate 555). Theodore Roszak (b. 1907) invented a language of potent new sculptural symbols analogous to clutching tree roots or bone and skeletal structure, and his violent images acquired a special power and durability in welded steel (plate 556).

Like the Abstract Expressionist painters, these sculptors were driven by an ambivalent sense of forging urgent personal images while yet adhering to the main line of European modernism. For the younger generation that followed them, the unfinished character of their imagery

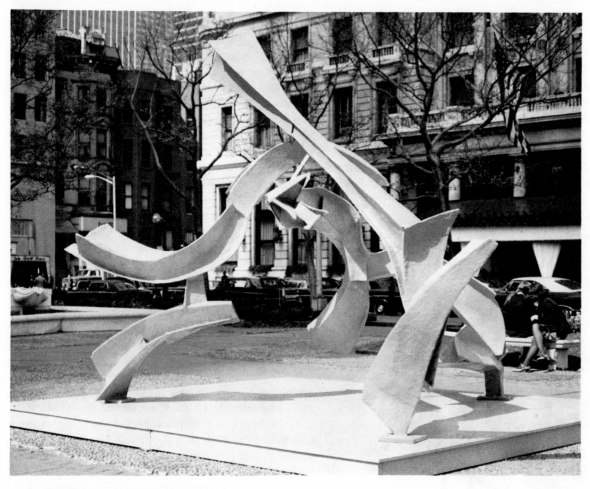

554 Herbert Ferber. *Three Arches*. 1966. Epoxy, 10′ 6″ × 15′.
André Emmerich Gallery, New York

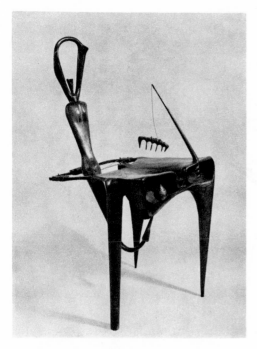

555 David Hare. *Magician's Game*. 1944.
Bronze, height 40¼″. The Museum of
Modern Art, New York. Gift of the artist

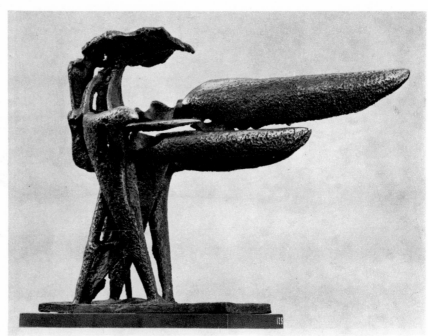

556 Theodore Roszak. *Whaler of Nantucket*.
1952. Steel, 35 × 48″.
The Art Institute of Chicago

and their technical laissez faire, in defiance of traditional sculpture methods, proved most liberating.

Another pioneer figure who exercised some influence on the work of young sculptors was Reuben Nakian (b.1897). Like so many American avant-garde artists, he had been a technically accomplished traditionalist until the early 1940s and then underwent a revolution in style. Later in that decade, he began to improvise freely in plaster, developing mythological subjects in baroque, twisting

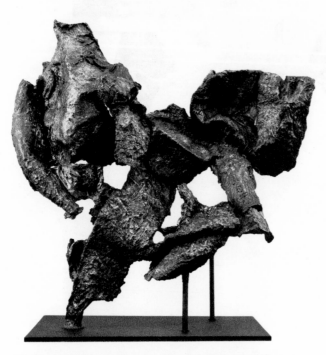

557 Reuben Nakian. *Olympia*. 1961. Bronze, height 72".
Whitney Museum of American Art, New York.
Gift of the Friends of the Whitney Museum

diagonals, which he gouged, pressed, and kneaded until they functioned as loose, amorphous, abstract forms. Then, in 1953, he experimented with burlap stretched on chicken wire, dipped in glue and quick-setting plaster. His forms were close in spirit to de Kooning's, and their impermanence of surface, casualness of technique, and materials seem now to have perhaps anticipated the primitivist, glued-paper constructions of Claes Oldenburg. His inventions, later cast in bronze (plate 557), represented a major departure from the direct metal techniques and the alternately linear or Cubist structural forms of the leading sculptors of his generation.

DAVID SMITH AND DI SUVERO

When David Smith (1906–1965) died, he was already recognized as the major American sculptor of his generation. His achievement is not diminished by the fact that, with the passage of time, his work now seems more the triumphant end of a Cubist and Constructivist tradition than the beginning of a new set of attitudes. In the late 1940s Smith produced a number of open-form linear sculptures which paralleled the cage structures of Lassaw and some aspects of Surrealism. *Royal Bird* (1948, plate 558) synthesizes a Constructivist diagramming of space and a fanciful bird presence which verges on the grotesque, evoking the totems of Surrealist invention. Within his open constructions, Smith managed to create a fantastic anatomical imagery without stylistic disunity. Also, adding another element to the identifiable amalgam of his highly personal and expressive style, he began to incorporate into his work "found" forms of machine and farm-equipment parts.

In 1956 Smith experimented with modular sculpture, or stacks of boxlike shapes (*Four Units Equal, Five Units*

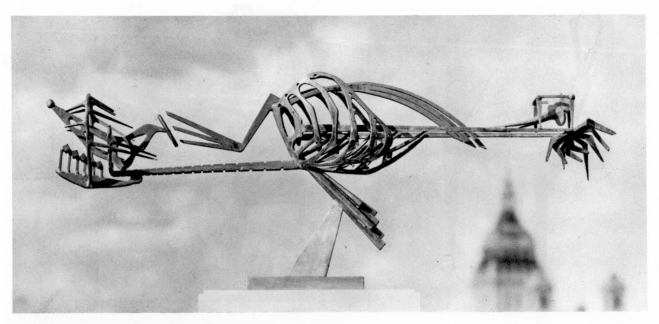

558 David Smith. *Royal Bird*. 1948. Stainless steel, 21¾ × 59".
Walker Art Center, Minneapolis.
T. B. Walker Foundation Acquisition, 1952

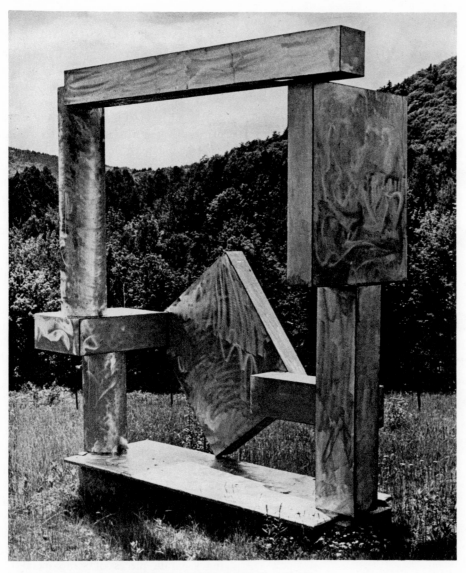

559 David Smith. *Cubi XXVIII*. 1965. Stainless steel, 9′ × 9′ 4⅛″.
Norton Simon, Inc., Foundation, Los Angeles

Equal, and others), but he was temperamentally unsuited to such uniformity, and to the absence of compositional tensions that the Minimalists and primary structurists were later to develop into a new kind of aesthetic. In his *Cubis* (plate 559), the most significant series he invented, cubes and rectangular boxes were piled up and balanced in precarious alignment with cylinders and disks so that their unstable, top-heavy quality, or skewed, random arrangements, became emphasized. The *Cubis* were impressive not only as balanced sculpture masses, but also they dealt as much with the quality of light on surface as with shape. Smith wrote of this monumental series: "They are conceived for bright light, preferably the sun, to develop the illusion of surface and depth." Like much of his painted polychromed sculpture (colorplate 83), in which he emphasized brushstroke almost to the point of painterly illusion, the stainless-steel surfaces of the *Cubis*

are burnished with a wire brush, and their swirls produce a pictorial pattern in dynamic opposition to their sculptural mass.

Smith's interest in a machine aesthetic (he called his studio the Terminal Iron Works, naming it after a factory where he had welded tanks during the war) and his respect for industrial techniques link him perhaps even more to the later generation of Minimalist sculptors than does his essentially Cubist and conservative treatment of volumes in space. His name and inspiration are frequently mentioned in connection with the unadorned floor boxes, the serial units of composition, and the modular styles of such artists as Don Judd (b. 1928), Sol LeWitt (b. 1928), and Carl Andre (b. 1935). Actually, however, Smith has little to do with their aesthetic. The only direct heir of his spirit, if not precisely of his formal ideas, is Mark di Suvero (b. 1933), whose huge cantilevered wooden-beam

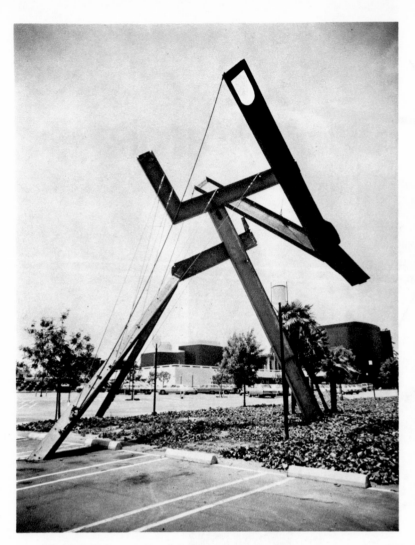

560 Mark di Suvero. *Untitled*. 1971.
Steel, height c. 30′. Collection the artist

ABSTRACT EXPRESSIONISM IN SCULPTURE

In 1950, the same year that Barnett Newman made his painting *The Wild*, in a radically narrow format, he also made the first primitive version of his *Here* sculpture series (plate 561), which comprised three works carried out over the next decade. *Here I* consisted of wooden planks covered with rough plaster, resourcefully mounted on a dilapidated wooden box. This unlikely creation was cast in bronze many years later, in the late sixties. Its early version surprisingly anticipated the unitary single-image of Minimalist sculpture. Newman's famous linear band in his painting, or his "zip," as the artist liked to call it, equating velocity with both luminous and kinetic effects, has been divorced from the canvas surface and transformed into imposing hierarchical sculpture form. Controlled emotion, an antithesis valued by the Periclean Greeks, is consciously resurrected in Newman's rare sculpture. *Here I* is one of only a half-dozen sculptures Newman made in his lifetime. The contrast of a freely handled edge and a solid bar of bronze derives from such paintings as *The Promise*, in which a feathery brushstroke opposes a hard, machined contour edge. The sculpture is eight feet high, exactly the same height as the vertical divisions in the painting *Vir Heroicus Sublimis* (colorplate 78).

In the late 1950s there were other notable attempts to translate the spirit and imagery of Abstract Expressionism into three dimensions. One of the first major assimilations of the energy and spontaneity of the New York school of painting was the recognition by John Chamberlain (b. 1927) of the sculptural possibilities of crushed automobile-body parts. Although his technique of welding separate pieces of scrap metal together remained within the tradition of Cubist "assemblage," Chamberlain transformed the basically planar format of the Cubists into an overwhelmingly three-dimensional sculptural statement. By limiting the manipulation of materials to fitting and welding, Chamberlain allowed the materials themselves to play a major role in determining form and expression. In his first phase, Chamberlain crossed his sculpture with a painterly rhetoric derived from de Kooning's jarring mixture of chromatic dazzle and painterly opulence. He never allowed the observer to forget, however, that he was bending sheets of a real automobile chassis. Recently Chamberlain has moved from the preoccupation with junk objects to a sparer kind of assemblage with homogeneous, galvanized aluminum (plate 562), after experimenting briefly with soft polyurethane foam and transparent plastic.

NOGUCHI

While sculptors using welded metals have dominated the American scene, there has also been vigorous creative work with more traditional materials. One of the most unusual abstract sculptors as early as the late 1920s was

sculptures—with occasional "junk" additions of chains, buckets, and ladders—can be directly related, like Smith's own sculptures, to the formal structure of paintings by Kline and de Kooning.

Di Suvero has succeeded in adapting in sculpture the heroic vision and the bold, dynamic forms of the Action Painters (plate 560). His early work combined the thrusting imagery and powerful gesture typical of Franz Kline's paintings, with a sense of monumental scale characteristic of the California landscape in which he grew up. His use of unrefined materials and found objects increased the expression of raw energy and power suggested by natural scale. Constructivist qualities of geometric form and careful engineering, always present in di Suvero's works, have become increasingly evident in recent years, when he has limited his materials to industrially fabricated steel plates and I-beams. As his work has evolved from the massive forms of the early period to the structural clarity and linear elegance of his recent pieces, di Suvero has continued to utilize the Constructivist compositional elements of strong diagonals, tetrahedral forms, and precise suspension systems.

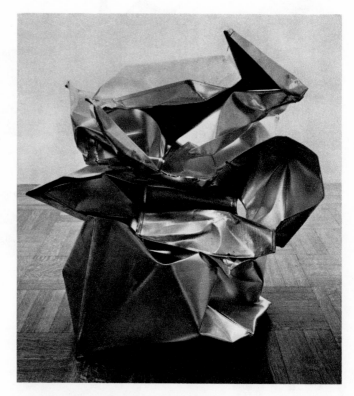

562 John Chamberlain. *Tippecanoe*. 1967.
Galvanized steel and aluminum, height 40".
David Whitney Collection, New York

Isamu Noguchi (b. 1904), the immensely gifted Japanese-American, who studied in Paris with Brancusi and returned to New York in 1928. There he held the first one-man show of his distinguished abstract forms, which a half century later he continues to produce with undiminished vitality and invention. Noguchi's open-form metal sculptures of the thirties were closer in spirit to the Constructivists than to Brancusi, and they also interestingly recall his childhood memories of kites and the paper objects so common in Japan. During the forties Noguchi worked in a variety of polished stones (plate 563). He demonstrated a suave and fluent mastery of abstract idioms with Surrealist overtones, deftly creating interlocking systems of flattened biomorphic forms derived perhaps from Arp or Miró. His stage properties and designs for the dance company of Martha Graham paved the way for many such interarts collaborations later in the century. He has also made freestanding terra cottas in rounded, doll-like shapes and has ingeniously grouped on a vertical post varied *kasama* forms, the durable earthenware that has for centuries been used in Japan for kitchen vessels. The tension between the naive conventions of popular art forms and a sophisticated modernity give these playful inventions a distinctive individuality. Noguchi is a master of elegant form and refined materials, including a wide variety of carved stones, from whose surfaces he seems able to coax a special sensuous poetry,

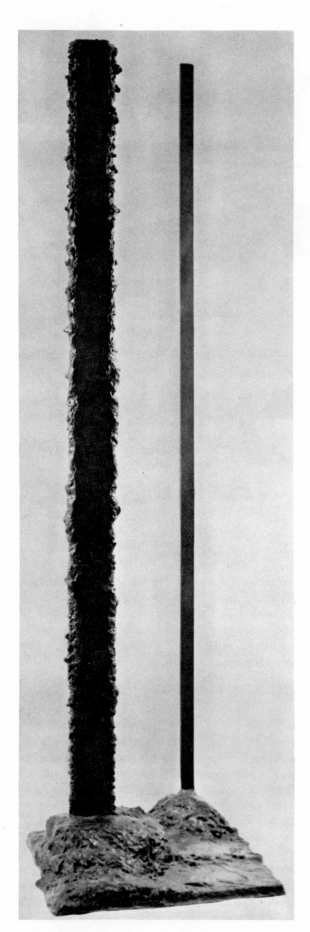

561 Barnett Newman. *Here*. 1950. Bronze, height 8' 11¼".
Collection Annalee G. Newman, New York

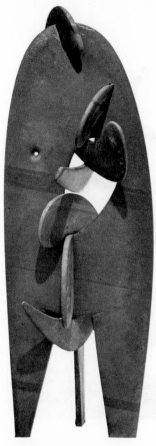

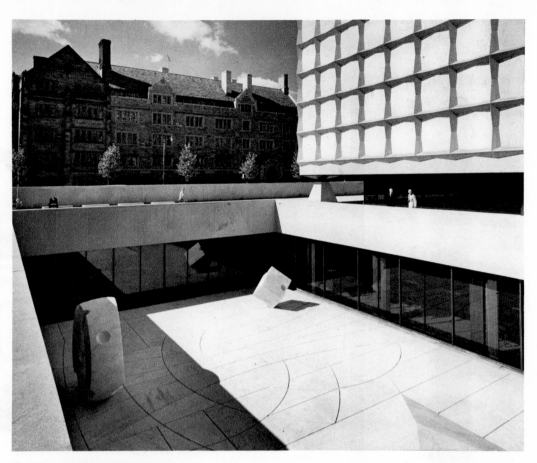

563 Isamu Noguchi.
Humpty-Dumpty. 1946.
Ribbon slate, height
58¾″. Whitney Museum
of American Art, New York

564 Isamu Noguchi. Courtyard,
Beinecke Rare Book and Manuscripts
Library, Yale University, New Haven, Conn. 1960–64

no matter how severely geometric his structure. He has roots deep in French modernist tradition as well as in the East.

In the past two decades Noguchi has become one of our most impressive public sculptors and shapers of environments. These have included the UNESCO gardens in Paris, the sunken sculpture court for the Beinecke Library at Yale (plate 564), the Billy Rose Sculpture Garden at the Israel National Museum in Jerusalem, and countless other projects. In his remarkable Yale library courtyard, Noguchi created a total environment of grace and architectural elegance, whose angled and curved geometric solids suggest a pristine absolutism. Despite their marble immaculateness and formal severity, they remain sensuous and poetic.

The experience of making sculpture gardens and environmental projects of heroic dimensions has influenced some of Noguchi's later large-scale private sculptures, which are less finished than his earlier work and show a more primitivist expressive force. Still carved and shaped to some degree with power tools, a piece such as *Rock of Inner Seeking* (c. 1970) suggests a new regard for a romantic, untamed nature. Its primitivism is qualified, however, by the subtle revelation of finely modelled interior cavities, which convert the rudimentary rough-hewn

boulder into a carefully deliberated structure, the obvious product of formal control.

Noguchi's Civic Center Plaza, in Detroit, is so far the most spectacular of his achievements in environmental space. Terraced down to the river and centering upon a gigantic stainless-steel structure that combines a play of lights and water jets, the complex is no longer simply sculpture but an experimental essay in sculpture, architecture, landscaping, and city planning.

CORNELL AND NEVELSON

A unique and mysterious figure in American sculpture was Joseph Cornell (1903–1972), who began in the thirties to make box constructions which deserve to be placed on the highest level of contemporary American creation. His work combined the structural austerities of Constructivism with the fantasies of Surrealism and utilized subtle painting and collage techniques. His mysterious boxes house the most surprising and entrancing romantic bric-à-brac: pasted fragments of nostalgic photographs, scenes from a Victorian "grand tour," a Surrealist "poetic object," or snatches of a counterfeit but somehow touching modern mythology culled from astrological illustrations. The fusion at poetic intensity of precious sentiment, bizarre imagery, and a stern formal rectitude gives Cornell's constructions a quality entirely their own (plate 565). He has become an honored precursor for works such as Louise Nevelson's "junk" assemblages, Jasper Johns's introduction of small anatomical casts into his paintings, and Lucas Samaras's boxed containers of fantasy and dream imagery.

The work of Louise Nevelson (b. 1900) also represents a sharp departure from the methods of the welder-sculptors with whom she is otherwise identified by age and achievement. Her "walls" contain commonplace objects in stacked and interconnected boxes and crates. Newel posts, finials, parts of balustrades, chair slats and barrel staves, bowling pins and rough-cut wood blocks, sprayed in a uniform white, black, or gold, are some of the myriad components which she cunningly sets in the shallow recesses of her additive, Cubistic constructions (colorplate 84). For all their intricacy and ingenuity of formal relation and dazzling variation of shape, her walls achieve both a powerfully unified impact and liberating possibilities of expansion. They operate forcefully upon the spectator and his own spatial environment. The rigorously formalized structures also have the air of being a collection of treasured trophies. Her ensembles function with the ambiguity of a de Chirico still life, where geometric style acts as a source of poetic mystery rather than of clarity and precision. The same unerring balance of expressive power and hermeticism continues to sustain Nevelson's inventions today. Even her large, public outdoor sculptures, usually erected in Cor-Ten steel, and the transparent Lucite structures of recent years carry the personal stamp of her early works, despite their monumental scale and look of impersonal fabrication.

ASSEMBLAGE AND POP SCULPTURE

A blatant use of subaesthetic materials containing an element of social commentary was a noticeable trend among both sculptors and painters about mid-century (see also Chapter 26). Artists began to call seriously into question the hierarchy of distinctions between the fine arts and extra-artistic materials drawn from the urban refuse heap. "Junk art" (so-called) gathered momentum in the late 1950s, and in the 1960s it was given added emphasis in the conglomerates of rusting boiler and machine parts used in the sculpture of Richard Stankiewicz (b. 1922) and in the crushed and shaped auto bodies of John Chamberlain (plate 562). Allan Kaprow, the prophet and advocate of literal experience in art, proposed in 1958 "a quite clear-headed decision to abandon craftsmanship and permanence" and "the use of obviously perishable media such as newspaper, string, adhesive tape, growing grass, or real food," so that "no one can mistake the fact that the work will pass into dust or garbage quickly."

The transformation of "assemblage," the apt rubric invented by critic William C. Seitz, into an expansive

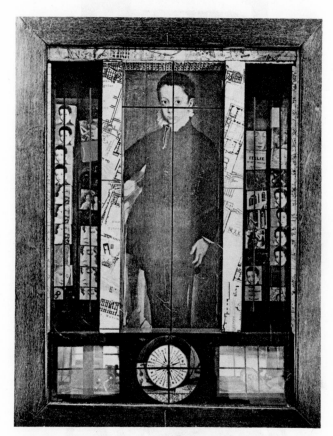

565 Joseph Cornell. *Medici Slot Machine*. 1942. Mixed media, 15½ × 12 × 4⅜". Private collection

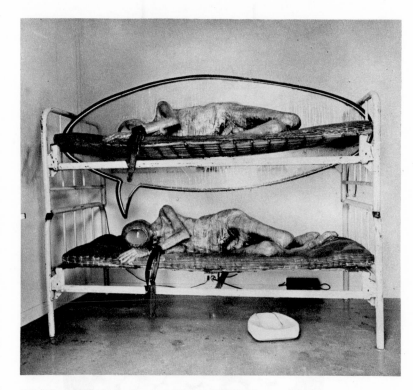

566 Edward Kienholz. *The State Hospital*. 1964–66. Mixed media, 8 × 12′. Moderna Museet, Stockholm

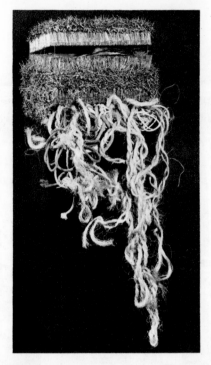

567 Lucas Samaras. *Untitled, Box No. 3*. 1963. Wood, pins, rope, and stuffed bird, $24\frac{1}{2} \times 11\frac{1}{2} \times 10\frac{1}{4}''$. Whitney Museum of American Art, New York. Gift of the Howard and Jean Lipman Foundation

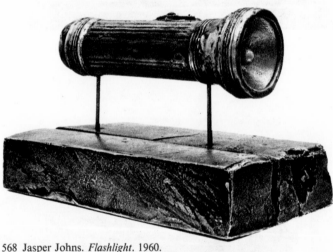

568 Jasper Johns. *Flashlight*. 1960. Bronze and glass, $4\frac{7}{8} \times 8 \times 4\frac{1}{2}''$. Collection Mr. and Mrs. Irving Blum, Los Angeles

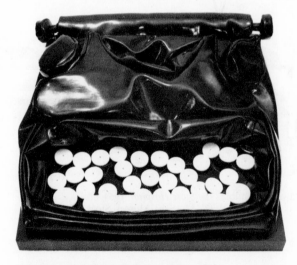

569 Claes Oldenburg. *Soft Typewriter*. 1963. Vinyl, kapok, cloth, and Plexiglas, $27\frac{1}{2} \times 26 \times 9''$. Collection Alan Powers, London

environmental art often with theatrical content was expressed with sharp dramatic tension in the mordant and memorable tableaux of Edward Kienholz (b. 1927). His vicious allegories can be viewed as the grotesque horror-film countercurrent to the mindless California fascination with a world of hot rods, baroque car designs, high-polish craftsmanship, and other evidences of shallow, ersatz visual culture. Kienholz's brutal creations belong to an American moralizing tradition, and comment on such topics as abortion, patriotism, eroticism, and even psychic disintegration, often with an almost unbearable literalism, as in his searing *State Hospital* (1964–66, plate 566).

Like certain aspects of Dada and Surrealist art, Lucas Samaras's *Boxes* (e.g., *No. 3*, 1963, plate 567) transform disparate objects and materials into new realities. His fascination with violence in his detailed photographic examination of his own body, as well as his exploration of magic and alchemy, places his work in the Surrealist tradition to a certain extent. Samaras (b. 1936) is aware that the spectator's involvement with his work is an integral part of its impact. The anticipation of pain in the touching of a pin box is an example of spectator involvement in the Duchampian aesthetic strategy of compelling the audience to complete the creative act.

The painter Jasper Johns (see also Chapter 26), who had a far-reaching effect on the innovations of the sixties, experimented among other things with assemblage. Johns's corpus includes bronze casts of a mounted flashlight (1960, plate 568), a light bulb, a toothbrush, eyeglasses, and a painted Savarin can with his studio brushes, all cast in bronze. His hand-painted bronze of Ballantine ale cans, entitled *Painted Bronze*, was made in response to de Kooning's ironic remark that the art dealer Leo Castelli could sell anything—even two beer cans. Johns used commercial Pop icons but transformed them by a veil of elegant, painterly gestures and marks or sculptural surface modeling similar to the handling of the Abstract Expressionists.

Toward the mid-sixties Claes Oldenburg (b. 1929), who had started as an Abstract Expressionist painter, began to produce a series of "soft sculptures" (1963, plate 569)—telephones, toasters, typewriters, fans, automobiles—that look freshly manufactured, slick, and grossly opulent instead of overripe or decayed. They entered into the context of art newly minted, vinyl-covered, preserved before they were caught up in the consumer cycle from use to junk. These creations remain outrageous in their immensity of scale and in their parody of the normal physical properties of the things they dissemble. Oldenburg's "soft" forms still exert a powerful influence on contemporary abstract sculpture.

In recent years Oldenburg has also executed a number of monumental hard sculptures, designing urban monuments from his food facsimiles and banal objects—a toilet ball for the Thames in London, a teddy bear for New

York's Central Park, a gargantuan Good Humor Bar for Manhattan's Park Avenue, a large clothespin which now actually stands on one of Philadelphia's most elegant and historic public squares. These bizarre inventions are grafts of the fantasies of childhood on an urban environment whose dehumanization, overcrowding, traffic congestion, crime, and pollution resist rational adult control.

It was perhaps inevitable that the obsession with visual facts precisely revealed through the photographic medium should open up the way for similar sculptural experiment. In the three-dimensional work of Duane Hanson (b. 1924) humanity is reborn as real and as bizarrely unreal as the subject matter in related Super-Realist painting. His figures in fact closely resemble those in Mme. Tussaud's waxworks, or the stuffed robots of Disney World's Hall of Presidents, with their accurate mimicry of human gesture. The fascination with duplications of reality, and particularly of the human form in life size, is an age-old obsession. But today, when originals and reproductions are no longer so easily distinguishable, owing to the manipulation of consumers by advertising ploys, sinister overtones are added to these counterfeit three-dimensional likenesses and to the artist's traditional deceptions and illusions. There is something uncanny about Hanson's *Woman with Suitcases* (1973, plate 570), which is both invented and utterly real in its polychrome plastic incarnation, capturing all the fatuous vulgarity of certain aspects of American life. Yet the more exact Hanson's facsimiles become, the more unreal they are—Frankenstein monsters of the contemporary culture.

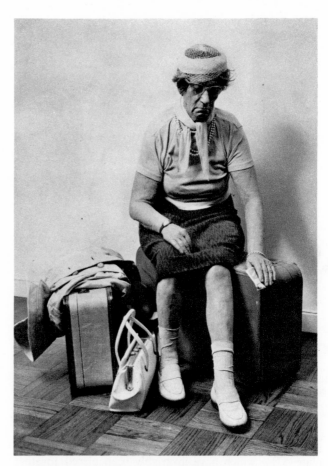

570 Duane Hanson. *Woman with Suitcases.* 1973.
Polyester resin and fiberglass, life size.
Morton G. Neumann Family Collection, Chicago

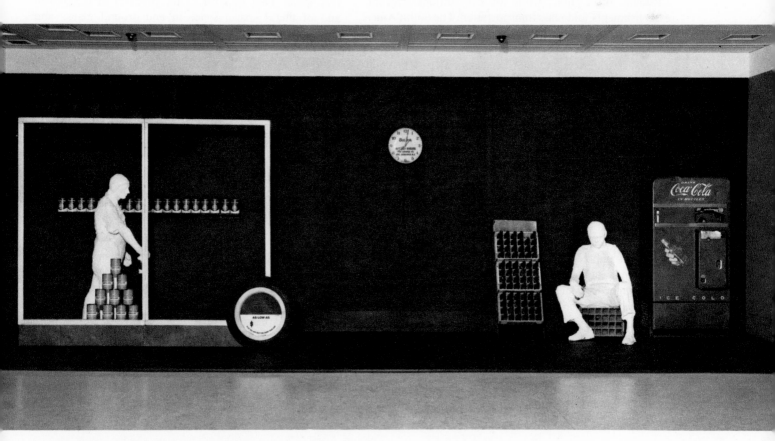

571 George Segal. *The Gas Station.* 1963. Assemblage, 8' 6" × 24' 2" × 4'.
The National Gallery of Canada, Ottawa

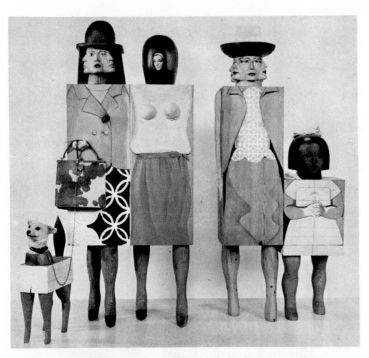

572 Marisol. *Women and Dog*. 1964. Wood, plaster, synthetic polymer paint, mixed media, 72 × 82 × 16″. Whitney Museum of American Art, New York. Gift of the Friends of the Whitney Museum

George Segal (b. 1924) creates equally literal but ghostly, white-plaster replicas of the human figure (1963, plate 571), which have invariably been pieced together from body casts of friends who patiently subjected themselves to his art. These stolid and unsensible dream figures dwell in the lonely limbo created by the chrome and neon vacancies of a public world of gas stations, cleaning establishments, and mass transportation. The South American-born Marisol (b. 1931) also treats the human figure in terms of personal fantasy and eroticism rooted both in Surrealist tradition and the imagery of Pop Art. Ambiguity and fantastic metamorphosis are hallmarks of Marisol's work in all media; the interaction of animate and inanimate, human and animal imagery in *Women and Dog* (1964, plate 572) recalls René Magritte's double-edged images of human/animal forms.

MINIMAL SCULPTURE

During the mid-sixties a new mood of self-scrutiny and reappraisal created a situation of uncertainty for avant-garde sculptors in which painting, sculpture, architecture, and engineering converged, often paradoxically, in unprecedented aesthetic objects which eluded traditional definitions. A stylistic synthesis emerged finally in the form of Minimal Art. Although this term also describes some examples of shaped canvas, monochrome painting, and a reductive, geometric pictorial art, it was identified especially with the severely structurist art which attained general public recognition in the exhibition "Primary Structures," organized by New York's Jewish Museum in the spring of 1966. The exhibition demon-

strated a new common sensibility and carried the weight of a visual manifesto for a new aesthetic viewpoint.

The museum exhibition had been preceded by a number of influential one-man shows in New York which already provided abundant evidence that a new type of easily perceived, yet mentally complex, geometric form—symmetrical, boxlike, set out in modular units, unadorned—had begun to comprise a new collective style. Walter de Maria (b. 1935) and Robert Morris (b. 1931) made what could be described as Minimal Art as early as 1961, some years before the term itself was invented. The first polyhedrons in painted plywood mock-ups by Tony Smith (b. 1912) preceded even these primitive ventures. The new reductive, impersonal trend in sculpture appeared officially in the first museum show devoted to art of this character, the Black, White, and Gray exhibition at the Wadsworth Atheneum in Hartford, Conn., in 1964.

Then, at the Jewish Museum exhibition, Donald Judd's standardized, repeated, boxy galvanized iron and aluminum permutations in colorful motorcycle paint; Morris's identical L-shaped volumes in gray-painted plywood; and Ronald Bladen's heroic and personal drama of untitled, thrice-repeated rectangular volumes in black-painted plywood and metal were singled out by critics as the enigmatic ciphers of a new artistic movement.

The best early rationale for Minimalism, with its rejection of pictorial illusionism and trust in real space, came from one of its leading exponents, Judd (b. 1928), who published prescient art criticism in the 1960s pinpointing the aesthetic issues involved. Describing his own practice, he wrote in 1965: "There dimensions are real space. That gets rid of the problem of illusionism and of literal space, space in and around marks and colors—which is riddance of one of the most salient and most objectionable relics of European art. . . . Actual space is intrinsically more powerful and specific than paint on a flat surface."

By the mid-1960s, Judd was fabricating metal forms either of a blocky, unitary character or in modular, repetitive serial schemes (plate 573), reflecting, to some degree, the influential anti-Cubist compositions of Frank Stella. Though Judd often used neutral, unadorned industrial surfaces, in more recent years he has experimented with a new kind of sensuousness based on fluorescent commercial colors. The asceticism of these elementary boxlike forms was countered by the play of colored surfaces as Judd continued to explore a wide range of expressive possibilities in new industrial materials and techniques.

Perhaps the most important pioneer of the new sensibility was Tony Smith, a member in good standing of the Abstract Expressionist community, though best known in his early years as a visionary architect and occasional painter. He did not make his first modular steel sculptures until 1962, but their impassive physical bulk and intense romantic presence almost instantly erased the

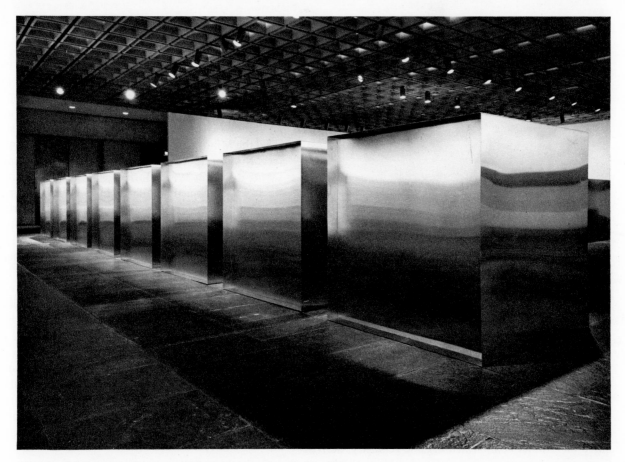

573 Don Judd. *Untitled* (8 boxes). 1968. Stainless steel, each 48″ cube.
Collection Miles Fiterman, Minneapolis

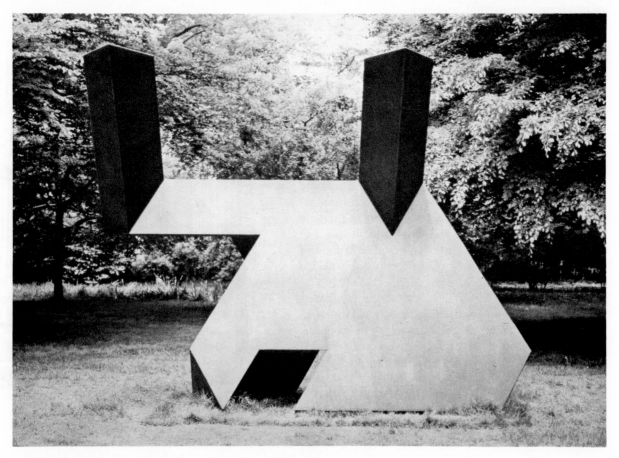

574 Tony Smith. *Moses*. 1969. Painted steel, height 15′. Princeton University,
Princeton, N.J. The Lt. John B. Putnam, Jr., Memorial Collection

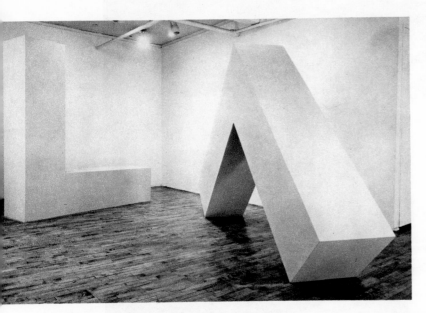

575 Robert Morris. *Untitled*. 1965. Painted plywood, height 96". Leo Castelli Gallery, New York

frivolous illusionism of the recent sculpture and decisively established new directions for three-dimensional construction (plate 574). Smith evolved a sculptural program based on a rather complicated organic geometry, derived from many sources, including Frank Lloyd Wright, an interest in topology and crystallography, the language inventions and puns of James Joyce, and some novel ideas about architectural sculpture. Smith wished to create new monuments which could coexist with such modern landmarks as massive oil tanks, smokestacks, airport runways, parking lots, and other constructions on a vast scale in the industrial landscape.

In the sixties Tony Smith and other Minimalist sculptors, given unusual opportunities for enlarging their work into monumental form by such skillful fabricators as Lippincott, in North Haven, Conn., began to execute commissions for public sculpture. Their invariably geometric, reductive forms in large scale have created a new and popular tradition of outdoor sculpture. During the past decade communities and corporations throughout the nation have acquired heroic-size works for civic and commercial plazas designed by abstract artists and fabricated industrially. Set on the ground, these immense sculptures are abstract and yet invite intimacy with the circulating, viewing public.

Another leading Minimalist sculptor was Robert Morris. Morris's approach to three-dimensional form was cerebral. By the mid-1960s he was working in geometric structures devoid of detail and obsessive in their emphasis on wholeness of vision, but he also showed a sense of irony, a game-playing cunning, closer in spirit to Marcel Duchamp than to the formal purists. His first one-man show in New York in 1963 consisted of lead and Sculptmetal reliefs with imagery clearly referring to Duchamp and to Jasper Johns. In the same year, however, he also

held a show of bland geometric forms in gray-painted plywood which reflected the paradoxical mental processes of the composer John Cage, a friend of Morris's who probably influenced the striking shift in visual aesthetics as much as any single figure. At this time, Cage summarized the Minimalist inspiration and its ironic vacuous effects with the aphorism: "I have nothing to say, and I am saying it." After 1965, Morris's work became more eclectic, but he remained unfailingly innovative in his modular sculpture (plate 575), experiments with soft materials and random pilings of "antiform" and process art, earthworks, steam environments, and other brilliantly original and daring projects in ecology, communications, and information systems (see also Chapter 27).

It was quite clear that the new structurist art engaged the most forceful rising talents. Exciting possibilities of invention were dramatically opened up, among them the compact monumental Cor-Ten steel disks poised in precarious equilibrium (plate 576) of Bernard Rosenthal (b. 1914) and the precious refinement of the more intimately scaled transparent boxes in fragile, coated optical glass (plate 577) by the West Coast artist Larry Bell (b. 1939). Other West Coast artists, including Ron Davis (b. 1937), have created a subtly inflected light and color

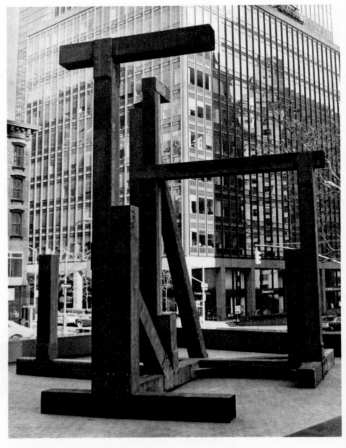

576 Bernard Rosenthal. *Hammarskjold*. 1977. Structural steel, 20 × 20 × 20'. Collection the artist

continuum from such varied materials as glass, vacuum plastic molds, and light projections, often discovering new expressive potential in the materials and processes of contemporary industry (plate 578).

ENVIRONMENTS AND EARTHWORKS

By the end of the 1960s the radical concept that came increasingly to dominate three-dimensional art forms was that of executing sculpture "in situ," as situational and therefore impermanent structures designed to function outside the studio environment. Carl Andre (b. 1935) was the first artist to use the term "post-studio sculpture" to rationalize what Robert Morris, Robert Irwin, Dan Flavin, and he had begun to do to break down conventional links between the artist's work and the studio.

Robert Irwin (b. 1929), in the 1960s, composed large, subtly curved disks set off the wall, whose overlapped shadows created a dematerialized illusion (plate 579). These evanescent shapes, spotlit at an angle, made a quatrefoil of shadows suspended between the contoured disk, the wall, and the observer's eye. From the disks, Irwin went on to work with scrims of fine white rope and cheesecloth mounted in galleries, creating in those spaces an environmental field and new presence of contained light. Irwin has been the most influential individual figure in Los Angeles art since the mid-sixties.

Dan Flavin (b. 1933), in his first one-man show in New York, in 1964, found a new and surprising use for commercial fluorescent light tubing. He proceeded to arrange his tubes in the gallery as if they were in his studio. As he wrote, "I knew that the actual space of a room could be broken down and played with by planting illusions of real light (electric light) at crucial junctures in the room's composition." Each of his succeeding exhibitions Flavin envisaged as a total ensemble and the exhibition space as an entity within which his fluorescent tubes, often radiating an austere white light but sometimes glowing with subtle color, created luminous zones related to each other and to the overall containment of the room. The meditative and chaste quality of his lights set him apart from the more sensational manipulators of pulsating light environments in a period dominated by the faddist interest in eye-popping intermedia shows. The artist's cleverly wrought intellectual propositions, acerbic wit, and sense of dedication to a highly principled art form were rivaled only by Ad Reinhardt's previous example of moral integrity. Flavin's speculative concerns were close to the theoretical interests of Morris, Judd, and Andre, and their work paralleled his own in providing a framework for new artistic practices and attitudes.

When Andre laid down his 34 feet of unattached firebricks on the floor of the Jewish Museum during the "Primary Structures" exhibition, or, in 1968, a much longer row of 184 bales of hay extending 500 feet across an open field, he was elaborating the idea of site as sculpture which had already been explored by Morris and Flavin. In these

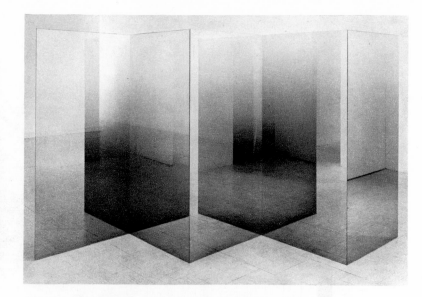

577 Larry Bell. *Untitled.* 1970. Glass with mineral coating, 5 panels, each 72 × 35½". Pace Gallery, New York

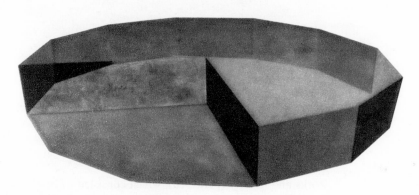

578 Ron Davis. *Vector.* 1968. Fiberglass, 5 × 12'. The Tate Gallery, London

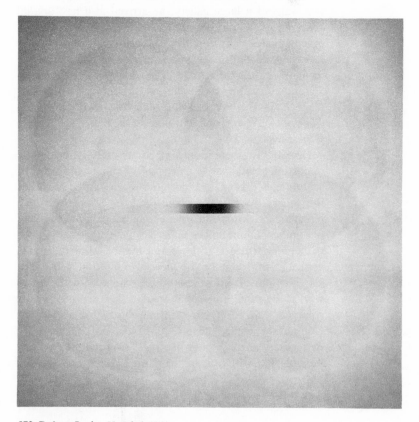

579 Robert Irwin. *Untitled.* 1968. Acrylic on cast acrylic, diameter 54". Collection The Fort Worth Art Museum

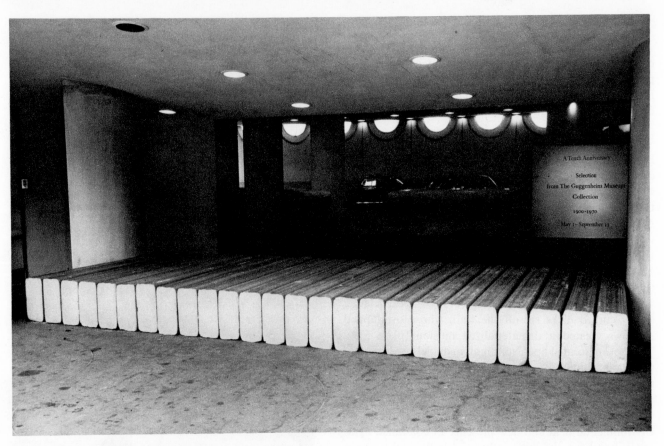

580 Carl Andre. *Reef*. 1969–70 (original 1966). Styrofoam, 20″ × 10′.
Collection Heiner Friedrich, Cologne

works and in *Reef* (plate 580), which consisted of brightly colored, identical styrofoam blocks placed side by side at the Whitney Museum's 1969 exhibition "Anti-Illusion: Procedures/Materials," filling the floor between two walls of a large gallery, he arrived at a new spatial concept. An admirably condensed and characteristically oracular statement described his indifference to materials as such and to their potential for aesthetic development in traditional terms: "The course of development/ Sculpture as form/Sculpture as structure/Sculpture as place." As the Whitney's catalog introduction notes: "The act of conceiving and placing the pieces takes precedence over the object quality of the works."

Horizontal orientation seemed to offer Andre more opportunity of spatial extension. "The ideal piece of sculpture is a road," he declared when he began to use the gallery floor as the plane for logs, Styrofoam bars, magnets, bricks, metal squares, and "scatter pieces" of old nails. Commonplace materials were laid on the floor to democratize art, to level and humble the traditional vertical, anthropomorphic view of sculpture. When artists later moved into the landscape literally with Earthworks, the same philosophy guided their sense of vastly enlarged scale and their essentially bird's eye viewpoint. Composing brute, nonart materials in checkerboard patterns of metal squares like rugs, Andre destroyed any possible identification of his flattened, ground-hugging

art with pedestal sculpture and with the human scale and orientation of a standing man. Instead, he forced the viewer into a new relationship with sculptural form, including thermal and bodily sensations produced by walking over slabs of aluminum, copper, steel, lead, or zinc, whose different conductive qualities were discernible even through the soles of one's shoes.

One of the most original and powerful sculptors to emerge from the atmosphere of site sculpture was Richard Serra (b. 1939). He began to fashion monumental pieces, described as "Props," in 1969, after an earlier phase of making molten lead floor pieces. In the later works, heavy sheets of lead and ponderous steel plate were balanced precariously against each other or supported against a wall with metal tubes. No parts were affixed to each other. The result was an aggressive sculptural experience, controlling great potential for both violence and disorder within its momentarily poised formal order. In recent environmental pieces of large dimension Serra's balance of conceptual idea and physical forces has been refined and amplified to include the subjective or perceptual experience of the viewer. His *Shift* (1970–72) consists of six rectilinear concrete sections, 5 feet high by 8 inches thick, set at angles in the contoured landscape. It creates a dialectic between the physical activity of walking around the slabs thrust into the earth, as an exercise in enforced, continuous perception, and the geometry of the entire formal configuration. The artist has said of it: "The work establishes a measure: one's relation to it and the land."

The emphasis by Morris, Andre, Flavin, and Serra on location, and their indifference to fine-arts quality in their materials, found a logical, if surprising, extension in the efforts of the young, idealistic avant-garde who reacted violently to the commercialism of the art world in the late 1960s by producing Earthworks, or Land Art. Many of the creators of Earthworks began their mature careers by making Minimalist sculpture in which the object itself became increasingly sublimated by serial emphasis or by geometric stereotyping of individual forms. The revived interest in deserts, mountains, geological strata, and primitive states of nature not only betrayed a certain romanticism but could also be rationalized in terms of the social conditions of a world in uneasy transition.

Spiral Jetty (plate 581) was perhaps the most picturesquely beautiful and ambitious of the Earthworks by Robert Smithson (1938–1973). The coil of rocks in the Great Salt Lake is 1,500 feet long and 15 feet in width, constructed of black rock moved by a bulldozer; to the coil, rock crystals, earth, and red water formed by algae have adhered. Rugged Earthworks of this type and scale were

essentially a romantic enterprise, antitechnological in spirit, a probing of the timeless wastes of geological nature. For Smithson and others, nature became their laboratory, and the whole earth was their studio.

After making Minimalist sculptures of elegant geometric perfection in polished stainless steel during the mid-1960s, Walter de Maria (b. 1935), in 1968, filled a Munich art gallery with dirt in a mode obviously close to the emerging Earthworks. He has also extended his own body in the landscape, had himself photographed, and created gargantuan line drawings on the desert terrain, as if it were a sheet of paper. Yet even his most ambitious landscape projects have a bizarre intellectual quality that relates them to Neo-Dada. His performance pieces develop from a premeditated program rather than an emotional commitment to conquering some aspect of nature.

Michael Heizer (b. 1944) was known in the late 1960s for his "depressions," or gigantic excavations, in the Nevada desert and mudflats. Often they curiously resembled the abandoned excavation sites he frequented in his youth with his father, a professional archaeologist. The new earth art that Heizer helped to originate was an attempt to escape from the gallery and the museum, and even from an object orientation, in order to confront

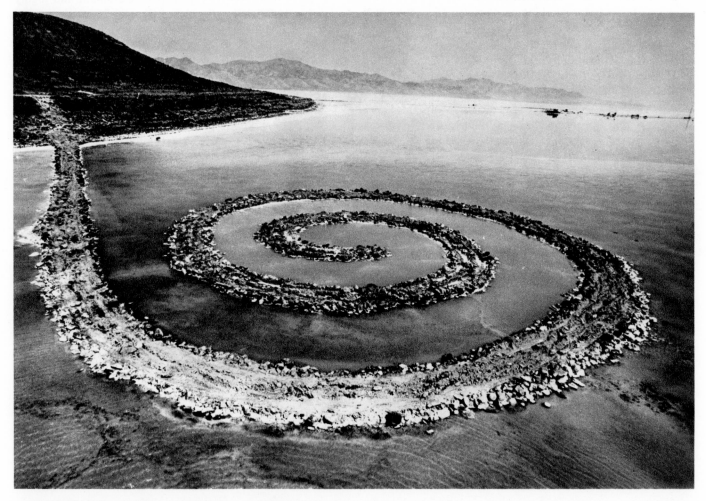

581 Robert Smithson. *Spiral Jetty*. 1970. Rock, salt crystals, earth, algae, coil length 1500'. Great Salt Lake, Utah

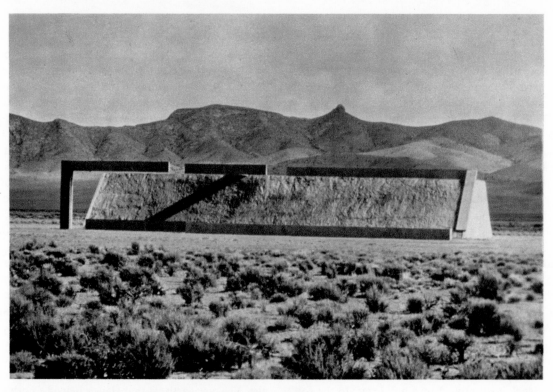

582 Michael Heizer. *Complex One*. 1972–76. Earth and concrete,
23' 6" × 140' × 110'. Courtesy Fourcade Gallery, New York

new issues on a vast scale of open, unstructured space and nonmaterialistic attitudes calling for a radical reorganization of our natural environment.

Heizer began working on *Complex One* (plate 582) in 1972 and completed it four years later. It is over 20 feet high and 140 feet long, inclined backward at a 45-degree angle. The architectural sources of the structure are Egyptian mastabas, for the mound form, and for the framing elements, the snake bands bordering the "ball court" at Chichén Itzá. However, these forms also evoke a lowlying factory building and modern architectural and pictorial elements, including large abstract American painting. The word "complex" suggests both the complicated spatiality of the work—its integration and disintegration of forms—as well as a plan for another similar structure which may ultimately face it. Together the ambitious ensemble will create a visionary urban plaza in the midst of the vacant Nevada desert.

Many other approaches have been made to working in the environment in recent years, and undoubtedly the most notorious have been the projects originated by Christo (b. 1935). Bulgarian by birth and a stateless Paris resident through much of the 1960s, Christo has now acquired American citizenship. When, in 1962, he blocked the rue Visconti in Paris outside his art gallery with a wall of oil drums, he turned the art of assemblage into an environmental experience with his gesture. Settling in New York in 1964, Christo began to create in drawings and collages visionary proposals for wrapping monuments and public buildings. Those ideas finally came to fruition on an environmental scale when he actually did wrap the Kunsthalle in Bern, Switzerland, in 1968, using 27,000 square feet of reinforced polyethylene tied with nylon rope. A more recent project was the dramatic and highly publicized *Running Fence* (see Chapter 27).

Plentiful precedents exist for working with land in traditions dating back to the Egyptian pyramids, the Middle Eastern ziggurats, Stonehenge, American Indian sand painting and burial mounds, and Zen rock gardens, not to mention Gutzon Borglum's presidential heads on Mount Rushmore. Perhaps even more important, as Willoughby Sharp pointed out in the catalog for his pioneering 1969 Earth Art exhibition at Cornell University, there were closer examples that directly influenced the American avant-garde; he cited Marcel Duchamp's *Large Glass*, the pebbles in Pollock's 1950 painting on glass, and Rauschenberg's so-called "nature paintings" of 1953. Other important contemporary influences were Kaprow's "happenings," with their emphasis on dispersive materials in environmental situations, and the speculative writings of Robert Morris, which questioned the nature of sculptural experience.

Earthworks and environmental art seek to remind us dramatically of man's indissoluble bonds with nature. A psychoanalyst quoted in *Art in America* (May–June, 1969, p. 34) remarked of these radical developments: "The works of these innovators are an attempt to be as big as the life we live today, the life of immensity and boundless geography. But it's also the manifestation of a desire to escape the city that is eating us alive, and perhaps a farewell to space and earth while there are still some left."

24
Photography Since World War II

During World War II, as photographers joined the Armed Forces and government withdrew its patronage of the arts, the documentary mode was eclipsed. When the style reappeared in the fifties, it had become the photography of "social landscape," uncommissioned and focused now on the gracelessness and glut of an affluent nation. The leading photographer of postwar social relationships was a young Swiss, Robert Frank (b. 1924), whose images of alienation, such as *Trolley, New Orleans* (plate 583), resulted from a ten-thousand-mile trip through his adopted country. Others who commented on contemporary culture in similar terms were Garry Winograd, Les Krims, Lee Friedlander, and Danny Lyon. Somewhat grotesque imagery characterizes the work of Jerome Liebling, Ralph Eugene Meatyard, and Diane Arbus (1923–1971), whose incisive image, *Mother Holding Her Child* (plate 584), is an ironic comment on one of the nation's most sanctified relationships. At the same time, a number of photographers viewed the social scene with greater compassion for the victimized individual, as in Roy de Carava's (b. 1919) image of tired misery, *Man on Subway Steps* (plate 585), George Krause's work, and Bruce Davidson's East 100th Street series. Contemporary interest in social relationships in the seventies has resulted in more idiosyncratic statements, as in the later work of Duane Michals, Emmett Gowin, and Lucas Samaras.

The publication of Frank's photographs, *The Americans*, in 1958, initiated a new attitude toward the photographic book. Publishers who had been reluctant to involve themselves with photographs realized that public interest in the medium warranted investment in the more expensive printing processes that the photographic image required, and several began to specialize in this area. In addition to books and portfolios of the work of contemporaries, historical images were unearthed from public and private collections, many becoming visible for the first time in mechanically printed form. The wide availability of the printed camera image, whether in offset or photoengraving, is a distinctive feature of our times.

Photojournalism was greatly stimulated during the 1930s by the advent of large-format picture magazines,

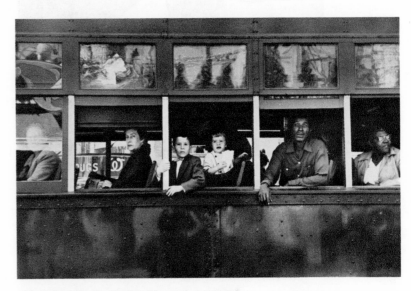

583 Robert Frank. *Trolley, New Orleans*. 1958.
The Art Institute of Chicago

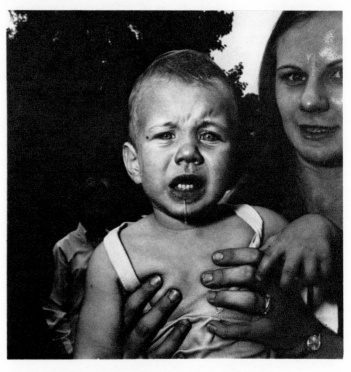

584 Diane Arbus. *Mother Holding Her Child*. 1967.
Estate of the photographer

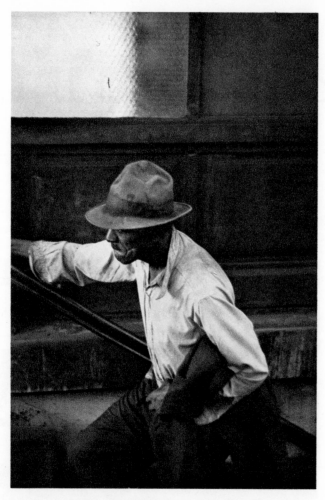

585 Roy de Carava. *Man on Subway Steps*. 1952.
Collection the photographer

Newman's (b. 1918) portraits, such as that of Mondrian (plate 587), and the work of Philippe Halsman, Irving Penn, and Richard Avedon. Fashion periodicals pioneered in the reproduction of color photography at this time, enabling photographers to gain experience with an expensive and temperamental material (see Color Photography, below).

During the same period both documentary and journalistic photography became more acceptable to museums, partly as a result of the "In and Out of Focus" exhibition held at the Museum of Modern Art in New York in 1948. This large show was organized by Edward Steichen, who had become head of the Museum's photography department in 1947, after the long tenure of Beaumont and, briefly, Nancy Newhall. The work of photojournalists, fashion photographers, documentarians, and art photographers was hung side by side without compartmentalization. Other museums began to follow this lead, setting up departments and/or staff to collect, exhibit, and publish photographs. To a great degree these events erased the distinction between artistic and documentary photography which had been so pro-

which featured photo essays of newsworthy events and world conditions. Along with the Leica and Ermanox, modern style in picture journalism had been introduced in Europe in the late twenties by Erich Salomon, Robert Capa, Werner Bischof, and Alfred Eisenstaedt. When, with the exception of Salomon, these men came to the United States to escape Fascism, they brought the same persistence and fearlessness to assignments for *Life* and *Look* magazines. The picture magazines offered unparalleled opportunities to native photojournalists as well, despite occasional disagreements over selection and editing. Margaret Bourke-White, W. Eugene Smith (1918 –1978), David Douglas Duncan, and Gordon Parks, among others, created memorable sequences and single images, such as Smith's *Spinner* (plate 586), from his Spanish Village series for *Life*.

Throughout the fifties and sixties publications such as *Vogue* and *Harper's Bazaar* also provided photographers with opportunities and commissions. A number of individuals continued the Steichen tradition of photographing models and celebrities with flair and inventiveness. Outstanding contributions of this nature are Arnold

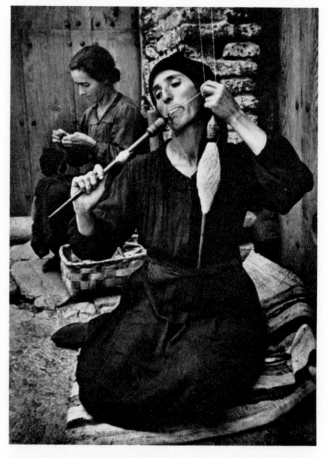

586 W. Eugene Smith. *The Spinner*, from the Spanish Village series. 1950. Collection the photographer

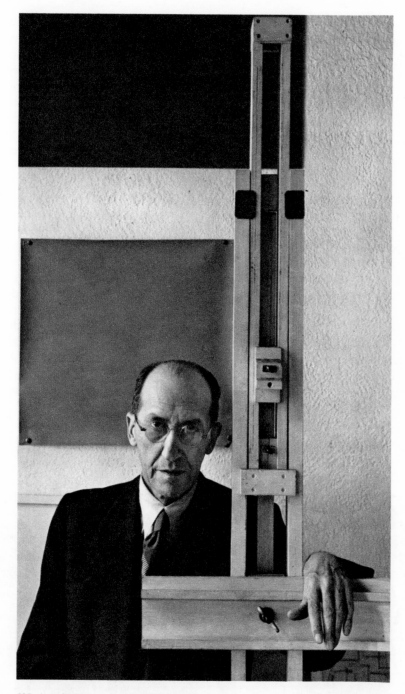

587 Arnold Newman. *Mondrian.* 1942.
Light Gallery, New York

nounced at the beginning of the century.

The documentary and journalistic mode had little effect on the work of Cunningham, Stieglitz, or Weston. Stieglitz's late images suggest his lingering attachment to New York, a city he now found incomprehensible. The poetic qualities of his late landscapes and "equivalents" inspired a group of younger photographers to conceive of photographic imagery in nonobjective terms, as metaphor rather than description. Weston, too, continued his intense preoccupation with landscape, shifting from concentration on the isolated object to concern for the larger view, while still emphasizing form and texture. In 1936 he received the first Guggenheim grant awarded to a photographer; it allowed him to photograph extensively throughout California for the following two years. Weston, along with Cunningham and Ansel Adams, had been part of a West Coast group formed in 1932 and known as "f64" because it was devoted to uniformly sharp, previsualized, large-camera imagery. Although Cunningham turned her attention to portraiture, photographing Hollywood notables and the dancer Martha Graham, she continued to work in this style throughout the thirties. Eventually she found the "f64" aesthetic too restricting, and her later images include multiple prints and other effects which give them a surreal, rather than purist, appearance.

The large-camera image, with sharp detail and long scale of values, is especially characteristic of the work of Ansel Adams (b. 1902). In the early thirties, while working in New Mexico, Adams had been inspired by seeing Strand's negatives to devote himself fully to photography. His efforts to achieve perfection through complete understanding and control of the technical process led him to develop the "Zone" system of exposure, developing, and printing, which he published in 1948. As a convinced conservationist, Adams has concentrated on photographing wilderness landscape, creating spectacular images of unspoiled nature such as *Frozen Lake and Cliffs* (plate 588). Others who work in the landscape tradition and sustain similar ideas are Brett Weston and William Garnett.

The European photographers who arrived in this country in the late thirties and early forties had a decided effect on American photography after World War II. As previously noted, European photojournalists were an invigorating influence on picture news stories, while small-camera enthusiasts such as Kertész and Lisette Model suggested uncommon ways of seeing picturesque (and sometimes horrifying) aspects of everyday life. Roman Vishniac and Fritz Goro made ingenious contributions to the field of scientific photography, and Bauhaus advocates brought the possibilities of photomanipulations such as montage and photograms to the attention of Americans. As in the past, native photographers integrated European ideas with their own experiences, creating an indigenous imagery that was both unique and forceful.

The most important center of avant-garde ideas in the forties and fifties was the Institute of Design in Chicago, where László Moholy-Nagy and Gyorgy Kepes (both refugees from the Dessau Bauhaus) held positions. In addition to influencing the appearance of graphic design and advertising art, these men were instrumental in directing photographers toward experimentation with nonliteral imagery. This emphasis came at a time when scientific photography was producing startling arrangements of shape and texture that are invisible to the naked human eye, as well as strange configurations created by aerial photographs of familiar landscape. While the Bauhaus was suggesting that the surfaces of the real world

588 Ansel Adams. *Frozen Lake and Cliffs, Sierra Nevada.*
c. 1936. Collection the photographer

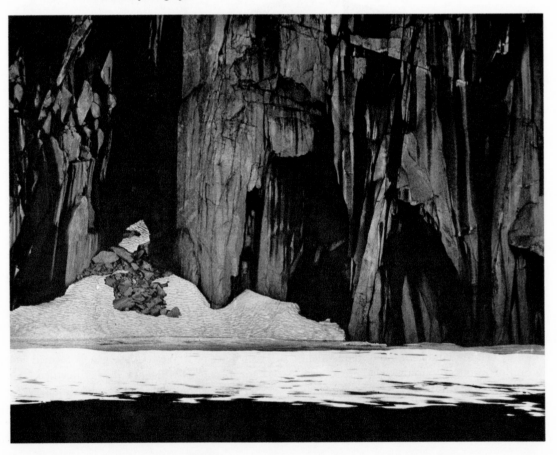

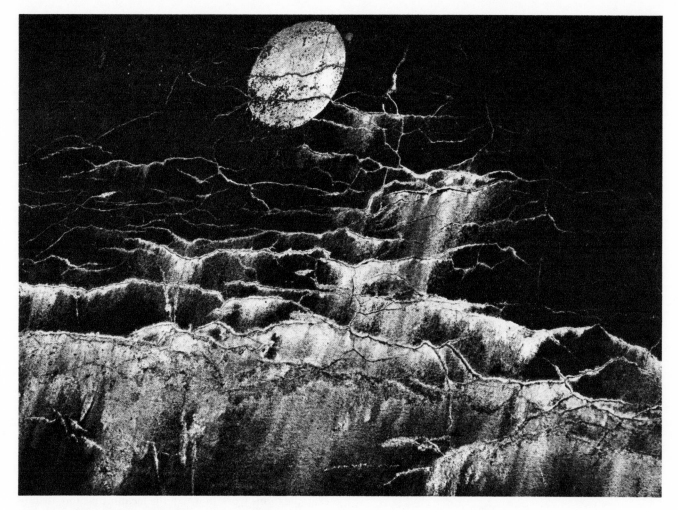

589 Minor White. *Moon and Wall Encrustations, Pultneyville, New York, 1964.* © 1978 Aperture, Inc., as published in *Minor White: Rites & Passages*

might serve as metaphors of personal feelings, the photographer's visual world was being expanded by the evidences of scientific photography. Responding to these new perceptions, Harry Callahan, Minor White, and Aaron Siskind related Bauhaus ideas to Stieglitz's concept of equivalency and searched for forms that would evoke feelings unconnected to the objects photographed.

Minor White (1908–1976) was undoubtedly the most influential photographer of the group convinced that the literal world could reveal forms capable of stimulating feelings similar to those aroused by music. In images such as *Moon and Wall Encrustations* (plate 589), the observer does not know what the object represents; the effect is achieved by linear and tonal qualities that suggest a sense of mystery and detachment. As a teacher and founding editor of the magazine *Aperture*, White reached a wide audience with his photographs and his ideas. Among the many who found his spiritual approach inspiring, Paul Caponigro (b. 1932), especially, conveys the enigmatic qualities of inert matter in *Rock Wall II* (plate 590).

The early photographs of Callahan (b. 1912) demonstrate strong Bauhaus influence in their intense simpli-

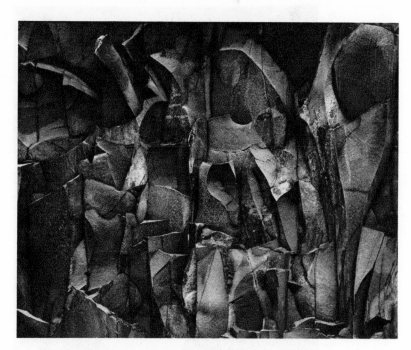

590 Paul Caponigro. *Rock Wall II.* 1959. Collection the photographer

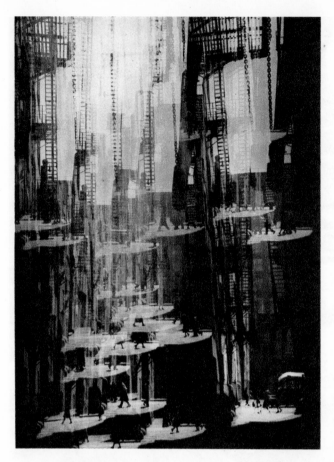

591 Harry Callahan. *Chicago Loop*. 1952.
Collection the photographer

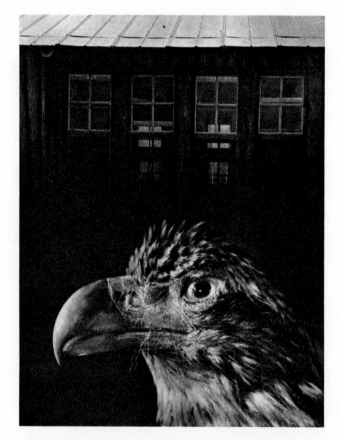

592 Jerry N. Uelsmann. *Bless Our Home and Eagle*. 1962.
Collection the photographer

fication, appearing almost as translations in visual terms of the dictum that "less is more." His use of multiple exposure in *Chicago Loop* (plate 591) creates a comprehensible metaphor of urban movement and tension, but in time his symbolism became more personal. Siskind, initially interested in documentary photography, became aware of the decorative possibilities of isolated shapes in a Martha's Vineyard series in the thirties. Eventually the flat plane became the focus of his concern. In endeavoring to create his own symbolic system through selection and exaggeration, Siskind paralleled similar efforts being made at the time by Abstract Expressionist painters of the New York school. Another for whom Bauhaus influence was especially stimulating is Arthur Siegel, who took an early interest in the cameraless photography advocated at the Institute of Design. A pronounced sense of design informs the work of Barbara Morgan and Clarence John Laughlin, as well.

Continuing efforts to deliteralize the camera image and obliterate its mechanical nature have resulted in images formed by restructuring the visible world or by manipulation of the process to create an imaginary content. Frederick Sommer works in both ways, finding and arranging objects and also intervening in the processing to invoke a strange, private world in which the observer finds his or her own meanings. Montage is the means by which Jerry Uelsmann (b. 1934) arrives at the enigmatic imagery of *Bless Our Home and Eagle* (plate 592), an example of his work in which the meaning is more readily accessible than in most.

COLOR PHOTOGRAPHY

For most of its existence the photograph had to register the colors of the objective world in shades of black and white. The absence of color was strongly felt and led to the addition of paint by hand to daguerreotypes and ambrotypes in order to impart a lifelike quality to the images. Throughout the late nineteenth century experimentation to find a way to capture color in the photographic process was carried on. The first success occurred in 1861, when British physicist James Clerk Maxwell devised a method of separately photographing red, blue, and green colors onto three negatives. An image in color was reconstituted when the three negatives were superimposed and projected through colored filters. Somewhat later, Charles Cros and Louis Ducos du Hauron, each working independently in France, discovered a different system. In their process the three negatives, each containing red, blue, or green colors, were transformed into three dye negatives that were, in turn, superimposed to produce a single print with all the colors. In 1877 Hauron used this process to make color prints, some of which still exist unfaded today.

The above system, known as "subtractive," eventually became the basis of modern color processing, but further experimentation on the earlier additive method was carried on by Frederic Ives in Philadelphia and John Joly in Dublin. Their work resulted in the first practical color film that could be used with ordinary equipment and even processed by dedicated individuals such as Stieglitz. This film, Autochrome, was invented by the Lumière brothers in France in 1907, and was used successfully by Steichen and Stieglitz. Transparencies occasionally had a spotted look, because the dyes were held by tiny grains of potato starch, but the color itself was rich and subtle, as is evident in Stieglitz's portrait *Mrs. Selma Schubart* (colorplate 85).

The search for simplification continued during the 1920s because of the complexity of processing Autochrome plates. Two young musicians, Leopold Mannes and Leopold Goldowsky, Jr., working under primitive conditions, were finally able to develop a two-layer plate, with each layer of emulsion sensitive to different portions of the spectrum. Eventually they joined forces with Eastman Kodak researchers, enabling the company to put Kodachrome film on the market in 1935, followed later by Ektachrome and Kodacolor. Somewhat earlier, Paul Outerbridge had experimented with a color print process called Carbro color (colorplate 86). It resulted in delicate tonalities, as seen in Outerbridge's work, but this process, used by Steichen also, entailed too much time and expense.

The invention of Kodachrome made color much more widely available to amateurs and professionals, but the processing had to be done by Eastman Kodak Company. In addition, the quality of the color print was not very good and the cost prohibitive, so that the consumer received a color transparency instead of a color print, resulting in reawakened interest in slides and slide projection. In efforts to improve the product, both negatives and prints, Kodak kept an eye on developments in the large German photochemical corporations, and following World War II, it was able to discover the secrets involved in the manufacture of Agfacolor, the German process. This method eventually became public property, and its technology became the basis for the manufacture of some color film, resulting in color that can be processed in individual darkrooms to provide negatives, prints, and transparent positives. A more recent development in the field is Edwin Land's Polacolor, the instantly developed material for use with Land camera equipment.

As was true of many technological advances in photography, color was developed mainly to provide the popular market with a more natural-looking image. It quickly became a resource of prime importance in the advertising, publicity, and fashion industries, where the ability to control exposure and processing soon resulted in elegant images of food, clothing, and personalities. Early fashion photographers such as George Platt Lynes,

Erwin Blumenfeld, Louise Dahl-Wolfe, Gjon Mili, and Irving Penn began to experiment with color as an expressive element, producing images in which the color not only described the objects, but was tastefully employed to suggest elegance, drama, or wholesomeness.

Although Eastman Kodak urged Strand, Adams, and Weston to experiment with Ektachrome after World War II, established art photographers were averse to using materials which had relatively short lives due to the instability of the dyes. Exceptions were Eliot Porter and Eliot Elisofon, who were among the first to attempt to recreate the subtle variations found in natural colors, an example of which is Porter's *Lichens on Round Stones* (colorplate 87). On the whole, however, photographers have come to regard the colored dyes of the negative material as an expressive rather than a descriptive device, to be used in the same manner as texture, shape, and pattern. Thus, color may underscore the mood and feeling of the city, as it does in the work of Jay Maisel, Ernst Haas (colorplate 88), and Helen Levitt. Color may create the mood entirely, as in Marie Cosindas's romantic portraits in Polacolor, or it may be used for itself alone, as in Syl Labrot's work.

In general, color seems most successful when it is integrated with other manipulations or when it is used in images which stress design, as in Haas's multiple image mentioned above. Another contemporary approach, inspired by the popularity of the snapshot and the group portrait (both of which have influenced the painter's vision in recent years), can be seen in the color photographs of Lucas Samaras and Neal Slavin.

Experimentation with multiple printing, solarization (in which the negative reverses to a positive through overdevelopment), photolithography, contrast control, and color are among the means that contemporary photographers such as Robert Heinecken, Naomi Savage, and Todd Walker use, producing works often indistinguishable from graphic art. At a time when many painters appear to draw inspiration from photographic images, a number of photographers are being stimulated by contemporary printmaking. Today, unlike the situation in the early years of the Photo-Secession, when photographers sought to emulate the more highly respected arts, photographic art has come to embrace a wide spectrum of styles and philosophies. Individual images are judged for their intrinsic expressiveness, no matter what purpose they may serve or in what manner they were executed. It has become obvious that what the photograph achieves is neither greater nor less than what is accomplished in other art media—only different. It is also true, however, that the kind of reality that the photograph creates "appeals," in Stieglitz's words, "to the consciousness of today."

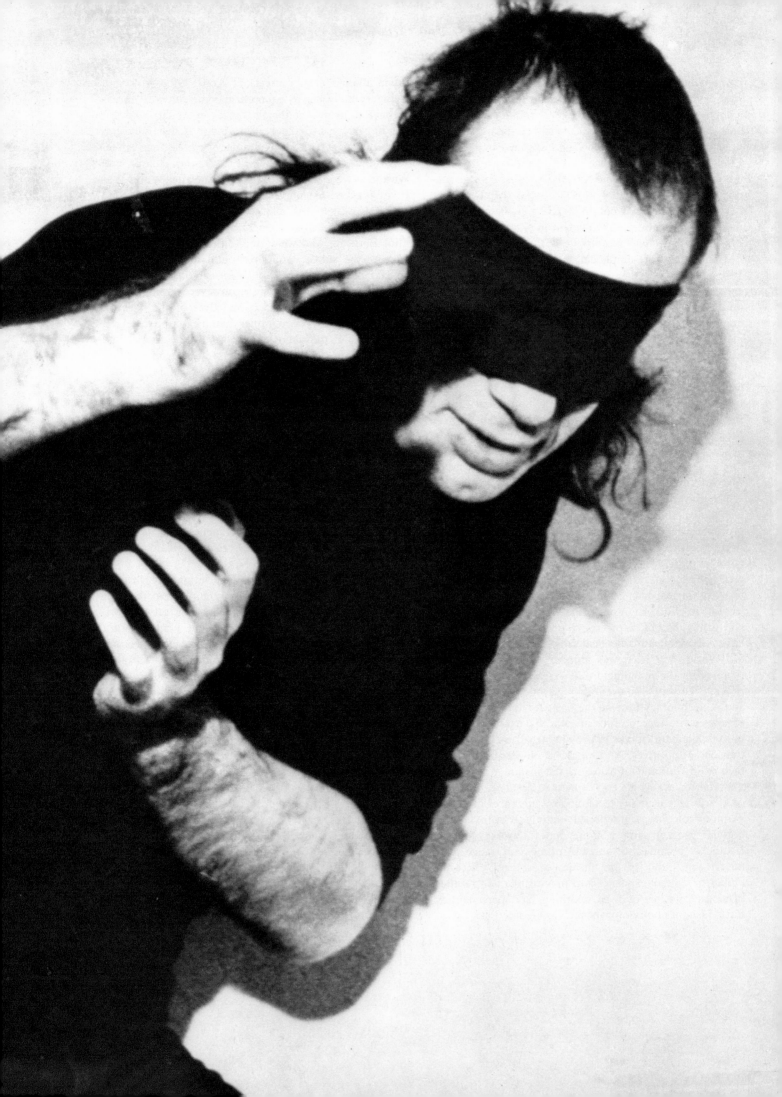

Part 8
THE ARTS SINCE 1960

Identifying an American architecture representative of the late twentieth century poses some formidable problems. The first of these is pluralism. In spite, or perhaps because, of the unanimous adoption of modernist, non-historical design, which laid to rest the various skeletons of the past shortly after 1945, there are now more style options than ever before. Today's formal architectural novelties occasionally echo the imagery of Pop Art sources in the real environment, and the forms of recent abstract painting find a scattering of correspondences in architectural design. In addition, there is the work of stubbornly independent figures whose personal style corresponds closely neither to current fashion nor to any immediately recognizable phase of traditional modernism. Much prestigious building design of the sixties and seventies, however, has retained a formal tradition stemming from the earlier International Style and its derivatives as established before 1960.

In other fields the rapidity of artistic change in the 1960s was unusual even in a period accustomed to the swift dispersal of short-lived styles into obsolescence. The accelerated pace of innovation may have reflected the sense, at large, of social despair and of impotence about solving critical human and environmental problems. There were widespread doubts about society's capacity to survive in the increasingly poisoned atmosphere of planet earth, and this new mood of global pessimism probably contributed to artistic novelty and uninhibited risk-taking in the use of art media.

In painting, the sense of urgent moral purpose and of difficulties overcome that characterized the "heroic" generation of Abstract Expressionists (not to mention the painters of centuries past) was no longer shared by the "post-painterly" abstractionists who followed them. These talented successors proposed an entirely new view of the artistic process—essentially anti-Expressionist, devoted to fact, and respectful of phenomena rather than responsive to urgent feeling. The younger abstract artists in the 1960s took as a point of departure the more impersonal painting of Newman and Reinhardt, rather than Rothko or Gottlieb, with their visible declaration of intimacy and sensibility. The Minimalist generation was more interested in the reductive character of color-field painting than in pursuit of the "sublime," and they found themselves most in accord with Reinhardt's insistence on anonymity.

From the 1960s on, the Pop artists, Minimalists, and color-field abstractionists have chosen, in the apt words of the critic Lucy R. Lippard, to restate their "commitment to a grueling, self-demanding ethic based on distrust of the accepted and the acceptable." The term "Neo-Dada," applied to Pop Art when it was first exhibited, indicates the parallels of disrespect for traditional standards of iconography and art materials that were perceived between the new manner and the earlier Dada movement (see Chapter 16). An important source and stimulus for Pop Art was the widespread interest in the whole field of communications in the 1960s. Mass media and popular culture were fashionable studies in sociology; by 1960 so much attention had been focused on them that an affirmative public response was almost assured when Pop paintings came to the public eye.

As Pop Art, and the geometric abstractions and color experiments called Op Art, became overnight successes in the art world of the sixties, and as paintings of the New York school of Action Painters began to fetch hundreds of thousands of dollars at auction, the new avant-garde reacted violently to the onslaught of commercialism. The atmosphere of inflated prices and falsified values brought about the demand that art no longer be treated as a commodity but find support as an act of inquiry of intrinsic worth to the human spirit. Only in recent years has this sort of idealism and protest on the part of artists been confirmed by a radical change in the nature of the work of art itself.

The effort of artists to protect their work from the profiteering of collectors in the marketplace has taken many turns in the past few years. Art materials have been reduced to junk, garbage, the evanescent, the self-destructive, the unrepeatable random spill. Artistic concepts have been outlined or programmed by documentary means (recorded or typewritten plans, sound and video tapes, computer printouts, mathematical schemes, preliminary notations and sketches, photographs, clippings, etc.) without ever being carried to completion in any collectible art materials. Great tracts of land (and sometimes water) have been manipulated to reveal temporarily or forever the mark of an artist's idea, and of the event of his creating it. It became clear that a dialogue existed between the conception and the actualization of a project in the landscape. John Gibson, a dealer who represented a number of Earthworks artists, described a Nevada desert scheme as a kind of "visionary sculpture" and himself in his promotional function as an "idea broker."

That final phrase still signals the financial dilemma of the Conceptual or Earthworks artist: he may have made his work noncollectible, but he still has to find someone who will pay for his doing it. And it is there that the age-old figure of the patron, the sponsor, is resurrected. In this day and age the patron may be an independently affluent magnate, a foundation, a tax-wary corporation, a government agency—in any case, an entity wealthy enough to buy something it can never own or resell at a profit.

Meanwhile, artists who remained throughout this period devoted to the realistic representation of American life clung steadfastly to their own manner, disregarding junk materials, evanescent art events, and abstractionist or conceptual tendencies. What they adopted was an enlargement of the fidelity of the camera eye, with every mole and whisker, every glint of glass or paint, every texture or tint of synthetic material painstakingly reproduced. Their work is a tribute to craftsmanship and a rebuke to the painterly "sloppiness" of Action Painting, but the message is unmistakable. The nudes of the New Realism, or Photo-Realism, are stripped of romantic overtones; they are clinical descriptions of the human figure. The objects represented with trompe-l'oeil accuracy are consumable. In short, while these painters are creating an unparalleled illusion of visual reality, they are also conveying a profound sense of disillusionment with the world as it exists.

New technical explorations in photography—holography, for example—continue to offer startling prospects for the future of the art, as they did from the beginning. When the camera temporarily robbed many late-nineteenth-century portraitists of their livelihood by taking over the Realist recording of the natural world, it may have stimulated the ascendancy of abstraction in painting. By now the mastery of the photographic process and the reproduction of the camera image have in turn entered the iconography of abstraction. Also, the circuit of exhibits and auctions embraces photographic prints and transparencies as well as paintings and other art objects. Multi-media works frequently include photographic images in silkscreen and other graphic techniques. Besides, almost the only way to capture the theme of vast Earthworks is aerial photography, and in Conceptual Art the basic concept is often conveyed by photographs of the projected elements. Photography has so far permeated the diffusion of knowledge of the arts today that this very book could not have been printed without it.

25
Contemporary Architecture and Planning Since 1960

Architecture has tended to remain the most conservative of the visual arts through much of the twentieth century, participating in few of the movements in painting, sculpture, and criticism, and these often in only a restricted way. There is no true architectural counterpart to American Scene Realism or to Action Painting; instead, for over a quarter-century a hefty segment of American building has been fussing with formal problems that were first stated by European abstract artists of the 1920s. And even those who rejected the limitations of this approach tended to look for support to earlier movements in design that had little or no correspondence with pictorial art.

In this context, the work of Paul Rudolph, beginning

593 Paul Rudolph. Art and Architecture Building, Yale University, New Haven, Conn. Exterior. 1958–64

with his design for the Yale Art and Architecture Building, New Haven, Connecticut (1958–64, plate 593), is especially illuminating. Its design and construction coincided with the period of his tenure as chairman of the Department of Architecture, and, in effect if not in fact, Rudolph was both client and architect on this project. The building, impressively sited on a street corner where the Yale campus touches a fringe of New Haven's downtown, was designed and redesigned, each time with an increasingly dramatic play of solids and voids, lights and shadows, resulting in an image of great power. The exposed concrete walls were developed into a surface of vertical striations that was even rougher than that inherent in raw, unfinished concrete. Everything about the design was forced and strained. Bulky sentinel towers collided with massive horizontal forms. Violent articulation of parts emphasized the deliberate overscaling of many elements. Altogether, the structure was a reaction to the precious detailing and graphic linearism of much American architecture of the past several decades.

Despite its novelty of expression, Yale Art and Architecture did not represent a new style. Rudolph had plundered some of the most memorable design features of the recent past and substituted a knowledgeable, emotional eclecticism for the hyperelegant refinements that characterized nearly every type of design about 1960. The concrete mass had a superficial resemblance to Le Corbusier's late mode; but Rudolph's design had a more calculated look. The interlocking of rectangular solids and voids seems closer to the studied patterns of De Stijl architecture, but at Yale the scale and rhetoric are vastly inflated. Moreover, one might superimpose on these previous sources the towered image of Wright's 1904 Larkin Building, Buffalo, thus obtaining an encyclopedic montage of modern masterworks. Finally, a comparison of Art and Architecture with Kahn's Richards Medical Research Building (plate 518) is inescapable: they were contemporaries, and both possessed sufficient similarities of bulky forms (clusters of vertical towers evocative of medieval San Gimignano) to suggest

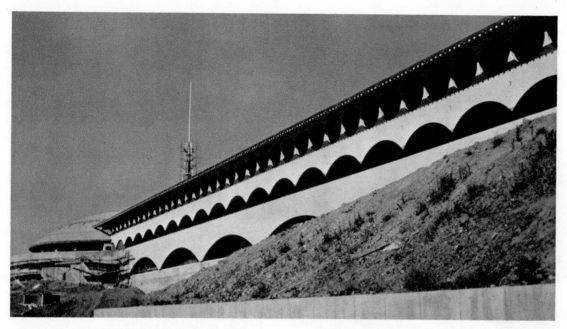

594 Frank Lloyd Wright. Marin County Center,
San Rafael, Calif. Designed 1957; completed 1963

that they represented a trend. Superficially they did,
though the two structures were fundamentally alien, Kahn
having no patience with the sort of convoluted eclecticism
that had snared Rudolph.

Rudolph's building seems, in retrospect, a furious
effort to rediscover a kind of stylistic integration, to
gather up, once and for all, the main architectural currents of the twentieth century. It was almost immediately
despised by those who had to work in it. Its spaces were
visually aggressive, overly large, or, conversely, cramped;
by the late sixties, when architectural students were finding social rather than aesthetic issues to be of greater
relevance, the learned formalism of Art and Architecture
seemed preposterous, the building an irritating anachronism, an example of what *not* to do. Ironically, Rudolph
had succeeded in creating one of the rare buildings of
effective monumentality in the contemporary American
idiom—an achievement that had eluded so many—merely
to be told by his critics and, loudest of all, by the younger
generation that monuments were obsolete in contemporary architecture.

The lesson of Art and Architecture remains. Once again
an American architect sought to measure himself against
a handful of past masterpieces, only to find himself in
check. Rudolph's problem here was fundamentally no
different from that faced earlier in the century by McKim,
Mead & White and by all those who sought refuge in a
style, whether old or new. The major dilemma of architecture in the sixties and seventies is the struggle between
the desire for a strong, indeed an overpowering, image,
one aspiring toward a megastructure or superbuilding,
and an increasing concern with a building's community
function, especially its social and environmental relevance.

Early twentieth-century figures such as Wright and Le
Corbusier tried in the beginning to give architecture over
to the common man, the individual tenant or house-
holder, but at the end of their careers they were often
designing monuments to their own fame as heroic creators. Thus Le Corbusier, at Harvard, created his only
authentic building in North America, Carpenter Center
for the Visual Arts, completed in 1964. It is a cryptic
building from the hand of an enigmatic architect whose
works often and incorrectly passed under the guise of
rational functionalism. Of rough, unfinished, poured-in-
place reinforced concrete (*beton brut*), it is tucked away
on an unsuitably cramped plot between two buildings
devoid of character. Le Corbusier's partly cubic form is
set askew—a bluff comment on the space he had to work
with. The relatively small building contains exhibition
and studio space above, below, and to both sides of an
open-air passage that extends through the middle of the
volume. This passage, together with the connecting
curved pedestrian ramps, is the key feature, functioning
not as a part of the building's interior volume but as a
part of the cityscape, linking the streets to the front and
to the rear.

Wright, too, in his final works sought to establish a new
relationship between the building and its setting, but the
setting that attracted him was rural rather than urban,
natural rather than man-made. The Marin County Center (plate 594), designed in 1957 and completed in 1963,
is a long, arcuated structure (suggestive of a Roman
aqueduct) stretched between two hills, the lower of which
Wright planed away in order to rebuild its contour in the
form of a domed pavilion. The misfortune of these noble
gestures, worthy of the century of Bernini and Le Nôtre,
was that many younger architects felt the need to emulate

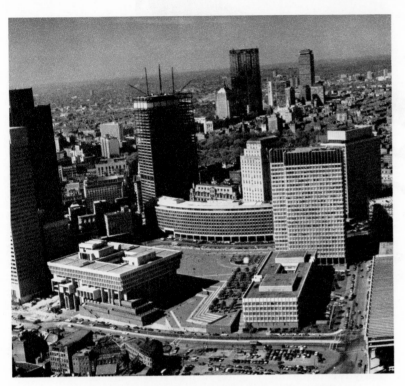

595 Government Center, Boston. City Hall (*lower left*), by Kallmann, McKinnell & Knowles. Designed 1962; constructed 1964–69

commercial power dwarfing the carefully restored mementos of Colonial and Federal days, not to mention Bulfinch's State House and the urbane residential streets of Beacon Hill and Louisburg Square. Such drastic surgery upon an ancient (by America's time scale) urban fabric of narrow winding streets, already overburdened with tall buildings that they were never meant to service, cannot heal easily or rapidly. It will probably always be something of a jolt to emerge from the narrow confines of Boylston Street into the vast paved expanse of City Hall Square. The greatest sin committed by the planners of Boston's Government Center is that they failed to provide for significant housing or for the development of shops, hotels, or places of entertainment in the area, thus ensuring the preservation of a characteristically American blight, the downtown abandoned at night and on weekends, an exclusively diurnal *cité des affaires*.

In spite of these major failings, Government Center is expertly designed and laid out. The space of the square is well defined by the surrounding towers and façades, and the light standards, trash containers, and other items of "furniture" are artfully contrived. City Hall comes straight out of the late Le Corbusier tradition of richly molded reinforced-concrete structures, jacked up on *pilotis* so that its profile expands toward the top, inadvertently a kind of upside-down ziggurat. The public spaces are grouped at the lower level (including accommodations for the collectors of taxes, license fees, and the like), and broad stairs lead upward to the mayor's office and the council chambers. Above these are three stories of offices, largely inaccessible to the public, and these layers of the building form the massive entablature of its exterior elevation.

Chicago, by way of contrast with Boston's extravagant design, solved the need for a new municipal building by erecting a Miesian skyscraper (by C. F. Murphy Associates, 1963–65) on a standard, unaltered rectangular site in the Loop, leaving an open plaza at street level with the happy addition of a fine sculpture by Picasso (plate 596). There was no need to disrupt the grid plan of historic downtown Chicago, whereas the city fathers of Boston had to gut a neighborhood rife with cow-path lanes to get their municipal plaza. Fortunately for Chicago, its street plan evolved as it did because its original settlement was of the early nineteenth, rather than the early seventeenth, century. Several other recent large office buildings are virtually indistinguishable from the Civic Center's sheer, rectangular tower, and those in the Loop continue, in their Miesian way, the blunt, foursquare silhouettes of earlier commercial blocks dating from the Sullivan era.

Of all the recent tall buildings in Chicago (or elsewhere, for that matter), one of the most distinctive is Marina City (1964–67, plate 597), a megastructure which actually looks like one, by Bertrand Goldberg (b. 1913). It comprises twin towers like Mies's boxy Lake Shore Drive Apartments (1949–51), but Goldberg's design belongs to

the scale and intensity of all-inclusive compositional grandeur.

Mies van der Rohe, as indicated earlier, went his own way in splendid isolation during the decade before his death in 1969, concerned not the slightest by issues lying beyond the limits of his profession, but within those limits seeking only to be, by his own admission, a good architect. Like other contemporaries, he was a treacherous model for the young. Not surprisingly, one of his last works was one of his finest: the Berlin National Gallery (1962–68). Situating the service areas of the structure out of sight in a massive podium, Mies was free to erect a stately glass pavilion with an enormous steel entablature carried on a mere eight isolated columns. Not since antiquity, not even in the most "ideal" of Renaissance or neoclassic buildings, had an architect sought and achieved a design in such complete equilibrium of parts.

It is clear that large office buildings no longer present the challenge for creative design that they did for nearly an entire century. This is true of government projects, insofar as they concern the housing of the bureaucracy, although city halls, if given a symbolic role to play, are another matter. Boston's City Hall (plate 595), the result of a 1962 competition won by Kallmann, McKinnell & Knowles, is the nucleus of the Government Center, an urban renewal project laid out according to a master plan by I. M. Pei (b. 1917). One of the most ambitious efforts to re-create an American center city, it confronts us with heroic-scaled contemporary monuments to civic and

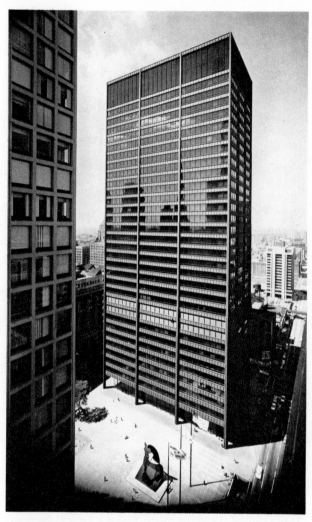

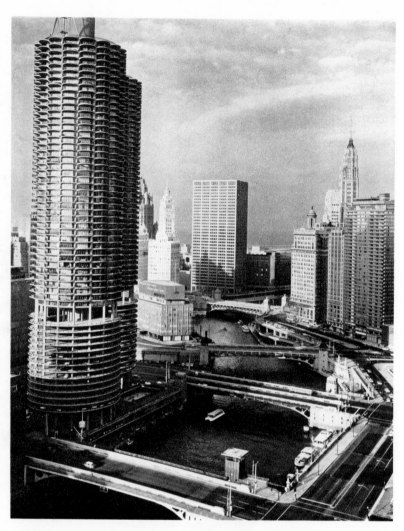

596 C. F. Murphy Associates. Civic Center, Chicago. 1963–65. Sculpture (*foreground*) by Picasso, installed 1967

597 View of downtown Chicago, north of the Loop. Marina City (*left*), 1964–67, by Bertrand Goldberg

another architectural culture entirely. At first glance the circular forms with their tiers of rippling, semicircular balconies, each projecting outward from a pie-shaped apartment, seem more in accord with the blithe stylishness of Los Angeles or the plastic elegance of Miami Beach. Yet the logic of the forms and the way, for example, the balcony curves depend upon the effective radius of the gantry crane that was used to construct the towers mark it as a Chicago product. Furthermore, the clarity with which the lower-level parking spiral is differentiated from the residential levels above is functionally appropriate, and no effort is made to gloss it over; the result is almost commonplace. Marina City, in spite of not fitting formally into the Chicago tradition, offers a number of construction features that establish its legitimacy.

New York has not been as fortunate as either Boston or Chicago in terms of its recent architectural renovation. The Pan American Building (plate 598), set astride Grand Central Station, is not an architectural amenity in the normal sense of the word, but a sadly inconclusive form with its corners planed down. The New York World

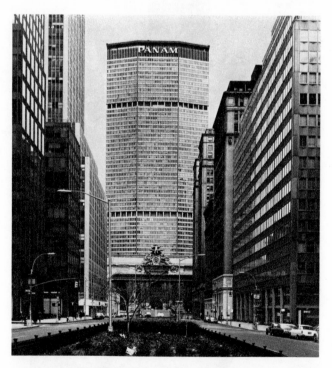

598 Emery Roth & Sons, Pietro Belluschi, and Walter Gropius. Pan American Building, New York. 1963. Facade of Grand Central Terminal (*below*), 1903–13

Contemporary Architecture and Planning Since 1960   537

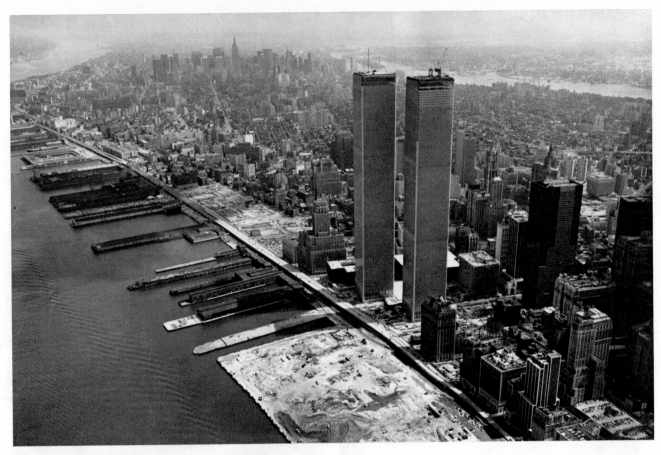

599 Minoru Yamasaki & Associates and Emery Roth & Sons. World Trade Center, New York. 1966–74

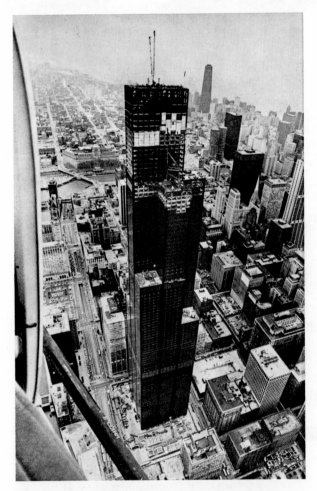

600 Skidmore, Owings & Merrill. Sears Roebuck Tower, Chicago. Topped out, May 3, 1973. In the distance, John Hancock Center, 1966–69, also by Skidmore, Owings and Merrill

Trade Center (1966–74, plate 599) is a typical instance of the ruthlessness with which that city's skyline and ground-level appearance have been treated by builders. On a huge site west of Church Street, along the Hudson River side of the downtown financial district, two identical towers rise 110 stories (1,350 feet), designed by Minoru Yamasaki (b. 1912) with Emery Roth & Sons as architects to be the highest buildings in the world, though now surpassed by Chicago's Sears Tower (plate 600). The plaza zone in which these towers are dropped again (like Lincoln Center) seems to turn its back on the historic neighborhood, and the blunt height and graceless profile of the towers have nothing to do with the once characteristic, now overpowered cluster of tapered spires that for decades dominated lower Manhattan and the harbor. The skyline of Chicago's Loop has fared better than this.

Los Angeles has been seen as the type par excellence of the late twentieth-century American metropolis. Architecturally, the region had been in the earlier days of the modern movement a major center of progressive design, though almost exclusively in the field of residential building. In the past decade, the architectural importance of Los Angeles waned as it failed to take the lead in the development of a characteristic architecture of a commercial or monumental sort. Typically, Los Angeles International Airport remains a pale version of what can be found elsewhere. In the midst of this southern California sprawl only three things stand out: Disneyland, with its architecture of escape into the past and the future; the unique Watts Towers (plate 601), a monument built out of junk, refuse, and solitary human ingenuity, a work without institutional or official initiative conceived and achieved in his spare time by Simon Rodia (c. 1875–1965), an immigrant laborer; and the retired Cunard liner *Queen Mary*, since the mid-1960s "beached" (actually docked) at the southern extremity of the Long Beach Freeway, serving as a convention center and tourist attraction—a monument of British design of the 1930s ending its days in a world of architectural Pop. The stupendous freeway system (plate 602) created for Los Angeles by the California Division of Highways represents one of the most ambitious, ongoing engineering projects of our age, comparable in scale (and almost analogous in urban function) to the aqueducts of Roman antiquity. This technological marvel, however, serves a wasteland of tract houses, roadside architecture, and ostentatiously styled public structures, whose component parts do not jell into a recognizable urban fabric. Autopia seems to spontaneously generate not conventional urban patterns of architectural density but endless linear highway strips, features of which have already been immortalized by the Pop artist Edward Ruscha. Viewed favorably, Los Angeles might prove to be the spawning ground of the city of the future as well as of a new architecture. Alas, too many as-yet-unsolved blights caused by the use of the automobile may finally stand in the way of realizing this particular urban dream.

Louis Kahn, though he made some studies for the historic center of Philadelphia in the 1950s, not only had no influence on recent urban building, but most of his work over the decade before his death was largely unrelated to it. He must certainly be ranked one of the greatest, most original designers of the second half of the century, yet his effect on the cityscape was nil. His Salk Research Institute, La Jolla, Calif. (1959–65, plate 603), is typical in that it is removed from a major center. Kahn had the knack of producing a formal design that manages not to look formalistic; that is, the final result does not appear to be a contrived package. With the Salk Institute he designed a double range of buildings on a raised podium containing a number of individual research areas. The duplication and reduplication of function become the basis of the building's recurring rhythmic dignity. The nature of the building is such that, while it is sited in a dramatic landscape overlooking the Pacific, it would be equally appropriate in an urban setting.

Kahn's plan for the government center (plate 604) at Dacca, now the capital of Bangladesh, was begun in 1966 and was the summit of his career; one can only regret that he was not commissioned to build something of this scale at home. At Dacca, Kahn's early background in Beaux-Arts planning served him well. Now that the modernist tradition can accept alternatives to open planning

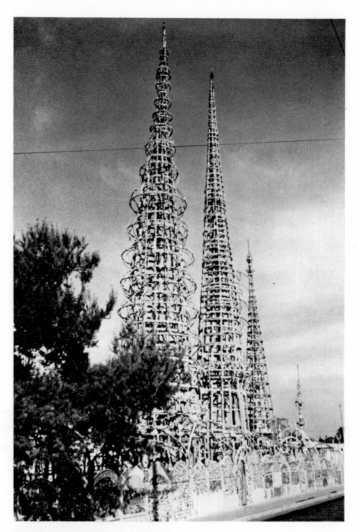

601 Simon Rodia. Watts Towers, Los Angeles. c. 1921–54

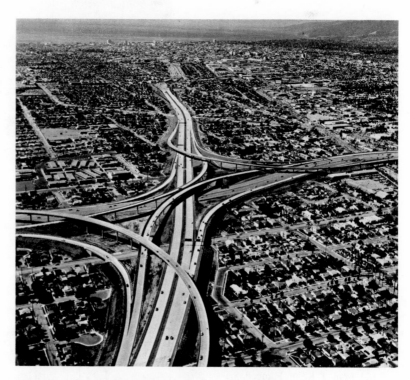

602 State of California, Division of Highways. Interchange, Santa Monica and San Diego Freeways, Los Angeles

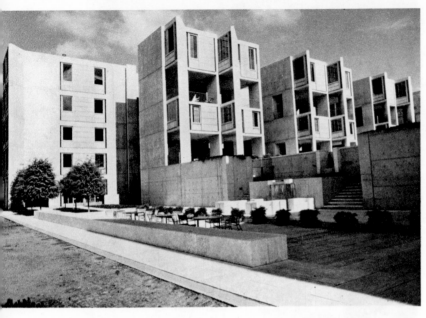

603 Louis I. Kahn. Salk Institute of
Biological Studies, La Jolla, Calif. 1959–65

and its free-flowing, integrated, overlapping spaces and interlocking forms, Kahn's self-contained capitol building, with its plazas and perspective axes, puts to shame the tentative, superficial formalism of Lincoln Center and like efforts. He worked diligently to realize a design based upon a traditional, academic central plan, employing plain brick walls akin more to Richardson than to Mies, and creating a monumental geometry of arches, circles, rectangular cubes, and cylinders that suggest a family relationship with the early brick traditions of the ancient Near East or of Rome rather than with the ubiquitous thin curtain walls of the twentieth century. Much of the quality of this rich heritage was similarly exploited by Kahn in the round-arched, cycloid-vaulted galleries of the Kimbell Art Museum (plate 605), Fort Worth, Texas (completed in 1972).

The probity, even a certain tediousness, that is at the heart of Kahn's monumental structures becomes immediately apparent when they are compared with the

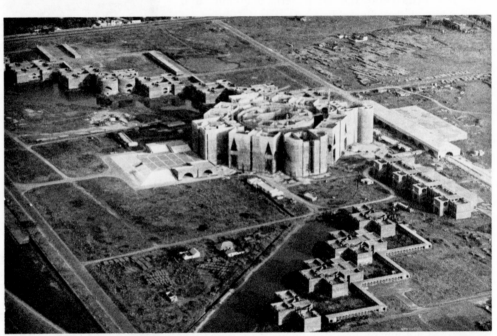

604 Louis I. Kahn. National Assembly
and Hostels, Dacca, Bangladesh

605 Louis I. Kahn. Kimbell Art
Museum, Fort Worth, Tex.
Cycloid vaulted chambers
with natural light fixtures.
Designed 1967; completed 1972

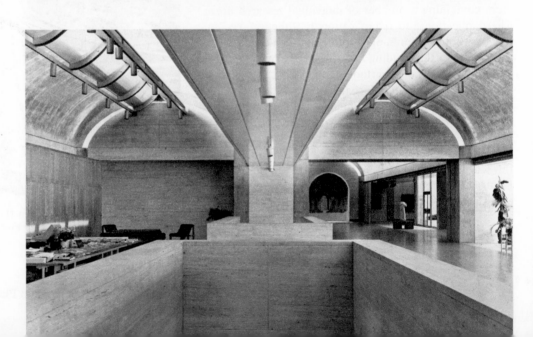

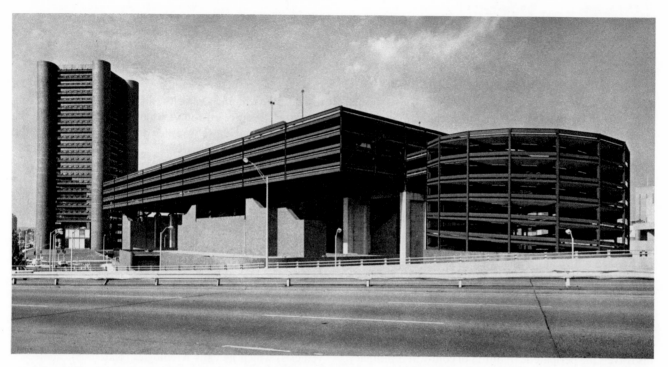

606 Kevin Roche and John Dinkeloo. Knights of Columbus Headquarters Building, 1966–70, and Veterans Memorial Coliseum (with superimposed parking structure), New Haven, Conn., 1962–72.

work of Kevin Roche (b. 1922) and John Dinkeloo (b. 1918), a partnership which represents the successor firm to the late Eero Saarinen. Their work has a discipline and control that their former employer lacked, but with them discipline becomes a constricting rather than a constructively ordering force. Their recently completed megastructure at New Haven, Conn., comprising an office tower for the Knights of Columbus and an arena with parking structure above (plate 606), is a fair index of the muscle-bound overdevelopment of their architecture. Seeking, with justification, to make a strong design statement in the midst of a weakly rebuilt area of a middle-sized downtown, in proximity to the intimidating forms of a freeway, they have employed grossly proportioned purple brick cylinders and massive steel beams to exaggerate the structure. First views of such designs normally provoke speechless wonder, but familiarity and reflective analysis demonstrate their underlying vulgarity and exhibitionism.

Most architects active today have been seeking an integrated, comprehensive design, a quest which often leads to the megastructure solution whether or not appropriate in a given circumstance. The most comprehensive designer on the scene in the late sixties seemed to be R. Buckminster Fuller (b. 1895). Not describable as an architect in the normal sense of the term, he has been designing archetypal buildings since 1927, when at the age of thirty-two he gave up a maverick career in industry to devote himself to design research. A prototypical dropout, twice separated from Harvard College, he combines the genius of the traditional Yankee tinkerer with a gift for contemporary modes of publicity and a restless, unrooted life style that keeps him on the move as visiting lecturer, consultant, and career gadfly. Perhaps better described as an inventor than as a creator, he does not so much design or build as provide systems for others. Having been stalemated in the development of industrialized housing types, he went further in his search for an ideal, comprehensive, universal building form with the "invention" of the geodesic dome in the 1940s. The dome was an ancient architectural form with cosmic implications, but Fuller was drawn to it for other reasons, such as its favorable ratio between area of surface and volume

607 R. Buckminster Fuller. American Pavilion, Expo '67, Montreal. Geodesic dome. 1967

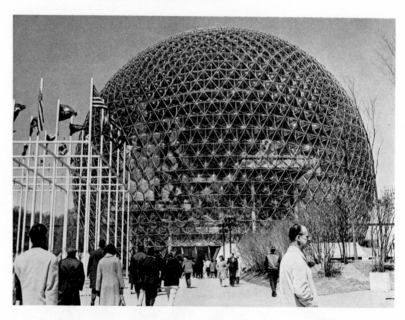

of enclosed space, and the simple rigidity of its structure in the geodesic mode. That it offered no logical opportunity for a door did not bother him in the least, though it irritated countless others in the architectural profession.

His greatest public and official success came with the construction of the American Pavilion (plate 607) at Montreal's Expo '67. Fuller has also enjoyed a considerable underground fame with the young and with the various counter-culture movements. To them he was a welcome guru, having for years blasted the traditional complacency of both industry and the design professions. He seemed a logical prophet as he wished to beat various "pentagons" and "rand corporations" with their own gamesmanship. Yet at the same time he has conferred with various Third World heads of state, has represented American interests abroad in places as different as Montreal, Moscow, and Afghanistan—in short, paralleling in his travels the peripatetic tradition of cold-war diplomacy. He professes to have rational, worldwide solutions that would wrap up social and environmental problems by the effective functional integration of energy sources, distribution channels, and the like. Paradoxically, many of today's disaffected found what they thought to be the means of achieving the framework for a freer life in the hands of a Philosopher-King, a Design-Scientist whose sovereignty would extend above and beyond national autonomy.

Fuller's comprehensive vision is typical of much modernist architectural theory. Wright's Broadacre City had the virtue of bringing certain ideal concepts to the point of being usefully realized in fragments or in limited aspects. Wright's onetime disciple Paolo Soleri (b. 1919) has found his mentor's Broadacre City to be absurdly wasteful of land and the radiant city of individual skyscrapers to be too inconclusive, and has proposed a solution of his own: spectacular megastructural cities for a variety of sites and landscapes (some even orbiting vehicles) which he calls Arcologies (plate 608).

Soleri's Arcologies (Architecture plus Ecology) are enormous cities-as-a-single-building, capable of accommodating anywhere from a few to many thousands—their dwellings, places of work and recreation, and public spaces—at an unheard-of density. Compartments and subdivisions for the entire gamut of human activity would be housed, racklike, on superimposed platforms, arranged so that crowding would not be visible yet communication would be facilitated by shortened distances. An Arcology is a kind of "new town" concept, but a world removed from the tentative, half-hearted schemes of Reston, Va. (plate 609), or Columbia, Md., both examples of an improved suburban subdivision with a few local industries and some of the public amenities of a resort or leisure-time community. Arcologies ask people to make certain fundamental adjustments in their life style, to give up the notion of the separate, detached suburban house and disassociate their daily activities from the automobile, so integral a part of our contemporary architectural plant system. Ecologically desirable because they halt the uncontrolled consumption of land through traditional development techniques, and heroically appealing, mind-boggling designs of undeniable power and beauty, Soleri's schemes are very likely sociologically impossible, even were there to occur in the near future a revolution of habit or an environmentally forced, survival-induced concentration of populations. Soleri's dream is just that, one of the most Leonardesque of architectural utopias created in our century. Not an impossible, but surely an unlikely pattern for the future, although a small Arcology (1977) was built on a site near Prescott, Ariz.

So far as it goes, the architectural vision of the common citizen, however, does not take in such images except as a brief entertainment on a late-night TV show. It has been the particular genius of Robert Venturi (b. 1925) to demonstrate that the architecture of the professional

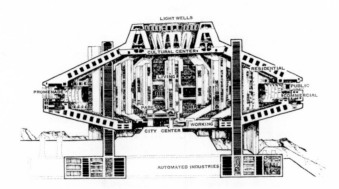

608 Paolo Soleri. Arcology "Babel II C." Section

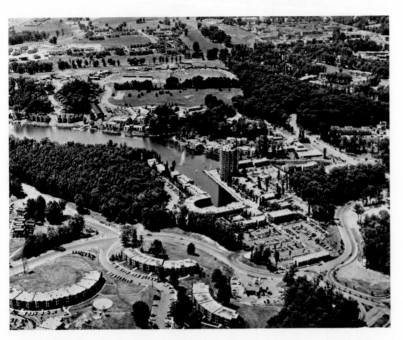

609 Conklin & Whittlesey. Village Center, Reston, Va. 1961

schools and magazines, of architects and critics, is not the architecture of all America. He has helped open our eyes to our characteristic everyday building shapes *as they exist*, and not as we would have them. Venturi has recoiled from any hint of a comprehensive solution in his own work. In his writings, such as *Learning from Las Vegas*, in collaboration with Denise Scott Brown and Steven Izenour, he has made it clear that America's true architectural vision lies with the fantopia of Las Vegas and Disneyland or with standardized, universally distributed, miniature versions of these places in the form of highway franchise design: for example, the twin yellow arches of McDonald's, a form known to, and representing the fulfillable aspirations of, anyone. This pop-culture architectural imagery is far removed from the similarly shaped, monumentally pretentious Jefferson Arch (plate 610), St. Louis, a Saarinen enigma that remains undecipherable in its meaning or association.

By recognizing the appositeness of roadside architecture and its display advertising techniques, Venturi has helped us to overcome the longing for the *big* civic monument—whether McKim's or Kahn's or Soleri's—and to settle for a conglomeration of the small-scaled, impermanent structures that have been, throughout history, among the most characteristic examples of native American building. A remarkable give-and-take has taken place between the buildings and ideas of Venturi and his circle, the aesthetic and sources of Pop Art, and even some recent abstract painting. Totally excluded

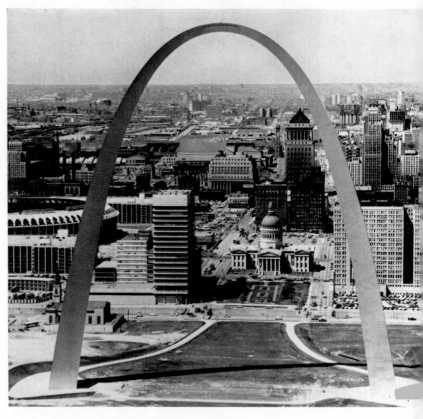

610 Eero Saarinen. Jefferson Arch, St. Louis, Mo. Designed 1949; completed 1965

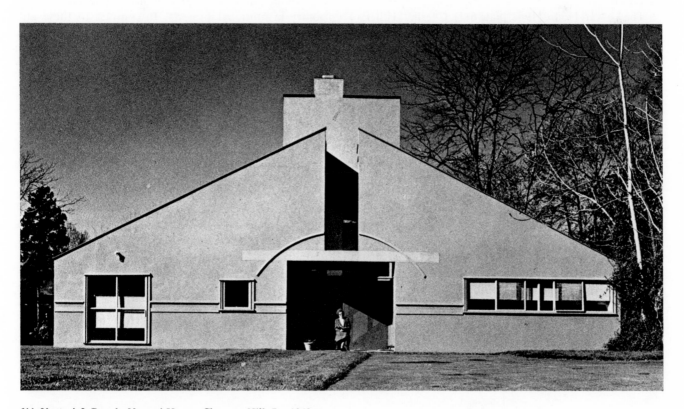

611 Venturi & Rauch. Venturi House, Chestnut Hill, Pa. 1962

Contemporary Architecture and Planning Since 1960   543

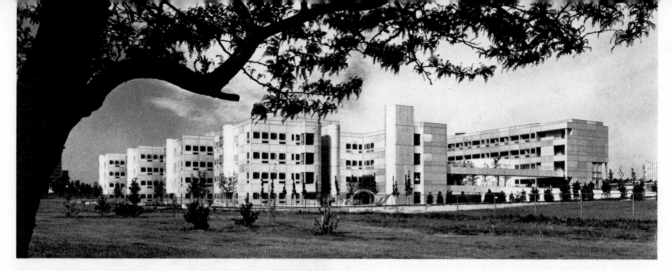

612 Richard Meier. Bronx Development Center, New York. Completed 1977

from Venturi's repertory is any (but for an ironic) reference to the once sacrosanct forms of the International Style and its American progeny. Venturi came to maturity in part under the influence of Louis Kahn, but his own designs are not reproductions or imitations; rather Venturi uses commonplace features with a cheerful wit, an offhand ease (an effect that actually must be very carefully calculated) that is disarming. His is a very artful architecture, if only in its clever dissimulation of the architect's creative role in transforming the environment. It is a matter of perceiving popular taste and then using it for benevolent ends, producing a market-tested product with hidden virtues instead of an architecturally virtuous (read: avant-garde, progressive, utopian, etc.) design that is likely to encounter consumer resistance and ultimately rejection.

The Venturi House (1962, plate 611), Chestnut Hill, Pa., is in the image of a Levittown model home. Yet it has never been demonstrated that this variant is especially acceptable to a mass audience, since the design has a number of quirks that surely set it apart from its common, Brand X prototype. Moreover, Venturi's species of architecture has irritated such establishment figures as Philip Johnson and Gordon Bunshaft (of Skidmore, Owings and Merrill); hence it finds only qualified acceptance in the professional quarter. Compared with a Wrightian Prairie House or a Breuer dwelling of the late 1940s, the Venturi house finds itself in familial company. The "round arch" over the portico is no mass-builder's device but a coy allusion to the form as used in American monumental design from Richardson to Kahn. Try as he may, Venturi cannot help being a perceptive trained architect, cannot attain a level of innocence, and so he does the next best thing.

Thanks to Venturi and to the influence of Pop Art in general, we have been awakened to the as-is realities of our built environment and can confront them objectively. We tend to remain blind, however, to the motivations behind our Levittown-to-Miami Beach civilization, with its axis drawn straight through the heated swimming pool of a Holiday Inn. It is well to comprehend the virtues of roadside, resort, and suburban tract architecture, to recognize it as fulfilling a broadly based taste and thus necessary; but it is equally vital to see this configuration as the display advertising of marginally legitimate commercial exploitations.

There are many architects who will have no part of this now respectable chaos. Sensitive house builders such as Richard Meier (b. 1934), Charles Gwathmey (b. 1938), and Michael Graves (b. 1934) have skillfully revived the Bauhaus and Purist image in numerous houses of the past decade. Their exquisitely designed planar forms and reductive geometric shapes show a nostalgia for the heroic age of European modernism. Meier, in his Bronx Development Center, New York (1977, plate 612), has evolved an original, if equally precisionist, mode for contemporary institutional projects. In contrast to these attitudes one finds the elaborate, whimsically romantic domestic designs of Charles Moore (b. 1925), redolent with historical memory, crammed with allusions to Pop imagery, and often constructed of common-place materials. The "complexity and contradiction" of Moore's work—to echo an assessment by Venturi—reveal an underlying instability and perhaps uncertainty on the part of the thoughtful architect of the seventies. The present is rich in choices and in perverse, contrary forces, and we can be sure that the future will offer still more.

Not only has architectural design become more pluralistic in the past decade; our awareness of it has increased by leaps and bounds, making the grasping and interpretation of a trend, now and perhaps forever, out of the question. We shall continue to get more of what we already have, from smart shopping plazas to delicately romanticized modernist villas. But now that there are common interests and themes between architecture and the imagery of painting, it seems likely that future architectural design, after a half-century of generally failing to recognize contemporary movements in painting and sculpture, will once again show a greater concern for pictorial values and conceptual forms.

26
Painting Since 1960: From Pop Art to Minimalism

Throughout the decade when American art was dominated by the Abstract Expressionists, unsympathetic critics looked vainly for a return to traditional, humanistic content which might reestablish connections with the past. It was assumed that as the more specialized styles of abstraction in due course lost impetus, references to common reality would be restored. The fragmentary human imagery of de Kooning's *Woman* series momentarily stimulated a new kind of improvisatory, abstract-figurative art among San Francisco Bay Region artists—most notably in the case of Richard Diebenkorn—and Pollock's fitful anatomical allusions encouraged the forlorn hope that a major trend, repudiating Action Painting, was gathering strength. In fact, what emerged at the end of the fifties and in the first years of the next decade was something quite different—an original and irreverent parody of the "vulgar" imagery and artifacts of commercial culture in the form of Pop Art.

POP ART: THE PRECURSORS

Pop Art did not appear *ex nihilo*, but was presaged by a gradual drift away from the gestural, painterly modes of Action Painting toward an environmental art. The first evidence of adulterations in art derived from the urban environment could be observed in de Kooning's women. His dominant image evolved in the late forties from a collage method that juxtaposed fragmentary commercial illustrations of lipsticked mouths with transpositions in paint of mass-culture sex idols and film stars.

In 1953, while de Kooning was working on that controversial series, Larry Rivers (b. 1923), first known as a second-generation de Kooning follower, had begun to reappraise the pictorial cliché with his equally controversial work, *Washington Crossing the Delaware* (plate 613). This large salon painting was inspired by American folklore and by Leutze's popular academic painting of the nineteenth century (plate 255). Its appearance signaled a general shift in outlook that made formerly scorned and banal themes admissible in "high" art. A new vernacular imagery drawn from popular sources and from nostalgic

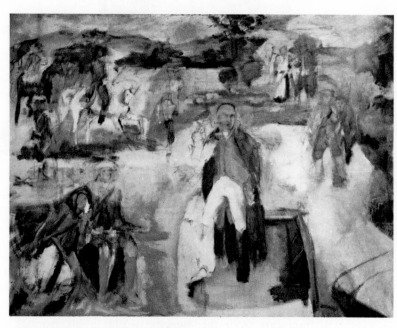

613 Larry Rivers. *Washington Crossing the Delaware*. 1953.
Oil on canvas, 6' 11⅝" × 9' 3⅝".
The Museum of Modern Art, New York

Americana began to establish itself as a provocative new current, in sharp opposition to the subjective preoccupations and idealism of Action Painting.

Robert Rauschenberg (b. 1925) treated the banal themes that Rivers introduced with even more formal radicalism outside the tradition of figurative realism; the results virtually transformed the values and the look of American painting in a few short years. In the mid-1950s Rauschenberg had begun to counter de Kooning's free brushstroke by loading his paintings with rags and tatters of cloth, reproductions, fragments of comic strips, and other collage elements of waste and discarded materials, Dadaist in their anti-art intensity. His packed surfaces were worked over with paint in the characteristic, spontaneous gestural language of Action Painting, but their painterly expressiveness was reduced in the context of an

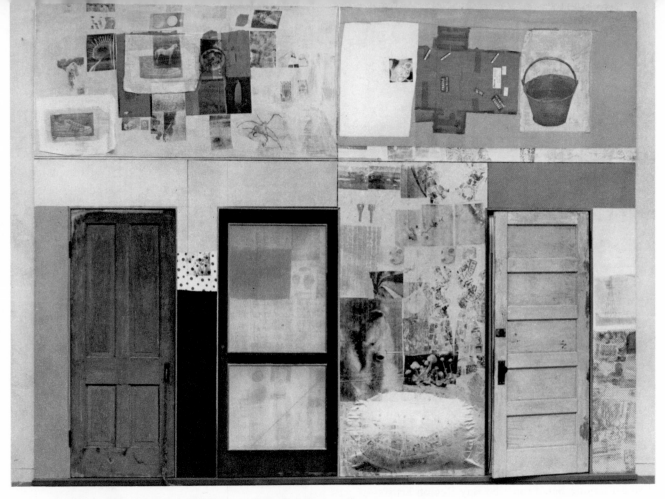

614 Robert Rauschenberg. *Rodeo Palace (Spread)*. 1975–76. Mixed media, 144 × 192 × 5½″. Collection Mr. and Mrs. Sidney Singer, Mamaroneck, N.Y.

artistic structure choked with alien matter.

The pillow and quilt in the *Bed* (1955, colorplate 89), which shocked taste when it was exhibited, serve ambiguously both as an Abstract Expressionist painterly experience and as a literal derelict object. Incorporating fragments from the domestic world in his paintings, Rauschenberg objectified and depersonalized the Action Painters' "gesture"; he thus managed to keep the dialogue between the sense of art and everyday reality open and unresolved. *Bed* was made at a time when he was short of canvas; he simply substituted the pillow, sheet, and patchwork quilt from his own bed. Hung straight up on the wall like a conventional stretched canvas, in contradiction to its original function, it was perhaps the first provocative assemblage by Rauschenberg; widely exhibited, it helped to earn the artist his reputation, which still persists, as an *enfant terrible*. Unlike the "poetic objects" of the Surrealists, to which Rauschenberg's conglomerates—or "combines," as he called them—have been compared, his "junk" compositions were actually not meant to offend by their incongruity. Rather, they were used in a matter-of-fact spirit anticipating the detachment of Pop Art. By forcing a confrontation with dilapidated object fragments, Rauschenberg effectively opposed a culture geared to the insatiable demand for new consumer products.

As his style evolved, Rauschenberg utilized silk-screened imagery taken from photojournalism, which in the sixties had begun radically to transform the art experience. New spatial and communication ideas infiltrated art through the process-oriented media of films, television, exhibitions, "Happenings," and other events, opening up unexpected creative opportunities and changing the forms of traditional painting. Rauschenberg was perhaps the first artist to test the new technical and aesthetic frontiers, now so familiar, in response to the communications dynamism of the contemporary electronic age. *Rodeo Palace (Spread)* (1975–76, plate 614), a work created for an exhibition in Texas devoted to the American rodeo, combines some of the synoptic, flashing juxtapositions of his silk-screened imagery of the sixties with collage techniques and material contrasts which allude to his earliest work. Here and there deliberately untidy contours and paint smears remind us that his work bridges the gap between Action Painting and Pop Art. Historical Dada and Surrealism, augmented by the continuing presence in America of Marcel Duchamp, became significant factors in the development of Rauschenberg's combines. They were sometimes described as "Neo-Dada" because of their anti-art character, and they were also linked to the phenomenon of the "Happening."

Allan Kaprow had invented the event called the Happening, and he intended to bring the creative artist into more fertile interaction with the actual world around him, by opening a new dialogue with overlooked commonplace materials of the environment. Many well-known artists, both painters and sculptors, gained their first significant public notice as originators of Happenings, among them Claes Oldenburg, Jim Dine, Red Grooms, and Robert Whitman; and the young Lucas Samaras performed in a number of them. The Happening became a kind of animated collage of events, involving persons and materials in a theatrical situation before an audience. There was no simulated time sequence in the events, no narrative, no playing of roles nor even an imaginative setting. People involved were treated literally as physical props. However, there was a program and a sequence of viewing, and both the dramatic action and the objects were often symbolic. Happenings were also loosely associated with the dance performances of Merce Cunningham and the music of John Cage, both of whom collaborated extensively with visual artists, and with the assemblage techniques widely adopted in the early sixties (see Chapter 23). Together these aesthetic developments, bridging a number of different mediums, had the effect of exposing the art scene to entirely new expressive possibilities.

The innovations of Jasper Johns (b. 1930) had a far-reaching influence on the artistic changes taking place in the 1960s. His historic paintings of flags and targets, first exhibited in 1957, and the subsequent maps, number series, rule-and-circle devices, and other themes created radically new forms of representation, utilizing commonplace imagery. Many of his subjects elucidated the creative process in a "do-it-yourself" spirit, breaking down and isolating constituent parts of illusion and literal fact, the visual and the tactile, and inviting the public to restructure the magical unities of the aesthetic experience. Johns's American flag motif (plate 615) in particular showed new and startling potentials of image-elaboration by making over a standard visual cliché that had seemed empty of content due to overfamiliarity.

Johns encompasses three major streams of contemporary expression: a modified Abstract Expressionist surface, the simplified composition of nonrelational abstract art, and post-Realist assemblage (see Chapter 23). Unlike Duchamp, who placed the "ready-made" object in the realm of art, Johns reversed the process and made the actual object into an elegantly crafted painting (colorplate 90). Sometimes one senses a certain quality of anxiety suppressed, and there is a shift in focus between the objective visual and subjective orientation. Johns makes veiled autobiographical references which are often as delicate, intriguing, and effective as those found in classical Cubism.

POP ART: DEBUT AND DIFFUSION
Pop Art made its dramatic public debut in 1962 with the individual exhibitions of Roy Lichtenstein, Claes Oldenburg, James Rosenquist, Andy Warhol, Tom Wesselmann,

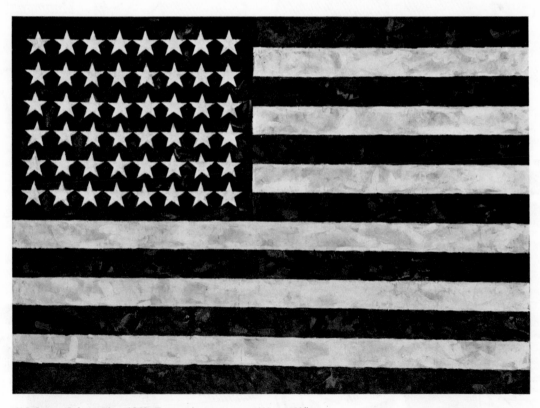

615 Jasper Johns. *Flag*. 1958. Encaustic on canvas, 41¼ × 60¾".
Collection Mr. and Mrs. Leo Castelli, New York

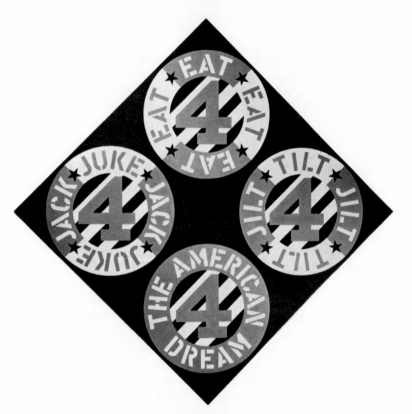

616 Robert Indiana. *The Beware-Danger American Dream #4.*
1963. Oil on canvas, 102 × 102".
Hirshhorn Museum and Sculpture Garden, Smithsonian
Institution, Washington, D.C.

and Robert Indiana. In November of that year most of these artists were represented in the now largely forgotten but then controversial exhibition entitled *New Realists*, which was held at the Sidney Janis Gallery in New York. The term "Pop Art" had been first coined by Lawrence Alloway in England in 1958, to describe the precocious English equivalent of the movement, and it soon became the most widely accepted American label, although "Neo-Dada" was also used for a brief time. Many artists and almost all older critics were shocked and offended when confronted by an imagery that seemed scarcely to transform its sources in the newspaper comic strip (Lichtenstein), the billboard (Rosenquist), repeated or isolated commercial brand symbols (Warhol), or food products in strong relief (Wesselmann). The more obviously aesthetic intention of the lettered signs and directional symbols of Robert Indiana (b. 1928) were found only slightly more acceptable, since he, too, took over explicit and routine commercial or industrial imagery, road signs, and mechanical type faces (plate 616).

By monumentally dilating a billboard detail, James Rosenquist (b. 1933) discovered iconic possibilities in the commercial advertising image and created confusing, alternative readings of his compartmented paintings. They relate both to the ambiguous legibility of contemporary abstraction and to the deliberate confusions of different

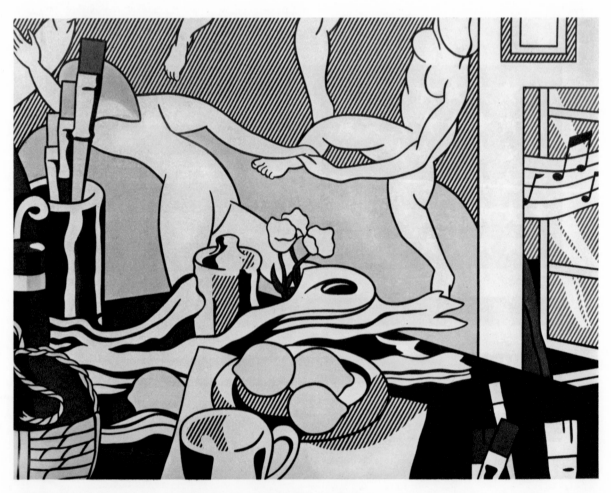

617 Roy Lichtenstein. *The Artist's Studio: The Dance.* 1974. Oil and magma
on canvas, 96 × 128". Leo Castelli Gallery, New York

realities by the Surrealists. Between 1954 and 1960 Rosenquist worked as a billboard painter, often on Times Square signs, and the experience of dealing with huge commercial images at close range and the use of Day-Glo paints were to become important in his paintings of the late 1960s and seventies. Some of those were large-scale canvases painted in a technique reminiscent of billboards but also prophetic of photo-Realism, which summarizes with epic grandeur America's taste for objects, material progress, and social optimism, despite the vulgarization of such impulses by the media and various forms of popular culture.

Roy Lichtenstein (b. 1923) decelerated the cartoon image by enlargement. He also conspicuously overstated the Ben Day screen dots in *As I Opened Fire* (1964, colorplate 91), as an integral part of his form, thus compelling our attention to medium and process as significant content and as an undoubtedly ironic commentary on the adolescent celebration of modern warfare. His work is about art and style, despite its lowbrow sources and extremely mechanical look. He achieved another kind of distancing effect by his choice of somewhat out-of-date comics for his early subjects. Modern life speeds up the sense of time's passage and makes us more sharply aware of changing styles and of the obsession with change and novelty through the communications media.

Lichtenstein's recent paintings represent an effort to reconcile his comic-strip style even with such admired twentieth-century masters as Matisse. In *The Artist's Studio: The Dance* (1974, plate 617) he discovered points of correspondence in taste between the Art Nouveau elements of Matisse's curvilinear style and his own deliberately vulgarized decoration and linear convolutions. He has often boldly tested "high art" values by contrasting them with a vernacular style and by introducing references both to fashionable art-historical models and to his own artistic evolution. Within his chosen scheme, he remains a constantly inventive artist, masterfully manipulating contour, color, shape, scale, and a variegated repertory of surface marks to create powerful abstract compositions.

Andy Warhol (b. 1925) presents repeated images of car crashes; movie stars, among them his famous variations on Marilyn Monroe (colorplate 92); and soup cans snatched from the daily unfolding of the press. The iconic gravity of his imagery arrests on canvas the accelerated transience of advertising or topical banalities. Like the assemblage sculptors (Chapter 23), he has constructed food, soap, and Brillo cartons of painted wood and stacked them to imitate a supermarket storeroom. These objects exist artistically by a nuance of contradiction between the actual product and its simulation and by the artist's fine calculation of his audience's differing responses to each.

Nothing actually happens in Warhol's art in the sense of conventional storytelling. Its point, at least in part, is to

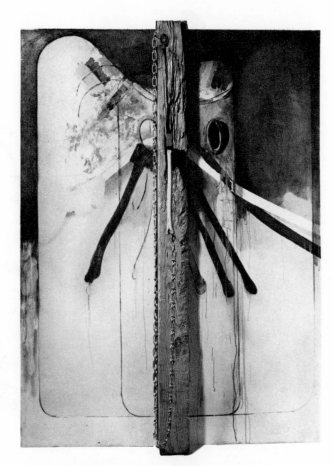

618 Jim Dine. *Hatchet with Two Palettes, State No. 2.* 1963. Oil on canvas with wood and metal, 72 × 54 × 12″. Private collection, New York

confront us with boredom as an issue, with a subject matter neutralized by a remorselessly mechanical presentation. His detached stance effectively thwarts any sense of emotional involvement or identification; yet despite the iconography of blankness and impassivity, Warhol operates in the area of public myth and parable. He may even be considered a modern history painter, since his dominant imagery and visual ironies are inextricably linked with the conditions and daily-newspaper events of urban life.

Jim Dine (b. 1935) occupies a unique position among the artists loosely associated with Pop Art. His paintings with object attachments and his "environments" have a brute physical presence that rebukes the indirection and muted poetic sentiment of Jasper Johns. Dine has extended the paradoxical play between literal experience and illusionistic representation by skillfully regenerating the painterly direction of Action Painting and then assimilating it to a wide repertory of objects rich in the human associations of personal use or admired strength (plate 618). His household furniture, room environments, bathroom cabinets, furniture, tools, palettes, and robes are meant to be enjoyed for their expressive power within the formal scheme of his construction as well as

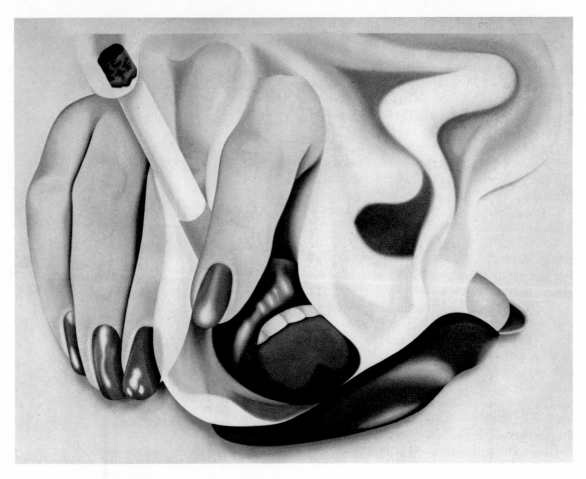

619 Tom Wesselmann. *Smoker No. 17*. 1975. Oil on canvas, 96 × 131″. Sidney Janis Gallery, New York

for personal or muted psychological association.

Claes Oldenburg (b. 1929) is one of the most inventive of the Pop artists and has had a wide influence on all manner of contemporary art expressions and ideas. He was educated to Abstract Expressionism but broke with that movement about 1959, opening paths to a variety of new concepts, including Pop sculpture (Chapter 23) and Happenings, but he is best known for the gigantic ersatz food compositions in painted canvas and plaster which he evolved after 1960. The surfaces of these bloated facsimiles of the lunch- and drugstore-counter were at first freely handled in the splatter-and-splash technique of Action Painting, but the reference to their real-life models was clear and inescapable. A repeated emphasis on foodstuffs seemed to draw on the preoccupation of advertising with the infantile oral obsessions of the American mass audience.

Tom Wesselmann (b. 1931) resorted to an essentially emblematic treatment of the female body in his first important series of paintings, the Great American Nudes, which grew out of his early student interest in cartoon illustration. He studied cartooning at the Cincinnati Art Academy, then in the late 1950s transferred to Cooper Union in New York. As early as 1961, when he started his Great American Nudes, he limited his palette to red, white, and blue, which clearly associated the erotic theme

with the American flag colors. Wesselmann's interest in singling out parts of the female body and in collage are visual factors closely linked to Surrealism, once again reaffirming the fantastic content of much American Pop Art. His impressive series of smokers (plate 619) also openly declare a provocative eroticism. Detached from the female body, the mouth becomes a huge orifice, waiting to receive the lighted cigarette. The fragmentation of the female form and the sexual candor were commonplace themes of Dada and Surrealist art, but Wesselmann's depiction of the disembodied parts of the female anatomy is usually a tough, blatant presentation that is fantastic in scale but not in mood.

A number of figurative artists of impressive accomplishment have been linked to Pop Art, because of their interest in popular culture and everyday life as image sources. Yet they are by no means strictly Pop artists. Although they use "vulgar" or vernacular subject matter, their work does not have the newly made, mass-produced, or standard-brands character of Pop. These works, in contrast to Pop Art, convey personal, poetic, and fantastic content. Foremost among these artists has been George Segal, whose uncanny, poignant sculptures dramatize the alienation in the urban environment (see Chapter 23). There is a comparable dramatic power and fantasy in the maenads of Richard Lindner (1901–1978), depicted in monumental isolation in *Hello* (1966, colorplate 93), but at other times participating in the gaudy parade of New York street life. Lindner's absorbing spectacle, however, is more irrational and hysterical in mood than Segal's somnolent world.

With our sense of super glut in the material environment, the general apprehension regarding world ecology, and the saturation of media salesmanship, Pop Art no longer seems quite so relevant to the concerns of the 1970s or so compelling. As a group style it began to lose its sense of collective discovery and some of its momentum by the late sixties. Individual artists associated with Pop Art, on the other hand, have become increasingly resourceful, even if they have lost touch with the original impulse that inspired them. Oldenburg, Lichtenstein, Warhol, Wesselmann, and Rosenquist in particular have all continued to develop and to expand their creative worlds in surprising ways. Also, the ersatz, commercial surfaces and synthetic textures of Pop Art have directly affected abstract and figurative artists, especially in sculpture, and have encouraged intermedia experiment. Reversing the process of influence, geometric and Minimalist sculptural forms have also affected a number of Pop artists. There is, in fact, a very lively interaction between apparently antithetical modes of abstraction and the representationalism of Pop Art, to their mutual benefit. If the results are as expansive and significant as many today believe, then obviously the actual contribution of the Pop artists, if not their original premises, is based on sound, formal values and will endure.

SUPER-REALISM

The attitudes of irony and wit established by Pop Art and its exploration of commonplace subject matter have been an influence in the rise of new forms of figurative art in recent years. This new Realism in painting and sculpture, sometimes called Super-Realism, often draws on photographic sources and commercial advertising for its imagery, but it has made trompe-l'oeil illusionism viable once again without going to the lengths of fantastic invention or satirical commentary often associated with Pop Art. Photographic adaptation was already implied by the simplified visual definitions of art-world personalities who were among the favorite subjects of Alex Katz (b. 1927) in the late 1950s. In the 1960s, an intense fidelity to photographic models and an equally insistent formal structuring identified Photographic Realism, or post-Pop Realism, as an art pushed to extremes. The powerful nude studies of Philip Pearlstein (b. 1924) are harsh, deliberately ugly, anti-idealistic in their anatomical elaboration, and brutally explicit in their sexuality (plate 620). The abrupt, angular croppings of his figures add a further tension to his compositions.

Chuck Close (b. 1941) does enlargements of the isolated human head to colossal proportions, as in *Kent* (1971, plate 621), painted painstakingly with acrylic. It

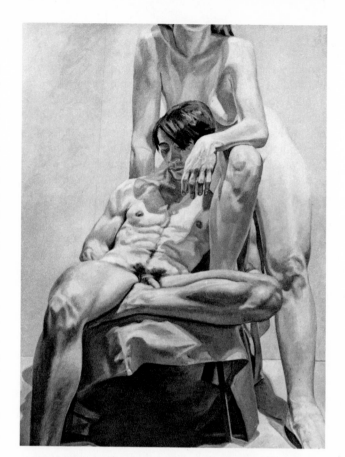

620 Philip Pearlstein. *Models in the Studio.* 1965. Oil on canvas, 72½ × 53¾". Allan Frumkin Gallery, New York

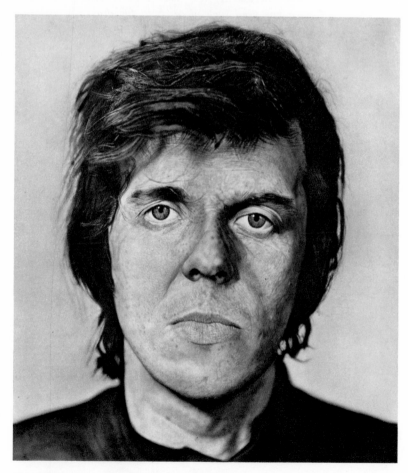

621 Chuck Close. *Kent.* 1971. Acrylic on canvas, 100 × 90". Art Gallery of Ontario, Toronto, Canada

Painting Since 1960   551

simulates the contemporary color photo even to the use of a grid of dots like those used in photomechanical reproductions. The meticulous technique of his Photo-Realism is designed to neutralize any possible emotional reaction to the object and to reduce the gargantuan image to nothing more than visual information about surface, depth of field, focus, and scale, rather than to psychological factors. English-born Malcolm Morley (b. 1931) actually painted his early works upside down, in order to deny the image importance and to concentrate on abstract elements of the painted surface.

Richard Estes (b. 1936) also began to forge novel expressive truths from the photographic image in the 1960s, concentrating on glistening showcases of shopping centers or upon theater marquees with a passion ironically contradicted by the dispassionate manner of his meticulous rendering (colorplate 94). Ralph Goings and Robert Bechtle (b. 1932) present the familiar world of motor vehicles. The gleam of their subjects is transplanted into an equally resplendent visual surface. The visual ironies stem from the vacuity of overfamiliar objects; the content is essentially uninteresting, but the artists are obsessed by the play of reflective surfaces and the magical illusion of even a commonplace subject.

(continued on page 569)

DECORATIVE ARTS

Jack Lenor Larsen (b. 1929) is one of the major practitioners of textile design for the power loom. Producing drapery and upholstery fabrics that are either made to order or available by the yard, he has brought his feel for texture and for mixtures of natural and synthetic yarns and his knowledge of the textiles of many cultures to a wide market. Such fabrics as Academia, *a design of small squares of platinum metallic fiber surrounded by raised natural wool (plate 622), have the feel of hand-woven material. Since his first success at New York's Lever House in 1952, Larsen has used such pieces both for draperies in large office buildings, and as upholstery material. His firm also produces carpeting that complements such designs.*

Another designer of contemporary fabrics is Louise Todd-Cope (b. 1930). Her wall hanging entitled Concerto *(plate 623) combines traditional weaving techniques with fibers used in an unconventional way and with nonfiber materials. Yet it is not unrelated to tradition; it preserves an interest in texture contrasts and the motif of a solid center with more delicate work thinning out and trailing off at the perimeter.*

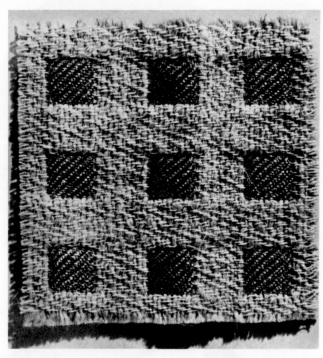

622 Jack Lenor Larsen, Inc. New York. *Academia.* Wool and metallic fiber upholstery in double twill weave, width c. 50″, repeat c. 2″.

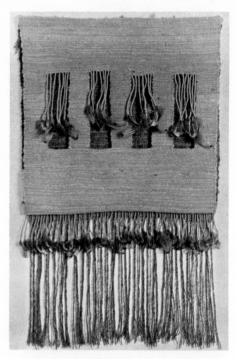

623 Louise Todd-Cope. *Concerto.* 1970. Wool, jute, and pheasant-feather wall hanging, 23 × 37″. Collection Helen Williams Drutt, Philadelphia

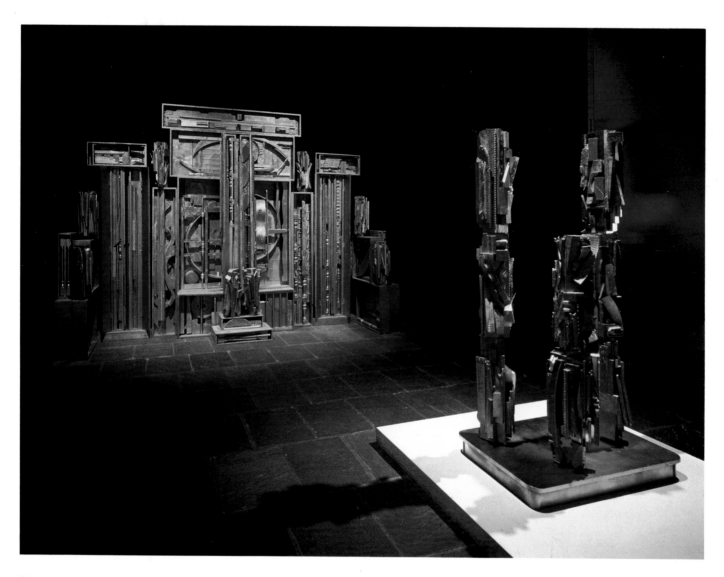

84 Louise Nevelson. *(left): An American Tribute to the British People.* 1960–65.
Painted wood, 10′2″ × 14′3″. The Tate Gallery, London. *(right): Sungarden No. 1.* 1964.
Painted wood, height 72″. Collection Mr. and Mrs. Charles M. Diker, New York

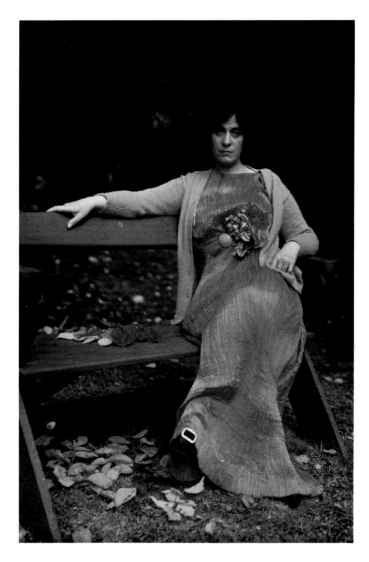

85 Alfred Stieglitz. *Mrs. Selma Schubart in a Yellow Dress.*
1907. Color photograph (Lumière Autochrome process).
The Metropolitan Museum of Art, New York.
The Alfred Stieglitz Collection, 1955

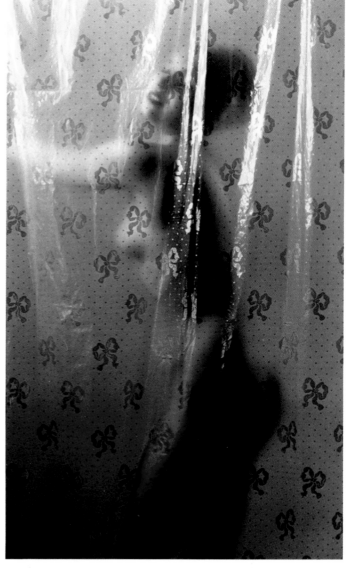

86 Paul Outerbridge. *Woman Behind Curtain.* 1937.
Color photograph (Carbro print).
Estate of Paul Outerbridge

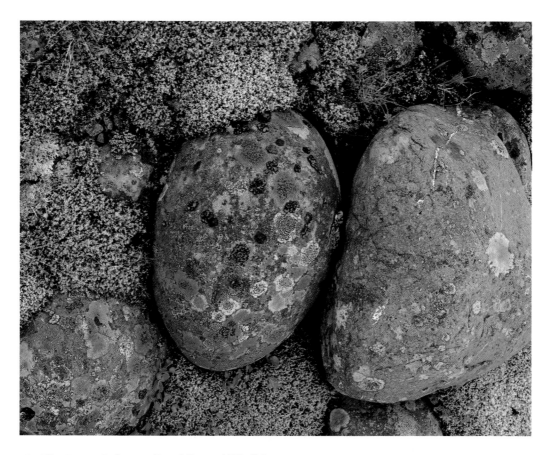

87   Eliot Porter. *Lichens on Round Stones*. 1972. Color
photograph (Carbro print). Courtesy the photographer

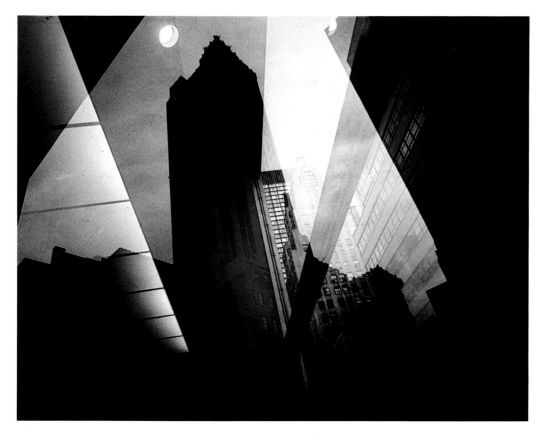

88   Ernst Haas. *New York Triangle*. 1965. Color photograph
(Polacolor). Magnum Photos, Inc.

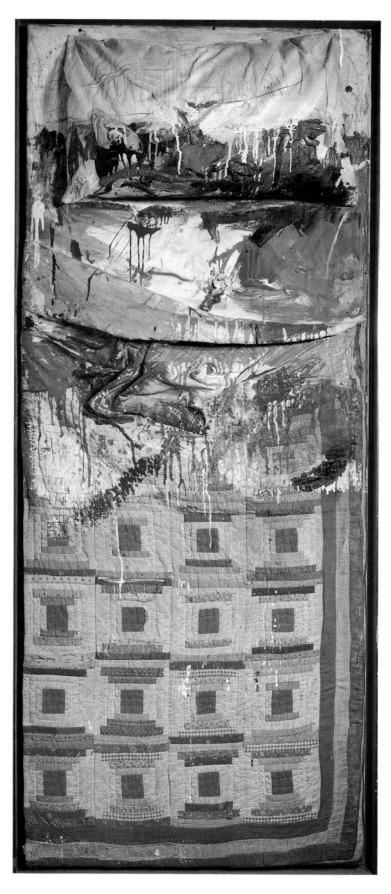

89   Robert Rauschenberg. *Bed*. 1955. Mixed media, 74 × 31″.
Collection Mr. and Mrs. Leo Castelli, New York

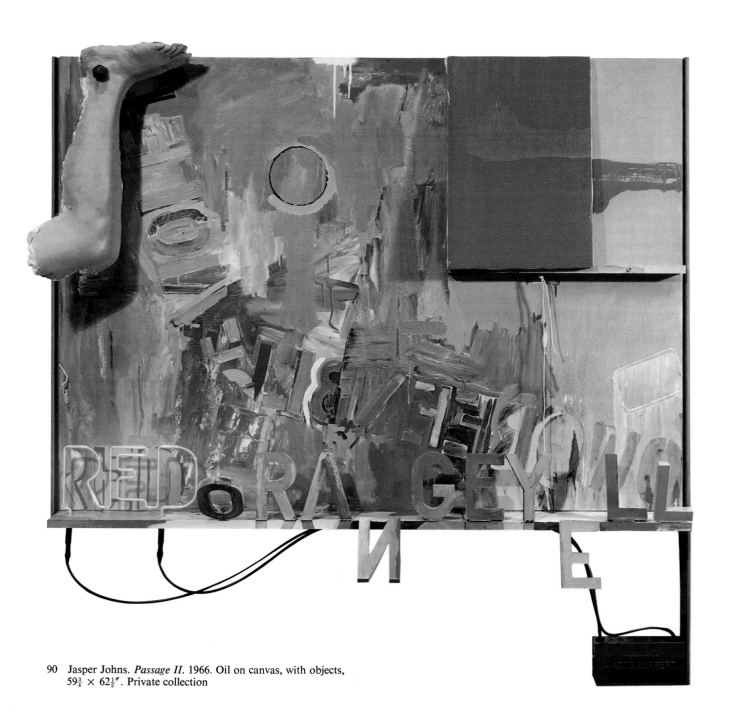

90   Jasper Johns. *Passage II*. 1966. Oil on canvas, with objects,
     59¾ × 62½″. Private collection

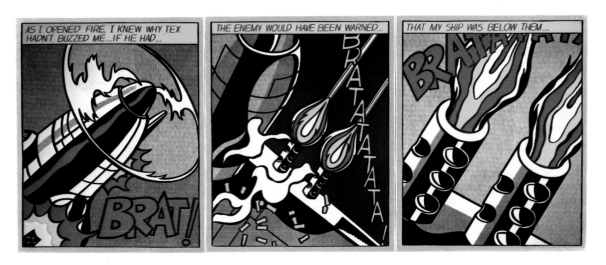

91 Roy Lichtenstein. *As I Opened Fire*. 1964. Magna on canvas, each panel 68 × 56″. Stedelijk Museum, Amsterdam

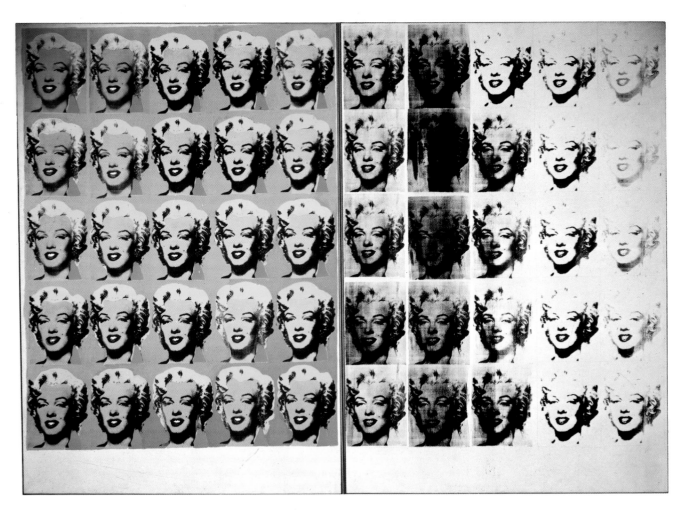

92 Andy Warhol. *Marilyn Monroe Diptych*. 1962. Acrylic on canvas, 82 × 144″. Collection Mr. and Mrs. Burton Tremaine, Meriden, Conn.

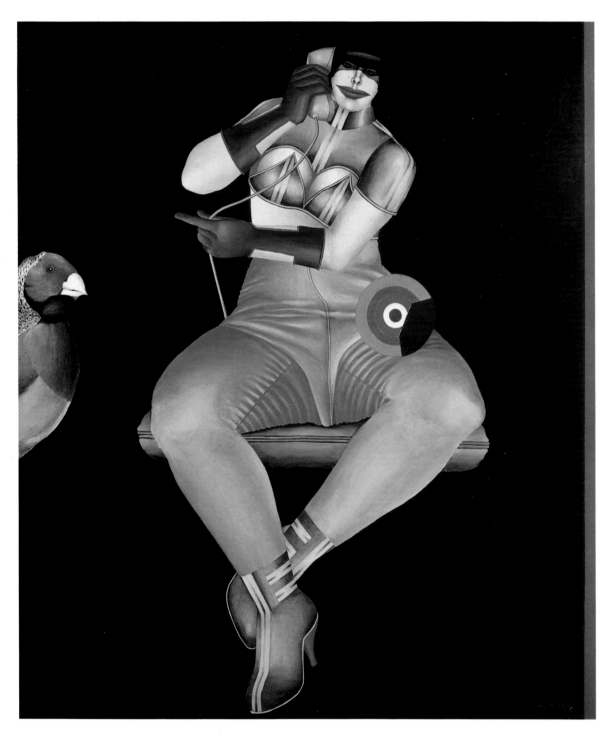

93   Richard Lindner. *Hello*. 1966. Oil on canvas, 70 × 60″.
Private collection

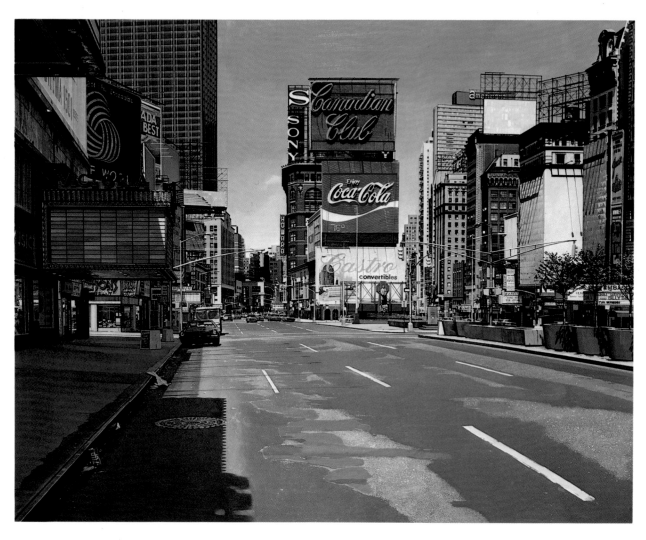

94   Richard Estes. *Canadian Club*. 1974. Oil on canvas, 48 × 60″.
     Collection Morton Neumann, Chicago

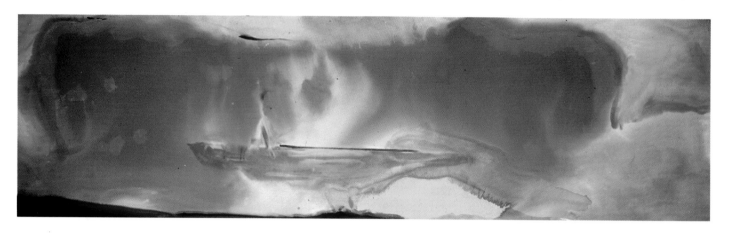

95 Helen Frankenthaler. *Movable Blue*. 1973. Acrylic on canvas,
70 × 243″. André Emmerich Gallery, New York

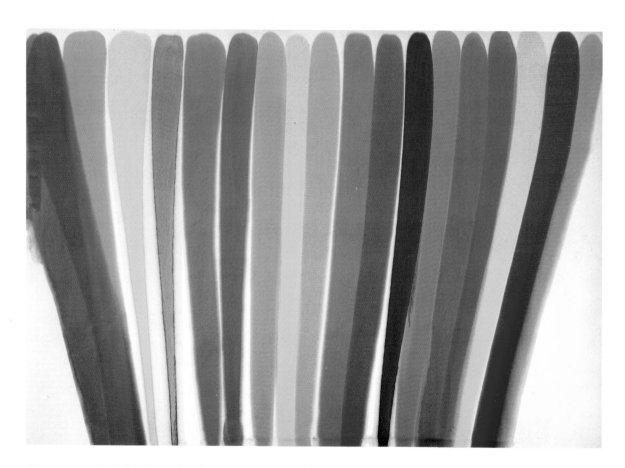

96 Morris Louis. *While*. 1960. Acrylic on canvas, $96\frac{1}{2} \times 136\frac{3}{8}″$.
Private collection

97 Kenneth Noland. *Burnt Beige*. 1975.
Magna on canvas, $96\frac{1}{2} \times 152\frac{1}{2}''$.
Leo Castelli Gallery, New York

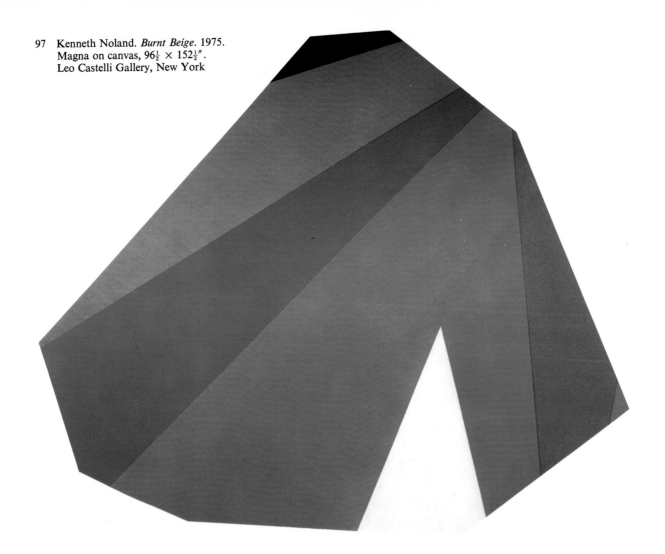

98 Ellsworth Kelly. *Two Panels: Black with Red Bar*. 1971.
Oil on canvas, 5'8″ × 10'. Leo Castelli Gallery, New York

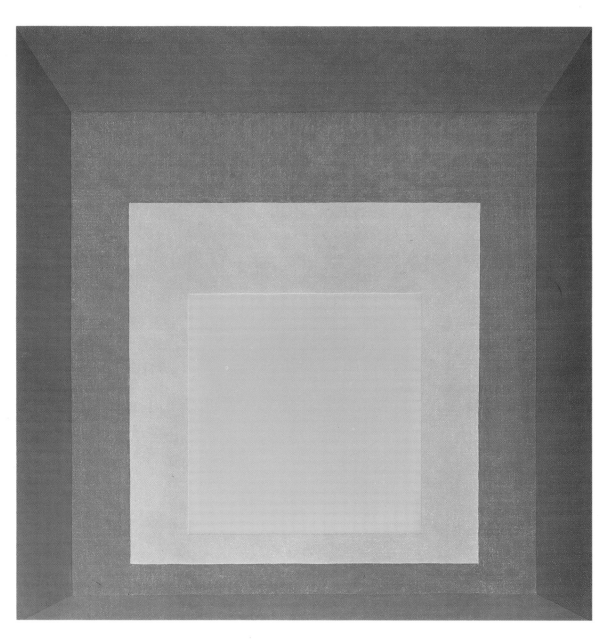

99   Josef Albers. *Homage to the Square: Apparition.* 1959. Oil on board,
      47½ × 47½″. The Solomon R. Guggenheim Museum, New York

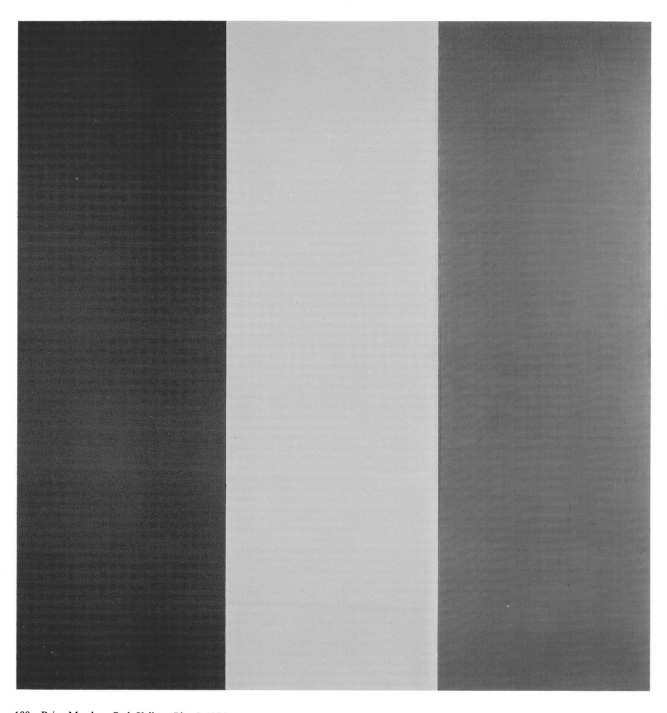

100   Brice Marden. *Red, Yellow, Blue I*. 1974.
Oil and wax on canvas, each panel 74 × 24″.
Albright-Knox Art Gallery, Buffalo, N.Y.

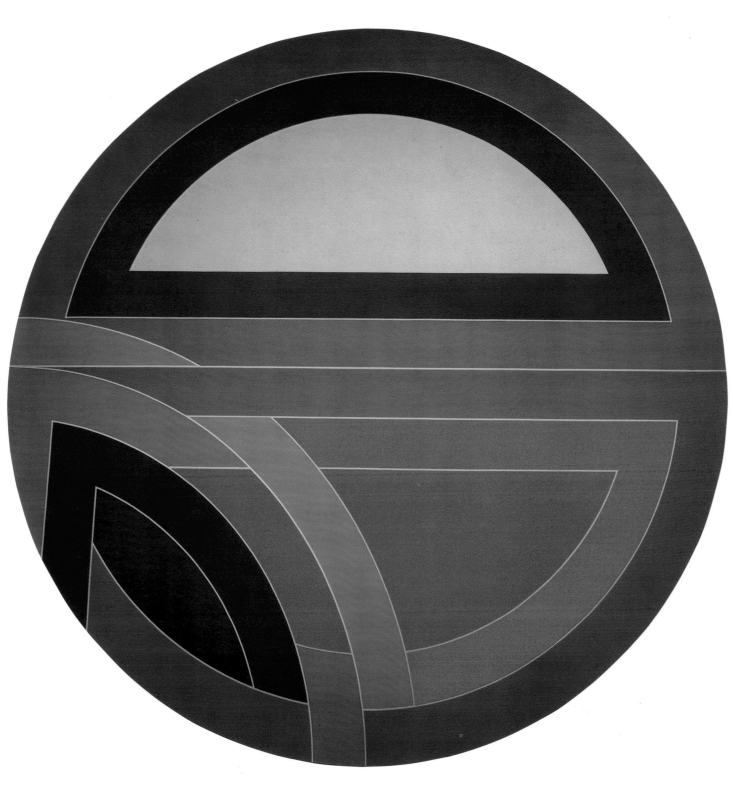

101 Frank Stella. *Sinjerli Variation I*. 1968. Fluorescent acrylic on canvas, diameter 10′.
Private collection

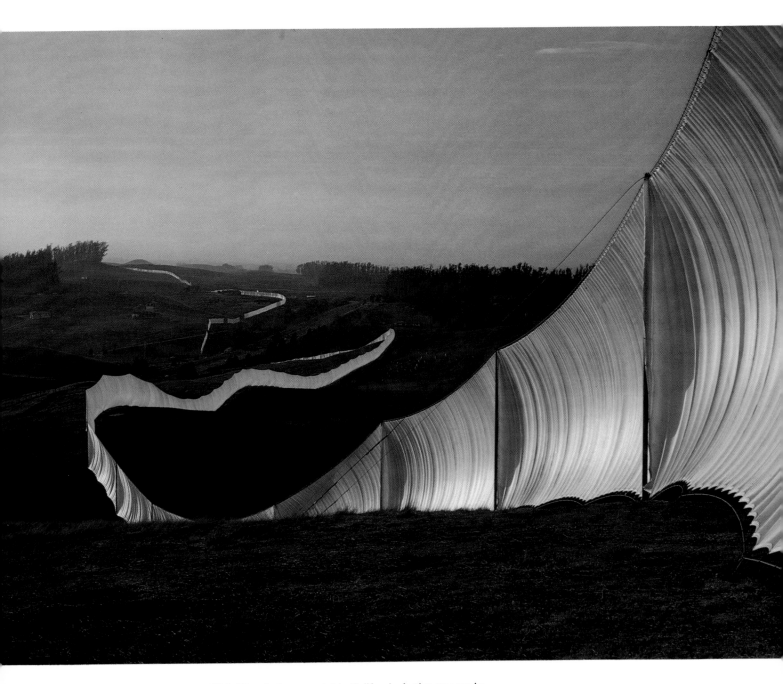

102   Christo. *Running Fence*. 1976. 24½-mile fence erected in California, lasting two weeks.
Courtesy the artist, New York

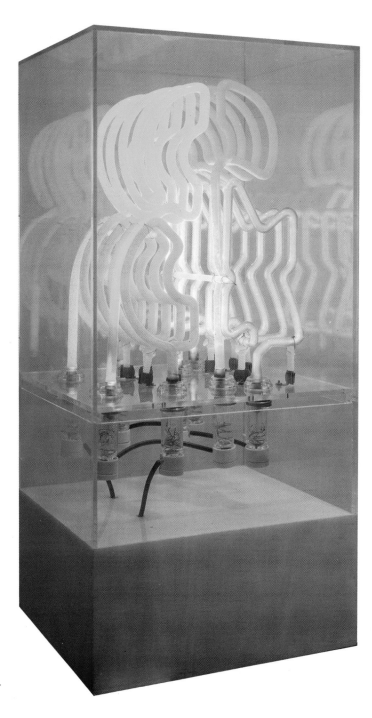

103 Chryssa. *Ampersand III*. 1965.
Neon lights in Plexiglas, height $30\frac{1}{4}''$.
Private collection

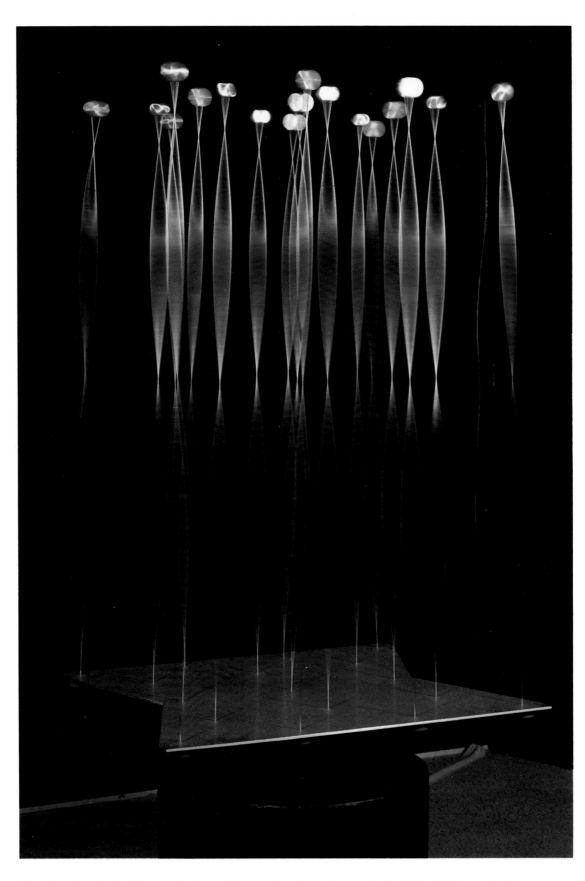

104 Wen-Ying Tsa'i. *Cybernetic Sculpture*. 1970. Stainless steel rods on motorized base, stroboscopic light, and microphone, height without base 45″. Collection the artist

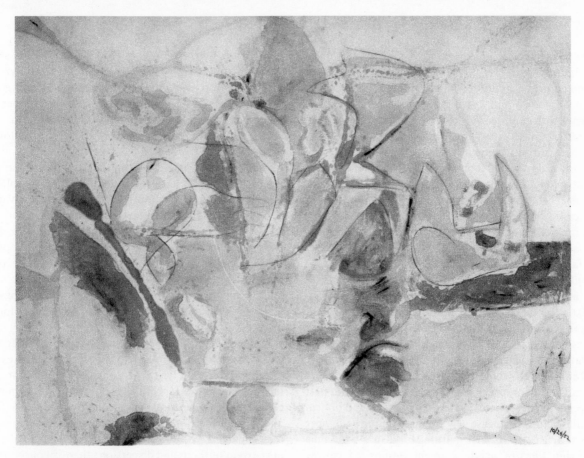

624 Helen Frankenthaler. *Mountains and Sea*. 1952. Oil on canvas, 7' 2⅞" × 9' 9¼". Collection the artist

(continued from page 552)
POST-PAINTERLY ABSTRACTION

While the new Realism and Pop Art were rather extreme reactions to Abstract Expressionism, the Post-Painterly Abstraction that emerged in the late 1950s and early 1960s was, at least in part, a continuation of certain of its important aspects. A radical new line of color-stain painting, opposed to de Kooning's opulent, loaded brushstrokes, made its appearance. It seemed to evolve through Sam Francis, or perhaps Helen Frankenthaler (see Chapter 22), to Morris Louis and then took a more rigorous geometric form in the work of Kenneth Noland. There was also an increasing interest among a large group of artists in symmetry, clear definition of shape, immaculate surface, and formal order, all of which opposed the free-wheeling invention, spontaneity, amorphous forms, and general messiness admired by the Action Painters. Soon the term "hard-edge" became current and popular. It was applied to Ellsworth Kelly (b. 1923), whose decisive development had taken place in Paris, removed entirely from the American experience of Action Painting; other artists, such as Leon Polk Smith, Alexander Liberman, and Al Held, made a loose group of related precisionist abstract artists.

These tendencies, however, were not identified with traditional geometric abstraction or with Constructivist examples based upon Mondrian and Malevich. The new American abstraction incorporated psychological ambiguity within its formal order and embodied the scale and energy associated with Action Painting. In place of the drama of personal creativity or physical engagement with medium, important new issues appeared in painting. A conceptual program and a depersonalized objectivity became decisive and controlling ideas for the younger artists. Barnett Newman provided a point of departure for color-field painting with romantic overtones, while Ad Reinhardt influenced a more self-contained, conventionalized, and repetitive or serial art in which color and atmosphere played only a marginal role.

Chromatic abstraction became a widespread trend only in the late 1950s. Beginning with her influential abstract landscape *Mountains and Sea* (1952, plate 624), Helen Frankenthaler pointed a new direction in American art. By pouring and running thinned paint washes down the canvas, she blurred and transformed the directional energies and brushstrokes of Action Painting. The wandering edges of her forms were determined only by gravity and the drying process. Thus color began to speak for itself, released from gesture and from romantic rhetoric of the "abstract sublime," and a new set of formal alternatives opened up to the artist.

A work such as *Movable Blue* (1973, colorplate 95) is distinguished by its monumental scale, mastery of color space and sheer aesthetic presence. The ease and confidence reflect a firm maturity, and her expression of an original color sensibility reminds us of both Matisse and Hans Hofmann. Frankenthaler combines spontaneity of handling with unexpected chromatic oppositions and evidence of an effusive, lyrical temperament under control. There are still vague metaphors of sky and water in her work today, even though pigment surface is more opulent, and they evoke the mood of her earliest paintings. She has recently abandoned the clearly defined shapes that recalled Matisse's large-scale cutouts for looser edges and a much thicker color paste on the unprimed canvas, modulated by a meandering line, which sometimes looks like a fault or crevice on a rock face.

Frankenthaler's development of her technical innovations into a strong personal style became a direct link in the sixties to the "stain" paintings of Morris Louis and Kenneth Noland, who later acknowledged her influence.

By age and origin Morris Louis (1912–1962) should be associated with the great pioneering generation of Pollock and Rothko, with whom he shared many formal characteristics. But his impact has been felt mainly in the past two decades, and his patent anonymity of style and optical dynamics helped to release new energies among a younger group of artists. In his first mature work, in 1954, Louis flowed thin films of acrylic pigment on unsized canvas to form faint, muted color shapes vaguely reminiscent of Action Painting, but less active and aggressive. The even

consistency of these diaphanous shapes, their slowed velocities, and relatively indeterminate flow paralyzed the urgent expressiveness of Action Painting. Defining edges resulted from the natural process of drying rather than from any expressive inflection of the hand. In *While* (1960, colorplate 96), transparent overlays of color give way to open and clearly differentiated ribbons of distinct hue and shape. Progressively in his art, individual color notes detached themselves from the flurry of soft tints and achieved a new chromatic limpidity and vividness. The large scale and boldness of color in his paintings derive from the Abstract Expressionist experience. However, their optical rather than material emphasis prophesied a new kind of color-field painting—more objective in character, liberated from the autographic marks and the emotionalism of the immediate pictorial past.

Louis's veils and overlapped washes of thin color led, in due course, to the structural rigor of the work of Kenneth Noland (b. 1924)—targets, chevrons, diagonals, and other emblem forms (plate 625). There was an evident progression from a lyrical art to a new iconic form, away from accident and profusion of means to symmetry, codification of gesture, and economy. Noland's forms and signs are clearly defined, simple, almost banal, and they expand to the limits of his field, creating an alternating current of focus and dispersion; there is concentration within the emblem form, and yet a peripheral sense of color expansion beyond the framing rectangle. His recent shaped canvases represent a significant departure from the formally ordered work of the past, in which ingratiating color and lucid geometric structure were elegantly synthesized, but the intellectual toughness of the work of the sixties persists, recalling the series of parallel stripes and overlapped rectangles of those years. In the new work (colorplate 97) there has been a deliberate and healthy intensification of emotion and of the sense of risk. Abrupt diagonal perimeters of color stripes create imbalance and spatial dislocation, and unexpectedly dissonant chromatic combinations represent a new mood of aggressiveness. Flat grounds of opaque color are relieved by a kind of granulated, atmospheric transparency; plunging spatial perspectives run off the edges of the canvas at extreme angles, creating a deliberate confusion of flatness and depth. The result reveals a capacity for emotional expression only hinted at in Noland's earlier paintings.

Whereas chance or irregularity was once equated with personal authenticity, by the 1960s formal decorum became the artist's marked preference, and it acquired unforeseen possibilities. Ellsworth Kelly (b. 1923) created hard-edge forms scrupulously clean of any detail and surface irregularity which might betray the individual hand. He managed a variety of inventions and new levels of sensuousness within his strict forms. Figure and field each became tangible realities, and the simplest configurations, in heroic scale, carried a dramatic impact without surrendering visual complexity (colorplate 98). In their

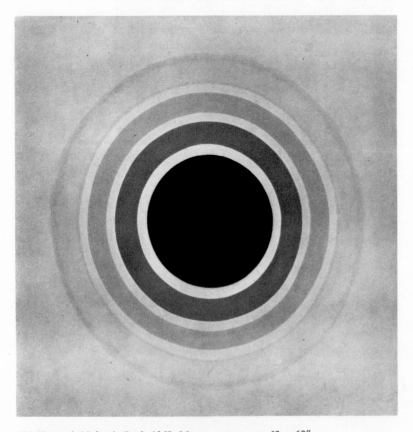

625 Kenneth Noland. *Rush.* 1960. Magma on canvas, 60 × 60″.
Collection Mrs. H. Gates Lloyd, Haverford, Pa.

"shaped canvases" Kelly, Charles Hinman, and Frank Stella in America, Richard Smith in England, and many others created an international mode of painting in three dimensions which opposed the Expressionist art of the Action Painters. The shaped canvas emphasized the ambiguities between the pictorial and the structural, between visual illusion and the three-dimensional object. The contoured stretcher provided one kind of definition, and the painted forms on the surface made another image and visual metaphor.

OP ART

Although color image and color-field painting became central aesthetic issues in American art of the sixties, the more conventional aspects of optical art, or Op Art, did not excite the American artistic imagination very deeply or for long. Josef Albers (1888–1976) was the primary exception to the rule, and he deserves priorities in the invention of the mode of perceptual art, which dates back to his Bauhaus experiments with illusionistic woodcuts in the early 1930s. From 1949 until his death, he repetitively painted nests of color squares in different dominant hues and sizes and identical modular formats. His celebrated *Homage to the Square* theme was the first unequivocal example of the "serial" composition in American art (colorplate 99). It occupied him exclusively as a compositional structure over the last two decades of his life and has no match for constancy of purpose, incorruptibility, and sheer obsessiveness except perhaps Mondrian's famous grid. Albers's squares of infinitely varied and nuanced color are, in effect, his *Art of Fugue*. Like Bach, he had a genius for stating and restating the same themes and variations, without exhausting their vitality or mercurial unpredictability. Although Albers's influence as a teacher was considerable, first at Black Mountain College and then at Yale, only one of his students, Richard Anuszkiewicz (b. 1930), has seriously and profitably pursued his investigations of the "interaction of colors" and perceptual ambiguities (plate 626).

PERCEPTUAL, MINIMALIST, AND POST-MINIMALIST PAINTING

Color-field painting of the sixties, even when of a more conventional nature, tended to divest itself of object status and to dematerialize the pictorial means. The large spray paintings of Jules Olitski (b. 1922) made their particular impact by diffusing the luminous effect of color so that both the rectangular boundaries of the frame and the material substance of the paint seem almost incidental to the perceived intensities of continuous color sensation. Structural accents and the internal formal complications of a meandering perimeter of agitated paint streaks play off against an alternately faint or subliminally bright color field, creating an impression of purity of feeling. Later Olitski began to employ less seductive visual effects in favor of opaque and materially insistent paint surface.

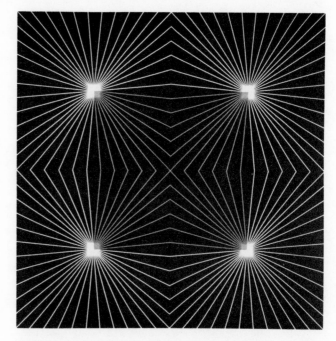

626 Richard Anuszkiewicz. *Coruscate*. 1965. Liquitex, 24 × 24″. Collection Harold and Alice Ladas, New York

He was followed in this challenging direction by Larry Poons (b. 1937) and a number of other color painters. In place of breathing color, subtle vibrations, and transparency, there was evidence of a new effort to explore pigment itself and to use its expressive, brute materiality for a more powerful emotional statement. In recent years Poons has cultivated deliberate gaucheries and a new crudeness of manner, presenting an obsessive downpour of melting, viscose color streaks in thickly textured paint. In some works the paint field seems at first glance positively ugly in its muddy coloration, conveying a sense of anarchy that contrasts dramatically with the lucidity and orderliness of his earlier exposition of optical energy in vibrant elliptical dots. His current "painterly" style, like that of Olitski, represents a fresh synthesis of the perceptual and material aspects of painting, probably in acute reaction to the popularity and facile pictorial effects of international Op Art.

Within the broad current of renewed "painterly" painting in the late sixties, one of the most interesting aspects was a more sensuous and material expressiveness (in contrast to the austerities of Minimal sculpture and geometric art) in the rediscovered work of Cy Twombly (b. 1929). His jumbled composite of painting and drawing synthesizes aspects of Expressionism, Surrealist automatism, and postwar Action Painting in an original amalgam. Today his work enjoys increasing respect after a period of relative neglect. The sketchbook freedom of his linear motifs affirms the spontaneous creative moment, but his nervous scribbles and paint marks are also like diaristic reminiscences. Handwriting acts as a half-way house between an identifiable imagery and geometric or biomorphic abstraction, recalling Jackson Pollock. For

627 Agnes Martin. *Untitled, No. 44.* 1974. Acrylic, pencil, and gesso, 6 × 6'.
Collection Harry and Linda Macklowe, New York

Twombly, drawing is an energizing source of visual creation and an autobiographical memory book of events. In fact, many of the finest artists of the 1970s have conferred upon drawing a new role, which mediates between painting's dual character as corporeal object and spatial diagram.

The paintings of Agnes Martin (b. 1912) represent another fascinating revival of a modified perceptual art which utilizes grids and simple visual systems. She has become increasingly admired in the late 1960s and the seventies as reductionist and perceptual modes of abstraction gained favor among younger artists. Martin's concern is only superficially with the activation of perception. She seems to wish to renew Constructivist tradition, but without its narrow ideological program. An explanation of the profound influence of her work may be her ability to resolve contradictory concerns. Her work is based on geometric structure, or parallel color bands, and it acknowledges surface in its material limits. Yet her form dematerializes into a visual field, a new presence of light (plate 627). The ability to balance the sense that the picture is no more than its physical attributes and yet has a subliminal spiritual life undoubtedly accounts for her importance in the minds of admiring contemporaries.

Among the outstanding "Post-Minimalist" artists who have been engaged by the same pictorial contradictions which Agnes Martin's paintings so elegantly straddle are

628 Robert Ryman. *Varese Wall.* 1975. Vinyl acetate emulsion on wood,
8 × 24'. John Weber Gallery, New York

629 Robert Mangold. *Circle Painting No. 7.* 1973.
Oil on composition board, diameter 6'.
Collection Mr. and Mrs. S. I. Newhouse, New York

Robert Ryman, Brice Marden, Robert Mangold, and Dorothea Rockburne. Like other leading figures of his generation, Ryman (b. 1930) has worked on such unconventional surfaces as steel and aluminum and used acrylics, mat enamel, and other materials to emphasize the importance of tangible surface. He is one of the most influential painters of early middle age, and his keen awareness of medium, support—whether metal, paper, or canvas—and brushstroke, and his consistent use of monochromes, usually white, reflect a new and fruitful preoccupation with the given physical conditions and internal syntax of painting. The result is an oeuvre that at first sight may look programmed and ideological in the narrowness of its controlling ideas, yet manages to emerge as a highly nuanced and optically rewarding exercise in sensibility. In recent years he has expanded his scale and tested environmental spaces with wall-like surfaces which stand physically away from the actual gallery walls, covered with razor-thin layers of mat white paint. Their scale is heroic, difficult to encompass as a single visual field within a confined gallery space. At the same time,

works such as *Varese Wall* (1975, plate 628) establish important, if elementary, distinctions between the art-making activity and dumb objects, art as an expansive environmental cliché and Ryman's stubbornly intact sense of the work of art as a rare and integral image.

Brice Marden (b. 1938) also accepts the condition of flatness of the canvas support, and surface as a physical reality, on which he works in a medium of wax and oil in muted colors, usually close to asphalt and putty in hue. Since his stretchers are massive in depth and streaked with visible, brushy paint built up to a palpable materiality, the effect locates the picture plane off the wall, as a wall-like surface in its own right (colorplate 100). In a recent series using primary colors in equal-sized, stacked rectangles, Marden abandoned his somber tones for a more aggressive chromatic scale. His independent and formally rigorous, yet intuitive, drawings of ambiguous spatial grids are integrated into his painting concepts and procedures.

Robert Mangold (b. 1937) uses tinted, shiny composition boards in eccentric shapes with ruled, subdivided interior circle segments to give the painting surface the mirrorlike opaqueness and finish of industrial products (plate 629). Yet the experience of his work is subtle, more like that of Martin or Marden than a commercial plastic artifact. Like the work of all the "Post-Minimalists" under discussion, his requires intense mental concentration on the part of the spectator and produces a slow and prolonged revelation. He paints on board with a spray gun and roller, always in monochrome. In whatever color key, he maintains the same objective of establishing a delicate equilibrium between atmospheric color space and his sense of art as a depersonalized, architectural structure.

In the past Dorothea Rockburne's drawings and paper folds created an intricate interplay of mathematical concepts and permutations of "set theory" ideas. Her art was both cerebral and sensuous in the care with which she manipulated her surfaces; as she has explained, it was based on "making parts that form units that go together to make larger units." Her more recent work takes advantage of the textured surface of raw linen and utilizes a natural brown hue to create a dramatic impact as a shaped canvas (plate 630). The subdivided, prismatic sections often recall Mangold's geometric art. Any sense of color and sensuous surface as a source of aesthetic pleasure is repudiated, however, as an accidental pictur-

esque feature in Rockburne's austere program. Her work brilliantly and delicately balances perceptual pleasure and logical structure in modified three-dimensional objects which aggressively intrude upon our own space.

Perhaps the most decisive impulse in creating the influential new genre of the painting as object has come from Frank Stella (b. 1936). Beginning with his black pinstripe paintings as far back as 1958–60, continuing more recently in his protractor patterns of segmented arcs in vivid color (colorplate 101), and then in his freely constructed reliefs and Expressionist abstractions, he has reversed the roles of geometry and Bauhaus design. His black paintings opened up new expressive possibilities which helped to force a fundamental change in artistic outlook. Subsequently, Stella's series paintings and shaped canvases in permutations of Vs, parallelograms, rhomboids, hexagons, and circle fragments have continued to play down traditional composition by repetition and standardization of shape, thus focusing on the painting as a single image and as an object (plate 631). The particular kinds of opacities and redundancies which make these surfaces and patterns look so predictable and impassive have, in fact, helped to generate contemporary forms in the realm of three-dimensional constructions perhaps even more than in the pictorial medium. Stella's painting is, in fact, more that of a structurist than a Post-Painterly

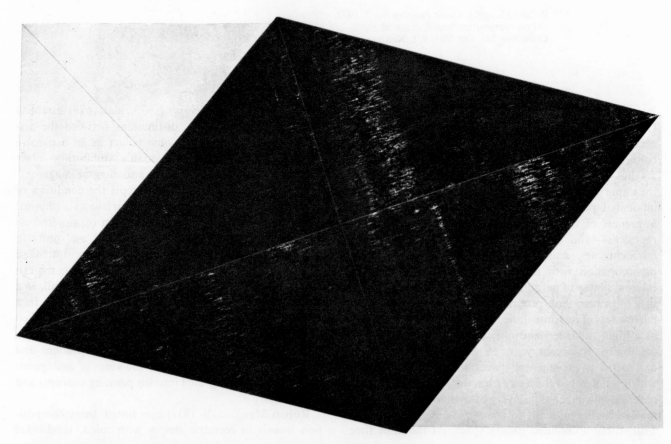

630 Dorothea Rockburne. *Golden Section Painting: Parallelogram and Square Separated.*
1974. Gesso and pencil on linen, 6′ 4⅜″ × 8′ 8½″. The Museum of Modern Art, New York.
Purchased with the aid of funds from the National Endowment for the Arts and an anonymous donor

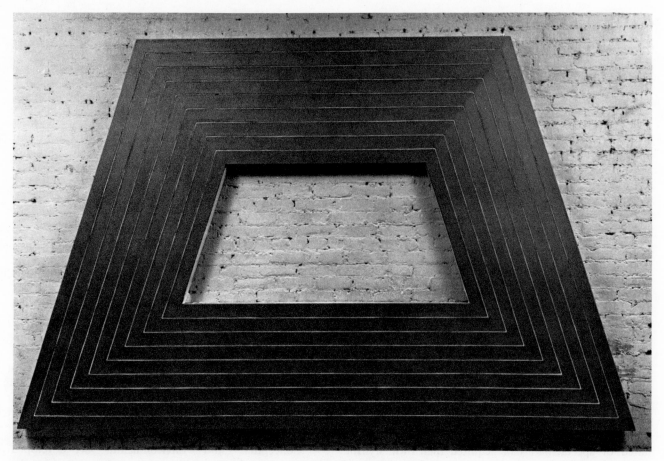

631 Frank Stella. *Ileana Sonnabend.* 1963. Oil on canvas, 7′ 5″ × 10′ 7″. Collection the artist

Abstractionist. His concern has been consistently not so much with color or pictorial illusion as with painting as an object—a thing of literal and denotative meaning which exists in its own right and is entirely self-referring.

In the late 1960s, the tenor of the arts, despite elaborate rationalizations of subjective aesthetic positions, was protest, an engagement with real, rather than ivory-tower, issues. For younger artists of that period, sculpture seemed a more attractive alternative than painting, because of its greater reality, its inescapable object quality, which only a few painters of the period, notably Stella, were able fully to realize. However, it was from his

example, and from the noncompositional field approach to painting found before him in the work of Pollock, Rothko, Newman, and Reinhardt, that a new and influential abstract art in three dimensions arose (see Chapter 23). Meanwhile, the revitalized status of painting-as-object was being challenged on ethical grounds. A radical younger generation felt that an artist in any medium might fare better if his work could be evaluated by criteria other than market price or role as a commodity in the museum and commercial gallery system (see Chapter 27).

27
The Dematerialized Object

In the late 1960s art in America and throughout the world began to expand its range of possibilities to unforeseen limits. The idea of a more flexible art seemed broad enough to include vast Earthworks projects, literally covering miles of terrain, videotape events, a series of photographs of parking lots, or cornflakes scattered in an open urban area. Art could be a computerized drawing of a nude or a web of laser beams covering three city blocks. It could be grease, dirt, leaves, or ice blocks melting on a gallery floor, or it could be merely verbal statements and print. All these kinds of art, whether modestly understated or spectacular, had acquired their own stylistic labels— "Land Art," "Performance Art," "Body Art," "Process Art," or whatever. What unites them is the drastic change from tradition that has been recognized under a number of more general rubrics, among them "Post-Studio Art" and "Conceptual Art."

The change in the nature of the work of art and in the way we regard its ultimate value came, to some extent, as a reaction to the commercialism of the art scene in the sixties, when the market for some paintings in fashion reached a peak of inflated prices and falsified values. In that atmosphere the new avant-garde began to demand that art no longer be treated as a commodity but find support in society as a self-justifying activity of intrinsic worth to the human spirit and to our scheme of civilized values. This sort of idealism and protest is not uncommon among artists, but only recently has there been a determination to create a dematerialized or nonobject art, freed from collectibility and profiteering by resale.

At the same time a change also took place in the structure of the art world. About 1967 nonobject art sprang up independently in several countries, and with it the transmission of art today has become truly global. Little time or energy is needed to transport entire exhibitions of statements by the artist (videotapes, photographs, and the like) anywhere in the world; and no particular exhibition center is required, since the work can exist simultaneously in various places. Furthermore, most of the artists concerned are extremely articulate, so that they need not await critical approval to sanction their efforts or make their work exportable.

The rapidity of artistic change in the 1960s was unusual even in a period accustomed to the swift dispersal of outmoded styles into inglorious obsolescence. The accelerated pace of innovation may have reflected the widespread sense of social despair and of governmental incapacity to halt wars or assure human survival in the poisoned atmosphere of planet earth. This new mood of global pessimism probably contributed to artistic innovation and the uninhibited risk-taking apparent on all sides.

"Conceptual" and "Environmental" art developed directly from structurist and Minimal sculpture of the 1960s. By the close of that decade, a remarkable variety of new sculpture and other three-dimensional forms had challenged the dominance of painting. Sculpture had so extended traditional definitions of medium that it could, with validity, be discussed as dust, literature, accident, nature, scientific illustration, theater, dance, or pedagogy. Increasingly, the articulated volumes or the physical presence traditionally associated with a sculptured object was abandoned in favor of a process in time, a performance, an idea, or an action, rather than a stable and tangible physical structure.

An example of the ephemeral physical object was Christo's *Running Fence* (1976, colorplate 102), a 24.5-mile-long, 18-foot-high translucent fabric fence erected by students, supervised by engineers, in northern California. Like so many of Christo's ambitious "packagings," whether of buildings or of landscape, the point of this temporary monument, which was dismantled after two weeks, was to widen public consciousness of the nature of art outside the museum context. The result was a financially extravagant work of spectacular beauty, undulating like a line drawing on a titanic scale in the changing light of the California landscape. But it also had significant sociological content, in bringing together so many elements of the planning of a contemporary art work in progress, with a direct effect on the lives of landowners, engineers, public officials, students, and casual observers.

THE CONCEPTUAL APPROACH

A German artist who has long worked in the United States, Hans Haacke, was one of the first to signal the significant change from object-making, which involved material processes, to the study and presentation of process and "systems" themselves in a purely conceptual approach (plate 632). As early as 1963 Haacke had conceived of new applications of the idea of "systems" to art and to natural phenomena, which he subjected to conditions of change in permissive environmental situations. Having abandoned the illusionism and willed artifice of conventional art, he turned to the forces of nature as his prime subject or "system." He was first known for his indoor "condensation boxes." Reacting to changing temperature conditions, these transparent cubes produced a continuous condensation of a little distilled water; the ever-varied patterns of droplets forming on the interior Plexiglas surfaces of his boxes became visible graphs of these conditions. His critical involvement with time and with patterns of physical transformation became an increasingly important factor in "Earth Art," "Process Art," and the emerging "Conceptual Art." The interest in systems (whether physical, biological, cybernetic, or finally societal) later continued with Haacke's serial photographs of seagulls and other natural phenomena.

Haacke also proposed a museum show listing property holdings in Manhattan, with photographs of slum and middle-class real estate—a system which inevitably would have revealed the interlocking character of ownership and might have embarrassed some church groups implicated as slumlords. Another recent exhibition contained pointed social ironies in presenting pious public-relations statements by well-known business leaders of corporations with aspirations to support the arts.

To an extraordinary degree, the last years of the 1960s saw idea rather than physical mass or visual definition become the controlling feature of art. Sol LeWitt (b. 1929) described the idea as "the machine that makes the work." The artist's aim, he wrote, is "not to instruct the viewer, but to give him information. Whether the viewer understands this information is incidental to the artist." The object became the visual residue or end product of a highly calculated and rationalized action. Much of the traditional satisfaction with sensuous form and structured composition was replaced by the pleasure of almost blindly working out an intellectual problem. Despite the value placed on cerebral process, the character of the end product nevertheless remained, in LeWitt's words, "intuitive."

Although probably best known for his austere, Minimalist sculptures (plate 633), LeWitt also began in the late 1960s to design influential large wall drawings, ex-

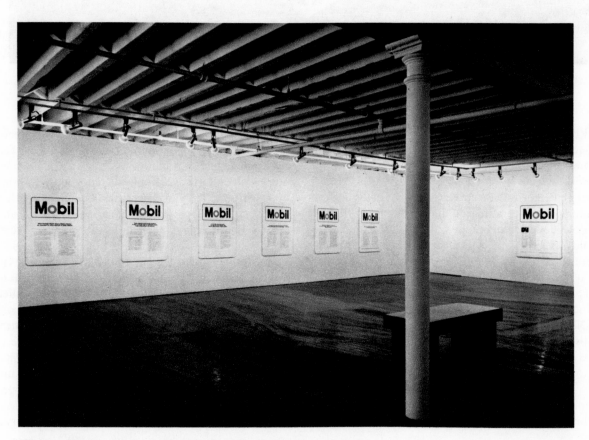

632 Hans Haacke. *The Good Will Umbrella.* 1976. Wall-mounted placards, reproduction, and text. John Weber Gallery, New York

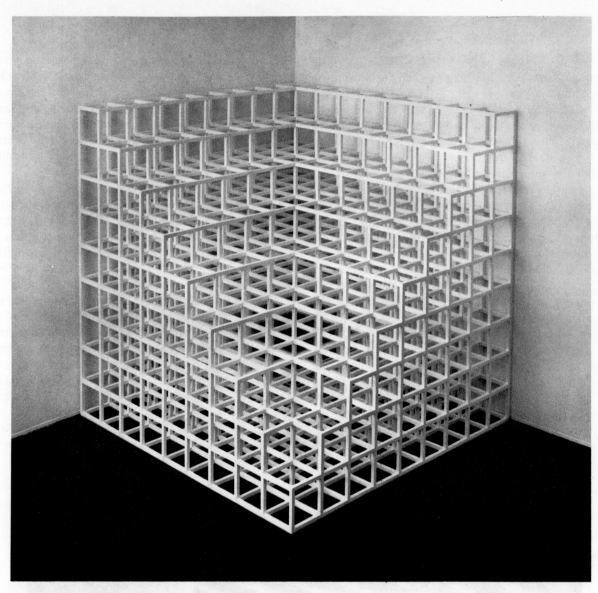

633 Sol LeWitt. *Corner Piece, No. 3.* 1976. White-painted wood, 43¼ × 43¼ × 43¼". Morton G. Neumann Family Collection, Chicago

ecuted by other hands, in which the consistent clarity of his concepts and ideas was equally evident. They were sometimes based on simple geometric figures, but he has also worked from a program of random lines, always following a detailed written prescription. Even though the governing ideas are stringent and methodical in their scrupulous documenting of idea, the results demonstrate sensibility as well as theoretical considerations. Of these wall drawings LeWitt wrote: "I wanted to do a work of art that was as two-dimensional as possible. It seems more natural to work directly on the walls than to make a construction, and then put the construction on the wall. . . . Different draftsmen produce lines darker or lighter and closer or farther apart. As long as they are consistent, there is no preference."

PERFORMANCE AND BODY ART

Conceptual Art has flourished not only in the realm of ideas but also in action, especially in performances of a

theatrical nature which involved the artist's awareness of his own body as topography or as an instrument for the ritual enactment of primitive feelings. In dramatic panto-mime and a narrative of body contortions, transmitted by video tape to TV screen, Bruce Nauman, Keith Sonnier, Vito Acconci, William Wegman, Peter Campus, Dennis Oppenheim, and many other artists have envisioned themselves as solitary performers. They seemed almost indifferent to the public audience, willfully cut off from it, like characters in the dramas of Beckett or Ionesco and acting out their private alienation and suffering. More recently they have adopted a mood of high comedy in a new kind of soliloquy utilizing the most elementary contact with their own physical existence. As the critic Michael Kirby wrote in his book *The Art of Time. . .* (1972): "In the new art form. . . the 'thing' has moved inside the body so to speak. The actions of the person himself become the object of his own attention."

The theatrical character of much contemporary performance art evolves from the Happenings of the late 1950s and from new ideas about the actual theater transmitted by Antonin Artaud, who remarked, in "The Theater of Cruelty" (a chapter in *The Theater and Its Double*, New York, 1958): "Instead of continuing to rely upon texts considered definitive and sacred, it is essential to put an end to the subjugation of the theater to the text, and to recover the notion of a kind of unique language halfway between gesture and thought." Another source of the unsettling sadomasochistic imagery that made its appearance in art of the late 1960s, besides the ritual "Theater of Cruelty," were violent public events such as the interminable Vietnam conflict, still dominating the TV screen. By the seventies, however, with the termination of the Vietnam conflict, the *Zeitgeist* in America began to change. The sense of commitment of the sixties turned to the post-Watergate disenchantment with the political process. A new kind of narcissistic and "loner" mentality began to permeate all areas of culture, and in the visual arts it dominated solitary video and performance art events, where analogies could be drawn to popular forms of meditation, withdrawal, and self-realization. The shift to more private and even solipsistic art forms became evident in the obsessive emphasis on artistic biography in videotapes.

Vito Acconci was one of the most intimately revealing and sensational of the first performance artists, who used their bodies as an expressive terrain in a manner strangely related to Earthworks. After he had executed several outdoor land pieces, Acconci began to treat his body as a "place" by creating a "sore" on his arm after rubbing it,

and then having it photographed periodically over a period of an hour. The willful infliction of pain and self-punishment have since figured prominently in his work. Some time ago the critic Max Kozloff defined "Body Art" as a condition wherein "the body is artistically dissociated from the person." Using the body for symbolic and expressive purposes, Acconci approaches in power and brutality the tortured imagery of Europe's most influential innovator in body works and performance art, Joseph Beuys. Acconci's self-referential dramas have magical and primitivist connotations (plate 634). They are ritualized enactments of feelings of protest, and they quite frequently contain elements of social and sexual content of a provocative nature that invites self-examination.

Dennis Oppenheim followed a pattern of development similar to Acconci's. After making Earthworks in the late sixties, and body works in the early seventies, Oppenheim attempted a varied expressive synthesis involving performance events, videotape, and film, as well as object art. Like Acconci, Oppenheim has connections with the more violent and sadistic tendencies of Surrealism. Because of the psychic intensity of his work, he has been called a "shaman."

Bruce Nauman's early work recorded the simple repetitive actions of his studio life, in films, videotape, and objects that displayed a Duchampian nonchalance. He characteristically employed casts in wax-covered cloth taken of his own body as an expressive field and involved them with the ambiguities of subjective feelings and ideas of extension and placement. His work questions his at-

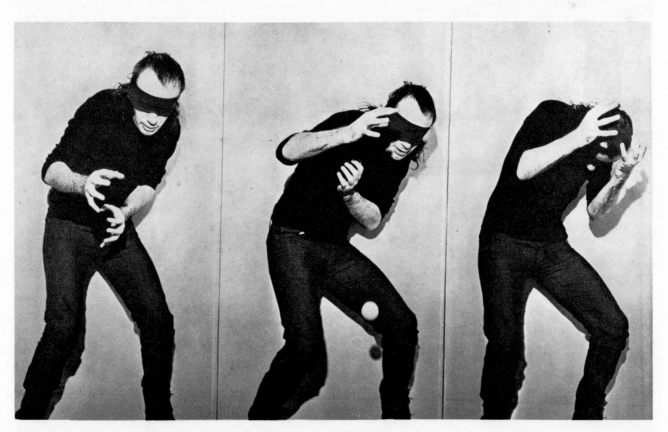

634 Vito Acconci. *Blindfolded Catching Piece.* 1970. Black-and-white Super-8 film, 16 mm., 3-minute exposure. John Gibson Gallery, New York

titudes toward his own body and his behavior as an artist. Wegman is a younger West Coast video artist who utilizes his own deadpan Buster Keaton image, his family, and very often his dog, called Man Ray, as well as other aspects of his domestic environment to create an eccentric and extremely comical visual narrative. His work is related to Conceptual Art in its perceptual interests, and to body and performance art in its spatial and personal concerns.

SPACE–TIME CONCERNS: PROCESS ART

Important aspects of performance and video art were anticipated between 1966 and 1969 by a number of significant exhibitions that explored unfamiliar materials and, by implication, the dimension of time. Although these exhibitions seemed opposed in spirit to the dematerialized art of the Conceptualists, they were, in fact, closely related to the space–time concerns of the more disembodied and cerebral art forms. Artists introduced flexible materials which lent themselves to visible manipulation, including even organic matter, which changed progressively in the course of an exhibition. Artistic "procedures," the "process," that went into the making of a work began to assume more critical interest than the end product. As early as 1966, the critic Lucy Lippard assembled an exhibition called *Eccentric Abstraction* at New York's Fischbach Gallery, and there a new kind of

material object—shabby, soft, perishable, and spatially unsubstantial—made its appearance. Such malleable materials, by their nature, preserved a visible record of process as the work evolved. Among the artists Miss Lippard showed were Eva Hesse, Keith Sonnier, Bruce Nauman, Louise Bourgeois, and Alice Adams. Two years later, in 1968, some of these artists and others exhibited even freer, more dispersive works in a show organized for the Leo Castelli warehouse spaces (plate 635) by Robert Morris, who rationalized the tendency in two *Artforum* articles under the designation of "antiform." Morris declared: "Random piling, loose stacking, handling, give passing form to the material. Chance is accepted and indeterminacy is implied."

Painting, too, began to approximate some of these antiformal effects and values. Richard Tuttle's unframed, dyed, nailed-up pieces of cloth (plate 636) seemed at the time to comment on painting as an "anxious object"—more object than framed pictorial enclosure of illusionistic space. Thus the development from art object to idea art was full of contradictions. Order and disorder, random and systemic effects, privacy and a legible public imagery couched in the traditional language of geometric abstraction competed for the ascendancy, as did the idea of collectible art and dematerialized art object. In idea art, a strong strain of subjectivism ranged from language play, in whimsical verbal constructs, to parody or mockery of introspection approaching slapstick.

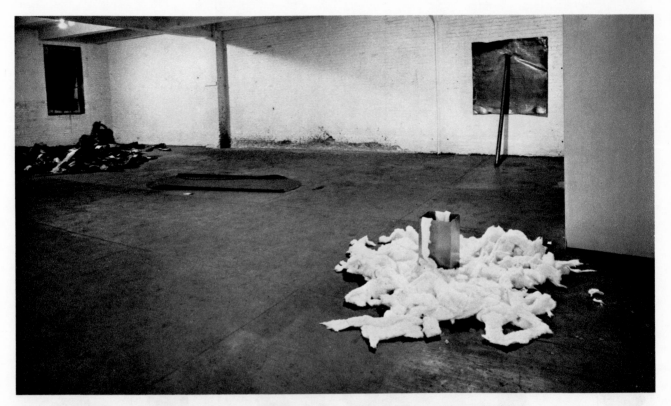

635 Installation view of group show *9 at Leo Castelli*. Works by Richard Serra (background, left and right), Steven Kaltenbach (center), and Giovanni Anselmo (foreground). Leo Castelli warehouse, New York. 1968

THE ABSURDIST MOOD:
STORY ART

While a great body of Conceptual Art is solemn, even grimly humorless in its exploration of contemporary formal, linguistic, and philosophical problems, there is a counter tendency of wildly comical impulse. The performance artist oscillates between the role of a clown and that of a grave professor dispensing obscure philosophical propositions. As examples of the absurdist mood, there are William Wegman's performance pieces; Lawrence Weiner's ironic propositions; John Baldessari's mixed verbal/visual narratives; the "Story Art" of Peter Hutchinson, Robert Cummings, and Bill Beckley; and such bits of whimsy as the following formulation by Robert Barry, offered (in Lucy Lippard, *Changing: Essays in Art Criticism*, New York, 1971) as a serious artistic commentary: "All the things I know/ But of which I am not/ At the moment thinking—/1:36 PM, June 1969." No matter how intrinsically negligible such proposals may at first glance appear, they pose an intellectual challenge that cannot be readily discounted. They cause us to reconsider our assumptions about the nature and the value of artistic work, and even the act of perception.

"Story Art" was the phrase adopted by the dealer John Gibson to characterize an offshoot of Conceptual Art which mixes verbal and visual means but discards the structuralist and philosophical pretensions of the more solemn Conceptualists. Instead of using theoretical ideas, verbal constructs, and photographic documentation to challenge the traditional, sensuous concerns of painting and sculpture, Story Artists as different as those mentioned above have made their mediums a vehicle for quixotic personal perceptions. The more hedonistic aspects of this development are indicated by the new emphasis on glossy color photography rather than on black-and-white visual material.

Baldessari, after a career in painting, began in 1966 to investigate new expressive forms of art inspired by Duchamp's conceptualist ironies, and he exhibited new narrative works that consisted merely of sign-painted verbal texts. These precocious examples of Story Art later became a seminal influence, and they, in turn, were modified by the artist in the form of combinations of photos and text. Each text represented a "moral" in a fantastic fable about the art-making activity, the politics of art, or the trials and tribulations of being an artist. More recently, Baldessari has discarded printed text, polemics, and ideology, using special effects in photography to make his points in a more inventive and purely visual manner. His photographic distortions break down normal sequences of movement and visual logic in reality, as if to demonstrate that any action reduced to its component parts must reveal a basic content of absurdity. Yet his bizarre visual shocks are balanced by the poetic action of his artistic synthesis, which has a way of becoming a

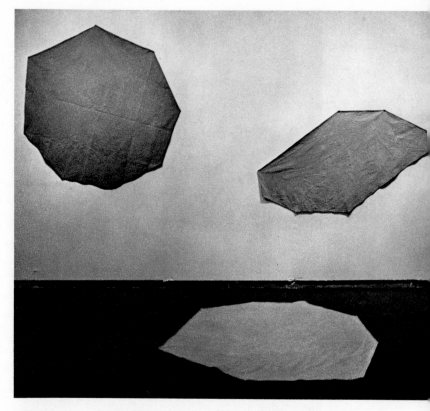

636 Richard Tuttle. *Violet Octagon; First Green Octagon; Red Octagon.* 1967. Dyed canvas, each piece c. 55 × 53″. Betty Parsons Gallery, New York

credible and convincing form of serious intellectual argument.

Peter Hutchinson was both an originator of Story Art and an innovator in developing the interaction between photographs and text. His work echoes a multiplicity of influences from Duchamp and Magritte to the hyped-up color photographs of contemporary commercial advertising. In his *Alphabet Series*, published in a limited edition of 1974, he observed and recorded everyday occurrences with an almost childlike simplicity in a brief handwritten documentation of apparently trivial events, which hangs beneath large letters upholstered in different materials. The series is plainly autobiographical and includes anecdotes about the artist's art activity, social life, and travels, along with casual stories about plants and animals, perhaps in ironic reference to his earlier conceptual concern with ecological systems.

So arresting are some of Bill Beckley's sumptuous color images, which he laboriously processes himself, that they re-establish affiliations with illusionistic painting. Photography is no longer a deliberately impoverished medium for routine information-gathering. In Beckley's case the photo images combine with abutting blocks of type that recount seemingly unimportant occurrences, but the guileless style of verbal narration betrays strange *double entendres* and operates on various levels of personal and formal meaning (plate 637).

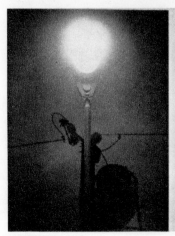
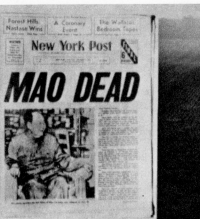
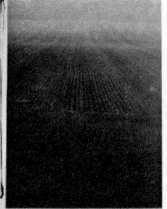

Some stories are short and some stories are long.
I was sitting in the living room reading the headlines on the first page of the newspaper. A streetlight faced the front of the house and a floor lamp stood inside. A shadow of a person with short curly hair fell on the paper. The pages ruffled, turning. The shadow was lost with the movement. The night air cooled and a mist fell over the countryside. The ruffling stopped, a weather report on the last page.

637 Bill Beckley. *Mao Dead*. 1977. Four photo panels, each 40 × 30″. Collection the artist

As narrative, Story Art plays a role today rather like that of Pop Art when it emerged in the early 1960s. Against the background of formalist abstraction and the ideological narrowness of Conceptual Art, it embraces a wider spectrum of real and imaginary life situations. In the words of one of its practitioners, James Collins, the current variation on traditional Realism offers us "a humanizing gesture of some significance."

FANTASY AND SCIENCE FICTION

Another, rather Gothic, aspect of Conceptual Art acknowledges earlier projects in nature, such as Earthworks, but breaks with that environmental form to introduce new kinds of content more in tune with the seventies: fantasy, acute sensory awareness, a more complex intellectual tension between bodily self-perception and external phenomena. There is a new integration of imaginative content within a structural style of purist aspiration.

Alice Aycock, as a notable example, constructs a rather formidable and illogical kind of Earthworks, on a scale of intimacy, in *A Simple Network of Underground Wells and Tunnels* (1975, plate 638), which compels the spectator to enter her game and participate in the experience of a maze. Besides excavating and drastically altering the earth's surface, she has added architectural and archaeological associations which draw on man-made antique ruins and evoke a startling subjective fantasy as well. Her structures are plausible and appear soundly made and constructed; yet they also become imaginary environ-

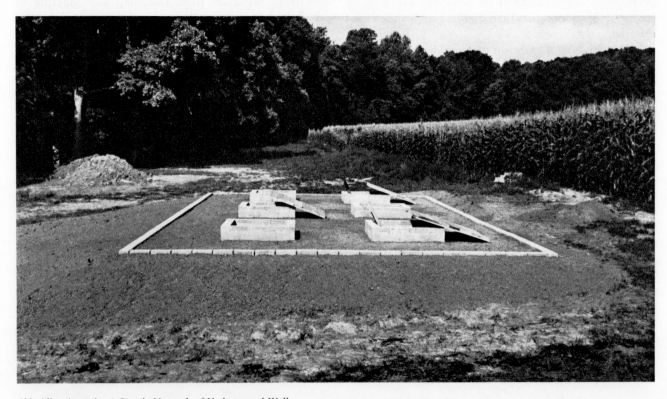

638 Alice Aycock. *A Simple Network of Underground Wells and Tunnels*. 1975. Merriewold West, Far Hills, N.J.

ments which challenge the viewer/participant to overcome obstacles and to transcend the traumas built into the experience. Aycock publishes elaborate notes for her projects, as an accompanying litany of literary and philosophical association.

A mood of estrangement is, indeed, characteristic of many of the solipsistic environmental projects of the 1970s. For the most part, however, Conceptual Art has presented itself in intellectually demanding and sober analytical forms, rather than as Gothic fantasy, or alternately as absurdist comedy. Its often maddening privatism contains elements of frustration and comments obliquely on a mass society which has learned to detest and fear strong forms of individualism. Political, cultural, and intellectual nonconformity pose a threat to current escapist illusions. The apparently contemptible "team spirit" and the faceless "plastic men," which, in Rebecca West's telling phrase, accounted for the Watergate fiasco have made the passive, mindless, and anti-individualist tendency of contemporary mass society all the more frightening. In a world whose capacity for self-deception seems unlimited and whose moral values are coming unstuck, the ironies (and even the infantile truancy) of Conceptual Art offer more hope about our condition of freedom than do some of the accomplished art objects of the past.

ART AND TECHNOLOGY

The dematerialization of the traditional work of art evident in various expressions of Conceptual and Performance art has found a parallel in another type of environmental art which perhaps even more dramatically captured popular imagination in recent years: the new union of art and technology. Vast areas of artistic expression have been assimilated to science and engineering, as artists boldly experimented with such materials as synthetics or plastics and embarked on the most complex imaginable collaborations with teams of technicians, working side by side with them in the research laboratory or factory.

The first solid evidence of the artist's gravitation to science came before the public with the appearance in the 1960s of Op Art, light art, the revival of motion sculpture, and intermedia experiments utilizing electronic technology. Op Art (see Chapter 26) now seems little more than a fad which exhausted its artistic invention almost at the moment it aroused the greatest public enthusiasm. Antecedents of Op Art in constructivist and kinetic traditions were remote from the more subjective traditions of postwar American art, despite the presence in this country of one of the inventors of perceptual art, Josef Albers. In the late 1960s Op Art played primarily a catalytic role, leading to new forms of collaboration with industry in esoteric technological form, and establishing new connections between optical and kinetic phenomena and art on an environmental scale.

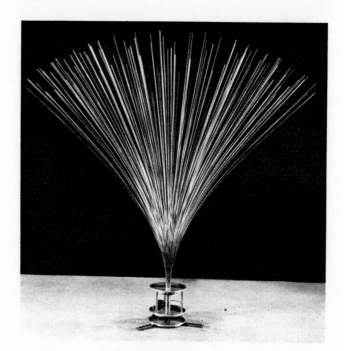

639 Len Lye. *Fountain II*. 1959.
Steel, motorized, height with base 89".
Howard Wise Collection, New York

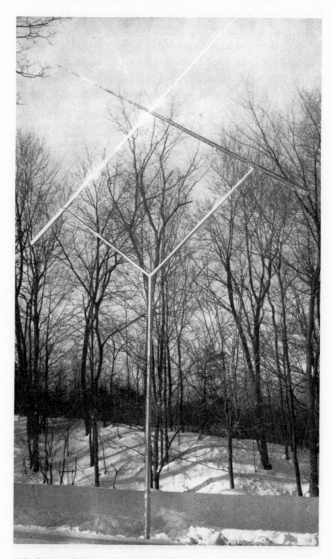

640 George Rickey. *Two Lines Oblique, Twenty-Five Feet*.
1967–68. Stainless steel, height 25'.
Collection the artist

A number of motion sculptors activated material forms with a movement so rapid that they created an optical imagery and the effect of disembodied energies. Perhaps the most remarkable of these has been New Zealand-born Len Lye. His "tangible motion sculptures," such as *Fountain II* (1959, plate 639), were, in essence, programmed machines constructed of exquisitely fine metal components of stainless steel. In motion, they created dematerialized tongues of light and images of flickering radiance. George Rickey has constructed on a large scale attenuated stainless-steel blade forms, eggbeater "space churns," and pairs and quartets of rectangular, uniform volumes that are driven gently, slowly, by air currents, but all their reflective, burnished surfaces also appear to melt away in motion. The sense of weightlessness and immateriality derives from the monumental scale, light play, and rhythmic control of movement that Rickey has mastered so admirably (plate 640).

In the changes that rapidly overtook art in the 1960s, Lye was more characteristic of new developments than the more conservative Rickey. The pervasiveness of environmental art systems, whether in kinetic, luminist, or filmic form, soon became more sophisticated than anything the original Constructivists or Bauhaus experimentalists might have fantasied. The new visual and mass-communications media, as Marshall McLuhan pointed out in his book *Understanding Media*, have restructured our normal perceptual patterns which are rapidly being superseded by a multisense involvement in a total "field" reality. The mixed-media art of the sixties fused motion, sound, and light, physical fact and psychic effect, in an environmental spectacle that encompassed the viewer and engaged his senses directly, instead of confronting him with an object or image.

LIGHT AND MOVEMENT ART

The twentieth-century pioneer in interpreting music visually, and in creating an abstract visual music, was the American Thomas Wilfred (1889–1968). Starting in May 1905 "with a cigar box, a small incandescent lamp, and some pieces of glass," Wilfred developed a large-scale, totally abstract, and new artistic medium, independent of music, that created flowing, variegated light compositions which he called "Lumia." For some time his pioneering *Lumia Suite* (plate 641) played as a curiosity at the Museum of Modern Art in New York and, producing mildly euphoric "light ballets," anticipated the optical experiments and the "psychedelic" art of the 1960s. There had, of course, been other authoritative precedents for electrified art, such as Moholy-Nagy's *Light-Space Modulator*, of 1922–30, around which a luminist tradition might have been built. However, it took a combination of McLuhanism and the new cult of technology in the 1960s—which included the interest in the retinal dynamics of perception in Op Art—to create the necessary climate in America for widespread experiments in light mediums.

Chryssa (b. 1933) was the first American artist to use emitted electric light and neon, rather than projected or screened light. Her imagery was also unique, since its sources were the lettered commercial signs of the urban environment, especially her preferred subjects—the neon signs of Times Square. Her best-known series contained delicate neon variations on the letters W and A and the ampersand (colorplate 103), aligned in refulgent, parallel banks. The repeated effect of the letters produced resonating light impulses which had the effect of oscillation, though the kinetic effect took place only in the eye of the beholder.

Many artists in America and Europe, later identified with an antiform tendency, employed light as an incidental element, among them Dan Flavin, Robert Morris, Bruce Nauman, and Keith Sonnier. Flavin uses fluorescent tubes of standardized commercial type in a completely straightforward, unsentimental manner. The familiar light fixtures bathe the gallery or museum space in their eerie glow; the rods of light are usually angled off the wall or presented in constructions of rectangular symmetry, and they create an unrelenting illumination which bleaches out the room's shadows and dissolves the silhouettes of the enclosing glass tubes. Their incandescence makes daylight, or even artificial room light, seem startlingly unreal.

A major portion of luminist and kinetic art originated in Europe, beginning with the formation in 1960 of

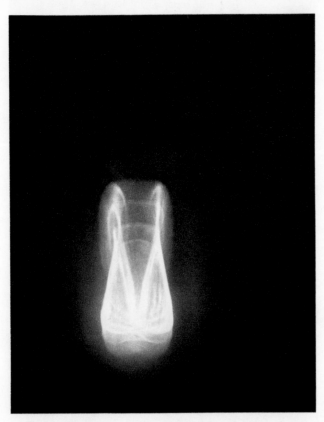

641 Thomas Wilfred. *Lumia Suite, Op. 158* (portion of screen shown). 1963–64. Motorized light sculpture, three movements lasting twelve minutes repeated continuously with variations, entire screen 6 × 8′. The Museum of Modern Art, New York. Mrs. Simon Guggenheim Fund

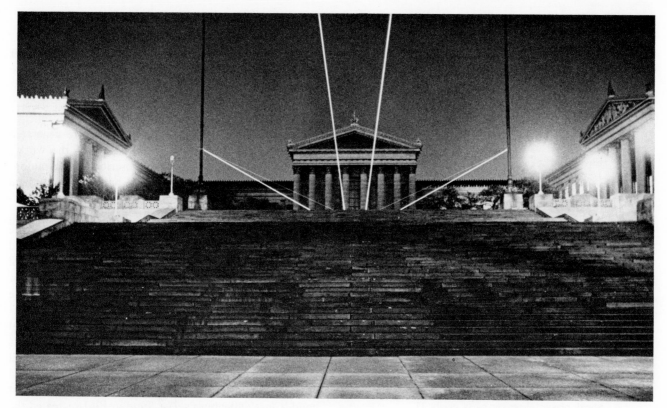

642 Rockne Krebs. *Sky Bridge Green.* 1973. Laser structure and city lights. Installed at the Philadelphia Museum of Art, 1973

GRAV (Groupe de Recherche de l'Art Visuel) by eleven artists of different nationalities, all resident in Paris. Wen-Ying Tsai is an associate who showed with that group at the Galerie Denise René, which made its reputation on technology art. Tsai is a Chinese-born sculptor now living in New York. The slender, stainless steel "cybernetic" rods of his sculpture (colorplate 104) vibrate in different patterns in response to electronic impulses, to the clapping of human hands, or to the flashes of a strobe light. In the artist's words, they are designed to simulate "the intensity of a living creature." While the contemporary interest in light and kinetic sculpture is in a sense traditional, and dates back at least to Naum Gabo, to Marcel Duchamp, Moholy-Nagy and the Bauhaus, only in the postwar era has the artist tried consciously to use available computer and electronic technology to create robot works of art which can be activated environmentally.

The subjective elements of videotape and Performance Art have increasingly absorbed the role of technological art. Rockne Krebs, one of the few contemporary survivors of the old marriage of art and technology, continues to work with projected images on an environmental scale. Krebs fashions sculpture from projected images and laser beams, utilizing space, light, and natural phenomena. *Sky Bridge Green* (1973, plate 642) was the first outdoor installation of laser beams in a new series, creating an abstract optical structure. The monumental network of light spatially linked the Philadelphia Museum of Art and the nearby City Hall by means of argon green lasers. The light beams made a purely formal structure but also managed to enclose the man-made and natural landscape of the city, as if in a pictorial frame. In subsequent work of the *Sky Bridge* series, this led to the ingenious device of combining abstract light structures with actual projections, in a *camera obscura* context of what the artist called a "living mural." Within an enclosed room projections of outdoor scenery were shown in full color, combining current optical technology, abstract structure, and literal representational elements.

ENVIRONMENTALISM

In his book *Beyond Modern Sculpture* (1968), Jack Burnham describes the artistic metamorphosis as an evolution "from the direct shaping of matter to a concern for organizing quantities of energy and information." Our total environmental sense today has little to do with the old concepts about the advantages or menace of machine culture. Machine-age art forms were officially recognized as superseded in 1968 by the collective works of a new group of artist-engineers who exhibited together for the first time at a Museum of Modern Art show in New York significantly entitled *The Machine As Seen at the End of the Mechanical Age.* Headed by Billy Klüver of the Bell Laboratories, the group sought to bridge the gap between science and art through the exchange of information and the creation of opportunities for joint experiment. They called their collaboration Experiments in Art and Tech-

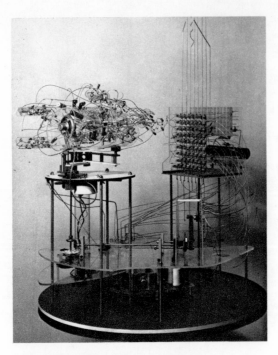

643 James Seawright. *Watcher*. 1965–66.
Metal, plastic, electronic parts, height 37″.
Collection Howard and Jean Lipman, New York

nology (EAT). The new development had actually begun two years earlier, with a series of brilliant performance spectacles organized by Klüver, Rauschenberg, dancers Yvonne Rainer, Alex Hay, and Steve Paxton, and the composer John Cage, among others. *Nine Evenings: Theater and Engineering* was presented in the fall of 1966 at the Sixty-ninth Regiment Armory in New York, the same one that had once held the Armory Show. There, participating artists and engineers invented a remote-control dance piece, self-performing musical machines, and infrared-ray television cameras which managed to reveal and transmit onto an enormously magnified video screen images of members of the audience performing simple activities on cue in the dark. With the success of *Nine Evenings*, EAT was established and the flowering of environmental and mixed-media art in the United States assured.

John Cage was the guru of the new environmentalism, for his electronic music had been intimately involved with technology since the 1940s. He had already composed music with radios, amplifiers, oscillators, contact microphones, and even sounds picked up from outer space. One of the memorable performances at *Nine Evenings* was the piece entitled *Bandoneon*, on which David Tudor collaborated with Cage. They left an ensemble of programmed and responsive audio circuits, moving loudspeakers, television images, and lights to make their own random music when activated by the audience, thus creating one of America's first autonomous artistic

machines. Such works-of-art-cum-robots were later developed by innumerable American visual artists who acquired familiarity with sophisticated electronic technology, transistors, and microcircuitry.

James Seawright created sculptures whose movements, electronic sounds, and light projections were generated by a visible circuitry that became part of the work's aesthetic (plate 643). He had described these autonomous machines as "sculpture that happens also to be a machine." Howard Jones also created lights and reflecting surfaces which the spectator activated both intentionally and unknowingly. Electronic technology made possible for the first time responsive environments and complex machines of this kind, set in motion by external environmental stimuli. Some of the early experiments of GRAV provided the models in the plastic arts for the American experiments.

Modern European precedents for such environmental art included the loose arrangements of collage materials in Kurt Schwitters's *Merzbau* environments and El Lissitsky's Constructivist *Proun* Rooms, which he called "the junction from architecture to painting." Closer at hand, Claes Oldenburg's *The Store* in 1961 recreated the interior of a Lower East Side store as an ironic commentary on derelict commercial culture. Allan Kaprow, the inventor of Happenings, had been drawn to Jackson Pollock's paintings as sources of energy that expanded the individual creator's private world into an activated space, engaging the spectator at new psychic and perceptual levels.

The environmental art that emerged in the mid-1960s contained a multitude of sensory phenomena—visual, aural, kinetic, and sometimes olfactory. Many of the most theatrical environments were essentially light shows, or entertainments, which tried to build an overload of sight and sound designed to disorient the senses, like a drug experience. A familiar and standard example was the euphoric light environments contrived by USCO (US Company of Garnerville), with flashing slide projections, pulsating strobe lights, Mylar sheets, and other devices which created heightened sensations and finally total immersion in an active field of pulsating sight and sound. A torrent of slide projections accompanied by high-decibel rock music made Andy Warhol's *Balloon Farm*, *Exploding Plastic Inevitable*, and the *Electric Circus* among the most popular ventures in discotheque multimedia of the 1960s. With visual imagery changing too rapidly to be followed coherently, and ear-splitting musical sound, the spectator experienced a sense of identity loss within the irresistibly energized room enclosure.

The character of artistic environments began to change markedly at the end of the decade. Robert Whitman's electronic environment *Pond* (plate 644) represents the shift to a more meditative mood. He was one of the pioneers in the early group of performance artists who

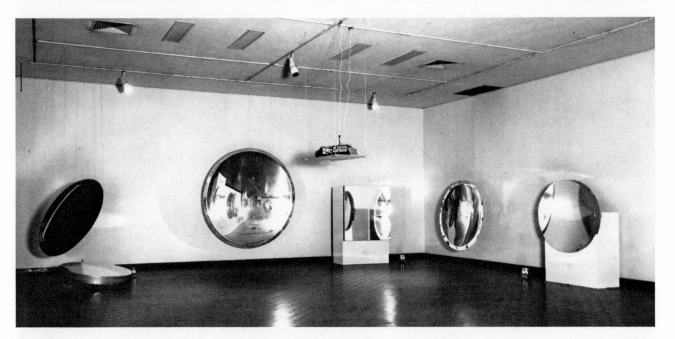

644 Robert Whitman. *Pond*. Environment photographed at the Jewish Museum, New York, in 1968. Lights, aluminum, plastic, electronic speakers. Dismantled

created the original Happenings. However, he went beyond them and beyond his mentor, Allan Kaprow, in utilizing technology and media as art materials. More recently, his art has paralleled other developments in intermedia works of a more abstract, cerebral, and self-consciously conceptual nature.

The electronic environment *Pond*, which has since been dismantled, incorporated eight vibrating concave Mylar mirrors, strobe lights, slide projectors, and a continuous tape-loop sound system repeating a sequence of single words and phrases of a banal character. The room was dark, but the viewer could make himself out in the mirrors. The oscillation of surface, sound, and light continually altered his perceptions in a mystifying manner. The experience was thus enigmatic and tended to move the viewer inward, into himself rather than outside to the world. This type of gentle narcissism, later to be amplified in different ways by the self-obsessed, erotic Polaroid imagery of Lucas Samaras (plate 645) and the energetic, more violent body works of Acconci and Nauman, attenuated the environmental impulse.

The Pulsa collaborative, a group of seven artists from Oxford, Conn., created extensive zones of sound, pulsating light, and heat out of doors, on golf courses (plate 646), and at the Museum of Modern Art garden. Pulsa's activities depended on chance stimuli in the environment interacting reciprocally with computer programming, and responding to such factors as human presence, traffic, and weather conditions. The group described their work as the "first . . . conceived on a scale and system of today." These sound and light performances show concern not only with immediate impact on the spectator but with ecology, both rural and urban, and even with the underlying rhythms of society itself.

The contemporary artist's interest in technology has inevitably led to ambitious and expensive collaborations within the industrial corporate structure. Art-conscious corporations have expanded the variety of types of assistance offered artists, which range from advice on materials to elaborate programs involving residence for creative individuals within industry. New synthetic materials have also significantly expanded the possibilities

645 Lucas Samaras. *Autopolaroids*. 1971. Polaroid prints, each $4\frac{1}{4} \times 3\frac{1}{4}''$. Pace Gallery, New York

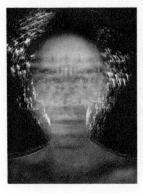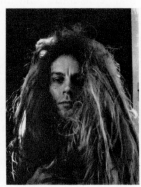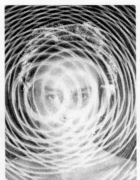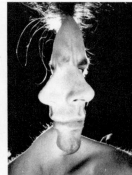

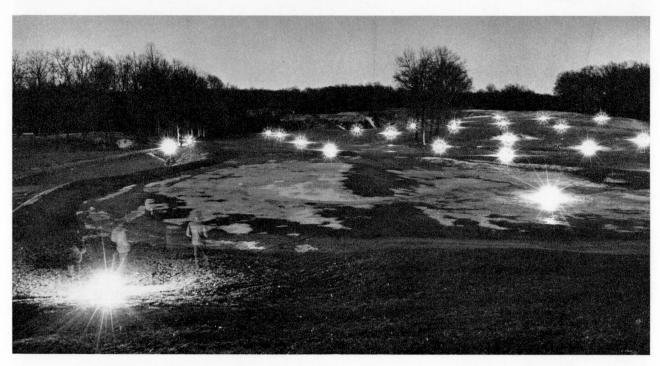

646 Pulsa Group (Oxford, Conn.). *Yale Golf Course Work.*
Environment photographed in New Haven, Conn., in 1969

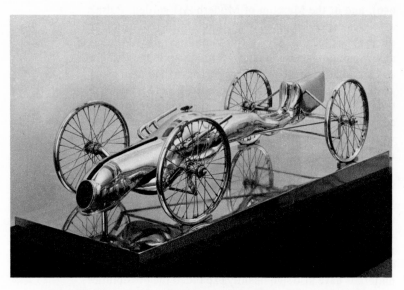

647 Ernest Trova. *Study: Falling Man.* 1966.
Polished silicone bronze and enamel, length 72″.
Whitney Museum of American Art, New York

of expression in painting and sculpture (see Chapters 23, 26).

The hybrid figures of Ernest Trova (b. 1927), which combine esoteric apparatuses and blandly generalized human figures in gleaming metals, are perhaps the most notable contemporary examples in sculpture of space-age imagery and technology, transcending even the cold perfection of Detroit aesthetics (plate 647).

Collaborations between artists and industry on a grand scale have been imaginative and bold, even though the new alliance has rarely been completely successful.

Still guided by the engineer Billy Klüver, the Experiments in Art and Technology group has continued imaginatively using computer and electronic technology to develop new artistic imagery and often spectacular multimedia techniques. At the Pepsi-Cola Pavilion at the World's Fair of 1970 in Osaka, Japan, his group designed and engineered the artificial "environments" inside and outside the Pavilion, from the cloud that floated above the dome to the responsive sound, light, and mirror systems inside triggered by the movement of the spectators (plate 648).

One of the most interesting and philosophically satisfying investigations of industrial technology was provided by the *Software* exhibition in 1970 at the Jewish Museum, New York, organized by Jack Burnham. There were, admittedly, a number of serious malfunctions in some of the most engrossing pieces, such as the MIT architecture group's *Seek*, a project in which a computer moved toy blocks around in interaction with an unpredictable and agitated team of gerbils who inhabited the man-made and constantly shifting environment. Exhibits were presented as a means of handling and relaying information and establishing patterns of environmental interaction within a systems structure rather than as a set of autonomous art objects. It signaled a movement, according to the catalog, away from art objects and toward artistic "concerns with natural and man-made systems, processes, ecological relationships, and the philosophic involvement of Conceptual Art."

A profound shift in attitude has inspired the continuing flow of innovation by some of the most fertile minds in

American art in the 1970s. New conceptions of art as idea and action, as information rather than a product, and even as a general state of awareness, have proved their viability. One of the assumptions underlying the most adventurous art of the contemporary period is rooted in the rejection of the status quo in art as well as in emotions and politics. Like other revolutionary twentieth-century art movements, the succession of dominant trends from 1945 to the end of the 1970s, from Abstract Expressionism to environmental systems and Conceptualism, has been motivated by the ingrained experimentalism of all modern art. The avant-garde's restless tendency to push ideas as far as possible, expanding the frontiers of artistic experience and individual consciousness, today continues to produce an unabated flow of significant art. The rate of major innovation and, perhaps, the stature of individuals of genius have diminished by comparison with some of the great names of the last few decades. Yet the energy level and the sheer numbers of serious, talented, and progressive artists today engaged in redefining the scope and meaning of the art enterprise is, if anything, more challenging intellectually and perceptually than it was thirty years ago, at the beginning of America's great postwar artistic renascence.

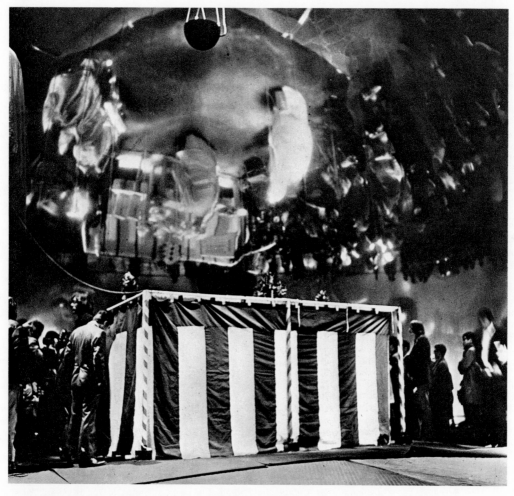

648 Mirror dome at the Pepsi-Cola Pavilion, Expo '70, Osaka, Japan, designed by Robert Breer, Forrest Myers, David Tudor, and Robert Whitman of the Experiments in Art and Technology Group. A Shinto ceremony is taking place.

BIBLIOGRAPHY

SOURCES

Battcock, Gregory, ed., *The New Art: A Critical Anthology*, New York: Dutton, 1966.

Benjamin, Samuel Greene, *Art in America: A Critical and Historical Sketch*, New York: Harper, 1880.

Dunlap, William, *A History of the Rise and Progress of the Arts of Design in the United States*, 3 vols., rev. ed., New York: Benjamin Blom, 1965.

Hill, Anthony, ed., *D.A.T.A.: Directions in Art Theory and Aesthetics*, London: Faber and Faber, 1968; anthology of artists' statements.

Jarves, James Jackson, *The Art-Idea* (1864), repr., Cambridge, Mass.: Belknap Press of Harvard University Press, 1960.

McCoubrey, John W., ed., *American Art 1700-1960: Sources and Documents*, Englewood Cliffs, N.J.: Prentice-Hall, 1965.

Rose, Barbara, ed., *Readings in American Art, 1900-1975*, New York: Praeger, 1975.

Tuckerman, Henry T., *Book of the Artists: American Artist Life* (1867), repr., New York: James F. Carr, 1966.

GENERAL

Art in America, vol. 53, no. 4, Aug./Sept., 1965; Archives of American Art issue.

The Art World: A 75-Year Treasury of ARTnews, Barbaralee Diamonstein, ed.; foreword, Harold Rosenberg; intro., Richard Shepard, New York: ARTnews, Rizzoli, 1977.

Baur, John I. H., *Revolution and Tradition in Modern American Art*, Cambridge, Mass.: Harvard University Press, 1951.

Blesh, Rudi, *Modern Art U.S.A.: Men, Rebellion, Conquest, 1900-1956*, New York: Knopf, 1956.

Cahill, Holger, and Alfred H. Barr, Jr., eds., *Art in America: A Complete Survey*, New York: Reynal & Hitchock, 1935.

Cummings, Paul, *Dictionary of Contemporary American Artists*, 3d. ed., New York: St. Martin, 1966.

Fielding, Mantle, *Dictionary of American Painters, Sculptors, and Engravers*, with addendum by James F. Carr, New York: J.F. Carr, 1965.

Goodrich, Lloyd, *Three Centuries of American Art*, New York: published for the Whitney Museum of American Art by Praeger, 1966.

Green, Samuel M., *American Art: A Historical Survey*, New York: Ronald Press, 1966.

Groce, George, and David Wallace, *The New-York Historical Society's Dictionary of Artists in America, 1564-1860*, New Haven: Yale University Press, 1957.

Hartmann, Sadakichi, *A History of American Art*, 2 vols., rev. ed., Boston: L.C. Page, 1932.

Hunter, Sam, and John Jacobus, *American Art of the 20th Century: Painting, Sculpture, Architecture*, New York: Abrams, 1973.

La Follette, Suzanne, *Art in America, from Colonial Times to the Present Day*, New York and London: Harper, 1929.

Larkin, Oliver W., *Art and Life in America*, rev. and enl. ed., New York: Holt, Rinehart and Winston, 1960.

Lipman, Jean, *What Is American in American Art?* New York: McGraw-Hill, 1963.

———, and Helen Franc, *Bright Stars: American Painting and Sculpture Since 1776*, New York: Dutton, 1976.

McCoy, Garnett, *Archives of American Art: A Directory of Resources*, New York: Bowker, 1972.

McLanathan, Richard, *The American Tradition in the Arts*, New York: Harcourt, Brace, and World, 1968.

Mendelowitz, Daniel M., *A History of American Art*, 2d ed., New York: Holt, Rinehart and Winston, 1970.

Pierson, William H., Jr., and Martha Davidson, *Arts of the United States: A Pictorial Survey*, New York: McGraw-Hill, 1960, repr., Athens, Ga.: University of Georgia Press, 1966.

Rose, Barbara, *American Art Since 1900: A Critical History*, New York: Praeger, 1967.

Rosenberg, Harold, *Discovering the Present: Three Decades in Art, Culture, and Politics*, Chicago: University of Chicago Press, 1973.

Taylor, Joshua C., *America As Art*, Washington, D.C.: National Collection of Fine Arts, 1976.

Walker, John A., *Glossary of Art, Architecture and Design Since 1945: Terms and Labels Describing Movements, Styles and Groups Derived from the Vocabulary of Artists and Critics*, 2d. rev. ed., London: Clive Bengley; Hamden, Conn.: Linnet Books, 1977.

Wheeler, Monroe, *Painters and Sculptors of Modern America*, New York: Crowell, 1942.

Wilmerding, John, *American Art*, Harmondsworth, England, and New York: Penguin Books, 1976.

SPECIAL TOPICS

Dover, Cedric, *American Negro Art*, Greenwich, Conn.: New York Graphic Society, 1960.

Driskell, David C., *Two Centuries of Black American Art*, New York: Knopf, 1976.

Fairman, Charles, *Art and Artists of the Capitol of the United States of America*, Washington, D.C.: United States Government Printing Office, 1927.

Greene, Carroll, Jr., *The Evolution of Afro-American Artists: 1800-1950*. New York: City University of New York, 1967.

Harris, Neil, *The Artist in American Society: The Formative Years, 1790-1860*, New York: Braziller, 1966.

Kaiser, Elizabeth, *From Pedestal to Pavement: The Image of Woman in American Art, 1875-1975*, South Hadley, Mass.: Mount Holyoke College, 1976.

Kouwenhoven, John, *Made in America: The Arts in Modern Civilization*, New York: Norton, 1967.

Lippard, Lucy R., ed., *From the Center: Feminist Essays on Women's Art*, New York: Dutton, 1976.

Lynes, Russell, *The Art-Makers of Nineteenth-Century America*, New York: Atheneum, 1970.

———, *The Tastemakers*, New York: Harper, 1954.

McCabe, Cynthia Jaffee, and Daniel J. Boorstin, *The Golden Door: Artist-Immigrants of America, 1876-1976*, Washington, D.C.: Hirshhorn Museum and Sculpture Garden, 1976.

Miller, Lillian, *Patrons and Patriotism, The Encouragement of the Fine Arts in the United States, 1790-1860*, Chicago and London: University of Chicago Press, 1966.

Saarinen, Aline, *The Proud Possessors: The Lives, Times, and Tastes of Some Adventurous American Art Collectors*, New York: Random House, 1958.

Stein, Roger B., *John Ruskin and Aesthetic Thought in America, 1840-1900*, Cambridge, Mass.: Harvard University Press, 1967.

ARCHITECTURE: GENERAL

Andrews, Wayne, *Architecture, Ambition and Americans*, New York: Harper, 1955.

———, *Architecture in America; A Photographic History from the Colonial Period to the Present*, New York: Atheneum, 1960.

Burchard, John, and Albert Bush-Brown, *The Architecture of America; A Social and Cultural History*, Boston: Little, Brown, 1961.

Coles, William A., and Henry Hope Reed, Jr., eds., *Architecture in America: A Battle of Styles*, New York: Appleton-Century-Crofts, 1961.

Early, James, *Romanticism and American Architecture*, New York: Barnes, 1965.

Fein, Albert, *Frederick Law Olmsted and the American Environmental Tradition*, New York: Braziller, 1972.

Fitch, James Marston, *American Building: The Historical Forces That Shaped It*, 2d ed., Boston: Houghton, Mifflin, 1966; rev. and enl., New York: Schocken, 1973.

———, *Architecture and the Aesthetics of Plenty*, New York: Columbia University Press, 1961.

Giedion, Siegfried, *Space, Time and Architecture*, 5th ed., Cambridge: Harvard University Press, 1967.

Gowans, Alan, *Images of American Living; Four Centuries of Architecture and Furniture as Cultural Expression*, Philadelphia: Lippincott, 1964.

Hitchcock, Henry-Russell, *Architecture, Nineteenth and Twentieth Centuries*, Harmondsworth, England, and Baltimore: Penguin Books, 1958.

Kaufmann, Edgar, Jr., ed., *The Rise of an American Architecture*, New York: Praeger, 1970.

Kimball, Sidney Fiske, *American Architecture*, Indianapolis: Bobbs-Merrill, 1928; repr. New York: AMS Press, 1970.

Kostof, Spiro, ed., *The Architect: Chapters in the History of the Profession*, New York: Oxford University Press, 1977.

Moore, Charles, Gerald Allen, and Donlyn Lyndon, *The Place of Houses*, New York: Holt, Rinehart and Winston, 1974.

Reps, John William, *The Making of Urban America; A History of City Planning in the United States*, Princeton: Princeton University Press, 1965.

Sanford, Trent, *The Architecture of the Southwest; Indian, Spanish, American*, New York: Norton, 1950.

Sky, Alison, and Michelle Stone, *Unbuilt America*, New York: McGraw-Hill, 1976.

Tallmadge, Thomas E., *The Story of Architecture in America*, new ed., New York: Norton, 1936.

Wrenn, Tony P., and Elizabeth D. Mulloy, *America's Forgotten Architecture*, by the National Trust for Historic Preservation, New York: Pantheon, 1976.

ARCHITECTURE: SPECIAL TOPICS

Colonial

Briggs, Martin S., *The Homes of the Pilgrim Fathers in England and America (1620–1685)*, London: Oxford University Press, 1932.

Downing, Antoinette F., *Early Homes of Rhode Island*, Richmond, Va.: Garrett & Massie, 1937.

———, and Vincent J. Scully, Jr., *The Architectural Heritage of Newport, Rhode Island, 1640–1915*, Cambridge: Harvard University Press, 1952; 2d ed., New York: Potter, 1970.

Eberlein, Harold D., *The Manors and Historic Houses of the Hudson Valley*, Philadelphia and London: Lippincott, 1924.

———, and Cortland Hubbard, *American Georgian Architecture*, Bloomington, Ind.: Indiana University Press, 1952.

Forman, Henry, *The Architecture of the Old South: The Medieval Style, 1585–1850*, Cambridge: Harvard University Press, 1948.

Garvan, Anthony, *Architecture and Town Planning in Colonial Connecticut*, New Haven: Yale University Press, 1951.

Hitchcock, Henry-Russell, *Rhode Island Architecture*, Providence: Rhode Island Museum Press, 1939.

Howells, John M., *Lost Examples of Colonial Architecture*, New York: Helburn, 1931.

Johnston, Frances, and Thomas T. Waterman, *The Early Architecture of North Carolina*, Chapel Hill: University of North Carolina Press, 1941.

Kimball, Sidney Fiske, *Domestic Architecture of the American Colonies and of the Early Republic*, New York: Scribner's, 1927; Dover, 1966.

Kubler, George, *The Religious Architecture of New Mexico in the Colonial Period and Since the American Occupation*, Colorado Springs: Taylor Museum, 1940.

Morrison, Hugh, *Early American Architecture, from the First Colonial Settlements to the National Period*, New York: Oxford University Press, 1952.

Newcomb, Rexford, *Spanish-Colonial Architecture in the United States*, New York: J.J. Augustin, 1937.

Pierson, William H., *American Buildings and Their Architects*, vol. 1 (the Colonial and Neoclassical Styles), Garden City, N.Y.: Doubleday, 1970.

Reynolds, Helen W., *Dutch Houses in the Hudson Valley before 1776*, New York: Payson & Clarke, 1929.

Waterman, Thomas T., *The Dwellings of Colonial America*, Chapel Hill: University of North Carolina Press, 1950.

———, and John A. Barrows, *Domestic Colonial Architecture of Tidewater Virginia*, New York: Scribner's, 1932; Da Capo, 1968.

———, *The Mansions of Virginia, 1706–1776*, Chapel Hill: University of North Carolina Press, 1946.

Nineteenth Century

Aidaca, Thomas, *The Great Houses of San Francisco*, New York: Knopf, 1974.

Barlow, Elizabeth, *Frederick Law Olmsted's New York*, New York: Praeger, 1972.

Condit, Carl W., *American Building Art: The Nineteenth Century*, New York: Oxford University Press, 1960.

———, *The Chicago School of Architecture; A History of Commercial and Public Building in the Chicago Area, 1875–1925*, Chicago: University of Chicago Press, 1964.

———, *The Rise of the Skyscraper*, Chicago: University of Chicago Press, 1952.

Coolidge, John, *Mill and Mansion: A Study of Architecture and Society in Lowell, Massachusetts, 1820–1865*, New York: Columbia University Press, 1942.

Frary, Ihna T., *They Built the Capitol*, Richmond, Va.: Garrett & Massie, 1940.

Gifford, Don, ed., *The Literature of Architecture: the Evolution of Architectural Theory and Practice in Nineteenth-Century America*, New York: Dutton, 1966.

Hamlin, Talbot F., *Greek Revival Architecture in America*, London: Oxford University Press, 1944.

Huxtable, Ada Louise, *The Architecture of New York: A History and Guide*, vol. 1 (Classic New York: Georgian Gentility to Greek Elegance), Garden City, N.Y.: Anchor Books, 1964.

Jackson, John Brinkerhoff, *American Space: The Centennial Years: 1865–1876*, New York: Norton, 1972.

Kidney, Walter C., *The Architecture of Choice: Eclecticism in America, 1880–1930*, New York: Braziller, 1974.

Kilham, Walter H., *Boston After Bulfinch; An Account of Its Architecture 1800–1900*, Cambridge: Harvard University Press, 1946.

Lancaster, Clay, "Oriental Forms in American Architecture, 1800–1870," *Art Bulletin*, vol. 29, Sept. 1947, pp. 83-93.

Meeks, Carroll, *The Railroad Station: An Architectural History*, New Haven: Yale University Press, 1956.

———, "Romanesque Before Richardson in the United States," *Art Bulletin*, vol. 35, March 1953, pp. 17-33.

Mumford, Lewis, *The Brown Decades; A Study of the Arts in America, 1865–1895*, 2d rev. ed., New York: Dover, 1955.

———, *Sticks and Stones; A Study of American Architecture and Civilization*, 2d rev. ed., New York: Dover, 1955.

Noffsinger, James P., *The Influence of the École des Beaux-Arts on the Architecture of the United States*, Washington, D.C.: Catholic University of America Press, 1955.

Peisch, Mark L., *The Chicago School of Architecture*, New York: Random House, 1965.

Schuyler, Montgomery, *American Architecture and Other Writings*, 2 vols., William H. Jordy and Ralph Coe, eds., Cambridge: Belknap Press of Harvard University Press, 1961.

Scully, Vincent J., *The Shingle Style: Architectural Theory and Design from Richardson to the Origins of Wright*, New Haven: Yale University Press, 1955.

Stanton, Phoebe B., *The Gothic Revival and American Church Architecture; An Episode in Taste, 1840–1856*, Baltimore: Johns Hopkins Press, 1968.

Teitelman, Edward, and Richard W. Longstreth, *Architecture in Philadelphia*, Cambridge, Mass.: M.I.T. Press, 1974.

Whiffen, Marcus, *American Architecture Since 1780: A Guide to the Styles*, Cambridge: M.I.T. Press, 1969.

Twentieth Century

Banham, Reyner, *Los Angeles: the Architecture of Four Ecologies*, New York: Harper and Row, 1971.

Blake, Peter, *God's Own Junkyard: the Planned Deterioration of America's Landscape*, New York: Holt, Rinehart, 1964.

Brooks, H. Allen, *The Prairie School: Frank Lloyd Wright and His Midwest Contemporaries*, Toronto: University of Toronto Press, 1971.

Cheney, Sheldon, *Art and the Machine: an Account of Industrial Design in Twentieth-Century America*, New York: McGraw-Hill, 1936.

Edgell, George H., *The American Architecture of Today*, New York: Scribner's, 1928.

Five Architects: Eisenman, Graves, Gwathmey, Hejduk, Meier, New York: Wittenborn, 1972.

Hall, Ben M., *The Best Remaining Seats: the Story of the Golden Age of the Movie Palace*, New York: Potter, 1961.

Hitchcock, Henry-Russell and Arthur Drexler, eds., *Built in U.S.A.: Post-War Architecture*, New York: Museum of Modern Art, 1952.

Jacobs, Jane, *The Death and Life of Great American Cities*, New York: Random House (Vintage), 1961.

Jacobus, John, *Twentieth-Century Architecture: the Middle Years 1940–65*, New York: Praeger, 1966.

Jordy, William H., *American Buildings and Their Architects: Progressive and Academic Ideals at the Turn of the Twentieth Century*, vol. 3, Garden City, N.Y.: Doubleday, 1970–72.

————, *American Buildings and Their Architects: the Impact of European Modernism in the Twentieth Century*, vol. 4, Garden City, N.Y.: Doubleday, 1970–72.

McCallum, Ian, *Architecture U.S.A.*, New York: Reinhold, 1959.

McCoy, Esther, *Five California Architects*, New York: Reinhold, 1960.

Mock, Elizabeth, ed., *Built in U.S.A., 1932–1944*, New York: Museum of Modern Art, 1944.

Mumford, Lewis, ed., *Roots of Contemporary American Architecture*, New York: Reinhold, 1952.

————, *The Highway and the City*, New York: Harcourt, Brace, 1963.

Scully, Vincent, *American Architecture and Urbanism*, New York: Praeger, 1969.

Stern, Robert A.M., *New Directions in American Architecture*, New York: Braziller, 1969.

Tunnard, Christopher, and Boris Pushkarev, *Man-Made America: Chaos or Control?* New Haven: Yale University Press, 1963.

ARCHITECTS

BUCKLAND: Beirne, Rosamond, and John Henry Scarff, *William Buckland, 1734–1774, Architect of Virginia and Maryland*, Baltimore: Maryland Historical Society, 1958.

BULFINCH: Place, Charles A., *Charles Bulfinch, Architect and Citizen*, Boston and New York: Houghton Mifflin, 1925.

BURNHAM: Hines, Thomas S., *Burnham of Chicago, Architect and Planner*, New York: Oxford University Press, 1974.

   Moore, Charles, *Daniel H. Burnham, Architect, Planner of Cities*, Boston and New York: Houghton Mifflin, 1921.

FULLER: Marks, Robert W., *The Dymaxion World of Buckminster Fuller*, New York: Reinhold, 1960.

FURNESS: O'Gorman, James F., *The Architecture of Frank Furness*, Philadelphia: Philadelphia Museum of Art, 1973.

GROPIUS: Giedion, Siegfried, *Walter Gropius, Work and Teamwork*, New York: Reinhold, c. 1954.

GRUEN: Gruen, Victor, *The Heart of Our Cities*, New York: Simon and Schuster, 1964.

HARRISON: Bridenbaugh, Carl, *Peter Harrison, First American Architect*, Chapel Hill: University of North Carolina Press, 1949.

JEFFERSON: Frary, Ihna T., *Thomas Jefferson, Architect and Builder*, Richmond, Va.: Garrett & Massie, 1939.

   Jefferson, Thomas, *Thomas Jefferson, Architect; Original Designs in the Collection of Thomas Jefferson Coolidge, Jr., with an Essay and Notes by Fiske Kimball*, Cambridge: Riverside Press, 1916.

   Lehmann, Karl, *Thomas Jefferson, American Humanist*, New York: Macmillan, 1947.

JOHNSON: Hitchcock, Henry-Russell, *Architecture 1949–1965 by Philip Johnson*, New York: Holt, Rinehart and Winston, 1966.

   Jacobus, John, *Philip Johnson*, New York: Braziller, 1962.

KAHN: Scully, Vincent, *Louis Kahn*, New York: Braziller, 1962.

LAFEVER: Landy, Jacob, *The Architecture of Minard Lafever*, New York: Columbia University Press, 1970.

LATROBE: Hamlin, Talbot, *Benjamin Henry Latrobe*, New York: Oxford University Press, 1955.

McINTIRE: Kimball, Sidney Fiske, *Mr. Samuel McIntire, Carver, The Architect of Salem*, Portland, Me.: published for the Essex Institute of Salem, Mass., by the Southworth-Anthoensen Press, 1940.

McKIM: Granger, Alfred H., *Charles Follen McKim; A Study of His Life and Work*, Boston: Houghton Mifflin, 1913.

   Moore, Charles, *The Life and Times of Charles Follen McKim*, Boston: Houghton Mifflin, 1929.

   McKim, Mead and White, *A Monograph of the Work of McKim, Mead and White, 1879–1915*, 4 vols., New York: Architectural Book Publishing Company, 1915.

MIES VAN DER ROHE: Blaser, Werner, *Mies van der Rohe: the Art of Structure*, New York: Praeger, 1972.

   Johnson, Philip, *Mies van der Rohe*, New York: Museum of Modern Art, 1947; 2d ed. rev. 1953.

MILLS: Gallagher, Helen, *Robert Mills, Architect of the Washington Monument, 1781–1855*, New York: Columbia University Press, 1935.

NEUTRA: Boesiger, Willy, ed., *Richard Neutra: Buildings and Projects*, 3 vols., New York: Praeger, 1951–66.

PURCELL & ELMSLIE: Gebhard, David, *The Work of Purcell and Elmslie, Architects*, Park Forest, Ill.: Prairie School Press, 1965.

RICHARDSON: Hitchcock, Henry-Russell, *The Architecture of H. H. Richardson and His Times*, New York: The Museum of Modern Art, 1936.

RUDOLPH: Moholy-Nagy, Sibyl, introd., *The Architecture of Paul Rudolph*, New York: Praeger, 1970.

SAARINEN: Saarinen, Aline B., ed., *Eero Saarinen on His Work*, New Haven: Yale University Press, 1962; rev. ed. 1968.

   Temko, Allan, *Eero Saarinen*, New York: Braziller, 1962.

SCHINDLER: Gebhard, David, *Schindler*, New York: Viking, 1971.

SOLERI: Soleri, Paolo, *Arcology: the City in the Image of Man*, Cambridge, Mass.: M.I.T. Press, 1969.

STONE: Stone, Edward Durell, *The Evolution of an Architect*, New York: Horizon Press, 1962.

STRICKLAND: Gilchrist, Agnes Addison, *William Strickland, Architect and Engineer, 1788–1854*, enl. ed., New York: Da Capo, 1969.

SULLIVAN: Bush-Brown, Albert, *Louis Sullivan*, London: Mayflower, 1960.

   Duncan, Hugh Dalziel, *Culture and Democracy; The Struggle for Form in Society and Architecture in Chicago and the Middle West During the Life and Times of Louis H. Sullivan*, Totowa, N.J.: Bedminster Press, 1965.

   Morrison, Hugh, *Louis Sullivan, Prophet of Modern Architecture*, New York: Peter Smith, 1952.

   Paul, Sherman, *Louis Sullivan, An Architect in American Thought*, Englewood Cliffs, N.J.: Prentice-Hall, 1962.

   Sullivan, Louis, *Kindergarten Chats*, Lawrence, Kans.: Scarab Fraternity Press, 1934; New York: Wittenborn, Schultz, 1947.

   ————, *The Autobiography of an Idea*, New York: American Institute of Architects, 1924.

TOWN & DAVIS: Newton, Roger Hale, *Town and Davis, Architects, Pioneers in American Revivalist Architecture, 1812–70*, New York: Columbia University Press, 1962.

UPJOHN: Upjohn, Everard M., *Richard Upjohn, Architect and Churchman*, New York: Columbia University Press, 1939.

VENTURI: Venturi, Robert, Denise Scott Brown, and Stephen Izenour, *Learning from Las Vegas*, Cambridge, Mass.: M.I.T. Press, 1972.

WHITE: Baldwin, Charles, *Stanford White*, New York: Dodd, Mead, 1931.

WRIGHT: Drexler, Arthur, *The Drawings of Frank Lloyd Wright*, New York: Museum of Modern Art, 1962.

   Eaton, Leonard K., *Two Chicago Architects and Their Clients: Frank Lloyd Wright and Howard Van Doren Shaw*, Cambridge, Mass.: M.I.T. Press, 1969.

   Frank Lloyd Wright, introd. and notes by Martin Pawley, New York: Simon and Schuster, 1970.

   Manson, Grant, *Frank Lloyd Wright to 1910: The First Golden Age*, New York: Reinhold, 1958.

   Scully, Vincent, *Frank Lloyd Wright*, New York: Braziller, 1960.

   Storrer, William Allin, *The Architecture of Frank Lloyd Wright*, Cambridge, Mass.: M.I.T. Press, 1974.

   Twombly, Robert C., *Frank Lloyd Wright: An Interpretive Biography*, New York: Harper and Row, 1973.

   Wright, Frank Lloyd, *An Autobiography*, New York: Longmans, Green, 1932; Duell, Sloan and Pearce, 1943.

PAINTING: GENERAL

Barker, Virgil, *American Painting: History and Interpretation*, New York: Macmillan, 1950.

Baur, John I.H., ed., *The New Art in America: 50 American Painters in the 20th Century*, New York: New York Graphic Society and Praeger, 1957.

Caffin, Charles, *The Story of American Painting: The Evolution of Painting in America from Colonial Times to the Present*, New York: Johnson Reprint Corporation, 1970.

Gardner, Albert Ten Eyck, and Stuart P. Feld, *American Paintings: a Catalogue of the Collection of The Metropolitan Museum of Art*, vol. I, New York: Metropolitan Museum of Art, 1965.

Geldzahler, Henry, *American Painting in the Twentieth Century*, New York: Metropolitan Museum of Art, 1965.

Howat, John K., and John Wilmerding, *Nineteenth-Century America: Paintings and Sculpture*, Greenwich, Conn.: New York Graphic Society, 1970.

Isham, Samuel, *The History of American Painting*, new ed. with supplemental chapters by Royal Cortissoz, New York: Macmillan, 1927.

McCoubrey, John, *American Tradition in Painting*, New York: Braziller, 1963.

————, and the Editors of Time-Life Books, *American Painting, 1900–1970*, New York: Time, Inc., 1970.

Prown, Jules David, *American Painting: From Its Beginnings to the Armory Show*, vol. 1, Geneva, Switzerland: Skira, 1969.

Richardson, Edgar, *Painting in America: The Story of 450 Years*, New York: Crowell, 1956.

Rose, Barbara, *American Painting: The Twentieth Century*, vol. 2, Geneva, Switzerland: Skira, 1969.

Wilmerding, John, *The Genius of American Painting*, London: Weidenfeld and Nicholson, 1973.

PAINTING: SPECIAL TOPICS

The Arcadian Landscape: Nineteenth-Century American Painters in Italy, Lawrence, Kans.: University of Kansas Museum of Art, 1972.

Baur, John I. H., *American Painting in the Nineteenth Century: Main Trends and Movements*, New York: Praeger, 1953.

Bearden, Romare, and Harry Henderson, *Six Black Masters of American Art*. Garden City, N.Y.: Doubleday, 1972.

Bermingham, Peter, *American Art in the Barbizon Mood*, Washington, D.C.: Smithsonian Institution Press, 1975.

Black, Mary, and Jean Lipman, *American Folk Painting*, New York: Potter, 1966.

Blashfield, Edwin Howland, *Mural Painting in America*, New York: Scribner's, 1913.

Born, Wolfgang, *American Landscape Painting; An Interpretation*, New Haven: Yale University Press, 1948.

————, *Still-life Painting in America*, New York: Oxford University Press, 1947.

Boyle, Richard J., *American Impressionism*, Greenwich, Conn.: New York Graphic Society, 1974.

Burroughs, Alan, *Limners and Likenesses: Three Centuries of American Painting*, Cambridge: Harvard University Press, 1936.

Callow, James T., *Kindred Spirits; Knickerbocker Writers and American Artists, 1807–1855*, Chapel Hill: University of North Carolina Press, 1967.

Curry, Larry, *The American West: Painters from Catlin to Russell*, New York: Viking, 1972.

Dickson, Harold E., *Arts of the Young Republic; The Age of William Dunlap*, Chapel Hill: University of North Carolina Press, 1968.

Domit, Moussa M., *American Impressionist Painting*, Washington, D.C.: National Gallery of Art, 1973.

Drepperd, Carl, *American Pioneer Arts and Artists*, Springfield, Mass.: Pond-Ekberg, 1942.

Ewers, John C., *Artists of the Old West*, New York: Doubleday, 1973.

Fink, Lois, *Academy: The Academic Tradition in American Art*, Washington, D.C.: Smithsonian Institution Press, 1975.

Flexner, James, *First Flowers of Our Wilderness*, Boston: Houghton Mifflin, 1947.

————, *The Light of Distant Skies, 1760–1835*, New York: Harcourt, Brace, 1954.

————, *That Wilder Image; The Painting of America's Native School from Thomas Cole to Winslow Homer*, Boston: Little, Brown, 1962.

Frankenstein, Alfred, *The Reality of Appearance: The Trompe l'Oeil Tradition in American Painting*, Greenwich, Conn.: New York Graphic Society, 1970.

Gerdts, William H., *The Great American Nude: A History in Art*, New York: Praeger, 1974.

————, and Russell Burke, *American Still-life Painting*, New York: Praeger, 1971.

Goodrich, Lloyd, *American Genre; The Social Scene in Paintings and Prints (1800–1935)*, New York: Whitney Museum of American Art, 1935.

Hagen, Oskar, *The Birth of the American Tradition in Art*, New York: Scribner's, 1940.

Hills, Patricia, *The American Frontier: Images and Myths*, New York: Whitney Museum of American Art, 1973.

————, *The Painters' America, Rural and Urban Life, 1810–1910*, New York: Praeger, 1974.

Hollmann, Clide Anne, *Five Artists of the Old West: George Catlin, Karl Bodmer, Alfred Jacob Miller, Charles M. Russell, and Frederic Remington*, New York: Hastings House, 1965.

Hoopes, Donelson F., *The American Impressionists*, New York: Watson-Guptill, 1972.

————, *American Watercolor Painting*, New York: Watson-Guptill, 1977.

————, *The Beckoning Land: Nature and the American Artist: A Selection of Nineteenth-Century Paintings*, Atlanta, Ga.: The High Museum of American Art, 1971.

————, and Wend von Kalnein, *The Düsseldorf Academy and the Americans*, Atlanta, Ga.: The High Museum of American Art, 1972.

Landgren, Marchal E., *American Pupils of Thomas Couture*, College Park: University of Maryland, 1970.

Lipman, Jean, and Alice Winchester, eds., *Primitive Painters in America*, New York: Dodd, Mead, c. 1950.

Little, Nina Fletcher, *American Decorative Wall Painting, 1700–1850*, New York: Old Sturbridge Village, published in cooperation with Studio, 1952.

McShine, Kynaston, ed., *The Natural Paradise: Painting in America, 1800–1950*, New York: Museum of Modern Art, 1976.

Novak, Barbara, *American Painting of the Nineteenth Century*, New York: Praeger, 1969.

Parry, Ellwood, *The Image of the Indian and the Black Man in American Art, 1590–1900*, New York: Braziller, 1974.

Quick, Michael, *American Expatriate Painters of the Late Nineteenth Century*, Dayton, Ohio: The Dayton Art Institute, 1976.

Richardson, Edgar, *American Romantic Painting*, New York: E. Weyhe, 1944.

Sears, Clara Endicott, *Highlights Among the Hudson River Artists*, Boston: Houghton Mifflin, 1947.

Soby, James Thrall, and Dorothy C. Miller, *Romantic Painting in America*, New York: Museum of Modern Art, 1943.

Stebbins, Theodore E., *American Master Drawings and Watercolors*, New York: Harper and Row, 1976.

Stein, Roger B., *Seascape and the American Imagination*, New York: Potter, 1975.

Sweet, Frederick A., *The Hudson River School and the Early American Landscape Tradition*, Chicago: Art Institute of Chicago, 1945.

Taft, Robert, *Artists and Illustrators of the Old West 1850–1900*, New York: Scribner's, 1953.

Williams, Herman Warner, Jr., *Mirror of the American Past; A Survey of American Genre Painting: 1750–1900*, Greenwich, Conn.: New York Graphic Society, 1973.

Wilmerding, John, *A History of American Marine Painting*, Salem and Boston: Peabody Museum and Little, Brown, 1968.

Wright, Louis B., George B. Tatum, John W. McCoubrey, and Robert C. Smith, *The Arts in America: The Colonial Period*, New York: Scribner's, 1966.

Twentieth Century

ACA Heritage Gallery, New York, *Commemorating the 50th Anniversary of "The Forum Exhibition of Modern American Painters," March 1916*, 1966.

Agee, William, "New York Dada, 1910–30," *Art News Annual XXXIV: The Avant Garde*, 1968, pp. 105–113.

————, *The 1930's: Painting and Sculpture in America*, New York: Whitney Museum of American Art, 1968.

————, *Synchromism and Color Principles in American Painting*, New York: Knoedler & Co., 1965.

Aldrich, Larry, *Lyrical Abstraction*, New York: Whitney Museum of American Art, 1971.

Alfieri, Bruno, "USA: Towards the End of 'Abstract' Painting," *Metro*, no. 4/5, 1962, pp. 4–13.

Alloway, Lawrence, *American Pop Art*, New York: Collier Books in association with the Whitney Museum of American Art, 1974.

————, *The Photographic Image*, New York: Solomon R. Guggenheim Museum, 1966.

————, *The Shaped Canvas*, New York: Solomon R. Guggenheim Museum, 1964.

————, *Six Painters and the Object*, New York: Solomon R. Guggenheim Museum, 1963.

————, *Systemic Painting*, New York: Solomon R. Guggenheim Museum, 1966.

————, *Topics in American Art Since 1945*, New York: Norton, 1975.

Amaya, Mario, *Pop Art...and After*, New York: Viking, 1965.

American Abstract Artists, eds., *The World of Abstract Art*, New York: Wittenborn, 1957.

American Federation of Arts, New York, *The Realist Revival*, 1972.

The Armory Show: International Exhibition of Modern Art, 1913, 3 vols., New York: Arno, 1972.

Arnason, H. H., *American Abstract Expressionists and Imagists*, New York: Solomon R. Guggenheim Museum, 1961.

Artforum, "Special Issue: The New York School," vol. 4, Sept., 1965.

————, "Special Painting Issue," vol. 14, Sept., 1975.

Art in America, "The Silent Decade: American Art, 1900–1910," Special Issue, vol. 61, July/Aug., 1973.

————, "Special Issue: Photo Realism," vol. 60, Nov./Dec., 1972, pp. 58–107.

Arts Magazine, "Special Issue: New York Dada and the Arensberg Circle," vol. 51, May, 1977.

Ashbery, John, *The New Realists*. New York: Sidney Janis Gallery, 1962.

Ashton, Dore, *The New York School: A Cultural Reckoning*, New York: Viking, 1973.

————, *The Unknown Shore: A View of Contemporary Art*, Boston: Little, Brown, 1962.

————, and Bernard Dorival, *New York and Paris: Painting in the Fifties*, Houston: Museum of Fine Arts, 1959.

Association of American Painters and Sculptors, Inc., New York, *Catalogue of the International Exhibition of Modern Art*, New York: Sixty-Ninth Regiment Armory, 1913.

Baigell, Matthew, *The American Scene: American Painting of the 1930s*, New York: Praeger, 1974.

————, "The Beginnings of the 'American Wave' and the Depression," *Art Journal*, vol. 27, Summer, 1968, pp. 387–396.

Barr, Alfred H., Jr., *Fantastic Art, Dada, Surrealism*, 3d ed., New York: Museum of Modern Art, Simon and Shuster, 1947.

————, *The New American Painting as Shown in Eight European Countries 1958–1959*, New York: Museum of Modern Art International Program, 1958–1959.

————, and Dorothy Miller, eds., *American Realists and Magic Realists*, New York: Museum of Modern Art, 1943.

Barrett, Cyril, *Op Art*, New York: Viking, 1970.

Battcock, Gregory, *Why Art: Casual Notes on the Aesthetics of the Immediate Past*, New York: Dutton, 1977.

————, ed., *Minimal Art: A Critical Anthology*, New York: Dutton, 1968.

————, *Super Realism: A Critical Anthology*, New York: Dutton, 1975.

Baur, John I. H., *The Eight*, New York: Brooklyn Museum, 1943.

———, *Nature in Abstraction*, New York: Whitney Museum of American Art, 1958.

———, *The New Decade: 35 American Painters and Sculptors*, New York: Whitney Museum of American Art, 1955.

———, Lloyd Goodrich, James Thrall Soby, and Frederick S. Wight, *New Art in America*, Greenwich, Conn.: New York Graphic Society; New York: Praeger, 1957.

Bonito-Oliva, Achille, *Europe/America: The Different Avant-Gardes*, New York, Deco Press, 1976.

Breeskin, Adelyn, *Roots of Abstract Art in America, 1910–30*, Washington, D.C.: National Collection of Fine Arts, 1965.

Brown, Milton W., *American Painting from the Armory Show to the Depression*, Princeton, N.J.: Princeton University Press, 1955.

———, "Cubist-Realism: An American Style," *Marsyas*, vol. 3, 1943/45, pp. 138–160.

———, "The Early Realism of Hopper and Burchfield," *College Art Journal*, vol. 7, Autumn, 1947, pp. 3–11.

———, *The Modern Spirit: American Painting, 1908–1935*, London: Arts Council of Great Britain in association with the Edinburgh Festival Society and the Royal Scottish Academy, 1977.

———, *1913, Armory Show: 1963, 50th Anniversary Exhibition*, Utica: Munson-Williams Proctor Institute; New York: Sixty-Ninth Regiment Armory, 1963.

———, *The Story of the Armory Show*, New York: Joseph H. Hirshhorn Foundation, 1963.

Bruce, Edward, and Forbes Watson, *Art in Federal Buildings*, vol. 1: *Mural Designs, 1934–36*, Washington, D.C.: Art in Federal Buildings, Inc., 1936.

Cahill, Holger, *American Art Today*, New York: National Art Society, 1939.

Calas, Nicolas, *Art in the Age of Risk and Other Essays*, New York: Dutton, 1971.

———, and Elena Calas, *Icons and Images of the Sixties*, New York: Dutton, 1971.

Carmean, E.A., Jr., *The Great Decade of American Abstraction*, Houston Museum of Fine Arts, 1974.

Caudill, Mariea, *The American Scene: Urban and Rural Regionalists of the '30s and '40s*, Minneapolis: University Gallery, University of Minnesota, 1976.

Chase, Linda, *Photo Realism*, New York: Eminent Publications, 1975.

Clifford, Henry, John Sloan, and Everett Shinn, *Artists of the Philadelphia Press*, Philadelphia Museum of Art, 1946.

Colt, Priscilla, *Color and Field 1890–1970*, Buffalo: Albright-Knox Art Gallery, 1970.

Compton, Michael, *Pop Art*, London and New York: Hamlyn, 1970.

Cowart, Jack, *New/Photo Realism: Painting and Sculpture of the 1970's*, Hartford, Conn.: Wadsworth Atheneum, 1974.

Dasburg, Andrew, "Cubism—Its Rise and Influence," *The Arts*, vol. 4, Nov., 1923, pp. 279–84.

Delaware Art Museum, Wilmington, *Avant-Garde Painting and Sculpture in America, 1910–25*, 1975.

D'Harnoncourt, René, and Alfred H. Barr, Jr., *The New American Painting*, New York: Museum of Modern Art, 1959.

Donnell, Radka Zagaroff, "Space in Abstract Expressionism," *Journal of Aesthetics*, vol. 23, Winter, 1964, pp. 239–49.

Doty, Robert, *Contemporary Black Artists in America*, New York: Whitney Museum of American Art, 1971.

Dreier, Katherine, *Collection of the Société Anonyme: Museum of Modern Art: 1920*, New Haven: Yale University Press, 1950.

Eddy, Arthur J., *Cubists and Post-Impressionists*, London: Grant Richards, 1915.

Egbert, Donald Drew, *Socialism and American Art*, Princeton, N.J.: Princeton University Press, 1967.

Elderfield, John, "Painterliness Redefined: Jules Olitski and Recent Abstract Art" (2 parts), *Art International*, vol. 16, Dec., 1972, pp. 22–26; vol. 17, April, 1973, pp. 36–41, 101.

Everitt, Anthony, *Abstract Expressionism*, London: Thames and Hudson, 1975.

Finch, Christopher, *Pop Art: Object and Image*, London: Studio Vista, 1968.

Fine Arts Gallery, San Diego, *Color and Form 1909–1914: The Origin and Evolution of Abstract Painting in Futurism, Orphism, Rayonnism, Synchromism and the Blue Rider*, 1971.

Forum Exhibition of Modern Painters . . . on View at the Anderson Galleries, New York: Hugh Kennerly, 1916; rep. New York: Arno, 1968.

Fried, Michael, *Three American Painters: Kenneth Noland, Jules Olitski, Frank Stella*, Cambridge, Mass.: Fogg Art Museum, 1965.

Friedman, B.H., *School of New York: Some Younger Artists*, New York: Grove Press, 1959.

Friedman, Martin, *The Precisionist View in American Art*, Minneapolis: Walker Art Center, 1960.

Geldzahler, Henry, *Ellsworth Kelly, Helen Frankenthaler, Roy Lichtenstein, and Jules Olitski*, Venice: 33rd Venice Biennale, United States Pavilion, 1966.

———, ed., *New York Painting and Sculpture: 1940–1970*, New York: Metropolitan Museum of Art, 1969.

Glaser, Bruce, "Oldenburg, Lichtenstein, Warhol: A Discussion," *Artforum*, vol. 4, Feb., 1966, pp. 20–24.

Goldwater, Robert, *50th Annual Exhibition: 50 Paintings, 1905–13*, Buffalo: Albright-Knox Art Gallery, 1955.

———, "Reflections on the New York School," *Quadrum*, no. 8, 1960, pp. 17–36.

Goodall, D., and M. Kasanin, *Partial Bibliography of American Abstract-Expressive Painting, 1943–1956*, Los Angeles: University of Southern California, 1956.

Goodrich, Lloyd, *American Genre*, New York: Whitney Museum of American Art, 1935.

———, *Pioneers of Modern Art in America: The Decade of the Armory Show, 1910–1920*, New York: Whitney Museum of American Art, 1946.

Gordon, John, *Geometric Abstraction in America*, New York: Whitney Museum of American Art, 1962.

Greenberg, Clement, *Art and Culture: Critical Essays*, Boston: Beacon, 1961.

———, "The 'Crisis' of Abstract Painting,' *Arts Yearbook 7: The Art World*, 1964, pp. 89–92.

———, "New York Painting Only Yesterday," *Art News*, vol. 56, Summer, 1957, pp. 58–59; 84–86.

———, *Post Painterly Abstraction*, Los Angeles County Museum of Art, 1964.

———, "The Present Prospects of American Painting and Sculpture," *Horizon*, no. 93/94, Oct., 1947, pp. 20–30.

Guggenheim, Peggy, ed., *Art of This Century: Objects, Drawings, Photographs, Sculpture, Collages, 1910 to 1942*, New York: Art of This Century, 1942.

Hamilton, George Heard, "Painting in Contemporary America," *Burlington Magazine*, vol. 102, May, 1960, pp. 192–97.

Harrison, Charles, "Abstract Expressionism," *Studio International*, Jan., 1973, pp. 9–18; Feb., 1973, pp. 53–60.

Heller, Nancy, and Julia Williams, *The Regionalists*, New York: Watson-Guptill, 1976.

Henning, Edward B., "Plane, Structure, Color and Content," *Bulletin of the Cleveland Museum of Art*, vol. 61, Sept., 1974, pp. 222–39.

———, "Colour and Field," *Art International*, vol. 15, May, 1971, pp. 46–50.

Hess, Thomas B., *Abstract Painting—Background and American Phase*, New York: Viking, 1950.

———, "U.S. Painting: Some Recent Directions," *Art News Annual*, XXV, 1956, pp. 74–98ff.

———, and Harold Rosenberg, *Action Painting . . . 1958*, Dallas: Museum for Contemporary Arts, 1958.

Hills, Patricia, *Turn-Of-The-Century America: Paintings, Graphics, Photographs, 1890–1910*, New York: Whitney Museum of American Art, 1977.

Homer, William Inness, *Alfred Stieglitz and the American Avant-Garde*, Boston: New York Graphic Society, 1977.

———, "The Exhibition of the Eight: Its History and Significance," *American Art Journal*, vol. 1, no. 1, 1972, pp. 53–64.

Hunter, Sam, "Abstract Expressionism Then and Now," *Canadian Art*, vol. 21, Sept./Oct., 1964, pp. 266–69.

———, "American Art Since 1945," in *New Art Around the World: Painting and Sculpture*, New York: Abrams, 1966, pp. 9–58.

———, *Art Since 1950*, Seattle: Seattle World's Fair, 1962.

———, *New Directions in American Painting*, Waltham, Mass.: Poses Institute, Brandeis University, 1963.

———, "Painting by Another Name," *Art in America*, vol. 42, Dec., 1954, pp. 291–95.

———, "USA," in *Art Since 1945*, New York: Abrams, 1958.

Janis, Sidney, *Abstract and Surrealist Art in America*, New York: Reynal and Hitchcock, 1944.

Johnson, Ellen H., *Modern Art and the Object: A Century of Changing Attitudes*, London: Thames and Hudson, 1976.

Kingsbury, Martha, *Art of the Thirties: The Pacific Northwest*, Seattle: University of Washington Press, 1972.

Kozloff, Max, "The Critical Reception of Abstract Expressionism," *Arts Magazine*, vol. 40, Dec., 1965, pp. 27–33.

———, "The Dilemma of Expressionism," *Artforum*, vol. 3, Nov., 1964, pp. 32–35.

———, "The New American Painting," in *The New American Arts*, Richard Kostelanetz, ed., New York: Horizon, 1965.

———, *Renderings: Critical Essays on a Century of Modern Art*, New York: Simon and Schuster, 1969.

Kramer, Hilton, *The Age of the Avant-Garde: An Art Chronicle of 1956–1972*, New York: Farrar, Straus and Giroux, 1973.

———, "Notes on Painting in New York," *Arts Yearbook 7: The Art World*, 1964, pp. 9–20.

Kuh, Katherine, *The Artist's Voice: Talks with Seventeen Artists*, New York: Harper & Row, 1962.

Kuhn, Walt, *The Story of the Armory Show*, New York: The Author, 1938.

Kultermann, Udo, *The New Painting*, new ed., Boulder, Col.: Westview Press, 1977.

———, *New Realism*, Greenwich, Conn.: New York Graphic Society, 1972.

Kutner, Janet, "Brice Marden, David Novros, Mark Rothko: The Urge to Communicate through Non-Imagistic Painting," *Arts Magazine*, vol. 50, Sept., 1975, pp. 61–63.

Lawrence, Ellen, *Graham, Gorky, Smith and Davis in The Thirties*, Providence: Brown University Art Gallery, 1977.

Levin, Gail, *Synchromism*, New York: Whitney Museum of American Art, 1978.

Levine, Edward M., "Abstract Expressionism: the Mystical Experience," *Art Journal*, vol. 31, Fall, 1971, pp. 22–25.

Levy, Julien, *Surrealism*, New York: Black Sun Press, 1936; rep. New York: Arno, 1968.

Licht, Jennifer, *Eight Contemporary Artists*, New York: Museum of Modern Art, 1974.

Lippard, Lucy R., *Changing: Essays in Art Criticism*, New York: Dutton, 1971.

———, "Homage to the Square," *Art in America*, vol. 55, July/Aug., 1967, pp. 50–57.

———, "Perverse Perspectives," *Art International*, vol. 11, March/April, 1967, pp. 28–33, 44.

———, "The Third Stream: Constructed Paintings and Painted Structures," *Art Voices*, vol. 4, Spring, 1965, pp. 44–49.

———, *Twenty-Six Contemporary Women Artists*. Ridgefield, Conn.: Aldrich Museum of Contemporary Art, 1971.

———, ed., *Dadas on Art*, Englewood Cliffs, N.J.: Prentice-Hall, 1971.

———, *Pop Art*, New York: Praeger, 1966.

Lucie-Smith, Edward, "Abstract Expressionism," in his *Late Modern: The Visual Arts Since 1945*, New York: Praeger, 1969, pp. 25–51.

———, *Art Now: Abstract Expressionism to Superrealism*, New York: Morrow, 1977.

Lynton, Robert, *Order and Experience*, London: Arts Council of Great Britain, 1975.

MacAgy, Douglas, *Pop Goes the Easel*, Houston: Contemporary Art Museum, 1963.

———, ed., *The Western Round Table on Modern Art*, San Francisco: San Francisco Art Association, 1949.

Maroney, James H., *Lines of Power*, New York: Hirschl & Adler Galleries, 1977.

Mather, Frank J., "The Forum Exhibition," *The Nation*, vol. 102, March 23, 1916, p. 340.

———, "Old and New Art," *The Nation*, vol. 96, March 6, 1913, pp. 240–43.

McKinzie, Richard D., *The New Deal for Artists*, Princeton, N.J.: Princeton University Press, 1973.

Miller, Dorothy, *Americans 1942: 18 Artists from Nine States*. New York: Museum of Modern Art, 1942.

———, ed., *Americans: 1942–1963; Six Group Exhibitions*, rep. New York: Museum of Modern Art, 1972.

———, *Fifteen Americans*, New York: Museum of Modern Art, 1952.

———, *Fourteen Americans*, New York: Museum of Modern Art, 1946.

Monroe, G.M., "The 30s: Art, Ideology, and the WPA," *Art in America*, vol. 63, Nov./Dec., 1975, pp. 64–67.

Monte, James K., *22 Realists*, New York: Whitney Museum of American Art, 1970.

Morris, George L.K., *American Abstract Art*, New York: St. Etienne Gallery, 1940.

Motherwell, Robert, ed. *The Dada Painters and Poets: An Anthology*. New York: Wittenborn, 1951, 1967.

———, and Ad Reinhardt, eds., *Modern Artists in America: First Series*, New York: Wittenborn, Schultz, 1951.

Mulas, Ugo, and Alan Solomon, *New York: The New Art Scene*, New York: Holt, Rinehart and Winston, 1967.

Müller, Gregoire, *The New Avant-Garde: Issues for the Art of the Seventies*, London: Pall Mall Press, 1972.

Murdock, Robert M., *Modular Painting*, Buffalo: Albright-Knox Art Gallery, 1970.

Museum of Modern Art, New York, *Two Decades of American Painting*. 1966.

Nemser, Cindy, *Art Talk: Conversations with 12 Women Artists*, New York: Scribner's, 1975.

Nochlin, Linda, "The Realist Criminal and the Abstract Law," *Art in America*, vol. 61, Sept./Oct., 1973, pp. 54–61.

O'Connor, Francis V., *Federal Support for the Visual Arts: The New Deal and Now*, Greenwich, Conn.: New York Graphic Society, 1969.

———, *W.P.A.: Art For the Millions*, Boston: New York Graphic Society, 1975.

———, ed., *The New Deal Art Projects: An Anthology of Memoirs*, Washington, D.C.: Smithsonian Institution Press, 1972.

O'Doherty, Brian, "Inside the White Cube, Part II: The Eye and the Spectator," *Artforum*, vol. 14, April, 1976, pp. 26–33.

O'Hara, Frank, *Art Chronicles, 1954–1966*, New York: Braziller, 1975.

Parola, René, *Optical Art: Theory and Practice*, New York: Reinhold, 1969.

Perlman, Bernard, *The Immortal Eight: American Painting from Eakins to the Armory Show (1870–1913)*, New York: Exposition Press, 1962.

Pellegrini, Aldo, *New Tendencies in Art*, New York: Crown, 1966.

Perreault, John, "Classic Pop Revisited," *Art in America*, March/April, 1974, pp. 64–68.

———, "Issues in Pattern Painting," *Artforum*, vol. 14, Nov., 1977, pp. 32–36.

Pincus-Witten, Robert, "Rosenquist and Samaras: The Obsessive Image and Post-Minimalism," *Artforum*, vol. 11, Sept., 1972, pp. 63–69.

———, "Ryman, Marden, Manzoni: Theory, Sensibility, Meditation," *Artforum*, vol. 10, June, 1972, pp. 50–53.

———, "'Systemic' Painting," *Artforum*, vol. 5, Nov., 1966, pp. 42–45.

Plagens, Peter, *Sunshine Muse: Contemporary Art on the West Coast*, New York: Praeger, 1974.

Purcell, Ralph, *Government and Art*, Washington, D.C.: Public Affairs Press, 1956.

Ratcliff, Carter, "The New Informalists," *Art News*, vol. 68, Feb., 1970, pp. 46–50.

Read, Helen Appleton, *New York Realists, 1900–1914*, New York: Whitney Museum of American Art, 1937.

Read, Herbert, "An Art of Internal Necessity," *Quadrum*, no. 1, 1956, pp. 7–22.

Rose, Barbara, "ABC Art," *Art in America*, vol. 53, Oct./Nov., 1965, pp. 57–69.

———, "Abstract Illusionism," *Artforum*, vol. 6, Oct., 1967, pp. 33–37.

———, "Dada Then and Now," *Art International*, vol. 7, Jan., 1963, pp. 23–28.

———, "Lee Krasner and the Origins of Abstract Expressionism," *Arts Magazine*, vol. 51, Feb., 1977, pp. 96–100.

———, "The Primacy of Color," *Art International*, vol. 8, May, 1964, pp. 22–26.

———, "The Second Generation: Academy and Breakthrough," *Artforum*, vol. 4, Sept. 1965, pp. 53–63.

Rosenberg, Bernard, and Norris Fliegel, *The Vanguard Artist: Portrait and Self-Portrait*, Chicago: Quadrangle Press, 1965.

Rosenberg, Harold, "The American Action Painters," *Art News*, vol. 51, Dec., 1952, pp. 22–23.

———, *Art on the Edge: Creators and Situations*, New York: Macmillan, 1975.

———, *Artworks and Packages*, New York: Horizon, 1969.

———, *The Anxious Object: Art Today and Its Audience*, New York: Horizon, 1966.

———, *The De-Definition of Art: Action to Pop to Earthworks*, New York: Horizon, 1972.

———, "Tenth Street: A Geography of Modern Art," *Art News Annual*, no. 28, 1959, pp. 120–143ff.

———, *The Tradition of the New*, New York: Horizon, 1959.

Rosenblum, Robert, "Abstract Expressionism," in his *Modern Painting and the Northern Romantic Tradition: Friedrich to Rothko*, New York: Harper and Row, 1975.

———, "The Abstract Sublime," *Art News*, vol. 59, Feb., 1961, pp. 38–41ff.

———, "Cubism in England and America," in his *Cubism and Twentieth-Century Art*, New York: Abrams, 1961.

———, "Pop Art and Non-Pop Art," *Art and Literature*, no. 5, Summer, 1965, pp. 80–93.

Rosenfeld, Paul, *Port of New York: Essays on Fourteen American Moderns*, New York: Harcourt, Brace, 1924.

Rubin, William S., *Dada and Surrealist Art*, New York: Abrams, 1969.

———, *Dada, Surrealism, and Their Heritage*, New York: Museum of Modern Art, 1968.

———, "Younger American Painters," *Art International*, vol. 4, Jan., 1960, pp. 24–31.

Rublowsky, John, *Pop Art*. New York: Basic Books, 1965.

Rudikoff, Sonya, "New Realists in New York," *Art International*, vol. 7, Jan., 1963, pp. 39–41.

Russell, John, and Suzi Gablik, *Pop Art Redefined*, New York: Praeger, 1969.

Sandler, Irving, *The Triumph of American Painting: A History of Abstract Expressionism*, New York: Praeger, 1970.

———, "The Surrealist Emigrés in New York," *Artforum*, vol. 6, May, 1968, pp. 9, 24–31.

Schapiro, Meyer, "The Liberating Quality of Avant-Garde Art," *Art News*, Summer, 1957, pp. 36–42.

———, "The Nature of Abstract Art," *Marxist Quarterly*, no. 1, Jan./March, 1937, pp. 77–98.

———, "Rebellion in Art," in Aaron, Daniel, ed., *America in Crisis*, New York: Knopf, 1952.

———, "The Younger American Painters of Today," *The Listener*, vol. 60, Jan. 26, 1956, pp. 146–47.

Schwarz, Arturo, *New York Dada: Duchamp, Man Ray, Picabia*, Munich: Prestel-Verlag, 1973.

Seitz, William C., "The Real and the Artificial: Painting of the New Environment," *Art in America*, vol. 40, Nov./Dec., 1972, pp. 58–72.

———, *The Responsive Eye*, New York: Museum of Modern Art, 1965.

———, "Spirit, Time and Abstract Expressionism," *Magazine of Art*, vol. 46, Feb., 1953, pp. 80–87.

Selz, Peter, "A Symposium of Pop Art," *Arts Magazine*, vol. 37, April, 1963, pp. 36–45.

Shapiro, David, ed., *Social Realism: Art As a Weapon*, New York: Ungar, 1973.

Sloan, John, *Gist of Art*, New York: American Artists Group, 1939.

Solomon, Alan, *American Painting Now*, Montreal: Expo '67, United States Pavilion, 1967.

———, *Painting in New York: 1944 to 1969*, Pasadena: Pasadena Art Museum, 1969.

———, *Toward a New Abstraction*, New York: Jewish Museum, 1963.

Sweeney, James Johnson, *Younger American Painters: A Selection*, New York: Solomon R. Guggenheim Museum, 1954.

———, ed., "Eleven Europeans in America," *Bulletin of the Museum of Modern Art*, Sept., 1946, pp. 1–39.

Swenson, G.R., "The New American 'Sign Painters'," *Art News*, vol. 61, Sept., 1962, pp. 44–47, 60–62.

———, "What is Pop Art?: Answers from 8 Painters," 2 parts, *Art News*, vol. 62, Nov., 1963, pp. 24–27; Feb., 1964, pp. 40–43, 66–67.

Tashjian, Dickran, *Skyscraper Primitives: Dada and the American Avant-Garde, 1910–1925*, Middletown, Conn.: Wesleyan University Press, 1975.

Tillim, Sidney, "Dissent on the Armory Show," *Arts Magazine*, vol. 37, May/June, 1963, pp. 96–101.

———, "Scale and the Future of Modernism," *Artforum*, vol. 6, Oct., 1967, pp. 14–18.

———, "A Variety of Realisms," *Artforum*, vol. 7, Summer, 1969, pp. 42–47.

Trapp, Frank Anderson, "Armory Show: A Review," *Art Journal*, vol. 23, Fall, 1963, pp. 2–9.

———, *The 1913 Armory Show in Retrospect*, Amherst, Mass.: Amherst Fine Arts Gallery, 1958.

Tuchman, Maurice, *The New York School: Abstract Expressionism in the 40's and 50's*, London: Thames and Hudson, 1969.

Tuchman, Phyllis, "Pop: Interviews with George Segal, Andy Warhol, Roy Lichtenstein, James Rosenquist and Robert Indiana," *Art News*, vol. 73, May, 1974, pp. 24–29.

Tucker, Marcia, *The Structure of Color*, New York: Whitney Museum of American Art, 1971.

Washington Gallery of Modern Art, Washington, D.C., *Formalists*, 1963.

Werner, Alfred, "WPA and Social Realism," *Art and Artists*, vol. 10, Oct., 1975, pp. 24–31.

Wright, Willard Huntington, *American Painting and Sculpture*, New York: Museum of Modern Art, 1932.

———, "Forum Exhibition at the Anderson Galleries," *Forum*, vol. 55, April, 1916, pp. 457–71.

———, *Modern Painting: Its Tendency and Meaning*, New York: Lane, 1915.

Young, Mahonri Sharp, *Early American Moderns: Painters of the Stieglitz Group*, New York: Watson-Guptill, 1974.

———, *The Eight: The Realist Revolt in American Painting*, New York: Watson-Guptill, 1973.

PAINTERS

Pre-1900

ALLSTON: Richardson, Edgar, *Washington Allston, a Study of the Romantic Artist in America*, Chicago: University of Chicago Press, 1948.

AUDUBON: Adams, Alexander B., *John James Audubon, a Biography*, New York: Putnam, 1966.

Audubon, John James, *Audubon and His Journals*, Maria Audubon, ed., 2 vols., New York: Dover, 1960.

Ford, Alice, *John James Audubon*, Norman: University of Oklahoma Press, 1964.

BIERSTADT: Hendricks, Gordon, *Albert Bierstadt: Painter of the American West*, New York: Abrams, 1975.

Trump, Richard Shafer, *The Life and Works of Albert Bierstadt*, unpubl. Ph.D. diss., Columbus: Ohio State University, 1963.

BINGHAM: Bloch, E. Maurice, *George Caleb Bingham*, Berkeley: University of California Press, 1967.

Christ-Janer, Albert, *George Caleb Bingham of Missouri; The Story of an Artist*, New York: Dodd, Mead, 1940.

BLAKELOCK: Geske, Norman A., *Ralph Albert Blakelock, 1847–1919*, Lincoln: Nebraska Art Association, 1974.

BLYTHE: Chambers, B. W., *David Gilmour Blythe: An Artist at Urbanization's Edge*, unpubl. Ph.D. diss., Philadelphia: University of Pennsylvania, 1974.

Miller, Dorothy, *The Life and Work of David G. Blythe*, Pittsburgh: University of Pittsburgh Press, 1950.

CASSATT: Breeskin, Adelyn, *Mary Cassatt: A Catalogue Raisonné of the Oils, Pastels, Water-Colors and Drawings*, Washington, D.C.: Smithsonian Institution Press, 1970.

Bullard, E. John, *Mary Cassatt: Oils and Pastels*, New York: Watson-Guptill, 1972.

Carson, Julia, *Mary Cassatt*, New York: McKay, 1966.

Sweet, Frederick, *Miss Mary Cassatt, Impressionist from Philadelphia*, Norman: University of Oklahoma Press, 1966.

CATLIN: Haberly, Lloyd, *Pursuit of the Horizon, a Life of George Catlin, Painter and Recorder of the American Indian*, New York: Macmillan, 1948.

CHASE: Art Association of Indianapolis, John Herron Art Institute, *Chase Centennial Exhibition, Commemorating the Birth of William Merritt Chase*, Indianapolis, Ind., 1949.

Roof, Katherine Metcalf, *The Life and Art of William Merritt Chase*, 1917, reissued by Hacker Art Books, Inc., 1975.

CHURCH: Huntington, David C., *The Landscapes of Frederic Edwin Church; Vision of an American Era*, New York: Braziller, 1966.

COLE: Noble, Louis L., *The Course of Empire, Voyage of Life and Other Pictures of Thomas Cole, N.A.* (1853), republ., Cambridge: Belknap Press of Harvard University Press, 1964, as *The Life and Works of Thomas Cole*.

Wadsworth Atheneum, *Thomas Cole, 1801–1848, One Hundred Years Later*, Hartford, Conn., 1948.

COPLEY: Prown, Jules David, *John Singleton Copley*, 2 vols., Cambridge: published for the National Gallery of Art by Harvard University Press, 1966.

DURAND: Durand, John, *The Life and Times of A. B. Durand*, New York: Scribner's, 1894.

Lawall, David B., *A. B. Durand, 1796–1886*, Montclair, N.J.: Montclair Art Museum, 1971.

———, *Asher Brown Durand and His Art Theory in Relation to His Times*, unpubl. Ph.D. diss., Princeton, N.J.: Princeton University, 1966.

DURRIE: Wadsworth Atheneum, *George Henry Durrie, 1820–1863, Connecticut Painter of American Life*, Hartford, Conn., 1947.

DUVENECK: Cincinnati Museum Association, *Exhibition of the Work of Frank Duveneck*, Cincinnati Art Museum, 1936.

Duveneck, Josephine W., *Frank Duveneck, Painter-Teacher*, San Francisco: J. Howell, 1970.

EAKINS: Goodrich, Lloyd, *Thomas Eakins, His Life and Work*, New York: Whitney Museum of American Art, 1933.

Hendricks, Gordon, *The Life and Work of Thomas Eakins*, New York: Grossman, 1974.

Hoopes, Donelson F., *Eakins Watercolors*, New York: Watson-Guptill, 1971.

Porter, Fairfield, *Thomas Eakins*, New York: Braziller, 1959.

Schendler, Sylvan, *Eakins*, Boston: Little, Brown, 1967.

EARL: Goodrich, Laurence B., *Ralph Earl, Recorder for an Era*, Albany: State University of New York Press, 1967.

Sawitzky, William, *Ralph Earl, 1751–1801*, New York: Whitney Museum of American Art, 1945.

FEKE: Foote, Henry Wilder, *Robert Feke, Colonial Portrait Painter*, Cambridge: Harvard University Press, 1930.

Whitney Museum of American Art, *Robert Feke*, New York, 1946.

HARNETT: Frankenstein, Alfred, *After the Hunt; William Harnett and Other American Still Life Painters, 1870–1900*, rev. ed., Berkeley: University of California Press, 1969.

HEADE: McIntyre, Robert G., *Martin Johnson Heade, 1819–1904*, New York: Pantheon, 1948.

Stebbins, Theodore E., *The Life and Works of Martin Johnson Heade*, New Haven: Yale University Press, 1975.

HESSELIUS: Philadelphia Museum of Art, *Gustavus Hesselius, 1682–1755*, Philadelphia, 1938.

HOMER: Gardner, Albert Ten Eyck, *Winslow Homer, American Artist, His World and His Work*, New York: Potter, 1961.

Goodrich, Lloyd, *Winslow Homer*, New York: published for the Whitney Museum of American Art by Macmillan, 1944.

———, *Winslow Homer*, New York: Whitney Museum of American Art, 1973.

Hoopes, Donelson F., *Winslow Homer Watercolors*, New York: Watson-Guptill, 1969.

Wilmerding, John, *Winslow Homer*, New York: Praeger, 1972.

HUNT: Knowlton, Helen M., *Art Life of William Morris Hunt*, Boston: Little, Brown, 1900.

INNESS: Cikovsky, Nicolai, *George Inness*, New York: Praeger, 1971.

Ireland, LeRoy, *The Works of George Inness; An Illustrated Catalogue Raisonné*, Austin: University of Texas Press, 1965.

McCausland, Elizabeth, *George Inness, An American Landscape Painter 1825–1894*, New York: American Artists Group, 1946.

JOHNSON: Baur, John I. H., *An American Genre Painter, Eastman Johnson, 1824–1906*, Brooklyn: Brooklyn Institute of Arts and Sciences, Brooklyn Museum, 1940.

Hills, Patricia, *Eastman Johnson*, New York: Potter, 1972.

KENSETT: Howat, John K., *John Frederick Kensett, 1866–1872*, New York: Whitney Museum of American Art, 1968.

LA FARGE: Cortissoz, Royal, *John LaFarge: A Memoir and a Study*, Boston: Houghton Mifflin, 1911.

Weinberg, Helene Barbara, *The Decorative Work of John LaFarge*, unpubl. Ph.D. diss., New York: Columbia University, 1972.

LANE: Wilmerding, John, *Fitz Hugh Lane*, New York: Praeger, 1971.

LEUTZE: Groseclose, Barbara, *Emanuel Leutze, 1816–1868: A German American History Painter*, unpubl. Ph.D. diss., Madison, Wisc.: University of Wisconsin, 1973.

MORAN: Wilkins, Thurman, *Thomas Moran, Artist of the Mountains*, Norman: University of Oklahoma Press, 1966.

MORSE: Larkin, Oliver, *Samuel F. B. Morse and American Democratic Art*, Boston: Little, Brown, 1954.

MOUNT: Cowdrey, Mary Bartlett, and Herman Warner Williams, Jr., *William Sidney Mount,*

1807–1868, An American Painter, New York: published for the Metropolitan Museum of Art by Columbia University Press, 1944.

Frankenstein, Alfred, *William Sidney Mount*, New York: Abrams, 1975.

NEWMAN: Landgren, Marchal E., *Robert Loftin Newman, 1827–1912*, Washington, D. C.: Smithsonian Institution Press, 1974.

PEALE: Detroit Institute of Arts, *The Peale Family: Three Generations of American Artists*, Detroit, 1967.

Sellers, Charles Coleman, *Charles Willson Peale*, rev. ed., New York: Scribner's, 1969.

REMINGTON: McCracken, Harold, *Frederic Remington, Artist of the Old West*, Philadelphia: Lippincott, 1947.

ROBINSON: Johnston, Sona, *Theodore Robinson, 1852–1896*, Baltimore: The Baltimore Museum of Art, 1973.

RYDER: Goodrich, Lloyd, *Albert P. Ryder*, New York: Braziller, 1959.

SARGENT: Hoopes, Donelson F., *Sargent Watercolors*, New York: Watson-Guptill, 1970.

Mount, Charles Merrill, *John Singer Sargent; A Biography*, New York: Norton, 1955, reprinted by Kraus Reprint Company, 1969.

Ormond, Richard, *John Singer Sargent*, New York: Harper & Row, 1970.

Sweet, Frederick, *Sargent, Whistler, and Mary Cassatt*, Chicago: Art Institute, 1954.

SMIBERT: Foote, Henry Wilder, *John Smibert, Painter*, Cambridge: Harvard University Press, 1950.

STUART: Flexner, James, *Gilbert Stuart; A Great Life In Brief*, New York: Knopf, 1955.

Park, Lawrence, *Gilbert Stuart; An Illustrated Descriptive List of His Works*, 4 vols., New York: Rudge, 1926.

TRUMBULL: Jaffe, Irma B., *John Trumbull*, Boston: New York Graphic Society, 1975.

Sizer, Theodore, *The Works of Colonel John Trumbull, Artist of the American Revolution*, rev. ed., New Haven: Yale University Press, 1967.

Trumbull, John, *The Autobiography of Colonel John Trumbull, Patriot Artist, 1756–1843*, New Haven: Yale University Press, 1953.

VANDERLYN: Lindsay, Kenneth C., *The Works of John Vanderlyn, From Tammany to the Capitol*, Binghamton, N.Y.: Niles & Phipps, 1970.

WEIR: Young, Dorothy Weir, *The Life and Letters of J. Alden Weir*, New Haven: Yale University Press, 1960.

WEST: Evans, Grose, *Benjamin West and the Taste of His Times*, Carbondale: Southern Illinois University Press, 1959.

WHISTLER: McMullen, Roy, *Victorian Outsider: A Biography of J. A. M. Whistler*, New York: Dutton, 1973.

Pennell, Elizabeth, and Joseph Pennell, *The Life of James McNeill Whistler*, 2 vols., London: Heinemann, 1908.

Sutton, Denys, *Nocturne: The Art of James McNeill Whistler*, London: Country Life, 1963.

Weintraub, Stanley, *Whistler: A Biography*, New York: Weybright and Talley, 1974.

Twentieth Century

ALBERS: Albers, Josef, *Interaction of Color*, 2 vols., New Haven and London: Yale University Press, 1963.

Comringer, Eugen, *Josef Albers*, New York: Wittenborn, 1968.

Spies, Werner, *Josef Albers*, New York: Abrams, 1970.

ANUSZKIEWICZ: Lunde, Karl, *Anuszkiewicz*, New York: Abrams, 1977.

AVERY: Breeskin, Adelyn D., *Milton Avery*, Washington, D.C.: National Collection of Fine Arts, 1969.

Kramer, Hilton, *Milton Avery: Paintings, 1930–1960*, New York: Yoseloff, 1962.

Wight, Frederick S., *Milton Avery*, Baltimore: Baltimore Museum of Art, 1952.

BAZIOTES: Alloway, Lawrence, *Baziotes*, New York: Solomon R. Guggenheim Museum, 1965.

Sandler, Irving, "Baziotes: Modern Mythologist," *Art News*, vol. 63, Feb., 1965, pp. 28–31.

BEARDEN: Bearden, Romare, and Carl Holty, *The Painter's Mind*, New York: Crown, 1969.

Greene, Carroll, *Romare Bearden: The Prevalence of Ritual*, New York: Museum of Modern Art, 1970.

Washington, M. Bunch, and John A. Williams, *Romare Bearden*, New York: Abrams, 1973.

BELLOWS: Braider, Donald, *George Bellows and the Ashcan School of Painting*, New York: Doubleday, 1971.

Morgan, Charles H., *George Bellows: Painter of America*, New York: Reynal, 1965.

Young, Mahonri Sharp, *The Paintings of George Bellows*, New York: Watson-Guptill, 1973.

BENTON: Baigell, Matthew, *Thomas Hart Benton*, New York: Abrams, 1974.

Benton, Thomas Hart, *An American in Art: A Professional and Technical Autobiography*. Lawrence: University of Kansas Press, 1969.

Fath, Creekmore, ed., *The Lithographs of Thomas Hart Benton*, Austin: University of Texas Press, 1969.

BURCHFIELD: Baur, John I. H., *Charles Burchfield*, New York: Whitney Museum of American Art, 1956.

————, *Charles E. Burchfield at Kennedy Galleries: The Early Years, 1915–1929*, New York: Kennedy Galleries, 1977.

Jones, Edith H., ed., *The Drawings of Charles Burchfield*, New York: Praeger in association with The Drawing Society, 1968.

DAVIES: Ackerman, Martin S., and Diane L. Ackerman, eds., *Arthur B. Davies: Essays on His Art*, New York: Arco, 1974.

Cortissez, Royal, *Arthur B. Davies*, American Artists Series, New York: Whitney Museum of American Art, 1931.

DAVIS: Arnason, H. H., *Stuart Davis, 1894–1964: Memorial Exhibition*, Washington, D.C.: National Collection of Fine Arts, 1965.

Blesh, Rudi, *Stuart Davis*, New York: Grove Press, 1960.

Goossen, E. C., *Stuart Davis*, New York: Braziller, 1959.

Kelder, Diane, ed., *Stuart Davis*, New York: Praeger, 1971.

Sweeney, James Johnson, *Stuart Davis*, New York: Museum of Modern Art, 1945.

DE KOONING: Hess, Thomas B., *Willem De Kooning*, New York: Braziller, 1959.

————, *Willem De Kooning*, New York: Museum of Modern Art, 1968.

Janis, Harriet, and Rudi Blesh, *De Kooning*, New York: Grove Press, 1960.

Larson, Phillip, and Peter Scheldahl, *De Kooning: Drawings/Sculpture*, New York: Dutton, 1974.

Rosenberg, Harold, *De Kooning*, New York: Abrams, 1974.

DEMUTH: Farnham, Emily, *Charles Demuth: Behind a Laughing Mask*, Norman: University of Oklahoma Press, 1971.

Gebhard, David, and Phyllis Plous, *Charles Demuth: The Mechanical Encrusted on the Living*, Santa Barbara: Art Galleries, University of California at Santa Barbara, 1971.

Ritchie, Andrew C., *Charles Demuth*, New York: Museum of Modern Art, 1950.

DILLER: Larson, Phillip, *Burgoyne Diller*, Minneapolis: Walker Art Center, 1972.

Phillips, Harlan, "Burgoyne Diller Talks with Harlan Phillips," *Archives of American Art Journal*, vol. 16, no. 2, 1976, pp. 14–21.

DOVE: Haskell, Barbara, *Arthur Dove*, San Francisco: San Francisco Museum of Art, 1974.

Johnson, Dorothy Rylander, *Arthur Dove: The Years of Collage*, College Park, Md.: University of Maryland, 1967.

Solomon, Alan, *Arthur G. Dove, 1880–1946: A Retrospective Exhibition*, Ithaca, N.Y.: Andrew Dickson White Museum of Art, Cornell University, 1954.

Wight, Frederick S., *Arthur G. Dove*, Berkeley and Los Angeles: University of California Press, 1958.

EILSHEMIUS: Karlstrom; Paul J., *The Romanticism of Eilshemius*, New York: Bernard Danenberg Galleries, 1973.

Schack, William, *And He Sat Among the Ashes*, New York: American Artists Group, 1939.

Stix, Hugh, *Masterpieces of Eilshemius*, New York: Artists Gallery, 1959.

FRANCIS: Selz, Peter, *Sam Francis*, with an essay on his prints by Susan Einstein, New York: Abrams, 1975.

Sweeney, James J., *Sam Francis*, Houston: Houston Museum of Fine Arts, 1967.

FRANKENTHALER: Baro, Gene, "The Achievement of Helen Frankenthaler," *Art International*, vol. 11, Sept., 1967, pp. 33–38.

Goossen, E. C., *Helen Frankenthaler*, New York: Whitney Museum of American Art, 1969.

Rose, Barbara, *Helen Frankenthaler*, New York: Abrams, 1971.

GLACKENS: Du Bois, Guy Pène, *William Glackens*, American Artists Series, New York: Whitney Museum of American Art, 1931.

Glackens, Ira, *William Glackens and the Ashcan Group*, New York: Crown, 1957.

Katz, Leslie, *William Glackens in Retrospect*, St. Louis: City Art Museum, 1966.

GORKY: Levy, Julien, *Arshile Gorky*, New York: Abrams, 1966.

Reiff, Robert F., *A Stylistic Analysis of Arshile Gorky's Art from 1943–1948*, New York: Garland, 1976.

Rosenberg, Harold, *Arshile Gorky: The Man, the Time, the Idea*, New York: Horizon Press, 1962.

Schwabacher, Ethel, *Arshile Gorky*, New York: Macmillan, 1957.

GOTTLIEB: Doty, Robert, and Diane Waldman, *Adolf Gottlieb*, New York: Whitney Museum of American Art and Solomon R. Guggenheim Museum, 1968.

Greenberg, Clement, *Adolf Gottlieb*, New York: Jewish Museum, 1957.

Friedman, Martin, *Adolf Gottlieb*, Minneapolis: Walker Art Center, 1963.

Sandler, Irving, *Adolf Gottlieb: Paintings 1945–1974*, New York: André Emmerich Gallery, 1977.

GRAVES: Rexroth, Kenneth, "The Visionary Paintings of Morris Graves," *Perspectives USA*, no. 10, Winter, 1955, pp. 58–66.

Rubin, Ida E., *The Drawings of Morris Graves*, Boston: New York Graphic Society, 1974.

Wight, Frederick S., *Morris Graves*, Berkeley and Los Angeles: University of California Press, 1956.

GUSTON: Arnason, H. H., *Philip Guston*, New York: Solomon R. Guggenheim Museum, 1962.

Ashton, Dore, *Yes, But . . . : A Critical Study of Philip Guston*, New York: Viking, 1976.

Hunter, Sam, and Harold Rosenberg, *Philip Guston*, New York: Jewish Museum, 1966.

HARTLEY: Hartley, Marsden, *Adventures in the Arts: Informal Chapters on Painters, Vaudeville, and Poets*, New York: Boni & Liverwright, 1921.

McCausland, Elizabeth, *Marsden Hartley*, Minneapolis: University of Minnesota Press, 1952.

Miller, Dorothy C., *Lyonel Feininger and Marsden Hartley*, New York: Museum of Modern Art, 1944.

HENRI: Henri, Robert, *The Art Spirit*, compiled by Margery Ryerson, new ed., Philadelphia: Lippincott, 1960.

Homer, William Inness, *Robert Henri and His Circle*, Ithaca: Cornell University Press, 1969.

Read, Helen Appleton, *Robert Henri*, American Artists Series, New York: Whitney Museum of American Art, 1931.

HESSE: Lippard, Lucy R., *Eva Hesse*, New York: New York University Press, 1976.

Pincus-Witten, Robert, and Linda Shearer, *Eva Hesse: A Memorial Exhibition*, New York: Solomon R. Guggenheim Museum, 1972.

HOFMANN: Bannard, Walter Darby, *Hans Hofmann: A Retrospective Exhibition*, Houston: Museum of Fine Arts, 1976.

Greenberg, Clement, *Hans Hofmann*, Paris: Georges Fall, 1961.

Hofmann, Hans, *Search for the Real and Other Essays*, rev. ed., Cambridge, Mass.: M.I.T. Press, 1967.

Hunter, Sam, *Hans Hofmann*, New York: Abrams, 1963.

Seitz, William C., *Hans Hofmann*, New York: Museum of Modern Art, 1963.

HOPPER: Barr, Alfred H., Jr., and Charles Burchfield, *Edward Hopper Retrospective*, New York: Museum of Modern Art, 1933.

Goodrich, Lloyd, *Edward Hopper*, New York: Whitney Museum of American Art, 1964.

————, *Edward Hopper*, New York: Abrams, 1971; new concise NAL ed., 1976.

INDIANA: Alasko, Richard-Raymond, *Robert Indiana Graphics*, Notre Dame, Ind.: St. Mary's College, Notre Dame, 1969.

McCoubrey, John, *Robert Indiana*, Philadelphia: Institute of Contemporary Art, 1968.

University of Texas at Austin, Art Museum, *Robert Indiana*, 1977.

JOHNS: Crichton, Michael, *Jasper Johns*, New York: Abrams in association with the Whitney Museum of American Art, 1977.

Kozloff, Max, *Jasper Johns*, New York: Abrams, 1967.

Solomon, Alan, and John Cage, *Jasper Johns*, New York: Jewish Museum, 1964.

Steinberg, Leo, *Jasper Johns*, New York: Wittenborn, 1963.

KELLY: Coplans, John, *Ellsworth Kelly*, New York: Abrams, 1972.

Goossen, E.C., *Ellsworth Kelly*, New York: Museum of Modern Art, 1973.

Waldman, Diane, *Ellsworth Kelly: Drawings, Collages, Prints*, Greenwich, Conn.: New York Graphic Society, 1971.

KLINE: Dawson, Fielding, *An Emotional Memoir of Franz Kline*, New York: Pantheon, 1967.

De Kooning, Elaine, *Franz Kline*, Washington, D.C.: Washington Gallery of Fine Art, 1962.

Gordon, John, *Franz Kline: 1910–1962*, New York: Whitney Museum of American Art, 1968.

Sylvester, David, "Franz Kline, 1910–1962: An Interview with David Sylvester," *Living Arts*, vol. 1, Spring, 1963, pp. 2–13.

KUHN: Adams, Philip Rhys, and William Steadman, *Painter of Vision: Walt Kuhn*, Tucson: Art Gallery, University of Arizona, 1966.

Adams, Philip Rhys, *Walt Kuhn: 1877–1949*, Cincinnati: Cincinnati Art Museum, 1960.

LAWRENCE: Brown, Milton W., *Jacob Lawrence*, New York: Whitney Museum of American Art, 1974.

Saarinen, Aline B., *Jacob Lawrence*, New York: American Federation of Arts, 1960.

LEVINE: Getlein, Frank, *Jack Levine*, New York: Abrams, 1966.

Wight, Frederick S., and Lloyd Goodrich, *Jack Levine*, New York: Whitney Museum of American Art, 1955.

LICHTENSTEIN: Alloway, Lawrence, and Richard Hamilton, "Roy Lichtenstein," *Studio International*, vol. 175, Jan., 1968, pp. 20–31.

Coplans, John, *Roy Lichtenstein*, New York: Praeger, 1972.

Waldman, Diane, *Roy Lichtenstein: Drawings and Prints*, New York: Chelsea House, 1969.

————, *Roy Lichtenstein*. New York: Abrams, 1972.

LINDNER: Ashton, Dore, *Richard Lindner*, New York: Abrams, 1969.

Kramer, Hilton, *Richard Lindner*, Boston: New York Graphic Society, 1975.

Tillim, Sidney, *Lindner*, Chicago: William and Noma Copley Foundation, 1960.

LOUIS: Alloway, Lawrence, *Morris Louis: 1912–1962*, New York: Solomon R. Guggenheim Museum, 1963.

Carmean, E.A., Jr., *Morris Louis: Major Themes & Variations*, Washington, D.C.: National Gallery of Art, 1976.

Elderfield, John, *Morris Louis*, London: Hayward Gallery, 1974.

Fried, Michael, *Morris Louis: 1912–1962*, Boston: Museum of Fine Arts, 1967.

————, *Morris Louis*, New York: Abrams, 1970.

LUKS: Cary, Elisabeth Luther, *George Luks*, American Artists Series, New York: Whitney Museum of American Art, 1931.

Heritage Gallery, New York, *George Luks, 1867–1933: Retrospective Exhibition*, 1967.

MACDONALD-WRIGHT: *American Art Review*, "MacDonald Wright: Special Issue," vol. 1, Jan./Feb., 1974.

Brown, Richard F., *A Retrospective Showing of the Work of Stanton MacDonald-Wright*. Los Angeles: Los Angeles County Museum of Art, 1956.

MacDonald-Wright, Stanton, *A Treatise on Color*, Los Angeles: The Author, 1934.

Scott, David W., *The Art of Stanton MacDonald-Wright*, Washington, D.C.: National Collection of Fine Arts, 1967.

Wight, Frederick S., *Stanton MacDonald-Wright: A Retrospective Exhibition*, Los Angeles: Art Galleries, University of California at Los Angeles, 1970.

MARIN: Benson, Emanuel M., *John Marin: The Man and His Work*, New York: Museum of Modern Art, 1935.

Gray, Cleve, ed., *John Marin by John Marin*, New York: Holt, Rinehart and Winston, 1977.

Norman, Dorothy, ed., *The Selected Writings of John Marin*, New York: Pellegrini and Cudahy, 1949.

Reich, Sheldon, *John Marin: Drawings, 1886–1951*, Salt Lake City: University of Utah Press, 1969.

————, *John Marin: A Stylistic Analysis and Catalogue Raisonné*, 2 vols. Tucson: University of Arizona Press, 1970.

MARSH: Goodrich, Lloyd, *Reginald Marsh*, New York: Whitney Museum of American Art, 1955.

————, *Reginald Marsh*, New York: Abrams, 1972.

Laning, Edward, *The Sketchbooks of Reginald Marsh*, Greenwich, Conn.: New York Graphic Society, 1973.

Sasowsky, Edward, *Reginald Marsh: Etchings, Engravings, Lithographs*, New York: Praeger, 1956.

MAURER: McCausland, Elizabeth, *A. H. Maurer*, New York: published for the Walker Art Center by A. A. Wyn, 1951.

Reich, Sheldon, *Alfred H. Maurer: 1868–1932*, Washington, D.C.: National Collection of Fine Arts, 1973.

MOTHERWELL: Arnason, H. H., *Robert Motherwell*, New York: Abrams, 1977.

Carmean, E. A., Jr., *The Collages of Robert Motherwell*, Houston: Museum of Fine Arts, 1972.

Hunter, Sam, *Robert Motherwell Collages*, Paris: Berggruen Galerie, 1960.

O'Hara, Frank, *Robert Motherwell*, New York: Museum of Modern Art, 1965.

NEWMAN: Alloway, Lawrence, *Barnett Newman: The Stations of the Cross, lema sabachthani*, New York: Solomon R. Guggenheim Museum, 1966.

Hess, Thomas B., *Barnett Newman*, New York: Walker, 1969.

————, *Barnett Newman*, New York: Museum of Modern Art, 1971.

Rosenberg, Harold, *Barnett Newman: Broken Obelisk and other Sculptures*, Seattle: University of Washington Press, 1971.

————, *Barnett Newman*, New York: Abrams, 1978.

NOLAND: Fried, Michael, *Kenneth Noland*, New York: The Jewish Museum, 1965.

Moffett, Kenworth, *Kenneth Noland*, New York: Abrams, 1977.

Waldman, Diane, *Kenneth Noland: A Retrospective*, New York: Solomon R. Guggenheim Museum, 1977.

O'KEEFFE: Goodrich, Lloyd, and Doris Bry, *Georgia O'Keeffe*, New York: Whitney Museum of American Art, 1970.

O'Keeffe, Georgia, *Georgia O'Keeffe*, New York: Viking, 1976.

Rich, Daniel Catton, *Georgia O'Keeffe*, Worcester, Mass.: Worcester Art Museum, 1960.

Wilder, Mitchell, *Georgia O'Keeffe: An Exhibition of the Work of the Artist from 1915 to 1966*, Fort Worth, Tex.: Amon Carter Museum of Western Art, 1966.

OLITSKI: Fried, Michael, "Jules Olitski's New Paintings," *Artforum*, vol. 4, Nov., 1965, pp. 36–40.

Krauss, Rosalind, *Jules Olitski: Recent Paintings*, Philadelphia: Institute of Contemporary Art, 1968.

Moffett, Kenworth, *Jules Olitski*, Boston: Museum of Fine Arts, 1973.

————, *Olitski: New Sculpture*. Boston: Museum of Fine Arts, 1977.

POLLOCK: Friedman, B. H., *Jackson Pollock: Energy Made Visible*, New York: McGraw-Hill, 1972.

Hunter, Sam, *Jackson Pollock*, New York: Museum of Modern Art, 1956.

O'Connor, Francis V., *Jackson Pollock*, New York: Museum of Modern Art, 1967.

O'Hara, Frank, *Jackson Pollock*, New York: Braziller, 1959.

Robertson, Bryan, *Jackson Pollock*, New York: Abrams, 1960.

Rose, Bernice, *Jackson Pollock: The Works on Paper*, New York: Museum of Modern Art in association with The Drawing Society, 1969.

Rubin, William S., "Jackson Pollock and the Modern Tradition" (4 parts), *Artforum*, vol. 5, Feb., 1967, pp. 14–22; March, 1967, pp. 28–37; April, 1967, pp. 18–31; May, 1967, pp. 28–33.

PRENDERGAST: Green, Eleanor, *Maurice Prendergast: Art of Impulse and Color*, College Park: University of Maryland Art Galleries, 1976.

Rhys, Hedley Howell, *Maurice Prendergast: 1859–1924*, Boston: Museum of Fine Arts, 1960.

Sawyer, Charles H., *Paintings and Watercolors by Maurice Prendergast*, New York: Knoedler & Co., 1966.

RAUSCHENBERG: Alloway, Lawrence, *Robert Rauschenberg*, Washington, D.C.: National Collection of Fine Arts, 1976.

Forge, Andrew, *Robert Rauschenberg*, New York: Abrams, 1969.

Rauschenberg, Robert, *Illustrations for Dante's Inferno*, New York: Abrams, 1964.

Solomon, Alan, *Robert Rauschenberg*, New York: Jewish Museum, 1963.

Whitechapel Art Gallery, London, *Robert Rauschenberg: Paintings, Drawings, and Combines, 1949–1964*, 1964.

RAY: Langsner, Jules, *Man Ray*, Los Angeles: Los Angeles County Museum of Art, 1966.

Penrose, Roland, *Man Ray*, Boston: New York Graphic Society, 1975.

———, and Mario Amaya, *Man Ray: Inventor/Painter/Poet*, New York: New York Cultural Center, 1974.

Pincus-Witten, Robert, "Man Ray: The Homonymic Pun and American Vernacular," *Artforum*, vol. 13, April, 1975, pp. 54–59.

Ray, Man, *Alphabet for Adults*, Beverley Hills: Copley Galleries, 1948.

———, *Self Portrait*, Boston: Little, Brown, 1963.

REINHARDT: Arnason, H. H., and Barbara Rose, *Ad Reinhardt: The Black Paintings, 1951–1967*, New York: Marlborough-Gerson Gallery, 1970.

Hunter, Sam, and Lucy R. Lippard, *Ad Reinhardt Paintings*, New York: The Jewish Museum, 1966.

Reinhardt, Ad, "Ad Reinhardt on His Art," *Studio International*, vol. 174, Dec., 1967, pp. 265–73.

RIVERS: Hunter, Sam, *Larry Rivers*, New York: Abrams, 1969.

Selle, Carol, *Larry Rivers: Drawings 1949–1969*, Chicago: Art Institute of Chicago, 1970.

ROSENQUIST: Smith, Brydon, and Ivan C. Karp, *James Rosenquist*, Ottawa: National Gallery of Canada, 1968.

Swenson, G. R., "The Figure a Man Makes" (2 parts), *Art and Artists*, vol. 3, April, 1968, pp. 26–29; May, 1968, pp. 42–45.

Tucker, Marcia, *James Rosenquist*, New York: Whitney Museum of American Art, 1972.

ROTHKO: Alloway, Lawrence, "Notes on Rothko," *Art International*, vol. 6, Summer, 1966, pp. 90–94.

Goldwater, Robert, "Reflections on the Rothko Exhibition," *Arts Magazine*, vol. 35, March, 1961, pp. 42–45.

O'Doherty, Brian, "The Rothko Chapel," *Art in America*, vol. 61, Jan./Feb., 1973, pp. 14–20.

Robertson, Bryan, *Mark Rothko*, London: Whitechapel Art Gallery, 1961.

Selz, Peter, *Mark Rothko*, New York: Museum of Modern Art, 1961.

Waldman, Diane, *Mark Rothko, 1903–1970, A Retrospective*, New York: Abrams, for the Solomon R. Guggenheim Museum, 1978.

SHAHN: Morse, John D., ed., *Ben Shahn*, New York: Praeger, 1972.

Shahn, Ben, *The Shape of Content*, Cambridge, Mass.: Harvard University Press, 1957; New York: Vantage Press, 1960.

Shahn, Bernarda Bryson, *Ben Shahn*, New York: Abrams, 1972.

Soby, James Thrall, *Ben Shahn: Paintings*, New York: Braziller, 1963.

SHEELER: Friedman, Martin, *Charles Sheeler: Paintings, Drawings, Photographs*, New York: Watson-Guptill, 1975.

National Collection of Fine Arts, Washington, D.C., *Charles Sheeler*, 1968.

Rourke, Constance, *Charles Sheeler: Artist in the American Tradition*, New York: Harcourt, Brace, 1938.

SHINN: DeShazo, Edith, *Everett Shinn, 1876–1953: A Figure in His Time*, New York: Potter, 1974.

Kent, N., "The Versatile Art of Everett Shinn," *American Artist*, vol. 9, Oct., 1945, pp. 8–13, 35–37.

New Jersey State Museum, Trenton, *Everett Shinn, 1873–1953*, 1973.

SLOAN: Brooks, Van Wyck, *John Sloan: A Painter's Life*, New York: Dutton, 1955.

Morse, Peter, *John Sloan's Prints: A Catalogue Raisonné of the Etchings, Lithographs, and Posters*, New Haven: Yale University Press, 1969.

St. John, Bruce, *John Sloan*, New York: Praeger, 1971.

———, ed., *John Sloan's New York Scene*, New York: Harper and Row, 1965.

Scott, David, *John Sloan*, New York: Watson-Guptill, 1975.

SOYER: Cole, Sylvan, Jr., *Raphael Soyer: 50 Years of Printmaking, 1917–1967*, New York: Da Capo, 1967.

Goodrich, Lloyd, *Raphael Soyer*, New York: Whitney Museum of American Art, 1967.

———, *Raphael Soyer*, New York: Abrams, 1972.

Gutman, Walter K., *Raphael Soyer: Paintings and Drawings*, New York: Sherwood, 1960.

STELLA, FRANK: Fried, Michael, *Frank Stella: An Exhibition of Recent Paintings*, Pasadena: Pasadena Art Museum, 1966.

Richardson, Brenda, *Frank Stella: The Black Paintings*, Baltimore: Baltimore Museum of Art, 1976.

Rosenblum, Robert, *Frank Stella*, Penguin New Art, vol. 1, Baltimore: Penguin, 1970.

Rubin, William S., *Frank Stella*, New York: Museum of Modern Art, 1970.

STELLA, JOSEPH: Baur, John I. H., *Joseph Stella*, New York: Whitney Museum of American Art, 1963.

———, *Joseph Stella*, New York: Praeger, 1971.

Jaffe, Irma B., *Joseph Stella*, Cambridge, Mass.: Harvard University Press, 1970.

STILL: Goossen, E. C., "Painting as Confronta-

tion: Clyfford Still," *Art International*, vol. 4, Jan., 1960, pp. 39–43.

Museum of Modern Art, San Francisco, *Clyfford Still*, 1976.

Sharpless, Ti-Grace, *Clyfford Still*, Philadelphia: Institute of Contemporary Art, 1963.

———, *Clyfford Still: Thirty-Three Paintings in the Albright-Knox Art Gallery*, Buffalo: Albright-Knox Art Gallery, 1966.

TOBEY: Breeskin, Adelyn D., *Tribute to Mark Tobey*, Washington, D.C.: National Collection of Fine Arts, 1974.

Roberts, Colette, *Mark Tobey*, New York: Evergreen Press, 1959.

Schmied, Wieland, *Tobey*, New York: Abrams, 1966.

Seitz, William C., *Mark Tobey*, New York: Museum of Modern Art, 1962.

TOMLIN: Ashbery, John, "Tomlin: The Pleasures of Color," *Art News*, vol. 56, Oct., 1957, pp. 22–25.

Baur, John I. H., *Bradley Walker Tomlin*, New York: Whitney Museum of American Art, 1957.

Sandler, Irving, and Jeanne Chenault, *Bradley Walker Tomlin: A Retrospective View*, Hempstead, N.Y.: Emily Lowe Gallery, Hofstra University, 1975.

WARHOL: Coplans, John, *Andy Warhol*, Greenwich, Conn.: New York Graphic Society, 1971.

Crone, Rainer, *Andy Warhol*, New York: Praeger, 1970.

Warhol, Andy, *The Philosophy of Andy Warhol (From A to B and Back Again)*, New York: Harcourt, Brace, Jovanovich, 1975.

———, and others, *Andy Warhol*, 2d ed., New York: Worldwide Books, 1969.

WEBER: Goodrich, Lloyd, *Max Weber: Retrospective Exhibition*, New York: Whitney Museum of American Art, 1949.

University of California at Santa Barbara Art Gallery, *Max Weber*, 1968.

Werner, Alfred, *Max Weber*, New York: Abrams, 1975.

WOOD: Dennis, James M., *Grant Wood: A Study in American Art and Culture*, New York: Viking, 1975.

Garwood, Darrell, *Artist in Iowa: A Life of Grant Wood*, New York: Norton, 1944.

WYETH: Corn, Wanda, and others, *The Art of Andrew Wyeth*, San Francisco: Fine Arts Museums of San Francisco, 1973.

Fraser, Joseph T., Jr., *Andrew Wyeth: Temperas, Watercolors, Dry Brush, Drawings, 1938 to 1966*, Philadelphia: Pennsylvania Academy of Fine Arts, 1966.

Hoving, Thomas, *Two Worlds of Andrew Wyeth: Kuerners and Olsons*, New York: Metropolitan Museum of Art, 1976.

Wyeth, Andrew, and Richard Meryman, *Andrew Wyeth*, New York: Houghton-Mifflin, 1968.

SCULPTURE: GENERAL

Andersen, Wayne, *American Sculpture in Process, 1930–1970*, Boston: New York Graphic Society, 1975.

Armstrong, Tom, and others, *200 Years of American Sculpture*, Boston: Godine, 1976.

Ashton, Dore, *Modern American Sculpture*, New York: Abrams, 1968.

Brumme, C. Ludwig, *Contemporary American Sculpture*, New York: Crown, 1948.

Craven, Wayne, *Sculpture in America*, New York: Crowell, 1968.

Gardner, Albert Ten Eyck, *American Sculpture: A*

Catalogue of the Collection of the Metropolitan Museum of Art, Greenwich, Conn.: New York Graphic Society, 1965.

Giedion-Welcker, Carole, *Contemporary Sculpture: An Evolution in Volume and Space*, New York: Wittenborn, 1955.

Goldwater, Robert, *What Is Modern Sculpture?*, New York: Museum of Modern Art, 1969.

Krauss, Rosalind, *Passages in Modern Sculpture*, New York: Viking, 1977.

Maillard, Robert, ed., *New Dictionary of Modern Sculpture*, New York: Tudor, 1971.

Ritchie, Andrew, *Sculpture of the Twentieth Century*, New York: Museum of Modern Art, 1952.

Schnier, Jacques, *Sculpture in Modern America*, Berkeley: University of California Press, 1948.

Seymour, Charles, Jr., *Tradition and Experiment in Modern Sculpture*, Washington, D.C.: American University Press, 1949.

Taft, Lorado, *The History of American Sculpture*, 2 vols., new ed., New York: Macmillan, 1930.

SCULPTURE: SPECIAL TOPICS

Adrian, Dennis, *John De Andrea, Duane Hanson: The Real and the Ideal in Figurative Sculpture*, Chicago: Museum of Contemporary Art, 1974.

Artforum, "American Sculpture: Special Issue," vol. 5, Summer, 1967.

Arts Magazine, "Special Issue: Sculpture," vol. 49, Jan., 1975.

Battcock, Gregory, ed., *Minimal Art: A Critical Anthology*, New York: Dutton, 1968.

———, *The New Art: A Critical Anthology*, Dutton, 1966.

Brewington, Marion, *Shipcarvers of North America*, Barre, Mass.: Barre Publishing Company, 1962.

Bullard, Frederic, *Lincoln in Marble and Bronze*, New Brunswick, N.J.: Rutgers University Press, 1952.

Burnham, Jack, *Beyond Modern Sculpture: The Effects of Science and Technology on the Sculpture of This Century*, New York: Braziller, 1970.

Contemporary Arts Center, Cincinnati, *Monumental Art*, 1970.

Crane, Sylvia, *White Silence: Greenough, Powers, and Crawford, American Sculptors in Nineteenth-Century Italy*, Coral Gables, Fla.: University of Miami Press, 1972.

Foote, Nancy, "Three Sculptors: Mark Di Suvero, Richard Nonas, Charles Ginnever," *Artforum*, vol. 14, Feb., 1976, pp. 46–51.

Forbes, Harriette, *Gravestones of Early New England, and the Men Who Made Them*, New York: Da Capo, 1967.

Friedman, Martin, *Scale & Environment: 10 Sculptors*, Minneapolis: Walker Art Center, 1977.

Gardner, Albert Ten Eyck, *Yankee Stonecutters: The First American School of Sculpture, 1800–1850*, Freeport, N.Y.: Books for Libraries Press, 1968.

Gerdts, William, *American Neo-Classic Sculpture; The Marble Resurrection*, New York: Viking Press, 1973.

Goossen, E. C., *The Art of the Real*, New York: Museum of Modern Art, 1968.

Green, Eleanor, *Scale as Content: Ronald Bladen, Barnett Newman, Tony Smith*, Washington, D.C.: Corcoran Gallery of Art, 1967.

Green, Samuel Adams, *7 Sculptors*, Philadelphia: Institute of Contemporary Art, 1965.

Hess, Thomas B., "U.S. Sculpture: Some Recent Directions," *Portfolio and Art News Annual*, no. 1, 1959, pp. 112–27, 146–52.

Kultermann, Udo, *The New Sculpture: Environments and Assemblages*, London: Thames and Hudson, 1968.

Ludwig, Allan I., *Graven Images; New England Stone Carving and Its Symbols, 1650–1815*, Middletown, Conn.: Wesleyan University Press, 1966.

McShine, Kynaston, *Primary Structures: Younger American and British Sculptors*, New York: Jewish Museum, 1966.

Pinckney, Pauline, *American Figureheads and Their Carvers*, New York: Norton, 1940.

Rose, Barbara, "Blowup—The Problem of Scale in Sculpture," *Art in America*, vol. 56, July/Aug., 1968, pp. 80–91.

———, "Looking at American Sculpture," *Artforum*, vol. 3, Feb., 1965, pp. 29–36.

———, *Sculpture Off the Pedestal*, Grand Rapids, Mich.: Grand Rapids Art Museum, 1973.

Sandler, Irving, *Three American Sculptors*, New York: Grove Press, 1959.

Seitz, William C., ed., *Contemporary Sculpture: Arts Yearbook 8*, New York: Art Digest, 1965.

Selz, Peter, ed., *Directions in Kinetic Sculpture*, Berkeley: Art Museum, University of California at Berkeley, 1966.

Sharp, Lewis I., *New York Public Sculpture by 19th-Century American Artists*, New York: The Metropolitan Museum of Art, 1974.

Smithson, Robert, "Entropy and the New Monuments," *Artforum*, vol. 4, June, 1966, pp. 26–31.

Thorp, Margaret Farrand, *The Literary Sculptors*, Durham, N.C.: Duke University Press, 1965.

Tuchman, Maurice, *American Sculpture of the Sixties*, Los Angeles: Los Angeles County Museum of Art, 1967.

Walker Art Center, Minneapolis, *14 Sculptors: The Industrial Edge*. 1969.

Wasserman, Jeanne L., ed., *Metamorphoses in Nineteenth-Century Sculpture*, Cambridge: Harvard University Press, 1975.

Weeren Giek, Hans van, *Recent American Sculpture*, New York: Jewish Museum, 1966.

Whittemore, Frances, *George Washington in Sculpture*, Boston: Marshall Jones, 1933.

SCULPTORS

ANDRE: Waldman, Diane, *Carl Andre*, New York: Solomon R. Guggenheim Museum, 1970.

BALL: Ball, Thomas, *My Three Score Years and Ten, An Autobiography*, Boston: Roberts Brothers, 1892.

BARNARD: Dickson, Harold, "Barnard and Norway," *Art Bulletin*, vol. 44, March, 1962, pp. 55–59.

———, "Barnard's Sculptures for the Pennsylvania Capitol," *Art Quarterly*, vol. 22, 1959, pp. 127–47.

BROWN: Craven, Wayne, "Henry Kirke Brown: His Search for an American Art in the 1840's," *American Art Journal*, vol. 4, Nov, 1972, pp. 44–58.

———, "Henry Kirke Brown in Italy, 1842–1846," *American Art Journal*, vol. 1, Spring, 1869, pp. 65–77.

CALDER: Arnason, H. H., *Alexander Calder*, Princeton, N.J.: Van Nostrand, 1966.

Lipman, Jean, *Calder's Universe*, New York: Viking Press in cooperation with the Whitney Museum of American Art, 1976.

CORNELL: Ashton, Doré, *A Joseph Cornell Album*, New York: Viking, 1974.

Waldman, Diane, *Joseph Cornell*, New York: Braziller, 1977.

CRAWFORD: Gale, Robert, *Thomas Crawford, American Sculptor*, Pittsburgh: University of Pittsburgh Press, 1964.

FERBER: Andersen, Wayne V., *The Sculpture of Herbert Ferber*, Minneapolis: Walker Art Center, 1962.

Rubin, William S., "Herbert Ferber's Sculpture in the Seventies," *Art International*, vol. 20, Feb./March, 1976, pp. 28–33.

FLANNAGAN: Flannagan, John B., *Letters of John B. Flannagan*, New York: Valentin, 1942.

Forsyth, Robert, J., *John B. Flannagan*, Notre Dame: University of Notre Dame Press, 1963.

Miller, Dorothy C., ed., *The Sculpture of John B. Flannagan*, New York: Museum of Modern Art, 1942.

FRENCH: Cresson, Margaret French, *Journey into Fame: The Life of Daniel Chester French*, Cambridge: Harvard University Press, 1947.

Richman, Michael, *Daniel Chester French: An American Sculptor*, New York: The Metropolitan Museum of Art, 1976.

GREENOUGH: Greenough, Horatio, *Form and Function*, Berkeley: University of California Press, 1947.

———, *Letters of Horatio Greenough, American Sculptor*, Madison: University of Wisconsin Press, 1972.

———, *The Travels, Observations, and Experiences of a Yankee Stonecutter* (1852), part 1, a facsimile reproduction, Gainesville, Fla.: Scholars' Facsimiles and Reprints, 1958.

Wright, Nathalia, *Horatio Greenough, The First American Sculptor*, Philadelphia: University of Pennsylvania Press, 1963.

GROSS: Flint, Janet A., *Chaim Gross: Sculpture and Drawings*, Washington, D.C.: National Collection of Fine Arts, 1974.

Getlein, Frank, *Chaim Gross*, New York: Abrams, 1974.

JUDD: Judd, Donald, "Specific Objects," in *Contemporary Sculpture, Arts Yearbook 8*, New York: *Art Digest*, 1965.

Smith, Brydon, ed., *Donald Judd*, Ottawa: National Gallery of Canada, 1975.

LACHAISE: Kramer, Hilton. *The Sculpture of Gaston Lachaise*, New York: Eakins Press, 1967.

Nordland, Gerald, *Gaston Lachaise: The Man and His Work*, New York: Braziller, 1974.

LASSAW: Hunter, Sam. *The Sculpture of Ibram Lassaw*, Detroit: Gertrude Kasle Gallery, 1968.

LAURENT: Hope, Henry R., *Laurent: Fifty Years of Sculpture*, Bloomington: Indiana University, 1961.

Moak, Peter W., *The Robert Laurent Memorial Exhibition, 1972–1973*, Durham, N.H.: New Hampshire University, 1972.

LeWITT: Legg, Alicia, ed., *Sol LeWitt*, New York: Museum of Modern Art, 1978.

LIPTON: Atkinson, Tracy, *Seymour Lipton: A Decade of Recent Works*, Milwaukee: Milwaukee Art Center, 1969.

Elsen, Albert, *Seymour Lipton*, New York: Abrams, 1972.

MANSHIP: Murtha, Edwin, *Paul Manship*. New York: Macmillan, 1957.

NADELMAN: Baur, John I. H., *The Sculpture and Drawings of Elie Nadelman*, New York: Whitney Museum of American Art, 1975.

Kirstein, Lincoln, *Elie Nadelman*, New York: Eakins Press, 1973.

NAKIAN: Goldwater, Robert, "Reuben Nakian," *Quadrum*, no. 11, 1961, pp. 95–102.

O'Hara, Frank, *Nakian*, New York: Museum of Modern Art, 1966.

NEVELSON: Glimcher, Arnold B., *Louise Nevelson*, New York: Praeger, 1972.

Gordon, John, *Louise Nevelson*, New York: Whitney Museum of American Art, 1967.

Nevelson, Louise, *Dawns + Dusks: Taped Conversations with Diana MacKown*, New York: Scribner's, 1976.

NOGUCHI: Gordon, John, *Isamu Noguchi*, New York: Whitney Museum of American Art, 1966.

Noguchi, Isamu, *A Sculptor's World*, New York: Harper and Row, 1968.

OLDENBURG: Oldenburg, Claes, *Store Days*, New York: Something Else Press, 1967.

———, *Raw Notes*, New York: Something Else Press, 1974.

Rose, Barbara, *Claes Oldenburg*, New York: Museum of Modern Art, 1970.

POWERS: Wunder, Richard P., *Hiram Powers, Vermont Sculptor*, Taftsville, Vt.: The Countryman Press, 1974.

———, "The Irascible Hiram Powers," *American Art Journal*, vol. 4, Nov., 1972, pp. 10–15.

REMINGTON: McCracken, Harold, *Frederic Remington, Artist of the Old West*, Philadelphia: Lippincott, 1947.

RICKEY: Rickey, George, *Constructivism: Origins and Evolution*, New York: Braziller, 1967.

Rosenthal, Nan, *George Rickey*, New York: Abrams, 1977.

RIMMER: Whitney Museum of American Art, *William Rimmer, 1816–1879*, New York, 1946.

RINEHART: Rusk, William, *William Henry Rinehart, Sculptor*, Baltimore: N.T.A. Munder, 1939.

ROGERS: Rogers, Millard F., *Randolph Rogers; American Sculptor in Rome*, Amherst: University of Massachusetts Press, 1971.

Wallace, David, *John Rogers, the People's Sculptor*, Middletown, Conn.: Wesleyan University Press, 1967.

ROSZAK: Arnason, H. H., *Theodore Roszak*, New York: Whitney Museum of American Art, 1956.

Roszak, Theodore, "Problems of Modern Sculpture," *7 Arts*, no. 3, 1955, pp. 58–68.

RUSH: Marceau, Henri, *William Rush, 1756–1833, The First Native American Sculptor*, Philadelphia: Museum of Art, 1937.

SAINT-GAUDENS: Cortissoz, Royal, *Augustus Saint-Gaudens*, Boston: Houghton Mifflin, 1907.

Saint-Gaudens, Augustus, *The Reminiscences of Augustus Saint-Gaudens*, 2 vols., ed. and amplified by Homer Saint-Gaudens, New York: Century Company, 1913.

Tharp, Louise Hall, *Saint-Gaudens and the Gilded Era*, Boston: Little, Brown, 1969.

SMITH, DAVID: Cone, Jane Harrison, *David Smith: A Retrospective Exhibition*, Cambridge, Mass.: Fogg Art Museum, 1966.

Fry, Edward F., *David Smith*, New York: Solomon R. Guggenheim Museum, 1969.

Gray, Cleve, ed., *David Smith by David Smith*, New York: Holt, Rinehart and Winston, 1968.

Hunter, Sam, "David Smith," *Museum of Modern Art Bulletin*, vol. 5, no. 2, 1957, pp. 3–36.

Kramer, Hilton, *David Smith: A Memorial Exhibition*, Los Angeles: Los Angeles County Museum of Art, 1965.

Krauss, Rosalind, *Terminal Iron Works: The Sculpture of David Smith*, Cambridge, Mass.: MIT Press, 1971.

McCoy, Garnett, ed., *David Smith*, New York: Praeger, 1973.

SMITH, TONY: Lippard, Lucy R., *Tony Smith*, London: Thames and Hudson, 1972.

———, *Tony Smith: Recent Sculpture*, New York: Knoedler & Co., 1971.

STORY: James, Henry, *William Wetmore Story and His Friends*, Boston: Houghton Mifflin, 1903.

WARD: Sharp, Lewis I., "John Quincy Adams Ward; Historical and Contemporary Influences," *American Art Journal*, vol. 4, Nov., 1972, pp. 71–83.

ZORACH: Baur, John, I. H., *William Zorach*, New York: Praeger, 1959.

Hoopes, Donelson F., *William Zorach: Paintings, Watercolors, and Drawings, 1911–1922*. New York: Brooklyn Museum, 1969.

Zorach, William, *Art Is My Life*, Cleveland: World, 1967.

NEW ART FORMS

Alloway, Lawrence, "Interfaces and Options: Participatory Art in Milwaukee and Chicago," *Arts Magazine*, vol. 43, Sept., 1968, pp. 25–29.

———, "Site Inspection," *Artforum*, vol. 15, Oct., 1976, pp. 49–55.

———, and Allan Kaprow, *New Forms—New Media I*, New York: Martha Jackson Gallery, 1960.

Antin, David. *Earth, Air, Fire, Water*, Boston: Museum of Fine Arts, 1971.

Artaud, Antonin, "The Theater of Cruelty (First Manifesto)," in *The Theater and Its Double*, New York: Grove Press, 1958.

"Art Outdoors," *Studio International*, vol. 193, March/April, 1977.

Art without Boundaries, 1950–1970, Gerald Woods, Philip Thompson, and John Williams, eds., New York: Praeger, 1972.

Baker, Elizabeth C., "Artworks on the Land," *Art in America*, vol. 64, Jan., 1976, pp. 92–96.

———, "The Light Brigade," *Art News*, vol. 66, March, 1967, pp. 52–55; 63; 66.

Baldwin, R., "Kinetic Art: On Producing Illusions by Photo-Stimulation of Alpha Brainwaves with Flashing Lights," *Leonardo*, vol. 5, Spring, 1972, pp. 147–49.

Battcock, Gregory, ed., *Idea Art: A Critical Anthology*, New York: Dutton, 1973.

Beardsley, John, *Probing the Earth: Contemporary Land Projects*, Washington, D.C.: Hirshhorn Museum and Sculpture Garden, 1977.

Bochner, Mel, "Excerpts from Speculations (1967–1970)," *Artforum*, vol. 8, May, 1970, pp. 70–73.

Borden, Lizzie, "Three Modes of Conceptual Art," *Artforum*, vol. 10, June, 1972, pp. 68–71.

Bornstein, M. H., "On Light and the Aesthetics of Color: Lumia Kinetic Art," *Leonardo*, vol. 8, Summer, 1975, pp. 203–12.

Brett, Guy, *Kinetic Art: The Language of Movement*, New York: Reinhold, 1968.

Brooklyn Museum, New York, *Some More Beginnings: An Exhibition of Submitted Works Involving Technical Materials and Processes*, 1968.

Burnham, Jack, *Great Western Salt Works: Essays in the Meaning of Post-Formalist Art*, New York: Braziller, 1974.

Celant, Germano, *Art Povera*, New York: Praeger, 1969.

Chandler, John N., "Art in the Electric Age," *Art International*, vol. 13, Feb., 1969, pp. 19–25.

Cincinnati Art Museum, *Laser Light—A New Visual Art*, 1969.

Davis, Douglas, *Art and the Future: A History/Prophecy of the Collaboration between Science,* *Technology and Art*, New York: Praeger, 1973.

———, and Allison Simmons, eds., *A New Television: A Public/Private Art*, Cambridge, Mass: M.I.T. Press, 1977.

"Discussions with Heizer, Oppenheim, Smithson," *Avalanche*, no. 1, Fall, 1970, pp. 48–71.

Doty, Robert, *Light: Object and Image*, New York: Whitney Museum of American Art, 1968.

Franke, Herbert W., *Computer Graphics-Computer Art*, London: Phaidon, 1971.

Goldin, Amy, "Art and Technology in a Social Vacuum," *Art in America*, vol. 60, March, 1972, pp.46–51.

———, and Robert Kushner, "Concept Art as Opera," *Art News*, vol. 69, April, 1970, pp. 40–43.

Gottlieb, Carla, *Beyond Modern Art*, New York: Dutton, 1976.

Hansen, Al, *A Primer of Happenings and Time/Space Art*, New York: Something Else Press, 1965.

Henri, Andrian, *Total Art, Environments, Happenings, and Performance*, New York: Praeger, 1974.

Higgins, Dick, *The Computer and the Arts*, New York: Abyss, 1970.

Hulten, K. G. Pontus, *The Machine as Seen at the End of the Mechanical Age*, New York: Museum of Modern Art, 1968.

Hutchinson, Peter, "Earth in Upheaval: Earthworks and Landscapes," *Arts Magazine*, vol. 43, Sept., 1968, pp. 44–50.

Jewish Museum, New York, *Software*, 1970.

Kaprow, Allan, *Assemblage, Environments & Happenings*, New York: Abrams, 1966.

———, "Non-Theatrical Performance," *Artforum*, vol. 14, May, 1976, pp. 45–51.

Karshan, Donald, *Conceptual Art and Conceptual Aspects*, New York: New York Cultural Center, 1970.

Kepes, Gyorgy, ed., *The Nature and Art of Motion*, New York: Braziller, 1965.

Kirby, Michael, *The Art of Time: Essays on the Avant-Garde*, New York: Dutton, 1969.

———, *Happenings: An Illustrated Anthology*, New York: Dutton, 1965.

Kluver, Billy, *Nine Evenings: Theatre and Engineering*, New York: Foundation for the Performing Arts, 1966.

———, Julie Martin, and Barbara Rose, *Pavilion, by Experiments in Art and Technology*, New York: Dutton, 1972.

Kozloff, Max, "Men and Machines," *Artforum*, vol. 7, Feb., 1969, pp. 22–29.

———, "Pygmalion Reversed," *Artforum*, vol. 14, Nov., 1975, pp. 30–37.

———, "The Trouble with Art-as-Idea," *Artforum*, vol. 11, Sept., 1973, pp. 33–37.

Kranz, Stewart, *Science & Technology in the Arts: A Tour Through the Realm of Science/Art*, New York: Van Nostrand Reinhold, 1974.

LeWitt, Sol, "Paragraphs on Conceptual Art," *Artforum*, vol. 5, June, 1967, pp.79–83.

———, ed., "Time: A Panel Discussion," *Art International*, vol. 13, Nov., 1969, pp. 20–23.

Licht, Jennifer, *Spaces*, New York: Museum of Modern Art, 1969.

Lippard, Lucy R., *Focus on Light*, Trenton: New Jersey State Museum, 1967.

———, ed., *Six Years: The Dematerialization of the Art Object from 1966 to 1972*, New York: Praeger, 1973.

Malina, Frank, *Kinetic Art: Theory and Practice. Selections from the Journal 'Leonardo,'* New York: Dover, 1974.

Marck, Jan van der, *Art by Telephone*, Chicago:

Museum of Contemporary Art, 1969.

McHale, John, *The Future of the Future*, New York: Braziller, 1969.

McLuhan, Marshall, *The Mechanical Bride*, Boston: Beacon, 1967.

McShine, Kynaston, ed., *Information*, New York: Museum of Modern Art, 1970.

Meyer, Ursula, *Conceptual Art*, New York: Dutton, 1972.

Mumford, Louis, *The Myth of the Machine: The Pentagon of Power*, New York: Harcourt, 1970.

O'Doherty, Brian, "Inside the White Cube: Notes on the Gallery Space," Part I, *Artforum*, vol. 14, March, 1976, pp. 24–30.

Perreault, John, "Literal Light," *Art News Annual XXXV: Light: From Aten to Laser*, 1969, pp. 129–41.

Piene, Otto, "Proliferation of the Sun: on Art, Fine Arts, Present Art, Kinetic Art, Light, Light Art, Scale, Now and Then," *Arts Magazine*, vol. 41, Summer, 1967, pp. 24–31.

Pierce, John, *Science, Art and Communication*, New York: Potter, 1968.

Pincus-Witten, Robert, *Against Order: Chance and Art*, Philadelphia: Institute of Contemporary Art, University of Pennsylvania, 1970.

———, "Anglo-American Standard Reference Works: Acute Conceptualism," *Artforum*, vol. 10, Oct., 1971, pp. 82–85.

———, "Theater of the Conceptual: Autobiography and Myth," *Artforum*, vol. 12, Oct., 1973, pp. 40–46.

Popper, Frank, *Art—Action and Participation*, New York: New York University Press, 1975.

———, *Origins and Development of Kinetic Art*, Greenwich, Conn.: New York Graphic Society, 1968.

Reichardt, Jasia, ed., *Cybernetic Serendipity: The Computer and the Arts*, New York: Praeger, 1968.

Rickey, George, "Kinesis Continued," *Art in America*, vol. 53, Dec., 1965/Jan., 1966, pp. 45–55.

———, "The Morphology of Movement," *College Art Journal*, vol. 22, Summer, 1963, pp. 220–31.

Reiser, Dolf, *Art and Science*, London: Studio Vista; New York: Van Nostrand Reinhold, 1972.

Schneider, Ira, and Beryl Korot, *Video Art: An Anthology*, New York: Harcourt, Brace, Jovanovich, 1976.

Seitz, William C., *The Art of Assemblage*, New York: Museum of Modern Art, 1961.

Sharp, Willoughby, *Air Art*, New York: Kineticism Press, 1968.

———, *Light, Motion, Space*, Minneapolis: Walker Art Center, 1967.

———, ed., *Kineticism*, New York: Kineticism Press, 1968.

Shirey, David L., "Impossible Art: What It Is," *Art in America*, vol. 57, May/June, 1969, pp. 32–47.

Sondheim, Alan, *Individuals: Post-Movement Art in America*, New York: Dutton, 1977.

Spear, Athena T., *Art in the Mind*, Oberlin, Ohio: Allen Memorial Art Museum, Oberlin College, 1970.

Tucker, Marcia, and James Monte, *Anti-Illusion: Procedures/Materials*, New York: Whitney Museum of American Art, 1969.

Walker Art Center, Minneapolis, *Projected Images*, 1974.

Worcester Art Museum, Worcester, Mass., *Light and Motion*, 1968.

SELECTED ARTISTS

CHRISTO: Bourdon, David, *Christo*, New York: Abrams, 1971.

Hunter, Sam, *Christo: Oceanfront*, Princeton, N.J.: Princeton University Art Museum, 1975.

FLAVIN: Flavin, Dan, "'...In Daylight or Cool White,' An Autobiographical Sketch," *Artforum*, vol. 4, Dec., 1965, pp. 20–24.

Smith, Brydon, *Dan Flavin, Fluorescent Light, etc.* Ottawa: National Gallery of Canada, 1969.

KIENHOLZ: Hopps, Walter, *Edward Kienholz: Work from the 1960's*, Washington, D.C.: Washington Gallery of Modern Art, 1968.

Kienholz, Edward, and K. G. Pontus Hulten, *Edward Kienholz: 11 + 11 Tableau*, Stockholm: Moderna Museet, 1970.

Tillim, Sidney, "The Underground Pre-Raphaelitism of Edward Kienholz," *Artforum*, vol. 4, April, 1965, pp. 38–40.

Tuchman, Maurice, "A Decade of Edward Kienholz," *Artforum*, vol. 4, April, 1965, pp. 41–45.

MORRIS: Compton, Michael, and David Sylvester, *Robert Morris*, London: Tate Gallery, 1971.

Michelsen, Annette, *Robert Morris*, Washington, D.C.: Corcoran Gallery of Art, 1969.

Morris, Robert, "Anti-Form," *Artforum*, vol. 6, April, 1968.

———, "Notes on Sculpture" (4 parts), *Artforum*, vol. 4, Feb., 1966, pp. 42–44; vol. 5, Oct., 1966, pp. 20–23; vol. 5, Summer, 1967, pp. 24–29; vol. 7, April, 1969, pp. 50–54.

Tucker, Marcia, *Robert Morris*, New York: Whitney Museum of American Art, 1970.

NAUMAN: Livingston, Jane, and Marcia Tucker, *Bruce Nauman: Work from 1965 to 1972*, Los Angeles: Los Angeles County Museum of Art, 1972.

Nauman, Bruce, "An Interview with the Artist," *Avalanche*, vol. 1, Winter, 1971, pp. 22–31.

Tucker, Marcia, "PheNAUMANology," *Artforum*, vol. 9, Dec., 1970, pp. 38–44.

SAMARAS: Alloway, Lawrence, *Samaras: Selected Works, 1960–1966*, New York: Pace Gallery, 1966.

Levin, Kim, *Lucas Samaras*, New York: Abrams, 1975.

Samaras, Lucas, *Samaras Album: Autointerview, Autobiography, Autopolaroid*, New York: Whitney Museum of American Art, 1971.

SERRA: Krauss, Rosalind, "Richard Serra: Sculpture Redrawn," *Artforum*, vol. 10, May, 1972, pp. 38–43.

Pincus-Witten, Robert, "Slow Information: Richard Serra," *Artforum*, vol. 8, Sept., 1969, pp. 34–39.

Serra, Richard, "Play It Again Sam," *Arts Magazine*, vol. 44, Feb., 1970, pp. 24–27.

———, "Shift," *Arts Magazine*, vol. 47, April, 1973.

SMITHSON: Ginsburg, Susan, and Joseph Maschek, *Robert Smithson: Drawings*, New York: New York Cultural Center, 1974.

Louw, Roelof, "Sites/Non Sites: Smithson's Influence on Recent Landscape Projects," *Tracks*, no. 3, Spring, 1977, pp. 5–15.

Robbins, Anthony, "Smithson's Non-Site Sights," *Art News*, vol. 67, Feb., 1969, pp. 50–53.

Smithson, Robert, "A Sedimentation of the Mind: Earth Projects," *Artforum*, vol. 7, Sept., 1968, pp. 44–50.

PHOTOGRAPHY: GENERAL

Andrews, Ralph W., *Picture Gallery Pioneers*, New York: Bonanza Books, 1964.

———, *Photographers of the Frontier West: Their Lives and Works, 1875–1915*, New York: Bonanza Books, 1965.

The Art of Photography, Life Library of Photography, New York: Time/Life, Inc., 1971.

Caffin, Charles C., *Photography as a Fine Art*, Hastings-on-Hudson, N.Y.: Morgan and Morgan, 1971.

Coke, Van Deren, *The Painter and the Photograph: from Delacroix to Warhol*, Albuquerque, N.M.: University of New Mexico Press, 1972.

Darrah, William C., *The World of Stereographs*, Gettysburg, Pa., 1977.

Documentary Photography, Life Library of Photography, New York: Time/Life, Inc., 1972.

Doherty, Robert J., *Social Documentary Photography in the USA*, Garden City, N.Y.: Amphoto, 1976.

Doty, Robert, *Photography in America*, New York: Ridge Press, Random House, 1974.

———, *Stieglitz and the Fine Art Movement in Photography*, repr., New York: Dover, 1978.

The Great Photographers, Life Library of Photography, New York: Time/Life, Inc., 1971.

The Great Themes, Life Library of Photography, New York: Time/Life, Inc., 1970.

Green, Jonathan, ed., *Camera Work: A Critical Anthology*, Millerton, N.Y.: Aperture, Inc., 1973.

Hurley, F. Jack, *Portrait of a Decade: Roy Stryker and the Development of Documentary Photography in the Thirties*, Baton Rouge: Louisiana State University Press, 1972.

Ivins, William M., *Prints and Visual Communication*, Cambridge, Mass.: M.I.T. Press, 1973.

Lyons, Nathan, ed., *Photographers on Photography*, Englewood Cliffs, N.J.: Prentice-Hall, 1966.

Moholy-Nagy, László, *Painting, Photography, Film*, Boston: New York Graphic Society, 1973.

Naef, Weston J., *Era of Exploration: The Rise of Landscape Photography in the American West, 1860–1885*, Buffalo: Albright-Knox Art Gallery, and New York: Metropolitan Museum of Art, 1975.

Newhall, Beaumont, *The History of Photography from 1839 to the Present Day*, New York: Museum of Modern Art, 1964.

———, *The Daguerreotype in America*, repr., New York: Dover, 1976.

Rudisill, Richard, *Mirror Image: The Influence of the Daguerreotype on American Society*, Albuquerque, N.M.: University of New Mexico Press, 1971.

Scherer, Joanna Cohan, *Indians: The Great Photographs that Reveal North American Indian Life, 1847–1929*, New York: Ridge Press, Crown, 1973.

Szarkowski, John, *Looking at Photographs*, New York: Museum of Modern Art, 1973.

———, *The Photographer and the American Landscape*, New York: Museum of Modern Art, 1963.

Taft, Robert, *Photography and the American Scene*, repr., New York: Dover, 1964.

Tucker, Anne, ed., *The Woman's Eye*, New York: Knopf, 1973.

Wall, E. J., *History of Three-Color Photography*, London: Focal Library, 1976.

Welling, William, *Photography in America: The Formative Years, 1839–1900, A Documentary History*, New York: Crowell, 1978.

Women of Photography, An Historical Survey, San Francisco: San Francisco Museum of Art, 1975.

The Years of Bitterness and Pride: FSA Photographs, 1935–1943, New York: McGraw-Hill, 1975.

PHOTOGRAPHERS

ABBOTT: Abbott, Berenice, *New York in the Thirties (Changing New York)*, New York: Dover, 1973.

ADAMS: Newhall, Nancy, *Ansel Adams: The Eloquent Light*, San Francisco: The Sierra Club, 1963.

BARNARD: Barnard, George N., *Photographic Views of Sherman's Campaign*, New York: Dover, 1977.

BOURKE-WHITE: Sean Callahan, ed., *The Photographs of Margaret Bourke-White*, Boston: New York Graphic Society, 1972.

BRADY: Kunhardt, Dorothy Meserve and Philip B., Jr., *Mathew Brady and His World*, New York: Time/Life Books, 1977.

BRUGUIÈRE: Enyeart, James, *Bruguière: His Photography and His Life*, New York: Knopf, 1977.

CUNNINGHAM: *Imogen Cunningham: Photographs*, intro. by Margery Mann, Seattle: University of Washington Press, 1970.

CURTIS: Graybill, Florence Curtis, and Victor Boesen, *Edward Sheriff Curtis: Visions of A Vanishing Race*, New York: Crowell, 1976.

EVANS: *Walker Evans*, New York: Museum of Modern Art, 1971.

GARDNER: Gardner, Alexander, *Gardner's Photographic Sketchbook of the Civil War*, New York: Dover, 1959.

HINE: Hine, Lewis W., *Men at Work: Photographic Studies of Modern Men and Machines*, New York: Dover, and Rochester: International Museum of Photography, 1977.

Rosenblum, Walter, and Alan Trachtenberg, *America and Lewis Hine*, Millerton, N.Y.: Aperture, Inc., 1977.

JACKSON: Newhall, Beaumont, and Diana E. Edkins, *William H. Jackson*, Ft. Worth, Tex.: Amon Carter Museum, and Dobbs Ferry, N.Y.: Morgan and Morgan, 1974.

LANGE: *Dorothea Lange*, New York: Museum of Modern Art, 1968.

O'SULLIVAN: Newhall, Beaumont and Nancy, *T.H. O'Sullivan, Photographer*, Rochester, N.Y.: George Eastman House, 1966.

RIIS: Alland, Alexander, Sr., *Jacob A. Riis: Photographer and Citizen*, Millerton, N.Y.: Aperture, Inc., 1974.

Riis, Jacob A., *How the Other Half Lives*. New York: Dover, 1971.

SISKIND: Lyons, Nathan, ed., *Aaron Siskind, Photographer*, Rochester, N.Y.: George Eastman House, 1965.

SMITH: *W. Eugene Smith, An Aperture Monograph*, Millerton, N.Y.: Aperture, Inc., 1969.

SOUTHWORTH and HAWES: Sobieszek, Robert, and Odette M. Appel, *The Spirit of Fact: The Daguerreotypes of Southworth and Hawes, 1843–1862*, Boston: Godine, and Rochester, N.Y.: International Museum of Photography, 1976.

STEICHEN: Steichen, Edward, *A Life in Photography*, Garden City, N.Y.: Doubleday, 1963.

STIEGLITZ: Norman, Dorothy, *Alfred Stieglitz: An American Seer*, New York: Random House, 1973.

STRAND: *Paul Strand: Sixty Years of Photographs*, Millerton, N.Y.: Aperture, Inc., 1976.

WESTON: Maddow, Ben, *Edward Weston*, Millerton, N.Y.: Aperture, Inc., 1973.

WHITE, CLARENCE: *Symbolism of Light: The Photographs of Clarence H. White*, Wilmington, Del.: Delaware Art Museum, 1977.

WHITE, MINOR: *Minor White: Rites and Passages*, Millerton, N.Y.: Aperture, Inc., 1977.

DECORATIVE ARTS: GENERAL

Christensen, Erwin O., *The Index of American Design*, New York: Macmillan, 1950.

Crane, Lucy, *Art and the Formation of Taste*, 1882, repr. in Aesthetic Movements Series, vol. 9, New York: Garland, 1977.

Hornung, Clarence Pearson, *Treasury of American Design*, 2 vols., New York: Abrams, 1972.

DECORATIVE ARTS: SPECIAL TOPICS

Barber, E. A., *The Pottery and Porcelain of the United States: An Historical Review of American Ceramic Art from the Earliest Times to the Present Day, to Which Is Appended a Chapter on the Pottery of Mexico*, 3d ed., rev. and enl., New York: Feingold and Lewis, 1976.

Clark, Robert Judson, ed., *The Arts and Crafts Movement in America, 1876–1916*, Princeton, N.J.: Princeton University Press, 1972.

Comstock, Helen, *American Furniture: Seventeenth, Eighteenth, and Nineteenth Century Styles*, New York: Viking, 1962.

————, ed., *The Concise Encyclopedia of American Antiques*, 2 vols., New York: Hawthorn, 1958.

Currier, Ernest M., *Marks of Early American Silversmiths*, Harrison, N.Y.: R.A. Green, 1970.

Fales, Dean A. *American Painted Furniture, 1660–1880*, New York: Dutton, 1972.

Holstein, Jonathan, *The Pieced Quilt: An American Design Tradition*, Greenwich, Conn.: New York Graphic Society, 1973.

Hood, Graham, *American Silver: A History of Style, 1650–1900*, New York: Praeger, 1971.

Kauffman, Henry J., *American Copper and Brass*, Camden, N.J.: Nelson, 1968.

Laughlin, Ledlie Irwin, *Pewter in America: Its Makers and Their Marks*, new ed., Barre, Mass.: Barre Publishers, 1969.

Lee, Ruth Webb, *Handbook of Early American Pressed Glass Patterns*, Northboro, Mass.: Author, 1946.

————, *Sandwich Glass Handbook*, Northboro, Mass.: Author, 1947.

Little, Frances, *Early American Textiles*, New York: Century, 1931.

McKearin, George S. and Helen, *American Glass*, New York: Crown, 1941.

————, *Two Hundred Years of American Blown Glass*, Garden City, N.Y.: Doubleday, 1950.

Metropolitan Museum of Art, New York, *19th Century America: Furniture and Other Decorative Arts*, 1970.

Miller, Edgar G., Jr., *American Antique Furniture*, 2 vols., New York: Dover, 1966.

Montgomery, Charles F., *A History of American Pewter*, New York: Praeger, 1973.

Nutting, Wallace, *Furniture Treasury*, 3 vols., Framingham, Mass.: Old America Company, 1928–33.

Quimby, Ian M.G., *Winterthur Conference Report, 1973: Technological Innovation and the Decorative Arts*, Charlottesville: University Press of Virginia, 1974.

Ramsay, John, *American Potters and Pottery*, New York: Tudor, 1947.

Raycraft, Don and Carol, *American Country Pottery*, Des Moines: Wallace-Homestead, 1975.

Safford, Carleton L., and Robert Bishop, *America's Quilts and Coverlets*, New York: Weathervane Books, 1974.

Schwartz, Marvin D., ed., *American Glass*, New York: Scribner's, 1974.

Stillinger, Elizabeth, *The "Antiques" Guide to Decorative Arts in America, 1600–1875*, New York: Dutton, 1972.

Watkins, Lura, *Early New England Potters and Their Wares*, 1950, repr. Hamden, Conn.: Shoe String, 1968.

Wyler, Seymour B., *The Book of Old Silver, English, American, Foreign; With All Available Hallmarks Including Sheffield Plate Marks*, New York: Crown, 1971.

SELECTED CRAFTSMEN

DUMMER: Clarke, Herman Frederick, and Henry Wilder Foote, *Jeremiah Dummer: Colonial Craftsman and Merchant*, Boston: Houghton Mifflin, 1935.

HURD: French, Hollis, *Jacob Hurd and His Sons, Nathaniel and Benjamin, Silversmiths, 1702–1781*, Cambridge, Mass.: Riverside Press, 1939.

PHYFE: Cornelius, Charles Over, *Furniture Masterpieces of Duncan Phyfe*, Garden City, N.Y.: Doubleday, Page, 1923.

REVERE: Buhler, Kathryn C., *Paul Revere: Goldsmith, 1735–1818*, Boston: Museum of Fine Arts, 1956.

ROOKWOOD: Peck, Herbert, *The Book of Rookwood Pottery*, New York: Crown, 1968.

SEYMOUR: Stoneman, Vernon C., *John and Thomas Seymour: Cabinetmakers in Boston, 1794–1816*, Boston: Special Publications, 1959.

STICKLEY: Freeman, John Crosby, *The Forgotten Rebel: Gustav Stickley and His Craftsman Mission Furniture*, Watkins Glen, N.Y.: Century House, 1966.

STIEGEL: Hunter, Frederick W., *Stiegel Glass*, New York: Dover, 1950.

TIFFANY: Bing, Samuel, *Artistic America: Tiffany Glass, and Art Nouveau*, Cambridge, Mass.: M.I.T. Press, 1970.

Koch, Robert, *Louis C. Tiffany, Rebel in Glass*, New York: Crown, 1964.

INDEX

PHOTOGRAPH CREDITS

The authors and publisher wish to thank the museums and private collectors for permitting the reproduction of paintings and sculptures in their collections. Photographs have been supplied by the owners or custodians of the works of art, except for the following plates:

Berenice Abbott, Abbott, Me.: 283; Aerial Photos of New England, Inc., Boston: 595; Wayne Andrews, Grosse Pointe, Mich.: 12, 38, 40, 44, 57, 58, 60, 64, 65, 66, 128, 131, 137, 150, 200, 203, 204, 211, 214, 224, 279, 298, 300, 366, 368, 373, 374, 449, 453; Doon Arbus, New York: 584; Avery Architectural Library, Columbia University, New York: 235; E. Irving Blomstrann, New Britain, Conn.: 389; Bodleian Library, Oxford University, England: 36, 37; Bostonian Society, Mass.: 201; Bowdoin College, Brunswick, Me.: 226; Milton W. Brown, New York: 294, 297; Rudolph Burckhardt, New York: 573; Barney Burstein, Boston: 394; Clayton Carlson, Wyoming, N.Y.: 218; Carolina Art Association, Charleston, S.C.: 115, 156, 209; Leo Castelli Gallery, New York: 617; Samuel Chamberlain, Marblehead, Mass.: 54; Chicago Architectural Photographing Service: 285, 287, 290; Chicago Historical Society: 292; Jeanne-Claude Christo, New York: colorplate 102; Geoffrey Clements, New York: 336, 463, 569, colorplates 26, 28, 90, 93, 96; Culver Pictures, Inc., New York: 233; George M. Cushing, Boston: 262; Robert Damora, Bedford, N.Y.: 517; Dartmouth College, Hanover, N.H.: 365,

369, 370, 372, 438, 450, 501, 508; James L. Dillon, Philadelphia: 196; Terry Dintenfass, Inc., New York: 457; Eastern National Park and Monument Association, Philadelphia: 39; André Emmerich Gallery, New York: 95; Herman Emmet, New York: 265; Essex Institute, Salem, Mass.: 53, 129, 154; Federal Hall Memorial Association, New York: 202; Philip Gendreau, New York: 237; General Motors Corp., Detroit: 443; Gianfranco Gorgoni, New York: 582; Pedro E. Guerrero, New York: 549; Harvard University, Cambridge, Mass.: 43; Hedrich-Blessing, Chicago: 288, 596; Helga Photo Studio, Upper Montclair, N.J.: 8; Historical Society of Pennsylvania, Philadelphia: 48, 216; Historical Society of Wilmington, Del.: 23; Michael E. Hoffman, Aperture, Inc., Millerton, N.Y.: 414; Cortland V.D. Hubbard, Philadelphia: 19; Sam Hunter, Princeton, N.J.: 570, 576, colorplate 94; Illinois Department of Conservation, Springfield: 84; John Jacobus, Hanover, N.H.: 363, 364, 367, 371, 431, 433, 444, 445, 452, 505, 509, 512, 518, 594; Peter A. Juley and Son, New York: 536; Ellsworth Kelly, Chatham, N.Y.: colorplate 98; Kentucky Historical Society, Frankfort: 205; M. Knoedler and Co., New York: 182; Balthazar Korab, Troy, Mich.: colorplate 82; Landmarks Preservation Commission, New York: 206, 219; Library of Congress, Washington, D.C.: 16, 21, 62, 67, 85, 145, 147, 163, 194, 197, 199, 210, 221, 227, 338; Long Island Historical Society, Brooklyn, N.Y.: 20;

Louisiana State Museum, New Orleans: 86; Manley Commercial Photography, Inc., Tucson, Ariz.: 83; C.M. Manthorpe, S. Charleston, W.Va.: colorplate 2; Marblehead Historical Society, Mass.: 55; Maryland Historical Society, Baltimore: 136, 148; Massachusetts Historical Society, Boston: 142; Laurin McCracken, Los Angeles: 603; Rollie McKenna, New York: 151; Richard Merrill, Melrose, Mass.: 130; The Metropolitan Museum of Art, New York: 230; Marshall Meyers, Philadelphia: 605; Michigan Department of State Archives, Lansing: 212; Museum of the City of New York: 22, 232, 236; Museum of Contemporary Crafts, New York: 551; Museum of Fine Arts, Boston: 166; Museum of Modern Art, New York: 284, 492, 533; National Archives, Washington, D.C.: 143; National Collection of Fine Arts, Smithsonian Institution, Washington, D.C.: 614; National Gallery of Art, Washington, D.C.: 624; National Park Service, Department of the Interior, Philadelphia: 157; National Park Service, Department of the Interior, Washington, D.C. (Fred Bell): 153; National Trust for Historic Preservation, Washington, D.C.: 222, 278; New Mexico Department of Development, Santa Fe: 25; New-York Historical Society, New York: 276; New York Public Library, New York: 146; Richard Nickel, Park Ridge, Ill.: 291; Philadelphia Historical Commission: 198; Philadelphia Museum of Art: 59, 61, 192, 310, 642; James Pierce, Brunswick, Me.: colorplate 7; Pittsburgh Historical and

Landmarks Foundation, Pa.: 282; Eric Pollitzer, New York: 240, 527; Preservation Society of Newport County, R.I.: 42, 301; Princeton University, Department of Public Information, N.J.: 228; Seymour Rosen, Los Angeles: 601; Naomi Rosenblum, Long Island City, N.Y.: 497; Walter Rosenblum, Long Island City, N.Y.: 547; St. Augustine Historical Society, Fla.: 24; Sandak, Inc., Stamford, Conn.: 2, 3, 10, 11, 15, 27, 45, 50, 63, 68, 81, 132, 156, 162, 164, 215, 217, 229, 280, 281, 289, 295, 337, 340, colorplate 4; Sleepy Hollow Studios, Tarrytown, N.Y.: 223; Les Smith, Natick, Mass.: 339; Society for the Preservation of New England Antiquities, Boston: 9, 13, 17, 18, 46, 47, 135; Ezra Stoller Associates, Mamaroneck, N.Y.: 507, 564; Taylor and Dull, N.Y.: 167; Texas Parks and Wildlife Department, Austin: 82; United Press International, New York: 600; United States Geodetic Service, Washington, D.C.: 144; University of Virginia, Information Services, Charlottesville: 152; Virginia Chamber of Commerce, Richmond (P. Flournoy): 184; Virginia Museum of Fine Arts, Richmond: 207; Wakefield Historical Society, Mass. (Donald T. Young): 114; John Weber Gallery, New York: 632, 633, 638; F. Peter Weil, Chicago: 286; Worcester Art Museum, Mass.: 186; Richard Wurts, Litchfield, Conn.: 299; Wurtz Brothers, New York: 51, 220; A.J. Wyatt, Philadelphia: 191; Kurt Wyss, Basel: 604; Yale University Art Gallery, New Haven, Conn.: 516, 593.